Oxford
Learner's Pocket
Dictionary

third edition

D0187910

OXFORD
UNIVERSITY PRESS

OXFORD
UNIVERSITY PRESS

Great Clarendon Street, Oxford OX2 6DP

Oxford University Press is a department of the University of Oxford.
It furthers the University's objective of excellence in research,
scholarship, and education by publishing worldwide in

Oxford New York

Auckland Cape Town Dar es Salaam Hong Kong Karachi
Kuala Lumpur Madrid Melbourne Mexico City Nairobi
New Delhi Shanghai Taipei Toronto

With offices in

Argentina Austria Brazil Chile Czech Republic France Greece
Guatemala Hungary Italy Japan Poland Portugal Singapore
South Korea Switzerland Thailand Turkey Ukraine Vietnam

OXFORD and OXFORD ENGLISH are registered trade marks of Oxford
University Press in the UK and in certain other countries

© Oxford University Press 1983

Database right Oxford University Press (maker)

First published 1983
Second edition 1991
Third edition 2003
2009 2008 2007
11 10 9 8 7

ISBN-13: 978 0 19431589 0

Data capture and processing by Oxford University Press

Printed in China

Contents

Guide to the dictionary

headword	**break¹** /breɪk/ v (pt **broke** /brəʊk/, pp **broken** /ˈbrəʊkən/) **1** [I, T] (cause sth to) be damaged and separated into pieces: *Glass ~s easily.* ◇ *~ a plate* **2** [I, T] (cause sth to) stop working as a result of being damaged: *My*	irregular verb forms
examples		
preposition that usually follows the headword	etc **4** [I] **~(for)** stop doing sth for a while, esp when it is time to eat or have a drink: *Let's ~ for lunch.* **5** [T] interrupt sth: *~ your journey.* **5** (= stop	
idioms	voice) become deeper **12** [T] do better than a previous record **13** [T] solve sth secret: *~ a code* [IDM] **break the back of sth** finish the largest or most difficult part of sth **break even** make neither a loss nor a profit **break fresh/new ground** introduce	idioms
phrasal verbs	succeed **PV** **break away (from sb/sth)** go away from sb/sth; leave eg a political party **break down 1** (of machinery) stop working **2** fail; collapse: *Talks between the two sides have broken down.* **3** lose control of your feelings **break sth down 1** destroy sth: *~ down resist-*	phrasal verbs
derivative	*Their marriage is ~ing up.* ▶ **breakable** *adj* easily broken ■ **'breakaway** *adj* (of a political group, or an organization) having separated from a larger group ■ **'break-in** *n*	derivative
compound nouns and adjectives		
words with the same spelling but different meanings and parts of speech	**brief¹** /briːf/ *adj* **1** lasting only a short time **2** using few words **3** (of clothes) short **in brief** in a few words ▶ **briefly** *adv*	different meanings of a word
word with a similar meaning to the headword, but a different part of speech	**brief²** /briːf/ *n* **1** instructions and for a barrister **3** (*GB, infml*) solicitor or defence lawyer: *I want to see my ~.* ● **brief** v [T] **1** give sb information about sth so that they are prepared to deal with it **2** (*GB, law*) give a barrister the main facts	degree of formality
		subject area in which the word is used
differences in meaning between British and American English	**bureau** /ˈbjʊərəʊ/ *n* (*pl* **~x** or **~s** /-rəʊz/) **1** (*GB*) writing desk with drawers **2** (*US*) = CHEST OF DRAWERS **3** office or organization that provides information on a particular subject **4** (*esp US*) government department	irregular plurals
help with spelling	**cancel** /ˈkænsl/ *v* (**-ll-**, *US* **-l-**) [T] **1** say that sth already arranged will not be done or happen: *The meeting was ~led.* **2** mark a ticket or stamp so that	differences between British and American spelling

A a

A, a /eɪ/ n [C,U] (pl **A's, a's** /eɪz/) the first letter of the English alphabet ● **A** abbr amp(s) ■ **'A level** n [C,U] (GB) exam in a particular subject at about the age of 18 and necessary for entrance to a university

a /ə; strong form eɪ/ (also an /ən; strong form æn/) indefinite article (an is used before a vowel sound) **1** one: a book ◇ a million pounds **2** used of number, quantity, groups, etc: a lot of money **3** each: 70 miles an hour

aback /ə'bæk/ adv [IDM] be taken aback (by sb/sth) be shocked or surprised by sb/sth

abacus /'æbəkəs/ n frame with small balls which slide on rods, used for counting

abandon /ə'bændən/ v [T] **1** leave sb/sth with no intention of returning **2** stop doing or having sth: ~ an idea **3** (lit) ~ yourself to feel an emotion so strongly that you can feel nothing else ▶ **abandoned** adj **1** no longer used **2** (of behaviour) wild ▶ **abandonment** n [U]

abashed /ə'bæʃt/ adj embarrassed; ashamed

abate /ə'beɪt/ v [I] (fml) (esp of wind or pain) become less strong ▶ **abatement** n [U]

abattoir /'æbətwɑː(r)/ n place where animals are killed for food

abbess /'æbes/ n woman who is the head of a convent

abbey /'æbi/ n building in which monks or nuns live

abbot /'æbət/ n man who is the head of a monastery or an abbey

abbreviate /ə'briːvieɪt/ v [T] make a word, phrase, etc shorter ▶ **abbreviation** /ə,briːvi'eɪʃn/ n short form of a word or phrase

abdicate /'æbdɪkeɪt/ v [I,T] give up a high position, responsibility, etc ▶ **abdication** /,æbdɪ'keɪʃn/ n [U]

abdomen /'æbdəmən/ n part of the body containing the stomach ▶ **abdominal** /æb'dɒmɪnl/ adj

abduct /æb'dʌkt/ v [T] take sb away illegally, using force ▶ **abduction** /æb'dʌkʃn/ n [U]

aberration /,æbə'reɪʃn/ n [C,U] action or way of behaving that is not normal

abet /ə'bet/ v (-tt-) [IDM] aid and abet → AID

abhor /əb'hɔː(r)/ v (-rr-) [T] (fml) hate sth ▶ **abhorrence** /əb'hɒrəns/ n [U] ▶ **abhorrent** /-ənt/ adj

abide /ə'baɪd/ v **1** [T] tolerate sb/sth **2** [I] ~ by keep or obey a law, promise, etc ▶ **abiding** adj (written) lasting for a long time and not changing

ability /ə'bɪləti/ n [C,U] (pl -ies) skill or power

abject /'æbdʒekt/ adj (fml) **1** terrible and without hope: ~ poverty **2** not having pride or respect for yourself ▶ **abjectly** adv

ablaze /ə'bleɪz/ adj (written) **1** burning; on fire **2** shining brightly

able /'eɪbl/ adj (~r, ~st) **1** ~to having the power, means or opportunity to do sth: Are you ~ to come with us? **2** clever; skilled ■ ,able-'bodied adj physically strong ▶ **ably** adv

abnormal /æb'nɔːml/ adj unusual in a way that is worrying, harmful, etc ▶ **abnormality** /,æbnɔː'mæləti/ n [C,U] (pl -ies) ▶ **abnormally** adv

aboard /ə'bɔːd/ adv, prep on or onto a ship, an aircraft, a train or a bus

abode /ə'bəʊd/ n [sing] (fml) house or home: people of no fixed ~ (= with no permanent home)

abolish /ə'bɒlɪʃ/ v [T] put an end to sth ▶ **abolition** /,æbə'lɪʃn/ n [U]

abominable /ə'bɒmɪnəbl/ adj extremely unpleasant and causing disgust ▶ **abominably** adv

Aboriginal /,æbə'rɪdʒənl/ (also **Aborigine** /,æbə'rɪdʒəni/) n member of the race of people who were the original inhabitants of Australia ▶ **Aboriginal** adj

abort /ə'bɔːt/ v [I, T] **1** (cause sb to) end a pregnancy early in order to prevent a baby from developing **2** end sth before it is completed ▶ **abortion** /ə'bɔːʃn/ n [C,U] (instance of) aborting(1): have an ~ ▶ **abortive** adj not successful; failed

abound /ə'baʊnd/ v [I] ~(in/with) have or exist in large numbers or quantities

about /ə'baʊt/ prep on the subject of: a book ~ flowers **2** in many directions: walking ~ the town **3** concerned or occupied with: And while you're ~ it, … (= while you are doing that) [IDM] be about to do sth be going to do sth very soon **how/what about … ? 1** used when making a suggestion: How ~ some more tea? **2** used when asking for information: What ~ the money – do we have enough? ● **about** adv **1** a little more or less than: It costs ~ £100. **2** in many different directions: The children were rushing ~. **3** here and there: papers lying ~ the room **4** able to be found in a place: There was no one ~. ■ a,bout-'turn n [sing] complete change of position or opinion

above /ə'bʌv/ prep, adv **1** at or to a higher place or position than sb/sth: the shelf ~ **2** more than sth; greater in number, level or age

abrasion than sb/sth **3** of greater importance or of higher quality than sb/sth: *I rate her ~ most players of her age.* **4** earlier in sth written or printed: *See ~, page 16.* **5** too good or too honest to do sth: *be ~ suspicion* [IDM] **above all** most important of all ● **above** *adj* mentioned or printed previously in a letter, book, etc: *Write to us at the ~ address.* ▶ **the above** *n* [sing, with sing or pl verb]: *Please notify us if the ~ is not correct.*

abrasion /əˈbreɪʒn/ *n* (tech) **1** [C] injury where the skin has been scraped **2** [U] scraping or rubbing

abrasive /əˈbreɪsɪv/ *adj* **1** that scrapes or rubs sth away; rough **2** rude and harsh: harsh ~ *manner*

abreast /əˈbrest/ *adv* side by side [IDM] **keep abreast of sth** remain well informed about sth

abridge /əˈbrɪdʒ/ *v* [T] make a book, etc shorter ▶ **abridgement** *n* [C,U]

abroad /əˈbrɔːd/ *adv* in or to another country: *travel* ~

abrupt /əˈbrʌpt/ *adj* **1** sudden and unexpected: *an* ~ *stop* **2** (of behaviour) rude and unfriendly ▶ **abruptly** *adv* ▶ **abruptness** *n* [U]

abscess /ˈæbses/ *n* painful swelling in the body, containing thick yellowish liquid (**pus**)

abscond /əbˈskɒnd/ *v* [I] (fml) **1** escape from a place that you are not allowed to leave without permission **2** leave secretly, esp with money that does not belong to you

abseil /ˈæbseɪl/ *v* [I] go down a steep hill or rock while attached to a rope, pushing against the slope with your feet

absence /ˈæbsəns/ *n* [U,C] (occasion or period of) being away: ~ *from school* **2** [U] fact of sb/sth not existing; lack: *the* ~ *of information*

absent /ˈæbsənt/ *adj* ~ **(from)** not present in a place ■ **absent-minded** *adj* with your mind on other things; forgetful

absentee /ˌæbsənˈtiː/ *n* person who is not present

absolute /ˈæbsəluːt/ *adj* **1** complete; total: ~ *trust* **2** not limited or restricted: *an* ~ *ruler* **3** not measured in relation to other things: *an* ~ *standard* ▶ **absolutely** *adv* **1** completely **2** /ˌæbsəˈluːtli/ (infml) used to emphasize that you agree with sth

absolve /əbˈzɒlv/ *v* [T] ~ **from/of** (fml) declare sb to be free from blame, a duty, etc

absorb /əbˈsɔːb/ *v* [T] **1** take in a liquid, heat, light, etc **2** hold sb's interest and attention: ~*ed in her work* ▶ **absorbent** *adj* that absorbs liquid easily ▶ **absorption** /əbˈsɔːpʃn/ *n* [U]

abstain /əbˈsteɪn/ *v* [I] **1** vote neither for nor against a proposal **2** ~ **(from)** keep yourself from drinking alcohol, etc

abstemious /əbˈstiːmiəs/ *adj* not eating or drinking a lot; moderate

abstention /əbˈstenʃn/ *n* [C,U] instance of abstaining(1)

abstinence /ˈæbstɪnəns/ *n* [U] practice of abstaining(2), esp from alcohol

abstract /ˈæbstrækt/ *adj* **1** existing as an idea, rather than having a physical or practical existence: *Beauty is ~.* **2** (of art) not showing objects in a realistic way **3** (of a noun) that refers to an abstract quality or state, eg *freedom* ● **abstract** *n* short account of a book, etc; summary

absurd /əbˈsɜːd/ *adj* unreasonable; ridiculous ▶ **absurdity** *n* [U,C] (pl -ies) ▶ **absurdly** *adv*

abundance /əˈbʌndəns/ *n* [U,sing] quantity that is more than enough ▶ **abundant** /əˈbʌndənt/ *adj* ▶ **abundantly** *adv*

abuse /əˈbjuːz/ *v* [T] **1** make bad or wrong use of sth **2** treat sb in a cruel or violent way, esp sexually **3** say rude things to or about sb ● **abuse** /əˈbjuːs/ *n* **1** [U,sing] wrong or bad use of sth: *the* ~ *of power* **2** [U] unfair, cruel or violent treatment of sb: *child* ~ **3** [U] rude or cruel words: *hurl* ~ *at sb* ▶ **abusive** *adj* using rude or cruel words

abysmal /əˈbɪzməl/ *adj* very bad: *an* ~ *failure* ▶ **abysmally** *adv*

abyss /əˈbɪs/ *n* hole so deep that it seems to have no bottom

academic /ˌækəˈdemɪk/ *adj* **1** (of teaching or learning in) schools, colleges, etc **2** involving a lot of reading or studying rather than practical skills ● **academic** *n* teacher at a university, college, etc ▶ **academically** /-kli/ *adv*

academy /əˈkædəmi/ *n* (pl -ies) **1** school for special training: *a music* ~ **2** society for people interested in the arts, etc

accede /əkˈsiːd/ *v* [I] ~ **(to)** (fml) agree to a request, suggestion, etc

accelerate /əkˈseləreɪt/ *v* [I, T] (cause sth to) move faster ▶ **acceleration** /əkˌseləˈreɪʃn/ *n* [U] ▶ **accelerator** /əkˈseləreɪtə(r)/ *n* pedal in a car, etc that is pressed with the foot to increase the car's speed

accent /ˈæksent; -sənt/ *n* **1** individual, local or national way of speaking **2** mark written over or under a letter, eg the symbol on the *e*'s in *résumé* **3** special emphasis or force given to sth

accentuate /əkˈsentʃueɪt/ *v* [T]

emphasize sth or make it more noticeable

accept /ək'sept/ v [I, T] agree to take sth offered; say yes to an invitation, etc – *a present* **2** [T] agree to sth; recognize or believe sth: ~ *the truth* ► **acceptable** *adj* agreed or approved of by most people in a society **2** that sb agrees is satisfactory or allowed ► **acceptance** *n* [U,C]

access /'ækses/ *n* [U] ~(to) **1** way into a place **2** opportunity or right to use sth ● **access** *v* [T] open a computer file in order to get or add information ► **accessible** /ək-'sesəbl/ *adj* easy to reach, use, etc

accession /æk'seʃn/ *n* [U] act of becoming a ruler of a country

accessory /ək'sesəri/ *n* (*pl* **-ies**) **1** something extra that is useful but not essential: *car accessories* **2** (*law*) person who helps another in a crime

accident /'æksɪdənt/ *n* event that happens unexpectedly, esp causing injury or damage [IDM] **by accident** in a way that is not planned ► **accidental** /ˌæksɪ'dentl/ *adj* happening by chance ► **accidentally** /-təli/ *adv* ■ **accident and emergency** (*abbr* **A & E**) *n* = CASUALTY(2)

acclaim /ə'kleɪm/ *v* [T] (*fml*) praise or welcome sb/sth publicly ● **acclaim** *n* [U] (*fml*) enthusiastic welcome or approval

acclimatize (*also* -**ise**) /ə'klaɪmə-taɪz/ *v* [I, T] ~(**yourself**) get used to a new climate or new conditions

accolade /'ækəleɪd/ *n* (*fml*) praise or approval

accommodate /ə'kɒmədeɪt/ *v* [T] **1** provide sb with a place to live **2** do a favour to sb; oblige sb ► **accommodating** *adj* helpful ► **accommodation** /əˌkɒmə'deɪʃn/ *n* [U] room(s), esp for living in

accompaniment /ə'kʌmpəni-mənt/ *n* **1** [C,U] music played to support a singer or another instrument **2** [C] something that you eat, drink or use together with sth else

accompanist /ə'kʌmpənɪst/ *n* person who plays music to support a singer or another instrument

accompany /ə'kʌmpəni/ *v* (*pt, pp* -**ied**) [T] **1** go somewhere with sb **2** happen or appear with sth else: *wind accompanied by rain* **3** play music to support a singer or another instrument

accomplice /ə'kʌmplɪs/ *n* person who helps another do sth wrong

accomplish /ə'kʌmplɪʃ/ *v* [T] succeed in doing sth ► **accomplished** *adj* skilled ► **accomplishment** *n* **1** [C] thing done or achieved after a lot of hard work **2** [C,U] skill or

special ability **3** [U] successful completing of sth

accord /ə'kɔːd/ *n* [IDM] **in accord (with sth/sb)** (*fml*) in agreement with sth/sb **of your own accord** without being asked or forced ● **accord** *v* [I] ~(**with**) (*fml*) agree with or match sth

accordance /ə'kɔːdns/ *n* [IDM] **in accordance with sth** in agreement with sth

accordingly /ə'kɔːdɪŋli/ *adv* because of sth just mentioned; for that reason

according to /ə'kɔːdɪŋ tə; *before vowels* tu/ *prep* **1** as stated by sb; as shown in sth: *A~ to the report, we don't take enough exercise.* **2** following or agreeing with sth: *act ~ to your principles*

accordion /ə'kɔːdiən/ *n* musical instrument with bellows and a keyboard

accost /ə'kɒst/ *v* [T] go up to and speak to sb, esp a stranger

account /ə'kaʊnt/ *n* **1** [C] arrangement that sb has with a bank to keep money there: *open a bank ~* **2** [usu pl] written record of money that is owed to a business and of money that has been paid by it: *the ~s department* **3** [C] written or spoken description of sth that has happened: *I gave the police a full ~ of the incident.* **4** [C] regular customer: *to lose an important ~* **5** [C] arrangement that sb has with a company that allows them to use the Internet, send emails, etc [IDM] **of no/little account** (*fml*) not important **on account of sth** because of sth **on no account** not for any reason **take account of sth / take sth into account** consider particular facts, etc when making a decision about sth ● **account** *v* [PV] **account for sth 1** be an explanation of sth **2** give an explanation of sth: *How do you ~ for the play's success?* **3** be a particular amount or part of sth ► **accountable** *adj* responsible

accountant /ə'kaʊntənt/ *n* person whose job is to keep or check financial accounts ► **accountancy** /-tənsi/ *n* [U] profession of an accountant

accredited /ə'kredɪtd/ *adj* officially recognized: *our ~ representative* ► **accreditation** /-'teɪʃn/ *n* [U] official approval given when sb/sth achieves a certain standard

accrue /ə'kruː/ *v* [I] (*fml*) come as an (esp financial) increase

accumulate /ə'kjuːmjələt/ *v* [I, T] become or make sth greater in quantity over a period of time ► **accumulation** /-'leɪʃn/ *n* [U,C]

accurate /'ækjərət/ *adj* exact;

correct ▶ **accuracy** /-rəsi/ n [U] ▶ **accurately** adv

accusation /ˌækjuˈzeɪʃn/ n statement accusing sb of having done wrong

accuse /əˈkjuːz/ v [T] ~(of) say that sb has done wrong: ~ *sb of theft* ▶ **the accused** n (pl **the accused**) person on trial for committing a crime ▶ **accuser** n

accustom /əˈkʌstəm/ v [T] ~to make yourself/sb get used to sth ▶ **accustomed** adj usual

ace /eɪs/ n 1 playing card with a large single symbol on it 2 (infml) person who is extremely skilled: an ~ *footballer* 3 (in tennis) serve that is so good that your opponent cannot reach the ball

ache /eɪk/ v [I] have a continuous dull ache: My head ~s. 2 (written) want sth very much ● **ache** n (often in compounds) continuous dull pain in a part of the body: a tummy ~

achieve /əˈtʃiːv/ v [T] gain or reach sth by effort; get sth done: ~ *your aim* ▶ **achievement** n [C,U]

Achilles heel /əˌkɪliːz ˈhiːl/ n [sing] weak point or fault in sb's character, which can be attacked by other people ■ **A,chilles 'tendon** n tendon joining the muscles at the back of the leg to the heel

acid /ˈæsɪd/ n [U,C] (chem) substance that contains hydrogen and has a pH of less than seven ● **acid** adj 1 sour 2 (of remarks) very unkind ■ **acid 'rain** n [U] rain containing harmful chemicals that kills trees, crops, etc ■ **acid 'test** n [sing] way of deciding whether sth is successful or true

acknowledge /əkˈnɒlɪdʒ/ v [T] 1 accept that sth is true 2 accept that sb/sth has a particular authority or status 3 tell sb that you have received sth (eg a letter) 4 show that you have noticed sth to sb 5 publicly express thanks for help you have been given ▶ **acknowledgement** (also **acknowledgment**) n [U,C]

acne /ˈækni/ n [U] spots on the face and neck

acorn /ˈeɪkɔːn/ n fruit of the oak tree

acoustic /əˈkuːstɪk/ adj of sound ▶ **acoustics** n [pl] qualities that make a room good or bad for hearing music or speeches in 2 [U] study of sound

acquaint /əˈkweɪnt/ v [T] ~with make sb/yourself familiar with sth ▶ **acquaintance** n 1 [C] person that you know slightly 2 [U,C] (with) (esp slight) knowledge of sb/sth **make sb's acquaintance** (fml) meet sb for the first time ▶ **acquainted** adj ~(with) knowing sb personally

acquiesce /ˌækwiˈes/ v [I] ~(in) (fml) accept sth without protest ▶ **acquiescence** n [U]

acquire /əˈkwaɪə(r)/ v [T] gain sth by your own ability, efforts, etc; obtain sth ▶ **acquisition** /ˌækwɪˈzɪʃn/ n 1 [U] act of getting sth, especially knowledge, a skill, etc 2 [C] something that sb buys to add to what they already own ▶ **acquisitive** /əˈkwɪzətɪv/ adj (fml, disapprov) wanting very much to get or keep new possessions

acquit /əˈkwɪt/ v (-tt-) 1 [T] declare that sb is not guilty 2 ~ yourself behave in the way that is stated ▶ **acquittal** n [C,U]

acre /ˈeɪkə(r)/ n measure of land: 4840 square yards (about 4050 square metres) ▶ **acreage** /ˈeɪkərɪdʒ/ n [U,C] area measured in acres

acrid /ˈækrɪd/ adj (esp of smell or taste) sharp or bitter

acrimonious /ˌækrɪˈməʊniəs/ adj (fml) (esp of quarrels) bitter ▶ **acrimony** /ˈækrɪməni/ n [U]

acrobat /ˈækrəbæt/ n person who can do skilful physical acts, eg walking on a rope, esp at a circus ▶ **acrobatic** /-ˈbætɪk/ adj ▶ **acrobatics** n [pl]

acronym /ˈækrənɪm/ n word formed from the first letters of a name, eg NATO

across /əˈkrɒs/ adv, prep 1 from one side to the other side: swim ~ *the lake* 2 on the other side of sth: My house is just ~ *the street.*

acrylic /əˈkrɪlɪk/ adj made of a substance or fabric produced by chemical processes from a type of acid: ~ *fibres/paints*

act¹ /ækt/ v 1 [I] do sth; behave: We must ~ *quickly.* 2 [I, T] perform a part in a play or film 3 ~**as/like sth** perform a particular role or function ▶ **acting** n [U] skill or work of performing in plays, etc ▶ **acting** adj doing the work of another person for a short time: the ~*ing manager*

act² /ækt/ n 1 particular thing that sb does: an ~ *of kindness* 2 law made by a government: an A~ *of Parliament* 3 way of behaving that is not sincere: to put on an ~ 4 main division of a play 5 one of a series of short performances: a circus ~ [IDM] **act of God** (law) event caused by natural forces beyond human control (eg a storm) **in the act (of doing sth)** while you are doing sth

action /ˈækʃn/ n 1 [U] process of doing sth: take ~ *to stop the rise in crime* 2 [C] something sb does 3 [C, U] legal process to stop sb from doing sth, to make them pay for a mistake, etc: bring a libel ~ *against him* 4 [U] fighting in war: He was killed in

~. 5 [U] events in a story, play, etc [IDM] **actions speak louder than words** what a person actually does means more than what they say they will do **into action** into operation **out of action** no longer working

activate /ˈæktɪveɪt/ v [T] start sth working

active /ˈæktɪv/ adj 1 doing things; busy or energetic 2 (gram) of the verb form used when the subject of a sentence does the action, as in 'She *drove* the car.' ▶ **the active** (also '**active voice**') n [sing] active(2) form of a verb ▶ **actively** adv

activist /ˈæktɪvɪst/ n person who works to achieve political or social change

activity /ækˈtɪvəti/ n (pl -**ies**) 1 [U] situation in which sth is happening or a lot of things are being done: *a lot of ~ in the street* 2 [C, usu pl] something done for interest or pleasure: *leisure/social activities*

actor /ˈæktə(r)/ n (fem **actress** /ˈæktrəs/) person who acts in plays, films, etc

actual /ˈæktʃuəl/ adj existing in fact; real ▶ **actually** adv 1 really; in fact: *what ~ly happened* 2 used for showing surprise: *He ~ly expected me to pay!*

acumen /ˈækjəmən/ n [U] (fml) ability to understand and judge things clearly

acupuncture /ˈækjupʌŋktʃə(r)/ n [U] treatment of illness by sticking small needles into the body

acute /əˈkjuːt/ adj 1 very great; severe: *suffer ~ hardship* 2 very sensitive: *an ~ sense of hearing* ■ a,cute '**accent** n mark written over a letter, as over the *e* in *resumé* ■ a,cute '**angle** n angle of less than 90° ▶ **acutely** adv ▶ **acuteness** n [U]

AD /ˌeɪ ˈdiː/ abbr (in the Christian calendar) since the birth of Jesus Christ

ad /æd/ n (infml) = ADVERTISEMENT

adamant /ˈædəmənt/ adj (fml) refusing to change your opinion

Adam's apple /ˌædəmz ˈæpl/ n lump at the front of the throat

adapt /əˈdæpt/ v 1 [T] make sth suitable for a new use 2 [I, T] change your behaviour to deal with a new situation ▶ **adaptable** adj able to change ▶ **adaptation** /-ˈteɪʃn/ n [C, U] result or process of adapting: *an ~ation of the play for television* ▶ **adaptor** n kind of electrical plug that allows several plugs to be connected to one socket

add /æd/ v [T] 1 put sth together with sth else: *~ the flour to the milk* 2 put numbers together to get a total 3 say sth more [PV] **add up** (infml)

seem reasonable; make sense **add up to** sth result in sth; show sth

adder /ˈædə(r)/ n small poisonous snake

addict /ˈædɪkt/ n 1 person who cannot stop taking drugs, alcohol, etc 2 person strongly interested in sth: *a TV ~* ▶ **addicted** /əˈdɪktɪd/ adj ~(**to**) unable to stop taking or using sth ▶ **addiction** /əˈdɪkʃn/ n [U,C] ▶ **addictive** /əˈdɪktɪv/ adj

addition /əˈdɪʃn/ n 1 [U] process of adding numbers together to find their total 2 [C] thing that is added to sth else [IDM] **in addition (to sb/sth)** as an extra person, thing, etc ▶ **additional** /-ʃənl/ adj extra ▶ **additionally** adv

additive /ˈædətɪv/ n substance added to sth, esp food

address /əˈdres/ n 1 details of where sb lives or works and where letters, etc can be sent: *What's your name and ~?* ◇ *an email ~* 2 formal speech ● **address** v [T] 1 write a name and address on sth 2 give a speech to sb

adept /əˈdept/ adj ~(**at/in**) skilled at (doing) sth

adequate /ˈædɪkwət/ adj enough; satisfactory ▶ **adequately** adv

adhere /ədˈhɪə(r)/ v [I] ~(**to**) stick firmly to sth [PV] **adhere to sth** (fml) act according to a law, rule, etc; follow a set of beliefs ▶ **adherent** /ədˈhɪərənt/ n supporter of a person, group, etc ▶ **adherence** /-rəns/ n [U]

adhesive /ədˈhiːsɪv/ adj able to stick to sth ▶ **adhesion** /ədˈhiːʒn/ n [U] ▶ **adhesive** n [C, U] substance, eg glue, that makes things stick together

ad hoc /ˌæd ˈhɒk/ adj, adv made or arranged for a particular purpose; not planned

adjacent /əˈdʒeɪsnt/ adj ~(**to**) next to sth

adjective /ˈædʒɪktɪv/ n (gram) word that describes a noun, eg *green* in *green grass* ▶ **adjectival** /ˌædʒekˈtaɪvl/ adj

adjoin /əˈdʒɔɪn/ v [I] (fml) be next to: *~ing rooms*

adjourn /əˈdʒɜːn/ v [I, T] stop a meeting for a time, esp in a court of law ▶ **adjournment** n [C,U]

adjudicate /əˈdʒuːdɪkeɪt/ v [I, T] (fml) make an official decision or judgement on sth ▶ **adjudication** /-ˈkeɪʃn/ n [U] ▶ **adjudicator** n

adjunct /ˈædʒʌŋkt/ n 1 (gram) adverb or phrase that adds meaning to the verb, eg *yesterday* in *She left home yesterday.* 2 (fml) thing that is attached to sth larger or more important

adjust /əˈdʒʌst/ v **1** [T] change or correct sth to make it right **2** [I, T] ~ **(to)** get used to a new situation ▸ **adjustable** adj ▸ **adjustment** n [C,U]

ad lib /ˌæd ˈlɪb/ adj, adv spoken, performed, etc without preparation ● **ad lib** v (**-bb-**) [I] speak, perform, etc without preparation

administer /ədˈmɪnɪstə(r)/ v [T] **1** control or manage sth: ~ a hospital **2** (fml) give sth: ~ a drug ▸ **administration** /-ˈstreɪʃn/ n **1** [U] activities done in order to plan, organize and run a business, school, etc **2** [U] process of organizing the way that sth is done **3** (often **Administration**) [C] the government of a country, esp the US: the Bush A~ ▸ **administrative** /ədˈmɪnɪstrətɪv/ adj ▸ **administrator** /ədˈmɪnɪstreɪtə(r)/ n

admirable /ˈædmərəbl/ adj deserving admiration; excellent ▸ **admirably** adv

admiral /ˈædmərəl/ n officer of very high rank in the navy

admire /ədˈmaɪə(r)/ v [T] have a good opinion of sb/sth; look at sb/sth with pleasure ▸ **admiration** /ˌædməˈreɪʃn/ n [U] feeling of respect, approval or pleasure ▸ **admirer** n ▸ **admiring** adj

admissible /ədˈmɪsəbl/ adj **1** (law) that can be allowed: ~ evidence **2** (fml) acceptable

admission /ədˈmɪʃn/ n **1** [U] entering or being allowed to enter a building, school, etc **2** [U] money charged for being admitted to a public place **3** [C] statement that sth is true; confession

admit /ədˈmɪt/ v (**-tt-**) [T] **1** allow sb/sth to enter; let sb/sth in **2** agree that sth bad is true: I ~ that I was wrong. ▸ **admittance** n [U] right to enter ▸ **admittedly** adv used when you are accepting that sth is true

admonish /ədˈmɒnɪʃ/ v [T] (fml) tell sb firmly that they have done sth wrong

ad nauseam /ˌæd ˈnɔːziæm/ adv so often as to become annoying: She played the same CDs ~.

ado /əˈduː/ n [U] trouble; delay: without further ~

adolescent /ˌædəˈlesnt/ adj, n (of a) young person who is developing from a child into an adult ▸ **adolescence** /-ˈlesns/ n [U]

adopt /əˈdɒpt/ v [T] **1** take sb else's child into your family, making them legally your son or daughter **2** take and use a method, way of life, etc ▸ **adoption** /əˈdɒpʃn/ n [U,C] ▸ **adoptive** adj related by adoption

adore /əˈdɔː(r)/ v [T] **1** love sb very much **2** (infml) like sth very much ▸ **adorable** adj easy to feel love for:

an adorable child ▸ **adoration** /ˌædəˈreɪʃn/ n [U]

adorn /əˈdɔːn/ v [T] decorate sth/sb ▸ **adornment** n [C,U]

adrenalin /əˈdrenəlɪn/ n [U] substance produced in the body by anger, fear, etc and which makes the heart beat faster

adrift /əˈdrɪft/ adj (of boats) floating freely; not fastened

adulation /ˌædjuˈleɪʃn/ n [U] (fml) too much praise or admiration

adult /ˈædʌlt; also əˈdʌlt/ n, adj (person or animal) grown to full size or strength ▸ **adulthood** n [U] state of being an adult

adulterate /əˈdʌltəreɪt/ v [T] make food or drink less pure by adding another substance

adultery /əˈdʌltəri/ n [U] sex between a married person and sb who is not their husband or wife ▸ **adulterer** n person who commits adultery ▸ **-teress** /-tərəs/ adj

advance /ədˈvɑːns/ n **1** [C,U] forward movement; progress **2** [C, usu sing] money paid for work before it has been done **3** (**advances**) [pl] attempts to start a sexual relationship with sb [IDM] **in advance (of sth)** before the time that is expected ● **advance** adj done or given before sth: an ~ warning ● **advance** v **1** [I] move forward **2** [T] give sb money before the time it would usually be paid ▸ **advanced** adj **1** having the most modern and recently developed ideas, etc: ~d technology **2** at a high or difficult level: ~d studies [IDM] **of advanced years** very old ▸ **advancement** n [U] act of advancing; progress or promotion

advantage /ədˈvɑːntɪdʒ/ n [C,U] **1** something special that puts you in a better or more favourable position than other people **2** quality that makes sth better or more useful [IDM] **take advantage of sth/sb 1** make good use of sth (eg an opportunity) **2** make use of sb/sth in a way that is unfair or dishonest to get what you want ▸ **advantageous** /ˌædvənˈteɪdʒəs/ adj

advent /ˈædvent/ n (**the advent**) [sing] ~**of** the coming of an important event

adventure /ədˈventʃə(r)/ n **1** [C] exciting or dangerous journey or experience **2** [U] excitement; risk ▸ **adventurer** n person who likes adventures ▸ **adventurous** adj **1** fond of adventures **2** exciting

adverb /ˈædvɜːb/ n (gram) word that adds information to a verb, adjective, phrase, or another adverb, eg quickly in run quickly ▸ **adverbial** /ˌædˈvɜːbiəl/ adj, n

adversary /ˈædvəsəri/ n (pl -ies) (fml) enemy; opponent

adverse /ˈædvɜːs/ adj negative and unpleasant: ~ weather conditions ▸ **adversely** adv ▸ **adversity** /ədˈvɜːsəti/ n [C,U] (pl -ies) trouble

advert /ˈædvɜːt/ n (infml) = ADVERTISEMENT

advertise /ˈædvətaɪz/ v [T] make sth, esp sth for sale, known to people by notices in newspapers, etc ▸ **advertisement** /ədˈvɜːtɪsmənt/ n notice in a newspaper, on television, etc, telling people about a product, job or service ▸ **advertiser** n ▸ **advertising** n [U]

advice /ədˈvaɪs/ n [U] opinion given to sb about what they should do

advise /ədˈvaɪz/ v [T] **1** give advice to sb **2** ~(of) (business) inform sb about sth: ~ sb of a delivery date ▸ **advisable** adj sensible or wise ▸ **adviser** (esp US advisor) n ▸ **advisory** adj giving advice

advocate /ˈædvəkət/ n person who speaks in favour of sb (esp in a law court) or an idea ● **advocate** /ˈædvəkeɪt/ v [T] support sth publicly

aerial /ˈeəriəl/ adj in, through or from the air: an ~ photograph ● **aerial** n wire or rod that receives television or radio signals

aerobics /eəˈrəʊbɪks/ n [U] physical exercise done to strengthen the heart and lungs

aerodynamics /ˌeərəʊdaɪˈnæmɪks/ n [U] science which deals with the forces that act on objects moving through the air ▸ **aerodynamic** adj

aeronautics /ˌeərəˈnɔːtɪks/ n [U] scientific study or practice of flying aircraft

aeroplane /ˈeərəpleɪn/ n flying vehicle with wings and one or more engines

aerosol /ˈeərəsɒl/ n small container from which a liquid is forced out as a fine spray

aerospace /ˈeərəʊspeɪs/ n [U] industry of building aircraft and equipment to be sent into space

aesthetic /iːsˈθetɪk/ adj concerned with (the enjoyment of) beauty ▸ **aesthetically** /-kli/ adv ▸ **aesthetics** n [U] branch of philosophy dealing with beauty

afar /əˈfɑː(r)/ adv [IDM] **from afar** from a long distance away

affable /ˈæfəbl/ adj friendly and easy to talk to ▸ **affably** adv

private business and financial matters b [sing] something that sb is responsible for: How I spend my money is my ~.

affect /əˈfekt/ v [T] have an influence on sb/sth: The cold climate ~ed her health. ▸ **affectation** /ˌæfekˈteɪʃn/ n [C,U] behaviour or an action that is not natural or sincere ▸ **affected** adj not natural; artificial

affection /əˈfekʃn/ n [U] feeling of love; fondness ▸ **affectionate** /-ʃənət/ adj ▸ **affectionately** adv

affidavit /ˌæfəˈdeɪvɪt/ n (law) sworn written statement used as evidence

affiliate /əˈfɪliət/ v [I, T] (esp of an organization) join a larger organization ▸ **affiliation** /-ˈeɪʃn/ n [C,U]

affinity /əˈfɪnəti/ n [C,U] (pl -ies) **1** close relationship **2** strong liking: She feels a strong ~ for him.

affirm /əˈfɜːm/ v [T] (fml) state or declare that sth is true ▸ **affirmation** /ˌæfəˈmeɪʃn/ n [C,U] ▸ **affirmative** n, adj (word, reply, etc) meaning 'yes' or showing agreement: I answered in the ~ (= I said yes).

affix /əˈfɪks/ v [T] (fml) stick or attach sth to sth else ● **affix** /ˈæfɪks/ n (gram) prefix or suffix, eg un- or -ly

afflict /əˈflɪkt/ v [T] cause pain or trouble to sb/sth ▸ **affliction** /-ʃn/ n [C,U] (fml) (cause of) suffering

affluent /ˈæfluənt/ adj rich; wealthy ▸ **affluence** /-ns/ n [U]

afford /əˈfɔːd/ v [T] **1** have enough money or time for sth **2** be able to do sth without risk to yourself: We can't ~ to lose such experienced workers.

affront /əˈfrʌnt/ v [T] insult or offend sb ● **affront** n insult

afield /əˈfiːld/ adv [IDM] **far/farther/further afield** far away from home

afloat /əˈfləʊt/ adj **1** floating on water **2** (of a business, etc) able to pay its debts

afoot /əˈfʊt/ adj being planned; happening

aforementioned /əˌfɔːˈmenʃənd/ (also **aforesaid** /əˈfɔːsed/) adj (fml) mentioned earlier

afraid /əˈfreɪd/ adj ~(of/to) frightened of sb/sth or that sth bad will happen: ~ of spiders ◊ ~ to go out in the dark [IDM] **I'm afraid** (spoken) I'm sorry: I'm ~ we'll arrive late.

afresh /əˈfreʃ/ adv (fml) again

after /ˈɑːftə(r)/ prep **1** later than sth: leave ~ lunch **2** following sth/sb: Year ~ year he would visit her. **3** because of sth: A~ what he said, I never want to see him again. **4** searching for sth or chasing sth: The police are ~ him. **5** in spite of sth: A~ all I've done for you, you're leaving me! **6** in the style of sb/sth; following the example of sb/sth: *We named the baby ~ my mother.* [IDM] **after all** in spite of what has been said or expected ● **after** *adv, conj* later in time (than sth) ■ **'after-effect** *n* [usu pl] (esp unpleasant) effect that is experienced later ■ **'afterthought** *n* idea that comes later

aftermath /'ɑːftəmæθ; -mɑːθ/ *n* result of a war or other bad event

afternoon /ˌɑːftə'nuːn/ *n* [U,C] part of the day from 12 midday until about 6 o'clock

afterwards /'ɑːftəwədz/ (*US also* **afterward**) *adv* at a later time

again /ə'gen; ə'gem/ *adv* **1** once more; another time: *try ~ later* ◇ *I've told you ~ and ~* (= many times) *not to do that.* **2** in return to the original place or condition: *I was glad to be home ~.* **3** in addition: *I'd like the same ~* (= the same amount or thing as before).

against /ə'genst; ə'gemst/ *prep* **1** in contact with: *The ladder was leaning ~ the wall.* **2** opposing: *Are you for or ~ the death penalty?* ◇ *swim ~ the current* ◇ *the law* **3** in contrast to: *The trees were black ~ the sky.* **4** in order to prevent sth from happening or causing harm: *an injection ~ measles*

age¹ /eɪdʒ/ *n* [C,U] length of time sb has lived or sth has existed **2** [U] state of being old: *Wisdom comes with ~.* **3** [C] period of history: *the Elizabethan ~* (= the time of Queen Elizabeth I) **4** (ages) [pl] (*infml*) very long time: *I waited for ~s.* [IDM] **come of age** become an adult in law **under age** not legally old enough ■ **'age group** *n* people of a similar age ▸ **ageism** /'eɪdʒɪzəm/ *n* [U] unfair treatment of people because they are considered too old ▸ **ageist** *adj* ■ **'age limit** *n* oldest or youngest age at which you are allowed to do sth ■ **,age-'old** *adj* having existed for a very long time

age² *v* (*pres pt* **ageing** *or* **aging** **aged** /eɪdʒd/) [I, T] (cause sb to) become old ▸ **aged** *adj* **1** /eɪdʒd/ of the age of: *a boy ~d ten* **2** /'eɪdʒɪd/ very old ▸ **the aged** /'eɪdʒɪd/ *n* [pl] very old people

agency /'eɪdʒənsi/ *n* (*pl* **-ies**) business or organization that provides a particular service esp on behalf of other businesses or organizations: *a travel ~*

agenda /ə'dʒendə/ *n* list of things to be discussed at a meeting

agent /'eɪdʒənt/ *n* **1** person who arranges business for other people: *an estate ~* **2** person who finds work for an actor, a musician, etc **3** person or thing that has an important effect on a situation

aggravate /'ægrəveɪt/ *v* [T] **1** make sth worse **2** (*infml*) annoy sb ▸ **aggravation** /ˌægrə'veɪʃn/ *n* [C,U]

aggregate /'ægrɪgət/ *n* total amount

aggression /ə'greʃn/ *n* [U] **1** angry feelings **2** violent attack or threats by one country against another ▸ **aggressor** /ə'gresə(r)/ *n* person or country that attacks first

aggressive /ə'gresɪv/ *adj* **1** having angry feelings **2** behaving in a way that is forceful and determined in order to succeed: *an ~ salesman* ▸ **aggressively** *adv* ▸ **aggressiveness** *n* [U]

aggrieved /ə'griːvd/ *adj* (*written*) feeling angry and bitter, esp because of unfair treatment

aghast /ə'ɡɑːst/ *adj* filled with horror or shock

agile /'ædʒaɪl/ *adj* able to move quickly and easily ▸ **agility** /ə'dʒɪləti/ *n* [U]

aging → AGE²

agitate /'ædʒɪteɪt/ *v* **1** [T] make sb anxious or nervous **2** [I] ~ **for/against** argue publicly in favour of/against sth **3** [T] (*tech*) shake a liquid strongly ▸ **agitation** /ˌædʒɪ'teɪʃn/ *n* [U] ▸ **agitator** *n* person who tries to persuade people to take part in political protest

AGM /ˌeɪ dʒiː 'em/ *abbr* (*esp GB*) annual general meeting; meeting held once a year by a company, club, etc

agnostic /æg'nɒstɪk/ *n, adj* (person who is) not sure whether God exists or not

ago /ə'ɡəʊ/ *adv* before now: *The train left five minutes ~.*

agog /ə'ɡɒg/ *adj* excited and interested to find out sth

agonize (*also* **-ise**) /'ægənaɪz/ *v* [I] ~ **(over/about)** spend a long time thinking and worrying about sth ▸ **agonized** (*also* **-ised**) *adj* expressing great pain ▸ **agonizing** (*also* **-ising**) *adj* causing great pain

agony /'ægəni/ *n* [U,C] (*pl* **-ies**) great pain ■ **'agony aunt** *n* (*GB*) person who writes in a newspaper, etc giving advice in reply to people's letters about their personal problems

agoraphobia /ˌægərə'fəʊbiə/ *n* [U] fear of being in public places where there are a lot of people ▸ **agoraphobic** *adj*

agrarian /ə'greəriən/ *adj* of land, esp farmland

agree /ə'griː/ *v* **1** [I] ~ **(with)** have the same opinion as sb: *I ~ with you that money is the problem.* **2** [I] ~ **to** be willing to do sth; say yes to sth: *My boss ~d to let me go home early.* **3** [I, T] ~ **(on)** decide sth **4** [I, T] ~

(with) approve of or accept sth **5** [I] be the same as sth; match: *The two descriptions do not ~.* **6** [I] ~(with) (*gram*) (of verbs, etc) have the same number, person, etc as another word in the same sentence [IDM] **be agreed** have the same opinion about sth [PV] **be agreed with sb** (of food) make you feel ill ▶ **agreeable** *adj* **1** pleasant **2** willing ▶ **agreeably** *adv* **agreement** *n* **1** [C] arrangement, promise or contract made with sb **2** [U] state of sharing the same opinion

agriculture /ˈægrɪkʌltʃə(r)/ *n* [U] science or practice of farming ▶ **agricultural** /ˌægrɪˈkʌltʃərəl/ *adj*

aground /əˈɡraʊnd/ *adv, adj* (of ships) touching the ground in shallow water

ahead /əˈhed/ *adv* further forward in space or time: *go/plan ~* ■ a**head of** *prep* **1** further forward in space or time than **2** further advanced than: *be years ~ of your rivals*

aid /eɪd/ *n* **1** [U] food, money, etc sent to a country in need **2** [U] help: *with the ~ of a friend* **3** [C] thing or person that helps: *visual ~s* [IDM] **what is ... in aid of?** (*GB, spoken*) used to ask why sth is happening ● **aid** *v* [T] (*fml*) help sb/sth [IDM] **aid and abet** (*law*) help or encourage sb to do wrong

aide /eɪd/ *n* assistant to sb with an important government job: *presidential ~s*

Aids (also **AIDS**) /eɪdz/ *abbr* Acquired Immune Deficiency Syndrome; serious illness which destroys the body's ability to fight infection

ailing /ˈeɪlɪŋ/ *adj* (*fml*) ill and not improving ▶ **ailment** /ˈeɪlmənt/ *n* illness, esp a slight one

aim /eɪm/ *v* **1** [I] ~(at/for) direct your efforts at sth; plan to achieve: *~ at increasing exports* **2** [I, T] ~(at) point a weapon or object towards sth **3** [T] direct a comment, etc at sb ● **aim** *n* **1** [C] purpose; intention: *Her ~ is to be famous.* **2** [U] action of pointing a weapon at sb/sth ▶ **aimless** *adj* having no purpose ▶ **aimlessly** *adv*

ain't /eɪnt/ (used in non-standard spoken English) *short for* AM NOT, IS NOT, ARE NOT, HAS NOT, HAVE NOT

air /eə(r)/ *n* **1** [U] mixture of gases that we breathe **2** [U] earth's atmosphere: *travel by ~* (= in an aircraft) **3** [C] impression or appearance: *an ~ of importance* **4** (**airs**) [pl] (*disapprov*) way of behaving that shows that sb thinks that they are more important, educated, etc than they really are: *I hate the way she puts on ~s.* [IDM] **in the air** felt by a number of people to exist or be

happening **on/off** (the) **air** broadcasting/not broadcasting on television or the radio **up in the air** not yet decided ■ **'air bag** *n* safety device in a car that fills with air if there is an accident, to protect the people in the car ■ **'airborne** *adj* **1** (of a plane or passengers) in the air **2** carried through the air ■ **'air conditioning** *n* [U] system of machines that supply a room or building with cool dry air ▶ **'air-conditioned** *adj* ■ **'aircraft** *n* (*pl* **aircraft**) any vehicle that can fly and carry goods or passengers ■ **'aircraft carrier** *n* large ship that carries aircraft which use it as a base to land on and take off from ■ **'airfield** *n* area of open ground where aircraft can take off and land ■ **'air force** *n* part of a country's military forces that is organized for fighting in the air ■ **'air hostess** *n* woman whose job is to look after the passengers in an aircraft ■ **'airlift** *n* transport of people or supplies by air ▶ **airlift** *v* [T] ■ **'airline** *n* company that carries passengers or goods by plane ■ **'airliner** *n* large passenger plane ■ **'airmail** *n* [U] system of sending letters, etc by air ■ **'airplane** *n* (US) = AEROPLANE ■ **'airport** *n* place where aircraft land and take off, with buildings for passengers to wait in, etc ■ **'air raid** *n* attack by aircraft ■ **'airship** *n* large aircraft without wings, filled with a gas which is lighter than air, and driven by engines ■ **'airspace** *n* [U] part of the earth's atmosphere above a country, considered to belong to that country ■ **'airstrip** *n* piece of land cleared for aircraft to take off and land ■ **'air terminal** *n* building at an airport that provides services for passengers travelling by plane ■ **'airtight** *adj* not allowing air to get in or out ■ **'air-to-'air** *adj* (fired) from one aircraft to another while flying ■ **'air traffic con'troller** *n* person whose job is to give radio instructions to pilots about taking off and landing ■ **'airway** *n* passage from the nose and throat to the lungs ■ **'airworthy** *adj* (of an aircraft) safe to fly

air *v* **1** [I, T] put clothes, etc in a warm place to dry completely **2** [T] let fresh air into a room **3** [T] express your opinions publicly ▶ **airing** *n* [sing]: *give the blankets a good ~ing* ■ **'airing cupboard** *n* warm cupboard for drying clean sheets, towels, etc

airless /ˈeələs/ *adj* not having enough fresh air

airy /ˈeəri/ *adj* (**-ier, -iest**) **1** with plenty of fresh air because there is a lot of space **2** not serious ▶ **airily** *adv*

aisle /aɪl/ n passage between rows of seats in a theatre, church, plane, etc or between shelves in a supermarket

ajar /əˈdʒɑː(r)/ adj (of a door) slightly open

akin /əˈkɪn/ adj ~to (fml) similar to

à la carte /ˌɑː lɑː ˈkɑːt/ adj (of a restaurant meal) ordered as separate items from the menu and not as a fixed price for the complete meal

alacrity /əˈlækrəti/ n [U] (fml) great willingness or enthusiasm

alarm /əˈlɑːm/ n 1 [U] sudden feeling of fear, caused by danger 2 [C] (device that gives a) warning sound: a fire ~ ◇ sound/raise the ~ ● **alarm** v [T] make sb anxious or afraid ■ a'larm clock n clock that can be set to make a noise at a particular time to wake you up ► **alarming** adj causing fear

albatross /ˈælbətrɒs/ n large white seabird

albeit /ˌɔːlˈbiːɪt/ conj (fml) although: a useful, ~ brief, report

albino /ælˈbiːnəʊ/ n (pl ~s) person or animal with white skin and hair and pink eyes

album /ˈælbəm/ n 1 book in which a collection of photographs, stamps, etc can be kept 2 long-playing record

alcohol /ˈælkəhɒl/ n [U] (pure colourless liquid in) drinks such as beer, wine and whisky ► **alcoholic** /ˌælkəˈhɒlɪk/ adj of or containing alcohol ► **alcoholic** n person who drinks too much alcohol and cannot stop drinking, so it has become an illness ► **alcoholism** /ˈælkəhɒlɪzəm/ n [U] (disease caused by) regular heavy drinking of alcohol

alcove /ˈælkəʊv/ n small area in a room formed by part of the wall being set back

ale /eɪl/ n [U,C] kind of strong beer

alert /əˈlɜːt/ adj fully awake and ready to act ● **alert** n 1 [sing, U] situation in which people are ready to deal with possible danger: Be on the ~ for suspicious packages. 2 [C] warning of danger ● **alert** v [T] ~ to warn sb of danger

algae /ˈældʒiː; ˈælgiː/ n [U] mass of very simple plants that are mainly found in water

algebra /ˈældʒɪbrə/ n [U] branch of mathematics in which letters represent quantities

algorithm /ˈælgərɪðəm/ n (computing) process or set of rules that must be followed when solving a particular problem

alias /ˈeɪliəs/ n false name, used esp by a criminal ● **alias** adv also

(falsely) called: Joe Sykes, ~ John Smith

alibi /ˈæləbaɪ/ n evidence that proves that sb was somewhere else when a crime was committed

alien /ˈeɪliən/ n 1 person who is not a citizen of the country in which they live or work 2 creature from another world ● **alien** adj 1 strange and frightening 2 foreign

alienate /ˈeɪliəneɪt/ v [T] cause sb to become unfriendly ► **alienation** /ˌeɪliəˈneɪʃn/ n [U]

alight /əˈlaɪt/ adj on fire ● **alight** v [I] (fml) 1 get off a bus, etc 2 (of a bird) come down from the air and settle

align /əˈlaɪn/ v 1 [T] place sth in a straight line 2 ~ yourself with join or publicly support sb/sth ► **alignment** n [C,U]

alike /əˈlaɪk/ adj like one another ● **alike** adv in the same way

alimentary canal /ˌælɪmentəri kəˈnæl/ n passage in the body that carries food from the mouth to the anus

alimony /ˈælɪməni/ n [U] money that sb has to pay regularly to a former wife or husband after they have been divorced

alive /əˈlaɪv/ adj 1 living 2 excited; lively **continuing to exist** [IDM] **alive to sth** aware of sth **alive with sth** full of living things

alkali /ˈælkəlaɪ/ n [C,U] (chem) substance that forms a salt when combined with an acid

all /ɔːl/ det, pron 1 the whole of a thing or of a period of time: We've lost ~ (of) the money. ◇ I've been here ~ day. 2 every one of a group: A - the people have come. ◇ They were ~ broken. 3 the only thing that; everything that: A - I want is some peace! 4 any whatever: beyond ~ doubt [IDM] **all in all** when everything is considered (**not**) **at all** (not) in any way: I don't enjoy it at ~. **in all** as a total **not at all** used as a polite reply when receiving thanks ● **all** adv 1 completely: dressed ~ in black 2 ~**too** used to show that sth is more than you would like: I'm ~ too aware of the problems. 3 (in games) to each side: The score was four ~. [IDM] **all along** (infml) all the time **all the better, harder, etc** so much better, harder, etc: We'll have to work ~ the harder with two people off sick. **all in** very tired **all over** everywhere **all the same → SAME all there** having a healthy mind; thinking clearly **be all for (doing) sth** believe strongly that sth should be done **be all the same to sb** not be important to sb: It's ~ the same to me when you go. **not all that good, well, etc** not very good, etc ■ the ,all-'clear n [sing] signal that the danger has ended ■ ,all-'in adj with everything included: an ~-in price ■ ,all-'out adj using all possible strength: an ~-out attack on the opposition ▶ 'all out adv: The team is going ~ out to win. ■ ,all 'right (also infml alright) adj, adv **1** satisfactory; in a satisfactory manner **2** safe and well **3** that can be allowed: Is it ~ to leave early? ■ ,all 'right exclam used to show that you agree to do what sb has asked ■ ,all-'rounder n person with a wide range of abilities

Allah /ˈælə/ n [sing] name of God among Muslims

allay /əˈleɪ/ v [T] (fml) make fears, doubts, etc less

allegation /ˌæləˈɡeɪʃn/ n statement that is made without proof, accusing sb of doing wrong

allege /əˈledʒ/ v [T] (fml) state sth as a fact but without proof ▶ **alleged** adj ▶ **allegedly** adv

allegiance /əˈliːdʒəns/ n [U] support or loyalty to a ruler, belief, etc

allegory /ˈæləɡəri/ n (pl -ies) story in which people are symbols of qualities such as truth or patience ▶ **allegorical** /ˌæləˈɡɒrɪkl/ adj

allergy /ˈælədʒi/ n (pl -ies) medical condition that causes you to react badly or feel ill when you eat or touch a particular substance ▶ **allergic** /əˈlɜːdʒɪk/ adj

alleviate /əˈliːvieɪt/ v [T] make pain or suffering less ▶ **alleviation** /əˌliːviˈeɪʃn/ n [U]

alley /ˈæli/ n narrow passage between or behind buildings

alliance /əˈlaɪəns/ n relationship or agreement between countries, groups, etc to work together for the same purpose

allied /əˈlaɪd; ˈælaɪd/ adj **1** (often **Allied**) of countries that unite to fight a war together: ~ forces/troops **2** ~ (to/with sth) (written) connected to sth; similar

alligator /ˈælɪɡeɪtə(r)/ n large reptile of the crocodile family that lives in rivers and lakes in America and China

alliteration /əˌlɪtəˈreɪʃn/ n [U] use of the same letter or sound at the beginning of words that are close together, as in 'He built a big boat.'

allocate /ˈæləkeɪt/ v [T] give sth officially for a particular purpose ▶ **allocation** /ˌæləˈkeɪʃn/ n [C,U]

allot /əˈlɒt/ v (-tt-) [T] give sth as a share ▶ **allotment** n **1** (GB) small area of land rented for growing vegetables **2** amount of sth that is given or allowed to have; the process of giving sth to sb

allow /əˈlaʊ/ v [T] **1** give permission to sb to do sth; let sth be done: You're not ~ed to smoke in this room. **2** make sure you have enough of sth for a particular purpose [PV] **allow for sth/sb** include sth/sb when calculating sth: ~ for traffic delays ▶ **allowable** adj ▶ **allowance** n money given to sb regularly [IDM] **make allowances (for sb)** allow sb to behave in a way that you would not usu accept, because of a problem or because of a special reason **make allowance(s) for sth** consider sth when making a decision

alloy /ˈælɔɪ/ n [C,U] mixture of metals

allude /əˈluːd/ v [PV] **allude to sb/sth** mention sth indirectly ▶ **allusion** /əˈluːʒn/ n [C,U] indirect reference to sth/sth

alluring /əˈlʊərɪŋ/ adj attractive; charming

ally /ˈælaɪ/ n (pl -ies) person or country that has agreed to support another ● **ally** /əˈlaɪ/ v (pt, pp -ied) [I, T] ~ (yourself) with sb/sth give your support to another group or country

almanac /ˈɔːlmənæk/ n book published every year with information about the sun, moon, tides, etc

almighty /ɔːlˈmaɪti/ adj (infml) very great ▶ the Almighty n [sing] God

almond /ˈɑːmənd/ n flat pale sweet nut of the almond tree

almost /ˈɔːlməʊst/ adv very nearly: ~ everywhere/impossible

alone /əˈləʊn/ adj, adv **1** without other people: living ~ **2** only: You ~ can help me. [IDM] **go it alone** do sth without help from anyone

along /əˈlɒŋ/ prep **1** from one end to the other end of sth: walk ~ the street **2** close to or on: a path ~ the river ● **along** adv **1** on; forward: Come ~! **2** with others: Can I bring some friends ~? [IDM] **along with sb/sth** together with sb/sth ■ a,long'side adv, prep close to the side of sth

aloof /əˈluːf/ adj not friendly or interested in other people ▶ **aloofness** n [U]

aloud /əˈlaʊd/ adv in a voice loud enough to be heard: to read ~

alphabet /ˈælfəbet/ n set of letters arranged in order, used when writing a language ▶ **alphabetical** /ˌælfəˈbetɪkl/ adj in the order of the alphabet ▶ **alphabetically** /-kli/ adv

already /ɔːlˈredi/ adv **1** before now: I've ~ told them what happened. **2** earlier than expected: You're not leaving us ~, are you?

alright = ALL RIGHT (ALL)

Alsatian /ælˈseɪʃn/ n large dog, often trained to help the police

also /'ɔːlsəʊ/ *adv* in addition; too

altar /'ɔːltə(r)/ *n* a table used in a religious service

alter /'ɔːltə(r)/ *v* [I, T] (cause sb/sth to) become different; change sb/sth ▶ **alteration** /-'reɪʃn/ *n* [C, U]

alternate /ɔːl'tɜːnət/ *adj* 1 (of two things) happening or following one after the other 2 every second: *on ~ days* (= eg on Monday, Wednesday and Friday) ▶ **alternately** *adv*
● **alternate** /'ɔːltəneɪt/ *v* [I, T] ~ (between/with) (cause things or people to) follow one another in a repeated pattern: *The weather will ~ between sunshine and rain.* ■ **alternating 'current** *n* [U] electric current that regularly changes direction ▶ **alternation** /-'neɪʃn/ *n* [C, U]

alternative /ɔːl'tɜːnətɪv/ *adj* 1 that may be used or done instead: *an ~ means of transport* 2 not based on the usual methods or standards: *~ medicine* ● **alternative** *n* thing that you choose to do out of two or more possibilities ▶ **alternatively** *adv*

alternator /'ɔːltəneɪtə(r)/ *n* device, used esp in a car, that produces an alternating current

although /ɔːl'ðəʊ/ *conj* though

altitude /'æltɪtjuːd/ *n* height above sea level

alto /'æltəʊ/ *n* (*pl* ~s) 1 (music for a singer with the) highest adult male or lowest female voice 2 musical instrument with the second highest range of notes in its group

altogether /ˌɔːltə'geðə(r)/ *adv* 1 completely: *It's not ~ surprising that I failed.* 2 including everything

altruism /'æltruːɪzəm/ *n* [U] (*fml*) fact of caring about the needs of other people more than your own ▶ **altruistic** /ˌæltru'ɪstɪk/ *adj*

aluminium /ˌæljə'mɪniəm/ ; ˌælə- / (*US* **aluminum** /ə'luːmɪnəm/) *n* [U] light silver-grey metal used for making pans, etc

always /'ɔːlweɪz/ *adv* 1 at all times: *You should ~ wear a seat belt.* 2 for ever: *I'll ~ love her.*

Alzheimer's disease /'æltshaɪməz dɪziːz/ *n* [U] serious disease, esp affecting older people, that prevents the brain from functioning normally

a.m. /ˌeɪ 'em/ *abbr* between midnight and midday

am /əm; *strong form* æm/ → BE

amalgamate /ə'mælgəmeɪt/ *v* [I, T] (cause two or more things to) join together to form one ▶ **amalgamation** /-'meɪʃn/ *n* [U, C]

amass /ə'mæs/ *v* [T] collect sth, esp in large quantities

amateur /'æmətə(r)/ *n* person who does sth as a hobby, without receiving money for it ▶ **amateurish** *adj* without skill

amaze /ə'meɪz/ *v* [T] surprise sb greatly: *~d at the news* ▶ **amazement** *n* [U] ▶ **amazing** *adj*

ambassador /æm'bæsədə(r)/ *n* official who represents his/her own country in a foreign country

amber /'æmbə(r)/ *n* [U] 1 hard yellowish-brown substance used for making jewels 2 yellowish-brown colour

ambidextrous /ˌæmbi'dekstrəs/ *adj* able to use the right hand and left hand equally well

ambiguous /æm'bɪɡjuəs/ *adj* having more than one meaning ▶ **ambiguity** /ˌæmbɪ'ɡjuːəti/ *n* [U, C] (*pl* -ies)

ambition /æm'bɪʃn/ *n* 1 [U] strong desire to be successful 2 [C] object of such a desire: *achieve your ~* ▶ **ambitious** /æm'bɪʃəs/ *adj*

ambivalent /æm'bɪvələnt/ *adj* (*written*) having or showing both good and bad feelings about sth/sb ▶ **ambivalence** *n* [U, sing]

amble /'æmbl/ *v* [I] walk at a slow relaxed speed

ambulance /'æmbjələns/ *n* vehicle for carrying sick people to hospital

ambush /'æmbʊʃ/ *n* [U, C] (waiting in a hidden position to make a) sudden attack ● **ambush** *v* [T] attack sb/sth from a hidden position

ameba (*US*) = AMOEBA

amen /ɑː'men; eɪ'men/ *exclam* used at the end of a prayer, meaning 'may it be so'

amenable /ə'miːnəbl/ *adj* willing to be guided by sth or to do sth

amend /ə'mend/ *v* [T] change sth slightly in order to correct it ▶ **amendment** *n* [C, U]

amends /ə'mendz/ *n* [pl] [IDM] **make amends (to sb)** (**for (doing) sth**) do sth for sb to show that you are sorry for sth wrong or unfair you have done

amenity /ə'miːnəti/ *n* (*pl* -ies) feature that makes a place pleasant or easy to live in

American /ə'merɪkən/ *n* person from America, esp the USA ▶ **American** *adj* ■ **A‚merican 'football** (*US* **football**) *n* [U] American game of football, similar to rugby

amethyst /'æməθɪst/ *n* purple precious stone

amiable /'eɪmiəbl/ *adj* pleasant and friendly ▶ **amiably** *adv*

amicable /'æmɪkəbl/ *adj* friendly and peaceful ▶ **amicably** *adv*

amid /ə'mɪd/ (*also* **amidst** /ə'mɪdst/) *prep* (*fml*) in the middle of; among

amiss /ə'mɪs/ *adj, adv* wrong; not as

it should be [IDM] **take sth amiss** be offended by sth

ammonia /əˈməʊniə/ n [U] gas with a strong smell, used in making explosives, fertilizers, etc

ammunition /ˌæmjuˈnɪʃn/ n [U] supply of bullets, bombs, etc, fired from weapons

amnesia /æmˈniːziə/ n [U] loss of memory

amnesty /ˈæmnəsti/ n (pl **-ies**) general pardon, esp for political offences

amoeba (US also **ameba**) /əˈmiːbə/ n (pl **~s** or **-ae** /-biː/) very small living creature consisting of only one cell

amok /əˈmɒk/ adv [IDM] **run amok →** RUN[1]

among /əˈmʌŋ/ (also **amongst** /əˈmʌŋst/) prep **1** surrounded by: a house ~ the trees **2** in the number of; included in: ~ the best in the world **3** (in parts) to each member of: distribute the books ~ the class

amorous /ˈæmərəs/ adj showing (esp sexual) love ▶ **amorously** adv

amount /əˈmaʊnt/ n total or quantity: a large ~ of money ● **amount** v [PV] **amount to sth** add up to or be equal to sth

amp /æmp/ n **1** (also **ampere** /ˈæmpeə(r)/) (abbr **A**) unit for measuring electric current **2** (infml) = AMPLIFIER

ampersand /ˈæmpəsænd/ n the symbol (&) used to mean 'and'

amphetamine /æmˈfetəmiːn/ n [C, U] illegal drug that makes you feel excited and full of energy

amphibian /æmˈfɪbiən/ n animal, eg a frog, that can live both on land and in water ▶ **amphibious** adj

amphitheatre (US **-ter**) /ˈæmfɪθɪətə(r)/ n round building without a roof and with rows of seats rising round an open space

ample /ˈæmpl/ adj (more than) enough ▶ **amply** adv

amplify /ˈæmplɪfaɪ/ v (pt, pp **-ied**) [T] **1** increase sth in strength, esp sound **2** add details to sth ▶ **amplification** /ˌæmplɪfɪˈkeɪʃn/ n [U] ▶ **amplifier** n device that makes sounds or radio signals louder

amputate /ˈæmpjuteɪt/ v [I, T] cut off an arm or a leg ▶ **amputation** /ˌæmpjuˈteɪʃn/ n [U, C]

amulet /ˈæmjulət/ n object worn to protect you from evil, etc

amuse /əˈmjuːz/ v [T] **1** make sb laugh or smile **2** make time pass pleasantly for sb ▶ **amusement** n **1** [C] something that makes time pass pleasantly **2** [U] state of being amused ▶ **amusing** adj causing you to laugh or smile

an → A

anachronism /əˈnækrənɪzəm/ n person or thing thought to be out of date

anaemia /əˈniːmiə/ n [U] lack of red cells in the blood, causing a person to look pale ▶ **anaemic** adj

anaesthesia /ˌænəsˈθiːziə/ n [U] state of being unable to feel pain ▶ **anaesthetic** /ˌænəsˈθetɪk/ n [C, U] substance that stops you feeling pain ▶ **anaesthetist** /əˈniːsθətɪst/ n person who is trained to give anaesthetics to patients ▶ **anaesthetize** (also **-ise**) /əˈniːsθətaɪz/ v [T] give sb an anaesthetic

anagram /ˈænəgræm/ n word made by changing the order of the letters of another word: 'Stare' is an ~ of 'tears'.

analgesic /ˌænəlˈdʒiːzɪk/ n (med) substance that reduces pain

analogue (US **analog**) /ˈænəlɒg/ adj (tech) **1** (of an electronic process) using a continuously changing range of physical quantities to measure or store data: an ~ computer/signal **2** (of clock or watch) showing the time using hands on a dial and not with a display of numbers

analogy /əˈnælədʒi/ n (pl **-ies**) **1** [C] comparison of one thing with another that has similar features: draw an ~ between the heart and a pump **2** [U] explaining one thing by comparing it to sth else ▶ **analogous** /əˈnæləgəs/ adj similar

analyse (US **analyze**) /ˈænəlaɪz/ v [T] examine or study sth, esp by separating sth into its parts

analysis /əˈnæləsɪs/ n (pl **-yses** /-əsiːz/) **1** [U] study of sth by examining its parts **2** [C] result of such study ▶ **analyst** /ˈænəlɪst/ n **1** person who makes (esp chemical) analyses: a political/food ~ **2** = PSYCHOANALYST ▶ **analytical** /ˌænəˈlɪtɪkl/ (also **analytic** /-ˈlɪtɪk/) adj

analyze (US) = ANALYSE

anarchy /ˈænəki/ n [U] absence of government; disorder ▶ **anarchist** n person who favours anarchy

anatomy /əˈnætəmi/ n [U,C] (pl **-ies**) (study of the) structure of human or animal bodies ▶ **anatomical** /ˌænəˈtɒmɪkl/ adj

ancestor /ˈænsestə(r)/ n person in your family who lived a long time ago ▶ **ancestral** /ænˈsestrəl/ adj or from your ancestors ▶ **ancestry** /-tri/ n (pl **-ies**) line of ancestors

anchor /ˈæŋkə(r)/ n heavy piece of metal lowered from a ship into the water in order to stop the ship from moving ● **anchor** v [I, T] lower a ship's anchor to stop it from moving

▶ **anchorage** /'æŋkərɪdʒ/ *n* [C,U] place where ships may anchor safely

anchovy /'æntʃəvi/ *n* (*pl* -ies) small fish with a strong salty flavour

ancient /'eɪnʃənt/ *adj* 1 belonging to times long ago: ~ *Greece* 2 very old: ~ *monuments*

ancillary /æn'sɪləri/ *adj* giving support; additional

and /ənd; æn; *strong form* ænd/ *conj* 1 also; in addition to: *bread* ~ *butter* 2 then; following this: *She came in* ~ *sat down.* 3 as a result of this: *Work hard* ~ *you'll succeed.* 4 used between repeated words to show that sth is repeated or continuing: *for hours* ~ *hours* 5 (*infml*) used instead of *to* after certain verbs: *Try* ~ *come early.*

anecdote /'ænɪkdəʊt/ *n* short interesting story about a real person or event

anemia, anemic (*US*) = ANAEMIA, ANAEMIC

anemone /ə'neməni/ *n* small plant with star-shaped flowers

anesthesia (*US*) = ANAESTHESIA

angel /'eɪndʒl/ *n* 1 messenger of God 2 beautiful or very kind person ▶ **angelic** /æn'dʒelɪk/ *adj*

anger /'æŋgə(r)/ *n* [U] feeling that makes people want to quarrel or fight ● **anger** *v* [T] make sb angry

angina /æn'dʒaɪnə/ *n* [U] very bad pain in the chest caused by a low supply of blood to the heart

angle /'æŋgl/ *n* 1 space between two lines that meet 2 corner 3 point of view [IDM] **at an angle** not straight ● **angle** *v* 1 [T] move or place sth so that it is not straight or not directly facing sb/sth 2 [T] present information, etc from a particular point of view 3 [I] catch fish with a line and hook [PV] **angle for sth** try to get a particular reaction from sb, without directly asking for what you want: ~ *for compliments* ▶ **angler** *n* person who catches fish (= goes angling) as a hobby ▶ **angling** *n* [U]

anglicize (*also* -**ise**) /'æŋglɪsaɪz/ [T] make sb/sth English in character

Anglo- /'æŋgləʊ/ *prefix* English or British: ~*American*

angry /'æŋgri/ *adj* (-**ier**, -**iest**) 1 filled with anger 2 (of a wound) red and infected ▶ **angrily** *adv*

angst /æŋst/ *n* [U] feeling of anxiety and worry about a situation

anguish /'æŋgwɪʃ/ *n* [U] great mental or physical pain ▶ **anguished** *adj*

angular /'æŋgjələ(r)/ *adj* 1 (of a person) thin and bony 2 having sharp corners

animal /'ænɪml/ *n* 1 living creature that can move and feel 2 any such creature other than a human being 3 unpleasant wild person ● **animal** *adj* physical; basic

animate /'ænɪmeɪt/ *v* [T] give life and energy to sth ● **animate** /'ænɪmət/ *adj* living ▶ **animated** /'ænɪmeɪtɪd/ *adj* 1 lively 2 (of pictures, drawings, etc in a film) made to look as if they are moving: ~*d cartoons* ▶ **animation** *n* /,ænɪ'meɪʃn/ 1 [U] energy and enthusiasm 2 [U] process of making animated cartoons 3 [C] animated film

animosity /,ænɪ'mɒsəti/ *n* [U,C] (*pl* -**ies**) strong hatred

ankle /'æŋkl/ *n* joint connecting the foot with the leg

annals /'ænlz/ *n* [pl] historical records

annex /ə'neks/ *v* [T] take control of a country, etc, esp by force ▶ **annexation** /-'seɪʃn/ *n* [U,C]

annexe (*esp US* **annex**) /'æneks/ *n* building added to a larger one

annihilate /ə'naɪəleɪt/ *v* [T] destroy sb/sth completely ▶ **annihilation** /-'leɪʃn/ *n* [U]

anniversary /,ænɪ'vɜːsəri/ *n* (*pl* -**ies**) day remembered for sth special which happened on that date in a previous year: *a wedding* ~

annotate /'ænəteɪt/ *v* [T] add notes to a book, etc ▶ **annotation** /,ænə'teɪʃn/ *n* [C,U]

announce /ə'naʊns/ *v* [T] make sth known publicly ▶ **announcement** *n* public statement ▶ **announcer** *n* person who introduces programmes on radio or television

annoy /ə'nɔɪ/ *v* [T] make sb slightly angry; cause trouble to sb ▶ **annoyance** *n* [U,C]

annual /'ænjuəl/ *adj* 1 happening once every year 2 calculated for the year: ~ *income* ● **annual** *n* 1 book published once a year, having the same title but different contents 2 plant that lives for one year ▶ **annually** *adv*

annuity /ə'njuːəti/ *n* (*pl* -**ies**) fixed sum of money paid to sb every year

annul /ə'nʌl/ *v* (-**ll**-) [T] declare sth no longer legally valid ▶ **annulment** *n* [C,U]

anode /'ænəʊd/ *n* place on a battery or other electrical device where the electric current enters

anoint /ə'nɔɪnt/ *v* [T] put oil or water on sb's head, esp as a religious ceremony

anomaly /ə'nɒməli/ *n* (*pl* -**ies**) (*fml*) something different from what is normal ▶ **anomalous** /-ləs/ *adj*

anonymous /ə'nɒnɪməs/ *adj* with a name that is not made known; without a name: *The author wishes* to remain ~. ▶ **anonymity** /ˌænə-ˈnɪməti/ n [U]

anorak /ˈænəræk/ n waterproof jacket with a hood

anorexia /ˌænəˈreksiə/ (also **anorexia nervosa** /nɜːˈvəʊsə/) n [U] mental illness that causes fear of gaining weight and eating and leads to dangerous loss of weight ▶ **anorexic** /ˌænəˈreksɪk/ adj

another /əˈnʌðə(r)/ adj, pron **1** an additional (one): have ~ cup of tea **2** a different (one): do that ~ time **3** a similar (one): ~ Einstein

answer /ˈɑːnsə(r)/ n **1** thing said or written in response to sb/sth; reply **2** solution: Do you know the answer to question 8? ● **answer** v [I, T] give an answer to sth/sb: Think before you ~. ◇ ~ the phone (= lift the receiver and speak to the person calling) ◇ ~ the door (= open the door when sb has knocked at it) [PV] **answer (sb) back** reply rudely to sb **answer for sb/sth 1** accept responsibility for sth **2** speak in support of sb/sth ▶ **answerable** adj responsible: ~ for your actions

ant /ænt/ n small insect that lives in organized groups

antagonism /ænˈtæɡənɪzəm/ n [U] opposition; dislike ▶ **antagonist** /-nɪst/ n opponent ● **antagonistic** /-ˈnɪstɪk/ adj

antagonize (also **-ise**) /ænˈtæɡənaɪz/ v [T] do sth to make sb angry with you

Antarctic /ænˈtɑːktɪk/ n [sing] (the Antarctic) very cold regions around the South Pole ● **Antarctic** adj

antecedent /ˌæntiˈsiːdnt/ n **1** [C] (fml) thing or event that comes before another **2** (antecedents) [pl] ancestors

antelope /ˈæntɪləʊp/ n animal like a deer

antenatal /ˌæntiˈneɪtl/ adj relating to the medical care given to pregnant women: an ~ clinic

antenna /ænˈtenə/ n **1** (pl ~e /-niː/) insect's feeler (= one of two long thin parts on its head) **2** (pl ~s, ~e) (esp US) = AERIAL

anthem /ˈænθəm/ n piece of music sung in churches or written for a special occasion

anthology /ænˈθɒlədʒi/ n (pl -ies) collection of writings, esp poems

anthrax /ˈænθræks/ n [U] serious disease that affects sheep and cows and sometimes people

anthropology /ˌænθrəˈpɒlədʒi/ n [U] study of the human race ▶ **anthropologist** n

anti- /ˈænti/ prefix opposed to; against

antibiotic /ˌæntibaɪˈɒtɪk/ n, adj (powerful substance, eg penicillin) that can destroy bacteria

antibody /ˈæntibɒdi/ n (pl -ies) substance formed in the blood which destroys harmful bacteria

anticipate /ænˈtɪsɪpeɪt/ v [T] **1** expect sth: We ~ trouble. **2** see what might happen in the future and take action ▶ **anticipation** /ænˌtɪsɪ-ˈpeɪʃn/ n [U]

anticlimax /ˌæntiˈklaɪmæks/ n disappointing end to sth exciting

anticlockwise /ˌæntiˈklɒkwaɪz/ adv, adj in the direction opposite to the movement of the hands of a clock

antics /ˈæntɪks/ n [pl] strange or amusing behaviour

anticyclone /ˌæntiˈsaɪkləʊn/ n area of high pressure that produces calm weather conditions

antidepressant /ˌæntidɪˈpresnt/ n drug used to treat depression

antidote /ˈæntidəʊt/ n substance that acts against the effects of a poison or disease

antifreeze /ˈæntifriːz/ n [U] substance added to water to stop it freezing, esp in car radiators

antihistamine /ˌæntiˈhɪstəmiːn/ n [C.U] drug used to treat allergies

antiperspirant /ˌæntiˈpɜːspərənt/ n [U.C] substance that prevents or reduces sweat

antiquated /ˈæntɪkweɪtɪd/ adj old-fashioned

antique /ænˈtiːk/ adj, n old and valuable (object): ~ furniture

antiquity /ænˈtɪkwəti/ n (pl -ies) **1** [U] ancient times **2** [C.usu pl] ancient building, painting, etc **3** [U] great age

antiseptic /ˌæntiˈseptɪk/ n, adj (substance) preventing disease by destroying bacteria

antisocial /ˌæntiˈsəʊʃl/ adj **1** not liking to meet other people; unfriendly **2** harmful to other people

antithesis /ænˈtɪθəsɪs/ n (pl -ses /-siːz/) (fml) direct opposite

antler /ˈæntlə(r)/ n horn of a deer

antonym /ˈæntənɪm/ n word that is opposite in meaning to another

anus /ˈeɪnəs/ n hole through which solid waste matter leaves the body

anvil /ˈænvɪl/ n heavy iron block on which metals are hammered into shape

anxiety /æŋˈzaɪəti/ n (pl -ies) **1** [U, C] concern and fear, esp about what might happen **2** [U] strong desire: ~ to please

anxious /ˈæŋkʃəs/ v **1** feeling anxiety **2** causing anxiety: an ~ time **3** ~ for/to strongly wishing sth: He's ~ to meet you. ▶ **anxiously** adv

any /ˈeni/ adj, pron **1** some amount

(of): Have you got ~ milk? ◇ I haven't read ~ books by Tolstoy. **2** no matter which: Take ~ card you like. ● any adv at all: I can't run ~ faster.

anybody /'enɪbɒdɪ/ (also **anyone** /'eniwʌn/) pron **1** used instead of somebody in negative sentences and questions: Did ~ see you? **2** any person at all: A ~ will tell you.

anyhow /'enɪhaʊ/ adv **1** = ANYWAY **2** carelessly: do the work ~

anyone = ANYBODY

anyplace /'enɪpleɪs/ (US) = ANY-WHERE

anything /'enɪθɪŋ/ pron **1** used instead of something in negative sentences and questions: Has ~ unusual happened? **2** any thing at all (whatever it is): I'm so hungry; I'll eat ~! [IDM] **anything but** definitely not

anyway /'enɪweɪ/ adv **1** in spite of everything **2** used to change the subject of conversation

anywhere /'eniweə(r)/ adv used instead of somewhere in negative sentences and questions [IDM] **get anywhere** → GET

aorta /eɪ'ɔːtə/ n main artery that carries blood from the heart to the rest of the body

apart /ə'pɑːt/ adv **1** separated by a distance, of space or time: The houses are 500 metres ~. **2** separate(ly): They're living ~. **3** into pieces: It fell ~. ■ **a'part from** prep **1** except for **2** as well as

apartment /ə'pɑːtmənt/ n (esp US) = FLAT² **2** set of rooms rented for a holiday

apathy /'æpəθɪ/ n [U] lack of interest or enthusiasm ► **apathetic** /ˌæpə'θetɪk/ adj

ape /eɪp/ n large animal like a monkey, with no tail, eg chimpanzee or gorilla ● **ape** v [T] copy sb's speech or behaviour

aperitif /əˌperə'tiːf/ n alcoholic drink before a meal

aperture /'æpətʃə(r)/ n (tech) narrow hole or opening, eg in a camera lens

apex /'eɪpeks/ n (pl **~es** or **apices** /'eɪpɪsiːz/) highest point: the ~ of a triangle

apiece /ə'piːs/ adv each

apologetic /əˌpɒlə'dʒetɪk/ adj saying or feeling sorry for doing sth wrong ► **apologetically** /-klɪ/ adv

apologize (also **-ise**) /ə'pɒlədʒaɪz/ v [I] say that you are sorry: I must ~ for being late.

apology /ə'pɒlədʒɪ/ n (pl **-ies**) statement saying that you are sorry for having done wrong, hurt sb's feelings, etc

apostle /ə'pɒsl/ n **1** (**Apostle**) any

of the twelve men sent out by Christ to spread his teaching **2** leader of a new faith or movement

apostrophe /ə'pɒstrəfɪ/ n sign (') used to show that one or more letters have been left out, as in I'm or I am

appal (US also **appall**) /ə'pɔːl/ v (-**ll**-) [T] fill sb with horror; shock sb deeply: We were ~led at the news. ► **appalling** adj

apparatus /ˌæpə'reɪtəs/ n [U] set of tools or equipment used for a purpose: laboratory ~

apparent /ə'pærənt/ adj **1** clearly seen: for no ~ reason **2** seen but not necessarily real: an ~ lack of knowledge ► **apparently** adv

apparition /ˌæpə'rɪʃn/ n ghost

appeal /ə'piːl/ v [I] **1** make a formal request to a higher court, etc for a new decision **2** ~**to** attract or interest sb: The design does not ~ to me. **3** ~**(for)** make a serious and urgent request: ~ for help/money ● **appeal** n **1** [C] formal request to a court of law, etc **2** [U] quality that makes sb/sth attractive or interesting: sex ~ **3** [C] urgent request ► **appealing** adj **1** attractive **2** wanting sb to show you pity

appear /ə'pɪə(r)/ v [I] **1** give the impression of being; seem: That explanation ~s (to be) absurd. **2** come into view; become visible: A ship ~ed on the horizon. **3** arrive **4** be published or broadcast: Her latest book ~s in the spring. **5** be present in a law court ► **appearance** n **1** [C] act of arriving, esp unexpectedly **2** [C,U] way sb/sth looks to other people: She was determined to keep up ~s (=hide the true situation and pretend that everything is going well). [IDM] **put in an appearance** go to a meeting, party, etc, esp for a short time ● **to all appearances** so far as can be seen

appease /ə'piːz/ v [T] make sb calm or stop sb being angry, esp by satisfying demands ► **appeasement** n [U]

append /ə'pend/ v [T] (fml) add or attach sth, esp in writing ► **appendage** /-dɪdʒ/ n something added to or joined to sth larger

appendicitis /əˌpendɪ'saɪtɪs/ n [U] painful swelling of the appendix that can be very serious

appendix /ə'pendɪks/ n **1** (pl **~es**) small organ attached to the large intestine **2** (pl **-dices** /-dɪsiːz/) section giving extra information at the end of a book

appetite /'æpɪtaɪt/ n [C,U] strong desire, esp for food

appetizer (also **-iser**) /'æpɪtaɪzə(r)/ n small amount of food or drink

that you have before a meal
▶ **appetizing** (also **-ising**) adj
making you feel hungry

applaud /ə'plɔːd/ v [I, T] show
approval of sb/sth by clapping
your hands **2** [T] express praise
for sb/sth because you approve of
them/it ▶ **applause** /ə'plɔːz/ n [U]

apple /'æpl/ n round fruit with
shiny red or green skin and white
flesh

applet /'æplət/ n (computing) program which is run from within
another program, eg from within
a web browser

appliance /ə'plaɪəns/ n device;
machine: *electrical/household ~s*

applicable /ə'plɪkəbl; 'æplɪkəbl/
adj ~(to) that can be said to be
true in the case of sb/sth

applicant /'æplɪkənt/ n person
who applies for a job, etc

application /ˌæplɪ'keɪʃn/ n **1** [C,
U] request: *an ~ (form) for a job* **2** [U,
C] act of putting sth to practical
use: *the practical ~ of the invention*
3 [U] hard work; great effort **4** [C]
(computing) program designed to
do a particular job: *a database ~*

apply /ə'plaɪ/ v (pt, pp **-ied**) **1** [I] ~
(for) ask officially for sth: ~ *for a
job/visa* **2** [I] ~(to) concern or relate
to sb/sth: *This rule does not ~ to you.*
3 [T] work at sth or study sth hard
4 [T] put sth into operation; use sth:
~ *the brakes* **5** [T] put or rub sth
onto a surface: ~ *ointment to the cut*
▶ **applied** adj put to practical use:
applied science

appoint /ə'pɔɪnt/ v [T] **1** choose sb
for a job **2** (fml) fix or decide sth:
the ~ed time ▶ **appointment** n **1** [C]
formal arrangement to meet sb,
esp with a reason connected with
their work: *make an ~* **2** [C] job to
which sb is appointed **3** [C,U] act
of appointing sb for a job

appraise /ə'preɪz/ v [T] (fml) consider the value of sb/sth ▶ **ap-
praisal** n [C,U] judgement of
the value of sth: *staff ~s*

appreciable /ə'priːʃəbl/ adj large
enough to be noticed: *an ~ difference* ▶ **appreciably** adv

appreciate /ə'priːʃieɪt/ v [T] recognize the good qualities of
sb/sth: *Her family doesn't ~ her.*
2 [T] be grateful for sth/sth: *I really
~ all your help.* **3** [T] understand
sth completely: *I ~ your problems,
but am not able to help.* **4** [I] (of
land, etc) increase in value
▶ **appreciation** /əˌpriːʃi'eɪʃn/ n [U,
C] ▶ **appreciative** /ə'priːʃətɪv/ adj

apprehend /ˌæprɪ'hend/ v [T]
(fml) (of the police) arrest sb

apprehension /ˌæprɪ'henʃn/ n
[U,C] worry or fear ▶ **apprehen-
sive** /ˌæprɪ'hensɪv/ adj worried

apprentice /ə'prentɪs/ n person
learning a skilled trade ▶ **appren-
ticeship** /ə'prentɪʃɪp/ n [C,U]
(time of) being an apprentice

approach /ə'prəʊtʃ/ v **1** [I, T] come
near(er) to sb/sth **2** [T] make a
request or offer to sb: ~ *the manager for a pay rise* **3** [T] begin to
deal with a problem, task, etc
● **approach** n [C] **1** way of dealing
with sb/sth **2** [usu sing] act of
approaching **3** road, way, etc ▶
approachable adj friendly and
easy to talk to

appropriate /ə'prəʊpriət/ adj
suitable; correct ▶ **appropriately**
adv ● **appropriate** /ə'prəʊprieɪt/ v
[T] **1** take sth that does not belong
to you for your own use **2** set sth
aside for a particular purpose
▶ **appropriation** /əˌprəʊpri'eɪʃn/ n [C,U]

approval /ə'pruːvl/ n [U] feeling or
showing that you think sb/sth is
good or acceptable: *Your plans
have my ~.* [IDM] **on approval** (of
goods) to be returned without
paying if not satisfactory

approve /ə'pruːv/ v **1** [I] ~(of) feel
or show that sb/sth is good or
acceptable **2** [T] agree to sth formally ▶ **approvingly** adv

approximate /ə'prɒksɪmət/ adj
almost correct or exact, but not
completely so ▶ **approximately**
adv: ~ly 100 students ● **approximate** /ə'prɒksɪmeɪt/ v [I] ~ to
come very near to sth ▶ **approxi-
mation** /əˌprɒksɪ'meɪʃn/ n [C]

apricot /'eɪprɪkɒt/ n **1** [C] small
round orange-yellow fruit with a
stone **2** [U] orange-yellow colour

April /'eɪprəl/ n [U,C] the fourth
month of the year: *on A~ the first* ◇
on the first of A~ ◇ *(US) on A~ first*
◇ *She was born in A~.* ◇ *last A~*

apron /'eɪprən/ n piece of clothing
worn round the front part of your
body to keep your clothes clean,
eg when cooking

apt /æpt/ adj **1** suitable: *an
~ remark* **2** ~ to likely to do sth:
~ *to be forgetful* **3** quick to learn
▶ **aptly** adv ▶ **aptness** n [U]

aptitude /'æptɪtjuːd/ n [C,U] natural ability or skill

aqualung /'ækwəlʌŋ/ n breathing
unit for underwater swimming

aquamarine /ˌækwəmə'riːn/ n
1 [C] bluish-green precious stone
2 [U] bluish-green colour

aquarium /ə'kweəriəm/ n (building with a) large glass tank for
keeping live fish

aquatic /ə'kwætɪk/ adj **1** (of

A

animals or plants) living or growing in water **2** (of sports) taking place on or in water

aqueduct /'ækwɪdʌkt/ n bridge that carries water across a valley

Arabic /'ærəbɪk/ n [U], adj (language) of the Arabs ■ Arabic 'numeral n symbol 0, 1, 2, 3, etc used for writing numbers in many countries

arable /'ærəbl/ adj (of land) used or suitable for growing crops

arbitrage /'ɑːbɪtrɑːʒ; -trɪdʒ/ n [U] (business) the practice of buying sth (eg shares or foreign money) in one place and selling it in another place where the price is higher ► **arbitrageur** /ˌɑːbɪtrɑːʒ 'ɜː(r)/ (also **arbitrager** /'ɑːbɪtrɪdʒə(r)/) n

arbitrary /'ɑːbɪtrəri/ adj based on chance, not reason ► **arbitrarily** adv

arbitrate /'ɑːbɪtreɪt/ v [I, T] ~ (between) settle a dispute, argument, etc between two groups ► **arbitration** /ˌɑːbɪ'treɪʃn/ n [U] settlement of a dispute by sb chosen as a judge ► **arbitrator** n

arc /ɑːk/ n part of the curved line of a circle

arcade /ɑː'keɪd/ n covered passage with shops

arch /ɑːtʃ/ n curved structure, eg one that is part of the support of a bridge ● **arch** v [I, T] form an arch: The cat ~ed its back.

archaeology /ˌɑːki'ɒlədʒi/ n [U] study of the remains of ancient buildings, etc ► **archaeological** /ˌɑːkiə'lɒdʒɪkl/ adj ► **archaeologist** n

archaic /ɑː'keɪɪk/ adj (esp of words) no longer in use; very old

archbishop /ˌɑːtʃ'bɪʃəp/ n chief bishop

archer /'ɑːtʃə(r)/ n person who shoots with a bow and arrows ► **archery** n [U] skill or sport of shooting with a bow and arrows

archipelago /ˌɑːkɪ'peləgəʊ/ n (pl ~s or ~es) group of many small islands

architect /'ɑːkɪtekt/ n person who designs buildings ► **architecture** /'ɑːkɪtektʃə(r)/ n [U] art of building; style of building ► **architectural** /ˌɑːkɪ'tektʃərəl/ adj

archives /'ɑːkaɪvz/ n [pl] (collection of) historical records

Arctic /'ɑːktɪk/ adj **1** of the very cold region around the North Pole **2** (arctic) very cold ► **the Arctic** n [sing] the very cold region around the North Pole

ardent /'ɑːdnt/ adj (written) very enthusiastic ► **ardently** adv

arduous /'ɑːdjuəs; -dʒu-/ adj needing a lot of effort or energy: an ~ journey ► **arduously** adv

are /ə(r); strong form ɑː(r)/ → BE

area /'eəriə/ n **1** [C] part of a place,

town, etc, or a region of a country or the world: desert ~s **2** [C,U] extent or measurement of a surface **3** [C] range of activity: different ~s of human experience

arena /ə'riːnə/ n **1** enclosed area used for sports, etc **2** area of activity: in the political ~

aren't /ɑːnt/ = ARE NOT (BE)

argue /'ɑːgjuː/ v **1** [I] express disagreement; quarrel **2** [I, T] ~for/ against give reasons for/against sth **3** [T] (fml) discuss sth: The lawyers ~d the case. ► **arguable** /'ɑːgjuəbl/ adj not certain; questionable ► **arguably** adv

argument /'ɑːgjumənt/ n **1** [C] disagreement **2** [C,U] discussion; reason for or against sth ► **argumentative** /ˌɑːgjuː'mentətɪv/ adj fond of arguing

aria /'ɑːriə/ n song for one voice in an opera, etc

arid /'ærɪd/ adj **1** (of land) very dry **2** dull; uninteresting

arise /ə'raɪz/ v (pt arose /ə'rəʊz/ pp ~n /ə'rɪzn/) [I] (fml) come into existence: A difficulty has ~n.

aristocracy /ˌærɪ'stɒkrəsi/ n (pl -ies) people born in the highest social class, who have special titles ► **aristocrat** /'ærɪstəkræt/ n member of the aristocracy ► **aristocratic** /ˌærɪstə'krætɪk/ adj

arithmetic /ə'rɪθmətɪk/ n [U] branch of mathematics that deals with the adding, multiplying, etc of numbers ► **arithmetical** /ˌærɪθ-'metɪkl/ adj

ark /ɑːk/ n (in the Bible) Noah's ship

arm /ɑːm/ n **1** either of the two long parts of your body that connect your shoulder to your hand **2** piece of clothing that covers this; sleeve **3** part of a chair where you rest your arms [IDM] **arm in arm** (of two people) with their arms linked ■ **'armchair** n chair with supports for the arms ■ **'armpit** n hollow part under the arm where it joins the shoulder ● **arm** v [I, T] supply sb with weapons [IDM] **armed to the teeth** having many weapons ■ the **armed 'forces** n [pl] a country's army, navy and air force

armada /ɑː'mɑːdə/ n large group of ships sailing together

armadillo /ˌɑːmə'dɪləʊ/ n (pl ~s) American animal with a hard shell made of pieces of bone

armament /'ɑːməmənt/ n **1** [C, usu pl] weapons, esp large guns **2** [U] process of equipping military forces for war

armistice /'ɑːmɪstɪs/ n agreement during a war to stop fighting for a time

armour (US **-or**) /ˈɑːmə(r)/ n [U] **1** protective metal covering for the body in battle **2** metal covering for tanks, ships, etc ▶ **armoured** (US **-or-**) adj ▶ **armoury** (US **-or-**) n (pl **-ies**) place where weapons are kept

arms /ɑːmz/ n [pl] weapons [IDM] **take up arms** (against sb) (fml) (prepare to) go to war (**be**) **up in arms** (about/over sth) (infml) be very angry about sth and ready to protest strongly about it

army /ˈɑːmi/ n [C, with sing or pl verb] (pl **-ies**) **1** military forces of a country which fight on land: join the ~ **2** large group: an ~ of helpers

aroma /əˈrəʊmə/ n pleasant smell ▶ **aromatic** /ˌærəˈmætɪk/ adj

aromatherapy /əˌrəʊməˈθerəpi/ n [U] use of natural oils for controlling pain or for massage ▶ **aromatherapist** n

arose pt of ARISE

around /əˈraʊnd/ adv, prep **1** approximately: It's ~ six o'clock. **2** on all sides of sb/sth; surrounding sb/sth: He put his arms ~ her. **3** on, to or from the other side of sb/sth: The bus came ~ the bend. **4** with a circular movement round sth: The earth moves ~ the sun. **5** in or to many places in an area: We walked all ~ the town. **6** to fit in with particular people, ideas, etc: I can't plan everything ~ your timetable! **7** present in a place; available: Is anyone ~?

arouse /əˈraʊz/ v [T] **1** cause sth to appear or become active: ~ suspicion **2** excite sb sexually

arraign /əˈreɪn/ v [T] (law) bring sb to court to formally accuse them of a crime ▶ **arraignment** n [C,U]

arrange /əˈreɪndʒ/ v [I, T] plan or organize sth in advance: We ~d to meet at one o'clock. ◊ I've ~d a loan with the bank. **2** [T] put sth in order; make sth attractive: ~ flowers **3** [T] adapt a piece of music for a particular instrument ▶ **arrangement** n **1** [C,usu pl] plan or preparation that you make so that sth can happen: travel ~ments **2** [C,usu pl] the way things are done or organized: new security ~ments **3** [C,U] agreement that you make with sb that you can both accept **4** [C] group of things that are arranged or placed in a particular order: a flower ~ment **5** [U] piece of music that has been adapted for a particular instrument

array /əˈreɪ/ n large impressive series of things

arrears /əˈrɪəz/ n [pl] money that is owing [IDM] **be in arrears** | **get/fall into arrears** be late in paying money that you owe

arrest /əˈrest/ v [T] **1** seize sb by the authority of the law **2** (fml) stop a process **3** attract sb's attention ● **arrest** n act of arresting [IDM] **under arrest** held prisoner by the police

arrival /əˈraɪvl/ n **1** [U] act of arriving **2** [C] person or thing that arrives: The new ~ (= baby) is a girl.

arrive /əˈraɪv/ v [i] **1** reach a place: ~ home **2** come: The great day has ~d! **3** (infml) become successful [PV] **arrive at** sth reach sth: ~ at a decision

arrogant /ˈærəgənt/ adj behaving in a proud and rude way ▶ **arrogance** /-ns/ n [U] ▶ **arrogantly** adv

arrow /ˈærəʊ/ n **1** pointed stick shot from a bow **2** sign (→) used for showing direction

arse /ɑːs/ n (GB, ⚠, sl) **1** buttocks; bottom(2) **2** stupid person ● **arse** v [PV] **arse about/around** (GB, ⚠, sl) behave in a silly way

arsenal /ˈɑːsənl/ n **1** collection of weapons **2** place where weapons and explosives are stored or made

arsenic /ˈɑːsnɪk/ n [U] very strong poisonous substance

arson /ˈɑːsn/ n [U] crime of setting fire to property

art /ɑːt/ n **1** [U] use of the imagination to express ideas or feelings, particularly in painting, drawing or sculpture **2** (**arts**) [pl] subjects of study, eg languages or history, that are in contrast to science **3** [C,U] skill in doing sth ■ '**art gallery** (pl **-ies**) n building where works of art are shown to the public

artefact (esp US **artifact**) /ˈɑːtɪfækt/ n thing made by a human being

artery /ˈɑːtəri/ n (pl **-ies**) **1** one of the tubes that carry blood from the heart to other parts of the body **2** main road, railway, etc ▶ **arterial** /ɑːˈtɪəriəl/ adj

artful /ˈɑːtfl/ adj clever at getting what you want, sometimes by not telling the truth ▶ **artfully** adv

arthritis /ɑːˈθraɪtɪs/ n [U] pain and swelling in a joint in the body ▶ **arthritic** /ɑːˈθrɪtɪk/ adj

artichoke /ˈɑːtɪtʃəʊk/ n **1** (also ˌglobe 'artichoke) kind of plant with a lot of thick, green leaves, the bottom part of which can be eaten when cooked **2** = JERUSALEM ARTICHOKE

article /ˈɑːtɪkl/ n **1** piece of writing in a newspaper, etc **2** (law) separate part of an agreement or a contract **3** separate thing: ~s of clothing **4** (gram) word a, an or the

articulate /ɑːˈtɪkjələt/ adj **1** (of a person) good at expressing ideas or feelings clearly in words **2** (of speech) clearly pronounced ● **articulate** /ɑːˈtɪkjuleɪt/ v [I, T] express sth clearly ▶ **articulated**

adj (of a lorry) having two parts connected by a joint which allows it to turn easily ▶ **articulation** /ɑːˌtɪkjuˈleɪʃn/ *n* [U]

artifact (*esp US*) = ARTEFACT

artificial /ˌɑːtɪˈfɪʃl/ *adj* **1** not natural; made by human beings **2** false; not what it appears to be ■ **artificial in'telligence** *n* [U] (*abbr* **AI**) (*computing*) area of study concerned with making computers copy intelligent human behaviour ■ **artificial respi'ration** *n* [U] process of helping a person who has stopped breathing begin to breathe again, usually by blowing into their mouth or nose ▶ **artificially** *adv*

artillery /ɑːˈtɪləri/ *n* [U] **1** (branch of the army that uses) large heavy guns

artisan /ˌɑːtɪˈzæn/ *n* (*fml*) person who does skilled work, making things with their hands

artist /ˈɑːtɪst/ *n* **1** person who creates works of art, esp paintings **2** = ARTISTE ▶ **artistic** /ɑːˈtɪstɪk/ *adj* **1** of art and artists **2** having or showing skill in art ▶ **artistically** /-kli/ *adv* ▶ **artistry** *n* [U] skill of an artist

artiste /ɑːˈtiːst/ *n* professional singer, dancer, actor, etc

arty /ˈɑːti/ *adj* (*infml*) pretending to be artistic

arugula /əˈruːgjələ/ *n* [U] (*US*) = ROCKET(3)

as /əz; strong form æz/ *prep* **1** appearing to be sb: *dressed as a policeman* **2** having the function or character of sb/sth: *a career as a teacher* ◇ *Treat me as a friend.* ● *as adv* (**as ... as**) (used in comparisons) equally ... as sb/sth: *as tall as his father* ◇ *Run as fast as you can!* ● *as conj* **1** during the time when: *I saw her as I was leaving.* **2** since; because: *As you were out, I left a message.* **3** though: *Young as I am, I know what I want to be.* **4** in the way which: *Do as I say.* [IDM] **as for sb/sth** used to start talking about sb/sth **as from | as of** showing the time from which sth starts **as if | though** in a way that suggests sth **as it is** in reality as it were as it might be expressed **as much as**: *I thought as much.* **as per** according to: *Work as per instructions.* **as to sth | as regards sth** used when you are referring to sth

asbestos /æsˈbestəs/ *n* [U] soft grey material that does not burn

ascend /əˈsend/ *v* [I, T] (*fml*) go up sth [IDM] **ascend the throne** (*fml*) become king or queen ▶ **ascendancy** *n* [U] (*fml*) power; influence ▶ **ascendant** *n* [IDM] **in the ascendant** being or becoming more powerful or popular

ascent /əˈsent/ *n* act of climbing or moving up; way up

ascertain /ˌæsəˈteɪn/ *v* [T] (*fml*) find out or make certain about sth

ASCII /ˈæski/ *n* [U] (*computing*) American Standard Code for Information Interchange; standard code used so that data can be moved between computers that use different programs

ascribe /əˈskraɪb/ *v* [T] ~ **to** consider sth to be caused by or to belong to sth/sb: *He ~d his failure to bad luck.*

aseptic /ˌeɪˈseptɪk/ *adj* free from harmful bacteria

asexual /ˌeɪˈsekʃuəl/ *adj* **1** without sex or sex organs **2** having no interest in sexual relations

ash /æʃ/ *n* **1** [U] grey or black powder left after sth has burnt: *cigarette* ~ **2** (**ashes**) [pl] what is left after sth has been destroyed by burning **3** (**ashes**) [pl] remains of a dead human body after burning **4** (*also* '**ash tree**) [C,U] forest tree with grey bark **5** [U] hard pale wood of the ash tree ■ '**ashtray** *n* small dish for tobacco ash

ashamed /əˈʃeɪmd/ *adj* feeling shame or embarrassment for sth you have done

ashore /əˈʃɔː(r)/ *adv* towards, onto or on land, having come from water

aside /əˈsaɪd/ *adv* to one side; out of the way: *He laid the book* ~. ● *aside n* remark that others are not supposed to hear

ask /ɑːsk/ *v* [I, T] **1** put a question to sb in order to get information: *I ~ed him where he lived.* ◇ *'What time is it?' she ~ed.* **2** [I, T] say to sb that you want them to do sth: *I ~ed them to close the window.* **3** [T] invite sb: ~ *him to the party* [IDM] **ask for it/trouble** (*infml*) behave in such a way that trouble is likely [PV] **ask after sb** ask about sb's health **ask for sb/sth** say that you want to speak to sb or be given sth ■ '**asking price** *n* price that sb wants to sell sth for

askew /əˈskjuː/ *adj, adv* not in a straight or level position

asleep /əˈsliːp/ *adj* **1** sleeping **2** (of an arm or leg) having no feeling

asp /æsp/ *n* small poisonous snake of N Africa

asparagus /əˈspærəgəs/ *n* [U] plant whose green shoots are eaten as a vegetable

aspect /ˈæspekt/ *n* **1** particular part or side of sth being considered **2** [T] direction in which a building faces

aspersions /əˈspɜːʃnz/ *n* [pl] (*fml*)

critical or unpleasant remarks or judgements: cast ~ on sb's honesty

asphalt /'æsfælt/ n [U] black sticky substance for making road surfaces

asphyxiate /əs'fiksieɪt/ v [T] cause sb to become very ill or die by preventing them from breathing ▸ **asphyxiation** /əs,fiksi'eɪʃn/ n [U]

aspirate /'æspərət/ n sound of the letter 'h' ● **aspirate** /'æspəreɪt/ v [T] pronounce sth with an 'h' sound

aspire /ə'spaɪə(r)/ v [I] ~(to) have a strong desire to achieve sth ▸ **aspiration** /,æspə'reɪʃn/ n [C,U] strong desire

aspirin /'æsprɪn; 'æspərɪn/ n [U,C] (pl **aspirin** or ~s) drug used to reduce pain and fever

ass /æs/ n [C] (US, ∆, sl) = ARSE (GB, infml) stupid person

assailant /ə'seɪlənt/ n (fml) person who attacks sb, esp physically

assassin /ə'sæsɪn/ n person who murders sb important or famous ▸ **assassinate** /ə'sæsɪneɪt/ v [T] murder sb important or famous, esp for political reasons ▸ **assassination** /ə,sæsɪ'neɪʃn/ n [C,U]

assault /ə'sɔ:lt/ n [C,U] sudden violent attack ● **assault** v [T] attack sb violently, esp when this is a crime

assemble /ə'sembl/ v 1 [I, T] come together as a group; bring people or things together 2 [T] fit together the parts of sth

assembly /ə'sembli/ n (pl **-ies**) 1 [C] (**Assembly**) group of people who have been elected to meet and make decisions or laws for a region or country: UN General A~ 2 [C] group of people coming together for a purpose 3 [C,U] meeting of teachers and students in a school, usually at the start of the day 4 [U] process of fitting the parts of sth together ■ as**'sembly line** n arrangement of machines and workers along which a product moves as it is put together in stages

assent /ə'sent/ n 1 [U] (fml) agreement ● **assent** v [I] ~(to) (fml) agree to sth

assert /ə'sɜ:t/ v [T] 1 state sth firmly 2 make others recognize your authority, etc by behaving firmly 3 ~ yourself behave in a confident and forceful way ▸ **assertion** /-ʃn/ n [U,C] ▸ **assertive** adj confident and forceful

assess /ə'ses/ v [T] 1 judge the importance, worth, etc of sb/sth 2 calculate the value of sth ▸ **assessment** n [C,U] ▸ **assessor** n

asset /'æset/ n [C] 1 valuable person or quality 2 [usu pl] thing owned, esp property, that can be sold to pay debts ■ **'asset-stripping**

n [U] (business) practice of buying a failing company at a low price and then selling all its assets(2) in order to make a profit

assign /ə'saɪn/ v [T] 1 give sth as a share or task 2 provide sb for a task or position 3 fix sth as a time, place, etc; name sth ▸ **assignment** n [1] piece of work that sb is given to do; task 2 [U] act of giving sth to sb as a share or task

assimilate /ə'sɪməleɪt/ v 1 [T] take in or absorb food, information, ideas, etc 2 [I, T] (allow sb to) become part of another group or state ▸ **assimilation** /-'leɪʃn/ n [U]

assist /ə'sɪst/ v [I, T] (fml) help sb to do sth ▸ **assistance** n [U] (fml) help ▸ **assistant** n person who helps or supports sb, usually in their job

associate /ə'səʊʃieɪt/ v 1 [T] ~ (with) make a connection between people or things in your mind: I always ~ the smell of baking with my childhood. 2 [I] ~with spend time with sb: I don't want to ~ with those people. ● **associate** /ə'səʊʃiət/ n person you work with or do business with: business ~s

association /ə,səʊsi'eɪʃn/ n 1 [C] official group of people joined together for a purpose 2 [C,U] connection or relationship between people or organizations 3 [C,U] connection in the mind [IDM] in association with sb together with sb

assorted /ə'sɔ:tɪd/ adj of different kinds; mixed ▸ **assortment** /ə-'sɔ:tmənt/ n collection of different things or different types of the same thing

assume /ə'sju:m/ v [T] 1 believe sth to be true without proof 2 begin to use, take or have sth: ~control ◇ ~ a greater importance 3 pretend to have a particular feeling or quality ▸ **assumption** n 1 [C] something believed to be true without proof 2 [U] act of assuming

assurance /ə'ʃɔ:rəns/ n 1 [U] belief in your own abilities 2 [U] promise: give an ~ 3 [U] (GB) insurance: life ~

assure /ə'ʃʊə(r); -ʃɔ:(r)/ v [T] 1 tell sb that sth is definitely true: I ~ you that the money will be safe with me. 2 ~ yourself (of sth) make yourself certain of sth 3 (GB) insure sth, esp against sb's death ▸ **assured** adj 1 confident 2 certain to happen

asterisk /'æstərɪsk/ n star-shaped symbol (*)

asteroid /'æstərɔɪd/ n any one of the small planets which go around the sun

asthma /'æsmə/ n [U] chest illness that causes difficulty in breathing ▸ **asthmatic** /æs'mætɪk/ adj

astonish /ə'stɒnɪʃ/ v surprise sb

greatly ▶ **astonishing** adj very surprising ▶ **astonishment** n [U]

astound /əˈstaʊnd/ v [T] shock or surprise sb very much

astray /əˈstreɪ/ adv away from the right path

astride /əˈstraɪd/ adj, prep with one leg on each side (of)

astrology /əˈstrɒlədʒi/ n [U] study of the stars in the belief that they influence human affairs ▶ **astrological** /-ˈlɒdʒɪkl/ adj ▶ **astrologer** n

astronaut /ˈæstrənɔːt/ n person who travels in a spacecraft

astronomy /əˈstrɒnəmi/ n [U] scientific study of the stars, planets, etc ▶ **astronomer** n ▶ **astronomical** /ˌæstrəˈnɒmɪkl/ adj 1 of astronomy 2 (infml) (of an amount, a price, etc) very large

astute /əˈstjuːt/ adj clever at seeing quickly how to gain an advantage ▶ **astutely** adv ▶ **astuteness** n [U]

asylum /əˈsaɪləm/ n [U] (also fml po,litical a'sylum) protection that a government gives to people who have left their own countries, usually because they were in danger for political reasons: the rights of ~ seekers (= people asking for political asylum)

at /ət; strong form æt/ prep 1 used to show where sb/sth is: at the station ◇ She's at Yale (= Yale university). 2 used to say when sth happens: at two o'clock ◇ at the end of the week 3 used to state the age at which sb does sth: He got married at (the age of) 24. 4 in the direction of or towards sb/sth: look at her ◇ He pointed a gun at him. 5 used to state the distance away from sth: hold sth at arm's length 6 used to show the situation sb/sth is in: The country is now at war. 7 used to show a rate, speed, etc: driving at 70mph ◇ exports valued at £1 million 8 used after an adj expressing ability: good at music 9 used after an adj to show the cause of sth: shocked at the news

ate pt of EAT

atheism /ˈeɪθiɪzəm/ n [U] belief that there is no God ▶ **atheist** n

athlete /ˈæθliːt/ n person trained for physical games ▶ **athletic** /æθˈletɪk/ adj 1 physically strong and fit 2 of athletics ▶ **athletics** n [U] sports that people compete in, esp running, jumping and throwing

atlas /ˈætləs/ n book of maps

ATM /ˌeɪ tiː ˈem/ n (US) automated teller machine = CASH MACHINE

atmosphere /ˈætməsfɪə(r)/ n [sing] 1 (the atmosphere) gases surrounding the earth 2 air in a room or enclosed space 3 general impression of a place: a friendly ~ ▶ **atmospheric** /ˌætməsˈferɪk/ adj of the atmosphere

atom /ˈætəm/ n smallest unit of an element that can take part in chemical change ▶ **atomic** /əˈtɒmɪk/ adj of atoms ■ a,tomic 'bomb (also 'atom bomb) n bomb whose explosive power comes from splitting atoms

atrocious /əˈtrəʊʃəs/ adj 1 very bad: ~ weather 2 very cruel ▶ **atrociously** adv

atrocity /əˈtrɒsəti/ n [C, usu pl, U] (pl -ies) cruel violent act, esp in a war

attach /əˈtætʃ/ v 1 [T] fasten or join sth to sth 2 [T] join sth as a companion or member 3 [I, T] ~to (cause sth to) connect with sth: ~ importance to her speech ▶ **attached** adj 1 ~ (to) be very fond of sb/sth 2 ~to forming part of an organization: The research unit is ~ed to the university. 3 joined to sth ▶ **attachment** n 1 [U] ~ (to) strong feeling of affection for sb/sth 2 [C] thing that can be fixed onto a machine to make it do another job 3 [C] (computing) document that you send to sb using email

attaché /əˈtæʃeɪ/ n person who works on the staff of an embassy ■ at'taché case n small case for documents

attack /əˈtæk/ n 1 [C, U] attempt to hurt or defeat sb/sth using force 2 [C, U] strong criticism in speech or writing 3 [C] short period when you suffer badly from a disease, etc ● **attack** v 1 [I, T] try to hurt or defeat sb/sth using force 2 [T] criticize sb/sth severely 3 [T] have a harmful effect on sth: a disease that ~s the brain 4 [T] deal with sth with a lot of energy and determination ▶ **attacker** n

attain /əˈteɪn/ v [T] (fml) succeed in getting sth; achieve sth ▶ **attainable** adj ▶ **attainment** n 1 [C] skill or ability 2 [U] success in achieving sth

attempt /əˈtempt/ v [T] try to do sth: ~ to escape ● **attempt** n effort to do sth [IDM] an attempt on sb's life an act of trying to kill sb

attend /əˈtend/ v 1 [T] be present at an event: ~ a meeting 2 [T] go regularly to a place: ~ school 3 [I] ~(to) (fml) pay attention to sb/sth [PV] attend to sb/sth deal with sb/sth; take care of sb/sth ▶ **attendance** n 1 [U,C] act of being present at a place, eg a school 2 [C,U] number of people present at an organized event ▶ **attendant** n person whose job is to serve people in a public place

attention /əˈtenʃn/ n [U] 1 careful thought: pay ~ 2 interest in sb/sth 3 special care or action: in need of medical ~ **4** position of a soldier standing upright and still

attentive /əˈtentɪv/ *adj* giving attention to sb/sth ▸ **attentively** *adv*

attest /əˈtest/ *v* [I, T] ~ **(to)** (*fml*) show or prove that sth is true

attic /ˈætɪk/ *n* room in the roof of a house

attitude /ˈætɪtjuːd/ *n* **1** way of thinking or behaving **2** (*fml*) position of the body

attn (*esp US* **attn.**) *abbr* (*business*) (in writing) for the attention of: *Sales Dept, attn A Waters*

attorney /əˈtɜːni/ *n* (*US*) lawyer

attract /əˈtrækt/ *v* [T] **1** get sb's attention or interest: *a display that ~s customers* **2** make sb/sth come somewhere: *The warm air ~s mosquitoes*. **3** cause people to have a particular reaction: *His remarks were bound to ~ criticism*. ▸ **attraction** /əˈtrækʃn/ *n* **1** [U, sing] feeling of liking sb, esp sexually **2** [C] interesting place to go or thing to do **3** [C, U] feature or quality that makes sth seem interesting ▸ **attractive** *adj* pleasing or interesting

attribute /əˈtrɪbjuːt/ *v* [T] ~ **to** say or believe that sth is caused by sb/sth: *He ~s his success to hard work.* ● **attribute** /ˈætrɪbjuːt/ *n* quality or feature of sth/sb

attributive /əˈtrɪbjətɪv/ *adj* (*gram*) coming in front of a noun

aubergine /ˈəʊbəʒiːn/ *n* [C, U] large dark purple fruit, used as a vegetable

auburn /ˈɔːbən/ *adj* (esp of hair) reddish-brown

auction /ˈɔːkʃn/ *n* [C, U] public sale at which goods are sold to the person who offers the most money ● **auction** *v* [T] sell sth at an auction ▸ **auctioneer** /ˌɔːkʃəˈnɪə(r)/ *n* person in charge of an auction

audacious /ɔːˈdeɪʃəs/ *adj* willing to take risks or do sth shocking ▸ **audaciously** *adv* ▸ **audacity** /ɔːˈdæsəti/ *n* [U] brave but rude or shocking behaviour

audible /ˈɔːdəbl/ *adj* able to be heard ▸ **audibly** *adv*

audience /ˈɔːdiəns/ *n* **1** group of people gathered together to hear or watch sb/sth **2** number of people who watch or listen to a broadcast programme **3** formal meeting with sb important

audio /ˈɔːdiəʊ/ *adj* of hearing or sound ■ **,audio-'visual** *adj* using both sound and pictures

audit /ˈɔːdɪt/ *n* official examination of business accounts ● **audit** *v* [T] examine accounts ▸ **auditor** *n*

audition /ɔːˈdɪʃn/ *n* short performance by an actor, singer, etc to test

ability ● **audition** *v* [I, T] (ask sb to) give an audition

auditorium /ˌɔːdɪˈtɔːriəm/ *n* part of a building in which an audience sits

augment /ɔːgˈment/ *v* [T] (*fml*) increase the amount, value, etc of sth

augur /ˈɔːgə(r)/ *v* [IDM] **augur well/ill for sb/sth** (*fml*) be a good/bad sign for sb/sth in the future

August /ˈɔːgəst/ *n* [U, C] the eighth month of the year (See examples of use at *April*.)

aunt /ɑːnt/ *n* sister of your father or mother; wife of your uncle ▸ **auntie** (*also* **aunty**) *n* (*infml*) aunt

au pair /ˌəʊ ˈpeə(r)/ *n* young person who lives with a family in a foreign country in order to learn the language and take care of the children

aura /ˈɔːrə/ *n* quality or feeling that seems to be produced by a person or place

aural /ˈɔːrəl/ *adj* of the ear or hearing

auspices /ˈɔːspɪsɪz/ *n* [pl] [IDM] **under the auspices of sb/sth** (*fml*) with the help or support of sb/sth

auspicious /ɔːˈspɪʃəs/ *adj* (*fml*) showing signs of future success; favourable

austere /ɒˈstɪə(r), ɔːˈst-/ *adj* **1** without decoration; simple and plain **2** (used about a person) strict and serious **3** allowing nothing that gives pleasure; not comfortable ▸ **austerely** *adv* ▸ **austerity** /ɒˈsterəti, ɔːˈst-/ *n* (*pl* **-ies**)

authentic /ɔːˈθentɪk/ *adj* known to be real or true ▸ **authentically** /-kli/ *adv* ▸ **authenticate** *v* [T] prove that sth is genuine, real or true ▸ **authentication** /-ˈkeɪʃn/ *n* [U] ▸ **authenticity** /-ˈtɪsəti/ *n* [U] quality of being genuine or true

author /ˈɔːθə(r)/ *n* **1** writer of a book **2** person who creates or begins sth ▸ **authoring** *n* [U] (*computing*) creating computer programs without using programming language, for use in multimedia products ▸ **authorship** *n* [U] identity of the person who wrote sth

authoritative /ɔːˈθɒrətətɪv/ *adj* having or showing authority; that can be trusted ▸ **authoritatively** *adv*

authority /ɔːˈθɒrəti/ *n* (*pl* **-ies**) **1** [U] power to give orders **2** [U] official permission to do sth **3** [C, usu pl] people or group with this power **4** [C] expert: *He's an ~ on criminal law.*

authorize (*also* **-ise**) /ˈɔːθəraɪz/ *v* [T] give official permission for sth ▸ **authorization** (*also* **-isation**) /ˌɔːθəraɪˈzeɪʃn/ *n* [U]

autobiography /ˌɔːtəbaɪˈɒgrəfi/ *n* (*pl* **-ies**) story of a person's life, written by that person ▸ **autobiographical** /ˌɔːtəˌbaɪəˈɡræfɪkl/ *adj*

autocrat /'ɔːtəkræt/ n **1** ruler who has complete power **2** person who expects to be obeyed ▶ **autocratic** /ˌɔːtə'krætɪk/ adj

autograph /'ɔːtəgrɑːf/ n signature of sb famous ● **autograph** v [T] write your signature on sth

automate /'ɔːtəmeɪt/ v [T] use machines and computers instead of people to do a job

automatic /ˌɔːtə'mætɪk/ adj **1** (of a machine) working by itself without human control **2** (of an action) done without thought ● **automatic** n **1** gun that fires bullets continuously as long as the trigger is pressed **2** (GB) car with a system of gears that operate without direct action from the driver ▶ **automatically** /-kli/ adv

automation /ˌɔːtə'meɪʃn/ n [U] use of machines to do work previously done by people

automobile /'ɔːtəməbiːl/ n (US) = CAR

autonomous /ɔː'tɒnəməs/ adj **1** (of a country, region, etc) able to govern itself **2** (of a person) able to do things without help from anyone else ▶ **autonomy** n [U] **1** freedom for a country, region, etc to govern itself independently **2** ability to act without being controlled by anyone else

autopsy /'ɔːtɒpsi/ n (pl -ies) medical examination of a body to find the cause of death

autumn /'ɔːtəm/ n [U,C] season of the year between summer and winter ▶ **autumnal** /ɔː'tʌmnəl/ adj

auxiliary /ɔːg'zɪliəri/ adj (of workers) giving help or support to the main group of workers: ~ nurses ▶ **auxiliary** n (pl -ies) ■ **au,xiliary 'verb** n verb used with main verbs to show tense, etc and to form questions, eg do and has in: Do you know where he has gone?

avail /ə'veɪl/ v (fml) ~ **yourself of** make use of sth ● **avail** n [IDM] **of little/no avail** (fml) of little or no use **to little/no avail** with little or no success

available /ə'veɪləbl/ adj **1** that you can find or buy: There are no tickets ~. **2** (of a person) free to see or talk to people ▶ **availability** /-'bɪləti/ n [U]

avalanche /'ævəlɑːnʃ/ n mass of snow that falls down the side of a mountain

avarice /'ævərɪs/ n [U] (fml) extreme desire for money ▶ **avaricious** /ˌævə'rɪʃəs/ adj

avenge /ə'vendʒ/ v [T] hurt or punish sb for a wrong they have done to you: ~ his father's murder

avenue /'ævənjuː/ n **1** (abbr Ave.) street in a town or city (GB) road,

esp one with trees on either side **3** choice or way of achieving sth: explore every ~s

average /'ævərɪdʒ/ n **1** [C] result of adding several amounts together and dividing the total by the number of amounts **2** [U] usual level ▶ **average** adj: the ~ age ● **average** v **1** [I, T] find the average of sth **2** [T] be or do sth as an average: Drivers ~ 12 miles an hour.

averse /ə'vɜːs/ adj ~**to** (fml) opposed to sth: not ~ to new ideas

aversion /ə'vɜːʃn/ n [C,U] ~(to) strong dislike of sb/sth

avert /ə'vɜːt/ v [T] **1** prevent sth unpleasant from happening **2** (fml) turn away your eyes, etc

aviary /'eɪviəri/ n (pl -ies) large cage or building in which birds are kept

aviation /ˌeɪvi'eɪʃn/ n [U] science or practice of flying aircraft

avid /'ævɪd/ adj very enthusiastic; keen ▶ **avidly** adv

avocado /ˌævə'kɑːdəʊ/ n (pl ~s) pear-shaped green tropical fruit

avoid /ə'vɔɪd/ v [T] **1** prevent sth bad from happening **2** keep away from sb/sth; try not to do sth ▶ **avoidable** adj that can be avoided ▶ **avoidance** n [U]

avow /ə'vaʊ/ v [T] (fml) declare sth openly

await /ə'weɪt/ v [T] (fml) wait for sb/sth

awake /ə'weɪk/ adj not asleep ● **awake** v (pt awoke /ə'wəʊk/ pp awoken /ə'wəʊkən/) [I, T] (cause sb to) wake up

awaken /ə'weɪkən/ v **1** [I, T] (cause sb to) wake up **2** [T] cause sth to become active: ~ sb's interest [PV] **awaken (sb) to sth** (cause sb to) become aware of sth ▶ **awakening** n [sing] act of realizing sth

award /ə'wɔːd/ v [T] make an official decision to give sth to sb: ~ her first prize ● **award** n something awarded: an ~ for bravery

aware /ə'weə(r)/ adj ~**of/that** knowing or realizing sth: I'm well ~ of the problem. ▶ **awareness** n [U]

away /ə'weɪ/ adv **1** to or at a distance from sth: The sea is two miles ~. **2** to a different place or in a different direction: Go ~! ◇ Put your toys ~. **3** not present: He's ~ this week. **4** continuously: He was working ~. **5** until disappearing completely: The water boiled ~. **6** (sport) at the ground of your opponents: play the next match ~

awe /ɔː/ n [U] respect and fear ■ **'awe-inspiring** adj impressive; making you feel respect ▶ **awesome** /'ɔːsəm/ adj **1** very impressive or difficult and perhaps rather frightening **2** (*US, infml*) very good, enjoyable, etc

awful /'ɔːfl/ *adj* **1** very bad or unpleasant: *~ weather* ◊ (*spoken*) used to emphasize that there is a large amount or too much of sth: *It cost an ~ lot of money.* ► **awfully** /'ɔːfli/ *adv* very: *~ly hot*

awkward /'ɔːkwəd/ *adj* **1** embarrassing: *an ~ silence* **2** difficult to deal with: *an ~ customer* **3** not convenient: *arrive at an ~ time* **4** difficult or dangerous because of its shape or design **5** not graceful; not comfortable: *to sleep in an ~ position* ► **awkwardly** *adv* ► **awkwardness** *n* [U]

awning /'ɔːnɪŋ/ *n* sheet of cloth that stretches out from above a door or window to keep off the rain or sun

awoke *pt of* AWAKE

awoken *pp of* AWAKE

axe (*esp US as* **ax**) /æks/ *n* tool for cutting wood [IDM] **have an axe to grind** have private reasons for doing sth ● **axe** *v* [T] greatly reduce jobs or services

axiom /'æksɪəm/ *n* statement accepted as true ► **axiomatic** /-'mætɪk/ *adj* true in such an obvious way that you do not need to prove it

axis /'æksɪs/ *n* (*pl* **axes** /'æksiːz/) **1** imaginary line through the centre of a turning object: *the earth's ~* **2** (*tech*) fixed line against which the positions of points are measured, esp on a graph: *horizontal ~*

axle /'æksl/ *n* rod on which a wheel turns

azure /'æʒə(r); 'æʒjʊə(r)/ *adj, n* [U] (*written*) bright blue

B b

B, b /biː/ *n* [C,U] (*pl* **B's, b's** /biːz/) the second letter of the English alphabet

b. *abbr* born

babble /'bæbl/ *v* [I] talk quickly or in an excited way ► **babble** *n* [sing]

baboon /bə'buːn/ *n* kind of large monkey

baby /'beɪbi/ *n* (*pl* **-ies**) **1** very young child or animal **2** (*sl, esp US*) word used affectionately to address your wife, husband or lover ► **babyish** *adj* or like a baby ■ **babysit** *v* (**-tt-** *pt, pp* **-sat**) [I] look after a child or children while the parents are out ■ **babysitter** *n*

bachelor /'bætʃələ(r)/ *n* **1** unmarried man **2** (**Bachelor**) holder of a first university degree: *a B~ of Arts*

back¹ /bæk/ *n* **1** [C] part of a

person's or an animal's body between the neck and the bottom **2** [*usu sing*] part or side of sth that is furthest from the front: *sit in the ~ of the car* ◊ *Write your number on the ~ of the cheque.* **3** [C] part of a chair that supports your upper body [IDM] **back to front** with the back where the front should be: *You've got your jumper on ~ to front.* **behind sb's back** without sb's knowledge **get/ put sb's back up** (*infml*) annoy sb **get off sb's back** (*infml*) stop annoying sb **put your back into sth** work very hard at sth ● **back** *adj* **1** situated behind or at the back of sth: *the ~ door* **2** owed from a time in the past: *~ pay* ■ **backache** *n* [U,C] continuous pain in the back ■ **back'bencher** *n* (*GB*) member of Parliament who does not hold a senior position in the government or opposition ■ **'backbone** *n* **1** [C] line of bones down the middle of the back **2** [*sing*] most important part of a system, an organization, etc that gives it support **3** [U] strength of character ■ **back-breaking** *adj* (of physical work) very hard and tiring ■ **'background** *n* **1** [C] details of a person's family, education, etc **2** [C, *usu sing*, U] circumstances or past events which explain why sth is how it is; information about these **3** [C, *usu sing*] part of a scene behind the main objects, people, etc **4** [sing] position in which sb/sth can be seen/heard etc, but is not the centre of attention ■ **'backhand** *n* stroke in tennis, etc with the back of the hand forward ■ **back'handed** *adj* indirect or sarcastic: *rather a ~handed compliment* ■ **'backlog** *n* work still to be done ■ **'backpack** *n* = RUCKSACK ■ **'backpack** *v* [I] travel on holiday carrying your equipment and clothes in a backpack: *go ~ing* ■ **'backside** *n* (*infml*) part of the body that you sit on ■ **'backslash** *n* mark (\) used in computer commands ■ **,back'stage** *adv* behind the scenes in a theatre ■ **'backstroke** *n* [U] swimming stroke done on your back ■ **'backwater** *n* **1** part of a river away from the main current **2** place not affected by progress, new ideas, etc

back² /bæk/ *adv* **1** towards or at the back; away from the front or centre: *Stand ~, please.* **2** in(to) an earlier position or condition: *Put the book ~ on the shelf.* **3** (of time) in the past: *a few years ~* ◊ *hit him ~* ◊ *I'll phone you ~.* [IDM] **back and forth** backwards and forwards ■ **'back-biting** *n* [U] unkind talk about sb who is not present ■ **,back'date** *v* [T] declare that sth is valid from an earlier date in the past ■ **'back'fire** v [I] have the opposite effect to the one intended, with bad or dangerous results ■ **'backlash** n [sing] extreme, esp violent, reaction to an event

back³ /bæk/ v **1** [I, T] move (sth) backwards: *a car into a space* **2** [T] ~ **onto** (of a building) face sth at the back: *The house ~s onto the park.* **3** [T] give help or support to sb/sth **4** [T] bet money on a horse, etc **5** [T] cover the back of sth [PV] **back down** withdraw a claim, etc made earlier; admit defeat **back out (of sth)** withdraw from an agreement **back sb/sth up 1** support or encourage sb **2** give evidence to prove sth **3** (*computing*) make a spare copy of a file, etc ▶ **backer** n person who gives (esp financial) support ▶ **backing** n [U] **1** support or help **2** material that forms the back of sth ■ **'backup** n [U, C] **1** extra help or support (*computing*) spare copy of a file, etc that can be used if the original is lost or damaged

backgammon /'bækgæmən/ n [U] game played with dice on a board marked with long thin triangles

backward /'bækwəd/ adj **1** directed towards the back: *a ~ glance* **2** having made less than normal progress: *a ~ child* ▶ **backwards** (*esp US* **backward**) adv **1** towards a place or position that is behind **2** with the back or end first: *say the alphabet ~s*

bacon /'beɪkən/ n [U] salted or smoked meat from the back or sides of a pig

bacteria /bæk'tɪəriə/ n [pl] (sing **-ium** /-ɪəm/) very small living organisms, often the cause of disease ▶ **bacterial** /-riəl/ adj

bad /bæd/ adj (**worse** /wɜːs/, **worst** /wɜːst/) **1** not good; unpleasant: *~ news* **2** of poor quality: *a ~ actor* **3** ~ **at** (of a person) not able to do sth well or easily: *He's ~ at maths* **4** serious; severe: *a ~ mistake* ◇ *in a ~ mood* **5** (of food) not fresh or fit to eat; rotten: *The fish has gone ~.* **6** unhealthy; painful: *a ~ back* **7** (of a person) wicked; immoral **8** harmful: *Smoking is ~ for you.* **9** inappropriate: *a ~ time to phone* [IDM] **be bad luck** to be unfortunate **go from bad to worse** to get even worse **not bad** (*spoken*) quite good **too bad** (*spoken*) unfortunate; regrettable: *It's too ~ she's ill.* ■ **bad 'debt** n money owed that is unlikely to be paid back ▶ **baddy** n (pl **-ies**) (*infml*) bad person in a film, etc ■ **bad 'language** [U] rude or offensive words ▶ **badly** adv (**worse**, **worst**) **1** in a bad way; not good enough **2** seriously; severely: *~ly wounded* **3** very much: *need some*

money *~ly* [IDM] **badly off** poor; not having enough of sth ■ **bad-'tempered** adj often angry; in an angry mood

bade pt of BID(3)

badge /bædʒ/ n something worn to show occupation, membership, rank, etc

badger /'bædʒə(r)/ n small animal with black and white stripes on its head that lives in holes in the ground and is active at night ● **badger** v [T] put pressure on sb by repeatedly asking them questions

badminton /'bædmɪntən/ n [U] game similar to tennis, played by hitting a shuttlecock across a high net

baffle /'bæfl/ v [T] confuse sb; be too difficult for sb to understand

bag¹ /bæɡ/ n **1** [C] flexible container with an opening at the top: *a paper/shopping ~* **2** (**bags**) [pl] *~of* (*GB, infml*) plenty of sth [IDM] **in the bag** (*infml*) certain to be won, achieved, etc ● **bag** v (**-gg-**) [T] **1** put sth into bags **2** catch or kill an animal **3** (*GB, infml*) claim sth as yours

baggage /'bæɡɪdʒ/ n [U] (*esp US*) = LUGGAGE

baggy /'bæɡi/ adj (**-ier**, **-iest**) (of clothing) hanging loosely: *~ trousers*

bagpipes /'bæɡpaɪps/ n [pl] musical instrument with pipes and a bag to store air

bail /beɪl/ n **1** [U] money that sb agrees to pay if an accused person fails to appear at their trial. When bail has been arranged, the accused person is allowed to go free until the trial: *He was released on ~.* **2** [C, usu pl] (in cricket) either of the two small pieces of wood over the wicket ● **bail** (*GB also* **bale**) v [PV] **bail out (of sth)** jump out of a plane that is going to crash **bail sb out 1** pay sb's bail for them **2** help sb out of (esp financial) difficulties **bail (sth) out** empty water from a boat using your hands or a container

bailiff /'beɪlɪf/ n **1** law officer who takes goods, etc from sb who owes money **2** (*GB*) person who manages land for sb else **3** (*US*) official who keeps order in a law court

bait /beɪt/ n **1** food put on a hook or in a trap to catch fish or animals **2** thing used to tempt or attract sb ● **bait** v [T] **1** put bait on or in sth **2** deliberately try to make sb angry

bake /beɪk/ v **1** [I, T] cook sth in an oven **2** [I, T] (cause sth to) become hard by heating **3** [I] (*infml*) be or become very hot: *It's baking today!* ▶ **baker** n person whose job is to bake and sell bread, etc ▶ **bakery** n (pl **-ies**) place where bread is baked and/or sold ■ **'baking powder** n [U] powder used for making cakes, etc rise and become light

balance¹ /'bæləns/ n **1** [U, sing] condition when two opposites are equal or in correct proportions: *a ~ between work and play* **2** [U] ability to keep steady with an equal amount of weight on each side of the body: *keep/lose your ~* **3** [C, usu sing] amount of money in a bank account **4** [C, usu sing] amount of money owed after a part payment **5** [C] instrument used for weighing things [IDM] **in the balance** uncertain or undecided **on balance** having considered everything ■ **'balance sheet** n (*business*) record of money received and paid out

balance² /'bæləns/ v **1** [I, T] put your body or sth else into a position where it is steady and does not fall: *How long can you ~ on one leg?* **2** [T] compare two objects, plans, etc; give equal importance to two contrasting things **3** [T] (*business*) show that in an account the total money spent is equal to the total money received

balcony /'bælkəni/ n (pl **-ies**) **1** platform built onto the outside of a building with a wall or rail around it **2** area of seats upstairs in a theatre

bald /bɔːld/ adj **1** having little or no hair on the head **2** without any extra explanation or detail: *a ~ statement* ▶ **balding** adj starting to lose the hair on your head ▶ **baldly** adv in a few words with nothing extra or unnecessary ▶ **baldness** n [U]

bale /beɪl/ n large bundle of hay, cloth, etc tied tightly together ● **bale** v [T] **1** make sth into bales **2** (*GB*) = BAIL

balk (*esp US*) = BAULK

ball /bɔːl/ n [C] **1** round object used in games **2** round mass: *~ of wool* **3** round part of the body: *the ~ of your foot* **4** [usu pl] (*infml*) testicle **5** large formal party with dancing [IDM] **get/start/keep the ball rolling** begin/ continue an activity **have a ball** (*infml*) have a very good time **(be) on the ball** (*infml*) be alert and aware of new ideas, etc ■ **'ball game** n **1** any game played with a ball **2** (*US*) game of baseball [IDM] **a (whole) different/new ball game** (*infml*) a completely different kind of situation ■ **'ballpoint** (*also* **,ballpoint 'pen**) n pen that uses a tiny ball at its point to roll ink onto the paper ■ **'ballroom** n large room used for dancing on formal occasions

ballad /'bæləd/ n song or poem that tells a story

ballast /'bæləst/ n [U] heavy material placed in a ship or hot-air balloon to keep it steady

ballerina /,bælə'riːnə/ n female ballet dancer

ballet /'bæleɪ/ n **1** [U] style of dancing that tells a story with music but no talking or singing **2** [C] story performed by a group of ballet dancers **3** [C, with sing or pl verb] group of dancers who work and perform ballet together

ballistics /bə'lɪstɪks/ n [U] scientific study of the movement of objects shot or fired through the air ■ **bal,listic 'missile** n missile that is at first powered and guided but then falls freely

balloon /bə'luːn/ n **1** brightly coloured rubber bag filled with air **2** (*also* **hot-'air balloon**) large rounded bag filled with air or gas to make it rise in the air, with a basket to carry passengers ● **balloon** v [I] **1** suddenly swell out or get bigger **2** travel in a hot-air balloon as a sport: *go ~ing* ▶ **balloonist** n person who flies in a balloon as a sport

ballot /'bælət/ n **1** [U,C] system of voting in secret; occasion on which such a vote is held **2** (*GB* **'ballot paper**) [C] piece of paper on which sb marks who they are voting for **3** (*the ballot*) [sing] total number of votes in an election ● **ballot** v **1** [T] ask sb to vote secretly about sth **2** [I] vote secretly about sth ■ **'ballot box** n box into which ballot papers are put

balm /bɑːm/ n [U] oil or cream that is used to make wounds less painful or skin softer ▶ **balmy** adj (**-ier, -iest**) (of the air, weather, etc) warm and pleasant

balsa /'bɔːlsə/ (*also* **'balsa wood**) n [U] light wood of the tropical American balsa tree

balustrade /,bælə'streɪd/ n row of posts, joined together at the top, built along the edge of a balcony, bridge, etc

bamboo /,bæm'buː/ n [C,U] (pl **~s**) tall plant of the grass family with hard hollow stems

ban /bæn/ v (**-nn-**) [T] forbid sth officially ● **ban** n ~(**on**) official rule that forbids sth

banal /bə'nɑːl/ adj ordinary and uninteresting: *~ remarks*

banana /bə'nɑːnə/ n long yellow tropical fruit

band /bænd/ n **1** group of musicians who play popular music **2** group of people: *a ~ of robbers* **3** thin flat strip of material for tying things together or putting round an object **4** range of numbers, amounts, etc within limits ● **band** v [I] ~**together** unite in a group ■ **'Band-Aid™** n (*esp US*) =

PLASTER(3) ■ **'bandstand** n covered platform outdoors, where musicians, esp a brass or military band, can play ● **'bandwagon** n [IDM] climb/ jump on the bandwagon (infml) join others in doing sth fashionable and successful

bandage /'bændɪdʒ/ n strip of cloth that is wrapped round a wound ● **bandage** v [T] wrap a bandage round sth

bandit /'bændɪt/ n member of an armed group of thieves who attack travellers

bandwidth /'bændwɪdθ,-wɪtθ/ n [C, U] (computing) measurement of the amount of information that a particular computer network or Internet connection can send in a particular time. It is often measured in bits per second.

bandy /'bændi/ adj (-ier, -iest) (of the legs) curving outwards at the knees ● **bandy** v (pt, pp -ied) [PV] **bandy sth about** mention a name, word, story, etc frequently

bang /bæŋ/ n 1 sudden loud noise 2 violent blow to a part of the body: a ~ on the head ● **bang** v 1 [I, T] (cause sth to) make a loud noise: The door ~ed shut. 2 [T] hit a part of the body against sth: She ~ed her knee on the desk. [IDM] be banging your head against a brick wall → HEAD.¹ ● **bang** adv (infml) exactly: ~ in the middle

banger /'bæŋə(r)/ n (GB, infml) 1 sausage 2 noisy firework 3 noisy old car

bangle /'bæŋgl/ n jewellery in the form of a large ring that is worn round the wrist

banish /'bænɪʃ/ v [T] 1 order sb to leave a place, esp as a punishment 2 (written) make sb/sth go away; get rid of sb/sth ▶ **banishment** n [U]

banister (also bannister) /'bænɪstə(r)/ n [C, usu pl] posts and rail at the side of a staircase

banjo /'bændʒəʊ/ n (pl ~s) musical instrument with a round body, played by plucking the strings

bank /bæŋk/ n 1 place where money is kept safely 2 place for storing supplies: a blood ~ 3 land sloping up beside a river, etc 4 raised area of ground that slopes at the sides 5 mass of snow, clouds, etc 6 row or series of similar objects, esp machines: a ~ of switches ● **bank** v 1 [T] put money into a bank account 2 [I] have an account with a particular bank 3 [I] (of an aircraft) travel with one side higher than the other, while turning [PV] **bank on sb/sth** rely on sb/sth ▶ **banker** n owner, director or manager of a bank ■ **bank 'holiday** n (GB) official public holiday ▶ **banking** n [U] business activity of banks ■ **banknote** n piece of paper money

bankrupt /'bæŋkrʌpt/ adj 1 unable to pay your debts 2 completely lacking in anything good ▶ **bankrupt** n (law) person who is declared bankrupt in a court of law ▶ **bankruptcy** /'bæŋkrʌptsi/ n [C, U] (pl -ies) state of being bankrupt

banner /'bænə(r)/ n long strip of cloth with a message on it, carried by marchers

bannister = BANNISTER

banns /bænz/ n [pl] public announcement in church of an intended marriage

banquet /'bæŋkwɪt/ n large formal dinner

bantam /'bæntəm/ n type of small chicken

banter /'bæntə(r)/ n [U] playful joking talk ● **banter** v [I] joke with sb

baptism /'bæptɪzəm/ n ceremony of sprinkling water on sb or dipping sb in water, often giving them a name as well, as a sign of membership of the Christian Church [IDM] baptism of fire difficult introduction to a new job or activity ▶ **baptize** (also -ise) /bæp'taɪz/ v [T] give sb baptism

bar /bɑː(r)/ n 1 [C] room or counter where drinks and food are served 2 [C] piece of sth with straight sides: a ~ of chocolate 3 [C] long straight piece of wood or metal, esp across a door, window, etc: be behind ~s (= be in prison) 4 [C] narrow band of colour, light, etc 5 [C, usu sing] thing that stops sb from doing sth: Poor health is a ~ to success. 6 [C] (music) series of notes 7 (the Bar) [sing] (GB) the profession of barrister: be called to the B~ (= become a qualified barrister) 8 (the Bar) [sing] (US) the profession of any kind of lawyer ■ **'bar code** n group of thick and thin parallel lines printed on goods for sale, containing information that a computer ■ **'barman** n (pl -men) (fem 'barmaid) (US 'bartender) person who serves drinks at a bar(1) ● **bar** v (-rr-) [T] 1 fasten sth with a bar or bars(3) 2 obstruct sb/sth: ~ the way 3 prevent sb from doing sth: She was ~red from entering the competition. ● **bar** prep except for sb/sth [IDM] bar none without exception

barb /bɑːb/ n sharp curved point of an arrow or a hook ▶ **barbed** adj with short sharp points: ~ed wire

barbarian /bɑː'beəriən/ adj, n uncivilized (person) ▶ **barbaric** /bɑː'bærɪk/ adj cruel and violent and not as expected from civilized people ▶ **barbarity** /bɑː'bærəti/ n [U,C] (pl -ies) great cruelty

B

▶ **barbarous** /ˈbɑːbərəs/ adj (written) cruel and shocking

barbecue /ˈbɑːbɪkjuː/ n (abbr BBQ) **1** metal frame for cooking food outdoors **2** party at which food is cooked on a barbecue ▶ **barbecue** v [T] cook food on a barbecue

barber /ˈbɑːbə(r)/ n person whose job is to cut men's hair

barbiturate /bɑːˈbɪtʃʊrət/ n powerful drug that causes sleep

bare /beə(r)/ adj (~r, ~st) **1** without clothing or covering **2** empty: ~ cupboards **3** just enough; basic ● **bare** v [T] uncover sth; reveal sth ■ **bareback** adj, adv on a horse without a saddle ■ **barefaced** adj shameless; very rude ■ **barefoot** adj, adv without shoes or socks ▶ **barely** adv only just ▶ **bareness** n [U]

bargain /ˈbɑːgən/ n **1** something sold cheaply **2** agreement between two or more people to do sth for each other [IDM] **into the bargain** also; as well ● **bargain** v [I] discuss prices, conditions, etc with sb in order to reach a satisfactory agreement [PV] **bargain for/on sth** expect and be prepared for sth to happen: I got more than I had ~ed for.

barge /bɑːdʒ/ n flat-bottomed boat ● **barge** v (infml) [I] move awkwardly, pushing people out of the way or crashing into them [PV] **barge in (on sb/sth)** interrupt rudely

baritone /ˈbærɪtəʊn/ n (man with a) singing voice between tenor and bass

bark /bɑːk/ n [U,C] **1** short loud sound made by a dog **2** outer covering of a tree ● **bark** v **1** [I] (of dogs) make a short loud sound **2** [T] say sth in a loud unfriendly way

barley /ˈbɑːli/ n [U] (plant producing) grain used for food and for making beer and whisky

barmy /ˈbɑːmi/ adj (-ier, -iest) (GB, infml) slightly crazy

barn /bɑːn/ n building for storing hay, etc on a farm

barnacle /ˈbɑːnəkl/ n small shellfish that attaches itself to objects under water

barometer /bəˈrɒmɪtə(r)/ n instrument for measuring air pressure to show changes in the weather: (fig) a ~ of public feeling

baron /ˈbærən/ n **1** British nobleman of the lowest rank **2** person who owns or controls a large part of a particular industry ▶ **baroness** n **1** woman with the same rank as a baron **2** wife of a baron ▶ **baronet** /ˈbærənət/ n man with the lowest hereditary rank in Britain, below a baron but above a knight

baroque /bəˈrɒk/ adj used to describe European architecture, art and music of the 17th and early 18th centuries that has a grand and highly decorated style

barrack /ˈbærək/ v [I, T] shout loudly at sb to interrupt him/her

barracks /ˈbærəks/ n [C] (pl barracks) [with sing or pl verb] large building(s) for soldiers to live in

barrage /ˈbærɑːʒ/ n **1** heavy continuous gunfire **2** large number of questions or comments that are directed at sb quickly and aggressively: a ~ of complaints **3** artificial barrier across a river

barrel /ˈbærəl/ n **1** round container for liquids **2** contents of or the amount contained in a barrel **3** tube of a gun through which the bullet is fired ▶ **barrel organ** n mechanical instrument from which music is produced by turning a handle

barren /ˈbærən/ adj **1** (of soil or plants) not able to produce crops or fruit **2** not producing anything useful or successful

barricade /ˌbærɪˈkeɪd/ n barrier of objects built to block a street, etc ▶ **barricade** v [T] block a street, etc

barrier /ˈbæriə(r)/ n **1** something that prevents or controls movement or progress: the removal of trade ~s **2** thing that keeps people apart: the language ~

barring /ˈbɑːrɪŋ/ prep except for

barrister /ˈbærɪstə(r)/ n lawyer in Britain who has the right to argue cases in higher courts

barrow /ˈbærəʊ/ n **1** (GB) small cart, moved by hand, from which fruit and vegetables are sold in the street **2** = WHEELBARROW (WHEEL)

barter /ˈbɑːtə(r)/ v [I, T] exchange goods for other goods, without using money ▶ **barter** n [U]

base /beɪs/ n **1** lowest part of sth, on which it stands **2** idea, fact, situation, etc from which sth is developed **3** main part to which other parts are added: a drink with a rum ~ **4** place from which the armed forces operate: a naval ~ ● **base** v [T] **1** ~ **on** develop sth using sth else as a starting point: a story ~d on real life **2** use a particular city, town, etc as the main place for a business, holiday, etc: a company ~d in Cairo ▶ **baseless** adj (fml) without cause or reason ● **base** adj (~r, ~st) (fml) immoral; dishonourable ▶ **base 'metal** n metal that is not a precious metal such as gold

baseball /ˈbeɪsbɔːl/ n [U] American game played with a bat and ball by two teams of nine players

basement /'beɪsmənt/ *n* lowest floor of a building, below ground level

bases **1** *plural of* BASIS **2** *plural of* BASE

bash /bæʃ/ *v* [T] (*infml*) hit sb/sth very hard ● **bash** *n* (*infml*) **1** hard hit [IDM] **have a bash (at sth)** (*GB*, *spoken*) try to do sth

bashful /'bæʃfl/ *adj* shy ▶ **bashfully** *adv*

BASIC /'beɪsɪk/ *n* [U] simple language, using familiar English words, for writing computer programs

basic /'beɪsɪk/ *adj* simplest or most important; fundamental: *the ~ facts* ▶ **basically** *adv* most importantly ▶ **basics** *n* [pl] basic parts or facts

basil /'bæzl/ *n* [U] sweet-smelling herb

basin /'beɪsn/ *n* **1** = WASHBASIN (WASH) **2** round open bowl for liquids or food **3** area of land by a large river with streams running down into it: *the Amazon ~* **4** hollow place where water collects

basis /'beɪsɪs/ *n* (*pl* **bases** /'beɪsiːz/) **1** [sing] reason why people take a particular action: *She was chosen for the job on the ~ of her qualifications.* **2** [sing] way in which sth is done: *a service run on a commercial ~* **3** [C, usu sing, U] most important part of sth from which it is developed; foundation: *arguments that have a firm ~*

bask /bɑːsk/ *v* [I] ~ **(in)** sit or lie, esp in the sunshine, enjoying the warmth: (*fig*) *~ in sb's approval*

basket /'bɑːskɪt/ *n* container made of woven strips of wood: *a shopping ~* ■ **'basketball** *n* [U] game in which two teams of five players try to throw a ball into a high net hanging from a ring

bass¹ /beɪs/ *n* **1** [U] lowest tone or part in music, for instruments or voices **2** [C] (man with the) lowest singing voice **3** = DOUBLE BASS (DOUBLE¹) ● **bass** *adj* low in tone

bass² /bæs/ *n* [C, U] (*pl* **bass**) kind of sea or freshwater fish, eaten as food

bassoon /bə'suːn/ *n* wind instrument made of wood, producing very low sounds

bastard /'bɑːstəd/ *n* **1** (⚠, *sl*) used to insult sb, esp a man, who is rude, unpleasant or cruel **2** (*sl*) word that some people use to refer to sb, esp a man, who they feel jealous of or sorry for

baste /beɪst/ *v* [T] pour fat over meat while cooking

bastion /'bæstiən/ *n* **1** group of people or system that protects a way of life or belief that is threatened **2** place that military forces are defending

bat /bæt/ *n* **1** piece of wood with a handle for hitting the ball in cricket, baseball, etc **2** animal like a mouse with wings that flies and feeds at night [IDM] **off your own bat** (*infml*) without being encouraged or helped by anyone else ● **bat** *v* (**-tt-**) [I] hit a ball with a bat(1) [IDM] **not bat an eyelid** (*infml*) show no sign of surprise ■ **'batsman** *n* (*pl* **-men**) (in cricket) player who is hitting the ball

batch /bætʃ/ *n* **1** group of things or people **2** (*computing*) set of jobs processed together on a computer: *process a ~ job ◇ a ~ file/program*

bath /bɑːθ/ *n* (*pl* **~s** /bɑːðz/) **1** large container for water in which you sit to wash your body **2** water in a bath, ready to use: *a long soak in a hot ~* **3** act of washing your body while sitting in the bath ● **bath** *v* [T] give a bath to sb: *~ a baby* ■ **'bathrobe** *n* **1** loose piece of clothing worn before or after taking a bath **2** (*US*) = DRESSING GOWN ■ **'bathroom** *n* **1** room in which there is a bath, a washbasin and often a toilet **2** (*esp US*) = TOILET ■ **'bathtub** *n* (*esp US*) bath(1)

bathe /beɪð/ *v* **1** [T] wash sth with water, esp a part of the body: *B~ the wound.* **2** [T] (*US*) give a bath to sb **3** [I] (*old-fash*) swim in the sea, etc ● **bathe** *n* [sing] (*GB*) swim in the sea, etc ▶ **bather** *n* swimmer

baton /'bætɒn; -tɒ/ *n* **1** short thin stick used by the conductor of an orchestra **2** (*esp GB*) police officer's short thick stick used as a weapon

battalion /bə'tæliən/ *n* (*GB*) large group of soldiers that form part of a brigade

batten /'bætn/ *n* long narrow wooden board ● **batten** *v* [T] ~ **down** fasten sth with battens

batter /'bætə(r)/ *v* [T] hit sb/sth hard and often ▶ **battered** *adj* out of shape because of old age, great use, etc ■ **'battering ram** *n* large heavy log formerly used for breaking down walls, etc ● **batter** *n* **1** [U] mixture of flour, eggs, milk, etc: *fish fried in ~* **2** [C] (*US*) (in baseball) player who is hitting the ball

battery /'bætri; -təri/ *n* (*pl* **-ies**) **1** [C] device for supplying electricity **2** [C] large number of things or people of the same type: *a ~ of cameras/reporters* **3** [C] number of big guns that are used together **4** [C] series of cages in which hens are kept: *~ hens/eggs* **5** [U] (*law*) crime of attacking sb physically

battle /'bætl/ *n* **1** [C, U] fight between armed forces **2** [C] competition, argument or struggle between people trying to win power or control: *a legal ~ for compensation* ● **battle** *v* [I] fight; struggle: *battling* against poverty ■ **'battlefield** n place where a battle is fought ■ **'battleship** n large warship with big guns and heavy armour

battlements /'bætlmənts/ n [pl] low wall around the top of a castle, with openings for shooting through

batty /'bæti/ adj (-ier, -iest) (infml) slightly crazy

bauble /'bɔːbl/ n cheap showy ornament

baulk (esp US **balk**) /bɔːk/ v [I] ~(at) be very unwilling to try or do sth

bawdy /'bɔːdi/ adj (-ier, -iest) rude and amusing about sexual matters

bawl /bɔːl/ v [I, T] 1 shout loudly 2 cry loudly: the ~s ing his eyes out.

bay /beɪ/ n 1 area of the coast where the land curves widely inwards 2 area or division used for a particular purpose: a loading ~ [IDM] hold/ keep sb/sth at bay prevent an enemy from coming near or a problem from having a bad effect ■ **'bay tree** n tree whose dark green leaves are used in cooking ■ **bay 'window** n window, with glass on three sides, that projects from an outside wall ● **bay** n [I] (of large dogs) make a deep loud sound, esp when hunting

bayonet /'beɪənət/ n long sharp blade fixed to the end of a rifle ▶ **bayonet** /'beɪənət/, ˌbeɪə'net/ v [T] stab sb with a bayonet

bazaar /bə'zɑː(r)/ n 1 (in some eastern countries) street or area where there are many small shops 2 (in Britain, the US, etc) sale of goods to raise money for charity

bazooka /bə'zuːkə/ n long portable gun that rests on the shoulder and fires rockets esp against tanks

BBC /ˌbiː biː 'siː/ abbr British Broadcasting Corporation

BBQ abbr = BARBECUE

BC /ˌbiː 'siː/ abbr (in the year) before the birth of Jesus Christ

be¹ /bi; strong form biː/ v (I **am** (I'm), you **are** (you're), he/she/it **is** (he's/ she's/it's), we **are** (we're), you **are** (you're), they **are** (they're). Past tense: I **was**, you **were**, he/she/it **was**, we **were**, you **were**, they **were**. Past participle: **been**, present participle: **being**, negative short forms: **aren't**, **isn't**, **wasn't**, **weren't**.) 1 linking verb (**there is/are**) exist; be present: Is there a God? 2 [I] be situated: The lamp is on the table. 3 linking verb used to give the date or age of sb/sth or to talk about time: Today's Tuesday April 9th. ◇ She'll be 39 this month. ◇ It's two thirty. 4 linking verb used when you are giving the name of people or things, describing them or giving more information about them: This is Mrs

Waters. ◇ The film was very funny. ◇ She's from Thailand. ◇ 'How is your wife?' 'She's fine, thanks.' 5 [I] (used only in the perfect tenses) go to a place; visit sth: I've never been to Japan. ◇ Has the doctor been yet? 6 linking verb used to show possession: The money's not yours, it's Mark's. ◇ The letter is for you. 7 linking verb used to show equivalence in value, number, etc: That will be £80.95. ◇ Two and two is four.

be² /bi; strong form biː/ aux v (for full present and past tense forms → BE¹) 1 used with a present participle to form the continuous tense: They are reading. 2 used with a past participle to form the passive: They were sacked. 3 (**be to do sth**) used to show that sth must happen or that sth has been arranged: You are to report to the police at 10 o'clock.

beach /biːtʃ/ n area covered by sand or small stones (**shingle**) beside the sea or a lake ● **beach** v [T] move a boat onto the shore from the water

beacon /'biːkən/ n light or fire used as a signal or warning

bead /biːd/ n 1 small piece of glass, wood, etc with a hole through it, that can be put on a string with others of the same type and worn as jewellery, etc 2 drop of liquid: ~s of sweat

beady /'biːdi/ adj (-ier, -iest) (of eyes) small and bright

beak /biːk/ n hard pointed or curved outer part of a bird's mouth

beaker /'biːkə(r)/ n 1 tall narrow cup for drinking from 2 glass container used in chemistry

beam /biːm/ n 1 line of light, electric waves or particles: ~s of sunlight ◇ a laser ~ 2 long piece of wood, metal, etc used to support weight, esp as part of the roof in a building 3 wooden bar that is used in gymnastics for people to move and balance on 4 wide and happy smile ● **beam** v 1 [I] ~(at) smile happily 2 [T] send out radio or television signals 3 [I] send out light and warmth

bean /biːn/ n 1 seeds or seed containers (**pods**) from a climbing plant, eaten as vegetables: soya ~s 2 seed from a coffee plant or similar plant: coffee/cocoa ~s [IDM] **full of beans** (infml) having a lot of energy; lively

bear /beə(r)/ v (pt **bore** /bɔː(r)/; pp **borne** /bɔːn/) 1 [T] (used with can/ could in negative sentences and questions) be able to accept and deal with sth unpleasant: I can't ~ the smell of fish. ◇ She couldn't ~ the pain any more. 2 [T] (used in negative sentences) be fit for sth: The

plan will not ~ close examination.
3 [T] (fml) take responsibility for sth:
We'll ~ the cost of the improvements.
4 [T] (written) have a particular feeling, esp a negative feeling: I ~ them
no resentment. **5** [T] support sb/sth:
The ice is too thin to ~ your weight.
6 [T] (fml) show sth; carry sth so it
can be seen: The letter bore her signature. **7** [T] (written) give birth to a
child **8** [T] (fml) (of trees and plants)
produce flowers or fruit **9** [I] go or
turn in the direction mentioned: The
road ~s left. [IDM] **bear the brunt of
sth** suffer the main force of sth: ~ the
brunt of an attack/sb's anger **bear sth
in mind → MIND[1] bear witness to sth**
show evidence of sth **bring sth to
bear (on sb/sth)** (fml) use pressure,
influence, etc to try to achieve sth or
make sb do sth: Pressure was
brought to ~ on him to finish the job.
[PV] **bear down on sb/sth** move
quickly and threateningly towards
sb/sth **bear sb/sth out** show that sth
is right or that sth is true **bear up** be
as cheerful as possible in difficult
times **bear with sb** be patient with
sb ▶ **bearable** adj that can be tolerated ● **bear** n heavy animal
with thick fur and sharp claws

beard /bɪəd/ n [C, U] hair that grows
on the chin and cheeks of a man's
face ▶ **bearded** adj

bearer /ˈbeərə(r)/ n **1** person who
carries sth, esp at a ceremony: coffin ~s **2** person who brings a letter
or message (fml) person who has
a cheque for payment

bearing /ˈbeərɪŋ/ n [U] **1** ~ on
relevance; connection: That has no
~ on the subject. **2** [sing] way of
standing or behaving **3** [C] (tech)
direction shown on a compass [IDM]
get/find your bearings become
familiar with where you are **be lose
your bearings → LOSE**

beast /biːst/ n **1** (old-fash or fml)
large or dangerous animal **2** cruel
person

beat[1] /biːt/ v (pt **beat** pp ~**en** /ˈbiːtn/)
1 [T] defeat sb; be better than sb:
She ~ me at chess. **2** [I, T] hit sth
many times, usually very hard
3 [I, T] make a regular sound or
movement: His heart ~ faster. **4** [T]
mix sth thoroughly with a fork:
~ eggs **5** [T] change the shape of sth,
esp metal, by hitting it [IDM] **beat
about the bush** talk indirectly
about sth **beat it** (sl) go away **beat a
(hasty) retreat** go away or back
quickly **beat time (to sth)** mark the
rhythm of music by making regular
movements **off the beaten track** far
away from other people, houses, etc
[PV] **beat down (on sb/sth)** (of the
sun) shine with great heat **beat sb**

down persuade a seller to reduce a
price **beat sb up** hit and kick sb hard,
many times: He was badly ~en up.
▶ **beat** adj very tired: I'm dead ~.
▶ **beater** n tool for beating: a carpet
~er ◇ an egg ~er ▶ **beating** n **1** punishment by hitting **2** very heavy defeat

beat[2] /biːt/ n **1** (sound of a) repeated
stroke: the ~ of a drum **2** rhythm in
music or poetry **3** route along which
a police officer goes regularly

beautician /bjuːˈtɪʃn/ n person
whose job is to give beauty treatments

beautiful /ˈbjuːtɪfl/ adj very pretty
or attractive; giving pleasure to the
senses ▶ **beautifully** adv ▶ **beautify**
/ˈbjuːtɪfaɪ/ v (pt, pp -**ied**) [T] make
sb/sth beautiful

beauty /ˈbjuːti/ n (pl -**ies**) **1** [U]
quality or state of being beautiful
2 [C] person or thing that is beautiful ■ **beauty salon** (also **beauty
parlour**) n place where you can pay
for treatment to your face, hair,
nails, etc ■ **beauty spot** n (GB)
place famous for its scenery

beaver /ˈbiːvə(r)/ n animal with a
flat wide tail and strong teeth that
lives on land and in water and that
builds barriers (**dams**) across rivers
● **beaver** v [PV] **beaver away (at sth)**
(infml) work hard at sth

became pt of BECOME

because /bɪˈkɒz/ conj for the reason that: I did it ~ they asked me.
● **because of** prep by reason of: He
couldn't walk fast ~ of his bad leg.

beckon /ˈbekən/ v [I, T] call sb to
come nearer by waving your hand
or finger

become /bɪˈkʌm/ v (pt **became** /bɪˈkeɪm/ pp **become**) (usu used with an
adj) **1** linking verb begin to be sth:
They soon became angry. ◇ He wants
to ~ a doctor. **2** [T] look attractive
on sb: Short hair ~s you. [IDM] **what
became, has become, will become of
sb/sth?** used to ask what has happened or will happen to sb/sth

bed[1] /bed/ n **1** piece of furniture that
you sleep on **2** bottom of the sea or a
river **3** piece of ground for growing
plants **4** layer of clay, rock,
etc in the ground [IDM] **go to bed
with sb** (infml) have sex with sb
■ **bedclothes** (pl) sheets, blankets,
etc on a bed ▶ **bedding** n [U] bedclothes ■ **bedpan** n container for
use as a toilet by sb ill in bed
■ **bedridden** adj having to stay in
bed all the time because of illness,
old age, etc ■ **bedroom** n room for
sleeping in ■ **bedside** n [sing] area
beside a bed ■ **bedsit** (also **bedsitter**) n (GB) rented room for both
living and sleeping in ■ **bedspread**
n decorative top cover for bed

■ **'bedstead** *n* wooden or metal frame of a bed ■ **'bedtime** *n* [U] time that sb normally goes to bed

bed² /bed/ *v* (**-dd-**) [T] place or fix sth firmly in sth: *The bricks are ~ded in the concrete.* [PV] **bed down** sleep in a place where you do not usu sleep

bedevil /bɪˈdevl/ *v* (**-ll-** *US* **-l-**) [T] (*fml*) cause a lot of problems for sb/sth

bedlam /ˈbedləm/ *n* [U] scene of noisy confusion

bedraggled /bɪˈdrægld/ *adj* made wet, dirty or untidy by rain, mud, etc

bee /biː/ *n* black and yellow stinging insect that makes honey [IDM] **have a bee in your bonnet (about sth)** think or talk about sth a lot and think that it is very important ■ **'beehive** *n* box for bees to live in ■ **'beeline** *n* [IDM] **make a beeline for sth/sb** (*infml*) go directly towards sth/sb

beech /biːtʃ/ *n* **1** [C] tree with smooth bark, shiny leaves and small nuts **2** [U] wood of this tree

beef /biːf/ *n* **1** [U] meat of a cow **2** [C] (*infml*) complaint ● **beef** *v* [I] (*infml*) complain about sth/sb ▶ **beefy** *adj* (**-ier, -iest**) (*infml*) big or fat

been /biːn; bɪn/ *pp of* BE

beer /bɪə(r)/ *n* [U,C] alcoholic drink made from malt and flavoured with hops ▶ **beery** *adj* smelling of or like beer

beet /biːt/ *n* [U,C] **1** plant with a fleshy root that is used as a vegetable, esp for feeding animals or for making sugar **2** (*US*) = BEETROOT ■ **'beetroot** *n* [U,C] dark red fleshy root of beet, eaten as a vegetable

beetle /ˈbiːtl/ *n* insect, often large and black, with a hard case on its back, covering its wings

before /bɪˈfɔː(r)/ *prep* **1** earlier than sb/sth: *the day ~ yesterday* **2** in front of sb/sth; ahead of sb/sth: *B comes ~ C in the alphabet.* ● **before** *conj* **1** earlier than the time when: *Do it ~ you forget.* **2** until: *It was some time ~ I realized the truth.* ● **before** *adv* at an earlier time; already: *I've seen that film ~.*

beforehand /bɪˈfɔːhænd/ *adv* in advance; earlier

befriend /bɪˈfrend/ *v* [T] make a friend of sb

beg /beg/ *v* [I, T] (**-gg-**) **1** ask sb for sth anxiously because you want or need it very much: *He ~ged for forgiveness.* **2** ~ (**for**) ask sb for food, etc, esp in the street [IDM] **go begging** (*GB, spoken*) (of things) be unwanted **I beg your pardon 1** (*fml*) I am sorry **2** I used to ask sb to repeat sth because you did not hear it

beggar /ˈbegə(r)/ *n* person who

lives by asking people for money, food, etc

begin /bɪˈɡɪn/ *v* (**-nn-** *pt* began /bɪˈɡæn/ *pp* begun /bɪˈɡʌn/) [I, T] start: *~ to read a new book* ◇ *The film ~s at ten.* ◇ *~ to feel ill* [IDM] **to begin with** at first; firstly ▶ **beginner** *n* person who is just starting to learn sth ▶ **beginning** *n* [C,U] starting point

begrudge /bɪˈɡrʌdʒ/ *v* [T] feel envy or resentment at sb/sth: *I do not ~ them their success.*

behalf /bɪˈhɑːf/ *n* [IDM] **on behalf of sb | on sb's behalf** be the representative of sb: *I'm speaking on Ann's ~.*

behave /bɪˈheɪv/ *v* **1** [I] act in a particular way: *well/badly* **2** [I] ~ **yourself** act in the correct or appropriate way ▶ **behaviour** (*US* **-ior**) *n* [U] way of behaving

behead /bɪˈhed/ *v* [T] cut off sb's head

behind /bɪˈhaɪnd/ *prep* **1** at, in or to the back of sb/sth: *Hide ~ the tree.* **2** later or less good than sb/sth; making less progress than sb/sth: *He's ~ the rest of the class.* **3** supporting or agreeing with sb/sth **4** responsible for causing or starting sth: *What's ~ that happy smile, then?* ● **behind** *adv* **1** at or towards the back of sb/sth; further back: *The others are a long way ~.* **2** remaining after others have gone: *stay ~ after school* **3** ~ (**with/in**) late in paying money or completing work: *be ~ with the rent* ● **behind** *n* (*infml*) person's bottom

beige /beɪʒ/ *adj, n* [U] (of a) very light yellowish-brown colour

being¹ /ˈbiːɪŋ/ *pres part* BE

being² /ˈbiːɪŋ/ *n* **1** [U] existence: *The society came into ~ in 2001.* **2** [C] living creature: *human ~s*

belated /bɪˈleɪtɪd/ *adj* coming or happening late ▶ **belatedly** *adv*

belch /beltʃ/ *v* **1** [I] let air come up noisily from your stomach and out through your mouth **2** [T] send out a lot of smoke, etc ▶ **belch** *n*

belfry /ˈbelfri/ *n* (*pl* **-ies**) tower for bells

belief /bɪˈliːf/ *n* **1** [U] ~(**in**) feeling that sth/sb is real and true and can be trusted **2** [C] something accepted as true: *religious ~s*

believe /bɪˈliːv/ *v* **1** [T] be sure of the truth of sth or that sb is telling the truth: *I don't ~ you!* **2** [T] think that sth is true or possible: *I ~ they have moved house.* **3** (in negative sentences) [T] used to show anger or surprise at sth **4** [I] have religious faith [PV] **believe in sb/sth 1** feel certain that sb/sth exists: *I don't ~ in ghosts.* **2** be sure of the value of sth: *He ~s in getting plenty of exercise.* ▶ **believable** *adj* that can be believed ▶ **believer** *n* person who believes in the existence or truth of sth, esp a religious faith

belittle /bɪˈlɪtl/ v [T] make sb/sth seem unimportant: *Don't ~ your achievements.*

bell /bel/ n **1** metal object that makes a ringing sound when struck: *church ~s* **2** electrical device that makes a ringing sound when a button on it is pushed; the sound that it makes: *Ring the ~ and see if they're in.*

belligerent /bəˈlɪdʒərənt/ adj **1** unfriendly and aggressive **2** (fml) (of a country) fighting a war

bellow /ˈbeləʊ/ v [I, T] shout in a deep loud voice

bellows /ˈbeləʊz/ n [pl] device for blowing air into sth, eg a fire

belly /ˈbeli/ n (pl -ies) part of the body below the chest, containing the stomach ■ **'bellyache** n [C,U] (infml) stomach pain ■ **'bellyache** v [I] (infml) complain constantly ■ **'bellyful** n (infml) enough; too much: *I've had a ~ful of your moaning.*

belong /bɪˈlɒŋ/ v [I] **1 ~to** be owned by sb: *These books ~ to me.* **2 ~to** be a member of sth: *~ to a political party* **3** have a right or usual place: *The plates ~ in this cupboard.* ▶ **belongings** n [pl] personal articles; possessions

beloved adj /bɪˈlʌvd/ before a noun /bɪˈlʌvɪd/ much loved: *He was ~ by all who knew him.* ◇ my ~ husband

below /bɪˈləʊ/ prep, adv at or to a lower place or level than sb/sth: *We saw the sea ~ us.* ◇ *The temperature fell ~ freezing.* ◇ *For details, see ~.*

belt /belt/ n **1** strip of material worn round the waist **2** circular piece of material that drives machinery or carries things along **3** area that has a particular feature or where a particular group of people live: *the commuter ~* [IDM] **below the belt** (infml) unfair or cruel ● **belt** v **1** [T] (infml) hit sb/sth very hard **2** [I] (infml) move very fast: *~ing along the road* **3** [T] fasten sth with a belt: *The dress was ~ed at the waist.* [PV] **belt up** (spoken) used to tell sb rudely to be quiet

bemoan /bɪˈməʊn/ v [T] (fml) complain about sth

bench /bentʃ/ n **1** [C] long wooden or metal seat for two or more people **2** (**the bench**) [sing] (law) judge or place where a judge sits in a law court: *address the ~* **3** [C,usu pl] (in British Parliament) seat where a particular group of politicians sit: *the Opposition ~es* **4** (**the bench**) [sing] (sport) seats where players sit when they are not playing in the team

bend /bend/ v (pt, pp **bent** /bent/) **1** [T] make sth that was straight into a curved shape: *~ the wire* ◇ *It hurts when I ~ my arm.* **2** [I] be or become curved: *The road ~s to the left here.*

3 [I] move your body forwards and downwards: *Slowly ~ from the waist and touch your toes.* [IDM] **bend over backwards (to do sth)** make a great effort ● **bend** n **1** [C] curve or turn: *a ~ in the road* **2** (**the bends**) [pl] pain suffered by divers coming to the surface too quickly [IDM] **round the bend** (infml) crazy

beneath /bɪˈniːθ/ prep, adv (fml) **1** below; under **2** not good enough for sb/sth: *~ contempt*

benediction /ˌbenɪˈdɪkʃn/ n [C,U] religious blessing

benefactor /ˈbenɪfæktə(r)/ n person who gives money or help to an organization such as a charity or school

beneficial /ˌbenɪˈfɪʃl/ adj having a good effect; useful

beneficiary /ˌbenɪˈfɪʃəri/ n (pl -ies) person who receives sth, esp money, from a will

benefit /ˈbenɪfɪt/ n **1** [U,C] advantage; helpful or useful effect: *have the ~ of a good education* **2** [U,C] (GB) money given by the government to people who are ill, poor, unemployed, etc: *sickness ~* **3** [C, usu pl] advantages that you get from a company in addition to the money you earn: *a company car and other ~s* [IDM] **for sb's benefit** for sb's advantage **give sb the benefit of the doubt** accept that sb is right because there is no clear proof that they are not ● **benefit** v **1** [T] be useful to sb/sth **2** [I] be in a better position because of sth

benevolent /bəˈnevələnt/ adj kind and helpful ▶ **benevolence** /bəˈnevələns/ n [U]

benign /bɪˈnaɪn/ adj **1** (fml) (of a person) kind and gentle **2** (med) (of tumours growing in the body) not dangerous

bent¹ pt, pp of BEND

bent² /bent/ adj **1** not straight: *with your knees ~* **2** (GB, infml) dishonest [IDM] **be bent on (doing) sth** be determined to do sth, esp sth bad ● **bent** n [C,usu sing] natural skill: *have a ~ for languages*

bequeath /bɪˈkwiːð/ v [T] (fml) leave property, etc to sb after your death ▶ **bequest** /bɪˈkwest/ n (fml) something bequeathed to sb

berate /bɪˈreɪt/ v [T] (fml) speak angrily to sb

bereaved /bɪˈriːvd/ adj (fml) having lost a relative or friend by death ▶ **bereavement** /bɪˈriːvmənt/ n [C,U]

bereft /bɪˈreft/ adj **~of** completely without sth: *~ of all hope*

beret /ˈbereɪ/ n soft flat round hat

berry /ˈberi/ n (pl -ies) small soft fruit with seeds: *black~*

berserk /bə'zɜːk/ adj very angry: My father will go ~ when he finds out.

berth /bɜːθ/ n 1 place for sleeping on a ship or train 2 place in a harbour where ships tie up ● **berth** v [I, T] tie up a ship

beseech /bɪ'siːtʃ/ v (pt, pp besought /bɪ'sɔːt/ or ~ed) [T] (fml) ask sb for sth anxiously because you want or need it very much

beset /bɪ'set/ v (-tt- pt, pp beset) [T] (fml) (usu passive) trouble sb/sth constantly: ~ by problems

beside /bɪ'saɪd/ prep next to or at the side of sb/sth: Sit ~ me. [IDM] **beside yourself (with sth)** unable to control yourself because of the strength of emotion you are feeling

besides /bɪ'saɪdz/ prep 1 in addition to sb/sth; apart from sb/sth ● **besides** adv moreover; also

besiege /bɪ'siːdʒ/ v [T] surround a place with armed forces: (fig) The actress was ~d by reporters.

bespoke /bɪ'spəʊk/ adj (of a product) made specially, according to the needs of the customer

best¹ /best/ adj superlative of GOOD¹ 1 of the most excellent type or quality: the ~ dinner I've ever tasted 2 most enjoyable; happiest: the ~ years of my life 3 most suitable or appropriate: It's ~ if you go now. ■ **best 'man** n man who helps the bridegroom at a wedding ● **best** adv superlative of WELL¹ 1 most; to the greatest extent: Which one do you like ~? 2 in the most excellent way: I work ~ in the mornings. 3 in the most suitable or appropriate way [IDM] **as best you can** not perfectly, but as well as you are able ■ **best-'seller** n book, etc that sells in very large numbers

best² /best/ n [sing] 1 most excellent thing or person: We want the ~ for our children. 2 highest standard that sb/sth can reach: do your ~ 3 something that is as close as possible to what you need or want: That's the ~ I can do. [IDM] **all the best** (infml) used when saying goodbye to sb to give them your good wishes **at best** taking the most favourable view **the best of both worlds** the benefits of two completely different situations that you can enjoy at the same time **make the best of sth** do as well as you can in a difficult situation

bestial /'bestiəl/ adj cruel and disgusting ▸ **bestiality** /ˌbesti'æləti/ n [U]

bestow /bɪ'stəʊ/ v [T] (fml) give sth to sb: ~ an honour on him

bet /bet/ v (-tt- pt, pp bet) [I, T] 1 ~(on) risk money on a race or event by trying to predict the result 2 (spoken) used to say you are almost sure sth will happen: I ~ they'll come late.

● **bet** n 1 arrangement to risk money on a future event 2 money risked in this way

betray /bɪ'treɪ/ v [T] 1 give information about sb/sth to an enemy; make a secret known 2 hurt sb who trusts you by not being faithful to them 3 show sth unintentionally: His face ~ed his guilt. ▸ **betrayal** /bɪ'treɪəl/ n [C,U]

better¹ /'betə(r)/ adj comparative of GOOD¹ 1 of a higher standard or less poor quality; not as bad as sth else: He's in a much ~ mood. 2 more able or skilled: She's ~ at cooking than I am. 3 more suitable or appropriate 4 less ill or unhappy: He is slowly getting ~.

better² /'betə(r)/ adv comparative of WELL¹,² 1 in a more excellent or pleasant way; not as badly: You play tennis ~ than I do. 2 more; to a greater degree: Wait till you get to know her ~. 3 used to suggest that sth would be a suitable or appropriate thing to do: Some things are ~ left unsaid. [IDM] **be better off** in a better position, esp financially **had better (do sth)** should; ought to: You'd ~ go soon. **know better (than to do sth)** be sensible enough not to do sth

better³ /'betə(r)/ n [sing, U] something that is better: I expected ~ of him. [IDM] **get the better of sb/sth** defeat sb/sth or gain an advantage

better⁴ /'betə(r)/ v [T] 1 be better or do sth better than sth/sb else 2 ~ **yourself** improve your social position through education, etc

between /bɪ'twiːn/ prep 1 in or into the space or time that separates two points: Q comes ~ P and R in the alphabet. ◇ Children must go to school ~ 5 and 16. 2 from one place to another and back again: We fly ~ Paris and Rome daily. 3 used to show a connection or relationship: the link ~ unemployment and crime 4 shared by two or more people or things: We drank a bottle of wine ~ us. 5 by putting together the actions of two or more people: B~ them, they collected £500. ● **between** adv (usu in between) in the space or time that separates two points, objects, dates, etc

bevelled /'bevld/ (US beveled) adj having a sloping edge or surface: a ~ mirror

beverage /'bevərɪdʒ/ n (fml) any kind of drink except water

bevy /'bevi/ n [sing] (infml) large group

beware /bɪ'weə(r)/ v 1 ~(of) be careful about sb/sth dangerous or harmful: B~ of the dog!

bewilder /bɪ'wɪldə(r)/ v [T] confuse sb: ~ed by the noise and lights ▸ **bewildering** adj

bewitch /bɪ'wɪtʃ/ v [T] **1** attract sb so much that they cannot think in a sensible way **2** put a magic spell on sb ▶ **bewitching** adj

beyond /bɪ'jɒnd/ prep **1** on or to the further side of sth: *The path continues ~ the village.* **2** further than the limits of: *What happened was ~ my control.* [IDM] **be beyond sb** (*infml*) too difficult for sb to understand ● **beyond** adv on the other side; further on

bias /'baɪəs/ n [U,C] tendency to be unfair in your decisions by strongly favouring one side, person, etc ● **bias** v (-s-, -ss-) [T] (*esp passive*) unfairly influence sb's opinions or decisions: *The jury was ~ed against her.*

bib /bɪb/ n piece of cloth or plastic that you put under babies' chins while they eat

bible /'baɪbl/ n **1** (**the Bible**) [sing] holy book of the Jewish and Christian religions **2** [C] copy of this holy book **3** [C] authoritative book: *the gardener's ~* ▶ **biblical** /'bɪblɪkl/ adj

bibliography /ˌbɪbli'ɒɡrəfi/ n (pl -ies) list of books and writings about one subject ▶ **bibliographer** /-'ɒɡrəfə(r)/ n

bicentenary /ˌbaɪsen'ti:nəri/ n (pl -ies) (*US* **bicentennial**) (celebration of the) 200th anniversary of an event

bicentennial /ˌbaɪsen'teniəl/ n (*US*) = BICENTENARY ● **bicentennial** adj

biceps /'baɪseps/ n (pl **biceps**) large muscle in the upper arm

bicker /'bɪkə(r)/ v [I] argue about unimportant things

bicycle /'baɪsɪkl/ v (*also infml* **bike**) road vehicle with two wheels that you ride by pushing the pedals with your feet: *Let's go for a ~ ride.*

bid /bɪd/ v (-dd- pt, pp **bid**) (usu in sense 3: pt **bade** /bæd/ pp **bidden** /'bɪdn/) **1** [I, T] offer to pay a particular price for sth, esp at an auction **2** [I] offer to do work or provide a service for a particular price, in competition with other companies **3** [T] (*fml*) say 'good morning', etc to sb ● **bid** n **1** price offered to buy sth **2** offer to do work or provide a service for a particular price, in competition with other companies **3** attempt to do sth: *a desperate ~ to escape* ▶ **bidder** n **bidding** n [U]

bide /baɪd/ v [IDM] **bide your time** wait for a good time to do sth

bidet /'bi:deɪ/ n low bowl in the bathroom that you fill with water and sit on to wash your bottom

biennial /baɪ'eniəl/ adj happening every two years

bifocals /ˌbaɪ'fəʊklz/ n [pl] pair of

glasses with lenses that are designed for both distant and near vision ▶ **bifocal** adj

big /bɪɡ/ adj (~ger, ~gest) **1** large in size, importance, etc: *~ feet* ◇ *a ~ match* **2** (*infml*) popular [IDM] **a big noise/shot** (*infml*) important person ■ **big game** [U] large wild animals, hunted for sport ■ **big-head** n (*infml*) person who is too proud ■ **big-headed** adj (*infml*) too proud ■ **bigwig** n (*infml*) important person

bigamy /'bɪɡəmi/ n [U] crime of marrying a person when you are legally married to sb else ▶ **bigamist** n person guilty of bigamy ▶ **bigamous** adj

bigot /'bɪɡət/ n person who holds strong unreasonable opinions and will not change them ▶ **bigoted** adj intolerant and narrow-minded ▶ **bigotry** n [U]

bike /baɪk/ n (*infml*) short for BICYCLE

bikini /bɪ'ki:ni/ n two-piece swimming costume worn by women

bilateral /ˌbaɪ'lætərəl/ adj between two sides: *a ~ agreement*

bile /baɪl/ n [U] liquid produced by the liver

bilge /bɪldʒ/ n **1** [C] (*also* **bilges** [pl]) almost flat part of the bottom of a boat or a ship **2** [U] dirty water that collects in a ship's bilge

bilingual /ˌbaɪ'lɪŋɡwəl/ adj speaking or using two languages

bill /bɪl/ n **1** statement of money owed for goods and services **2** proposed law to be discussed by parliament **3** (*US*) piece of paper money **4** printed notice **5** bird's beak [IDM] **fill/fit the bill** be suitable for a particular purpose ■ **bill of exchange** (pl **~s of exchange**) (*business*) written order to pay a particular person a sum of money on a particular date ■ **bill of lading** n (pl **~s of lading**) (*business*) list giving details of the goods that a ship, etc is carrying ● **bill** v [T] **1** send a bill(1) to sb **2** announce sb/sth in a programme: *He is ~ed to appear as Othello.*

billet /'bɪlɪt/ n private house in which soldiers are put to live temporarily ▶ **billet** v [T]

billiards /'bɪliədz/ n [U] game played on a table, using balls and long sticks

billion /'bɪljən/ number one thousand million

billow /'bɪləʊ/ v [I] **1** (of a sail, skirt, etc) fill with air and swell out **2** (of smoke, cloud, etc) rise and move in a large mass ● **billow** n moving mass of smoke, cloud, etc

billy goat /'bɪli ɡəʊt/ n male goat

bin /bɪn/ n large container for storing things in or for rubbish

binary /'baɪnəri/ adj of a system of

numbers that uses only the digits 0 and 1

bind /baɪnd/ (pt, pp **bound** /baʊnd/) v **1** [T] tie or fasten sth/sb with a string or rope: ~ *the prisoner's legs to the chair* **2** [T] unite people, organizations, etc: *bound by friendship* **3** [T] fasten a book to a cover: *a book bound in leather* **4** [T] make sb obey a duty or promise: *He bound her to secrecy.* **5** [I, T] (cause sth to) stick together in a solid mass ▪ **bind** n [sing] (GB, infml) annoying situation that is difficult to avoid ▶ **binder** n **1** hard cover that holds sheets of paper together **2** person or machine that binds books ▶ **binding** n book cover

binge /bɪndʒ/ n (infml) short time of doing too much of a particular activity, esp eating or drinking alcohol: *go on a ~* ▪ **binge** [I] **~(on)**

bingo /ˈbɪŋɡəʊ/ n [U] gambling game using numbers

binoculars /bɪˈnɒkjələz/ n [pl] instrument with a lens for each eye, making distant objects seem nearer

biochemistry /ˌbaɪəʊˈkemɪstri/ n [U] study of the chemistry of living things ▶ **biochemist** n scientist who studies biochemistry

biodata /ˈbaɪəʊdeɪtə/ n [U] (esp US) = CURRICULUM VITAE

biodegradable /ˌbaɪəʊdɪˈɡreɪdəbl/ adj that can be taken back into the earth naturally and so not harm the environment

biodiversity /ˌbaɪəʊdaɪˈvɜːsəti/ n [U] existence of many different kinds of animals and plants which make a balanced environment

biography /baɪˈɒɡrəfi/ n (pl **-ies**) story of a person's life, written by sb else ▶ **biographer** /baɪˈɒɡrəfə(r)/ n person who writes a biography ▶ **biographical** /ˌbaɪəˈɡræfɪkl/ adj

biology /baɪˈɒlədʒi/ n [U] scientific study of living things ▶ **biological** /ˌbaɪəˈlɒdʒɪkl/ adj ▶ **biologist** n scientist who studies biology

birch /bɜːtʃ/ n [U,C] (hard wood of a) kind of tree with smooth bark and thin branches

bird /bɜːd/ n creature with feathers and wings, usu able to fly **2** (GB, sl sometimes offens) young woman ▪ **bird of 'prey** n bird that kills other animals for food

Biro™ /ˈbaɪrəʊ/ n (pl **~s**) kind of ballpoint pen

birth /bɜːθ/ n **1** [C,U] (process of) being born **2** [U] family origin: *Russian by ~* **3** [sing] beginning: *the ~ of socialism* [IDM] **give birth (to sb/sth)** produce a baby or young animal ▪ **'birth control** n [U] practice of preventing pregnancy ▪ **'birthday** n

anniversary of the day on which you were born ▪ **'birthmark** n unusual mark on the skin from birth ▪ **'birth rate** n number of births in one year to every thousand people

biscuit /ˈbɪskɪt/ n (US **cookie**) small flat thin crisp cake

bisect /baɪˈsekt/ v [T] divide sth into two parts

bishop /ˈbɪʃəp/ n **1** Christian clergyman of high rank **2** chess piece ▶ **bishopric** /ˈbɪʃəprɪk/ n office or district of a bishop

bison /ˈbaɪsn/ n (pl **bison**) American buffalo; European wild ox

bistro /ˈbiːstrəʊ/ n (pl **~s**) small restaurant

bit[1] pt of BITE

bit[2] /bɪt/ n **1** (**a bit**) [sing] rather; a little: *a ~ tired* **2** [sing] short time or distance: *Move up a ~.* **3** [C] **~of** small piece, amount or part of sth: *useful ~s of information* ◇ *Which ~ of the film did you like best?* **4** (**a bit**) [sing] (infml) a lot: *He earns quite a ~.* **5** [C] (computing) smallest unit of information **6** [C] metal bar that is put inside a horse's mouth so that the rider can control it **7** [C] part of a tool for drilling holes [IDM] **bit by bit** gradually **do your bit** (infml) do your share of a task **every bit as good, bad, etc (as sth)** just as good, etc **not a bit | not one (little) bit** not at all

bitch /bɪtʃ/ n **1** female dog **2** (sl, disapprov) unpleasant woman

bite /baɪt/ v (pt bit /bɪt/ pp **bitten** /ˈbɪtn/) **1** [I, T] cut into or through sth with your teeth **2** [I, T] (of an insect or snake) wound sb by making a small hole or mark in their skin **3** [I] (of fish) take the food from the hook of a fishing line **4** [I] have an unpleasant effect: *The recession is beginning to ~.* [IDM] **bite sb's head off** (infml) answer sb angrily **bite off more than you can chew** try to do too much ▪ **bite** n **1** [C] act of biting **2** [C] piece cut off by biting **3** [sing] (infml) small amount of food: *have a ~ to eat* **4** [C] wound made by an animal or insect ▶ **biting** adj sharp; painful: *a biting wind*

bitmap /ˈbɪtmæp/ n (computing) way in which an image is stored with a fixed number of bits (= units of information) ▶ **bitmap** v (**-pp-**) [T]

bitter /ˈbɪtə(r)/ adj **1** having a sharp unpleasant taste; not sweet **2** filled with anger or hatred: *~ enemies* **3** causing unhappiness or anger for a long time: *a ~ disappointment* **4** very cold: *a ~ wind* ▪ **bitter** n [U] (GB) type of dark beer that is popular in Britain ▶ **bitterly** adv: *~ly cold| disappointed* ▶ **bitterness** n

bitumen /ˈbɪtʃəmən/ n [U] sticky

black substance used in making roads

bivouac /'bɪvuæk/ n temporary camp or shelter, built without using a tent ► **bivouac** v (-ck-) [I]

bizarre /bɪ'zɑː(r)/ adj very strange or unusual

blab /blæb/ v (-bb-) [I] (infml) tell a secret, usu through talking carelessly

black /blæk/ adj **1** of the darkest colour **2** of a dark-skinned race **3** (of coffee or tea) without milk or cream **4** very angry: give sb a ~ look **5** without hope; depressing: The future looks ~. **6** very dirty **7** (of humour) funny, but about unpleasant events: a ~ comedy ● **black** n [U] the darkest colour **2** [C] person belonging to a race of people with dark skin ● **black** v [T] (GB) refuse to handle goods or do business with sb as a political protest: The strikers ~ed the cargo. [PV] **black out** lose consciousness **black sth out** switch off lights and cover windows ■ '**blackberry** n (pl -ies) small dark fruit growing wild on bushes ■ '**blackbird** n common European bird with black or brown feathers ■ '**blackboard** n board used in schools for writing on ■ ,black'currant n small black fruit that grows on a bush ► **blacken** v **1** [I, T] become or make sth black **2** [T] say harmful things about sb ■ ,black 'eye n dark-coloured bruise around the eye caused by a blow ■ '**blackhead** n small spot on the skin, with a black top ■ ,black 'ice n [U] clear thin layer of ice on a road ■ '**blackleg** n (GB, disapprov) person who works when other workers are on strike ■ '**blacklist** n list of people considered dangerous or who are to be punished ► **blacklist** v [T] ■ ,black 'magic n [U] magic used for evil purposes ■ '**blackmail** n [U] **1** crime of demanding money from sb by threatening to tell sb else a secret about them **2** use of threats to influence sb: emotional/moral ~ ► '**blackmail** v [T] ~(into) force sb to give you money or do sth for you by threatening them ► '**blackmailer** n ■ ,black 'market n [C, usu sing] illegal buying and selling of goods ► '**blackness** n [U] ■ '**blackout** n **1** period of darkness caused by electrical failure **2** period in a war when all lights must be switched off and windows covered **3** short loss of consciousness **4** prevention of the reporting of information: a news ~ ■ ,black 'sheep n person who is different from the rest of their family ■ '**blacksmith** n person whose job is to make things out of iron

bladder /'blædə(r)/ n organ in the body in which urine collects

blade /bleɪd/ n **1** sharp cutting edge of a knife, razor, etc **2** flat wide part of an oar, a propeller, etc **3** long narrow leaf of grass

blame /bleɪm/ v [T] consider sb/sth to be responsible for sth bad [IDM] **be to blame (for sth)** be responsible for sth bad ● **blame** n [U] responsibility for sth bad: lay/put the ~ on sb ► **blameless** adj not having done anything wrong ► **blameworthy** adj having done sth wrong

blanch /blɑːntʃ/ v **1** [I] become pale because you are shocked or frightened **2** [T] prepare food by putting it into boiling water for a short time

blancmange /blə'mɒnʒ/ n [C, U] jelly-like dessert made with milk

bland /blænd/ adj **1** ordinary or not very interesting **2** (of food) having little flavour **3** not showing any emotion ► **blandly** adv ► **blandness** n [U]

blank /blæŋk/ adj **1** (of paper) with nothing written on it **2** without expression; empty: a ~ look ● **blank** n **1** empty space in a document, etc **2** cartridge without a bullet ■ ,blank 'cheque n cheque that is signed but which has a space so that the amount can be written in later ► **blankly** adv ■ ,blank 'verse n [U] (tech) poetry that has a regular rhythm but which does not rhyme

blanket /'blæŋkɪt/ n **1** piece of thick cloth used as a warm covering on a bed **2** thick covering of sth: a ~ of snow ● **blanket** v [T] cover sth ► **blanket** adj including all people or things in a group: a ~ ban on tobacco

blare /bleə(r)/ v [I, T] make a loud unpleasant noise ► **blare** n [sing]

blasé /'blɑːzeɪ/ adj showing no excitement or interest in things because you have experienced them before

blaspheme /blæs'fiːm/ v [I, T] speak in a bad or disrespectful way about God or holy things ► **blasphemous** /'blæsfəməs/ adj ► **blasphemy** /'blæsfəmi/ n [U,C] (pl -ies)

blast /blɑːst/ n **1** explosion, esp one caused by a bomb **2** sudden strong rush of air **3** loud sound made by a musical instrument, etc [IDM] **(at) full blast** at the greatest possible volume or power ● **blast** v [T] **1** break sth apart or destroy sth with explosives **2** direct water, air, etc at sb/sth with a lot of force [PV] **blast off** (of spacecraft) leave the ground ● **blast** exclam (infml) used for showing anger or annoyance ■ '**blast furnace** n large structure like an oven for melting ore (= rock containing iron) ■ '**blast-off** n [U] moment when a spacecraft leaves the ground

blatant /'bleɪtnt/ adj very obvious; shameless ▸ **blatantly** adv

blaze /bleɪz/ n 1 [C] large dangerous fire 2 [sing] strong bright flames in a fire 3 [sing] ~of bright show of light or colour; impressive show of sth: a ~ of publicity ● **blaze** v [I] 1 burn brightly 2 shine brightly 3 show strong feeling: blazing with anger ▸ **blazing** adj

blazer /'bleɪzə(r)/ n jacket, often showing the colours of a school or team

bleach /bliːtʃ/ v [I, T] become or make sth white or lighter in colour by using a chemical or by leaving it in the sun ● **bleach** n [U] strong chemical used to bleach cloth or to clean sth well

bleak /bliːk/ adj 1 (of a situation) not hopeful or encouraging: The future looks ~. 2 cold and unpleasant: a ~ night ▸ **bleakly** adv

bleary /'blɪəri/ adj (-ier, -iest) (of eyes) sore and tired ▸ **blearily** adv

bleat /bliːt/ v [I] n (make the) sound of a sheep or goat

bleed /bliːd/ v (pt, pp **bled** /bled/) 1 [I] lose blood 2 [T] draw liquid or air from sth

blemish /'blemɪʃ/ n mark that spoils the good appearance of sth ● **blemish** v [T] spoil sth: The defeat has -ed the team's record.

blend /blend/ v [I, T] mix together (two substances): ~ in mix well, so that you cannot notice separate parts ● **blend** n mixture ▸ **blender** n electric machine for mixing soft food or liquid

bless /bles/ v (pt, pp ~ed /blest/) [T] 1 ask for God's favour for sb/sth 2 make sth holy ▸ **blessed** /'blesɪd/ adj 1 holy 2 giving pleasure ▸ **blessing** n [C] 1 something you are grateful for 2 [usu sing] approval 3 [usu sing] (prayer asking for) God's favour

blew pt of BLOW¹

blight /blaɪt/ n 1 [U,C] disease of plants 2 [U,sing] bad influence ▸ **blight** v [T] spoil or damage sth

blind¹ /blaɪnd/ adj 1 unable to see 2 ~(to) unwilling to notice sth: ~ to the dangers involved 3 without reason or thought: ~ obedience [IDM] (as) blind as a bat unable to see well ■ blind drunk (infml) very drunk ▸ the blind n [pl] blind people ■ blind 'alley n course of action that does not produce useful results ▸ **blindly** adv ▸ **blindness** n [U] ■ 'blind spot n 1 part of a road that a motorist cannot see 2 subject that sb is unwilling or unable to understand ■ **blind** v [T] 1 make sb blind 2 take away sb's reason, judgement, etc: ~ed by love

blind² /blaɪnd/ n roll of cloth pulled down to cover a window

blindfold /'blaɪndfəʊld/ v [T] cover sb's eyes with a strip of cloth ● **blindfold** n strip of cloth to cover the eyes ● **blindfold** adj, adv (as if) with the eyes covered

blink /blɪŋk/ v [I, T] shut and open your eyes quickly 2 [I] (of light) shine with an unsteady light ● **blink** n act of blinking [IDM] **on the blink** (infml) (of a machine) not working properly

blinkers /'blɪŋkəz/ n [pl] leather pieces fixed at the side of a horse's eyes to stop it from looking sideways

bliss /blɪs/ n [U] perfect happiness ▸ **blissful** adj ▸ **blissfully** adv

blister /'blɪstə(r)/ n 1 swelling on the surface of the skin, containing watery liquid 2 swelling on the surface of paint, etc ● **blister** v [I, T] (cause sth to) form blisters

blitz /blɪts/ n ~(on) sudden attack: (fig) have a ~ on the house (= clean it very thoroughly)

blizzard /'blɪzəd/ n severe snowstorm

bloated /'bləʊtɪd/ adj swollen

blob /blɒb/ n drop of liquid; small round mass

bloc /blɒk/ n group of countries, etc united by a common interest

block /blɒk/ n 1 large solid piece: a ~ of ice/stone 2 large building divided into separate parts: a ~ of flats 3 group of buildings with streets on four sides: walk round the ~ 4 quantity of things considered as a unit: a ~ of shares 5 obstruction: a ~ to progress ● **block** v [T] 1 make movement on or in sth difficult or impossible: roads -ed by snow 2 prevent sb/sth from moving ■ **block 'capitals** (also **,block 'letters**) n [pl] separate capital letters

blockade /blɒ'keɪd/ n action of surrounding a place to prevent goods or people from coming in or out ▸ **blockade** v [T]

blockage /'blɒkɪdʒ/ n thing that blocks; obstruction: a ~ in a pipe

bloke /bləʊk/ n (GB, infml) man

blonde (also **blond**) /blɒnd/ n, adj (person) having golden or pale-coloured hair

blood /blʌd/ n [U] 1 red liquid that flows through your body 2 (fml) family origins: a woman of noble ~ [IDM] **make sb's blood boil** make sb very angry **make sb's blood run cold** make sb very frightened **new/fresh blood** new members or employees with new ideas, etc ■ 'bloodbath n violent killing of many people ■ 'blood-curdling adj filling you with horror ■ 'blood donor n person who gives their blood for transfusions ■ 'blood group (esp US 'blood type) n

class of human blood ■ **'bloodhound**
n large dog, used for tracking down
▶ **bloodless** adj 1 without any killing 2 very pale ■ **'blood poisoning** n
[U] infection of the blood with
harmful bacteria ■ **'blood pressure**
n [U] measured force of blood as it
travels round the body ■ **'bloodshed**
n [U] killing or wounding of people
■ **'bloodshot** adj (of eyes) red
■ **'blood sport** n [C,usu pl] sport in
which animals or birds are killed
■ **'bloodstained** adj covered with
blood ■ **'bloodstream** n blood flowing through the body ■ **'bloodthirsty**
adj wanting to kill or wound; showing interest in violence ■ **'blood
vessel** n tube in the body through
which blood flows

bloody /ˈblʌdi/ adj, adv (△, GB,
spoken) swear word that is used for
adding emphasis: You ~ idiot!
● **bloody** adj (**-ier, -iest**) 1 covered
with blood 2 with a lot of violence
and killing ● **bloody** adv ■ **bloody-
'minded** adj (GB, infml) deliberately
unhelpful

bloom /bluːm/ n flower [IDM] **in (full)
bloom** with the flowers fully open
● **bloom** v [I] 1 produce flowers 2
become healthy, happy or confident

blossom /ˈblɒsəm/ n flower,
esp of a fruit tree: The trees are in ~.
● **blossom** v [I] 1 produce blossom
2 become more healthy, confident
or successful

blot /blɒt/ n 1 spot of ink, etc 2 fault:
a ~ on his character ● **blot** v [T]
1 make a blot on sth 2 dry wet ink
with blotting paper [PV] **blot sth out**
cover or hide sth: Thick cloud ~ed
out the view. ▶ **blotter** n large piece of
blotting paper ■ **'blotting paper** n [U]
absorbent paper for drying wet ink

blotch /blɒtʃ/ n irregular dis-
coloured mark or spot

blouse /blaʊz/ n piece of clothing
like a shirt, worn by women

blow¹ /bləʊ/ v (pt **blew** /bluː/, pp ~n
/bləʊn/) 1 [I, T] send out air from the
mouth 2 [I, T] (of the wind) be moving
3 [I, T] move sth or be moved by the
wind, sb's breath, etc: The wind blew
my hat off. ◊ The door blew open.
4 [I, T] produce sound from a brass
instrument, whistle, etc 5 [T] clear
your nose by forcing air out of it 6 [T]
make or shape sth by blowing:
~ bubbles 7 [I, T] (cause a fuse to)
melt because the electric current is
too strong: A fuse has ~n. 8 [T] (infml)
spend or waste a lot of money on sth
[IDM] **blow your/sb's brains out**
(infml) kill yourself/sb by shooting
yourself/them through the head
blow your mind (infml) produce a
pleasant or shocking feeling **blow
your own trumpet** (infml) praise

your own abilities and achievements [PV] **blow (sth) out** (cause sth
to) be extinguished by the wind, sb's
breath, etc: ~ out a candle **blow over**
pass away without serious effect:
The argument will soon ~ over. **blow
up 1** explode **2** start suddenly and
with force: A storm is ~ing up. **3**
(infml) get angry with sb **blow sth up
1** destroy sth by an explosion **2** fill
sth with air or gas **3** make a photograph bigger ■ **'blowlamp** (US
'blowtorch) n burner for directing a
flame onto a surface, eg to remove
old paint ■ **'blowout** n 1 bursting of a
tyre on a motor vehicle 2 sudden
uncontrolled escape of oil or gas
from a well 3 (infml) large meal
■ **'blow-up** n enlargement of a
photograph

blow² /bləʊ/ n 1 hard hit with your
hand or a weapon 2 unexpected
misfortune 3 action of blowing:
Give your nose a good ~. [IDM] **come
to blows** start fighting ■ **,blow-by-
'blow** adj giving all the details of an
event as they occur

blown pp of BLOW¹

blubber /ˈblʌbə(r)/ n [U] fat of
whales

bludgeon /ˈblʌdʒən/ v [T] (written)
1 hit sb several times with a heavy
object 2 force sb to do sth, esp by
arguing with them

blue /bluː/ adj 1 having the colour
of a clear sky on a sunny day
2 (infml) sad; depressed 3 (of films,
jokes, etc) about sex: a ~ film ● **blue**
n 1 [C,U] colour of a clear sky on a
sunny day 2 (**the blues**) [with sing or
pl verb] slow sad music from the
southern US 3 (**the blues**) [pl]
(infml) sadness [IDM] **out of the blue**
unexpectedly ■ **'bluebell** n plant
with blue bell-shaped flowers
■ **,blue-'blooded** adj from a royal or
noble family ■ **'bluebottle** n large
fly with a blue body ■ **,blue-'collar**
adj of manual workers ■ **'blueprint**
n detailed description of a plan

bluff /blʌf/ v [I, T] try to make sb
believe that you will do sth that you
do not really intend to do ● **bluff**
n [U,C] (act of) bluffing ● **bluff** adj (of
a person) very direct and cheerful

blunder /ˈblʌndə(r)/ n stupid or
careless mistake ● **blunder** v [I] 1
make a mistake 2 move clumsily or
uncertainly

blunt /blʌnt/ adj 1 without a sharp
edge or point 2 (of a person) very
direct; not trying to be polite
● **blunt** v [T] make sth less sharp
▶ **bluntness** n [U]

blur /blɜː(r)/ n something that cannot be seen clearly ● **blur** v (**-rr-**)
[I, T] become or make sth unclear

blurb /blɜːb/ n short description of the contents of a book

blurt /blɜːt/ v [PV] **blurt sth out** say sth suddenly and thoughtlessly

blush /blʌʃ/ v [I] become red in the face because of embarrassment or shame ▸ **blush** n

bluster /ˈblʌstə(r)/ v [I] **1** talk in a noisy, angry way but with little effect **2** (of the wind) blow violently ▸ **bluster** n [U] ▸ **blustery** adj (of the weather) with strong winds

boa constrictor /ˌbəʊə kənˈstrɪktə(r)/ (also **boa**) n large South American snake that crushes animals to death

boar /bɔː(r)/ n **1** male pig **2** wild pig

board¹ /bɔːd/ n **1** [C] long thin flat piece of wood: a floor~ **2** [C] flat piece of wood, etc used for a special purpose: a notice~ **3** [C] surface marked with patterns on which certain games are played: Chess is a ~ game. **4** [C] group of people controlling a business: the ~ of directors **5** [U] food in rented accommodation: pay for ~ and lodging [IDM] **across the board** affecting or including all members, groups, etc: an across-the-~ wage increase **be above board** be honest and open **go by the board** be rejected or ignored **on board** on or in a ship, an aircraft or a train **take sth on board** (infml) accept sth

board² /bɔːd/ v **1** [T] get on to a ship, plane, train, etc **2** [T] (**be boarding**) [I] (of a plane, train, etc) be ready for passengers to get on **3** [I] live and take meals in sb's home, in return for payment **4** [I] live at a school during the term [PV] **board sth up** cover a window, door, etc with wooden boards ▸ **boarder** n pupil who lives at a boarding school during the term ■ **'boarding card** n card allowing a person to board a ship or an aircraft ■ **'boarding house** n private house providing meals and accommodation ■ **'boarding school** n school where pupils live during the term

boast /bəʊst/ v **1** [I, T] ~(**about/of**) talk about your own achievements, possessions, etc with too much pride: ~ about your new car **2** [T] possess sth that you are proud of: The hotel ~s a fine swimming pool. ▸ **boast** n ▸ **boastful** adj (disapprov) talking about yourself in a very proud way ▸ **boastfully** adv

boat /bəʊt/ n **1** vehicle (smaller than a ship) for travelling on water: a rowing ~ **2** any ship ■ **'boathouse** n building beside a river in which boats are stored ▸ **boating** n [U] activity of using a small boat for pleasure: go ~ing on the lake

bob /bɒb/ v (**-bb-**) **1** [I] move up and down, esp in water: a cork ~bing on

the water **2** [T] cut sb's hair so that it is the same length all the way around ● **bob** n woman's hairstyle in which the hair is cut the same length all the way around

bobbin /ˈbɒbɪn/ n small device on which you wind thread, used eg on a sewing machine

bobsleigh /ˈbɒbsleɪ/ (also **bobsled** /ˈbɒbsled/) n sledge for racing on snow

bode /bəʊd/ v [IDM] **bode well/ill (for sb/sth)** (written) be a good/bad sign for sb/sth

bodice /ˈbɒdɪs/ n upper part of a woman's dress

bodily /ˈbɒdɪli/ adj of the human body; physical ● **bodily** adv **1** by moving the whole of sb's body; by force **2** in one piece; completely

body /ˈbɒdi/ n (pl **-ies**) **1** whole physical structure of a person or an animal **2** main part of a human body without the head, arms or legs **3** dead body **4** main part of sth: the ~ of a car **5** group of people doing sth together: a parliamentary ~ **6** large amount of sth; mass: a ~ of water **7** (fml) object: heavenly bodies (= stars and planets) ■ **'bodyguard** n person or group of people who protect sb important ■ **'bodywork** n [U] main outside structure of a motor vehicle

bog /bɒg/ n **1** area of soft wet ground **2** (GB, sl) toilet ● **bog** v (**-gg-**) [IDM] **be/get bogged down (in sth)** be/get stuck so that you cannot make progress: get ~ged down in small details ▸ **boggy** adj (of land) soft and wet

bogey (also **bogy**) /ˈbəʊgi/ n (pl **-ies**) thing that causes fear, often without reason

boggle /ˈbɒgl/ v [I] ~(**at**) (infml) find sth difficult to imagine or accept: The mind ~s (at the idea).

bogus /ˈbəʊgəs/ adj not real

bogy ⇨ BOGEY

boil /bɔɪl/ v [I, T] (of a liquid) (cause sth to) bubble and change into steam or vapour by being heated: The kettle (= the water in the kettle) is ~ing. ◇ She left the gas on and the pan ~ed dry (= the water boiled until there was none left). **2** [T] cook sth in boiling water: ~ an egg **3** [I] (written) be very angry [PV] **boil away** (of a liquid) boil until there is none left **boil down to sth** have sth as its main point: It all ~s down to what you really want. **boil over** (of a liquid) boil and flow over the side of a pan **2** (of a situation, an emotion, etc) change into sth more dangerous or violent ● **boil** n [sing] period of boiling; point at which liquid boils: Bring the soup to the ~, then allow it to simmer. **2** [C] red infected swelling under the skin ▸ **boiling** (also **boiling 'hot**) adj very hot ● **'boiling point** *n* temperature at which a liquid begins to boil

boiler /'bɔɪlə(r)/ *n* device in which water is heated, eg for the central heating in a house ■ **'boiler suit** *n* one-piece garment worn for doing dirty work

boisterous /'bɔɪstərəs/ *adj* (of a person) noisy and full of life and energy

bold /bəʊld/ *adj* **1** (of a person) brave and confident; not afraid to take risks **2** (of shape, colour, lines, etc) that can be clearly seen: ~ *designs* ▶ **boldly** *adv* ▶ **boldness** *n* [U]

bollard /'bɒlɑːd/ *n* short thick post used to stop motor vehicles from going on to a road

bolster /'bəʊlstə(r)/ *n* long pillow ● **bolster** *v* [T] ~ **(up)** improve sth or make it stronger

bolt /bəʊlt/ *n* **1** metal bar that slides into a socket to lock a door, etc **2** metal screw used with a nut for holding things together **3** flash of lightning **4** act of running away quickly: *make a ~ for it* ● **bolt** *v* **1** [I] fasten sth with a bolt **2** [I] (esp of a horse) run away quickly **3** [T] ~ **(down)** swallow food quickly ● **bolt** *adv* [IDM] **sit/stand bolt upright** sit or stand with your back straight

bomb /bɒm/ *n* **1** [C] weapon designed to explode when it is thrown or dropped **2** **(the bomb)** [sing] nuclear weapons (atomic or hydrogen bombs) **3** **(a bomb)** [GB, *infml*] [sing] a lot of money: *This dress cost a ~.* ● **bomb** *v* [T] attack sb/sth with bombs ▶ **bomber** *n* **1** aircraft that drops bombs **2** person who throws or puts bombs in place ■ **bombshell** *n* (*infml*) great shock

bombard /bɒm'bɑːd/ *v* **1** attack sb/sth with bombs or shells from big guns **2** attack sb with a lot of questions, criticism, etc ▶ **bombardment** *n* [U,C]

bona fide /ˌbəʊnə 'faɪdɪ/ *adj, adv* genuine(ly)

bond /bɒnd/ *n* **1** [C] something that unites people or groups: ~*s of friendship* **2** [C] (*fml*) written agreement that has legal force **3** [C] certificate stating that money has been lent to a government, etc and will be paid back with interest **4** **(bonds)** [pl] (*fml*) ropes or chains used for tying up a prisoner ● **bond** *v* **1** [T] join sth together **2** [I, T] develop a relationship of trust and affection with sb

bone /bəʊn/ *n* [C,U] any of the hard parts that form the skeleton of an animal's body [IDM] **feel (it) in your bones** (that ...) feel certain about sth ● **have a bone to pick with sb** have sth to complain about to sb ● **make no bones about (doing) sth** not hesitate to do sth ● **bone** *v* [T] take bones

out of sth ■ **bone 'dry** *adj* completely dry ■ **bone 'idle** *adj* (*GB*) very lazy ■ **bone marrow** *n* [U] soft substance that fills the hollow parts of bones: *a ~ marrow transplant*

bonfire /'bɒnfaɪə(r)/ *n* large outdoor fire

bonnet /'bɒnɪt/ *n* **1** cover over the engine of a motor vehicle **2** baby's or woman's hat tied under the chin

bonus /'bəʊnəs/ *n* **1** payment in addition to what is usual **2** anything pleasant in addition to what is expected

bony /'bəʊni/ *adj* (**-ier, -iest**) **1** full of bones: *This fish is ~.* **2** very thin; having bones that are close to the skin

boo /buː/ *exclam, n* (*pl* **~s**) sound made to show disapproval ● **boo** *v* [I, T] shout 'boo' at sb/sth

booby prize /'buːbi praɪz/ *n* prize given to sb who comes last in a competition

booby trap /'buːbi træp/ *n* object that looks harmless but that will kill or injure sb when touched ● **booby-trap** *v* (**-pp-**) [T] place a booby trap in sth

book¹ /bʊk/ *n* **1** [C] number of printed sheets of paper fastened together in a cover **2** [C] set of things fastened together like a book: *a ~ of stamps* **3** **(books)** [pl] business accounts **4** [C] main division of a large written work, eg the Bible [IDM] **be in sb's good/bad books** (*infml*) used to say that sb is pleased/annoyed with you ■ **'bookcase** *n* piece of furniture with shelves for books ■ **'book club** *n* organization that sells books cheaply to its members ▶ **'bookkeeper** *n* person whose job is to keep an accurate record of the accounts of a business ▶ **'bookkeeping** *n* [U] ■ **'bookmaker** (*also infml* **'bookie**) *n* person whose job is to take bets on horse races ■ **'bookmark** *n* **1** something put in a book to mark the reader's place **2** (*computing*) record of the address of a file, a Web page, etc that enables you to find it quickly ▶ **bookmark** *v* [T]: *Do you want to ~ this site?* ■ **'bookshop** *n* shop that sells mainly books ■ **'bookstall** *n* small shop that is open at the front and which sells newspapers, etc ■ **'book token** *n* card with a voucher, usu given as a gift, that can be exchanged for books ■ **'bookworm** *n* person who is very fond of reading

book² /bʊk/ *v* **1** [T] order tickets, etc in advance; reserve sth **2** [T] write down the name of sb when bringing a legal charge: *be ~ed for speeding* ▶ **bookable** *adj* that can be reserved ▶ **booking** *n* [C,U] arrangement that is made in advance to buy a ticket to travel somewhere, etc: *No advance ~ is necessary.* ■ '**booking office** *n* office where tickets are sold

bookie /'bʊki/ *n* (*infml*) *short for* BOOKMAKER (BOOK¹)

booklet /'bʊklət/ *n* small thin book with paper covers

boom /buːm/ *n* **1** ~ (**in**) sudden increase in trade and economic activity **2** long pole that the bottom of a boat's sail is attached to **3** long pole that carries a microphone ● **boom** *v* **1** [I] make a loud deep sound **2** [I, T] ~(**out**) say sth in a loud deep voice **3** [I] (of business or the economy) have a period of rapid growth: *Sales are ~ing.*

boomerang /'buːməræŋ/ *n* curved wooden stick (used by Australian Aborigines) that returns to the thrower

boon /buːn/ *n* something that is helpful and makes life easier for you

boost /buːst/ *v* [T] increase the strength or value of sth ● **boost** *n* ► **booster** *n* **1** something that gives extra strength or power to sth **2** additional injection of a drug: *a polio/tetanus ~er*

boot /buːt/ *n* **1** shoe that covers the foot and ankle, and sometimes also the lower leg **2** space for luggage at the back of a car [IDM] **be given/get the boot** (*infml*) be told that you must leave your job **put the boot in** (*infml*) kick sb hard, esp when they are on the ground ● **boot** *v* **1** [T] kick sb/sth **2** [I, T] (*computing*) prepare a computer for use by loading its operating system [PV] **boot sb out** (**of sth**) (*infml*) force sb to leave a job or place

booth /buːð/ *n* **1** small stall where goods are sold **2** small enclosed area: *a telephone ~*

booze /buːz/ *n* [U] (*infml*) alcoholic drink ● **booze** *v* [I] (*infml*) drink alcohol, esp in large quantities ► **boozer** *n* (*infml*) **1** person who boozes **2** (*GB*) pub ■ '**booze-up** *n* (*GB, infml*) party, event, etc at which a lot of alcohol is drunk

bop /bɒp/ *n* [C, U] (*GB, infml*) dance to pop music ● **bop** *v* (**-pp-**) [I] (*infml*) dance to pop music

border /'bɔːdə(r)/ *n* **1** (land near the) dividing line between two countries **2** edge of sth **3** (in a garden) strip of soil along the edge of the grass for planting flowers ● **border** *v* [I, T] ~(**on**) be next to another country or area [PV] **border on sth** come very close to being sth: *a state of excitement ~ing on madness* ■ '**borderline** *n* division between two qualities or conditions ■ '**borderline** *adj* not clearly

belonging to a particular condition or group: *a ~line candidate* (= one that may or may not pass an exam)

bore¹ /bɔː(r)/ *v* **1** [T] make sb feel tired and uninterested, esp by talking too much **2** [I, T] ~**into/through** make a long deep hole in sth with a special tool ● **bore** *n* **1** person or thing that bores or annoys sb **2** (diameter of the) hollow part inside a tube, eg a pipe or gun **3** deep hole made in the ground, esp to find water or oil ► **boredom** /'bɔːdəm/ *n* [U] state of being bored ► **boring** *adj* uninteresting; dull

bore² *pt of* BEAR

born /bɔːn/ *v* (**be born**) (used only in the passive, without *by*) come out of your mother's body at the beginning of your life: *He was ~ in 1954.* ● **born** *adj* having a particular natural ability: *be a ~ leader* ► **-born** (in compounds) born in the order, way, place, etc mentioned: *Dutch-~* ■ ,**born-a'gain** *adj* having renewed and very strong faith in sth, esp a religion: *a ~-again Christian*

borne *pp of* BEAR

borough /'bʌrə/ *n* town or part of a city that has its own local government

borrow /'bɒrəʊ/ *v* [I, T] have or use sth that belongs to sb else, with the promise that it will be returned ► **borrower** *n*

bosom /'bʊzəm/ *n* **1** [C] a woman's chest or breasts **2** (**the bosom of sth**) [sing] loving care and protection of sth: *in the ~ of your family* ■ ,**bosom 'friend** *n* very close friend

boss /bɒs/ *n* person who is in charge of others at work and tells them what to do ● **boss** *v* [T] ~(**about/around**) (*infml*) tell sb what to do in an aggressive and/or annoying way ► **bossy** *adj* (**-ier, -iest**) always telling people what to do

botany /'bɒtəni/ *n* [U] scientific study of plants ► **botanical** /bə'tænɪkl/ *adj* ► **botanist** *n* scientist who studies botany

botch /bɒtʃ/ *v* [T] spoil sth by doing it badly ● **botch** *n* piece of badly-done work

both /bəʊθ/ *adj, pron* the two; the one as well as the other: *B~ (the) books are expensive.* ◇ *His parents are ~ dead.* ● **both** *adv* with equal truth in two cases: *She has houses in ~ London and Paris.*

bother /'bɒðə(r)/ *v* **1** [T] cause trouble or annoyance to sb: *Is something ~ing you?* **2** [I, T] take the time or trouble to do sth: *Don't ~ to stand up.* ● **bother** *n* [U] trouble or difficulty: *I don't want to put you to any ~* (= cause you any trouble).

bottle /'bɒtl/ *n* **1** [C] container with

a narrow neck, for liquids **2** [C] amount contained in this **3** [C, usu sing] baby's feeding bottle; milk from this: *It's time for her ~.* **4** [U] (*GB, infml*) courage: *She didn't have the ~ to ask him.* ● **bottle** *v* [T] put sth in bottles [PV] **bottle sth up** not allow your feelings to be shown ■ **'bottleneck** *n* **1** narrow or restricted stretch of road that causes traffic to slow down **2** anything that slows down movement or progress

bottom /'bɒtəm/ *n* **1** [C, usu sing] ~(of) lowest part of sth **2** [C] (*esp GB*) part of the body that you sit on **3** [sing] ground under a sea, lake, etc **4** [sing] part that is furthest from you, your house, etc: *the ~ of the garden* **5** [sing] lowest position in a class, organization, etc [IDM] **get to the bottom of sth** be/lie at the **bottom of sth** be the original cause of sth **get to the bottom of sth** discover the real cause of sth ● **bottom** *v* [PV] **bottom out** (of prices, a bad situation, etc) stop getting worse ▶ **bottomless** *adj* very deep; unlimited ■ **the ˌbottom 'line** *n* **1** most important or deciding point **2** (*business*) amount of money that is profit or loss after everything has been calculated

bough /baʊ/ *n* large branch of a tree

bought *pt, pp of* BUY

boulder /'bəʊldə(r)/ *n* large rock

bounce /baʊns/ *v* **1** [I, T] (cause e g a ball to) move quickly back from a surface it has just hit **2** [I, T] (cause sb/sth to) move up and down in a lively way: *She ~d the child on her lap.* **3** [I] move in the direction that is mentioned in a lively way: *She ~d into the room.* **4** [I, T] (*infml*) (of a cheque) be returned by a bank because there is not enough money in an account **5** [I, T] (of an email) be returned to the sender because the system could not deliver it ● **bounce** *n* action of bouncing ▶ **bouncer** *n* person employed by a club, pub, etc to throw out troublemakers ● **bouncing** *adj* strong and healthy: *a ~ baby boy*

bound¹ *pt, pp of* BIND

bound² /baʊnd/ *adj* ~**to** certain or likely to happen, or to do or be sth: *He is ~ to win.* **2** forced to do sth by law or duty **3** ~**(for)** travelling to a place: *a ship ~ for Rotterdam* [IDM] **bound up in sth** very busy with sth **bound up with sth** closely connected with sth

bound³ /baʊnd/ *v* **1** [I] jump; run with jumping movements **2** [T] (*usu passive*) (*fml*) form the boundary of sth: *an airfield ~ed by woods* ▶ **bound** *n*

boundary /'baʊndri/ *n* (*pl* -**ies**) line that marks a limit

boundless /'baʊndləs/ *adj* without limits

bounds /baʊndz/ *n* [pl] limits [IDM] **out of bounds (to sb)** (of a place) not allowed to be entered by sb

bounty /'baʊnti/ *n* (*pl* -**ies**) **1** [U,C] (*lit*) generous actions **2** [C] money given as a reward ▶ **bountiful** *adj* giving generously

bouquet /buˈkeɪ/ *n* **1** [C] bunch of flowers **2** [C, U] smell of wine

bourgeois /'bʊəʒwɑː, ˌbʊəʒˈwɑː/ *n, adj* **1** (person) belonging to the middle class **2** (*disapprov*) (person who is) concerned with material possessions and social status ▶ **bourgeoisie** /ˌbʊəʒwɑːˈziː/ *n* [sing, with sing or pl verb] (**the bourgeoisie**) middle classes

bout /baʊt/ *n* short period of activity or an illness

boutique /buːˈtiːk/ *n* small shop, esp one that sells fashionable clothes

bow¹ /baʊ/ *v* [I, T] bend your head or the upper part of your body forward as a sign of respect or as a greeting [PV] **bow out (of sth)** stop taking part in sth **bow to sth** agree unwillingly to do sth because other people want you to ● **bow** *n* **1** act of bending your head or body forward as a sign of respect or as a greeting **2** front part of a boat or ship

bow² /bəʊ/ *n* **1** weapon used for shooting arrows, consisting of a long piece of wood curved by a tight string **2** long thin piece of wood with thin string stretched along it, used for playing the violin, etc **3** knot with two loops, often in ribbon, for decoration ▶ **bow-legged** /ˌbəʊ ˈleɡɪd/ *adj* having legs that curve outward at the knees ■ **ˌbow 'tie** *n* man's tie formed as a bow(3)

bowel /'baʊəl/ *n* [C, usu pl] **1** intestine **2** deepest part: *in the ~s of the earth*

bowl¹ /bəʊl/ *n* **1** [C] deep round container for food or liquid **2** [C] amount contained in this **3** [C] part of some objects that is shaped like a bowl **4** [C] heavy ball used for playing bowls or tenpin bowling **5** (**bowls**) [U] game played on an area of very smooth grass, in which players try to roll bowls as near as possible to a small ball

bowl² /bəʊl/ *v* **1** [I, T] roll a ball in the game of bowls or bowling **2** [I, T] throw a ball to the batsman in cricket **3** [T] ~**(out)** get a batsman out of a game of cricket by hitting the wicket behind them with the ball [PV] **bowl sb over 1** run into sb and knock them down **2** surprise or impress sb a lot

bowler /'bəʊlə(r)/ n **1** (in cricket) person who bowls **2** (also **bowler 'hat**) man's hard round hat

bowling /'bəʊlɪŋ/ n **1** game in which heavy balls (**bowls**) are rolled along a track towards a group of bottle-shaped objects (**pins**) to knock them down

box /bɒks/ n **1** [C] container made of wood, cardboard, etc, usu with a lid, used for holding solid things **2** [C] box and its contents: *a ~ of chocolates* **3** [C] separate enclosed area or compartment: *a ~ in a theatre* **4** [C] small hut used for a particular purpose: *a telephone ~* **5** [C] small square on a form, to be filled in **6** (**the box**) [sing] (*infml*) television ● **box** v [T] put sth into a box **2** [I, T] fight sb with the fists, wearing large thick gloves, as a sport [PV] **box sb/sth in** prevent sb from being able to move by surrounding them with people, vehicles, etc ▸ **boxer** n **1** person who boxes(2) **2** breed of bulldog ▸ **boxing** n [U] sport in which two people fight each other with their fists ■ **'box number** n number used as an address in a newspaper advertisement, to which replies may be sent ■ **'box office** n office at a theatre, etc where tickets are sold

Boxing Day /'bɒksɪŋ deɪ/ n [U,C] (GB) the first weekday after Christmas Day

boy /bɔɪ/ n male child; young man ■ **'boyfriend** n man or boy with whom sb has a romantic and/or sexual relationship ▸ **boyhood** n [U] the time of being a boy ▸ **boyish** adj looking or behaving like a boy

boycott /'bɔɪkɒt/ v [T] refuse to be involved with or take part in sth as a way of protesting ● **boycott** n

bra /brɑː/ n (also fml **brassière**) piece of women's underwear worn to support the breasts

brace /breɪs/ v **1** ~ **sb/yourself (for)** prepare sb/yourself for sth difficult or unpleasant **2** [T] tighten the muscles in your body or part of your body before doing sth that is physically difficult **3** [T] (tech) make sth stronger or more solid ● **brace** n **1** [C] wire device used esp by children to straighten the teeth **2** [C] device that straightens or supports sth **3** (**braces**) [pl] (GB) straps that pass over the shoulders to hold trousers up ▸ **bracing** adj giving energy: *the bracing sea air*

bracelet /'breɪslət/ n piece of jewellery worn around the wrist

bracken /'brækən/ n [U] wild plant with large leaves that grows on hills and in woods

bracket /'brækɪt/ n **1** [usu pl] either of a pair of marks, (), placed

around extra information in a piece of writing **2** wood or metal support for a shelf **3** group within particular limits: *the 20-30 age ~* ● **bracket** v [T] **1** put sth in brackets **2** group sb/sth together

brackish /'brækɪʃ/ adj (of water) slightly salty

brag /bræg/ v (-**gg**-) [I, T] talk with too much pride about sth

braid /breɪd/ n **1** [U] thin coloured rope that is used to decorate furniture and military uniforms **2** [C] (esp US) = PLAIT ● **braid** v [T] (US) plait

Braille /breɪl/ n [U] system of writing for blind people, using raised dots

brain /breɪn/ n **1** [C] organ in the body that controls thought, feeling, etc **2** [U, C, usu pl] mind; intelligence: *have a good ~* **3** [C, usu sl] (infml) clever person [IDM] **have sth on the brain** (infml) think about sth constantly ● **brain** v [T] kill sb with a heavy blow on the head ■ **'brainchild** n [sing] person's original idea or invention ■ **'brain drain** n [sing] (infml) movement of skilled clever people to other countries where they can earn more money ▸ **brainless** adj stupid ■ **brainstorm** n (GB) sudden mental disturbance ■ **'brainstorming** n [U] way of making a group of people all think about sth at the same time, esp in order to solve a problem or to create good ideas ■ **'brainwash** v [T] force sb to accept new beliefs by use of extreme mental pressure ■ **'brainwave** n sudden clever idea ▸ **brainy** adj (-ier, -iest) (infml) clever

braise /breɪz/ v [T] cook meat or vegetables slowly in a covered container

brake /breɪk/ n device for reducing the speed of or stopping a vehicle ● **brake** v [I, T] slow down or stop a vehicle using a brake

bramble /'bræmbl/ n prickly wild bush on which blackberries grow

bran /bræn/ n [U] outer covering of grain which is left when the grain is made into flour

branch /brɑːntʃ/ n **1** part of a tree growing out from a trunk **2** local office or shop belonging to a large company or organization: *a ~ office* **3** smaller or less important part of a river, road, railway, etc ● **branch** v [I] divide into two or more parts [PV] **branch off** turn from one road into a smaller one **branch out (into sth)** start to do an activity that you have not done before, esp in your work or business

brand /brænd/ n **1** type of product made by a particular company: *the* cheapest ~ of margarine ◇ Sportswear manufacturers owe their success to ~ image. **2** particular kind: a strange ~ of humour **3** mark burn onto the skin of an animal to show ownership ● **brand** v [T] **1** mark an animal with hot metal to show who owns it **2** give a bad name to sb: He was ~ed (as) a thief. ■ **'brand name** (also **'trade name**) n name given to a product by the company that produces it ■ **brand 'new** adj completely new

brandish /'brændɪʃ/ v [T] wave sth, esp a weapon, threateningly in the air

brandy /'brændi/ n [U,C] (pl **-ies**) strong alcoholic drink made from wine

brash /bræʃ/ adj confident in a rude or aggressive way

brass /brɑːs/ n **1** [U] bright yellow metal; objects made of brass **2** (**the brass**) [U, with sing or pl verb] (people who play) musical instruments made of metal that form a band or section of an orchestra ■ **,brass 'band** n group of musicians who play brass instruments

brassiere /'bræziə(r)/ n (fml) = BRA

brat /bræt/ n (disapprov) badly-behaved child

bravado /brə'vɑːdəʊ/ n [U] unnecessary or false show of courage

brave /breɪv/ adj (~r, ~st) **1** (of a person) willing to do things which are dangerous or painful; not afraid **2** (of an action) requiring or showing courage ● **brave** v [T] have to deal with sth difficult or unpleasant in order to achieve sth ▶ **bravely** adv ▶ **bravery** /'breɪvəri/ n [U]: an award for outstanding ~

bravo /ˌbrɑː'vəʊ/ exclam, n (pl **~s**) shout meaning 'Well done!'

brawl /brɔːl/ n noisy argument, usu in a public place ▶ **brawl** v [I]

brawny /'brɔːni/ adj (infml) strong and muscular

bray /breɪ/ v [I] **1** (of a donkey) make a loud harsh sound **2** [I, T] (of a person) talk or laugh in a loud unpleasant voice ▶ **bray** n

brazen /'breɪzn/ adj open and without shame, usu about sth that people find shocking

brazier /'breɪziə(r)/ n metal container for holding a charcoal or coal fire

breach /briːtʃ/ n **1** [C,U] breaking or neglect of a law, an agreement, etc: a ~ of contract ◇ a ~ of the peace = the crime of fighting in a public place) **2** [C] break in a friendly relationship **3** [C] (fml) opening, eg in a wall ● **breach** v [T] **1** not keep to an agreement or not keep a

promise **2** (fml) make a hole in a wall, fence, etc, so that sb/sth can go through it

bread /bred/ n [U] food made of flour, water and usu yeast, baked in an oven: a loaf of brown ~ ■ **'breadcrumbs** n [pl] tiny pieces of bread ■ **'breadline** n [IDM] **on the breadline** very poor ■ **'breadwinner** n person who supports their family with the money they earn

breadth /bredθ/ n [U,C] **1** distance from side to side; width **2** wide range (of knowledge, interests, etc)

break¹ /breɪk/ v (pt **broke** /brəʊk/, pp **broken** /'brəʊkən/) **1** [I, T] (cause sth to) be damaged and separated into pieces: Glass ~s easily. ◇ ~ a plate **2** [I, T] (cause sth to) stop working as a result of being damaged: My watch has broken. **3** [T] do sth that is against the law; not keep a promise, etc **4** [I] ~(**for**) stop doing sth for a while, esp when it is time to eat or have a drink: Let's ~ for lunch. **5** [T] interrupt sth: ~ your journey **6** [I] stop somewhere on the way to your destination) ◇ ~ the silence ◇ A tree broke his fall (= stopped him as he was falling). **6** [I, T] ~**free** (of a person or an object) escape from a position in which they are trapped: He broke free from his attacker. **7** [I, T] (cause sb/sth to) be weakened or destroyed: ~ the power of the unions ◇ His wife's death broke him. **8** [I] (of the weather) change suddenly after a settled period **9** [I] begin: Day was ~ing. **10** [T] become or make sth known: ~ the news **11** [I] (of a boy's voice) become deeper **12** [T] do better than a previous record **13** [T] solve sth secret: ~ a code [IDM] **break the back of sth** finish the largest or most difficult part of sth **break even** make neither a loss nor a profit **break fresh/new ground** introduce or discover a new method, activity, etc **break the ice** make people feel friendly towards one another, eg at the beginning of a party **break wind** let out air from the bowels **make or break sb/sth** cause sb/sth to either succeed or fail [PV] **break away (from sb/sth)** go away from sb/sth; leave eg a political party **break down 1** (of machinery) stop working **2** fail; collapse: Talks between the two sides have broken down. **3** lose control of your feelings **break sb/sth down 1** destroy sth: ~ down resistance **2** analyse sth; classify: ~ down expenses **break in 1** enter a building by force **2** ~(**on**) interrupt or disturb sth **break sb/sth in 1** train sb/sth in sth new that they must do **2** wear sth, esp new shoes, until they become comfortable **break into sth 1** enter a building or open a car, etc by force **2** suddenly begin sth: *~ into laughter/a run* **3** start to use sth, esp money, that has been kept for an emergency **break off** stop speaking **break (sth) off** (cause to) separate by force **break sth off** end sth suddenly: *They've broken off their engagement.* **break out 1** (of sth bad) start suddenly: *Fire broke out.* **2 ~(of)** escape from a prison **3 ~(in)** suddenly become covered in sth: *~ out in spots* **break through (sth) 1** force a way through sth **2** (of the sun) appear from behind clouds **break up 1** (of a group of people) go away in different directions **2** (*GB*) (of a school or its pupils) begin the holidays **3 ~ (with)** end a relationship with sb **break (sth) up 1** (cause sth to) separate into smaller pieces **2** (cause sth to) come to an end: *Their marriage is ~ing up.* ▶ **breakable** *adj* easily broken ■ **breakaway** *adj* (of a political group, or an organization) having separated from a larger group ■ **'break-in** *n* entry into a building by force, esp to steal sth ■ **'breakout** *n* escape from a prison ■ **'breakthrough** *n* important development or discovery ■ **'break-up** *n* end, esp of a relationship

break² /breɪk/ *n* **1** rest; pause: *a lunch ~* **2** short holiday: *a weekend ~* **3** interruption or end of sth that has existed for a long time: *a ~ with tradition* **4** space or gap between two or more things **5** (*infml*) piece of luck that leads to success: *a lucky ~* **6** place where sth, esp a bone, is broken [IDM] **break of day/dawn** (*lit*) moment in the early hours of the morning when it begins to get light **make a break for sth/for it** run towards sth in order to try and escape

breakage /'breɪkɪdʒ/ *n* **1** [C] object that has been broken **2** [U,C] act of breaking sth

breakdown /'breɪkdaʊn/ *n* **1** failure in machinery **2** failure of a relationship, discussion or system **3** analysis of statistics: *a ~ of expenses* **4** weakness or collapse of sb's mental health: *a nervous ~*

breaker /'breɪkə(r)/ *n* large wave that breaks into foam

breakfast /'brekfəst/ *n* **1** [C,U] first meal of the day ● **breakfast** *v* [I] eat breakfast

breakneck /'breɪknek/ *adj* dangerously fast: *at ~ speed*

breakwater /'breɪkwɔːtə(r)/ *n* wall built out into the sea to protect a harbour

breast /brest/ *n* **1** either of the two parts of a woman's body that produce milk **2** upper front part of the body ■ **'breastbone** *n* thin flat vertical bone in the chest between the ribs ■ **'breaststroke** *n* [U,sing] kind of swimming style that you do on your front

breath /breθ/ *n* **1** [U] air taken into and sent out of the lungs **2** [C] amount of air that enters the lungs at one time: *Take a deep ~.* **3** [sing] slight movement of air [IDM] **get your breath (back)** breathe normally again after running, etc **out of breath** having difficulty breathing after exercise **take sb's breath away** be very surprising or beautiful **under your breath** quietly so that people cannot hear ▶ **breathless** *adj* **1** having difficulty breathing **2 ~(with)** experiencing a strong emotional reaction: *~less with terror* ▶ **breathlessly** *adv* ■ **'breathtaking** *adj* amazing

breathalyser™ /'breθəlaɪzə(r)/ (*US* **Breathalyzer**) *n* device used by the police for measuring the amount of alcohol in a driver's breath

breathe /briːð/ *v* **1** [I, T] take air into the lungs and send it out again **2** [T] say sth very quietly; whisper **3** [T] (*fml*) be full of a particular feeling or quality [IDM] **breathe again** feel calm or relaxed after a difficult or anxious time **breathe down sb's neck** (*infml*) watch sb too closely ▶ **breather** *n* (*infml*) short rest

breed /briːd/ *v* (*pt, pp* **bred** /bred/) **1** [T] keep animals for the purpose of producing young: *~ horses/cattle* **2** [I] (of animals) produce young **3** [T] bring sb up; educate sb in a particular way: *a well-bred child* **4** [T] be the cause of sth: *Dirt ~s disease.* ● **breed** *n* **1** particular type of animal: *a ~ of cattle/dog* **2** particular kind of person: *a new ~ of manager* ▶ **breeder** *n* person who breeds animals ▶ **breeding** *n* [U] **1** producing of animal young **2** good manners: *a man of good ~ing*

breeze /briːz/ *n* [C,U] light wind ● **breeze** *v* [I] move in a cheerful and confident way in a particular direction: *She just ~d into the office and sat down.* ▶ **breezy** *adj* **1** windy **2** having a cheerful and relaxed manner ▶ **breezily** *adv*

brevity /'brevəti/ *n* [U] (*fml*) fact of lasting a short time: *the ~ of life*

brew /bruː/ *v* **1** [I, T] prepare tea, coffee or beer **2** [I] (of sth unpleasant) develop ● **brew** *n* result of brewing ▶ **brewer** *n* ▶ **brewery** /'bruːəri/ *n* (*pl -ies*) place where beer is brewed

bribe /braɪb/ *n* something (esp money) given to sb to persuade them to help, usu by doing sth dishonest ● **bribe** *v* [T] give a bribe to sb ▶ **bribery** /'braɪbəri/ *n* [U] the giving or taking of bribes

bric-a-brac /'brɪkəbræk/ n [U] small ornaments of little value

brick /brɪk/ n [C,U] (block of) baked clay used for building ● **brick** v [PV] **brick sth in/up** fill or block an opening with bricks ■ **'bricklayer** n person whose job is to build walls, etc with bricks ■ **'brickwork** n [U] bricks in a wall, building, etc

bridal /'braɪdl/ adj of a bride or wedding

bride /braɪd/ n woman on her wedding day; newly married woman ■ **'bridegroom** n man on his wedding day; newly married man ■ **'bridesmaid** n woman or girl helping the bride on her wedding day

bridge /brɪdʒ/ n **1** [C] structure providing a way across a river, etc **2** [C] thing which links two or more different things **3** [C] part of a ship where the captain and officers stand to control and steer it **4** [sing] upper part of the nose **5** [C] part on a violin, etc over which the strings are stretched **6** [U] card game for four players ● **bridge** v [T] build a bridge across sth

bridle /'braɪdl/ n part of a horse's harness that goes on its head ● **bridle** v **1** [T] put a bridle on a horse **2** [I] show anger or annoyance by moving your head up and back

brief¹ /briːf/ adj **1** lasting only a short time **2** using few words **3** (of clothes) short ▶ **in brief** in a few words ▶ **briefly** adv

brief² /briːf/ n **1** instructions and information for a particular task **2** (GB, law) legal case given to a lawyer to argue in court; piece of work for a barrister **3** (GB, infml) solicitor or defence lawyer: I want to see my ~. ● **brief** v [T] **1** give sb information about sth so that they are prepared to deal with it **2** (GB, law) give a barrister the main facts of a legal case so that it can be argued in a court of law ■ **'briefcase** n flat leather case for papers, etc

briefs /briːfs/ n [pl] pants or knickers

brigade /brɪ'ɡeɪd/ n **1** army unit usu of three battalions **2** organization for a particular purpose: the fire ~ ▶ **brigadier** /ˌbrɪɡə'dɪə(r)/ n officer commanding a brigade(1)

bright /braɪt/ adj **1** giving out or reflecting a lot of light; shining **2** (of colour) strong **3** cheerful; happy **4** clever **5** likely to be successful: The future looks ~. ▶ **brighten** v [I, T] become or make sth/sb brighter ▶ **brightly** adv ▶ **brightness** n [U]

brilliant /'brɪliənt/ adj **1** very clever or impressive **2** (of light or colours) very bright **3** (spoken) very good ▶ **brilliance** /'brɪliəns/ n [U] ▶ **brilliantly** adv

brim /brɪm/ n **1** edge of a cup, etc **2** bottom edge of a hat ● **brim** v (-mm-) [I] ~(with) be full of sth [PV] **brim over (with sth)** overflow

brine /braɪn/ n [U] salt water, esp for preserving food

bring /brɪŋ/ v (pt, pp brought /brɔːt/) [T] **1** come to a place with sb/sth: Please ~ a dictionary to class. ◊ He brought his mother with him. **2** cause sth: The story brought tears to her eyes. **3** cause sb/sth to be in a particular condition or place: ~ the water to the boil (= boil it) ◊ ~ the meeting to a close **4** ~(against) (law) officially accuse sb of a crime: a charge against sb **5** force yourself to do sth: I can't ~ myself to tell him. [IDM] **bring sth to a head** → HEAD¹ **bring sth to mind** → MIND¹ [PV] **bring sth about** cause sth to happen **bring sb/sth back 1** return sb/sth: ~ back a book ◊ I brought the children back (= home). **2** cause sb/sth to be remembered **3** introduce sth again: ~ back the death penalty **bring sb/sth down 1** cause sb/sth to fall: ~ down the government ◊ I brought him down with a rugby tackle. **2** lower or reduce sth: ~ prices down **3** cause an aircraft to fall out of the sky or to land **bring sth forward 1** move sth to an earlier date or time: ~ the meeting forward **2** propose sth for discussion **bring sth/sb in 1** introduce a new law: ~ in new legislation **2** attract sb/sth to a place or business **3** use sb's services as an adviser, etc: ~ in a scientist to check pollution **bring sth off** succeed in doing sth difficult **bring sth on** make sth develop, usu sth unpleasant: The rain brought on his cold. **bring sth out 1** make sth appear: A crisis ~s out the best in him. **2** make sth easy to see or understand **3** produce or publish sth: ~ out a new type of computer **bring sb round 1** cause sb to regain consciousness **2** persuade sb to agree to sth **bring sb up** care for a child, teaching him or her how to behave, etc: We were brought up to be polite. **bring sth up 1** call attention to sth; mention sth: ~ up the subject of salaries **2** vomit sth **3** make sth appear on a computer screen

brink /brɪŋk/ n [sing] edge of a steep or dangerous place: (fig) on the ~ of war

brisk /brɪsk/ adj moving quickly; lively: walk at a ~ pace ▶ **briskly** adv

bristle /'brɪsl/ n [C,U] short stiff hair, esp on a brush ● **bristle** v **1** suddenly become annoyed or offended at what sb says or does **2** (of animal's fur) stand up stiffly [PV] **bristle with sth** have a large number of sth

brittle /'brɪtl/ adj hard but easily broken

broach /brəʊtʃ/ v [T] begin a discussion of a subject

broad /brɔːd/ adj **1** measuring a large amount from one side to the other; wide: ~ shoulders **2** including a great variety of people or things: a ~ range of subjects **3** not detailed; general: a ~ outline of a speech **4** (of speech) with a strong accent **5** clear; obvious: a ~ hint [IDM] **in broad daylight** in the full light of day ■ '**broadband** adj, n [U] (of a) communications network that allows several channels of information to pass through a single cable at the same time, eg cable TV and Internet access ▶ **broaden** v [I, T] become or make sth wider ▶ **broadly** adv generally: ~ly speaking ■ **broad-'minded** adj liberal and tolerant

broadcast /'brɔːdkɑːst/ n radio or television programme ● **broadcast** v (pt, pp **broadcast**) [I, T] send out radio or television programmes ▶ **broadcaster** n ▶ **broadcasting** n [U]

broadside /'brɔːdsaɪd/ n fierce attack in words ● **broadside** adv sideways

broccoli /'brɒkəli/ n [U] kind of cauliflower with dark green or purple flower heads

brochure /'brəʊʃə(r)/ n booklet containing information or advertisements

broil /brɔɪl/ v [T] (US) grill meat or fish

broke[1] pt of BREAK[1]

broke[2] /brəʊk/ adj (infml) having no money: flat/stony ~ (= completely broke)

broken[1] pp of BREAK[1]

broken[2] /'brəʊkən/ adj **1** that has been damaged or injured; no longer whole or working correctly: a ~ arm ◇ a ~ marriage **2** not continuous; interrupted: ~ sleep **3** (of a person) weakened by illness or difficulties **4** (of a foreign language) spoken slowly and with a lot of mistakes ■ ,broken 'home n family in which the parents have divorced or separated

broker /'brəʊkə(r)/ n person who buys and sells eg business shares for others

brolly /'brɒli/ n (pl **-ies**) (GB, infml) = UMBRELLA

bronchial /'brɒŋkiəl/ adj of the tubes of the windpipe

bronchitis /brɒŋ'kaɪtɪs/ n [U] illness that affects the bronchial tubes

bronze /brɒnz/ n **1** [U] metal that is a mixture of copper and tin **2** [U] dark reddish-brown colour **3** [C] something made of bronze; bronze medal ■ ,bronze 'medal n medal awarded as third prize in a competition, esp a sports contest

brooch /brəʊtʃ/ n piece of jewellery with a pin on the back of it, that can be fastened to your clothes

brood /bruːd/ n **1** young birds produced at one hatching or birth **2** (hum) large family of children ● **brood** v [I] **1** think a lot about sth that makes you annoyed, anxious or upset: ~ing over her problems **2** sit on eggs to hatch them ▶ **broody** adj **1** (of a woman) wanting very much to have babies **2** (of a hen) wanting to brood **3** sad and very quiet

brook /brʊk/ n small stream

broom /bruːm/ n brush with a long handle for sweeping floors

broth /brɒθ/ n [U] kind of soup

brothel /'brɒθl/ n house of prostitutes

brother /'brʌðə(r)/ n **1** son of the same parents as yourself or another person mentioned **2** man who is a member of the same society, profession, etc **3** (also **Brother**) (pl **brethren** /'breðrən/ or **brothers**) male member of a religious group, esp a monk ▶ **brotherhood** n **1** [U] (feeling of) friendship and understanding between people **2** [C] organization formed for a particular purpose, esp a religious or political one **3** [U] relationship between brothers ■ '**brother-in-law** n (pl **~s-in-law**) brother of your husband or wife; your sister's husband ▶ **brotherly** adj

brought pt, pp of BRING

brow /braʊ/ n **1** forehead **2** = EYEBROW **3** top part of a hill

browbeat /'braʊbiːt/ v (pt **browbeat**, pp **~en** /-biːtn/) [T] frighten sb into doing sth

brown /braʊn/ adj, n [C,U] (having the) colour of earth or coffee with milk ● **brown** v [I, T] become or make sth brown

browse /braʊz/ v [I] **1** look at a lot of things in a shop rather than looking for one particular thing **2** look through a book, newspaper, etc without reading everything **3** (computing) look for information on a computer **4** (of cows, goats, etc) feed on grass, leaves, etc ▶ **browse** n [sing] ▶ **browser** n **1** (computing) program that lets you look at or read documents on the Internet: a Web ~r **2** person who browses

bruise /bruːz/ n blue, brown or purple mark caused by a blow to the body ● **bruise** v [I, T] develop a bruise, or make a bruise appear on the skin of sb/sth

brunette /bruː'net/ n white-skinned woman with dark brown hair

brunt /brʌnt/ n [IDM] **bear the brunt of sth** → BEAR

brush¹ /brʌʃ/ n **1** [C] tool with bristles for cleaning, painting, etc: *a tooth~ 2* [sing] act of brushing **3** [C] short unfriendly meeting with sth; unpleasant experience of sth: *a nasty ~ with his boss* **4** [U] land covered by small trees and shrubs

brush² /brʌʃ/ v [T] **1** clean sth with a brush **2** touch sb/sth lightly when passing [PV] **brush sth aside** pay little or no attention to sth **brush sth up| brush up on sth** study or practise sth forgotten: *~ up (on) your French*

brusque /bruːsk/ adj using few words and sounding rude ▶ **brusquely** adv ▶ **brusqueness** n [U]

Brussels sprout /ˌbrʌslz 'spraʊt/ n kind of vegetable that looks like a very small cabbage

brutal /'bruːtl/ adj violent and cruel ▶ **brutality** /bruː'tæləti/ n [U,C] (pl -ies) ▶ **brutally** adv

brute /bruːt/ n **1** cruel insensitive man **2** large strong animal ● **brute** adj involving physical strength only and not thought or intelligence: *~ force* ▶ **brutish** adj of or like a brute

BSE /ˌbiː es 'iː/ n (also infml ˌmad 'cow disease) n [U] bovine spongiform encephalopathy; brain disease of cows that causes death

bubble /'bʌbl/ n **1** (in the air) floating ball of liquid containing air or gas **2** (in a liquid) ball of air or gas ● **bubble** v [I] **1** send up, rise in or make the sound of bubbles (~ **with**) be full of a particular feeling ▶ **'bubblegum** n [U] chewing gum that can be blown into bubbles ▶ **bubbly** adj (-ier, -iest) **1** full of bubbles **2** happy and lively

buck¹ /bʌk/ n **1** [C] (esp US, infml) US or Australian dollar **2** [C] male deer, hare or rabbit **3** (**the buck**) [sing] (infml) responsibility: *pass the ~* (= make sb else responsible)

buck² /bʌk/ v **1** [I] (of a horse) jump up with all four feet together [PV] **buck up** hurry **buck (sb) up** (cause sb to) become more cheerful

bucket /'bʌkɪt/ n **1** round open container with a handle, for carrying liquids **2** (also '**bucketful**) amount a bucket contains ● **bucket** v [I] ~ (**down**) (GB, infml) rain heavily

buckle /'bʌkl/ n **1** metal or plastic fastener for a belt, etc ● **buckle** v [I, T] **1** fasten with a buckle **2** (cause

sth to) become bent, esp because of force or heat [PV] **buckle down (to sth)** (infml) start to do sth seriously

bud /bʌd/ n flower or leaf before it opens ● **bud** v (-**dd-**) [I] produce buds ▶ **budding** adj beginning to develop or become successful

Buddhism /'bʊdɪzəm/ n [U] Asian religion based on the teaching of Gautama Siddhartha (or Buddha) ▶ **Buddhist** /'bʊdɪst/ n, adj

buddy /'bʌdi/ n (pl -**ies**) (infml) friend

budge /bʌdʒ/ v [I, T] (cause sb/sth to) move slightly: *The stone won't ~.*

budgerigar /'bʌdʒərɪgɑː(r)/ n (also infml **budgie**) brightly-coloured bird, often kept as a pet

budget /'bʌdʒɪt/ n [C,U] amount of money that is available to a person or an organization and a plan of how it will be spent over a period of time: *The work was finished within ~* (= did not cost more money than was planned). ● **budget** v [I] ~ (**for**) plan the amount of money to be spent on sth ● **budget** adj cheap: *~ holidays*

buff /bʌf/ n **1** [C] person who knows a lot about the subject that is mentioned: *a computer ~ 2* [U] pale yellow-brown colour ● **buff** v [T] polish sth with a soft cloth

buffalo /'bʌfələʊ/ n (pl **buffalo** or ~**es**) kind of large wild ox

buffer /'bʌfə(r)/ n **1** device on a railway engine, etc to reduce the effect of a collision **2** (computing) area in a computer's memory where data can be stored for a short time ● **buffer** v (computing) (of a computer) hold data for a short time before using it

buffet¹ /'bʊfeɪ/ n **1** counter where food and drink may be bought and eaten, eg at a railway station **2** meal at which guests serve themselves from a number of dishes

buffet² /'bʌfɪt/ v [T] push or knock sb/sth roughly from side to side: *~ed by the wind*

bug /bʌg/ n **1** any small insect **2** (infml) infectious illness that is usu fairly mild: *a stomach ~ 3* (infml) great interest in sth mentioned: *He's got the travel ~! 4* (infml) small hidden microphone **5** (infml) fault in a machine, esp a computer ● **bug** v (-**gg-**) **1** fit sb/sth with a bug(4) **2** (infml) annoy sb constantly

bugbear /'bʌgbeə(r)/ n thing that is disliked or causes annoyance

bugger /'bʌgə(r)/ n (GB, △, sl) **1** annoying person or thing **2** person that you feel sorry for: ● **bugger exclam** (GB, △, infml) used for expressing anger or annoyance

bugle /'bjuːgl/ n musical instrument like a small trumpet, used in the army for giving signals ▶ **bugler** n

build¹ /bɪld/ v (pt, pp **built** /bɪlt/) [T] **1** make sth by putting parts, etc together **2** create or develop sth: ~ a *better future* [PV] **build on sth** use sth as a basis for further progress **build sth on sth** base sth on sth **build (sth) up** (cause sth) to become greater; increase: *Traffic is ~ing up.* ◇ ~ *up a business* **build sb/sth up** speak with great praise about sb/sth ▶ **builder** n ■ **'build-up** n **1** gradual increase **2** favourable description of sb/sth that is going to happen, which is intended to make people excited about it ■ **built-'in** adj included to form part of a structure: ~ *wardrobes* ■ **built-'up** adj (of an area of land) covered with buildings

build² /bɪld/ n [U,C] shape and size of the human body

building /'bɪldɪŋ/ n **1** [C] structure with a roof and walls **2** [U] (business of) constructing houses, etc ■ **'building society** n (GB) organization that accepts money to be invested and lends money to people who want to buy houses

bulb /bʌlb/ n **1** (also **light bulb**) glass part that fits into an electric lamp **2** thick rounded underground stem of certain plants ▶ **bulbous** adj round and fat

bulge /bʌldʒ/ v [I] stick out from sth in a round shape ● **bulge** n round lump that sticks out from sth

bulk /bʌlk/ n **1** (**the bulk of sth**) [sing] the main part of sth **2** [U] (large) size or quantity of sth: *It's cheaper to buy in ~.* **3** [sing] large shape or mass ▶ **bulky** adj (-**ier**, -**iest**) large; difficult to move

bull /bʊl/ n **1** the male of any animal in the cow family **2** male of the elephant, whale and some other large animals [IDM] **a bull in a china shop** person who is clumsy where skill or care is needed **take the bull by the horns** face difficulty or danger directly and with courage ■ **bulldog** n strong dog with a large head and a short thick neck ■ **bullseye** n centre of the target used in archery and darts ■ **bullshit** n [U] (△, sl) nonsense

bulldozer /'bʊldəʊzə(r)/ v [T] **1** destroy buildings, trees, etc with a bulldozer **2** force sb to do sth ▶ **bulldozer** n powerful tractor for moving large quantities of earth

bullet /'bʊlɪt/ n small round or pointed piece of metal shot from a gun ■ **'bulletproof** adj that can stop bullets passing through it: *a ~proof vest*

bulletin /'bʊlətɪn/ n short official news report

bullion /'bʊliən/ n [U] gold or silver in large amounts or in the form of bars

bullock /'bʊlək/ n young bull that has been castrated

bully /'bʊli/ n (pl -**ies**) person who uses their strength to frighten or hurt weaker people: *the school* ~ ● **bully** v (pt, pp -**ied**) [T] frighten or hurt a weaker person; use your strength or power to make sb do sth

bulrush /'bʊlrʌʃ/ n tall strong plant that grows in or near water

bulwark /'bʊlwək/ n **1** person or thing that defends or protects·sth **2** wall built as a defence

bum /bʌm/ n (infml) **1** (GB) the part of the body that you sit on; buttocks **2** (esp US) homeless person who asks other people for money or food **3** lazy person ● **bum** v [PV] **bum around** (infml) spend your time doing nothing in particular

bumblebee /'bʌmblbiː/ n large hairy bee that makes a loud noise as it flies

bump /bʌmp/ v [I] hit sb/sth accidentally: *I ~ed into the chair in the dark.* **2** [T] hit sth against or on sth by accident: *I ~ed my head on the door frame.* **3** [I] move across a rough surface: *The bus ~ed along the mountain road.* [PV] **bump into sb** (infml) meet sb by chance **bump sb off** (infml) kill sb **bump sth up** (infml) increase sth ● **bump** n **1** action or sound of sth hitting a hard surface **2** swelling on the body **3** uneven area on a road surface ▶ **bumpy** adj (-**ier**, -**iest**) not smooth; uneven

bumper /'bʌmpə(r)/ n bar on the front and back of a motor vehicle to protect it from damage ● **bumper** adj unusually large: *a ~ harvest*

bun /bʌn/ n **1** small round sweet cake **2** (esp woman's) hair twisted round into a tight knot at the back of the head

bunch /bʌntʃ/ n **1** number of similar things fastened or growing together: *a ~ of flowers/grapes* **2** (infml) group of people ● **bunch** v [PV] **bunch (sb/sth) up/together** (cause sb/sth to) move closer and form into a group

bundle /'bʌndl/ n **1** [C] number of things fastened or wrapped together: *old clothes tied into a ~* **2** [sing] ~**of** a mass of sth: *He's a ~ of nerves* (= he is very nervous). ● **bundle** v [T] **1** ~(up/together) make or tie sth into a bundle **2** push or send sth somewhere quickly and roughly: *They ~d him into a taxi.*

bung /bʌŋ/ v [T] (GB, infml) throw or put sth somewhere carelessly and quickly [PV] **bung sth up (with sth)** block sth: *My nose is all ~ed up.*

● **bung** n stopper for closing the hole in a barrel or jar

bungalow /'bʌŋgələʊ/ n house built all on one level

bungee jumping /'bʌndʒi dʒʌmpɪŋ/ n [U] sport in which a person jumps from a high place, such as a bridge, with a long elastic rope (**a bungee**) tied to their feet

bungle /'bʌŋgl/ v [I, T] do sth badly or clumsily; fail at sth

bunion /'bʌnjən/ n painful swelling on the foot, usu on the big toe

bunk /bʌŋk/ n **1** narrow bed fixed to a wall, eg on a ship or train **2** (also '**bunk bed**) one of a pair of beds fixed one above the other, usu for children [IDM] **do a bunk** (*GB, infml*) run away

bunker /'bʌŋkə(r)/ n **1** strongly built underground shelter for soldiers or guns **2** container for storing coal **3** small area filled with sand on a golf course

bunny /'bʌni/ n (*pl* **-ies**) child's word for a rabbit

buoy /bɔɪ/ n floating object attached to the sea bottom to show danger, rocks, etc ● **buoy** v [T] **1** ~(**up**) make sb feel cheerful or confident **2** ~ (**up**) keep sb/sth afloat **3** ~(**up**) keep prices at a high level

buoyant /'bɔɪənt/ adj **1** (of prices, business activity, etc) tending to increase or stay at a high level, usu showing financial success: *a ~ economy* **2** cheerful and optimistic **3** able to float or keep things afloat ▶ **buoyancy** /-ənsi/ n [U] **buoyantly** adv

burden /'bɜːdn/ n **1** responsibility or duty that causes worry or is hard to deal with: *the ~ of taxation* **2** (*fml*) heavy load ● **burden** v [T] **1** put a burden on sb **2 be ~ed** with be carrying sth heavy

bureau /'bjʊərəʊ/ n (*pl* **-x** or **-s** /-rəʊz/) **1** (*GB*) writing desk with drawers **2** (*US*) = CHEST OF DRAWERS **3** office or organization that provides information on a particular subject **4** (*esp US*) government department

bureaucracy /bjʊə'rɒkrəsi/ n (*pl* **-ies**) **1** [U] (*disapprov*) unnecessary and complicated official rules **2** [U, C] (country with) a system of government in which there are a large number of state officials who are not elected ▶ **bureaucrat** /'bjʊərəkræt/ n (*often disapprov*) person who works in a government department ▶ **bureaucratic** /ˌbjʊərə'krætɪk/ adj

burglar /'bɜːglə(r)/ n person who breaks into a building to steal things ▶ **burglary** n [U, C] (*pl* **-ies**) crime of entering a building in order to steal things ▶ **burgle** (*US* **burglarize**) /'bɜːgləraɪz/ n [T] break into a building to steal things

burial /'beriəl/ n [C,U] act or ceremony of burying a dead body

burly /'bɜːli/ adj (**-ier, -iest**) (of a man) having a strong heavy body

burn /bɜːn/ v (*pt, pp* ~**t** /bɜːnt/ or ~**ed** /bɜːnd/) **1** [I] be on fire; produce flames and heat **2** [I, T] (cause sb/sth to) be destroyed, damaged, injured or killed by fire: *~ old papers* ◇ *The house ~ed to the ground.* **3** [T] use sth for heating or lighting: *~ coal in a fire* **4** [I, T] (cause food to) become spoilt because it gets too hot: *Sorry, I've ~t the toast.* **5** [I, T] (cause sb/sth to) be damaged or injured by the sun, heat, acid, etc: *My skin ~s easily* (= in the sun). **6** [I] (of part of the body) feel hot and painful **7** [I] ~**with** (*written*) experience a strong emotion or desire [PV] **burn** (**sth**) **down** (cause sth to) be completely destroyed by fire **burn** (**itself**) **out** (of a fire) stop burning because there is no more fuel **burn** (**yourself**) **out** exhaust yourself or ruin your health by working too hard **burn sth out** destroy sth completely by burning so that only the frame remains: *the ~t-out wreck of a car* ● **burn** n injury or mark caused by fire, heat or acid ▶ **burner** n part of a cooker, etc that produces a flame ▶ **burning** adj **1** intense: *a ~ing thirst/desire* **2** very important; urgent: *the ~ing question*

burnish /'bɜːnɪʃ/ v [T] (*fml*) polish metal by rubbing it

burp /bɜːp/ v [I] (*infml*) let out air from the stomach through the mouth, making a noise ▶ **burp** n

burrow /'bʌrəʊ/ n hole made in the ground by rabbits, etc ● **burrow** v [I, T] dig a hole

bursar /'bɜːsə(r)/ n person who manages the money in a school or college ▶ **bursary** n (*pl* **-ies**) money given to sb so that they can study, usu at a college or university

burst /bɜːst/ v (*pt, pp* burst) **1** [I, T] (cause sth to) break open or apart, esp because of pressure from inside: *The tyre ~.* ◇ *The river ~ its banks.* **2** [I] ~(**with**) be full of sth to the point of breaking open: *She was ~ing with pride.* [IDM] **be bursting to do sth** be very eager to do sth **burst** (**sth**) **open** open (sth) suddenly or violently: *The door ~ open.* [PV] **burst in on sb/sth** interrupt sb/sth by entering a place suddenly **burst into sth** suddenly start producing sth: *~ into tears/laughter* **burst into, out of, etc sth** move suddenly and forcefully in the direction that is mentioned **burst out 1** speak suddenly and loudly **2** begin doing sth suddenly: *~ out crying* ● **burst** n **1** short period of an activity or a strong emotion: *a ~ of energy* **2** occasion when sth bursts;

the hole left where sth has burst **3** short series of shots from a gun

bury /'beri/ v (pt, pp **-ied**) [T] **1** put a dead body in a grave **2** put sth underground; hide sth from view: *buried treasure* ◊ *She buried* (= hid) *her face in her hands.* **3** ~ **yourself** in give all your attention to sth [IDM] **bury the hatchet | bury your differences** stop arguing and become friends again

bus /bʌs/ *n* large motor vehicle that carries passengers ● **bus** *v* (-s- also -ss-) [I, T] go or take sb/sth by bus ■ **'bus stop** *n* regular stopping place for a bus

bush /bʊʃ/ *n* **1** [C] low plant that grows thickly: *a rose* ~ **2** (**the bush**) [U] wild uncultivated land, esp in Africa and Australia ▶ **bushy** *adj* (**-ier, -iest**) growing thickly: ~*y eyebrows*

business /'bɪznəs/ *n* **1** [U] activity of buying and selling; commerce or trade **2** [U] work that is part of your job: *He's away on* ~. **3** [U] amount of work done by a company, etc; the rate or quality of this: *How's* ~? **4** [C] organization that sells goods or provides a service **5** [sing] something that concerns a particular person or organization: *My private life is none of your* ~ (= does not concern you)! **6** [U] important matters that need to be dealt with **7** [sing] matter; affair: *Let's forget the whole* ~. [IDM] **get down to business** start the work that must be done **go out of business** become bankrupt **have no business to do sth** have no right to do sth ■ **'businesslike** *adj* well organized; efficient ■ **'businessman | 'businesswoman** (*pl* **-men** /-mən/ | **-women** /-wɪmɪn/) *n* person who works in business

busker /'bʌskə(r)/ *n* (*infml*) person who plays music in the street, etc to try to earn money

bust /bʌst/ *v* (*pt, pp* **bust** or **~ed**) [T] (*infml*) **1** break sth **2** (of the police) enter a place and search it or arrest sb: *He's been ~ed for drugs.* ● **bust** *n* **1** sculpture of a person's head and shoulders **2** woman's breasts ● **bust** *adj* (*infml*) broken [IDM] **go bust** (of a business) become bankrupt

bustle /'bʌsl/ *v* [I] move busily and energetically ▶ **bustle** *n* [U]

busy /'bɪzi/ *adj* (**-ier, -iest**) **1** having a lot to do; already working on sth: *I'm ~ all day so I won't be able to help you.* **2** full of activity: *a* ~ *day* **3** (of a telephone line) being used ▶ **busily** *adv* ● **busy** *v* (*pt, pp* **-ied**) [T] ~ **yourself** fill your time doing an activity

but /bət; *strong form* bʌt/ *conj* used for showing a contrast: *Tom went to the party,* ~ *his brother didn't.* ● **but** *prep*

apart from; except: *nothing to eat* ~ *bread and cheese* ◊ *I came last* ~ *one* (= next to last) *in the race* (= wasn't last but next to last). ● **but** *adv* only: *We can* ~ *try.*

butcher /'bʊtʃə(r)/ *n* **1** person whose job is to cut up and sell meat in a shop or to kill animals for this purpose **2** cruel murderer ● **butcher** *v* [T] **1** kill sb/sth cruelly and violently **2** kill and prepare animals for meat ▶ **butchery** *n* [U] unnecessary cruel killing

butler /'bʌtlə(r)/ *n* chief male servant in a house

butt /bʌt/ *n* **1** thick end of a weapon or tool **2** unburned end of a cigarette or cigar **3** large barrel for storing liquids **4** person who is often joked about or criticized: *She's always the* ~ *of their jokes.* ● **butt** *v* [T] hit or push sb/sth hard with your head [PV] **butt in** (**on** sb/sth) interrupt sb's conversation rudely

butter /'bʌtə(r)/ *n* yellow fatty food made from cream, spread on bread, etc ● **butter** *v* [T] spread butter on sth [PV] **butter sb up** (*infml*) flatter sb ■ **'buttercup** *n* wild plant with small yellow flowers ■ **'butterscotch** *n* hard pale brown sweet made by boiling sugar and butter together

butterfly /'bʌtəflaɪ/ *n* (*pl* **-ies**) insect with a long thin body and large colourful wings

buttock /'bʌtək/ *n* [C, usu *pl*] either of the two round soft parts at the top of a person's legs

button /'bʌtn/ *n* **1** small round piece of metal, plastic, etc that is sewn onto a piece of clothing as a fastener: *Your top* ~ *is undone.* **2** small knob that is pressed to operate a machine, bell, etc ● **button** *v* [I, T] fasten sth with buttons ■ **'buttonhole** *n* **1** hole through which a button is passed **2** flower worn on a coat or jacket ■ **'buttonhole** *v* [T] stop sb and make them listen to you

buttress /'bʌtrəs/ *n* support built against a wall ● **buttress** *v* [T] support or strengthen sth

buxom /'bʌksəm/ *adj* (of a woman) large in an attractive way, and with large breasts

buy /baɪ/ *v* (*pt, pp* **bought** /bɔːt/) [T] **1** get sth by paying money for it **2** (*infml*) believe that sth is true [PV] **buy sb out** pay sb to give up a share in a business so that you can gain control ● **buy** *n* thing bought: *a good* ~ ▶ **buyer** *n* person who buys sth, esp sb who chooses goods to be sold in a large shop

buzz /bʌz/ *v* **1** [I] (of a bee) make a low sound **2** [I] make a sound like a bee buzzing: *The doorbell* ~*ed.* **3** [I] ~ (**with**) be full of excited talk **4** [I, T] call sb with a buzzer: *The doctor ~ed for her next patient.* [PV] **buzz off** (*infml*) go away ● **buzz** *n* 1 [C] buzzing sound 2 [sing] (*infml*) feeling of pleasure or excitement [IDM] **give sb a buzz** (*infml*) telephone sb ▶ **buzzer** *n* electrical device that produces a buzzing sound as a signal

buzzard /'bʌzəd/ *n* large European bird of prey of the hawk family

by /baɪ/ *prep* 1 at the side of sb/sth; near sb/sth: *Sit by me.* 2 used, usu after a passive verb, to show who or what does, creates or causes sth: *The soldiers were shot by terrorists.* ◇ *a play by Shaw* 3 used to show how or in what way sth is done: *pay by cheque* ◇ *travel by train* ◇ *Switch it on by pressing this button.* 4 as a result of sth; because of sth: *meet by chance* 5 not later than the time mentioned; before: *finish the work by tomorrow* 6 past sb/sth: *She walked by me.* 7 during sth: *travel by day/night* 8 used to show the degree or amount of sth: *The bullet missed him by ten millimetres.* 9 according to sth: *By law, his parents should be informed.* 10 used to show the part of sb/sth that sb touches, holds, etc: *take sb by the hand* 11 using sth as a standard or unit: *get paid by the hour* ◇ *sell material by the metre* 12 used to state the rate at which sth happens: *He did it bit by bit.* 13 used to show the measurements of sth: *The room measures 18 feet by 20 feet.* ● **by** *adv* past: *Let me get by.*

bye /baɪ/ (*also* **bye-bye** /ˌbaɪbaɪ/) *exclam* (*infml*) goodbye

by-election /'baɪ ɪlekʃn/ *n* election of a new Member of Parliament in a place when the member has died or resigned

bygone /'baɪɡɒn/ *adj* past: *in ~ days* ▶ **bygones** *n* [pl] [IDM] **let bygones be bygones** forgive and forget past quarrels

by-law (*also* **bye-law**) /'baɪ lɔː/ *n* (*GB*) law made by a local authority

bypass /'baɪpɑːs/ *n* 1 main road that goes round a town instead of through it 2 medical operation on the heart to redirect the flow of blood in order to avoid a part that is damaged or blocked ● **bypass** *v* [T] 1 go around or avoid a place 2 ignore a rule, an official person, etc, esp in order to get sth done quickly

by-product /'baɪ prɒdʌkt/ *n* substance produced during the process of making or destroying sth else

bystander /'baɪstændə(r)/ *n* person who sees sth that is happening but is not involved

byte /baɪt/ *n* (*computing*) unit of information stored in a computer,

equal to 8 bits. A computer's memory is measured in bytes.

byword /'baɪwɜːd/ *n* 1 **~ for** person or thing that is well known for a particular quality 2 common word or expression

C c

C, c /siː/ *n* [C,U] (*pl* **C's, c's** /siːz/) the third letter of the English alphabet ● **C** *abbr* 1 Celsius; Centigrade 2 (*also* **c**) Roman numeral for 100

c (*also* **c.**) *abbr* 1 cent(s) 2 (*also* **C**) century 3 (*also* **ca**) (esp before dates)

cab /kæb/ *n* 1 taxi 2 place where the driver sits in a bus, train or lorry

cabaret /'kæbəreɪ/ *n* [U,C] singing and dancing provided in a restaurant or nightclub

cabbage /'kæbɪdʒ/ *n* [C,U] vegetable with a round head of thick green leaves

cabin /'kæbɪn/ *n* 1 small room or compartment in a ship or an aircraft 2 small wooden hut ■ **'cabin cruiser** *n* = CRUISER(2)

cabinet /'kæbɪnət/ *n* [C] 1 piece of furniture with drawers or shelves for storing things 2 (**the Cabinet**) [with sing or pl verb] group of chief ministers of a government

cable /'keɪbl/ *n* 1 [U,C] thick strong metal rope, used on ships, for supporting bridges, etc 2 [C,U] set of wires for carrying electricity, telephone signals, etc 3 [U] = CABLE TELEVISION ■ **'cable car** *n* 1 vehicle like a box that hangs on a moving cable and carries passengers up and down a mountain 2 (*esp US*) vehicle that runs on tracks and is pulled by a moving cable ■ **,cable 'television** [U] system of broadcasting television programmes along wires rather than by radio waves

cache /kæʃ/ *n* 1 hidden store of things such as weapons 2 (*computing*) part of a computer's memory that stores copies of data that can be accessed very quickly

cackle /'kækl/ *n* 1 [U] loud clucking noise that a hen makes 2 [C] loud laugh ● **cackle** *v* [I] 1 (of a chicken) make a loud unpleasant noise 2 (of a person) laugh noisily

cactus /'kæktəs/ *n* (*pl* **~es** or **-ti** /-taɪ/) plant that grows in hot dry regions, esp one with thick stems and prickles

cadet /kə'det/ *n* young person training to become an officer in the police or armed forces

cadge /kædʒ/ v [I, T] (*infml*) ask sb for food, money, etc, esp because you do not want to pay for sth yourself

cafe /'kæfeɪ/ n place where you can buy drinks and simple meals

cafeteria /ˌkæfə'tɪəriə/ n restaurant where you choose and pay for your meal at a counter and carry it to your table

caffeine /'kæfiːn/ n [U] stimulating drug found in tea and coffee

cage /keɪdʒ/ n structure of bars or wires in which birds or animals are kept ● **cage** v [T] put or keep an animal in a cage

cagey /'keɪdʒi/ adj (*infml*) secretive

cagoule /kə'guːl/ n (GB) light long waterproof jacket with a hood

cairn /keən/ n pile of stones as a landmark(1) or memorial

cajole /kə'dʒəʊl/ v [T] make sb do sth by saying nice things to them

cake /keɪk/ n 1 [C,U] sweet food made from a mixture of flour, eggs, butter, etc baked in an oven 2 [C] other food mixture cooked in a round flat shape: *fish~s* ● **cake** v [T] cover sth thickly with mud, etc

calamity /kə'læməti/ n (*pl* **-ies**) great disaster

calcium /'kælsiəm/ n [U] (*symb* **Ca**) chemical element which is found as a compound in bones, teeth and chalk

calculable /'kælkjələbl/ adj that can be calculated

calculate /'kælkjuleɪt/ v [I, T] use numbers to find out a total number, amount, etc: ~ *the cost* **IDM** **be calculated to do sth** be intended to do sth: ~*d to attract attention* ▶ **calculating** adj (*disapprov*) using deceit or trickery to get what you want ▶ **calculation** /ˌkælkju'leɪʃn/ n [C,U] ▶ **calculator** n small electronic device for making calculations

calendar /'kælɪndə(r)/ n 1 chart showing the days, weeks and months of a particular year 2 system by which time is divided: *the Islamic* ~

calf /kɑːf/ n (*pl* **calves** /kɑːvz/) 1 [C] back part of the leg, between the knee and the ankle 2 [C] young cow 3 [C] young of the seal, whale and certain other animals 4 (*also* **'calfskin**) [U] leather made from the skin of calves(2)

calibre (US **-ber**) /'kælɪbə(r)/ n 1 [U] quality; ability: *Her work is of the highest* ~. 2 [C] diameter of the inside of a tube or gun

caliper = CALLIPER

call¹ /kɔːl/ v 1 [T] give sb/sth a name; use a particular name when talking to sb: *His name's Hiroshi but everyone ~s him Hiro.* 2 [T] describe sth/sb in a particular way; consider sb/sth

to be sth: *I wouldn't ~ it a great film.* 3 [I, T] say sth loudly; shout 4 [T] order or ask sb to come by telephoning, shouting, etc: ~ *the police* 5 [I, T] telephone sb 6 [I] make a short visit to a person or place: *Let's ~ on Jane.* 7 [T] order sth to happen; announce sth: ~ *a meeting/an election/a strike* **IDM** **call sb's bluff** invite sb to do what they are threatening to do **call it a day** (*infml*) decide to stop doing sth **call sb names** insult sb **call the shots/tune** (*infml*) be the person who controls a situation **call sth to mind** → MIND¹ **PV** **call for sb/sth** 1 visit a house, etc to collect sb/sth 2 demand or need sth: *The problem ~s for immediate action.* **call sb in** ask for the services of sb: ~ *in the experts* **call sb/sth off** order a dog or person to stop attacking, searching, etc **call sth off** cancel a planned event **call on/upon sb** formally ask or invite sb to do sth **call sb out** 1 ask sb to come, esp in an emergency: ~ *out the fire brigade* 2 order or advise workers to go on strike **call sb up** 1 (*esp US*) telephone sb 2 order sb to join the armed forces ▶ **caller** n person who makes a telephone call or a short visit ■ **'call-up** n [U,C] order to join the armed forces

call² /kɔːl/ n 1 [C] (*also* **'phone call**) telephone conversation 2 [C] loud sound made by a bird or an animal, or by a person to attract attention 3 [C] short visit 4 [C] request, order or demand for sb to do sth or to go somewhere: ~*s for the minister to resign* 5 [U] (**no~for sth**) no need or demand for sth 6 [C] (*infml*) decision: *It's your* ~. **IDM** **(be) on call** (of a doctor, etc) available for work if needed ■ **call box** n = TELEPHONE BOX

calligraphy /kə'lɪgrəfi/ n [U] (art of) beautiful handwriting

calling /'kɔːlɪŋ/ n strong desire or feeling of duty to do a certain job

calliper (*also* **caliper**) /'kælɪpə/ n 1 (**callipers**) [pl] instrument for measuring the diameter of round objects 2 (GB) (**usu pl**) metal support for weak or injured legs

callous /'kæləs/ adj cruelly unkind and insensitive

callow /'kæləʊ/ adj (*disapprov*) young and inexperienced

callus /'kæləs/ n area of thick hardened skin

calm /kɑːm/ adj 1 not excited, nervous or upset 2 (of the sea) without large waves 3 (of the weather) not windy ● **calm** n [U,C] calm state or period ● **calm** v [I, T] ~(**down**) become or make sb/sth calm ▶ **calmly** adj ▶ **calmness** n [U]

calorie /'kæləri/ n 1 unit of heat 2 unit of the energy value of food

calve /kɑːv/ v [I] (of a cow) give birth to a calf

calves *plural of* CALF

calypso /kəˈlɪpsəʊ/ n [C,U] (*pl* ~s) Caribbean song; this type of music

camber /ˈkæmbə(r)/ n slight rise in the middle of a road surface

camcorder /ˈkæmkɔːdə(r)/ n portable video camera that records pictures and sound

came *pt of* COME

camel /ˈkæml/ n animal with a long neck and one or two humps on its back

cameo /ˈkæmiəʊ/ n (*pl* ~s) **1** short part in a film or play for a famous actor: *a ~ role* **2** short piece of descriptive writing **3** piece of jewellery with a raised design, usu of a head

camera /ˈkæmərə/ n piece of equipment for taking photographs or moving pictures

camouflage /ˈkæməflɑːʒ/ n [C,U] (use of) colour, nets, branches, etc that help to hide sb/sth: *soldiers in ~* ● **camouflage** v [T] hide sb/sth by camouflage

camp /kæmp/ n **1** place where people live in tents or huts for a short time **2** group of people with the same, esp political, ideas ● **camp** v [I] put up a tent; spend a holiday in a tent: *We go ~ing every summer.* ▶ **camper** n person who camps

campaign /kæmˈpeɪn/ n **1** series of planned activities with a particular aim: *an advertising ~* **2** series of military operations in a war ● **campaign** v [I] take part in a campaign ▶ **campaigner** n

campus /ˈkæmpəs/ n grounds of a university, college or school

can¹ /kən; *strong form* kæn/ *modal v* (*neg* **cannot** /ˈkænɒt/, *short form* **can't** /kɑːnt/, *pt* **could** /kəd; *strong form* kʊd/, *neg* **could not**, *short form* **couldn't** /ˈkʊdnt/) **1** used to say that it is possible for sb/sth to do sth, or for sth to happen: *The building ~ be emptied in 2 minutes.* **2** be able to or know how to do sth: *C~ you ski?* **3** used with the verbs 'feel', 'hear', 'see', 'smell', 'taste': *C~ you hear a funny noise?* **4** used to show that sb is allowed to do sth: *You ~ borrow my car if you want.* **5** (*spoken*) used to ask permission to do sth: *C~ I use your phone?* **6** (*spoken*) used to ask sb to do sth for you: *C~ you close the door, please?* **7** used when you are sure sth is not true: *That ~'t be Dan—he's in Chicago.*

can² /kæn/ n **1** metal container for food or liquids: *a ~ of beans* **2** con-

tents of such a container ● **can** v (**-nn-**) [T] put food, etc in a can ▶ **cannery** n (*pl* **-ies**) factory where food is canned

canal /kəˈnæl/ n man-made waterway for boats to travel along or for irrigation

canary /kəˈneəri/ n (*pl* **-ies**) small yellow bird, often kept in a cage as a pet

cancel /ˈkænsl/ v (**-ll-**, *US* **-l-**) [T] **1** say that sth already arranged will not be done or happen: *The meeting was ~led.* **2** mark a ticket or stamp so that it cannot be used again [PV] **cancel (sth) out** be equal to sth in effect; balance: *Recent losses have ~led out any profits made earlier.* ▶ **cancellation** /ˌkænsəˈleɪʃn/ n [C,U]

cancer /ˈkænsə(r)/ n [U,C] very serious disease in which lumps form in the body and kill normal cells ▶ **cancerous** *adj*: *~ cells*

candid /ˈkændɪd/ *adj* saying what you think openly: *a ~ discussion* ▶ **candidly** *adj*

candidate /ˈkændɪdət/ n **1** person being considered for a job or in an election **2** person taking an exam

candle /ˈkændl/ n stick of wax with a string (**wick**) through it, which gives out light when it burns ■ **'candlestick** n holder for a candle

candour (*US* **-dor**) /ˈkændə(r)/ n [U] quality of being candid

candy /ˈkændi/ n [U,C] (*pl* **-ies**) (*US*) (piece of) sweet food made of sugar and/or chocolate, eaten between meals

cane /keɪn/ n **1** [C] hollow stem of certain plants, eg bamboo or sugar **2** [U] such stems as a material for making furniture **3** [C] length of cane, etc, used as a support, for a plant or as a walking stick **4** (**the cane**) [sing] punishment of children by being hit with a cane ● **cane** v [T] hit a child with a cane as a punishment

canine /ˈkeɪnaɪn/ *adj* of or like a dog

canister /ˈkænɪstə(r)/ n **1** small (usu metal) box with a lid **2** cylinder fired from a gun

canker /ˈkæŋkə(r)/ n **1** [U] disease of trees **2** [U] disease that causes ulcers **3** [C] bad influence that spreads

cannabis /ˈkænəbɪs/ n [U] drug made from the hemp plant, smoked for its relaxing effect

cannery → CAN²

cannibal /ˈkænɪbl/ n **1** person who eats human flesh **2** animal that eats its own kind ▶ **cannibalism** /ˈkænɪbəlɪzəm/ n [U] ▶ **cannibalize** (*also* **-ise**) /ˈkænɪbəlaɪz/ v [T] use a machine, vehicle, etc to provide spare parts for another

cannon /'kænən/ n (pl **cannon**) **1** old type of large heavy gun firing solid metal balls **2** automatic gun firing shells(2) from an aircraft

cannot → CAN¹

canoe /kə'nu:/ n light narrow boat which you move along in the water with a paddle ● **canoe** v [I] travel by canoe ▸ **canoeist** n person travelling in a canoe

canon /'kænən/ n **1** priest with special duties in a cathedral **2** (fml) generally accepted standard or principle: offend the ~ of taste ▸ **canonical** /kə'nɒnɪkl/ adj according to the law of the Christian Church ▸ **canonize** (also **-ise**) /'kænənaɪz/ v [T] (of the Pope) officially declare sb to be a saint ‖ **canon 'law** n [U] law of the Christian Church

canopy /'kænəpi/ n (pl **-ies**) **1** cover that hangs above a bed, throne, etc **2** cover for the cockpit of an aircraft

can't cannot → CAN¹

cant /kænt/ n [U] insincere talk

cantankerous /kæn'tæŋkərəs/ adj bad-tempered and always complaining

canteen /kæn'ti:n/ n **1** place, eg in a factory, an office or a school, where food is served **2** (GB) box containing a set of knives, forks and spoons

canter /'kæntə(r)/ n [C, usu sing] horse's movement that is faster than a trot but slower than a gallop ● **canter** v [I, T] (cause a horse to) move at a canter

cantilever /'kæntɪli:və(r)/ n long piece of metal or wood that sticks out from a wall to support the end of a bridge

canvas /'kænvəs/ n **1** [U] strong coarse cloth used for making tents, sails, etc and by artists for painting on **2** [C] piece of canvas used for painting on; an oil painting

canvass /'kænvəs/ v [I, T] go round an area asking people for their political support or opinions ▸ **canvasser** n

canyon /'kænjən/ n deep valley ▸ **canyoning** n [U] sport of jumping into a fast-flowing mountain stream and being carried downstream

cap /kæp/ n **1** soft flat hat with a peak (= hard curved part sticking out at the front) **2** top covering sth eg on a bottle or tube of toothpaste ● **cap** v (**-pp-**) [T] **1** cover the top or end of sth **2** do or say sth better than sth previously done or said **3** choose a player for a national team

capability /ˌkeɪpə'bɪləti/ n [C,U] (pl **-ies**) **1** ability or qualities necessary to do sth **2** the power or weapons that a country has for war or for military action: Britain's nuclear ~

capable /'keɪpəbl/ adj **1** ~ of having the ability necessary for sth: You are ~ of producing better work than this. **2** having the ability to do things well ▸ **capably** adv

capacity /kə'pæsəti/ n (pl **-ies**) **1** [U, C, usu sing] number of people or things that a container or space can hold: a hall with a seating ~ of 750 **2** [C,U] power or ability **3** [C] official position that sb has: in my ~ as manager

cape /keɪp/ n **1** loose sleeveless garment like a short cloak **2** piece of land that sticks out into the sea

capillary /kə'pɪləri/ n (pl **-ies**) (anat) any of the smallest tubes in the body that carry blood

capital /'kæpɪtl/ n **1** [C] town or city that is the centre of government of a country, etc **2** [U] wealth or property owned by a person or business; money with which a business is started **3** [C] (also ˌcapital 'letter) large letter, eg A [IDM] **make capital (out) of sth** use a situation for your advantage ● **capital** adj involving punishment by death

capitalism /'kæpɪtəlɪzəm/ n [U] economic system in which a country's trade and industry are controlled by private owners and not the state ▸ **capitalist** /'kæpɪtəlɪst/ n **1** person who supports capitalism **2** person who owns capital(2) ▸ **capitalist** adj

capitalize (also **-ise**) /'kæpɪtəlaɪz/ v [T] **1** write a letter of the alphabet as a capital; begin a word with a capital letter **2** (business) sell possessions in order to change them into money **3** (business) provide a company, etc with the money it needs to function [PV] **capitalize on/upon sth** gain a further advantage for yourself from a situation

capitulate /kə'pɪtʃuleɪt/ v [I] ~(to) surrender to sb ▸ **capitulation** /kəˌpɪtʃu'leɪʃn/ n [U]

capsize /kæp'saɪz/ v [I, T] (cause a boat to) turn over in the water

capsule /'kæpsju:l/ n **1** very small container of medicine that is swallowed **2** compartment for people or instruments in a spacecraft

captain /'kæptɪn/ n **1** person in charge of a ship or an aircraft **2** officer of fairly high rank in the army **3** leader of a sports team ● **captain** v [T] be captain of a sports team or a ship

caption /'kæpʃn/ n words printed underneath a picture or cartoon in order to explain it

captivate /'kæptɪveɪt/ v [T] fascinate sb: ~d by her beauty

captive /'kæptɪv/ n, adj (person or animal) taken prisoner ▶ **captivity** /kæp'tɪvəti/ n [U] state of being kept as a prisoner

captor /'kæptə(r)/ n person who captures a person or an animal

capture /'kæptʃə(r)/ v [T] **1** catch a person or an animal and keep them as a prisoner **2** take control of a place, building, etc using force **3** succeed in accurately expressing a feeling, etc in a picture, film, etc ● **capture** n [U] act of capturing sb/sth or of being captured: *data* ~

car /kɑː(r)/ n **1** motor vehicle for carrying passengers **2** railway carriage of a particular type: *a dining* ~ ■ **car 'boot sale** n (GB) outdoor sale at which people sell unwanted goods from the backs of their cars ■ **'car park** n (GB) area where cars may be parked

carafe /kə'ræf/ n glass container in which water or wine is served

caramel /'kærəmel/ n **1** [U] burnt sugar used for colouring and flavouring food **2** [C] chewy sweet of boiled sugar

carat /'kærət/ n **1** unit of weight for precious stones **2** unit for measuring the purity of gold

caravan /'kærəvæn/ n **1** small home on wheels, pulled by a car **2** covered cart for living in **3** group of people and animals travelling across a desert

carbohydrate /,kɑːbəʊ'haɪdreɪt/ n [C,U] substance found in food, eg sugar and potatoes, that provides energy

carbon /'kɑːbən/ n [U] (symb **C**) non-metallic element found in diamonds, coal and all living matter ■ ,**carbon 'copy** (also **carbon**) n copy of a document, etc made with carbon paper ■ '**carbon paper** n [C,U] (sheet of) thin paper coated with a dark substance, used for making copies

carbuncle /'kɑːbʌŋkl/ n large painful swelling under the skin

carburettor /,kɑːbə'retə(r)/ (US **-t-**) n part of a car engine in which petrol and air are mixed

carcass /'kɑːkəs/ n dead body of an animal

card /kɑːd/ n **1** [U] thick stiff paper **2** [C] piece of stiff paper or plastic with information on it: *an identity* ~ ◇ *a business/credit* ~ **3** [C] piece of card with a picture on it that you use for sending a greeting to sb: *a Christmas/birthday* ~ **4** [C] = PLAYING CARD (PLAY¹) **5** [C] (computing) small electronic circuit that is part of a computer, enabling it to perform certain functions: *a sound* ~ [IDM] **lay/**

put your cards on the table be honest about your intentions **on the cards** (infml) likely

cardboard /'kɑːdbɔːd/ n [U] thick stiff kind of paper: *a* ~ *box*

cardiac /'kɑːdiæk/ adj of the heart

cardigan /'kɑːdɪɡən/ n knitted woollen jacket with buttons or a zip at the front

cardinal /'kɑːdɪnl/ n **1** senior Roman Catholic priest **2** (also ,**cardinal 'number**) number, eg 1, 2, or 5, used to show quantity rather than order ● **cardinal** adj (fml) most important

care¹ /keə(r)/ n **1** [U] protection: *The child was left in his sister's* ~. **2** [U] serious attention or thought: *arrange the flowers with* ~ ◇ *Take* ~ *when crossing the road.* **3** [C, esp sing, U] feeling of worry or anxiety: *without a* ~ *in the world* **in care** (GB) (of children) living in an institution run by the local authority rather than with their parents: *The boys were taken into* ~ *when their mother died.* **take care of yourself/sb/sth 1** keep yourself/sb/sth safe from injury, illness, damage, etc; look after sb/sth/yourself **2** be responsible for sth ■ '**carefree** adj without worries ▶ **careful** adj **1** (of a person) cautious; thinking about what you are doing **2** giving a lot of attention to details: *a* ~*ful piece of work* ▶ **carefulness** n [U] ▶ **careless** adj **1** not taking care; thoughtless **2** resulting from lack of attention and thought: *a* ~ *mistake* **3** ~of (fml) not at all worried about sth ▶ **carelessly** adv ▶ **carelessness** n [U]

care² /keə(r)/ v [I] **1** ~(about) feel that sth is important and worth worrying about: *I* ~ *about this country's future.* **2** ~(about) like or love sb and worry about what happens to them **3** ~for/to (fml) like to have sth or do sth: *Would you* ~ *for a drink?* [PV] **care for sb 1** look after sb who is ill, very old, etc **2** love or like sb very much

career /kə'rɪə(r)/ n **1** series of jobs that a person has in a particular area of work **2** the period of time that you spend in your life working ● **career** v [I] rush wildly: ~ *down the hill*

caress /kə'res/ n loving touch ● **caress** v [T] give a caress to sb/sth

caretaker /'keəteɪkə(r)/ n person whose job is to look after a building

cargo /'kɑːɡəʊ/ n [C,U] (pl ~**es** US also ~**s**) goods carried in a ship or an aircraft

caricature /'kærɪkətʃʊə(r)/ n picture or description of a person that emphasizes certain features to cause amusement or ridicule

● **caricature** v [T] produce a caricature of sb

carnage /'kɑːnɪdʒ/ n [U] killing of a lot of people

carnal /'kɑːnl/ adj (fml) connected with the body or with sex

carnation /kɑː'neɪʃn/ n white, pink or red flower, often worn as a decoration

carnival /'kɑːnɪvl/ n public festival

carnivore /'kɑːnɪvɔː(r)/ n any animal that eats meat ▶ **carnivorous** /kɑː'nɪvərəs/ adj

carol /'kærəl/ n Christian religious song sung at Christmas

carp /kɑːp/ n (pl carp) large freshwater fish ● **carp** v [I] ~(at/about) complain continually about sth in an annoying way

carpenter /'kɑːpəntə(r)/ n person whose job is to make and repair wooden objects ▶ **carpentry** /'kɑːpəntri/ n [U] work of a carpenter

carpet /'kɑːpɪt/ n [U,C] (piece of) thick woollen or artificial fabric for covering floors ● **carpet** v [T] cover sth with or as if with a carpet

carriage /'kærɪdʒ/ n 1 [C] separate section of a train for carrying passengers 2 [C] vehicle pulled by a horse 3 [U] act or cost of transporting goods 4 [C] moving part of a machine: a typewriter ~ ■ **carriageway** n one of the two sides of a motorway, etc, intended for traffic moving in one direction

carrier /'kæriə(r)/ n 1 person or company that carries goods 2 person or animal that can pass a disease to others without suffering from it ■ **carrier bag** n paper or plastic bag for carrying shopping

carrot /'kærət/ n long pointed orange root vegetable

carry /'kæri/ v (pt, pp -ied) 1 [T] support the weight of sb/sth and take them or it from one place to place: ~ the boxes upstairs 2 [T] have sth with you and take it wherever you go: I never ~ much money. 3 [T] (of pipes, wires, etc) contain and direct the flow of water, electricity, etc 4 [T] support the weight of sth: The pillars ~ the whole roof. 5 [T] have sth as a result: Power carries great responsibility. 6 [I] (of a sound) be able to be heard at a distance: His voice doesn't ~ very far. 7 [T] (usu passive) approve of sth in a vote: The proposal was carried. 8 [T] (of a newspaper) include or contain a particular story [IDM] be/get carried away become so excited that you lose self control [PV] carry sth off 1 win sth 2 succeed in doing sth difficult carry on (with/doing sth) continue doing sth: ~ on reading carry sth on 1 do sth that you have

said you will do or have been asked to do: ~ out a promise/threat 2 do and complete a task: ~ out a survey **carry sth through** complete sth successfully **carry sb through sth** help sb to survive a difficult period

cart /kɑːt/ n vehicle for carrying loads, usu pulled by a horse [IDM] **put the cart before the horse** do things in the wrong order ● **cart** v [T] 1 carry sth in a cart or other vehicle 2 (infml) carry sth large, heavy or awkward ■ **carthorse** n large strong horse used for heavy work ■ **cartwheel** n sideways somersault with arms and legs stretched out

carte blanche /ˌkɑːt 'blɑːnʃ/ n [U] complete freedom to do whatever you like

cartilage /'kɑːtɪlɪdʒ/ n [U,C] strong white flexible tissue found between the joints in the body

carton /'kɑːtn/ n cardboard or plastic box for holding esp food or liquid

cartoon /kɑː'tuːn/ n 1 amusing drawing or series of drawings in a newspaper, etc 2 film made by photographing a series of drawings: a Walt Disney ~ ▶ **cartoonist** n person who draws cartoons

cartridge /'kɑːtrɪdʒ/ n 1 tube or case containing explosive and a bullet, for firing from a gun 2 case containing sth that is used in a machine, eg photographic film for a camera, ink for a printer, etc 3 thin tube containing ink which you put in a pen

carve /kɑːv/ v [I, T] 1 make objects, patterns, etc by cutting away material from stone or wood: ~ your initials on a tree 2 cut cooked meat into slices for eating [PV] **carve sth out (for yourself)** work hard in order to have a successful career, reputation, etc ▶ **carving** n object or pattern carved in stone, etc ■ **carving knife** n large sharp knife used for carving meat

cascade /kæ'skeɪd/ n small waterfall ● **cascade** v [I] fall downwards in large amounts

case /keɪs/ 1 [C] particular situation or a situation of a particular type: In most ~s, no extra charge is made. 2 (the case) [sing] the true situation: If that is the ~, we need more staff. 3 [C] matter being investigated by the police 4 [C] matter to be decided in a law court: a court ~ 5 [C, usu sing] set of facts, etc that support one side in a law court, discussion, etc 6 [C] box or other container for storing things: a pencil ~ 7 [C] = SUITCASE 8 [C] instance of a disease or injury 9 [C,U] (in some languages) form of a word that shows its relationship to another word [IDM] **a case in point** clear example that is relevant to the matter being discussed **in any case** whatever happens (just) **in case** (...) because of the possibility of sth happening: *Take an umbrella in ~ it rains.* **in case of sth** if sth happens: *In ~ of emergency, phone the police.* **in that case** if that is the situation ■ **,case 'history** *n* record of a person's background, health, etc

casement /ˈkeɪsmənt/ *n* window that opens like a door

cash /kæʃ/ *n* [U] **1** money in coins or notes **2** (*infml*) money in any form ● **cash** *v* [T] exchange a cheque for cash [PV] **cash in (on sth)** take advantage of sth; profit from sth ■ **'cash cow** (*business*) part of a business that always makes money for the rest of the business ■ **'cash crop** *n* crop grown for selling ■ **'cash machine** (*also* **'cash dispenser**, **'Cashpoint™**) *n* machine outside a bank from which you can get money from your bank account using a special plastic card ■ **'cash register** *n* machine in a shop for recording and storing money received

cashew /ˈkæʃuː; kæˈʃuː/ *n* (*tropical American tree and*) small curved nut, used in cooking

cashier /kæˈʃɪə(r)/ *n* person whose job is to receive and pay out money in a bank, shop, etc

cashmere /ˈkæʃmɪə(r); ˌkæʃˈm-/ *n* [U] fine soft wool

casing /ˈkeɪsɪŋ/ *n* covering that protects sth

casino /kəˈsiːnəʊ/ *n* (*pl* ~s) public building or room where people play gambling games for money

cask /kɑːsk/ *n* barrel for storing liquids

casket /ˈkɑːskɪt/ *n* **1** small box for holding jewellery, letters, etc **2** (*US*) = COFFIN

cassava /kəˈsɑːvə/ *n* [U] roots of a tropical plant from the thick roots of a tropical plant

casserole /ˈkæsərəʊl/ *n* **1** [C,U] hot dish made with meat, vegetables, etc that are cooked slowly in liquid in an oven **2** [C] container in which such food is cooked

cassette /kəˈset/ *n* small sealed case containing magnetic tape or film: *a ~ recorder/player*

cassock /ˈkæsək/ *n* long outer garment worn by some Christian priests

cast¹ /kɑːst/ *v* (*pt, pp* **cast**) [T] **1** throw sth; allow sth to fall: *~ a net* ◇ *The tree ~ a long shadow.* ◇ *~ a glance at sb ◇ ~ doubt on his claims ◇ ~ aspersions on his reputation* **2** give an actor a part in a play

3 make an object by pouring metal into a mould (= a specially shaped container): *a statue ~ in bronze* [IDM] **cast an eye/your eyes over sth** look at or examine sth quickly **cast light on sth** → LIGHT¹ **cast lots (for sth/to do sth)** → LOT³ [PV] **cast sb/sth aside** (*fml*) get rid of sb/sth **cast sth off** untie the ropes of a boat **cast sth off** (*written*) get rid of sth ► **casting** *n* **1** [U] process of choosing actors for a play or film **2** [C] object made by pouring metal into a mould ■ **,casting 'vote** *n* vote given to decide a matter when votes on each side are equal ■ **,cast 'iron** *n* [U] hard alloy of iron made by pouring hot liquid metal into a mould ► **,cast-'iron** *adj* **1** made of cast iron **2** very strong or certain: *a ~-iron excuse* ■ **'cast-off** (*GB*) *n* [C, usu *pl*] *adj* (piece of clothing) no longer wanted by its original owner

cast² /kɑːst/ *n* **1** all the actors in a play, etc **2** object made by pouring hot liquid metal, etc into a mould (= a specially shaped container) **3** shaped container used for this **4** act of throwing sth, esp a fishing line

castanets /ˌkæstəˈnets/ *n* [*pl*] musical instrument, consisting of two small round pieces of wood, hit together with the fingers, used esp in Spanish dances

castaway /ˈkɑːstəweɪ/ *n* shipwrecked person

caste /kɑːst/ *n* any one of the Hindu social classes

caster sugar (*also* **castor sugar**) /ˈkɑːstə(r)/ *n* [U] very fine white sugar

castigate /ˈkæstɪgeɪt/ *v* [T] (*fml*) criticize sb severely

castle /ˈkɑːsl/ *n* **1** old large building with thick walls, made for protection from enemies **2** chess piece

castor (*US* **caster**) /ˈkɑːstə(r)/ *n* small wheel fixed to a chair, etc

castor oil /ˌkɑːstər ˈɔɪl/ *n* [U] thick yellowish oil used as a medicine

castor sugar *n* [U] = CASTER SUGAR

castrate /kæˈstreɪt/ *v* [T] remove the testicles of a male animal ► **castration** /kæˈstreɪʃn/ *n* [U, C]

casual /ˈkæʒuəl/ *adj* **1** not showing much care or thought; seeming not to be worried **2** informal: *~ clothes* **3** not permanent or regular: *~ work* **4** happening by chance: *a ~ meeting* ► **casually** *adv*

casualty /ˈkæʒuəlti/ *n* (*pl* **-ies**) **1** [C] person injured or killed in a war or an accident **2** [U] (*GB* also **'casualty department**) part of a hospital where people who need urgent treatment are taken

cat /kæt/ *n* **1** small furry animal

C

often kept as a pet **2** wild animal of the cat family, eg lion or tiger ■ 'cat **burglar** n burglar who enters buildings by climbing up walls, etc ■ 'catcall n [usu pl] loud shrill whistle expressing disapproval ■ 'catnap n short sleep

catacombs /'kætəkuːmz/ n [pl] series of underground tunnels for burying dead bodies

catalogue (US also **-log**) /'kætəlɒg/ n list of items, eg goods for sale ● **catalogue** v [T] list sth in a catalogue

catalyst /'kætəlɪst/ n something that speeds up or causes a change without itself changing

catalytic converter /ˌkætəˌlɪtɪk kən'vɜːtə(r)/ n device used in the exhaust system of motor vehicles to reduce the damage caused to the environment

catapult /'kætəpʌlt/ n Y-shaped stick with a piece of elastic, for shooting stones, etc ● **catapult** v [I, T] throw sb/sth or be thrown suddenly and violently through the air

cataract /'kætərækt/ n **1** disease of the eye, causing blindness **2** (lit) large steep waterfall

catarrh /kə'tɑː(r)/ n thick liquid (phlegm) in the nose and throat, caused by a cold

catastrophe /kə'tæstrəfi/ n sudden great disaster or misfortune ▶ **catastrophic** /ˌkætə'strɒfɪk/ adj

catch¹ /kætʃ/ v (pt, pp caught /kɔːt/) **1** [T] stop and hold sth moving, esp in the hands: ~ a ball **2** [T] capture a person or an animal: ~ a thief **3** [T] find or discover sb doing sth: ~ sb stealing **4** [T] be in time for or get on a train, etc **5** [I, T] (cause sb/sth to) become trapped: I caught my fingers in the door. **6** [T] become ill with sth: ~ a cold **7** [T] hear sth; understand sth: I didn't quite ~ your name. **8** [T] hit sb/sth: The stone caught him on the head. [IDM] **catch sb's eye** attract sb's attention **catch sb's fancy →** FANCY¹ **catch fire** begin to burn **catch napping** (infml) find sb not paying attention **catch sb red-handed** discover sb in the act of doing wrong **catch sight of sb/sth** see sb/sth for a moment [PV] **catch on** (infml) become popular **catch on (to sth)** (infml) understand sth **catch sb out** show that sb is ignorant or is doing sth wrong **catch up (with sb)** (GB also) **catch sb up** reach the same level as sb **catch up on sth** spend extra time doing sth **be/get caught up in sth** be/get involved in sth ▶ **catching** adj (of a disease) infectious ■ 'catchment area n area from which people are sent to a particular school, hospital, etc ■ 'catchphrase n popular word or phrase

connected with the politician or entertainer who made it famous ▶ **catchy** adj (-ier, -iest) (of music or the words of an advertisement) easy to remember

catch² /kætʃ/ n **1** act of catching sth, esp a ball **2** (amount of) fish caught: a huge ~ of fish **3** device for fastening sth **4** hidden difficulty: There must be a ~ in this somewhere.

categorical /ˌkætə'gɒrɪkl/ adj (of a statement) unconditional; absolute ▶ **categorically** /-kli/ adv

category /'kætəgəri/ n (pl **-ies**) group in a complete system; class ▶ **categorize** (also **-ise**) /'kætəgəraɪz/ v [T] put sb/sth in a category

cater /'keɪtə(r)/ v [I] **~(for) 1** provide food and services for sb, esp at social functions **2** provide what is needed or desired by sb: videos ~ing for all tastes ● **caterer** n

caterpillar /'kætəpɪlə(r)/ n small creature like a worm with legs, which develops into a butterfly or moth

catgut /'kætgʌt/ n [U] thin strong cord used in making the strings of musical instruments

cathedral /kə'θiːdrəl/ n main church of a district, under the care of a bishop

cathode /'kæθəʊd/ n (tech) negative electrode in a battery, etc

catholic /'kæθlɪk/ adj **1** (Catholic) = ROMAN CATHOLIC (ROMAN) **2** (fml) including many things; general: have ~ tastes ● **Catholic** n = ROMAN CATHOLIC (ROMAN) ▶ **Catholicism** /kə'θɒləsɪzəm/ n [U] teaching, beliefs, etc of the Roman Catholic Church

cattle /'kætl/ n [pl] cows and bulls that are kept as farm animals

catty /'kæti/ adj (-ier, -iest) (infml) (of a woman) saying unkind things about others

caught pt, pp of CATCH¹

cauldron /'kɔːldrən/ n large deep pot for boiling things in: a witch's ~

cauliflower /'kɒlɪflaʊə(r)/ n [C, U] vegetable with a large white flower head

cause /kɔːz/ n **1** [C] person or thing that makes sth happen: the ~ of the fire **2** [U] ~ (for) reason: There's no ~ for concern. ◇ have ~ for complaint **3** [C] organization or idea that is strongly supported: the ~ of world peace ● **cause** v [T] make sth happen, esp sth bad: What ~d his death?

causeway /'kɔːzweɪ/ n raised road or path across water or wet ground

caustic /'kɔːstɪk/ adj **1** able to burn by chemical action: ~ soda **2** (of remarks) very bitter or critical ▶ **caustically** /-kli/ adv

caution /'kɔːʃn/ n **1** [U] great care

2 [C] (GB) warning given by the police to sb who has committed a minor crime **3** [U,C] warning words ● **caution** v [T] **1** warn sb of possible danger **2** (GB, law) warn sb that anything they say may be used in evidence against them in a law court ▶ **cautionary** /'kɔ:ʃənəri/ adj giving a warning: a ~ary tale

cautious /'kɔ:ʃəs/ adj very careful about what you do, esp to avoid danger ▶ **cautiously** adv

cavalcade /ˌkævl'keɪd/ n procession of people on horseback, in cars, etc

cavalry /'kævlri/ n [C, with sing or pl verb] (pl ~ies) soldiers fighting on horseback (esp in the past), or in armoured vehicles

cave /keɪv/ n large hole in the side of a hill, or under the ground ● **cave** v [PV] **cave in (on sb/sth)** (of a roof, wall, etc) fall inwards; collapse

cavern /'kævən/ n large cave ▶ **cavernous** adj (written) (of a space or space) large and often empty and/or dark

caviar (also **caviare**) /'kæviɑ:(r)/ n [U] salted eggs of certain types of large fish, eaten as food

caving /'keɪvɪŋ/ n [U] (GB) sport or activity of going into caves under the ground

cavity /'kævəti/ n (pl ~ies) (fml) small hole in sth solid, eg a tooth

cayenne /keɪ'en/ (ˌcayenne 'pepper) n [U] kind of hot red powdered pepper

CB /ˌsi: 'bi:/ abbr Citizens' Band; range of waves on a radio on which people can talk to each other, esp when driving

cc /ˌsi: 'si:/ abbr cubic centimetre, a measure of the power of an engine

CCTV /ˌsi: si: ti: 'vi:/ abbr = CLOSED-CIRCUIT TELEVISION (CLOSE¹)

CD /ˌsi: 'di:/ abbr compact disc; small disc on which information or sound is recorded and reproduced by laser action. CDs are played on a special machine called a **CD player**.

CD-ROM /ˌsi: di: 'rɒm/ n [C,U] compact disc read-only memory; CD on which large amounts of information, sound and pictures can be stored, for use on a computer: The encyclopedia is available on ~. ◇ a ~ drive (= in a computer)

cease /si:s/ v [I, T] (fml) (cause sth to) stop happening or existing ■ **'ceasefire** n agreement to stop fighting ▶ **ceaseless** adj (fml) not stopping ▶ **ceaselessly** adv

cedar /'si:də(r)/ n **1** [C] tall evergreen tree with wide spreading branches **2** [U] hard sweet-smelling wood of this tree

ceiling /'si:lɪŋ/ n **1** top inside surface of a room **2** official upper limit: a price/wage ~

celebrate /'selɪbreɪt/ v **1** [I, T] mark a special occasion by enjoying yourself **2** [T] (fml) praise sb/sth ▶ **celebrated** adj famous ▶ **celebration** /ˌselɪ'breɪʃn/ n [C, U]

celebrity /sə'lebrəti/ n (pl ~ies) **1** [C] famous person **2** [U] fame

celery /'seləri/ n [U] plant whose white stems are eaten raw

celestial /sə'lestiəl/ adj (fml) of the sky; of heaven

celibate /'selɪbət/ adj not married and not having sex, esp for religious reasons ▶ **celibacy** /-bəsi/ n [U]

cell /sel/ n **1** small room: a prison ~ **2** smallest unit of living matter that can exist on its own: red blood ~s **3** device for producing electric current by chemical action **4** small group of people, eg in a secret organization

cellar /'selə(r)/ n underground room for storing things: a wine ~

cello /'tʃeləʊ/ n (pl ~s) kind of large violin, held between the knees ▶ **cellist** /'tʃelɪst/ n person who plays a cello

Cellophane™ /'seləfeɪn/ n [U] thin transparent plastic material used for wrapping things in

cellphone /'selfəʊn/ n (esp US) = MOBILE PHONE (MOBILE)

cellular /'seljələ(r)/ adj **1** connected with or consisting of plant or animal cells **2** connected to a telephone system that works by radio instead of wires **3** (GB) (of blankets, etc) loosely woven ■ ˌcellular 'phone n (esp US) = MOBILE PHONE (MOBILE)

cellulite /'seljulaɪt/ n [U] type of fat just below the skin which stops the surface of the skin looking smooth

Celsius /'selsiəs/ (also **centigrade**) (abbr **C**) adj, n [U] (of or using the) temperature scale in which water freezes at 0° and boils at 100°

cement /sɪ'ment/ n [U] **1** grey powder that when mixed with water becomes hard like stone, used in building **2** kind of glue ● **cement** v [T] **1** join sth with cement **2** make a relationship, agreement, etc stronger

cemetery /'semətri/ n (pl ~ies) place where dead people are buried

cenotaph /'senətɑ:f/ n monument built in memory of soldiers killed in war

censor /'sensə(r)/ n person whose job is to examine books, films, etc and remove parts considered indecent, offensive, etc ● **censor** v [T] examine or remove parts of a book, film, etc ▶ **censorship** n [U] act or policy of censoring books, etc

censure /'senʃə(r)/ v [T] criticize sb strongly for sth they have done ▶ **censure** n [U]

census /'sensəs/ n official counting of sth, esp of the population of a country

cent /sent/ n one 100th part of a main unit of money, eg a dollar

centaur /'sentɔ:(r)/ n (in Greek mythology) creature that is half man and half horse

centenarian /ˌsentɪ'neəriən/ n person who is 100 years old or more

centenary /sen'ti:nəri/ n (pl -ies) 100th anniversary

centennial /sen'teniəl/ n (esp US) centenary

center (US) = CENTRE

centigrade /'sentɪɡreɪd/ adj, n [U] = CELSIUS

centimetre (US -meter) /'sentɪmi:tə(r)/ n metric unit of length; 100th part of a metre

centipede /'sentɪpi:d/ n small crawling creature with many legs

central /'sentrəl/ adj 1 most important; main 2 at or of the centre ■ **central 'heating** n [U] system of heating a building from one main source through pipes and radiators ▶ **centrally** adv ■ **central 'processing unit** n = CPU

centralize (also -ise) /'sentrəlaɪz/ v [I, T] (cause sth to) come under the control of one central authority ▶ **centralization** (also -isation) /ˌsentrəlaɪ'zeɪʃn/ n [U]

centre (US **center**) /'sentə(r)/ n 1 [C] middle point or part of sth 2 [C] building or place for a particular activity: a shopping ~ 3 [C, usu sing] point towards which people direct their attention: the ~ of attention 4 (usu the centre) [sing] moderate political position, between the extremes of left and right ● **centre** v [T] move sth so that it is in the centre of sth else [PV] **centre** (**sth**) **around/on/round/upon sth** (cause sth to) have sb/sth as its main concern

centrifugal /ˌsentrɪ'fju:ɡl; sen'trɪfjəɡl/ adj (tech) moving away from a centre: ~ force

century /'sentʃəri/ n (pl -ies) 1 period of 100 years 2 (in cricket) 100 runs by one player

ceramic /sə'ræmɪk/ n 1 [C, usu pl] object made of clay that has been made permanently hard by heat 2 (**ceramics**) [U] art of making and decorating ceramics ▶ **ceramic** adj: ~ tiles

cereal /'sɪəriəl/ n [U,C] 1 (edible grain produced by a kind of grass, eg wheat or barley 2 food made from cereal grain: breakfast ~s

ceremonial /ˌserɪ'məʊniəl/ adj relating to or used in a ceremony: a ~ occasion ● **ceremonial** n [C,U] system of rules, etc for ceremonies ▶ **ceremonially** /-niəli/ adv

ceremonious /ˌserɪ'məʊniəs/ adj (written) very formal and polite ▶ **ceremoniously** adv

ceremony /'serəməni/ n (pl -ies) 1 [C] formal act(s), religious service, etc on a special occasion: a wedding ~ 2 [U] formal behaviour

certain /'sɜ:tn/ adj 1 having no doubts; sure 2 ~(to) sure to happen: They're ~ to win the game. 3 particular, but not named: on ~ conditions 4 slight; noticeable: a ~ coldness in his attitude [IDM] **make certain** (**that …**) find out whether sth is definitely true: Make ~ that no bones are broken. ▶ **certainly** adv 1 without doubt 2 (in answer to questions) of course; yes ▶ **certainty** n (pl -ies) 1 [C] thing that is certain 2 [U] state of being sure

certificate /sə'tɪfɪkət/ n official paper that states certain facts: a birth/marriage ~

certify /'sɜ:tɪfaɪ/ v (pt, pp -ied) [T] state officially, esp in writing, that sth is true

cessation /se'seɪʃn/ n [U,C] (fml) the stopping of sth

cesspit /'sespɪt/ (also **cesspool** /'sespu:l/) n underground hole for collecting waste from a building, esp the toilets

CFC /ˌsi: ef 'si:/ n [C,U] chlorofluorocarbon; type of gas used esp in aerosols. CFCs are harmful to the layer of the gas ozone in the earth's atmosphere.

chafe /tʃeɪf/ v 1 [I, T] (cause sth to) become sore by rubbing: The rope ~d her wrists. 2 [I] ~(at/under) become impatient because of sth

chaff /tʃɑ:f/ n [U] outer covering of grain, removed before the grain is used as food

chagrin /'ʃæɡrɪn/ n [U] (fml) disappointment or annoyance

chain /tʃeɪn/ n 1 [C] length of metal rings joined together 2 [C] series of connected things: a ~ of mountains/shops/events ● **chain** v [T] fasten sb/sth to another person or thing with a chain ■ **chain re'action** n series of events, each of which causes the next ■ **'chain-smoke** v [I, T] smoke cigarettes continuously ▶ **'chain-smoker** n ■ **'chain store** n one of several similar shops owned by the same company

chair /tʃeə(r)/ n 1 [C] moveable seat with a back, for one person 2 (**the chair**) [sing] (position of the) person in charge of a meeting or committee 3 [C] position of a professor at a university ● **chair** v [T] be in charge of a meeting ■ '**chairman** | '**chairperson** | '**chairwoman** n person in charge of a meeting, committee, etc

chalet /'ʃæleɪ/ n 1 Swiss mountain hut built of wood 2 (GB) small house in a holiday camp

chalk /tʃɔːk/ n 1 [U] kind of soft white rock 2 (pl **chalks**) substance similar to chalk made into white or coloured sticks for writing or drawing ● **chalk** v [I, T] write or draw sth with chalk [PV] **chalk up sth** (infml) achieve a success, points in a game, etc ▶ **chalky** adj (-ier, -iest) containing or like chalk

challenge /'tʃælɪndʒ/ n 1 difficult or demanding task 2 invitation to take part in a game, fight, etc ● **challenge** v [T] 1 invite sb to take part in a game, fight, etc 2 question the truth, rightness, etc of sth ▶ **challenger** n ● **challenging** adj difficult and demanding

chamber /'tʃeɪmbə(r)/ n 1 [C] large room in a public building used for formal meetings: the council ~ 2 (**chambers**) [pl] set of rooms used by judges and barristers 3 [C, with sing or pl verb] one of the parts of a parliament 4 [C] room used for the particular purpose mentioned: a burial ~ 5 [C] enclosed space: the ~s of the heart ■ '**chambermaid** n woman whose job is to clean bedrooms in a hotel ■ '**chamber music** n [U] classical music written for a small group of instruments ■ ,**Chamber of 'Commerce** n group of business people organized to support or promote local trade interests

chameleon /kə'miːliən/ n small lizard whose skin colour changes to match its surroundings

chamois /'ʃæmwɑː/ n (pl **chamois**) animal like a small deer, that lives in the mountains of Europe and Asia ● **chamois** /'ʃæmi/ n [C, U] (piece of) soft leather cloth from the skin of goats, etc, used esp for cleaning windows

champ /tʃæmp/ v [I] 1 (esp of horses) bite noisily 2 be impatient

champagne /ʃæm'peɪn/ n [U, C] sparkling white French wine

champion /'tʃæmpiən/ n 1 person, team, etc that wins a competition 2 ~ (**of**) person who supports or defends sb or a principle: a ~ of women's rights ● **champion** v [T] fight for or speak in support of a group of people or a belief ▶ '**championship** n [C] 1 (also **championships** [pl]) competition to find the best player or team in a particular sport 2 position of being a champion

chance /tʃɑːns/ n 1 [C, U] possibility

of sth happening, esp sth that you want: no ~ of winning 2 [C] suitable time when you have the opportunity to do sth: have a ~ to apologize 3 [C] unpleasant or dangerous possibility: Don't take any ~s. 4 [U] way in which things happen without any cause that can be seen; luck: I met her by ~ at the station. [IDM] **on the off chance (that)** because of the possibility of sth happening, although it is unlikely **take a chance (on sth)** decide to do sth, though it may not be the right choice ● **chance** v [T] 1 (infml) take a risk 2 [I] (written or fml) happen by chance ● **chance** adj not planned: a ~ meeting ▶ **chancy** adj (infml) risky

chancel /'tʃɑːnsl/ n eastern part of a church, containing the altar

chancellor (also **Chancellor**) /'tʃɑːnsələ(r)/ n 1 head of government in Germany or Austria 2 honorary head of a university in Britain ■ ,**Chancellor of the Ex'chequer** n (GB) government minister responsible for finance

chandelier /,ʃændə'lɪə(r)/ n decorative hanging light with branches for several bulbs or candles

change[1] /tʃeɪndʒ/ v 1 [I, T] become or make sb/sth different: Our plans have ~d. ◇ Water ~s into steam. ◇ ~ your attitude 2 [T] replace one thing or person with another: ~ a light bulb 3 [I, T] take off your clothes and put others on 4 [I, T] go from one train, bus, etc to another 5 [T] give and receive money in exchange for money of smaller value or in a foreign currency [IDM] **change hands** pass to another owner **change your/ sb's mind** change a decision or opinion **change your tune** (infml) express a different opinion or behave differently when your situation changes [PV] **change over (from sth) (to sth)** change from one system or position to another ▶ **changeable** adj likely to change ■ '**changeover** n change from one system or method of working to another

change[2] /tʃeɪndʒ/ n 1 [C, U] act or result of sth becoming different 2 (a **change**) [sing] fact of a situation, place, etc being different and therefore nice to be interesting, enjoyable, etc: Let's stay in for a ~. 3 [C] something used in place of another: ~ of name/clothes 4 [U] money returned when the price of sth is less than the amount given 5 [U] coins of low value

channel /'tʃænl/ n 1 television station 2 way by which news or information may travel: Your complaint must be made through the proper ~s. 3 [C] passage along which a liquid flows **4** narrow passage of water: *the English C—* ● **channel** *v* (**-ll-**, *US also* **-l-**) **1 ~(into)** direct money, feelings, ideas, etc towards a particular thing or purpose: *~ all our resources into the new scheme* **2** carry or send water, light, etc through a passage

chant /tʃɑːnt/ *v* [I, T] **1** sing or shout the same words many times **2** sing a religious song or prayer using very few words that are repeated many times ▸ **chant** *n*

chaos /'keɪɒs/ *n* [U] complete disorder or confusion ▸ **chaotic** /keɪ-'ɒtɪk/ *adj*

chap /tʃæp/ *n* (GB, *infml*) man or boy ● **chap** *v* (**-pp-**) [I, T] (of the skin) (cause sth to) become cracked, rough and sore: *~ped lips*

chapel /'tʃæpl/ *n* **1** place used for Christian worship, eg in a school or hospital **2** separate part of a church or cathedral, with its own altar

chaplain /'tʃæplɪn/ *n* priest or Christian minister in the armed forces, a hospital, prison, etc

chapter /'tʃæptə(r)/ *n* **1** (usu numbered) main division of a book **2** period of time

char /tʃɑː(r)/ *v* (**-rr-**) [I, T] (cause sth to) become black by burning

character /'kærəktə/ *n* **1** [C] qualities that make sb, a country, etc different from others: *The ~ of the town has changed over the years.* **2** [U] particular quality of sth: *buildings that were simple in ~* **3** [C] interesting or unusual quality that a person or place has: *houses with no ~* **4** [C] moral strength: *a woman of ~* **5** [C] person in a play, novel, etc **6** [C] (*infml*) person, esp an unpleasant or a strange one **7** [C] letter or sign used in writing or printing: *Chinese ~s* [IDM] **in/out of character** typical/not typical of sb's character ▸ **characterless** *adj* uninteresting; ordinary

characteristic /ˌkærəktə'rɪstɪk/ *adj* typical of sb or sb's character ● **characteristic** *n* typical quality or feature ▸ **characteristically** /-kli/ *adv*

characterize (*also* **-ise**) /'kærəktəraɪz/ *v* [T] (*fml*) **1** be typical of sb/ sth **2** describe the qualities of sb/sth

charade /ʃə'rɑːd/ *n* **1** [C] absurd and obvious pretence (*charades*) [U] party game in which one team acts a word that has to be guessed by the other team

charcoal /'tʃɑːkəʊl/ *n* [U] black substance of burnt wood, used as a fuel, for drawing, etc

charge¹ /tʃɑːdʒ/ *v* **1** [I, T] ask an amount of money for goods or a service: *They ~d me £50 for the repair.* **2** [T] **~to** record sth as a debt to be paid by sb/sth: *C~ it to his account.* **3** [T] **~**

(**with**) accuse sb of sth, esp in a law court: *He was ~d with murder.* **4** [I, T] rush forward and attack sb/sth **5** [T] put electricity into a battery **6** [T] **~ with** (esp passive) (*written*) fill sth with an emotion: *a voice ~d with tension* **7** [T] **~with** (*fml*) give sb a duty or responsibility

charge² /tʃɑːdʒ/ *n* **1** [C] price asked for goods or services **2** [C] formal claim that sb has done wrong: *a ~ of murder* **3** [U] responsibility and control: *She's in ~ of the accounts.* ◇ *take ~ of the department* **4** [C, U] sudden rush or violent attack **5** [C] amount of electricity put into a battery or carried by a substance [IDM] **bring/press/prefer charges against sb** (*law*) accuse sb formally of a crime so that there can be a trial in a court of law

chariot /'tʃæriət/ *n* open vehicle with two wheels, pulled by horses, used in ancient times in battle and for racing ▸ **charioteer** /ˌtʃæriə-'tɪə(r)/ *n* driver of a chariot

charisma /kə'rɪzmə/ *n* [U] power to inspire devotion and enthusiasm ▸ **charismatic** /ˌkærɪz'mætɪk/ *adj*: *a ~tic politician*

charitable /'tʃærətəbl/ *adj* **1** kind in your attitude to others **2** of or connected with a charity(1) ▸ **charitably** /-bli/ *adv*

charity /'tʃærəti/ *n* (*pl* **-ies**) **1** [C] organization that helps people in need **2** [U] money, food, etc given to people in need **3** [U] kindness towards others

charlatan /'ʃɑːlətən/ *n* person who falsely claims to have a special skill or knowledge

charm /tʃɑːm/ *n* **1** [U] power of pleasing or attracting people **2** [C] pleasing quality **3** [C] object worn for good luck **4** [C] magic spell ● **charm** *v* [T] **1** please or attract sb **2** influence sb/sth (as if) using magic ▸ **charming** *adj* very pleasant or attractive

chart /tʃɑːt/ *n* **1** [C] diagram, graph, etc giving information **2** [C] map of the sea **3** (**the charts**) [pl] (*esp GB*) weekly list of the best-selling pop music records ● **chart** *v* [T] **1** record or follow the progress or development of sb/sth **2** plan a course of action **3** make a map of an area

charter /'tʃɑːtə(r)/ *n* **1** [C] official written statement giving certain rights, privileges, principles, etc **2** [U] hiring of an aircraft or a ship ▸ **'charter flight** *n* flight in an aircraft in which all the seats are paid for by a travel company and then sold to their customers at a low price ● **charter** *v* [T] hire an aircraft, a boat, etc for a particular purpose

▶ **chartered** adj qualified according to the rules of a certain profession: a ~ed accountant/surveyor

chase /tʃeɪs/ v [I, T] ~ (after) run, drive, etc after sb in order to catch them or make them go away ● **chase** n act of chasing sb/sth

chasm /ˈkæzəm/ n 1 deep opening in the ground 2 (fml) great difference in attitude, etc between two people

chassis /ˈʃæsi/ n (pl chassis /-siz/) frame that a vehicle is built on

chaste /tʃeɪst/ adj 1 (old-fash) avoiding sexual activity 2 not expressing sexual feeling 3 (fml) simple and plain in style

chasten /ˈtʃeɪsn/ v [T] (usu passive) (fml) make sb feel sorry for sth they have done

chastise /tʃæˈstaɪz/ v [T] (fml) criticize sb for doing sth wrong ▶ **chastisement** n [U]

chastity /ˈtʃæstəti/ n [U] state of not having sex with anyone or only with the person you are married to

chat /tʃæt/ n [C,U] friendly informal talk ● **chat** v (-tt-) [I] talk to sb in an informal way [PV] **chat sb up** (GB, infml) talk in a friendly way to sb you are sexually attracted to ▶ **chatty** adj (-ier, -iest) talking a lot in a friendly way ■ **'chat room** n area on the Internet where people can communicate with each other

chateau (also **château**) /ˈʃætəʊ/ n (pl -x /-təʊz/) castle or large country house in France

chatter /ˈtʃætə(r)/ v [I] 1 talk quickly and continuously about unimportant things 2 (of birds or monkeys) make short repeated high-pitched noises 3 (of the teeth) strike together from cold or fear ● **chatter** n 1 continuous quick talk 2 series of high sounds that some animals make ■ **'chatterbox** n person who talks a lot

chauffeur /ˈʃəʊfə(r)/ n person whose job is to drive a car, esp for sb rich ● **chauffeur** v [T] drive sb in a car, usu as your job

chauvinism /ˈʃəʊvɪnɪzəm/ n [U] 1 excessive and unreasonable belief that your own country is the best 2 = MALE CHAUVINISM (MALE) ▶ **chauvinist** n ▶ **chauvinistic** /ˌʃəʊvɪˈnɪstɪk/ adj

cheap /tʃiːp/ adj 1 costing little money 2 (of poor quality: - and nasty 3 unkind and unfair: a ~ joke ▶ **cheapen** v [T] 1 make sb lose respect for himself or herself 2 lower the price of sth 3 make sth appear to have less value ▶ **cheaply** adv ▶ **cheapness** n [U]

cheat /tʃiːt/ v [I] act dishonestly: ~ in

an examination [PV] **cheat sb (out) of sth** prevent sb from having sth by dishonest behaviour ● **cheat** n person who cheats

check¹ /tʃek/ v 1 [T] examine sth to make sure it is correct, safe, satisfactory, etc 2 [T] find out if sth is correct or true, or if sth is how you think it is 3 [T] stop sb/sth to stop; control sth: ~ the enemy's progress [PV] **check in** inform sb of your arrival at an airport, a hotel, etc **check sb in** leave bags or cases with an official to be put on a plane **check out (of ...)** pay your bill and leave a hotel **check sth out** find out if sth is correct, true or acceptable 2 (infml) look at or examine sth that seems interesting or attractive **check up on sb** make sure that sb is doing what they should be doing **check up on sth** examine sth to discover if it is true, safe, correct, etc ■ **'check-in** n 1 [C,U] place where you go first when you arrive at an airport 2 [U] act of showing your ticket, etc when you arrive at an airport: the --in desk ■ **'checkout** n 1 [C] place where customers pay for goods in a supermarket 2 [U] time when you leave a hotel at the end of your stay ■ **'checkpoint** n place, eg on a frontier, where travellers and vehicles are inspected ■ **'check-up** n medical examination to make sure that you are healthy

check² /tʃek/ n 1 [C,U] ~(on) examination to make sure that sth is correct, safe, satisfactory, etc 2 [U] (fml) control: hold/keep your emotions in ~ 3 [U,C] pattern of squares, usu two colours: a ~ shirt 4 [C] (US) = CHEQUE 5 [C] (US) bill in a restaurant 6 [U] (in chess) position in which a player's king can be directly attacked 7 [C] (US) = TICK(1)

checkered (esp US) = CHEQUERED

checkers /ˈtʃekəz/ n [U] (US) = DRAUGHTS(3)

checkmate /ˌtʃekˈmeɪt/ n (in chess) situation in which one player cannot prevent the capture of his/her king and therefore loses the game 2 total defeat

cheek /tʃiːk/ n 1 [C] either side of the face below the eyes 2 [U] rude and disrespectful behaviour or talk ● **cheek** v [T] (GB, infml) speak to sb in a rude way that shows a lack of respect ▶ **cheeky** adj (-ier, -iest) (GB) rude and disrespectful ▶ **cheekily** adv

cheer /tʃɪə(r)/ v 1 [I, T] give shouts of praise, support, etc to sb 2 [T] give hope, comfort or encouragement to sb: -ing news [PV] **cheer (sb/sth) up** (cause sb/sth to) become more cheerful

cheer² /tʃɪə(r)/ n **1** [C] shout of praise, support, etc **2** [U] (old-fash) happiness ▶ **cheerful** /tʃɪəfl/ adj **1** happy **2** giving you a feeling of happiness: a bright, ~ restaurant ▶ **cheerfully** adv ▶ **cheerless** adj sad; gloomy

cheerio /ˌtʃɪəriˈəʊ/ exclam (GB, infml) goodbye

cheers /tʃɪəz/ exclam **1** word that people say to each other as they lift up their glasses to drink **2** (GB, infml) thank you

cheery /tʃɪəri/ adj (-ier, -iest) lively and happy ▶ **cheerily** adv

cheese /tʃiːz/ n [U,C] solid food made from milk ● **cheesecake** n [C, U] cold sweet dish made with cream cheese on a base of crushed biscuits ● **cheesecloth** n [U] loosely woven cotton cloth

cheetah /tʃiːtə/ n spotted African wild animal of the cat family, able to run very fast

chef /ʃef/ n chief cook in a restaurant, hotel, etc

chemical /ˈkemɪkl/ adj **1** of or relating to chemistry **2** produced by or using processes which involve changes to atoms or molecules: a ~ reaction ● **chemical** n substance obtained by or used in a chemical process ▶ **chemically** /-kli/ adv

chemist /ˈkemɪst/ n **1** person whose job is to prepare and sell medicines, and who works in a shop **2** student of or expert in chemistry

chemistry /ˈkemɪstri/ n [U] scientific study of the structure of substances and how they combine together

cheque /tʃek/ n written order to a bank to pay money ● **chequebook** n book of printed cheques ■ **cheque card** n card issued by a bank to sb who has an account with it, guaranteeing payment of his/her cheques up to a stated amount

chequered /ˈtʃekəd/ adj having good and bad parts: a ~ history

cherish /ˈtʃerɪʃ/ v [T] (written) **1** love sb/sth very much and want to protect them/it **2** keep an idea, a hope, etc in your mind for a long time: ~ed memories

cherry /ˈtʃeri/ n (pl -ies) small round red or black fruit with a stone inside

cherub /ˈtʃerəb/ n **1** (in art) kind of angel **2** (infml) pretty young child; child who behaves well

chess /tʃes/ n [U] board game for two players

chest /tʃest/ n **1** upper front part of the body **2** large strong box [IDM] **get sth off your chest** (infml) say sth that you have wanted to say for

a long time ■ **chest of 'drawers** n (pl ~s of drawers) piece of furniture with drawers for keeping clothes in

chestnut /ˈtʃesnʌt/ n (tree producing a) smooth reddish-brown nut ● **chestnut** adj reddish-brown in colour

chew /tʃuː/ v [I, T] **1** bite food into small pieces in your mouth with your teeth **2** bite sth continuously, eg because you are nervous: Don't ~ your nails. [PV] **chew sth over** think about sth slowly and carefully ● **chew** n ● **chewing gum** n type of sweet that you chew but do not swallow ▶ **chewy** adj (-ier, -iest) (of food) needing to be chewed a lot

chic /ʃiːk/ adj fashionable; elegant

chick /tʃɪk/ n young bird, esp a young chicken

chicken /ˈtʃɪkɪn/ n **1** [C] large bird, often kept for its eggs or meat **2** [U] meat from a chicken ● **chicken** adj (sl) not brave; cowardly ● **chicken** v [PV] **chicken out (of sth/doing sth)** (infml) decide not to do sth because you are afraid ■ **chickenpox** n [U] disease, esp of children, causing red spots on the skin

chicory /ˈtʃɪkəri/ n [U,C] small pale green plant with bitter leaves that can be eaten raw in salads. The root can be dried and used with coffee.

chief /tʃiːf/ n highest official; leader or ruler ● **chief** adj **1** most important; main **2** having the highest rank ■ **chief 'constable** n (GB) head of the police force in a particular area ▶ **chiefly** adv mainly ■ **-in-'chief** (in compound nouns) highest in rank

chieftain /ˈtʃiːftən/ n leader of a tribe

child /tʃaɪld/ n (pl children /ˈtʃɪldrən/) **1** young human being **2** son or daughter of any age ■ **childbirth** n [U] act of giving birth to a baby ▶ **childhood** n [U,C] state or time of being a child ▶ **childish** adj (of an adult) behaving like a child ▶ **childless** adj having no children ▶ **childlike** adj simple; innocent ■ **childminder** n (GB) person whose job is to care for children while their parents are at work

chill /tʃɪl/ v **1** [I, T] become or make sb/sth cold **2** [T] (lit) frighten sb ● **chill** n **1** [sing] feeling of being cold **2** [C] illness caused by cold and damp **3** [sing] feeling of fear: It sent a ~ down my spine. ▶ **chilly** adj (-ier, -iest) **1** too cold to be comfortable **2** unfriendly

chilli (US chili) /ˈtʃɪli/ n [C,U] (pl ~es) small green or red fruit of a type of pepper plant used in cooking to give a hot taste to food, often dried or made into powder (**chilli powder**) ■ **chilli con carne** /ˌtʃɪli kɒn ˈkɑːni/ n [U] hot spicy Mexican dish made with meat, beans and chillies

chime /tʃaɪm/ n ringing sound, esp one made by a bell ● **chime** v [I, T] (of a bell or clock) ring; show the time by making a ringing sound

chimney /ˈtʃɪmni/ n structure through which smoke is carried away from a fire and through the roof of a building ■ **chimney pot** n (GB) short pipe fitted to the top of a chimney ■ **chimney stack** n part of the chimney that is above the roof of a building ■ **chimney sweep** n person whose job is to clean the inside of chimneys

chimpanzee /ˌtʃɪmpænˈziː/ (also infml **chimp**) n small intelligent African ape

chin /tʃɪn/ n part of the face below the mouth

china /ˈtʃaɪnə/ n [U] 1 white clay which is baked and used for making delicate cups, plates, etc 2 cups and plates, etc made from china

chink /tʃɪŋk/ n 1 narrow opening in sth 2 small area of light shining through a narrow opening 3 light ringing sound that is made when glass objects or coins touch ● **chink** v [I] make a ringing sound when glass objects, coins, etc hit together

chip /tʃɪp/ n [C] 1 (GB [usu pl] long thin piece of potato fried in oil or fat: fish and ~s 2 place from which a small piece of wood, glass, etc has broken from an object: a cup with a ~ in it 3 small piece of wood, glass, etc which has broken from an object 4 (US) = CRISP 5 = MICROCHIP 6 flat piece of plastic used in gambling to represent an amount of money [IDM] **have a chip on your shoulder** (about sth) (infml) be sensitive about sth that happened in the past because you think you were treated unfairly ● **chip** v (-pp-) [I, T] (cause sth to) become damaged by breaking a small piece off the edge of sth [PV] **chip in** (with sth) (infml) join in or interrupt a conversation: She ~ped in with a couple of useful comments. 2 give money so a group of people can buy sth together

chiropodist /kɪˈrɒpədɪst/ n person whose job is to treat minor problems people have with their feet ▶ **chiropody** /kɪˈrɒpədiː/ n [U]

chirp /tʃɜːp/ v [I], n (make the) short sharp sound of small birds ▶ **chirpy** adj (-ier, -iest) (infml) lively and happy

chisel /ˈtʃɪzl/ n tool with a sharp end for cutting wood or stone ● **chisel** v (-ll-, US also -l-) [T] cut or shape sth with a chisel

chit /tʃɪt/ n note showing an amount of money owed

chivalry /ˈʃɪvəlri/ n [U] 1 rules and customs of knights in the Middle Ages 2 good manners, eg honour and politeness, esp as shown by men towards women ▶ **chivalrous** /ˈʃɪvlrəs/ adj

chlorine /ˈklɔːriːn/ n [U] (symb Cl) strong-smelling greenish-yellow gas often used in swimming pools to keep the water clean

chlorofluorocarbon /ˌklɔːrəˌfluərəʊˈkɑːbən/ n → CFC

chlorophyll /ˈklɒrəfɪl/ n [U] green substance in plants that absorbs energy from sunlight to help them grow

chocolate /ˈtʃɒklət/ n 1 [U] hard brown sweet food made from cocoa beans 2 [C] sweet made of or covered with chocolate 3 [U] hot drink made from chocolate ● **chocolate** n [U], adj (of a) dark brown colour

choice /tʃɔɪs/ n 1 [C] act of choosing between two or more possibilities 2 [U] right or possibility of choosing: I had no ~ but to leave. 3 [C] variety from which to choose: a large ~ of restaurants 4 [C] person or thing chosen: She was the right ~ for the job. ● **choice** adj of high quality: ~ fruit

choir /ˈkwaɪə(r)/ n [C] 1 [with sing or pl verb] group of singers 2 part of a church where the choir sits

choke /tʃəʊk/ v 1 [I, T] (cause sb to) be unable to breathe because the windpipe is blocked 2 [T] block or fill a passage, space, etc: The drains are ~d with dead leaves. [PV] **choke sth back** prevent your feelings from showing: He ~d back the tears. ● **choke** n device that controls the amount of air flowing into the engine of a vehicle

cholera /ˈkɒlərə/ n [U] infectious and often fatal disease caught from infected water

cholesterol /kəˈlestərɒl/ n [U] fatty substance found in blood, fat and most tissues of the body

choose /tʃuːz/ v (pt chose /tʃəʊz/, pp chosen /ˈtʃəʊzn/) 1 [I, T] decide which thing or person you want out of the ones available: You can't have all of the sweets, you must ~ one. 2 [T] prefer or decide to do sth: She chose to become a doctor.

chop /tʃɒp/ v [T] (-pp-) cut sth into pieces with an axe, a knife, etc ● **chop** n 1 thick slice of meat, esp pork or lamb, with a bone attached to it 2 act of chopping sth

chopper /ˈtʃɒpə(r)/ n 1 (infml) = HELICOPTER 2 heavy knife or small axe

choppy /'tʃɒpi/ adj (-ier, -iest) (of the sea) with a lot of small waves; not calm

chopstick /'tʃɒpstɪk/ n [usu pl] either of a pair of thin sticks used for eating with, esp in Asian countries

choral /'kɔːrəl/ adj of or for a choir

chord /kɔːd/ n 1 musical notes played together 2 (maths) straight line that joins two points on a curve

chore /tʃɔː(r)/ n ordinary or boring task

choreography /ˌkɒriˈɒɡrəfi/ n [U] art of designing and arranging steps for dances on stage ▶ **choreographer** /ˌkɒriˈɒɡrəfə(r)/ n

chorister /'kɒrɪstə(r)/ n person, esp a boy, who sings in a church choir

chorus /'kɔːrəs/ n 1 [C] part of a song that is sung after each verse 2 [C] (piece of music for a) large group of singers 3 [sing] ~of something said by many people together: a ~ of approval ● **chorus** v [I] sing or say sth all together

chose pt of CHOOSE

chosen pp of CHOOSE

Christ /kraɪst/ (also Jesus, Jesus 'Christ) n [sing] founder of the Christian religion

christen /'krɪsn/ v [T] 1 give a name to a baby at his/her baptism to welcome him/her into the Christian church 2 give a name to sb/sth 3 (infml) use sth for the first time ▶ **christening** n

Christian /'krɪstʃən/ n person who believes in the Christian religion ● **Christian** adj 1 of Christianity 2 showing the qualities of a Christian; kind ▶ **Christianity** /ˌkrɪstiˈænəti/ n [U] religion based on the belief that Christ was the son of God, and on his teachings ■ **'Christian name** n (GB) first name

Christmas /'krɪsməs/ (also Christmas 'Day) n [U,C] yearly celebration of the birth of Christ; 25 December

chrome /krəʊm/ n [U] hard shiny metal used esp as a protective covering on other metals; chromium

chromium /'krəʊmiəm/ n [U] (symb Cr) metallic element used esp as a shiny protective covering on other metals

chromosome /'krəʊməsəʊm/ n (biol) one of the fine threads in animal and plant cells, carrying genes

chronic /'krɒnɪk/ adj 1 (of an illness) lasting a long time 2 (GB, infml) very bad ▶ **chronically** /-kli/ adv

chronicle /'krɒnɪkl/ n written record of events in the order in which they happened ● **chronicle** v [T] record events in the order in which they happened

chronology /krəˈnɒlədʒi/ n [U,C]

(pl **-ies**) order in which a series of events happened; list of these events in order ▶ **chronological** /ˌkrɒnəˈlɒdʒɪkl/ adj (of a number of events) arranged in the order in which they happened: Present the facts in chronological order. ▶ **chronologically** /-kli/ adv

chronometer /krəˈnɒmɪtə(r)/ n very accurate clock

chrysalis /'krɪsəlɪs/ n form of an insect, esp a butterfly or moth, while it is changing into an adult inside a hard case

chrysanthemum /krɪˈsænθəməm/ n garden plant with brightly coloured flowers

chubby /'tʃʌbi/ adj (-ier, -iest) slightly fat

chuck /tʃʌk/ v [T] (esp GB, infml) 1 throw sth carelessly 2 give up or stop doing sth 3 leave your boyfriend/girlfriend and stop having a relationship with him/her 4 (spoken) throw sth away ● **chuck** n part of a tool such as a drill that can be adjusted to hold sth tightly

chuckle /'tʃʌkl/ v [I] laugh quietly ● **chuckle** n

chum /tʃʌm/ n (infml) friend ▶ **chummy** adj (-ier, -iest) friendly

chunk /tʃʌŋk/ n 1 thick piece or lump: a ~ of cheese 2 (infml) fairly large amount of sth ▶ **chunky** adj (-ier, -iest) 1 thick and heavy; ~y jewellery 2 having a short strong body 3 (of food) containing thick pieces

church /tʃɜːtʃ/ n 1 [C] building for public Christian worship 2 (Church) [C] particular group of Christians: the Anglican C~ 3 ((the) Church) [sing] ministers of the Christian religion; the institution of the Christian religion: go into/ enter the C~ (= become a Christian minister) ■ **'churchyard** n enclosed area of land around a church, often used for burying people

churn /tʃɜːn/ n 1 container in which milk or cream is shaken to make butter 2 (GB) large metal container in which milk is carried ● **churn** v 1 [T] beat milk or cream to make butter 2 [I, T] move (sth) around violently [PV] **churn sth out** (infml) produce sth in large amounts

chute /ʃuːt/ n tube or passage down which people or things can slide

chutney /'tʃʌtni/ n [U] cold thick sauce made from fruit, spices, sugar and vinegar, eaten with cheese, etc

cider /'saɪdə(r)/ n [U,C] alcoholic drink made from apples

cigar /sɪˈɡɑː(r)/ n roll of dried

tobacco leaves that people smoke, like a cigarette but bigger

cigarette /ˌsɪgəˈret/ n thin tube of paper filled with tobacco, for smoking

cinder /ˈsɪndə(r)/ n [C, usu pl] small piece of partly burnt coal, etc

cinema /ˈsɪnəmə/ n (*GB*) **1** [C] place where films are shown **2** (**the cinema**) [sing] films as an art or industry

cinnamon /ˈsɪnəmən/ n [U] yellowish-brown spice used in cooking

cipher (*also* **cypher**) /ˈsaɪfə(r)/ n **1** [C,U] secret system of writing in which symbols or letters represent other letters **2** [C] (*fml, disapprov*) person or thing of no importance

circa /ˈsɜːkə/ prep (*abbr* **c**) (used with dates) about: *born ~ 150 BC*

circle /ˈsɜːkl/ n **1** [C] (space enclosed by) a curved line, every point on which is the same distance from the centre **2** ring **3** group of people: *our ~ of friends* **4** upstairs seats in a theatre, etc ● **circle** v **1** [I, T] move in a circle, esp in the air **2** [T] draw a circle around sth

circuit /ˈsɜːkɪt/ n **1** line or journey round a place: *a racing ~* **2** complete path along which an electric current flows **3** series of places or events: *a lecture ~* ▸ **circuitous** /səˈkjuːɪtəs/ *adj* (*fml*) long and indirect: *a ~ous route*

circular /ˈsɜːkjələ(r)/ *adj* **1** shaped like a circle; round **2** moving around in a circle: *a ~ route* ● **circular** n printed letter, advertisement, etc sent to many people

circulate /ˈsɜːkjəleɪt/ v **1** (cause sth to) go around continuously; move about freely **2** pass (sth) from one person to another ▸ **circulation** /ˌsɜːkjəˈleɪʃn/ n **1** [U] movement of blood round the body **2** [U] passing of sth from one person to another: *the circulation of money* **3** [U] fact that sb takes part in social activities at a particular time: *He's been out of circulation for months with a bad back.* **4** [C, usu sing] usual number of copies of a newspaper or magazine that are sold each day, week, etc

circumcise /ˈsɜːkəmsaɪz/ v [T] cut off the skin at the end of the penis of a man or boy ▸ **circumcision** /ˌsɜːkəmˈsɪʒn/ n [C,U]

circumference /səˈkʌmfərəns/ n [C,U] (length of the) line that goes around a circle or any other curved shape: *the earth's ~*

circumflex /ˈsɜːkəmfleks/ n mark over a vowel, as in French: *the ~ accent*

circumnavigate /ˌsɜːkəmˈnævɪgeɪt/ v [T] (*fml*) sail all the way around

sth, esp the world ▸ **circumnavigation** /ˌsɜːkəmˌnævɪˈgeɪʃn/ n [C,U]

circumspect /ˈsɜːkəmspekt/ *adj* (*fml*) cautious

circumstance /ˈsɜːkəmstəns/ n **1** [C, usu pl] condition connected with an event or action: *the ~s of his death* **2** (**circumstances**) [pl] conditions of a person's life, esp the money they have **3** [U] situations and events that affect you but are not in your control: *a victim of ~* [IDM] **in/under the circumstances** this being the case **in/under no circumstances** never

circumstantial /ˌsɜːkəmˈstænʃl/ *adj* **1** (*law*) (of evidence) having details that strongly suggest sth but do not prove it **2** (*fml*) connected with particular circumstances

circus /ˈsɜːkəs/ n **1** [C] group of entertainers, sometimes with trained animals, who perform in a show that travels around to different places **2** (**the circus**) [sing] show performed by circus entertainers, usu in a large tent **3** (*GB*) (in some place names) open space where several streets meet: *Piccadilly C~*

cistern /ˈsɪstən/ n water tank, eg above a toilet

cite /saɪt/ v [T] (*fml*) **1** mention sth as an example or to support an argument **2** quote sb/sth **3** order sb to appear in court; name sb officially in a legal case ▸ **citation** /saɪˈteɪʃn/ n **1** [C] quotation **2** [U] act of citing sb/sth

citizen /ˈsɪtɪzn/ n **1** person who has full rights as a member of a country **2** person who lives in a town or city ■ **Citizens' Band** n = CB ▸ **citizenship** n [U] legal rights, duties and state of being a citizen

citric acid /ˌsɪtrɪk ˈæsɪd/ n [U] kind of weak acid from such fruits as oranges and lemons

citrus /ˈsɪtrəs/ n any of a group of related trees including the lemon, lime and orange: *~ fruit*

city /ˈsɪti/ n (*pl* **-ies**) **1** [C] large important town **2** [C, with sing or pl verb] all the people living in a city **3** (**the City**) [sing] financial and business centre of London

civic /ˈsɪvɪk/ *adj* of a town or city or its citizens

civil /ˈsɪvl/ *adj* **1** of the citizens of a country **2** connected with the state rather than with religion or with the armed forces: *a ~ marriage ceremony* **3** polite in a formal way ■ **civil engineering** n [U] design and building of roads, bridges, etc ▸ **civility** /səˈvɪləti/ n (*fml*) (*pl* **-ies**) **1** [U] polite behaviour **2** [C] (**civilities**) [pl] polite remarks ▸ **civilly** /ˈsɪvəli/ *adv* ■ **civil 'rights** n [pl] rights of each citizen to freedom and equality ■ ,civil 'servant *n* person who works in the civil service ■ the ,civil 'service *n* [sing] all government departments in a country, except the armed forces, and the people who work for them ■ ,civil war *n* [C, U] war between groups of people in the same country

civilian /sə'vɪliən/ *n, adj* (person) not of the armed forces

civilization (also **-isation**) /ˌsɪvəlaɪ-'zeɪʃn/ *n* **1** [U] (esp advanced) state of human social development and organization **2** [C, U] culture and way of life of a society at a particular time and place: *the history of western ~*

civilize (also **-ise**) /'sɪvəlaɪz/ *v* [T] educate and improve a person or society; make sb's behaviour or manners better: *the ~d world*

CJD /ˌsiː dʒeɪ 'diː/ *abbr* = CREUTZFELDT-JAKOB DISEASE

clad /klæd/ *adj* (written) ~(in) wearing a particular type of clothing

claim /kleɪm/ *v* [T] **1** say that sth is true, without being able to prove it: *He ~s to be a British citizen.* **2** ask for or demand sth as your legal right **3** (written) (of a disaster, etc) cause sb's death: *The earthquake ~ed thousands of lives.* ● **claim** *n* **1** [C] statement that sth is true, without being able to prove it **2** [C, U] legal right that sb believes they have to sth, esp land or property **3** [C] request for money that you believe you have a right to, esp from the government, a company, etc: *an insurance ~* ▶ **claimant** *n* person who claims sth as their legal right

clairvoyance /kleə'vɔɪəns/ *n* [U] supposed power of seeing future events in the mind ▶ **clairvoyant** *n, adj* (person) having such power

clam /klæm/ *n* large edible shellfish that has a shell in two parts that can open and close ● **clam** *v* (-mm-) [PV] **clam up (on sb)** (infml) refuse to speak

clamber /'klæmbə(r)/ *v* [I] climb with difficulty

clammy /'klæmi/ *adj* (-ier, -iest) unpleasantly damp and sticky

clamour (US -or) /'klæmə(r)/ *n* [C, U] (fml) loud confused noise ● **clamour** [I] ~(for) demand sth noisily

clamp /klæmp/ *n* tool for holding things tightly together, usu with a screw ● **clamp** *v* [T] fasten two things together with a clamp [PV] **clamp down (on sb/sth)** take strict action in order to prevent sth, esp crime ▶ '**clampdown** *n* [usu sing] sudden action taken to stop an illegal activity

clan /klæn/ *n* large family group, esp in Scotland

clandestine /klæn'destɪn/ *adj* (fml) secret: *a ~ organization*

clang /klæŋ/ *v* [I, T] (cause sth to) make a loud ringing sound like that of metal being hit ▶ **clang** *n*

clank /klæŋk/ *v* [I, T] (cause sth to) make a sound like pieces of metal hitting each other ▶ **clank** *n*

clap /klæp/ *v* (-pp-) **1** [I, T] hit your open hands together several times to show your approval of sth **2** [T] hit sb lightly with your open hand: *~ sb on the back/shoulder* **3** [T] (infml) put sth/sb somewhere quickly and suddenly: *She ~ped her hand over her mouth.* ● **clap** *n* **1** act or sound of clapping **2** sudden loud noise, esp of thunder ■ ,**clapped 'out** *adj* (GB, infml) (of a car or machine) old and in bad condition

claret /'klærət/ *n* [C, U] kind of red French wine ● **claret** *adj* dark red

clarify /'klærəfaɪ/ *v* (pt, pp **-ied**) make sth clearer and easier to understand ▶ **clarification** /ˌklærəfɪ-'keɪʃn/ *n* [U, C]

clarinet /ˌklærə'net/ *n* musical instrument of the woodwind group ▶ **clarinettist** (also **clarinetist**) *n* person who plays the clarinet

clarity /'klærəti/ *n* [U] **1** quality of being expressed clearly **2** ability to think about or understand sth clearly

clash /klæʃ/ *v* **1** [I] fight or argue with sb **2** [I] (of ideas, personalities, etc) be very different and opposed to one another **3** [I] (of events) happen at the same time so that you cannot go to or see them both **4** [I] (of colours, patterns, etc) look ugly when put together **5** [I, T] hit sth together with a harsh ringing noise ● **clash** *n* **1** short fight, argument or disagreement **2** difference between two opposing things: *a personality ~ with his boss* **3** loud noise made by two metal objects being hit together: *a ~ of cymbals*

clasp /klɑːsp/ *n* **1** device for fastening things together: *the ~ of a necklace* **2** firm hold with your hand ● **clasp** *v* [T] **1** hold sb/sth tightly **2** fasten sth with a clasp(1)

class /klɑːs/ *n* **1** [C, with sing or pl verb] group of students taught together **2** [C, U] period of time when a group of students are taught **3** [C, with sing or pl verb] social group at a particular level: *the working/middle/upper ~* **4** [U] way that people are divided into different social and economic groups **5** [C] group of people, animals or things with similar qualities **6** [U] (infml) elegance ● **class** *v* [T] think or decide that sb/sth is a particular type of person or thing: *Immigrant workers are ~ed as aliens.* ■ 'classroom *n* room in a school in which a class of students is taught ▶ **classy** *adj* (**-ier, -iest**) (*infml*) fashionable; stylish

classic /'klæsɪk/ *adj* **1** typical: *a ~ example* **2** of very high quality: *a ~ film/novel* ● **classic** *n* [C] book, film or song of high quality and lasting value: *The novel will become a modern ~.* **2** (**Classics**) [U] (study of the) languages and literature of ancient Greece and Rome

classical /'klæsɪkl/ *adj* **1** traditional **2** of the style of ancient Greece and Rome **3** (of music) serious, and having a value that lasts ▶ **classically** /-kli/ *adv*

classify /'klæsɪfaɪ/ *v* (*pt, pp* **-ied**) [T] arrange sth into groups according to the features that they have in common ▶ **classification** /ˌklæsɪfɪ'keɪʃn/ [C,U] ▶ **classified** *adj* officially secret: *classified information*

clatter /'klætə(r)/ *n* [sing] loud noise made by hard objects hitting each other: *the ~ of horses' hoofs* ▶ **clatter** *v* [I]

clause /klɔːz/ *n* **1** (*gram*) group of words that contains a subject and a verb **2** (*law*) section of a legal document

claustrophobia /ˌklɔːstrə'fəʊbiə/ *n* [U] extreme fear of being in an enclosed space

claw /klɔː/ *n* **1** hard curved nail at the end of the foot of an animal or a bird **2** long, sharp, curved part of the body of some shellfish **3** device like a claw for gripping and lifting things ● **claw** *v* [I, T] ~(**at**) tear or scratch sb/sth with claws or with your fingernails [PV] **claw sth back 1** get sth back that you have lost, usu by using a lot of effort **2** (of a government) get back money that has been paid to people, usu by taxing them ■ 'clawback *n* (*GB, business*) act of getting money back from people it has been paid to; money that is paid back

clay /kleɪ/ *n* [U] stiff sticky earth that becomes hard when baked, used for making bricks, pots, etc

clean¹ /kliːn/ *n* **1** not dirty **2** (of paper) with nothing written on it **3** not offensive or referring to sex: *a ~ joke* **4** not having any record of doing sth that is against the law: *a ~ driving licence* **5** smooth; regular: *a ~ cut* [IDM] **make a clean breast of sth** make a full confession of sth ● **clean** *adv* (*infml*) completely: *I ~ forgot about it.* [IDM] **come clean (with sb) (about sth)** make a full and honest confession ■ ˌclean-'cut

adj (*esp of a man*) looking neat and clean and therefore socially acceptable ■ ˌclean-'shaven *adj* not having a beard or moustache

clean² /kliːn/ *v* [T] make sth clean [PV] **clean sb out** (*infml*) take all sb's money **clean sth out** clean the inside of sth thoroughly: *He ~ed out the fish tank.* **clean** (**sth**) **up 1** remove dirt, rubbish, etc from a place **2** (*infml*) make or win a lot of money **clean sth up** remove crime and immoral behaviour from a place or an activity ▶ **clean** *n* [sing]: *The car needs a good ~.* ▶ **cleaner** *n* **1** person whose job is to clean other people's houses, offices, etc **2** machine or substance that cleans: *a vacuum ~* ◇ *window ~* **3** (**cleaner's**) (*also* ˌdry-'cleaner's) shop where clothes, etc are cleaned with chemicals, not water

cleanliness /'klenlinəs/ *n* [U] state of being clean

cleanly /'kliːnli/ *adv* easily; smoothly

cleanse /klenz/ *v* [T] clean your skin or a wound ▶ **cleanser** *n* substance that cleanses

clear¹ /klɪə(r)/ *adj* **1** easy to see through: *~ glass* **2** easy to understand, see or hear: *a ~ explanation of the problems* **3** obvious; definite: *a ~ case of cheating* **4** without error or confusion; certain: *I'm not ~ about what I should do.* **5** free from obstructions *sth* **7** without cloud or mist: *a ~ sky* **8** without spots: *~ skin* **9** free from guilt: *a ~ conscience* **10** (of a sum of money) with nothing to be taken away: *~ profit* [IDM] **make sth/ yourself clear** express sth/yourself in such a way that your wishes, etc are fully understood ● **clear** *n* [IDM] **in the clear** (*infml*) no longer in danger or suspected of sth ● **clear** *adv* **1** away from sth; not near or touching sth: *Stand ~ of the doors.* **2** (*esp US*) all the way to sth that is far away [IDM] **keep/stay/steer clear (of sb/sth)** avoid a person or thing because they/it may cause problems ■ ˌclear-'cut *adj* definite and easy to see or identify ■ ˌclear-'headed *n* able to think clearly ▶ **clearly** *adv* in a way that is easy to see, hear or understand; obviously ■ ˌclear-'sighted *adj* understanding or thinking clearly

clear² /klɪə(r)/ *v* **1** [T] remove sth unwanted from a place **2** [I] move freely again; no longer be blocked: *The traffic took ages to ~ after the accident.* **3** [I] (of sky or weather) become brighter and free of cloud, fog or rain **4** [T] approve sth officially **5** [T] ~(**of**) declare sb to be not guilty of a crime **6** [T] get past or over sth without touching it: *The horse ~ed the fence.* [IDM] **clear the air** remove fears, suspicions, etc by talking about them openly [PV] **clear (sth) away** remove objects in order to leave a place tidy **clear off** (*infml*) go away **clear out** (*of* …) (*infml*) leave a place quickly **clear sth out** make sth empty or tidy by removing unwanted things: ~ *out the cupboards* **clear up** (of the weather) become bright or fine **clear (sth) up** make sth clean and tidy **clear sth up** remove doubt about sth; solve: ~ *up a mystery*

clearance /ˈklɪərəns/ *n* 1 [C,U] removal of unwanted things 2 [C, U] clear space between two things: *There's not much ~ for vehicles passing under the bridge.* 3 [U] official approval or permission

clearing /ˈklɪərɪŋ/ *n* open space from which trees have been cleared in a forest

cleavage /ˈkliːvɪdʒ/ *n* 1 space between a woman's breasts 2 (*fml*) division or split

clef /klef/ *n* musical symbol showing the pitch of the notes

clemency /ˈklemənsi/ *n* [U] (*fml*) kindness shown to sb when they are being punished; mercy

clench /klentʃ/ *v* [T] close sth tightly: press sth firmly together: ~ *your fists*

clergy /ˈklɜːdʒi/ *n* [pl] (often **the clergy**) priests and ministers of a religion, esp of the Christian Church ■ **clergyman** /ˈklɜːdʒimən/ *n* (*pl* **-men** /-mən/) Christian priest or minister

clerical /ˈklerɪkl/ *adj* 1 connected with office work 2 of or for the clergy

clerk /klɑːk/ *n* 1 person whose job is to keep the records or accounts in an office, a shop, etc 2 (*US*) (*also* **'sales clerk**) = SHOP ASSISTANT

clever /ˈklevə(r)/ *adj* 1 quick at learning and understanding; intelligent 2 showing skill; effective: *a ~ scheme* ▶ **cleverly** *adv* ■ **cleverness** *n* [U]

cliché /ˈkliːʃeɪ/ *n* idea or expression that is used so often that it no longer has any meaning

click /klɪk/ *v* 1 [I, T] (cause sth to) make a short sharp sound: *He ~ed his fingers at the waiter.* 2 ~(*on*) [I, T] choose a particular function or item on a computer screen, etc by pressing one of the buttons on the mouse: *Just ~ on the link to our website.* 3 [I] (*infml*) suddenly become understood ▶ **click** *n*

client /ˈklaɪənt/ *n* 1 person who receives help or advice from a professional person: *a well-known*

lawyer *with many famous ~s* 2 (*computing*) computer that is linked to a server

clientele /ˌkliːɒnˈtel/ *n* [*sing*, with sing or pl *verb*] all the customers or clients of a shop, a restaurant, an organization, etc

cliff /klɪf/ *n* steep rock face, esp by the sea

climactic /klaɪˈmæktɪk/ *adj* (*written*) (of an event or a point in time) very exciting, most important

climate /ˈklaɪmət/ *n* 1 [C,U] general weather conditions of a place 2 [C] general attitude or feeling ▶ **climatic** /klaɪˈmætɪk/ *adj*

climax /ˈklaɪmæks/ *n* most exciting or interesting moment in a story, etc, usu near the end ● **climax** *v* [I] reach a climax

climb /klaɪm/ *v* 1 [I, T] go up sth, esp using your hands and feet 2 [I] move in the direction mentioned, with difficulty: ~ *out of the lorry* 3 [I] (of aircraft) go higher in the sky 4 [I] (of plants) grow up a wall or frame [IDM] **climb on the bandwagon →** BAND [PV] **climb down** (**over** *sth*) (*infml*) admit that you have made a mistake or were wrong ● **climb** *n* 1 act of climbing 2 mountain or rock which people climb for sport ■ **'climbdown** *n* act of admitting you were wrong ▶ **climber** *n* 1 person who climbs 2 climbing plant

clinch /klɪntʃ/ *v* [T] 1 succeed in achieving or winning sth: *to ~ an argument/a deal* 2 provide the answer to sth; settle sth that was not certain ● **clinch** *n* (*infml*) tight embrace

cling /klɪŋ/ *v* (*pt, pp* **clung** /klʌŋ/) [I] ~(*on*) hold on tightly to sb/sth ■ **'cling film** *n* [U] clear thin plastic material used for wrapping food

clinic /ˈklɪnɪk/ *n* building or part of a hospital where people go for special medical treatment or advice: *a children's ~* ▶ **clinical** *adj* 1 of clinics or medical treatment 2 cold and unfeeling 3 (of a room or building) very plain and undecorated

clink /klɪŋk/ *n* sound of small pieces of glass, etc knocking together ● **clink** *v* [I, T] (cause sth to) make this sound

clip /klɪp/ *v* (-**pp**-) 1 [I, T] fasten sth to sth else with a clip 2 [T] cut sth with scissors, etc 3 [T] hit the edge or side of sth ● **clip** *n* 1 [C] small metal or plastic object used for holding things together: *a hair/paper ~* 2 [*sing*] act of cutting sth to make it shorter 3 [C] short part of a film that is shown separately: *Here's a ~ from her latest film.* 4 [C] (*infml*) quick hit with your hand: *She gave him a ~ round the ear.* ■ **'clipboard** *n*

clique 1 portable board with a clip at the top for holding papers 2 (*computing*) place where information from a computer file is stored temporarily before it is added to another file ► **clippers** *n* [pl] tool for cutting small pieces off things: *nail ~pers* ► **clipping** *n* [C] 1 piece that is cut off sth 2 (*esp US*) = CUTTING(1)

clique /kliːk/ *n* (*often disapprov*) closely united group of people

cloak /kləʊk/ *n* 1 [C] type of loose coat that has no sleeves and fastens at the neck 2 [sing] (*lit*) thing that hides or covers sth: *a ~ of secrecy* ● **cloak** *v* [T] cover or hide sth ■ **cloakroom** *n* 1 (*esp GB*) place in a public building where coats, bags, etc may be left 2 (*GB*) room in a public building where there are toilets

clock /klɒk/ *n* instrument for measuring and showing the time [IDM] **around/round the clock** all day and all night **put/turn the clock back** 1 return to a situation that existed in the past 2 return to old-fashioned ideas, etc ● **clock** *v* [T] reach a particular time or speed [PV] **clock in/on** record the time that you arrive at work, esp by putting a card into a machine **clock out/off** record the time that you leave work, esp by putting a card into a machine **clock sth up** win or achieve a particular number or amount ■ **clockwise** *adv*, *adj* in the direction of the movement of the hands of a clock ■ **clockwork** *n* [U] machinery wound up with a key [IDM] **go/run like clockwork** happen according to plan and without problems

clod /klɒd/ *n* lump of earth or clay

clog /klɒɡ/ *v* (**-gg-**) [I, T] ~ (**up**) (cause sth to) become blocked ● **clog** *n* wooden shoe

cloister /ˈklɔɪstə(r)/ *n* covered passage round a square in a convent, college, cathedral, etc ► **cloistered** *adj* protected from the dangers and problems of normal life

clone /kləʊn/ *n* 1 (*biol*) exact copy of a plant or animal, which is produced artificially from the cells of another plant or animal 2 (*computing*) computer designed to work in exactly the same way as another, usu one made by a different company ● **clone** *v* [T] produce an exact copy of an animal or a plant from its cells

close[1] /kləʊz/ *v* [I, T] 1 (cause sth to) shut: *~ the door* ◇ *The shop ~s at 5pm*. 2 (cause sth to) come to an end: *~ a case/an investigation* [IDM] **close your eyes to sth** pretend you have not noticed sth so that you do not have to deal with it [PV] **close (sth) down** (of

a factory, business, etc) stop (sth) operating as a business **close in (on sb/sth)** move nearer to sb/sth, esp in order to attack them ● **close** *n* [sing] (*fml*) end of a period of time or activity: *I brought the meeting to a ~*. ■ **closed-circuit 'television** (*abbr* CCTV) *n* [U] television system that works within a limited area, eg a public building, to protect it from crime ■ **'close-down** *n* [U, sing] stopping of work, esp permanently, in an office, a factory, etc ■ **closed 'shop** *n* place of work where the employees must all be members of a particular trade union

close[2] /kləʊs/ *adj* (**~r, ~st**) 1 ~ (**to**) near 2 knowing sb very well and liking them very much: *a ~ friend* 3 near in a family relationship: *~ relatives* 4 careful and thorough: *on ~ inspection* 5 won by a small difference: *a ~ race* 6 uncomfortably hot and without fresh air [IDM] **a close call/shave** (*infml*) situation in which a disaster or failure is only just avoided ● **close** *adv* near; not far away: *follow ~ behind* ■ **close-fitting** *adj* (of clothes) fitting tightly to the body ■ **close-knit** *adj* (of a group of people) joined together closely by shared beliefs, activities, etc ► **closely** *adv* ► **closeness** *n* [U] ■ **close-set** *adj* situated very close together: *~-set eyes* ■ **close-up** *n* photograph taken very near to sb/sth

close[3] /kləʊs/ *n* 1 (*GB*) (esp in street names) street closed at one end 2 grounds of a cathedral

closet /ˈklɒzɪt/ *n* (*esp US*) small room or space in a wall, used for storing things ● **closet** *adj* secret ● **closet** *v* [T] shut sb in a room away from other people

closure /ˈkləʊʒə(r)/ *n* [C,U] situation when a factory, school, etc shuts permanently

clot /klɒt/ *n* lump formed from a liquid, esp blood ● **clot** *v* (**-tt-**) [I, T] (cause sth to) form into clots

cloth /klɒθ/ *n* 1 [U] material made by weaving cotton, wool, etc 2 [C] piece of cloth used for a special purpose: *a table~* ◇ *Wipe the table with a damp ~*.

clothe /kləʊð/ *v* [T] provide clothes for sb

clothes /kləʊðz/ *n* [pl] things that you wear, eg trousers, dresses, etc ■ **'clothes hanger** *n* = HANGER ■ **'clothes horse** *n* frame on which clothes are hung to dry, esp indoors ■ **'clothes line** *n* rope stretched between posts on which washed clothes are hung to dry ■ **'clothes peg** *n* wooden or plastic clip for fastening clothes to a clothes line

C

clothing /ˈkləʊðɪŋ/ n [U] clothes

cloud /klaʊd/ n 1 [C,U] (mass of) visible water vapour floating in the sky 2 [C] mass of sth, eg dust or smoke, in the air 3 [C] thing that makes you feel sad or anxious: **under a cloud** in a state of disgrace; under suspicion ● **cloud** v 1 [T] confuse sth: *His judgement was ~ed by jealousy.* 2 [I, T] ~(**over**) (of the sky) to fill with clouds ▸ **cloudy** adj (**-ier, -iest**) 1 covered with clouds 2 (of liquids) not clear

clout /klaʊt/ v [T] (infml) hit sb, esp with your hand ● **clout** n (infml) 1 [U] power and influence 2 [C] heavy blow, esp with the hand

clove /kləʊv/ n 1 dried flower of a tropical tree, used in cooking as a spice 2 one of the small separate sections of a bulb of garlic: *Crush two ~s of garlic.*

clover /ˈkləʊvə(r)/ n [U,C] small wild plant with (usu) three leaves on each stalk

clown /klaʊn/ n 1 performer in a circus who does silly things to make people laugh 2 (*disapprov*) person who acts in a stupid way ● **clown** v [I] ~(**around**) behave foolishly

club /klʌb/ n [C] 1 group of people who meet for sport, social entertainment, etc 2 building that a particular club uses 3 place where esp young people go to listen to music, dance, etc 4 thick heavy stick used as a weapon 5 stick for hitting the ball in golf 6 (**clubs**) [pl, U] one of the four sets of playing cards (**suits**) with black three-leaved shapes: *the queen of ~s* ● **club** (**-bb-**) 1 [T] hit sb with a heavy stick: *The victim was ~ed to death with a baseball bat.* 2 [I] (**go clubbing**) (GB, infml) spend time dancing and drinking in a club(3) [PV] **club together** (GB) join together to give money for sth

cluck /klʌk/ v [I], n (make the) noise of a hen

clue /kluː/ n something that gives help in finding an answer to a problem: *The police are looking for ~s.* [IDM] **not have a clue** (infml) not know anything ▸ **clueless** adj (infml, *disapprov*) stupid

clump /klʌmp/ n small group (of trees or plants) ● **clump** v 1 [I] walk heavily and awkwardly 2 [I, T] (cause sth to) come together to form a tight group

clumsy /ˈklʌmzi/ adj (**-ier, -iest**) 1 lacking in skill and ungraceful in movement 2 (of actions and statements) tactless 3 difficult to use ▸ **clumsily** adv ▸ **clumsiness** n [U]

clung pt, pp of CLING

cluster /ˈklʌstə(r)/ n group of

things close together ● **cluster** v [I] ~(**together**) form a close group

clutch /klʌtʃ/ v [I, T] (try to) hold sb/sth tightly, esp with the hands ● **clutch** n 1 [C] pedal in a car, etc that you press with your foot in order to change gear 2 [C] device in a machine that connects and disconnects the engine and the gears 3 (**clutches**) [pl] (infml) power or control: *be in sb's ~es* 4 [C] tight hold of sb/sth 5 [C] group of bird's eggs that hatch together

clutter /ˈklʌtə(r)/ n (esp unnecessary or unwanted) things lying about untidily ● **clutter** v [T] fill a place with too many things so that it is untidy

cm abbr (pl **cm** or **~s**) centimetre

Co. abbr company(1)

c/o /siː ˈəʊ/ abbr (on letters, etc addressed to sb staying at sb else's house) care of

coach /kəʊtʃ/ n 1 person who trains sb or a team in sport 2 bus for carrying passengers on long journeys 3 railway carriage 4 large carriage with four wheels, pulled by horses 5 (US) cheapest seats in a plane ● **coach** v [T] teach sb, esp for an examination or in a sport

coagulate /kəʊˈæɡjuleɪt/ v [I, T] (cause sth to) change from a liquid to a thick semi-solid state

coal /kəʊl/ n [C,U] (piece of) black mineral that is burnt as a fuel ■ **'coalface** n surface in a coal mine from which coal is cut ■ **'coalfield** n district in which coal is mined ■ **'coal mine** n place underground where coal is dug ▸ **'coal miner** n person whose job is digging coal in a coal mine

coalesce /ˌkəʊəˈles/ v [I] (fml) come together to form one larger group, substance, etc

coalition /ˌkəʊəˈlɪʃn/ n union of political parties for a special purpose

coarse /kɔːs/ adj (**~r, ~st**) 1 rough; not fine 2 rude and offensive ▸ **coarsely** adv ▸ **coarsen** /ˈkɔːsn/ v [I, T] become or make sb/sth coarse ▸ **coarseness** n [U]

coast /kəʊst/ n land next to the sea [IDM] **the coast is clear** (infml) there is no danger of being seen or caught ● **coast** v [I] move, esp downhill, without using power ▸ **coastal** adj ■ **'coastguard** n [C, with sing or pl verb] (one of a) group of people on police duty on the coast ■ **'coastline** n shape or outline of a coast

coat /kəʊt/ n 1 piece of outdoor clothing worn over other clothes to keep warm or dry 2 fur or hair on an animal 3 layer on a surface: *a ~ of paint* ● **coat** v [T] cover sth with

a layer of sth ■ 'coat hanger n =
HANGER ▶ 'coating n thin layer
■ ,coat of 'arms n design on a
shield used as a sign by a noble
family, town, etc

coax /kəʊks/ v [T] persuade sb gently or gradually [PV] **coax sth out of/
from sb** obtain sth from sb by persuading them gently

cob /kɒb/ n 1 = CORNCOB (CORN) 2
strong short-legged horse 3 male
swan

cobble /'kɒbl/ v [PV] **cobble sth
together** put sth together quickly
or roughly

cobbles /'kɒblz/ (also 'cobblestones) n [pl] small round stones
used to make the surfaces of roads,
esp in the past ▶ **cobbled** adj

cobra /'kəʊbrə/ n poisonous snake
of India and Africa

cobweb /'kɒbweb/ n spider's web

cocaine /kəʊ'keɪn/ n [U] powerful,
illegal drug taken for pleasure by
some people

cock[1] /kɒk/ n 1 male bird, esp an
adult male chicken 2 = STOPCOCK

cock[2] /kɒk/ v [T] 1 raise or turn part
of the body upwards: *The horse ~ed
its ears.* 2 raise the hammer of a
gun ready for firing [PV] **cock sth
up** (GB, sl) spoil or ruin sth ■ '**cock-
up** n (GB, spoken) bad mistake that
spoils people's arrangements

cockatoo /ˌkɒkə'tuː/ n (pl ~s) kind
of parrot with a large crest

cockerel /'kɒkərəl/ n young male
chicken

cock-eyed /ˌkɒk 'aɪd/ adj (infml) 1
not straight or level; crooked 2 not
practical: *a ~ scheme*

cockle /'kɒkl/ n small edible shellfish

cockney /'kɒkni/ n 1 [C] person
from the East End of London 2 [U]
way of speaking that is typical of
cockneys: *a ~ accent*

cockpit /'kɒkpɪt/ n part of a plane,
boat or racing car where the pilot
or driver sits

cockroach /'kɒkrəʊtʃ/ n large
brown insect that lives esp in
damp rooms

cocktail /'kɒkteɪl/ n 1 mixed alcoholic drink 2 mixture of fruit or
shellfish: *a prawn ~*

cocky /'kɒki/ adj (-ier, -iest) (infml)
too self-confident

cocoa /'kəʊkəʊ/ n 1 [U] brown powder tasting like bitter chocolate
2 [U,C] hot drink made from this

coconut /'kəʊkənʌt/ n large nut
with a hard hairy shell and an
edible white lining and filled with
milky juice

cocoon /kə'kuːn/ n silky covering

made by an insect larva to protect
itself while it is a chrysalis

cod /kɒd/ n [C,U] (pl **cod**) large sea
fish with white flesh that is used
for food

coddle /'kɒdl/ v [T] treat sb with too
much care and attention

code /kəʊd/ n 1 [C,U] system of
words, letters, numbers or symbols
that represent a message or record
information secretly or in a shorter
form: *break the ~ the enemy use to
send messages* 2 [U] (computing)
system of computer programming
instructions 3 [C] system of rules
and principles: *a ~ of behaviour*
● **code** v [T] 1 put sth into code
2 (computing) write a computer
program by putting one system of
numbers, words and symbols into
another system

co-educational /ˌkəʊedʒu'keɪʃnl/
(also infml **coed** /ˌkəʊ'ed/) adj (of a
school or an educational system)
where boys and girls are taught
together ▶ **coeducation** n [U]

coerce /kəʊ'ɜːs/ v [T] (fml) force sb
to do sth ▶ **coercion** /kəʊ'ɜːʃn/ n [U]
▶ **coercive** /-'ɜːsɪv/ adj

coexist /ˌkəʊɪg'zɪst/ v [I] (fml) exist
together at the same time or in the
same place ▶ **coexistence** n [U] state
of being together in the same place
at the same time: *peaceful ~ence*

coffee /'kɒfi/ n 1 [U,C] (powder
obtained by grinding the roasted)
seeds of the coffee tree 2 [U,C] hot
drink made from coffee powder
and boiling water

coffer /'kɒfə(r)/ n 1 [C] large strong
box used in the past for holding
money, etc 2 (**coffers**) [pl] (written)
money that a government, etc has
available to spend

coffin /'kɒfɪn/ n (esp GB) box in
which a dead body is buried or cremated

cog /kɒg/ n 1 one of the teeth on a
wheel that moves the teeth of a
similar wheel 2 = COGWHEEL [IDM] **a
cog in the machine** unimportant
but necessary person in a large
organization ■ '**cogwheel** (also **cog**)
n wheel with teeth round the edge

cogent /'kəʊdʒənt/ adj (fml)
strongly and clearly expressed;
convincing

cognac /'kɒnjæk/ n [U,C] kind of
brandy

cohabit /kəʊ'hæbɪt/ v [I] (fml) (usu
of an unmarried couple) live
together as husband and wife ▶
cohabitation /ˌkəʊˌhæbɪ'teɪʃn/ n [U]

cohere /kəʊ'hɪə(r)/ v [I] (fml) 1 (of
ideas, etc) be connected logically
2 (of people) work closely together
▶ **coherent** /kəʊ'hɪərənt/ adj (of

ideas, arguments, etc) connected logically; clear and easy to understand ▶ **coherence** /kəʊ'hɪərəns/ n [U] ▶ **coherently** adv

cohesion /kəʊ'hiːʒn/ n [U] tendency to stick together; unity ▶ **cohesive** /kəʊ'hiːsɪv/ adj

coil /kɔɪl/ v [I, T] (cause sth to) wind into a series of circles ● **coil** n 1 series of circles formed by winding up a length of rope, wire, etc 2 one circle of rope, wire, etc in a series

coin /kɔɪn/ n piece of metal used as money ● **coin** n [T] 1 invent a new word or phrase 2 make coins ▶ **coinage** /'kɔɪnɪdʒ/ n [U] coins in use in a country

coincide /ˌkəʊɪn'saɪd/ v [I] 1 (of events) happen at the same time 2 (of opinions or ideas) agree 3 (fml) (of objects) meet; share the same space

coincidence /kəʊ'ɪnsɪdəns/ n [C, U] fact of two or more things happening at the same time by chance: *It was pure ~ that we were both travelling on the same plane.* ▶ **coincidental** /kəʊˌɪnsɪ'dentl/ adj happening by chance ▶ **coincidentally** adv

coke /kəʊk/ n [U] 1 (infml) = COCAINE 2 black substance produced from coal and used as a fuel

colander /'kʌləndə(r)/ n bowl with many small holes in it, used to drain water from food

cold¹ /kəʊld/ adj 1 of low temperature 2 (of food) not heated; having cooled after being heated 3 unfriendly; unfeeling: *a ~ stare/welcome* 4 unconscious: *knock sb out* – [IDM] **get/have cold feet** (infml) become afraid to do sth you had planned to do **give sb the cold shoulder** (infml) treat sb in an unfriendly way **in cold blood** deliberately cruel and without feeling: *kill sb in ~ blood* **pour/throw cold water on sth** be discouraging or not enthusiastic about sth ■ ˌcold-'blooded adj 1 (of people and their actions) without pity; cruel 2 (biol) (of animals) having a blood temperature that varies with the surroundings ■ ˌcold 'cash n [U] (US) = HARD CASH (HARD¹) ■ ˌcold-'hearted adj not showing any love or sympathy for other people ▶ **coldly** adj ▶ **coldness** n [U] ■ ˌcold 'war n [sing] very unfriendly relationship between two countries who are not actually fighting each other

cold² /kəʊld/ n 1 [U] lack of heat or warmth; low temperature 2 [C] common illness of the nose or throat [IDM] **leave sb out in the cold** not include sb in a group or an activity

coleslaw /'kəʊlslɔː/ n [U] finely chopped raw cabbage, carrots, etc mixed with mayonnaise

colic /'kɒlɪk/ n [U] severe pain in the stomach and bowels

collaborate /kə'læbəreɪt/ v [I] 1 ~ (with) work together 2 ~(with) help the enemy ▶ **collaboration** /kəˌlæbə'reɪʃn/ n [U] ▶ **collaborator** n

collage /'kɒlɑːʒ/ n picture made by sticking pieces of paper, cloth, etc onto a surface

collapse /kə'læps/ v 1 [I] fall down suddenly: *The building ~d in the earthquake.* 2 [I] fall down (and become unconscious) because of illness or tiredness 3 [I] fail suddenly and completely 4 [I, T] fold sth into a flat compact shape: *The table ~s to fit into the cupboard.* ● **collapse** n [C, usu sing, U]: *the ~ of the company* ▶ **collapsible** adj that can be folded for packing, etc: *a collapsible chair/table*

collar /'kɒlə(r)/ n 1 part around the neck of a shirt, jacket or coat 2 band of leather, etc put round the neck of a dog or other animal ● **collar** v [T] seize or catch sb ■ 'collarbone n either of the two bones that go from the base of the neck to the shoulders

collate /kə'leɪt/ v [T] gather information to examine and compare it

collateral /kə'lætərəl/ n [U] (business) property or money used as security for a loan

colleague /'kɒliːɡ/ n person that you work with

collect /kə'lekt/ v 1 [I, T] come together; bring sth/sb together: *A crowd ~ed at the scene of the accident.* ◇ *~ the empty glasses* 2 [T] save stamps, etc as a hobby 3 [I, T] ~(for) obtain money from a number of people for sb/sth: *~ money for charity* 4 [T] fetch sb/sth: *~ a child from school* [IDM] **collect yourself/your thoughts** control your emotions; prepare yourself mentally for sth ● **collect** adj, adv (US) (of a phone call) paid for by the person who receives the call ▶ **collected** adj calm and self-controlled ▶ **collection** /kə'lekʃn/ n 1 [C] group of objects collected 2 [C,U] act of collecting sb/sth 3 [C] sum of money collected ▶ **collective** adj of a group or society as a whole; shared ▶ **collectively** adv ▶ **collector** n person who collects sth, either as a hobby, or as a job: *a theatre/ticket ~or*

college /'kɒlɪdʒ/ n 1 institution for higher education; part of a university 2 (fml) organized group of professional people

collide /kə'laɪd/ v [I] 1 ~(with) (of moving objects or people) hit each

colliery /ˈkɒliəri/ n (pl -ies) (GB) coal mine

collision /kəˈlɪʒn/ n [C,U] **1** accident in which two vehicles or people crash into each other **2** (written) strong disagreement

colloquial /kəˈləʊkwiəl/ adj (of words and language) used in conversation but not in formal speech or writing ▶ **colloquialism** n colloquial word or phrase ▶ **colloquially** adv

collude /kəˈluːd/ v [I] ~(with) (fml) work with sb secretly and dishonestly ▶ **collusion** /kəˈluːʒn/ n [U]

colon /ˈkəʊlən/ n **1** punctuation mark (:) **2** (anat) lower part of the large intestine (= part of the bowels)

colonel /ˈkɜːnl/ n middle-ranking officer in the army or US air force

colonial /kəˈləʊniəl/ adj connected with or belonging to a colony(1) ● **colonial** n person living in a colony(1) ▶ **colonialism** n [U] policy of having colonies ▶ **colonialist** n, adj

colonist /ˈkɒlənɪst/ n person who settles in an area and colonizes it

colonize (also **-ise**) /ˈkɒlənaɪz/ v [T] establish an area as a colony(1) ▶ **colonization** (**-isation**) /-ˈzeɪʃn/ n [U]

colonnade /ˌkɒləˈneɪd/ n row of columns(1)

colony /ˈkɒləni/ n (pl -ies) **1** country lived in and controlled by another country **2** group of people with the same interests, etc living in the same place

color (US) = COLOUR

colossal /kəˈlɒsl/ adj very large

colour¹ /ˈkʌlə(r)/ n **1** [C,U] appearance that things have that results from the way in which they reflect light. Red, green and orange are colours. **2** [U] appearance of the skin on sb's face: *The fresh air brought some ~ to her cheeks.* **3** [U,C] colour of a person's skin, when it shows the race they belong to **4** [C] interesting details or qualities **5** (colours) [pl] flag, badge, etc worn to show that sb is a member of a particular team, school, etc [IDM] **off colour** (infml) unwell; ill **with flying colours** with great success ■ **colour-blind** adj unable to distinguish between colours(1) ▶ **colourful** adj **1** brightly coloured **2** interesting or exciting ▶ **colourless** adj **1** without colour(1) **2** dull and uninteresting ■ **colour supplement** n (GB) magazine printed in colour, given free esp with a Sunday newspaper

colour² /ˈkʌlə(r)/ v **1** [T] give colour to sth, using paint, coloured pens, etc **2** [I] become red with embarrassment; blush **3** [T] affect sth, esp

in a negative way [PV] **colour sth in** fill a picture, etc with colour ▶ **coloured** adj having a particular colour or different colours ▶ **colouring** n **1** [U,C] substance used to give a particular colour to food **2** [U] colours of sb's skin, eyes and hair **3** [U] colours that exist in sth, esp a plant or an animal

colt /kəʊlt/ n young male horse

column /ˈkɒləm/ n **1** tall vertical post supporting part of a building or standing alone **2** something shaped like a column: *a ~ of smoke* **3** (abbr col.) vertical division of a printed page **4** part of a newspaper or magazine which appears regularly: *a gossip ~* **5** long moving line of people or vehicles ▶ **columnist** /ˈkɒləmnɪst/ n person who writes regular articles for a newspaper

coma /ˈkəʊmə/ n state of deep unconsciousness

comb /kəʊm/ n [C] **1** piece of plastic or metal with teeth, used for tidying your hair **2** [usu sing] act of using a comb on your hair: *give your hair a ~* **3** n [C,U] = HONEYCOMB ● **comb** v [T] **1** tidy your hair with a comb **2** search sth carefully in order to find sb/sth

combat /ˈkɒmbæt/ n [U,C] fighting or a fight, esp during a time of war ● **combat** v (-t- or -tt-) [T] **1** stop sth unpleasant or harmful from happening or getting worse **2** (fml) fight against an enemy ▶ **combatant** /ˈkɒmbətənt/ n person who fights

combination /ˌkɒmbɪˈneɪʃn/ n [C] number of things or people joined or mixed together: *a ~ of traditional and modern architecture* **2** act of joining two or more things together to form a single unit **3** [C] series of numbers or letters needed to open the lock of a safe, etc

combine¹ /kəmˈbaɪn/ v [I, T] join two or more things together

combine² /ˈkɒmbaɪn/ n **1** (also ˌcombine ˈharvester) machine that both cuts and threshes grain **2** group of people or organizations acting together in business

combustible /kəmˈbʌstəbl/ adj that can catch fire and burn easily

combustion /kəmˈbʌstʃən/ n [U] process of burning

come /kʌm/ v (pt came /keɪm/, pp come) [I] **1** move towards the speaker or the place to which he/she is referring: *~ and talk to me* **2** arrive at or reach a place **3** reach; extend: *The path ~s right up to the gate.* **4** travel a specified distance: *We've ~ thirty miles since lunch.* **5** happen; take place: *Christmas ~s once a year.* **6** ~to/into reach a particular state: *~ to an end* **7** *~(in)* (of goods, products, etc) exist; be available: *This dress ~s in several different colours.* **8** become: *The button came undone.* **9** *~to* begin: *~ to realize the truth* [IDM] **come to grips with sth →** GRIP **come to a head →** HEAD¹ **come to nothing | not come to anything** be unsuccessful **come what may** in spite of any problems or difficulties you may have **how come** (…)? (spoken) why? **come in for** sth: *for several years to ~* [PV] **come about happen come across** (also **come over**) **1** be understood: *He spoke for ages but his meaning didn't really ~ across.* **2** make a particular impression: *She ~s across well in interviews.* **come across sb/sth** find sth or meet sb by chance **come along 1** arrive; appear: *When the right job ~s along, she'll take it.* **2** progress, develop or improve: *Her work is coming along nicely.* **3** = COME ON(3) **come apart** fall to pieces **come around/round 1** (also **come to**) become conscious again **2** occur again: *Christmas seems to ~ round quicker every year.* **come around/round (to …)** visit for a short time: *C~ round to my place for the evening.* **come around/round (to sth)** change your mood or your opinion **come at sb** move towards sb to attack them: *He came at me with a knife.* **come back** return **come back (to sb)** return to sb's memory **come before sb/sth** (fml) be presented to sb/sth for discussion or a decision: *The case ~s before the court next week.* **come between A and B** interfere **come by sth** obtain or receive: *Good jobs are hard to ~ by these days.* **come down 1** collapse **2** (of rain, prices, etc) fall **3** decide and say publicly that you support or oppose sth **4** reach down to a particular point: *Her hair ~s down to her waist.* **come down (to sb)** have come from a long time in the past **come down to sth** be able to be explained by a single important point: *What it ~s down to is that if your work doesn't improve you'll have to leave.* **come in 1** (of the tide) move towards the land **2** become fashionable **3** arrive somewhere; be received **4** have a part to play: *Where do I ~ in?* **come in for sth** be the object of punishment, criticism, etc **come into sth** inherit sth **come of/from sth** be the result of sth **come off 1** be able to be removed: *Will these dirty marks ~ off?* **2** (infml) take place; happen **3** (infml) (of plans, etc) be successful: *The experiment did not ~ off.* **come off (sth) 1** fall from sth: *~ off your bicycle/horse* **2** become separated

from sth: *The button ~s off my coat.* **come on 1** (of an actor) walk onto the stage **2** improve or develop in the way you want **3** used in orders to tell sb to hurry or to try harder: *C~ on, if we don't hurry we'll be late.* **4** (of rain, night, illness, etc) begin: *I think he has a cold coming on.* **come on/upon sb/sth** (fml) meet or find sb/sth by chance **come out 1** become visible; appear: *The rain stopped and the sun came out.* **2** become known; be published: *The truth came out eventually.* **3** (of workers) strike **4** be clearly revealed, eg in a photograph **come out (of sth)** be removed from sth: *Will the stains ~ out?* **come out in sth** become (partly) covered in spots, etc: *~ out in a rash* **come out with sth** say sth: *He ~s out with the strangest remarks.* **come over 1** (GB, infml) suddenly become sth: *She came over all shy.* **2** = COME ACROSS **come over (to …)** move from one place to another, esp for a visit: *~ over to Scotland for a holiday* **come over sb** (of feelings, etc) affect sb: *A feeling of dizziness came over him.* **come round (to sth)** = COME AROUND **come through** (of a message, signal, etc) arrive **come through (sth)** recover from a serious illness or escape injury **come to** = COME AROUND(1) **come to sb** (of an idea) enter your mind: *The idea came to me in a dream.* **come to sth 1** add up to sth: *The bill came to £20.* **2** reach a particular situation, esp a bad one: *The doctors could operate, but it might not ~ to that.* **come under sth 1** be in a certain category, etc **2** be subjected to sth: *~ under her influence* **come up 1** (of plants, etc) appear above the soil **2** happen: *Something urgent has ~ up so I'll be late home.* **3** be mentioned: *The question hasn't ~ up yet.* **come up against sb/sth** be faced with or opposed by sb/sth **come up to sth** reach sth: *The water came up to my waist.* **come up with sth** produce or find: *~ up with a solution* **come upon sb/sth** = COME ON SB/STH ■ **'comeback** n [C, usu sing] return to a previous successful position: *an ageing pop star trying to make a ~back* ■ **'comedown** n [C, usu sing] situation in which a person is not as important as before, or does not get as much respect from others ▶ **coming** adj future: *in the coming months* ▶ **coming** n [sing] arrival: *the coming of spring* [IDM] **comings and goings** arrivals and departures

comedian /kəˈmiːdiən/ n (old-fash fem **comedienne** /kəˌmiːdiˈen/) entertainer who makes people laugh by telling jokes, etc

comedy /ˈkɒmədi/ n (pl -ies) **1** [C,U]

amusing play, film, etc **2** [U] amusing aspect of sth

comet /'kɒmɪt/ n bright object, like a star with a long tail, that moves round the sun

comfort /'kʌmfət/ n **1** [U] state of being relaxed and free from pain or worry: *They had enough money to live in ~ For the rest of their lives.* **2** [U] feeling of not suffering or worrying so much; feeling of being less unhappy: *to take ~ from sb's words* [sing] person or thing that brings you help or relief **4** [C, usu pl] thing that gives physical ease and makes life more pleasant ● **comfort** v [T] make sb feel less unhappy or worried ▶ **comfortable** /'kʌmftəbl/ adj **1** (of clothes, furniture, etc) pleasant to sit on, wear, etc: *a ~able chair* **2** feeling pleasantly relaxed; warm enough, without pain, etc: *Make yourself ~able while I make some coffee.* **3** (infml) fairly rich **4** quite large; allowing you to win easily ▶ **comfortably** adv

comic /'kɒmɪk/ adj amusing and making you laugh **2** connected with comedy ● **comic** n **1** comedian **2** magazine, esp for children, with stories told in pictures ▶ **comical** adj (old-fash) funny or amusing because of being strange or unusual ■ '**comic strip** (also **cartoon**) *n* series of drawings that tell a story and are often printed in newspapers

comma /'kɒmə/ *n* punctuation mark (,)

command /kə'mɑːnd/ v **1** [I, T] order sb to do sth **2** [T] be in charge of a group of people in the army, navy or air force: *~ a regiment* **3** [T] deserve and get sth: *~ respect* **4** [T] (fml) have a clear view of a place: *a ~ing position over the valley* ● **command** *n* **1** [C] order given to a person or an animal **2** [C] instruction given to a computer **3** [U] control; authority over a situation or group of people: *in ~ of a ship* **4** (**Command**) [C] part of an army, air force, etc **5** [U, sing] *~(of)* ability to use sth: *a good ~ of French*

commandant /'kɒməndænt/ *n* officer in command of a military group or an institution

commandeer /ˌkɒmən'dɪə(r)/ *v* [T] take possession or control of sth for official, esp military, purposes

commander /kə'mɑːndə(r)/ *n* **1** person who is in charge of sth, esp an officer in charge of a group of soldiers or a military operation **2** (abbr **Cdr**) officer of fairly high rank in the British or American navy

commandment /kə'mɑːndmənt/ *n* law given by God

commando /kə'mɑːndəʊ/ *n* (pl **~s**

or **~es**) (member of a) group of soldiers trained to make quick attacks in enemy areas

commemorate /kə'meməreɪt/ *v* [T] honour the memory of sb, an event, etc ▶ **commemoration** /kəˌmeməˈreɪʃn/ *n* [C,U] ▶ **commemorative** /kə'memərətɪv/ *adj*

commence /kə'mens/ *v* [I, T] (fml) begin; start ▶ **commencement** *n* [U]

commend /kə'mend/ *v* [T] (fml) **1** praise sb/sth publicly; recommend sb/sth to sb **2** be approved of by sb: *His outspoken behaviour did not ~ itself to his colleagues.* ▶ **commendable** *adj* deserving praise ▶ **commendation** /-'deɪʃn/ *n* [U,C]

commensurate /kə'menʃərət/ *adj* ~**with** (fml) matching sth in size, importance, etc: *pay ~ with the importance of the job*

comment /'kɒment/ *n* [C,U] written or spoken statement which gives an opinion on or explains sth ● **comment** *v* [I] ~(on) give your opinion on sth

commentary /'kɒməntri/ *n* (pl -ies) **1** [C,U] spoken description of an event given as it happens, esp on the radio or television: *a sports ~* [C] written explanation of a book, play, etc

commentate /'kɒmənteɪt/ *v* [I] ~(on) give a commentary(1) ▶ **commentator** *n*

commerce /'kɒmɜːs/ *n* [U] trade, esp between countries; the buying and selling of goods

commercial /kə'mɜːʃl/ *adj* **1** of or relating to commerce **2** making a profit **3** (of television or radio) paid for by advertisements ● **commercial** *n* advertisement on television or radio ▶ **commercialized** (also **-ised**) *adj* concerned mainly with making a profit: *Their music has become very ~ized in recent years.* ▶ **commercially** /-ʃəli/ *adv*

commiserate /kə'mɪzəreɪt/ *v* [I] ~(**with**) (fml) show sympathy to sb: *I ~d with her on the loss of her job.* ▶ **commiseration** /kəˌmɪzəˈreɪʃn/ *n* [C,U]

commission /kə'mɪʃn/ *n* **1** [C] (often **Commission**) official group of people asked to find out about sth and to report on it **2** [U,C] amount of money paid to sb who sells goods for making a sale **3** [C] formal request to sb to design a piece of work such as a building or painting **4** [C] officer's position in the armed forces ● **commission** *v* [T] **1** officially ask sb to do a piece of work for you **2** choose sb as an officer in one of the armed forces

commissioner /kə'mɪʃənə(r)/ *n* **1** (usu **Commissioner**) member of a commission(1) **2** (esp US '**police**

commissioner) head of a particular police force in some countries **3** head of a government department in some countries

commit /kə'mɪt/ v (**-tt-**) [T] **1** do sth wrong or illegal: ~ *murder/adultery/ suicide* **2** ~(**to**) promise sincerely that you will do sth: *The government has ~ted itself to fighting inflation.* **3** ~ **yourself** give your opinion openly so that it is then difficult to change it **4** be completely loyal to one person, organization, etc **5** ~**to** order sb to be sent to a prison or hospital ▸ **commitment** *n* **1** [C] something that you have promised to do **2** [U] loyalty

committee /kə'mɪti/ *n* [C, with sing or pl verb] group of people chosen to deal with a particular matter

commodity /kə'mɒdəti/ *n* (*pl* **-ies**) useful thing, esp an article of trade; product

common[1] /'kɒmən/ *adj* **1** happening or found often and in many places; usual **2** shared or used by two or more people: *a* ~ *interest* ◇ ~ *knowledge* (*GB, disapprov*) typical of sb from a low social class and not having good manners ■ ,**common 'ground** *n* [U] shared opinions or aims ■ ,**common 'law** *n* [U] (in England) system of laws developed from customs and decisions made by judges, not created by Parliament ▸ '**common-law** *adj* ■ '**commonplace** *adj* done very often or existing in many places ■ ,**common 'sense** *n* [U] ability to think about things in a practical way and make sensible decisions

common[2] /'kɒmən/ *n* area of open land which everyone may use [IDM] **have sth in common** share interests, ideas, etc **in common with** sb/sth together with sb/sth

commoner /'kɒmənə(r)/ *n* person who does not come from a noble family

Commons /'kɒmənz/ *n* [sing] (**the Commons**) = THE HOUSE OF COMMONS (HOUSE[1])

commonwealth /'kɒmənwelθ/ *n* **1** (**the Commonwealth**) [sing] organization consisting of the UK and most of the countries that used to be part of the British Empire **2** (usu **Commonwealth**) [C] used in the names of some groups of countries or states that have chosen to be politically linked

commotion /kə'məʊʃn/ *n* [sing, U] noisy confusion

communal /kə'mju:nl; 'kɒmjənl/ *adj* shared by a group of people

commune[1] /'kɒmju:n/ *n* **1** group of people who live together and

share property and responsibilities **2** (in France, etc) smallest division of local government

commune[2] /kə'mju:n/ *v* [PV] **commune with** sb/sth (*fml*) share your emotions and feelings with sb/sth without speaking: *He spent his time communing with nature.*

communicate /kə'mju:nɪkeɪt/ *v* **1** [I, T] make your ideas, feelings, etc known to other people **2** [T] pass on a disease **3** [I] (of rooms) be connected: *a communicating door* ▸ **communication** /kə,mju:nɪ'keɪʃn/ *n* **1** [U] activity of expressing ideas and feelings or of giving people information **2** [U] (*also* **communications** [pl]) methods of sending information, esp telephones, radio, computers, etc or roads and railways **3** [C] (*fml*) message, letter or telephone call ▸ **communicative** /kə-'mju:nɪkətɪv/ *adj* willing to give information or talk

communion /kə'mju:niən/ *n* **1** (*also* **Communion**, ,**Holy Com'munion**) Christian ceremony of sharing bread and wine **2** (*fml*) state of sharing thoughts, feelings, etc

communiqué /kə'mju:nɪkeɪ/ *n* official announcement

communism /'kɒmjunɪzəm/ *n* [U] **1** social and economic system in which there is no private ownership and the means of production belongs to all members of society **2** (**Communism**) system of government by a ruling Communist Party, such as in the former Soviet Union ▸ **communist** (*also* **Communist**) /'kɒmjunɪst/ *n, adj*

community /kə'mju:nəti/ *n* (*pl* **-ies**) **1** [sing] all the people living in one place **2** [C, with sing or pl verb] group of people who share the same religion, race, job, etc **3** [U] feeling of sharing or having things in common

commute /kə'mju:t/ *v* **1** [I] travel regularly by car, train, etc between your place of work and home **2** [T] (*law*) replace a punishment with one that is less severe ▸ **commuter** *n* person who travels into a city to work each day, usu from near or far away

compact[1] /kəm'pækt/ *adj* closely packed together; neatly fitted in a small space ▸ **compactly** *adv* ▸ **compactness** [U]

compact[2] /'kɒmpækt/ *n* small flat box with a mirror, containing face powder

compact disc *n* = CD

companion /kəm'pæniən/ *n* person who spends time or travels with another ▸ **companionship** *n* [U] relationship between friends or companions

company /'kʌmpəni/ n (pl **-ies**) **1**
[C] (abbr **Co.**) business organization **2** [C] group of people who
work or perform together: an opera
~ **3** [U] fact of being with sb else
and not alone: He is good/bad ~ (=
he is pleasant/unpleasant to be
with). **4** [U] (fml) guests in one's
house **5** [U] (fml) group of people
together **6** [C] group of soldiers
that forms part of a battalion [IDM]
keep sb company stay with sb so
that they are not alone

comparable /'kɒmpərəbl/ adj that
can be compared; similar

comparative /kəm'pærətɪv/ adj **1**
connected with studying things to
find out how similar or different
they are **2** measured by comparing;
relative: living in ~ comfort **3** (gram)
of adjectives and adverbs expressing a greater degree or 'more', eg
better, worse: 'Better' is the ~ form of
'good'. ● **comparative** n (gram)
comparative form of an adjective
or adverb ▶ **comparatively** adv

compare /kəm'peə(r)/ v **1** [T] ~
(**with/to**)(abbr **cf.**) examine things
to see how they are alike and how
they are different: ~ the results of
one test with the results of another **2**
[I] ~**with/to** be similar to sb/sth else,
either better or worse **3** [T] ~**A to B**
show the similarity between sth and
sb/sth else [IDM] **compare notes**
(**with sb**) exchange opinions with sb

comparison /kəm'pærɪsn/ n **1** [C,
U] ~(**with**) process of comparing
sb/sth: There is no ~ between them. **2**
[C] ~(**of A and/to sth with B**); ~(**between
A and B**) occasion when two or
more people or things are compared [IDM] **by/in comparison** (**with
sb/sth**) when compared with sb/sth

compartment /kəm'pɑːtmənt/ n **1**
section of a railway carriage **2** separate section in a piece of furniture, etc for keeping things in

compass /'kʌmpəs/ n **1** [C] device
for finding direction, with a needle
that points north **2** (also **com-
passes** [pl]) V-shaped instrument
for drawing circles **3** [C] (fml)
range; scope

compassion /kəm'pæʃn/ n [U]
feeling of pity for the suffering of
others ▶ **compassionate** /kəm-
'pæʃənət/ adj showing or feeling
compassion ▶ **compassionately** adv

compatible /kəm'pætəbl/ adj ~
(**with**) **1** (of machines, esp computers) able to be used together
2 (eg of people, ideas or principles)
able to exist together ▶ **compatibil-
ity** /kəm,pætə'bɪləti/ n [U]

compatriot /kəm'pætriət/ n person
from the same country as sb else

compel /kəm'pel/ v (**-ll-**) [T] (fml)

force sb to do sth ▶ **compelling** adj
convincing

compensate /'kɒmpenseɪt/ v [I, T]
~(**for**) pay or give sb sth to balance
or lessen the bad effect of damage,
loss, etc ▶ **compensation** /,kɒmpen-
'seɪʃn/ n [U,C] ~(**for**) something,
esp money, that sb gives you
because they have hurt you, or
damaged sth of yours; act of giving
this to sb **2** [C,usu pl] things that
make a bad situation better

compère /'kɒmpeə(r)/ n person
who introduces the performers or
guests in a radio or television show
● **compère** v [T] act as a compère
for a show

compete /kəm'piːt/ v [I] take part in a
race, contest, etc; try to win by defeating others: ~against/with others

competence /'kɒmpɪtəns/ n [U] **1**
ability to do sth well **2** (law) legal
authority ▶ **competent** /'kɒmpɪtənt/
adj having the ability, skill, knowledge, etc to do sth well ▶ **compe-
tently** adv

competition /,kɒmpə'tɪʃn/ n **1** [U]
situation in which people compete
for sth that not everyone can have
2 [C] event in which people compete to find out who is the best at
sth: a photography ~ **3** (**the competition**) [sing, with sing or pl verb] people
who are competing against sb
▶ **competitive** /kəm'petətɪv/ adj **1**
of or involving competition **2** (of a
person) trying hard to be better
than others

competitor /kəm'petɪtə(r)/ n person who competes

compile /kəm'paɪl/ v [T] **1** produce
a book, report, etc by collecting
information **2** (computing) translate a set of instructions into a language that a computer will understand ▶ **compilation** /,kɒmpɪ'leɪʃn/
n **1** [C] collection of items taken
from different places and put
together **2** [U] process of compiling
▶ **compiler** n

complacent /kəm'pleɪsnt/ adj
(disapprov) calmly satisfied ▶ **com-
placency** /kəm'pleɪsnsi/ n [U] ▶
complacently adv

complain /kəm'pleɪn/ v [I] say that
you are dissatisfied or unhappy
about sb/sth: ~about the food

complaint /kəm'pleɪnt/ n **1** [C,U]
(statement of) complaining **2** [C]
illness; disease

complement /'kɒmplɪmənt/ n **1**
something that goes well with sth
else, making it complete: Wine is the
perfect ~ to a meal. **2** total number
needed **3** (gram) word(s), esp
adjectives and nouns, used after a
verb such as be or become describing the subject of the verb: In

'I'm unhappy', 'unhappy' is the ~. ● **complement** /'kɒmplɪment/ v [T] go well with sth to form a whole ▶ **complementary** /ˌkɒmplɪ'mentri/ adj going well with each other to form a whole

complete /kəm'pli:t/ adj 1 having all its parts; whole 2 finished; ended 3 in every way; total: a ~ surprise ● **complete** v [T] finish sth; make sth whole 2 fill in a form ▶ **completely** adv in every way ▶ **completeness** n [U] ▶ **completion** /kəm'pli:ʃn/ n [U] act of finishing sth; state of being complete

complex /'kɒmpleks/ adj made up of many different parts; difficult to understand or explain ● **complex** n 1 group of similar buildings or things that are connected: a sports ~ 2 abnormal mental state: suffer from a guilt ~ ▶ **complexity** /kəm'pleksəti/ n [C,U] (pl -ies)

complexion /kəm'plekʃn/ n [C] 1 natural colour and condition of the skin on a person's face: a spotty ~ 2 [usu sing] general character of sth

compliance /kəm'plaɪəns/ n [U] (written) practice of obeying rules made by those in authority ▶ **compliant** /kəm'plaɪənt/ adj obedient

complicate /'kɒmplɪkeɪt/ v [T] make sth difficult to do, understand or deal with ▶ **complicated** adj difficult to understand or explain because there are many different parts ▶ **complication** /ˌkɒmplɪ'keɪʃn/ n something that makes a situation more difficult

complicity /kəm'plɪsəti/ n [U] (fml) taking part with another person in a crime

compliment /'kɒmplɪment/ n 1 [C] remark that expresses praise, admiration, etc 2 (**compliments**) [pl] (fml) greetings or good wishes ● **compliment** /'kɒmplɪment/ v [T] express praise or admiration of sb/sth ▶ **complimentary** /-'mentri/ adj 1 expressing admiration 2 given free of charge: ~ary tickets

comply /kəm'plaɪ/ v (pt, pp -ied) [I] ~ (with) (fml) obey a rule, an order, etc

component /kəm'pəʊnənt/ n any of the parts of which sth is made ▶ **component** adj

compose /kəm'pəʊz/ v 1 [I, T] write music, a poem, a letter, etc 2 [T] (fml) manage to control your feelings or expression: She made a real effort to ~ herself. ● **composed** adj 1 (**be composed of sth**) made or formed from several parts, things or people 2 calm ▶ **composer** n person who writes music

composite /'kɒmpəzɪt/ n, adj (thing) made up of different parts or materials

composition /ˌkɒmpə'zɪʃn/ n 1 [C] sth, eg a piece of music, that is composed 2 [U] action of composing sth 3 [C] short piece of written work done at school 4 [U] parts of which sth is made: the chemical ~ of the soil

compost /'kɒmpɒst/ n [U] mixture of decayed plants, manure, etc, added to soil to help plants grow

composure /kəm'pəʊʒə(r)/ n [U] (fml) calmness

compound¹ /'kɒmpaʊnd/ n 1 thing made up of two or more parts 2 (chem) substance formed by a chemical reaction of two or more elements 3 (gram) word made up of two or more words, eg travel agent, dark-haired 4 enclosed area with buildings, etc: a prison ~ ● **compound** adj (tech) formed of two or more parts ■ ,compound 'interest n [U] interest(4) paid on both the original amount of money and on the interest added to it

compound² /kəm'paʊnd/ v [T] (fml) 1 make sth become even worse 2 mix sth together (tech)

comprehend /ˌkɒmprɪ'hend/ v [T] (fml) understand sth fully

comprehension /ˌkɒmprɪ'henʃn/ n 1 [U] ability to understand sth 2 [C] exercise that trains students to understand a language: a reading/ listening ~ ▶ **comprehensible** /-'hensəbl/ adj that can be understood by sb

comprehensive /ˌkɒmprɪ'hensɪv/ adj 1 including (nearly) everything: a ~ description 2 (GB) (of education) for pupils of all abilities in the same school ● **comprehensive** (also **compre'hensive school**) n (in Britain) large secondary school which teaches pupils of all abilities

compress /kəm'pres/ v [T] 1 force sth into a small(er) space; press sth together 2 put ideas, etc into fewer words ▶ **compression** /-'preʃn/ n [U]

comprise /kəm'praɪz/ v [T] have sth/sb as parts or members; be composed of sb/sth

compromise /'kɒmprəmaɪz/ n [C, U] settling of an argument by which each side gives up sth it had asked for ● **compromise** v 1 [I] make a compromise 2 [T] put sb/sth into a dangerous or embarrassing position

compulsion /kəm'pʌlʃn/ n 1 [U,C] strong pressure that makes sb do sth they do not want to do 2 [C] strong desire to do sth

compulsive /kəm'pʌlsɪv/ adj 1 (of behaviour) that is difficult to stop or control: ~ eating/spending 2 (of people) not being able to control their behaviour: a ~ liar 3 that makes you pay attention to it because it is so interesting and exciting: *The programme makes ~ viewing.*

compulsory /kəm'pʌlsəri/ *adj* that must be done; required by the law, etc

compunction /kəm'pʌŋkʃn/ *n* [U] (*fml*) feeling of guilt

compute /kəm'pju:t/ *v* [T] (*fml*) calculate ▶ **computation** /ˌkɒmpju-'teɪʃn/ *n* [C,U] act or process of calculating sth

computer /kəm'pju:tə(r)/ *n* electronic device that can store, organize and find information, do calculations and control other machines ▶ **computerize** (*also* **-ise**) *v* [T] 1 provide a computer to do the work of sth 2 store information on a computer: *~ized records* ■ **computerization** (*also* **-isation**) /kəmˌpju:tərar-'zeɪʃn/ *n* [U] ■ **com,puter-'literate** *adj* able to use computers well

comrade /'kɒmreɪd/ *n* person who is a member of the same communist or socialist political party as the speaker ▶ **comradeship** *n* [U]

Con *abbr* (in British politics) Conservative

con /kɒn/ *v* (-**nn**-) [T] (*infml*) trick sb ● **con** *n* (*infml*) trick: *He's a real ~ artist* (= someone who regularly cheats others). ■ **'con man** *n* (*infml*) man who tricks others into giving him their money, etc

concave /'kɒnkeɪv/ *adj* curved inwards

conceal /kən'si:l/ *v* [T] hide sb/sth ▶ **concealment** *n* [U] (*fml*)

concede /kən'si:d/ *v* 1 [T] admit that sth is true 2 [T] give sth away, esp unwillingly; allow sb to have sth 3 [I, T] admit that you have lost a game, etc

conceit /kən'si:t/ *n* [U] too high an opinion of yourself ▶ **conceited** *adj*

conceive /kən'si:v/ *v* [I, T] 1 ~ (**of**) form an idea, etc in your mind; imagine sth 2 become pregnant ▶ **conceivable** *adj* that you can imagine ▶ **conceivably** *adv*

concentrate /'kɒnsntreɪt/ *v* 1 [I] ~ (**on**) give your full attention to sth: *~ on your work* 2 [T] bring sth together in one place 3 [T] (*tech*) increase the strength of a substance by reducing its volume ● **concentrate** *n* [C,U] substance or liquid that is made stronger because water or other substances have been removed

concentration /ˌkɒnsn'treɪʃn/ *n* 1 [U] ability to give your full attention to sth 2 [U] ~ (**on**) process of people directing their full attention to a particular thing 3 [C] ~ (**of**) a lot of

sth in one place ■ **concen'tration camp** *n* prison for political prisoners

concentric /kən'sentrɪk/ *adj* (of circles) having the same centre

concept /'kɒnsept/ *n* general idea

conception /kən'sepʃn/ *n* 1 [U] process of forming an idea or a plan 2 [C,U] understanding or belief of what sth is 3 [U,C] act of conceiving(2)

concern /kən'sɜ:n/ *v* [T] 1 involve sb; affect sb 2 be about sth 3 worry sb: *I'm ~ed about her safety.* 4 ~ **yourself with/about sth** take an interest in sth [IDM] **as/so far as I am concerned** → FAR¹ ▶ **concerning** *prep* (*fml*) about sth; involving sb/sth ● **concern** *n* 1 [U,C] worry 2 [C] something that is important to sb 3 [C] business or company: *a profitable ~*

concert /'kɒnsət/ *n* musical performance: *Oasis in ~ at Wembley Arena* [IDM] **in concert with sb/sth** (*fml*) working together with sb/sth

concerted /kən'sɜ:tɪd/ *adj* arranged or done by people working together: *make a ~ effort*

concertina /ˌkɒnsə'ti:nə/ *n* musical instrument like a small accordion ▶ **concertina** *v* [i] fold up by being pressed together from each end

concerto /kən'tʃɜ:təʊ/ *n* (*pl* **~s**) musical composition for one instrument supported by an orchestra

concession /kən'seʃn/ *n* 1 [C,U] something that you allow or do, or allow sb to have, in order to end an argument, etc 2 [U] act of conceding 3 [C, *usu pl*] (*GB*) reduction in the amount of money that has to be paid; ticket sold at a reduced price to a particular group of people: *Adults £2.50, ~s £2, family £5* 4 [C] special right given to sb to do sth: *a ~ to drill for oil*

conciliate /kən'sɪlieɪt/ *v* [T] (*fml*) make sb less angry or more pleasant ▶ **conciliation** /kənˌsɪli'eɪʃn/ *n* [U] ▶ **conciliatory** /kən'sɪliətəri/ *adj* having the intention or effect of making angry people calm

concise /kən'saɪs/ *adj* giving a lot of information in a few words ▶ **concisely** *adv* ▶ **conciseness** *n* [U]

conclude /kən'klu:d/ *v* 1 [T] come to believe sth as a result of what you have heard or seen: *The report ~d that the road should be closed to traffic.* 2 [I, T] (*fml*) come or bring sth to an end 3 [T] arrange and settle an agreement with sb formally ▶ **conclusion** /kən'klu:ʒn/ *n* 1 decision; settlement 2 end of sth ▶ **conclusive** /kən'klu:sɪv/ *adj* proving sth and allowing no doubt: *~ evidence* ▶ **conclusively** *adv*

concoct /kən'kɒkt/ *v* [T] 1 make

C

sth, esp food or drink, by mixing several things together **2** invent a story, an excuse, etc ► **concoction** /kənˈkɒkʃn/ n strange or unusual mixture of things, esp drinks or medicines

concord /ˈkɒŋkɔːd/ n [U] (fml) agreement or harmony

concourse /ˈkɒŋkɔːs/ n large open part of a public building, esp an airport or a train station

concrete /ˈkɒŋkriːt/ adj **1** made of concrete: a ~ wall/floor **2** based on facts, not on ideas or guesses **3** existing in material form; that can be touched, etc ● **concrete** n [U] building material made by mixing cement with sand, gravel, etc ● **concrete** v [T] cover sth with concrete

concur /kənˈkɜː(r)/ v (-rr-) [I] (fml) agree ► **concurrence** /kənˈkʌrəns/ n [U, sing] agreement **2** [sing] example of two or more things happening at the same time ► **concurrent** /kənˈkʌrənt/ adj existing or happening at the same time ► **concurrently** adv

concuss /kənˈkʌs/ v [T] hit sb on the head, making them unconscious or confused for a short time ► **concussion** /kənˈkʌʃn/ n [U]

condemn /kənˈdem/ v [T] **1** say that you disapprove of sb/sth **2** ~to (law) say what sb's punishment will be: He was ~ed to death. **3** ~to make sb accept sth unpleasant: ~ed to a job she hates **4** say officially that a building, etc is unfit for use ► **condemnation** /ˌkɒndemˈneɪʃn/ n [U, C]

condense /kənˈdens/ v **1** [I, T] (cause a gas) to change into a liquid **2** [I, T] (cause a liquid) to become thicker and stronger because it has lost some of its water **3** [T] put sth into fewer words: a speech ► **condensation** /ˌkɒndenˈseɪʃn/ n [U] **1** drops of liquid formed on a cool surface when warm water vapour condenses **2** process of a gas changing to a liquid ► **condenser** n

condescend /ˌkɒndɪˈsend/ v [T] ~(to) (disapprov) do sth that you think is below your social or professional position to do ► **condescending** adj ► **condescension** /ˌkɒndɪˈsenʃn/ n [U]

condiment /ˈkɒndɪmənt/ n seasoning, eg salt or pepper

condition /kənˈdɪʃn/ n **1** [U, sing] what sth is like; state of sth: a car in good ~ **2** [U, sing] state of sb's health or physical fitness: be out of ~ **3** [C] illness or medical problem: He has a heart ~. **4** (**conditions**) [pl] circumstances **5** [C] rule or decision that you must agree to, esp as part of an agreement or contract: They agreed to lend

us the car on ~ that (= only if) we returned it the next day. **6** [C] situation that must exist in order for sth else to happen: One of the ~s of the job is that you can drive. ● **condition** v [T] **1** train sb/sth to behave or think in a certain way **2** have an important effect on sb/sth; influence the way sth happens ► **conditioner** n [C, U] liquid that makes hair healthy and shiny after washing ► **conditioning** n [U]

conditional /kənˈdɪʃənl/ adj **1** ~(on) depending on sth: Payment is ~ on satisfactory completion of the work. **2** (gram) (of a clause) beginning with if or unless ► **conditionally** /-ʃənəli/ adv

condolence /kənˈdəʊləns/ n [C, usu pl, U] expression of sympathy

condom /ˈkɒndɒm/ n rubber covering worn by a man on his penis during sex, as a contraceptive

condone /kənˈdəʊn/ v [T] accept behaviour that is morally wrong as if it were not serious

conducive /kənˈdjuːsɪv/ adj ~to (written) allowing or helping sth to happen

conduct¹ /kənˈdʌkt/ v [T] **1** organize and do a particular activity: ~ a survey **2** [I, T] direct a group of people who are singing or playing music **3** [T] lead or guide sb through or around a place **4** ~yourself (fml) behave in a certain way **5** [T] allow heat, electricity, etc to pass along or through sth ► **conduction** /kənˈdʌkʃn/ n [U] conducting of heat or electricity ► **conductor** n **1** person who conducts an orchestra, etc **2** (GB) person who sells tickets on a bus **3** substance that conducts heat or electricity

conduct² /ˈkɒndʌkt/ n [U] **1** behaviour: The sport has a strict code of ~. **2** way in which a business or an activity is organized and managed

cone /kəʊn/ n **1** solid body that narrows to a point from a circular flat base **2** solid or hollow object that is shaped like a cone: an ice-cream ~ **3** fruit of certain evergreen trees, eg fir or pine

confection /kənˈfekʃn/ n (fml) cake or other sweet food that looks very attractive ► **confectioner** /kənˈfekʃənə(r)/ n person who makes and sells sweets and cakes ► **confectionery** n [U] (written) sweets, cakes, etc

confederacy /kənˈfedərəsi/ n [sing] union of states, groups of people or political parties with the same aim

confederate /kənˈfedərət/ n person who helps sb, esp to do sth illegal or secret

confederation /kənˌfedəˈreɪʃn/ n organization of countries, businesses, etc that have joined together to help each other

confer /kənˈfɜː(r)/ v (-rr-) (*fml*) **1** [I] ~ (**with**) discuss sth with sb **2** [T] ~ (**on**) give sb an award, a university degree or a particular honour or right

conference /ˈkɒnfərəns/ n **1** large official meeting, usu lasting for a few days, at which people with the same work or interests come together for discussion or exchange of opinions **2** meeting at which people have formal discussions: *He was in ~ with his lawyers all day.*

confess /kənˈfes/ v [I, T] **1** admit, esp formally or to the police, that you have sth done wrong or illegal **2** admit sth that you feel ashamed or embarrassed about **3** (esp in the Roman Catholic Church) tell your sins formally to a priest ▸ **confession** /kənˈfeʃn/ n [C,U] **1** statement admitting that you have done sth wrong **2** telling of your sins to a priest ▸ **confessional** /kənˈfeʃənl/ n private enclosed place in a church where a priest hears confessions

confetti /kənˈfeti/ n [U] small pieces of coloured paper thrown at weddings

confidant (*fem* **confidante**) /ˈkɒnfɪdænt; ˌkɒnfɪˈdɑːnt/ n person that you trust and who you talk to about private or secret things

confide /kənˈfaɪd/ v [T] tell secrets and personal information that you do not want others to know [PV] **confide in sb** tell sb secrets, etc because you feel you can trust them

confidence /ˈkɒnfɪdəns/ n **1** [U] ~ (**in**) firm trust in the abilities or good qualities of sb/sth: *I have every ~ in her ability.* **2** [U] belief in your own ability to do things and be successful **3** [U] feeling that you are certain about sth **4** [U] feeling of trust that sb will keep information private: *He told me this in the strictest ~.* **5** [C] (*fml*) secret that you tell sb [IDM] **take sb into your confidence** tell sb a secret ▸ **confident** /ˈkɒnfɪdənt/ *adj* very sure ▸ **confidently** *adv*

confidential /ˌkɒnfɪˈdenʃl/ *adj* **1** meant to be kept secret **2** trusted with secrets ▸ **confidentiality** /ˌkɒnfɪˌdenʃiˈæləti/ n [U] ▸ **confidentially** /-ˈdenʃəli/ *adv*

configuration /kənˌfɪɡəˈreɪʃn/ n **1** (*fml*) arrangement of the parts of sth **2** (*computing*) equipment and programs that form a computer system and the way these are set up to run

confine /kənˈfaɪn/ v [T] **1** ~ (**to**) keep sb/sth within certain limits: *The ill-*

ness was ~d to the village. **2** keep sb shut in: ~d to bed with a fever ▸ **confined** *adj* (of space) limited; restricted ▸ **confinement** n [U] state of being shut in a closed space, prison, etc; act of putting sb there ▸ **confines** /ˈkɒnfaɪnz/ n [pl] (*fml*) limits; borders

confirm /kənˈfɜːm/ v [T] **1** show or say that sth is true: *The announcement ~ed my suspicions.* **2** say or write that sth is definite: *Please write to ~ the details.* **3** (usu passive) make sb a full member of the Christian Church ▸ **confirmation** /ˌkɒnfəˈmeɪʃn/ n [C,U] ▸ **confirmed** *adj* unlikely to change: *a ~ed bachelor*

confiscate /ˈkɒnfɪskeɪt/ v [T] officially take sth away from sb, esp as a punishment ▸ **confiscation** /ˌkɒnfɪˈskeɪʃn/ n [C,U]

conflagration /ˌkɒnfləˈɡreɪʃn/ n (*fml*) large and destructive fire

conflict /ˈkɒnflɪkt/ n [C,U] **1** struggle, fight or serious disagreement **2** (of opinions, etc) opposition; difference ▸ **conflict** /kənˈflɪkt/ v [I] be in opposition

conform /kənˈfɔːm/ v [I] **1** ~ (**to**) keep to generally accepted rules, standards, etc **2** ~ **with/to** agree with sth ▸ **conformist** n person who conforms ▸ **conformity** n [U]

confront /kənˈfrʌnt/ v [T] **1** ~ (**with**) make sb face sth unpleasant or difficult **2** meet sb face to face; oppose sb ▸ **confrontation** /ˌkɒnfrʌnˈteɪʃn/ n [U,C] (instance of) angry opposition between two or more people

confuse /kənˈfjuːz/ v [T] **1** make sb unable to think clearly **2** mistake sb/sth for sb/sth else: *Don't ~ quality with quantity.* **3** make sth unclear ▸ **confusion** /kənˈfjuːʒn/ n [U]

congeal /kənˈdʒiːl/ v [I] (of blood, fat, etc) become thick and solid

congenial /kənˈdʒiːniəl/ *adj* **1** pleasant: *a ~ atmosphere* **2** having similar interests ▸ **congenially** *adv*

congenital /kənˈdʒenɪtl/ *adj* (of a disease or medical condition) present from or before birth

congested /kənˈdʒestɪd/ *adj* too full; overcrowded: *streets ~ with traffic* ▸ **congestion** /kənˈdʒestʃən/ n [U]

conglomerate /kənˈɡlɒmərət/ n (*business*) large business organization consisting of several different firms ▸ **conglomeration** /kənˌɡlɒməˈreɪʃn/ n mixture of different things that are found all together

congratulate /kənˈɡrætʃuleɪt/ v [T] tell sb you are pleased about their success or achievements: ~ *sb on good exam results* ▸ **congratulations** /kənˌɡrætʃuˈleɪʃnz/ *exclam* used for congratulating sb

congregate /'kɒŋgrɪgeɪt/ v [I] come together in a group ▶ **congregation** /ˌkɒŋgrɪ'geɪʃn/ n group of people who regularly attend a church ▶ **congregational** adj

congress /'kɒŋgres/ n [C, with sing or pl verb] **1** large formal meeting for discussion **2** (**Congress**) (in the US, etc) group of people elected to make laws ▶ **congressional** /kən-'greʃənl/ adj ● '**Congressman**, '**Congresswoman** n member of the US Congress

congruent /'kɒŋgruənt/ adj (of triangles) having the same size and shape

conical /'kɒnɪkl/ adj shaped like a cone

conifer /'kɒnɪfə(r); 'kəʊn-/ n tree, eg pine or fir, that produces hard dry fruit (**cones**) ▶ **coniferous** /kə-'nɪfərəs/ adj

conjecture /kən'dʒektʃə(r)/ v [I, T] (fml) guess sth ● **conjecture** n [U, C] (fml) guessing ▶ **conjectural** adj

conjugal /'kɒndʒəgl/ adj (fml) of the relationship between a husband and wife

conjunction /kən'dʒʌŋkʃn/ n **1** (gram) word, eg and, but or or that joins words, phrases or sentences **2** (fml) combination of events, etc that causes a particular result [IDM] **in conjunction with** (fml) together with

conjure /'kʌndʒə(r)/ v [I] do clever tricks that appear magical [PV] **conjure sth up** cause sth to appear as a picture in the mind ▶ **conjuror** (also **-er**) n person who performs conjuring tricks

conk /kɒŋk/ [PV] **conk out** (infml) **1** (of a machine) stop working: His old car has ~ed out. **2** (esp US) (of a person) fall asleep

connect /kə'nekt/ v **1** [I, T] come or bring two or more things together; join sth: ~ two wires **2** [I, T] (cause sb/sth to) have a link with sth/sb: be ~ed by marriage ◇ There's nothing to ~ him with the crime.

connection (GB **connexion**) /kə-'nekʃn/ n **1** [C] something that connects two facts, ideas, etc **2** [U] act of connecting or state of being connected **3** [C] train, aircraft, etc that takes passengers on the next stage of their journey **4** [C, usu pl] person you know who can help or advise you in your social or professional life: He's one of my business ~s. [IDM] **in connection with sb/sth** for reasons connected with sb/sth

connive /kə'naɪv/ v [I] (disapprov) **1** ~ **at** seem to allow sth wrong to happen **2** work with sb to do sth wrong or illegal ▶ **connivance** n [U]

connoisseur /ˌkɒnə'sɜː(r)/ n expert, eg on food or art

connotation /ˌkɒnə'teɪʃn/ n idea or quality suggested by a word in addition to its main meaning: negative ~s

conquer /'kɒŋkə(r)/ v [T] **1** take control of a country, city, etc by force **2** defeat sb or overcome sth ▶ **conqueror** n

conquest /'kɒŋkwest/ n **1** [U] conquering, eg of a country or people **2** [C] something gained by conquering

conscience /'kɒnʃəns/ n [C,U] sense of right and wrong: have a clear/guilty ~ (= feel that you have done right/wrong) [IDM] **on your conscience** making you feel guilty for doing or failing to do sth

conscientious /ˌkɒnʃi'enʃəs/ adj (of a person or their actions) very careful ▶ **conscientiously** adv ▶ **conscientiousness** n [U]

conscious /'kɒnʃəs/ adj **1** awake **2** ~(**of**) aware of sth **3** intentional: make a ~ effort ▶ **consciously** adv ▶ **consciousness** n [U]: regain ~ness after an accident

conscript /kən'skrɪpt/ v [T] force sb by law to serve in the armed forces ▶ **conscript** /'kɒnskrɪpt/ n person who has been conscripted ▶ **conscription** /kən'skrɪpʃn/ n [U]

consecrate /'kɒnsɪkreɪt/ v [T] **1** officially declare sth to be holy or sb to be a priest: ~ a church **2** reserve sth for a special (esp religious) purpose ▶ **consecration** /ˌkɒnsɪ'kreɪʃn/ n [U]

consecutive /kən'sekjətɪv/ adj coming one after the other without interruption ▶ **consecutively** adv

consensus /kən'sensəs/ n [C,U] general opinion

consent /kən'sent/ v [I] ~(**to**) give agreement to or permission for sth ▶ **consent** n [U] agreement; permission

consequence /'kɒnsɪkwəns/ n **1** [C] result or effect: the political ~s of the decision **2** [U] (fml) importance: It is of no ~.

consequent /'kɒnsɪkwənt/ adj (fml) following as a result ▶ **consequently** adv therefore

consequential /ˌkɒnsɪ'kwenʃl/ adj (fml) **1** consequent **2** important

conservation /ˌkɒnsə'veɪʃn/ n [U] **1** (fml) protection of the natural environment **2** prevention of loss, waste, etc: ~ of energy ▶ **conservationist** n person interested in protecting the natural environment

conservative /kən'sɜːvətɪv/ adj **1** opposed to great or sudden change **2** (**Conservative**) of the Conservative Party **3** cautious; moderate:

a ~ estimate ● **conservative** *n*
1 conservative person **2** (**Conservative**) member of the Conservative Party ▶ **conservatively** *adv* ■ **the Conservative Party** *n* [sing, with sing or pl verb] one of the main British political parties, on the political right, which supports capitalism ▶ **conservatism** /kənˈsɜːvətɪzəm/ *n* [U]

conservatory /kənˈsɜːvətri/ *n* (*pl -ies*) **1** (*GB*) room with glass walls and roof that is built at the side of a house for growing plants in, etc **2** (*esp US*) school of music, drama, etc

conserve /kənˈsɜːv/ *v* [T] prevent sth from being changed, lost or destroyed ● **conserve** /ˈkɒnsɜːv/ *n* [C,U] (*fml*) jam, with quite large pieces of fruit

consider /kənˈsɪdə(r)/ *v* [T] **1** think about sth carefully **2** think of sb/sth in a particular way: *We ~ this (to be) very important.* **3** take sth into account: *~ the feelings of others* ▶ **considered** *adj* as a result of careful thought: *a ~ed opinion*

considerable /kənˈsɪdərəbl/ *adj* great in amount or size ▶ **considerably** /kənˈsɪdərəbli/ *adv* (*fml*) much; a lot: *It's considerably colder today.*

considerate /kənˈsɪdərət/ *adj* kind and thinking of the needs of others ▶ **considerately** *adv*

consideration /kənˌsɪdəˈreɪʃn/ *n* **1** [U] careful thought **2** [C] something that must be thought about, esp when deciding sth: *Cost is just one of the ~s.* **3** [U] quality of being thoughtful towards others **4** [C] (*fml*) reward; payment [IDM] **take sth into consideration** think about and include a particular thing or fact when forming an opinion or making a decision

considering /kənˈsɪdərɪŋ/ *prep, conj* used to show that you are thinking about and are influenced by a particular fact when you make a statement about sth: *She's very active, ~ her age.*

consign /kənˈsaɪn/ *v* (*fml*) [T] put sth/sb somewhere in order to get rid of them: *~ the letter to the wastepaper basket* **2** give or send sth to sb ▶ **consignment** *n* [C] quantity of goods sent or delivered somewhere **2** [U] act of sending or delivering

consist /kənˈsɪst/ *v* [I] [PV] **consist in sth** have sth as the main or only part **consist of sth** be made up of sth: *a meal ~ing of soup and bread*

consistency /kənˈsɪstənsi/ *n* (*pl -ies*) *n* **1** [U] quality of being consistent(1) **2** [C,U] degree of thickness, smoothness, etc, esp of a liquid

consistent /kənˈsɪstənt/ *adj* **1** (*approv*) always behaving in the same way, having the same opinions, standards, etc **2** ~(**with**) in agreement: *injuries ~ with the accident* ▶ **consistently** *adv*

consolation /ˌkɒnsəˈleɪʃn/ *n* [U,C] person or thing that makes you feel better when you are unhappy

console[1] /kənˈsəʊl/ *v* [T] give sb comfort or sympathy

console[2] /ˈkɒnsəʊl/ *n* panel for the controls of electronic equipment

consolidate /kənˈsɒlɪdeɪt/ *v* [I, T] **1** become or make sth stronger, more secure, etc **2** (*tech*) join things together or become joined into one: *~ all his debts* ▶ **consolidation** /kənˌsɒlɪˈdeɪʃn/ *n* [U]

consommé /kənˈsɒmeɪ/ *n* [U] clear meat soup

consonant /ˈkɒnsənənt/ *n* **1** speech sound made by (partly) stopping the breath with the tongue, lips, etc **2** letter of the alphabet that represents a consonant sound, eg *b*, *c* and *d*

consort /ˈkɒnsɔːt/ *n* husband or wife, esp of a ruler ● **consort** /kənˈsɔːt/ *v* [I] ~**with** (*fml*) spend time with sb that others disapprove of: *~ing with criminals*

consortium /kənˈsɔːtiəm/ *n* (*pl -s* or **-tia** /-tiə/) [C, with sing or pl verb] group of businesses, banks, etc with a common purpose

conspicuous /kənˈspɪkjuəs/ *adj* easily seen; noticeable ▶ **conspicuously** *adv*

conspiracy /kənˈspɪrəsi/ *n* (*pl -ies*) [C,U] secret plan by a group of people to do sth harmful or illegal

conspire /kənˈspaɪə(r)/ *v* [I] **1** ~ (**with; against**) secretly plan with other people to do sth harmful or illegal: *He ~d with others against the government.* **2** ~**against** (*written*) (of events) seem to work together to make sth bad happen: *Circumstances ~d against them.* ▶ **conspirator** /kənˈspɪrətə(r)/ *n* person who conspires

constable /ˈkʌnstəbl/ *n* = POLICE CONSTABLE ▶ **constabulary** /kənˈstæbjələri/ *n* [C, with sing or pl verb] (*pl -ies*) (in Britain) police force of a particular area

constant /ˈkɒnstənt/ *adj* **1** continuing all the time: *~ noise* **2** not changing: *a ~ temperature* ▶ **constancy** *n* [U] state of being constant(2)

constellation /ˌkɒnstəˈleɪʃn/ *n* group of stars with a name

consternation /ˌkɒnstəˈneɪʃn/ *n* [U] feeling of surprise, fear and worry

constipated /ˈkɒnstɪpeɪtɪd/ *adj* not able to empty waste matter from the bowels easily ▶ **constipation** /ˌkɒnstɪˈpeɪʃn/ n [U]

constituency /kənˈstɪtjuənsi/ n [C, with sing or pl verb] (pl **-ies**) (in Britain) (voters living in an) area that sends a representative to Parliament

constituent /kənˈstɪtjuənt/ adj **1** being part of a whole **2** (of an assembly, etc) having the power or right to alter a political constitution ● **constituent** n **1** member of a constituency **2** part of a whole

constitute /ˈkɒnstɪtjuːt/ linking verb **1** be considered to be sth: The decision to build the road ~s a real threat to the countryside. **2** be the parts that together form sth: Twelve months ~ a year.

constitution /ˌkɒnstɪˈtjuːʃn/ n **1** set of laws and principles according to which a country is governed **2** person's physical structure and condition: a strong ~ **3** general structure of sth ▶ **constitutional** adj conforming to the laws, etc by which a country is governed ▶ **constitutionally** adv

constrain /kənˈstreɪn/ v [T] (fml) **1** make sb do sth by force or strong persuasion: I felt ~ed to obey. **2** restrict or limit sth/sb

constraint /kənˈstreɪnt/ n **1** [C] thing that limits or restricts sth, or your freedom to do sth: One of the ~s on the project will be the money available. **2** [U] strict control over the way you behave

constrict /kənˈstrɪkt/ v **1** [I, T] become or make sth tighter, smaller or narrower: Her throat ~ed and she swallowed hard. **2** [T] limit or restrict what sb is allowed to do ▶ **constriction** /kənˈstrɪkʃn/ n [U,C]

construct /kənˈstrʌkt/ v [T] build sth or put sth together

construction /kənˈstrʌkʃn/ n **1** [U] way or act of building sth: The new bridge is still under ~. **2** [C] (fml) structure; building **3** [C] way in which words are put together and arranged to form a sentence, phrase, etc: grammatical ~s

constructive /kənˈstrʌktɪv/ adj helpful; useful: ~ suggestions ▶ **constructively** adv

consul /ˈkɒnsl/ n official sent by his/her government to live in a foreign country and help people from his/her own country who are living there ▶ **consular** /ˈkɒnsjələ(r)/ adj of a consul or his/her work ▶ **consulate** /ˈkɒnsjələt/ n consul's office

consult /kənˈsʌlt/ v **1** [T] go to a person, book, etc for information, advice or help: ~ the doctor about a sore throat **2** [I, T] ~ **with** sb discuss sth with sb to get their permission for sth or to help you make a decision:

You should have ~ed me before going ahead.

consultant /kənˈsʌltənt/ n **1** person who is paid to give expert advice **2** (GB) senior hospital doctor who specializes in a particular branch of medicine

consultation /ˌkɒnslˈteɪʃn/ n **1** [U] act of discussing sth with sb before making a decision about it **2** [C] meeting with an expert, esp a doctor, to get advice or treatment

consume /kənˈsjuːm/ v [T] **1** use sth: Some types of car ~ less petrol than others. **2** (fml) eat or drink sth **3** ~(**with**) fill sb with a strong feeling: She was ~d with guilt. **4** (of fire, etc) destroy sth ▶ **consuming** adj very strong

consumer /kənˈsjuːmə(r)/ n person who buys goods ■ **con,sumer durables** n [pl] (business) goods expected to last for a long time, such as cars, televisions, etc ■ **con'sumer goods** n [pl] goods bought by individual customers, such as food, clothes, etc

consummate¹ /ˈkɒnsəmət; ˈkɒnsəmət/ adj (fml) very skilled; perfect

consummate² /ˈkɒnsəmeɪt/ v [T] (fml) **1** make a marriage or relationship complete by having sex **2** make sth perfect ▶ **consummation** /ˌkɒnsəˈmeɪʃn/ n [C,U]

consumption /kənˈsʌmpʃn/ n [U] act of using food, resources, etc amount used: This food is not fit for human ~. ◇ measure a car's fuel ~

contact /ˈkɒntækt/ n **1** [U] act of communicating with sb, esp regularly: Stay in ~ with your parents. **2** [U] state of touching sth: This substance should not come into ~ with food. **3** [C, usu pl] instance of meeting or communicating with sb: a job involving ~s with other companies **4** [C] person that you know, esp sb who can be helpful to you in your work: He has several ~s in the building trade. **5** [C] electrical connection ● **contact** v [T] communicate with sb, eg by telephone or letter: Where can I ~ you next week? ■ '**contact lens** n thin piece of plastic that you put on your eye to help you see better

contagion /kənˈteɪdʒən/ n [U] spreading of disease by being close to or touching other people ▶ **contagious** /kənˈteɪdʒəs/ adj **1** (of a disease) spread by people touching each other: Scarlet fever is highly ~. ◇ (fig) a ~ laugh **2** (of a person) having a disease that can be spread to others by touch

contain /kənˈteɪn/ v [T] **1** have or hold sth inside: a bottle ~ing two litres of milk **2** (written) keep your feelings under control **3** (*written*) prevent sth harmful from spreading or getting worse: ~ *an epidemic*

container /kən'temnə(r)/ n **1** bottle, box, etc for holding sth: *a ~ for sugar* **2** large metal box, etc for transporting goods

contaminate /kən'tæmment/ v [T] make sth dirty or impure: *~d food* ▶ **contamination** /-'neɪʃn/ n [U]

contemplate /'kɒntəmpleɪt/ v [T] **1** think carefully about sth; consider doing sth: ~ *visiting London* **2** (*fml*) look at sth thoughtfully: *a picture to ~* ▶ **contemplation** /ˌkɒntəm'pleɪʃn/ n [U] act of contemplating sth; deep thought ▶ **contemplative** /kən-'templətɪv/ adj thoughtful

contemporary /kən'temprəri/ adj **1** belonging to the same time: *a play by Shakespeare accompanied by ~ music* **2** of the present time; modern ▶ **contemporary** n (pl **-ies**) person who lived or lives at the same time as another person: *Shakespeare and his contemporaries*

contempt /kən'tempt/ n [U] ~ (**for**) **1** feeling that sb/sth is of no value and cannot be respected: *feel ~ for people who are cruel to animals* **2** lack of respect for rules, danger, etc: *her ~ for the risks* ▶ **contemptible** /kən'temptəbl/ adj not deserving any respect at all ■ con**,tempt of 'court** n [U] crime of not obeying a court or judge: *He was in ~ of court.* ▶ **contemptuous** /kən'temptʃuəs/ adj feeling or showing contempt

contend /kən'tend/ v **1** [I,T] say that sth is true, esp in an argument: ~ *that the theory was wrong* **2** [I] compete against sb in order to gain sth [PV] **contend with sth** have to deal with a problem or difficult situation ▶ **contender** n person who tries to win sth in competition with others

content¹ /kən'tent/ adj satisfied; happy: ~ *to stay at home* ● **content** v [T] ~ **yourself** with sth be satisfied with sth ▶ **contented** adj satisfied ▶ **contentedly** adv ▶ **contentment** (*also* **content**) n [U] state of being content

content² /'kɒntent/ n **1** (**contents**) [pl] what is contained in sth: *the ~s of her bag* **2** (**contents**) [pl] list of chapters in a book **3** [sing] subject written or spoken about in a book, programme, etc **4** [sing] amount of sth contained in a substance, etc: *the silver ~ of a coin*

contention /kən'tenʃn/ n **1** [U] (*fml*) angry disagreement between people **2** [C] opinion expressed, esp in an argument ▶ **contentious** /kən'tenʃəs/ adj liking or causing argument

contest¹ /'kɒntest/ n fight; competition

contest² /kən'test/ v [T] **1** take part in and try to win a competition, etc: ~ *an election* **2** formally oppose a decision, etc because you think it is wrong ▶ **contestant** n person who takes part in a competition

context /'kɒntekst/ n [C,U] **1** situation in which an event happens **2** sentence, phrase, etc in which a word appears

continent /'kɒntɪnənt/ n **1** [C] one of the main land masses (Europe, Asia, Africa, etc) **2** (**the Continent**) [sing] (*GB*) the main part of the continent of Europe, not including Britain and Ireland ▶ **continental** /ˌkɒntɪ'nentl/ (*also* **Continental**) (*GB*) of or in the continent of Europe, not including Britain and Ireland: ~ *a holiday* **2** of or typical of a continent

contingency /kən'tɪndʒənsi/ n (pl **-ies**) event that may or may not happen: *make ~ plans*

contingent /kən'tɪndʒənt/ n [C, with sing or pl verb] **1** group of people at a meeting or an event who have sth in common **2** group of soldiers that are part of a larger force ● **contingent** adj ~ (**on/upon**) (*fml*) dependent on chance

continual /kən'tɪnjuəl/ adj happening all the time or very frequently: ~ *rain* ◇ ~ *interruptions* ▶ **continually** adv again and again; without stopping

continuation /kənˌtɪnju'eɪʃn/ n **1** [U,sing] act of continuing **2** [C] thing which continues beyond or extends something else: *This road is a ~ of the motorway.*

continue /kən'tɪnju:/ v **1** [I, T] (cause sth to) keep existing or happening without stopping: ~ *running* ◇ *She ~d her visits to the hospital.* **2** [I] go or move further in the same direction: ~ *up the hill* **3** [I] remain in a particular job or condition **4** [I, T] start (sth) again after stopping

continuity /ˌkɒntɪ'nju:əti/ n [U] **1** state of being continuous **2** logical connection between parts of a whole: *The story lacks ~.*

continuous /kən'tɪnjuəs/ adj going on without stopping: *a ~ line/ noise/flow* ▶ **continuously** adv ■ con**,tinuous tense** n (*gram*) phrase formed from part of the verb *be* and a verb ending in *-ing*, used to show an action that continues over a period of time, as in *I am singing.*

contort /kən'tɔ:t/ v [I, T] (cause sth to) become twisted out of its normal shape: *a face ~ed with pain* ▶ **contortion** /kən'tɔ:ʃn/ n [C,U]

contour /'kɒntʊə(r)/ n **1** outline of

a coast, a human figure, etc **2** (*also* '**contour line**') line on a map showing points that are the same height above sea level

contraband /ˈkɒntrəbænd/ *n* [U] goods brought illegally into or out of a country

contraception /ˌkɒntrəˈsepʃn/ *n* [U] preventing of pregnancy ► **contraceptive** /ˌkɒntrəˈseptɪv/ *n, adj* (device, drug, etc for) preventing pregnancy

contract¹ /ˈkɒntrækt/ *n* [C,U] official written agreement: *a ~ between buyer and seller* ◇ *The builder is under ~ to finish the house by the end of June.* ► **contractual** /kənˈtræktʃuəl/ *adj* of or in a contract

contract² /kənˈtrækt/ *v* **1** [I, T] (cause sth to) become less or smaller: *Metal ~s as it cools.* **2** [T] (*written*) catch a disease **3** [I, T] make a legal agreement with sb: *She's ~ed to work 35 hours a week.* [PV] **contract out (of sth)** (GB) agree not to take part in sth ► **contraction** /kənˈtrækʃn/ *n* **1** [U] process of becoming smaller **2** [C] tightening of the muscles around a woman's womb before birth **3** [C] (*ling*) short form of a word: *'Can't' is a ~ion of 'cannot'.*

contradict /ˌkɒntrəˈdɪkt/ *v* [T] **1** say that a person has said is wrong and that the opposite is true: *Don't ~ your mother.* **2** (of statements or pieces of evidence) be so different from each other that one of them must be wrong: *Her account ~s what you said.* ► **contradiction** *n* [C,U] ► **contradictory** *adj* not agreeing: *~ory accounts of the accident*

contraflow /ˈkɒntrəfləʊ/ *n* (GB) system used when one half of a large road is closed for repairs, and the traffic going in both directions has to use the other half

contralto /kənˈtræltəʊ/ *n* [C,U] = ALTO

contraption /kənˈtræpʃn/ *n* (*infml*) strange or complicated device

contrary¹ /ˈkɒntrəri/ *adj* ~(to) opposite; quite different: *~ to what you believe* ► **contrary** *n* (**the contrary**) [sing] the opposite: *The ~ is true.* [IDM] **on the contrary** used to introduce a statement that says the opposite of the last one: *'It must have been awful.' 'On the ~, I loved every minute.'* **to the contrary** showing or proving the opposite: *I shall continue to believe this until I get evidence to the ~.*

contrary² /kənˈtreəri/ *adj* (*fml*) (usu of children) behaving badly; doing the opposite of what is expected ► **contrariness** *n* [U]

contrast /kənˈtrɑːst/ *v* **1** [T] compare two things so that differences are made clear **2** [I] show a clear difference: *bright, ~ing colours* ● **contrast** /ˈkɒntrɑːst/ *n* [C,U] clear difference between two or more people or things

contravene /ˌkɒntrəˈviːn/ *v* [T] break a law, rule, etc ► **contravention** /ˌkɒntrəˈvenʃn/ *n* [C,U]

contretemps /ˈkɒntrətɒ̃/ (*pl* **contretemps**) *n* unfortunate event or embarrassing disagreement with sb

contribute /kənˈtrɪbjuːt; GB also ˈkɒntrɪbjuːt/ *v* **1** [I, T] ~(to/towards) join with others in giving help, money, ideas, etc **2** [I] ~to help to cause sth: *~ to her success* **3** [I, T] write articles, etc for newspapers, etc ► **contribution** /ˌkɒntrɪˈbjuːʃn/ *n* [C,U] ► **contributor** /kənˈtrɪbjətə(r)/ *n* person who contributes ► **contributory** /kənˈtrɪbjətəri/ *adj*

contrite /ˈkɒntraɪt; kənˈtraɪt/ *adj* (*fml*) very sorry for sth bad that you have done ► **contritely** *adv* ► **contrition** /kənˈtrɪʃn/ *n* [U]

contrive /kənˈtraɪv/ *v* [T] (*fml*) **1** find a way of doing sth: *~ to live on a small income* **2** invent, plan or design sth: *a way of avoiding paying tax* ► **contrivance** *n* **1** [C,U] something that sb has done or written that does not seem natural; fact of seeming artificial **2** [C] clever or complicated device or tool

control /kənˈtrəʊl/ *n* **1** [U] power to make decisions about how a country, an organization, etc is run: *A military junta took ~ of the country.* **2** [U] ability to make sb/sth do what you want: *She lost ~ of the car on the ice.* **3** [U,C] means of restricting, limiting or managing sth: *traffic ~* **4** [usu pl] means by which a machine, etc is operated or regulated **5** [C] (*tech*) standard of comparison for the results of an experiment [IDM] **be in control (of sth)** manage, direct or rule sth **be/get/run/etc out of control** be or become impossible to manage or to control: *The children are out of ~ since their father left.* **bring/get/keep sth under control** succeed in dealing with sth so that it does not cause any harm: *The fire was brought under ~.* ● **control** *v* (**-ll-**) [T] **1** have power or authority over sb/sth: *~ your temper* **2** limit sth or make it happen in a particular way: *drugs to ~ the pain* **3** make a machine or system work in the way that you want it to: *This dial ~s the volume.* ► **controller** *n* person who manages or directs sth, esp part of a large organization

controversy /ˈkɒntrəvɜːsi; GB also kənˈtrɒvəsi/ *n* (*pl* **-ies**) [C,U] public argument or debate about sth many

C

people do not agree with: ~ *over the site of the new airport* ▶ **controversial** /ˌkɒntrə'vɜːʃl/ *adj* causing controversy ▶ **controversially** *adv*

conundrum /kə'nʌndrəm/ *n* [C, usu sing] **1** confusing problem **2** question, usu involving a trick with words, asked for fun

conurbation /ˌkɒnɜː'beɪʃn/ *n* large urban area formed by several towns which have spread towards each other

convalesce /ˌkɒnvə'les/ *v* [I] become healthy and strong again after an illness ▶ **convalescence** *n* [sing, U] (period of) recovery from an illness ▶ **convalescent** *n, adj* (person who is) recovering from illness

convene /kən'viːn/ *v* [I, T] (arrange for people to) come together for a meeting, etc ▶ **convener** (*also* **-venor**) *n* person who arranges meetings

convenience /kən'viːniəns/ *n* **1** [U] quality of being useful, easy or suitable for sb **2** [C] device, tool, etc that is useful, suitable, etc: *Central heating is one of the ~s of modern houses.*

convenient /kən'viːniənt/ *adj* fitting in well with sb's needs; suitable: *a ~ place to stay* ▶ **conveniently** *adv*

convent /'kɒnvənt/ *n* building where a community of nuns lives

convention /kən'venʃn/ *n* **1** [C,U] general, usu unspoken, agreement on how people should behave: *social ~s* **2** [C] meeting of the members of a profession, political party, etc: *a scientists' ~* **3** [C] official agreement between countries or leaders ▶ **conventional** *adj* based on or following convention(1); normal and ordinary, and perhaps not very interesting ▶ **conventionally** *adv*

converge /kən'vɜːdʒ/ *v* [I] (of lines, moving objects) come towards each other and meet at a point: *a village where two roads ~* ▶ **convergence** *n* [U] ▶ **convergent** *adj*

conversant /kən'vɜːsnt/ *adj* ~ with having knowledge or experience of sth: *~ with modern methods*

conversation /ˌkɒnvə'seɪʃn/ *n* [C, U] informal talk involving a small group of people or only two; activity of talking in this way: *I had a long ~ with her yesterday.* ◇ *He was deep in ~ with his boss.* ▶ **conversational** *adj* not formal; as used in conversation: *a ~ tone/style*

converse¹ /kən'vɜːs/ *v* [I] (*fml*) have a conversation with sb

converse² /'kɒnvɜːs/ *n* (**the converse**) *n* [sing] the opposite or reverse of a fact or statement ▶ **converse¹** *adj* ▶ **conversely** *adv*

conversion /kən'vɜːʃn/ *n* [C,U] (instance of) converting sb/sth: *the ~ of the barn into a house*

convert¹ /kən'vɜːt/ *v* [I, T] **1** (cause sth to) change from one form, use, etc to another: *~ a house into flats* **2** change or make sb change their religion or beliefs: *He ~ed to Islam.* ▶ **convertible** /kən'vɜːtəbl/ *adj* that can be changed to a different form or use ▶ **convertible** *n* car with a roof that can be folded down or removed

convert² /'kɒnvɜːt/ *n* person who has converted, esp to a different religion

convex /'kɒnveks/ *adj* curved outwards: *~ mirror*

convey /kən'veɪ/ *v* [T] **1** ~ (**to**) make feelings, ideas, etc known to sb: *She ~ed her fears to her friends.* **2** take, carry or transport sb/sth from one place to another: *goods ~ed by rail* ▶ **conveyance** *n* [C,U] (vehicle for) transporting ▶ **conveyancing** *n* [U] (*law*) branch of law concerned with moving property from one owner to another ▶ **conveyor** (*also* **-veyer**) *n* person or thing that conveys sth ● **con'veyor belt** *n* (eg in a factory) continuous moving band used for transporting products, etc

convict /kən'vɪkt/ *v* [T] (of a judge, court, etc) declare that sb is guilty of a crime: *She was ~ed of theft.* ● **convict** /'kɒnvɪkt/ *n* person who has been convicted and sent to prison

conviction /kən'vɪkʃn/ *n* [C,U] **1** (instance of the) convicting of a person for a crime **2** firm belief: *a ~ that what she said was true*

convince /kən'vɪns/ *v* [T] **1** ~ (**of**) make sb/yourself believe that sth is true: *You'll need to ~ them of your enthusiasm for the job.* **2** persuade sb to do sth ▶ **convincing** *adj* that makes sb believe that sth is true: *a convincing argument* ▶ **convincingly** *adv*

convivial /kən'vɪviəl/ *adj* cheerful and friendly: *a ~ person/evening* ▶ **conviviality** /kənˌvɪvi'æləti/ *n* [U]

convoluted /'kɒnvəluːtɪd/ *adj* **1** extremely complicated and difficult to follow **2** having many twists or curves

convolution /ˌkɒnvə'luːʃn/ *n* [C, usu pl] (*fml*) **1** thing that is very complicated and difficult follow: *the ~s of the plot* **2** twist; curve

convoy /'kɒnvɔɪ/ *n* group of vehicles or ships travelling together, esp when soldiers, etc travel with them for protection [IDM] **in convoy** (of travelling vehicles) as a group; together: *to drive in ~*

convulse /kən'vʌls/ *v* [I, T] (cause

sb to) make a violent shaking movement: *A violent shiver ~d him.* ▶ **convulsion** /kənˈvʌlʃn/ *n* [C] 1 [usu pl] sudden uncontrollable and violent body movement 2 sudden important change ● **convulsive** *adj*

coo /kuː/ *v* 1 [I] make a soft quiet sound like that of a dove 2 [T] say sth in a soft quiet voice ▶ **coo** *n*

cook /kʊk/ *v* 1 [I] prepare food by heating it: ~ *breakfast/dinner* 2 [i] (of food) be prepared by boiling, baking, frying, etc [IDM] **cook the books** (*infml*) change facts or figures dishonestly ● **cook** *n* person who cooks food ▶ **cooker** *n* device for cooking food by heating it ▶ **cookery** *n* [U] art or activity of preparing and cooking food ▶ **cooking** *n* [U] process of preparing and cooking food

cookie /ˈkʊki/ *n* 1 (*esp US*) biscuit 2 (*US, infml*) person: *a tough ~* 3 (*computing*) computer file with information in it that is sent to the central server each time sb uses a network or the Internet

cool[1] /kuːl/ *adj* 1 not hot or cold; fairly cold: *It feels ~ in the shade.* 2 calm; not excited: *stay ~ in spite of danger* 3 showing no interest, enthusiasm, etc: *He was ~ about the suggestion.* 4 used about a sum of money to emphasize how large it is 5 (*infml*) very good; fine ● **cool** *n* **the cool** [sing] cool air or place; coolness: *sitting in the ~* [IDM] **keep/lose your cool** (*infml*) remain/not remain calm ■ **cool-headed** *adj* not easily excited or worried; calm ▶ **coolly** *adv* **coolness** *n* [U]

cool[2] /kuːl/ *v* [I, T] ~ **(down/off)** become or make sth cooler: *Have a drink to ~ down.* [PV] **cool down/off** become calm or less excited

coop /kuːp/ *n* cage, esp for hens ● **coop** *v* [PV] **coop sb/sth up** confine sb/sth in a small space: *prisoners ~ed up in cells*

cooperate (*also* **co-operate**) /kəʊˈɒpəreɪt/ *v* [I] 1 work or act together to achieve sth: *They ~d on the project.* 2 be helpful by doing what sb asks you to do ▶ **cooperation** (*also* **co-operation**) /kəʊˌɒpəˈreɪʃn/ *n* [U] 1 acting or working together with a common purpose 2 willingness to be helpful ▶ **cooperative** (*also* **co-operative**) /kəʊˈɒpərətɪv/ *adj* 1 joint 2 willing to co-operate ● **cooperative** (*also* **co-operative**) *n* business that is owned and run by the people involved, and they share the profits

co-opt /kəʊˈɒpt/ *v* [T] make sb a member of a committee, etc by voting for them

coordinate[1] (*also* **co-ordinate**) /kəʊˈɔːdɪneɪt/ *v* [T] ~ **(with)** make actions,

limbs, etc work together: *~ efforts to get the project finished* ▶ **coordination** (*also* **co-ordination**) /kəʊˌɔːdɪˈneɪʃn/ *n* [U] ▶ **coordinator** (*also* **co-ordinator**) *n*

coordinate[2] (*also* **co-ordinate**) /kəʊˈɔːdɪnət/ *n* 1 [C] either of the two numbers or letters used to fix the position of a point on a map, etc 2 **(coordinates)** [pl] pieces of clothing in matching colours for wearing together

cop /kɒp/ *n* (*infml*) police officer ● **cop** *v* (**-pp-**) [T] (*sl*) receive sth unpleasant: *~ a bang on the head* [PV] **cop out (of sth)** (*infml*) avoid or stop doing sth because you are afraid, lazy, etc ■ **cop-out** *n* (*infml, disapprov*) act of or excuse for doing sth

cope /kəʊp/ *v* [I] ~ **(with)** deal successfully with sth difficult: *She couldn't ~with all her work.*

copier → COPY[2]

copious /ˈkəʊpiəs/ *adj* (*fml*) in large amounts: *I took ~ notes.* ▶ **copiously** *adv*

copper /ˈkɒpə(r)/ *n* 1 [U] (*symb* Cu) a chemical element. Copper is a soft reddish-brown metal: ~ *wire* ◊ *~-coloured hair* 2 **(coppers)** [pl] (*GB*) brown coins, of very low value 3 [C] (*GB, infml*) police officer

copse /kɒps/ *n* small area of shrubs and trees

copulate /ˈkɒpjuleɪt/ *v* [I] ~ **(with)** (*tech*) have sex ▶ **copulation** /ˌkɒpjuˈleɪʃn/ *n* [U]

copy[1] /ˈkɒpi/ *n* (*pl* **-ies**) 1 thing made to be like another, esp a reproduction of a letter, pictures, etc: *Put a ~ of the letter in the file.* 2 one example of a book, newspaper, etc of which many have been made: *The library has two copies of this book.* ■ **copycat** *n* (*infml, disapprov*) person who imitates another's behaviour, etc

copy[2] /ˈkɒpi/ *v* (*pt, pp* **-ied**) 1 [T] make sth that is exactly like sth else: *~ a document on the photocopier* 2 [T] write sth exactly as it is written somewhere else: *I copied out several poems.* 3 [T] behave or do sth in the same way as sb else: *She copies everything her sister does.* 4 [I] cheat in an exam, etc by copying what sb else has done, written, etc

copyright /ˈkɒpiraɪt/ *n* [U,C] author's legal right to print, publish and sell his/her work ▶ **copyright** *v* [T] get the copyright for sth

coral /ˈkɒrəl/ *n* [U] hard red, pink or white substance formed on the sea bed by small creatures: *a ~ reef* ● **coral** *adj* made of coral

cord /kɔːd/ *n* 1 [C,U] (piece of)

strong thick string or thin rope **2** [C, U] (esp US) = FLEX **3** [U] = CORDUROY

cordial /'kɔːdiəl/ adj (fml) warm and friendly ▸ **cordially** adv ● **cordial** n [U] (GB) non-alcoholic sweet drink: lime ~

cordon /'kɔːdn/ n ring or line of police officers, soldiers, etc guarding sth or stopping people entering or leaving an area: a police ~ ● **cordon** v [PV] **cordon sth off** stop people getting into an area by surrounding it with police, soldiers, etc: The army ~ed off the area.

corduroy /'kɔːdərɔɪ/ n [U] thick cotton cloth with soft ridged marks

core /kɔː(r)/ n **1** usu hard centre of some fruits, eg the apple **2** central or most important part of anything: the ~ of the problem [IDM] **to the core** completely: shocked to the ~ ● **core** v [T] take the core out of sth, eg an apple

cork /kɔːk/ n **1** [U] light springy bark from a type of oak tree: ~ table mats **2** [C] round piece of this used to seal bottles, esp wine bottles ● **cork** v [T] seal a bottle with a cork ■ **'corkscrew** n tool for pulling corks from bottles

corn /kɔːn/ n **1** [U] (GB) the grain of) any plant that is grown for its grain, such as wheat **2** [U] (US) = MAIZE **3** [C] small painful area of hard skin on the foot ■ **'corncob** n hard part at the top of a maize stalk on which the grains grow ▸ **'cornflour** n [U] flour made from maize ■ **corn on the 'cob** n corn that is cooked with all the parts still attached to the inner part and eaten as a vegetable

cornea /'kɔːniə/ n (anat) transparent protective covering of the eye

corned beef /ˌkɔːnd 'biːf/ n [U] beef preserved in salt

corner /'kɔːnə(r)/ n **1** place where two lines or surfaces meet **2** place where two streets join **3** region: from all ~s of the earth **4** (infml) difficult or awkward situation: get out of a tight ~ **5** (in sports such as football) free kick taken from the corner of your opponent's end of the field [IDM] **turn the corner** pass a very important point in an illness or a difficult situation and start to improve ● **corner** v **1** [T] trap a person or an animal: ~ed by the police **2** [I] turn a corner on a road, etc: a car designed for fast ~ing

cornet /'kɔːnɪt/ n **1** small musical instrument like a trumpet **2** cone-shaped container of thin biscuit for ice cream, etc

cornice /'kɔːnɪs/ n ornamental border around a ceiling or at the top of a column

corny /'kɔːni/ adj (-ier, -iest) (infml) not original; used too often to sound interesting or sincere

coronary /'kɒrənri/ adj (med) of the arteries carrying blood to the heart ■ **coronary throm'bosis** (also infml **coronary**) n (med) blocking of an artery in the heart by a clot of blood, often damaging the heart or causing death

coronation /ˌkɒrə'neɪʃn/ n ceremony of crowning a king or queen

coroner /'kɒrənə(r)/ n (GB) official whose job is to find the cause of any accidental or suspicious death by holding an inquest

coronet /'kɒrənet/ n small crown worn by princes, princesses, etc

corporal /'kɔːpərəl/ n (abbr **Cpl**) non-commissioned officer below the rank of sergeant in the army ● **corporal** adj involving physical punishment: ~ punishment

corporate /'kɔːpərət/ adj **1** of or belonging to a corporation(1) **2** of or shared by all the members of a group: ~ responsibility

corporation /ˌkɔːpə'reɪʃn/ n [C, with sing or pl verb] **1** large business or company **2** (GB) group of people elected to govern a town

corps /kɔː(r)/ n (pl **corps** /kɔːz/) **1** military force formed from part of the full army, etc **2** one of the technical branches of an army **3** group of people involved in a particular activity: the diplomatic ~

corpse /kɔːps/ n dead body, esp a human being

corpulent /'kɔːpjələnt/ adj (fml) fat

corpuscle /'kɔːpʌsl/ n (anat) one of the red or white cells in the blood

corral /kə'rɑːl/ n (in N America) fenced area for horses, cattle, etc on a farm or ranch ● **corral** v (-ll- US -l-) [T] force horses or cattle into a corral

correct¹ /kə'rekt/ adj **1** true; right; accurate: the ~ answer ◇ the ~ way to do it **2** (of manners, dress, etc) proper; decent ▸ **correctly** adv ▸ **correctness** n [U]

correct² /kə'rekt/ v [T] **1** make sth correct; remove the mistakes from sth: ~ sb's spelling **2** change sth so that it is accurate: glasses to ~ your eyesight ▸ **correction** /kə'rekʃn/ n **1** [C] change that corrects sth: ~ions written in red ink **2** [U] act of correcting sth ▸ **corrective** n, adj (something) that makes sth right

correlate /'kɒrəleɪt/ v [I, T] ~(with) (of two things) to be closely related or connected; show such a relation between two things: The results of the two tests do not ~. ▸ **correlation** /ˌkɒrə'leɪʃn/ n [C,U] connection between two things in which one thing changes as the other does

correspond /ˌkɒrəˈspɒnd/ v [I] 1 ~ (to/with) be the same or similar; be in agreement: *Your account doesn't ~ with hers.* 2 ~(with) (*fml*) exchange letters with sb ▸ **corresponding** adj ~(to) matching or connected with sth that you have just mentioned ▸ **correspondingly** adv

correspondence /ˌkɒrəˈspɒndəns/ n 1 [C,U] agreement; similarity: *a close ~ between the two texts* 2 [U] letter writing; letters ▸ **correspondent** n 1 person who reports for a newspaper, radio or TV station, usu from abroad 2 person who writes letters to another person

corridor /ˈkɒrɪdɔː(r)/ n long narrow passage from which doors open into rooms

corroborate /kəˈrɒbəreɪt/ v [T] confirm the correctness of a belief, statement, etc: *I can ~ what she said.* ▸ **corroboration** /kəˌrɒbəˈreɪʃn/ n [U]

corrode /kəˈrəʊd/ v [I, T] be destroyed or destroy sth slowly, esp by chemical action: *Acid ~s metal.* ▸ **corrosion** /kəˈrəʊʒn/ n [U] ▸ **corrosive** /kəˈrəʊsɪv/ n,adj (substance) that corrodes sth: *corrosive acid*

corrugated /ˈkɒrəɡeɪtɪd/ adj shaped into a series of regular folds that look like waves: ~ *iron*

corrupt /kəˈrʌpt/ adj 1 immoral: *a ~ society/mind* 2 dishonest, esp because of taking bribes: *a business deal* 3 (*computing*) containing changes or faults, and no longer in the original state: ~ *software* ● **corrupt** v [I, T] become or make sb/sth corrupt: ~*ing people* ▸ **corruption** /kəˈrʌpʃn/ n [U] ▸ **corruptly** adv

corset /ˈkɔːsɪt/ n piece of women's underwear worn esp in the past to make the waist look smaller

cortège (*esp US* **cortege**) /kɔːˈteʒ; ˈtɜːʒ/ n funeral procession

cosh /kɒʃ/ n (*GB*) length of pipe, rubber tubing filled with metal, etc used as a weapon

cosmetic /kɒzˈmetɪk/ n [C, usu pl] substance put on the body, esp the face, to make it beautiful ● **cosmetic** adj 1 improving only the outside appearance of sth and not its basic character: *These reforms are not merely* ~. 2 of medical treatment that is intended to improve a person's appearance: ~ *surgery*

cosmic /ˈkɒzmɪk/ adj of the whole universe or cosmos

cosmopolitan /ˌkɒzməˈpɒlɪtən/ adj 1 of or from all parts of the world: *a ~ city* 2 having or showing a wide experience of people and things from many different countries

cosmos /ˈkɒzmɒs/ (**the cosmos**) n [sing] the universe

cost¹ /kɒst/ n 1 [C,U] price paid for a thing: *the high ~ of repairs* 2 (**costs**) [pl] total amount of money that needs to be spent by a business 3 [U,sing] effort, loss or damage that is involved in order to do or achieve sth: *the ~ of victory* 4 (**costs**) [pl] sum of money that sb is ordered to pay for lawyers, etc in a court case [IDM] **at all cost/costs** whatever is needed to achieve sth **to your cost** to your loss or disadvantage ▸ **costly** adj (**-ier, -iest**) 1 costing a lot of money 2 causing problems or the loss of sth: *a ~ly mistake*

cost² /kɒst/ v (pt, pp **cost**, in sense 3 ~**ed**) [T] 1 have as a price; be obtainable at the price of: *shoes ~ing £20* 2 cause the loss of sth; require sth: *a mistake that ~ him his life ◊ ~ a great deal of effort* 3 (*business*) estimate the cost of sth ▸ **costing** n [C, U] (*business*) estimate of how much money will be needed for sth

co-star /ˈkəʊ stɑː(r)/ n well-known actor who appears in a film, etc with other actors of the same status ● **co-star** v (**-rr-**) [I] appear as a co-star

costume /ˈkɒstjuːm/ n [C,U] 1 clothes worn by people from a particular place or during a particular historical period: *Welsh national ~* 2 clothes worn by actors on stage or worn by sb to make them look like sth else

cosy (*US* **cozy**) /ˈkəʊzi/ adj (**-ier, -iest**) 1 warm and comfortable: *a ~ room/feeling* 2 friendly and private: *a ~ chat* ▸ **cosily** (*US* **cozily**) adv ▸ **cosiness** (*US* **coziness**) n [U]

cot /kɒt/ n 1 (*GB*) small bed for a young child 2 (*US*) simple narrow bed, eg on a ship

cottage /ˈkɒtɪdʒ/ n small house, esp in the country

cotton /ˈkɒtn/ n [U] 1 plant grown in warm countries for the soft, white hairs around its seeds that are used to make fabric and thread 2 fabric made from the cotton plant: *a ~ dress* 3 thread used for sewing: *a reel of ~* ■ **cotton 'wool** n [U] soft mass of white material used for cleaning the skin or a wound ● **cotton** v [PV] **cotton on (to sth)** (*infml*) begin to understand or realize sth without being told

couch /kaʊtʃ/ n long comfortable seat like a bed ● **couch** v [T] ~(**in**) (*fml*) say or write sth in a particular style or manner: *a reply ~ed in friendly terms*

couchette /kuːˈʃet/ n narrow folding bed on a train

cougar /ˈkuːɡə(r)/ n (*esp US*) = PUMA

cough /kɒf/ v 1 [I] force air out from

the lungs violently and noisily: *The smoke made me ~.* **2** [T] **~(up)** force sth out of your lungs or throat by coughing ● **cough** *n* **1** [C] act or sound of coughing **2** [sing] illness that makes you cough

could /kəd; *strong form* kʊd/ *modal v* (*neg* **could not** *short form* **couldn't** /'kʊdnt/) **1** used as the past tense of 'can': *I ~ hear her crying.* **2** used in requests: *C~ I use your phone?* ◇ *C~ you babysit on Friday?* **3** used to show that sth is or might be possible: *You ~ be right.* **4** used to suggest sth: *You ~ ask her to go with us.* [IDM] **could do with sth** (*spoken*) need sth: *I ~ do with a cold drink!*

council /'kaʊnsl/ *n* [C, with *sing* or *pl verb*] group of people elected to manage the affairs of a city, town, etc, give advice, make rules, etc: *a ~ meeting* ■ **'council house**, **'council flat** *n* (*GB*) house or flat rented from the local council ■ **'council tax** *n* [sing, U] (in Britain) tax charged by local councils, based on the value of a person's home ▶ **councillor** (*US* **councilor**) /'kaʊnsələ(r)/ *n* member of a council

counsel /'kaʊnsl/ *n* **1** [U] (*fml*) advice **2** [C] (*pl* **counsel**) (*law*) barrister acting in a law case ● **counsel** *v* (**-ll-** *US* **-l-**) (*fml*) **1** listen to and give support to sb who needs help: *Therapists were brought in to ~ the victims.* **2** (*fml*) advise sb ▶ **counselling** (*US* **-l-**) *n* [U] professional advice about a problem: *marriage guidance ~* ▶ **counsellor** (*US* **-l-**) *n* **1** person who has been trained to advise people with problems **2** (*US*) lawyer

count¹ /kaʊnt/ *v* **1** [I] say numbers in order: *C~ from 1 to 10.* **2** [I, T] **~(up)** find the total number of people, things etc in a particular group: *~ the people in the room* **3** [T] include sb/sth: *ten people, ~ing me* **4** [T] consider sb to be sth: *~ yourself lucky* **5** [I] be important: *every minute ~s* **6** [I, T] be officially accepted: *That goal didn't ~ because the game was over.* [PV] **count (sth) against sb** be to the disadvantage of sb: *Will my past mistakes ~ against me?* **count on sb/sth** rely on or depend on sb/sth: *I'm ~ing on you to help.* **count sb/sth out 1** count things one after the other as you put them somewhere **2** not include sb: *C~ me out, I'm not going.* ▶ **countable** *adj* that can be counted: *'House'* is a *~able* noun. ■ **'countdown** *n* action of counting seconds backwards to zero, eg before a rocket is launched

count² /kaʊnt/ *n* **1** [usu sing] act of counting; total number reached by counting: *There were 50 at the last ~.* **2** (*law*) crime that sb is

accused of: *He is guilty on all ~s.* **3** (in some European countries) nobleman of high rank [IDM] **keep/lose count (of sth)** know/not know how many there are of sth

countenance /'kaʊntənəns/ *n* [C] (*fml*) person's face or expression **2** [U] support; approval: *give/lend ~ to a plan* ● **countenance** *v* [T] (*fml*) support sth or agree to sth happening: *I cannot ~ violence.*

counter /'kaʊntə(r)/ *n* **1** flat surface where goods are shown, items sold, etc in a shop, bank, etc **2** small disc used for counting games, etc **3** thing that can be exchanged for sth else: *a bargaining ~* ● **counter** *v* [I, T] **~(with)** respond to an attack, etc with an opposing view, etc: *~ his arguments with her own opinion* ● **counter** *adv* **~ to** in the opposite direction; against sth: *Her theories ran ~ to the evidence.*

counter- /'kaʊntə(r)/ *prefix* (in compounds) **1** against; opposite: *~productive* **2** corresponding: *~part*

counteract /ˌkaʊntər'ækt/ *v* [T] do sth to reduce the bad or harmful effects of sth

counter-attack /'kaʊntər ətæk/ *n*, *v* [I] (make an) attack in response to an enemy's attack

counterbalance /ˌkaʊntə'bæləns/ *v* [T] (*fml*) have an equal but opposite effect to sth else ● **counterbalance** /'kaʊntəbæləns/ *n* thing that has an equal but opposite effect to sth else and can be used to lessen the bad effects of sth

counter-espionage /ˌkaʊntər 'espiənɑːʒ/ *n* [U] secret action taken by a country to prevent an enemy country from finding out its secrets

counterfeit /'kaʊntəfɪt/ *adj* (of money and goods for sale) made to look exactly like sth else in order to deceive people: *~ banknotes* ▶ **counterfeit** *v* [T] make an exact copy of sth in order to deceive people ▶ **counterfeiter** *n* person who counterfeits money

counterfoil /'kaʊntəfɔɪl/ *n* detachable part of a cheque, etc that can be kept as a record

countermand /ˌkaʊntə'mɑːnd/ *v* [T] cancel or change a command you have already given

counterpart /'kaʊntəpɑːt/ *n* person or thing similar or corresponding to another

counterproductive /ˌkaʊntəprə'dʌktɪv/ *adj* producing the opposite effect to what is intended: *Increasing taxes would be ~.*

countersign /'kaʊntəsaɪn/ *v* [T] (*tech*) sign a document, etc that has already been signed, esp to make it valid

C

countess /ˈkaʊntəs; -es/ n 1 woman who has the rank of a count or an earl 2 wife of a count or an earl

countless /ˈkaʊntləs/ adj very many: I've been there ~ times.

country /ˈkʌntri/ n (pl -ies) 1 [C] area of land that forms a politically independent unit; nation 2 (**the country**) [sing] the people of a country: a politician loved by the whole ~ 3 (**the country**) [sing] land outside towns; fields, woods, etc used for farming, etc ~ life/people [IDM] **go to the country** (of a government) call a general election

countryman /ˈkʌntrimən/ (fem **countrywoman** /ˈkʌntriwʊmən/) n 1 person born or living in the same country as sb else 2 person who lives in the country(3)

countryside /ˈkʌntrisaɪd/ n [U] land outside towns and cities, with fields, woods, etc

county /ˈkaʊnti/ n (pl -ies) (abbr **Co.**) area of Britain, Ireland or the US that has its own local government

coup /kuː/ n (pl -s /kuːz/) 1 (also **coup d'état** /ˌkuː deɪˈtɑː/) illegal seizing of power in a state, often by violence 2 fact of achieving sth that was difficult to do: This deal was a ~ for her.

couple¹ /ˈkʌpl/ n 1 two people or things, seen together or associated: a married ~ 2 ~(of) a few: a ~ of drinks/days

couple² /ˈkʌpl/ v 1 [T] fasten or join two parts of sth, eg two vehicles or pieces of equipment 2 [I] (fml) (of two people or animals) have sex [PV] **couple sb/sth with sb/sth** link one thing, situation, etc to another: His illness, ~d with his lack of money, prevented him leaving.

coupon /ˈkuːpɒn/ n 1 ticket which gives the holder the right to receive or do sth 2 printed form, often cut out from a newspaper, used to enter a competition, order goods, etc

courage /ˈkʌrɪdʒ/ n [U] ability to face danger, pain, etc without showing fear; bravery: show ~ in a battle ▶ **courageous** /kəˈreɪdʒəs/ adj ▶ **courageously** adv

courgette /kɔːˈʒet/ n small green marrow(2), eaten as a vegetable

courier /ˈkʊriə(r)/ n 1 person or company whose job is to take packages, documents, etc somewhere 2 (GB) person employed by a travel company to give help and advice to groups of tourists on holiday

course /kɔːs/ n 1 [C] series of lessons, lectures, etc: a French ~ ◇ a degree ~ 2 [C] path or direction followed by sth: the ~ of a river/ aircraft 3 [sing] way sth develops:

the ~ of history 4 [C] one of several parts of a meal: the fish ~ 5 [C] (often in compounds) area where sports events, esp races, are held: a golf ~ ◇ a race ~ 6 [C] (med) series of treatments, etc: a ~ of injections [IDM] (**as**) **a matter of course** (as) sth that is quite normal and expected **in due course** at the right time **of course** naturally; certainly **run/ take its course** develop and end in the usual way ● **course** v [I] (fml) (of liquids) move quickly: The blood ~ed through his veins.

court¹ /kɔːt/ n 1 [C,U] place where legal cases are heard 2 (**the court**) [sing] those present in a court, esp the judges, etc 3 [C] (often in compounds) space marked out for certain ball games: a tennis ~ 4 [C,U] (residence of) a king or queen, their family and the people who work for them 5 [C] = COURTYARD

court² /kɔːt/ v 1 [T] try to gain the favour or support of sb: ~ sb's favour 2 [T] (fml) risk trouble, etc: ~ disaster 3 (old-fash) [T] try to win sb's affection, esp when hoping to marry them

courteous /ˈkɜːtiəs/ adj having good manners; polite: a ~ person/ request ▶ **courteously** adv

courtesy /ˈkɜːtəsi/ n (pl -ies) 1 [U] polite behaviour 2 [C] polite remark, action, etc [IDM] (**by**) **courtesy of sb/sth** with the permission of sb/sth and as a favour

courtier /ˈkɔːtiə(r)/ n (esp in the past) member of a king or queen's court¹(4)

court martial /ˌkɔːt ˈmɑːʃl/ n (pl **courts martial**) court for trying crimes against military law; trial in such a court ● **court martial** v (-ll- US -l-) [T] ~(**for**) try sb in a court martial

courtyard /ˈkɔːtjɑːd/ n open space surrounded by walls but with no roof: the central/inner ~

cousin /ˈkʌzn/ n child of your uncle or aunt

cove /kəʊv/ n small bay

cover¹ /ˈkʌvə(r)/ v 1 [T] ~(**up/over**) place one thing over or in front of another; hide or protect sth in this way: ~ a table with a cloth ◇ ~ your face ◇ ~ (up) the body 2 [T] ~(**in/ with**) (esp passive) spread, etc a layer of sth on the surface of sth: hills ~ed with snow ◇ boots ~ed in mud 3 [T] travel a certain distance: ~ 100 miles in a day 4 [T] (of money) be enough for sth: Will £20 ~ your expenses? 5 [T] include sth; deal with sth: The survey ~s all aspects of the business. 6 [T] (of a journalist) report an event: I've been asked to ~ the election. 7 [I] ~ **for** do sb's work, etc while they are away 8 [I] ~ **for**

invent a lie or an excuse that will stop sb from getting into trouble **9** [T] keep a gun aimed at sb: *We've got him ~ed.* [IDM] **cover your tracks** leave no evidence of where you have been or what you have been doing [PV] **cover sth up** (*disapprov*) keep a scandal, an embarrassment, etc secret | reporting of news and sport in the media ▶ **covered** *adj* **~in/with** having a layer or amount of sth on it: *His face was ~ed in blood.* ■ **'cover-up** *n* [*usu sing*] act of hiding a mistake or crime from the public

cover² /'kʌvə(r)/ *n* **1** [C] thing that is put over sth on another thing, usu to protect or decorate it: *a cushion ~.* **2** [U] place or area giving shelter: *We ran for ~ under some trees.* **3** [C] thick outside pages of a book, magazine, etc **4** [U] insurance against loss, damage, etc **5** [U] protection from attack: *Aircraft gave the infantry ~.* **6** (**the covers**) [*pl*] sheets, blankets, etc on a bed **7** [C, *usu sing*] **~(for)** means of keeping sth secret: *a business that is a ~ for drug dealing* [IDM] **under (the) cover of** hidden or protected by sth: *under ~ of darkness*

covert /'kʌvət/ *adj* half-hidden; not open; secret: *a ~ glance/threat* ▶ **covertly** *adv*

cow¹ /kaʊ/ *n* **1** large female animal kept on farms to produce milk or beef **2** female of the elephant, whale and some other large animals **3** (*disapprov, sl*) offensive word for a woman: *You silly ~!* ■ **'cowboy** *n* **1** man who looks after cattle in the western part of the US **2** (*GB, infml*) dishonest person in business, esp sb whose work is of bad quality

cow² /kaʊ/ *v* frighten sb into doing what you want: *He was ~ed into giving them all his money.*

coward /'kaʊəd/ *n* (*disapprov*) person who is not brave or does not have the courage to do things that other people do not consider very difficult ▶ **cowardly** *adj* ▶ **cowardice** /'kaʊədɪs/ *n* [U] (*disapprov*) fear or lack of courage

cower /'kaʊə(r)/ *v* [I] lower the body or move back from fear, cold, etc

cowl /kaʊl/ *n* **1** large loose covering for the head, worn esp by monks **2** metal cover for a chimney, etc

cox /kɒks/ (*also fml* **coxswain** /'kɒksn/) *n* person who controls the direction of a rowing boat while other people are rowing ● **cox** *v* [I, T] act as a cox

coy /kɔɪ/ *adj* (pretending to be) shy, modest, etc: *a ~ smile* **2** not willing to give information, answer questions, etc: *She was ~ about her past.* ▶ **coyly** *adv* ▶ **coyness** *n* [U]

coyote /'kaɪəʊtɪ; kɔɪ-/ *n* small wolf of western N America

cozy (*US*) = COSY

CPU /ˌsiː piː 'juː/ *abbr* (*computing*) central processing unit; part of a computer that controls all the other parts of the system

crab /kræb/ *n* **1** [C] shellfish with eight legs and two pincers that moves sideways on land **2** [U] meat from a crab, eaten as food

crabby /'kræbi/ *adj* (**-ier, -iest**) (*infml*) bad-tempered; irritable

crack¹ /kræk/ *v* **1** [I, T] (cause sth to) break without dividing into separate parts: *a plate ◇ The cup ~ed.* **2** [T] break sth open or into pieces: *a safe ◇ ~ nuts* **3** [T] hit sth/sb sharply: *~ your head on the door* **4** [I, T] (cause sth to) make a sharp sound: *~ a whip* **5** [I] (of the voice) suddenly change in depth, volume, etc in a way that you cannot control: *in a voice ~ing with emotion* **6** [I] no longer be able to function normally because of pressure: *She finally ~ed and told the truth.* **7** [T] solve a problem, etc: *~ a code* **8** [T] (*infml*) tell a joke [IDM] **get cracking** (*infml*) start work immediately [PV] **crack down (on sb/sth)** become more severe in preventing illegal activity: *~ down on crime* **crack up** (*infml*) **1** become ill because of pressure **2** start laughing ■ **'crackdown** *n* sudden strict or severe measures: *a police ~down on vandalism* ▶ **cracked** *adj* **1** damaged with lines in its surface: *a ~ed mirror* **2** (*infml*) slightly mad

crack² /kræk/ *n* **1** [C] **~(in)** line where sth has broken, but not into separate parts: *a ~ in a cup/the ice* **2** [C] narrow space or opening: *a ~ in the curtains* **3** [C] sudden loud noise: *the ~ of a whip/rifle* **4** [C] sharp blow: *a ~ on the head* **5** [C] **~(at)** (*infml*) attempt to do sth: *to have a ~ at the world record* **6** (*also* **,crack 'cocaine**) [U] very strong pure form of cocaine **7** [C] (*infml*) joke, esp a critical one: *She made a ~ about his baldness.* [IDM] **at the crack of dawn** (*infml*) very early in the morning ● **crack** *adj* excellent; very skilful: *She's a ~ shot.*

cracker /'krækə(r)/ *n* **1** thin dry biscuit, often eaten with cheese **2** (*also* **,Christmas 'cracker**) tube of coloured paper that makes a cracking noise when pulled apart by two people and has toys, presents, etc inside it

crackers /'krækəz/ *adj* (*GB, infml*) mad; crazy

crackle /'krækl/ *v* [I] make a series of short sharp sounds, as when dry sticks burn: *Dry leaves ~d under our*

C

feet. ● **crackle** *n* [U,C] series of short sharp sounds

crackpot /'krækpɒt/ *n* (*infml*) eccentric or mad person: *a ~ idea/ person*

cradle /'kreɪdl/ *n* [C] **1** small bed for a baby which can be pushed from side to side **2** [*usu sing*] ~**of** place where sth begins: *the ~ of Western culture* **3** place where sth is made ▶ **cradle** *v* [T] hold sb/sth gently in your arms or hands

craft /krɑːft/ *n* **1** [C] (activity needing) skill at making things with your hands: *traditional ~s like basketweaving* **2** [U] (*fml, disapprov*) skill in deceiving people **3** [C] (*pl* **craft**) ship, boat, aircraft or spacecraft ■ **'craftsman** *n* (*pl* **-men**) skilled worker who practises a craft ■ **'craftsmanship** *n* [U] skill as a craftsman

crafty /'krɑːfti/ *adj* (**-ier, -iest**) clever at getting what you want, esp by dishonest methods ▶ **craftily** *adv* ▶ **craftiness** *n* [U]

crag /kræg/ *n* high steep mass of rock ▶ **craggy** *adj* (**-ier, -iest**) **1** having many crags **2** (of sb's face) having strong features and deep lines

cram /kræm/ *v* (**-mm-**) [T] ~ (**into/ onto**) push too much of sth into sth: *~ the clothes into the suitcase* ▶ **crammed** *adj* ~(**with**) full of things or people: *shelves ~med with books*

cramp /kræmp/ *n* **1** [U,C] sudden and painful tightening of the muscles **2** (**cramps**) [*pl*] severe pain in the stomach ● **cramp** *v* [T] (*usu passive*) give too little space to; prevent the movement or development of: *feel ~ed by the rules* [IDM] **cramp sb's style** (*infml*) stop sb doing things in the way they want to ▶ **cramped** *adj* having too little space: *~ conditions*

crampon /'kræmpɒn/ *n* iron plate with spikes, worn over shoes for climbing on ice

cranberry /'krænbəri/ *n* small red slightly sour berry, used for making jelly and sauce

crane /kreɪn/ *n* **1** machine with a long arm, used for lifting heavy weights **2** large wading bird with long legs and neck ● **crane** *v* [I, T] stretch your neck, eg to see better: *He ~d his neck to see over the crowd.*

cranium /'kreɪniəm/ *n* (*pl* **~s** *or* **crania** /'kreɪniə/) (*anat*) bone structure that forms the head and protects the brain ▶ **cranial** *adj*

crank /kræŋk/ *n* **1** (*disapprov*) person with fixed strange ideas **2** L-shaped handle for turning things ● **crank** *v* [T] ~ (**up**) make sth move by turning a crank: *~ the engine* (= start it with a crank) ■ **'crankshaft** *n*

(*tech*) metal rod in a vehicle that helps turn the engine's power into movement ▶ **cranky** *adj* (**-ier, -iest**) (*infml*) **1** strange; eccentric **2** (*esp US*) bad-tempered

cranny /'kræni/ *n* very small hole or opening in a wall [IDM] **every nook and cranny** → NOOK

crap /kræp/ *v* (**-pp-**) [I] (*sl*, △) empty solid waste from the bowels ● **crap** *n* (△) **1** [U] nonsense; rubbish **2** [U] excrement **3** [sing] act of emptying the bowels ▶ **crappy** *adj* (**-ier, -iest**) (*sl*) of very bad quality

crash¹ /kræʃ/ *n* [C] **1** accident involving a vehicle in collision with sth: *a car ~* **2** (*usu sing*) sudden loud noise made by sth falling: *The dishes fell with a ~ to the floor.* **3** sudden fall in the price or the value of sth; collapse of a business, etc: *the 1997 stock market ~* **4** sudden failure of a computer or system ● **crash** *adj* done to achieve quick results: *a ~ course in French* ■ **'crash helmet** *n* hard hat worn by a motorcyclist to protect the head ■ **,crash-'land** *v* [I, T] land an aircraft in an emergency ■ **,crash 'landing** *n* emergency landing

crash² /kræʃ/ *v* **1** [I, T] (cause sth) to collide with sth: *~ the car (into a wall)* **2** [I, T] (cause sb/sth to) hit sth hard while moving, causing noise and/or damage: *The tree ~ed through the window.* **3** [I] make a loud noise: *The thunder ~ed.* **4** [I] (of prices, a business, shares, etc) lose value or fail suddenly **5** [I, T] (cause a computer to) stop working

crass /kræs/ *adj* very stupid and showing no sympathy or understanding: *a ~ question*

crate /kreɪt/ *n* large wooden container for goods ● **crate** *v* [T] pack sth in a crate

crater /'kreɪtə(r)/ *n* **1** opening at the top of a volcano **2** hole made by a bomb

cravat /krə'væt/ *n* piece of cloth worn by men round the neck

crave /kreɪv/ *v* [T] ~ (**for**) have a strong desire for sth: *~ for a cigarette* ▶ **craving** *n*

crawl /krɔːl/ *v* [I] **1** move slowly along the ground or on the hands and knees: *The baby ~ed along the floor.* **2** move very slowly: *traffic ~ing into London* **3** ~**with** (esp in the continuous tense) be covered with or full of things that crawl, etc: *a floor ~ing with ants* **4** ~**to** (*infml*) try to gain sb's favour by doing what they want, flattering them, etc [IDM] **make your skin crawl** → SKIN ● **crawl** *n* **1** [sing] very slow speed **2** (**the crawl**) [sing,U] fast swimming stroke ▶ **crawler** *n* (*infml, disapprov*) person who crawls(4)

crayon /'kreɪən/ *n* pencil of soft coloured chalk or wax ● **crayon** *v* [T] draw sth with crayons

craze /kreɪz/ *n* enthusiastic, usu brief, popular interest in sth; object of such an interest

crazed /kreɪzd/ *adj* ~(with) (*fml*) full of strong feelings, esp anger

crazy /'kreɪzi/ *adj* (**-ier, -iest**) (*infml*) **1** foolish; not sensible: *a ~ idea* **2** very angry: *The noise is driving me ~!* **3** wildly excited or enthusiastic: *~ about football* **4** ~ **about** in love with sb: *He's ~ about you!* **5** mentally ill; insane ▶ **crazily** *adv* ▶ **craziness** *n* [U]

creak /kri:k/ *v* [I] *n* (make a) sound like a door that needs oil: *a ~ing door/floorboard* ▶ **creaky** *adj* (**-ier, -iest**) making creaks

cream /kri:m/ *n* **1** [U] thick yellowish fatty liquid that rises to the top of milk: *strawberries and ~* **2** [C] a sweet that has a soft substance like cream inside **3** [U,C] any soft substance used on your skin to protect it, etc or used for cleaning things: *hand ~* **4** [U] pale yellowish-white colour **5** (**the cream**) [sing] the best part: *the ~ of society* ● **cream** *adj* yellowish-white ● **cream** *v* [T] mix things together into a soft paste [PV] **cream sb/sth off** take the best part away ▶ **creamy** *adj* (**-ier, -iest**) like cream; containing cream

crease /kri:s/ *n* **1** line made on cloth, paper, etc by crushing, folding or pressing **2** wrinkle on the skin **3** white line near the wicket on a cricket pitch ● **crease** *v* [I, T] (cause sth to) develop creases

create /kri'eɪt/ *v* [T] **1** make sth happen or exist **2** produce a particular feeling or impression: *The company wants to ~ a good image.*

creation /kri'eɪʃn/ *n* **1** [U] act of making sth new or of causing sth to exist **2** (usu **the Creation**) [sing] making of the world, esp by God as described in the Bible **3** [U] the world and all the living things in it

creative /kri'eɪtɪv/ *adj* **1** able to produce sth new or a work or art: *a ~ person who writes and paints* **2** involving the use of skill and the imagination to produce sth new: *the ~ arts* ▶ **creatively** *adv* ▶ **creativity** /ˌkriːeɪ'tɪvəti/ *n* [U]

creator /kri'eɪtə(r)/ *n* **1** [C] person who creates: *the ~ of this novel* **2** (**the Creator**) [sing] God

creature /'kri:tʃə(r)/ *n* living animal or person

crèche (*also* **creche**) /kreʃ/ *n* (*GB*) place where babies are cared for while their parents are at work, etc

credentials /krə'denʃlz/ *n* [pl] **1** qualities, etc that make you suitable to sth **2** documents showing that you are who you claim to be

credible /'kredəbl/ *adj* that can be believed or trusted: *a ~ story/ explanation* ▶ **credibility** /ˌkredə'bɪləti/ *n* [U] quality of being credible: *to gain/lose credibility* ▶ **credibly** /-əbli/ *adv*

credit¹ /'kredɪt/ *n* **1** [U] agreement to buy sth and pay later: *buy a car on ~* **2** [U] belief of others that a person, company, etc can pay debts: *have good/poor ~* **3** [U] sum of money in a bank account **4** [U] sum of money lent by a bank, etc **5** [C] entry in an account for money received **6** [U] belief; trust: *give ~ to her story* **7** [U] praise; approval: *get/ be given all the ~ for sth* **8** [sing] ~ **to** person or thing that makes sb have a reputation better: *She's a ~ to her family.* **9** [C] (*US*) unit of study at a college or university [IDM] **to sb's credit** make sb deserve praise or respect ■ **'credit card** *n* card allowing the holder to buy goods on credit(1) ■ **'creditworthy** *adj* able to be trusted to repay money owed ▶ **'creditworthiness** *n* [U]

credit² /'kredɪt/ *v* [T] **1** ~(with) think that sb has sth: *I ~ed you with more sense.* **2** add an amount of money to sb's bank account **3** believe sth: *Would you ~ it?*

creditable /'kredɪtəbl/ *adj* deserving praise (although not perfect): *a ~ piece of work* ▶ **creditably** *adv*

creditor /'kredɪtə(r)/ *n* person, company, etc that sb owes money to

credulous /'kredjələs/ *adj* too willing to believe things ▶ **credulity** /krɪ'dju:ləti/ *n* [U]

creed /kri:d/ *n* set of beliefs, esp religious ones

creek /kri:k/ *n* **1** (*GB*) narrow stretch of river cutting into a coast or river bank **2** (*US*) small river

creep /kri:p/ *v* [I] (*pt, pp* **crept** /krept/) **1** move along slowly or quietly, esp keeping the body close to ground: *The thief crept along the corridor.* **2** (of plants, etc) grow over the surface of a wall, etc **3** ~ (**to**) (*GB, infml, disapprov*) try to gain sb's favour by doing what they want, flattering them, etc [IDM] **make your flesh creep** ⇒ FLESH [PV] **creep up on sb** move slowly nearer to sb, usu from behind, without being seen or heard: (*fig*) *Old age is ~ing up on me.* ● **creep** *n* (*infml, disapprov*) unpleasant person, esp one who tries to gain sb's favour by doing what they want, flattering them, etc [IDM] **give sb the creeps** (*infml*) make sb feel fear or dislike

▶ **creeper** n plant that grows along the ground, up walls, etc

creepy /'kri:pi/ adj (-ier, -iest) (infml) causing or feeling fear: a ~ house/atmosphere

creepy-crawly /'kri:pi 'krɔ:li/ n (infml) insect, worm, etc when you think of it as unpleasant

cremate /krə'meɪt/ v [T] burn the body of a dead person esp as part of a funeral ceremony ▶ **cremation** /krə'meɪʃn/ n [C,U] (act of) cremating sb ▶ **crematorium** /ˌkreməˈtɔ:riəm/ n (pl ~s or -oria /-ɔ:riə/) place where bodies are burned

creosote /'kri:əsəʊt/ n [U] brown oily liquid used for preserving wood

crêpe (also **crepe**) /kreɪp/ n 1 [U] any of various types of wrinkled cloth or paper 2 [U] rubber with a wrinkled surface, used for making the soles of shoes 3 [C] thin pancake

crept pt, pp of CREEP

crescendo /krə'ʃendəʊ/ n (pl ~s) 1 (music) gradual increase in loudness 2 gradual increase in intensity, noise, etc to a climax ● **crescendo** adj, adv of or with increasing loudness: a ~ passage

crescent /'kresnt; 'kreznt/ n 1 (something shaped like this) curve of the new moon 2 row of houses built in a curve

cress /kres/ n [U] small plant with very small leaves, used in salads

crest /krest/ n 1 top of a hill or wave 2 design used as the symbol of a particular family, organization, etc, esp one with a long history 3 group of feathers that stand up on top of a bird's head ● **crest** v [T] (written) reach the top of a hill, etc

crestfallen /'krestfɔ:lən/ adj very sad or disappointed

Creutzfeldt-Jakob disease /ˌkrɔɪtsfelt 'jækɒb dɪz:z/ n [U] (abbr CJD) fatal disease of the brain and nervous system, thought to be linked to BSE in cows.

crevasse /krə'væs/ n deep open crack in thick ice

crevice /'krevɪs/ n narrow opening or crack in a rock, wall, etc

crew /kru:/ n 1 all the people working on a ship or aircraft; these people, except the officers 2 group of people working together: a camera ~ ● **crew** v [I, T] be part of a crew, esp on a ship

crib /krɪb/ n 1 (US) small bed for a small child 2 long open box for holding an animal's food 3 (infml) written information such as answers to questions, often used dishonestly by students in tests: a ~ sheet ·

crick /krɪk/ n [sing] painful stiff feeling in your neck

cricket /'krɪkɪt/ n 1 [U] ball game played on grass by two teams of eleven players, in which a ball is bowled at a wicket and a batsman tries to hit it: a ~ match/club/ball 2 [C] small brown jumping insect that makes a shrill noise ▶ **cricketer** n cricket player

cried pt, pp of CRY[1]

cries 1 third pers sing pres tense CRY[1] 2 plural of CRY[2]

crime /kraɪm/ n 1 [U] activities that involve breaking the law 2 [C] ~ (against) illegal act for which there is a punishment by law: commit a ~ 3 (a crime) [sing] act that you think is immoral or foolish: It's a ~ to waste money like that.

criminal /'krɪmɪnl/ adj 1 of or concerning crime or the laws that deal with it: a ~ offence ◇ ~ law 2 morally wrong: a ~ waste of resources ● **criminal** n person who commits a crime or crimes ▶ **criminally** /-nəli/ adv

crimson /'krɪmzn/ adj, n [U] (of a) deep red

cringe /krɪndʒ/ v [I] 1 move back and away from sb/sth in fear 2 feel very embarrassed about sth: I ~ when I think of the poems I wrote then.

crinkle /'krɪŋkl/ v very thin fold or line made on paper, fabric or skin ▶ **crinkle** v [I, T] (cause sth to) form crinkles: ~d paper

cripple /'krɪpl/ v [T] (usu passive) 1 damage sb's body so that they are no longer able to walk or move normally: ~d by a back injury 2 seriously damage or harm sb/sth: ~d by debt

crisis /'kraɪsɪs/ n [C,U] (pl crises /-si:z/) time of difficulty, danger, etc; decisive moment: an economic ~ ◇ a country in ~

crisp /krɪsp/ adj 1 (also **crispy**) (of food) pleasantly hard and dry: a ~ biscuit 2 (also **crispy**) (of fruit and vegetables) fresh and firm: a ~ lettuce 3 (of paper or fabric) new and slightly stiff: ~ banknotes 4 (of the weather) frosty, cold: a ~ winter morning 5 (of sb's way of speaking) quick and confident and not very friendly: a ~ reply ● **crisp** (GB also **po̱tato 'crisp**) n [C, usu pl] thin slice of potato, fried and dried and sold in packets ● **crisp** v [I, T] become or make sth crisp ▶ **crisply** adv ▶ **crispness** n [U] ● **crispy** adj (-ier, -iest) (infml) = CRISP(1),(2)

criss-cross /'krɪs krɒs/ adj with crossed lines: a ~ pattern ● **criss-cross** v [I, T] form or make a criss-cross pattern on sth: roads ~ing the country

criterion /kraɪ'tɪəriən/ n (pl -ria /-riə/) standard by which sb/sth is judged

critic /'krɪtɪk/ n 1 person who gives opinions about the good and bad qualities of books, music, etc: *The ~s liked the play.* 2 person who expresses disapproval of sb/sth publicly

critical /'krɪtɪkl/ adj 1 expressing disapproval of sb/sth publicly: *a ~ remark* 2 extremely important for the future: *a ~ decision* 3 serious, uncertain and possibly dangerous: *The fire victim is in a ~ condition.* 4 giving fair, careful judgements, esp about art, literature, etc: *a ~ review* ▶ **critically** /ɪkli/ adv *to be ~ly ill*

criticism /'krɪtɪsɪzəm/ n 1 [U,C] (of) act of expressing disapproval of sb/sth and opinions about their bad qualities; statement showing disapproval: *I can't stand her constant ~.* 2 [U] work or activity of making fair, careful judgements about the good and bad qualities of sb/sth, esp books, music, etc: *literary ~*

criticize (also **-ise**) /'krɪtɪsaɪz/ v 1 [I, T] point out the faults of sb/sth; express disapproval of sb/sth: *Don't ~ my work.* 2 [T] (GB) judge the good and bad qualities of sth

critique /krɪ'tiːk/ n piece of written criticism of a set of ideas, work of art, etc

croak /krəʊk/ n deep, hoarse sound as made by a frog ● **croak** v 1 [I] make a deep hoarse sound 2 [I, T] speak or say sth in a croaking voice

crockery /'krɒkəri/ n [U] plates, cups, dishes, etc

crocodile /'krɒkədaɪl/ n 1 [C] large river reptile with a long body and tail, found in hot countries 2 [U] crocodile skin made into leather 3 [C] (GB) long line of people, esp children, walking in pairs [IDM] **crocodile tears** insincere sorrow

crocus /'krəʊkəs/ n small plant with white, yellow purple flowers appearing early in spring

croissant /'krwæsɒ̃/ n small sweet roll with a curved shape, eaten esp at breakfast

crony /'krəʊni/ n (pl **-ies**) (disapprov) friend or companion

crook /krʊk/ n 1 (infml) criminal 2 bend in sth: *the ~ of your arm* (= the place where it bends at the elbow) 3 stick with a hook at one end, esp as used by a shepherd ● **crook** v bend your finger or arm

crooked /'krʊkɪd/ adj 1 not straight: *a ~ line* 2 (infml) dishonest: *a ~ politician* ▶ **crookedly** adv

crop¹ /krɒp/ n 1 [C] plant that is grown in large quantities, esp as food 2 [C] amount of grain, grass, fruit, etc produced in a year or

season: *a good ~ of wheat* 3 [sing] ~ **of** group of people or things

crop² /krɒp/ v (-**pp**-) [T] 1 cut sb's hair very short 2 (of animals) bite off and eat the tops of plants, esp grass [PV] **crop up** appear or happen, esp unexpectedly: *A new problem has ~ped up.*

croquet /'krəʊkeɪ/ n [U] game played on grass with balls that are knocked through hoops

cross¹ /krɒs/ n 1 [C] mark made by drawing one line across another, (x or +) 2 [C] long upright piece of wood with a shorter piece across it near the top. In the past people were hung on crosses and left to die as a punishment. 3 **(the Cross)** [sing] the cross that Jesus Christ died on, used as a symbol of Christianity 4 [C] piece of jewellery, etc in the shape of a cross, used as a symbol of Christianity 5 (usu **Cross**) [C] small cross-shaped decoration awarded to sb for doing sth very brave 6 [C] mixture of two different things, breeds of animal, etc 7 [C] (in football or hockey) kick or hit of the ball across the field [IDM] **have a (heavy) cross to bear** have a difficult problem to deal with

cross² /krɒs/ v 1 [I, T] go across sth; extend from one side to the other of sth: *a bridge ~ing the road* 2 [I] pass across each other: *The letters ~ed in the post.* 3 [T] put or place sth across or over sth else: *~ your arms/legs* (= place one arm or leg over the other) 4 [T] oppose sb or speak against them or their plans, etc: *You shouldn't ~ her in business.* 5 [T] ~ **(with)** cause two different types of animal or plant to produce young: *A mule is the product of a horse ~ed with a donkey.* 6 [I] (in football, etc) pass the ball sideways across the field 7 [T] draw a line across sth: *~ a cheque* (= draw two lines on it to show that it must be paid into a bank account) 8 ~ **yourself** make the sign of a cross (= the Christian symbol) on your chest [IDM] **cross your mind** (of ideas, etc) come into your head [PV] **cross sb/sth off** draw a line through a person's name or an item on a list because they/it is no longer required: *C~ her off the list; she's not coming.* **cross sth out/through** draw a line through a word, usu because it is wrong

cross³ /krɒs/ adj annoyed; angry: *I was ~ with him for being late.* ◊ *She's ~ about this.* ▶ **crossly** adv

crossbow /'krɒsbəʊ/ n weapon consisting of a bow²(1) that is fixed onto a larger piece of wood, and that shoots short heavy arrows (**bolts**)

C

cross-breed /'krɒs briːd/ v [I, T] (cause an animal or plant to) breed with an animal or plant of a different breed: *cross-bred sheep* ● **cross-breed** n animal or plant that is the result of cross-breeding

cross-check /ˌkrɒs 'tʃek/ v [I, T] make sure that information, figures, etc are correct by using a different method or system to check them ▶ **cross-check** /'krɒs tʃek/ n

cross-country /ˌkrɒs 'kʌntri/ *adj, adv* across the country or fields, not on roads: *a ~ race*

cross-examine /ˌkrɒs ɪg'zæmɪn/ v [T] question sb closely, esp to test answers already given, esp in a law court ▶ **cross-e**ˌ**xami'nation** n [C,U]

cross-eyed /ˌkrɒs 'aɪd/ *adj* with one or both eyes turned towards the nose

crossfire /'krɒsfaɪə(r)/ n [U] firing of guns from two or more points, so that the bullets cross

crossing /'krɒsɪŋ/ n 1 place where you can safely cross a road, river, etc or from one country to another 2 place where two roads, railways, etc meet 3 journey across the sea or a wide river: *a six-hour ferry ~*

cross-legged /ˌkrɒs 'legd; -'legɪd/ *adj, adv* with one leg over the other

crosspiece /'krɒspiːs/ n (tech) piece of a structure or tool that lies or is fixed across another piece

cross purposes /ˌkrɒs 'pɜːpəsɪz/ n [IDM] **at cross purposes** (of two people or groups) misunderstanding what the other is talking about

cross-reference /ˌkrɒs 'refrəns/ n note directing the reader to another part of the book, file, etc

crossroads /'krɒsrəʊdz/ n (pl **crossroads**) place where two roads meet and cross each other [IDM] **at a/the crossroads** at a point where an important decision is to be taken

cross section /ˌkrɒs 'sekʃn/ n 1 [C,U] (drawing of a) surface formed by cutting or slicing through sth 2 [C,usu sing] group of people or things that are typical of a larger group: *a ~ of society*

crosswind /'krɒswɪnd/ n wind blowing across the direction you are moving in

crossword /'krɒswɜːd/ n puzzle in which words have to be guessed from clues and written in spaces in a grid

crotch /krɒtʃ/ n place where a person's legs, or trouser legs, join

crouch /kraʊtʃ/ v [I] lower your body by bending your knees: *~ down on the floor* ● **crouch** n [sing] crouching position

croupier /'kruːpɪeɪ/ n person in charge of a table where people gamble money on cards, etc

crow¹ /krəʊ/ n 1 large black bird with a harsh cry 2 sound like that of a cock crowing [IDM] **as the crow flies** in a straight line: *It's ten miles away, as the ~ flies.* ■ **crow's feet** n [pl] lines on the skin near the corner of the eye ■ **crow's-nest** n lookout platform at the top of a ship's mast

crow² /krəʊ/ v [I] 1 (of a cock) make loud high sounds, esp early in the morning 2 ~(about/over) talk too proudly about your own success or achievements: *~ing over her profits*

crowbar /'krəʊbɑː(r)/ n straight iron bar used as a lever for opening crates, moving heavy objects, etc

crowd /kraʊd/ n [C, with sing or pl verb] 1 large number of people together: *a ~ of tourists* 2 (infml) particular group of people: *the usual ~* (= people who often meet each other) ● **crowd** v 1 [I] come together in a crowd: *~ around the stage* 2 [T] fill a place so there is little room to move: *Tourists ~ed the beach.* 3 [T] (infml) stand close to sb so that they feel nervous ▶ **crowded** *adj* (too) full of people: *a ~ room*

crown¹ /kraʊn/ n 1 [C] circular ornamental headdress of a king or queen 2 (**the Crown**) [sing] royal power 3 [C] top of a hill, head, hat, etc

crown² /kraʊn/ v [T] 1 put a crown on a new king or queen 2 ~(with) (usu passive) form or cover the top of sth: *His head was ~ed with a mop of curly hair.* 3 ~ (with) (usu passive) make sth complete or perfect: *a project ~ed with success* [IDM] **to crown it all** (GB) to be the last in a series of bad events ▶ **crowning** *adj* making sth perfect or complete: *a ~ing achievement*

crucial /'kruːʃl/ *adj* of decisive importance: *a ~ decision* ▶ **crucially** /-ʃəli/ *adv*

crucifix /'kruːsəfɪks/ n model of the Cross with a figure of Christ on it

crucifixion /ˌkruːsə'fɪkʃn/ n [C,U] (act of) crucifying sb

crucify /'kruːsɪfaɪ/ v (*pt, pp* -ied) [T] 1 kill sb as a punishment by nailing them to a cross 2 (infml) criticize or punish sb very severely

crude /kruːd/ *adj* 1 simple and not very accurate but giving a general idea of sth 2 (of objects or works of art) simply made: *~ tools* 3 rude and vulgar: *~ jokes* 4 (of materials) in a natural state and not refined: *~ oil* ▶ **crudely** *adv*

cruel /'kruːəl/ *adj* (**-ler, -lest**) 1 (of people) enjoying the suffering of others 2 causing suffering: *~ treatment* ▶ **cruelly** *adv* ▶ **cruelty** n 1 [U] behaviour that causes pain and suffering to others **2** [C, usu pl] (pl **-ies**) cruel action

cruet /ˈkruːɪt/ n small stand for salt and pepper, oil and vinegar, etc on a table

cruise /kruːz/ v [I] **1** travel in a ship visiting different places, esp as a holiday **2** (of cars, aircraft, etc) travel at a steady speed: ~ *along at 50 miles an hour* ● **cruise** n journey by sea, visiting different places: *go on a round-the-world* ~ ▶ **cruiser** n **1** fast warship **2** motor boat with sleeping accommodation ■ '**cruise missile** n missile that flies low and can guide itself

crumb /krʌm/ n **1** very small piece of dry food, esp bread **2** very small amount

crumble /ˈkrʌmbl/ v [I, T] (cause sth to) break into very small pieces **2** [I] begin to fail or come to an end: *Their marriage ~d.* ▶ **crumbly** adj (**-ier, -iest**) that breaks easily into small pieces: ~ *cheese/soil*

crumple /ˈkrʌmpl/ v ~ **(-up)** [I, T] **1** (cause sth to) be crushed into folds: *material that ~s easily* **2** [I] fall down; collapse

crunch /krʌntʃ/ v [T] ~ **(-up)** crush sth noisily between your teeth when eating **2** [I, T] crush sth or be crushed noisily: *The snow ~ed under our feet.* ● **crunch** n [C, usu sing] **1** noise like the sound of sth firm being crushed **2** (**the crunch**) [sing] important, often unpleasant situation: *when the* ~ *comes*

crusade /kruːˈseɪd/ n ~ **(against)** long struggle for sth good or against sth bad ● **crusade** v [I] take part in a crusade ▶ **crusader** n

crush[1] /krʌʃ/ v [T] press sth so hard there is breakage or injury: *Some people were ~ed to death in the accident.* **2** [I] push or press sb/sth into a small space: *Crowds ~ed into the theatre.* **3** [T] break sth into small pieces or powder by pressing hard **4** [I, T] (cause sth to) become full of creases: *clothes ~ed in a suitcase* **5** [T] defeat sb completely ▶ **crushing** adj used to emphasize how bad or severe sth is: *a ~ing defeat/blow*

crush[2] /krʌʃ/ n **1** [sing] crowd of people pressed together **2** ~ **(on)** strong feeling of love, that usu does not last very long: *She's got a* ~ *on her teacher.*

crust /krʌst/ n [C, U] **1** hard outer surface of bread, pastry, etc **2** hard layer or surface: *the earth's* ~ ▶ **crusty** adj (**-ier, -iest**) **1** having a crust; like a crust: ~*y bread* **2** (infml) bad-tempered

crustacean /krʌˈsteɪʃn/ n (tech) shellfish

crutch /krʌtʃ/ n **1** stick used as a support under the arm to help an injured person walk **2** (disapprov) person or thing that you depend on for help and support **3** = CROTCH

crux /krʌks/ n most important or difficult part of a problem

cry[1] /kraɪ/ v (pt, pp **-ied**) **1** [I] ~ **(for; about/over; with)** produce tears from the eyes because you are unhappy or hurt: *The baby was ~ing for his mother.* ◇ ~ *with pain* **2** [I, T] ~ **(for)** shout loudly: *to* ~ *for help* ◇ '*Get out!*' *he cried.* **3** [I] (of animals) make a loud harsh noise [PV] **cry off** (GB) cancel an appointment, etc **cry out for** sth need sth urgently ■ '**crybaby** n person who cries too easily or for no good reason

cry[2] /kraɪ/ n (pl **-ies**) **1** [C] loud sound expressing a strong feeling: *a* ~ *of anguish/despair* **2** sound made by a bird or animal: *the* ~ *of the thrush* **3** [sing] act or period of crying: *have a good* ~ **4** [C] ~**(for)** urgent demand or request for sth: *a* ~ *for help* [IDM] **a far cry from** very different experience from

crypt /krɪpt/ n room under a church

cryptic /ˈkrɪptɪk/ adj having a hidden meaning

crystal /ˈkrɪstl/ n **1** [C] regular shape taken naturally by certain substances: *salt* ~*s* **2** [U,C] transparent colourless mineral, eg quartz, used in making jewellery, etc **3** [U] high quality glass **4** [C] (US) glass or plastic cover on the face of a watch ▶ **crystalline** /ˈkrɪstəlaɪn/ adj **1** made of crystal(s); like crystal **2** (fml) very clear: ~ *water* ▶ **crystallize** (also **-ise**) /ˈkrɪstəlaɪz/ v **1** [I, T] (cause ideas, plans, etc to) become clear and definite **2** [I, T] (cause sth to) form into crystals

cub /kʌb/ n young lion, bear, fox, etc

cubbyhole /ˈkʌbɪhəʊl/ n small enclosed space or room

cube /kjuːb/ n **1** solid figure with six equal square sides **2** (maths) result of multiplying a number by itself twice ● **cube** v [T] (usu passive) (maths) multiply a number by itself twice: *3* ~*d is 27.* ■ **cubic** /ˈkjuːbɪk/ adj **1** (abbr **cu**) produced by multiplying length, width and height: *a* ~ *metre* **2** having the shape of a cube; of a cube

cubicle /ˈkjuːbɪkl/ n small space formed by dividing a larger room

cuckoo /ˈkʊkuː/ n bird whose call is like its name, and which lays its eggs in the nests of other birds

cucumber /ˈkjuːkʌmbə(r)/ n [C, U] long green vegetable, eaten raw, esp in salads

cud /kʌd/ n [U] food which cows, etc

bring back from the stomach and chew again

cuddle /'kʌdl/ v [T] hold sb close and lovingly in your arms: ~ *a child* [PV] **cuddle up (to/against sb/sth)| cuddle up (together)** sit or lie very close to sb/sth: *She* ~*d up to her father.* ● **cuddle** /*n* [usu sing] act of cuddling sb to show love or affection ▶ **cuddly** *adj* (-**ier**, -**iest**) (*infml*) pleasant to cuddle: *a* ~ *toy*

cudgel /'kʌdʒl/ *n* short thick stick used as a weapon ● **cudgel** *v* (-**ll-** US **-l-**) [T] hit sb with a cudgel

cue /kjuː/ *n* **1** ~(**for**) action or event that is a signal for sb to do sth: *Jon's arrival was the* ~ *for more drinks.* **2** few words or an action in a play that is a signal for another actor to do sth **3** long thin stick used for hitting the ball in games of snooker, billiards, or pool

cuff¹ /kʌf/ *n* **1** end of a coat or shirt sleeve at the wrist **2** light hit with an open hand [IDM] **off the cuff** of a remark, etc) said without previous thought or preparation ▪ **'cufflink** *n* decorative object for fastening shirt cuffs

cuff² /kʌf/ *v* [T] hit sb quickly and lightly with an open hand

cuisine /kwɪ'ziːn/ *n* [U] (style of) cooking

cul-de-sac /'kʌl də sæk/ *n* street that is closed at one end

culinary /'kʌlɪnəri/ *adj* (*fml*) of or for cooking

culminate /'kʌlmɪneɪt/ *v* [I] ~**in/with** have as a final result or highest point: ~ *in success* ▶ **culmination** /ˌkʌlmɪ'neɪʃn/ *n* [sing] final result or highest point

culpable /'kʌlpəbl/ *adj* deserving blame ▶ **culpability** /ˌkʌlpə'bɪləti/ *n* [U] ▶ **culpably** *adv*

culprit /'kʌlprɪt/ *n* person who has done sth wrong

cult /kʌlt/ *n* **1** system of religious worship **2** devotion to a person, thing, practice, etc **3** popular fashion: *a* ~ *film*

cultivate /'kʌltɪveɪt/ *v* [T] **1** prepare and use land for growing plants or crops **2** grow plants and crops **3** try to get sb's friendship or support **4** develop a way of talking, behaving, etc: ~ *her interest in literature* ▶ **cultivated** *adj* showing a high level of education and good manners ▶ **cultivation** /ˌkʌltɪ'veɪʃn/ *n* [U]

culture /'kʌltʃə(r)/ *n* **1** [U] customs, beliefs, art, way of life, etc of a particular country or group: *Greek* ~ **2** [C] country, group, etc with its own beliefs, etc **3** [U] art, music, literature, etc thought of as a group **4** [U] (*tech*) cultivating of crops, etc

5 [C] (*biol, med*) group of cells grown for study ▶ **cultural** *adj* concerning culture ▶ **cultured** *adj* (of people) able to appreciate art, literature, etc ▪ **'culture shock** *n* feeling of confusion and anxiety that sb may feel when they go to live in or visit another country

cumbersome /'kʌmbəsəm/ *adj* **1** heavy and awkward to carry **2** slow and inefficient

cumulative /'kjuːmjələtɪv/ *adj* increasing in amount, force, etc by one addition after another

cunning /'kʌnɪŋ/ *adj* having or showing skill in deceiving people: *a* ~ *trick* ● **cunning** *n* [U] quality of being cunning ▶ **cunningly** *adv*

cunt /kʌnt/ *n* (*offens*, △, *sl*) **1** female sexual organs **2** very offensive word used to insult sb

cup¹ /kʌp/ *n* **1** small bowl with a handle for drinking tea, coffee, etc **2** contents of a cup **3** gold or silver vessel given as a prize in a competition **4** something shaped like a cup [IDM] **not sb's cup of tea** (*infml, spoken*) not what sb likes ▶ **cupful** *n* amount that a cup will hold

cup² /kʌp/ *v* (-**pp-**) [T] put your hands in the shape of a cup; hold sth as if in a cup: ~ *your chin in your hands*

cupboard /'kʌbəd/ *n* set of shelves with doors in the front

curable /'kjʊərəbl/ *adj* (of an illness) that can be cured

curate /'kjʊərət/ *n* clergyman who helps a parish priest

curative /'kjʊərətɪv/ *adj* (*fml*) able to cure illness

curator /kjʊə'reɪtə(r)/ *n* person in charge of a museum, art gallery, etc

curb /kɜːb/ *n* **1** ~(**on**) something that controls and limits sth **2** (*esp US*) = KERB ● **curb** *v* [T] control or limit sth, esp sth bad: *to* ~ *your temper*

curd /kɜːd/ *n* [U] (*also* **curds** [pl]) thick soft substance formed when milk turns sour

curdle /'kɜːdl/ *v* [I, T] (cause a liquid to) separate into solid and liquid parts

cure /kjʊə(r)/ *v* [T] **1** ~(**of**) bring sb back to health: ~*d of a serious illness* **2** put an end to sth: *a policy to* ~ *inflation* **3** stop sb doing sth unpleasant, foolish, etc: ~ *sb of an obsession* **4** treat meat, fish, etc in order to preserve it ● **cure** *n* **1** ~(**for**) medicine or medical treatment that cures an illness: *a* ~ *for arthritis* **2** return to health

curfew /'kɜːfjuː/ *n* time or signal for people to stay indoors

curio /'kjʊəriəʊ/ *n* (*pl* ~**s**) rare or unusual small object

curiosity /ˌkjʊəri'ɒsəti/ *n* (*pl* **-ies**) **1**

[U,sing] strong desire to know about sth **2** [C] strange or rare object

curious /'kjʊəriəs/ adj **1** ~about eager to know about sth: ~ about how a machine works **2** strange and unusual ▶ **curiously** adv

curl /kɜːl/ n something that forms a curved or round shape, esp a small bunch of hair ● **curl** v [I, T] **1** form into a curl or curls **2** [I] grow into curls; coil: a plant ~ing round a post [PV] **curl up** lie or sit with a curved back and legs close to the body ▶ **curly** adj (-ier, -iest) having curls

currant /'kʌrənt/ n **1** small dried grape used in cakes, etc **2** (used in compounds) (bush with) small black, red or white fruit: black~s

currency /'kʌrənsi/ n (pl -ies) **1** [U, C] money in use in a country **2** [U] state of being generally used or believed

current[1] /'kʌrənt/ adj **1** of the present time; happening now: ~ affairs **2** in general use; generally accepted ■ **current ac'count** n bank account from which money can be drawn without notice ▶ **currently** adv at the present time; now

current[2] /'kʌrənt/ n **1** movement of water or air in a particular direction **2** flow of electricity **3** fact of particular feelings, opinions, etc being present

curriculum /kə'rɪkjələm/ n (pl -la or -la /-lə/) subjects included in a course of study or taught in a school, college, etc ▶ **curriculum vitae** /kə,rɪkjələm 'viːtaɪ/ (abbr CV) (GB) n written record of your education and employment used when you apply for jobs

curry /'kʌri/ n [C,U] (pl -ies) Indian dish of meat, fish, vegetables, etc cooked with hot spices ● **curry** v (pt, pp -ied) [T] make curry out of meat or vegetables [IDM] **curry favour (with sb)** (disapprov) try to get sb to like or support you by praising or helping them a lot ▶ **curried** adj cooked with hot spices

curse[1] /kɜːs/ n **1** offensive word or phrase used to express anger, etc **2** word or phrase that has a magic power to make sth bad happen: The witch put a ~ on him. **3** sth that causes harm or evil

curse[2] /kɜːs/ v **1** [I] swear: cursing her bad luck **2** [T] say rude things to sb or think rude things about sb **3** [T] use a magic word or phrase against sb to harm them [PV] **be cursed with sth** continuously suffer from or be affected by sth bad

cursor /'kɜːsə(r)/ n (computing) small movable mark on a computer screen that shows the position you are at

cursory /'kɜːsəri/ adj often (disapprov) done quickly and without much attention to detail ▶ **cursorily** adv

curt /kɜːt/ adj (of a speaker or sth spoken) abrupt; brief: a ~ refusal ▶ **curtly** adv ▶ **curtness** n [U]

curtail /kɜːteɪl/ v [T] (fml) shorten or limit sth: ~ sb's spending ▶ **curtailment** n [U]

curtain /'kɜːtn/ n **1** [C] piece of cloth, etc hung up to cover a window, divide a room, etc: draw the ~s **2** [sing] sheet of heavy material across the front of a stage in a theatre **3** [C, usu sing] anything that screens, covers, protects, etc: a ~ of mist [IDM] **be curtains (for sb)** (infml) be a hopeless situation or one that you cannot escape from: ● **curtain** v [T] provide with curtains for a window or room

curtsy (also **curtsey**) /'kɜːtsi/ n (pl -ies or ~s) act of bending the knees (by a woman) to show respect ● **curtsy** v (pt, pp -ied) (also **curtsey**): [I] She ~ied to the Queen.

curve /kɜːv/ n line or surface that bends gradually; smooth bend ● **curve** v [I, T] **1** (cause sth to) move in a curve or curves **2** [I] be in the shape of a curve

cushion /'kʊʃn/ n **1** small bag filled with soft material, to make a seat more comfortable, to kneel on, etc **2** something like a cushion: a ~ of air ● **cushion** v [T] **1** reduce the force of a blow, etc **2** ~(from) protect sb from sth unpleasant

cushy /'kʊʃi/ adj (-ier, -iest) usu (disapprov) (of a job, etc) not needing much effort; easy

custard /'kʌstəd/ n [U] sweet yellow sauce made from eggs, sugar, flour and milk

custodian /kʌ'stəʊdiən/ n person who is in charge of sth, esp a public building

custody /'kʌstədi/ n [U] **1** (legal right or duty of) caring for or keeping sb/sth: ~ of her child **2** imprisonment while waiting for trial: be in ~

custom /'kʌstəm/ n **1** [U] generally accepted behaviour among members of a social group **2** [sing] (fml) way of a person always behaves; habit: ancient ~s **3** [U] (GB, fml) regular use of a shop, etc: We've lost a lot of ~ since prices went up. ▶ **customary** /'kʌstəməri/ adj according to custom, usual ■ **custom-'built** (,custom-'made) adj designed and made for a particular person

customer /'kʌstəmə(r)/ n person who buys sth in a shop, etc, uses a service, etc

customs /'kʌstəmz/ n [pl] **1** (Customs)

government department that collects taxes on goods brought into the country, etc **2** place at an airport, etc where your bags are checked as you come into a country **3** taxes payable on imported goods

cut¹ /kʌt/ v (-tt- *pt*, *pp* cut) [I, T] **1** make an opening or wound in sth with sth sharp: *I ~ my hand with a knife.* **2** [T] remove sth from sth larger with a knife, etc; divide sth into two or more pieces: ~ *a piece of cake* ◇ ~ *the cake into four* **3** [T] shorten sth by cutting it: ~ *sb's hair* **4** [I] be capable of cutting or being cut: *This knife won't* ~. ◇ *Sandstone ~s easily* **5** [T] reduce sth: ~ *prices/ taxes* **6** [T] remove sth from sth: ~ *some scenes from a film* **7** [I, T] remove part of a text on a computer screen in order to place it elsewhere: *You can ~ and paste between different programs.* **8** [T] prepare a film or tape by removing parts of it, etc; edit sth **9** [I] stop filming or recording **10** [I] (in films, radio or television) move quickly from one scene to another **11** [T] (*infml, esp US*) stay away from a class that you should go to **12** [T] (*written*) hurt sb emotionally: *His remarks ~ me deeply.* **13** [T] (of a line) cross another line [IDM] **cut and dried** decided in a way that cannot be changed or argued about **cut both/ two ways** having two opposite effects or results **cut corners** do things in the easiest and quickest way, often by being careless **cut sb dead** (*GB*) pretend not to have seen sb; refuse to greet sb **cut it/things fine** (*infml*) leave yourself just enough time to do sth **cut your losses** stop doing sth that is not successful knowing the situation gets even worse **cut no ice (with sb)** not impress or influence sb **cut sb to the quick** hurt sb's feelings [PV] **cut across sth** **1** affect different groups that you remain separate: ~ *across social barriers* **2** go across a field, etc to shorten your journey **cut sth back; cut back (on sth)** **1** reduce sth: ~ *back on the number of workers* **2** cut shrubs, etc close to the stem **cut sth down** cause sth to fall by cutting it at the base: ~ *down a tree* **cut sth down; cut down (on sth)** reduce the size, amount or number of sth: ~ *down on your smoking* **cut in (on sb/sth)** **1** interrupt a conversation, etc **2** move in front of another vehicle, leaving too little space **cut sb off** interrupt sb: ~ *off while talking on the phone* **cut sb/sth off** stop the supply of sth to sb: ~ *off the gas* **cut sth off** **1** remove sth by cutting: *He ~ off his finger.* **2** block or obstruct their

retreat **cut out** (of an engine, etc) stop working **cut sth out** **1** remove sth by cutting **2** make or shape sth by cutting: ~ *out a dress* **3** leave sth out of a piece of writing, etc **4** (*infml*) stop doing or using sth: ~ *out cigarettes* **not be cut out for sth/to be sth** (not) have the abilities needed for sth: *I'm not ~ out to be a teacher.* **cut sth up** (*infml*) upset sb emotionally **cut sth up** cut sth into small pieces ▪ **'cutback** *n* reduction in sth ▪ **'cut-out** *n* **1** shape cut out of paper, wood, etc **2** safety device that stops the flow of electric current through sth ▪ **,cut·price** *adj* reduced in price; cheap

cut² /kʌt/ n **1** wound caused by sth sharp **2** hole or opening made with a knife, etc **3** ~ (**in**) reduction in amount, size, supply, etc: *a ~ in taxes* **4** act of cutting sth: *Your hair needs a ~.* **5** style in which clothes, hair, etc is cut: *a suit with a loose ~* **6** share in sth: *a ~ of the profits* **7** act of removing part of sth: *make some ~s in the film* **8** part that is cut from sth larger: *a ~ of beef* [IDM] **a cut above sb/sth** better than sb/sth

cute /kju:t/ *adj* **1** attractive, pretty or charming **2** (*infml, esp US*) too clever; sharp-witted ▶ **cutely** *adv* ▶ **cuteness** *n* [U]

cuticle /'kju:tɪkl/ *n* layer of skin at the base of a fingernail or toenail

cutlery /'kʌtləri/ *n* [U] knives, forks, etc used for eating

cutlet /'kʌtlət/ *n* slice of meat or fish

cutter /'kʌtə(r)/ *n* **1** [C] person or thing that cuts (**cutters**) [pl] (used esp in compounds) tool for cutting **3** [C] type of small sailing boat

cut-throat /'kʌt θrəʊt/ *adj* (of an activity) in which people compete in aggressive and unfair ways

cutting /'kʌtɪŋ/ *n* **1** article or a story cut from a newspaper or magazine **2** short piece of the stem of a plant, used for growing a new plant **3** (*GB*) narrow open passage cut in high ground for a road, railway or canal ● **cutting** *adj* (of remarks, etc) unkind; hurtful

CV /ˌsiː 'viː/ *abbr* curriculum vitae

cyanide /'saɪənaɪd/ *n* [U] strong poison

cyber- /'saɪbə(r)/ *prefix* connected with electronic communication networks, esp the Internet

cybercafe /'saɪbəkæfeɪ/ *n* a cafe with computers on which customers can use the Internet, send emails, etc

cyberspace /'saɪbəspeɪs/ *n* [U] imaginary place where electronic messages, pictures, etc exist while they are being sent between computers

cycle /ˈsaɪkl/ n **1** (infml) bicycle or motorcycle: go for a ~ ride **2** series of events in a regularly repeated order: the ~ of the seasons ● **cycle** v [I] ride a bicycle ▶ **cyclical** /ˈsaɪklɪkl; ˈsɪk-/ adj repeated many times and always happening in the same order ▶ **cyclist** n person who cycles

cyclone /ˈsaɪkləʊn/ n violent tropical storm in which winds move in a circle

cygnet /ˈsɪɡnət/ n young swan

cylinder /ˈsɪlɪndə(r)/ n **1** long solid or hollow body with circular ends and straight sides **2** hollow tube in an engine, shaped like a cylinder, inside which the piston moves ▶ **cylindrical** /səˈlɪndrɪkl/ adj cylinder-shaped

cymbal /ˈsɪmbl/ n musical instrument in the form of a round metal plate, which is hit with a stick or against another cymbal to make a ringing sound

cynic /ˈsɪnɪk/ n person who believes that people only do things to help themselves, rather than for good or sincere reasons ▶ **cynical** adj of or like a cynic: a ~al remark ▶ **cynically** /-kli/ adv ▶ **cynicism** /ˈsɪnɪsɪzəm/ n [U]

cypher = CIPHER

cypress /ˈsaɪprəs/ n any of various types of evergreen tree with dark leaves and hard wood

cyst /sɪst/ n swelling or lump filled with liquid in the body or under the skin

cystitis /sɪˈstaɪtɪs/ n [U] infection of the bladder

czar, czarina = TSAR, TSARINA

Dd

D, d /diː/ n [C,U] (pl **D's, d's** /diːz/) **1** the fourth letter of the English alphabet **2** Roman numeral for 500

d. abbr died: d. 1924

dab /dæb/ v (-**bb**-) [T] touch sth lightly or gently: ~ your face dry ● **dab** n small quantity of paint, etc put on a surface

dabble /ˈdæbl/ v **1** [I] ~(in) interested in a subject in a way that is not serious **2** [T] move your hands or feet gently about in water

dachshund /ˈdæksnd/ n small dog with very short legs

dad /dæd/ n (infml) father

daddy /ˈdædi/ n (pl -**ies**) (used by children) father

daffodil /ˈdæfədɪl/ n yellow trumpet-shaped flower that grows in spring

daft /dɑːft/ adj (infml) silly

dagger /ˈdæɡə(r)/ n short sharp knife used as a weapon

daily /ˈdeɪli/ adj, adv happening or appearing every day or every weekday ● **daily** n (pl -**ies**) newspaper that is published every day

dainty /ˈdeɪnti/ adj (-**ier**, -**iest**) pretty and delicate ▶ **daintily** adv

dairy /ˈdeəri/ n (pl -**ies**) **1** building on a farm where butter and cheese are made **2** company that sells milk, butter, eggs, etc ▶ **dairy** adj **1** made from milk: ~ products **2** connected with the production of milk: ~ cattle

daisy /ˈdeɪzi/ n (pl -**ies**) small flower with a yellow centre and white petals

dale /deɪl/ n (lit) valley

dam /dæm/ n wall built to keep back water ● **dam** v (-**mm**-) [T] build a dam across sth

damage /ˈdæmɪdʒ/ n **1** [U] harm; loss: The fire caused great ~. **2** (**damages**) [pl] (law) money claimed from a person who has caused loss or injury ● **damage** v [T] harm or spoil sb/sth

dame /deɪm/ n (**Dame**) title given to a woman as a special honour because of the work she has done

damn /dæm/ exclam (infml) used for showing anger or annoyance ● **damn** (also **damned**) adj, adv (infml) **1** swear word people use to show anger or annoyance: You know ~ well what I mean! **2** swear word people use to emphasize what they are saying: He was ~ lucky to survive. ● **damn** v [T] **1** used when swearing at sb/sth to show that you are angry **2** (of God) decide sb must suffer in hell **3** criticize sb/sth very strongly ● **damn** n [IDM] **not care/give a damn (about sb/sth)** (infml) not care at all about sb/sth ▶ **damnation** /dæmˈneɪʃn/ n [U] state of being in hell; act of sending sb to hell

damp¹ /dæmp/ adj slightly wet: a ~ cloth ● **damp** n [U] state of being damp; areas on a wall, etc that are damp ▶ **dampness** n [U]

damp² /dæmp/ v = DAMPEN [PV] **damp sth down** make a fire burn more slowly

dampen /ˈdæmpən/ v [T] **1** make sth slightly wet **2** make a feeling or a reaction less strong: ~ his enthusiasm

damper /ˈdæmpə(r)/ n small flat piece of metal that controls the flow of air into a fire [IDM] **put a damper on sth** (infml) make sth less enjoyable, successful, etc

damson /ˈdæmzn/ n (tree producing a) small purple plum

dance /dɑːns/ n **1** [C] movements and steps in time to music **2** [U] art of dancing **3** [C] act of dancing: *He asked her for a* ~. **4** [C] social event at which people dance ● **dance** v **1** [I] move with steps in time to music **2** [T] do a particular type of dance ▶ **dancer** n ● **dancing** n [U]: *dancing classes/shoes*

dandelion /ˈdændɪlaɪən/ n small wild plant with yellow flowers

dandruff /ˈdændrʌf/ n [U] small pieces of dead skin in a person's hair

danger /ˈdeɪndʒə(r)/ n **1** [U] possibility of being hurt or killed **2** [C] thing or person that may cause danger [IDM] **in danger** likely to be hurt or killed **out of danger** no longer seriously ill ▶ **dangerous** adj likely to cause danger ▶ **dangerously** adv

dangle /ˈdæŋɡl/ v [I, T] hang or swing loosely

dank /dæŋk/ adj unpleasantly damp and cold: *a* ~ *cellar/cave*

dare /deə(r)/ v **1** (*pres tense, all persons* **dare**, *neg* **dare not**, **daren't** /ˈdeənt/ *or* **do not/does not dare**, *short form* **don't/doesn't dare**) [I] ~(**to**) (*usu in negative sentences*) have enough courage to do sth: *No one* ~(*to*) *speak.* ◇ *I* ~*n't ask him.* ◇ *We didn't* ~ (*to*) *go into the room.* **2** [T] ~(**to**) challenge sb to do sth dangerous or difficult: *I* ~ *you to jump off the tree.* ● **dare** n [usu sing] something dangerous, difficult, etc that you try to persuade sb to do, to see if they will do it: *He climbed onto the roof for a* ~. ■ **daredevil** n person who likes to do dangerous things

daring /ˈdeərɪŋ/ adj brave; willing to take risks ▶ **daringly** adv

dark¹ /dɑːk/ adj **1** with no or very little light: *a* ~ *night/room* **2** (*of colour*) nearer black than white: ~ *blue* **3** (*of the skin*) not fair **4** hopeless; sad: *look on the* ~ *side of things* [IDM] **a dark horse** person who hides special abilities ▶ **darken** v [I, T] become or make sth dark ▶ **darkly** adv ▶ **darkness** n [U]

dark² /dɑːk/ n [U] lack of light: *sit in the* ~ [IDM] **after/before dark** after/before the sun goes down **in the dark (about sth)** knowing nothing about sth

darling /ˈdɑːlɪŋ/ n person who is loved very much

darn /dɑːn/ v [I, T] repair a hole in sth by sewing: ~ *sb's socks* ● **darn** n hole repaired by darning

dart /dɑːt/ n **1** [C] small pointed object used in the game of darts **2** (**darts**) [U] game in which darts are thrown at a target ● **dart** v [I] move suddenly and quickly

dash¹ /dæʃ/ n **1** [sing] sudden quick movement: *make a* ~ *for the bus* **2** small amount of sth added: *a* ~

of pepper **3** punctuation mark (—) ■ **'dashboard** n part of a car in front of the driver that has instruments and controls in it

dash² /dæʃ/ v **1** [I] go somewhere quickly: ~ *across the road* **2** [T] throw sth violently onto a hard surface [IDM] **dash sb's hopes** destroy sb's hopes ▶ **dashing** adj (*written*) attractive and confident

data /ˈdeɪtə/ n [U] information or facts, esp to be analysed by a computer ■ **database** n organized store of computer data ■ **data processing** n [U] (*computing*) series of actions that a computer performs on data to produce an output (= information that has been analysed)

date¹ /deɪt/ n **1** [C] particular day of the month or year: *Her* ~ *of birth is 24 April 1983.* **2** [sing] a particular time: *We'll discuss this at a later* ~. **3** [C] arrangement to meet sb, esp a boyfriend or girlfriend **4** [C] (*esp US*) boyfriend or girlfriend with whom you have arranged a date **5** [C] sweet sticky brown fruit that grows on a tree [IDM] **out of date 1** old-fashioned; no longer useful: *out-of-* ~ *methods/machinery* **2** no longer valid: *My passport's out of* ~. **to date** until now **up to date 1** completely modern **2** with all the latest information: *I'll bring you up to* ~ *with the latest news.*

date² /deɪt/ v **1** write a date on sth: *The letter was* ~*d 23 July.* **2** [T] say when sth old existed or was made **3** [I] become old-fashioned **4** [T] (*US*) have a romantic relationship with sb [PV] **date back (to ...)|date from ...** have existed since ...: *The church* ~*s from the twelfth century.* ▶ **dated** /ˈdeɪtɪd/ adj old-fashioned

daub /dɔːb/ v [T] put paint, plaster, etc roughly on a surface

daughter /ˈdɔːtə(r)/ n person's female child ■ **'daughter-in-law** n (*pl* ~**s-in-law**) wife of your son

daunting /ˈdɔːntɪŋ/ adj making you feel nervous and less confident

dawdle /ˈdɔːdl/ v [I] go somewhere very slowly

dawn /dɔːn/ n **1** [C,U] first light of day **2** [sing] beginning of sth ● **dawn** v [I] begin to become light [PV] **dawn on sb** become clear to sb: *The truth began to* ~.

day /deɪ/ n **1** [C] period of 24 hours **2** [U] time between sunrise and sunset: *It rained all* ~ *long.* **3** [C, usu sing] hours of the day when you are awake, working, etc **4** [C,usu pl] period of time or history: *in the* ~*s of the Roman Empire* [IDM] **any day (now)** (*spoken*) very soon **day after day | day in, day out** every day for a long time **day and night** → NIGHT

sb's/sth's days are numbered person or thing will soon die, fail, etc **make sb's day** (*infml*) make sb very happy **one day** at some time in the future or at a particular time in the past ■ **daybreak** *n* [U] first light of day; dawn ■ **daydream** *v* [I] *n* (have) pleasant thoughts that make you forget about the present ■ **daylight** *n* [U] light from the sun during the day ■ **daytime** *n* [U] time between sunrise and sunset

daze /deɪz/ *n* [IDM] **in a daze** unable to think clearly

dazed /deɪzd/ *adj* unable to think or react normally

dazzle /'dæzl/ *v* [T] **1** make sb unable to see clearly because of too much strong light **2** impress sb with your beauty, skill, etc

DDT /ˌdiː diː 'tiː/ *n* [U] powerful dangerous insecticide

dead /ded/ *adj* **1** (of people, animals or plants) no longer alive **2** belonging to the past; no longer used or believed in **3** (of machines, etc) not working: *The phone suddenly went ~.* **4** without activity: *The town is ~ after 10 o'clock.* **5** (*infml*) extremely tired; not well **6** (of part of the body) unable to feel because of cold, etc **7** complete; absolute: *a ~ silence/calm* ● **dead** *adv* completely; absolutely: *~ certain/accurate* ► **the dead** *n* [pl] people who have died ■ **dead 'end** *n* place or situation where more progress is impossible ■ **deadline** *n* fixed date for completing a task: *meet/miss a ~line* ■ **dead 'loss** *n* [usu sing] (*GB, infml*) person or thing that is not useful or helpful

deaden /'dedn/ *v* [T] make a sound, feeling, etc less strong

deadlock /'dedlɒk/ *n* [C, U] total failure to reach agreement

deadly /'dedli/ *adj* (-ier, -iest) **1** causing or likely to cause death: *a ~ poison* **2** extreme; complete: *I'm in ~ earnest.* **3** (*GB, infml*) boring ● **deadly** *adv* (*infml*) extremely: *~ serious*

deaf /def/ *adj* **1** unable to hear **2 ~to** unwilling to listen ■ **the deaf** *n* [pl] deaf people ► **deafness** *n* [U]

deafen /'defn/ *v* [T] make it difficult for sb to hear sth: *~ed by the noise*

deal[1] /diːl/ *v* (*pt, pp* **~t** /delt/) [I, T] **1** give out playing cards to a number of players ■ buy and sell illegal drugs [IDM] **deal sb/sth a blow** | **deal a blow to sb/sth** (*fml*) be very shocking or harmful to sb/sth [PV] **deal in sth** buy and sell goods; trade in sth: *In second-hand cars deal with sb/sth* **1** take appropriate action in a particular situation: *She has to ~ with difficult customers in her job.* **2** do business with a per-

son, a company or an organization **deal with sth 1** solve a problem, carry out a task, etc **2** be about sth: *poems that ~ with the subject of death* ► **dealer** *n* **1** person whose business is buying and selling a particular product: *an antiques/art ~* **2** person who sells illegal drugs **3** person who deals out playing cards ► **dealings** *n* [pl] business activities: *have ~ings with sb*

deal[2] /diːl/ *n* [sing] (**a good/great ~**) much; a lot: *a good ~ of money* ◇ *I see a great ~ of him.* **2** [C] (*business*) agreement **3** [C, usu sing] way that sb/sth is treated: *They'd had a rough/raw ~* (= been treated unfairly). **4** [C] action of giving out playing cards in a card game

dean /diːn/ *n* **1** priest of high rank in charge of other priests **2** head of a university department

dear /dɪə(r)/ *adj* **1 ~ (to)** loved by or important to sb (*Dear*) used at the beginning of letters: *D~ Madam/Sir* **3** (*GB*) expensive ● **dear** *exclam* used for expressing surprise, impatience, etc: *Oh ~! ◇ D~ me!* ● **dear** *n* **1** (*GB, spoken*) kind person **2** used when speaking kindly to sb: *Yes, ~.* ● **dear** *adv* (*GB*) at a high price ► **dearly** *adv* **1** very much **2** with great loss, damage, etc

dearth /dɜːθ/ *n* [sing] ~(**of**) (*fml*) shortage of sth

death /deθ/ *n* **1** [C] dying; being killed **2** [U] end of life; state of being dead **3** [U] ~**of** permanent end or destruction of sth [IDM] **put sb to death** kill sb; execute sb to **death** extremely; very much: *be bored/frightened to ~* ► **deathly** *adj, adv* like death ■ **death penalty** *n* [sing] punishment of being killed for a crime ■ **death trap** *n* (*infml*) road, vehicle, etc that is dangerous and could cause sb's death ■ **death warrant** *n* official order for sb to be killed as punishment for a crime

debacle /deɪ'bɑːkl/ *n* event or situation that is a complete failure

debase /dɪ'beɪs/ *v* [T] lower the value or quality of sth ► **debasement** *n* [U]

debate /dɪ'beɪt/ *n* [C, U] formal discussion at a public meeting or in Parliament ► **debate** *v* [I, T] discuss sth formally; consider sth ► **debatable** *adj* not certain; open to question

debauched /dɪ'bɔːtʃt/ *adj* (*fml*) immoral ► **debauchery** /dɪ'bɔːtʃəri/ *n* [U] wild immoral behaviour

debilitating /dɪ'bɪlɪteɪtɪŋ/ *adj* making sb weak: *a ~ illness*

debit /'debɪt/ *n* written note in a bank account of money owed or spent ● **debit** *v* [T] take money from an account to pay for sth

debris /'debriː; 'deɪ-/ *n* [U] pieces of

metal, wood, etc left after sth has been destroyed

debt /det/ n **1** [C] sum of money owed to sb **2** [U] state of owing money: *be in/out of* ~ **3** [C, usu sing] fact of feeling grateful to sb for their help or kindness: *to owe a* ~ *of gratitude to sb* ▶ **debtor** n person who owes money to sb

debut /'deɪbjuː/ n **1** first public appearance of an actor, musician, etc: *make your* ~

decade /'dekeɪd; dɪ'keɪd/ n period of ten years

decadent /'dekədənt/ adj (*disapprov*) showing a fall in moral standards: ~ *behaviour/society* ▶ **decadence** /'dekədəns/ n [U]

decaffeinated /ˌdiː'kæfɪneɪtɪd/ adj (of coffee) with the caffeine removed

decant /dɪ'kænt/ v [T] pour wine, etc from a bottle into another container ▶ **decanter** n glass bottle with a stopper, for wine

decapitate /dɪ'kæpɪteɪt/ v [T] cut off sb's head

decay /dɪ'keɪ/ v [I, T] (cause sth to) be destroyed gradually by natural processes: ~*ing teeth/food* **2** [I] lose strength, power, etc; deteriorate ▶ **decay** n [U]

deceased /dɪ'siːst/ ▶ **the deceased** n (pl **the deceased**) (*fml*) person who has recently died

deceit /dɪ'siːt/ n [U, C] dishonest behaviour that causes sb to believe sth that is false ▶ **deceitful** adj behaving dishonestly by making people believe things which are false ▶ **deceitfully** adv ▶ **deceitfulness** n [U]

deceive /dɪ'siːv/ v [T] make sb believe sth that is false ▶ **deceiver** n

December /dɪ'sembə(r)/ n [U, C] twelfth month of the year (See examples of use at *April*.)

decent /'diːsnt/ adj **1** of a good enough standard or quality: *a ~ meal* **2** (of people) honest and fair **3** acceptable to people in a particular situation: *That dress isn't* ~. ▶ **decency** /-nsi/ n [U] ▶ **decently** adv

deception /dɪ'sepʃn/ n **1** [U] act of deceiving sth: *obtain sth by* ~ **2** [C] trick intended to make sb believe sth that is false

deceptive /dɪ'septɪv/ adj misleading: *a ~ appearance* ▶ **deceptively** adv

decibel /'desɪbel/ n unit for measuring the loudness of sounds

decide /dɪ'saɪd/ v **1** [I] think about sth and choose between the possibilities available: *I ~d to leave.* **2** [I] (*law*) make an official or legal judgement **3** affect the result of sth **4** [T] be the reason why sb does sth

▶ **decided** adj obvious and definite
▶ **decidedly** adv definitely

deciduous /dɪ'sɪdʒuəs; -dju-/ adj (of trees) losing their leaves every autumn

decimal /'desɪml/ adj based on or counted in tens or tenths: *the ~ system* ■ **decimal** n fraction expressed in tenths, hundredths, etc, eg 0·25 ■ **decimal 'point** n dot placed after the unit figure in decimals: *10·25*

decimate /'desɪmeɪt/ v [T] **1** kill large numbers of animals, plants or people **2** (*infml*) severely damage or weaken sth

decipher /dɪ'saɪfə(r)/ v [T] succeed in finding the meaning of sth that is difficult to read: *to ~ a code*

decision /dɪ'sɪʒn/ n **1** [C] choice or judgement made after careful thought: *come to/reach/make a ~* **2** [U] ability to decide sth quickly **3** [U] process of deciding sth ▶ **decisive** /dɪ'saɪsɪv/ adj **1** important for the final result of sth: *a ~ factor/victory* **2** able to decide sth quickly and with confidence ▶ **decisively** adv ▶ **decisiveness** n [U]

deck¹ /dek/ n **1** floor in a ship, bus, etc **2** (*esp US*) pack of playing cards **3** (*esp US*) wooden floor that is built outside the back of a house where you can sit and relax **4** part of a music system that records and/or plays sounds on a disc or tape ■ **'deckchair** n folding canvas chair, used outside

deck² /dek/ v [T] ~**(out)** decorate sb/sth: *streets ~ed out with flags*

declare /dɪ'kleə(r)/ v **1** say sth officially or publicly **2** state sth firmly and clearly **3** tell the authorities about money you have earned or goods you have imported, on which you have to pay tax ▶ **declaration** /ˌdeklə'reɪʃn/ n

decline¹ /dɪ'klaɪn/ n [C, U] gradual and continuous loss of quality, importance, power, etc: *a ~ in population* ● **decline** v **1** [I] become smaller, fewer, weaker, etc **2** [I, T] (*fml*) refuse politely to do or accept sth

decode /ˌdiː'kəʊd/ v [T] find the meaning of a message written in code

decompose /ˌdiːkəm'pəʊz/ v [I, T] be destroyed gradually by natural chemical processes: *a ~d body* ▶ **decomposition** /ˌdiːˌkɒmpə'zɪʃn/ n [U]

decor /'deɪkɔː(r)/ n [U, C, usu sing] style in which the inside of a room is decorated

decorate /'dekəreɪt/ v **1** [T] make sth more attractive by putting things on it: *The room was ~d with flowers and balloons.* **2** [I, T] put paint or wallpaper on the walls of a room or building **3** [T] give a medal

decoy /ˈdiːkɔɪ/ n **1** (real or imitation) bird used to attract others so that they can be caught or shot **2** person or thing that is used to tempt sb into a trap

decrease /dɪˈkriːs/ v [I, T] become or make sth smaller in size, number, etc: *Sales are decreasing.* ● **decrease** /ˈdiːkriːs/ n [C,U] process of reducing sth or the amount that sth is reduced by: *a small ~ in exports*

decree /dɪˈkriː/ n **1** official order that has the force of the law: *by royal ~* **2** decision made in a law court ● **decree** v [T] order, judge or decide sth officially

decrepit /dɪˈkrepɪt/ adj very old and not in good condition

dedicate /ˈdedɪkeɪt/ v [T] **~to** give a lot of your time, energy, etc an activity because you think it is important **2** (of an author) write sb's name at the beginning of a book as a sign of friendship or respect ▶ **dedicated** adj working hard at sth because it is important to you ▶ **dedication** /ˌdedɪˈkeɪʃn/ n [U,C]

deduce /dɪˈdjuːs/ v [T] reach a conclusion, theory, etc by reasoning

deduct /dɪˈdʌkt/ v [T] take away an amount or part from sth: *~ £50 from her salary*

deduction /dɪˈdʌkʃn/ n **1** [U,C] conclusion reached by reasoning **2** process of deducting sth; amount deducted: *tax ~s*

deed /diːd/ n **1** (fml) something done; act **2** (law) signed agreement, esp about ownership

deem /diːm/ v [T] consider sth to be sth: *The party was ~ed a great success.*

deep[1] /diːp/ adj **1** going a long way down from the top or surface: *a ~ river ◇ a hole one metre ~* **2** (of sounds) low **3** (of colours or feelings) strong; intense: *~ trouble* **4** (of sleep) from which it is difficult to wake **5** serious; profound: *a ~ book* **6 ~ in** absorbed in sth: *~ in thought/ a book* [IDM] **go off the deep end** (infml) become very angry **in deep water(s)** (infml) in trouble ▶ **deeply** adv very much; intensely: *~ly hurt by your remarks*

deep[2] /diːp/ adv far down or in sth ■ ˌdeep ˈfreeze n = FREEZER ■ ˌdeep-ˈrooted (also ˌdeep-ˈseated) adj (of

feelings and beliefs) very fixed and strong; difficult to change or destroy: *~-rooted suspicions*

deepen /ˈdiːpən/ v [I, T] become or make sth deep, deeper or more intense

deer /dɪə(r)/ n (pl **deer**) fast graceful animal, the male of which has branching horns (**antlers**)

deface /dɪˈfeɪs/ v [T] damage the appearance of sth, esp by drawing or writing on it

defame /dɪˈfeɪm/ v [T] (fml) attack the good reputation of sb ▶ **defamation** /ˌdefəˈmeɪʃn/ n [U]

default /dɪˈfɔːlt/ v [I] **1** fail to pay a debt, perform a duty or appear (eg in a law court) when required **2** (computing) **~(to)** happen when you do not make any other choice or change. ● **default** n [U,C] **1** failure to do sth, appear, etc: *win a game by ~* **2** (computing) what happens if you do not make any other choice or change ▶ **defaulter** n

defeat /dɪˈfiːt/ v [T] **1** win a victory over sb **2** stop sb from being successful: *Looking at the answers ~s the object of the exercise!* ● **defeat** n [C,U] instance of defeating sb/sth or being defeated

defect[1] /ˈdiːfekt/ n fault; imperfection ▶ **defective** /dɪˈfektɪv/ adj

defect[2] /dɪˈfekt/ v [I] leave your country, political party, etc and join an opposing one ▶ **defection** /dɪˈfekʃn/ n [C,U] ▶ **defector** n person who defects

defence (US **defense**) /dɪˈfens/ n **1** [U] act of protecting sb/sth from attack, criticism, etc **2** [C,U] something that provides protection against attack: *the country's ~s* **3** [C, U] (law) (act of presenting an) argument used in a law court to prove that a person did not commit a crime **4** (**the defence**) [sing, with sing or pl verb] the lawyer(s) acting in court for an accused person ▶ **defenceless** adj unable to defend yourself

defend /dɪˈfend/ v [T] **1 ~(from/ against)** protect sb/sth from attack **2** [T] speak or write in support of sb/sth: *~ a decision* **3** [I, T] act as a lawyer for sb who has been charged with a crime ▶ **defendant** n person against whom a case is brought in a law court ▶ **defender** n **1** person who defends sth/sb **2** (in sport) player who guards the goal area ▶ **defensible** /dɪˈfensəbl/ adj able to be defended

defensive /dɪˈfensɪv/ adj **1** protecting sb/sth against attack **2** behaving in a way that shows that you feel that people are criticizing you ● **defensive** n [IDM] **on/onto the**

defensive ready to protect yourself against criticism ▶ **defensively** adv

defer /dɪˈfɜː(r)/ v (-rr-) 1 [I] **~ to** accept sb's decision, opinion, etc, because you respect him or her: I ~ to her experience. 2 [T] delay sth until a later time: ~ payment ▶ **deference** /ˈdefərəns/ n [U] behaviour that shows you respect sb/sth

defiance /dɪˈfaɪəns/ n [U] open refusal to obey sb/sth: in ~ of my orders ▶ **defiant** /dɪˈfaɪənt/ adj openly and aggressively disobedient ▶ **defiantly** adv

deficiency /dɪˈfɪʃnsi/ n [C,U] (pl -ies) state of not having, or not having enough of, sth that is essential ▶ **deficient** /dɪˈfɪʃnt/ adj not having enough of sth

deficit /ˈdefɪsɪt/ n amount by which sth, esp a sum of money, is too small

defile /dɪˈfaɪl/ v [T] (fml) make sth dirty or impure

define /dɪˈfaɪn/ v [T] **1** say or explain what the meaning of a word or phrase is **2** describe or show sth clearly ▶ **definable** adj

definite /ˈdefɪnət/ adj **1** sure or certain; not likely to change **2** easily seen or understood; obvious ■ **definite 'article** n (gram) the word the ▶ **definitely** adv **1** without doubt: ~ly not true **2** (infml) (used in answer to a question): certainly

definition /ˌdefɪˈnɪʃn/ n **1** [C] explanation of the meaning of a word or phrase, esp in a dictionary **2** [U] quality of being clear and easy to see: The photograph lacks ~.

definitive /dɪˈfɪnətɪv/ adj final; not able to be changed

deflate v [I, T] /dɪˈfleɪt, diː-/ make a tyre, etc smaller by letting out air or gas **2** /dɪˈfleɪt/ make sb feel less important or confident **3** /dɪˈfleɪt/ reduce the amount of money in circulation in an economy ▶ **deflation** /dɪˈfleɪʃn/ n [C,U]

deflect /dɪˈflekt/ v [I, T] (cause sth to) change direction, esp after hitting sth: ~ a bullet/criticism ▶ **deflection** /dɪˈflekʃn/ n [C,U]

deform /dɪˈfɔːm/ v [T] change or spoil the natural shape of sth: a ~ed foot ▶ **deformity** n [C,U] (pl -ies)

defraud /dɪˈfrɔːd/ v [T] **~(of)** get money illegally by tricking sb: ~ him of £100

defrost /ˌdiːˈfrɒst/ v [T] remove ice from a refrigerator, frozen food, etc

deft /deft/ adj **~(at)** quick and skilful, esp with your hands ▶ **deftly** adv ▶ **deftness** n [U]

defunct /dɪˈfʌŋkt/ adj (fml) no longer existing or being used

defuse /ˌdiːˈfjuːz/ v [T] **1** reduce the dangerous tension in a difficult

situation **2** remove the fuse from a bomb

defy /dɪˈfaɪ/ v (pt, pp **-ied**) [T] **1** refuse to obey sb or respect sb in authority, a law, a rule, etc **2** (almost) impossible to believe, explain, describe, etc: ~ description **3** challenge sb to do sth

degenerate v [I] /dɪˈdʒenəreɪt/ become worse in quality or strength, etc ● **degenerate** /dɪˈdʒenərət/ adj having lost good moral or mental qualities ▶ **degenerate** /dɪˈdʒenərət/ n

degrade /dɪˈɡreɪd/ v [T] show or treat sb in a way that makes them seem unworthy of respect: This poster ~s women. ▶ **degradation** /ˌdeɡrəˈdeɪʃn/ n [U]

degree /dɪˈɡriː/ n **1** [C] unit for measuring angles: an angle of 30 ~s (30°) **2** [C] unit for measuring temperature: ten ~s Celsius (10°C) **3** [C, U] amount or level of sth: a high ~ of accuracy ◊ I agree with you to a certain ~. **4** [C] qualification given by a university or college to sb who has completed a course [IDM] **by degrees** gradually

dehydrate /diːˈhaɪdreɪt/ v **1** [T] remove water from sth, esp food, in order to preserve it **2** [I, T] (cause sb to) lose too much water from the body

de-ice /ˌdiː ˈaɪs/ v [T] remove the ice from sth

deign /deɪn/ v [T] (disapprov) do sth in a way that shows you think you are too important to do it: She didn't ~ to speak to me.

deity /ˈdeɪəti/ n (pl -ies) god or goddess

dejected /dɪˈdʒektɪd/ adj sad and disappointed ▶ **dejection** /-ʃn/ n [U]

delay /dɪˈleɪ/ v **1** [T] not do sth until a later time or make sth happen at a later time **2** [T] be or make sb slow to do sth: I was ~ed by the traffic. ● **delay** n [C,U] (instance of) delaying sth or being delayed

delectable /dɪˈlektəbl/ adj (written) (of food) extremely pleasant to taste, look at, etc

delegate /ˈdelɪɡət/ n person chosen by others to express their views at a meeting ● **delegate** /ˈdelɪɡeɪt/ v [I, T] **1** give part of your work, power, etc to sb in a lower position than you **2** [T] choose sb to do sth ▶ **delegation** /ˌdelɪˈɡeɪʃn/ n **1** [C] group of representatives of an organization, a country, etc **2** [U] process of delegating

delete /dɪˈliːt/ v [T] remove sth written, printed or stored in a computer ▶ **deletion** /dɪˈliːʃn/ n [C,U]

deliberate¹ /dɪˈlɪbərət/ adj **1**

intentional: *a ~ insult* **2** (of a movement or an action) slow and cautious ▶ **deliberately** *adv*

deliberate² /dɪˈlɪbəreɪt/ *v* [I, T] ~ **(about/on)** (*fml*) think very carefully about sth

deliberation /dɪˌlɪbəˈreɪʃn/ *n* **1** [U, C, *usu pl*] careful thought **2** [U] slowness of action or speech

delicacy /ˈdelɪkəsi/ *n* (*pl* -**ies**) **1** [U] quality of being delicate **2** [C] tasty food: *a local ~*

delicate /ˈdelɪkət/ *adj* **1** needing careful handling or treatment: *a ~ vase/situation* **2** (of a person) becoming ill easily: *in ~ health* **3** small and pretty **4** able to show very small changes or differences: *a ~ instrument* **5** (of colours, flavours and smells) light and pleasant; not strong ▶ **delicately** *adv*

delicatessen /ˌdelɪkəˈtesn/ *n* shop selling prepared, esp unusual or imported food

delicious /dɪˈlɪʃəs/ *adj* having a very pleasant taste or smell

delight¹ /dɪˈlaɪt/ *n* **1** [U] great pleasure: *take ~ in being a parent* **2** [C] cause or source of great pleasure ▶ **delightful** *adj* ▶ **delightfully** *adv*

delight² /dɪˈlaɪt/ *v* [T] give sb a lot of pleasure [PV] **delight in (doing) sth** enjoy doing sth very much ▶ **delighted** *adj* very pleased

delineate /dɪˈlɪnieɪt/ *v* [T] (*fml*) describe, draw or explain sth in detail

delinquent /dɪˈlɪŋkwənt/ *n, adj* (person) behaving badly or committing crimes ▶ **delinquency** /dɪˈlɪŋkwənsi/ *n* [C, U] (*pl* -**ies**) bad or criminal behaviour, usu of young people

delirious /dɪˈlɪriəs; -ˈlɪəriəs/ *adj* **1** in a confused and excited state, usu because of fever **2** very excited and happy ▶ **deliriously** *adv*

delirium /dɪˈlɪriəm; -ˈlɪəriəm/ *n* [U] mental disturbance, esp during illness

deliver /dɪˈlɪvə(r)/ *v* **1** [I, T] take letters, goods, etc to houses or buyers: *~ milk/newspapers* **2** [T] give a speech in public: *~ a lecture* **3** [T] help a woman in the birth of a baby [IDM] **deliver the goods →** GOODS

delivery /dɪˈlɪvəri/ *n* (*pl* -**ies**) **1** [U,C] act of delivering letters, goods, etc: *When can you take ~ of* (= be available to receive) *the car?* **2** [C, U] process of giving birth to a child: *The mother had an easy ~.* **3** [sing] way sb speaks, sings a song, etc in public

delta /ˈdeltə/ *n* land in the shape of a triangle where a river separates into branches

delude /dɪˈluːd/ *v* [T] deceive sb

deluge /ˈdeljuːdʒ/ *n* **1** heavy fall of rain **2** great quantity of sth: *a ~ of letters* ● **deluge** *v* [T] send or give sb/sth with a lot of things at once: *We were ~d with applications.*

delusion /dɪˈluːʒn/ *n* [C,U] false belief: *~s of grandeur* (= a belief that you are more important than you really are)

de luxe /də ˈlʌks; ˈlʊks/ *adj* of very high quality: *a ~ hotel*

delve /delv/ *v* [I] search for sth inside a bag, container, etc [PV] **delve into sth** try hard to find out more information about sth

Dem. *abbr* (in politics in the US) Democrat(ic)

demand¹ /dɪˈmɑːnd/ *n* **1** [C] very firm request for sth; sth that sb needs: *~s for higher pay* **2** [U,C] people's desire for sth/sb that they want to buy/employ: *Our goods are in great ~.* (= many people want them) [IDM] **on demand** when asked for

demand² /dɪˈmɑːnd/ *v* [T] **1** ask for sth very firmly **2** need sth: *work ~ing great care* ▶ **demanding** *adj* **1** needing much skill, effort, etc: *a ~ing job* **2** making others work hard: *a ~ing boss*

demarcate /ˈdiːmɑːkeɪt/ *v* [T] (*fml*) fix the limits of sth ▶ **demarcation** /ˌdiːmɑːˈkeɪʃn/ *n* [U, C]

demean /dɪˈmiːn/ *v* [T] (*fml*) **1** ~ **yourself** do sth that makes people have less respect for you **2** make people have less respect for sb/sth

demeanour (*US* **-or**) /dɪˈmiːnə(r)/ *n* [C, *usu sing*] (*fml*) way sb looks or behaves

demented /dɪˈmentɪd/ *adj* mad

demerara sugar /ˌdeməˈreərə ˈʃuːgə(r)/ *n* [U] (*GB*) type of rough brown sugar

demilitarize (*also* **-ise**) /ˌdiːˈmɪlɪtəraɪz/ *v* [T] remove military forces from an area

demise /dɪˈmaɪz/ *n* [sing] **1** end or failure of an institution, an idea, etc **2** (*fml*) death

demist /ˌdiːˈmɪst/ *v* [T] remove the condensation from a car's windows

democracy /dɪˈmɒkrəsi/ *n* (*pl* -**ies**) **1** [C,U] (country with) a system of government in which all the people of a country can vote to elect their representatives **2** [U] fair and equal treatment of everyone in an organization, etc

democrat /ˈdeməkræt/ *n* **1** person who favours or supports democracy **2** (**Democrat**) (*US*) member of the Democratic Party ▶ **democratic** /ˌdeməˈkrætɪk/ *adj* of or supporting democracy ▶ **democratically** *adv*

demolish /dɪˈmɒlɪʃ/ *v* [T] **1** pull or knock down a building **2** destroy an argument, theory, etc ▶ **demolition** /ˌdeməˈlɪʃn/ n [C,U]

demon /ˈdiːmən/ n **1** evil spirit **2** (infml) person with great skill or energy ▶ **demonic** /diˈmɒnɪk/ adj

demonstrable /ˈdemənstrəbl/ adj that can be shown or proved ▶ **demonstrably** adv

demonstrate /ˈdemənstreɪt/ v **1** [T] show sth clearly by giving proof or evidence **2** [T] show and explain how sth works or how to do sth **3** [I] take part in a public meeting or march, usu as a protest ▶ **demonstrator** n **1** person who demonstrates(3) **2** person whose job is to show or explain how sth works or is done

demonstration /ˌdemənˈstreɪʃn/ n **1** [C] public meeting or march at which people show that are protesting against or supporting sth **2** [C,U] (also infml **demo**) act of showing how sth works or is done **3** [C,U] act of giving proof or evidence for sth ▶ **demonstrative** /diˈmɒnstrətɪv/ adj **1** showing feelings openly **2** (gram) used to identify the person or thing being referred to, eg this, those

demoralize (also **-ise**) /diˈmɒrəlaɪz/ v [T] destroy sb's courage, confidence, etc: ~d students

demote /ˌdiːˈməʊt/ v [T] move sb to a lower position or rank

demure /diˈmjʊə(r)/ adj (of a woman) quiet, serious and shy ▶ **demurely** adv

den /den/ n **1** a wild animal's hidden home: a lion's ~ **2** (disapprov) place where people meet in secret, esp for some illegal or immoral activity: a ~ of thieves

denationalize (also **-ise**) /ˌdiːˈnæʃnəlaɪz/ v [T] sell a company so that it is no longer owned by the government; privatize sth ▶ **denationalization** (also **-isation**) /ˌdiːˌnæʃnəlaɪˈzeɪʃn/ n [U]

denial /diˈnaɪəl/ n **1** statement that sth is not true **2** [C,U] refusal to allow sb to have sth they have a right to expect

denigrate /ˈdenɪɡreɪt/ v [T] claim unfairly that sb/sth is inferior, worthless, etc

denim /ˈdenɪm/ n [U] strong cotton cloth, that is usu blue and is used for making clothes, esp jeans: a ~ jacket

denomination /dɪˌnɒmɪˈneɪʃn/ n **1** religious group **2** unit of money or measurement ▶ **denominational** adj of religious groups

denominator /dɪˈnɒmɪneɪtə(r)/ n number below the line in a fraction, eg 4 in ¾

denote /dɪˈnəʊt/ v [T] **1** be a sign of sth: Red ~s danger. **2** mean sth

denounce /dɪˈnaʊns/ v [T] ~ (as) speak publicly against sth/sb

dense /dens/ adj (~r, ~st) **1** (of people and things) crowded together: ~ traffic **2** difficult to see through: ~ fog **3** (infml) stupid ▶ **densely** adv

density /ˈdensəti/ n (pl **-ies**) **1** [U] the quality of being dense **2** [C,U] (physics) relation of mass to volume **3** [U] (computing) amount of space available on a disk: a high ~ floppy

dent /dent/ n hollow place in a hard surface made by sth hitting it ● **dent** v [T] make a dent in sth

dental /ˈdentl/ adj of or for the teeth

dentist /ˈdentɪst/ n person whose job is to take care of people's teeth ▶ **dentistry** n [U] work of a dentist

denunciation /dɪˌnʌnsiˈeɪʃn/ n [C,U] act of publicly criticizing sth/sb

deny /dɪˈnaɪ/ v (pt, pp **-ied**) [T] **1** say that sth is not true **2** refuse to give sth asked for or needed by sb

deodorant /diˈəʊdərənt/ n [C,U] substance that hides or removes body odours

dep. abbr (in writing) depart(s); departure

depart /dɪˈpɑːt/ v [I] (fml) go away; leave: The train ~s from platform 3.

department /dɪˈpɑːtmənt/ n one of several divisions of a government, business, shop, university, etc ■ de**partment store** n large shop where many kinds of goods are sold in different departments

departure /dɪˈpɑːtʃə(r)/ n [C,U] **1** act of leaving a place **2** plane, train, etc leaving a place at a particular time: the ~s board

depend /dɪˈpend/ v [IDM] **that depends | it (all) depends** used to say that you are not certain about sth because other things must be considered [PV] **depend on/upon sb/sth 1** rely on sb/sth; be certain about sth: You can ~ on John not to be late. **2** need the support of sb/sth in order to survive: Children ~ on their parents. **3** be affected or decided by sth: Our success ~s on how hard we work. ▶ **dependable** adj that can be relied on: a ~able friend

dependant (esp US **-ent**) /dɪˈpendənt/ n person who depends on another for a home, food, etc

dependence /dɪˈpendəns/ n [U] state of needing sth in order to survive, esp when this is not normal or necessary: ~ on drugs

dependent /dɪˈpendənt/ adj **1** ~ (on/upon) needing sb/sth for support: ~ on her parents **2** ~ on/upon affected or decided by sth: ~ on *your passing the exam* ▶ **dependent** *n (esp US)* = DEPENDANT

depict /dɪˈpɪkt/ *v* [T] show an image of sb/sth in a picture; describe sth in words ▶ **depiction** /-kʃn/ *n* [U,C]

deplete /dɪˈpliːt/ *v* [T] reduce sth by a large amount: *Our supplies are badly ~d.* ▶ **depletion** /dɪˈpliːʃn/ *n* [U]

deplore /dɪˈplɔː(r)/ *v* [T] express strong disapproval of sth ▶ **deplorable** *adj* very bad; deserving strong disapproval

deploy /dɪˈplɔɪ/ *v* [T] *(tech)* move soldiers or weapons into position for battle

deport /dɪˈpɔːt/ *v* [T] force sb unwanted to leave a country ▶ **deportation** /ˌdiːpɔːˈteɪʃn/ *n* [C,U]

depose /dɪˈpəʊz/ *v* [T] remove a ruler from power

deposit¹ /dɪˈpɒzɪt/ *n* **1** payment of part of a larger sum, the rest of which is to be paid later **2** amount of money that sb pays when beginning to rent sth **3** amount of money paid into a bank account **4** layer of a substance left by a river, etc ■ **de'posit account** *n* account at a bank, etc in which the money earns interest

deposit² /dɪˈpɒzɪt/ *v* [T] **1** put sth or put sth down **2** (eg of a river) leave mud, etc on sth **3** put money into a bank, esp to earn interest; put sth valuable in a safe place

depot /ˈdepəʊ/ *n* **1** storehouse; warehouse *(GB)* place where vehicles, eg buses, are kept **2** *(US)* small railway or bus station

depraved /dɪˈpreɪvd/ *adj (fml)* morally bad ▶ **depravity** /dɪˈprævəti/ *n* [U]

deprecate /ˈdeprəkeɪt/ *v* [T] *(fml)* feel and show disapproval of

depreciate /dɪˈpriːʃieɪt/ *v* [I] become less valuable over a period of time ▶ **depreciation** /dɪˌpriːʃiˈeɪʃn/ *n* [U]

depress /dɪˈpres/ *v* [T] **1** make sb sad: *feel very ~ed* **2** make trade, business, etc less active: *The recession has ~ed the housing market.* **3** lower the value of prices or wages **4** *(fml)* press or push sth down ▶ **depressing** *adj* making you feel sad: *a ~ing film*

depression /dɪˈpreʃn/ *n* **1** [U,C] state of feeling very sad and anxious: *clinical ~* **2** [C] period of little economic activity and poverty and unemployment **3** [C] *(written)* part of a surface that is lower than the parts around it **4** [C] *(tech)* weather condition in which the air pressure becomes lower

deprive /dɪˈpraɪv/ *v* [PV] **deprive sb/sth of sth** prevent sb from having or doing sth: *~ people of free-*

dom ▶ **deprivation** /ˌdeprɪˈveɪʃn/ *n* [U] ▶ **deprived** *adj* without enough food, housing, health care, etc

Dept *abbr* Department

depth /depθ/ *n* **1** [C,U] distance from the top to the bottom or from the front to the back **2** [U] deep thought, feeling, etc: *a writer of great ~* [IDM] **in depth** in detail; thoroughly **out of your depth 1** in water that is deeper than your height **2** in a situation that is beyond your understanding or control

deputation /ˌdepjuˈteɪʃn/ *n* [C, with sing or pl verb] group of people with the right to act or speak for others

deputize (*also* -**ise**) /ˈdepjutaɪz/ *v* [I] ~ (**for**) act as deputy: *~ for the manager*

deputy /ˈdepjuti/ *n* (*pl* -**ies**) person immediately below a business manager, a head of a school, a political leader, etc and who does the person's job when he or she is away

derail /dɪˈreɪl/ *v* [T] cause a train to leave the track ▶ **derailment** *n* [C,U]

deranged /dɪˈreɪndʒd/ *adj* unable to act and think normally, esp because of mental illness

derelict /ˈderəlɪkt/ *adj* left to fall into ruin: *a ~ house* ▶ **dereliction** /ˌderəˈlɪkʃn/ *n* [U]

derision /dɪˈrɪʒn/ *n* [U] unkind laughter or remarks

derisory /dɪˈraɪsəri/ *adj* too small to be considered seriously

derivation /ˌderɪˈveɪʃn/ *n* [C,U] origin or development of a word ▶ **derivative** /dɪˈrɪvətɪv/ *adj, n* (something, esp a word) developed from another

derive /dɪˈraɪv/ *v* [PV] **derive sth from sth** *(fml)* get sth from sth: *~ pleasure from sth* **derive from sth|be derived from sth** develop from sth: *words ~d from Latin*

derogatory /dɪˈrɒɡətri/ *adj* showing a lack of respect for sb/sth

derrick /ˈderɪk/ *n* **1** large crane for moving cargo on a ship **2** framework over an oil well to hold the drilling machinery, etc

descend /dɪˈsend/ *v* [I, T] *(fml)* come or go down sth [IDM] **be descended from sb** be related to sb who lived a long time ago [PV] **descend on/upon sb/sth** visit or attack sb/sth in large numbers, usu unexpectedly ▶ **descendant** *n* person or animal that is descended from another

descent /dɪˈsent/ *n* **1** [C, usu sing] action of coming or going down **2** [C] downward slope **3** [U] family; origin: *of French ~*

describe /dɪˈskraɪb/ *v* [T] **1** say what sb/sth is like **2** *(fml)* *(tech)* form a particular shape: *~ a circle*

description /dɪˈskrɪpʃn/ *n* **1** [C,U]

D

(giving a) statement of what sb/sth is like 2 [C] kind or type: *boats of every* ~ ▶ **descriptive** /dɪˈskrɪptɪv/ *adj* saying what sb/sth is like

desecrate /ˈdesɪkreɪt/ *v* [T] spoil or damage a sacred thing or place ▶ **desecration** /ˌdesɪˈkreɪʃn/ *n* [U]

desert¹ /dɪˈzɜːt/ *v* **1** [T] leave sb without help or support: ~ *your family* **2** [T] go away from a place and leave it empty **3** [I] leave the armed forces without permission ▶ **deserter** *n* person who deserts(3) ▶ **desertion** /dɪˈzɜːʃn/ *n* [U]

desert² /ˈdezət/ *n* [C, U] large area of land, without water and trees, often covered with sand ■ **desert 'island** *n* tropical island where no people live

deserts /dɪˈzɜːts/ *n* [pl] [IDM] **sb's (just) deserts** what sb deserves, esp sth bad

deserve /dɪˈzɜːv/ *v* [T] earn sth, either good or bad, because of sth you have done: *She ~d to win.*

design /dɪˈzaɪn/ *n* **1** [U] general arrangement of the parts of a machine, building, etc **2** [U] art of deciding how sth will look, work, etc by drawing plans **3** [C] drawing from which sth may be made **4** [C] decorative pattern of lines, shapes, etc **5** [U, C] plan; intention ● **design** *v* [T] **1** prepare a plan or drawing of sth to be made **2** make, plan or intend sth for a particular purpose or use: *a room ~ed for children* ▶ **designer** *n* person whose job is to decide how clothes, buildings, etc will look by making drawings, plans, etc

designate /ˈdezɪgneɪt/ *v* [T] **1** choose sb for a particular job or purpose **2** mark sth out clearly

desirable /dɪˈzaɪərəbl/ *adj* worth having or doing ▶ **desirability** /dɪˌzaɪərəˈbɪləti/ *n* [U]

desire /dɪˈzaɪə(r)/ *n* [C, U] strong wish to have or do sth: *no ~ to be rich/for wealth* **2** [C, sing] person or thing that is wished for ● **desire** *v* [T] (*fml*) want sb/sth very much

desist /dɪˈzɪst/ *v* [I] ~ (*from*) (*fml*) stop doing sth

desk /desk/ *n* table, usu with drawers in it, that you sit at to read, write or work ■ **desktop com'puter** (*also* **desktop**) *n* computer with a keyboard, screen and main processing unit, that fits on a desk ■ **desktop 'publishing** *n* [U] (*abbr* DTP) use of a small computer and a printer to produce a small book, a magazine, etc

desolate /ˈdesələt/ *adj* **1** (of a place) empty and without people **2** lonely and sad ▶ **desolation** /ˌdesəˈleɪʃn/ *n* [U]

despair /dɪˈspeə(r)/ *n* [U] feeling of

having lost all hope ● **despair** *v* [I] ~ (*of*) stop having any hope: ~ *of ever getting better*

despatch = DISPATCH

desperate /ˈdespərət/ *adj* **1** having little hope and ready to do anything without caring about danger to yourself and others: *The prisoners grew increasingly* ~. **2** (of an action) tried when everything else has failed: *a* ~ *attempt to save her* **3** in great need: ~ *for money* **4** extremely serious or dangerous: *a* ~ *situation* ▶ **desperately** *adv* ▶ **desperation** /ˌdespəˈreɪʃn/ *n* [U]

despicable /dɪˈspɪkəbl/ *adj* very unpleasant or evil

despise /dɪˈspaɪz/ *v* [T] dislike and have no respect for sb/sth

despite /dɪˈspaɪt/ *prep* used to introduce a contrast: *still a clear thinker,* ~ *his old age*

despondent /dɪˈspɒndənt/ *adj* sad, without hope ▶ **despondency** /-dənsi/ *n* [U] ▶ **despondently** *adv*

despot /ˈdespɒt/ *n* ruler with great power, esp one who rules unfairly ▶ **despotic** /dɪˈspɒtɪk/ *adj*: ~ *rule*

dessert /dɪˈzɜːt/ *n* [U, C] sweet food eaten at the end of a meal ■ **des'sertspoon** *n* medium-sized spoon

destination /ˌdestɪˈneɪʃn/ *n* place to which sb/sth is going

destined /ˈdestɪnd/ *adj* **1** intended or certain: ~ *to become famous* **2** ~ *for* on the way to a place

destiny /ˈdestəni/ *n* (*pl* -ies) **1** [C] what happens to sb, or what will happen to them in the future, esp things beyond their control **2** [U] fate

destitute /ˈdestɪtjuːt/ *adj* without food, money, shelter, etc ▶ **destitution** /ˌdestɪˈtjuːʃn/ *n* [U]

destroy /dɪˈstrɔɪ/ *v* [T] **1** break or damage sth so badly it no longer exists, works, etc **2** kill an animal, usu because it is sick ▶ **destroyer** *n* **1** small fast warship **2** person or thing that destroys

destruction /dɪˈstrʌkʃn/ *n* [U] act of destroying sth or of being destroyed ▶ **destructive** /dɪˈstrʌktɪv/ *adj* causing destruction or damage

detach /dɪˈtætʃ/ *v* [I, T] remove sth from sth larger; become separated from sth ▶ **detached** *adj* **1** (of a house) not joined to another **2** not involved; unemotional ▶ **detachment** *n* **1** [U] state of not being emotionally involved **2** [C] group of soldiers sent away from the main group

detail /ˈdiːteɪl/ *n* **1** [C, U] small particular fact or item: *describe sth in* ~ **2** (**details**) [pl] information about sth: *Further ~s are available on* *request.* ● **detail** v [T] **1** give a list of facts or information about sth **2** appoint a soldier for special duty

detain /dɪ'teɪn/ v [T] **1** keep sb in an official place, eg a police station, and prevent them from leaving **2** (*fml*) delay sb ▸ **detainee** /ˌdiːteɪ'niː/ n person who is kept in prison, esp for political reasons

detect /dɪ'tekt/ v [T] discover the existence or presence of sth ▸ **detection** n [U] ▸ **detective** n person, esp a police officer, whose job is to investigate crimes ▸ **detector** n device for detecting sth: *a metal/smoke ~*

detention /dɪ'tenʃn/ n **1** [U,C] act of detaining sb, esp for political reasons **2** [U,C] punishment of being kept at school after school hours

deter /dɪ'tɜː(r)/ v (-rr-) [T] ~ (**from**) prevent or discourage sb from doing sth

detergent /dɪ'tɜːdʒənt/ n [C,U] liquid or powder used for washing clothes or plates, etc

deteriorate /dɪ'tɪəriəreɪt/ v [I] become worse: *His health* ~. ▸ **deterioration** /dɪˌtɪəriə'reɪʃn/ n [U]

determination /dɪˌtɜːmɪ'neɪʃn/ n [U] **1** quality that makes you continue trying to do sth even when this is difficult: *her* ~ *to win* **2** process of deciding sth officially

determine /dɪ'tɜːmɪn/ v [T] (*fml*) **1** discover the facts about sth: ~ *what happened* **2** control sth or cause sth to happen: *Our living standards are* ~*d by our income.* **3** officially decide sth: ~ *party policy* **4** decide firmly to do sth ▸ **determined** *adj* showing a serious wish to do sth successfully: ~*d to improve your English*

deterrent /dɪ'terənt/ n something that makes sb less likely to do sth: *the nuclear* ~ (= nuclear weapons that are intended to stop an enemy from attacking)

detest /dɪ'test/ v [T] hate sb/sth very much ▸ **detestable** *adj* that deserves to be hated

dethrone /ˌdiː'θrəʊn/ v [T] remove a king, queen or ruler from power

detonate /'detəneɪt/ v [I,T] (cause a bomb, etc to) explode ▸ **detonation** /ˌdetə'neɪʃn/ n [C,U] ▸ **detonator** n device that makes a bomb explode

detour /'diːtʊə(r)/ n longer way round sth: *make a* ~ *round the floods*

detract /dɪ'trækt/ v [PV] **detract** (**sth**) **from sth** make sth seem less good or enjoyable

detriment /'detrɪmənt/ n damage; harm: *to the* ~ *of her health* ▸ **detrimental** /ˌdetrɪ'mentl/ *adj* ~ (**to**) harmful

deuce /djuːs/ n (in tennis) score of 40 points to each player

devalue /ˌdiː'væljuː/ v [I,T] make the value of a currency less ▸ **devaluation** /ˌdiːˌvæljuː'eɪʃn/ n [C,U]

devastate /'devəsteɪt/ v [T] **1** completely destroy a place or an area **2** make sb very shocked and sad ▸ **devastation** /ˌdevə'steɪʃn/ n [U]

develop /dɪ'veləp/ v **1** [I,T] become or make sth larger, more advanced, stronger, etc: *The argument* ~*ed into a fight.* **2** [I,T] begin to have sth, eg a disease or a problem; start to affect sb/sth: ~ *a cough* **3** [T] build houses, etc on an area of land and so increase its value **4** [I] treat an exposed film so that the photograph can be seen ▸ **developer** n person or company that develops land ▸ **development** n **1** [U] gradual growth of sth **2** [C] new event or situation **3** [C] area of land with new buildings on it

deviate /'diːvieɪt/ v [I] ~ **from** turn away from what is usual, accepted, etc ▸ **deviation** /ˌdiːvi'eɪʃn/ n [C,U]

device /dɪ'vaɪs/ n **1** object designed to do a particular job **2** plan or trick

devil /'devl/ n **1** (**the Devil**) most powerful evil being; Satan **2** evil spirit **3** (*infml*) person who behaves badly, esp a child ● **devil's advocate** n person who expresses views that admires and is enthusiastic about sb/sth ▸ **devotion** /dɪ'vəʊʃn/ n **1** [U] great love, care and support for sb/sth **2** [pl] prayers

devious /'diːviəs/ *adj* behaving in a dishonest or indirect way in order to get sth

devise /dɪ'vaɪz/ v [T] invent sth new

devoid /dɪ'vɔɪd/ *adj* ~ **of** without sth: ~ *of any ability*

devolution /ˌdiːvə'luːʃn/ n [U] transfer of power from central to regional government

devote /dɪ'vəʊt/ v [PV] **devote sth to sth** give an amount of time, attention, etc to sth: *D~ an hour a day to the project.* **devote yourself to sb/sth** give most of your time, energy, etc to sb/sth ▸ **devoted** *adj* ~ (**to**) very loving or loyal to sb/sth ▸ **devotee** /ˌdevə'tiː/ n person who admires and is enthusiastic about sb/sth ▸ **devotion** /dɪ'vəʊʃn/ n **1** [U] great love, care and support for sb/sth **2** [pl] prayers

devour /dɪ'vaʊə(r)/ v [T] **1** eat all of sth quickly and hungrily **2** (*fml*) destroy sb/sth: *forests* ~*ed by fire*

devout /dɪ'vaʊt/ *adj* (of a person) believing strongly in a particular religion and obeying its laws

dew /djuː/ n [U] tiny drops of water that form on the ground during the night ▸ **dewy** *adj* ● **dewdrop** n drop of dew

dexterity /dek'sterəti/ n [U] skill, esp with your hands ▸ **dexterous** (*also* **dextrous**) /'dekstrəs/ *adj*

diabetes /ˌdaɪə'biːtiːz/ n [U] disease

in which the body cannot control the level of sugar in the blood ▶ **diabetic** /ˌdaɪə'betɪk/ *adj*, *n* (of or for a) person with diabetes

diabolical /ˌdaɪə'bɒlɪkl/ *adj* **1** (*infml, esp GB*) very bad: ~ *weather* **2** evil and wicked

diagnose /ˈdaɪəgnəʊz/ *v* [T] say exactly what an illness or the cause of a problem is ▶ **diagnosis** /ˌdaɪəg-ˈnəʊsɪs/ *n* [C,U] (*pl* -**noses** /-siːz/) act of identifying the exact cause of an illness or problem ▶ **diagnostic** /ˌdaɪəgˈnɒstɪk/ *adj*

diagonal /daɪˈægənl/ *n*, *adj* (straight line) joining two opposite sides of sth at an angle ▶ **diagonally** *adv* /-nəli/

diagram /ˈdaɪəgræm/ *n* drawing, design or plan used for explaining or illustrating sth ▶ **diagrammatic** /ˌdaɪəgrəˈmætɪk/ *adj*

dial /ˈdaɪəl/ *n* **1** marked face of a clock, watch or measuring instrument **2** round part on older telephones, that you move round to call a number ● **dial** *v* (-**ll-** *US* -**l-**) [I, T] use a telephone by turning the dial or pushing buttons to call a number ■ **dialling tone** *n* sound heard on the telephone before you dial the number

dialect /ˈdaɪəlekt/ *n* [C,U] form of a language used in part of a country

dialogue (*US* -**log**) /ˈdaɪəlɒg/ *n* [C, U] **1** conversations in a book, play or film **2** formal discussion between two groups or countries ■ **dialogue box** (*US*, *GB also* **'dialog box**) *n* box that appears on a computer screen asking the user to choose what they want to do next

diameter /daɪˈæmɪtə(r)/ *n* length of a straight line drawn from side to side through the centre of a circle

diametrically /ˌdaɪə'metrɪkli/ *adv* completely: ~ *opposed*

diamond /ˈdaɪəmənd/ *n* **1** [U,C] very hard clear colourless precious stone: *a* ~ *ring* **2** [C] shape with four equal sides whose angles are not right angles **3** (**diamonds**) [pl] one of the four suits in a pack of cards, marked with red diamond shapes ■ **diamond 'jubilee** *n* 60th anniversary of an important event

diaper /ˈdaɪpə(r)/ (*US*) = NAPPY

diaphragm /ˈdaɪəfræm/ *n* **1** (*anat*) muscle between the lungs and the stomach **2** (*tech*) thin vibrating disc or plate in an instrument

diarrhoea (*US* **diarrhea**) /ˌdaɪə'rɪə/ *n* [U] too frequent and too watery emptying of the bowels

diary /ˈdaɪəri/ *n* (-**ies**) book used for a daily record of events, future appointments, etc: *keep* (= write regularly in) *a* ~ ◇ *a desk* ~

dice /daɪs/ *n* (*pl* **dice**) small cube marked with spots to indicate numbers, used in games ● **dice** *v* [T] cut food into small cubes [IDM] **dice with death** (*infml*) risk your life

dictate /dɪk'teɪt/ *v* [I, T] **1** say words aloud for sb else to write down **2** order sb to do sth **3** control or influence how sth happens ▶ **dictation** /dɪk'teɪʃn/ *n* **1** [U] act of saying words aloud so that sb can write it down **2** [C,U] test in which students write down what is being read aloud to them

dictator /dɪk'teɪtə(r)/ *n* (*disapprov*) ruler who has complete power over a country ▶ **dictatorial** /ˌdɪktə'tɔːriəl/ *adj* ▶ **dictatorship** *n* [C,U] (country with) government ruled by a dictator

diction /ˈdɪkʃn/ *n* [U] way that sb pronounces words

dictionary /ˈdɪkʃənri/ *n* (*pl* -**ies**) book containing the words of a language, with their meanings, arranged in alphabetical order

did *pt* of DO

didn't *short for* DID NOT

die /daɪ/ *v* (*pres p* **dying** /ˈdaɪɪŋ/) [I] **1** stop living **2** stop existing; disappear: *love that will never* ~ [IDM] **be dying for sth/to do sth** (*infml*) want (to do) sth very much: *I'm dying for a drink.* ◇ *I'm dying to tell her.* **die laughing** (*infml*) find sth very funny [PV] **die away** become weaker and disappear **die down** become less strong **die out** disappear completely ● **die** *n* metal block used to stamp designs on coins, medals, etc

diesel /ˈdiːzl/ *n* **1** [U] (*also* **'diesel oil**) type of heavy oil used as a fuel used instead of petrol **2** [C] vehicle that uses diesel: *Our new car's a* ~.

diet /ˈdaɪət/ *n* **1** [C,U] food that you eat and drink regularly **2** [C] limited variety or amount of food that you eat to lose weight or for medical reasons: *be/go on a* ~ ● **diet** *v* [I] eat less food or special food in order to lose weight

differ /ˈdɪfə(r)/ *v* [I] **1** ~ (**from**) be different from sb/sth else **2** disagree with sb ▶ **difference** /ˈdɪfrəns/ *n* **1** [C,U] way in which two people or things are not like each other; way in which sb/sth has changed: *the* ~ *in their ages* **2** [sing, U] amount that sth is greater or smaller than sth else: *The* ~ *between 7 and 18 is 11.* **3** [C] disagreement between people: *It's time to settle your* ~*s.* [IDM] **make a, no, some, etc. difference** (**to/in sb/sth**) have an effect/ no effect on sth/sb: *The rain made no* ~ *to the game.*

different /ˈdɪfrənt/ *adj* **1** ~ (**from/to/**

than) not the same as sb/sth; not like sb/sth **2** separate and individual: *several ~ people*

differentiate /ˌdɪfəˈrenʃieɪt/ v [I, T] ~ **between A and B**/~**A from B** show the difference between two or more things; distinguish one thing from others

difficult /ˈdɪfɪkəlt/ adj **1** not easy; needing effort or skill: *find sth ~ to understand* **2** full of problems; causing trouble: *be in a ~ position/ situation* **3** (of people) not easy to please; not helpful ▶ **difficulty** n (pl -ies) **1** [C, usu pl, U] problem, thing or situation that causes problems: *We've run into ~ies with the project.* **2** [U] state or quality of being difficult to do or understand; effort that sth involves: *He stood up with great ~.*

diffident /ˈdɪfɪdənt/ adj lacking confidence; shy ▶ **diffidence** /-dəns/ n [U]

diffuse /dɪˈfjuːz/ v [I, T] (cause sth to) spread widely in all directions ▶ **diffuse** /dɪˈfjuːs/ adj **1** spread over a wide area: *~ light* **2** unclear or easy to understand; using a lot of words ▶ **diffusion** /dɪˈfjuːʒn/ n [U]

dig¹ /dɪg/ v (-gg- pt, pp dug /dʌg/) **1** [I, T] make a hole in the ground or move soil from one place to another using your hands, a tool or a machine **2** [T] remove sth from the ground with a tool: *~ potatoes* [PV] **dig sb/sth out** (of sth) **1** remove sb/sth from sth by digging the ground around them/it **2** find sth that has been hidden or forgotten for a long time: *I dug these old photo albums out of the attic.* **dig sth up** remove or find sth by digging or careful searching

dig² /dɪg/ n **1** small push with your fingers or elbow: *a ~ in the ribs* **2** ~ (**at**) critical remark: *That was a ~ at Ray.* **3** archaeological excavation

digest /daɪˈdʒest/ v [T] **1** change food in your stomach so that it can be used by your body **2** [I] (of food) be changed in this way **3** [T] understand sth fully ▶ **digest** /ˈdaɪdʒest/ n short concise report; summary

digit /ˈdɪdʒɪt/ n **1** any of the ten numbers from 0 to 9 **2** (*anat*) finger or toe ▶ **digital** adj using an electronic system that uses the numbers 1 and 0 to record sound or store information, and that gives high-quality results **1** (of clocks, watches, etc) showing information by using numbers

dignified /ˈdɪgnɪfaɪd/ adj calm and serious and deserving respect

dignitary /ˈdɪgnɪtəri/ n (pl -ies) (*fml*) person with an important official position

dignity /ˈdɪgnəti/ n [U] **1** calm serious manner, that deserves respect **2** fact of being given honour and respect by people [IDM] **beneath your dignity** below what you see as your own importance or worth

digress /daɪˈgres/ v [I] ~(**from**) turn from the main topic of discussion ▶ **digression** /daɪˈgreʃn/ n [U, C]

dike n = DYKE

dilapidated /dɪˈlæpɪdeɪtɪd/ adj (of buildings) old and falling to pieces

dilate /daɪˈleɪt/ v [I, T] become or make sth wider, larger or more open

dilemma /dɪˈlemə/ n difficult situation in which you have to choose between two things

diligent /ˈdɪlɪdʒənt/ adj hardworking; showing care and effort: *a ~ worker* ▶ **diligence** /ˈdɪlɪdʒəns/ n [U] ▶ **diligently** adv

dilute /daɪˈluːt; GB also -ˈljuːt/ v [T] ~ (**with**) make a liquid weaker by adding water or another liquid ▶ **dilution** /daɪˈluːʃn; GB also -ˈljuːʃn/ n [U]

dim /dɪm/ adj (-mer, -mest) **1** not bright: *in a ~ light* **2** not easy to see **3** unclear; vague: *~ memories* **4** (*infml*) not intelligent [IDM] **take a dim view of sth/sb** disapprove of sb/sth ● **dim** v (-mm-) [I, T] become or make sth less bright or strong ▶ **dimly** adv ▶ **dimness** n [U]

dime /daɪm/ n coin of USA and Canada worth ten cents

dimension /dɪˈmenʃn/ n [C] **1** measurement of length, width or height of sth **2** [usu pl] size and extent of a situation: *the ~s of the problem* **3** aspect or way of looking at sth **4** (-dimensional) /-ʃənəl/ (in compound adjectives) having the number of dimensions that is mentioned: *two-~al*

diminish /dɪˈmɪnɪʃ/ v [I, T] become or make sth smaller, weaker, etc

diminutive /dɪˈmɪnjətɪv/ adj (*fml*) very small

dimple /ˈdɪmpl/ n small natural hollow in sb's cheek or chin

din /dɪn/ n [U, sing] loud unpleasant noise

dine /daɪn/ v [I] (*fml*) eat dinner [PV] **dine out** eat dinner in a restaurant, hotel, etc **■ 'dining car** n railway carriage in which meals are served **■ 'dining room** n room in which meals are eaten

dinghy /ˈdɪŋi/ n (pl -ies) small open boat

dingy /ˈdɪndʒi/ adj (-ier, -iest) dark and dirty ▶ **dinginess** n [U]

dining → DINE

dinner /ˈdɪnə(r)/ n [U, C] main meal of the day, eaten either at midday or in the evening **■ 'dinner jacket** n (GB) man's black jacket worn at formal evening events

dinosaur /'daɪnəsɔː(r)/ n large prehistoric reptile that no longer exists

diocese /'daɪəsɪs/ n area for which a bishop is responsible

dip /dɪp/ v (-pp-) 1 [T] put sth into a liquid for a short time: *D~ your hand in to test the water.* 2 [I, T] (cause sth to) go downwards or to a lower level: *The sun ~ped below the horizon.* 3 [T] (GB) lower a beam of light: *Motorists should ~ their headlights.* [PV] **dip into sth** 1 put your hand into a container to take sth out 2 read parts of sth 3 take an amount from money you have saved ● **dip** n 1 [C] (infml) quick swim 2 [C] decrease in the amount or success of sth 3 [C] downward slope 4 [U,C] creamy sauce into which food is dipped

diphtheria /dɪf'θɪəriə/ n [U] serious disease of the throat

diphthong /'dɪfθɒŋ/ n union of two vowels, eg /aɪ/ in *pipe* /paɪp/

diploma /dɪ'pləʊmə/ n official paper showing that a student has passed an examination, etc

diplomacy /dɪ'pləʊməsi/ n [U] 1 management of relations between countries 2 skill in dealing with people; tact

diplomat /'dɪpləmæt/ n person whose job is to represent his or her country in a foreign country ▶ **diplomatic** /,dɪplə'mætɪk/ adj 1 of diplomacy(1): *work in the ~ic service* 2 having or showing diplomacy(2); tactful ▶ **diplomatically** adv

dire /'daɪə(r)/ adj terrible

direct¹ /də'rekt; dɪ-; daɪ-/ adj 1 with nothing or nobody in between: *a ~ result* ◇ *Avoid ~ sunlight.* 2 going straight between two places without stopping: *a ~ route* 3 exact: the *~ opposite* 4 frank and honest ● **direct** adv without interrupting a journey: *fly ~ to Hong Kong* ■ **direct 'current** n [U] (abbr DC) electric current that flows in one direction only ■ **di,rect 'debit** n (in Britain) instruction to your bank that allows sb else to take money from your account ▶ **directness** n [U] ■ **di,rect 'object** n (gram) noun, noun phrase or pronoun that is affected by the action of the verb, eg *the money* in *He took the money.* ■ **di,rect 'speech** n [U] speaker's actual words

direct² /də'rekt; dɪ-; daɪ-/ v [T] 1 aim sth in a particular direction or at a particular person: *Was that remark ~ed at me?* 2 control or be in charge of sb/sth: *~ a project/film* 3 tell how to get somewhere: *Can you ~ me to the station, please?* 4 (fml) give an official order

direction /də'rekʃn; dɪ-; daɪ-/ n 1 [C] general position a person or thing

moves or points towards: *run off in the opposite ~* 2 [C, usu pl] instructions about where to go, etc 3 [U] organization or management of sb/sth: *under my ~*

directive /də'rektɪv; dɪ-; daɪ-/ n (fml) official instruction

directly /də'rektli; dɪ-; daɪ-/ adv 1 in a direct manner; exactly 2 immediately ● **directly** conj as soon as: (GB) *I came ~ I knew.*

director /də'rektə(r); dɪ-; daɪ-/ n 1 person who manages sth, esp a company 2 person who directs a play or a film ▶ **directorship** n position of a company director

directory /də'rektəri; dɪ-; daɪ-/ n (pl **-ies**) 1 book with a list of names, addresses and telephone numbers 2 file containing a group of other files or programs on a computer

dirt /dɜːt/ n [U] 1 unclean matter, eg dust or mud 2 (infml) scandal 3 (infml) = EXCREMENT ■ **dirt 'cheap** adj, adv (infml) very cheap

dirty /'dɜːti/ adj (-ier, -iest) 1 not clean: *~ water* 2 unpleasant or dishonest: *a ~ trick* 3 connected with sex in an offensive way: *a ~ joke* [IDM] **give sb a dirty look** look at sb in a way that shows you are annoyed with them ● **dirty** v (pt, pp -ied) [T] make sth dirty

disable /dɪs'eɪbl/ v [T] injure or affect sb permanently so that they cannot walk or use a part of their body ▶ **disability** /,dɪsə'bɪləti/ n (pl **-ies**) 1 [C] physical or mental condition that disables sb 2 [U] state of being disabled ▶ **disabled** adj ▶ **disablement** n [U]

disabuse /,dɪsə'bjuːz/ v [T] ~of sb that what they think is true is, in fact, false

disadvantage /,dɪsəd'vɑːntɪdʒ/ n something that causes problems: *I hope my lack of experience won't be to my ~.* ▶ **disadvantaged** adj not having the things, eg education or money, that people need to succeed in life ▶ **disadvantageous** /,dɪsædvæn'teɪdʒəs/ adj

disagree /,dɪsə'griː/ v [I] 1 have different opinions: *I ~ with you/with what you say.* 2 be unhelpful [PV] **disagree with sb** (of food) make sb feel ill ▶ **disagreeable** adj unpleasant ▶ **disagreeably** adv ▶ **disagreement** n [C,U] difference of opinion

disappear /,dɪsə'pɪə(r)/ v [I] 1 go out of sight 2 stop existing ▶ **disappearance** n [U,C]

disappoint /,dɪsə'pɔɪnt/ v [I, T] fail to do or be what sb hoped for ▶ **disappointed** adj sad at not getting what was hoped for: *He was bitterly ~ed by the result.* ▶ **disappointing** adj: *a ~ing result* ▶ **disappointingly**

disapprove

adv ▶ **disappointment** *n* **1** [U] state of being disappointed **2** [C] person or thing that disappoints sb

disapprove /ˌdɪsəˈpruːv/ *v* [I] **1** ~(of) say or think that sth/sb is bad ▶ **disapproval** *n* [U]

disarm /dɪsˈɑːm/ *v* **1** [T] take away all weapons from sb **2** [I] (of a country) give up all or some (esp nuclear) weapons **3** [T] (written) make sb feel less angry or critical ▶ **disarmament** *n* [U] act of disarming(2)

disarray /ˌdɪsəˈreɪ/ *n* [U] (*fml*) state of confusion a lack of organization: *in* ~

disassociate /ˌdɪsəˈsəʊʃɪeɪt/; -ˈsəʊs-/ = DISSOCIATE

disaster /dɪˈzɑːstə(r)/ *n* serious sudden misfortune; terrible accident ▶ **disastrous** /dɪˈzɑːstrəs/ *adj* ▶ **disastrously** *adv*

disband /dɪsˈbænd/ *v* [I, T] break up a group of people or an organization

disbelieve /ˌdɪsbɪˈliːv/ *v* [T] refuse to believe sb/sth ▶ **disbelief** /ˌdɪsbɪ-ˈliːf/ *n* [U] feeling of not being able to believe sb/sth

disc (*esp US* **disk**) /dɪsk/ *n* **1** thin flat circular object **2** = CD **3** (*GB, old-fash*) = RECORD(2) **4** one of the layers of cartilage between the bones of the back: *a slipped* ~ ▪ '**disc jockey** *n* (*abbr* DJ) person whose job is to introduce and play popular recorded music on the radio or at a club

discard /dɪsˈkɑːd/ *v* [T] get rid of sth; throw sth away

discern /dɪˈsɜːn/ *v* [T] (*fml*) **1** know, recognize or understand sth, esp sth that is not obvious **2** see or hear sth, but not very clearly ▶ **discernible** *adj* ▶ **discerning** *adj* (*approv*) showing good judgement about the quality of sth ▶ **discernment** *n* [U] ability to judge the quality of sb/sth well

discharge /dɪsˈtʃɑːdʒ/ *v* **1** [T] give sb official permission to leave a place or a job; make sb leave a job **2** [I, T] send out a liquid or gas **3** [T] (*fml*) do everything necessary to perform and complete a particular duty: *to ~ a debt* (= pay it) ● **discharge** /ˈdɪstʃɑːdʒ/ *n* **1** [U, C] action of releasing a gas, liquid, etc; substance that comes out of inside somewhere **2** [U, C] act of officially allowing sb to leave a place, etc **3** [U] (*fml*) act of performing a duty or paying money owed

disciple /dɪˈsaɪpl/ *n* follower of a religious, political, etc leader

discipline /ˈdɪsəplɪn/ *n* **1** [U] practice of training people to obey rules and punishing them if they do not; controlled behaviour that results from such training **2** [U] ability to control your behaviour or the way you live, work, etc **3** [C]

(*fml*) area of knowledge ● **discipline** *v* [T] **1** punish sb for sth they have done **2** train sb to be obedient

disclaim /dɪsˈkleɪm/ *v* [T] (*fml*) say that you have no knowledge of or responsibility for sth

disclose /dɪsˈkləʊz/ *v* [T] **1** make sth known **2** allow sth that was hidden to be seen ▶ **disclosure** /dɪs-ˈkləʊʒə(r)/ *n* [U, C]

disco /ˈdɪskəʊ/ (*also old-fash* **discotheque** /ˈdɪskətek/) *n* (*pl* ~**s**) club, party, etc where people dance to pop records

discolour (*US* -**or**) /dɪsˈkʌlə(r)/ *v* [I, T] (cause sth to) change colour in an unpleasant way ▶ **discoloration** /dɪsˌkʌləˈreɪʃn/ *n* [U, C]

discomfort /dɪsˈkʌmfət/ *n* **1** [U] lack of comfort; slight pain **2** [U] feeling of worry or embarrassment **3** (*fml*) something that causes slight pain or lack of comfort

disconcert /ˌdɪskənˈsɜːt/ *v* [T] embarrass, upset or worry sb

disconnect /ˌdɪskəˈnekt/ *v* [T] ~**A** (**from B**) detach sth from sth; undo a connection ▶ **disconnected** *adj* **1** not related to the things or people around **2** (of speech or writing) badly ordered

disconsolate /dɪsˈkɒnsələt/ *adj* (*fml*) very unhappy and disappointed ▶ **disconsolately** *adv*

discontent /ˌdɪskənˈtent/ (*also* **discontentment** /ˌdɪskənˈtentmənt/) *n* [U,C] ~(**with**) lack of satisfaction ▶ **discontented** *adj* not satisfied

discontinue /ˌdɪskənˈtɪnjuː/ *v* [T] (*fml*) put an end to sth; stop doing sth

discord /ˈdɪskɔːd/ *n* **1** [U] (*fml*) disagreement; quarrelling **2** [C,U] (*music*) combination of musical notes that sound harsh together ▶ **discordant** /dɪsˈkɔːdənt/ *adj*

discotheque = DISCO

discount /ˈdɪskaʊnt/ *n* reduction in price ● **discount** /dɪsˈkaʊnt/ *v* [T] consider sth to be unimportant or untrue

discourage /dɪsˈkʌrɪdʒ/ *v* [T] **1** take away sb's hope or enthusiasm: *~d by failure* **2** persuade sb not to do sth: *~ children from smoking* ▶ **discouragement** *n* [U,C]

discourse /ˈdɪskɔːs/ *n* [C,U] (*fml*) long and serious speech

discourteous /dɪsˈkɜːtiəs/ *adj* (*fml*) impolite; rude ▶ **discourtesy** /dɪsˈkɜːtəsi/ *n* [U]

discover /dɪˈskʌvə(r)/ *v* [T] **1** find or learn about sth for the first time **2** come to know or realize sth; find out about sth ▶ **discoverer** *n*: *the ~er of penicillin* ▶ **discovery** /dɪˈskʌvəri/ *n* (*pl* -**ies**) [C,U] act of finding sb/sth or learning sth that was unknown before **2** [C] something that is found or learned about for the first time

discredit /dɪsˈkredɪt/ v [T] **1** cause people to stop respecting sb/sth **2** cause to appear untrue or doubtful ● **discredit** n [U] (*fml*) loss of respect; damage to sb's reputation

discreet /dɪˈskriːt/ adj careful in what you say or do, in order to keep sth secret ▸ **discreetly** adv

discrepancy /dɪsˈkrepənsi/ n (pl -ies) difference between two things that should be the same

discretion /dɪˈskreʃn/ n [U] **1** freedom to decide what should be done: *use your ~* **2** care in what you say and do, eg in order to keep sth secret

discriminate /dɪˈskrɪmɪneɪt/ v [I] **1** ~(between) see or show a difference between people or things **2** ~against/in favour of treat sb worse/better than another in an unfair way ▸ **discriminating** adj ▸ **discrimination** n [U]

discus /ˈdɪskəs/ n heavy round disc thrown as a sport

discuss /dɪˈskʌs/ v [T] talk or write about sth ▸ **discussion** n [C, U]

disdain /dɪsˈdeɪn/ n [U] feeling that sb/sth is not good enough to deserve respect ● **disdain** v [T] **1** think that sb/sth does not deserve your respect **2** refuse to do sth because you think you are too important to do it ▸ **disdainful** adj

disease /dɪˈziːz/ n illness ▸ **diseased** adj having a disease

disembark /ˌdɪsɪmˈbɑːk/ v [I] leave a ship or an aircraft ▸ **disembarkation** /ˌdɪsˌembɑːˈkeɪʃn/ n [U]

disenchanted /ˌdɪsɪnˈtʃɑːntɪd/ adj ~(with) having lost your good opinion of sb/sth

disengage /ˌdɪsɪnˈgeɪdʒ/ v **1** [T] ~ (from) free sb/sth from something or thing that is holding them or it **2** [I] (*tech*) (of an army) stop fighting

disentangle /ˌdɪsɪnˈtæŋgl/ v [T] **1** ~ (from) free sb/sth from complicated or confused **2** make string, etc free of knots

disfigure /dɪsˈfɪgə(r)/ v [T] spoil the appearance of sb/sth ▸ **disfigurement** n [C, U]

disgorge /dɪsˈgɔːdʒ/ v [I, T] (*written*) (cause sth to) flow or pour out of sth

disgrace /dɪsˈgreɪs/ n **1** [U] loss of other people's respect because of sb's bad behaviour **2** [sing] person or thing that is so bad that it causes shame to others: *He's a ~ to the legal profession.* ● **disgrace** v [T] behave badly in a way that makes you or other people feel ashamed ▸ **disgraceful** adj very bad; that people should feel ashamed about

disgruntled /dɪsˈgrʌntld/ adj annoyed and dissatisfied

disguise /dɪsˈgaɪz/ v [T] **1** change your appearance so that people cannot recognize you **2** hide sth or change it, so that it cannot be recognized: ~ *your anger* ● **disguise** n **1** [C, U] thing you wear in order to disguise yourself **2** [U] art of changing your appearance

disgust /dɪsˈgʌst/ n [U] strong dislike or disapproval of sb/sth ● **disgust** v [T] make sb feel shocked and almost ill ▸ **disgusted** adj feeling disgust ▸ **disgusting** adj causing disgust

dish /dɪʃ/ n **1** [C] flat shallow container for serving food **2** [C] particular kind of food in a meal **3** (**the dishes**) [pl] plates, bowls, cups, etc used for a meal ● **dish** v [PV] **dish sth out** (*infml*) give away a lot of sth: ~ *out leaflets/compliments* **dish (sth) up** serve food onto plates ■ **dishcloth** n cloth for washing dishes ■ **dishwasher** n machine that washes plates, bowls, etc

dishearten /dɪsˈhɑːtn/ v [T] (*written*) make sb lose hope or confidence

dishevelled (*US* -l-) /dɪˈʃevld/ adj (of clothes or hair) very untidy

dishonest /dɪsˈɒnɪst/ adj not honest; intending to deceive people ▸ **dishonestly** adv ▸ **dishonesty** n [U]

dishonour (*US* -or) /dɪsˈɒnə(r)/ n [U] (*fml*) loss of respect because you have done sth immoral or unacceptable ● **dishonour** v [T] (*fml*) make sb/sth lose people's respect **1** or immoral or **2** refuse to keep an agreement or promise ▸ **dishonourable** adj immoral or unacceptable

disillusion /ˌdɪsɪˈluːʒn/ v [T] destroy sb's belief in or good opinion of sb/sth ▸ **disillusioned** adj ▸ **disillusionment** n [U]

disinclined /ˌdɪsɪnˈklaɪnd/ adj ~ (to) (*fml*) not willing

disinfect /ˌdɪsɪnˈfekt/ v [T] clean sth with a substance that kills bacteria: ~ *a wound* ▸ **disinfectant** n [U, C] substance that disinfects

disinformation /ˌdɪsɪnfəˈmeɪʃn/ n [U] false information, esp from a government

disinherit /ˌdɪsɪnˈherɪt/ v [T] prevent sb from inheriting your property

disintegrate /dɪsˈɪntɪgreɪt/ v [I] break into small pieces ▸ **disintegration** /dɪsˌɪntɪˈɡreɪʃn/ n [U]

disinterested /dɪsˈɪntrəstɪd/ adj not influenced by personal interests

disjointed /dɪsˈdʒɔɪntɪd/ adj not communicated in a logical way; not connected

disk /dɪsk/ n **1** (*esp US*) = DISC

2 (*computing*) device for storing information on a computer, with a magnetic surface that records information received in electronic form: *a floppy ~* ■ **disk drive** *n* device in a computer that transfers information to and from a disk(2) ► **dis'kette** *n* = FLOPPY DISK (FLOP)

dislike /dɪsˈlaɪk/ *v* [T] not like sb/sth ● **dislike** *n* **1** [U] feeling of not liking sb/sth **2** [C] something that you dislike

dislocate /ˈdɪsləkeɪt/ *v* [T] **1** put a bone out of its usual position **2** stop a system, plan, etc from working ► **dislocation** /ˌdɪsləˈkeɪʃn/ *n* [C, U]

dislodge /dɪsˈlɒdʒ/ *v* [T] force or knock sth out of its position

disloyal /dɪsˈlɔɪəl/ *adj* not loyal ► **disloyalty** *n* [U]

dismal /ˈdɪzməl/ *adj* sad; miserable ► **dismally** *adv*

dismantle /dɪsˈmæntl/ *v* [T] take sth to pieces: ~ *a machine/engine*

dismay /dɪsˈmeɪ/ *n* [U] worried, sad feeling after you have received an unpleasant surprise ● **dismay** *v* [T] shock and disappoint sb

dismember /dɪsˈmembə(r)/ *v* [T] **1** cut or tear the arms and legs off a dead body **2** divide a country, etc into smaller parts

dismiss /dɪsˈmɪs/ *v* [T] **1** decide that sb/sth is not important, not worth thinking about **2** put thoughts and feelings out of your mind **3** officially remove sb from their job **4** send sb away or allow them to leave **5** (*law*) end a court case ► **dismissal** *n* [C, U]

disobedient /ˌdɪsəˈbiːdiənt/ *adj* failing or refusing to obey ► **disobedience** /ˌdɪsəˈbiːdiəns/ *n* [U]

disobey /ˌdɪsəˈbeɪ/ *v* [I, T] refuse to do what a person, law, etc tells you to do

disorder /dɪsˈɔːdə(r)/ *n* **1** [U] lack of order; confusion **2** [U] violent behaviour of large groups of people **3** [C, U] illness of the mind or body ► **disorderly** *adj*

disorganized (*also* **-ised**) /dɪsˈɔːɡənaɪzd/ *adj* badly planned; not able to organize well ► **disorganization** /ˌdɪsˌɔːɡənaɪˈzeɪʃn/ *n* [U]

disorientate /dɪsˈɔːrientert/ (*esp US* **disorient** /dɪsˈɔːrient/) *v* [T] cause sb to lose all sense of direction; confuse sb ► **disorientation** /dɪsˌɔːrienˈteɪʃn/ *n* [U]

disown /dɪsˈəʊn/ *v* [T] say that you no longer want to be connected with sb/sth

disparaging /dɪsˈpærɪdʒɪŋ/ *adj* suggesting that sb/sth is not important; scornful

disparate /ˈdɪspərət/ *adj* (*fml*) made up of parts or people that are very different from each other **2** (of two things) so different that they cannot be compared ► **disparity** /dɪsˈpærəti/ *n* [U, C] difference

dispassionate /dɪsˈpæʃənət/ *adj* not influenced by emotion; fair ► **dispassionately** *adv*

dispatch (*GB also* **despatch**) /dɪsˈpætʃ/ *v* [T] **1** send sb/sth somewhere **2** finish sth quickly ● **dispatch** *n* **1** [U] (*fml*) act of dispatching sb/sth **2** [C] message or report that is sent

dispel /dɪsˈpel/ *v* (**-ll-**) [T] cause sth to disappear: ~ *doubts*

dispense /dɪsˈpens/ *v* [T] **1** (*fml*) give sth out to people; provide sth **2** prepare medicine and give it to people, as a job [PV] **dispense with sb/sth** get rid of sb/sth that is not necessary ► **dispensary** /dɪsˈpensəri/ *n* (*pl* **-ies**) place where medicines are dispensed ► **dispensation** /ˌdɪspenˈseɪʃn/ *n* [C, U] special permission to do sth usually forbidden **2** [U] (*fml*) act of dispensing sth

disperse /dɪsˈpɜːs/ *v* [I, T] (cause to) move away and spread out ► **dispersal** *n* [U]

dispirited /dɪsˈpɪrɪtɪd/ *adj* without enthusiasm; discouraged

displace /dɪsˈpleɪs/ *v* [T] **1** take the place of sb/sth **2** move sth from its usual position ► **displacement** *n* [U]

display /dɪsˈpleɪ/ *v* [T] show sth; exhibit sth ● **display** *n* **1** act of being displayed; something displayed **2** words, pictures, etc shown on a computer screen

displease /dɪsˈpliːz/ *v* [T] annoy sb ► **displeasure** /dɪsˈpleʒə(r)/ *n* [U] annoyance

dispose /dɪsˈpəʊz/ *v* [PV] **dispose of sb/sth** get rid of sth/sb unwanted ► **disposable** /dɪsˈpəʊzəbl/ *adj* **1** made to be thrown away after use: ~ *nappies* **2** available for use: ~ *income* ► **disposal** *n* **1** [U] action of getting rid of sth **2** [C] (*business*) sale of part of a business, property, etc [IDM] **at your/sb's disposal** available for use as you prefer/sb prefers ► **disposed** *adj* ~(**to**) willing to do sth: *She seems favourably ~d to the move.* ► **disposition** /ˌdɪspəˈzɪʃn/ *n* (*fml*) person's natural character

dispossess /ˌdɪspəˈzes/ *v* [T] ~(**of**) take sb's property, etc away from them

disproportionate /ˌdɪsprəˈpɔːʃənət/ *adj* too large or too small ► **disproportionately** *adv*

disprove /ˌdɪsˈpruːv/ *v* [T] show sth to be wrong or false

dispute /dɪsˈpjuːt; ˈdɪspjuːt/ *n* [C, U] disagreement or argument

● **dispute** /dɪsˈpjuːt/ v **1** [T] question whether sth is true and valid **2** [I, T] ~(with) argue with sb, esp about who owns sth

disqualify /dɪsˈkwɒlɪfaɪ/ v (pt, pp -ied) [T] ~(from) prevent sb from doing sth because they have broken a rule ▸ **disqualification** /dɪsˌkwɒlɪfɪˈkeɪʃn/ n [C,U]

disquiet /dɪsˈkwaɪət/ n [U] (fml) worry or anxiety

disregard /ˌdɪsrɪˈɡɑːd/ v [T] not consider sth; treat sth as unimportant ● **disregard** n [U] lack of attention or care

disrepair /ˌdɪsrɪˈpeə(r)/ n [U] state of needing repair

disrepute /ˌdɪsrɪˈpjuːt/ n [U] state of having lost the good opinion of people: *bring the sport into* ▸ **disreputable** /dɪsˈrepjətəbl/ adj not respectable: *a disreputable nightclub*

disrespect /ˌdɪsrɪˈspekt/ n [U] lack of respect for sb/sth ▸ **disrespectful** adj

disrupt /dɪsˈrʌpt/ v [T] cause disorder in sth: ~ *a public meeting* ▸ **disruption** /dɪsˈrʌpʃn/ n [C,U] ▸ **disruptive** adj causing disruption: *a ~ive influence*

dissatisfied /dɪsˈsætɪsfaɪd; dɪˈsæt-/ adj ~(with) not happy or satisfied with sth ▸ **dissatisfaction** /dɪsˌsætɪsˈfækʃn/ n [U]

dissect /dɪˈsekt; daɪ-/ v [T] cut up a dead body to examine it ▸ **dissection** /dɪˈsekʃn/ n [U,C]

disseminate /dɪˈsemɪneɪt/ v [T] (fml) spread information, etc widely ▸ **dissemination** /dɪˌsemɪˈneɪʃn/ n [U]

dissension /dɪˈsenʃn/ n [U] disagreement

dissent /dɪˈsent/ n [U] fact of having opinions that differ from those that are officially accepted ● **dissent** v [I] ~(from) (fml) disagree with an opinion ▸ **dissenter** n person who dissents

dissertation /ˌdɪsəˈteɪʃn/ n ~(on) long piece of writing

disservice /dɪsˈsɜːvɪs/ n [sing] [IDM] **do sb a disservice** do sth that harms sb

dissident /ˈdɪsɪdənt/ n person who disagrees with official government views

dissimilar /dɪˈsɪmɪlə(r)/ adj not the same ▸ **dissimilarity** /ˌdɪsɪmɪˈlærəti/ n [C,U] (pl -ies)

dissipated /ˈdɪsɪpeɪtɪd/ adj (disapprov) enjoying activities that are harmful, esp drinking too much

dissociate /dɪˈsəʊʃieɪt; -siət/ (also **disassociate**) v [T] **1** ~ yourself/sth from sb/sth say that you do not support sb/sth **2** ~(from) separate two

people or things in your mind ▸ **dissociation** /dɪˌsəʊʃiˈeɪʃn; -səʊs-/ n [U]

dissolve /dɪˈzɒlv/ v **1** [I] (of a solid) become liquid: *Salt ~s in water.* **2** [T] make a solid become liquid: *D~ the salt in water.* **3** [T] bring to an end to sth: ~ *parliament* [IDM] **dissolve into** tears/laughter suddenly start crying/laughing ▸ **dissolution** /ˌdɪsəˈluːʃn/ n [U] (written) act of officially ending a marriage, parliament, etc

dissuade /dɪˈsweɪd/ v [T] ~(from) advise sb not to do sth

distance /ˈdɪstəns/ n **1** [C,U] amount of space between two points or places **2** [U] being far away in space or time **3** [C,U] distant place or point: *listen from a ~* [IDM] **go the (full) distance** continue to run, fight, etc until the end of the contest ● **distance** v [T] ~(from) become less involved or connected with sb/sth

distant /ˈdɪstənt/ adj **1** far away **2** (of people) not closely related: *a ~ cousin* **3** unfriendly ▸ **distantly** adv

distaste /dɪsˈteɪst/ n [U, sing] dislike ▸ **distasteful** adj unpleasant or offensive

distil (US **distill**) /dɪsˈtɪl/ v (-ll-) [T] **1** ~(from) change a liquid to gas by heating it, and then cool the gas and collect drops of liquid **2** make whisky, etc in this way **3** ~(from/into) get the essential meaning from thoughts, information, etc ▸ **distillation** /ˌdɪstɪˈleɪʃn/ n [C,U] ▸ **distillery** /dɪˈstɪləri/ n factory where whisky, etc is distilled

distinct /dɪsˈtɪŋkt/ adj **1** clearly different; separate **2** easily heard or seen ▸ **distinctly** adv

distinction /dɪsˈtɪŋkʃn/ n **1** [C] ~(between A and B) clear difference between two people or things **2** [U] excellence **3** separation of people or things into different groups **4** [C,U] mark of honour or high achievement

distinctive /dɪsˈtɪŋktɪv/ adj marking sth as clearly different ▸ **distinctively** adv

distinguish /dɪsˈtɪŋɡwɪʃ/ v **1** [I, T] ~(between) A and B | ~A from B recognize the difference between two people or things **2** [T] ~A (from B) be a characteristic that makes two people or things different **3** [T] be able to see or hear sth **4** ~ yourself do sth very well ▸ **distinguishable** adj ▸ **distinguished** adj successful and admired

distort /dɪsˈtɔːt/ v [T] **1** pull or twist sth out of its usual shape **2** give a false account of sth: ~ *the facts* ▸ **distortion** /dɪsˈtɔːʃn/ n [C,U]

distract /dɪsˈtrækt/ v [T] take sb's attention away from sth ▸ **distracted** adj unable to pay attention to sb/sth because you are worried, etc ▶ **distraction** /dɪ'stræk∫n/ n 1 [C,U] something, esp a noise, that distracts sb's attention 2 [C] activity that amuses or entertains you

distraught /dɪ'strɔːt/ adj very upset and worried

distress /dɪ'stres/ n [U] 1 great worry, suffering or unhappiness 2 state of danger: a ship in ~ ● **distress** v [T] make sb feel worried or unhappy ▶ **distressing** adj making you feel upset: ~ing news

distribute /dɪ'strɪbjuːt/ v [T] 1 give sth out 2 send goods to shops and businesses to be sold 3 spread sth over an area ▶ **distribution** /ˌdɪstrɪ'bjuːʃn/ n [U,C] ▶ **distributor** /dɪ'strɪbjətə(r)/ n 1 person or company that supplies goods to shops, etc 2 device in an engine that sends electric current to the spark plugs

district /'dɪstrɪkt/ n part of a town or country

distrust /dɪs'trʌst/ n [U] have no trust in sb ▶ **distrust** n [U,sing] lack of trust; suspicion ▶ **distrustful** adj

disturb /dɪ'stɜːb/ v [T] 1 interrupt sb when they are trying to work, etc 2 move sth or change its position 3 worry sb ▶ **disturbance** n 1 [U,C] act of disturbing sb/sth 2 [C] violent public disorder ▶ **disturbed** adj emotionally or mentally ill

disunity /dɪs'juːnəti/ n [U] (fml) lack of agreement between people

disuse /dɪs'juːs/ n [U] state of not being used: fall into ~ ▶ **disused** /ˌdɪs'juːzd/ adj

ditch /dɪtʃ/ n long channel dug at the side of a road to hold or take away water ● **ditch** v [T] (infml) get rid of sth unwanted: She ~ed her boyfriend.

dither /'dɪðə(r)/ v [I] be unable to decide what to do

ditto /'dɪtəʊ/ n (symb ") used in lists to avoid repeating a word, etc

ditty /'dɪti/ n (pl -ies) short simple song

divan /dɪ'væn/ n long low seat without a back

dive /daɪv/ v (pt, pp **dived** US also pt **dove** /dəʊv/) [I] 1 go head first into water 2 go under water 3 (of an aircraft) go steeply downwards 4 move quickly in the direction that is mentioned: ~ under the bed [PV] **dive into sth** (infml) put your hand quickly into such as a bag or pocket ● **dive** n 1 act of diving into water 2 (infml) bar, club, etc that is cheap, and perhaps dark or dirty ▶ **diver** n person who dives, esp one who works under water ■ **'diving board** n board from which people dive into a swimming pool

diverge /daɪ'vɜːdʒ/ v [I] separate; differ ▶ **divergence** /-dʒəns/ n [C,U] ▶ **divergent** /-dʒənt/ adj

diverse /daɪ'vɜːs/ adj of different kinds: ~ interests ▶ **diversity** n [U,C, usu sing] range; variety

diversify /daɪ'vɜːsɪfaɪ/ v (pt, pp -ied) [I, T] (esp of a business) develop a wider range of products, interests, etc ▶ **diversification** /-fɪˌkeɪʃn/ n [U]

diversion /daɪ'vɜːʃn/ n 1 [C,U] act of changing direction: the ~ of a river 2 [C] something that draws attention away from sth that you do not want to be noticed: create a ~ 3 [C] different route for traffic ▶ **diversionary** adj: ~ary tactics

divert /daɪ'vɜːt/ v [T] 1 ~ (from, to) turn sth from one direction, use, etc to another: ~ traffic 2 take sb's attention away from sth

divide /dɪ'vaɪd/ v 1 [I, T] separate; break sth into parts 2 [T] cause people to disagree 3 [T] ~ by find out how many times one number is contained in another: 30 ~d by 6 is 5. ● **divide** n [usu sing] something that divides sb/sth ▶ **dividers** n [pl] instrument for measuring lines, angles, etc

dividend /'dɪvɪdend/ n part of the profits paid to people who have shares in a company

divine¹ /dɪ'vaɪn/ adj 1 of or like God or a god 2 (infml) wonderful ▶ **divinely** adv ▶ **divinity** /dɪ'vɪnəti/ n 1 [U] quality of being a god or like God 2 [C] god or goddess 3 [U] study of religion

divine² /dɪ'vaɪn/ v [T] (fml) discover sth by guessing

divisible /dɪ'vɪzəbl/ adj that can be divided: 4 is ~ by 2

division /dɪ'vɪʒn/ n 1 [U,sing] process or result of dividing or being divided 2 [U] process of dividing numbers 3 [C,U] disagreement 4 [C] big part of an organization: the sales ~ 5 [C] group of sports teams 6 [C] (tech) (in British Parliament) vote ▶ **divisional** /dɪ'vɪʒənl/ adj

divisive /dɪ'vaɪsɪv/ adj causing disagreement

divorce /dɪ'vɔːs/ n 1 [C,U] legal ending of a marriage 2 [C] (fml) ending of a relationship between two things ● **divorce** v 1 [T] end your marriage to sb by law: get ~d 2 [T] ~ from separate sth from sth else ▶ **divorcee** /dɪˌvɔː'siː/ n (GB) divorced person

divulge /daɪ'vʌldʒ/ v [T] (fml) give sb secret information

DIY /ˌdiː aɪ 'waɪ/ n [U] (GB) abbreviation for 'do it yourself'; activity of doing house repairs, decorating rooms, etc yourself

dizzy /'dɪzi/ adj (-ier, -iest) 1 (of a

person) feeling as if everything is turning round and round; unable to balance **2** of or causing this feeling ▸ **dizzily** adv ▸ **dizziness** n [U]

DJ /ˌdiː ˈdʒeɪ/ n = DISC JOCKEY

do[1] /duː/ v (third pers sing pres tense **does** /dʌz/ pt **did** /dɪd/ pp **done** /dʌn/) **1** [T] perform an action, activity or job: What are you doing now? ◊ What do you do (= What's your job)? ◊ do your hair ◊ do the cooking **2** [I] progress or develop: She's doing well at school. **3** [T] produce or make sth: do a drawing **4** [T] provide a service: Do you do eye tests here? **5** [T] study sth or find the answer to sth: do a puzzle ◊ do French/a course/a degree **6** [T] travel a certain distance or at a certain speed: How many miles did you do? **7** [T] have a particular effect: The fresh air will do you good. ◊ do a lot of damage **8** [I, T] be enough or suitable: If you haven't got a pen, a pencil will do. [IDM] be/have to do with sb/sth be connected with sb/sth: The letter is to do with the trip to France. how do you do? (fml) used when meeting sb for the first time [PV] do away with yourself/sb (infml) kill yourself/sb do away with sth (infml) get rid of sth; abolish sth do sth down (GB, infml) criticize sth unfairly do sb/sth for sb/sth (infml) (usu passive) ruin or kill sb/sth: If we can't borrow the money, we're done for. do sb/yourself in (infml) **1** kill sb/yourself **2** make sb very tired: You look done in! do sth in (infml) injure a part of the body: to do your back in do sb out of sth (infml) stop sb having sth, esp by cheating do sb over (infml, esp GB, disapprov) attack and beat sb severely do sth up **1** be fastened: The skirt does up at the back. do sth up **1** fasten a coat, skirt, etc **2** repair and decorate an old house, etc do with sth with sth (usu in negative sentences and questions with what): What does he do with himself (= how does he pass the time) at weekends? ◊ What have you done with (= where have you put) my keys? do without (sb/sth) manage without sb/sth: She can't do without a secretary. ◊ do without

do[2] /də; strong form duː/ aux v (neg **do not**, short form **don't** /dəʊnt/; third pers sing pres tense **does** /dəz; strong form dʌz/, neg **does not**, short form **doesn't** /ˈdʌznt/; pt **did**, neg **did not**, short form **didn't** /ˈdɪdnt/; pp **done** /dʌn/) **1** used before a full verb to form negative sentences and questions: I don't like fish. ◊ Do you believe him? **2** used at the end of a sentence to form a

question tag: You live in Hastings, don't you? **3** used to avoid repeating a full verb: She runs faster than I do. **4** used for emphasizing that a verb is positive: He 'does look tired. ◊ Do shut up!

do[3] /duː/ n (pl **dos** or **do's** /duːz/) (GB, infml) party [IDM] **do's and don'ts** (infml) rules that you should follow

docile /ˈdəʊsaɪl/ adj quiet and easy to control

dock /dɒk/ n **1** part of a port where ships are loaded and unloaded, or repaired **2** (US) = JETTY **3** part of a law court where the prisoner stands ● **dock** v **1** [I, T] (of a ship) come or be brought into a dock **2** [I, T] (of two spacecraft) join or be joined together in space **3** [T] take away part of sb's wages, etc **4** [T] cut an animal's tail short ▸ **docker** n person who loads and unloads ships ■ **dockland** n [U] (also **docklands** [pl]) (GB) district near docks ■ **dockyard** n place where ships are built or repaired

docket /ˈdɒkɪt/ n (business) document or label showing what is in a package, which goods have been delivered, etc

doctor /ˈdɒktə(r)/ n (abbr Dr) **1** person who has been trained in medicine **2** person who has received the highest university degree ● **doctor** v **1** [T] change sth in order to deceive people: ~ the figures **2** (infml) remove part of the sex organs of an animal ▸ **doctorate** /ˈdɒktərət/ n highest university degree

doctrinaire /ˌdɒktrɪˈneə(r)/ adj (disapprov) strictly applying a theory without thinking about practical problems: ~ attitudes

doctrine /ˈdɒktrɪn/ n [C,U] set of teachings; belief(s) ▸ **doctrinal** /dɒkˈtraɪnl/ adj

document /ˈdɒkjumənt/ n **1** official paper giving information, evidence, etc **2** computer file that contains text and has a name that identifies it ● **document** v [T] record the details of sth; prove or support sth with documents ▸ **documentation** /ˌdɒkjumenˈteɪʃn/ n [U] documents used as evidence or proof

documentary /ˌdɒkjuˈmentri/ adj (pl **-ies**) film, radio or television programme that gives information and facts ▸ **documentary** adj of documents: ~ evidence

docusoap /ˈdɒkjusəʊp/ n television programme about the lives of real people, presented as entertainment

dodge /dɒdʒ/ v **1** [I, T] move suddenly to one side in order to avoid sb/sth **2** [T] avoid sth by dishonesty: tax dodging ● **dodge** n **1** sudden movement to avoid sb/sth **2** clever trick ▶ **dodger** n (*infml*) person who dishonestly avoids doing sth ▶ **dodgy** /'dɒdʒi/ adj (*infml*, GB) dishonest; risky

doe /dəʊ/ n adult female deer, reindeer, rabbit or hare

does /dʌz/ → DO

doesn't /'dʌznt/ short for DOES NOT

dog¹ /dɒg/ n [C] **1** common animal kept by people for hunting, guarding, etc or as a pet **2** male dog, fox or wolf **3** (**the dogs**) [pl] (GB, *infml*) greyhound racing [IDM] (**a case of**) **dog eat dog** situation in business, politics, etc where people are willing to harm each other in order to succeed **a dog in the manger** person who stops others enjoying sth even though he/she does not need or want it **a dog's life** an unhappy life **go to the dogs** (*infml*) get into a very bad state ■ **dog collar** n **1** collar for a dog **2** (*infml*) stiff white collar worn by a clergyman ■ **'dog-eared** adj (of a book) used so much that the corners of many pages are turned down ■ **doghouse** n (*US*) = KENNEL [IDM] **be in the doghouse** (*infml*) be in disgrace because of sth bad you have done ■ **dog-'tired** adj (*infml*) very tired

dog² /dɒg/ v (**-gg-**) [T] **1** (of a problem or bad luck) cause you trouble for a long time: *~ged by illness* **2** follow sb/sth closely

dogged /'dɒgɪd/ adj (*approv*) not giving up easily; determined ▶ **doggedly** adv

dogma /'dɒgmə/ n [U,C] (esp religious) belief(s) to be accepted without questioning ▶ **dogmatic** /dɒg'mætɪk/ adj giving opinions forcefully, without thinking that different opinions might be right ▶ **dogmatically** /-kli/ adv

do-gooder → DO¹

dogsbody /'dɒgzbɒdi/ n (pl **-ies**) (GB, *infml*) person who does boring and unpleasant jobs for others

doldrums /'dɒldrəmz/ n [pl] (**the doldrums**) **1** state of feeling sad or depressed: *He's been in the ~ since she left him.* **2** lack of activity or improvement

dole /dəʊl/ n (**the dole**) [sing] (GB, *infml*) money paid regularly by the government to people without jobs: *be/go on the ~* (= receive such money) ● **dole** v [PV] **dole sth out** give out an amount of money, food, etc to a group of people

doleful /'dəʊlfl/ adj sad; unhappy ▶ **dolefully** adv

doll /dɒl/ n child's toy in the shape of a person, esp a baby or a child ● **doll** v [PV] **doll yourself up** (*infml*)

make yourself look attractive for a party, etc

dollar /'dɒlə(r)/ n **1** (symb **$**) unit of money in the USA, Canada, Australia, etc **2** banknote or coin worth one dollar

dollop /'dɒləp/ n (*infml*) soft shapeless mass of sth, esp food

dolphin /'dɒlfɪn/ n intelligent animal that looks like a large fish and lives in the sea

domain /də'meɪn/ n (*fml*) **1** area of activity or knowledge **2** (*computing*) set of Internet addresses that end with the same group of letters **3** area under sb's control

dome /dəʊm/ n round roof with a circular base ▶ **domed** adj shaped like a dome

domestic /də'mestɪk/ adj **1** of the home, house or family: *~ duties* **2** within a particular country; not foreign: *~ policies/flights* **3** (of animals) not wild; kept in a house or on a farm ▶ **domesticated** adj **1** (of animals) tame **2** (of people) enjoying housework and home life

dominant /'dɒmɪnənt/ adj most important or powerful: *a ~ position* ▶ **dominance** /'dɒmɪnəns/ n [U]

dominate /'dɒmɪneɪt/ v **1** [I, T] have control or power over sb/sth, esp in an unpleasant way **2** [T] be the most important feature of sth **3** [T] be most noticeable thing in a place: *The castle ~s the whole city.* ▶ **domination** /ˌdɒmɪ'neɪʃn/ n [U]

domineering /ˌdɒmɪ'nɪərɪŋ/ adj trying to control other people in an unpleasant way

dominion /də'mɪniən/ n **1** [U] (*fml*) authority to rule; control **2** [C] land controlled by a ruler

domino /'dɒmɪnəʊ/ n (pl **~es**) [C] small flat piece of wood marked with spots, used for playing games **2** (**dominoes**) [U] game played with a set of dominoes

don /dɒn/ n (GB) teacher at a university

donate /dəʊ'neɪt/ v [T] **1** ~(**to**) give money, clothes, etc to sb, esp a charity ▶ **donation** /dəʊ'neɪʃn/ n [C,U]

done¹ /dʌn/ pt of DO¹

done² /dʌn/ adj **1** finished **2** (of food) cooked enough **3** socially correct

donkey /'dɒŋki/ n animal like a small horse, but with longer ears [IDM] **donkey's years** (GB, *infml*) a very long time

donor /'dəʊnə(r)/ n **1** person who gives sth to charity **2** person who gives blood or part of his body to help sick people: *a blood ~*

don't short for DO NOT

doodle /'duːdl/ v [I] do small drawings

while you are thinking about sth else ► **doodle** n

doom /duːm/ n [U] death or destruction; any terrible event that you cannot avoid ► **doomed** adj certain to fail, suffer, die, etc ■ **'doomsday** n [sing] the end of the world

door /dɔː(r)/ n 1 piece of wood, etc used for closing the entrance to a building, room, etc 2 = DOORWAY [IDM] **be on the door** work at the entrance to a theatre, club, etc, eg collecting tickets (**from**) **door to door** from building to building: *The journey takes an hour.* ~ *to* ~ **out of doors** in the open air ■ **'doorbell** n bell that is rung by visitors to a house ■ **'doorstep** n step in front of a door ■ **'doorway** n opening for a door

dope /dəʊp/ n 1 [U] (*infml*) harmful drug 2 [C] stupid person ● **dope** v [T] give a drug to a person or an animal ► **dopey** adj (*infml*) 1 stupid 2 sleepy, as if drugged

dormant /'dɔːmənt/ adj not active: *a* ~ *volcano*

dormitory /'dɔːmɪtri/ n (pl -**ies**) large bedroom where several people sleep

dormouse /'dɔːmaʊs/ n (pl dormice /-maɪs/) small animal like a mouse

dosage /'dəʊsɪdʒ/ n [C, usu sing] amount of medicine

dose /dəʊs/ n 1 amount of medicine to be taken at one time 2 experience of sth unpleasant: *a* ~ *of flu* ● **dose** v [T] ~(**with**) give sb/yourself a medicine

doss /dɒs/ v [I] (*GB, sl*) ~(**down**) sleep somewhere, esp somewhere uncomfortable or not in a proper bed ■ **'dosshouse** n (*GB, sl*) cheap place to stay for homeless people

dossier /'dɒsieɪ/ n ~(**on**) set of papers containing information about a person or event

dot /dɒt/ n small round mark, esp one that is printed [IDM] **on the dot** at the exact time mentioned ■ **dot-com** (*also* **dot.'com**) n company that sells goods and services on the Internet ● **dot** v (**-tt-**) [T] 1 put a dot above or next to a letter or word 2 (usu passive) spread things or people all over an area: *The sky was ~ted with stars.*

dotage /'dəʊtɪdʒ/ n [IDM] **be in your dotage** be old and not able to think clearly

dote /dəʊt/ v [PV] **dote on/upon sb** show too much love for sb, ignoring their faults

double¹ /'dʌbl/ adj 1 twice as much, big, good, etc: *Her income is* ~ *what it was a year ago.* 2 having two parts or uses: ~ *doors* ◇ *'Otter' is spelt with a* ~ *t.* 3 made for two people: *a* ~ *bed*

■ **double 'bass** n largest instrument of the violin family, that plays very low notes ■ **double 'chin** n fold of fat below the chin ■ **double-'dealing** n [U] deceitful behaviour ■ **double-'decker** n bus with two floors ■ **double 'Dutch** n [U] (*GB, infml*) speech or writing that is impossible to understand

double² /'dʌbl/ det twice as much or as many as: *He earns* ~ *what I do.* ● **double** adv in two or in two parts: *I had to bend* ~ *to get under the table.* ■ **double-'barrelled** adj (of a gun) having two barrels ■ **double-'book** v [T] reserve a ticket, hotel room, etc for more than one person at a time ■ **double-'breasted** adj (of a coat) made to cross over at the front with two rows of buttons ■ **double-'check** v [I, T] check sth for a second time or with great care ■ **double-'click** v (*computing*) ~ (**on**) choose a particular function or item on a computer screen, etc, by pressing one of the mouse buttons twice quickly ■ **double-'cross** v [T] cheat or deceive sb who trusts you ■ **double-'edged** adj (of a comment) having two possible meanings ■ **double 'glazing** n [U] windows that have two layers of glass, designed to reduce noise, heat loss, etc ■ **double-'jointed** adj having joints in your fingers, arms, etc that can bend backwards as well as forwards ■ **double 'quick** adv (*infml*) very quickly ► **double-'quick** adj

double³ /'dʌbl/ n 1 [U] twice the quantity: *He's paid* ~ *for the same job.* 2 [C] person who looks exactly like another 3 (**doubles**) [pl] game with two players on each side [IDM] **at the double** (*infml*)

double⁴ /'dʌbl/ v 1 [I, T] become or make sth become twice as much or as many: *the price has* ~*d* 2 [T] bend or fold sth to make two layers [PV] **double** (**up**) **as sth** have a second use or function **double back** turn back in the opposite direction **double** (**sb**) **up/over** (cause sb to) bend the body over quickly: *be* ~*d up with laughter/pain*

doubly /'dʌbli/ adv (used before an adj) more than usual: *make* ~ *sure*

doubt /daʊt/ n [U,C] feeling of uncertainty or not believing sth [IDM] **be in doubt** be uncertain **no doubt** very probably **without/ beyond doubt** certainly ● **doubt** v [I, T] feel uncertain about sth/sb; not believe sb/sth ► **doubtful** adj 1 uncertain 2 unlikely ► **doubtless** adv almost certainly, probably

dough /dəʊ/ n [U, sing] mixture of flour, water, etc for making bread

■ 'doughnut *n* small round cake made of fried dough

douse (also **dowse**) /daʊs/ *v* [T] put out a fire by pouring water over it; put out a light **2** pour a lot of liquid over sb/sth: *The car was ~d in petrol and set alight.*

dove[1] /dʌv/ *n* **1** kind of pigeon. The white dove is a symbol of peace. **2** person in favour of peace ▶ **dovecote** /'dʌvkɒt, -kəʊt/ *n* small building for doves to live in

dove[2] /dəʊv/ (*US*) *pt of* DIVE

dovetail /'dʌvteɪl/ *v* [I, T] fit together well ● **dovetail** *n* joint for fixing two pieces of wood together

dowdy /'daʊdi/ *adj* (**-ier, -iest**) **1** (of a woman) not attractive or fashionable **2** (of a thing) dull or boring

down[1] /daʊn/ *adv, prep* **1** to or at a lower level or place; from the top towards the bottom of sth: *jump* ~ ◇ *roll* ~ *the hill* **2** (of flat places) along: *live* ~ *the street* **3** to a sitting or horizontal position: *I think I'll lie* ~. **4** to or in the south: *We went* ~ *to London.* **5** used to show a reduction in level, amount, strength, etc: *Turn the heating* ~ ◇ *calm/settle* ~ **6** (written) on paper: *Copy/Take this* ~. [IDM] **be down to sb** (*infml*) be the responsibility of sb **be/go down with sth** have or catch an illness **down under** (*infml*) in Australia **down with sb/sth** used to say you are opposed to sb/sth: *D~ with fascism!* ● **'down-and-out** *n* person with no job, money or home ● **down-to-earth** *adj* (of a person) practical; sensible

down[2] /daʊn/ *adj* **1** sad: *feel* ~ **2** lower than before: *Interest rates are* ~. **3** (of a computer or computer system) not working: *Our computers have been* ~ *all day.* ● **down 'payment** *n* part of the total cost of sth paid at the time of buying, with the rest to be paid later

down[3] /daʊn/ *v* [T] (*infml*) **1** finish a drink quickly **2** force sb/sth to the ground

down[4] /daʊn/ *n* [U] very soft feathers or hair: *duck* ~

downcast /'daʊnkɑːst/ *adj* **1** sad; depressed **2** (of eyes) looking down

downfall /'daʊnfɔːl/ *n* [sing] fall from power or success; cause of such a fall

downgrade /,daʊn'greɪd/ *v* [T] **1** move sb/sth to a lower rank or level **2** make sth/sb seem less important or valuable

downhearted /,daʊn'hɑːtɪd/ *adj* sad; depressed

downhill /,daʊn'hɪl/ *adv* towards the bottom of a thing: *run/walk* ~ [IDM] **go downhill** get worse in quality,

health, etc ● **downhill** *adj* going down a slope

download /,daʊn'ləʊd/ *v* [T] (*computing*) copy a file or files from one computer to another ● **download** /'daʊnləʊd/ *n* (*computing*) **1** [U] act of copying data from one computer to another **2** [C] computer file that is copied in this way

downpour /'daʊnpɔː(r)/ *n* heavy fall of rain

downright /'daʊnraɪt/ *adj* (of sth bad) complete: *a* ~ *lie* ● **downright** *adv* thoroughly: ~ *rude*

downs /daʊnz/ *n* (**the downs**) [pl] area of low hills

downspout /'daʊnspaʊt/ (*US*) = DRAINPIPE

downstairs /,daʊn'steəz/ *adv, adj* to or on a lower floor

downstream /,daʊn'striːm/ *adv* in the direction in which a river flows

downtown /,daʊn'taʊn/ *adv, adj* (*esp US*) to or in the centre of a city, esp its main business area

downtrodden /'daʊntrɒdn/ *adj* treated badly: ~ *workers*

downward /'daʊnwəd/ *adj* moving or pointing towards a lower level ▶ **downwards** (*esp US* **downward**) *adv* towards the ground or a lower level: *He lay face* ~ *on the grass.*

dowry /'daʊri/ *n* (**-ies**) property or money that a bride's father gives to her husband

dowse = DOUSE

doz. *abbr* DOZEN

doze /dəʊz/ *v* [I] sleep lightly for a short time ● **doze** *n* [sing] light sleep ▶ **dozy** *adj* (**-ier, -iest**) (*infml*) **1** sleepy **2** (*GB*) stupid; not intelligent

dozen /'dʌzn/ *n, det* (*pl* **dozen**) **1** [C] (*abbr* **doz.**) set of twelve of the same thing: *two* ~ *eggs* **2** [C] group of approximately twelve people or things: *a couple of* ~ *workers* **3** (**dozens**) [pl] ~ (**of**) (*infml*) a lot of people or things: *I've told her* ~ *s of times.* [IDM] **talk, etc nineteen to the dozen** → NINETEEN

Dr (also **Dr.**) *abbr* **1** Doctor: *Dr (John) Waters* **2** (in street names) Drive

drab /dræb/ *adj* (~**ber**, ~**best**) without interest or colour; dull ▶ **drabness** *n* [U]

draft /drɑːft/ *n* **1** [C] rough written plan of sth **2** [C] written order for payment of money by a bank **3** (**the draft**) [sing] (*esp US*) = CALL-UP (CALL[1]) **4** [C] (*US*) = DRAUGHT ● **draft** *v* [T] **1** write the first rough version of sth **2** send people somewhere for a special task **3** (*US*) = CONSCRIPT: *He was* ~*ed into the army.* ▶ **'draftsman, 'draftswoman** *n* (*pl* **-men, -women**) **1** (*US*) = DRAUGHTSMAN, DRAUGHTSWOMAN

2 person who writes official or legal documents

drafty /'drɑːfti/ adj (US) = DRAUGHTY (DRAUGHT)

drag /dræg/ v (-gg-) **1** [T] pull sb/sth along with effort and difficulty **2** [I] move yourself slowly and with effort: *I ~ged myself out of bed.* **3** [T] force sb to go somewhere: *I'm sorry to ~ you all this way.* **4** [I] (of time) pass slowly **5** [T] search the bottom of a river, lake, etc with nets, etc **6** (*computing*) [T] move some text, an icon, etc across a computer screen using the mouse [IDM] **drag your feet/heels** deliberately do sth slowly [PV] **drag on** (*disapprov*) go on for too long **drag sth out** cause a meeting, etc to last longer than necessary **drag sth out of sb** force sb to say sth they do not want to say **drag sth up** mention an unpleasant or embarrassing event ● **drag** n **1** [sing] (*infml*) boring thing or person **2** [sing] **~on** (*infml*) person or thing that makes progress difficult **3** [C] (*infml*) act of breathing in smoke from a cigarette, etc **4** [U] (*infml*) women's clothes worn by a man: *in ~*

dragon /'drægən/ n **1** (in stories) large animal with wings and claws, able to breathe out fire **2** fierce unpleasant old woman

drain /dreɪn/ n [C] **1** pipe or channel for carrying away water or sewage **2** [sing] **~on** thing that uses a lot of money, time, etc that could be used for sth else: *a ~ on the country's resources* [IDM] **(go) down the drain | (go) down the plughole** (*infml*) be wasted; (get) much worse ● **drain** v **1** [I, T] become or make sth dry and empty by removing all the liquid from it: *Leave the dishes to ~.* ◇ *D~ the pasta.* **2** [I, T] **~(away/off)~ (from)** (cause liquid to) flow away: *The water ~ed away.* **3** [T] empty a glass or cup by drinking everything in it **4** [T] make sb/sth weaker or poorer: *The experience left her emotionally ~ed.* ● **drainage** n [U] process by which water, etc is drained from an area **2** system of drains ■ **'draining board** (*US* **'drainboard**) n surface next to a sink, on which dishes, etc drain ■ **'drainpipe** n pipe for carrying water from the roof of a building to the ground

drake /dreɪk/ n male duck

drama /'drɑːmə/ n **1** [C] play for the theatre, radio or television **2** [U] plays in general: *Elizabethan ~* **3** [C,U] series of exciting events ▶ **dramatic** /drə'mætɪk/ adj exciting or impressive: *a ~tic rise/fall* ◇ *~tic developments* **2** of the theatre **3** exaggerated in order to attract people's attention: *Don't be so ~tic!*

▶ **dramatically** /-kli/ adv ▶ **dramatics** /drə'mætɪks/ n [pl] exaggerated behaviour that does not seem sincere ▶ **dramatist** /'dræmətɪst/ n writer of plays ▶ **dramatize** (also **-ise**) /'dræmətaɪz/ v [T] **1** present a book, an event, etc as a play or film **2** make sth seem more exciting or important than it really is ▶ **dramatization** (also **-isation**) /ˌdræmətaɪ'zeɪʃn/ n [U, C]: *a ~tization of the novel*

drank pt of DRINK

drape /dreɪp/ v [T] **1** hang clothes, fabric, etc loosely on sth/sb **2** **~(in/with)** cover or decorate sb/sth with material **3** **~round/over** allow part of your body to rest loosely on sth: *His arm was ~d round her shoulders.* ● **drape** n [usu pl] (*esp US*) long thick curtain ▶ **drapery** /'dreɪpəri/ n (pl -ies) **1** [U] (also **draperies** [C, usu pl] (*US*) = DRAPE

drastic /'dræstɪk/ adj extreme; very significant: *a ~ shortage of food* ▶ **drastically** /-kli/ adv

draught /drɑːft/ (*US* **draft** /dræft/) n **1** [C] current of cool air in a room: *to sit in a ~* **2** [C] (*fml*) amount of liquid swallowed at one time **3** (**draughts**) [U] game for two players using 24 round pieces on a board [IDM] **on draught** (*GB*) (of beer) taken from a barrel ● **draught** adj **1** served from a barrel rather than a bottle: *~ beer* **2** used for pulling heavy loads: *a ~ horse* ■ **'draughtsman, 'draughtswoman** (*US* **'drafts-**) n (pl **-men, -women**) **1** person whose job is to draw detailed plans of machinery, buildings, etc **2** person who is skilled at drawing ▶ **draughty** adj (**-ier, -iest**) with currents of cold air blowing through

draw /drɔː/ v (pt **drew** /druː/ pp **~n** /drɔːn/) **1** [I, T] make a picture with a pen, pencil, etc **2** [T] move sb/sth by pulling it/them: *The horses drew the coach along.* ◇ *~ the curtains* (= pull them across a window to cover or uncover it) **3** [I] (*written*) move in the direction mentioned: *The train drew into the station.* **4** [T] **~from/out of** take or pull sth out of sth: *~ a gun from your pocket* **5** [T] attract or interest sb: *~ a crowd* **6** [T] make or obtain sth by study, reasoning, etc: *~ a conclusion/comparison* **7** [I, T] decide sth by picking cards, tickets, numbers, etc by chance: *~ the winning ticket* **8** [I, T] finish a game with neither side winning: *They drew 3-3.* **9** [T] obtain sth from a source: *~ water from a well* ◇ *Draw out £100 out of my account.* **10** [I, T] breathe in smoke or air [IDM] **draw a blank** get no response or result **draw lots** →

LOT³ draw the line (at sth/doing sth) refuse to do sth [PV] **draw back (from sth/doing sth)** not take action, esp because you feel nervous **draw in** (of the day) become shorter **draw sb in| draw sb into sth/doing sth** make sb take part in sth, esp when they do not want to **draw on** (written) (of time) pass **draw on/upon sth** use a supply of sth: ~ *on sb's experience* **draw out** (of the day) become longer **draw sb out** encourage sb to talk **draw sth out** make sth last longer than usual or necessary **draw up** (of a vehicle) arrive and stop **draw yourself up** stand up very straight **draw sth up** write out a list, etc.

draw³ /drɔː/ n [C] **1** [usu sing] ~(**for**) act of choosing tickets, etc by chance; lottery or raffle **2** result of a game in which neither side wins **3** person or thing that attracts many people

drawback /ˈdrɔːbæk/ n disadvantage; problem

drawer /drɔː(r)/ n box-like container that slides in and out of a desk, chest, etc

drawing /ˈdrɔːɪŋ/ n **1** [C] picture **2** [U] art or skill of making pictures, plans, etc using a pen or pencil ■ **'drawing pin** n short pin with a flat top ■ **'drawing room** n (fml) room in which guests are received

drawl /drɔːl/ v [I, T] speak or say sth slowly, making the vowels longer ▶ **drawl** n [sing]

drawn¹ pp of DRAW¹

drawn² /drɔːn/ adj (of a person or their face) looking very tired or worried

dread /dred/ v [T] be very afraid of sth ● **dread** n [U] great fear and anxiety ▶ **dreaded** adj causing fear ▶ **dreadful** adj very bad; terrible ▶ **dreadfully** adv terribly; very

dream /driːm/ n **1** [C] series of images and events that happen in your mind while you are asleep **2** [C] wish to have or be sth, esp one that seems difficult to achieve: *his* ~ *of becoming president* **3** [sing] (infml) wonderful person or thing: *The car goes like a* ~. ● **dream** v (pt, pp ~t /dremt/ or ~ed) **1** [I, T] ~(**of/about**) have experience sth in a dream **2** [I, T] ~(**of/about**) imagine sth that you would like to happen [IDM] **not dream of sth/doing sth** (spoken) not consider doing sth; never do sth: *I wouldn't* ~ *of allowing you to pay* [PV] **dream sth up** (infml) have an idea, esp a silly one ● **dream** adj (infml) wonderful: *a* ~ *house* ▶ **dreamer** n **1** person with impractical ideas **2** person who dreams ▶ **dreamless**

adj (of sleep) without dreams ▶ **dreamlike** adj like a dream; strange and unreal ▶ **dreamy** adj (-ier, -iest) **1** thinking about other things and not paying attention to what is happening **2** imaginative, but not realistic **3** pleasant and peaceful ▶ **dreamily** adv

dreary /ˈdrɪəri/ adj (-ier, -iest) dull or boring; making you feel depressed ▶ **drearily** /ˈdrɪərəli/ adv ▶ **dreariness** n [U]

dredge /dredʒ/ v [T] clear mud, stones, etc from the bottom of a river, etc using a dredger [PV] **dredge sth up** mention sth unpleasant that has been forgotten ▶ **dredger** n boat that can clear mud, etc from the bottom of rivers, canals, etc

dregs /dregz/ n [pl] **1** little bits of solid material that sink to the bottom of liquid: *coffee* ~ **2** (disapprov) worst and most useless parts of sth: *the* ~ *of society*

drench /drentʃ/ v [T] make sb/sth completely wet

dress¹ /dres/ n **1** [C] piece of woman's clothing made in one piece that covers the body down to the legs **2** [U] clothes: *formal* ~ ■ **'dressmaker** n person who makes women's clothes, esp as a job ■ **dress re'hearsal** n final practice of a play, with costumes, lighting, etc

dress² /dres/ v **1** [I, T] put clothes on yourself/sb **2** [T] ~(**for/in/as**) wear a particular type or style of clothes: ~ *for dinner* ◇ *She was* ~*ed in black.* **3** [T] clean, treat and cover a wound **4** [T] prepare food for cooking or eating: *to* ~ *a salad* (= put oil or vinegar, etc on it) **5** [T] decorate or arrange sth: *a shop window* [IDM] **dressed to kill** (infml) wearing clothes that will make you noticed and admired [PV] **dress sb down** criticize sb angrily **dress sb up** put on smart clothes **2** put on special clothes for fun: *Children love* ~*ing up.*

dresser /ˈdresə(r)/ n **1** (esp GB) piece of kitchen furniture with shelves for dishes, and cupboards below **2** (US) = CHEST OF DRAWERS

dressing /ˈdresɪŋ/ n **1** [C,U] sauce of oil, vinegar, etc put on salads **2** [U] (US) = STUFFING(2) **3** [C] bandage for protecting a wound ■ **'dressing gown** n long loose piece of clothing worn indoors over your night clothes ■ **'dressing table** n table with drawers and a mirror, in a bedroom

drew pt of DRAW¹

dribble /ˈdrɪbl/ v **1** [I, T] let saliva or another liquid come out of your mouth **2** [I] (cause a liquid to) fall in small drops or a thin stream **3** [I, T] (in football, etc) move the ball along with many short kicks ▶ **dribble** n [C,U]

dried pt, pp of DRY

drier → DRY

drift /drɪft/ v [I] **1** move along in a current of air or water **2** (of people) live or move somewhere without any purpose ● **drift** n [sing,U] **1** slow steady movement from one place to another; a gradual change or development **2** [C] mass of snow piled up by the wind **3** [sing] general meaning: the ~ of her argument ▶ **drifter** n person who moves from one place or job to another with no real purpose

drill /drɪl/ n **1** [C] tool for making holes **2** [C,U] way of learning sth by means of repeated exercises: pronunciation ~s **3** [C,U] practice of what to do in an emergency: a fire ~ **4** [U] method of training soldiers ● **drill** v [I, T] **1** make a hole in sth, using a drill **2** train or teach sb with drills

drily adv = DRYLY

drink /drɪŋk/ v (pt **drank** /dræŋk/ pp **drunk** /drʌŋk/) **1** [I, T] take liquid into your mouth and swallow it **2** [I] drink alcohol (GB) wish sb good health as you lift your glass to drink it from it **drink like a fish** (infml) drink a lot of alcohol regularly [PV] **drink sth in** watch or listen to sth with great interest **drink to sb/sth** wish sb/sth happiness, etc as you lift your glass to drink it from it ● **drink** n [C,U] **1** liquid for drinking; amount of liquid that you drink **2** alcohol or an alcoholic drink; sth that you drink on a social occasion: Let's go for a ~. ▶ **drinkable** adj ▶ **drinker** n person who drinks too much alcohol

drip /drɪp/ v (-pp-) (of liquid) to fall in small drops [IDM] **dripping wet** very wet ● **drip** n **1** series of drops of falling liquid **2** (med) device that puts liquid food, etc directly into a patient's veins **3** (infml) dull weak person ■ **,drip-'dry** adj (of clothes) made of fabric that will dry easily when you hang it up ▶ **dripping** n [U] fat from roasted meat

drive¹ /draɪv/ v (pt **drove** /drəʊv/ pp **~n** /'drɪvn/) **1** [I, T] operate and control a vehicle **2** [T] take sb somewhere in a car, etc **3** [T] force animals or people to move somewhere **4** [T] be the power for a machine **5** [T] hit a ball with force **6** [T] force sth to go into sth mentioned: a nail into wood **7** [T] force sb to be in a certain state: You're driving me mad! [IDM] **what sb is driving at** the thing sb is trying to say **drive a hard bargain** argue aggressively and force sb to agree on the best possible price, etc ■ **'drive-by** (esp US)

done from a moving car: a ~-by shooting ■ **'drive-in** n place where you can watch films, eat, etc without leaving your car ▶ **driver** n **1** person who drives a vehicle **2** (computing) software that controls the sending of data between a computer and a piece of equipment attached to it, eg a printer ■ **'driving licence** (US **driver's license**) n official document that shows you are qualified to drive

drive² /draɪv/ n **1** [C] journey in a car or other vehicle **2** [C] (also **'driveway**) private road leading to a house **3** [C] organized effort by a group of people: an export/ economy ~ **4** [C,U] strong desire or need **5** [U] energy **6** [C] hard stroke in golf, tennis, etc

drivel /'drɪvl/ n [U] silly nonsense

drizzle /'drɪzl/ n [U] fine light rain ● **drizzle** v [I] rain lightly

drone /drəʊn/ v [I] make a continuous low noise [PV] **drone on** (about sth) talk for a long time in a boring way ● **drone** n [C] **1** low continuous low noise **2** male bee

drool /druːl/ v [I] **1** let saliva come out or your mouth **2** ~(over) (disapprov) show in a silly way how much you like sb/sth: teenagers ~ing over photos of movie stars

droop /druːp/ v [I] hang or bend downwards because of weakness

drop¹ /drɒp/ v (-pp-) **1** [I, T] fall or allow sth to fall **2** [I, T] become or make sth weaker or less **3** [T] ~(off) stop so that sb can get out of a car, etc; deliver sth **4** [T] ~(from) leave sb/sth out: He's been ~ped from the team. **5** [T] stop doing or discussing sth (infml) **drop sb a line** (infml) write a short letter to sb [PV] **drop back/ behind| drop behind sb** move slowly and so get behind other people **drop by/in/round| drop in on sb** visit sb informally **drop off** (GB, infml) fall asleep **drop out (of sth)** **1** no longer take part in sth **2** leave college, etc without finishing your course ■ **,drop-down 'menu** n (computing) = PULL-DOWN MENU (PULL¹) ▶ **'dropout** n **1** person who leaves college, etc without finishing their course **2** person who rejects the ideas, behaviour, etc accepted by the rest of society ▶ **droppings** n [pl] solid waste matter of animals and birds

drop² /drɒp/ n **1** [C] small round mass of liquid **2** [C, usu sing] fall or reduction in sth: a ~ in prices **3** [sing] steep or vertical distance: a ~ of 500 metres **4** (**drops**) [pl] liquid medicine taken in drops **5** [C] small round sweet [IDM] **at the drop of a hat** immediately; without hesitating

drought /draʊt/ n [C, U] long period of very dry weather

drove¹ pt of DRIVE¹

drove² /drəʊv/ n [usu pl] very large group: ~s of visitors

drown /draʊn/ v **1** [I, T] die in water because you cannot breathe; kill sb in this way **2** [T] ~(out) (of a sound) be louder than other sounds so that you cannot hear them [IDM] **drown your sorrows** get drunk in order to forget your problems

drowsy /ˈdraʊzi/ adj (-ier, -iest) feeling sleepy ▸ **drowsily** /-əli/ adv ▸ **drowsiness** n [U]

drudge /drʌdʒ/ n person who does hard boring work ▸ **drudgery** /ˈdrʌdʒəri/ n [U] hard boring work

drug /drʌg/ n **1** illegal substance, eg cocaine or heroin, used for pleasure: He's on ~s. ◇ She's a ~ addict (= cannot stop taking drugs). **2** substance used as a medicine ● **drug** v (-gg-) [T] **1** give drugs to a person or an animal, esp to make them unconscious **2** add a drug to sb's food or drink ■ **drugstore** n (US) chemist's shop that sells medicines and other types of goods, eg cosmetics

drum /drʌm/ n **1** musical instrument made of skin stretched tightly across a hollow round frame **2** large round metal container: an oil ~ ● **drum** v (-mm-) [I] **1** play a drum [I, T] make a sound by hitting a surface again and again: to ~ your fingers on the table [PV] **drum sth into sb** make sb remember sth by repeating it often **drum sth up** try hard to get support, customers, etc ▸ **drummer** n person who plays a drum ■ **drumstick** n stick used for beating a drum

drunk¹ pp of DRINK

drunk² /drʌŋk/ adj excited or confused by alcoholic drink ● **drunk** (also old-fash **drunkard** /ˈdrʌŋkəd/) n person who often gets drunk ▸ **drunken** adj **1** showing the effects of too much alcohol **2** drunk ▸ **drunkenly** adv ▸ **drunkenness** n [U]

dry /draɪ/ adj (drier, driest) **1** not wet: a ~ cloth ◇ ~ paint ◇ ~ weather **2** (of wine) not sweet **3** (of humour) pretending to be serious; ironic **4** boring; dull: a ~ speech ● **dryer** (also **drier**) /ˈdraɪə(r)/ n machine that dries sth: a hair ~er ● **dry** v (pt, pp **dried**) [I, T] (cause sb/sth to) become dry [PV] **dry (sth) out** (cause sth) to become dry, in a way that is not wanted **dry up 1** (of a supply) come to an end **2** suddenly stop talking because you do not want to say next **dry (sth) up** dry dishes, etc with a cloth after washing them ■ **dry-clean** v [T] clean clothes using chemicals instead of water

■ **dry-ˈcleaner's** n = CLEANER'S (CLEAN²) ■ **dry-ˈcleaning** n [U] ■ **dry ˈdock** n part of a port from which water is removed, so that a ship may be repaired ▸ **dryly** (also **drily**) /ˈdraɪli/ adv ▸ **dryness** n [U] ■ **dry ˈrot** n [U] fungus that causes wood to decay and turn to powder

dual /ˈdjuːəl/ adj having two parts; double ▸ [U] ■ **dual ˈcarriageway** n road divided down the centre by a barrier or grass

dub /dʌb/ v (-bb-) [T] **1** give sb/sth a particular name **2** replace the original speech in a film with words in another language

dubious /ˈdjuːbiəs/ adj causing or feeling doubt ▸ **dubiously** adv

duchess /ˈdʌtʃəs/ n **1** wife of a duke **2** woman who has the rank of a duke

duchy /ˈdʌtʃi/ n (pl **-ies**) land owned by a duke or duchess

duck /dʌk/ n (pl **duck** or ~s) [C] **1** common bird that lives on or near water **2** [C] female duck **3** [U] meat from a duck **4** (**a duck**) [sing] (in cricket) batsman's score of 0 ● **duck** /dʌk/ v [I, T] **1** move your head or body down quickly **2** [T] push sb underwater for a short time **3** [I, T] ~ (**out of**) try to avoid a responsibility

duckling /ˈdʌklɪŋ/ n young duck

duct /dʌkt/ n tube or channel carrying liquids or air

dud /dʌd/ n, adj (infml) (something) that is useless: a ~ cheque

due /djuː/ adj **1** ~ **to** because of sb/sth; caused by sb/sth: Her success is ~ to hard work. **2** arranged or expected: The train is ~ (to arrive) at 1.30. **3** needing to be paid; owed **4** suitable; right ● **due** adv (of points of the compass) exactly: ~ east ● **due** n **1** [U] thing that should be given to sb by right **2** (**dues**) [pl] charges, eg for membership of a club

duel /ˈdjuːəl/ n **1** (in the past) formal fight with weapons between two people **2** contest between two people or groups ● **duel** v (-ll- US -l-) [I] fight a duel

duet /djuˈet/ n piece of music for two players or singers

duffel coat (also **duffle coat**) /ˈdʌfl kəʊt/ n coat made of a heavy woollen fabric, usu with a hood

dug pt, pp of DIG¹

dugout /ˈdʌgaʊt/ n **1** rough shelter for soldiers, made by digging a hole in the ground **2** canoe made by cutting out the inside of a tree trunk

duke /djuːk/ n nobleman of the highest rank ▸ **dukedom** n **1** position or rank of a duke **2** = DUCHY

dull /dʌl/ adj **1** not exciting; boring **2** not bright or shiny **3** (of pain) not severe, but continuous: a ~ ache

D

4 slow in understanding ● **dull** v [I, T] become or make sb/sth dull ▶ **dullness** n [U] ▶ **dully** /'dʌlli/ adv

duly /'djuːli/ adv **1** in the correct manner; at the proper time

dumb /dʌm/ adj **1** (old-fash) unable to speak **2** temporarily not speaking: *to be struck ~ with amazement* **3** (infml, esp US) stupid ▶ **dumbly** adv ▶ **dumbness** n [U]

dumbfounded /dʌm'faʊndɪd/ adj unable to speak because of surprise

dummy /'dʌmi/ n (pl -ies) **1** model of a person, used esp for showing clothes in a shop (GB) rubber or plastic object for a baby to suck ■ **dummy 'run** n (GB) practice attempt before the real performance

dump /dʌmp/ v **1** get rid of sth unwanted: *~ rubbish in the river* **2** put sth down carelessly **3** (business) get rid of goods by selling them at a very low price, often abroad **4** (computing) copy information and move it somewhere to store it ● **dump** n **1** place where rubbish may be left (infml, disapprov) dirty unattractive place **3** store of military supplies **4** (computing) (act of making a) copy of data stored in a computer: *a screen ~* (= copy of what is on the screen) [IDM] **down in the dumps** (infml) unhappy ■ **dumper truck** n vehicle for carrying earth, etc

dumpling /'dʌmplɪŋ/ n ball of cooked dough, eaten with meat

dumpy /'dʌmpi/ adj (-ier, -iest) short and fat

dunce /dʌns/ n (disapprov) person, esp at school, who is slow to learn

dune /djuːn/ n (also 'sand dune) n small hill of sand formed by the wind

dung /dʌŋ/ n [U] solid waste matter from animals

dungarees /ˌdʌŋɡə'riːz/ n [pl] trousers with an extra piece of fabric covering the chest, held up by straps

dungeon /'dʌndʒən/ n dark underground prison

dunk /dʌŋk/ v [T] dip food into liquid before eating it

duo /'djuːəʊ/ n (pl **~s**) pair of performers

dupe /djuːp/ v [T] trick or cheat sb ● **dupe** n (fml) person who is duped

duplex /'djuːpleks/ n (esp US) **1** semi-detached house **2** flat on two floors

duplicate[1] /'djuːplɪkeɪt/ v [T] make an exact copy of sth ▶ **duplication** /ˌdjuːplɪ'keɪʃn/ n [U, C]

duplicate[2] /'djuːplɪkət/ adj exactly like sth else; made as a copy of sth else ● **duplicate** n something that is exactly the same as sth else [IDM]

in duplicate (of documents, etc) as two copies that are exactly the same

durable /'djʊərəbl/ adj lasting for a long time ▶ **durable 'goods** n [pl] (US) = CONSUMER DURABLES

duration /dju'reɪʃn/ n [U] time during which sth lasts

duress /dju'res/ n [U] (fml) threats or force: *under ~*

during /'djʊərɪŋ/ prep **1** all through a period of time **2** at some point in a period of time: *He died ~ the night.*

dusk /dʌsk/ n [U] time just before night ▶ **dusky** adj (-ier, -iest) (lit) not very bright; dark in colour

dust /dʌst/ n [U] fine dry powder of earth or other matter ● **dust** v [I, T] clean furniture, etc by removing dust from surfaces with a cloth **2** [T] cover sth with fine powder ■ **dustbin** n container for household rubbish ■ **dust bowl** n area that has no vegetation because of drought, etc ■ **dustcart** n lorry for collecting rubbish from dustbins ▶ **duster** n cloth for removing dust from furniture ■ **dust jacket** n loose paper cover for a book ■ **dustman** n (pl **-men**) person whose job is to empty dustbins ■ **dustpan** n small flat container into which dust is swept ■ **dust sheet** n large sheet for covering furniture, to protect it from dust ▶ **dusty** adj (-ier, -iest) covered with dust

Dutch /dʌtʃ/ adj of the Netherlands (Holland), its people or their language [IDM] **go Dutch** (with sb) share the cost of sth

duty /'djuːti/ n [C, U] (pl -ies) **1** something that you must do **2** tax: *customs duties* **3** (of nurses, police officers, etc) working/not working: **on/off duty** (of nurses, police officers, etc) working/not working ▶ **dutiful** adj showing respect and obedience ▶ **dutifully** adv ▶ **,duty-'free** adj, adv (of goods) able to be taken into a country without payment of tax

duvet /'duːveɪ/ n large bag filled with soft feathers used as a bed covering

DVD /ˌdiː viː 'diː/ n 'digital versatile disc'; disk on which large amounts of information, esp photographs and video, can be stored, for use on a computer: *a ~ player* ◇ *a ~-ROM drive*

dwarf /dwɔːf/ n (pl **~s**) person, animal or plant that is much smaller than usual ● **dwarf** v [T] make sb/sth seem small

dwell /dwel/ v (pt, pp **dwelt** or **dwelled**) [I] (fml, lit) live somewhere [PV] **dwell on/upon sth** think or talk a lot about sth that would be better to forget ▶ **dweller** n (in compound nouns) person who lives in the place mentioned: *city ~ers* ▶ **dwelling** n (fml) home

dwindle /ˈdwɪndl/ v [I] become gradually less, fewer or smaller

dye /daɪ/ v (pres pt **-ing**) [T] change the colour of sth by dipping it in a liquid ● **dye** n [C,U] substance used to dye cloth, etc ■ **dyed in the 'wool** adj totally fixed in your opinions

dying pres part DIE

dyke (also **dike**) /daɪk/ n **1** long wall of earth, for holding back water **2** (esp GB) channel that carries water away from the land

dynamic /daɪˈnæmɪk/ adj **1** energetic and forceful **2** (physics) (of a force or power) producing movement ▶ **dynamics** n [pl] way in which people or things react to each other **2** [U] branch of physics dealing with movement and force ▶ **dynamism** /ˈdaɪnəmɪzəm/ n [U] energy and enthusiasm

dynamite /ˈdaɪnəmaɪt/ n [U] **1** powerful explosive **2** person or thing that is likely to shock or excite ● **dynamite** v [T] blow sth up with dynamite

dynamo /ˈdaɪnəməʊ/ n (pl **~s**) machine that uses the movement of sth, eg water, to produce electricity

dynasty /ˈdɪnəsti/ n (pl **-ies**) series of rulers belonging to the same family

dysentery /ˈdɪsəntri/ n [U] painful disease of the bowels

dyslexia /dɪsˈleksiə/ n [U] abnormal difficulty in reading and spelling ▶ **dyslexic** /dɪsˈleksɪk/ n, adj (person) with dyslexia

Ee

E abbr **1** East(ern): E Sussex **2** (sl) the illegal drug Ecstasy

E, e /iː/ n [C,U] (pl **E's, e's** /iːz/) the fifth letter of the English alphabet ■ **'E-number** n number used for showing an artificial substance added to food

e- /iː/ prefix connected with electronic communication, esp the Internet, for sending information, doing business, etc: e-commerce

each /iːtʃ/ det, pron used to refer to every one of two or more people or things, when you are thinking about them separately: a ring on ~ finger ◇ ~ of the girls ◇ They cost £10 ~. ■ **each 'other** pron used as the object of a v or as a prep to show that each member of a group does sth to or for the other members: Paul and Sue helped ~ other (= Paul helped Sue and Sue helped Paul).

eager /ˈiːgə(r)/ adj **~(for)~(to)** wanting to have sth or to do sth very much: ~ for success ▶ **eagerly** adv ▶ **eagerness** n [U]

eagle /ˈiːgl/ n large strong bird that eats small animals ■ **eagle-'eyed** adj good at noticing small details

ear /ɪə(r)/ n **1** [C] part of the body on each side of the head used for hearing **2** [sing] ability to recognize and copy sounds well: She has a good ~ for music. **3** [C] top part of wheat, barley, etc that contains the seeds [IDM] **be all ears** is listening with great interest ■ **be up to your ears in sth** have a lot of sth to deal with ■ **'earache** n [U,C] pain inside the ear ■ **'eardrum** n [C] tightly stretched skin inside the ear which vibrates when sounds reach it ■ **'ear lobe** n soft part at the bottom of the ear ■ **'earring** n piece of jewellery fastened on or in the ear ■ **'earshot** n [U] [IDM] **out of/within earshot (of sb/sth)** not close/close enough to hear sb/sth or be heard

earl /ɜːl/ n nobleman of high rank

early /ˈɜːli/ adj, adv (**-ier, -iest**) **1** near to the beginning of sth: in the ~ morning **2** before the usual or expected time: The bus arrived ~. [IDM] **an early bird** (hum) person who gets up or arrives early **at the earliest** time before which sth cannot happen **at your earliest convenience** (written, business) as soon as possible ■ **early 'warning** n [U,sing] thing that tells you that sth dangerous is going to happen: an ~ warning system (= of enemy attack)

earmark /ˈɪəmɑːk/ v [T] decide sth will be used for a special purpose

earn /ɜːn/ v **1** [I,T] get money by working **2** [T] get sth you deserve because of sth good you have done or the respect of sb ▶ **earner** n ▶ **earnings** n [pl] money earned

earnest /ˈɜːnɪst/ adj serious and sincere ● **earnest** n [U] [IDM] **in earnest** serious(ly) ▶ **earnestly** adv ▶ **earnestness** n [U]

earth /ɜːθ/ n **1** (also **Earth**, the **Earth**) the world; the planet we live on **2** [U,sing] the surface of the world; land **3** [U] soil **4** [C] hole where an animal, esp a fox, lives **5** [C, usu sing] (GB) wire for electrical contact with the ground [IDM] **charge, cost, pay, etc the earth** (infml) charge, etc a lot of money **how, why, etc on earth** (infml) used to emphasize the question: What on ~ are you doing? ● **earth** v [T] (GB) (usu passive) make electrical equipment safe by connecting it to the ground with a wire ▶ **earthly** adj **1** (written) of this world; not spiritual **2** possible: no ~ly use ■ **earthquake** /ˈɜːθkweɪk/ n sudden violent movement of the earth's surface

■ 'earthworm *n* worm that lives in the soil ▶ **earthy** *adj* (**-ier, -iest**) **1** connected with the body, sex, etc, in a way some people find rude: *an ~y sense of humour* **2** of like soil

earthenware /'ɜːθnweə(r)/ *n* [U] *adj* (bowls, etc) made of very hard baked clay

ease /iːz/ *n* [U] **1** lack of difficulty: *do sth with ~* **2** comfort [IDM] *at* (**your**) **ease** comfortable and relaxed ● **ease** *v* [I, T] become or make sth less unpleasant, painful, severe, etc **2** [T] move sb/sth slowly and carefully: ~ *the injured man out of the car* [PV] **ease off/up** become less intense or severe

easel /'iːzl/ *n* wooden frame to hold a picture while it is being painted

east /iːst/ *n* [U, sing] (*abbr* **E**) **1** (**the east**) direction you look towards to see the sun rise; one of the four main points of a compass **2** (also **East**) eastern part of a country, region or city **3** (**the East**) countries of Asia, esp China, Japan and India ● **east** *adj, adv* **1** (also **East**) (*abbr* **E**) in or towards the east: *the ~ coast* ◇ *The house faces ~.* **2** (of winds) blowing from the east ■ **'eastbound** *adj* travelling towards the east ▶ **'easterly** *adj* **1** in or towards the east **2** (of winds) blowing from the east ▶ **'eastern** (also **Eastern**) (*abbr* **E**) *adj* situated in the east or facing east: *E~ Europe* ▶ **'eastward** *adj* towards the east ▶ **eastward(s)** *adv*

Easter /'iːstə(r)/ *n* [U] day when Christians celebrate the resurrection of Christ

easy /'iːzi/ *adj* (**-ier, -iest**) **1** not difficult **2** free from anxiety, pain or trouble ▶ **easily** *adv* **1** without problems or difficulty **2** without doubt: *easily the best* ● **easy** *adv* [IDM] **go easy on sb** (*infml*) to be severe with sb **go easy on/with sb** (*infml*) used to tell sb not to use too much of sth: **take it/things easy** relax and not work too hard ■ **easy-'going** *adj* relaxed and happy to accept things without worrying

eat /iːt/ *v* (*pt* **ate** /et/ *pp* **~en** /'iːtn/) [I, T] **1** put food into your mouth and swallow it **2** [I] have a meal: *Where shall we ~ tonight?* [IDM] **eat your heart out** (*spoken*) used to compare two things and say that one of them is better: *Look at him dance. E~ your heart out John Travolta!* (= he dances even better than John Travolta) **eat your words** admit that you were wrong [PV] **eat away destroy sth** gradually **eat into sth 1** use up money, time, etc **2** destroy or damage the surface of sth ▶ **eatable** *adj* that can be eaten ▶ **eater** *n* person who eats in a particular way: *a big ~er* (= a person who eats a lot)

eaves /iːvz/ *n* [pl] overhanging edges of a roof

eavesdrop /'iːvzdrɒp/ *v* (**-pp-**) [I] ~ (**on**) listen secretly to a private conversation ▶ **eavesdropper** *n*

ebb /eb/ *v* [I] **1** (of the tide in the sea) move away from the land **2** become less or weaker ● **ebb** *n* (**the ebb**) [usu sing] flowing out of the tide

ebony /'ebəni/ *n* [U] hard black wood ● **ebony** *adj* black in colour

eccentric /ɪk'sentrɪk/ *adj* considered by other people to be strange or unusual ▶ **eccentric** *n* ▶ **eccentricity** /ˌeksen'trɪsəti/ *n* [C, U] (*pl* **-ies**) (example of) eccentric behaviour

ecclesiastical /ɪˌkliːzi'æstɪkl/ *adj* of the Christian Church

echo /'ekəʊ/ *n* (*pl* **~es**) sound reflected off a surface so that it seems to be repeated ● **echo** *v* **1** [I] be sent back as an echo **2** [T] (*written*) repeat or agree with sb's words

eclair /ɪ'kleə(r)/ *n* long thin cream-filled cake with chocolate on top

eclipse /ɪ'klɪps/ *n* **1** (of the sun) blocking of the sun's light by the moon **2** (of the moon) blocking of the moon's light when the earth's shadow falls on the moon ● **eclipse** *v* [T] make sb/sth seem less important by comparison

ecology /i'kɒlədʒi/ *n* [U] (study of the) relations of living things to their surroundings ▶ **ecological** /ˌiːkə'lɒdʒɪkl/ *adj* ▶ **ecologist** /i'kɒlədʒɪst/ *n* expert in ecology

economic /ˌiːkə'nɒmɪk; ˌekə-/ *adj* **1** connected with trade and industry; of economics **2** profitable ▶ **economical** /ˌiːkə'nɒmɪkl; ˌekə-/ *adj* careful in using money, time, etc ▶ **economically** /-kli/ *adv*

economics /ˌiːkə'nɒmɪks; ˌekə-/ *n* [U] study of how a society organizes its money, trade and industry ▶ **economist** /ɪ'kɒnəmɪst/ *n* student of or expert in economics

economize (also **-ise**) /ɪ'kɒnəmaɪz/ *v* [I] save money; spend less than before

economy /ɪ'kɒnəmi/ *n* (*pl* **-ies**) **1** (often **the economy**) [C] economic system of a country **2** [C,U] use of money, time, etc available in a way that avoids waste: *fly ~ class* (= by the cheapest class of air travel)

ecotourism /ˌiːkəʊ'tʊərɪzəm/ *n* [U] organized travel to unspoiled natural environments, when some of the money paid by the tourists is used to protect the area and the animals that live there

ecstasy /'ekstəsi/ n [U,C] (pl -ies) feeling of great happiness ▶ **ecstatic** /ɪk'stætɪk/ adj ▶ **ecstatically** /-kli/ adv

eddy /'edi/ n (pl -ies) circular movement of water or air ● **eddy** v (pt, pp -ied) [I] move around in a circle

edge /edʒ/ n [C] 1 outer limit of an object or surface: the ~ of the bed 2 sharp cutting part of a knife, etc 3 [sing] ~(on/over) slight advantage over sb/sth [IDM] **be on edge** be nervous or tense **take the edge off sth** make sth less strong, bad, etc ● **edge** v [I, T] 1 move (sth) slowly and carefully in a particular direction: She ~d (her way) along the cliff. 2 [T] put sth round the edge of sth ▶ **edging** n [C,U] narrow border ▶ **edgy** adj (infml) nervous

edible /'edəbl/ adj that can be eaten

edit /'edɪt/ v [T] 1 prepare sb else's writing for publication 2 direct the publishing of a newspaper, magazine, etc 3 prepare a film, television programme, etc by choosing and putting together different parts ▶ **editor** n person who edits a newspaper, book, etc

edition /ɪ'dɪʃn/ n 1 form in which a book is printed: a paperback ~ 2 total number of copies of a book, etc published at one time

editorial /,edɪ'tɔːriəl/ adj of an editor ▶ **editorial** n article in a newspaper giving the editor's opinion

educate /'edʒukeɪt/ v [T] teach sb ▶ **education** /,edʒu'keɪʃn/ n [U] 1 process of teaching, training and learning 2 (usu Education) institutions or people involved in teaching or training ▶ **educational** /,edʒu'keɪʃənl/ adj

eel /iːl/ n long fish like a snake

eerie /'ɪəri/ adj (~r, ~st) strange and frightening ▶ **eerily** /'ɪərəli/ adv

effect /ɪ'fekt/ n 1 [C,U] change that sb/sth causes in sb/sth else; result 2 [C,U] particular look, sound or impression that sb, eg an artist, wants to create 3 [pl] (fml, written) personal possessions [IDM] **bring/put sth into effect** put sth into use or operation **in effect** 1 in fact; really 2 (of a law or rule) in use **take effect** 1 start to produce the results that are intended: The aspirin finally took ~. 2 come into use ● **effect** v [T] (fml) make sth happen

effective /ɪ'fektɪv/ adj 1 producing the result that is wanted or intended: the most ~ method 2 (fml) (of laws, etc) coming into use ▶ **effectively** adv ▶ **effectiveness** n [U]

effectual /ɪ'fektʃuəl/ adj (fml) (of things) producing the result that was intended: an ~ remedy

effeminate /ɪ'femɪnət/ adj (disapprov) (of a man) like a woman

effervescent /,efə'vesnt/ adj 1 (of a person) excited and full of energy; bubbly 2 (of a liquid) having or producing small bubbles of gas ▶ **effervescence** /,efə'vesns/ n [U]

efficient /ɪ'fɪʃnt/ adj 1 able to work well: an ~ manager 2 (of a machine, etc) producing good results ▶ **efficiency** /-ʃnsi/ n [U] ▶ **efficiently** adv

effigy /'efɪdʒi/ n (pl -ies) figure or model of a person

effort /'efət/ n 1 [U] use of strength: a waste of time and ~ 2 [C] attempt ▶ **effortless** adj done easily, without effort ▶ **effortlessly** adv

effrontery /ɪ'frʌntəri/ n [U] (fml) behaviour that is confident and rude without shame

effusive /ɪ'fjuːsɪv/ adj showing too much feeling ▶ **effusively** adv

EFL /,iː ef 'el/ abbr (GB) English as a Foreign Language

eg /,iː 'dʒiː/ abbr for example

egg¹ /eg/ n 1 [C] round object with a hard shell, containing a baby bird 2 [C,U] hen's egg used as food 3 [C] female reproductive cell [IDM] **put all your eggs in one basket** risk all your money, time, etc on one single opportunity ■ **egg cup** n small container for a boiled egg ■ **egghead** n (infml, disapprov) very intellectual person ■ **eggplant** n [C,U] (US) = AUBERGINE

egg² /eg/ v [PV] **egg sb on** encourage sb to do sth, esp sth bad

ego /'iːgəʊ; 'egəʊ/ n (pl ~s) sense of your own value and importance

egocentric /,egəʊ'sentrɪk/ adj thinking only about yourself

egoism /'egəʊɪzəm; 'iːg-/ (also **egotism** /'egətɪzəm; 'iːg-/) n [U] self-centredness; selfishness ▶ **egoist** /'egəʊɪst; 'iːg-/ (also **egotist** /'egətɪst; 'iːg-/) n (disapprov) person who thinks they are better than other people and who thinks and talks too much about himself/herself

eiderdown /'aɪdədaʊn/ n thick, warm bed covering

eight /eɪt/ number 8 ▶ **eighth** /eɪtθ/ ordinal number, n 8th; each of eight equal parts of sth

eighteen /,eɪ'tiːn/ number 18 ▶ **eighteenth** /,eɪ'tiːnθ/ ordinal number

eighty /'eɪti/ n number 80 2 (**the eighties**) n [pl] numbers, years or temperatures from 80 to 89 ▶ **eightieth** ordinal number

either /'aɪðə(r); 'iːðə(r)/ det, pron 1 one or the other of two: park on ~ side of the road 2 each of two: The offices on ~ side are empty. ● **either** adv, conj 1 used after negative verbs: You can't go and I can't ~. 2 (**either ... or ...**)

used to show a choice of two things: *E- you go or I do.*

eject /ɪ'dʒekt/ *v* [T] ~(**from**) push or send sb/sth out of a place, usu with force ▶ **ejection** /ɪ'dʒekʃn/ *n* [U] ● **e'jector seat** *n* seat that throws the pilot out of an aircraft in an emergency

eke /i:k/ *v* [PV] **eke sth out** make a small supply of sth last as long as possible

elaborate /ɪ'læbərət/ *adj* complicated; very detailed ▶ **elaborately** *adv* ● **elaborate** /ɪ'læbəreɪt/ *v* [I, T] ~(**on**) explain or describe sth in more detail ▶ **elaboration** /ɪ,læbə'reɪʃn/ *n* [U, C]

elapse /ɪ'læps/ *v* [I] (*fml*) (of time) pass

elastic /ɪ'læstɪk/ *n* [U] material made with rubber that can stretch and then return to its original size ● **elastic** *adj* **1** made with elastic **2** able to stretch and then return to its original size **3** not fixed: *Our plans are fairly ~.* ● **e,lastic 'band** *n* (*GB*) = RUBBER BAND ▶ **elasticity** /,i:læ'stɪsəti/ *n* [U]

elated /i'leɪtɪd/ *adj* ~(**at/by**) very happy and excited ▶ **elation** /i-'leɪʃn/ *n* [U]

elbow /'elbəʊ/ *n* **1** joint where the arm bends **2** part of a piece of clothing that covers the elbow ● **elbow** *v* [T] push sb with your elbow, usu in order to get past them: *He ~ed his way through the crowd.* ■ **'elbow grease** *n* [U] (*infml*) effort used in physical work ■ **'elbow room** *n* [U] (*infml*) enough space to move in

elder /'eldə(r)/ *adj* (of two members of a family) older: *my ~ brother* ● **elder** *n* **1** (**elders**) [pl] people of greater age and authority **2** (**my, etc elder**) [sing] (*fml*) person older than me, etc **3** [C] official in some Christian churches **4** [C] small tree with white flowers and black berries ▶ **elderly** *adj* (of people) used as a polite word for 'old' ■ **elder 'statesman** *n* old and respected politician

eldest /'eldɪst/ *adj, n* (of three or more people) oldest (person)

elect /ɪ'lekt/ *v* [T] **1** choose sb by voting **2** (*fml*) choose to do sth: *They ~ed to stay.* ● **elect** *adj* (*fml*) chosen but not yet doing the job: *the president ~* ▶ **elector** *n* person with the right to vote in an election ▶ **electoral** /ɪ'lektərəl/ *adj* of elections ▶ **electorate** /ɪ'lektərət/ *n* [C, with sing or pl verb] all the electors

election /ɪ'lekʃn/ *n* [C, U] process of choosing representatives by voting

electric /ɪ'lektrɪk/ *adj* **1** using, produced by or producing electricity:

an ~ fire **2** exciting ▶ **electrical** *adj* using, producing or connected with electricity ▶ **electrically** /-kli/ *adv* ■ **the e,lectric 'chair** *n* [sing] (esp in the US) chair in which criminals are killed by passing a strong electric current through their bodies ● **e,lectric 'shock** *n* sudden pain caused by electricity passing through your body

electrician /ɪ,lek'trɪʃn/ *n* person whose job is to fit and repair electrical equipment

electricity /ɪ,lek'trɪsəti/ *n* [U] **1** form of energy used for heating, lighting, driving machines, etc **2** supply of such energy: *Don't waste ~.*

electrify /ɪ'lektrɪfaɪ/ *v* (*pt, pp* -**ied**) [T] **1** (usu passive) provide sth with electricity **2** (*written*) make sb excited

electrocute /ɪ'lektrəkju:t/ *v* [T] injure or kill sb using an electric current ▶ **electrocution** /ɪ,lektrə-'kju:ʃn/ *n*

electrode /ɪ'lektrəʊd/ *n* point by which an electric current enters or leaves a battery, etc

electromagnetic /ɪ,lektrəʊmæg-'netɪk/ *adj* (*physics*) having both electrical and magnetic characteristics (**properties**): *an ~ wave/field*

electron /ɪ'lektrɒn/ *n* tiny particle of matter inside an atom, with a negative electric charge ▶ **electronic** /ɪ,lek'trɒnɪk/ *adj* **1** (of a device) having many small parts, eg microchips, that control and direct a small electric current **2** concerned with electronic equipment, eg computers ▶ **electronically** /-kli/ *adv* ▶ **electronics** *n* [U] science and development of electronic technology

elegant /'elɪɡənt/ *adj* showing good taste; graceful and attractive ▶ **elegance** /'elɪɡəns/ *n* [U] ▶ **elegantly** *adv*

element /'elɪmənt/ *n* **1** [C] ~(**in/of**) necessary or typical part of sth: *Justice is only one ~ in good government.* **2** [C, usu sing] small amount of sth: *an ~ of truth in their story* **3** [C] chemical substance that cannot be divided into simpler substances **4** [C] one of the four substances: earth, air, fire and water **5** (**the elements**) [pl] bad weather **6** (**elements**) [pl] basic principles of a subject **7** [C] part of a piece of electrical equipment that gives out heat [IDM] **in/out of your element** doing/not doing what you are good at and enjoy

elementary /,elɪ'mentri/ *adj* **1** of the basic and first stages of sth: *~ maths* **2** simple; not advanced ■ **ele'mentary school** *n* (*US*) school for children aged about 6 to 12

elephant /'elɪfənt/ *n* very large

animal with thick grey skin, two tusks and a trunk

elevate /'eliveit/ v [T] **1** (fml) or (tech) raise sb/sth to a higher position **2** (fml) improve sb's mind or morals

elevation /,eli'veiʃn/ n **1** [U] (fml) process of raising sb/sth to a higher position **2** [C, usu sing] (tech) height of a place above sea level **3** [C] (fml) piece of land that is higher than the area around **4** [C] (in architecture) (drawing of) one side of a building

elevator /'eliveitə(r)/ n (US) = LIFT

eleven /i'levn/ number 11 ► **eleventh** /i'levnθ/ ordinal number

elf /elf/ n (pl **elves** /elvz/) (in stories) creature with pointed ears and magic powers

elicit /i'lisit/ v [T] ~ (from) (written) get information or a reaction from sb

eligible /'elidʒəbl/ adj ~ (for)/(to) suitable; having the right qualifications: ~ for a job ► **eligibility** /,elidʒə'biləti/ n [U]

eliminate /i'limineit/ v [T] remove or get rid of sb/sth ► **elimination** /i,limi'neiʃn/ n [U,C]

elite /ei'li:t; I'li:t/ n [C, with sing or pl verb] group of powerful important people in society ► **elitism** /-tızəm/ n [U] often (disapprov) (belief in a) system that aims to develop an elite ► **elitist** /-tıst/ n, adj

elk /elk/ n very large deer

ellipse /I'lıps/ n (tech) regular oval shape ► **elliptical** /I'lıptıkl/ adj

elm /elm/ n **1** [C,U] (also **elm tree**) tall tree with broad leaves **2** [U] hard wood of the elm tree

elocution /,elə'kju:ʃn/ n [U] art of speaking clearly

elongate /'i:lɒŋgeit/ v [I, T] become or make sth longer

elope /I'ləʊp/ v [I] run away secretly to get married ► **elopement** n [C,U]

eloquence /'eləkwəns/ n [U] skilful use of language to express yourself or to persuade others ► **eloquent** /'eləkwənt/ adj ► **eloquently** adv

else /els/ adv in addition to sth already mentioned; different: Have you got anything - to do? ◇ I saw Bob and no one -. [IDM] **or else** otherwise; if not: Run or - you'll be late. ■ **else-'where** adv in, at or to another place

ELT /,i:; el 'ti:/ abbr (GB) English Language Teaching

elucidate /i'lu:sideit/ v [T] (fml) make sth clearer by explaining it ► **elucidation** /i,lu:sr'deiʃn/ n [U,C]

elude /i'lu:d/ v [T] **1** avoid or escape from sb/sth **2** be difficult for sb to achieve, remember or understand: Sleep -d him. ► **elusive** /i'lu:siv/ adj hard to find, describe or achieve

elves plural of ELF

emaciated /i'meiʃieitid/ adj very thin and weak ► **emaciation** /i,meisi'eiʃn/ n [U]

email (also **e-mail**) n **1** [U] way of sending electronic messages or data from one computer to another **2** [C,U] message(s) sent by email ● **email** v [T] send a message to sb by email

emanate /'eməneit/ v [I] ~from (fml) come or flow from sb/sth

emancipate /i'mænsipeit/ v [T] set sb free, esp politically or socially ► **emancipation** /i,mænsi'peiʃn/ n [U]

embalm /im'ba:m/ v [T] preserve a dead body with chemicals, etc

embankment /im'bæŋkmənt/ n wall of earth, etc that holds back water or supports a railway or road

embargo /im'ba:gəʊ/ n (pl **-es**) (on) official order that forbids trade with another country ● **embargo** v (pt, pp -ed) [T] put an embargo on sth

embark /im'ba:k/ v [I] go on board a ship [PV] **embark on/upon sth** start sth new or difficult ► **embarkation** /,emba:'keiʃn/ n [U,C]

embarrass /im'bærəs/ v [T] make sb feel shy, awkward or ashamed: His behaviour ~ed her. ► **embarrassing** adj: an ~ing mistake ► **embarrassingly** adv ► **embarrassment** n [U,C]

embassy /'embəsi/ n (pl **-ies**) office of an ambassador and his/her staff

embed /im'bed/ v (-dd-) [T] ~ (in) (usu passive) fix sth firmly into a substance or solid object

embellish /im'belıʃ/ v [T] **1** ~ (with) (usu passive) make sth attractive by adding decorations **2** add details to a story to make it more interesting ► **embellishment** n [C,U]

ember /'embə(r)/ n [C, usu pl] piece of hot coal, etc in a dying fire

embezzle /im'bezl/ v [I, T] steal money that you are responsible for or that belongs to your employer

embitter /im'bitə(r)/ v [T] (usu passive) make sb feel angry and disappointed about sth

emblem /'embləm/ n design or symbol that represents sth: The dove is an ~ of peace.

embody /im'bɒdi/ v (pt, pp -ied) [T] ~ (in) (fml) express an idea or feature; include ► **embodiment** n [usu sing]: She is the embodiment of honesty.

emboss /im'bɒs/ v [T] put a raised design or type of writing on paper, leather, etc ► **embossed** adj: ~ed stationery

embrace /im'breis/ v **1** [I, T] (written) take sb into your arms as a sign of affection **2** [T] (fml) accept an idea, religion willingly **3** [T] (*fml*) include sth ► **embrace** *n* [C,U]

embroider /ɪmˈbrɔɪdə(r)/ *v* **1** [I, T] decorate fabric with needlework **2** [T] add untrue details to a story to make it more interesting ► **embroidery** *n* [U,C]

embryo /ˈembriəʊ/ *n* (*pl* ~**s**) young animal before birth [IDM] **in embryo** existing but not yet fully developed ► **embryonic** /ˌembriˈɒnɪk/ *adj*

emerald /ˈemərəld/ *n* bright green precious stone ► **emerald** (*also* ˌemerald ˈgreen) *adj* bright green in colour

emerge /iˈmɜːdʒ/ *v* [I] **1** come out; come into view **2** (of facts) become known ► **emergence** /-dʒəns/ *n* [U] ► **emergent** /iˈmɜːdʒənt/ *adj* beginning to develop; new

emergency /iˈmɜːdʒənsi/ *n* [C,U] (*pl* -**ies**) sudden serious and dangerous situation needing quick action ■ **eˈmergency room** (*abbr* **ER**) (*US*) = CASUALTY(2)

emigrate /ˈemɪɡreɪt/ *v* [I] leave your own country to go and live in another ► **emigrant** /ˈemɪɡrənt/ *n* person who emigrates ► **emigration** /ˌemɪˈɡreɪʃn/ *n* [U]

eminent /ˈemɪnənt/ *adj* (of a person) famous and respected ► **eminence** /ˈemɪnəns/ *n* [U] ► **eminently** *adv* (*fml*) very; extremely: ~*ly* qualified

emir /eˈmɪə(r)/; ˈemɪə(r)/ *n* Muslim ruler ► **emirate** /ˈemɪərət; ˈemɪrət/ *n* lands, etc ruled by an emir

emit /iˈmɪt/ *v* (**-tt-**) [T] (*fml*) send out sth such as light, heat, sound, gas, etc: ~ *heat* ► **emission** /iˈmɪʃn/ *n* [U,C]

emoticon /iˈməʊtɪkɒn/ *n* group of keyboard symbols that represent the expression on sb's face, used in email, etc. to show the feelings of the person sending the message, eg :-) represents a smiling face

emotion /iˈməʊʃn/ *n* [C,U] strong feeling, eg love, joy, fear or hate ► **emotional** /iˈməʊʃənl/ *adj* **1** of the emotions **2** causing emotion: *an* ~*al speech* **3** showing (too much) emotion ► **emotionally** *adv*

emotive /iˈməʊtɪv/ *adj* causing strong feelings

emperor /ˈempərə(r)/ *n* ruler of an empire

emphasis /ˈemfəsɪs/ *n* [U,C] (*pl* -**ases** /-əsiːz/) **1** special importance given to sth **2** extra force given to a word or words, esp to show that it is important ► **emphasize** (*also* -**ise**) /ˈemfəsaɪz/ *v* [T] put emphasis on sth ► **emphatic** /ɪmˈfætɪk/ *adj* having or using emphasis ► **emphatically** /-kli/ *adv*

empire /ˈempaɪə(r)/ *n* group of countries controlled by one ruler or government

empirical /ɪmˈpɪrɪkl/ *adj* (of knowledge) based on experiments or experience rather than theory

employ /ɪmˈplɔɪ/ *v* [T] **1** give work to sb for payment **2** (*fml*) use sth ► **employable** *adj* having the skills that will make sb want to employ you ► **employee** /ɪmˈplɔɪiː/ *n* person who is paid to work for sb ► **employer** *n* person or company that employs people ► **employment** *n* **1** [U,C] regular paid work; state of being employed **2** [U] act of employing sb

empower /ɪmˈpaʊə(r)/ *v* [T] (*fml*) (usu passive) give sb the power or authority to do sth

empress /ˈempres/ *n* female ruler of an empire; wife of an emperor

empty /ˈempti/ *adj* (-**ier**, -**iest**) **1** containing nothing or no one **2** having no value or meaning: ~ *promises* ► **empties** *n* [pl] empty bottles or glasses ► **emptiness** /ˈemptinəs/ *n* [U, sing] ● **empty** *v* (*pt, pp* -**ied**) [I, T] become or make sth empty ■ ˌempty-ˈhanded *adj* bringing or taking nothing ■ ˌempty-ˈheaded *adj* foolish; silly

emu /ˈiːmjuː/ *n* large Australian bird that cannot fly

emulate /ˈemjuleɪt/ *v* [T] (*fml*) try to do sth as well as sb because you admire them ► **emulation** /ˌemjuˈleɪʃn/ *n* [U,C]

emulsion /iˈmʌlʃn/ *n* [U,C] creamy liquid mixture, esp paint

enable /iˈneɪbl/ *v* [T] ~ **to** make sb able to do sth

enamel /iˈnæml/ *n* [U] **1** shiny substance that is melted onto metal, pots, etc **2** hard covering of the teeth ► **enamelled** (*US* -**l**-) *adj* covered or decorated with enamel

enamoured (*US* -**ored**) /iˈnæməd/ *adj* ~ **of/with** liking sth a lot

enchant /ɪnˈtʃɑːnt/ *v* [T] (*fml*) attract sb strongly ► **enchanted** /ɪnˈtʃɑːntɪd/ *adj* placed under a magic spell ► **enchanting** *adj* attractive and pleasing ► **enchantment** *n* [U,C]

encircle /ɪnˈsɜːkl/ *v* [T] surround sb/sth completely

encl. *abbr* (*business*) enclosed; used on business letters to show that another document is being sent in the same envelope

enclave /ˈenkleɪv/ *n* part of a country or a city surrounded by another

enclose /ɪnˈkləʊz/ *v* [T] **1** build a wall, etc round sth **2** put sth in the same envelope as sth else ► **enclosure** /ɪnˈkləʊʒə(r)/ *n* **1** area of land surrounded by a fence or wall **2** something put in the same envelope as a letter

encode /ɪnˈkəʊd/ v [T] **1** change ordinary language into letters, symbols, etc in order to send secret messages **2** (computing) change information into a form that can be processed by a computer

encore /ˈɒŋkɔː(r)/ exclam, n (used by an audience to ask for a) repeated performance

encounter /ɪnˈkaʊntə(r)/ v [T] (fml) meet sth/sb difficult or unexpected ● **encounter** n unexpected (esp unpleasant) meeting

encourage /ɪnˈkʌrɪdʒ/ v [T] give sb support, confidence or hope: They ~d him to come. ▶ **encouragement** n [C,U] ▶ **encouraging** adj

encroach /ɪnˈkrəʊtʃ/ v [I] ~(on) (fml) take more than what is right or natural: ~ on sb's rights

encyclopedia (also **-paedia**) /ɪn-ˌsaɪklə'piːdiə/ n book(s) or a CD-ROM giving information on all subjects or on one subject, usu in alphabetical order ▶ **encyclopedic** (also **-paedic**) /-ˈpiːdɪk/ adj complete and thorough

end /end/ n point where sth stops; last part of sth: at the ~ of the street/war **2** small piece that remains: cigarette ~s **3** aim or purpose: with this ~ in view [IDM] **in the end** at last; finally **make (both) ends meet** earn just enough money to live on **no end of sth** (spoken) a lot of sth **on end 1** upright **2** continuously: rain for days on ~ **put an end to sth** stop sth ● **end** v [I, T] (cause sth to) finish [PV] **end up** reach a certain place or state finally ▶ **ending** /ˈendɪŋ/ n last part of a word, story, etc ▶ **endless** /ˈendləs/ adj having no end ▶ **endlessly** adv

endanger /ɪnˈdeɪndʒə(r)/ v [T] cause danger to sb/sth

endear /ɪnˈdɪə(r)/ v [T] [PV] **endear sb/yourself to sb** make sb/yourself popular ▶ **endearment** n [C,U] expression of affection

endeavour (US **-or**) /ɪnˈdevə(r)/ v [I] ~to (fml) try to do sth ● **endeavour** n [U,C] (fml) attempt to do sth, esp sth new or difficult

endemic /enˈdemɪk/ adj often found in a particular place: Malaria is ~ in many hot countries.

endive /ˈendaɪv; -dɪv/ (US) = CHICORY

endorse /ɪnˈdɔːs/ v [T] **1** approve of or support sth/sb publicly **2** write your name on the back of a cheque **3** (GB) (usu passive) record a driving offence on a driving licence ▶ **endorsement** n [C,U]

endow /ɪnˈdaʊ/ v [T] give money that provides a regular income for a school, etc [PV] **be endowed with sth** naturally have a particular feature, quality, etc ▶ **endowment** n [C,U]

endure /ɪnˈdjʊə(r)/ v **1** (written) [T] suffer pain, etc patiently **2** [I] (fml) continue to exist for a long time ▶ **endurance** n [U] ability to endure sth ▶ **enduring** adj lasting

enemy /ˈenəmi/ n (pl **-ies**) **1** [C] person who hates sb or who acts against sb/sth **2** (the enemy) [sing, with sing or pl verb] (armed forces of a) country that you are fighting against

energy /ˈenədʒi/ n **1** [U] ability to act or work with strength or enthusiasm **2** (energies) [pl] physical and mental effort you use to do sth **3** [U] power used for operating machinery, etc: atomic ~ ▶ **energetic** /ˌenə'dʒetɪk/ adj having or needing a lot of energy and enthusiasm ▶ **energetically** /-kli/ adv

enfold /ɪnˈfəʊld/ v [T] (fml) hold sb in your arms

enforce /ɪnˈfɔːs/ v [T] force people to obey a law, etc ▶ **enforceable** adj ▶ **enforcement** n [U]

engage /ɪnˈgeɪdʒ/ v **1** [T] (fml) succeed in keeping your attention and interest **2** [T] (fml) employ sb **3** [I, T] (part of a machine) fit (sth) together [PV] **engage (sb) in sth** (make sb) take part in sth ▶ **engaged** adj **1** having agreed to marry sb **2** being used; busy ▶ **engagement** n **1** agreement to marry sb **2** arrangement to do sth at a particular time **3** (fml) battle ▶ **engaging** adj pleasant; charming

engine /ˈendʒɪn/ n **1** machine that changes energy into movement **2** vehicle that pulls a train

engineer /ˌendʒɪ'nɪə(r)/ n **1** person who designs machines, engines, railways, etc **2** person whose job is to control and repair engines ▶ **engineer** v [T] arrange sth, esp secretly or indirectly ▶ **engineering** n [U] work of an engineer; study of engineering as a subject

English /ˈɪŋglɪʃ/ n **1** [U] the English language **2** (the English) [pl] the people of England ▶ **English** adj

engrave /ɪnˈgreɪv/ v [T] ~A on B/B (with A) cut words or designs on a hard surface [IDM] **be engraved on/in your heart, memory, mind, etc** be sth that you will never forget because it affected you so strongly ▶ **engraver** n person whose job is to cut words or designs on wood, metal, etc ▶ **engraving** n **1** [C] picture printed from an engraved metal plate **2** [U] work of an engraver

engross /ɪnˈgrəʊs/ v [T] (usu passive) take all sb's attention: ~ed in her work

engulf /ɪnˈgʌlf/ v [T] (written) surround

or cover sb/sth completely: *The hotel was ~ed in flames.*

enhance /ɪnˈhɑːns/ v [T] improve the good qualities of sb/sth ▶ **enhancement** n [U,C]

enigma /ɪˈnɪgmə/ n mystery ▶ **enigmatic** /ˌenɪgˈmætɪk/ adj ▶ **enigmatically** /-kli/ adv

enjoy /ɪnˈdʒɔɪ/ v [T] 1 get pleasure from sth 2 ~ **yourself** be happy 3 (written) be lucky to have sth: ~ *good health* ▶ **enjoyable** adj pleasant ▶ **enjoyably** adv ▶ **enjoyment** n [U,C]

enlarge /ɪnˈlɑːdʒ/ v [I, T] become or make sth bigger [PV] **enlarge on/upon sth** (fml) say or write more about sth ▶ **enlargement** n [C,U]

enlighten /ɪnˈlaɪtn/ v [T] give sb more knowledge or understanding of sth ▶ **enlightenment** n [U]

enlist /ɪnˈlɪst/ v [T] 1 persuade sb to help you or join you in doing sth 2 [I, T] (make sb) join the armed forces ▶ **enlistment** n [U,C]

enormity /ɪˈnɔːməti/ n (pl -ies) 1 [U] very great size, effect, etc of sth 2 [C, usu pl] (fml) very serious crime

enormous /ɪˈnɔːməs/ adj very large ▶ **enormously** adv very; very much

enough /ɪˈnʌf/ det, pron as many or as much as sb needs or wants: *Is £100 ~?* ● **enough** adv sufficiently: *not old* ~ [IDM] **funnily, oddly, strangely, etc enough** used to show that sth is very surprising

enquire (also **inquire**) /ɪnˈkwaɪə(r)/ v [I, T] ~(**about**) ask sb for information about sth: ~ *about trains to Oxford* [PV] **enquire after sb** ask about sb's health **enquire into sth** investigate sth ▶ **enquiring** adj showing an interest in learning: *an enquiring mind*

enquiry (also **inquiry**) /ɪnˈkwaɪəri/ n (pl -ies) 1 [C] request for information about sth; investigation 2 [U] act of asking questions or collecting information about sth

enrage /ɪnˈreɪdʒ/ v [T] (written) make sb very angry

enrich /ɪnˈrɪtʃ/ v [T] 1 ~(**with**) improve sth by adding sth to it: *soil ~ed with fertilizer* 2 make sb/sth richer ▶ **enrichment** n [U]

enrol (esp US **enroll**) /ɪnˈrəʊl/ v (-ll-) [I, T] become or make sb a member of a college or course ▶ **enrolment** (US **enrollment**) n [U,C]

en route /ˌɒ ˈruːt; ˌɒn/ adv (GB) (from French) on the way

ensemble /ɒnˈsɒmbl/ n 1 group of things considered as a whole 2 small group of musicians who often play together

ensign /ˈensən/ n 1 ship's flag 2 junior officer in the US navy

ensue /ɪnˈsjuː/ v [I] (written) happen after or as a result of another event

en suite /ˌɒ ˈswiːt/ adj, adv (GB) (of a bathroom) joined onto a bedroom and for use only by people in that bedroom

ensure (esp US **insure**) /ɪnˈʃʊə(r); -ˈʃɔː(r)/ v [T] make certain of sth

entail /ɪnˈteɪl/ v [T] involve sth that cannot be avoided: *Your plan ~s a lot of work.*

entangled /ɪnˈtæŋgld/ adj ~(**in**) twisted or caught in sth ▶ **entanglement** n [C,U]

enter /ˈentə(r)/ v 1 [I, T] (fml) come or go into sth 2 [T] become a member of an institution; join a profession: ~ *university* 3 [T] write details of sb/sth in a book or list 4 [I, T] take part in a competition, examination, etc [PV] **enter into sth** 1 begin to deal with sth 2 take an active part in sth; form part of sth **enter on/upon sth** (fml) begin sth

enterprise /ˈentəpraɪz/ n 1 [C] company or business 2 [C] large (esp difficult) project 3 [U] business activity: *private* ~ 4 [U] ability to think of new projects ▶ **enterprising** adj having or showing enterprise(4)

entertain /ˌentəˈteɪn/ v 1 [I, T] invite people to eat or drink with you in your home 2 [I, T] amuse and interest sb 3 [T] (fml) consider an idea, a hope, feeling, etc ▶ **entertainer** n person whose job is to amuse or interest people, eg by singing ▶ **entertaining** adj amusing ▶ **entertainment** n 1 [C] films, music, etc used to entertain people 2 [U] act of entertaining sb

enthral (esp US **enthrall**) /ɪnˈθrɔːl/ v (-ll-) [T] capture sb's complete attention

enthuse /ɪnˈθjuːz/ v [I] ~(**about/over**) talk about sth with great enthusiasm

enthusiasm /ɪnˈθjuːziæzəm/ n [U] great excitement or interest in sth and a desire to become involved in it ▶ **enthusiast** /ɪnˈθjuːziæst/ n person with a strong interest in sth ▶ **enthusiastic** /ɪnˌθjuːziˈæstɪk/ adj full of enthusiasm ▶ **enthusiastically** /-kli/ adv

entice /ɪnˈtaɪs/ v [T] persuade sb/sth to go somewhere or do sth, by offering them sth ▶ **enticement** n [C,U]

entire /ɪnˈtaɪə(r)/ adj complete ▶ **entirely** adv ▶ **entirety** /-rəti/ n

entitle /ɪnˈtaɪtl/ v 1 ~**to** give sb the right to have or do sth 2 give a title to a book, etc ▶ **entitlement** n [C,U]

entity /ˈentəti/ n (pl -ies) (fml) something that has a separate existence

entourage /ˈɒntʊrɑːʒ/ n [C, with sing

or pl verb] people who travel with an important person

entrance¹ /'entrans/ n 1 [C] door, gate, etc used for entering a room, building or place 2 [C, usu sing] act of entering 3 [U] right to enter a building or place

entrance² /ɪn'trɑːns/ v [T] make sb feel pleasure and give sb/sth all their attention: ~d by the music

entrant /'entrant/ n person who enters a competition, profession, etc

entreat /ɪn'triːt/ v [T] (fml) ask sb to do sth in a serious way ► **entreaty** n [C, U] (pl -**ies**) serious, often emotional, request

entrenched /ɪn'trentʃt/ adj (of ideas, etc) firmly fixed

entrepreneur /ˌɒntrəprə'nɜː(r)/ n person who starts a business

entrust /ɪn'trʌst/ v [T] ~ **with**/~ **to** give sth to sb to look after: ~ the job to him ◇ ~ him with the job

entry /'entri/ n (pl -**ies**) 1 [C] act of coming or going in a place 2 [U] right to take part in or join sth 3 [C] item written in a dictionary, diary, etc 4 [C] door, gate or passage where you enter a building

enumerate /ɪ'njuːməreɪt/ v [T] name things on a list one by one

enunciate /ɪ'nʌnsieɪt/ v [I, T] say words clearly ► **enunciation** /ɪˌnʌnsi'eɪʃn/ n [U]

envelop /ɪn'veləp/ v [T] wrap sb/sth up or cover them or it completely

envelope /'envələʊp; 'ɒn-/ n paper covering for a letter

enviable /'enviəbl/ adj desirable; causing envy

envious /'enviəs/ adj feeling or showing envy ► **enviously** adv

environment /ɪn'vaɪrənmənt/ n 1 [C, U] physical conditions that sb/sth exists in 2 **(the environment)** [sing] the natural world in which people, plants and animals live ► **environmental** /ɪnˌvaɪrən'mentl/ adj ► **environmentalist** /ɪnˌvaɪrən'mentəlɪst/ n person who wants to protect the environment(2) ► **environmentally** /-təli/ adv: ~ally friendly packaging

envisage /ɪn'vɪzɪdʒ/ v [T] have an idea of sth as a future possibility

envoy /'envɔɪ/ n messenger or representative of a government or an organization

envy /'envi/ n [U] feeling of wanting sth that sb else has [IDM] **be the envy of sb/sth** be a person or thing that others admire and that causes envy ● **envy** v (pt, pp -**ied**) [T] wish you had the same qualities, possessions, etc, as sb else

enzyme /'enzaɪm/ n chemical substance formed in living cells that causes chemical change

epaulette (esp US -**let**) /'epəlet/ n decoration on the shoulder of a uniform

ephemeral /ɪ'femərəl/ adj lasting for a very short time

epic /'epɪk/ n long poem, film, etc about the actions of great heroes ● **epic** adj impressive; grand

epidemic /ˌepɪ'demɪk/ n disease that spreads quickly among many people

epilepsy /'epɪlepsi/ n [U] disease that causes sb to become unconscious and to have sudden fits ► **epileptic** /ˌepɪ'leptɪk/ adj, n

epilogue (US -**log**) /'epɪlɒg/ n last part of a book or play

episode /'epɪsəʊd/ n 1 one important event or period of time in sb's life 2 one of several parts of a story on television, etc

epitaph /'epɪtɑːf/ n words on a tombstone

epithet /'epɪθet/ n adjective used to describe sb

epitome /ɪ'pɪtəmi/ n person or thing that is the perfect example of a quality or type: She is the ~ of kindness. ► **epitomize** (also -**ise**) /ɪ'pɪtəmaɪz/ v [T] be a perfect example of sth

epoch /'iːpɒk/ n period of time marked by important events or characteristics

equable /'ekwəbl/ adj moderate; not changing much: an ~ climate/temper

equal /'iːkwəl/ adj 1 the same in size, number, value, etc 2 ~ **to** having the ability or strength for sth: ~ to the task ● **equal** n person or thing equal to another ● **equal** v (-**ll**- US -**l**-) [T] be equal to sb/sth ► **equality** /ɪ'kwɒləti/ n [U] fact of being equal in rights, status, advantages, etc ► **equalize** (also -**ise**) v [I, T] become or make sb/sth equal ► **equally** adv 1 to the same degree; in the same way 2 in equal parts, amounts, etc

equate /ɪ'kweɪt/ v [T] consider sth to be the same or as important as sth else: You cannot ~ these two systems of government.

equation /ɪ'kweɪʒn/ n (maths) statement that two amounts or values are equal: $2x + 5 = 11$ is an ~.

equator /ɪ'kweɪtə(r)/ n **(the equator)** [sing] imaginary line round the earth, halfway between the North and South Poles ► **equatorial** /ˌekwə'tɔːriəl/ adj

equestrian /ɪ'kwestriən/ adj connected with horse riding

equilibrium /ˌiːkwɪ'lɪbriəm; ˌek-/ n [U, sing] (fml) state of being balanced

equinox /'i:kwɪnɒks; 'ek-/ n one of the two times in the year when day and night are of equal length: *the spring/autumn ~*

equip /ɪ'kwɪp/ v (-pp-) [T] ~(with) supply sb with sth needed for a particular purpose ▸ **equipment** n [U] things needed for a particular purpose: *office ~ment*

equitable /'ekwɪtəbl/ adj fair and reasonable ▸ **equitably** adv

equity /'ekwəti/ n 1 value of a company's shares; value of a property after all debts have been paid 2 (**equities**) [pl] shares in a company on which fixed interest is not paid 3 [U] (fml) fairness

equivalent /ɪ'kwɪvələnt/ adj, n (thing) that is equal in value, amount, importance, etc to sth else

equivocal /ɪ'kwɪvəkl/ adj (fml) not having one clear or definite meaning: *an ~ answer* ▸ **equivocate** /-'kwɪvəkeɪt/ v [I] (fml) speak about sth in a way that is not clear in order to hide the truth

era /'ɪərə/ n period in history marked by an important event or development

eradicate /ɪ'rædɪkeɪt/ v [T] destroy sth bad ▸ **eradication** /-'keɪʃn/ n [U]

erase /ɪ'reɪz/ v [T] remove sth completely: *~ the event from his memory* ▸ **eraser** n (esp US) = RUBBER(2)

erect /ɪ'rekt/ v [T] 1 (fml) build sth 2 fix or set sth upright: *~ a tent* ● **erect** adj in an upright position: *stand ~* ▸ **erection** /ɪ'rekʃn/ n 1 [C] swelling and hardening of a man's penis 2 [U] (fml) act of erecting sth 3 [C] (fml) building

erode /ɪ'rəʊd/ v [T] (of the sea, wind, etc) gradually destroy the surface of sth ▸ **erosion** /ɪ'rəʊʒn/ n [U]

erotic /ɪ'rɒtɪk/ adj causing sexual excitement

err /ɜ:(r)/ v [I] (old-fash, fml) make a mistake

errand /'erənd/ n short journey, eg to buy goods from a shop

erratic /ɪ'rætɪk/ adj not regular or reliable ▸ **erratically** /-kli/ adv

erroneous /ɪ'rəʊniəs/ adj (fml) (of beliefs, etc) incorrect

error /'erə(r)/ n [C,U] mistake: *The accident was due to human ~.*

erudite /'erudaɪt/ adj (fml) having or showing great knowledge

erupt /ɪ'rʌpt/ v [I] 1 (of a volcano) throw out lava 2 break out violently: *Fighting ~ed on the streets.* ▸ **eruption** /ɪ'rʌpʃn/ n [C,U]

escalate /'eskəleɪt/ v [I, T] become or make sth bigger or more serious ▸ **escalation** /ˌeskə'leɪʃn/ n [U]

escalator /'eskəleɪtə(r)/ n moving staircase for carrying people up or down

escapade /'eskəpeɪd/ n exciting and possibly dangerous adventure

escape /ɪ'skeɪp/ v 1 [I] ~(from) get free from prison or sb's control 2 [I, T] get away from sth unpleasant 3 [I] ~(from) (of gases, liquids, etc) find a way out 4 [T] be forgotten or not noticed: *Her name ~s me* (=I can't remember it). ● **escape** n 1 [C,U] act or method of escaping from somewhere 2 [C] leaking of a gas or liquid ▸ **escapism** n [U] activity that helps you forget your problems, etc ▸ **escapist** adj

escort /'eskɔ:t/ n person or group of people or vehicles that travel with sb to protect them ● **escort** /ɪ'skɔ:t/ v go with sb as an escort

esophagus (US) = OESOPHAGUS

esoteric /ˌesə'terɪk; ˌi:sə-/ adj (fml) understood by only a small group of people

especially /ɪ'speʃəli/ adj (abbr **esp.**) 1 in particular: *I love Paris, ~ in spring.* 2 for a particular purpose, person, etc 3 very much; to a great degree: *This is ~ true of the old.*

espionage /'espiənɑ:ʒ/ n [U] activity of spying

essay /'eseɪ/ n short piece of writing on one subject ▸ **essayist** n writer of essays

essence /'esns/ n 1 [U] most important quality of sth 2 [C,U] flavouring in concentrated liquid form [IDM] **in essence** really

essential /ɪ'senʃl/ adj 1 extremely important; completely necessary 2 fundamental: *an ~ part of the English character* ● **essential** n [C, usu pl] most important or necessary thing: *Pack the bare ~s.* ▸ **essentially** /ɪ'senʃəli/ adv basically or really

establish /ɪ'stæblɪʃ/ v [T] 1 start or create a business, system, etc meant to last for a long time 2 settle yourself firmly in a position or activity 3 show a fact, etc to be true; prove ▸ **establishment** n 1 [C] (fml) organization, large institution or a hotel 2 (usu the **Establishment**) [sing, with sing or pl verb] often (disapprov) people in positions of power 3 [U] act of starting or creating sth

estate /ɪ'steɪt/ n 1 land in the country, with one owner 2 (GB) large area of land with factories or houses on it: *a housing ~* 3 (law) all of a person's money and property, esp after their death ■ **e'state agent** n person who buys and sells houses for others ■ **e'state car** n car with an area for luggage behind the back seats and a door at the back

esteem /ɪ'sti:m/ n [U] (fml) good

opinion; respect ● **esteem** v [T] (*fml*) respect sb/sth greatly

esthetic (*US*) = AESTHETIC

estimate /'estɪmeɪt/ v [T] form an idea of the cost, size, value, etc of sth, but without calculating it exactly ● **estimate** /'estɪmət/ n approximate calculation of cost, size, etc of sth ▶ **estimation** /ˌestɪ'meɪʃn/ n [U] judgement or opinion about value or quality of sb/sth

estuary /'estʃuəri/ n (*pl* -ies) mouth of a river into which the tide flows

etc /ˌet 'setərə/, ˌit-/ *abbr* (short for 'et cetera') and other similar things; and the rest

etch /etʃ/ v [I, T] cut lines into a piece of glass, metal, etc in order to make words or a picture ▶ **etching** n [C,U] picture printed from an etched metal plate; art of making these pictures

eternal /ɪ'tɜːnl/ *adj* 1 lasting for ever 2 (*disapprov*) seeming never to stop ▶ **eternally** /ɪ'tɜːnəli/ *adv*

eternity /ɪ'tɜːnəti/ n 1 [U] (*fml*) time without end, esp after death 2 (an eternity) [sing] (*infml*) a very long time

ether /'iːθə(r)/ n [U] colourless liquid made from alcohol ▶ **ethereal** /i'θɪəriəl/ *adj* very delicate and light

Ethernet /'iːθənet/ n [U] system for connecting a number of computer systems to form a network

ethic /'eθɪk/ n 1 (ethics) [pl] moral principles 2 [sing] system of moral principles: *the Christian ~* 3 (ethics) [U] study of moral principles ▶ **ethical** *adj* 1 of morals 2 morally correct ▶ **ethically** *adv* -kli/

ethnic /'eθnɪk/ *adj* of a national, racial or tribal group ▶ **ethnically** /-kli/ *adv*

etiquette /'etɪket/ n [U] rules for polite behaviour in society

etymology /ˌetɪ'mɒlədʒi/ n [U] study of the history of words

eucalyptus /ˌjuːkə'lɪptəs/ n tall evergreen tree from which an oil, used as medicine, is obtained

euphemism /'juːfəmɪzəm/ n [C,U] use of an indirect word or phrase to express sth unpleasant: *'Pass away' is a ~ for 'die'.* ▶ **euphemistic** /ˌjuːfə'mɪstɪk/ *adj*

euphoria /juː'fɔːriə/ n [U] feeling of great happiness and excitement ▶ **euphoric** /juː'fɒrɪk/ *adj*

euro /'jʊərəʊ/ n (*pl* ~s) n (*symb* €) (since 1999) unit of money of many countries of the European Union

Euro- /'jʊərəʊ/ *prefix* of Europe or the European Union

euthanasia /ˌjuːθə'neɪziə/ n [U] painless killing of people who have a painful incurable disease

evacuate /ɪ'vækjueɪt/ v [T] move people from a place of danger to a safer place: *~ the building* ▶ **evacuation** /ɪˌvækju'eɪʃn/ n [C,U]

evade /ɪ'veɪd/ v [T] 1 escape from or avoid meeting sb/sth 2 find a way of not doing or dealing with sth: *~ (answering) a question*

evaluate /ɪ'væljueɪt/ v [I] decide on the value or quality of sb/sth ▶ **evaluation** /ɪˌvælju'eɪʃn/ n [C,U]

evangelical /ˌiːvæn'dʒelɪkl/ *adj* of a Christian group that emphasizes salvation by belief in Christ

evangelist /ɪ'vændʒəlɪst/ n 1 person who travels around holding meetings to persuade people to become Christians 2 one of the four writers of the Gospels in the Bible ▶ **evangelistic** /ˌiːvændʒə'lɪstɪk/ *adj*

evaporate /ɪ'væpəreɪt/ v 1 [I, T] (cause a liquid to) change into gas, esp steam, and disappear 2 [I] gradually disappear ▶ **evaporation** /ɪˌvæpə'reɪʃn/ n [U]

evasion /ɪ'veɪʒn/ n [C,U] act of avoiding sb/sth ▶ **evasive** /ɪ'veɪsɪv/ *adj* not willing to give clear answers to a question ▶ **evasively** *adv*

eve /iːv/ n [C, usu sing] day before an event, esp a religious festival: *Christmas E~*

even¹ /'iːvn/ *adv* 1 used for emphasizing sth unexpected or surprising: *E~ a child can understand it* (= so adults certainly can). 2 used to make a comparison between two things stronger: *You know ~ less than I do.* [IDM] **even if/ though** in spite of the fact that: *I'll get there ~ if I have to walk.* **even now/so/then** in spite of what (had) happened: *I told him, but ~ then he didn't believe me.*

even² /'iːvn/ *adj* 1 level and smooth: *an ~ surface* 2 not changing much in amount, speed, etc: *an ~ temperature* 3 (of amounts) equal or the same for each person, team, etc 4 (of two people or teams) equally balanced: *The two teams are ~.* 5 (of numbers) that can be divided by two [IDM] **be/get even (with sb)** (*infml*) cause sb the same amount of harm as they have caused you **on an even keel** calm, with no sudden changes ● **even** v [PV] **even (sth) out/up** become or make sth level, equal or balanced ▶ **even-handed** *adj* fair ▶ **evenly** *adv* ▶ **evenness** n [U] ▶ **even-tempered** *adj* not easily made angry

evening /'iːvnɪŋ/ n [C, U] part of the day between the afternoon and bedtime ■ **'evening dress** n 1 [U] clothes worn for formal occasions in the evening 2 [C] woman's long formal dress

event /ɪ'vent/ n **1** something that happens, esp important **2** one race, competition, etc in a sports programme [IDM] **at all events** whatever happens **in the event of sth** (fml) if sth happens ▶ **eventful** /ɪ'ventfl/ adj full of interesting or important events

eventual /ɪ'ventʃuəl/ adj happening at the end of a period of time or of a process ▶ **eventuality** /ɪ,ventʃu'æləti/ n (pl -ies) (fml) possible event or result ▶ **eventually** adv in the end: They ~ly agreed to pay.

ever /'evə(r)/ adv **1** at any time: Nothing ~ happens here. ◇ Do you ~ wish you were rich? ◇ the best work you've ~ done **2** all the time or every time; always: the ~-increasing number of students ◇ He said he'd love her for ~. **3** (used for showing surprise in questions): What ~ do you mean? [IDM] **ever since** (...) continuously since the time mentioned: She's liked reading ~ since she was a child. **ever so/ such a** (spoken, esp GB) very; really: ~ so rich

evergreen /'evəɡri:n/ n, adj (tree or bush) that has green leaves throughout the year

everlasting /,evə'lɑ:stɪŋ/ adj lasting for ever

every /'evri/ adj **1** each (one): E~ child passed the exam. **2** all possible: You have ~ reason to be satisfied. **3** used for showing that sth happens regularly: She phones ~ week. [IDM] **every other** each alternate one: ~ other day = (Monday, Wednesday and Friday, etc) ■ **everybody** also **'everyone** pron every person; all people ■ **everyday** adj ordinary; daily ■ **everything** pron all things: E~thing was destroyed. ■ **everywhere** adv in or to every place

evict /ɪ'vɪkt/ v [T] force sb to leave a house or land, esp by official authority of the law ▶ **eviction** /ɪ'vɪkʃn/ n [C,U]

evidence /'evɪdns/ n [U] **1** facts, signs or objects that make you believe sth is true **2** information used in a law court to try to prove sth: I was asked to give ~. [IDM] **(be) in evidence** (be) present and clearly seen

evident /'evɪdənt/ adj plain and clear; obvious ▶ **evidently** adv

evil /'i:vl/ adj wicked; cruel ● **evil** n (fml) **1** [U] force that causes wicked things to happen **2** [C, usu pl] very bad or harmful thing: the ~s of alcohol ▶ **evilly** /'i:vəli/ adv

evocative /ɪ'vɒkətɪv/ adj that brings memories, feelings, etc of sth: an ~ picture

evoke /ɪ'vəʊk/ v [T] produce a memory, feeling, etc

evolution /,i:və'lu:ʃn/ n [U] (theory of) gradual development, esp of animals and plants from earlier simpler forms

evolve /ɪ'vɒlv/ v [I, T] (cause sth to) develop gradually

ewe /ju:/ n female sheep

exacerbate /ɪɡ'zæsəbeɪt/ v [T] (fml) make sth worse, esp a disease or problem

exact¹ /ɪɡ'zækt/ adj correct in every detail; precise: the ~ time ▶ **exactitude** /ɪɡ'zæktɪtju:d/ n [U] (fml) correctness ▶ **exactly** adv precisely **2** used to agree with what sb just said ▶ **exactness** n [U]

exact² /ɪɡ'zækt/ v [T] (fml) demand and obtain sth from sb: to ~ a promise from her ▶ **exacting** adj requiring or demanding hard work and care

exam /ɪɡ'zæm/ n short for EXAMINATION(1)

examination /ɪɡ,zæmɪ'neɪʃn/ n **1** [C] (fml) formal test of knowledge or ability, esp at school: take/sit/do an ~ **2** [U,C] action of looking at or considering sth carefully

examine /ɪɡ'zæmɪn/ v [T] **1** consider or study an idea, subject, etc carefully **2** look at sb/sth to see if there is anything wrong **3** question sb in order to test their knowledge or ability ▶ **examiner** n person who tests knowledge or ability

example /ɪɡ'zɑ:mpl/ n **1** fact, thing, etc that shows a general rule or represents a group: a fine ~ of Norman architecture **2** person or quality to be copied: His bravery is an ~ to us all. [IDM] **for example** (abbr **eg**) used to emphasize sth that explains or supports what you are saying: There is a similar word in many languages, ~ French and Italian. **make an example of sb** punish sb as a warning to others

exasperate /ɪɡ'zæspəreɪt/ v [T] annoy sb very much ▶ **exasperation** /ɪɡ,zæspə'reɪʃn/ n [U]

excavate /'ekskəveɪt/ v [T] make or uncover sth by digging in the ground: ~ a buried city ▶ **excavation** /,ekskə'veɪʃn/ n [C,U] ▶ **excavator** n person or machine that excavates sth

exceed /ɪk'si:d/ v [T] (fml) **1** be greater than a particular number or amount **2** go beyond a limit or rule: ~ the speed limit = (drive faster than is allowed) ▶ **exceedingly** adv (fml) extremely

E

excel /ɪk'sel/ v (-ll-) [I] ~at/in be very good at sth

Excellency /'eksələnsɪ/ n (pl -ies) title of some officials, eg ambassadors or governors

excellent /'eksələnt/ adj very good ▶ **excellence** /-ləns/ n [U] ▶ **excellently** adv

except /ɪk'sept/ prep not including; apart from: The shop is open every day ~ Sunday. ● **except** v [T] (fml) (usu passive) not include sb/sth

exception /ɪk'sepʃn/ n person, thing, etc that is not included [IDM] **make an exception (of sb/sth)** treat sb/sth as a special case **take exception to sth** be annoyed by sth **with the exception of** except; not including ▶ **exceptional** /-ʃənl/ adj very good; unusual ▶ **exceptionally** /-ʃənəlɪ/ adv

excerpt /'eksɜːpt/ n piece taken from a book, film, etc

excess /ɪk'ses/ n 1 [sing] ~of more than is necessary, reasonable or acceptable: an increase in ~ of (= more than) 2%. ◇ drink to ~ (= too much) 2 (**excesses**) [pl] (US) unacceptable, illegal or immoral behaviour ● **excess** /'ekses/ adj in addition to the usual or legal amount: ~ baggage ▶ **excessive** adj too much ▶ **excessively** adv

exchange /ɪks'tʃeɪndʒ/ v [T] give and receive sth in return: ~ euros for dollars ● **exchange** n 1 [C,U] act of exchanging sth 2 [C] (angry) conversation 3 [U] process of changing an amount of one currency for an equal value of another: the ~ rate ◇ get a good rate of ~ 4 [C] place where people meet for business: the London Stock E~ 5 = TELEPHONE EXCHANGE

exchequer /ɪks'tʃekə(r)/ n (the **Exchequer**) [sing] (GB) government department in charge of public money: the Chancellor of the E~ (= the minister at the head of this department)

excise /'eksaɪz/ n [U] tax on certain goods produced inside a country

excite /ɪk'saɪt/ v [T] 1 cause strong, esp pleasant feelings in sb 2 cause a particular feeling or response in sb ▶ **excitable** adj easily excited ▶ **excited** adj full of strong happy feelings ▶ **excitedly** adv ▶ **excitement** n [U,C] ▶ **exciting** adj causing great interest and excitement

exclaim /ɪk'skleɪm/ v [I, T] (written) say sth suddenly or loudly, esp because of strong emotion or pain ▶ **exclamation** /ˌeksklə'meɪʃn/ n sound(s) or word(s) exclaimed ■ **excla'mation mark** (US **excla'mation point**) n mark (!) written after an exclamation

exclude /ɪk'skluːd/ v [T] 1 deliberately not include sb/sth; keep sb/sth out of sth 2 decide that sth is not possible: Police have ~d theft as a possible motive. ▶ **exclusion** /ɪk'skluːʒn/ n [U,C]

exclusive /ɪk'skluːsɪv/ adj 1 only to be used by or given to one particular person or group 2 (of a group) admitting only carefully chosen people 3 of a high quality and expensive and therefore not used by many people ● **exclusive** n report published by only one newspaper ▶ **exclusively** adv only

excommunicate /ˌekskə'mjuːnɪkeɪt/ v [T] exclude sb from the Christian church ▶ **excommunication** /ˌekskəˌmjuːnɪ'keɪʃn/ n [U,C]

excrement /'ekskrɪmənt/ n [U] (fml) solid waste matter from the body

excrete /ɪk'skriːt/ v [T] pass solid waste matter from the body

excruciating /ɪk'skruːʃɪeɪtɪŋ/ adj very painful ▶ **excruciatingly** adv

excursion /ɪk'skɜːʃn/ n short journey, esp for pleasure

excuse /ɪk'skjuːs/ n reason given to explain or defend your behaviour ▶ **excusable** /ɪk'skjuːzəbl/ adj forgivable ● **excuse** /ɪk'skjuːz/ v [T] 1 ~ (for) forgive sb for sth they have done 2 justify sb's behaviour: Nothing can ~ such rudeness. 3 ~ (from) set sb free from a duty [IDM] **excuse me 1** used as an apology when you interrupt sb, disagree, etc 2 (US) used to ask sb to repeat sth they said

execute /'eksɪkjuːt/ v [T] 1 kill sb, esp as a legal punishment 2 (fml) do a piece of work, perform a duty, etc: ~ a plan ▶ **execution** /ˌeksɪ'kjuːʃn/ n 1 [U,C] act of killing sb, esp as a legal punishment 2 [U] (fml) act of carrying out of a plan, doing a piece of work, etc ▶ **executioner** /ˌeksɪ'kjuːʃənə(r)/ n official who executes criminals

executive /ɪg'zekjətɪv/ adj concerned with managing, and putting laws and decisions into effect ● **executive** n [C] person with an important job as a manager of a company or an organization 2 (**the executive**) [sing, with sing or pl verb] branch of government responsible for putting laws into effect

executor /ɪg'zekjətə(r)/ n (tech) person chosen to carry out the instructions in sb's will

exemplify /ɪg'zemplɪfaɪ/ v (pt, pp **-ied**) [T] be or give an example of sth ▶ **exemplification** /ɪgˌzemplɪfɪ'keɪʃn/ n [U,C]

exempt /ɪg'zempt/ adj ~(from) free from a duty or obligation ● **exempt** v [T] (fml) ~(from) give or get sb's official permission not to do or pay sth ▶ **exemption** /ɪgˈzempʃn/ *n* [U,C]

exercise /ˈeksəsaɪz/ *n* **1** [U] physical or mental activity that keeps you healthy: *Jogging is good* ~. **2** [C] activity intended for training or testing sb: *relaxation* ~*s* ◇ *maths* ~*s* **3** [U] careful use or practice: *the* ~ *of power* ● **exercise** *v* **1** [T] use your power, authority or a right in order to achieve sth **2** [I, T] keep your body healthy by doing sports, etc ■ **'exercise book** *n* small book for students to write in

exert /ɪgˈzɜːt/ *v* [T] **1** use power or influence to affect sb/sth: ~ *pressure on sb to do sth* **2** ~ *yourself* make a big effort ▶ **exertion** /ɪgˈzɜːʃn/ *n* [C, U]

exhale /eksˈheɪl/ *v* [I, T] breathe out the air, smoke, etc in your lungs ▶ **exhalation** /ˌekshəˈleɪʃn/ *n* [U]

exhaust /ɪgˈzɔːst/ *v* [T] **1** make sb very tired **2** use all of sth ● **exhaust** *n* **1** [U] waste gases that come out of a vehicle, engine, etc **2** [C] (*also* **ex'haust pipe**) pipe through which exhaust gases come out ▶ **exhausted** *adj* very tired ▶ **exhaustion** /ɪgˈzɔːstʃən/ *n* [U] ▶ **exhaustive** *adj* thorough

exhibit /ɪgˈzɪbɪt/ *v* **1** [I, T] show sth publicly for people to enjoy or to give them information **2** [T] (*written*) show clearly that you have a particular feeling, quality or ability ● **exhibit** *n* something shown in a museum, etc **2** something shown as evidence in a law court ▶ **exhibitor** *n* person who shows their works or products to the public

exhibition /ˌeksɪˈbɪʃn/ *n* **1** (*US* **exhibit**) public show of pictures, etc **2** (*usu sing*) act of showing a skill, a feeling or kind of behaviour ● **exhibitionism** /-ʃənɪzəm/ *n* [U] behaviour intended to attract attention to yourself ▶ **exhibitionist** *n*

exhilarate /ɪgˈzɪləreɪt/ *v* [T] (*usu passive*) make sb feel happy and excited ▶ **exhilaration** /-ˈreɪʃn/ *n* [U]

exhort /ɪgˈzɔːt/ *v* [T] (*fml*) ~ (**to**) urge sb to do sth: ~ *them to try harder* ▶ **exhortation** /ˌegzɔːˈteɪʃn/ *n* [C, U]

exile /ˈeksaɪl/ *n* **1** [U] being sent to live in a country that is not your own, esp for political reasons: *live in* ~ **2** [C] person who is sent away from their own country ● **exile** *v* [T] send sb into exile

exist /ɪgˈzɪst/ *v* [I] be real be; continue living ▶ **existence** *n* **1** [U] state of existing: *believe in the* ~*ence of God* **2** [C] way of life: *a miserable* ~*ence* ▶ **existent** *adj* (*fml*) living; real

exit /ˈeksɪt/ *n* **1** way out of a public building or vehicle **2** act of leaving a place, esp of an actor from the stage ● **exit** *v* [I] **1** go out; leave a

building, stage, etc **2** finish using a computer program

exonerate /ɪgˈzɒnəreɪt/ *v* [T] (*fml*) free sb from blame ▶ **exoneration** /ɪgˌzɒnəˈreɪʃn/ *n* [U]

exorbitant /ɪgˈzɔːbɪtənt/ *adj* (of a price) much too high ▶ **exorbitantly** *adv*

exorcize (*also* **-ise**) /ˈeksɔːsaɪz/ *v* [T] drive out an evil spirit by prayer ▶ **exorcism** /ˈeksɔːsɪzəm/ *n* [U,C] ▶ **exorcist** *n*

exotic /ɪgˈzɒtɪk/ *adj* **1** from another country, esp a tropical one: ~ *fruits* **2** attractive or pleasing because unusual

expand /ɪkˈspænd/ *v* [I, T] become or make sth greater in size, number or importance: *Metals* ~ *when heated.* ◇ ~ *a business* [PV] **expand on/upon sth** give more information about sth

expanse /ɪkˈspæns/ *n* wide open area (of land, sea, etc)

expansion /ɪkˈspænʃn/ *n* [U] action of expanding ▶ **expansionism** /ɪkˈspænʃənɪzəm/ *n* [U] esp (*disapprov*) policy of expanding your land or business ▶ **expansionist** *adj*

expansive /ɪkˈspænsɪv/ *adj* **1** covering a large area **2** (of people) willing to talk a lot

expatriate /ˌeksˈpætriət/ (*also infml* **expat**) *n* (person) living outside his/her own country

expect /ɪkˈspekt/ *v* [T] think or believe that sth will happen [IDM] **be expecting a baby/child** be pregnant ▶ **expectancy** *n* [U] state of expecting sth to happen, esp sth good ▶ **expectant** *adj* **1** expecting sth to happen, esp sth good **2** pregnant ▶ **expectation** /ˌekspekˈteɪʃn/ *n* [C,U] strong hope or belief that sth will happen

expedient /ɪkˈspiːdiənt/ *adj, n* (*fml*) (action that is) useful for a particular purpose, but not always fair or moral ▶ **expediency** /-ənsi/ *n* [U]

expedition /ˌekspəˈdɪʃn/ *n* **1** organized journey for a purpose, eg exploration **2** people who go on an expedition ■ **expe'ditionary force** *n* group of soldiers sent to another country to fight

expel /ɪkˈspel/ *v* (**-ll-**) [T] **1** to force sb to leave a school or an organization **2** (*tech*) force air or water out of a part of the body or a container

expend /ɪkˈspend/ *v* [T] (*fml*) spend or use a lot of money, time or energy ▶ **expendable** *adj* (*fml*) that may be got rid or or destroyed when no longer needed

expenditure /ɪkˈspendɪtʃə(r)/ *n* [U, C] **1** amount of money spent on sth

2 act of spending or using money, energy, etc

expense /ɪkˈspens/ *n* **1** [U,C] thing that makes you spend money; amount of money spent on sth **2** (**expenses**) [pl] money used for a particular purpose: *travelling ~s* [IDM] **at sb's expense 1** paid for by sb **2** (of a joke) intended to make sb look foolish

expensive /ɪkˈspensɪv/ *adj* costing a lot of money ► **expensively** *adv*

experience /ɪkˈspɪəriəns/ *n* **1** [U] knowledge or skill gained by doing or seeing things: *learn by ~* **2** [C] event or activity that affects you in some way: *a happy ~* ● **experience** *v* [T] have an experience of sth; feel a particular emotion or physical sensation: *~ difficulty/pain* ► **experienced** *adj* having a lot of experience(1)

experiment /ɪkˈsperɪmənt/ *n* [C,U] (esp in science) test done carefully to find out what happens ● **experiment** *v* [I] do a scientific experiment; try or test new ideas, methods, etc ► **experimental** /ɪkˌsperɪˈmentl/ *adj* of or using experiments ► **experimentation** /ɪkˌsperɪmenˈteɪʃn/ *n* [U]

expert /ˈekˈspɜːt/ *n ~*(**at/in**) person with special knowledge or skill ● **expert** *adj ~*(**at/in**) having or involving great knowledge or skill ► **expertly** *adv*

expertise /ˌekspɜːˈtiːz/ *n* [U] great knowledge or skill in a particular subject or job

expire /ɪkˈspaɪə(r)/ *v* [I] **1** (of a document, an agreement, etc) be no longer valid: *My passport has ~d.* **2** (*lit*) die ► **expiry** /ɪkˈspaɪəri/ *n* [U] ending of the period when a contract, etc is valid

explain /ɪkˈspleɪn/ *v* **1** [I,T] make sth clear, give the meaning of sth **2** [T] give reasons for sth: *~ your behaviour* [PV] **explain sth away** give reasons why sth is not your fault or not important ► **explanation** /ˌekspləˈneɪʃn/ *n* **1** [C] statement that explains sth **2** [U] act of explaining sth ► **explanatory** /ɪkˈsplænətri/ *adj* giving the reasons for sth; intended to explain sth

explicit /ɪkˈsplɪsɪt/ *adj* **1** (of statements) clear and easy to understand **2** (of people) saying sth clearly and openly ► **explicitly** *adv* ► **explicitness** *n* [U]

explode /ɪkˈspləʊd/ *v* **1** [I,T] (cause sth to) burst loudly and violently, usu causing damage **2** [I] (of people) show strong feelings suddenly

exploit¹ /ɪkˈsplɔɪt/ *v* [T] **1** treat sb selfishly and unfairly, for profit **2** use or develop sth, esp for profit:

~ oil reserves ► **exploitation** /ˌeksplɔɪˈteɪʃn/ *n* [U]

exploit² /ˈeksplɔɪt/ *n* brave or exciting act

explore /ɪkˈsplɔː(r)/ *v* [T] **1** travel through a country to learn about it **2** examine sth carefully: *~ different possibilities* ► **exploration** /ˌekspləˈreɪʃn/ *n* [U,C] ► **exploratory** /ɪkˈsplɔrətri/ *adj* done in order to find out sth ► **explorer** *n* person who travels to unknown places to find out more about them

explosion /ɪkˈspləʊʒn/ *n* **1** sudden loud noise caused by sth exploding; act of causing sth to explode **2** sudden burst of anger **3** great and sudden increase: *the population ~*

explosive /ɪkˈspləʊsɪv/ *n, adj* (substance) that can explode: *an ~ device* (= a bomb) ► **explosively** *adv*

exponent /ɪkˈspəʊnənt/ *n* person who supports and explains a belief, etc

export /ɪkˈspɔːt/ *v* [I,T] sell and send goods to another country ● **export** /ˈekspɔːt/ *n* **1** [U] (business of) exporting goods **2** [C, usu pl] product sold to another country ► **exporter** *n* person, company or country that exports goods

expose /ɪkˈspəʊz/ *v* [T] **1** show sth that is usu hidden **2** tell the true facts about sb/sth and show them/it to be immoral, illegal, etc **3** put sb/sth in a place or situation where they are unprotected against harm or danger **4** (in photography) allow light to reach film ► **exposure** /ɪkˈspəʊʒə(r)/ *n* [U,C]

expound /ɪkˈspaʊnd/ *v* [I,T] (*fml*) *~* (**on**) explain sth by talking about it in detail: *~ a theory*

express¹ /ɪkˈspres/ *v* [T] **1** make known a feeling, an opinion, etc by words or looks: *~ an opinion* **2** *~* **yourself** speak or write clearly your thoughts or feelings

express² /ɪkˈspres/ *adj* **1** going quickly: *an ~ letter* **2** (*fml*) clearly stated: *his ~ wish* ● **express** *adv* (*esp GB*) by express post: *send a letter* *~* ● **express** (*also* **ex'press train**) *n* fast train ► **expressly** *adv* definitely; clearly ■ **ex'press·way** *n* (*US*) = MOTORWAY

expression /ɪkˈspreʃn/ *n* **1** [C,U] things that people say, write or do to show their feelings, opinions or ideas **2** [C] look on sb's face that shows a feeling: *an angry ~* **3** [C] word or phrase: *a polite ~* **4** [U] feeling shown when acting, singing, etc ► **expressionless** *adj* not showing your feelings, thoughts, etc

expressive /ɪkˈspresɪv/ *adj* showing your feelings or thoughts ► **expressively** *adv* ► **expressiveness** *n* [U]

expropriate /eks'prəupriett/ v [T] **1** (fml) or (law) (of a government) take away private property for public use **2** (fml) take sb's property and use it without permission

expulsion /ik'spʌlʃn/ n [C,U] (act of) expelling sb

exquisite /ik'skwizit; 'ekskwizit/ adj very beautiful; skilfully made ▶ **exquisitely** adv

extend /ik'stend/ v **1** [T] make sth longer or larger: ~ the house **2** [i] cover a particular area, distance or length of time: The Park ~s to the river. **3** [T] stretch out part of your body fully **4** [T] (fml) offer or give sth to sb: ~ an invitation

extension /ik'stenʃn/ n **1** [U,C] act of extending sth **2** [C] new part that is added to a building: a new ~ to the hospital **3** [C] extra telephone line inside a house or an organization

extensive /ik'stensiv/ adj large in area or amount ▶ **extensively** adv

extent /ik'stent/ n [sing, U] **1** how large, important, serious, etc sth is: the ~ of the damage **2** degree: to some ~

extenuating /ik'stenjueitiŋ/ adj (fml) making bad behaviour less serious by giving reasons for it: ~ circumstances

exterior /ik'stiəriə(r)/ n outside surface of sth or appearance of sth ▶ **exterior** adj on the outside of sth; done outdoors

exterminate /ik'stɜ:mineit/ v [T] kill all the members of a group of people or animals ▶ **extermination** /ik,stɜ:mi'neiʃn/ n [U]

external /ik'stɜ:nl/ adj outside: ~ injuries (= not inside the body) ▶ **externally** /-nəli/ adv

extinct /ik'stiŋkt/ adj **1** (of a kind of animal) no longer existing **2** (of a volcano) no longer active ▶ **extinction** /ik'stiŋkʃn/ n [U] situation in which a plant, animal, etc stops existing

extinguish /ik'stiŋgwiʃ/ v [T] (fml) **1** cause a fire, etc to stop burning **2** destroy hope, love, etc ▶ **extinguisher** = FIRE EXTINGUISHER (FIRE)

extol /ik'stəul/ v (-ll-) [T] (fml) praise sb/sth greatly

extort /ik'stɔ:t/ v [T] obtain sth from sb using violence, threats, etc ▶ **extortion** /ik'stɔ:ʃn/ n [U,C] ▶ **extortionate** /ik'stɔ:ʃənət/ adj (disapprov) (of prices, etc) much too high

extra /'ekstrə/ adj more than usual or necessary; additional: ~ pay ● **extra** adv more than usually: an ~ strong box **2** in addition: price £1.75, postage ~ ● **extra** n **1** additional thing **2** person employed for a small part in a film

extract /ik'strækt/ v [T] **1** remove or obtain a substance from sth, eg using an industrial process **2** obtain sth by force: ~ money from sb **3** pull sth out, esp with effort ● **extract** /'ekstrækt/ n **1** short part of a book, film, etc **2** substance obtained by extracting: beef ~ ▶ **extraction** /ik'strækʃn/ n **1** [U,C] act of removing or obtaining sth from sth else: the ~ion of information/a tooth **2** [U] having a particular family origin: of French ~ion

extra-curricular /,ekstrə kə'rikjələ(r)/ adj outside the regular course of work at a school or college

extradite /'ekstrədait/ v [T] send sb accused of a crime to the country where the crime was said to have been committed ▶ **extradition** /,ekstrə'diʃn/ n [U,C]

extramarital /,ekstrə'mæritl/ adj happening outside marriage: an ~ affair

extraneous /ik'streiniəs/ adj (fml) not directly connected with what is being dealt with

extraordinary /ik'strɔ:dnri/ adj **1** beyond what is usual or ordinary; remarkable: ~ beauty **2** very strange ▶ **extraordinarily** adv

extrapolate /ik'stræpəleit/ v [i, T] (fml) estimate sth unknown from facts that are already known ▶ **extrapolation** /ik,stræpə'leiʃn/ n [U]

extraterrestrial /,ekstrətə'restriəl/ adj of or from outside the planet Earth

extravagant /ik'strævəgənt/ adj **1** wasting money, etc **2** (of ideas or behaviour) impressive but not reasonable ▶ **extravagance** /-gəns/ n [U,C] ▶ **extravagantly** adv

extravaganza /ik,strævə'gænzə/ n large expensive and impressive entertainment

extreme /ik'stri:m/ adj **1** very great in degree: in ~ pain **2** not ordinary or usual; serious or severe: ~ sports (= dangerous sports, eg bungee jumping) **3** far from what people consider normal; not moderate: ~ opinions **4** furthest possible: the ~ north of the country ● **extreme** n **1** opposite feeling or condition: Love and hate are ~s. **2** greatest degree of sth: the ~s of heat in the desert ▶ **extremely** adv very

extremist /ik'stri:mist/ n, adj (disapprov) (person) holding extreme(3) political opinions

extremity /ik'streməti/ n (pl -ies) **1** furthest point, end or limit of sth **2** [C,U] degree to which a situation, feeling, action, etc is extreme **3** (extremities) [pl] (fml) parts of your body furthest from the centre, esp the hands and feet

F

extricate /ˈekstrɪkeɪt/ v [T] ~(from) (enable sb to) escape from a difficult situation

extrovert /ˈekstrəvɜːt/ n lively cheerful person

exuberant /ɪgˈzjuːbərənt/ adj full of energy and excitement; lively ▶ **exuberance** /-rəns/ n [U] ▶ **exuberantly** adv

exude /ɪgˈzjuːd/ v (fml) 1 [I] express a feeling strongly: ~ happiness 2 [I, II] (of drops of liquid, etc) (cause sth to) come out slowly

exult /ɪgˈzʌlt/ v [I] (fml) show great happiness ▶ **exultant** adj ▶ **exultation** /ˌegzʌlˈteɪʃn/ n [U]

eye /aɪ/ n 1 [C] either of the two organs of sight 2 [C, usu sing] a particular way of seeing sth: She can do no wrong in his ~s. 3 [C] hole in a needle 4 [C] calm area in the centre of a storm [IDM] **be all eyes** be watching sb/sth with great attention **have an eye for sth** be good at judging if things look attractive, valuable, etc. *have a good ~ for detail* **in the eyes of the law, world, etc** according to the law, most people in the world, etc **make eyes at sb** (*infml*) look at sb in a way that shows you find them attractive **with your eyes open** fully aware of what you are doing ● **eye** v [T] look at sb/sth carefully ■ **eyeball** n the whole of the eye, including the part inside the head that cannot be seen ■ **eyebrow** n line of hair above each eye ■ **eyelash** (*also* **lash**) n one of the hairs growing on the edge of the eyelid ■ **eyelid** n one of the two folds of skin that cover the eyes when they close ■ **eye-opener** n [usu sing] surprising or revealing event or experience ■ **eyesight** n [U] ability to see ■ **eyesore** n something that is ugly, eg a building ■ **eyewitness** n = WITNESS(1)

Ff

F *abbr* Fahrenheit

F, f /ef/ n [C, U] (*pl* **F's, f's** /efs/) the sixth letter of the English alphabet

fable /ˈfeɪbl/ n 1 [C] traditional short story, esp with animals as characters, that teaches a moral lesson 2 [U,C] statement or account of sth that is not true ▶ **fabled** adj famous and often talked about

fabric /ˈfæbrɪk/ n 1 [C,U] woven cloth **(the fabric (of sth))** [sing] the basic structure of sth: *the ~ of society/a building*

fabricate /ˈfæbrɪkeɪt/ v [T] invent a false story 2 (*tech*) make or

manufacture sth ▶ **fabrication** /ˌfæbrɪˈkeɪʃn/ n [C,U]

fabulous /ˈfæbjələs/ adj 1 (*infml*) wonderful 2 (*written*) very great: ~ *wealth* ▶ **fabulously** adv extremely: ~*ly rich*

facade /fəˈsɑːd/ n 1 front of a building 2 false appearance: *behind a ~ of respectability*

face /feɪs/ n 1 front part of the head 2 expression shown on sb's face 3 surface or (front) side of sth: *the north ~ of the mountain* [IDM] **face to face (with sb)** close to and looking at sb or looking sb in the face in a situation where you have to accept that sth is true and deal with it **lose face** = LOSE **make/pull faces/a face (at sb)** produce an expression on your face to show your dislike of sb/sth or to make sb laugh **to sb's face** openly and directly in sb's presence ● **face** v 1 [I, T] be opposite sb/sth; have or turn the face towards sb/sth 2 [T] accept and deal with a difficult situation: ~ *danger* ◇ *the problems that ~ the government* 3 [T] cover a surface with another material [IDM] **face the music** (*infml*) accept criticism or punishment for sth you have done [PV] **face up to sth** accept and deal with sth bravely ▶ **faceless** adj with no clear character or identity ■ **facelift** n 1 medical operation performed to make the face look younger 2 improvement in the appearance of a building, etc ■ **face value** n [U, sing] value shown on a coin or postage stamp [IDM] **take sth at face value** believe that sth is what it appears to be

facet /ˈfæsɪt/ n 1 particular part or aspect of sth 2 any of the many sides of a cut stone or jewel

facetious /fəˈsiːʃəs/ adj trying to be amusing, esp cleverly or at the wrong time ▶ **facetiously** adv

facial /ˈfeɪʃl/ adj of or for the face

facile /ˈfæsaɪl/ adj (*disapprov*) produced easily but without careful thought: ~ *comments*

facilitate /fəˈsɪlɪteɪt/ v [T] (*fml*) make sth possible or easier

facility /fəˈsɪləti/ n 1 (**facilities**) [pl] buildings, services and equipment that are provided for a particular purpose: *sports facilities* 2 [C] special extra feature of a machine, service, etc: *a bank account with an overdraft ~* 3 [sing, U] natural ability to do sth easily

facsimile /fækˈsɪməli/ n [C] exact copy of sth 2 [C, U] = FAX

fact /fækt/ n 1 [sing] ~(that ...) used to refer to a particular situation that exists: *Despite the ~ that he felt* *ill,* he went to work. **2** [C] thing that is known to be true, esp when it can be proved **3** [U] truth; reality [IDM] **the facts of life** details of sex and how babies are born in (*actual*) **fact** **1** used to give extra details about sth **2** really

faction /'fækʃn/ n small group in a larger group, esp in politics

factor /'fæktə(r)/ n fact, circumstance, etc that helps to produce a result: *a major ~ in the decision*

factory /'fæktri, -təri/ n (*pl* -ies) building(s) where goods are made

factual /'fæktʃuəl/ adj based on or containing facts ▶ **factually** adv

faculty /'fæklti/ n (*pl* -ies) **1** [usu pl] natural ability of the body or mind: *mental faculties* **2** university department **3** [with sing or pl verb] all the teachers in a faculty

fade /feɪd/ v [I, T] (cause sth to) become paler and less bright **2** [I] (*away*) disappear gradually [PV] **fade away** (of people) become weaker; die

faeces /'fi:si:z/ n [pl] (*fml*) solid waste matter passed from the bowels

fag /fæg/ n **1** [C] (*GB, infml*) = CIGARETTE **2** [C] (*US, △, sl*) offensive word for a male homosexual **3** [sing] (*GB*) something that is boring and tiring to do

faggot (*US* **fagot**) /'fægət/ n **1** (*GB*) ball of chopped meat **2** (*US* also **fag**) (*infml,* △) offensive word for a male homosexual **3** bundle of sticks for burning

Fahrenheit /'færənhaɪt/ adj, n [U] (*abbr* F) (of or using a) temperature scale in which water freezes at 32° and boils at 212°

fail /feɪl/ v [I, T] be unsuccessful: *I'm going to ~ the exam.* **2** [I] not do sth: *~ to keep an appointment* **3** [T] decide that sb/sth has not passed an exam **4** [I] (of health, eyesight, etc) become weak **5** [I, T] not be enough for sb/sth; disappoint sb: *The crops ~ed because of drought.* ◇ *He felt he had ~ed his family.* **6** [I] become bankrupt: *The company ~ed.* ● **fail** n failure in an examination [IDM] **without fail** definitely

failing /'feɪlɪŋ/ n fault or weakness in sb/sth ● **failing** prep used to make a suggestion that could be considered if the one mentioned first is not possible

failure /'feɪljə(r)/ n **1** [U] lack of success **2** [C] person or thing that fails **3** [C, U] (instance of) not doing sth: *His ~ to help us was disappointing.* **4** [U, C] (instance of) not operating normally: *engine/heart ~*

faint /feɪnt/ adj **1** that cannot be

clearly seen, heard or smelt: *~ sounds* **2** very small or weak; possible but unlikely: *a ~ hope* **3** (of people) about to lose consciousness ● **faint** v [I] become unconscious, usu because of the heat, a shock, etc ■ **faint** n [sing] act of fainting ■ **'faint-'hearted** adj not brave or confident ▶ **faintly** adv ▶ **faintness** n [U]

fair[1] /feə(r)/ adj **1** acceptable and appropriate; just: *a ~ decision* **2** quite good: *a ~ chance of success* **3** (of the weather) dry and fine **4** (of the skin or hair) light in colour: *a ~-haired boy* [IDM] **fair play** fact of acting honestly and according to the rules ● **fair** adv according to the rules; in a way that is considered to be acceptable [IDM] **fair enough** (*esp GB, spoken*) used to say that an idea, etc seems reasonable ▶ **fairly** adv **1** moderately: *~ly easy* **2** honestly ▶ **fairness** n [U]

fair[2] /feə(r)/ n **1** (also **'funfair**) outdoor entertainment with machines to ride on, games, shows, etc **2** (*GB*) = FÊTE **3** large exhibition of goods: *a world trade ~* ◇ *a book ~* **4** (*GB*) (in the past) market at which animals were sold ■ **'fairground** n open area where funfairs are held

fairy /'feəri/ n (*pl* -ies) small imaginary creature with magical powers ■ **'fairy tale** | **'fairy story** n **1** story about fairies, magic, etc usu for children **2** untrue story; lie

fait accompli /ˌfeɪt ə'kɒmpli:/ n (from French) something that has already happened and cannot be changed

faith /feɪθ/ n **1** [U] ~ (*in*) strong trust and confidence in sb/sth **2** [U, sing] strong religious belief **3** [C] religion: *the Muslim ~* [IDM] **in good faith** with honest intentions

faithful /'feɪθfl/ adj **1** ~ (*to*) loyal to sb/sth **2** accurate: *a ~ description* ▶ **the faithful** n [pl] true believers in a religion or a political party ▶ **faithfully** /'feɪθfəli/ adv [IDM] **Yours faithfully** (*GB*) used to end a formal letter before you sign your name ▶ **faithfulness** n [U]

faithless /'feɪθləs/ adj not loyal; false

fake /feɪk/ adj **1** not genuine **2** made to look like sth else: *a ~ fur jacket* ● **fake** n **1** object, eg a work of art, made to appear genuine **2** person who pretends to be what they are not in order to deceive ● **fake** v [T] **1** make sth false appear to be genuine **2** pretend to have a particular feeling, illness, etc

falcon /'fɔ:lkən/ n small bird that can be trained to hunt and kill other birds and animals

fall[1] /fɔ:l/ v (*pt* **fell** /fel/ *pp* ~en

fall /'fɔːlən/ [I] **1** drop down from a higher level to a lower level: *Leaves ~ in autumn.* ◇ ~ *off a ladder* **2** suddenly stop standing: *I fell over and hurt my knee.* ◇ *Her hair ~s over his shoulders.* **4** (of land) slope downwards **5** decrease in amount, number or strength: *The temperature fell sharply.* **6** be captured or defeated; die in battle **7** pass into the state that is mentioned; become sth: ~ *asleep* ◇ ~ *into disuse* **8** happen or occur as a date: *Christmas ~s on a Friday this year.* [IDM] **fall flat** (eg of a joke or act) fail to produce the effect that was wanted **fall foul of sb/sth** get into trouble with sb/sth because of doing sth wrong or illegal **fall in love with sb** feel a sudden strong attraction for sb **fall on your feet** → FOOT **fall short of sth** fail to reach the necessary standard [PV] **fall apart** break into pieces **fall back** retreat **fall back on sth** use sth, when other things have been tried without success **fall behind (sb/sth)** fail to keep level with sb/sth **fall behind with sth** not do or pay sth at the right time: *He's fallen behind with his school work.* **fall for sb** (*infml*) be very attracted to sb **fall for sth** (*infml*) be tricked into believing sth **fall in** collapse: *The roof fell in.* **fall off** become less: *Attendance has ~en off.* **fall on/upon sb/sth 1** attack or take hold of sb/sth with great enthusiasm **2** be the responsibility of sb **fall out (with sb)** (*GB*) quarrel with sb **fall through** fail to be completed: *The business deal fell through.*

fall² /fɔːl/ *n* [C] **1** act of falling **2** amount of sth that has fallen: *a heavy ~ of snow* **3** distance through which sth falls **4** (*also* **falls** [pl]) waterfall **5** (*US*) = AUTUMN

fallacy /'fæləsi/ *n* [C,U] (*pl* -**ies**) false belief or argument ▸ **fallacious** /fə'leɪʃəs/ *adj* (*fml*) wrong; based on a false idea

fallen *pp* of FALL¹

fallible /'fæləbl/ *adj* liable to make mistakes ▸ **fallibility** /-'bɪləti/ *n* [U]

fallout /'fɔːlaʊt/ *n* [U] radioactive dust in the air after a nuclear explosion

fallow /'fæləʊ/ *adj* (of farm land) not used for growing crops, esp to improve the quality of the land

false /fɔːls/ *adj* **1** wrong; incorrect **2** not real; artificial: ~ *teeth* **3** deceitful; disloyal: *a ~ friend* [IDM] **by/on/under false pretences** by pretending to be sb else in order to gain an advantage for yourself ■ **false a'larm** *n* warning about a danger that does not happen ▸ **falsehood** *n* [C,U] untrue statement; lie; lying ▸ **falsely** *adv* ■ **false 'start 1** unsuccessful beginning to sth **2** (in a race) start before the signal has been given

falsify /'fɔːlsɪfaɪ/ *v* (*pt, pp* -**ied**) [T] alter a document, etc so it is false ▸ **falsification** /ˌfɔːlsɪfɪ'keɪʃn/ *n* [C,U]

falsity /'fɔːlsəti/ *n* (*pl* -**ies**) [U] state of not being true or genuine

falter /'fɔːltə(r)/ *v* [I] **1** become weaker or less effective **2** walk or speak in a way that shows you are not confident ▸ **falteringly** *adv*

fame /feɪm/ *n* [U] state of being well known ▸ **famed** *adj* famous

familiar /fə'mɪliə(r)/ *adj* **1** ~(**to**) well known to sb; often seen or heard **2** ~**with** having a good knowledge of sth **3** close and (too) friendly ▸ **familiarity** /fəˌmɪli'ærəti/ *n* [C,U] (*pl* -**ies**) ▸ **familiarly** *adv*

familiarize (*also* -**ise**) /fə'mɪliəraɪz/ *v* [T] ~ **yourself/sth** (**with sth**) make yourself/sb well informed about sth in order to understand it

family /'fæməli/ *n* (*pl* -**ies**) **1** [C, with sing or pl verb] group consisting of one or two parents and their children **2** [C, with sing or pl verb, U] group consisting of one or two parents, their children and close relations **3** [C, with sing or pl verb] all the people descended from the same ancestor: *This painting has been in our ~ for generations.* **4** [C, with sing or pl verb, U] couple's or person's children: *to start a ~* (= have children) **5** [C] group of related animals or plants: *the cat ~* [IDM] **run in the family** be a common feature in a particular family: *Red hair runs in the ~.* ■ **family 'planning** *n* [U] controlling the number of children in a family by using contraception ■ **family 'tree** *n* chart showing the relationship of family members over a long period of time

famine /'fæmɪn/ *n* [C,U] serious shortage of food

famished /'fæmɪʃt/ *adj* (*infml*) very hungry

famous /'feɪməs/ *adj* known about by many people ▸ **famously** *adv* in a way that is famous

fan /fæn/ *n* **1** object for making a current of air, eg to cool a room **2** very keen supporter: *football ~* ◇ ~ *mail* (= letters from fans to a famous person) ● **fan** *v* (-**nn-**) [T] send a current of air onto sth/sb [PV] **fan out** spread out from a central point: *The troops ~ned out across the field.* ■ **'fan belt** *n* rubber belt used to turn the fan that cools a car engine

fanatic /fə'nætɪk/ *n* **1** (*infml*) person who is very enthusiastic about sth: *a fitness ~* **2** (*disapprov*) person holding extreme or dangerous opinions:

F

a religious ~ ▶ **fanatical** /-kl/ adj ▶ **fanatically** /-kli/ adv ▶ **fanaticism** /fə'nætɪsɪzəm/ n [U]

fanciful /'fænsɪfl/ adj (written) **1** based on imagination, not reason **2** (of things) unusually decorated ▶ **fancifully** /-fali/ adv

fancy¹ /'fænsi/ v (pt, pp -**ied**) [T] (GB, infml) want sth or want to do sth: I ~ going out tonight. **2** (infml) find sb sexually attractive: I think she fancies you. **3** (GB, infml) ~ **yourself** (**as**) think you are very popular, intelligent, etc; believe that you are sth: They ~ themselves as serious actors. ● **fancy** n (pl -**ies**) **1** [C,U] something that you imagine; your imagination **2** [sing] liking or desire: a ~ for some cake [IDM] **take a fancy to sb/sth** start liking sb/sth

fancy² /'fænsi/ adj (-**ier**, -**iest**) **1** unusually complicated, often in an unnecessary way: a kitchen full of ~ gadgets **2** decorated and colourful; not plain: ~ cakes ■ **fancy 'dress** n [U] (GB) clothes worn for a party to make you appear to be a different character: fancy-dress guests in a ~ dress

fanfare /'fænfeə(r)/ n short piece of music played on trumpets

fang /fæŋ/ n long sharp tooth

fanny /'fæni/ n (pl -**ies**) **1** (GB, △, infml) female sex organs **2** (sl, esp US) person's bottom

fantasize (also -**ise**) /'fæntəsaɪz/ v [I, T] ~(**about**) imagine sth you are doing sth you would like to do

fantastic /fæn'tæstɪk/ adj **1** (infml) wonderful: a ~ party **2** (infml) very large **3** strange and imaginative **4** (of ideas) not practical ▶ **fantastically** /-kli/ adv

fantasy /'fæntəsi/ n [C,U] (pl -**ies**) (pleasant idea or dream of the) imagination: childhood ~ids

far¹ /fɑː(r)/ adv (~**ther** /'fɑːðə(r)/ or **further** /'fɜːðə(r)/ ~**thest** /'fɑːðɪst/ or **furthest** /'fɜːðɪst/) **1** at or to a great distance: How ~ is it to London? **2** very much; to a great degree: fallen ~ behind in his work ◇ ~ richer **3** used to talk about how much progress has been made: I got as ~ as chapter 4. [IDM] **as/so far as** | **in so far as** to the degree that: As ~ as I know, they're still coming. **as/so far as** used to give your personal opinion on sth: As ~ as I'm concerned, you can do what you like. **far from sth** almost the opposite of sth: F~ from hating the music, I love it! ◇ The work is ~ from easy (= it is very difficult). **go far** | **go a long way** (of people) be very successful in the future **go too far** behave in a way that is beyond reasonable limits

not go far 1 (of money) not be enough to buy many things **2** (of a supply of sth) not be enough **so far** | **thus far** until now ● **faraway** adj **1** distant **2** (of a look in sb's eyes) dreamy ■ **far-'fetched** adj difficult to believe ■ **'far-off** adj long distance away ■ **far-'reaching** adj having a wide influence: a ~-reaching decision ■ **far-'sighted** adj seeing what may happen in the future and so making wise plans

far² /fɑː(r)/ adj (~**ther** /'fɑːðə(r)/ or **further** /'fɜːðə(r)/ ~**thest** /'fɑːðɪst/ or **furthest** /'fɜːðɪst/) **1** more distant; at the furthest point in a particular direction: the ~ end of the street ◇ on the ~ right of the party (= with extreme right-wing political views) **2** (old-fash or lit) distant: a ~ country ■ **the Far 'East** n [sing] China, Japan and several countries of E and SE Asia

farce /fɑːs/ n [C,U] funny play for the theatre, with unlikely ridiculous situations; this type of writing or performance **2** [C] series of actual ridiculous events: The whole ~ was a complete ~. ▶ **farcical** adj

fare /feə(r)/ n [C,U] money charged for a journey by bus, train, etc: bus ~s ● **fare** v [I] (fml) progress; get on: ~ well/badly

farewell /ˌfeə'wel/ exclam, n (old-fash or fml) goodbye

farm /fɑːm/ n area of land and buildings for growing crops and raising animals ● **farm** v [I, T] use land for growing crops and raising animals ▶ **farmer** n person who owns or manages a farm ■ **'farmhand** n person who works for a farmer ■ **'farmhouse** n main house on a farm, where the farmer lives ■ **'farmyard** n area surrounded by farm buildings

fart /fɑːt/ v [I] (△, sl) let air from the bowels out through the anus ● **fart** n (△, sl) **1** act of letting air out through the anus **2** unpleasant, boring or stupid person

farther, farthest adv, adj → FAR

fascinate /'fæsɪneɪt/ v [T] attract or interest sb greatly ▶ **fascinating** adj ▶ **fascination** /-'neɪʃn/ n [U,C]

fascism (also **Fascism**) /'fæʃɪzəm/ n [U] extreme right-wing political system ▶ **fascist** (also **Fascist**) adj, n

fashion /'fæʃn/ n **1** [U,C] popular style of clothes, hair, etc at a particular time: Flared trousers are in ~ again. ◇ Some styles never go out of ~. **2** [C] popular way of behaving, doing sth, etc **3** [U] business of making and selling clothes: a ~ designer/show [IDM] **after a fashion** not very well ● **fashion** v [T] make or shape sth, esp with your hands

fashionable /ˈfæʃnəbl/ adj **1** following a style that is popular at a particular time **2** used by many (esp rich) people: a ~ restaurant ▶ **fashionably** adv

fast¹ /fɑːst/ adj **1** quick: ~ cars **2** (of a watch or clock) showing a time later than the true time **3** (of a boat, etc) firmly fixed **4** (of colours) not likely to fade or spread when washed ● **fast** adv **1** quickly; without delay **2** firmly; completely: She was ~ asleep (= sleeping deeply). [IDM] **stand fast** → STAND²(11) ■ **fast food** n [U] hot food, that is served very quickly in special restaurants and is often taken away to be eaten in the street

fast² /fɑːst/ v [I] go without food, esp for religious reasons ● **fast** n period of fasting

fasten /ˈfɑːsn/ v [I, T] become or make sth joined together, closed or fixed: ~ your seat belt [PV] **fasten on(to) sb/sth** choose or follow sb/sth in a determined way ▶ **fastener** (also **fastening**) n device, eg a button or a zip, that fasten things together

fastidious /fæˈstɪdiəs/ adj difficult to please; not liking things to be dirty or untidy ▶ **fastidiously** adv

fat¹ /fæt/ adj (**-ter**, **-test**) **1** (of sb's body) large; weighing too much **2** thick or wide **3** (infml) large in quantity: ~ profits ▶ **fatness** n [U]

fat² /fæt/ n **1** [U] substance in the body of animals and humans, stored under the skin **2** [C,U] substance from animals or plants used in cooking

fatal /ˈfeɪtl/ adj **1** causing or ending in death: a ~ accident **2** causing disaster: a ~ mistake ▶ **fatally** adv

fatalism /ˈfeɪtəlɪzəm/ n [U] belief that events are controlled by fate(2) ▶ **fatalist** n

fatality /fəˈtæləti/ n (pl **-ies**) **1** [C] death caused by accident or violence **2** [U] fact that a particular disease will end in death: the ~ rate of this type of cancer **3** [U] belief that we have no control over what happens to us

fate /feɪt/ n **1** [C] person's future, esp death **2** [U] power believed to control all events ▶ **fateful** adj important: that ~ day

father /ˈfɑːðə(r)/ n **1** male parent **2** (**fathers**) [pl] (lit) person's ancestors **3** first leader: city ~s **4** (**Father**) title of a priest **5** (**Father**) God ● **father** v be the father of sth ■ **Father Christmas** n old man who is believed by children to bring presents at Christmas ■ **father-in-law** n (pl **~s-in-law**) father of your wife or husband ▶ **fatherly** adj of or like a father

fathom /ˈfæðəm/ n measurement of the depth of water (1·8 metres or 6 feet) ● **fathom** v [T] **~(out)** understand sth fully

fatigue /fəˈtiːɡ/ n **1** [U] great tiredness **2** [U] weakness in metals, etc caused by constant stress **3** (**fatigues**) [pl] clothes worn by soldiers when cleaning, cooking, etc

fatten /ˈfætn/ v [I, T] become or make sb/sth fatter, esp an animal before killing it for food

fatty /ˈfæti/ adj (**-ier**, **-iest**) containing a lot of fat; consisting of fat ▶ **fatty** n (pl **-ies**) (infml, disapprov) fat person

fatuous /ˈfætʃuəs/ adj silly: ~ remarks ▶ **fatuously** adv

faucet /ˈfɔːsɪt/ n (US = TAP(1))

fault /fɔːlt/ n **1** [sing] responsibility for sth wrong that has happened or been done: It's my ~. ◊ The owners are at ~ (= responsible) for this. **2** [C] mistake or imperfection: an electrical ~ **3** [C] crack in the surface of the earth ● **fault** v [T] find a weakness in sb/sth: I cannot ~ her performance. ▶ **faultless** adj perfect ▶ **faultlessly** adv ▶ **faulty** adj (esp of a machine) not working properly

fauna /ˈfɔːnə/ n [U] all the animals living in an area or of a period of history

faux pas /ˌfəʊ ˈpɑː/ n (pl **faux pas** /-ˈpɑːz/) (from French) embarrassing mistake

favour (US **-or**) /ˈfeɪvə(r)/ n **1** [C] thing you do to help sb: Do me a ~ and lend me your pen. **2** [U] approval or support for sb/sth: She's back in ~ with the boss again (= the boss likes her again). **3** [U] treatment of sb more generously than others: show ~ to sb [IDM] **in favour (of sb/sth)** supporting sb/sth **in sb's favour** to the advantage of sb ● **favour** v [T] **1** support sb/sth **2** treat sb/sth more generously than others ▶ **favourable** adj **1** getting or showing approval **2** helpful ▶ **favourably** adv

favourite (US **favor-**) /ˈfeɪvərɪt/ n **1** person or thing liked more than others **2** horse, competitor, team, etc expected to win a race ● **favourite** adj liked more than any other ▶ **favouritism** /ˈfeɪvərɪtɪzəm/ n [U] practice of being unfairly generous to one person or group

fawn /fɔːn/ n **1** [C] young deer **2** [U] light yellowish-brown colour ● **fawn** adj light yellowish-brown in colour ● **fawn** v [PV] **fawn on/over sb** (disapprov) try to gain sb's favour by pretending to like them

fax /fæks/ n **1** [C] (also **fax machine**) machine that sends and receives documents electronically along telephone wires and then prints them **2** [U] system for sending documents using a fax machine: *What's your ~ number?* **3** [C] letter or message sent by fax ● **fax** v [T] send sb a document, etc by fax

FBI /,ef bi: 'ai/ *abbr* (US) Federal Bureau of Investigation

fear /fɪə(r)/ n [C,U] bad feeling you have when you are in danger, when sth bad might happen or when sb/sth frightens you [IDM] **in fear of your life** afraid that you might be killed **no fear** (GB, spoken) certainly not ● **fear** v [T] **1** be afraid of sb/sth **2** feel that sth bad might have happened or will happen in the future [IDM] **fear for sb/sth** be worried about sb/sth: *began to ~ for his safety* ▶ **fearful** adj **1** (fml) nervous and afraid **2** (fml) terrible and frightening ▶ **fearless** adj not afraid ▶ **fearlessly** adv

feasible /'fi:zəbl/ adj that can be done ▶ **feasibility** /,fi:zə'bləti/ n [U]

feast /fi:st/ n **1** large or special meal, esp for a lot of people **2** religious festival **3** thing that brings great pleasure ● **feast** v [I] ~(on) eat a lot of food, with great enjoyment [IDM] **feast your eyes on sth** look at sth with pleasure

feat /fi:t/ n action that needs skill, strength or courage

feather /'feðə(r)/ n one of the many light parts that cover a bird's body: *a ~ pillow* (= one containing feathers) [IDM] **a feather in your cap** an action that you can be proud of ● **feather** v [IDM] **feather your (own) nest** make yourself richer or more comfortable ▶ **feathery** adj light and soft

feature /'fi:tʃə(r)/ n **1** noticeable part: *an important ~ of city life* **2** parts of sb's face, eg the eyes and mouth **3** ~(on) special article in a newspaper ● **feature** v [T] **1** include a particular person or thing as a special feature **2** [I] ~in have an important part in sth ▶ **featureless** adj uninteresting

February /'februəri/ n [U,C] second month of the year (See examples of use at *April*.)

feces (US) = FAECES

fed pt, pp of FEED

federal /'fedərəl/ adj **1** of a system of government in which several states unite, eg for defence **2** of the central government, not the government of states

federation /,fedə'reɪʃn/ n **1** union of states with a central federal government **2** similar union of clubs, trade unions, etc, etc

fed up /,fed 'ʌp/ adj (infml) ~(with) bored or unhappy

fee /fi:/ n **1** money paid for professional advice or services: *legal ~s* **2** money paid to join an organization or do sth: *an entrance ~*

feeble /'fi:bl/ adj (~r, ~st) weak ▶ **feebly** /-bli/ adv

feed /fi:d/ v (pt, pp fed /fed/) **1** [T] give food to sb/sth **2** [I] ~(on) (esp of animals) eat food **3** [T] ~ A with (B) | ~ B into A supply sth to sb/sth ● **feed** n **1** [C] meal for an animal or baby **2** [U] food for animals or plants **3** [C] pipe, channel, etc that carries material to a machine ■ **'feedback** n [U] advice, criticism, etc about how good or useful sth or sb's work is ■ **'feeding bottle** n plastic bottle from which a baby is given milk

feel /fi:l/ v (pt, pp felt /felt/) **1** linking verb experience a particular feeling or emotion: *~ happy/tired* **2** [T] notice or be aware of sth: *~ the sun on your face* ◇ *~ the tension in the atmosphere* **3** linking verb give you a particular feeling or impression: *These shoes ~ tight.* ◇ *It ~s strange to come back here again.* **4** linking verb have a particular physical quality which you discover by touching: *The water ~s warm.* **5** [T] move your fingers over sth to feel sth or to find out what sth is like: *Can you ~ the bump on my head?* **6** [T] think or believe that sth is the case: *He felt he would succeed.* **7** [T] experience the effects of sth, often strongly: *~ the cold* [IDM] **feel like (doing) sth** want (to do) sth: *~ like (having) a drink* [PV] **feel for sb** have sympathy for sb ● **feel** n [sing] **1** (the feel) sensation caused by touching sth or being touched **2** act of feeling or touching **3** general impression of a place, etc

feeler /'fi:lə(r)/ n long thin part of an insect's head, used for touching things [IDM] **put out feelers** ask questions, etc to test the opinions of others

feeling /'fi:lɪŋ/ n **1** [C] something felt through the mind or the senses **2** [sing] belief; vague idea: *a ~ that something awful is going to happen* **3** [U,C] attitude or an opinion **4** (**feelings**) [pl] sb's emotions rather than thoughts **5** [sing] sympathy or sensitivity **6** [U] ability to feel physically [IDM] **bad/ill feeling** anger between people, esp after an argument

feet plural of FOOT

feign /feɪn/ v [T] (written) pretend sth

feint /feɪnt/ n [C,U] (esp in sport) movement made to make your opponent think you are going to do one thing instead of another ● **feint** v [I] make a feint

felicity /fə'lɪsəti/ n [U] (fml) great happiness

feline /'fi:laɪn/ adj of or like a cat

fell¹ pt of FALL¹

fell² /fel/ n area of rocky moorland in N England

fell³ /fel/ v [T] **1** cut down a tree **2** (written) knock sb down

fellow /'feləʊ/ n [C] **1** (old-fash, infml) man **2** [usu pl] companion: school ~s **3** [C] senior member of a college or university **4** member of the same group or kind: ~ work-ers ▶ **fellowship** n **1** [U] feeling of friendship **2** [C] group or society **3** [C] position of a college fellow

felony /'feləni/ n [C,U] (pl -ies) (US or law) serious crime, eg murder ▶ **felon** /'felən/ n person guilty of a felony

felt¹ pt, pp of FEEL

felt² /felt/ n [U] thick cloth made from pressed wool, hair or fur ■ felt-tip 'pen (also 'felt tip) n pen with a pointed tip made of felt

female /'fi:meɪl/ adj **1** of the sex that produces young **2** (of a plant) producing fruit **3** (of part of a device) having a hollow part into which another part fits ● **female** n female person or animal

feminine /'femənɪn/ adj **1** of or like women **2** (gram) of a particular class of nouns, pronouns, etc ▶ **femininity** /ˌfemə'nɪnəti/ n [U] quality of being feminine

feminism /'femənɪzəm/ n [U] belief in the principle that women should have the same rights as men ▶ **feminist** n, adj

fen /fen/ n area of low flat wet land

fence /fens/ n wall made of wood or wire ● **fence** v [T] **1** ~ in/off surround or divide sth with a fence **2** [I] fight with a long thin sword as a sport **3** [I] avoid giving a direct answer to a question ▶ **fencing** n [U] **1** sport of fighting with long thin swords **2** material for making fences

fend /fend/ v [PV] **fend for yourself** look after yourself **fend sb/sth off** defend yourself from sb/sth

ferment¹ /fə'ment/ v [I, T] (make sth) change chemically so that glucose becomes alcohol, eg in wine ▶ **fermentation** /ˌfɜ:men'teɪʃn/ n [U]

ferment² /'fɜ:ment/ n [U,sing] state of political and social excitement

fern /fɜ:n/ n [C,U] flowerless plant with feathery green leaves

ferocious /fə'rəʊʃəs/ adj fierce or violent ▶ **ferociously** adv

ferocity /fə'rɒsəti/ n [U] quality of being ferocious

ferret /'ferɪt/ n small animal of the weasel family that hunts rabbits and rats ● **ferret** v [I] ~(about/

around) (infml) search for sth [PV] **ferret sb/sth out** (infml) find sb/sth by searching thoroughly

ferry /'feri/ (also 'ferry boat) n (pl -ies) boat that carries people and goods across a river or short stretch of sea ● **ferry** v (pt, pp -ied) [T] transport people or goods from one place to another

fertile /'fɜ:taɪl/ adj **1** (of land or soil) able to produce strong plants **2** (of a person's mind) full of new ideas **3** (of plants or animals) able to produce fruit or young ▶ **fertility** /fə'tɪləti/ n [U]

fertilize (also -ise) /'fɜ:təlaɪz/ v [T] make sth fertile ▶ **fertilization** (also -isation) /ˌfɜ:təlaɪ'zeɪʃn/ n [U] ▶ **fertilizer** (also -iser) n [U,C] substance added to soil to make it more fertile

fervent /'fɜ:vənt/ adj showing strong feeling: ~ belief/supporter ▶ **fervently** adv

fervour (US -or) /'fɜ:və(r)/ n [U] very strong feeling; enthusiasm

fester /'festə(r)/ v [I] **1** (of a wound) become infected **2** (of bad feelings or thoughts) become more bitter and angry

festival /'festɪvl/ n **1** organized series of performances of music, drama, etc **2** (day or time for a) public, esp religious, celebration

festive /'festɪv/ adj joyous

festivity /fe'stɪvəti/ n [U,C] (pl -ies) happy celebration

fetch /fetʃ/ v [T] **1** collect sb/sth from a place: ~ the children from school **2** be sold for a [particular price: The vase ~ed £1000.

fête /feɪt/ n outdoor entertainment, usu to collect money for a particular purpose ● **fête** v [T] (usu passive) honour sb in a special way

fetish /'fetɪʃ/ n something to which too much attention is given

fetter /'fetə(r)/ n **1** (usu pl) something that restricts sb's freedom: the ~s of government controls **2** chain for a prisoner's foot ● **fetter** v [T] **1** (usu passive) put chains on a prisoner **2** restrict sb's freedom

fetus (US) = FOETUS

feud /fju:d/ n long bitter quarrel ● **feud** v [I] carry on a feud

feudal /'fju:dl/ adj of the system of receiving land from a nobleman, and working and fighting for him in return, during the Middle Ages in Europe ▶ **feudalism** /-dəlɪzəm/ n [U]

fever /'fi:və(r)/ n **1** [C,U] very high temperature of the body **2** [U] disease causing a high body temperature **3** [sing] state of excitement ▶ **feverish** adj **1** excited; very fast **2** having a fever ▶ **feverishly** adv

F

few /fjuː/ *det, adj, pron* **1** not many people, things or places: *F~ people live to be 100.* **2** (**a few**) a small number of people or things; some [IDM] **few and far between** very rare

fiancé /fɪˈɒnseɪ/ *n* (*fem* **fiancée**) person you are engaged to (= have agreed to marry)

fiasco /fɪˈæskəʊ/ *n* (*pl* ~**s** US also ~**es**) complete failure

fib /fɪb/ *n* (*infml*) small lie, esp about sth unimportant ● **fib** *v* (**-bb-**) [I] tell a fib ▶ **fibber** *n*

fibre (US **fiber**) /ˈfaɪbə(r)/ *n* **1** [U] part of food that helps to keep a person healthy by keeping the bowels working: *a high-~ diet* **2** [U] material, eg rope, formed from a mass of fibres **3** [C] one of the many thin threads that form body tissue and other natural materials: *muscle/cotton ~s* **4** [U] person's character: *strong moral ~* ■ **fibreglass** (US **fiberglass**) *n* [U] material made from glass fibres, used for making boats, etc ■ **fibre optics** (US **fiber-**) *n* use of thin fibres of glass, etc to sending information in the form of light signals ▶ **fibrous** /ˈfaɪbrəs/ *adj* made of, or like, fibres

fickle /ˈfɪkl/ *adj* often changing

fiction /ˈfɪkʃn/ *n* **1** [U] writing that describes invented people and events, not real ones **2** [C] thing that is invented or not true ▶ **fictional** /-ʃənl/ *adj*

fictitious /fɪkˈtɪʃəs/ *adj* untrue; invented

fiddle /ˈfɪdl/ *v* **1** [I] ~ **with** keep touching or playing with sth in your hands **2** [T] (*infml*) change accounts dishonestly; get sth by cheating **3** [I] (*infml*) play the violin ● **fiddle** *n* (*infml*) **1** = VIOLIN **2** dishonest action ▶ **fiddler** *n* person who plays a violin ▶ **fiddly** *adj* difficult to do or use because small objects are involved

fidelity /fɪˈdeləti/ *n* [U] **1** faithfulness **2** accuracy of a translation, report, etc

fidget /ˈfɪdʒɪt/ *v* [I] move your body about restlessly ● **fidget** *n* person who fidgets ▶ **fidgety** *adj*

field¹ /fiːld/ *n* **1** area of land on which crops are grown or cattle are kept **2** open area: *a football/landing ~* **3** area of study or activity **4** area in which a force can be felt: *a magnetic ~* **5** (*computing*) part of a record that is a separate item of data ■ **field day** *n* [IDM] **have a field day** have great fun, success, etc ■ **field 'marshal** *n* officer of the highest rank in the British army

field² /fiːld/ *v* **1** (in cricket, etc) (stand ready to) catch or stop the ball **2** [T] put a team into the field

3 [T] deal with a question skilfully ▶ **fielder** *n* (in cricket, etc) person who fields

fiend /fiːnd/ *n* **1** very wicked person **2** person who is very keen on sth mentioned: *a health ~* ▶ **fiendish** *adj* ▶ **fiendishly** *adv* very

fierce /fɪəs/ *adj* (**~r, ~st**) **1** angry and violent **2** intense; strong: *~ heat* ▶ **fiercely** *adv* ▶ **fierceness** *n*

fiery /ˈfaɪəri/ *adj* (**-ier, -iest**) **1** of or like fire; flaming **2** (of a person) quickly made angry

fifteen /ˌfɪfˈtiːn/ *number* **15** ▶ **fifteenth** /ˌfɪfˈtiːnθ/ *ordinal number*

fifth /fɪfθ/ *ordinal number, n* 5th; ⅕

fifty /ˈfɪfti/ *number* **50 2** (**the fifties**) *n* [pl] numbers, years, or temperatures from 50 to 59 ▶ **fiftieth** *ordinal number* ■ **fifty-'fifty** *adj, adv* (*infml*) shared equally between two

fig /fɪg/ *n* (tree with a) soft sweet fruit full of small seeds

fig. *abbr* (written) **1** figure; illustration: *See fig. 3.* **2** figurative(ly)

fight /faɪt/ *v* (*pt, pp* **fought** /fɔːt/) **1** [I, T] use force with the hands or weapons against sb: *~ against poverty* **2** [T] take part in a war or battle against sb **3** [T] try hard to stop sth bad or to achieve sth **4** [I] quarrel or argue with sb [PV] **fight back** (**against sb/sth**) resist strongly or attack sb who has attacked you **fight sb/sth off** resist or repel sb/sth: *~ off an attacker/a cold* **fight sth out** fight or argue until the argument is settled ● **fight** *n* **1** [C] act of fighting against sb/sth **2** [U] desire or ability to keep fighting for sth ▶ **fighter** *n* **1** fast military aircraft **2** person who fights in war or in sport

figment /ˈfɪgmənt/ *n* [IDM] **a figment of sb's imagination** something not real

figurative /ˈfɪgərətɪv/ *adj* (of words) used not in the ordinary literal sense but in an imaginative way ▶ **figuratively** *adv*

figure /ˈfɪgə(r)/ *n* **1** symbol representing a number **2** price **3** human form or shape: *a ~ approaching in the darkness ◊ a good ~* (= slim body) **4** person: *important ~s in history* **5** form of a person that is drawn, carved, etc **6** diagram; illustration ● **figure** *v* **1** [I] ~ (**as/in**) be a part of a process, situation, etc, esp an important one **2** [T] think or decide that sth is true or will happen [IDM] **it/that figures** used to say that sth seems logical [PV] **figure on sth/doing sth** plan sth or to do sth; expect sth **figure sb/sth out** think about sb/sth until you understand them/it **2** calculate an amount ■ **figurehead** *n* person in a high position but with no real authority ■ **,figure of 'speech** *n* figurative expression

filament /'filəmənt/ *n* thin wire inside a light bulb; thin thread

file¹ /faɪl/ *n* **1** holder, box, cover, etc for keeping papers **2** organized computer data: *create/delete a ~* **3** papers and information contained in a file: *have a confidential ~ on sb* **4** metal tool with a rough surface for cutting or shaping hard substances **5** line of people or things one behind the other [IDM] **on file** kept in a file

file² /faɪl/ *v* **1** [T] put sth in a file **2** [I, T] ~ **(for)** *(law)* make a formal request, etc officially: *~ for divorce* **3** [I] walk in a line of people, one after the other: *~ out of the room* **4** [T] cut or shape sth with a file¹(4): *~ your nails* ► **filings** /'faɪlɪŋz/ *n* [pl] small pieces of metal removed by a file¹(4) ■ **filing cabinet** (*US* **file cabinet**) *n* piece of office furniture for holding files

fill /fɪl/ *v* **1** [I, T] become or make sth full of sth **2** [T] do a job, have a role or position, etc; put sb into a job: *~ a vacancy* [PV] **fill sb in (for sb)** do sb's job when they are away **fill sth in** (*esp US*) fill sb out complete a form, etc by writing information on it **fill out** become larger or fatter **fill (sth) up (with sth)** become or make sth completely full ● **fill** *n* [IDM] **your fill of sth/sb 1** as much of sth/sb as you can bear: *I've had my ~ of your rudeness!* **2** as much as you can eat or drink ► **filler** *n* material used to fill holes in walls, etc before painting ► **filling** *n* material used to fill a hole in a tooth

fillet /'fɪlɪt/ *n* [C,U] piece of meat or fish without bones ● **fillet** *v* [T] cut fish or meat into fillets

film /fɪlm/ *n* **1** [C] cinema picture; movie **2** [U,C] roll of thin plastic used in photography **3** [C, usu sing] thin layer of sth: *a ~ of oil* ● **film** *v* [I, T] make a film(1) ■ **'film star** *n* famous cinema actor

filter /'fɪltə(r)/ *n* **1** device used for holding back solid material in a liquid passed through it **2** coloured glass that allows light only of certain wavelengths to pass through ● **filter** *v* **1** [I, T] (cause sth to) flow through a filter **2** [I] pass or flow slowly; become known gradually

filth /fɪlθ/ *n* [U] **1** disgusting dirt **2** very rude and offensive words, pictures, etc ► **filthy** *adj* (**-ier, -iest**)

fin /fɪn/ *n* **1** wide thin wing-like part of a fish **2** thing shaped like this, eg on the back of an aircraft

final /'faɪnl/ *adj* **1** coming at the end; last **2** (of a decision) that cannot be changed [IDM] **final straw** → STRAW ● **final** *n* [C] **1** last of a series of competitions: *the tennis ~s* **2** (finals) [pl] last set of university examinations ► **finalist** /'faɪnəlɪst/ *n* player in a final competition ► **finalize** (*also* **-ise**) /'faɪnəlaɪz/ *v* [T] complete the last part of a plan, etc ► **finally** /'faɪnəli/ *adv* **1** eventually **2** conclusively: *settle the matter ~ly*

finale /fɪ'nɑːli/ *n* last part of a piece of music or drama

finance /'faɪnæns; faɪ'næns; fə-/ *n* **1** [U] management of (esp public) money **2** [U] money needed to pay for a project: *obtain ~ from the bank* **3** (finances) [pl] money available to a person, company, etc ● **finance** *v* [T] provide money for a project, etc ► **financial** /faɪ'nænʃl; fə-/ *adj* ► **financially** *adv* ► **financier** /faɪ'nænsiə(r); fə-/ *n* person who finances businesses

finch /fɪntʃ/ *n* small bird

find /faɪnd/ *v* (*pt, pp* **found** /faʊnd/) [T] **1** discover sth/sb unexpectedly **2** get back sth/sb that was lost **3** discover sth by searching, studying or testing **4** have a particular feeling or opinion about sth: *I ~ it difficult to understand him.* **5** have sth available for you to use: *~ time to study* **6** arrive at sth naturally: *Water always ~s its own level.* **7** exist in a particular place: *Tigers are found in India.* **8** (*fml*) decide sth in a court of law: *~ her guilty* [IDM] **find fault (with sth/sb)** look for mistakes in sth/sb; complain about sth [PV] **find out (sth) (about sth/sb)** learn sth by study or inquiry: *~ out when the next train leaves* ● **find** *n* something interesting or valuable that is found ► **finder** *n* ► **finding** *n* [C] **1** [usu pl] what is learnt by study or inquiry **2** (*law*) decision reached by a court

fine¹ /faɪn/ *adj* (**~r, ~st**) **1** enjoyable or pleasing: *a ~ view* **2** in good health **3** (of weather) bright; clear **4** made of very small particles: *~ powder* **5** delicate; carefully made **6** (able to be) seen or noticed only with difficulty or effort: *a ~ distinction* ● **fine** *adv* (*infml*) well: *We're all doing ~.* ■ **fine 'art** *n* [U] (*also* **fine 'arts** [pl]) paintings, sculptures, etc ► **finely** *adv* **1** into small pieces: *~ly cut meat* **2** beautifully; delicately ► **fineness** *n* [U]

fine² /faɪn/ *n* money paid as a punishment for breaking the law ● **fine** *v* [T] officially punish sb by making them pay a fine

finery /'faɪnəri/ *n* [U] beautiful clothes

finesse /fɪ'nes/ *n* [U] skilful way of dealing with a situation

finger /'fɪŋɡə(r)/ *n* **1** any of the five

parts at the end of each hand **2** part of a glove that fits over a finger [IDM] **get, pull, etc your finger out** (*infml*) stop being lazy; start to work hard **not put your finger on sth** not be able to find exactly what is wrong ● **finger** v [T] touch or feel sth with your fingers ■ **fingernail** *n* hard layer that covers the end of each finger ■ **fingerprint** *n* mark made by a finger when pressed on a surface ■ **fingertip** *n* end of a finger [IDM] **have sth at your fingertips** know sth very well

finish /'fɪnɪʃ/ v [I, T] come or bring sth to an end; reach the end of a task **2** [T] eat, drink or use what is left of sth **3** [T] make sth complete [PV] **finish sb/sth off** (*infml*) destroy sb/sth **finish with sb/sth** no longer be dealing with sb/sth; end a relationship with sb ● **finish** *n* **1** [C] last part of sth **2** [C, U] last covering of paint or polish: *a highly-polished* ~

finite /'faɪnaɪt/ *adj* **1** limited **2** (*gram*) (of a verb form) showing a particular tense, person and number: *'Is' and 'was' are* ~ *forms of 'be'.*

fir (*also* **'fir tree**) /fɜː(r)/ *n* evergreen tree with leaves like needles ■ **fir cone** *n* fruit of the fir tree

fire¹ /'faɪə(r)/ *n* **1** [C] fire that produces light and heat **2** [U,C] burning that causes destruction: *forest ~s* **3** [C] pile of burning fuel for heating, cooking, etc: *light a* ~ **4** [C] apparatus for heating a room: *a gas* ~ **5** [U] shots from guns [IDM] **on fire** burning **under fire** being shot at ■ **'fire alarm** *n* bell that warns people of a fire ■ **firearm** *n* [C, *usu pl*] gun ■ the **'fire brigade** *n* [*sing*] team of people who put out fires ■ **'fire drill** *n* [C] practice of leaving a burning building, etc safely ■ **'fire engine** *n* vehicle that carries firefighters and equipment to put out fires ■ **'fire escape** *n* outside staircase for leaving a burning building ■ **'fire extinguisher** *n* metal cylinder containing water or chemicals for putting out a small fire ■ **'firefighter** *n* person whose job is to put out fires ■ **'fireguard** *n* protective metal framework round a fire in a room ■ **'fireman** *n* (*pl* **-men**) person whose job is to put out fires ■ **'fireplace** *n* open space in a wall for a fire in a room ■ **'fireproof** *adj* unable to be damaged by fire ■ **'fireside** *n* [C, *usu sing*] part of a room beside the fire ■ **'fire station** *n* building for a fire brigade ■ **'firewall** *n* (*computing*) part of a computer system designed to prevent people from getting at information without authority but still allows them to receive information that is

sent to them ■ **'firewood** *n* [U] wood used for lighting fires or as fuel ■ **'firework** *n* device containing chemicals that burn or explode with coloured flames

fire² /'faɪə(r)/ v [I, T] shoot with a gun; shoot a bullet **2** [T] force sb to leave their job **3** [T] excite sb **4** [T] heat a clay object in a special oven ■ **'firing line** *n* [*sing*] front line of battle, nearest the enemy ■ **'firing squad** *n* [C, U] group of soldiers ordered to shoot a condemned person

firm¹ /fɜːm/ *adj* **1** fairly hard **2** strongly fixed in place **3** not likely to change **4** (of a person's voice or movements) strong and steady [IDM] **stand firm** → STAND²(11) ● **firm** v [I, T] become or make sth firm ● **firm** *n* business or company ▶ **firmly** *adv* in a strong or definite way ▶ **firmness** *n* [U]

first¹ /fɜːst/ *det, ordinal number* coming before all others [IDM] **at first sight** when seen for the first time ■ **first thing** as early as possible in the day ■ **first 'aid** *n* [U] treatment given immediately to an injured person before a doctor comes ■ **first 'class** *n* [U] *adv* (using) the best seats on a train, plane, etc or the fastest form of mail ■ **first-'class** *adj* of the best class ■ **first 'floor** *n* **1** (*GB*) floor immediately above the ground floor **2** (*US*) = GROUND FLOOR (GROUND¹) ■ **first-'hand** *adj, adv* (of information) (obtained) directly from the origin ▶ **firstly** *adv* (in giving a list) to begin with ■ **first name** *n* name that goes before your family name ■ the **first 'person** *n* [*sing*] (*gram*) set of pronouns, eg *I, we, me,* and the verb forms, eg *am, are, am*, used with them ■ **first-'rate** *adj* excellent

first² /fɜːst/ *adv* **1** before anyone or anything else: *She spoke* ~. **2** for the first time: *when I* ~ *came to London* **3** in preference to sth else [IDM] **at first** at or in the beginning

first³ /fɜːst/ *n* **1** (**the first**) [C] (*pl* **the first**) first person or thing: *the* ~ *to leave* **2** [C, *usu sing*] (*infml*) important new achievement **3** [C] (*GB*) highest level of university degree

fish /fɪʃ/ *n* (*pl* **fish** *or* **-es**) **1** [C] cold-blooded animal that lives in water **2** [U] flesh of a fish eaten as food: ~ *and chips* ● **fish** v [I] try to catch fish [PV] **fish for sth** try to obtain compliments, etc indirectly **fish sb/sth out** (*of sth*) take or pull sb/sth out of a place: *He* ~*ed a coin out of his pocket.* ■ **fisherman** *n* (*pl* **-men**) person who catches fish, as a job or as a sport ▶ **fishery** *n* [C, *usu pl*] (*pl* **-ies**) part of the sea where fish are caught ▶ **fishing** *n* [U] sport or job of catching fish: *go ~ing*

■ **fishmonger** /ˈfɪʃmʌŋgə(r)/ n person who sells fish in a shop ▸ **fishy** adj (-ier, -iest) **1** (infml) causing doubt: a ~y story **2** like fish

fission /ˈfɪʃn/ n [U] splitting, esp of an atom: nuclear ~.

fissure /ˈfɪʃə(r)/ n deep crack in rock

fist /fɪst/ n hand when tightly closed ▸ **fistful** n number or quantity that can be held in a fist

fit¹ /fɪt/ v (-tt-) **1** [I, T] be the right size and shape for sb/sth: These shoes don't ~ (me). **2** [T] (usu passive) put clothes on sb to make them the right size, shape, etc: have a new coat ~ed **3** [T] put or fix sth somewhere: ~ a new window **4** [I, T] (make sth) agree with, match or be suitable for sth: make the punishment ~ the crime [PV] **fit sb/sth in** find time or room for sb/sth **fit in (with sb/sth)** live, work, etc in an easy way with sb/sth **fit sb/sth out** equip sb/sth ▸ **fitted** adj fixed in place: ~ted carpets/cupboards ▸ **fitter** n **1** person whose job is to put together and fit machinery **2** person who cuts and fits clothes, carpets, etc

fit² /fɪt/ adj (~ter, ~test) **1** healthy and strong: keep ~ by jogging **2** ~for/~to suitable; good enough; right: not ~ to eat ◇ Do as you think ~. **3** ~to ready to do sth extreme: laughing ~ to burst ▸ **fitness** n [U] **1** state of being physically fit **2** ~for/~to suitability for sth

fit³ /fɪt/ n **1** sudden attack of an illness, eg epilepsy, in which you become unconscious and make violent movements **2** sudden short period of intense feeling or activity: a ~ of enthusiasm **3** way in which sth, esp clothing, fits: a tight ~ [IDM] **by/in fits and starts** not continuously over a period of time **have/throw a fit** (infml) be very shocked or angry ▸ **fitful** /ˈfɪtfl/ adj occurring irregularly ▸ **fitfully** /-fəli/ adv

fitting /ˈfɪtɪŋ/ adj (fml) right; suitable ● **fitting** n [C] **1** [usu pl] small part of equipment: electrical ~s **2** [usu pl] something, eg a cooker, that is fixed in a building but can be removed

five /faɪv/ number **5** ▸ **fiver** /ˈfaɪvə(r)/ n (GB, infml) £5 (note)

fix¹ /fɪks/ v **1** fasten sth firmly to sth **2** arrange or organize sth: ~ a date for a meeting **3** (esp US) prepare food or drink **4** repair sth **5** put sth in order: ~ your hair **6** unfairly influence the result of sth **7** direct your eyes, thoughts, etc onto sth [IDM] **fix sb with a look, a stare, etc** look directly at sb for a long time [PV] **fix on sb/sth** choose sb/sth **fix sb up (with sth)** (infml)

provide sb with sth ▸ **fixation** /fɪkˈseɪʃn/ n unhealthy interest in sth/sb; obsession

fix² /fɪks/ n [C] **1** [C] (infml) solution to a problem **2** [sing] (infml) injection of a narcotic drug **3** [sing] difficult situation **4** act of finding the position of a ship or an aircraft

fixture /ˈfɪkstʃə(r)/ n [C] **1** [usu pl] something, eg a bath, that is fixed in a building and cannot be removed **2** sporting event on an agreed date

fizz /fɪz/ v **1** make a hissing sound of bubbles of gas in a liquid ● **fizz** n [U, sing] small bubbles of gas in a liquid ▸ **fizzy** adj (-ier, -iest)

fizzle /ˈfɪzl/ v [I] make a weak hissing sound [PV] **fizzle out** come to a weak disappointing end

flab /flæb/ n [U] (infml) soft loose flesh on a person's body ▸ **flabby** adj (-ier, -iest) **1** having soft loose flesh; fat **2** feeble and weak

flabbergasted /ˈflæbəgɑːstɪd/ adj (infml) very shocked and surprised

flag /flæg/ n **1** piece of cloth used as a symbol of a country, or as a signal ● **flag** v (-gg-) [T] mark information to show you think it is important **2** [I] become tired or weak: Enthusiasm is ~ging. [PV] **flag sb/sth down** signal to a vehicle to stop ▸ **flagship** n **1** main ship in a fleet of ships in the navy **2** most important product, service, etc that an organization owns

flagon /ˈflægən/ n large round bottle for wine, cider, etc

flagrant /ˈfleɪgrənt/ adj openly bad: ~ disobedience ▸ **flagrantly** adv

flagstone /ˈflægstəʊn/ n large flat stone for a floor, path or pavement

flair /fleə(r)/ n [U, sing] natural ability to do sth well: She has a ~ for languages (= is quick at learning them).

flake /fleɪk/ n small thin layer; small piece of sth: snow~s ● **flake** v [I] fall off in flakes [PV] **flake out** (infml) collapse with exhaustion ▸ **flaky** adj (-ier, -iest) made of flakes; tending to flake

flamboyant /flæmˈbɔɪənt/ adj **1** (of a person) very confident and lively **2** brightly coloured ▸ **flamboyance** /-ˈbɔɪəns/ n [U] ▸ **flamboyantly** adv

flame /fleɪm/ n [C, U] hot bright stream of burning gas coming from sth on fire: The house was in ~s (= was burning). ● **flame** v [I] **1** burn with a bright flame **2** have the colour of flames; blaze ▸ **flaming** adj violent: a flaming argument

flamingo /fləˈmɪŋgəʊ/ n (pl ~s) large bird with long legs, a long neck and pink feathers

flammable /ˈflæməbl/ adj that can burn easily

flan /flæn/ n open pastry case with fruit, jam, etc in it

flank /flæŋk/ n 1 left or right side of an army 2 side of an animal between the ribs and the hip ● **flank** v [T] place sb/sth on one or both sides of sb/sth

flannel /ˈflænl/ n 1 [U] soft light fabric, containing cotton or wool 2 small piece of cloth used for washing yourself 3 (**flannels**) [pl] trousers made of flannel

flap /flæp/ n 1 flat piece of material that covers an opening 2 action or sound of flapping 3 part of the wing of an aircraft that can be lifted [IDM] **be in/get into a flap** (infml) be/become excited or confused ● **flap** v (-pp-) 1 [I, T] (of a bird's wings) move or be made to move quickly up and down: *The bird ~ped its wings.* 2 [I, T] (cause sth to) move up and down or from side to side: *sails ~ping in the wind* 3 [I] (GB, infml) become excited and anxious

flare /fleə(r)/ v 1 [I] burn brightly, but only for a short time 2 [I] (of clothes) become wider at the bottom: *~d trousers* [PV] **flare up** 1 burst into a bright flame 2 become more violent ● **flare** n [C] 1 [usu sing] bright unsteady light or flame that does not last 2 (device that produces a) flaring light used as a signal 3 shape that becomes gradually wider ■ **'flare-up** n [usu sing] 1 sudden appearance of violent feeling 2 (of illness) sudden attack

flash /flæʃ/ n 1 sudden bright burst of light: *a ~ of lightning* ◊ (*fig*) *a ~ of inspiration* 2 [C, U] (device that produces a) brief bright light for taking photographs indoors [IDM] **in/like a flash** very quickly ● **flash** adj (infml) expensive-looking; showy ● **flash** v 1 [I, T] (cause sth to) shine with a sudden bright light 2 [I] move quickly: *The train ~ed past us.* 3 [I] come suddenly into view or into the mind 4 [T] send information quickly by radio, computer, etc ■ **'flashback** n part of a film, etc that shows a scene in the past ■ **'flashbulb** n electric bulb in a flash(2) ■ **'flashlight** n (esp US) small electric torch ▸ **flashy** adj (-ier, -iest) attractive, but not in good taste: *~y clothes* ▸ **flashily** adv

flask /flɑːsk/ n 1 bottle with a narrow neck 2 (GB) = VACUUM FLASK 3 (esp US) = HIP FLASK (HIP)

flat¹ /flæt/ adj (~ter, ~test) 1 smooth and level, not curved or sloping 2 having a broad level surface but not high: *~ shoes* 3 dull; boring 4 absolute: *a ~ refusal* 5 (music) below the correct pitch 6 (of drinks) no longer fizzy 7 (of a battery) no longer producing electricity 8 (of a tyre) no longer having air inside ● **flat** adv 1 in or into a flat position: *Lie ~ and breathe deeply.* 2 exactly: *in 10 seconds ~* 3 (music) lower than the correct pitch [IDM] **flat out** (infml) as fast or as hard as possible ■ **flat-'footed** adj having feet with flat soles

flat² /flæt/ n [C] (esp GB) (esp US **apartment**) set of rooms on one floor of a building, used as a home 2 [sing] flat level part of sth 3 [C, usu pl] area of low level land 4 [C] (music) (symb ♭) note that is half a tone lower than the note named 5 [C] (esp US) flat tyre

flatten /ˈflætn/ v [I, T] become or make sth flat

flatter /ˈflætə(r)/ v [T] 1 praise sb too much or insincerely 2 make sb seem more attractive than they really are [IDM] **be/feel flattered** be pleased because sb has made you feel special ▸ **flatterer** n ▸ **flattery** n [U] insincere praise

flaunt /flɔːnt/ v [T] (disapprov) show sth valuable in order to gain admiration: *~ your wealth*

flautist /ˈflɔːtɪst/ n flute player

flavour (US **-or**) /ˈfleɪvə(r)/ n 1 [U] taste and smell of food: *add salt to improve the ~* 2 [C] particular taste: *six ~s of ice cream* 3 [sing] particular quality ● **flavour** v [T] give flavour to sth ▸ **flavouring** n [C, U] something added to food to give flavour ▸ **flavourless** adj

flaw /flɔː/ n fault or mistake; imperfection ▸ **flawed** adj having a flaw; damaged ▸ **flawless** adj perfect ▸ **flawlessly** adv

flax /flæks/ n [U] plant grown for its fibres, used for making linen

flea /fliː/ n small jumping insect that feeds on blood

fleck /flek/ n very small patch, spot or grain ● **fleck** v [T] cover or mark sth with flecks

flee /fliː/ v (pt, pp **fled** /fled/) [I, T] *~ (from)* run or hurry away from sb/sth; escape

fleece /fliːs/ n woolly coat of a sheep ● **fleece** v [T] (infml) rob sb by trickery, esp by charging too much money ▸ **fleecy** adj like fleece; woolly

fleet /fliːt/ n 1 group of ships under one commander 2 group of buses, cars, etc owned by one organization

fleeting /ˈfliːtɪŋ/ adj lasting only a short time: *a ~ glimpse*

flesh /fleʃ/ n 1 [U] soft part between the skin and bones of animal bodies 2 [U] soft juicy part of a fruit 3 (**the flesh**) [sing] the body, contrasted with the mind or the soul (IDM) **in the flesh** in person; in real life make **make your flesh creep** make you feel afraid or disgusted **your (own) flesh and blood** person you are related to ▸ **fleshy** *adj* fat

flew *pt of* FLY¹

flex /fleks/ *n* [C,U] wire for electric current, in a covering of plastic, etc ● **flex** *v* [T] bend or stretch your legs, muscles, etc

flexible /ˈfleksəbl/ *adj* **1** that can bend easily without breaking **2** easily changed: ~ *plans* ▸ **flexibility** /ˌfleksəˈbɪləti/ *n* [U]

flick /flɪk/ *n* **1** quick light blow **2** quick sharp movement: *with a ~ of his wrist* ● **flick** *v* [T] hit sth lightly with a sudden quick movement [PV] **flick through sth** turn over the pages of a book, etc quickly

flicker /ˈflɪkə(r)/ *v* **1** (of a light or flame) keep going on and off **2** (of an emotion) appear briefly **3** move with small quick movements ● **flicker** *n* [C, usu sing] **1** flickering movement **2** feeling or emotion only lasts for a short time: *a ~ of hope*

flier = FLYER

flight /flaɪt/ *n* **1** [C] journey made by air **2** [C] plane making a particular journey: ~ *BA 4793 from London* **3** [U] act of flying **4** [C] set of stairs between two floors **5** [U] fleeing or running away **6** [C] group of aircraft or birds flying together [IDM] **a flight of fancy/imagination** unrealistic imaginative idea ■ **flight path** *n* course of an aircraft through the air

flimsy /ˈflɪmzi/ *adj* (**-ier, -iest**) **1** light and thin; easily destroyed **2** difficult to believe: *a ~ excuse* ▸ **flimsily** *adv*

flinch /flɪntʃ/ *v* [I] move back because of shock, fear or pain

fling /flɪŋ/ *v* (*pt, pp* flung /flʌŋ/) [T] throw sb/sth violently somewhere [PV] **fling yourself into sth** do sth with a lot of energy and enthusiasm ● **fling** *n* short period of enjoyment and fun

flint /flɪnt/ *n* **1** [C,U] hard stone, used for making sparks **2** [C] piece of flint or hard metal that is used to make a spark

flip /flɪp/ *v* (**-pp-**) **1** [T] make sth move, esp through the air, by hitting it lightly: ~ *a coin* **2** [I] (*infml*) become very angry ● **flip** *n* quick light blow

flippant /ˈflɪpənt/ *adj* not showing enough respect ▸ **flippancy** /-ənsi/ *n* [U] ▸ **flippantly** *adv*

flipper /ˈflɪpə(r)/ *n* **1** broad flat limb of a seal, turtle, etc **2** large flat rubber shoe used when swimming underwater

flirt /flɜːt/ *v* [I] **1** ~ (**with**) behave towards sb in a romantic but not serious way **2** ~**with** think about sth, but not seriously ● **flirt** *n* person who flirts ▸ **flirtation** /flɜːˈteɪʃn/ *n* [C,U] ▸ **flirtatious** /flɜːˈteɪʃəs/ *adj* fond of flirting

flit /flɪt/ *v* (**-tt-**) [I] fly or move lightly and quickly

float /fləʊt/ *v* **1** [I, T] (cause sth to) stay on the surface of a liquid or up in the air **2** [T] (*business*) sell shares in a business or company for the first time **4** [I, T] (of a currency) (allow its value to) change according to the value of foreign currencies ● **float** *n* **1** large vehicle, esp one used in a procession: *a carnival* ~ **2** light object that floats (often used to support a heavier object in water) **3** amount of money used, esp by a shopkeeper to provide change ▸ **floating** *adj* not fixed

flock /flɒk/ *n* **1** group of sheep, birds or goats **2** large crowd of people **3** church congregation ● **flock** *v* [I] move in great numbers: *Crowds ~ed to the football match.*

flog /flɒg/ *v* (**-gg-**) [T] **1** beat sb severely as punishment **2** (*infml*) sell sth to sb [IDM] **flog a dead horse** (*infml*) waste your efforts doing sth that cannot succeed **flog sth to death** (*infml*) repeat a story, joke, etc too often ▸ **flogging** *n* [C,U] severe beating

flood /flʌd/ *n* **1** (coming of a) great quantity of water, esp water from a place that is usually dry **2** large quantity: *a ~ of tears/letters* ● **flood** *v* [I, T] **1** fill or cover sth with water **2** (of a feeling) affect sb suddenly and strongly: *A sense of relief ~ed over her.* **3** ~ **in/into/out of** arrive or go somewhere in large numbers ■ **flood tide** *n* [C,U] rising tide

floodlight /ˈflʌdlaɪt/ *n* [C, usu pl] large powerful light that produces a wide beam ● **floodlight** *v* (*pt, pp* floodlit /-lɪt/) [T] light sth with floodlights

floor /flɔː(r)/ *n* **1** [C] surface of a room that you walk on **2** [C] number of rooms on the same level in a building: *I live on the fourth* ~. **3** [C, usu sing] ground at the bottom of the sea, a forest, etc **4** (**the floor**) [sing] part of a building, esp in a parliament, where debates are held **5** [C, usu sing] area in a building used for a particular activity: *the dance* ~ ◇ *the factory/shop* ~ (= where the ordinary workers, not the managers work) ● **floor** *v* [T] **1** surprise or confuse sb so that they are not sure what to do **2** knock sb down **3** provide a building or room with a floor ■ **'floorboard** n wooden plank for a floor ■ **'floor show** n cabaret entertainment

flop /flɒp/ v (**-pp-**) [I] **1** move or fall clumsily or helplessly: ~ *exhausted into a chair* **2** (*infml*) (of a book, film, etc) fail ● **flop** n [C] **1** [usu sing] flopping movement or sound **2** (*infml*) failure of a book, film, etc ▶ **floppy** adj (**-ier**, **-iest**) hanging down loosely; soft and flexible: *a ~py hat* ■ **floppy 'disk** (*also* **floppy**) (*pl* **-ies**) (*also* **diskette**) n (*computing*) flexible disk used for storing data

flora /'flɔːrə/ n [U] (*tech*) all the plants of an area or period of time

floral /'flɔːrəl/ adj of flowers

florid /'flɒrɪd/ adj (*written*) **1** (of a person's face) red **2** (*disapprov*) decorated too much

florist /'flɒrɪst/ n person who has a shop that sells flowers

flotation /fləʊ'teɪʃn/ n [C,U] (*business*) act of floating(3) a company

flotilla /flə'tɪlə/ n group of small, esp military, ships

flounce /flaʊns/ v [I] move in a quick angry manner: *She ~d out of the room.*

flounder /'flaʊndə(r)/ v [I] **1** struggle to know what to say or do or how to continue with sth **2** struggle to move through water, mud, etc

flour /'flaʊə(r)/ n [U] fine powder made from grain, used for making bread, etc

flourish /'flʌrɪʃ/ v **1** [I] be successful: *Her business is ~ing.* **2** [I] grow healthily **3** [T] (*written*) wave sth about ● **flourish** n [C,usu sing] **1** exaggerated movement made to attract attention **2** short loud piece of music

flout /flaʊt/ v [T] disobey rules, etc openly and without respect

flow /fləʊ/ v [I] **1** (of liquid, gas or electricity) move steadily and continuously: (*fig*) *Keep the traffic ~ing.* **2** (of hair or clothes) hang loosely **3** (of the tide) come in from the sea to the land [PV] **flow from sth** (*fml*) come or result from sth ● **flow** n **1** [C,usu sing] flowing movement; constant stream or supply **2** movement of the sea towards the land: *the ebb and ~ of the tide*

flower /'flaʊə(r)/ n part of a plant that produces seeds, often brightly coloured [IDM] **the flower of sth** (*lit*) finest part of sth ● **flower** v [I] produce flowers ■ **'flower bed** n ground where flowers are grown ■ **'flowerpot** n pot in which a plant is grown ▶ **flowery** adj **1** having many flowers **2** (of language) too complicated

flown pp of FLY[1]

flu /fluː/ n [U] (*often* **the flu**) (*also fml* **influenza**) infectious disease with fever, aches and a bad cold

fluctuate /'flʌktʃueɪt/ v [I] change frequently in size, amount, quality, etc ▶ **fluctuation** /-'eɪʃn/ n [C,U]

fluent /'fluːənt/ adj **1** (of a person) able to speak a language easily and well: *He's ~ in Spanish.* **2** (of a language or an action) expressed in a smooth easy way: *speak ~ English* ▶ **fluency** /-ənsi/ n [U] ▶ **fluently** adv

fluff /flʌf/ n [U] **1** soft light pieces that come from woolly material **2** soft fur or hair on a young animal ● **fluff** v [T] **1** (*infml*) do sth badly or fail at sth: *The actor ~ed his lines.* **2** ~ **out/up** shake or brush sth so that it looks larger and/or softer: ~ *up a pillow* ▶ **fluffy** adj (**-ier**, **-iest**) soft and light; covered with fluff: *a ~y cat*

fluid /'fluːɪd/ adj **1** (of movements, designs, music, etc) smooth, graceful and flowing **2** (of a situation) not fixed; likely to change ● **fluid** n [C,U] liquid

fluke /fluːk/ n [usu sing] (*infml*) accidental good luck

flung pt, pp of FLING

fluorescent /flɔː'resnt/ adj giving out a bright glowing light when exposed to another light

fluoride /'flɔːraɪd/ n [U] chemical compound thought to prevent teeth from decaying

flurried /'flʌrid/ adj nervous and confused

flurry /'flʌri/ n [C] (*pl* **-ies**) **1** [usu sing] short burst of activity: *a ~ of activity/excitement* **2** sudden rush of wind, snow, etc

flush /flʌʃ/ n **1** [C,usu sing] redness of the face **2** [C,U] sudden strong feeling: *a ~ of anger/embarrassment* **3** [sing] act of cleaning a toilet with a sudden rush of water ● **flush** v [I, T] **1** (of the face) become red **2** clean sth with a rush of water: ~ *the toilet* ▶ **flushed** adj (of a person) red; with a red face ● **flush** adj **1** (*infml*) having plenty of money **2** ~ **with** (of two surfaces) level

fluster /'flʌstə(r)/ v [T] make sb nervous and confused ● **fluster** n [sing] nervous confused state

flute /fluːt/ n musical instrument like a thin pipe, played by blowing across a hole at one end

flutter /'flʌtə(r)/ v [I, T] (cause sth to) move about lightly and quickly: *curtains ~ing in the breeze* **2** [I, T] (of birds or insects) move the wings lightly and quickly up and down **3** [I] (of the heart) beat irregularly ● **flutter** n [C,usu sing] **1** quick light movement **2** [sing] state of nervous excitement

flux /flʌks/ n [U] continuous change: *in a state of ~*

fly¹ /flaɪ/ v (*pt* flew /fluː/ *pp* flown /fləʊn/) **1** [I] move through the air as a bird does, or in an aircraft **2** [T] control an aircraft **3** [I] go or move quickly: *It's late. I must ~.* **4** [T] raise a flag [IDM] **fly in the face of sth** (*written*) oppose or be the opposite of sth **fly into a rage, temper, etc** become suddenly very angry ■ **,flying 'saucer** n spacecraft believed to have come from another planet ■ **,flying 'start** n [sing] very good beginning ■ **,flying 'visit** n (*GB*) very short visit

fly² /flaɪ/ n [C] (*pl* **flies**) **1** insect with two wings **2** natural or artificial fly used as a bait in fishing **3** [*usu pl*] (*pl* **flies**) zip or buttoned opening on the front of a pair of trousers

flyer (*also* **flier**) /ˈflaɪə(r)/ n **1** (*infml*) pilot of an aircraft **2** person who travels in an aircraft **3** small sheet of paper that advertises sth

flyleaf /ˈflaɪliːf/ n (*pl* **-leaves**) blank page at the beginning or end of a book

flyover /ˈflaɪəʊvə(r)/ n bridge that carries one road over another

foal /fəʊl/ n young horse

foam /fəʊm/ n [U] **1** (*also* **foam 'rubber**) soft light rubber material used for seats, mattresses, etc **2** mass of small usu white air bubbles in a liquid ● **foam** v [I] (of a liquid) have or produce foam

fob /fɒb/ v (**-bb-**) [PV] **fob sth off** (**with sth**) trick sb into accepting sth of little or no value: *He ~bed me off with a weak excuse.*

focus /ˈfəʊkəs/ n [C] **1** [*usu sing*] centre of interest: *the ~ of attention* **2** point at which rays of light, heat, etc meet [IDM] **in/out of focus** giving/not giving a clear sharp picture ● **focus** v (**-s-** *or* **-ss-**) **1** [I, T] adjust a lens, etc to a clear sharp image **2** [T] **~(on)** give all your attention to sth/sb

fodder /ˈfɒdə(r)/ n [U] food for farm animals

foe /fəʊ/ n (*old-fash* or *fml*) enemy

foetus /ˈfiːtəs/ n young human or animal before it is born

fog /fɒɡ/ n [U,C] **1** thick cloud of tiny drops of water in the air: *I couldn't see through the ~.* **2** state of confusion ● **fog** v (**-gg-**) [I, T] **1** cover sth or become covered with fog: *The window has ~ged up.* **2** make sb/sth confused and less clear ▶ **foggy** *adj* (**-ier, -iest**) not clear because of fog: *a ~gy night* ■ **'foghorn** n instrument used for warning ships in a fog ■ **'fog lamp** (*also* **'fog light**) n powerful light on the front of a car for use in fog

foil /fɔɪl/ n **1** [U] metal cut into thin sheets, used for covering food **2** [C] person or thing that contrasts with another ● **foil** v [PV] prevent sb from doing sth, esp sth illegal

foist /fɔɪst/ v [PV] **foist sth on/ upon sb** force sb to accept sb/sth that they do not want

fold /fəʊld/ v **1** [T] bend one part of sth back on itself: *~ a letter* **2** [I] be able to be folded: *a ~ing bed* **3** [I] (of a business) come to an end; fail [IDM] **fold your arms** cross your arms over your chest ● **fold** n **1** part of fabric, etc that is folded **2** line made by folding sth **3** area surrounded by a wall where sheep are kept ▶ **folder** n holder, usu made of cardboard, etc

foliage /ˈfəʊliɪdʒ/ n [U] (*fml*) all the leaves of a tree or plant

folk /fəʊk/ n **1** [pl] people in general **2** (**folks**) [pl] (*infml*) relatives **3** [U] (*also* **'folk music**) music in the traditional style of a country or community ■ **'folk dance** n [C,U] (music for a) traditional popular dance ■ **folk-lore** /ˈfəʊklɔː(r)/ n [U] traditions and stories of a country or community ■ **'folk music** = FOLK(3) ■ **'folk song** n traditional popular song

follow /ˈfɒləʊ/ v **1** [I, T] come or go after sb/sth **2** [I] be the logical result of sth: *It ~s from what you say that …* **3** [T] go along a road, etc **4** [T] act according to advice, instructions, etc **5** [I, T] understand sth: *I don't ~ (your meaning).* **6** [T] watch or listen to sth carefully **7** [T] take an interest in sth: *~ all the football news* [IDM] **as follows** used to introduce a list **follow in sb's footsteps** do what sb else has done earlier **follow your nose** act instinctively **follow suit** do what sb else has just done [PV] **follow sth through** carry out or continue sth to the end **follow sth up 1** add to sth you have just done by doing sth else **2** investigate sth: *Police are ~ing up a new lead.* ▶ **follower** n supporter or admirer ■ **'follow-up** n something done to continue what has already been done: *a ~-up visit*

following /ˈfɒləʊɪŋ/ *adj* (**the following …**) **1** next **2** about to be mentioned: *Answer the ~ questions.* ● **following** n [*usu sing*] group of supporters ● **following** *prep* after or as a result of a particular event

folly /ˈfɒli/ n (*pl* **-ies**) [U,C] (action that shows) lack of judgement; foolishness

fond /fɒnd/ *adj* **1** **~of** having a great liking for sb/sth **2** loving: *a ~ embrace* **3** hoped for but not likely to happen: *~ hopes* ▶ **fondly** *adv* ▶ **fondness** n [U]

fondle /ˈfɒndl/ v [T] touch sb/sth lovingly

font /fɒnt/ n **1** basin in a church to hold water for baptism **2** (tech) size and style of a set of letters used for printing or computer documents

food /fuːd/ n **1** [U] things that people or animals eat: a shortage of ~ **2** [C,U] particular kind of food: health ~s [IDM] **food for thought** idea that makes you think seriously ■ **foodstuff** n [usu pl] any substance used as food

fool /fuːl/ n person who you think lacks intelligence or good judgement [IDM] **act/play the fool** behave in a stupid way to make people laugh **make a fool of yourself** do sth stupid ● **fool** v **1** [T] trick sb into believing sth that is not true **2** [I] ~ (**about/around**) behave in a silly way, often in order to make people laugh: Stop ~ing around! ● **fool** adj (infml) stupid ▶ **foolhardy** adj (disapprov) taking unnecessary risks ▶ **foolish** adj silly ▶ **foolishly** adv ▶ **foolishness** n [U] ▶ **foolproof** adj that cannot go wrong: a ~proof plan

foot /fʊt/ n (pl **feet** /fiːt/) **1** [C] lowest part of the leg, below the ankle **2** [sing] lowest part: at the ~ of the stairs **3** [C] (pl **feet** or **foot**) (abbr **ft**) measure of length equal to 12 inches (30.48 centimetres) [IDM] **fall/land on your feet** recover quickly esp through good luck, after being in difficulties **on foot** walking **put your feet up** rest **put your foot down** be firm in opposing sth/sb **put your foot in it** say or do sth that upsets or offends sb else ● **foot** v [IDM] **foot the bill** pay the bill ■ **foot-and-'mouth disease** n [U] disease that cows, sheep, etc. can die from, which causes sore places on the mouth and feet ■ **'football** n **1** [U] game played by two teams of 11 players. Each team tries to kick the ball into the other's goal. **2** [C] large round or oval ball ▶ **'footballer** n (GB) person who plays football ■ **'football pools** n [pl] system of betting money on the results of football matches ■ **'footer** n line of text that is automatically added to the bottom of every page that is printed from a computer ■ **'foothill** n [usu pl] low hill at the base of a mountain ■ **'foothold** n **1** firm place for the foot when climbing **2** strong position in a business, etc from which progress can be made ■ **'footnote** n note at the bottom of a page ■ **'footpath** n path made for people to walk along ■ **'footprint** n mark made by sb's foot/shoe ■ **'footstep** n [usu pl] sound or mark made each

time your foot touches the ground ■ **'footwear** n [U] shoes, etc

footing /ˈfʊtɪŋ/ n [sing] **1** secure placing of the feet **2** relationship with others: on an equal ~

for /fə(r); strong form fɔː(r)/ prep **1** used to show the person who is intended to have or use sth or where sth is intended to be put: a letter ~ you ◇ a table ~ the kitchen **2** in order to help sb/sth: What can I do ~ you? **3** concerning sb/sth: anxious ~ his safety **4** representing sb/sth; meaning: Speak ~ yourself! ◇ Red is ~ danger. **5** in support of sb/sth: Are you ~ or against nuclear arms? **6** used to show purpose or function: go ~ a walk ◇ What's this machine ~? **7** used to show a reason or cause: famous ~ its church **8** in order to obtain sth: pray ~ peace **9** in exchange for sth: buy a book ~ £15 ◇ trade your car in ~ a new one **10** considering what can be expected from sb/sth: She's tall ~ her age. **11** used to show where sb/sth is going: Is this the train ~ York? **12** used to show a distance or a length of time: walk ~ three miles ◇ stay ~ a few days **13** used to say how difficult, necessary, pleasant, etc sth is that sb might do or has done: It's impossible ~ me to go.

forage /ˈfɒrɪdʒ/ v [I] ~ (**for**) search for sth: birds foraging for food

foray /ˈfɒreɪ/ n sudden attack or rush: (fig) the company's first ~ into the computer market

forbear = FOREBEAR

forbearance /fɔːˈbeərəns/ n [U] (fml) quality of being patient and forgiving

forbid /fəˈbɪd/ v (pt **forbade** /fəˈbæd; fəˈbeɪd/ pp **~den** /fəˈbɪdn/) [T] ~ (**to**) order sb not to do sth; order that sth must not be done: I ~ you to go. ◇ Smoking is ~den. ▶ **forbidding** adj looking unfriendly; threatening

force /fɔːs/ n **1** [U] strength, power or violence **2** [C,U] power or influence: the ~s of nature ◇ economic ~s **3** [U] authority: the ~ of the law **4** [C] group of soldiers, etc: the police ~ ◇ a sales ~ **5** [C,U] power that causes movement: the ~ of gravity [IDM] **bring sth/come into force** (cause a law, rule, etc to) start being used **in force 1** (of people) in large numbers **2** (of a law, etc) being used ● **force** v [T] **1** ~ (**to**) make sb do sth they do not want to do: ~ him to talk **2** use physical strength to move sb/sth into a particular position: ~ a lock/door (= make it open using force) **3** make yourself laugh, smile, etc ▶ **forceful** /ˈfɔːsfl/ adj (of a person or an argument, etc) strong; convincing ▶ **forcefully**

/-fəli/ adv ► **forcible** /ˈfɔːsəbl/ adj involving the use of physical force ► **forcibly** adv

forceps /ˈfɔːseps/ n [pl] medical instrument used for holding things

ford /fɔːd/ n shallow place in a river where you can walk or drive across ● **ford** v [T] cross a river or stream

fore /fɔː(r)/ adj front ● **fore** n [IDM] **be/come to the fore** be/become important

forearm /ˈfɔːrɑːm/ n part of the arm from the elbow to the wrist

forebear (also **forbear**) /ˈfɔːbeə(r)/ n [C, usu pl] (fml) ancestor

foreboding /fɔːˈbəʊdɪŋ/ n [U,C] strong feeling that danger or trouble is coming

forecast /ˈfɔːkɑːst/ v (pt, pp ~ or ~ed) [T] say in advance what is expected to happen ● **forecast** n statement of expected future events: *weather* ~

forecourt /ˈfɔːkɔːt/ n open area in front of a building

forefinger /ˈfɔːfɪŋɡə(r)/ n finger next to the thumb

forefront /ˈfɔːfrʌnt/ n [sing] most forward or important position: *in the ~ of space research*

foregone /ˈfɔːɡɒn/ adj [IDM] **a foregone conclusion** result that is certain to happen

foreground /ˈfɔːɡraʊnd/ n [sing] **(the foreground)** 1 nearest part of a view or picture: *in the ~* 2 most important and noticeable position

forehand /ˈfɔːhænd/ adj, n (stroke in tennis, etc) made with the palm of your hand turned forward

forehead /ˈfɔːhed, ˈfɒrɪd/ n part of the face above the eyes

foreign /ˈfɒrən/ adj 1 of, in or from a country that is not your own 2 concerning other countries: *policy* 3 ~to (fml) not natural to sb/sth: *~ to his nature* 4 (fml) having entered sth by accident: *a ~ body* (= eg a hair) *in the eye* ► **foreigner** n foreign person ■ **foreign exchange** n [U] (system of buying and selling) foreign money

foreman /ˈfɔːmən/ n (pl -men /-mən/ fem **forewoman** /-wʊmən/ pl -women /-wɪmɪn/) 1 worker who is in charge of others 2 leader of a jury

foremost /ˈfɔːməʊst/ adj most important

forensic /fəˈrensɪk/ adj of or used in courts of law: *~ medicine*

forerunner /ˈfɔːrʌnə(r)/ n person or thing that prepares the way for the coming of another

foresee /fɔːˈsiː/ v (pt **foresaw** /fɔːˈsɔː/ pp ~n /fɔːˈsiːn/) [T] see in advance what is going to happen: *~ difficulties* ► **foreseeable** adj that

can be foreseen [IDM] **for/in the foreseeable future** for the time being; fairly soon

forest /ˈfɒrɪst/ n [C, U] large area of land covered with trees ► **forestry** n [U] science and practice of planting and caring for forests

forestall /fɔːˈstɔːl/ v [T] (written) prevent sth from happening by doing sth first

forethought /ˈfɔːθɔːt/ n [U] careful planning for the future

forever /fərˈevə(r)/ adv 1 (also **for ever**) always: *I'll love you ~ !* ◊ (infml) *It takes her ~* (= a very long time) *to get dressed.* 2 (spoken) constantly: *He is ~ complaining.*

forewarn /fɔːˈwɔːn/ v [T] ~(of) warn sb of a possible danger or problem

foreword /ˈfɔːwɜːd/ n short introduction to a book

forfeit /ˈfɔːfɪt/ v [T] lose sth as a punishment for or as a result of an action ● **forfeit** n something forfeited

forgave pt of FORGIVE

forge /fɔːdʒ/ n place where objects are made by heating and shaping metal ● **forge** v [T] 1 put a lot of effort into making sth successful: *~ a friendship/link* 2 make an illegal copy of sth, in order to deceive people: *~ banknotes* 3 shape metal by heating and hammering it [PV] **forge ahead (with sth)** advance or progress quickly ► **forger** n person who forges money, documents, etc ► **forgery** /ˈfɔːdʒəri/ n (pl -ies) 1 [U] forging of money, documents, etc 2 [C] forged banknote, document, etc

forget /fəˈɡet/ v (pt **forgot** /fəˈɡɒt/ pp **forgotten** /fəˈɡɒtn/) [i, t] 1 fail to remember sth: *Don't ~ to post the letters.* 2 stop thinking about sb/sth: *Let's ~ our differences.* ► **forgetful** /fəˈɡetfl/ adj in the habit of forgetting

forgive /fəˈɡɪv/ v (pt **forgave** /fəˈɡeɪv/ pp ~n /fəˈɡɪvn/) [T] ~(for) stop being angry with sb for sth they have done to you: *She forgave him his rudeness.* ► **forgivable** adj that can be forgiven ► **forgiveness** n [U] ► **forgiving** adj willing to forgive

forgo (also **forego**) /fɔːˈɡəʊ/ v (pt **forwent** /fɔːˈwent/ pp **-gone** /-ˈɡɒn/) [T] decide not to have or do sth that you would like

forgot pt of FORGET

forgotten pp of FORGET

fork /fɔːk/ n 1 tool with sharp points, used for lifting food to the mouth 2 gardening tool with metal points, used for digging 3 place where a road, tree, etc divides into two parts 4 thing shaped like a fork

with two or more long parts ● **fork**
v **1** [I] (of a road, etc) divide into two
parts **2** [I] (of a person) turn left or
right where a road, etc divides into
two **3** [T] move, dig or carry sth with
a fork [PV] **fork out (sth)** (*infml*) pay
money unwillingly ▸ **forked** *adj*
divided into two or more parts
■ **fork-lift truck** *n* small powerful
vehicle for lifting heavy goods

forlorn /fə'lɔːn/ *adj* lonely and
unhappy ▸ **forlornly** *adv*

form¹ /fɔːm/ *n* **1** [C] kind or type:
different ~s of government **2** [U]
shape; appearance **3** [C] printed
paper with spaces to be filled in:
application ~s **4** [U] general way in
which sth made is put together:
~ and content **5** [C,U] (*gram*) spelling or pronunciation of a word: *The
plural of 'goose' is 'geese'.* **6** [C]
(*GB, old-fash*) class in a school [IDM]
on/off form fit/unfit; performing
well/badly ▸ **formless** *adj* (*written*)
without shape

form² /fɔːm/ *v* **1** [I, T] (cause sth to)
come into existence: *a govern-
ment* **2** [T] produce or give shape to
sth **3** [I, T] be arranged or arrange
sb/sth in a certain order or shape:
~ a line **4** linking verb be sth: *It ~s
part of the course.*

formal /'fɔːml/ *adj* **1** showing or
expecting careful serious behaviour: *a ~ dinner* **2** (of clothes or
words) used in formal situations
3 regular in design: *~ gardens*
4 official: *a ~ declaration of war*
▸ **formality** /fɔː'mæləti/ *n* (*pl* **-ies**)
1 [U] attention to rules **2** [C] action
required by custom: *a legal ~ity*
▸ **formalize** (*also* **-ise**) /'fɔːməlaɪz/
v [T] make an
arrangement, a plan, etc official
▸ **formally** *adv*

format /'fɔːmæt/ *n* size, shape or
general arrangement of sth ▸ **format** *v* (**-tt-**) [T] arrange sth in a particular format, esp for a computer

formation /fɔː'meɪʃn/ *n* **1** [U] forming or shaping of sth **2** [C,U]
structure; arrangement

formative /'fɔːmətɪv/ *adj* influencing the development of sth or of
sb's character: *a child's ~ years*

former /'fɔːmə(r)/ *adj* of an earlier
period: *the ~ president* ▸ **the former**
pron the first of two people or
things mentioned ▸ **formerly** *adv* in
earlier times

formidable /'fɔːmɪdəbl/ *adj* (of
people, things or situations) causing fear and respect because they
are impressive or powerful or
because they seem very difficult: *a
~ opponent* ▸ **formidably** *adv*

formula /'fɔːmjələ/ *n* (*pl* **~s** or, in
scientific use **-mulae** /-mjuliː/) **1**
rule, fact, etc shown in letters, signs

or numbers: *a chemical ~* **2** method
or set of ideas to achieve sth: *a
peace ~* **3** list of things that sth is
made from **4** fixed group of words
used in a particular situation

formulate /'fɔːmjuleɪt/ *v* [T] **1** create or prepare sth carefully **2**
express sth in carefully chosen
words ▸ **formulation** /-'leɪʃn/ *n* [U,C]

forsake /fə'seɪk/ *v* (*pt* **forsook** /fə-
'sʊk/ *pp* **~n** /fə'seɪkən/) [T] (*fml*)
leave sb/sth

fort /fɔːt/ *n* building for military
defence

forte /'fɔːteɪ/ *n* [sing] something sb
does well: *Singing is not my ~.*

forth /fɔːθ/ *adv* (*lit*) away from a
place; out [IDM] **and (so on and) so
forth** and other things of the same
kind

forthcoming /,fɔːθ'kʌmɪŋ/ *adj* **1**
about to happen, be published, etc
very soon **2** ready when needed:
The money was not ~. **3** willing to
give information about sth

fortieth → FORTY

fortify /'fɔːtɪfaɪ/ *v* (*pt, pp* **-ied**) [T]
1 ~ (**against**) strengthen a place
against attack **2** make sb/sth
stronger: *cereal fortified with extra
vitamins* ▸ **fortification** /,fɔːtɪfɪ-
'keɪʃn/ *n* **1** [U] act of fortifying sth
2 [C, usu pl] tower, wall, etc built
for defence

fortnight /'fɔːtnaɪt/ *n* (*esp GB*) two
weeks ▸ **fortnightly** *adj, adv* happening every fortnight

fortress /'fɔːtrəs/ *n* large fort; castle

fortuitous /fɔː'tjuːɪtəs/ *adj* (*fml*)
happening by chance

fortunate /'fɔːtʃənət/ *adj* lucky ▸
fortunately *adv*

fortune /'fɔːtʃuːn/ *n* **1** [C,U] good or
bad luck; chance **2** [C] what will
happen to sb in the future: *tell sb's
~* **3** [C] large amount of money: *cost
a ~* ■ **'fortune teller** *n* person who
tells people's fortunes(2)

forty /'fɔːti/ *number* **1** 40 **2** (**the for-
ties**) *n* [pl] numbers, years or temperatures from 40 to 49 ▸ **fortieth**
/'fɔːtiəθ/ *ordinal number*

forum /'fɔːrəm/ *n* place for public
discussion

forward¹ /'fɔːwəd/ *adj* **1** directed
towards the front; at the front:
~ movements **2** of the future: *planning* **3** behaving in a way that is too
confident or informal ● **forward** *n*
attacking player in football, etc
● **forward** *v* [T] **1** send or pass
goods or information to sb **2** send
on a letter, etc to a new address
3 help to develop sth: *~ her career*
▸ **forwardness** *n* [U] behaviour that
is too confident or informal

forward² /'fɔːwəd/ *adv* (**forwards**)

towards the front; towards the future ■ **'forward-looking** adj (approv) having modern ideas

forwent pt of FORGO

fossil /'fɒsl/ n remains of an animal or plant that have hardened or turned into rock ▶ **fossilize** (also **-ise**) /'fɒsəlaɪz/ v [I, T] (cause sth to) become a fossil **2** (disapprov) (cause sth to) become fixed and unable to change

foster /'fɒstə(r)/ v [T] **1** encourage sth to develop **2** take care of a child without becoming his/her legal parent ● **foster** adj used with some nouns in connection with the fostering of a child: a ~ mother

fought pt, pp of FIGHT

foul /faʊl/ adj **1** dirty and smelling bad **2** very unpleasant; very bad: a ~ temper **3** (of language) obscene and offensive **4** (of weather) stormy ● **foul** n (sport) action against the rules ● **foul** v **1** [I, T] make sth dirty [PV] **foul sth up** (infml) spoil sth ■ **,foul 'play** n [U] **1** criminal violence that leads to murder **2** (sport) unfair play

found[1] pt, pp of FIND

found[2] /faʊnd/ v [T] **1** build or establish sth: ~ a hospital **2** (usu passive) base sth on sth: a novel ~ed on facts ▶ **founder** n person who establishes sth

foundation /faʊnˈdeɪʃn/ n [C, usu pl] layer of bricks, etc that form the strong base of a building **2** [C, U] an idea, etc on which sth is based **3** [C] organization that provides money for a charity, etc **4** [U] act of starting a new institution or organization

founder /'faʊndə(r)/ v [I] (written) **1** (of a plan, etc) fail **2** (of a ship) fill with water and sink

foundry /'faʊndri/ n (pl **-ies**) factory where metal or glass is melted and shaped into objects

fount /faʊnt/ n ~(**of**) (lit or hum) place where sth important comes from: the ~ of all knowledge

fountain /'faʊntən/ n **1** ornamental structure from which water is pumped into the air **2** powerful jet of liquid ■ **'fountain pen** n pen with a container from which ink flows to the nib

four /fɔː(r)/ number **4** [IDM] **on all fours** bent over with your hands and knees on the ground ▶ **fourth** /fɔːθ/ ordinal number, n **1** 4th **2** (esp US) = QUARTER

fourteen /ˌfɔːˈtiːn/ number **14** ▶ **fourteenth** ordinal number

fowl /faʊl/ n (pl **fowl** or **~s**) [C, U] bird, eg a chicken, kept for its meat or eggs

fox /fɒks/ n wild animal of the dog family with red fur and a bushy tail ● **fox** v [T] (infml) confuse or trick sb ■ **'fox-hunting** n [U] sport in which a fox is hunted by hounds and people on horses

foyer /'fɔɪeɪ/ n **1** large entrance hall in a theatre or hotel **2** (US) entrance hall in a private house or flat

fraction /'frækʃn/ n **1** division of a number, eg ½ **2** small part: a ~ of a second ▶ **fractional** /-ʃənl/ adj very small

fracture /'fræktʃə(r)/ n **1** breaking of sth, esp a bone ● **fracture** v [I, T] (cause sth to) break or crack

fragile /'frædʒaɪl/ adj **1** easily broken or damaged **2** (infml) weak; not healthy ▶ **fragility** /frəˈdʒɪləti/ n

fragment /'frægmənt/ n small part of sth that has broken off ▶ **fragment** /frægˈment/ v [I, T] (written) (cause sth to) break into pieces ▶ **fragmentary** adj incomplete ▶ **fragmentation** /ˌfrægmenˈteɪʃn/ n [U]

fragrance /'freɪɡrəns/ n [C, U] sweet smell ▶ **fragrant** /'freɪɡrənt/ adj sweet-smelling

frail /freɪl/ adj weak ▶ **frailty** n (pl **-ies**) **1** [U] quality of being frail **2** [U, C] fault in sb's character

frame /freɪm/ n [C] **1** border in which a picture, window, etc is set **2** main structure of a building, vehicle, etc that forms a support for its parts **3** [usu pl] structure that holds the lenses of a pair of glasses **4** [usu sing] human or animal body **5** single photograph on a cinema film [IDM] **a frame of mind**: way you feel about sth ● **frame** v [T] **1** put a frame(1) round sth **2** (infml) make an innocent person appear guilty of a crime **3** express sth in words ■ **'framework** n **1** structure giving shape and support **2** set of principles or ideas

franchise /'fræntʃaɪz/ n **1** [C, U] right to sell a product or service **2** [U] (fml) the right to vote

frank[1] /fræŋk/ adj showing thoughts and feelings openly ▶ **frankly** adv ▶ **frankness** n [U]

frank[2] /fræŋk/ v [T] mark a letter to show that postage has been paid

frankfurter /'fræŋkfɜːtə(r)/ n kind of small smoked sausage

frantic /'fræntɪk/ adj **1** wildly afraid or anxious **2** hurried but disorganized ▶ **frantically** /-kli/ adv

fraternal /frəˈtɜːnl/ adj brotherly ▶ **fraternally** adv

fraternity /frəˈtɜːnəti/ n (pl **-ies**) **1** [C] group of people with the same interests or job **2** [C] (US) society of male university students **3** [U] brotherly feeling

fraternize (also **-ise**) /'frætənaɪz/ v [I] ~(with) become friendly with sb: ~ *with the enemy* ▸ **fraternization** (also **-isation**) /,frætənaɪ'zeɪʃn/ n [U]

fraud /frɔːd/ n 1 [C,U] crime of deceiving sb in order to gain money illegally 2 [C] person who deceives others ▸ **fraudulent** /'frɔːdjələnt/ adj intended to deceive sb

fraught /frɔːt/ adj 1 ~with filled: ~ *with danger* 2 worried or anxious

fray /freɪ/ v [I, T] 1 (cause cloth, etc to) become worn, so that there are loose threads 2 (cause sth to) become strained: ~*ed nerves*

freak /friːk/ n 1 very unusual act or event: *a* ~ *storm* 2 person thought to be very abnormal 3 (infml) person who is very interested in sth mentioned: *a jazz* ~ ▸ **freakish** adj strange; unusual

freckle /'frekl/ n [C, usu pl] small brown spot on a person's skin ▸ **freckled** adj

free /friː/ adj (~r, ~st) 1 not in prison; allowed to go where you want 2 not controlled by sb else, rules, a government, etc: *a democracy with* ~ *speech and a* ~ *press* 3 costing nothing 4 not blocked; clear: *a* ~ *flow of water* 5 ~from/of without sth, usu sth unpleasant: ~ *from pain/blame* 6 without the thing mentioned: *tax* ~ 7 not fixed to sth: *the* ~ *end of a rope* 8 not being used: *a* ~ *seat* 9 (of a person) not busy 10 ~with ready to give sth, esp sth not wanted: *He's* ~ *with his opinions.* [IDM] **free and easy** relaxed **get/have a** ~ **hand** • **free** adv 1 without payment 2 no longer fixed or trapped [IDM] **make free with sth** use sth a lot, even though it does not belong to you • **free** v [T] make sb/sth free ■ **free 'enterprise** n [U] operation of business and trade without government control ■ **free-for-all** n [sing] quarrel, etc in which everyone joins in ■ **freehand** adj, adv (drawn) by hand, without instruments ■ **freelance** adj, adv done by a writer, artist, etc who works for several employers ■ **freelance** v [I] work in this way ▸ **freely** adv in a free manner; readily ■ **free-'range** adj produced by hens kept in natural conditions ■ **free 'trade** n [U] system of international trade without taxes or other controls ■ **freeway** n (US) = MOTORWAY ■ **free 'will** n [U] power to make your own decisions independently of God or fate [IDM] **of your own free will** because you want to do sth

freedom /'friːdəm/ n 1 [C,U] ~(to) right to do or say what you want without anyone stopping you: ~ *of speech* 2 [U] state of being free

freeze /friːz/ v (pt **froze** /frəʊz/ pp **frozen** /'frəʊzn/) 1 [I, T] (esp of water) change into ice 2 [I] (used with *it*) (of weather) be at or below 0° Celsius: *It's freezing today.* 3 [I] be very cold; be so cold you could die: *He froze to death on the mountain.* 4 [T] keep food, etc at a temperature below freezing point: *frozen peas* 5 [I] stop moving suddenly because of fear, etc: ~ *with terror* 6 [T] hold prices, wages, etc at a fixed level [PV] **freeze over/up** become covered/blocked with ice • **freeze** n 1 period of freezing weather 2 fixing of wages, prices, etc ▸ **freezer** n large refrigerator in which food is kept frozen ■ **'freezing point** n [U,C] temperature at which a liquid, esp water, freezes

freight /freɪt/ n [U] goods carried by ships, aircraft, etc • **freight** v [T] send or carry goods by air, sea or train ▸ **freighter** n ship or aircraft that carries freight

French /frentʃ/ adj of France, its people or their language ■ **French 'fry** n [usu pl] (esp US) = CHIP(1) ■ **French 'window** n [C, usu pl] glass door that opens onto a garden or balcony

frenzy /'frenzi/ n [C, usu sing, U] violent excitement ▸ **frenzied** adj

frequency /'friːkwənsi/ n (pl **-ies**) 1 [U] rate at which sth happens or is repeated 2 [C] rate at which a radio wave vibrates

frequent¹ /'friːkwənt/ adj happening often ▸ **frequently** adv

frequent² /frɪ'kwent/ v [T] (fml) go to a place often

fresco /'freskəʊ/ n (pl **-es** or **-s**) picture painted on a wall before the plaster is dry

fresh /freʃ/ adj 1 new or different: *make a* ~ *start* 2 newly made or produced; not stale: ~ *bread* 3 (of food) not tinned or frozen 4 (of water) not salty 5 (of weather) cool and windy 6 (of colours) clear and bright 7 full of energy 8 (infml) rude and too confident with sb 9 ~from having just left a place: *students* ~ *from college* ▸ **freshly** adv (usu with a pp) recently: ~*ly painted* ▸ **freshness** n [U] ■ **freshwater** adj living in or having water that is not salty

freshen /'freʃn/ v 1 [T] make sth fresh 2 [I] (of the wind) become stronger [PV] **freshen (yourself) up** wash and make yourself look clean and tidy

fret¹ /fret/ v (-tt-) [I, T] ~(about) (cause sb to) worry about sth

fret F 172

fret¹ ▶ **fretful** /ˈfretfl/ adj worried or complaining ▶ **fretfully** adv

fret² /fret/ n one of the metal bars across the neck of a guitar, etc

friar /ˈfraɪə(r)/ n male member of a certain Christian group

friction /ˈfrɪkʃn/ n 1 [U] rubbing of one thing against another 2 [C,U] disagreement between people

Friday /ˈfraɪdeɪ; -di/ n [C,U] the day of the week after Thursday and before Saturday (See examples of use at *Monday*.)

fridge /frɪdʒ/ n (also *fml* or *US* **refrigerator**) electrical appliance in which food is kept cold

fried pt, pp of FRY

friend /frend/ n 1 person you know well and like, but who is not a relative 2 helper or supporter: *a ~ of the arts* [IDM] **be/make friends (with sb)** be/become a friend of sb ▶ **friendless** adj without any friends ▶ **friendly** adj (-ier, -iest) 1 acting as a friend 2 (of an argument, game, etc) not as a serious competition ▶ **friendliness** n [C,U] ▶ **friendship** n [C,U] friendly relationship

frieze /friːz/ n band of decoration along the top of a wall

frigate /ˈfrɪɡət/ n small fast warship

fright /fraɪt/ n [U,C] feeling of sudden fear

frighten /ˈfraɪtn/ v [T] make sb suddenly feel afraid ▶ **frightened** adj afraid ▶ **frightening** adj causing fear ▶ **frighteningly** adv

frightful /ˈfraɪtfl/ adj (old-fash) very unpleasant; very bad ▶ **frightfully** /-fəli/ adv (old-fash) very

frigid /ˈfrɪdʒɪd/ adj 1 (of a woman) not able to enjoy sex 2 very cold ▶ **frigidity** /-ˈdʒɪdəti/ n [U] ▶ **frigidly** adv

frill /frɪl/ n 1 [C] decorative border on a dress, etc 2 [pl] unnecessary additions ▶ **frilly** adj

fringe /frɪndʒ/ n 1 hair hanging over the forehead 2 decorative edge of loose threads on a rug, etc 3 outer edge: *on the ~ of the crowd*

frisk /frɪsk/ n 1 [T] pass your hands over sb's body to search for hidden weapons, etc 2 [I] (of animals) jump and run about playfully ▶ **frisky** adj (-ier, -iest) lively

fritter /ˈfrɪtə(r)/ v [PV] **fritter sth away (on sth)** waste money or time on unimportant things ▶ **fritter** n piece of fried batter, with sliced fruit, meat, etc in it

frivolous /ˈfrɪvələs/ adj not serious; silly ▶ **frivolity** /frɪˈvɒləti/ n (pl -ies) [U,C] silly behaviour, esp when this is not suitable ▶ **frivolously** adv

frizzy /ˈfrɪzi/ adj (of hair) having small tight curls

fro /frəʊ/ adv [IDM] to and fro → TO³

frog /frɒɡ/ n small cold-blooded jumping animal that lives in water and on land ■ **frogman** n (pl -men) (GB) person who works underwater, wearing a rubber suit and breathing apparatus

frolic /ˈfrɒlɪk/ v (pt, pp ~ked) [I] play about in a lively way

from /frəm; strong form frɒm/ prep 1 used to show where sb/sth starts: *the train ~ Leeds* 2 used to show when sth starts: *on holiday ~ 1 May* 3 used to show who sent or gave sth: *a letter ~ my brother* 4 used to show what the origin of sb/sth is: *quotations ~ Shakespeare* 5 used to show the material that sth is made of: *Wine is made ~ grapes.* 6 used to show the distance between two places: *10 miles ~ the sea* 7 used to show the range of sth: *Tickets cost ~ £3 to £12.* 8 used to show change: *~ bad to worse* 9 used to show that sb/sth is separated or removed: *take the money ~ my purse* 10 used to show that sth is prevented: *save a boy ~ drowning* 11 used to show the reason for sth: *She felt sick ~ tiredness.* 12 used to show the reason for making a judgement: *reach a decision ~ the evidence*

front /frʌnt/ n 1 (usu the front) [C, sing] part or side of sth that faces forward: *the ~ of a building* 2 [sing] the part of sb's body that faces forward; the chest: *Lie on your ~.* 3 (the front) [sing] (GB) road beside the sea 4 (the front) [C,usu sing] (in war) area where fighting takes place 5 [C] particular area of activity: *on the financial ~* 6 [sing] (often fake) behaviour: *put on a brave ~* 7 [C,usu sing] ~ (for) person or organization that hides an illegal or secret activity 8 [C] line where cold air meets warm air [IDM] **in front** in the most forward position; ahead **in front of 1** ahead of sth 2 in the presence of sb ● **front** v [I, T] have the front facing sb: *hotels that ~ onto the sea* ■ **frontage** /ˈfrʌntɪdʒ/ n [U] extent of a piece of land or building along its front ▶ **frontal** adj of, from or in the front ■ **the front line** n [sing] line of fighting that is nearest the enemy ■ **front-page** adj appearing on the front page of a newspaper

frontier /ˈfrʌntɪə(r)/ n [C] 1 (land near) the border between two countries 2 [pl] extreme limit: *the ~s of science*

frost /frɒst/ n 1 [C,U] (period of) weather with the temperature below freezing point 2 [U] thin white layer of ice on the ground ● **frost** v 1 [I, T] **~over/up** (cause sth to) become covered with frost(2)

2 [T] give a rough surface to glass to make it opaque: *~ed windows* **3** [T] (*esp US*) cover a cake with powdered sugar ■ **'frostbite** n [U] injury to the fingers, toes, etc caused by extreme cold ► **'frostbitten** adj ► **frosty** adj (**-ier, -iest**) **1** cold with frost **2** unfriendly: *a ~y welcome*

froth /frɒθ/ n [U] **1** mass of small bubbles, eg on beer **2** (*disapprov*) light but worthless talk, ideas, etc ● **froth** v [I] have or produce froth ► **frothy** adj (**-ier, -iest**) like or covered with froth

frown /fraʊn/ v [I] bring your eyebrows together to express anger, thought, etc [PV] **frown on/upon sth** disapprove of sth ► **frown** n

froze pt of FREEZE

frozen pp of FREEZE

frugal /'fruːgl/ adj **1** not wasteful; economical **2** costing little; small

fruit /fruːt/ n **1** [C, U] part of a plant used as food, eg apple, banana **2** [C] (*tech*) part of a plant or tree which contains the seeds [IDM] **the fruit/fruits of sth** good results of hard work, etc ► **fruitful** adj producing useful results ► **fruitless** adj producing no useful results ► **fruity** adj (**-ier, -iest**) **1** of or like fruit **2** (*infml*) (of the voice) rich and deep

fruition /fru'ɪʃn/ n [U] (*fml*) successful result of a plan, process or activity: *Our plans finally came to ~.*

frustrate /frʌ'streɪt/ v [T] **1** make sb feel annoyed because they cannot achieve what they want **2** prevent sb from doing sth or sth from happening ► **frustrated** adj annoyed; not satisfied ► **frustration** /frʌ'streɪʃn/ n [U, C]

fry /fraɪ/ v (pt, pp **fried** /fraɪd/) [I, T] cook sth in hot fat or oil ■ **'frying pan** (US **frypan**) n shallow pan used for frying food [IDM] **out of the frying pan into the fire** from a bad situation to a worse one

ft (*also* **ft.**) abbr feet; foot

fuck /fʌk/ v [I, T] (△, sl) **1** have sex with sb **2** offensive swear word used to show anger or surprise [PV] **fuck off** go away ● **fuck** n (△, sl) act of having sex ■ **fuck 'all** n (△, sl) nothing ► **fucking** adj, adv (△, sl) offensive swear word used to emphasize a comment or remark

fudge /fʌdʒ/ n [U] soft brown sweet made of sugar, butter, milk, etc ● **fudge** v [T] (*infml*) avoid giving clear information or a clear answer

fuel /'fjuːəl/ n [U] material, eg coal or oil, burned to produce heat or power ● **fuel** v (**-ll-** *US* **-l-**) [T] **1** supply sth with fuel **2** make a

situation worse: *to ~ inflation* ■ **'fuel injection** n [U] system of putting fuel into a car engine under pressure so as to improve its performance

fugitive /'fjuːdʒətɪv/ n ~(**from**) person who is escaping from sth

fulfil (*US* **fulfill**) /fʊl'fɪl/ v (**-ll-**) [T] **1** do or achieve what was hoped for, expected or required: *~ an ambition* ◇ *~ a duty/promise* **2** make sb feel happy and satisfied with what they are doing or have done ► **fulfilment** n [U]

full /fʊl/ adj **1** holding as much or as many as possible: *a ~ bottle* **2** ~**of** thinking or talking a lot about sth: (*disapprov*) *He's ~ of himself* (= thinking only of himself). **3** having eaten enough **4** complete: *give ~ details* ◇ *Write your name in ~.* **5** to the highest level or greatest amount possible: *He came round the corner at ~ speed.* ◇ *enjoy life to the ~* **6** plump: *a ~ figure/face* **7** (of clothes) wide and loose: *a ~ skirt* ● **full** adv **1** exactly; directly: *hit him ~ in the face* **2** very: *You knew ~ well that he was lying.* ■ **,full 'board** n [U] hotel accommodation with all meals included ■ **,full-length** adj **1** (of a picture, mirror, etc) showing the whole of a person **2** (of clothing) reaching the ankles ■ **,full 'moon** n [C, usu sing] the moon appearing as a complete circle ► **fullness** n [U] ■ **,full-'scale** adj **1** (of drawings, plans, etc) of the same size as the object itself **2** complete: *a ~scale inquiry* ■ **,full 'stop** n (*GB*) mark (.) used esp at the end of a sentence [IDM] **come to a full stop** stop completely ■ **,full-'time** adj, adv working all the normal hours ► **fully** adv completely

fumble /'fʌmbl/ v [I] use your hands awkwardly

fume /fjuːm/ n [C, usu pl] strong-smelling smoke or gas ● **fume** v [I] **1** be very angry about sth **2** give off fumes

fun /fʌn/ n [U] **1** (source of) enjoyment; pleasure **2** playfulness [IDM] **for fun** for amusement **in fun** not seriously **make fun of sb/sth** laugh at sb/sth unkindly ■ **'funfair** n = FAIR²(1)

function /'fʌŋkʃn/ n **1** purpose of a thing or person **2** formal social event **3** (*computing*) part of a program, etc that carries out a basic operation ● **function** v [I] work in the correct way ► **functional** /-ʃənl/ adj **1** having a practical use, not decorative **2** working; able to work ► **functionality** /ˌfʌŋkʃə'næləti/ n **1** [U] quality in sth of being very suitable for the purpose it was designed for **2** [U,C] (*computing*) range of functions that a computer or other electronic system can perform

fund /fʌnd/ n **1** amount of money for a purpose **2** supply of sth: *a large ~ of experience* ● **fund** v [T] provide money for sth

fundamental /ˌfʌndəˈmentl/ adj very important; basic or essential ● **fundamental** n [C, usu pl] basic rule or principle ▶ **fundamentalism** /-təlɪzəm/ n [U] **1** practice of following very strictly the rules of any religion **2** (in Christianity) belief that everything written in the Bible is true ▶ **fundamentalist** n, adj ▶ **fundamentally** /-təli/ adv

funeral /ˈfjuːnərəl/ n ceremony of burying or cremating (= burning) a dead person ■ **'funeral parlour** n (GB) place where dead people are prepared for the funeral and where visitors can see the body

fungus /ˈfʌŋgəs/ n [C, U] (pl fungi /ˈfʌŋgiː, -gaɪ/) plant without leaves that grows on decaying matter, eg old wood

funnel /ˈfʌnl/ n **1** tube that is wide at the top and narrow at the bottom, used for pouring liquids through **2** chimney on a steam engine or ship ● **funnel** v (-ll- US -l-) [I, T] pour sth through a funnel or narrow space

funny /ˈfʌni/ adj (-ier, -iest) **1** causing laughter; amusing **2** strange ▶ **funnily** adv ■ **'funny bone** n sensitive part of the elbow

fur /fɜː(r)/ n **1** [U] soft thick hair covering a cat, rabbit, etc **2** [C] (coat, etc made from an) animal skin with the fur on it **3** [U] hard grey covering on the inside of kettles, pipes, etc ▶ **furry** adj (-ier, -iest) of, like or covered with fur

furious /ˈfjʊəriəs/ adj **1** very angry **2** very strong; wild: *a ~ storm* ▶ **furiously** adv

furlong /ˈfɜːlɒŋ/ n distance of 220 yards (201 metres)

furnace /ˈfɜːnɪs/ n enclosed fireplace used eg for heating metals

furnish /ˈfɜːnɪʃ/ v [T] **1** put furniture in a room, etc **2** (fml) provide sb/sth with sth ▶ **furnishings** n [pl] furniture, carpets, curtains, etc in a room or house

furniture /ˈfɜːnɪtʃə(r)/ n [U] large movable things, eg tables, chairs, etc in a house or office

furrier /ˈfʌriə(r)/ n person who prepares or sells fur clothing

furrow /ˈfʌrəʊ/ n **1** long mark cut into the ground by a plough **2** deep line in the skin of the face ● **furrow** v [T] make furrows in sth

furry → FUR

further /ˈfɜːðə(r)/ adv **1** at or to a

greater distance in space or time: *It's not safe to go any ~.* **2** to a greater degree or extent **3** in addition ● **further** adj more; additional: *~ information* ● **further** v [T] help sb/sth to advance ▶ **furtherance** n [U] (fml) advancement ■ **ˌfurther eduˈcation** n [U] (abbr FE) (GB) formal (but not university) education for people older than 16 ▶ **furthermore** adv (fml) in addition ▶ **furthermost** adj most distant

furthest /ˈfɜːðɪst/ superlative of FAR

furtive /ˈfɜːtɪv/ adj done or behaving secretly so as not to be noticed ▶ **furtively** adv ▶ **furtiveness** n [U]

fury /ˈfjʊəri/ n [U, C] violent anger

fuse /fjuːz/ n **1** short wire in an electrical appliance that melts to break the circuit if the current is too strong **2** long piece of string or paper which is lit to make a bomb or firework explode **3** (US also **fuze**) device in a bomb that makes it explode ● **fuse** v [I, T] **1** (cause two things to) join together to form a single thing **2** (GB) (cause sth to) stop working because a fuse melts: *~ the lights*

fuselage /ˈfjuːzəlɑːʒ/ n body of an aircraft

fusion /ˈfjuːʒn/ n [C, U] mixing or joining of different things into one

fuss /fʌs/ n [U, sing] unnecessary excitement, worry or activity [IDM] **make a fuss of/over sb** pay a lot of loving attention to sb ● **fuss** v [I] be worried or excited esp about small things ▶ **fussy** adj (-ier, -iest) **1** ~ (about) too concerned about unimportant details **2** showing nervous excitement **3** (of dress or style) decorated too much ▶ **fussily** adv

futile /ˈfjuːtaɪl/ adj useless; unsuccessful ▶ **futility** /fjuːˈtɪləti/ n [U]

future /ˈfjuːtʃə(r)/ n **1** (**the future**) [sing] the time that will come after the present: *in the ~* **2** [C] what will happen to sb/sth: *The company's ~ is uncertain* **3** [U] possibility of success: *There is no ~ in this job.* **4** (**futures**) [pl] (business) goods or shares bought at agreed prices but to be delivered and paid for later **5** (**the future**) (also **the ˌfuture ˈtense**) [sing] (gram) form of a verb that expresses what will happen after the present [IDM] **in future** from now onwards ● **future** adj of or happening in the future

futuristic /ˌfjuːtʃəˈrɪstɪk/ adj looking very modern and strange

fuzz /fʌz/ n [U] fluff ▶ **fuzzy** adj (-ier, -iest) **1** (of hair) tightly curled **2** (of cloth, etc) soft or fluffy **3** not clear in shape or sound ▶ **fuzzily** adv ▶ **fuzziness** n [U]

FYI *abbr* used in writing to mean 'for your information'

G g

G, g /dʒiː/ n [C,U] (pl **G's, g's** /dʒiːz/) the seventh letter of the English alphabet

g *abbr* gram(s): *500g*

gabble /'gæbl/ v [I, T] talk or say sth too quickly to be understood ● **gabble** n [U] very fast talk

gable /'geɪbl/ n triangular part of an outside wall, between the two sloping sides of the roof

gad /gæd/ v (-dd-) [PV] **gad about/ around** (*infml*) visit different places and have fun

gadget /'gædʒɪt/ n small useful tool or device ► **gadgetry** n [U] gadgets

Gaelic n [U] *adj* **1** /'geɪlɪk/ (language) of the Celtic people of Ireland **2** /'gælɪk; 'geɪlɪk/ (language) of the Celtic people of Scotland

gaffe /gæf/ n tactless remark or act

gag /gæg/ n **1** something put over sb's mouth to prevent them from speaking **2** joke ● **gag** v (-gg-) [T] put a gag(1) on sb

gaga /'gɑːgɑː/ *adj* (*infml*) senile

gage (*US*) = GAUGE

gaggle /'gægl/ n **1** group of geese **2** group of noisy people

gaily /'geɪli/ *adv* happily; cheerfully

gain /geɪn/ v [I, T] **1** obtain sth wanted or needed: *experience an advantage* **2** increase in speed, weight, etc **3** (of a clock or watch) go too fast: *My watch ~s two minutes a day.* [IDM] **gain ground** → GROUND¹ **gain time** obtain extra time by making excuses, talking slowly, etc [PV] **gain on sb/sth** come closer to sb/sth, eg in a race ● **gain** n [C,U] increase in amount or wealth; advantage ► **gainful** /-fl/ *adj* useful work that you are paid for: *~ful employment*

gait /geɪt/ n way of walking

gala /'gɑːlə/ n special public celebration or entertainment

galaxy /'gæləksi/ n (pl **-ies**) **1** [C] large group of stars **2** (**the Galaxy**) [sing] the system of stars that contains our sun and many planets, seen as a pale band in the sky **3** [C] (*infml*) group of people ► **galactic** /gə'læktɪk/ *adj*

gale /geɪl/ n **1** very strong wind **2** noisy outburst of laughter

gall¹ /gɔːl/ n [U] **1** rude behaviour showing lack of respect **2** (*fml*) bitter feeling of hatred ● **gall bladder** n organ attached to the liver that

stores bile ■ **gallstone** n hard painful mass that can form in the gall bladder

gall² /gɔːl/ v [T] annoy sb

gallant /'gælənt/ *adj* **1** (*old-fash* or *lit*) brave **2** (of a man) giving polite attention to women ► **gallantly** *adv* ► **gallantry** n [U]

galleon /'gælian/ n Spanish sailing ship (15th to 17th centuries)

gallery /'gæləri/ n (pl **-ies**) **1** room or building for showing works of art **2** raised area along an inner wall of a hall or church **3** highest seats in a theatre **4** passage in a mine

galley /'gæli/ n **1** (in the past) long flat ship with sails and oars **2** kitchen on a ship or plane

gallivant /'gælɪvænt/ v [PV] **gallivant about/around** (*old-fash*, *infml*) travel for pleasure

gallon /'gælən/ n measure for liquids equal to 4.5 litres in the UK and 3.8 litres in the US

gallop /'gæləp/ n fastest pace of a horse: *at full ~* ● **gallop** v **1** [I, T] (cause a horse to) go at a gallop **2** [I] (*infml*) hurry

gallows /'gæləʊz/ n structure on which people, eg criminals are killed by hanging

galore /gə'lɔː(r)/ *adv* (*infml*) in large quantities: *prizes ~*

galvanize (*also* **-ise**) /'gælvənaɪz/ v [T] **1** ~ (**into**) shock sb into taking action **2** (*tech*) cover iron with zinc to protect it from rust

gambit /'gæmbɪt/ n **1** thing said or done at the beginning of a conversation, etc, intended to give some advantage **2** opening move in chess, to produce an advantage later

gamble /'gæmbl/ v [I] play games of chance for money [PV] **gamble on sth** take a risk with sth ● **gamble** n risky attempt to win money or to be successful ► **gambler** n person who gambles ► **gambling** n [U]

gambol /'gæmbl/ v (-ll- *US also* -l-) [I] jump about playfully

game /geɪm/ n **1** [C] form of play or sport with rules **2** (**games**) [pl] sports, esp athletics competitions **3** [C] single part of a match in tennis, etc **4** [C] children's activity when they play with toys, pretend to be sb else, etc **5** [C] activity or business: *Politics is a power ~.* **6** [C] (*infml*) secret plan or trick **7** [U] (flesh of) animals or birds hunted for sport or food [IDM] **give the game away** carelessly reveal a secret ■ **gamekeeper** n man employed to breed and protect game(7), eg pheasants ● **game** adj willing to do sth risky ▸ **gamely** adv

gammon /ˈgæmən/ n [U] smoked or cured ham

gamut /ˈgæmət/ n (**the gamut**) [sing] complete range of sth

gander /ˈgændə(r)/ n male goose

gang /gæŋ/ n [C, with sing or pl verb] 1 organized group of criminals or workers 2 group of young people, usu males, who often fight against other groups: *a street* ~ ▸ **gang** v [PV] **gang up (on/against sb)** (*infml*) join together to hurt or frighten sb

gangling /ˈgæŋglɪŋ/ adj (of a person) tall, thin and awkward

gangrene /ˈgæŋgriːn/ n [U] decay of a part of the body because blood has stopped flowing to it ▸ **gangrenous** /ˈgæŋgrɪnəs/ adj

gangster /ˈgæŋstə(r)/ n member of a gang of armed criminals

gangway /ˈgæŋweɪ/ n 1 movable bridge from a ship to the land 2 passage between rows of seats

gaol (GB) = JAIL

gap /gæp/ n 1 empty space in sth or between two things 2 period of time when sth stops or between two things: *between school and university* 3 space where sth is missing: ~s *in your knowledge*

gape /geɪp/ v [I] 1 stare at sb/sth with your mouth open, usu in surprise 2 be or become wide open: *a gaping hole* ▸ **gape** n

garage /ˈgærɑːʒ; -rɑːdʒ; -rɪdʒ/ n 1 building in which a car is kept 2 place where cars are repaired ● **garage** v [T] put or keep a vehicle in a garage

garbage /ˈgɑːbɪdʒ/ n [U] (*esp US*) rubbish ▪ **garbage can** n (US) = DUSTBIN

garbled /ˈgɑːbld/ adj incomplete and confused: *a* ~ *message*

garden /ˈgɑːdn/ n 1 [C, U] piece of land next to or around your house used for growing flowers, vegetables, etc 2 (usu **gardens**) [pl] public park ● **garden** v [I] work in a garden ▪ **garden centre** n (GB) place that sells plants, seeds, garden equipment, etc ▸ **gardener** n person who works in a garden ▸ **gardening** n [U] ▪ **garden party** n formal social party in a garden

gargle /ˈgɑːgl/ v [I] wash the throat with liquid without swallowing ● **gargle** n 1 [C, U] liquid used for gargling 2 [sing] act of gargling

gargoyle /ˈgɑːgɔɪl/ n stone figure of an ugly creature on the roof of a church, etc, through which rainwater is carried away

garish /ˈgeərɪʃ/ adj unpleasantly bright ▸ **garishly** adv

garland /ˈgɑːlənd/ n circle of flowers or leaves as a decoration ● **garland** v [T] (*lit*) decorate sb/sth with a garland

garlic /ˈgɑːlɪk/ n [U] strong-smelling plant of the onion family, used in cooking

garment /ˈgɑːmənt/ n (*fml*) piece of clothing

garnish /ˈgɑːnɪʃ/ v [T] decorate a dish of food with a small amount of another food ● **garnish** n small amount of food used to decorate a larger dish

garret /ˈgærət/ n small room at the top of a house

garrison /ˈgærɪsn/ n [C, with sing or pl verb] group of soldiers living in a town or fort ● **garrison** v [T] defend a place with a garrison

garrulous /ˈgærələs/ adj (*fml*) talking too much

garter /ˈgɑːtə(r)/ n elastic band worn round the leg to keep up a sock or stocking

gas /gæs/ n (pl **~es** US also **~ses**) 1 [C, U] substance like air 2 [U] gas used for heating, cooking, etc 3 [U] (US) = PETROL ● **gas** v (**-ss-**) [T] kill sb with gas ▸ **gaseous** /ˈgæsiəs; ˈgeɪsiəs/ adj of or like gas ▪ **gaslight** n [C, U] light from burning gas ▪ **gasman** n (pl **-men**) (*infml*) official who reads gas meters and checks gas heaters, etc ▪ **gas mask** n breathing apparatus to protect the wearer against poisonous gas ▪ **gas station** n (US) = PETROL STATION (PETROL) ▸ **gassy** adj (**-ier, -iest**) of or like gas; full of gas: ~*y beer* ▪ **gasworks** n (pl **gasworks**) factory where coal is made into gas

gash /gæʃ/ n ~(**in**) long deep cut ● **gash** v [T] make a gash in sth

gasket /ˈgæskɪt/ n soft flat piece of material between two metal surfaces to prevent oil, steam, etc from escaping

gasoline (also **gasolene**) /ˈgæsəliːn/ n [U] (US) = PETROL

gasp /gɑːsp/ v 1 [I] breathe in quickly, because of surprise, pain, etc 2 [I, T] have difficulty breathing or speaking ● **gasp** n quick deep breath

gastric /ˈgæstrɪk/ adj of the stomach: ~ *ulcers*

gastro-enteritis /ˌgæstrəʊ ˌentəˈraɪtɪs/ n [U] (*med*) illness of the stomach that causes diarrhoea and vomiting

gate /geɪt/ n 1 [C] movable barrier that closes an opening in a wall, fence, etc 2 [C] way out from an airport building to a plane 3 [C, U] (money paid by) number of people attending a sports event

■ 'gatecrash v [I, T] go to a party without being invited ▶ 'gate-crasher n ■ 'gatepost n post on which a gate is hung ▶ 'gateway n [C] 1 opening with a gate 2 [usu sing] ~ to means of reaching sth: the ~way to success 3 (computing) device connecting two computer networks that cannot be connected in any other way

gateau /'gætəʊ/ n [C,U] (pl ~x or ~s) large rich cream cake

gather /'gæðə(r)/ v 1 [I, T] come or bring people or things together to form a group 2 [T] pick flowers, fruit, etc; cut and collect crops 3 [T] understand or believe sth: I ~ she's looking for a job. 4 [T] collect information from different sources 5 [T] increase in speed, force, etc 6 [T] pull a piece of clothing together in folds ▶ **gathering** n meeting

gauche /ɡəʊʃ/ adj socially awkward

gaudy /'ɡɔːdi/ adj (-ier, -iest) (disapprov) too bright and showy ▶ **gaudily** adv

gauge (US also **gage**) /ɡeɪdʒ/ n 1 instrument for measuring sth: a petrol ~ 2 measurement of the thickness of sth, esp sheet of metal or wire 3 distance between the rails on a railway 4 means of comparison; indication of: a ~ of her progress ● **gauge** v [T] 1 make a judgement about sth, esp people's feelings or attitudes 2 measure sth accurately 3 estimate sth

gaunt /ɡɔːnt/ adj (of a person) very thin, as from illness or hunger ▶ **gauntness** n [U]

gauntlet /'ɡɔːntlət/ n 1 strong glove with a wide covering for the wrist

gauze /ɡɔːz/ n [U] thin net material, used esp on wounds

gave pt of GIVE¹

gawky /'ɡɔːki/ adj (-ier, -iest) (esp of a tall young person) awkward and clumsy: a ~ teenager ▶ **gawkiness** n [U]

gawp /ɡɔːp/ v [I] (infml) stare rudely or stupidly at sb/sth

gay /ɡeɪ/ adj 1 homosexual 2 (old-fash) happy; cheerful ● **gay** n homosexual person

gaze /ɡeɪz/ v [I] ~(at) look steadily at sb/sth for a long time ● **gaze** n [sing] long steady look

gazelle /ɡə'zel/ n small graceful antelope (= an African animal like a deer)

gazette /ɡə'zet/ n official newspaper with legal notices, news, etc

gazump /ɡə'zʌmp/ v (GB, infml, disapprov) (usu passive) increase the price of a house after accepting an offer from a buyer

GB /ˌdʒiː 'biː/ abbr Great Britain

GCSE /ˌdʒiː siː es 'iː/ n (GB) General Certificate of Secondary Education; examination in a particular subject taken by school pupils aged about 16

GDP /ˌdʒiː diː 'piː/ abbr gross domestic product; total value of all the goods and services produced in a country in one year

gear /ɡɪə(r)/ n 1 [C,U] set of toothed wheels working together in a machine: The car has five ~s. ◇ change ~ 2 [U] equipment: camping ~ 3 [U] apparatus of wheels, levers, etc: the landing ~ of an aircraft ● **gear** v [PV] **gear sth to/towards sth** adapt or organize sth for a particular need: The whole city is ~ed to the needs of tourists. **gear (sb) up** (for/to sth) become or make sb ready for sth ■ '**gearbox** n case that contains the gears of a car or machine ■ 'gear lever (US 'gear shift) n handle used for changing gear(1)

geese plural of GOOSE

gelatin /'dʒelətɪn/ (also **gelatine** /'dʒelətiːn/) n [U] clear tasteless substance, used for making jelly

gelding /'ɡeldɪŋ/ n male horse whose sexual organs have been removed

gelignite /'dʒelɪɡnaɪt/ n [U] powerful explosive

gem /dʒem/ n 1 jewel 2 person, place or thing that is especially good

gender /'dʒendə(r)/ n [C,U] 1 fact of being male or female 2 (gram) grouping of nouns and pronouns into masculine, feminine and neuter

gene /dʒiːn/ n (biol) unit in a cell that controls a particular quality in a living thing that has been passed on from its parents

genealogy /ˌdʒiːni'ælədʒi/ n (pl -ies) 1 [U] study of family history 2 [C] diagram showing the history of a family ▶ **genealogical** /ˌdʒiːniə'lɒdʒɪkl/ adj

general /'dʒenrəl/ adj 1 affecting all or most people, places or things: of ~ interest ◇ a ~ strike 2 not exact or detailed: ~ impressions 3 not limited to a particular subject or use or to just one part or aspect of sb/sth: ~ knowledge ◇ a ~ anaesthetic 4 (in titles) chief [IDM] in general usually; mainly ● **general** n army officer of very high rank ■ **general e'lection** n election in which all the people of a country vote to choose a government ▶ **generality** /ˌdʒenə'ræləti/ n (pl -ies) 1 [C] general statement 2 [U] quality of being general ▶ **generally** adv 1 by or to most people: The plan was ~ly welcomed. 2 usually; in most cases: I ~ly get up early. 3 without discussing the details of sth: *~ly speaking* ■ ,general prac'titioner (*abbr* **GP**) *n* (*esp GB*) doctor trained in general medicine who treats patients in the local community rather than at a hospital

generalize (*also* **-ise**) /'dʒenrəlaɪz/ *v* [I] make a general statement about sth ▶ **generalization** (*also* **-isation**) /,dʒenrəlaɪ'zeɪʃn/ *n* [C,U] (statement based on) generalizing

generate /'dʒenəreɪt/ *v* [T] produce sth: *~ electricity* ▶ **generative** /'dʒenərətɪv/ *adj* (*fml*) able to produce sth ■ **generator** *n* machine that generates electricity

generation /,dʒenə'reɪʃn/ *n* [C] **1** all the people born at about the same time **2** [C] single stage in a family history **3** [U] act of generating sth

generic /dʒə'nerɪk/ *adj* shared by a whole group; not specific ▶ **generically** /-kli/ *adv*

generous /'dʒenərəs/ *adj* **1** giving freely; kind: *He's ~ with his money.* **2** larger than normal: *a ~ helping of food* ▶ **generosity** /,dʒenə'rɒsəti/ *n* [U] ▶ **generously** *adv*

genetic /dʒə'netɪk/ *adj* of genes or genetics ▶ **genetically** /-kli/ *adv* ■ ge,netically 'modified *adj* (*abbr* **GM**) (of food, plants, etc) grown from cells whose genes have been changed artificially ■ ge,netic engi'neering *n* [U] science of changing the way a human, an animal or a plant develops by changing the information in its genes ▶ **genetics** *n* [U] study of how characteristics are passed from one generation to the next

genial /'dʒiːniəl/ *adj* kind and pleasant ▶ **genially** *adv*

genie /'dʒiːni/ *n* (in stories) spirit with magic powers, esp one that lives in a bottle or a lamp

genital /'dʒenɪtl/ *adj* of the reproductive organs of people or animals ▶ **genitals** (*also* **genitalia** /,dʒenɪ'teɪliə/) *n* [pl] (*anat*) person's external sex organs

genius /'dʒiːniəs/ *n* **1** [U] very great intelligence or artistic ability **2** [C] unusually intelligent or artistic person **3** [sing] special skill or ability: *have a ~ for languages*

genocide /'dʒenəsaɪd/ *n* [U] killing of a whole race or group of people

genome /'dʒiːnəʊm/ *n* (*biol*) complete set of genes in a cell or living thing: *the human ~*

genre /'ʒɒnrə/ *n* (*fml*) particular style or type of literature, art, film or music

gent /dʒent/ *n* (*GB*) **1** [C] (*old-fash* or *hum*) gentleman **2** (a/the Gents) [sing] (*infml*) public toilet for men

genteel /dʒen'tiːl/ *adj* quiet and polite, esp in an exaggerated way

gentile /'dʒentaɪl/ *n, adj* (person who is) not Jewish

gentle /'dʒentl/ *adj* (*~r* /-lə(r)/ *~st* /-lɪst/) not rough or violent ▶ **gentleness** *n* [U] ▶ **gently** /-li/ *adv*

gentleman /'dʒentlmən/ *n* [C] (*pl* **-men** /-mən/) **1** [C] man who is polite and behaves well **2** [C, *usu pl*] (*fml*) used to address or refer to a man, esp one you do not know: *Ladies and ~men ...* **3** (*old-fash*) man of wealth and social position ▶ **gentlemanly** *adv* (*fml or old-fash*) behaving like a gentleman(1)

genuine /'dʒenjuɪn/ *adj* real; true ▶ **genuinely** *adv* ▶ **genuineness** *n* [U]

genus /'dʒiːnəs/ *n* (*pl* **genera** /'dʒenərə/) (*biol*) division of animals or plants within a family(5)

geography /dʒi'ɒɡrəfi/ *n* [U] **1** study of the earth's surface, climate, countries, population, etc **2** arrangement of features in a particular region ▶ **geographer** /-fə(r)/ *n* expert in geography ▶ **geographical** /,dʒiːə'ɡræfɪkl/ *adj* ▶ **geographically** /-kli/ *adv*

geology /dʒi'ɒlədʒi/ *n* [U] **1** scientific study of the earth's rocks, crust, etc **2** [sing] structure of rocks, etc, in a particular region ▶ **geological** /,dʒiːə'lɒdʒɪkl/ *adj* ▶ **geologically** /-kli/ *adv* ▶ **geologist** /dʒi'ɒlədʒɪst/ *n* expert in geology

geometry /dʒi'ɒmətri/ *n* [U] study of lines, angles and figures and their relationships ▶ **geometric** /,dʒiːə'metrɪk/ (*also* geometrical) *adj*

geranium /dʒə'reɪniəm/ *n* garden plant with red, pink or white flowers

geriatrics /,dʒeri'ætrɪks/ *n* [U] branch of medicine concerned with the care of old people ▶ **geriatric** *adj*

germ /dʒɜːm/ *n* **1** [C, *usu pl*] very small living thing that can cause disease **2** [*sing*] **~of** beginning: *the ~ of an idea*

German /'dʒɜːmən/ *adj* of Germany, its people or their language ▶ ,German 'measles *n* [U] mild infectious disease causing red spots all over the body

germinate /'dʒɜːmɪneɪt/ *v* [I, T] (cause seeds to) start growing ▶ **germination** /,dʒɜːmɪ'neɪʃn/ *n* [U]

gerund /'dʒerənd/ *n* the *-ing* form of a verb when used as a noun (as in 'fond of *swimming*')

gestation /dʒe'steɪʃn/ *n* [U, *sing*] process or period of a baby or young animal being carried in the womb

gesticulate /dʒe'stɪkjuleɪt/ *v* [I] (*fml*) move your hands and arms about to express yourself ▶ **gesticulation** /dʒe.stɪkjuˈleɪʃn/ *n* [C,U]

gesture /ˈdʒestʃə(r)/ *n* **1** [C,U] movement of the hand or head to show an idea, feeling, etc **2** [C] action done to show a particular feeling or intention: *a ~ of support/defiance*

get /get/ *v* (**-tt-** *pt, pp* **got** /gɒt/, *US pp* **gotten** /ˈgɒtn/) **1** [T] receive sth: *~ a letter* **2** [T] obtain sth: *~ a new car* **3** [T] fetch sth: *G~ your coat.* **4** [T] receive sth as a punishment: *~ six months* (= six months in prison) **5** [T] (begin to) suffer from an illness, etc: *~ flu/a headache* **6** [I, T] (cause sb/sth/yourself to) reach a particular state or condition: *~ wet/dressed* ◇ *~ the children ready for school* ◇ *~ your hair cut* ◇ *He got* (= was) *killed in a car accident.* **7** [I] reach the point at which you feel, know, are etc sth: *~ to know someone* **8** [T] make or persuade sb/sth to do sth: *I can't ~ her to understand.* ◇ *He got me to help him with his homework.* **9** [I] start doing sth: *We soon got talking.* **10** [I] arrive at or reach a place or point: *~ home early* ◇ *What time did you ~ to London?* **11** [I, T] (cause sb/sth to) move somewhere, sometimes with difficulty: *~ off the bus* ◇ *We can't ~ the piano downstairs.* ◇ *~ a message to sb* **12** [T] use a bus, train, etc: *~ a plane to Rome* **13** [T] prepare a meal **14** [T] (*spoken*) answer the telephone or a door when sb calls, knocks, etc: *Can you ~ the phone?* **15** [T] catch sb, esp in order to harm or punish them: *The police got the robber.* ◇ *I'll ~ you for that!* **16** [T] kill or wound sb: *The bullet got him in the neck.* **17** [T] (*infml*) understand sb/sth: *I don't ~ you.* ◇ *She didn't ~ the joke.* **18** [T] (*spoken*) confuse or puzzle sb: *That's got you!* **19** [T] (*spoken*) annoy sb: *What ~s me is having to listen to his problems all the time.* **IDM** **get (sb) anywhere/somewhere/nowhere** (*infml*) (cause sb to) achieve something/nothing: *I tried to persuade him but I got nowhere* (= I failed). **get to grips with sth** ⇒ GRIP **[PV]** **get (sth) across (to sb)** (cause sth to) be communicated or understood by others: *I tried to get this idea ~ to your work.* **get ahead (of sb)** make progress (further than others have done) **get along (with sb)** = GET ON (WITH SB) **get along with sth** = GET ON WITH STH **get at sb** (*infml*) criticize sb: *Stop ~ting at me!* **get at sth 1** reach or gain access to sth **2** learn or find out sth: *~ at the truth* **3** (only in the continuous tenses) suggest sth indirectly: *What are you ~ting at?* **get away 1** have a holiday: *~ away for two weeks in France* **2** (*from …*) escape from sth or a place: *Two prisoners got away.* **get away with sth 1** steal and

escape with it **2** receive a relatively light punishment: *to ~ away with just a fine* **3** do sth wrong and receive no punishment: *~ away with murder* **get by (on/in/with sth)** survive: *~ by on a small salary* **get sb down** (*infml*) make sb feel depressed **get sth down** swallow sth with difficulty **get down to sth** begin to do sth seriously: *~ down to work/business* **get in|get into sth** arrive at a place: *The train got in late.* **get sb in** call sb to your house to do a job: *~ someone in to fix the TV* **get sth in 1** collect or gather sth **2** buy a supply of sth: *~ some coal in for the winter* **3** manage to do or say sth: *He talks so much I can't ~ a word in.* **get in with sb** (*infml*) become friendly with sb, usu to gain an advantage **get into sth 1** put on a piece of clothing, esp with difficulty **2** start a career in a particular profession: *~ into journalism* **3** become involved in sth; start sth: *~ into a fight* ◇ *~ into conversation with sb* **4** develop a habit: *~ into the habit of going to bed early* ◇ *Don't ~ into drugs* (= Don't start taking them!) **5** (*infml*) become interested in sth: *I can't ~ into this book.* **get (yourself/sb) into sth** (cause yourself/sb) to reach a particular state or condition: *~ into trouble/difficulties* **get off (sb/sth)** used to tell sb to stop touching sb/sth: *get (sb) off* (help sb) leave a place or start a journey: *~ the children off to school* **get (sb) off (with sth)** (help sb to) receive little or no punishment: *She got off with just a fine.* **get on 1** progress or become successful in life, in a career, etc **2** (only in the continuous tenses) be getting old **3** (only in the continuous tenses) be getting late **get on/along (with sb)** have a friendly relationship with sb: *We don't ~ on.* ◇ *Do you ~ with your boss?* ◇ *We ~ along just fine.* **get on with sth** (*also* **get along with sth**) make progress: *How are you ~ting on with your new job?* **2** continue doing sth: *G~ on with your work.* **get out 1** become known: *The secret got out.* **2** (*of*) leave a place **get out of sth** avoid a responsibility or duty: *We can't ~ out of going to her wedding.* **get over sth 1** recover from an illness, a shock, the end of a relationship, etc **2** deal with or gain control of sth: *~ over your fears* **get sth over (to sb)** make sth clear to sb **get sth over** (*infml*) finish sth unpleasant: *I'm glad I've got my exams over with.* **get round/around sb** persuade sb to agree or do what you want, often by flattery, etc: *She knows how to ~ round her father.* **get round/around sth** deal with a

problem successfully **get round/ around to sth** find the time to do sth: *I didn't ~ round to phoning her.* **get through sth 1** use up a large amount of sth: *~ through £100 a week* **2** manage to do or complete sth **get through (sth)** (GB) be successful in an exam, etc **get through (to sb) 1** reach sb: *We must ~ the supplies through to the refugees.* **2** contact sb, esp by telephone **get (sth) through to sb** succeed in making sb understand sth: *I just can't ~ through to them (that this is wrong).* **get together (with sb)** meet sb socially or to discuss sth: *~ together and (get sb) up 1* (cause sb to) get out of bed 2 stand up after sitting, kneeling, etc **get up to sth 1** reach a particular point: *~ up to page ten* **2** be busy with sth, esp sth surprising or unpleasant: *What have the kids been ~ting up to?*
■ **'getaway** n escape: *a fast ~away*
■ **'get-together** n (old-fash, infml) informal social meeting ■ **,get-up-and-'go** n [U] (infml) energy and determination to get things done

geyser /'gi:zə(r)/ n natural spring sending up a column of hot water or steam

ghastly /'gɑːstli/ adj (-ier, -iest) **1** (of an event) causing horror: *a ~ accident* **2** (infml) very bad: *a ~ mistake* **3** very pale and ill

ghetto /'getəʊ/ n (pl ~s) area of a city where many people of the same race or background live, separately from the rest of the population. Ghettos are often crowded, with bad living conditions. ■ **'ghetto blaster** n (infml) large, powerful, portable radio and cassette player

ghost /gəʊst/ n **1** [C] spirit of a dead person that appears to sb living **2** [sing] very slight amount of sth that is left behind: *the ~ of a (= very little) chance* [IDM] **give up the ghost** die ▶ **ghostly** adj of or like a ghost ■ **'ghost town** n town that was once full of people but is now empty ■ **'ghostwriter** n person who writes material for sb else but does not use his/her own name

GI /ˌdʒiː 'aɪ/ n soldier in the US army

giant /'dʒaɪənt/ n (fem ~ess) (in stories) enormous and very strong person ▶ **giant** adj enormous

gibberish /'dʒɪbərɪʃ/ n [U] meaningless talk; nonsense

gibbon /'gɪbən/ n long-armed ape

gibe = JIBE

giblets /'dʒɪbləts/ n [pl] heart, liver, etc of a chicken or other bird, usu taken out before it is cooked

giddy /'gɪdi/ adj (-ier, -iest) feeling that everything is spinning around

and that you are going to fall ▶ **giddiness** n [U]

gift /gɪft/ n **1** something given freely; present **2** natural ability: *a ~ for languages* [IDM] **the gift of the gab** the ability to speak easily and persuasively ▶ **gifted** adj talented

gig /gɪg/ n live performance by pop or jazz musicians

gigantic /dʒaɪˈgæntɪk/ adj very big

giggle /'gɪgl/ v [I] ~(at) laugh in a silly way because you are amused, embarrassed, etc ● **giggle** n **1** [C] light silly laugh **2** [sing] (GB, infml) something done for amusement

gild /gɪld/ v [T] cover sth with gold leaf or gold paint

gill¹ /gɪl/ n [C, usu pl] organ through which a fish breathes

gill² /dʒɪl/ n measure for liquids; one quarter of a pint (0.142 litre)

gilt /gɪlt/ n [U] thin layer of gold that is used on a surface for decoration ■ **,gilt-edged** (business) very safe: *~-edged shares/stocks* (= investments considered very safe because they have been sold by the government)

gimmick /'gɪmɪk/ n often (disapprov) unusual trick or device used for attracting attention or persuading people to buy sth ▶ **gimmicky** adj

gin /dʒɪn/ n strong colourless alcoholic drink

ginger /'dʒɪndʒə(r)/ n [U] **1** root of the ginger plant used in cooking as a spice **2** orange-brown colour ■ **,ginger 'ale | ,ginger 'beer** n [U] non-alcoholic drink flavoured with ginger ■ **'gingerbread** n [U] sweet cake flavoured with ginger

gingerly /'dʒɪndʒəli/ adv with great care; hesitantly

gingham /'gɪŋəm/ n [U] cotton cloth with a pattern of squares or stripes

gipsy = GYPSY

giraffe /dʒəˈrɑːf/ n African animal with a very long neck and legs

girder /'gɜːdə(r)/ n long strong piece of iron or steel used for supporting a floor, roof, bridge, etc

girdle /'gɜːdl/ n piece of women's underwear that fits closely around the body from the waist to the thigh

girl /gɜːl/ n female child; daughter; young woman ▶ **'girlfriend** n **1** woman that sb is having a romantic relationship with **2** (esp US) woman's female friend ■ **Girl 'Guide** n = GUIDE(5) ▶ **girlish** adj of or like a girl ■ **Girl 'Scout** (US) = GUIDE(5)

giro /'dʒaɪrəʊ/ n (pl ~s) **1** [U,C] system for transferring money directly from one bank or post office account to another **2** [C] (GB) cheque issued by the government for a social security payment

girth /gɜːθ/ n 1 [C] measurement round sth, esp a person's waist 2 [C] leather strap fastened round the body of a horse to keep the saddle in place

gist /dʒɪst/ n (the gist) [sing] ~(of) general meaning or main points: get (= understand) the ~ of an argument

give¹ /ɡɪv/ v (pt gave /ɡeɪv/ pp given /ˈɡɪvn/) 1 [T] hand sth to sb so they can look at it, use it or keep it for a time: ~ her a cheque ◇ Have you been ~n the books you need? 2 [I, T] let sb have sth as a present: What did he ~ you for your birthday? ◇ They both ~ regularly to charity. 3 [T] provide sb with sth: They were thirsty so I gave them all a drink. ◇ I'll ~ you (= allow you to have) a week to decide. ◇ ~ an account of your journey 4 [T] ~ for pay money in exchange for sth: I gave her £500 for the car. 5 [T] ~to use time, energy, etc for sth sth: I gave the matter a lot of thought. 6 [T] make sb suffer a particular punishment: The judge gave him a suspended sentence. 7 [T] infect sb with an illness: You've ~n me your cold. 8 [T] provide a party, meal, etc as a host: ~ a dinner party 9 [T] perform sth in public: ~ a poetry reading 10 [T] used with a noun to describe an action, giving the same meaning as the related verb: She gave a smile (= smiled). ◇ ~ a cry ◇ He ~ her a kiss (= kissed her). ◇ ~ a wave 11 [I] bend or stretch under pressure: The plank gave a little when I stepped on it. [IDM] **give and take** be tolerant and willing to compromise: You have to ~ and take in a marriage. **give ground (to sb/sth)** → GROUND¹ **give or take (sth)** (infml) plus or minus: It takes an hour to get to Hastings, ~ or take a few minutes. [PV] **give sth away** give sth as a gift **give sth/sb away** betray sb or reveal a secret **give sb back sth| give sth back (to sb)** return sth to sb: ~ the book back (to him) ◇ ~ him back the book **give in (to sb/sth) 1** admit that you have been defeated by sb/sth **2** agree to do sth that you do not want to do **give sth off** produce sth, eg smoke, a smell, etc **give sth out 1** (of supplies, sb's strength, etc) come to an end **2** (of a motor, etc) stop working **give sth out** distribute sth to a lot of people: ~ out prizes/leaflets **give over (sth, spoken)** used to tell sb to stop doing sth **give sth up 1** (esp US **give up on sb**) believe that sth is never going to arrive, get better, etc: After so many years, they had ~n him up for dead. **2** stop having a relationship with sb **give sth up 1** stop doing or having sth: I've ~n up

smoking. ◇ I gave up my job. **2** allow sb else to have sth: He gave up his seat to the old man. **give yourself/sb up (to sb)** offer yourself/sb to be captured: He gave himself up to the police. **give up on sb** stop believing that sb will change, get better, etc **2** (esp US) = GIVE SB UP ➤ **given** adj agreed: at the ~n time ➤ **given** prep considering sth: G~n his size, he runs very fast. ■ **'giveaway** n (infml) **1** something that a company gives free of charge **2** something that reveals a secret

give² /ɡɪv/ n [U] ability of sth to bend and stretch under pressure: This rope has too much ~ in it. [IDM] **give and take** willingness to be tolerant and make compromises in a relationship

glacial /ˈɡleɪʃl; ˈɡleɪsiəl/ adj (geol) of ice or the Ice Age

glacier /ˈɡlæsiə(r)/ n mass of ice that moves slowly down a valley

glad /ɡlæd/ adj (~der, ~dest) **1** pleased; happy: ~ to hear the news ◇ I'd be ~ to help you. **2** grateful for sth: He was ~ of the warm coat. ➤ **gladly** adv happily; willingly: I will ~ly help you. ➤ **gladness** n [U]

glade /ɡleɪd/ n (lit) small open space in a forest

gladiator /ˈɡlædieɪtə(r)/ n (in ancient Rome) man trained to fight at public shows in an arena

glamour (US also **-or**) /ˈɡlæmə(r)/ n [U] **1** attractive and exciting quality: the ~ of Hollywood **2** physical beauty that suggests wealth and success ➤ **glamorize** (also **-ise**) v [T] make sth bad seem attractive and exciting ➤ **glamorous** adj

glance /ɡlɑːns/ v [I] take a quick look at sth/sb [PV] **glance off (sth)** hit sth and bounce off it at an angle ● **glance** n quick look [IDM] **at a (single) glance** at once

gland /ɡlænd/ n organ that produces a chemical substance for the body to use ➤ **glandular** /ˈɡlændjələ(r)/ adj

glare /ɡleə(r)/ v [I] **1** ~ (at) look at sb/sth angrily **2** shine very with a bright unpleasant light ● **glare** n **1** [U,sing] very bright unpleasant light **2** [C] angry look ➤ **glaring** adj **1** (of sth bad) very easily seen: a glaring mistake **2** (of light) very bright and unpleasant **3** angry; fierce

glass /ɡlɑːs/ n **1** [U] hard transparent substance used in windows, mirrors, etc **2** [C] a drinking container made of glass; its contents: a ~ of milk **3** (**glasses**) [pl] two lenses in a frame worn in front of the eyes to help a person to see better: a pair of ~es ■ **'glasshouse** n type of greenhouse ■ **'glassware** /-weə(r)/ n [U] objects made of glass ➤ **glassy**

adj (**-ier, -iest**) **1** smooth and shiny **2** showing no feeling or emotion

glaze /gleɪz/ *v* **1** ~**(over)** [I] (of sb's eyes) become dull and lifeless because of boredom or tiredness **2** [T] fit sheets of glass into sth: ~ *a window* **3** [T] cover sth with a thin shiny surface: ~ *pottery* ● **glaze** *n* [C,U] thin shiny coating ▶ **glazier** /ˈgleɪziə(r)/ *n* person who fits glass into windows, etc

gleam /gliːm/ *n* [C, usu sing] **1** pale clear light, often reflected from sth **2** small amount of sth: *a ~ of hope* ● **gleam** *v* [I] **1** shine softly **2** look very clean or bright

glean /gliːn/ *v* [I] obtain information, etc in small quantities and with difficulty

glee /gliː/ *n* [U] ~**(at)** feeling of happiness and satisfaction ▶ **gleeful** /-fl/ *adj* **gleefully** *adv*

glen /glen/ *n* narrow valley, esp in Scotland or Ireland

glib /glɪb/ *adj* (~**ber, ~best**) (*disapprov*) speaking or spoken easily and confidently but not sincerely: *a ~ answer* ▶ **glibly** *adv*

glide /glaɪd/ *v* [I] **1** move along smoothly and quietly **2** fly without engine power ● **glide** *n* continuous smooth movement ▶ **glider** *n* light aircraft without an engine ▶ **gliding** *n* [U] sport of flying in a glider

glimmer /ˈglɪmə(r)/ *v* [I] shine with a weak unsteady light ● **glimmer** *n* **1** weak unsteady light **2** (*also* **glimmering**) small sign of sth: *a ~ of interest*

glimpse /glɪmps/ *n* quick incomplete look at sb/sth: *He caught a ~ of her in the crowd.* ● **glimpse** *v* [T] see sb/sth for a moment, but not very clearly

glint /glɪnt/ *v* [I] produce small bright flashes of light ● **glint** *n* sudden flash of light or colour shining from a bright surface

glisten /ˈglɪsn/ *v* [I] (of sth wet) shine

glitter /ˈglɪtə(r)/ *v* [I] shine brightly with little flashes of light: ~*ing jewels* ● **glitter** *n* [U] **1** bright sparkling light **2** attractiveness; excitement: *the ~ of show business*

gloat /gləʊt/ *v* [I] ~**(about/at/over)** show selfish happiness at your own success or at sb else's failure

global /ˈgləʊbl/ *adj* **1** covering or affecting the whole world **2** considering or including all parts of sth ▶ **globally** /-bəli/ *adv* ■ **global 'village** *n* [sing] the whole world, considered as a single community connected by electronic communication systems ■ **global 'warming** *n* [U] increase in temperature of

the earth's atmosphere, caused by the increase of particular gases, esp carbon dioxide

globalize /ˈgləʊbəlaɪz/ *v* [I, T] (of business companies, etc) operate all around the world ▶ **globalization** *n* [U]: *the globalization of world trade*

globe /gləʊb/ *n* **1** [C] a model of the earth **2** (**the globe**) [sing] the world ■ **'globetrotter** *n* person who travels in many countries around the world

globule /ˈglɒbjuːl/ *n* (*fml*) tiny drop, esp of liquid

gloom /gluːm/ *n* **1** feeling of being sad and without hope **2** [U] (*lit*) almost total darkness ▶ **gloomy** *adj* (**-ier, -iest**) **1** almost dark **2** sad and without hope ▶ **gloomily** /-ɪli/ *adv*

glorify /ˈglɔːrɪfaɪ/ *v* (*pt, pp* **-ied**) [T] **1** often (*disapprov*) make sth seem better or more important than it really is: *This cottage is just a glorified barn.* **2** (*fml*) praise and worship God ▶ **glorification** /ˌglɔːrɪfɪˈkeɪʃn/ *n* [U]

glorious /ˈglɔːriəs/ *adj* (*fml*) **1** deserving or bringing great fame and success: *a ~ victory* **2** magnificent ▶ **gloriously** *adv*

glory /ˈglɔːri/ *n* (*pl* **-ies**) **1** [U] fame, praise or honour: *I do all the work and he gets all the ~.* **2** [U] praise and worship of God **3** [U] great beauty: *The house was restored to its former ~.* **4** [C] special cause for pride, respect or pleasure: *Her hair is her crowning ~.* ● **glory** *v* (*pt, pp* **-ied**) [I] *~* **in** take too much pleasure in sth

gloss /glɒs/ *n* **1** [U, sing] shine on a smooth surface **2** (*also* **gloss 'paint**) [U] paint that has a shiny surface when dry **3** [U, sing] deceptively good appearance **4** [C] ~**(on)** explanation of a word or phrase in a text ● **gloss** *v* [T] give an explanation of a word or phrase in a text [PV] **gloss over sth** avoid talking about sth unpleasant or embarrassing ▶ **glossy** *adj* (**-ier, -iest**) smooth and shiny: ~*y magazines* (= magazines printed on shiny paper)

glossary /ˈglɒsəri/ *n* (*pl* **-ies**) alphabetical list of explanations of words

glove /glʌv/ *n* covering for the hand

glow /gləʊ/ *v* [I] **1** ~**(with)** (esp of sth hot or warm) produce a dull, steady light: ~*ing coal* **2** be warm or red in the face **3** appear a strong, warm colour ● **glow** *n* [sing] **1** glowing light: *the ~ of a sunset* **2** warm colour ▶ **glowing** *adj* giving enthusiastic praise: *a ~ing report*

glower /ˈglaʊə(r)/ *v* [I] ~**(at)** look at sb angrily

glucose /'gluːkəʊs/ n [U] natural sugar found in fruit

glue /gluː/ n [U,C] sticky substance used for joining things together ● **glue** v [T] join two things together with glue [IDM] **be glued to sth** stay close to sth: *They were ~d to the TV.* ■ **'glue-sniffing** n [U] dangerous habit of breathing in the fumes of some kinds of glue as a drug

glum /glʌm/ adj (**~mer, ~mest**) sad; gloomy ▶ **glumly** adv

glut /glʌt/ v (**-tt-**) [T] supply sth with too much of sth: *The market is ~ted with cheap apples.* ● **glut** n [C, usu sing] **~(of)** situation in which there is more of sth than can be used

glutton /'glʌtn/ n 1 (disapprov) person who eats too much 2 person who enjoys doing difficult or unpleasant task: *a ~ for punishment* ▶ **gluttonous** /-tənəs/ adj very greedy ▶ **gluttony** n [U] habit of eating too much

glycerine /'glɪsəriːn/ (US **glycerin** /-rɪn/) n [U] thick colourless liquid used in eg medicines and explosives

GM /,dʒiː 'em/ abbr (GB) genetically modified: *GM foods*

gm (also **gm.**) abbr gram(s)

gnarled /nɑːld/ adj 1 (of trees) rough and twisted 2 (of a person or part of the body) bent and twisted because of age or illness

gnash /næʃ/ v [PV] **gnash your teeth** feel very angry or upset about sth, esp because you cannot get what you want

gnat /næt/ n small fly with two wings, that bites

gnaw /nɔː/ v [I, T] keep biting or chewing sth so that it gradually disappears: *The dog was ~ing a bone.* ◊ (fig) *Self-doubt had begun to ~ away at her confidence.*

gnome /nəʊm/ n 1 (in stories) small old man who lives under the ground 2 model of such a man used as a garden ornament

GNP /,dʒiː en 'piː/ abbr gross national product; total value of all the goods and services produced by a country in one year, including the total income from foreign countries

go¹ /ɡəʊ/ v (third pers sing pres tense **goes** /ɡəʊz/ pt **went** /went/ pp **gone** /ɡɒn/) [I] 1 move from one place to another: *go home/on a walk/on holiday/to the cinema* ◊ move or travel: *go five miles to get a doctor* 2 leave a place: *It's time for us to go.* 3 **~to** visit or attend a place for a particular purpose: *go to school* 4 **~to** visit or attend a place for a particular purpose: *go to school* 5 lead or extend from one place to

another: *This road goes to London.* 6 have as a usual or correct position: *The book goes on the shelf.* 7 fit into a place or space: *This key won't go in the lock.* 8 make progress: *How are things going?* ◊ *The party went very well.* 9 used to show that sb/sth has reached a particular state/is no longer in a particular state: *go to sleep* ◊ *go out of fashion* 10 linking verb become different in a particular way, esp a bad way: *go bald/blind/mad* 11 live or move around in a particular state: *go barefoot/hungry* 12 have a certain wording or tune: *How does the poem/song go?* 13 make a certain sound: *The bell went at 3 p.m.* ◊ *The clock goes 'tick-tock'.* 14 (esp in commands) begin an activity: *One, two, three, go!* 15 (of a machine) work: *This clock doesn't go.* 16 get worse; stop working: *My sight is going.* ◊ *The car battery has gone.* 17 be given, lost, spent, used up, etc: *Supplies of coal went very cheaply.* 18 **~(to, for)** be sold: *The car went to a dealer for £500.* 19 (of time) pass: *two hours to go before lunch* [IDM] **anything goes** (infml) anything is allowed **be going to do sth 1** intend; plan: *We're going to sell our house.* 2 be likely or about to happen: *It's going to rain.* **go and do sth** used to show that you are angry that sb has done sth stupid: *That stupid girl went and lost her watch.* **go to seed** → **SEED** **go to waste** → **WASTE** ²**there goes sth** (infml) used for showing regret that sth has been lost: *There goes my chance of getting the job* (=I will certainly not get it). [PV] **go about** move from place to place ◊ about sth start working on sth: *How do you go about writing a novel?* **go after sb** chase or follow sb **go after sb/sth** try to get sb/sth **go against sb/sth 1** oppose sb/sth: *Don't go against my wishes.* 2 be unfavourable to sb: *The verdict went against him.* **go ahead 1** travel in front of other people in your group and arrive before them 2 happen; be done: *The tennis match went ahead in spite of the bad weather.* **go along 1** continue with an activity: *He made up the story as he went along.* 2 make progress; develop **go along with sb/sth 1** accompany sb 2 agree with sb/sth: *Will they go along with the plan?* **go around/round 1** spin or turn: *go around in a circle* 2 be enough for everyone: *There aren't enough apples to go around.* 3 often be in a particular state or behave in a certain way: *You can't go around criticizing people like that.* **go around/round (to ...)** visit sb or a place that is near: *I'm going round to* *my sister's later.* **go around/round with sb** be often in the company of **go at sb/sth 1** attack sb 2 work hard at sth **go away 1** leave a person or place: *Go away and leave me alone!* **2** leave home for a period of time, esp for a holiday 3 disappear: *Has the pain gone away?* **go back 1** return 2 extend backwards in space or time: *Our family goes back 300 years.* **go back on sth** fail to keep a promise: *We went back on his word.* **go by** (of time) pass: *The days go by so slowly.* **go by sth** be guided by sth: *I always go by what my doctor says.* **go down 1** fall to the ground **2** (of a ship, etc) sink **3** (of the sun, moon, etc) set **4** (of food) be swallowed **5** (of the sea, wind, etc) become calm **6** (of prices, the temperature, etc) become lower **7** (computing) stop working temporarily: *The system went down for over an hour.* **go down (in sth)** be written or recorded in sth: *Her name will go down in history* **go down well/badly (with sb)** (of a comment, performance, etc) be well/badly received by sb **go down with sth** become ill with an illness: *go down with flu* **go for sb/sth 1** fetch sb/sth **2** attack sb: *The dog went for him.* **3** apply to sb/sth: *What she said goes for me too.* **4** (infml) like or prefer sb/sth **go in 1** enter a room, house, etc **2** (of the sun, moon, etc) disappear behind clouds **go in for sth 1** enter a competition, etc **2** have sth as an interest or hobby: *she doesn't go in for team games.* **go into sth 1** (of a car, etc) hit sth **2** join an organization, esp in order to pursue a career in it: *go into the Army* **3** examine sth carefully: *go into the details* **4** begin to do sth: *go into a long explanation* **go off 1** leave a place, esp in order to do sth: *She went off to get a drink.* **2** explode; be fired **3** (of an alarm, etc) suddenly make a loud noise **4** (of a light, the electricity, etc) stop working **5** (GB) (of food, etc) become unfit to eat: *The milk has gone off.* **6** proceed: *The party went off well.* **7** get worse in quality or health **go off sb/sth** stop liking sb/sth **go on 1** (of time) pass **2** (of a light, the electricity, etc) start to work **3** continue: *The meeting was on for hours.* **4** happen: *What's going on here?* **5** used to encourage sb: *Go on! Have a cake.* **go on (about sb/sth)** talk about sb/sth for a long time **go on (at sb)** criticize sb **go on (with sth/doing sth)** continue an activity **go on to sth/to do sth** do or say sth next **go out 1** leave your house to go to a social event: *I don't go out much at weekends.* **2** (of a fire, light, etc) stop burning or shining

3 become unfashionable **go out (together)| go out with sb** have a romantic or sexual relationship with sb: *How long have they been going out together?* **go over sth** examine or check sth carefully **go round** = GO AROUND **go round (to) =** GO AROUND (TO) **go round with sb =** GO AROUND WITH SB **go through 1** be officially accepted and completed: *The deal didn't go through.* **go through sth 1** study or consider sth in detail **2** examine sth carefully: *go through the papers* **3** experience or suffer sth **4** use up or finish sth completely **go through with sth** complete sth, esp sth unpleasant or difficult **go to/towards sth** be contributed to sth: *All profits go to charity.* **go under 1** sink **2** fail **go up 1** rise **2** be built **3** be destroyed by fire or in an explosion: *The petrol station went up in flames.* **4** (of prices, temperatures, etc) become higher **go up with sb** climb sth **go with sb** accompany sb **go together| go with sth** match: *Do green curtains go with a pink carpet?* **go without (sth)** manage without sth you usu have or need: *go without food for four days* ▪ **'go-ahead** *n* (the go-ahead) [sing] permission to start doing sth ▪ **go-ahead** *adj* willing to try new methods ▪ **,go-'slow** *n* industrial protest in which workers work more slowly than usual

go² /gəʊ/ *n* (pl **~es** /gəʊz/) **1** [C] (GB) person's turn to play in a game **2** [C] attempt: *'I can't lift this box.' 'Let me have a go.'* **3** [U] (GB, infml) energy and enthusiasm: *He's full of go.* [IDM] **be all go** (GB, infml) be very busy or full of activity **be on the go** (infml) be very active or busy **have a go (at sb)** criticize sb or attack sb **make a go of sth** (infml) make a success of sth

goad /gəʊd/ *v* **1** [T] ~ (into) annoy sb continually: *he ~ed me into an angry reply.* [PV] **goad sb on** urge sb to do sth ● **goad** *n* pointed stick for making cattle move

goal /gəʊl/ *n* **1** (in football, hockey, etc) pair of posts between which the ball has to go in order to score **2** point scored when the ball goes into the goal **3** something that you hope to achieve ▪ **'goalkeeper** *n* player who stands in the goal and tries to prevent the other team from scoring ▪ **'goalpost** *n* either of the two posts which form a goal(1)

goat /gəʊt/ *n* small horned animal with long hair that lives in mountain areas: *~'s milk/cheese* [IDM] **get sb's goat** (infml) annoy sb

gobble /'gɒbl/ *v* **1** [I, T] eat sth

quickly and greedily **2** [I] (of a turkey) make a sound in the throat

go-between /'ɡəʊ bɪtwiːn/ n person who takes messages between one group or person and another

goblet /'ɡɒblət/ n cup for wine, usu made of glass or metal, with a stem but no handle

goblin /'ɡɒblɪn/ n (in fairy stories) small ugly mischievous creature

god /ɡɒd/ n **1** (**God**) [sing] (in Christianity, Judaism and Islam) the maker and ruler of the universe **2** [C] (in some religions) being that is believed to have power over nature or to represent a particular quality **3** [C] person or thing that is greatly admired or loved **4** (**the gods**) [pl] (GB, infml) seats high up in a theatre [IDM] **God willing** (spoken) if everything goes as planned ■ **godchild** | **god-daughter** | **godson** n person for whom sb takes responsibility as a godparent ▶ **godchildren** /-ɡdɪz/ n female god ■ **godfather** | **godmother** | **godparent** n person who promises when a child is baptized to see that he/she is brought up as a Christian ■ **godforsaken** adj (of places) boring, depressing and ugly ■ **godless** adj not believing in God; wicked ■ **godlike** adj like God or a god in some quality ■ **godsend** n [sing] unexpected piece of good luck

goggle /'ɡɒɡl/ v [I] (old-fash) **~ (at)** look at sb/sth with wide round eyes ▶ **goggles** n [pl] glasses worn to protect the eyes from water, wind, dust, etc ▪ a pair of swimming/safety **~s**

going /'ɡəʊɪŋ/ n **1** (fml) departure **2** [U] (with an adjective) speed or difficulty involved in doing sth: It was good ~ to get to York so quickly. ● **going** adj [IDM] **a going concern** a profitable business **the going rate (for sth)** the usual price or cost of sth ▶ **goings-on** n [pl] (infml) unusual events or dishonest activities

go-kart (also **go-cart**) /'ɡəʊ kɑːt/ n small, low, open racing car

gold /ɡəʊld/ n **1** (symb **Au**) [U] yellow precious metal **2** [U] jewellery, money, etc made of gold **3** [U,C] bright yellow colour of gold **4** [C] = GOLD MEDAL ■ **goldfish** n (pl **goldfish**) small orange or red fish kept as a pet ■ **gold leaf** (also **gold foil**) n [U] very thin sheet of gold, used for decoration ■ **gold medal** n [C, U] (sport) prize given to the winner of a competition, esp a sports contest ■ **gold mine** n **1** place where gold is dug out of the ground **2** profitable business activity ■ **gold rush** n rush to a place where gold has been discovered in the ground

■ **goldsmith** n person who makes or sells objects made of gold

golden /'ɡəʊldən/ adj **1** of or like gold **2** special; wonderful: a ~ opportunity ■ **golden 'handshake** n large sum of money given to sb when they leave their job ■ **golden 'jubilee** n 50th anniversary of an important event ■ **golden 'rule** n very important rule of behaviour

golf /ɡɒlf/ n [U] outdoor game in which players hit a small ball into a series of 9 or 18 holes: play a round of ~ ■ **'golf club** n **1** (also **club**) long metal stick used for hitting the ball in golf **2** organization whose members play golf; place where these people meet ■ **'golf course** (also **course**) n large area of land designed for playing golf ▶ **golfer** n person who plays golf

gone pp of GO[1]

gong /ɡɒŋ/ n round piece of metal that makes a loud ringing sound when it is hit with a stick

gonorrhoea (US **gonorrhea**) /ˌɡɒnə-'rɪə/ n [U] sexually transmitted disease

good[1] /ɡʊd/ adj (**better** /'betə(r)/ **best** /best/) **1** of a high quality: very ~ exam results **2** pleasant; that you enjoy or want: ~ news/weather ◇ have a ~ time ◇ It's a ~ thing (= it is lucky) you are not a vegetarian. **3** able to do sth well; skilful: a ~ teacher ◇ ~ at languages **4** morally right or acceptable: ~ deeds **5** kind: They were very ~ to her when she was ill. **6** (esp of a child) well behaved **7** beneficial; suitable: Milk is ~ for you. **8** (spoken) used as an expression of approval, agreement, etc: 'I've finished!' 'G~!' **9** (spoken) used in exclamations: G~ Heavens! **10** great in number, amount or degree: a ~ many people **11** not less than: ~ three miles to the station **12** thorough: a ~ sleep **13** likely to provide sth: He's always ~ for a laugh. **14** used in greetings and farewells: G~ morning/afternoon. [IDM] **a good job** (spoken) used to show you are pleased about sth or that sb is lucky that sth happened (**all**) in **good time** (spoken) used to say that sth will happen or be done at the appropriate time and not before **as good as** very nearly: as ~ as finished **as good as gold** (of a child) very well behaved (**do sb**) **a good turn** (do) sth useful or helpful for sb **for good measure** as an extra amount of sth in addition to what has already been given **good and ...** (infml) completely: I won't go until I'm ~ and ready. **good for you, sb, them, etc** (infml) used to praise sb for doing sth well **good grief!** (infml) used to express surprise or shock **good 'luck (with sth)** used to wish sb success with sth **have a good mind to do sth** be very willing to do sth **in good time** early **make good** become rich and successful ■ **'good-for-nothing** n, adj (person who is) lazy and without any skills ■ **Good 'Friday** n [U,C] the Friday before Easter Sunday ■ **good-'humoured** (US **-humored**) adj cheerful ■ **good-'looking** adj handsome; beautiful ■ **good-'natured** adj kind and friendly ■ **good 'sense** n [U] ability to act wisely ■ **good-'tempered** adj not easily annoyed

good² /gʊd/ n [U] **1** behaviour which is morally right or acceptable: ~ *and evil* **2** something that helps sb/sth: *It's for your own ~.* [IDM] **be no much good | not be any| much good 1** not be useful: *have no useful effect: It's no ~ talking to them.* **2** not be interesting or enjoyable: *His new film's not much ~.* **do (sb) good** have a useful effect; help sb: *A walk will do you ~.* **for good** permanently **up to no good** (infml) doing sth wrong

goodbye /ˌgʊd'baɪ/ exclam, n used when you are leaving or when sb else is leaving

goodness /'gʊdnəs/ n [U] **1** (spoken) used to express surprise: *My ~!* **2** quality of being good **3** part of food that provides nourishment: *Brown bread is full of ~.*

goods /gʊdz/ n [pl] **1** things for sale; movable property: *electrical ~* **2** things carried by train: *a ~ train* [IDM] **come up with/deliver the goods** (infml) do what you have promised

goodwill /ˌgʊd'wɪl/ n [U] **1** friendly or helpful feeling towards other people or countries **2** financial value of the good reputation of a business, calculated when the business is sold

goody (also **goodie**) /'gʊdi/ n [C] (pl **-ies**) (infml) **1** [usu pl] something pleasant, esp to eat **2** hero of a book, film, etc

goose /guːs/ n (pl **geese** /giːs/) **1** [C] bird like a large duck with a long neck **2** [U] meat from a goose **3** [C] female goose ■ **'goose pimples** n [pl] (esp GB **'goose flesh** [U]) (also **'goose bumps**) small raised spots on the skin, caused by cold or fear

gooseberry /'gʊzbəri/ n (pl **-ies**) **1** (bush with a) green hairy sour berry

gorge /gɔːdʒ/ n narrow steep-sided valley ● **gorge** v [I, T] ~ (**yourself**) (**on**) eat a lot of sth until you cannot eat any more

gorgeous /'gɔːdʒəs/ adj (infml) very beautiful and attractive;

giving pleasure and enjoyment ▶ **gorgeously** adv

gorilla /gə'rɪlə/ n large powerful African ape

gorse /gɔːs/ n [U] bush with sharp thorns and yellow flowers

gory /'gɔːri/ adj (**-ier, -iest**) (infml) involving blood and violence

gosh /gɒʃ/ exclam (infml) used to express surprise

gosling /'gɒzlɪŋ/ n young goose

gospel /'gɒspl/ n **1** (**the Gospel**) [sing] life and teaching of Jesus **2** (**Gospel**) [C] any one of the first four books of the New Testament **3** [U] (infml) the complete truth **4** (also **'gospel music**) [U] style of religious singing popular among African Americans and other black people: *a ~ choir*

gossamer /'gɒsəmə(r)/ n [U] fine silky thread

gossip /'gɒsɪp/ n **1** [C,U] informal talk about other people, esp about their private lives **2** [C] (disapprov) person who likes gossip ■ **'gossip column** n piece of writing in a newspaper about the personal lives of famous people ● **gossip** v [I] talk gossip

got pt, pp of GET

gotten (US) pp of GET

gouge /gaʊdʒ/ n tool with a sharp semicircular cutting edge for cutting grooves in wood ● **gouge** v [T] make a hole in sth roughly [PV] **gouge sth out** force sth out with a sharp tool or your fingers

goulash /'guːlæʃ/ n [C,U] hot spicy Hungarian dish of meat cooked slowly in liquid with paprika

gourd /ɡʊəd/ n type of large fruit, not usu eaten, with hard skin and soft flesh. Gourds are often dried and used as containers.

gourmet /'ɡʊəmeɪ/ n expert in good food and drink

gout /ɡaʊt/ n [U] disease that causes painful swellings in joints, esp toes and fingers

govern /'ɡʌvn/ v **1** [I, T] legally control and run a country, city, etc **2** [T] control or influence sb/sth: *The law of supply and demand ~s the prices of goods.* ▶ **governing** /'ɡʌvənɪŋ/ adj having the power or right to govern sth: *the ~ing body of a school*

governess /'ɡʌvənəs/ n (esp in the past) woman employed to teach the children of a rich family and to live with them

government /'ɡʌvənmənt/ n **1** (**the Government**) (abbr **govt**) [C, with sing or pl verb] group of people who govern a country or state **2** [U] (method or system of) governing a country: *democratic ~*

G

governor /ˈgʌvənə(r)/ n **1** person who governs a province or (in the USA) a state **2** head of an institution; member of a governing body: *a prison/school ~*

gown /gaʊn/ n **1** woman's long dress for special occasions **2** loose usu black garment worn by judges, members of a university, etc

GP /ˌdʒiː ˈpiː/ *abbr* = GENERAL PRACTITIONER (GENERAL).

grab /græb/ v (**-bb-**) [I, T] take sth in your hand quickly or roughly ● **grab** n sudden attempt to grab sth [IDM] **up for grabs** (*infml*) available for anyone to take

grace /greɪs/ n **1** [U] simple beauty, esp in movement **2** [U] polite and pleasant behaviour, deserving respect **3** [U] extra time allowed to complete sth, pay money, etc: *give sb a week's ~* **4** [U,C] short prayer of thanks before or after a meal **5** [U] God's kindness towards people [IDM] **with (a) bad/good grace** unwillingly/willingly ● **grace** v [T] (*fml*) **1** make sth more attractive **2** bring honour to sb/sth; be kind enough to attend sth: *The Queen is gracing us with her presence.* ▸ **graceful** /-fl/ *adj* having grace(1); *a ~ful dancer* ▸ **gracefully** *adv* ▸ **graceless** *adj* without grace(2); rude

gracious /ˈgreɪʃəs/ *adj* **1** polite; kind **2** showing the comfort that wealth can bring: *~ living* ● **graciously** *adv* ▸ **graciousness** n [U]

grade /greɪd/ n **1** step or degree in quality, rank, etc: *different ~s of pay* **2** mark given for work in school **3** (*US*) class in a school **4** (*US*) gradient [IDM] **make the grade** (*infml*) reach the required standard ● **grade** v [T] **1** arrange people or things in groups according to their ability, size, etc **2** (*esp US*) mark schoolwork ▪ **'grade school** n (*US*) = ELEMENTARY SCHOOL

gradient /ˈgreɪdiənt/ n degree of slope of a road, railway, etc

gradual /ˈgrædʒuəl/ *adj* taking place slowly over a period of time; not sudden ▸ **gradually** /ˈgrædʒuəli/ *adv*

graduate¹ /ˈgrædʒuət/ n **1** person with a university degree **2** (*US*) person who has completed their school studies

graduate² /ˈgrædʒueɪt/ v [I] get a degree, esp a first degree, from a university: *~ in law* **2** (*US*) complete a course in education, esp at high school **3** [I] start doing sth more difficult or important than what you were doing before ▸ **graduated** *adj* **1** divided into groups or levels on a scale **2** (of a container, etc) marked with lines to show measurements ▸ **graduation** /ˌgrædʒuˈeɪʃn/ n **1** [U, C] (ceremony of) graduating at a university, etc **2** [C] mark showing a measurement

graffiti /grəˈfiːti/ n [U,pl] drawings or writing on a wall in a public place

graft /grɑːft/ n **1** [C] piece cut from a plant and fixed in another place to form a new growth **2** [C] (*med*) piece of skin, bone, etc transplanted to another body or another part of the same body **3** [U] (*GB, infml*) hard work ● **graft** v [T] attach sth to sth else as a graft

grain /greɪn/ n **1** [U,C] seeds of food plants such as wheat and rice **2** [C] small hard piece of particular substances: *~s of sand/sugar* **3** [C] very small amount: *a ~ of truth* **4** [U,C] pattern of the lines of fibres in wood, stone, etc [IDM] **be/go against the grain** be or do sth different from what is normal or natural

gram (*GB* **gramme**) /græm/ n metric unit of weight

grammar /ˈgræmə(r)/ n [C,U] (book that describes the) rules for forming words and making sentences ▸ **grammarian** /grəˈmeəriən/ n expert in grammar ▪ **'grammar school** n kind of British secondary school that provides academic courses ▸ **grammatical** /grəˈmætɪkl/ *adj* correct according to the rules of grammar ▸ **grammatically** /-kli/ *adv*

granary /ˈgrænəri/ n (*pl* **-ies**) building where grain is stored

grand /grænd/ *adj* **1** impressive and large or important: *a ~ palace* **2** full; final: *the ~ total* **3** proud; important **4** (*infml*) enjoyable ● **grand** n (*pl* **grand**) **1** (*infml*) $1000; £1000 **2** = GRAND PIANO ▸ **grandly** *adv* ▪ **grand 'piano** n large piano with horizontal strings ▪ **'grandstand** n large building with rows of seats for people watching sports

grand- *prefix* (used in compound nouns to show family relationships) ▪ **'grandchild** (*pl* **-children**) **'granddaughter** | **'grandson** n daughter or son of your child ▪ **'grandfather** | **'grandmother** | **'grandparent** n father or mother of either of your parents ▪ **'grandfather clock** n clock in a tall wooden case

grandad (*also* **granddad**) /ˈgrændæd/ n (*infml*) grandfather

grandeur /ˈgrændʒə(r), -djə(r)/ n [U] greatness; importance

grandiose /ˈgrændiəʊs/ *adj* seeming impressive but not practical

grandma /ˈgrænmɑː/ n (*infml*) grandmother

grandpa /ˈgrænpɑː/ n (*infml*) grandfather

granite /'grænɪt/ n [U] hard grey or red stone used for building

granny (also **grannie**) /'græni/ n (pl **-ies**) (infml) grandmother ■ '**granny flat** n (GB, infml) flat for an old person in a relative's house

grant /grɑːnt/ v [T] **1** (fml) agree to give sb what they ask for, esp formal or legal permission to do sth: ~ sb's request **2** (fml) admit that sth is true [IDM] **take it for granted (that …)** believe sth is true without first making sure that it is **take sb/sth for granted** be so familiar with sb/sth that you no longer value them/it ● **grant** n sum of money given by the government for a particular purpose

granulated sugar /,grænjuleɪtɪd 'ʃʊɡə(r)/ n [U] white sugar in the form of grains

granule /'grænjuːl/ n small hard piece of sth; small grain

grape /ɡreɪp/ n small green or purple fruit used for making wine ■ '**grapevine** n [IDM] **on/through the grapevine** by talking in an informal way to other people: I heard it on the ~-vine.

grapefruit /'ɡreɪpfruːt/ n (pl **grapefruit** or **~s**) large yellow fruit like an orange but usually not so sweet

graph /ɡrɑːf/ n diagram showing the relationship of two or more sets of numbers ■ '**graph paper** n [U] paper with small squares of equal size

graphic /'ɡræfɪk/ adj **1** connected with drawings and design: ~ design **2** (of descriptions) clear and detailed ▶ **graphically** /-kli/ adv clearly: ~ally described ● **graphics** n [pl] designs, drawings or pictures: computer ~s

graphite /'ɡræfaɪt/ n [U] soft black substance used in pencils

grapple /'ɡræpl/ v [I] **1** ~ (with) hold and struggle with sb/sth **2** try to deal with a problem

grasp /ɡrɑːsp/ v [T] **1** take a firm hold of sth/sb **2** understand sth fully [PV] **grasp at sth** try to take hold of sth in your hands **2** try to take an opportunity ● **grasp** n [C, usu sing] **1** firm hold of sth/sb **2** understanding ▶ **grasping** adj (disapprov) greedy for money

grass /ɡrɑːs/ n **1** [U] common wild short green plant eaten by cattle, etc **2** [C] any type of grass **3** (usu **the grass**) [sing, U] ground covered with grass: Don't walk on the ~. **4** [U] (sl) marijuana **5** [C] (GB, sl) person who grasses on sb [IDM] **not let the grass grow under your feet** not delay in doing sth ● **grass** (also **grass sb up**) v [I] (GB, infml) ~ (on) tell the police about sb's criminal

activities [PV] **grass sth over** cover an area with grass ■ **grass 'roots** n [pl] ordinary people rather than leaders or decision makers: the ~ roots of the party ▶ **grassy** adj (**-ier, -iest**) covered with grass

grasshopper /'ɡrɑːshɒpə(r)/ n jumping insect that makes a sound with its legs

grate /ɡreɪt/ n metal frame in a fireplace ● **grate** v **1** [T] rub food against a grater to cut it into small pieces: ~d cheese **2** [I] ~ (on/with) irritate or annoy sb: His voice ~s on me. **3** [I] make a rough unpleasant noise by rubbing together or against sth ▶ **grater** n kitchen utensil with a rough surface, used for grating food

grateful /'ɡreɪtfl/ adj **1** ~ (to) feeling or showing thanks: I'm ~ to you for your help. **2** used to make a request, esp in a letter: I would be ~ if you could send me … ▶ **gratefully** /-fəli/ adv

gratify /'ɡrætɪfaɪ/ v (pt, pp **-ied**) [T] (written) please or satisfy sb/sth ▶ **gratification** /,ɡrætɪfɪ'keɪʃn/ n [U,C] (fml) feeling of pleasure or satisfaction ▶ **gratifying** adj (fml) pleasing

grating /'ɡreɪtɪŋ/ n framework of bars across an opening, eg a window ● **grating** adj (of a person's voice) harsh and unpleasant

gratis /'ɡrætɪs/ adj, adv done or given without having to be paid for: a ~ copy of a book

gratitude /'ɡrætɪtjuːd/ n [U] ~(to; for) feeling of being grateful and wanting to express your thanks: feel ~

gratuitous /ɡrə'tjuːɪtəs/ adj (fml, disapprov) done without any good reason and often having harmful effects: ~ violence on television ▶ **gratuitously** adv

gratuity /ɡrə'tjuːəti/ n (pl **-ies**) **1** (fml) money given for a service done; tip **2** (GB) money given to a retiring worker

grave /ɡreɪv/ n hole in the ground for a dead body ■ '**gravestone** n stone over a grave ■ '**graveyard** n cemetery ● **grave** adj (~r, ~st) serious: a ~ situation ▶ **gravely** adv

gravel /'ɡrævl/ n [U] small stones, used to make the surface of paths and roads ● **gravel** v (-ll- US also **-l-**) [T] cover sth with gravel ▶ **gravelly** /'ɡrævəli/ adj **1** full of gravel **2** (of a voice) deep and rough

gravitate /'ɡrævɪteɪt/ v (written) [PV] **gravitate to/towards(s) sb/sth** move towards sb/sth that you are attracted to ▶ **gravitation** /,ɡrævɪ'teɪʃn/ n [U] (physics) force of attraction that causes objects to move towards each other

gravity /'grævəti/ n [U] **1** (abbr **g**) force that attracts objects towards the centre of the earth **2** (fml) seriousness: the ~ of the situation

gravy /'greivi/ n [U] juice that comes from meat while it is cooking

gray (esp US) = GREY

graze /greiz/ v **1** [I] (of cattle, sheep, etc) eat grass **2** [T] put cattle, etc in a field to eat grass **3** [T] break the surface of your skin by rubbing it against sth rough **4** [T] touch sth lightly while passing it ● **graze** n place where the surface of the skin has been broken

grease /gri:s/ n [U] **1** thick oily substance **2** soft animal fat ● **grease** v [T] rub grease or fat on sth [IDM] **like greased lightning** (infml) very fast ■ **greaseproof 'paper** n [U] paper used in cooking that does not let grease pass through it ▶ **greasy** adj (-ier, -iest) covered with grease

great /greit/ adj **1** very large in size, quantity or degree: of ~ importance **2** (infml) used for emphasis: Look at that ~ big tree! **3** very good in ability or quality: a ~ artist **4** (infml) very good or pleasant: a ~ time on holiday ◇ What a ~ idea! **5** important and impressive: The wedding was a ~ occasion. **6** healthy; fine: I feel ~ today. **7** used in compounds to show a further generation: my ~-aunt (= my father's or mother's aunt) ▶ **greatly** adv (fml) very much ▶ **greatness** n [U]

greed /gri:d/ n [U] strong desire for too much food, money, etc ▶ **greedy** adj (-ier, -iest) ▶ **greedily** adv

green¹ /gri:n/ adj **1** having the colour of grass **2** covered with grass or other plants **3** (of fruit) not yet ripe **4** (infml) (of a person) young and inexperienced **5** (of a person) pale; looking ill **6** esp (pol) concerned about protecting the environment: the G~ Party [IDM] **give sb/get the green light** give sb/get permission to do sth ● **green with envy** very jealous ■ **green 'bean** n long thin pod, cooked and eaten whole as a vegetable ■ **green 'belt** n [U,C, usu sing] (GB) area of open land round a city, where building is strictly controlled ■ **green 'fingers** n [pl] (US **green 'thumb**) (infml) skill in gardening ■ **greengrocer** n (esp GB) shopkeeper who sells fruit and vegetables ■ **greenhouse** n glass building used for growing plants ■ **greenhouse effect** n [sing] slow warming of the earth's atmosphere, caused by increased carbon dioxide ■ **'greenhouse gas** n any of the gases thought to cause the green-house effect, esp carbon dioxide ▶ **greenness** n [U]

green² /gri:n/ n **1** [U,C] colour of grass **2** (greens) [pl] green vegetables **3** [C] area of grass, eg in the middle of a town or village **4** [C] (in golf) area of grass cut short around a hole on a golf course

greenery /'gri:nəri/ n [U] attractive green leaves and plants

greet /gri:t/ v [T] **1** say hello to sb or welcome sb **2** react to sth/sb in a particular way **3** (of sights and sounds) be the first thing you see or hear ▶ **greeting** n [C,U] something you say or do to greet sb **2** (greetings) [pl] message of good wishes for sb: Christmas ~s

gregarious /gri'geəriəs/ adj **1** liking to be with other people **2** (biol) (of animals and birds) living in groups

grenade /grə'neid/ n small bomb thrown by hand

grew pt of GROW

grey (esp US **gray**) /grei/ adj **1** of the colour of black mixed with white **2** having grey hair ● **grey** n [U,C] grey colour ● **grey** v [I] (of hair) become grey ■ **'grey matter** n [U] (infml) person's intelligence

greyhound /'greihaund/ n thin dog able to run fast

grid /grid/ n **1** pattern of straight lines that cross each other to form squares **2** framework of bars: a cattle ~ (= one placed at a gate to stop cattle from leaving a field) **3** pattern of squares on a map, marked with numbers or letters: The ~ reference is C8. **4** (esp GB) system of wires for supplying electricity: the national ~ (= the electricity supply in a country)

grief /gri:f/ n **1** [U] ~ (over/at) great sadness, esp when sb dies **2** [C,U] thing that causes great sadness [IDM] **come to grief** (infml) **1** end in failure **2** be injured in an accident

grievance /'gri:vəns/ n ~ (against) real or imagined cause for complaint

grieve /gri:v/ v (fml) **1** ~ (for/over) [I] feel very sad, esp because sb has died **2** [T] (fml) make you feel sad: It ~d him that he could not help her.

grill /gril/ n **1** shelf in a cooker where food is cooked below direct heat **2** food, esp meat, cooked in this way: a mixed ~ ● **grill** v [I, T] **1** cook food under or over direct heat **2** [T] question sb severely

grille (also **grill**) /gril/ n **1** screen of metal bars in front of a window, door, etc, to protect it

grim /grim/ adj (~mer, ~mest) **1** looking or sounding serious:

--**faced 2** unpleasant; depressing: ~ *news* ▸ **grimly** *adv*

grimace /grɪˈmeɪs; ˈgrɪməs/ *n* ugly expression on the face, to show pain, disgust, etc ● **grimace** *v* [I] make an ugly expression with your face to show pain, etc

grime /graɪm/ *n* [U] dirt, esp on a surface ▸ **grimy** *adj* (-ier, -iest)

grin /grɪn/ *v* (-nn-) **1** smile widely [IDM] **grin and bear it** accept pain, disappointment, etc without complaining ● **grin** *n* wide smile

grind /graɪnd/ *v* (*pt, pp* **ground** /graʊnd/) **1** crush sth into powder: ~ *corn into flour* **2** make sth sharp or smooth by rubbing it against a hard surface: ~ *a knife* **3** press or rub sth into a surface: *He ground the cigarette into the ashtray.* [IDM] **grind to a halt** stop slowly [PV] **grind sb down** treat sb very cruelly or unfairly over a long period of time ● **grind** *n* [sing] **1** (*infml*) hard boring task **2** harsh noise made by machines ▸ **grinder** *n* person or thing that grinds sth ■ **'grindstone** *n* round stone used for sharpening tools

grip /grɪp/ *v* (-pp-) **1** [I, T] hold sth tightly **2** [T] interest or excite sb; hold sb's attention: *a ~ping film* ● **grip** *n* **1** [C, usu sing] tight hold of sb/sth **2** [sing] ~ **(on)** control or power over sth; understanding of sth **3** [U] ability of sth to move over a surface without slipping **4** [C] part of sth that has a special surface so that it can be held without the hands slipping [IDM] **come to grips with** begin to understand and deal with sth difficult

grisly /ˈgrɪzli/ *adj* causing horror or terror

gristle /ˈgrɪsl/ *n* [U] tough tissue in meat

grit /grɪt/ *n* [U] **1** very small pieces of stone or sand **2** courage and determination ● **grit** *v* (-tt-) [T] spread grit on an icy road [IDM] **grit your teeth 1** bite your teeth tightly together **2** show courage and determination ▸ **gritty** *adj* (-ier, -iest)

groan /grəʊn/ *v* [I] *n* (make a) long deep sound of pain or distress: *She ~ed with pain.*

grocer /ˈgrəʊsə(r)/ *n* shopkeeper who sells food and goods for the home ▸ **groceries** *n* [pl] food and other goods sold by a grocer or at a supermarket

groggy /ˈgrɒgi/ *adj* (-ier, -iest) (*infml*) weak and unsteady after illness, etc

groin /grɔɪn/ *n* part of the body where the legs meet

groom /gruːm/ *n* **1** person who looks after horses **2** bridegroom ● **groom** *v* [T] **1** clean and brush an animal **2** prepare sb for an important job or position ▸ **groomed** *adj* neat and tidy: *a well-~ed young man*

groove /gruːv/ *n* long narrow cut in a surface [IDM] **be (stuck) in a groove** (*GB*) become set in a particular way of life which has become boring ▸ **grooved** *adj* having grooves

grope /grəʊp/ *v* **1** [I] try and find sth that you cannot see, by feeling with your hands: ~ *for the light switch* **2** [T] (*infml, disapprov*) touch sb sexually, esp when they do not want you to

gross /grəʊs/ *adj* **1** being the total amount before anything is taken away: ~ *income* (= before tax has been deducted) **2** (*fml*) (of law) (of a crime etc) very obvious and unacceptable: ~ *injustice* **3** (*spoken*) very unpleasant **4** very rude **5** very fat and ugly ● **gross** *v* [T] earn sth as a total amount before tax is deducted ● **gross** *n* (*pl* **gross**) group of 144 things ▸ **grossly** *adv* (*disapprov*) **grossness** *n* [U]

grotesque /grəʊˈtesk/ *adj* strange, ugly and unnatural: *a ~ building/figure* ▸ **grotesquely** *adv*

grotto /ˈgrɒtəʊ/ *n* (*pl* **~es** or **~s**) small cave

ground¹ /graʊnd/ *n* **1** (often **the ground**) [sing] solid surface of the earth: *fall to the ~* **2** [U] soil: *stony/marshy ~* **3** [U] area of open land: *piece of waste ~* **4** [C] piece of land used for a particular purpose: *a football/sports ~* **5** (**grounds**) [pl] land or gardens round a building: *the palace ~s* **6** [U] area of interest, knowledge or ideas: *common ~ between the two sides* (= points on which they can agree) **7** [C, usu pl] reason: ~*s for divorce* **8** (**grounds**) [pl] small solid bits at the bottom of a liquid: *coffee ~s* [IDM] **gain/make up ground (on sb/sth)** gradually get closer to sb/sth who is ahead of you: *gain ~ on your competitors* **get off the ground** (of a project) make a successful start **give/lose ground (to sb/sth)** lose an advantage over sb/sth **hold/stand your ground** not change your position, opinion, etc; not yield ■ **ground 'floor** (*US* **first 'floor**) *n* [sing] (*GB*) floor of a building at ground level ▸ **groundless** *adj* without good reason: ~*less fears* ■ **'groundsheet** *n* large waterproof piece of material to spread on the ground in a tent, etc ■ **'groundwork** *n* [U] preparation for further study or work

ground² /graʊnd/ *v* **1** [I, T] (cause a) ship to) touch the sea bottom and

G

be unable to move **2** [T] prevent an aircraft from taking off **3** [T] punish a child by not allowing them to go out with their friends: *You're ~ed for a week!* **IDM** (**be**) **grounded in/ on sth** (be) based on sth ▶ **grounding** n [sing] teaching of the basic principles of a subject

ground³ *pt*, *pp* of GRIND

group /gruːp/ n [C, with sing or pl verb] **1** number of people or things together **2** (*business*) number of companies owned by the same person or organization ● **group** v [I, T] (cause sb/sth to) form into a group

grouse /graʊs/ v [I] (*infml*) complain about sb/sth in a way that people find annoying ● **grouse** n **1** (*pl* **grouse**) small fat bird, shot for sport and food **2** (*infml*) complaint

grove /grəʊv/ n group of trees

grovel /ˈɡrɒvl/ v (**-ll-** *US* **-l-**) [I] **1** (*disapprov*) show humility and respect towards sb, trying to gain his/her favour **2** move along the ground on your hands and knees ▶ **grovelling** adj: a ~ling letter of apology

grow /grəʊ/ v [I] n (make a) low threatening sound: *The dog ~ed at the burglars.*

grown /grəʊn/ adj mentally and physically an adult ▪ **grown-up** adj adult; mature ▪ **'grown-up** n adult person

growth /grəʊθ/ n **1** [U] process of growing; development **2** [U] increase in the size, amount or degree of sth **3** [C] lump caused by a disease that forms in or on the body **4** [U,C] something that has grown: *three days' ~ of beard*

grub /ɡrʌb/ n **1** [C] young form of an insect **2** [U] (*infml*) food ● **grub** v (**-bb-**) [I] look for sth, esp by digging

grubby /ˈɡrʌbi/ adj (**-ier, -iest**) dirty

grudge /ɡrʌdʒ/ v [T] do or give sth unwillingly: *I ~ paying so much tax.* ● **grudge** n feeling of anger towards sb because of sth bad they have done to you in the past: *bear/ have a ~ against sb* ▶ **grudging** adj unwilling ▶ **grudgingly** adv

gruelling (*US* **grueling**) /ˈɡruːəlɪŋ/ adj very tiring

gruesome /ˈɡruːsəm/ adj causing horror and disgust: a ~ murder ▶ **gruesomely** adv

gruff /ɡrʌf/ adj rough and unfriendly ▶ **gruffly** adv

grumble /ˈɡrʌmbl/ v [I] complain about sb/sth in a bad-tempered way ● **grumble** n complaint

grumpy /ˈɡrʌmpi/ adj (**-ier, -iest**) (*infml*) bad-tempered ▶ **grumpily** adv

grunt /ɡrʌnt/ v [I] **1** (esp of pigs) make a low sound in the throat **2** (of people) make a similar sound to show you are annoyed, bored, etc ● **grunt** n low sound made by a person or an animal

guarantee /ˌɡærənˈtiː/ n **1** firm promise that you will do sth or that sth will happen **2** written promise given by a company that sth you buy will be repaired without payment if it goes wrong: *The watch is still under ~.* **3** promise to be responsible for the payment of a debt ● **guarantee** v [T] **1** promise sth: *We cannot ~ that trains will arrive on time.* **2** give a guarantee for sth

guarantor /ˌɡærənˈtɔː(r)/ n (*fml*) or (*law*) person who agrees to be responsible for sb or for making sure that sth happens

guard /ɡɑːd/ n **1** [C] person, eg a soldier or police officer, who watches over sb or sth: a security ~ **2** [C, with sing or pl verb] group of people, eg soldiers or police officers, who protect sb/sth: a ~ of honour **3** [U] act or duty of protecting sb/sth from attack or danger, or of preventing prisoners from escaping: a soldier on ~ **4** [C] (esp in compounds) apparatus designed to protect sb/sth: fire- **5** [C] (*GB*) official in charge of a train ● **guard** v [T] **1** protect sb/sth **2** [T] prevent prisoners from escaping **[PV] guard against sth** take care to prevent sth: ~ against disease ▶ **guarded** adj not showing or saying too much

guardian /ˈɡɑːdiən/ n **1** person who protects sth **2** person legally responsible for the care of a child ▶ **guardianship** n [U] position of being responsible for sb/sth

guerrilla (*also* **guerilla**) /ɡəˈrɪlə/ n fighter in an unofficial army that attacks in small groups

guess /ɡes/ v **1** [I, T] try and give an answer or form an opinion about sth without being sure of all the facts **2** [T] suppose sth to be true or likely ● **guess** n ~ (**at**) attempt to give an answer or opinion when you cannot be certain you are right ■ **'guesswork** *n* [U] process of guessing sth

guest /gest/ *n* **1** person invited to your house or an event that you are paying for **2** person staying at a hotel, etc **3** famous person who takes part in a television show [IDM] **be my guest** (*infml*) used to give sb permission to do sth ■ **'guest house** *n* small hotel

guffaw /gə'fɔː/ *v* [I] *n* (give a) noisy laugh

guidance /'gaɪdns/ *n* [U] help or advice

guide /gaɪd/ *n* **1** book, magazine, etc that gives information about sth: *a ~ to plants* **2** (*also* **'guidebook**) book with information about a place for travellers **3** person who shows other people the way to a place, esp sb employed to show tourists around: *a tour ~* **4** something that gives you enough information to be able to form an opinion about sth: *As a rough ~, allow 1 cup of rice per person.* **5** (**Guide**) (*GB old-fash*, **Girl 'Guide**) (*US*, *Girl* **'Scout**) member of an organization for girls that aims to develop practical skills ● **guide** *v* [T] act as a guide to sb ▪ **,guided 'missile** *n* missile that can be guided in flight ■ **'guideline** *n* [C, usu pl] advice on how to do sth

guild /gɪld/ *n* society of people with similar jobs or interests

guile /gaɪl/ *n* [U] (*fml*) use of clever but dishonest behaviour to deceive people

guillotine /'gɪləti:n/ *n* **1** machine for cutting off the heads of criminals **2** machine for cutting sheets of paper **3** (*GB*, *pol*) time limit for a discussion in Parliament ● **guillotine** *v* [T] use a guillotine on sb/sth

guilt /gɪlt/ *n* [U] **1** feeling of shame for having done wrong **2** fact that sb has done sth illegal: *an admission of ~* **3** blame or responsibility for wrongdoing ▶ **guilty** *adj* (*-ier*, *-iest*) **1** feeling shame for having done wrong **2** having done sth illegal; being responsible for sth bad that has happened ▶ **guiltily** *adv*

guinea /'gɪni/ *n* old British gold coin worth 21 shillings (= £1.05)

guinea pig /'gɪni pɪɡ/ *n* **1** small animal with short ears and no tail, often kept as a pet **2** person used in an experiment

guise /gaɪz/ *n* (*fml*) outward appearance

guitar /ɡɪ'tɑː(r)/ *n* musical instrument with six strings played with the fingers ▶ **guitarist** *n*

gulf /ɡʌlf/ *n* **1** part of the sea almost surrounded by land: *the G~ of*

Mexico **2** ~ **(between)** big difference in opinion, lifestyle, etc

gull /ɡʌl/ *n* large seabird with long wings

gullet /'ɡʌlɪt/ *n* food passage from the mouth to the stomach

gullible /'ɡʌləbl/ *adj* easily deceived

gulp /ɡʌlp/ *v* [I, T] **1** swallow food or drink quickly **2** swallow because of a strong emotion, eg fear **3** breathe deeply because you need air ● **gulp** *n* act of gulping

gum /ɡʌm/ *n* **1** [C, usu pl] either of the firm areas of pink flesh around the teeth **2** [U] sticky substance produced by certain trees **3** [U] type of glue **4** [U] = CHEWING GUM (CHEW) **5** [C] fruit-flavoured sweet that you chew ● **gum** *v* (*-mm-*) [T] (*old-fash*) spread glue on sth; stick two things together with glue ■ **'gumboot** *n* (*old-fash*) = WELLINGTON ▶ **gummy** *adj* (*-ier*, *-iest*) sticky ■ **'gum tree** *n* eucalyptus tree

gun /ɡʌn/ *n* weapon that fires bullets or shells from a metal tube ● **gun** *v* (*-nn-*) [PV] **be gunning for sb** (*infml*) be looking for an opportunity to blame or attack sb **gun sb down** (*infml*) shoot sb, esp so as to kill them ■ **'gunboat** *n* small warship with heavy guns ■ **'gunfire** *n* [U] shooting of guns ■ **'gunman** (*pl* **-men**) man who uses a gun to rob or kill ■ **'gunner** *n* soldier who uses large guns ■ **'gunpoint** *n* [IDM] **at gunpoint** under the threat of being shot ■ **'gunpowder** *n* [U] explosive powder ■ **'gunshot** *n* **1** [C] shot fired from a gun **2** [U] distance that a bullet from a gun can travel ■ **'gunsmith** *n* person who makes and repairs guns

gurgle /'ɡɜːɡl/ *v* [I] *n* (make the) bubbling sound of flowing water

gush /ɡʌʃ/ *v* [I] **1** flow out of sth suddenly and in large amounts: *blood ~ing from a wound* **2** (*disapprov*) talk with too much enthusiasm ● **gush** *n* [sing] sudden outburst ▶ **gushing** *adj*

gust /ɡʌst/ *n* sudden rush of wind ▶ **gusty** *adj* (*-ier*, *-iest*)

gut /ɡʌt/ *n* **1** [C] intestine **2** (**guts**) [pl] organs in and around the stomach **3** (**guts**) [pl] (*infml*) courage and determination necessary to do sth difficult **4** (**guts**) [pl] most important part of sth: *the ~s of the problem/argument* **5** [U] = CATGUT ● **gut** *v* (*-tt-*) [T] **1** destroy the inside of a building or room: *a house ~ed by fire* **2** take the guts out of a fish, etc ● **gut** *adj* based on feelings rather than thought: *a ~ reaction*

gutter /'ɡʌtə(r)/ *n* **1** [C] channel under the edge of a roof, or at the side of a road, to carry away rainwater **2 (the gutter)** [sing] bad social conditions or lack of morals ■ the **gutter 'press** *n* [sing] (*disapprov*) newspapers that contain a lot of gossip and scandal

guy /gaɪ/ *n* **1** (*infml*) man **2** (in Britain) figure of a man dressed in old clothes burned on a bonfire on 5 November **3** (*also* **'guy rope**) rope used to keep a tent or a pole firmly in place

guzzle /'gʌzl/ *v* [I, T] (*infml*) eat or drink sth greedily

gym /dʒɪm/ *n* (*infml*) **1** (*also fml* **gymnasium**) [C] room or hall with apparatus for physical exercise **2** [U] physical exercises done in a gym, esp at school ■ **'gym shoe** *n* (*GB*) = PLIMSOLL

gymkhana /dʒɪm'kɑːnə/ *n* public competition of horse riding

gymnasium /dʒɪm'neɪziəm/ *n* (*pl* ~s or **gymnasia** /-ziə/) (*fml*) = GYM

gymnast /'dʒɪmnæst/ *n* expert in gymnastics

gymnastics /dʒɪm'næstɪks/ *n* [pl] physical exercises to train the body or show how agile it is ▸ **gymnastic** *adj*

gynaecology (*US* **gynec-**) /ˌgaɪnə-'kɒlədʒi/ *n* [U] study and treatment of disorders of the female reproductive system ▸ **gynaecological** (*US* **gynec-**) /ˌgaɪnəkə'lɒdʒɪkl/ *adj* ▸ **gynaecologist** (*US* **gynec-**) *n* expert in gynaecology

gypsy (*also* **gipsy**) /'dʒɪpsi/ *n* (*pl* **-ies**) (*sometimes offens*) member of a race of people who travel around and traditionaly live in caravans

gyrate /dʒaɪ'reɪt/ *v* [I, T] (cause sth to) move around in circles ▸ **gyration** /dʒaɪ'reɪʃn/ *n* [C, U]

H h

H, h /eɪtʃ/ *n* [C, U] (*pl* **H's, h's** /'eɪtʃɪz/) the eighth letter of the English alphabet

haberdasher /'hæbədæʃə(r)/ *n* **1** (*GB, old-fash*) shopkeeper who sells small articles for sewing, eg needles **2** (*US*) shopkeeper who sells men's clothing ▸ **haberdashery** /*n* [U] (*old-fash*) goods sold by a haberdasher

habit /'hæbɪt/ *n* **1** [C, U] thing that you do often and almost without thinking: *Smoking is a bad ~.* ◇ *Don't make a ~ of borrowing money.* **2** [C] long garment worn by a monk or nun

habitable /'hæbɪtəbl/ *adj* fit to be lived in

habitat /'hæbɪtæt/ *n* natural home of an animal or plant

habitation /ˌhæbɪ'teɪʃn/ *n* [U] act of living in a place: *houses unfit for human ~*

habitual /hə'bɪtʃuəl/ *adj* **1** usual or typical of sb/sth **2** doing sth by habit: *a ~ criminal* ▸ **habitually** *adv*

hack /hæk/ *v* [I, T] **1** cut sth roughly **2** ~(**into**) (*computing*) secretly look at and/or change information on sb else's computer system ■ **'hacksaw** *n* tool for cutting metal ● **hack** *n* (*disapprov*) writer, esp of newspaper articles, who does a lot of low quality work for little money

hacker /'hækə(r)/ *n* person who looks at computer data without permission

hackneyed /'hæknid/ *adj* (of a phrase, etc) meaningless because used too often

had /həd; əd; *strong form* hæd/ *pt, pp* of HAVE

haddock /'hædək/ *n* [C, U] (*pl* **haddock**) sea fish used for food

hadn't /'hædnt/ *short for* HAD NOT

haemophilia (*US* **hem-**) /ˌhiːmə-'fɪliə/ *n* [U] medical condition that causes a person to bleed badly from even a small injury ▸ **haemophiliac** (*US* **hem-**) /-'fɪliæk/ *n* person with haemophilia

haemorrhage (*US* **hem-**) /'hemərɪdʒ/ *n* [C, U] great flow of blood

haemorrhoids (*US* **hem-**) /'hemərɔɪdz/ *n* [pl] (*med*) swollen veins inside the anus

hag /hæg/ *n* (*offens*) ugly old woman

haggard /'hægəd/ *adj* looking tired, esp from worry

haggis /'hægɪs/ *n* [C, U] Scottish food made from parts of a sheep and cooked in a sheep's stomach

haggle /'hægl/ *v* [I] ~(**over/about**) argue about a price

hail /heɪl/ *n* **1** [U] small balls of ice that fall like rain **2** [sing] large number or amount of sth that is aimed at sb to harm them: *a ~ of bullets* ● **hail** *v* **1** [T] describe sb/sth as being very good or special, esp in newspapers, etc: *They ~ed them as their hero.* **2** [T] signal to a taxi or a bus to stop **3** [T] (*lit*) call out to sb, in order to attract attention **4** [I] (used with *it*) (of small balls of ice) fall like rain [PV] **hail from …** (*fml*) come from a particular place ■ **'hailstone** *n* small ball of ice that falls like rain ■ **'hailstorm** *n* storm with hail

hair /heə(r)/ *n* [C, U] substance that looks like a mass of fine threads growing esp on the head; one of these threads [IDM] (**by**) **a hair's breadth** (by) a very small distance **make sb's hair stand on end** shock

or frighten sb ■ '**haircut** n act or
style of cutting the hair ■ '**hairdo** n
(pl **-dos**) (*infml, old-fash*) act or
style of arranging a woman's hair
■ '**hairdresser** n person who cuts
and styles hair ■ '**hairgrip** n clip for
holding the hair in place ■ '**hairline**
n **1** edge of the hair above the forehead **2** (used as an adjective) very
thin line: *a ~line crack/fracture*
■ '**hairpin** n bent pin used for keeping the hair in place ■ ,**hairpin**
'**bend** n very sharp bend in a road
■ '**hair-raising** adj very frightening
■ '**hairstyle** n way of arranging or
cutting the hair ▷ **hairy** adj (**-ier**,
-iest) **1** covered with hair **2** (*infml*)
exciting but frightening ▷ **hairi-
ness** n [U]

hale /heɪl/ adj **hale and hearty**
strong and healthy

half¹ /hɑːf/ n (pl **halves** /hɑːvz/) **1**
one of two equal parts; ½ **2** either
of two periods of time into which a
sports match, concert, etc is divided **3** a ticket or drink that is half
the usual price or size: *Two halves
(= children's fares) to the station,
please.* [IDM] **go half and half | go
halves (with sb)** share the cost of
sth equally

half² /hɑːf/ det, pron **1** amount
equal to half of sth/sb: *~ an hour* **2**
the largest part of sth: *H~ the time,
you don't listen to what I say.* [IDM]
half past one, two, etc (*US also*)
half after one, two, etc thirty minutes after any hour on the clock
■ ,**half-and-'half** adj being half one
thing and another ■ ,**half
'board** n [U] (*GB*) hotel accommodation with breakfast and evening
meal included ■ ,**half 'mast** n [IDM]
at half mast (of a flag) flown halfway up a mast, as a sign of respect
for a dead person ■ ,**half-'term** n
(*GB*) short holiday in the middle of
a school term ■ ,**half-'time** n [U]
interval between the two halves of
a sports match ■ ,**half'way** adj, adv
between and at an equal distance
from two places ▷ ,**halfwit** n (*infml*)
stupid person ▷ ,**half-'witted** adj

half³ /hɑːf/ adv **1** to the extent of
half: *~ full* **2** partly: *~ cooked* [IDM]
not half (*GB, infml*) used to emphasize a statement or opinion: *It
wasn't ~ good* (= it was very good).
■ ,**half-'baked** adj (*infml*) not well
planned ■ ,**half-'hearted** adj showing little enthusiasm

hall /hɔːl/ n **1** space or passage
inside the entrance of a house
2 building or large room for meetings, concerts, meals, etc **3** building
for university students to live in: *a
~ of residence*

hallmark /'hɔːlmɑːk/ n **1** feature

that is typical of sb/sth **2** mark
stamped on gold or silver objects to
show the quality of the metal
● **hallmark** v [T] put a hallmark on
metal goods

hallo (*GB*) = HELLO

Halloween (*also* **Hallowe'en**) /ˌhæləʊ
'iːn/ n [U] 31 October, when children dress up as ghosts and witches

hallucination /həˌluːsɪ'neɪʃn/ n
[C,U] seeing sth that is not really there

halo /'heɪləʊ/ n (pl **-es**) **1** circle of
light round the head of a holy per-
son in a picture **2** circle of light
round the sun or moon

halt /hɔːlt/ v [I, T] (cause sb/sth to)
stop ● **halt** n [sing] stop: *The train
came to a ~ outside the station.*

halter /'hɔːltə(r)/ n rope or leather
strap put round a horse's head, for
leading the horse

halting /'hɔːltɪŋ/ adj slow and hesitating ▷ **haltingly** adv

halve /hɑːv/ v **1** [T] divide sth into
two equal parts **2** [I, T] (cause sth to)
reduce by a half: *~ the cost*

halves *plural of* HALF

ham /hæm/ n **1** [C,U] (meat from
the) top part of a pig's leg, that has
been salted or smoked to be eaten
as food **2** [C] (*infml*) amateur radio
operator **3** [C] (*infml*) bad actor
● **ham** v (**-mm-**) [PV] **ham it up**
(*infml*) (esp of actors) to act in an
exaggerated way ■ ,**ham-'fisted**
(*US* '**ham-handed**) adj (*infml*) lacking skill when using your hands or
dealing with people

hamburger /'hæmbɜːgə(r)/ n flat
round cake of minced meat, usu
fried and eaten in a bread roll

hamlet /'hæmlət/ n small village

hammer /'hæmə(r)/ n **1** tool with a
heavy metal head, used for hitting
nails, etc **2** (in a piano) part that
hits the strings ● **hammer** v [I, T]
hit sth with a hammer **2** [T] (*infml*)
defeat sb completely [PV] **hammer
away at sth** work hard at sth **hammer out sth** reach an agreement
about sth after long discussion

hammock /'hæmək/ n bed made of
cloth or rope net hung between
two posts

hamper /'hæmpə(r)/ v [T] (*written*)
prevent sb from easily doing or
achieving sth ● **hamper** n large
basket with a lid, used for carrying
food

hamster /'hæmstə(r)/ n small animal like a mouse, kept as a pet

hand¹ /hænd/ n **1** [C] part of the
human arm below the wrist **2** (a
hand) [sing] help in doing sth:
*Can you give me a ~ with the wash-
ing-up?* **3** [sing] **~in** role or influence that
sb/sth has in a particular situation:

She had a ~ in his downfall. **4** [C] pointer on a clock, dial, etc: *hour-~* **5** [C] worker: *a farm-* **6** [C] set of cards dealt to a player in a game [IDM] **(close/near) at hand** close to you **by hand 1** by a person, not a machine **2** (of a letter) brought by a person, not sent by post **give sb/get a big hand** show your approval of sb by clapping your hands; be applauded in this way **hand in hand 1** (of people) holding each other's hands **2** (of things) closely connected **have your hands full** be very busy in hand **1** available to be used; in control: *The situation is well in ~.* **2** that is being being dealt with: *the job in ~* **in/ out of sb's hands** in/no longer in sb's control or care **off/on your hands** no longer being your responsibility **on hand** available **on the one hand ... on the other (hand) ...** used for showing two opposite points of view **out of hand 1** out of control **2** without further thought: *All our suggestions were dismissed out of ~.* **(at) second, third, etc hand** being told about sth by sb else who has seen it, heard about it, etc, rather than experiencing it yourself ■ **'handbag** (*US* **purse**) *n* woman's bag for money, keys, etc ■ **'handbook** *n* book giving facts and instructions ■ **'handbrake** *n* brake in a car, van, etc operated by the driver's hand ■ **'handcuff** *v* [T] put handcuffs on sb ■ **'handcuffs** *n* [pl] metal rings joined by a chain, for fastening round a prisoner's wrists ■ **handful** *n* **1** [C] as much as can be held in one hand **2** [sing] small number **3** [sing] (*infml*) person or animal that is difficult to control ■ **,hand-'held** *adj* small enough to be held in the hands while being used ■ **hand-held** *n* ■ **,hand-'picked** *adj* carefully chosen ■ **,hands-'free** *adj* (esp of a telephone) that can be operated without using your hands ■ **'handshake** *n* shaking of sb's hand with your own, as a greeting, etc ■ **'handstand** *n* movement in which you balance yourself on your hands, with your feet in the air ■ **'handwriting** *n* [U] (style of) writing by hand

hand² /hænd/ *v* [T] pass or give to sb: *Please ~ me that book.* [IDM] **hand sth to sb on a plate → PLATE** [PV] **hand sth down (to sb)** give or leave sth to sb who is younger than you **hand sth in (to sb)** give sth to a person in authority, esp a piece of work: *~ in homework* **hand sth on (to sb)** give sth to another person to use or deal with **hand sth out (to sb) 1** give a number of things to members of a group **2** give advice, punishment, etc **hand sb/sth over (to sb)** give the responsibility for

sb/sth to sb: *a prisoner over to the authorities* ■ **'handout** *n* **1** something, eg food or money, given freely **2** sheet of information given out, eg by a teacher

handicap /'hændɪkæp/ *n* **1** (*old-fash*) disability in a person's body or mind **2** condition that makes it difficult to do sth **3** disadvantage given to a skilled competitor in a sport ● **handicap** *v* (**-pp-**) [T] make sth more difficult for sb to do ▶ **handicapped** *adj* (*old-fash*) having a handicap(1)

handicraft /'hændɪkrɑːft/ *n* work, eg pottery, that needs skill with the hands

handiwork /'hændiwɜːk/ *n* [U] **1** work done or something made using artistic skill **2** thing done by a particular person, esp sth bad

handkerchief /'hæŋkətʃɪf, -tʃiːf/ *n* square piece of cloth used for blowing your nose

handle /'hændl/ *n* part of a cup, door, tool, etc, by which it is held ● **handle** *v* **1** [T] deal with or control sb/sth **2** [T] touch, hold or move sth with your hands **3** [I, T] (esp of a vehicle) operate or control sth in the way that is mentioned: *This car ~s well.* ■ **'handlebars** *n* [pl] bar with a handle at each end for steering a bicycle or motorcycle ▶ **handler** *n* person who trains an animal, eg a police dog

handsome /'hænsəm/ *adj* **1** (esp of men) good-looking **2** (of gifts, behaviour, etc) generous ▶ **handsomely** *adv*

handy /'hændi/ *adj* (**-ier, -iest**) **1** useful; easy to use or do **2** easily reached; near **3** clever with your hands [IDM] **come in handy** be useful ▶ **handily** *adv* ■ **'handyman** *n* (*pl* **-men**) person skilled at doing small repairs

hang¹ /hæŋ/ *v* (*pt, pp* **hung** /hʌŋ/ ; in sense 2 **~ed**) **1** [I, T] attach sth or be attached at the top so that the lower part is free or loose: *~ the washing out to dry* **2** [T] kill sb by tying a rope around their neck and allowing them to drop **3** [T] stick wallpaper to a wall [PV] **hang about/ around** wait or stay near a place, not doing very much **hang back (from sth)** hesitate because you are nervous about doing sth **hang on 1** hold sth tightly **2** (*spoken*) wait for a short time **hang on to sth 1** hold sth tightly **2** (*infml*) keep sth **hang up** put down a telephone receiver **(be/get) hung up (on/about sth/sb)** (*infml*) (feel) very worried about sth/sb; (be) thinking about sth/sb too much ■ **'hang-gliding** *n* [U] sport of flying while hanging from a frame like a large kite ■ '**hang-glider** n **1** frame used in hang-gliding **2** person who goes hang-gliding ▶ **hanging** n **1** [U,C] death by hanging **2** [C, usu pl] large piece of material hung on a wall for decoration: *wall ~s* ■ '**hangman** /-mən/ n (pl **-men**) man whose job is to hang criminals ■ '**hang-up** n (*infml*) emotional problem about sth

hang³ /hæŋ/ n [IDM] **get the hang of sth** (*infml*) understand sth or learn how to do sth

hangar /'hæŋə(r)/ n building in which aircraft are kept

hanger /'hæŋə(r)/ n (*also* '**coat hanger**, '**clothes hanger**) piece of wood, wire, etc with a hook, used for hanging up clothes ■ **hanger-'on** n (pl **~s-on**) (*disapprov*) person who tries to be friendly, in the hope of personal gain

hangover /'hæŋəʊvə(r)/ n **1** unpleasant feeling after drinking too much alcohol on the previous night **2** something left from an earlier time

hanker /'hæŋkə(r)/ v [I] **~ after/for** have a strong desire for sth ▶ **hankering** n

hanky (*also* **hankie**) /'hæŋki/ n (pl **-ies**) (*infml*) = HANDKERCHIEF

haphazard /hæp'hæzəd/ adj with no particular plan or order ▶ **haphazardly** adv

happen /'hæpən/ v [I] **1** (of an event) take place, usu by chance **2** do or be sth by chance: *I ~ed to be out when she called.* ▶ **happening** n event

happy /'hæpi/ adj (**-ier, -iest**) **1** feeling, giving or expressing pleasure; pleased: *I'm happy – for you.* ◊ *a ~ marriage* ◊ *a ~ smile* **2** used in greetings to express good wishes: *H~ birthday!* **3** satisfied that sth is good or right; not anxious **4** willing or pleased to do sth [IDM] **a/the happy medium** a balance between two extremes ▶ **happily** adv ▶ **happiness** n [U] ■ **happy-go-'lucky** adj not worrying about the future

harangue /hə'ræŋ/ n long loud angry speech ● **harangue** v [I] speak loudly and angrily to sb in a way that criticizes them

harass /'hærəs/ v [T] worry or annoy sb by putting pressure on them ▶ **harassment** n [U]

harbour (*US* **-or**) /'hɑːbə(r)/ n place of shelter for ships ● **harbour** v [T] **1** hide and protect sb who is hiding from the police **2** (*written*) keep feelings in your mind for a long time: *~ secret fears*

hard¹ /hɑːd/ adj **1** firm and solid; not easy to bend, cut, etc: *as ~ as rock*

2 difficult: *a ~ exam* **3** needing or showing great effort: *~ work* ◊ *a ~ worker* **4** (of a person) showing no kindness; harsh **5** (*infml*) (of people) ready to fight and showing no fear **6** that can be proved to be definitely true: *~ evidence/facts* **7** (of the weather) very cold and severe: *a ~ winter* [IDM] **hard and fast** (of rules, etc) fixed **hard at it** working hard **hard luck** (*GB*) used to tell sb you feel sorry for them **hard of hearing** rather deaf ■ '**hardback** n book with a stiff cover ■ '**hardboard** n [U] thin board made of very small pieces of wood pressed together ■ **hard 'cash** (*US* **cold 'cash**) n [U] money in the form of coins and notes ■ **hard 'copy** n [U] (*computing*) information from a computer that has been printed on paper ■ '**hard core** n [sing] central most involved members of a group ■ **hard 'currency** n [U,C] money that is not likely to fall suddenly in value ■ **hard 'disk** n disk inside a computer that stores data and programs ■ **hard 'drug** n strong dangerous drug that is likely to lead to addiction ■ **hard-'headed** adj determined; not influenced by your emotions ■ **hard-'hearted** adj not kind or caring ■ **hard 'labour** (*US* **hard 'labor**) n [U] punishment in prison that involves hard physical work ■ **hard-'line** adj fixed in your beliefs ■ **hard 'shoulder** n [sing] hard surface at the side of a motorway, used in an emergency ■ '**hardware** n [U] **1** (*computing*) machinery and electronic parts of a computer system **2** tools and equipment used in the house and garden ■ **hard 'water** n [U] water that contains calcium and other minerals that make mixing with soap difficult ■ '**hardwood** n [U] hard heavy wood, eg oak or beech

hard² /hɑːd/ adv **1** with great effort; with difficulty: *try/work ~* ◊ *my ~-earned money* **2** carefully and thoroughly: *think/stare* **3** heavily; a lot: *raining ~* [IDM] **be/feel hard done by** be or feel unfairly treated **be hard pressed/pushed to do sth | be hard put (to it) (to do sth)** find it very difficult to do sth **be hard to say** be difficult to estimate **be hard up for sth** have too few or too little of sth **take sth hard** be very upset by sth ■ **hard-'boiled** adj (of eggs) boiled until the yellow part (yolk) is hard ■ **hard-'pressed** adj in difficulties, because of lack of time or money ■ **hard 'up** adj (*infml*) having little money ■ **hard-'wearing** adj (*GB*) (of cloth) tough and lasting for a long time

harden /'hɑːdn/ v [I, T] become or

make sth firm, solid, etc **2** [T] ~**(to)** make sb less sensitive to sth

hardly /'hɑːdli/ adv **1** almost no; almost not: ~ *ever* **2** used to emphasize that it is difficult to do sth: *I could ~ keep my eyes open*

hardship /'hɑːdʃɪp/ n [U,C] (cause of) severe suffering

hardy /'hɑːdi/ adj (-ier, -iest) able to endure cold, difficult conditions, etc ▶ **hardiness** n [U]

hare /heə(r)/ n animal like a large rabbit with strong back legs that can run very fast ● **hare** v [I] run fast ■ **'hare-brained** adj crazy and unlikely to succeed

harem /'hɑːriːm/ n (women living in the) separate women's part of a Muslim house

hark /hɑːk/ v [I] (old-fash) listen [PV] **hark back (to sth)** mention again an earlier subject or event

harm /hɑːm/ n [U] damage; injury [IDM] **out of harm's way** safe ● **harm** v [T] cause harm to sb/sth ▶ **harmful** adj causing harm ▶ **harmless** adj **1** not dangerous **2** unlikely to upset or offend people: ~*less fun*

harmonica /hɑː'mɒnɪkə/ n = MOUTH ORGAN (MOUTH[1])

harmonize (also **-ise**) /'hɑːmənaɪz/ v [I, T] **1** (cause two or more things to) match and look attractive together: *colours that ~ well* **2** (music) sing or play in harmony

harmony /'hɑːməni/ n (pl **-ies**) **1** [U] state of peaceful existence and agreement: *live together in perfect ~* **2** [U,C] (music) pleasing combination of musical notes **3** [C,U] pleasing combination of related things: *the ~ of colours* ▶ **harmonious** /hɑː'məʊniəs/ adj

harness /'hɑːnɪs/ n [C,U] **1** set of leather straps for fastening a horse to a cart, etc **2** set of straps for fastening sth to a person's body or to keep them from moving off or falling: *a safety ~* ● **harness** v [T] **1** put a harness on a horse or other animal **2** use the force strength of sth to produce power: ~ *the sun's rays as a source of energy*

harp /hɑːp/ n large upright musical instrument with vertical strings played with the fingers ● **harp** v [PV] **harp on (about) sth** keep talking about sth in a boring way ▶ **harpist** n person who plays the harp

harpoon /hɑː'puːn/ n spear on a rope, used for catching whales ● **harpoon** v [T] hit sth with a harpoon

harpsichord /'hɑːpsɪkɔːd/ n musical instrument like a piano,

but with strings that are plucked mechanically

harrowing /'hærəʊɪŋ/ adj very shocking or frightening

harsh /hɑːʃ/ adj **1** unpleasantly rough or sharp **2** cruel; severe: *a ~ punishment* ▶ **harshly** adv ▶ **harshness** n [U]

harvest /'hɑːvɪst/ n **1** [C,U] (season for) cutting and gathering of crops on a farm, etc **2** [C] crops, or amount of crops gathered: *a good wheat ~* ● **harvest** v [T] cut and gather a crop

has /həz; əz/ → HAVE

hash /hæʃ/ n **1** [U] cooked chopped meat **2** (infml) = HASHISH **3** (also **'hash sign**) (GB) [C] symbol (#), esp one on a telephone [IDM] **make a hash of sth** (infml) do sth badly

hashish /'hæʃiːʃ; hæ'ʃiːʃ/ n [U] drug from the hemp plant

hasn't /'hæznt/ has not → HAVE

hassle /'hæsl/ n [C,U] (infml) difficulty; trouble ● **hassle** v [T] (infml) annoy sb by continually asking them to do sth

haste /heɪst/ n [U] speed in doing sth, esp because there is not much time

hasten /'heɪsn/ v **1** [I] be quick to do or say sth: *I ~ to add that your child is safe*. **2** [T] (written) cause sth to happen sooner

hasty /'heɪsti/ adj **1** made or done too quickly: *a ~ meal* **2** (of a person) acting too quickly ▶ **hastily** adv

hat /hæt/ n covering for the head [IDM] **I take my hat off to sb | hats off to sb** (esp GB) used to show admiration for sb ■ **'hat-trick** n three similar successes made one after the other by one person

hatch /hætʃ/ v **1** [I, T] ~**(out)** (cause a young bird, fish, insect, etc to) come out of an egg: *The chicks have ~ed* (out). **2** [T] prepare a plan, etc, esp in secret ● **hatch** n (movable cover over an) opening in a floor, wall, etc: *an escape ~*

hatchback /'hætʃbæk/ n car with a sloping door at the back that opens upwards

hatchet /'hætʃɪt/ n small axe

hatchway /'hætʃweɪ/ n = HATCH

hate /heɪt/ v [T] **1** have a great dislike for sb/sth **2** be sorry: *I ~ to trouble you*. [IDM] **hate sb's guts** (infml) dislike sb very much ● **hate** n [U] great dislike ▶ **hateful** adj very unpleasant

hatred /'heɪtrɪd/ n [U] ~**(for/of)** hate

haughty /'hɔːti/ adj (-ier, -iest) unfriendly and too proud; arrogant ▶ **haughtily** adv ▶ **haughtiness** n [U]

haul /hɔːl/ v [I, T] pull sth/sb with a lot of effort ● **haul** n **1** large amount of sth stolen or illegal: *a ~ of weapons/ drugs* **2** distance covered in a particular journey: *a long~~ flight* **3** quantity of fish caught at one time ■ **haulage** *n* [U] (*GB*) business of transporting goods by road or railway

haunch /hɔːntʃ/ *n* [C, usu pl] part of the body between the waist and the thighs

haunt /hɔːnt/ *v* [T] **1** (of ghosts) appear in a place: *a ~ed house* **2** (of sth unpleasant) return repeatedly to your mind: *The memory still ~s me.* **3** continue to cause problems for sth ● **haunt** *n* place visited often

have¹ /həv; *əv; strong form* hæv/ (*third pers sing pres tense* has *pt* had *pp* had) (*GB* have got) *v* **1** (*also* **have got**) [T] (*also* **has got/have got**) own, hold or possess sth: *He has/has got a house in London.* ◇ *Has she (got)/Does she ~ blue eyes?* **2** (*also* **have got**) [T] let a feeling or thought come into your mind: *I ~ no doubt* (= I am sure) *that you are right.* ◇ *H~ you (got) any idea where he lives?* **3** (*also* **have got**) [T] suffer from an illness: *~ a headache* **4** [T] experience sth: *~ a good holiday* **5** [T] eat, drink or smoke sth: *~ breakfast/a cigarette* **6** [T] perform a particular action: *~ a swim/walk/ shower* **7** [T] give birth to sb/sth: *~ a baby* **8** [T] produce a particular effect: *~ a strong influence on sb* **9** [T] receive sth from sb: *I've had a letter from my aunt.* **10** [T] suffer the effects of what sb does to you: *They had their house burgled.* **11** [T] cause sth to be done or to be by sb else: *You should ~ your hair cut.* **12** [T] allow sth: *I won't ~ such behaviour here!* **13** [T] (*infml*) trick or deceive sb: *You've been had!* **14** [T] entertain sb in your home: *We're having friends to dinner.* [IDM] **have had it** (*infml*) **1** be in very bad condition; be unable to be repaired **2** be unable to accept a situation any longer: *I've had it (up to here) with his problems.* **have it in for sb** (*infml*) not like sb and be unpleasant to them **have it** (that) claim that it is a fact that ... *Rumour has it that ...* [PV] **have sb on** (*infml*) play a trick on sb **have (got) sth on** be wearing sth **have sth on sb** (*infml*) have information to show that sb has done sth wrong **have sth out** cause sth, esp part of the body, to be removed: *~ a tooth out* **have sth out (with sb)** settle a disagreement with sb by arguing about it openly **have sb up (for sth)** (*infml*) (*esp passive*) cause sb to appear in court for a crime: *He was had up for robbery.*

have² /həv; *əv; strong form* hæv/ *aux v* used for forming perfect tenses: *I ~/I've finished.* ◇ *She has/*

she's gone. ◇ (*fml*) *Had I known that* (= if I had known that) *I would never have come.*

haven /ˈheɪvn/ *n* place of safety or rest

haven't /ˈhævnt/ *short for* HAVE NOT

have to /ˈhæv tə; ˈhæf tə; *strong form and before vowels* ˈhæv tuː; ˈhæf tuː/ (*also* **have got to**) *modal v* used for saying that sb must do sth or that sth must happen: *I've got to go now.* ◇ *You don't have to* (= it is not necessary to) *go out.*

havoc /ˈhævək/ *n* [U] widespread damage

hawk /hɔːk/ *n* **1** large bird that catches and eats small birds and animals **2** person, esp a politician, who favours the use of military force

hay /heɪ/ *n* [U] grass cut and dried for use as animal food ■ **'hay fever** *n* [U] illness of the nose and throat, caused by pollen from plants ■ **'haystack** *n* large pile of hay firmly packed for storing ■ **'haywire** *adj* **go haywire** (*infml*) become disorganized or out of control

hazard /ˈhæzəd/ *n* ~ **(to)** danger; risk ● **hazard** *v* [T] **1** suggest or guess at sth that you know may be wrong **2** (*fml*) risk sth or put it in danger ▶ **hazardous** *adj* dangerous; risky

haze /heɪz/ *n* [U] **1** thin mist **2** confused mental state

hazel /ˈheɪzl/ *n* small tree that produces small edible nuts (**hazelnuts**) ● **hazel** *adj* (of eyes) greenish-brown or reddish-brown in colour

hazy /ˈheɪzi/ *adj* (**-ier, -iest**) **1** misty **2** not clear; vague: *~ memories* ▶ **hazily** *adv*

H-bomb /ˈeɪtʃ bɒm/ *n* = HYDROGEN BOMB (HYDROGEN)

he /hiː/ *pron* (used as the subject of a v) **1** male person or animal mentioned earlier: *I spoke to John before he left.* **2** (*old-fash*) (male or female) person: *Every child needs to know that he is loved.*

head¹ /hed/ *n* **1** [C] part of the body that contains the eyes, nose, brain, etc **2** [C] mind or brain: *The thought never entered my ~.* **3** (**heads**) [U] side of a coin with the head of a person on it **4** [C, usu sing] wider end of a long narrow object: *the ~ of a pin/ hammer* **5** [sing] top: *at the ~ of the page* **6** [sing] most important end: *at the ~ of the table* ◇ *the ~ of a bed* (= where your head rests) **7** [sing] front: *at the ~ of the queue* **8** [C] person in charge of a group of people or an organization: *~s of government* **9** [sing] pressure produced by steam [IDM] **a/per head** for each person: *dinner at £15 a ~* ● **be banging, etc**

your head against a brick wall keep trying to do sth without any success **bring sth/come to a head** bring sth to/reach the point at which action is essential **go to your head 1** make you slightly drunk **2** (of success) make you too confident **have a head for sth** be good at sth: *to have a ~ for business/figures* **have your head screwed on (the right way)** (*infml*) be sensible **head first 1** with your head before the rest of your body: *fall ~ first down the stairs* **2** without thinking before acting **head over heels in love** loving sb very much **keep/lose your head** stay calm/fail to stay calm in a crisis **laugh, scream, etc your head off** (*infml*) laugh, etc a lot and very loudly **over sb's head 1** too difficult to understand **2** to a higher position of authority than sb **put/our/put your heads together** discuss a plan, etc as a group ■ **headache** *n* **1** pain in the head **2** problem ■ **header** *n* **1** (in football) act of hitting the ball with your head **2** line of text that is automatically added to the top of every page printed from a computer ■ **headland** *n* high piece of land that sticks out into the sea ■ **headlight** (*also* **headlamp**) *n* bright light on the front of a vehicle ■ **headline** *n* **1** [C] words printed in large letters above a newspaper story **2** (**the headlines**) [*pl*] summary of the main points of the news on radio or television ■ **headmaster** (*fem* **headmistress**) *n* teacher who is in charge of a school ■ **head-on** *adj, adv* with the front parts hitting each other: *The cars crashed ~-on.* ■ **headphones** [*pl*] receivers that fit over the ears, for listening to music, etc ■ **head quarters** [*n*, *U*, *with sing or pl verb*] (*abbr* **HQ**) place from which an organization is controlled ■ **headrest** *n* part of a seat that supports a person's head, esp in a car ■ **headroom** *n* [U] clear space above a vehicle ■ **headstone** *n* stone that marks the head of a grave ■ **headway** *n* [U] [IDM] **make headway** make progress

head² /hed/ *v* **1** [T, I] move in the direction that is mentioned: *~ south/ for home* **2** [T] (*also* **head sth up**) lead or be in charge of sth: *She'll ~ the research team.* **3** [T] be at the front of a line of people or at the top of a list of names: *~ a procession* **4** [T] hit a football with your head [PV] **head sb off** get in front of sb and make them change direction **head sth off** take action to prevent sth from happening

heading /'hedɪŋ/ *n* words at the top of a page, as a title

headlong /'hedlɒŋ/ *adv, adj* **1** with

the head first **2** quickly and without thinking: *rush ~ into a decision*

headstrong /'hedstrɒŋ/ *adj* determined to do things your own way, refusing to listen to advice

heady /'hedi/ *adj* (**-ier, -iest**) having a strong effect on your senses, making you feel excited

heal /hi:l/ *v* [I, T] become or make sth healthy again: *The cut has ~ed.*

health /helθ/ *n* [U] **1** condition of a person's body or mind: *be in good/ poor ~* **2** state of being physically and mentally healthy **3** work of providing and maintaining health services: *the Department of ~* ■ **health farm** (*US* **'health spa**) *n* place where people can stay for short periods of time in order to improve their health by dieting, doing physical exercises, etc ▸ **healthy** *adj* (**-ier, -iest**) **1** having good health **2** good for your health: *a ~y diet* **3** showing that you are in good health: *a ~y appetite* **4** large and showing success: *~y profits* ▸ **healthily** *adv*

heap /hi:p/ *n* [C] **1** pile or mass of things or material: *a ~ of books/ sand* **2** (**heaps**) [*pl*] (*infml*) large quantity of sth: *~s of time* ● **heap** *v* [T] put sth in a large pile: *~ food on your plate*

hear /hɪə(r)/ *v* (*pt, pp* **~d** /hɜ:d/) **1** [I, T] be aware of sounds with your ears **2** [T] pay attention to sb: *You're not to go, do you ~ me?* **3** [T] be told about sth: *I ~ she's leaving.* **4** [T] listen and judge a case in a law court [IDM] **hear! hear!** used for expressing agreement at a meeting [PV] **hear from sb** receive a letter, news, etc from sb **hear of sb/sth** know about: *I've never ~d of the place.* **not hear of sth** refuse to allow sth: *He wouldn't ~ of my walking home alone.* **hear sb out** listen to sb until they finish speaking

hearing /'hɪərɪŋ/ *n* **1** [U] ability to hear **2** [C] official meeting at which the facts of a crime, complaint, etc are presented to a group of people and a course of action is decided **3** [*sing*] opportunity to defend your opinion, actions, etc: *get a fair ~* [IDM] **in/within (sb's) hearing** near enough to sb so that they can hear what is said ■ **hearing aid** *n* small device used for improving hearing

hearsay /'hɪəseɪ/ *n* [U] rumour

hearse /hɜ:s/ *n* car used for carrying the coffin to a funeral

heart /hɑ:t/ *n* [C] **1** organ that pumps blood around the body **2** centre of a person's feelings, esp love **3** centre or most important part of sth **4** something shaped like a heart **5** (**hearts**) [*pl*] one of the four sets of playing cards (**suits**), with red heart symbols on them [IDM] **break sb's heart** make sb feel very sad **by heart** from memory: *learn/know a poem by* ~ **from the (bottom of your) heart** sincerely **not have the heart (to do sth)** not be cruel enough to do sth **take/lose heart** become encouraged/discouraged **take sth to heart** be very upset by sth that sb says or does ■ **heartache** n [U,C] great sadness ■ **heart attack** n sudden serious illness in which the heart stops working ■ **heartbeat** n movement or sound of the heart as it pumps blood ■ **heartbreaking** adj causing deep sadness ■ **heartbroken** adj feeling great sadness ■ **heartburn** n [U] burning feeling in the chest, caused by indigestion ■ **heartfelt** adj sincere ■ **heartless** adj without pity ▶ **heartlessly** adv ■ **heartrending** adj causing deep sadness ■ **heart-to-heart** n open honest talk about personal matters

hearten /ˈhɑːtn/ v [T] make sb feel encouraged and more hopeful

hearth /hɑːθ/ n (area in front of the) fireplace

hearty /ˈhɑːti/ adj (-ier, -iest) 1 friendly: *a ~ welcome* 2 loud and (too) cheerful 3 (of a meal or appetite) big 4 showing that you feel strongly about sth: *a ~ dislike of sth* ▶ **heartily** adv 1 in a hearty way 2 very: *I'm heartily sick of this rain.*

heat¹ /hiːt/ n 1 [U,sing] quality of being hot 2 [U,C,usu sing] level of temperature: *increase/reduce the ~* 3 [U] hot weather 4 [U] great anger or excitement 5 [C] early stage in a competition [IDM] **be on heat** (US) **be in heat** (of female dogs, etc) be in a period of sexual excitement ■ **heatwave** n period of unusually hot weather

heat² /hiːt/ v [I, T] become or make sth hot ● **heated** adj angry; excited: *a ~ed argument* ● **heater** n machine used for heating a room or water ● **heating** n [U] system for heating a building

heath /hiːθ/ n area of open land covered with rough grass and heather

heathen /ˈhiːðn/ n (old-fash, offens) person who does not believe in one of the world's main religions

heather /ˈheðə(r)/ n [U] low wild plant with small purple, pink or white flowers

heave /hiːv/ v 1 [I, T] lift, pull or throw sth heavy with great effort 2 [I] rise and fall regularly: *Her shoulders ~d with laughter.* 3 [T] make a sound slowly: *a ~ a sigh of relief* 4 [I] get a tight feeling in your throat as though you are about to vomit [PV]

heave to (pt, pp **hove** /həʊv/) (of a ship) stop moving ● **heave** n act of heaving

heaven /ˈhevn/ n 1 (also **Heaven**) [U] place believed to be the home of God and of good people after death 2 [U,C] (infml) place or state of great happiness 3 (**Heaven**) [?] (fml) God 4 (**the heavens**) [pl] (lit) the sky [IDM] (**Good**) **Heavens!** (spoken) used for showing surprise ▶ **heavenly** adj 1 of or from heaven or the sky: *~ bodies* (= the sun, moon, stars and planets) 2 (infml) very pleasant

heavy /ˈhevi/ adj (-ier, -iest) 1 weighing a lot; difficult to lift or move 2 of more than the usual amount, force, etc: *~ rain* ◇ *a ~ smoker* (= a person who smokes a lot) 3 busy: *a ~ day/schedule* 4 (of work) hard; needing a lot of effort 5 (of food) large in amount or very solid 6 (of writing, music, etc) difficult and serious [IDM] **heavy going** difficult or boring **a heavy heart** feeling of great sadness **make heavy weather of sth** make sth more difficult than it really is ▶ **heavily** adv: *drink/sleep heavily* ● **heaviness** n [U] ● **heavy** n (pl -ies) (infml) big strong man employed as a bodyguard, etc ■ **heavy-duty** adj strong enough for rough use, bad weather, etc ■ **heavy industry** n [U,C] industry that produces metal, large machines, cars, etc ■ **heavyweight** n 1 boxer weighing 79·5 kilograms or more 2 important person

heckle /ˈhekl/ v [I, T] shout out rude remarks at a speaker in a meeting ▶ **heckler** /ˈheklə(r)/ n

hectare /ˈhekteə(r)/ n (abbr **ha**) metric measure of area; 10 000 square metres

hectic /ˈhektɪk/ adj very busy; full of activity: *lead a ~ life*

he'd /hiːd/ = HE HAD; HE WOULD

hedge /hedʒ/ n 1 row of bushes between fields, gardens, etc 2 ~ (**against**) defence: *a ~ against inflation* ● **hedge** v 1 [I] avoid giving a direct answer to a question 2 [T] put a hedge around a field, etc [IDM] **hedge your bets** protect yourself against loss by supporting more than one side in an argument, etc ■ **hedgerow** n row of bushes, etc planted along the edge of a road or field

hedgehog /ˈhedʒhɒg/ n small animal covered with spines

heed /hiːd/ v [T] (fml) pay careful attention to sb's advice or a warning ● **heed** n [U] [IDM] **give/pay heed (to sb/sth)** | **take heed (of sb/sth)** (fml) pay careful attention to sb/sth ▶ **heedless** adj ~(**of**) (fml) not paying attention to sb/sth

heel /hiːl/ n **1** back part of the human foot **2** part of a sock or shoe that covers this **3** raised part of a shoe under the back of the foot [IDM] **at/on sb's heels** following closely behind sb **come to heel 1** agree to obey sb **2** (of a dog) come close behind its owner **down at heel** untidy and poorly dressed ● **heel** v **1** [T] repair the heel of a shoe **2** [I] ~(**over**) (of a ship) lean over to one side

hefty /ˈhefti/ adj (-**ier**, -**iest**) (infml) big; powerful

heifer /ˈhefə(r)/ n young female cow

height /haɪt/ n **1** [U,C] measurement of how tall a person or thing is **2** [U] quality of being tall **3** [C,U] particular distance above the ground: gain/lose ~ **4** [C, usu pl] high place or position **5** [sing] highest degree or main point of sth: the ~ of folly/summer

heighten /ˈhaɪtn/ v [I, T] become or make a feeling or effect greater or more intense

heir /eə(r)/ n ~(**to; of**) person with the legal right to inherit property, etc when the owner dies ▶ **heiress** /ˈeəres/ n female heir ▶ **heirloom** /ˈeəluːm/ n valuable object that has belonged to the same family for many years

held pt, pp of HOLD¹

helicopter /ˈhelɪkɒptə(r)/ n aircraft with horizontal revolving blades (**rotors**) on the top

helium /ˈhiːliəm/ n [U] (symb **He**) light colourless gas, used in balloons and airships

hell /hel/ n **1** (usu **Hell**) [sing] place believed to be the home of wicked people after death **2** [U,sing] very unpleasant situation or experience causing great suffering **3** [U] (sl) swear word used to show anger or for emphasis: Who ~ is he? [IDM] (**just**) **for the hell of it** (infml) just for fun **give sb hell** (infml) make life unpleasant for sb **like hell 1** (infml) used for emphasis: drive like ~ (= very fast) **2** (spoken) used when you are refusing permission or denying sth ▶ **hellish** adj (infml, esp AmE) very unpleasant

he'll /hiːl/ short for HE WILL

hello (GB **hallo**, **hullo**) /həˈləʊ/ n, exclam (pl ~s) used as a greeting, to attract sb's attention or to express surprise

helm /helm/ n handle or wheel for steering a boat or ship [IDM] **at the helm** in control

helmet /ˈhelmɪt/ n protective covering for the head

help¹ /help/ v **1** [I, T] do part of the work of sb, be of use or service to sb: They ~ed me (to) lift the boxes. ◇ H~! I'm stuck! **2** [T] ~ **yourself/sb** (**to**) serve yourself/sb with food, drink, etc [IDM] **can (not) help (doing) sth | can not help but do sth** can not prevent or avoid sth: She couldn't ~ laughing. [PV] **help (sb) out** help sb in a difficult situation ▶ **helper** n person who helps ▶ **helping** n serving of food

help² /help/ n **1** [U] act of helping sb to do sth; fact of being useful **2** [U] advice, money, etc given to sb to solve their problems: medical ~ ◇ a ~ key/screen (= function on a computer that gives information on how to use the computer) **3** [sing] person or thing that helps sb: She's a great ~ to me. ■ **'help desk** n service in a business company that gives people information and help, esp if they are having problems with a computer ▶ **helpful** adj useful ▶ **helpfully** /-fəli/ adv ▶ **helpfulness** n [U] ▶ **helpless** adj needing the help of others; powerless ▶ **helplessly** adv ▶ **helplessness** n [U] ■ **'helpline** n (GB) telephone service that provides advice and information about particular problems

hem /hem/ n edge of a piece of cloth, turned under and sewn, esp on a piece of clothing ● **hem** v (-**mm**-) [T] make a hem on sth [PV] **hem sb/sth in** surround sb/sth, so that they cannot move easily ■ **'hemline** n lower edge of a skirt or dress

hemisphere /ˈhemɪsfɪə(r)/ n **1** one half of the earth: the northern ~ **2** (anat) either half of the brain **3** one half of a sphere

hemo- → HAEMO-

hemp /hemp/ n [U] plant used for making rope and cloth, and also to make the drug cannabis

hen /hen/ n **1** adult female chicken **2** female of any bird ■ **'hen party** (also **'hen night**) (GB) n party for women only which is held for a woman who will soon get married ■ **'henpecked** adj (infml) (of a man) ruled by his wife

hence /hens/ adv **1** for this reason **2** from now ▶ **hence'forth** (also ~**forward**) adv (fml) from now on

henchman /ˈhentʃmən/ n (pl -**men**) faithful supporter who always obeys his leader's orders

henna /ˈhenə/ n [U] plant producing a) reddish-brown dye, used esp on the hair and skin

her /hɜː(r)/ pron (used as the object of a v or prep) female person or animal mentioned earlier: I love ~. ◇ Give it to ~. ● **her** det of or belonging to her: *That's ~ book, not yours.* ▶ **hers** /hɜːz/ *pron* of or belonging to her: *Is that ~?*

herald /'herəld/ *n* **1** sign that sth else is going to happen soon **2** (in the past) person who carried messages from a ruler ● **herald** *v* [T] (*written*) be a sign that sth is going to happen ▶ **heraldry** /'herəldri/ *n* [U] study of coats of arms

herb /hɜːb/ *n* plant whose leaves or seeds are used in medicine or to add flavour to food ▶ **herbal** *adj* of herbs ▪ **herbalist** *n* person who grows or sells herbs for medical use

herbaceous /hɜː'beɪʃəs/ *adj* (*tech*) (of a plant) having a soft stem ▪ **her baceous 'border** *n* flower bed with plants that flower every year

herd /hɜːd/ *n* group of animals, esp cattle, together ● **herd** *v* [T] move sb/sth in a particular direction: *The prisoners were ~ed onto a train.* ▶ **herdsman** /'hɜːdzmən/ *n* (*pl* -men) man who looks after a herd

here /hɪə(r)/ *adv* **1** in, at or to this place: *I live ~.* ◇ *Come ~.* **2** now; at this point: *H~ the speaker paused.* [IDM] **here and there** in various places **here's to sb/sth** used when drinking to the health or success of sth/sb **neither here nor there** not important or relevant ▪ **here a'bouts** *adv* (*fml*) near this place ▪ **here'in** *adv* (*fml*) (*law*) in this place or document ▪ **here'with** *adv* (*written*) with this letter, book or document

hereafter /ˌhɪər'ɑːftə(r)/ *adv* (*fml*) **1** (in legal documents, etc) in the rest of this document **2** from this time; in future ▶ **the hereafter** *n* [sing] life after death

hereditary /hə'redɪtri/ *adj* (esp of illness) passed on from parent to child

heredity /hə'redəti/ *n* [U] passing on of characteristics from parents to children

heresy /'herəsi/ *n* [U,C] (*pl* -ies) (holding of a) belief that is completely different from what is generally accepted, esp in a religion ▶ **heretic** /'herətɪk/ *n* person guilty of heresy ▶ **heretical** /hə'retɪkl/ *adj*

heritage /'herɪtɪdʒ/ *n* [C, usu sing] all the things that have been passed on over many years in a country

hermit /'hɜːmɪt/ *n* person who lives a simple life alone for religious reasons

hernia /'hɜːniə/ *n* [C,U] medical condition in which the bowel pushes through the wall of the abdomen

hero /'hɪərəʊ/ *n* (*pl* ~es) **1** person admired for bravery or other good qualities **2** main male character in a story, play, etc ▶ **heroic** /hə'rəʊɪk/ *adj*

of heroes; very brave ▶ **heroically** /-kli/ *adv* ▶ **heroics** *n* [pl] (*disapprov*) talk or behaviour that is too brave or dramatic ▶ **heroine** /'herəʊɪn/ *n* female hero ▶ **heroism** /'herəʊɪzəm/ *n* [U] very great courage

heroin /'herəʊɪn/ *n* [U] drug made from morphine

herpes /'hɜːpiːz/ *n* [U] infectious disease that causes painful spots on the skin

herring /'herɪŋ/ *n* sea fish used for food ▪ **'herringbone** *n* [U] V-shaped pattern

hers → HER

herself /hɜː'self/ *pron* **1** used as a reflexive when the female doer of an action is also affected by it: *She hurt ~.* **2** used for emphasis: *She told me the news ~.* [IDM] **(all) by herself 1** alone **2** without help

he's /hiːz/ *short for* HE IS; HE HAS

hesitant /'hezɪtənt/ *adj* slow to speak or act because you are unsure ▶ **hesitancy** *n* [U]

hesitate /'hezɪteɪt/ *v* [I] be slow to speak or act because you are uncertain or nervous ▶ **hesitation** /ˌhezɪ'teɪʃn/ *n* [U,C]

heterogeneous /ˌhetərə'dʒiːniəs/ *adj* (*fml*) made up of different kinds

heterosexual /ˌhetərə'sekʃuəl/ *adj, n* (person who is) sexually attracted to people of the opposite sex

het up /ˌhet 'ʌp/ *adj* (*infml*, *GB*) upset

hexagon /'heksəgən/ *n* (*geom*) shape with six sides

heyday /'heɪdeɪ/ *n* [sing] time of greatest success

hi /haɪ/ *exclam* (*infml*) used as a greeting: *Hi guys!*

hiatus /haɪ'eɪtəs/ *n* [usu sing] space or pause when nothing happens or where something is missing

hibernate /'haɪbəneɪt/ *v* [I] (of animals) sleep during the winter ▶ **hibernation** /ˌhaɪbə'neɪʃn/ *n* [U]

hiccup (*also* **hiccough**) /'hɪkʌp/ *n* **1** sudden repeated stopping of the breath with a sound that you cannot control **2** (*infml*) small problem ● **hiccup** *v* [I] give a hiccup(1)

hide¹ /haɪd/ *v* (*pt* **hid** /hɪd/; *pp* **hidden** /'hɪdn/) **1** [T] put or keep sth out of sight **2** [I] get out of sight ▪ **'hideaway** *n* place where you can to to hide or be alone ▪ **'hideout** *n* place where sb goes where they do not want anyone to find them ▪ **'hiding place** *n* place where sb/sth can be hidden

hide² /haɪd/ *n* animal's skin

hideous /'hɪdiəs/ *adj* very ugly; horrible ▶ **hideously** *adv*

hiding /'haɪdɪŋ/ *n* **1** state of being hidden **2** [sing] (*infml*, *esp*

GB) physical punishment of being beaten

hierarchy /'haɪərɑːki/ n (pl **-ies**) organization with ranks of authority from lowest to highest

hi-fi /'haɪ faɪ/ adj, n [C,U] (of) equipment that reproduces recorded sound almost perfectly

high¹ /haɪ/ adj **1** measuring a long distance from the bottom to the top: a ~ fence **2** having the distance that is mentioned from the bottom to the top: The wall is six feet ~. **3** greater than normal in quantity, size or degree: a ~ price ◇ a ~ degree of accuracy **4** important: a ~ official **5** morally good: have ~ ideals **6** very favourable: have a ~ opinion of her **7** (of a sound) not deep **8** middle or most attractive part of a period of time: ~ summer **9** (of food) beginning to go bad and having a strong smell **10** ~(**on**) (infml) under the influence of alcohol or drugs [IDM] **be/get on your high horse** (infml) act proudly, thinking that you know best **high and dry** without help or support **it's high time** → **TIME¹** ■ **'highbrow** adj sometimes (disapprov) knowing a lot about or concerned with intellectual matters ■ **high-'class** adj of good quality ■ **High Com'missioner** n representative of one Commonwealth country in another ■ **High 'Court** n highest court of law for civil cases in England and Wales ■ **higher edu'cation** n [U] education at college and university, esp to degree level ■ **high fi'delity** adj, n (old-fash) = HI-FI ■ **high-'flyer** (also **high-'flier**) n person with the ambition and ability to be very successful ■ **high-'grade** adj of high quality ■ **high-'handed** adj using power without consideration for others ■ **the 'high jump** n [sing] sport of jumping over a high bar ■ **'highlands** /'haɪləndz/ n [pl] mountainous part of a country ■ **high-'level** adj **1** (of meetings, etc) involving senior people **2** advanced ■ **the 'high life** n [sing] fashionable luxurious way of living ■ **high-'minded** adj having strong moral principles ■ **high-'powered** adj having great power and influence; full of energy ■ **high-'profile** adj receiving a lot of media attention ■ **high-'rise** adj (of a building) very tall ■ **the 'high school** n (esp US) secondary school, for pupils aged 14–18 ■ **the high 'seas** n [pl] (fml) areas of the sea that do not belong to any particular country ■ **high 'season** n [U, sing] (esp GB) time of year when a hotel, resort, etc has most visitors ■ **high-'spirited** adj lively; excited ■ **high 'spot** n most enjoyable or important part of sth ■ **high 'street** n main

street of a town ■ **high 'tea** n (GB) early evening meal ■ **high-'tech** (also **hi-'tech**) adj (infml) **1** using the most modern methods and machines, esp electronic ones **2** (of designs, objects, etc) very modern in appearance ■ **high 'technology** n [U] use of the most modern methods and machines, esp electronic ones, in industry, etc ■ **high-'tension** adj carrying a powerful electrical current: ~-tension cables ■ **'highway** n **1** (esp US) main road, usu connecting large towns **2** (GB, fml) public road ■ **'highwayman** n (pl **-men**) (in the past) man who robbed travellers on roads

high² /haɪ/ n [C] **1** highest level or number: Profits reached a new ~. **2** (infml) feeling of intense pleasure: He was on a real ~ after winning. ● **high** adv at or to a high position: a desk piled ~ with papers

highlight /'haɪlaɪt/ n **1** most interesting part of sth **2** [pl] areas of the hair which are lighter than the rest, usu because they have been dyed **3** [pl] (tech) light part of a picture ● **highlight** v [T] give special attention to sth

highly /'haɪli/ adv **1** very; to a great extent: a ~ amusing film **2** very favourably: think ~ of sb ■ **highly-'strung** (US **high-'strung**) adj easily upset

Highness /'haɪnəs/ n title of a member of the royal family: His/Her (Royal) ~

hijack /'haɪdʒæk/ v [T] take control of a vehicle, esp an aircraft, by force ► **hijacker** n

hike /haɪk/ n, v [I] (go for a) long walk in the country ► **hiker** n

hilarious /hɪ'leəriəs/ adj very amusing ► **hilariously** adv ► **hilarity** /hɪ'lærəti/ n [U] loud happy laughter

hill /hɪl/ n **1** area of high land, not as high as a mountain **2** slope on a road, etc ■ **'hillside** n side of a hill ■ **'hilltop** n top of a hill ► **hilly** adj having many hills

hilt /hɪlt/ n handle of a sword [IDM] **(up) to the hilt** as much as possible

him /hɪm/ pron (used as the object of a v or prep) male person or animal mentioned earlier: I love ~.

himself /hɪm'self/ pron **1** used as a reflexive when the male doer of an action is affected by it: He cut ~. **2** used for emphasis: He told me the news ~. [IDM] **(all) by himself 1** alone **2** without help

hind /haɪnd/ adj at the back: the ~ legs of a horse ■ **hind 'quarters** n [pl] back parts of an animal with four legs ● **hind** n female deer

hinder /'hɪndə(r)/ v [T] make it

difficult for sb to do sth or for sth to happen: ~ sb from working ▶ **hindrance** /'hɪndrəns/ n person or thing that hinders sb/sth

hindsight /'haɪndsaɪt/ n [U] understanding of an event after it has happened

Hindu /'hɪnduː/ n person whose religion is Hinduism ● **Hindu** adj of the Hindus ▶ **Hinduism** /'hɪnduːɪzəm/ n [U] Indian religion involving the worship of several gods and belief in reincarnation

hinge /hɪndʒ/ n piece of metal on which a door, gate, etc swings ● **hinge** v [T] attach sth with a hinge [PV] **hinge on/upon sth** depend on sth completely: *Everything ~s on the result of these talks.*

hint /hɪnt/ n [C] 1 indirect suggestion: *Should I drop a ~ (= give a hint) to her?* 2 slight trace of sth: *a ~ of envy in his voice* 3 [usu pl] practical piece of advice: *helpful ~s* ● **hint** v [I, T] ~at suggest sth indirectly

hip /hɪp/ n part on either side of the body above the legs and below the waist ■ **'hip flask** n small flat bottle used for carrying alcohol

hippie (also **hippy**) /'hɪpi/ n (pl -ies) person who rejects usual social standards

hippo /'hɪpəʊ/ n (pl ~s) (infml) short for HIPPOPOTAMUS

hippopotamus /ˌhɪpə'pɒtəməs/ n (pl -muses or -mi /-maɪ/) large African river animal with thick skin

hire /'haɪə(r)/ v [T] 1 obtain the use of sth in return for payment: *a car for a week* 2 employ sb to do a job [PV] **hire sth out** allow the use of sth for a short time, in return for payment ● **hire** n [U] act of hiring sth for a short time: *bicycles for ~* ■ **hire 'purchase** n [U] (GB) agreement to pay small regular amounts for sth, having the use of it immediately

his /hɪz/ det of or belonging to him: *That's ~ book, not yours.* ● **his** pron of or belonging to him: *Is that ~?*

hiss /hɪs/ v [I, T] make a sound like that of a long 's', esp to show disapproval of sb/sth ● **hiss** n hissing sound

historian /hɪ'stɔːriən/ n student of, or expert in, history

historic /hɪ'stɒrɪk/ adj important in history: *a ~ event*

historical /hɪ'stɒrɪkl/ adj of or concerning history: *~ studies/novels* ▶ **historically** /-kli/ adv

history /'hɪstri/ n (pl -ies) 1 [U] study of past events 2 [C] description of past events 3 [sing] past events or experiences of sb/sth: *his medical ~* [IDM] **go down in/make**

history be or do sth so important that it will be remembered

hit¹ /hɪt/ v (-tt- pt, pp **hit**) [T] 1 bring sth forcefully against sb/sth: *He ~ me with a stick.* 2 come against sth/sb with force: *The car ~ a tree.* 3 have a bad effect on sb/sth: *The new law will ~ the poor.* 4 reach a place or level; find sth: ~ *the right road* [IDM] **hit it off (with sb)** (infml) have a good relationship with sb **hit the hay/sack** (infml) go to bed **hit the nail on the head** say sth that is exactly right **hit the roof** (infml) suddenly become very angry [PV] **hit back (at sb/sth)** reply forcefully to an attack **hit on/upon sth** think of a plan, solution, etc unexpectedly **hit out (at sb/sth)** attack sb/sth forcefully, esp with words ■ **hit-and-run** adj (of a road accident) caused by a driver who does not stop to help

hit² /hɪt/ n 1 act of hitting sb/sth 2 person or thing that is very popular: *Her new play is a great ~.* 3 result of a search on a computer, esp on the Internet ■ **'hit list** n (infml) list of people to be killed or against whom an action is planned ■ **hit man** n (infml) criminal who is paid to kill sb

hitch /hɪtʃ/ v 1 [I, T] get free rides in other people's cars; travel around in this way: ~ *round Europe* 2 [T] ~ (**up**) pull up a piece of your clothing 3 [T] fasten sth to sth with a loop or hook ● **hitch** n 1 small problem that causes a delay 2 kind of knot ■ **'hitch-hike** v [I] travel around by obtaining free rides in other people's cars ▶ **'hitch-hiker** n

hitherto /ˌhɪðə'tuː/ adv (fml) until now

HIV /ˌeɪtʃ aɪ 'viː/ abbr virus that causes AIDS: *to be ~ positive*

hive /haɪv/ n 1 box for bees to live in 2 place full of busy activity: *a ~ of activity* ● **hive** v [PV] **hive sth off (to/into sth)** separate one part of a group from the rest; sell part of a business

HMS /ˌeɪtʃ em 'es/ abbr (used before the name of British warships) Her/His Majesty's Ship

hoard /hɔːd/ n often secret store of money, food, etc ● **hoard** v [T] save and store food, money, etc, secretly

hoarding /'hɔːdɪŋ/ n (GB) large board on which advertisements are stuck

hoarse /hɔːs/ adj (~r, ~st) (of a voice) sounding rough ▶ **hoarsely** adv ▶ **hoarseness** n [U]

hoax /həʊks/ n trick played on sb for a joke: *a bomb ~* ● **hoax** v [T] deceive sb with a hoax

hob /hɒb/ n (GB) flat heating surface on a cooker

hobble /'hɒbl/ v [I] walk awkwardly, eg because your feet hurt

hobby /'hɒbi/ n (pl -ies) activity you do for pleasure in your free time

hobnail boot /ˌhɒbneɪl 'buːt/ n heavy boot with short nails in the sole

hockey /'hɒki/ n [U] 1 (GB) team game played on a field with curved sticks and a small hard ball 2 (US) = ICE HOCKEY (ICE¹)

hod /hɒd/ n box with a long handle, used for carrying bricks

hoe /həʊ/ n garden tool with a long handle, used for breaking up the soil ● **hoe** v [I, T] break up soil, remove plants, etc with a hoe

hog /hɒg/ n castrated male pig, kept for its meat ● **hog** v (-gg-) [T] have more than your fair share of sth and stop others from having it

Hogmanay /'hɒgməneɪ/ n [U] (in Scotland) New Year's Eve (31 December)

hoist /hɔɪst/ v [T] lift sth up, esp with ropes ● **hoist** n piece of equipment with ropes and pulleys for lifting heavy things

hold¹ /həʊld/ v (pt, pp held /held/) 1 [T] carry sth; have sb/sth in your hands 2 [T] keep sb/sth in a particular position: H~ your head up! 3 [T] support the weight of sb/sth: That beam won't ~ you. 4 [T] have enough room for sb/sth; contain sth/sb: This barrel ~s 25 litres. 5 [T] not allow sb to leave: H~ the thief until the police come. 6 [T] defend sth against attack 7 [I] remain firm or unchanged: How long will this fine weather ~? 8 [T] keep sb's attention or interest 9 [T] own or have sth: ~ shares 10 [T] have a particular job or position: ~ the post of Prime Minister 11 [T] have a belief, opinion, etc 12 [T] (fml) consider that sth is true: I ~ you responsible for the accident. 13 [T] cause a meeting, conversation, etc to take place 14 [T] (of a car, etc) keep a grip on a road [IDM] hold sb/sth at bay → BAY **hold your breath** stop breathing for a short time **hold the fort** look after sth while others are away **hold good** be true **hold your ground** → GROUND¹ **hold it** (spoken) used for asking sb to wait, or not to move **hold the line** keep a telephone connection open **hold your own (against sb)** not be defeated by sb **hold your tongue** not say anything **there's no holding sb** sb cannot be prevented from doing sth [PV] **hold sth against sb** allow sth bad to influence your opinion of sb **hold back** be unwilling to act

hold sb/sth back 1 control sb/sth: ~ back the crowd **2** keep sth secret **hold sb down** control the freedom of sb **hold sth down 1** keep sth at a low level: ~ down prices **2** keep a job for some time **hold forth (on sth)** speak for a long time about sth **hold off** (of rain, etc) be delayed **hold sb/sth off** resist an attack **hold off (doing)** delay sth **hold on 1** (spoken) used to tell sb to wait or stop **2** survive, even in a difficult situation **hold sb/sth on** keep sth in position **hold on to sth** keep sth **hold out 1** last **2** resist an attack or survive in a dangerous situation **hold sth out** offer sth **hold out for sth** refuse to accept an offer, and continue to demand sth better **hold sth over** postpone sth **hold sb to sth** make sb keep a promise **hold sb/sth up 1** delay sb/sth: Our flight was held up by fog. **2** use sb/sth as an example **hold up sth** rob a bank, etc by force ■ **hold-up** n **1** delay, eg in traffic **2** robbery by armed robbers

hold² /həʊld/ n **1** [sing] act of holding sb/sth **2** [C] way of holding an opponent, eg in wrestling **3** [sing] ~ (on/over) influence or power over sb/sth **4** [C] place where you can put your hands or feet when climbing **5** [C] part of a ship or plane where goods or luggage is stored [IDM] **catch, grab, take, etc (a) hold of sth** take sb/sth in your hands **get hold of sth/sb** (infml) **1** contact or find sb **2** find and use sth

holdall /'həʊldɔːl/ n (GB) large soft bag, used when travelling

holder /'həʊldə(r)/ n **1** person who owns or possesses sth: ticket ~ **2** thing that supports or holds sth: a cigarette ~

holding /'həʊldɪŋ/ n **1** ~ (in) number of shares that sb has in a company **2** something, eg land, that is owned

hole /həʊl/ n **1** [C] hollow space or gap in sth solid or in the surface of sth: a ~ in the road/wall **2** [C] small animal's home **3** [C] (infml) unpleasant place to live or to be in **4** [sing] (infml) difficult situation: be in a ~ **5** [C] place into which a ball must be hit in golf, etc [IDM] **make a hole in sth** (infml) use up a large part of your money, etc ● **hole** v [T] make a hole in sth **2** [T, T] ~ (out) hit a golf ball into the hole [PV] **hole up / be holed up** (infml) hide in a place

holiday /'hɒlədeɪ/ n **1** day(s) of rest from work: be/go on ~ **2** period of time spent travelling away from home: a camping ~ ● **holiday** v [I] spend a holiday somewhere ■ **'holidaymaker** n person visiting a place on holiday

holiness /'həʊlinəs/ n 1 [U] quality of being holy 2 [C] (His/Your Holiness) title of the Pope

hollow /'hɒləʊ/ adj 1 having a hole or empty space inside 2 curving inwards; sunken: ~ cheeks 3 (of sounds) echoing, as if coming from a hollow place 4 not sincere; false: ~ words ● hollow n area that is lower than the surface around it ● hollow v [PV] hollow sth out make a hole in sth by removing part of it: ~ out a tree trunk

holly /'hɒli/ n small evergreen tree with sharp-pointed leaves and red berries

holocaust /'hɒləkɔːst/ n large-scale destruction and the killing of many people, esp because of a war

holster /'həʊlstə(r)/ n leather holder for a small gun

holy /'həʊli/ adj (-ier, -iest) 1 associated with God or religion 2 pure and good: live a ~ life ■ the Holy 'Spirit (also the Holy 'Ghost) n [sing] (in Christianity) God in the form of a spirit

homage /'hɒmɪdʒ/ n [U,C, usu sing] (fml) ~(to) something said or done to show respect for sb

home¹ /həʊm/ n 1 [C,U] place where you live, esp with your family 2 [C] place for the care of old people or children 3 [C] place where an animal or plant lives naturally 4 [sing] place in which sth was first discovered, made or invented: Greece is the ~ of democracy. [IDM] at home 1 in a person's own house, etc 2 comfortable and relaxed: Make yourself at ~! ■ the Home 'Counties n [pl] the counties around London ■ home eco'nomics n [U] cooking and other skills needed at home, taught as a school subject ■ home-'grown adj (of food, etc) produced in your own country, garden, etc ■ home 'help n (GB) person whose job is to help old or sick people with cooking, cleaning, etc ■ 'homeland n country where a person was born ▶ homeless adj having no home ■ home-'made adj made at home ■ the 'Home Office n [sing] British government department dealing with the police, immigration, etc ■ 'home page n (computing) main page created by a company, an organization, etc on the World Wide Web from which connections to other pages can be made ■ 'homesick adj sad because you are away from home ■ homesickness n [U] ■ home 'truth n [usu pl] true but unpleasant fact about sb ■ homeward adj ▶ homeward adv going towards home ▶ homewards adv towards home ■ 'homework n [U] 1 work that a pupil does away from

school 2 (infml) work sb does to prepare for sth

home² /həʊm/ adj 1 of or connected with the place where you live 2 connected with your own country rather than foreign countries: ~ news 3 (sport) played on the team's own ground: a ~ match ● home adv 1 to or at your home: on her way ~ 2 into the correct position: drive a nail ~ [IDM] be home and dry have done sth difficult successfully ■ bring sth/come home to sb make sth/become fully understood ■ 'home coming n [C,U] act of returning to your home after being away for a long time ● home v [PV] home in on sth aim at sth and move straight towards it

homely /'həʊmli/ adj (-ier, -iest) 1 (approv, esp GB) comfortable; simple and good 2 (US, disapprov) (of a person's appearance) unattractive

homeopathy /ˌhəʊmi'ɒpəθi/ n [U] treatment of disease by giving small doses of drugs which in larger amounts would cause the same disease ▶ homeopathic /ˌhəʊmiə'pæθɪk/ adj

homicide /'hɒmɪsaɪd/ n [C,U] (esp US, law) crime of killing sb deliberately ▶ homicidal /ˌhɒmɪ'saɪdl/ adj

homing /'həʊmɪŋ/ adj 1 (of a pigeon, etc) having the ability to find its way home 2 (of a missile, etc) fitted with a device that guides it to the target

homogeneous /ˌhɒmə'dʒiːniəs/ adj (fml) consisting of things or people that are the same or of the same type

homogenized (also -ised) /hə'mɒdʒənaɪzd/ adj (of milk) treated so that the cream is mixed in with the rest

homonym /'hɒmənɪm/ n word spelt and pronounced like another word but with a different meaning, eg can meaning 'be able' and can meaning 'container'

homosexual /ˌhəʊmə'sekʃuəl; ˌhɒm-/ n, adj (person who is) sexually attracted to people of their own sex ▶ homosexuality /ˌhəʊməˌsekʃu'æləti; ˌhɒm-/ n [U]

honest /'ɒnɪst/ adj (of a person) telling the truth; not cheating or stealing 2 not hiding the truth about sth: an ~ opinion 1 ▶ honestly adv 1 in an honest way 2 (used for emphasis) really ▶ honesty n [U]

honey /'hʌni/ n 1 [U] sweet sticky substance made by bees 2 [C] (spoken, esp US) way of addressing sb that you like or love ■ 'honeycomb n [C,U] wax structure made by bees for holding their honey and eggs ■ 'honeysuckle n [U] climbing plant with sweet-smelling flowers

honeymoon /'hʌnimuːn/ n **1** holiday taken by a couple who have just got married **2** pleasant time at the start of a new job, etc: *The ~ period for the government is now over.* ● **honeymoon** v [I] spend your honeymoon somewhere

honk /hɒŋk/ v [I] n (make the) sound of a car horn

honorary /'ɒnərəri/ adj **1** (of a degree or rank) given as an honour **2** (of a person or an organization) unpaid: *~ president*

honour (US **-or**) /'ɒnə(r)/ n **1** [U] great respect and admiration for sb: *the guest of ~* (= the most important one) **2** [sing] (*fml*) something you are pleased and proud to do because of people's respect for you: *a great ~ to be invited* **3** [U] strong sense of right; reputation for good behaviour: *a man of ~* **4** [sing] person or thing that brings respect: *You are an ~ to your school.* **5** (**honours**) [pl] (*abbr* **Hons**) university course of a higher level than a basic course; high mark obtained on such a course: *an ~s degree* **6** (**His/Her/Your Honour**) [C] title of respect to a judge or a US mayor ● **honour** v [T] **1** do sth which shows great respect or praise for sb **2** do what you have agreed or promised to do

honourable (US **-or-**) /'ɒnərəbl/ adj **1** deserving or showing honour **2** (**the Honourable**) title given to certain high officials, etc ► **honourably** adv

hood /hʊd/ n **1** covering for the head and neck, fastened to a coat **2** folding cover of a car, pram, etc **3** (*US*) = BONNET(1) ► **hooded** adj having a hood

hoodwink /'hʊdwɪŋk/ v [T] trick sb

hoof /huːf/ n (pl **~s** or **hooves** /huːvz/) hard bony part of the foot of a horse, etc

hook /hʊk/ n **1** curved piece of metal, plastic, etc used for catching hold of sth or for hanging sth on **2** (in boxing) short blow with the elbow bent [IDM] **off the hook 1** (of a telephone receiver) not resting on the main part of the telephone **2** (*infml*) no longer in a difficult situation: *let/get sb off the ~* ● **hook** v [T] **1** fasten or catch sth with a hook **2** make sth into the form of a hook: *~ your foot round sth* ► **hooked** adj **1** curved; shaped like a hook **2** ~ (**on**) (*infml*) dependent on sth bad, esp a drug **3** enjoying sth very much so that you want to do it, see it, etc as much as possible

hooligan /'huːlɪɡən/ n noisy violent young person: *football ~s* ► **hooliganism** n [U]

hoop /huːp/ n circular band of wood or metal: *gold ~ earrings*

hooray /hu'reɪ/ exclam used to show happiness or approval of sth

hoot /huːt/ n [C] **1** short loud laugh or shout **2** [sing] very funny situation or person **3** sound of a car horn **4** cry of an owl [IDM] **not care/give a hoot/two hoots** (*infml*) not care at all ● **hoot** v [I] make a loud noise **2** [T] sound a car horn

Hoover™ /'huːvə(r)/ n = VACUUM CLEANER ● **hoover** v [I, T] (*GB*) clean sth with a vacuum cleaner

hooves plural of HOOF

hop /hɒp/ v (**-pp-**) [I] **1** (of a person) jump on one foot **2** (of an animal or bird) jump with all or both feet together **3** (*infml*) move quickly or easily: *~ on a bus* ● **hop** n **1** short jump **2** (*infml*) short journey, esp by plane **3** climbing plant used to flavour beer

hope /həʊp/ n **1** [C,U] desire and expectation that sth good will happen **2** [C,sing] person or thing that will help you get what you want: *You're my last ~.* [IDM] **be beyond hope (of sth)** have no chance of succeeding or recovering ● **hope** v [I, T] want sth to happen and think that it is possible: *I ~ (that) you win.* ► **hopeful** adj having or giving hope ► **hopefully** adv **1** used for expressing hope that sth will happen: *H~fully, she'll be here soon.* **2** in a hopeful way ► **hopeless** adj **1** giving no hope **2** ~ (**at**) (*infml*) very bad at sth; with no ability or skill: *~less at maths* ► **hopelessly** adv ► **hopelessness** n [U]

horde /hɔːd/ n very large crowd

horizon /hə'raɪzn/ n **1** (**the horizon**) [sing] the line at which the earth and sky seem to meet **2** [C] limit of your knowledge, experience, etc: *Travel broadens your ~s.*

horizontal /ˌhɒrɪ'zɒntl/ adj flat and level: *~ and vertical lines* ● **horizontal** [sing] horizontal line or position ► **horizontally** /-təli/ adv

hormone /'hɔːməʊn/ n substance produced in the body that encourages growth, etc

horn /hɔːn/ n **1** [C] hard pointed usu curved growth on the heads of cattle, deer, etc **2** [U] hard substance of which animal horns are made **3** [C] musical instrument with a trumpet-shaped end: *a French ~* **4** [C] device in a vehicle for making a warning sound: *blow the car horn* ► **horny** adj (**-ier, -iest**) (*infml*) sexually excited or exciting **2** made of or like horn

hornet /'hɔːnɪt/ n large wasp

horoscope /'hɒrəskəʊp/ n statement about sb's future based on the position of the stars and planets at the time of their birth

horrendous /hɒˈrendəs/ *adj* very unpleasant or shocking: ~ *injuries*

horrible /ˈhɒrəbl/ *adj* **1** (*spoken*) very bad or unpleasant: ~ *weather* **2** causing horror: *a* ~ *crime* ▶ **horribly** *adv*

horrid /ˈhɒrɪd/ *adj* (*old-fash* or *infml*) very unpleasant; nasty

horrific /həˈrɪfɪk/ *adj* extremely bad and shocking or frightening ▶ **horrifically** *adv*

horrify /ˈhɒrɪfaɪ/ *v* (*pt, pp* **-ied**) [T] fill sb with horror

horror /ˈhɒrə(r)/ *n* **1** [C, U] (something causing a) feeling of great shock, fear or disgust **2** [U] type of book, film, etc that is designed to frighten people: *a* ~ *story/film* **3** [C] (*infml*) naughty child ■ **'horror-struck** (*also* **-stricken**) *adj* very shocked

hors d'oeuvre /ˌɔː ˈdɜːv/ *n* [C, U] small amount of food served at the beginning of a meal

horse /hɔːs/ *n* large four-legged animal that people ride on or use for pulling carts, etc [IDM] **(straight) from the horse's mouth** (*infml*) (of information) directly from the person concerned ● **horse** *v* [PV] **horse about/around** (*infml*) behave in a noisy playful way ■ **'horseplay** *n* [U] rough noisy fun or play ■ **'horsepower** *n* [U] unit for measuring the power of an engine ■ **'horseshoe** *n* U-shaped metal shoe for a horse

horseback /ˈhɔːsbæk/ *n* [IDM] **on horseback** sitting on a horse ● **horseback** *adv* (*US*): ~ *riding*

horticulture /ˈhɔːtɪkʌltʃə(r)/ *n* [U] science of growing flowers, fruit, and vegetables ▶ **horticultural** /ˌhɔːtɪˈkʌltʃərəl/ *adj*

hose /həʊz/ (*also* **hosepipe**) *n* **1** [C, U] flexible tube used for directing water onto a garden or a fire **2** [pl] stockings, socks, etc ● **hose** *v* [T] ~ (**down**) wash sth with a hose

hosiery /ˈhəʊziəri/ *n* [U] used esp in shops as a word for tights, stockings and socks: *the* ~ *department*

hospice /ˈhɒspɪs/ *n* hospital for people who are dying

hospitable /hɒˈspɪtəbl; ˈhɒspɪtəbl/ *adj* **1** ~ (**to/towards**) giving a kind welcome to guests **2** (of places) pleasant to be in ▶ **hospitably** *adv*

hospital /ˈhɒspɪtl/ *n* place where people are treated for illness or injuries ▶ **hospitalize** (*also* **-ise**) *v* [T] send sb to hospital for treatment

hospitality /ˌhɒspɪˈtæləti/ *n* [U] **1** friendly and kind behaviour

towards guests **2** food, drink or services provided by an organization for guests, customers, etc: *the* ~ *industry* (= hotels, restaurants, etc)

host /həʊst/ *n* **1** person who entertains guests in their house **2** country, city or organization that holds a special event **3** person who introduces guests on radio or television programme **4** ~ **of** large number of people or things: *a* ~ *of different reasons* ● **host** *v* [T] act as a host at sth or to sth

hostage /ˈhɒstɪdʒ/ *n* prisoner kept by a person who threatens to hurt or kill them unless certain demands are obeyed

hostel /ˈhɒstl/ *n* **1** building providing cheap accommodation for students, travellers, etc **2** building where homeless people can stay

hostess /ˈhəʊstəs; -es/ *n* **1** female host **2** woman employed to welcome and entertain men at a nightclub

hostile /ˈhɒstaɪl/ *adj* ~ (**to/towards**) **1** unfriendly **2** belonging to a military enemy: ~ *aircraft* **3** (*business*) (of an offer to buy a company, etc) not wanted by the company that is to be bought: *a* ~ *takeover bid*

hostility /hɒˈstɪləti/ *n* **1** [U] unfriendly behaviour **2** (**hostilities**) [pl] acts of war

hot /hɒt/ *adj* (**-ter, ~test**) **1** having a high temperature **2** (of food) producing a burning taste: ~ *spices/curry* **3** (*infml*) new, exciting and very popular **4** (of news) very recent and usu exciting **5** strong; fierce: *He has a* ~ *temper* (= gets angry quickly). [IDM] **be in/get into hot water** (*infml*) be in/get into trouble **hot air** (*infml*) meaningless talk **(be) hot on sb's/sth's heels/tracks/trail** following sb/sth closely **not so hot** (*infml*) not good ● **hot** *v* (**-tt-**) [PV] **hot up** (*infml*) become more exciting or intense ■ **ˌhot-ˈblooded** *adj* easily angered; passionate ■ **ˌhot-ˈdesking** *n* [U] practice in an office of giving desks to workers when they are required, rather than giving each worker their own desk ■ **'hot dog** *n* hot sausage served in a long bread roll ■ **'hotfoot** *adv* (*written*) quickly and eagerly ■ **'hothead** *n* person who acts too quickly, without thinking ■ **ˌhot-ˈheaded** *adj* ■ **'hothouse** *n* heated glass building, for growing plants ■ **'hotline** *n* **1** special telephone line that people can use to get information or to talk about sth **2** direct telephone connection between heads of government ▶ **hotly** *adv* **1** passionately **2** closely: ~*ly pursued* ■ **'hot spot** *n* **1** place where fighting is common, esp for political reasons **2** place where there is a lot of activity or entertainment **3** (*computing*) area on a computer screen that you click on to start an operation, eg to load a file ■ **hot-'tempered** *adj* easily angered

hotel /həʊˈtel/ *n* building where rooms and meals are provided for travellers ▶ **hotelier** /həʊˈtelɪə(r); -lieɪ/ *n* person who owns or manages a hotel

hound /haʊnd/ *n* hunting or racing dog ● **hound** *v* [T] keep following sb and not leave them alone: *~ed by newspaper reporters*

hour /ˈaʊə(r)/ *n* **1** [C] period of 60 minutes: *London is only two ~s away* (= it takes two hours to get there). **2** [C, usu sing] period of about an hour: *a long lunch ~* **3** (**hours**) [pl] fixed period of time for work, etc: *Office ~s are from 9 a.m. to 5 p.m.* **4** (**the hour**) [sing] time when it is exactly 1 o'clock, 2 o'clock, etc: *Trains leave on the ~*. [IDM] **at the eleventh hour** at the last possible moment

hourly /ˈaʊəli/ *adj* **1** done or happening every hour: *an ~ bus service* **2** calculated by the hour: *an ~ rate of £20* ● **hourly** *adv* every hour

house¹ /haʊs/ *n* [C] (*pl* **~s** /ˈhaʊzɪz/) **1** building made for people to live in, usu for one family **2** [usu sing] people living in a house: *Be quiet or you'll wake the whole ~!* **3** building made for a purpose that is mentioned: *an opera ~* ◇ *a hen ~* **4** business firm: *a publishing ~* **5** (usu **House**) (building used by) people who discuss or pass laws: *the H~s of Parliament* ◇ *the H~ of Representatives* **6** part of a theatre where the audience sits; the audience at a particular performance: *a full ~* (= a large audience) **7** division of a school for competitions in sport, etc **8** (usu **the House of ...**) old and famous family [IDM] **bring the house down** (*infml*) make an audience laugh or clap loudly on the house paid for by the pub, firm, etc ■ **'housebound** *adj* not able to leave your house because of illness, etc ■ **'housebreaking** *n* [U] (*esp GB*) crime of entering a building by force ■ **'housekeeper** *n* person (*esp* a woman) whose job is to manage a household ■ **'housekeeping** *n* [U] **1** work of managing a household **2** money allowed for this ■ **'housemaster** (*fem* **'housemistress**) *n* (*esp GB*) teacher in charge of a group of children (**a house**) in a school ■ **the ,House of 'Commons** (**also the Commons**) (*GB*) *n* [sing, with sing or pl verb] (members of) the part of Parliament which is elected ■ **the**

,House of 'Lords (**also the Lords**) (*GB*) *n* [sing, with sing or pl verb] (members) of the non-elected part of Parliament ■ **'house music** (**also house**) *n* [U] type of popular dance music with a fast beat, played on electronic instruments ■ **'house-proud** *adj* giving great attention to the appearance of your home ■ **'housewife** *n* (*pl* **-wives** /-waɪvz/) woman who works at home looking after her family, cleaning, cooking, etc ■ **'housework** *n* [U] work done in a house, eg cleaning and cooking

house² /haʊz/ *v* [T] provide sb with a place to live

household /ˈhaʊshəʊld/ *n* all the people living in a house [IDM] **a household name/word** name of sb/sth that is very well known

housing /ˈhaʊzɪŋ/ *n* **1** [U] houses, flats, etc considered as a group: *poor ~ conditions* **2** [U] job of providing houses, flats, etc for people to live in: *a ~ committee/officer* **3** [C] cover that protects a machine

hove → HEAVE

hovel /ˈhɒvl/ *n* (*disapprov*) small dirty house or hut

hover /ˈhɒvə(r)/ *v* [I] **1** (of birds, helicopters, etc) stay in the air in one place **2** (of a person) wait about, in an uncertain manner ■ **'hovercraft** *n* (*pl* **hovercraft**) vehicle that moves over land or water supported by a cushion of air underneath it

how /haʊ/ *adv* **1** (used in questions) in what way or manner: *H~ is this word spelt?* **2** used to ask about sb's health: *H~ are you?* **3** used to ask whether sth is successful or enjoyable: *H~ was your trip?* **4** (used with an adj or adv) used to ask about the amount, degree, etc of sth or about sb's age: *H~ much are those earrings?* ◇ *H~ old is he?* **5** used to express surprise, pleasure, etc: *H~ kind of you to help!* ● **how** *conj* the way in which: *He told me ~ to get to the station.*

however /haʊˈevə(r)/ *adv* **1** to whatever degree: *He'll never succeed, ~ hard he tries.* **2** (used for adding a comment to what you have just said) although sth is true: *Sales are poor. H~, there may be an increase next month.* **3** (used in questions for showing surprise) in what way; how: *H~ did you get here without a car?* ● **however** *conj* in any way: *H~ you look at it, it's going to cost a lot.*

howl /haʊl/ *v* [I] *n* (make a) long loud cry

HQ /ˌeɪtʃ ˈkjuː/ *abbr* = HEADQUARTERS

hr *abbr* (*pl* **hrs**) = HOUR

HRH /ˌeɪtʃ ɑːr ˈeɪtʃ/ *abbr* His/Her Royal Highness

H

hub /hʌb/ n **1** central point of an activity **2** central part of a wheel ■ **'hubcap** n round metal cover over the hub of a car wheel

hubbub /'hʌbʌb/ n [sing] loud noise made by a lot of people talking at the same time

huddle /'hʌdl/ v [I, T] **1 ~(up)** crowd together, usu because of cold or fear **2** hold your arms and legs close to your body: *I ~d under a blanket.* ● **huddle** n number of people or things close together

hue /hju:/ n (fml) (shade of) colour [IDM] **hue and cry** loud angry public protest

huff /hʌf/ n [IDM] **in a huff** (infml) in a bad mood, esp because sb has upset you

hug /hʌg/ v (**-gg-**) [T] **1** put your arms round sb tightly, esp to show love **2** keep close to sth: *The boat ~ged the shore.* ● **hug** n act of hugging sb: *give sb a ~*

huge /hju:dʒ/ adj very large ▶ **hugely** adv very much

hulk /hʌlk/ n **1** broken old ship **2** large awkward person or thing ▶ **hulking** adj large and awkward

hull /hʌl/ n body of a ship

hullo = HELLO

hum /hʌm/ v (**-mm-**) **1** [I, T] sing a tune with your lips closed: *~ a tune* **2** [I] make a low continuous sound **3** [I] (infml) be full of activity ● **hum** n humming sound

human /'hju:mən/ adj **1** of people **2** showing the better qualities of people; kind ● **human** (also **human 'being**) n person ▶ **humanly** adv within human ability: *do all that is ~ly possible* ■ **human 'rights** n [pl] basic rights of freedom, equality, justice, etc

humane /hju:'meɪn/ adj showing kindness towards people and animals by making sure they do not suffer more than is necessary: *the ~ killing of animals* ▶ **humanely** adv

humanity /hju:'mænəti/ n **1** [U] people in general **2** [U] quality of being kind to people and animals **3** ((the) **humanities**) [pl] subjects of study concerned with the way people think and behave, eg literature, philosophy, etc

humble /'hʌmbl/ adj (**~r, ~st**) **1** having a modest opinion of yourself **2** low in rank; unimportant **3** (of things) not large or special in any way: *a ~ farmhouse* ● **humble** v [T] make sb feel humble ▶ **humbly** adv

humdrum /'hʌmdrʌm/ adj boring and always the same

humid /'hju:mɪd/ adj (of the air) warm and damp ▶ **humidity**

/hju:'mɪdəti/ n [U] (amount of) water in the air

humiliate /hju:'mɪlieɪt/ v [T] make sb feel ashamed or foolish ▶ **humiliating** adj: *a humiliating defeat* ▶ **humiliation** /-'eɪʃn/ n [C,U]

humility /hju:'mɪləti/ n [U] quality of being humble(1)

humorist /'hju:mərɪst/ n person who writes or tells jokes

humorous /'hju:mərəs/ adj funny; amusing ▶ **humorously** adv

humour (US **-or**) /'hju:mə(r)/ n [U] (ability to cause or feel) amusement: *have a sense of ~* ● **humour** v [T] keep sb happy by doing what they want

hump /hʌmp/ n round lump, esp on a camel's back ● **hump** v [T] (infml) carry sth heavy

hunch /hʌntʃ/ n (infml) feeling that sth is true, though without evidence to prove it ● **hunch** v [T] bend your back and shoulders into a rounded shape ■ **'hunchback** n (offens) person with a hump on their back

hundred /'hʌndrəd/ number **1** 100: *one, two, etc* ~ **2** (**a hundred** or **hundreds** (of …)) large amount: *~s of people* ▶ **hundredth** /'hʌndrədθ, -ətθ/ ordinal number 100th; the fraction ¹⁄₁₀₀; one of a hundred equal parts of sth

hundredweight /'hʌndrədweɪt/ n (pl **hundredweight**) measure of weight; one twentieth of one ton (50·8 kilograms)

hung pt, pp of HANG¹

hunger /'hʌŋɡə(r)/ n **1** [U] need or desire for food **2** [sing] **~for** (fml) strong desire ● **hunger for/after sth/sb** have a strong desire for sth/sb ■ **'hunger strike** n refusal to eat food as a protest

hungry /'hʌŋɡri/ adj (**-ier, -iest**) feeling hunger ▶ **hungrily** adv

hunk /hʌŋk/ n thick piece cut off sth: *a ~ of bread/cheese*

hunt /hʌnt/ v [I, T] **1** chase wild animals to catch or kill them for food or sport **2 ~for** (try to find sb/sth [PV] **hunt sb down** search for and find sb ● **hunt** n [sing] act of hunting **2** [C] group of people who hunt foxes ▶ **hunter** n person who hunts

hurdle /'hɜ:dl/ n **1** frame to be jumped over in a race **2** difficulty to be overcome

hurl /hɜ:l/ v [T] throw sth/sb violently in a particular direction: *(fig) ~ insults at sb*

hurly-burly /'hɜ:li bɜ:li/ n [U] noisy busy activity

hurrah /hə'rɑ:/ (also **hurray** /hu-'reɪ/) exclam = HOORAY

hurricane /'hʌrɪkən/ n violent storm with very strong winds

hurry /'hʌri/ v (pt, pp -ied) [I, T] (make sb) move or do sth (too) quickly [PV] **hurry (sb) up** (make sb) do sth more quickly: H~ up! It's late. ▸ **hurried** adj done (too) quickly ● **hurriedly** adv ● **hurry** n [U] need to do sth quickly [IDM] **in a hurry 1** very quickly **2** impatient to do sth

hurt /hɜːt/ v (pt, pp **hurt**) **1** [I, T] cause injury or pain to sb/yourself: He ~ himself. ◊ I ~ my hand. **2** [I, T] cause pain to a person or their feelings: My feet ~. ◊ It ~ his pride. [IDM] **it won't/wouldn't hurt (sb/sth) (to do sth)** used to say that sb should do a particular thing: It wouldn't ~ (you) to say sorry. ● **hurt** n [U, sing] unhappiness because sb has been unkind to you ▸ **hurtful** adj ▸ **hurtfully** adv

hurtle /'hɜːtl/ v [I] move violently or quickly

husband /'hʌzbənd/ n man that a woman is married to

hush /hʌʃ/ v [I, T] become or make sb/sth quiet [PV] **hush sth up** keep sth secret ● **hush** n [U, sing] silence

husk /hʌsk/ n dry outer covering of seeds, esp grain ▸ **husk** v [T] remove the husks from grain, seeds, etc

husky /'hʌski/ adj (**-ier, -iest**) (of a voice) deep and rough ● **huskily** adv ● **husky** n (pl **-ies**) dog used for pulling sledges across snow

hustle /'hʌsl/ v [T] **1** make sb move by pushing them roughly **2** ~ (**into**) make sb act quickly: ~ sb into a decision ● **hustle** n [U] busy lively activity ▸ **hustler** /'hʌslə(r)/ n (US) **1** (infml, esp US) person who tries to trick sb into giving them their money **2** (sl) prostitute

hut /hʌt/ n small roughly-built house or shelter

hutch /hʌtʃ/ n cage for rabbits, etc

hyacinth /'haɪəsɪnθ/ n plant with sweet-smelling flowers, growing from a bulb

hyaena = HYENA

hybrid /'haɪbrɪd/ n animal or plant produced from two different species

hydrant /'haɪdrənt/ n pipe connected to a water supply, esp in a street

hydraulic /haɪ'drɔːlɪk/ adj worked by the pressure of a liquid, esp water

hydroelectric /ˌhaɪdrəʊɪ'lektrɪk/ adj using the power of water to produce electricity: a ~ dam

hydrofoil /'haɪdrəfɔɪl/ n boat which rises above the surface of the water when travelling fast

hydrogen /'haɪdrədʒən/ n [U] (symb **H**) light colourless gas that combines with oxygen to form water ■ **hydrogen bomb** (also '**H-bomb**') n extremely powerful bomb that explodes when the central parts (**nuclei**) of hydrogen atoms join together

hyena (also **hyaena**) /haɪ'iːnə/ n wild animal with a laughing cry

hygiene /'haɪdʒiːn/ n [U] keeping yourself and your living area clean, in order to prevent disease ▸ **hygienic** /haɪ'dʒiːnɪk/ adj of hygiene; clean ▸ **hygienically** adv

hymn /hɪm/ n song of praise to God

hyperactive /ˌhaɪpər'æktɪv/ adj (esp of children) too active; unable to rest

hyperlink /'haɪpəlɪŋk/ n place in an electronic document on a computer that is linked to another electronic document: Click on the ~.

hypermarket /'haɪpəmɑːkɪt/ n (GB) very large supermarket

hyphen /'haɪfn/ n mark (-) used for joining two words or parts of words ▸ **hyphenate** /'haɪfəneɪt/ v [T] join two words with a hyphen

hypnosis /hɪp'nəʊsɪs/ n [U] state like deep sleep in which a person's actions may be controlled by another person ▸ **hypnotic** /hɪp'nɒtɪk/ adj **1** making you feel sleepy **2** of or produced by hypnosis ▸ **hypnotism** /'hɪpnətɪzəm/ n [U] practice of hypnotizing sb ▸ **hypnotist** /'hɪpnətɪst/ n ▸ **hypnotize** (also **-ise**) /'hɪpnətaɪz/ v [T] produce a state of hypnosis in sb

hypochondriac /ˌhaɪpə'kɒndriæk/ n person who worries too much about their health

hypocrisy /hɪ'pɒkrəsi/ n [U,C] (pl **-ies**) (disapprov) making yourself appear more moral, etc than you really are ▸ **hypocrite** /'hɪpəkrɪt/ n person who makes himself or herself appear better than they really are ▸ **hypocritical** /ˌhɪpə'krɪtɪkl/ adj

hypodermic /ˌhaɪpə'dɜːmɪk/ adj, n (of a) needle used for injecting a drug into a person: a ~ syringe

hypotenuse /haɪ'pɒtənjuːz/ n longest side of a right-angled triangle

hypothesis /haɪ'pɒθəsɪs/ n (pl **-theses** /-siːz/) idea that is suggested as a possible explanation of facts ▸ **hypothetical** /ˌhaɪpə'θetɪkl/ adj based on ideas or situations which are possible but not real

hysteria /hɪ'stɪəriə/ n [U] **1** state of extreme excitement, fear or anger, which causes loss of control **2**

uncontrolled excitement ▶ hyster-ical /hɪˈsterɪkl/ adj ▶ hysterics /hɪ-ˈsterɪks/ n [pl] attack(s) of hysteria

Ii

I, i /aɪ/ n [C,U] (pl **I's, i's** /aɪz/) **1** the ninth letter of the English alpha-bet **2** Roman numeral for 1

I /aɪ/ pron (used as the subject of a v) person who is the speaker or writer

ice¹ /aɪs/ n [U] **1** water that has frozen and become solid **2** pieces of ice used to keep food and drinks cold [IDM] **on ice 1** (of wine, etc) kept cold by being surrounded with ice **2** (of a plan, etc) waiting to be dealt with at a later time ■ **ice-berg** /ˈaɪsbɜːg/ n large mass of ice floating in the sea **,ice 'cream** (esp US **'ice cream**) n [U,C] (portion of) frozen flavoured creamy mixture ■ **'ice cap** n layer of ice perman-ently covering part of the earth, esp around the North and South Poles ■ **'ice hockey** n [U] team game played on ice with sticks and a hard rubber disc ■ **'ice ,lolly** n US **'ice ,lolly** flavoured ice on a stick ■ **'ice skate** n boot with a thin metal blade on the bottom, for skating on ice ■ **'ice-skate** v [I] skate on ice

ice² /aɪs/ v [T] cover a cake with icing [PV] **ice sth over/up** cover sth with ice; become covered with ice

icicle /ˈaɪsɪkl/ n pointed piece of ice, formed from when water freezes as it drips from a roof, etc

icing /ˈaɪsɪŋ/ n mixture of pow-dered sugar, flavouring, etc, used for decorating cakes

icy /ˈaɪsi/ adj (-ier, -iest) **1** very cold **2** covered with ice **3** unfriendly: an ~ stare ▶ **icily** adv

I'd /aɪd/ short for 1 I HAD; 2 I WOULD

idea /aɪˈdɪə/ n **1** [C] plan or thought: That's a good ~! **2** [U,sing] picture in the mind **3** [C] opinion or belief **4** [U,sing] feeling that sth is pos-sible: I've an ~ it will rain. **5** (**the idea**) [sing] the aim or purpose of doing sth: You'll soon get the ~ (= understand). [IDM] **have no idea** | **not have the faintest, first, etc idea** (spoken) used to emphasize that you do not know sth: He has no ~ how to manage people.

ideal /aɪˈdiːəl/ adj **1** perfect: ~ weather **2** existing only in the imag-ination: in an ~ world ● **ideal** n [C] **1** idea or standard that seems per-fect **2** [usu sing] person or thing con-sidered perfect ▶ **ideally** adv **1** suited to the job **2** if conditions were perfect

idealist /aɪˈdiːəlɪst/ n person who has (often impractical) ideals(1) and who tries to achieve them ▶ **idealism** n [U] ▶ **idealistic** /ˌaɪdɪə-ˈlɪstɪk/ adj

idealize (also **-ise**) /aɪˈdiːəlaɪz/ v [T] think of sb/sth as perfect ▶ **ideal-ization** (also **-isation**) /aɪˌdiːəlaɪ-ˈzeɪʃn/ n [U,C]

identical /aɪˈdentɪkl/ adj **1** the same **2** ~ (to/with) exactly alike: ~ twins ▶ **identically** adv

identify /aɪˈdentɪfaɪ/ v (pt, pp -ied) [T] show or prove who or what sb/sth is: Can you ~ the man who attacked you? [PV] **identify with sb** understand the feelings of sb **iden-tify yourself with sb/sth** support sb/sth; be closely connected with sb/sth ▶ **identification** /aɪˌdentɪfɪ-ˈkeɪʃn/ n (abbr ID) n **1** [U,C] act of identifying sb/sth **2** [U] official papers that can prove who you are

identity /aɪˈdentəti/ n (pl -ies) **1** [C, U] who or what sb/sth is: the ~ of the thief **2** [U] state of being very simi-lar to and able to understand sb/sth

ideology /ˌaɪdiˈɒlədʒi/ n [C,U] (pl -ies) set of (political) beliefs ▶ **ideological** /ˌaɪdiəˈlɒdʒɪkl/ adj

idiocy /ˈɪdiəsi/ n (pl -ies) **1** [U] extreme stupidity **2** [C] very stupid act, remark, etc

idiom /ˈɪdiəm/ n group of words with a meaning that is different from the meaning of all the individual words: 'Pull your socks up' is an ~ meaning 'improve your behaviour'. ▶ **idiom-atic** /ˌɪdiəˈmætɪk/ adj (of language) natural and correct

idiosyncrasy /ˌɪdiəˈsɪŋkrəsi/ n (pl -ies) way of behaving that is par-ticular to a person ▶ **idiosyncratic** /ˌɪdiəsɪŋˈkrætɪk/ adj

idiot /ˈɪdiət/ n (infml) very stupid person ▶ **idiotic** /ˌɪdiˈɒtɪk/ adj

idle /ˈaɪdl/ adj (~r, ~st) **1** (of people) lazy; not working hard **2** (of machines, etc) not in use **3** (of people) unemployed **4** useless: ~ gossip/promises ● **idle** v **1** [I, T] waste time: He ~d the days away, watching TV. **2** [I] (of an engine) run slowly in neutral gear ▶ **idleness** n [U] ▶ **idly** adv

idol /ˈaɪdl/ n **1** person or thing that is greatly loved or admired **2** statue that is worshipped as a god ▶ **idolize** (also **-ise**) /ˈaɪdəlaɪz/ v [T] admire or love sb very much

idyllic /ɪˈdɪlɪk/ adj peaceful and beautiful; perfect

ie /ˌaɪ ˈiː/ abbr that is: They arrived on the next day, ie Monday.

if /ɪf/ conj **1** on condition that: She will help you if you ask her. **2** whether: Do you know if he's work-ing today? **3** when; whenever; every time: *If you mix yellow and blue, you get green.* **4** used after verbs or adjectives expressing feelings: *I'm sorry if I'm disturbing you.* **5** used before an adjective to introduce a contrast: *The hotel was good value, if a little expensive.* ● **if** (*infml*) uncertainty: *No more ifs and buts—you're going to the party.*

igloo /'ɪglu:/ *n* (*pl* ~**s**) small round house made of blocks of snow by the Inuit people

ignite /ɪg'naɪt/ *v* [I, T] (*written*) (cause sth to) start to burn ▶ **ignition** /ɪg'nɪʃn/ *n* **1** [C] electrical apparatus that starts the engine of a car, etc **2** [U] (*tech*) process of igniting sth

ignorant /'ɪgnərənt/ *adj* lacking knowledge about sth ▶ **ignorance** /'ɪgnərəns/ *n* [U] ▶ **ignorantly** *adv*

ignore /ɪg'nɔː(r)/ *v* [T] take no notice of sb/sth

ill /ɪl/ *adj* **1** sick; suffering from an illness or disease: *She was taken ~ suddenly.* **2** bad: *~ health/luck* ◇ *~ feeling* (= anger, jealousy, etc) ● **ill** *n* **1** [C, usu *pl*] (*fml*) problem **2** [U] (*lit*) harm; bad luck ● **ill** *adv* **1** badly: *an ~-written book* **2** only with difficulty: *We can ~ afford the time.* [IDM] **ill at ease** uncomfortable; embarrassed **speak/think ill of sb** say or think bad things about sb ■ **ill-ad'vised** *adj* unwise ■ **ill-'bred** *adj* badly brought up ■ **ill-'treat** *v* [T] treat sb cruelly ■ **ill-'treatment** *n* [U] ■ **ill 'will** *n* [U] unkind feelings towards sb

I'll /aɪl/ *short for* I WILL

illegal /ɪ'liːɡl/ *adj* against the law; not legal ▶ **illegality** /ˌɪliː'ɡæləti/ *n* [U,C] ▶ **illegally** /-ɡəli/ *adv*

illegible /ɪ'ledʒəbl/ *adj* difficult or impossible to read

illegitimate /ˌɪlə'dʒɪtəmət/ *adj* **1** born to parents not married to each other **2** not allowed by the law ▶ **illegitimately** *adv*

illicit /ɪ'lɪsɪt/ *adj* not allowed by the law ▶ **illicitly** *adv*

illiterate /ɪ'lɪtərət/ *n, adj* (person who is) unable to read or write ▶ **illiteracy** /ɪ'lɪtərəsi/ *n* [U]

illness /'ɪlnəs/ *n* **1** [U] state of being ill **2** [C] specific kind of illness

illogical /ɪ'lɒdʒɪkl/ *adj* not logical; not reasonable ▶ **illogicality** /ɪˌlɒdʒɪ'kæləti/ *n* [C,U] ▶ **illogically** *adv*

illuminate /ɪ'luːmɪneɪt/ *v* [T] **1** shine light on sth **2** (*fml*) make sth clearer or easier to understand **3** decorate sth with lights ▶ **illuminated** *adj* (of

books, etc) decorated with gold, silver and bright colours ▶ **illuminating** *adj* explaining sth clearly: *an illuminating lecture* ▶ **illumination** /ɪˌluːmɪ'neɪʃn/ *n* **1** [U] lighting **2** (**illuminations**) [*pl*] (*GB*) bright colourful lights to decorate a town

illusion /ɪ'luːʒn/ *n* **1** false idea or belief **2** something that seems to exist but in fact does not: *an optical ~* ▶ **illusory** /ɪ'luːsəri/ *adj* not real, though seeming to be

illustrate /'ɪləstreɪt/ *v* [T] **1** use pictures, diagrams, etc in a book, etc: *~ a book* **2** explain sth by using examples, diagrams, etc ▶ **illustration** /ˌɪlə'streɪʃn/ *n* **1** [C] picture or drawing in a book, etc **2** [C,U] example of sth **3** [U] process of illustrating sth ▶ **illustrative** /'ɪləstrətɪv/ *adj* (*fml*) helping to explain sth ▶ **illustrator** *n* person who draws pictures for books, etc

illustrious /ɪ'lʌstriəs/ *adj* (*fml*) very famous and much admired

I'm /aɪm/ *short for* I AM (BE)

image /'ɪmɪdʒ/ *n* **1** [C,U] impression that a person, company, product etc gives to the public **2** [C] mental picture of sb/sth **3** [C] copy of sth, esp in wood or stone **4** [C] picture of sb/sth seen in a mirror, through a camera, etc [IDM] be the **(living/spitting) image of sb** (*infml*) look exactly like sb ▶ **imagery** *n* [U] use of figurative language to produce pictures in the mind

imaginary /ɪ'mædʒɪnəri/ *adj* unreal

imagine /ɪ'mædʒɪn/ *v* [T] **1** form a picture of sth in your mind: *Can you ~ life without electricity?* **2** suppose sth: *I ~ he'll be angry.* ▶ **imaginable** *adj* that can be imagined ▶ **imagination** /ɪˌmædʒɪ'neɪʃn/ *n* **1** [U,C] ability to form pictures or ideas in the mind, esp of interesting things **2** [U] something experienced in the mind, not in real life ▶ **imaginative** /ɪ'mædʒɪnətɪv/ *adj* having or showing imagination(1)

imaging /'ɪmɪdʒɪŋ/ *n* [U] (*computing*) process of capturing, storing and showing an image on a computer screen: *~ software*

imbalance /ɪm'bæləns/ *n* lack of equality or balance

imbecile /'ɪmbəsiːl/ *n* stupid person ▶ **imbecile** *adj*

imbue /ɪm'bjuː/ *v* [T] ~**with** (*fml*) fill sb with a feeling, etc

imitate /'ɪmɪteɪt/ *v* [T] **1** copy sb/sth **2** copy the way a person speaks or behaves ▶ **imitative** /'ɪmɪtətɪv/ *adj* (*fml*) that copies sb/sth ▶ **imitator** *n*

imitation /ˌɪmɪ'teɪʃn/ *n* **1** [C] copy of sth, esp sth expensive: *~ leather* **2** [C,U] act of copying sb/sth

immaculate /ɪˈmækjələt/ adj clean; perfect ► **immaculately** adv

immaterial /ˌɪməˈtɪərɪəl/ adj ~(to) **1** not important **2** (fml) not having a physical form

immature /ˌɪməˈtjʊə(r)/ adj **1** not sensible in behaviour **2** not fully developed ► **immaturity** n [U]

immeasurable /ɪˈmeʒərəbl/ adj too large to be measured

immediate /ɪˈmiːdɪət/ adj **1** happening or done at once: take ~ action **2** nearest: in the ~ future

immediately /ɪˈmiːdɪətlɪ/ adv **1** at once; without delay **2** being nearest; directly: the years ~ after the war ● **immediately** conj (esp GB) as soon as: I recognized her ~ I saw her.

immense /ɪˈmens/ adj very great ► **immensely** adv very much: I enjoyed the film ~ly. ►

immerse /ɪˈmɜːs/ v [T] ~(in) **1** put sth under the surface of a liquid **2** ~ yourself (in) involve yourself deeply in sth: ~ yourself in your work ► **immersion** /ɪˈmɜːʃn/ n [U] ► **immersion heater** n (GB) electric heater in a water tank

immigrant /ˈɪmɪɡrənt/ n person who has come to live in a country that is not their own ► **immigration** /ˌɪmɪˈɡreɪʃn/ n [U] moving of people from one country to come to live in another country

imminent /ˈɪmɪnənt/ adj likely to happen very soon ► **imminently** adv

immobile /ɪˈməʊbaɪl/ adj not moving; unable to move ► **immobility** /ˌɪməˈbɪlətɪ/ n [U] ► **immobilize** (also -ise) /ɪˈməʊbəlaɪz/ v [T] prevent sth from moving or working properly

immoral /ɪˈmɒrəl/ adj not moral; wrong **2** against usual standards of sexual behaviour ► **immorality** /ˌɪməˈrælətɪ/ n [U]

immortal /ɪˈmɔːtl/ adj **1** living or lasting for ever **2** famous and likely to be remembered for ever ● **immortal** n immortal being ► **immortality** /ˌɪmɔːˈtælətɪ/ n [U] ► **immortalize** (also -ise) /ɪˈmɔːtəlaɪz/ v [T] prevent sb/sth from being forgotten in the future: ~ized in a novel

immune /ɪˈmjuːn/ adj **1** ~(to/ against) that cannot be harmed by a disease: ~ to smallpox **2** ~(to) not affected by sth: ~ to criticism **3** (from) protected from sth: ~ from tax ► **immunity** n [U] ► **immunize** (also -ise) /ˈɪmjunaɪz/ v [T] ~ (against) make sb immune to a disease, esp by giving them an injection of a vaccine ► **immunization** (also -isation) /ˌɪmjunaɪˈzeɪʃn/ n [U,C]

imp /ɪmp/ n **1** (in stories) little devil **2** mischievous child

impact /ˈɪmpækt/ n [C, usu sing] ~ (on) strong effect that sth has on sb/sth: the ~ of computers on industry **2** [U] (force of sth) hitting an object against another: The bomb exploded on ~ (= when it hit sth). ● **impact** /ɪmˈpækt/ v [T] have an effect on sth **2** [I] hit sth with great force

impair /ɪmˈpeə(r)/ v [T] damage sth or make sth worse: Loud noise can ~ your hearing.

impale /ɪmˈpeɪl/ v [T] ~(on) push a sharp-pointed object through sth/sb

impart /ɪmˈpɑːt/ v [T] (fml) pass information, etc to other people

impartial /ɪmˈpɑːʃl/ adj just; fair: A judge must be ~. ► **impartiality** /ˌɪmˌpɑːʃɪˈælətɪ/ n [U]

impassable /ɪmˈpɑːsəbl/ adj (of a road, etc) impossible to travel on

impassioned /ɪmˈpæʃnd/ adj showing strong deep feeling: an ~ appeal

impassive /ɪmˈpæsɪv/ adj showing no sign of feeling ► **impassively** adv

impatient /ɪmˈpeɪʃnt/ adj **1** showing a lack of patience **2** very eager: ~ to leave school ► **impatience** /ɪmˈpeɪʃns/ n [U] ► **impatiently** adv

impeccable /ɪmˈpekəbl/ adj faultless ► **impeccably** adv

impede /ɪmˈpiːd/ v [T] delay or stop the progress of sth

impediment /ɪmˈpedɪmənt/ n **1** something that makes progress difficult **2** physical defect, esp in speech

impending /ɪmˈpendɪŋ/ adj about to happen: ~ disaster

impenetrable /ɪmˈpenɪtrəbl/ adj **1** that cannot be passed through **2** impossible to understand

imperative /ɪmˈperətɪv/ adj very urgent or important ● **imperative** n (gram) verb form that expresses a command, eg Go!

imperfect /ɪmˈpɜːfɪkt/ adj not perfect ● **imperfect** n (the imperfect) [sing] (gram) verb tense that shows incomplete action in the past, eg was speaking ► **imperfection** /ˌɪmpəˈfekʃn/ n [C,U] fault or weakness in sb/sth ► **imperfectly** adv

imperial /ɪmˈpɪərɪəl/ adj of an empire or its ruler ► **imperialism** n [U] (belief in) a political system of gaining economic or political control over other countries ► **imperialist** n, adj

impersonal /ɪmˈpɜːsənl/ adj **1** lacking friendly human feelings: a large ~ organization **2** not referring to any particular person ► **impersonally** /-nəlɪ/ adv

impersonate /ɪmˈpɜːsəneɪt/ v [T]

pretend to be another person ▶ **impersonation** /-ˌneɪʃn/ n [C, U]

impertinent /ɪmˈpɜːtɪnənt/ adj not showing proper respect ▶ **impertinence** /-əns/ n [U, sing] ▶ **impertinently** adv

impervious /ɪmˈpɜːviəs/ adj **1** not influenced by sth: ~ *to criticism* **2** (tech) not allowing a liquid or gas to pass through

impetuous /ɪmˈpetʃuəs/ adj acting quickly and without thinking

impetus /ˈɪmpɪtəs/ n **1** [U, sing] something that encourages a process to develop more quickly: *give a fresh ~ to trade* **2** [U] (tech) force with which sth moves

impinge /ɪmˈpɪndʒ/ v **1** ~(on) (fml) have an effect on sth/sb, esp a bad one

implacable /ɪmˈplækəbl/ adj that cannot be changed or satisfied

implant /ɪmˈplɑːnt/ v [T] ~(in/into) (written) **1** fix an idea, attitude, etc firmly in sb's mind **2** put sth, usu sth artificial, into a part of the body for medical purposes ● **implant** /ˈɪmplɑːnt/ n something that is put into sb's body during a medical operation

implement¹ /ˈɪmplɪment/ v [T] carry out a plan, promise, etc ▶ **implementation** /ˌɪmplɪmenˈteɪʃn/ n [U]

implement² /ˈɪmplɪmənt/ n tool or instrument

implicate /ˈɪmplɪkeɪt/ v [T] ~(in) show or suggest sb is involved in a crime, etc

implication /ˌɪmplɪˈkeɪʃn/ n [C, usu pl] possible effect of an action or decision **2** [C,U] something suggested or implied **3** [U] act of implicating sb, esp in a crime

implicit /ɪmˈplɪsɪt/ adj implied, but not expressed directly **2** unquestioning; complete: ~ *trust* ▶ **implicitly** adv

implore /ɪmˈplɔː(r)/ v [T] ask or beg sb strongly: *They ~d her to stay.*

imply /ɪmˈplaɪ/ v (pt, pp -ied) [T] **1** suggest that sth is true without actually saying it: *Are you ~ing that I stole your watch?* **2** suggest sth as a necessary result

impolite /ˌɪmpəˈlaɪt/ adj not polite; rude

import /ɪmˈpɔːt/ v [T] bring in goods, etc from another country ● **import** /ˈɪmpɔːt/ n **1** [C, usu pl] product or service that is imported **2** [U] (fml) importance ▶ **importation** /ˌɪmpɔːˈteɪʃn/ n [U,C] ▶ **importer** n person, company, etc that imports goods to sell

important /ɪmˈpɔːtnt/ adj **1** having a great effect or value: *an ~ decision*

2 (of a person) having great influence or authority ▶ **importance** /ɪmˈpɔːtns/ n [U] ▶ **importantly** adv

impose /ɪmˈpəʊz/ v **1** ~(on/upon) [T] put a tax, penalty, etc on sb/sth **2** [T] try to make sb accept an opinion, etc **3** expect sb to do sth for you when it may be inconvenient ▶ **imposing** adj large and impressive ▶ **imposition** /ˌɪmpəˈzɪʃn/ n [U,C]

impossible /ɪmˈpɒsəbl/ adj **1** not possible **2** very difficult to deal with: *an ~ situation* ▶ **impossibility** /ɪmˌpɒsəˈbɪləti/ n [U,C] ▶ **impossibly** adv

impostor /ɪmˈpɒstə(r)/ n person who pretends to be sb else, esp to deceive others

impotent /ˈɪmpətənt/ adj **1** powerless or helpless **2** (of a man) unable to have sex ▶ **impotence** /-əns/ n [U]

impound /ɪmˈpaʊnd/ v [T] take possession of sth by law

impoverish /ɪmˈpɒvərɪʃ/ v [T] make sb/sth poor

impracticable /ɪmˈpræktɪkəbl/ adj impossible to put into practice

impractical /ɪmˈpræktɪkl/ adj not sensible, useful or realistic

imprecise /ˌɪmprɪˈsaɪs/ adj not exact or accurate

impregnable /ɪmˈpreɡnəbl/ adj that cannot be entered by attack

impregnate /ˈɪmpreɡneɪt/ v [T] **1** cause one substance to be filled in every part with another substance: *cloth ~d with perfume* **2** (fml) make a woman or female animal pregnant

impresario /ˌɪmprəˈsɑːriəʊ/ n (pl ~s) manager of a theatre or music company

impress /ɪmˈpres/ v [T] **1** cause sb to feel admiration: *Her honesty ~ed me.* **2** ~on/upon (fml) fix sth in sb's mind: ~ *on him the importance of hard work*

impression /ɪmˈpreʃn/ n **1** idea, feeling or opinion that you get about sb/sth: *My general ~ was that she seemed a nice woman.* **2** lasting effect on sb's mind or feelings: *create a good ~* **3** funny imitation of sb's behaviour or way of talking **4** mark left when an object is pressed hard into a surface [IDM] **be under the impression** that ... have the (usu wrong) idea that ... ▶ **impressionable** /ɪmˈpreʃənəbl/ adj easily influenced ▶ **Impressionism** /ɪmˈpreʃənɪzəm/ n [U] style in painting that gives a general impression(1) of sth by using the effects of colour and light

impressive /ɪmˈpresɪv/ adj causing admiration: *an ~ building* ▶ **impressively** adv

imprint /ɪmˈprɪnt/ v [T] print or

press a mark or design onto a surface: *(fig) details ~ed on his memory* ● **imprint** /'ɪmprɪnt/ *n* 1 mark made by pressing sth onto a surface 2 lasting effect

imprison /ɪm'prɪzn/ *v* [T] put sb in prison ► **imprisonment** *n* [U]

improbable /ɪm'prɒbəbl/ *adj* not likely to be true or to happen ► **improbability** /ɪm,prɒbə'bɪləti/ *n* [U,C] (*pl* -ies) ► **improbably** *adv*

impromptu /ɪm'prɒmptjuː/ *adj, adv* (done) without preparation: *an ~ speech*

improper /ɪm'prɒpə(r)/ *adj* 1 dishonest or morally wrong: *~ business practices* 2 (*fml*) not suitable for the purpose, situation, etc: *~ behaviour/ dress* 3 wrong or incorrect: *~ use of the drug* ► **improperly** *adv*

improve /ɪm'pruːv/ *v* [I, T] become or make sth/sb better ► **improvement** *n* 1 [C,U] process of becoming or making sth better 2 [C] change that improves sth: *home ~ments*

improvise /'ɪmprəvaɪz/ *v* [I, T] 1 make sth from whatever is available, without preparation 2 compose music or speak or act without preparation ► **improvisation** /,ɪmprəvaɪ'zeɪʃn/ *n* [U,C]

impudent /'ɪmpjədənt/ *adj* very rude and disrespectful ► **impudence** /-əns/ *n* [U]

impulse /'ɪmpʌls/ *n* 1 [C,U] sudden desire to do sth 2 [C] (*tech*) force or movement of energy: *an electrical ~* [IDM] **on impulse** suddenly and without thought

impulsive /ɪm'pʌlsɪv/ *adj* acting suddenly without thinking carefully about the results of your actions ► **impulsively** *adv* ► **impulsiveness** *n* [U]

impunity /ɪm'pjuːnəti/ *n* [IDM] **with impunity** (*fml, disapprov*) without being punished

impure /ɪm'pjʊə(r)/ *adj* 1 mixed with sth else; not clean 2 (*old-fash*) morally wrong ► **impurity** *n* [U,C] (*pl* -ies)

in¹ /ɪn/ *adv* 1 (to a position) within a particular area or space: *He opened the bedroom door and went in.* 2 at home or at a place of work: *Nobody was in when we called.* 3 (of trains, buses, etc) at the station 4 (of letters) received: *Competition entries should be in by 31 May.* 5 (of the tide) at or towards its highest point on land 6 elected: *Labour came in after the war.* 7 (*sport*) batting 8 (*sport*) (of a ball) inside the line [IDM] **be in for sth** (*infml*) be about to experience sth, esp sth unpleasant **be/get in on sth** (*infml*) become involved in sth; share or know about sth **be (well) in with sb**

(*infml*) be (very) friendly with sb **have it in for sb** (*infml*) not like sb and be unpleasant to them ● **in** *adj* 1 (*infml*) popular and fashionable: *Exotic pets are the in thing.* 2 shared by a small group: *an in-joke*

in² /ɪn/ *prep* 1 at a point within an area or a space; surrounded by sth: *Rome is in Italy.* ◇ *play in the street* ◇ *lying in bed* ◇ *a pen in his pocket* 2 used to showing movement into sth: *Throw it in the fire.* 3 forming the whole or part of sth/sb: *seven days in a week* 4 during a period of time: *in June* 5 after a particular length of time: *Lunch will be ready in an hour.* 6 wearing sth: *the woman in white* 7 used to show physical surroundings: *go out in the cold* 8 used to show a state or condition: *in a mess* ◇ *in love* 9 used to show sb's job or profession: *a career in journalism* 10 used to show form or arrangement of sth: *a story in three parts* 11 used to show the language, material, etc used: *speak in English* ◇ *write in ink* 12 concerning sth: *lacking in courage* ◇ *3 metres in length* 13 used to show a rate or relative amount: *a slope of 1 in 5* (= 20%) [IDM] **in that** (*written*) for the reason that; because: *The chemical is dangerous in that it can kill.*

in³ /ɪn/ *n* [IDM] **the ins and outs (of sth)** all the details, esp the complicated ones

inability /,ɪnə'bɪləti/ *n* [U, sing] ~(**to**) fact of not being able to do sth

inaccessible /,ɪnæk'sesəbl/ *adj* impossible to reach

inaccurate /ɪn'ækjərət/ *adj* not correct ► **inaccuracy** /ɪn'ækjərəsi/ *n* [U,C] (*pl* -ies) ► **inaccurately** *adv*

inadequate /ɪn'ædɪkwət/ *adj* not (good) enough ► **inadequately** *adv*

inadmissible /,ɪnəd'mɪsəbl/ *adj* that cannot be allowed in a court of law: *~ evidence*

inadvertent /,ɪnəd'vɜːtənt/ *adj* done without thinking or accidentally ► **inadvertently** *adv*

inalienable /ɪn'eɪliənəbl/ *adj* (*fml*) that cannot be taken away from you: *the ~ right to decide your own future*

inane /ɪ'neɪn/ *adj* silly ► **inanely** *adv*

inanimate /ɪn'ænɪmət/ *adj* not living: *A rock is an ~ object.*

inapplicable /,ɪnə'plɪkəbl; ɪn-'æplɪkəbl/ *adj* ~(**to**) not applicable to sth

inappropriate /,ɪnə'prəʊpriət/ *adj* ~(**to/for**) not suitable for sb/sth ► **inappropriately** *adv*

inarticulate /,ɪnɑː'tɪkjələt/ *adj* 1 unable to express yourself clearly 2 (of speech) not clear

I

inasmuch as /ˌɪnəzˈmʌtʃ əz/ conj (fml) to the extent that; since

inaudible /ɪnˈɔːdəbl/ adj not loud enough to be heard

inaugural /ɪˈnɔːgjərəl/ adj (of an official speech, meeting, etc) first, and marking the beginning of sth important: the President's ~ speech

inaugurate /ɪˈnɔːgjəreɪt/ v [T] 1 introduce a new official or leader at a special ceremony 2 start or open an organization, exhibition, etc with a special ceremony 3 (fml) introduce a new development or important change ▸ **inauguration** /ɪˌnɔːgjəˈreɪʃn/ n [U,C]

inborn /ˌɪnˈbɔːn/ adj (of a quality) existing in a person from birth

inbred /ˌɪnˈbred/ adj 1 having ancestors closely related to one another 2 = INBORN ▸ **inbreeding** /ˈɪnbriːdɪŋ/ n [U] breeding among closely related people or animals

inbuilt /ˈɪnbɪlt/ adj (of a quality) existing as an essential part of sth

Inc. (also **inc**) /ɪŋk/ abbr Incorporated (used after the name of a company in the US)

incalculable /ɪnˈkælkjələbl/ adj too great to be calculated

incapable /ɪnˈkeɪpəbl/ adj ~of not able to do sth: ~ of telling a lie

incapacitate /ˌɪnkəˈpæsɪteɪt/ v [T] (fml) make sb unable to live or work normally ▸ **incapacity** /ˌɪnkəˈpæsəti/ n inability

incarcerate /ɪnˈkɑːsəreɪt/ v [T] (fml) put sb in prison ▸ **incarceration** /ɪnˌkɑːsəˈreɪʃn/ n [U]

incarnation /ˌɪnkɑːˈneɪʃn/ n 1 period of life in a particular form 2 person who represents a particular quality in human form: the ~ of evil

incendiary /ɪnˈsendiəri/ adj 1 designed to cause fires: an ~ device 2 causing strong feeling: an ~ speech ▸ **incendiary** n (pl -ies) incendiary bomb

incense¹ /ˈɪnsens/ n [U] substance that produces a pleasant smell when burnt

incense² /ɪnˈsens/ v [T] make sb very angry

incentive /ɪnˈsentɪv/ n [C,U] ~(to) something that encourages you to do sth

incessant /ɪnˈsesnt/ adj not stopping; continual: his ~ complaints ▸ **incessantly** adv

incest /ˈɪnsest/ n [U] sexual activity between close relatives ▸ **incestuous** /ɪnˈsestjuəs/ adj

inch /ɪntʃ/ n 1 measure of length; one twelfth of a foot (2.54 cm) 2 small amount: He escaped death by an ~. [IDM] **every inch** all; completely **within an inch of sth** very

close to sth ● **inch** v [I, T] move or make sth move slowly and carefully in the direction mentioned: He ~ed his way through the tunnel.

incidence /ˈɪnsɪdəns/ n [C, usu sing] number of times or way in which sth happens: a high ~ of crime

incident /ˈɪnsɪdənt/ n 1 [C] event, esp sth unusual or unpleasant 2 [C, U] serious or violent event, eg a crime or an accident: a shooting ~

incidental /ˌɪnsɪˈdentl/ adj happening in connection with sth else, but not as important as it, or not intended: ~ expenses ◊ ~ music for a film ▸ **incidentally** /ˌɪnsɪˈdentli/ adv used for introducing sth extra that you have just thought of

incinerate /ɪnˈsɪnəreɪt/ v [T] burn sth completely ▸ **incineration** /ɪnˌsɪnəˈreɪʃn/ n [U] ▸ **incinerator** n furnace, etc for burning rubbish

incipient /ɪnˈsɪpiənt/ adj (fml) just beginning

incision /ɪnˈsɪʒn/ n [C, U] (act of making a) sharp cut in sth, esp during a medical operation

incisive /ɪnˈsaɪsɪv/ adj clear and direct: ~ comments ▸ **incisively** adv

incisor /ɪnˈsaɪzə(r)/ n any one of the front cutting teeth

incite /ɪnˈsaɪt/ v [T] encourage sb to do sth violent, illegal or unpleasant: ~ workers to riot ▸ **incitement** n [U,C]

inclination /ˌɪnklɪˈneɪʃn/ n 1 [U,C] feeling that makes you want to do sth: I have no ~ to leave. 2 [C] tendency to do sth 3 [C,U sing, sing] (tech) angle of a slope

incline¹ /ɪnˈklaɪn/ v (fml) 1 [I, T] ~to/towards (persuade sb to) tend to think or behave in a particular way: He ~s to laziness. 2 [T] bend your head forward, esp as a sign of agreement, etc 3 [I, T] ~(towards) (cause sth to) lean or slope in a particular direction ▸ **inclined** adj ~(to) 1 wanting to do sth 2 tending to do sth; likely to do sth: I'm ~d to believe him.

incline² /ˈɪnklaɪn/ n (fml) slope

include /ɪnˈkluːd/ v [T] 1 have sth as part of a whole: Prices ~ delivery. 2 make sth/sb part of a larger group: ~ Chris in the team ▸ **inclusion** /ɪnˈkluːʒn/ n [U,C] ▸ **inclusive** /ɪnˈkluːsɪv/ adj including everything

incognito /ˌɪnkɒɡˈniːtəʊ/ adv, adj in a way that prevents other people from finding out who you are: travel ~

incoherent /ˌɪnkəʊˈhɪərənt/ adj not clear; not expressed clearly ▸ **incoherence** /-əns/ n [U] ▸ **incoherently** adv

income /ˈɪnkʌm; ˈɪnkəm/ n [C,U]

money received during a month, year, etc, esp as payment for work ■ **'income tax** n [U] money that you pay to the government according to how much you earn

incoming /'ɪnkʌmɪŋ/ adj **1** recently elected or appointed: the ~ president **2** arriving or being received: ~ mail

incomparable /ɪn'kɒmpərəbl/ adj so good or impressive that nothing can be compared to it

incompatible /,ɪnkəm'pætəbl/ adj not able or suitable to exist together: The hours of the job are ~ with family life. ▶ **incompatibility** /,ɪnkəm,pætə'bɪləti/ n [U]

incompetent /ɪn'kɒmpɪtənt/ adj not skilful enough to do your job or a task as it should be done ▶ **incompetence** /ɪn'kɒmpɪtəns/ n [U]

incomplete /,ɪnkəm'pliːt/ adj not complete ▶ **incompletely** adv

incomprehensible /ɪn,kɒmprɪ'hensəbl/ adj impossible to understand ▶ **incomprehension** /ɪn,kɒmprɪ'henʃn/ n [U] failure to understand sth

inconceivable /,ɪnkən'siːvəbl/ adj impossible to imagine or believe

inconclusive /,ɪnkən'kluːsɪv/ adj not leading to a definite decision or result: ~ evidence

incongruous /ɪn'kɒŋgruəs/ adj out of place: Modern buildings look ~ in an old village. ▶ **incongruity** /,ɪnkɒŋ'gruːəti/ n [U, C] (pl -ies)

inconsiderate /,ɪnkən'sɪdərət/ adj not caring about the feelings of other people ▶ **inconsiderately** adv

inconsistent /,ɪnkən'sɪstənt/ adj ~ (with) not in harmony with sth; likely to change ▶ **inconsistency** /-ənsi/ n [U,C] (pl -ies) ▶ **inconsistently** adv

inconspicuous /,ɪnkən'spɪkjuəs/ adj not attracting attention; not easy to notice ▶ **inconspicuously** adv

incontinent /-ənt/ adj unable to control the bladder or bowels ▶ **incontinence** /ɪn'kɒntɪnəns/ n [U]

incontrovertible /,ɪnkɒntrə'vɜː-təbl/ adj (fml) that is true and cannot be denied

inconvenience /,ɪnkən'viːniəns/ n [C,U] (cause of) trouble, difficulty or discomfort ● **inconvenience** n [T] cause trouble or difficulty for sb ▶ **inconvenient** /,ɪnkən'viːniənt/ adj causing inconvenience ▶ **inconveniently** adv

incorporate /ɪn'kɔːpəreɪt/ v [T] include sth so that it forms part of sth: ~ your ideas in the new plan ▶ **incorporated** adj (business) (abbr **Inc.**) formed into a business com-

pany with legal status ▶ **incorporation** /ɪn,kɔːpə'reɪʃn/ n [U]

incorrect /,ɪnkə'rekt/ adj not correct; wrong ▶ **incorrectly** adv ▶ **incorrectness** n [U]

incorrigible /ɪn'kɒrɪdʒəbl/ adj (of a person or bad behaviour) that cannot be corrected or improved

increase¹ /ɪn'kriːs/ v [I, T] become or make sth greater in amount, number, value, etc ▶ **increasingly** adv more and more: increasingly difficult

increase² /'ɪŋkriːs/ n [C,U] ~ (in) rise in the amount, number or value of sth

incredible /ɪn'kredəbl/ adj **1** impossible to believe **2** (infml) wonderful; amazing ▶ **incredibly** adv

incredulous /ɪn'kredjələs/ adj not believing sth; showing disbelief ▶ **incredulity** /,ɪnkrə'djuːləti/ n [U] ▶ **incredulously** adv

increment /'ɪŋkrəmənt/ n increase in money or value

incriminate /ɪn'krɪmɪneɪt/ v [T] make sb appear to be guilty of doing sth wrong or illegal

incubate /'ɪŋkjubeɪt/ v [I, T] keep eggs warm until they hatch ▶ **incubation** /,ɪŋkju'beɪʃn/ n **1** [U] hatching of eggs **2** [C] (also **incu'bation period**) period between infection and the first appearance of a disease ▶ **incubator** n **1** piece of hospital equipment for keeping alive weak or premature babies **2** machine for hatching eggs by artificial warmth

incumbent /ɪn'kʌmbənt/ adj ~on (fml) necessary as a part of sb's duty ● **incumbent** n person holding an official position

incur /ɪn'kɜː(r)/ v (-rr-) [T] cause yourself to suffer sth, esp sth bad: ~ large debts

incurable /ɪn'kjʊərəbl/ adj that cannot be cured ▶ **incurably** /-əbli/ adv

incursion /ɪn'kɜːʃn/ n (fml) sudden attack; invasion

indebted /ɪn'detɪd/ adj very grateful: ~ to him for his help

indecent /ɪn'diːsnt/ adj **1** likely to shock people; obscene **2** unsuitable; not right ▶ **indecency** /-nsi/ n [U] ▶ **indecently** adv

indecision /,ɪndɪ'sɪʒn/ n [U] state of being unable to decide

indecisive /,ɪndɪ'saɪsɪv/ adj **1** unable to make decisions **2** not giving a clear answer or result ▶ **indecisively** adv

indeed /ɪn'diːd/ adv **1** used to emphasize a positive statement or answer: 'Did he complain?' 'I~ he did.' **2** used after very to emphasize a statement: Thank you very much

~. **3** used to show that you are surprised at sth or that you find sth ridiculous: *'She thinks she got the job.' 'Does she ~!'*

indefensible /ˌɪndɪˈfensəbl/ *adj* impossible to defend: *~ rudeness*

indefinable /ˌɪndɪˈfaɪnəbl/ *adj* impossible to define or put in words

indefinite /ɪnˈdefɪnət/ *adj* **1** lasting for a period of time with no fixed end: *an ~ period of time* **2** not clearly defined ▶ **in**ˌ**definite 'article** *n* (*gram*) *a* or *an* ▶ **indefinitely** *adv*: *The meeting was postponed ~ly.*

indelible /ɪnˈdeləbl/ *adj* impossible to forget or remove ▶ **indelibly** *adv*

indelicate /ɪnˈdelɪkət/ *adj* (*fml*) rude or embarrassing

indemnify /ɪnˈdemnɪfaɪ/ *v* (*pt, pp* **-ied**) [T] (promise to) pay sb for loss, damage, etc

indemnity /ɪnˈdemnəti/ *n* (*pl* **-ies**) (*fml*) or (*law*) **1** [U] protection against damage or loss **2** [C] payment for damage or loss

indent /ɪnˈdent/ *v* [T] start a line of writing further in from the margin than the other lines ● **indent** /ˈɪndent/ *n* (*business*) official order for goods or equipment ▶ **indentation** /ˌɪndenˈteɪʃn/ *n* **1** [C] cut or mark on the edge of sth: *the ~ations of the coastline* **2** (*also* **indent**) [C,U] (act of) indenting sth

independent /ˌɪndɪˈpendənt/ *adj* **1** (of countries) having their own government: *an ~ nation* **2** able to work alone; self-confident **3** ~ (of) not needing money, etc from other people to live ● **independent** *n* politician who does not belong to a particular political party ▶ **independence** /ˌɪndɪˈpendəns/ *n* [U]: *a woman's financial independence* ▶ **independently** *adv*

indescribable /ˌɪndɪˈskraɪbəbl/ *adj* impossible to describe ▶ **indescribably** *adv*

indestructible /ˌɪndɪˈstrʌktəbl/ *adj* impossible to destroy

index /ˈɪndeks/ *n* (*pl* **~es**; in sense 3 **~es** *or* **indices** /ˈɪndɪsiːz/) **1** list of names, subjects, etc in alphabetical order at the end of a book **2** (*also* **'card index**) (*GB*) box of cards with information on them, arranged in alphabetical order **3** system that compares the level of prices, etc with that of a former time: *the cost-of-living ~* ◇ *the Dow Jones ~* ● **index** *v* [T] make an index of ■ **index finger** *n* finger next to the thumb

indicate /ˈɪndɪkeɪt/ *v* [T] **1** show sth, esp by pointing; be a sign of sth **2** [I, T] (*GB*) signal that your vehicle is about to change direction ▶ **indica-**

tion /ˌɪndɪˈkeɪʃn/ *n* [C,U] remark or sign that shows that sth is happening or what sb is thinking ▶ **indicative** /ɪnˈdɪkətɪv/ *adj* ~(of) (*fml*) showing or suggesting sth ▶ **indicator** *n* **1** something that gives information, eg a pointer on a machine **2** flashing light on a vehicle showing that it is about to change direction

indict /ɪnˈdaɪt/ *v* [T] ~(for) (*esp US, law*) officially charge sb with a crime: *~ed for murder* ▶ **indictable** *adj* (*esp US, law*) for which you can be indicted: *an ~able offence* ▶ **indictment** *n* **1** [C, *usu sing*] sign that a system, a society, etc is very bad or wrong **2** [C,U] (*esp US*) (act of making a) written statement accusing sb of a crime

indifferent /ɪnˈdɪfrənt/ *adj* **1** ~(to) not interested in sth **2** not very good: *an ~ meal* ▶ **indifference** /ɪnˈdɪfrəns/ *n* [U] ▶ **indifferently** *adv*

indigenous /ɪnˈdɪdʒənəs/ *adj* ~(to) belonging naturally to a place; native: *Kangaroos are ~ to Australia.*

indigestion /ˌɪndɪˈdʒestʃən/ *n* [U] (pain from) difficulty in digesting food

indignant /ɪnˈdɪɡnənt/ *adj* angry, esp at injustice ▶ **indignantly** *adv* ▶ **indignation** /ˌɪndɪɡˈneɪʃn/ *n* [U]

indignity /ɪnˈdɪɡnəti/ *n* [C,U] (*pl* **-ies**) treatment causing shame or loss of respect

indirect /ˌɪndəˈrekt; -daɪˈr-/ *adj* **1** not immediate; secondary: *an ~ cause* **2** avoiding saying sth in a clear way: *an ~ answer* **3** not going in a straight line: *an ~ route* ▶ **indirectly** *adv* ■ ˌ**indirect 'object** *n* (*gram*) person or thing to whom or to which an action is done: In *'Give him the book', 'him' is the ~ object* ■ ˌ**indirect 'speech** *n* [U] (*gram*) reporting of what sb has said, without using their actual words: In *~ speech, 'I'll come later' becomes 'He said he'd come later'.* ■ ˌ**indirect 'tax** *n* [C,U] tax that is included in the price of certain goods

indiscreet /ˌɪndɪˈskriːt/ *adj* not careful about what you say and do ▶ **indiscreetly** *adv* ▶ **indiscretion** /ˌɪndɪˈskreʃn/ *n* **1** [U] indiscreet behaviour **2** [C] indiscreet remark or act

indiscriminate /ˌɪndɪˈskrɪmɪnət/ *adj* acting or done without careful thought ▶ **indiscriminately** *adv*

indispensable /ˌɪndɪˈspensəbl/ *adj* absolutely necessary

indisposed /ˌɪndɪˈspəʊzd/ *adj* (*fml*) **1** ill **2** unwilling to do sth: *~ to help*

indisputable /ˌɪndɪˈspjuːtəbl/ *adj* that is true and cannot be denied ▶ **indisputably** *adv*

indistinguishable /ˌɪndɪˈstɪŋgwɪʃ-əbl/ *adj* ~(**from**) impossible to identify as different: *as different: ~ from her sister*

individual /ˌɪndɪˈvɪdʒuəl/ *adj* **1** single; separate **2** of or for one person ● **individual** *n* any one human being ▶ **individuality** /ˌɪndɪˌvɪdʒu-ˈælɪti/ *n* [U] all the characteristics that make a person different from others ▶ **individually** *adv*

indoctrinate /ɪnˈdɒktrɪneɪt/ *v* [T] ~ (**with**) (*disapprov*) fill sb's mind with fixed beliefs or ideas ▶ **indoctrination** /ɪnˌdɒktrɪˈneɪʃn/ *n* [U]

indolent /ˈɪndələnt/ *adj* (*fml*) lazy ▶ **indolence** /-əns/ *n* [U]

indoor /ˈɪndɔː(r)/ *adj* done or situated inside a building: *an ~ swimming pool* ▶ **indoors** /ˌɪnˈdɔːz/ *adv* inside or into a building

induce /ɪnˈdjuːs/ *v* [T] **1** (*fml*) persuade or influence sb to do sth **2** (*fml*) cause sth **3** (*med*) cause a woman to begin childbirth by giving her drugs ▶ **inducement** *n* [C,U] something, eg money, that encourages sb to do sth: *a pay rise as an ~ment to work harder*

induction /ɪnˈdʌkʃn/ *n* **1** [U] act of introducing sb to a new job **2** [U] (*tech*) method of reasoning in which general laws are produced from particular facts **3** [U,C] inducing of a pregnant woman

indulge /ɪnˈdʌldʒ/ *v* [I] **1** [I] ~(**in**) allow yourself to enjoy sth **2** [T] satisfy a desire **3** [T] allow sb to have whatever they like or want ▶ **indulgence** *n* **1** [C] something pleasant in which sb indulges **2** [U] indulging ▶ **indulgent** *adj* tending to indulge(3) sb ▶ **indulgently** *adv*

industrial /ɪnˈdʌstriəl/ *adj* of industry ■ **industrial 'action** *n* [U] refusing to work normally; striking ▶ **industrialism** *n* [U] system in which large industries have an important part ▶ **industrialist** *n* owner of a large industrial company ▶ **industrialize** (*also* **-ise**) *v* [I, T] develop a country with many industries ▶ **industrially** *adv*

industrious /ɪnˈdʌstriəs/ *adj* hardworking; busy

industry /ˈɪndəstri/ *n* (*pl* **-ies**) **1** [C, U] (branch of) manufacture or production of goods from raw materials: *the steel ~* **2** [U] (*fml*) quality of being hard-working

inebriated /ɪˈniːbrieɪtɪd/ *adj* (*fml or hum*) drunk

inedible /ɪnˈedəbl/ *adj* (*fml*) not suitable to be eaten

ineffective /ˌɪnɪˈfektɪv/ *adj* not producing the results that you want ▶ **ineffectively** *adv* ▶ **ineffectiveness** *n* [U]

ineffectual /ˌɪnɪˈfektʃuəl/ *adj* (*written*) without the ability to achieve much; weak: *an ~ teacher* ▶ **ineffectually** *adv*

inefficient /ˌɪnɪˈfɪʃnt/ *adj* not doing a job well and not making the best use of time, money, energy etc ▶ **inefficiency** /-ənsi/ *n* [U] ▶ **inefficiently** *adv*

ineligible /ɪnˈelɪdʒəbl/ *adj* ~(**for**) not having the suitable or necessary qualifications: *~ for the job*

inept /ɪˈnept/ *adj* acting or done with no skill ▶ **ineptitude** /ɪˈneptɪtjuːd/ *n* [U]

inequality /ˌɪnɪˈkwɒləti/ *n* [U,C] (*pl* **-ies**) unfair difference between groups of people in society

inert /ɪˈnɜːt/ *adj* **1** (*fml*) without power to move or act **2** (*tech*) without active chemical or other properties (= characteristics): *~ gases*

inertia /ɪˈnɜːʃə/ *n* [U] **1** lack of energy; lack of desire to move or change **2** (*physics*) tendency of an object to remain still or to continue moving unless another force acts on it

inescapable /ˌɪnɪˈskeɪpəbl/ *adj* impossible to avoid or ignore

inevitable /ɪnˈevɪtəbl/ *adj* **1** that you cannot avoid or prevent **2** (*infml*) familiar and expected ▶ **inevitability** /ɪnˌevɪtəˈbɪləti/ *n* [U] ▶ **inevitably** *adv*

inexact /ˌɪnɪɡˈzækt/ *adj* not exact or precise

inexcusable /ˌɪnɪkˈskjuːzəbl/ *adj* too bad to accept or forgive

inexpensive /ˌɪnɪkˈspensɪv/ *adj* not costing a lot of money

inexperience /ˌɪnɪkˈspɪəriəns/ *n* [U] lack of experience ▶ **inexperienced** *adj*

inexplicable /ˌɪnɪkˈsplɪkəbl/ *adj* that cannot be explained ▶ **inexplicably** *adv*

inextricable /ˌɪnɪkˈstrɪkəbl; ɪn-ˈekstrɪkəbl/ *adj* (*fml*) too closely linked to be separated

infallible /ɪnˈfæləbl/ *adj* **1** never wrong: *Nobody is ~.* **2** that never fails: *an ~ method* ▶ **infallibility** /ɪnˌfælə-ˈbɪləti/ *n* [U]

infamous /ˈɪnfəməs/ *adj* well known for being bad or evil ▶ **infamy** /ˈɪnfəmi/ *n* [C,U] (*pl* **-ies**) (instance of) infamous behaviour

infancy /ˈɪnfənsi/ *n* [U] **1** state or period of being a young child **2** early stage of development: *The project is still in its ~.*

infant /ˈɪnfənt/ *n* baby or very young child

infantile /ˈɪnfəntaɪl/ *adj* of an infant; childish: *~ behaviour*

infantry /ˈɪnfəntri/ n [U, with sing or pl verb] soldiers who fight on foot

infatuated /ɪnˈfætʃueɪtɪd/ adj ~ (with) having a very strong feeling of love or attraction for sb so that you cannot think clearly ▶ **infatuation** /ɪnˌfætʃuˈeɪʃn/ n [U, C]

infect /ɪnˈfekt/ v [T] ~(with) 1 make a disease or an illness spread to another person, animal or plant 2 make sb share a particular feeling ▶ **infection** /ɪnˈfekʃn/ n [C, U] 1 act or process of causing or getting a disease: danger of ~ion 2 [C] illness caused by bacteria or a virus: an ear ~ **infectious** /ɪnˈfekʃəs/ adj 1 (of a disease) caused by bacteria, etc that are passed from one person to another: (fig) ~ious laughter 2 (of a person or an animal) having a disease that can be spread to others

infer /ɪnˈfɜː(r)/ v (-rr-) [T] ~(from) reach an opinion from facts: What can be ~red from the election results? ▶ **inference** /ˈɪnfərəns/ n [C, U]

inferior /ɪnˈfɪəriə(r)/ adj ~(to) not as good as sb/sth else ● **inferior** n inferior person ▶ **inferiority** /ɪnˌfɪəriˈɒrəti/ n [U] ■ **inferiority complex** n feeling that you are not as good, important, etc as other people

inferno /ɪnˈfɜːnəʊ/ n (pl ~s) large destructive fire

infertile /ɪnˈfɜːtaɪl/ adj 1 (of people, animals and plants) not able to have babies or produce young 2 (of land) not able to produce good crops: ~ land

infest /ɪnˈfest/ v [T] ~(with) (of rats, insects, etc) live in large numbers in a particular place: shark-~ed waters

infidelity /ˌɪnfɪˈdeləti/ n [C, U] (pl -ies) (fml) (act of) being unfaithful to your wife, husband or partner by having sex with someone else

infighting /ˈɪnfaɪtɪŋ/ n [U] fierce competition between colleagues or rivals in an organization

infiltrate /ˈɪnfɪltreɪt/ v [T] enter a place or an organization secretly to get information, etc ▶ **infiltration** /ˌɪnfɪlˈtreɪʃn/ n [U] ▶ **infiltrator** n

infinite /ˈɪnfɪnət/ adj without limits; endless ▶ **infinitely** adv

infinitive /ɪnˈfɪnətɪv/ n (gram) basic form of a verb, without inflections, etc (in English used with or without to, eg 'let him go', 'allow him to go')

infinity /ɪnˈfɪnəti/ n [U] endless distance, space or quantity

infirm /ɪnˈfɜːm/ adj weak, esp from old age or illness ▶ **infirmity** n [U, C] (pl -ies)

infirmary /ɪnˈfɜːməri/ n (pl -ies) hospital

inflame /ɪnˈfleɪm/ v [T] make sb/sth very angry or overexcited ▶ **inflamed** adj (of a part of the body) red, hot and sore

inflammable /ɪnˈflæməbl/ adj easily set on fire; that can burn easily

inflammation /ˌɪnfləˈmeɪʃn/ n [C, U] condition in which a part of the body is red, swollen and sore

inflammatory /ɪnˈflæmətri/ adj likely to make people angry or overexcited: ~ remarks

inflate /ɪnˈfleɪt/ v 1 [I, T] fill sth or become filled with gas or air 2 [T] make sth appear to be more important that it really is 3 [I, T] (cause sth to) increase in price ▶ **inflation** /ɪnˈfleɪʃn/ n [U] 1 general rise in prices in a particular country, resulting in a fall in the value of money; rate at which this happens 2 process of filling sth with air or gas ▶ **inflationary** /ɪnˈfleɪʃənri/ adj of or causing inflation(1)

inflection (also **inflexion**) /ɪnˈflekʃn/ n [C, U] 1 (gram) change in the form of a word to show a past tense, plural, etc 2 rise and fall of the voice in speaking

inflexible 1 refusing to change or be influenced 2 (of a material) impossible to bend or turn ▶ **inflexibility** /ɪnˌfleksəˈbɪləti/ n [U] ▶ **inflexibly** adv

inflict /ɪnˈflɪkt/ v [T] ~(on) make sb/sth suffer sth unpleasant: ~ a defeat on the enemy ▶ **infliction** /ɪnˈflɪkʃn/ n [U]

in-flight adj provided or happening during a journey on a plane: an ~ magazine/movie

influence /ˈɪnfluəns/ n 1 effect that sb/sth has on the way sb thinks or behaves or on the way sth develops 2 [U] power to produce an effect on sb/sth 3 [C] somebody or something that affects the way people behave or think: She's a bad ~ on me. [IDM] **under the influence** drunk ● **influence** v [T] have an effect on sb/sth

influential /ˌɪnfluˈenʃl/ adj having a lot of influence on sb/sth

influenza /ˌɪnfluˈenzə/ n [U] = FLU

influx /ˈɪnflʌks/ n arrival, esp in large numbers or quantities

inform /ɪnˈfɔːm/ v [T] 1 tell sb about sth, esp in an official way 2 ~ yourself (of/about) find out information about sth [PV] **inform on sb** give information about sb's illegal activities to the police ▶ **informant** /ɪnˈfɔːmənt/ n person who gives secret information about sb/sth to the police or a newspaper ▶ **informed** adj having or showing knowledge ▶ **informer** n criminal who gives information to the police about other criminals

informal /ɪnˈfɔːml/ adj **1** not formal or serious: ~ clothes (= those worn when you are relaxing) **2** (of words) used when you can be friendly and relaxed ▶ **informality** /ˌɪnfɔːˈmæləti/ n [U] ▶ **informally** adv

information /ˌɪnfəˈmeɪʃn/ n [U] ~ (on/about) facts or details about sb/sth

informative /ɪnˈfɔːmətɪv/ adj giving a lot of information

infrared /ˌɪnfrəˈred/ adj (physics) of the invisible, heat-giving rays below red in the spectrum

infrastructure /ˈɪnfrəstrʌktʃə(r)/ n [C,U] basic systems and services necessary for a country or an organization, eg transport, power supplies, etc

infrequent /ɪnˈfriːkwənt/ adj not happening often; rare ▶ **infrequently** adv

infringe /ɪnˈfrɪndʒ/ v **1** [T] break a law or a rule **2** [I, T] ~(on) limit sb's legal rights: ~ on the rights of other people ▶ **infringement** n [U,C]

infuriate /ɪnˈfjʊərieɪt/ v [T] make sb very angry

infuse /ɪnˈfjuːz/ v **1** [T] (fml) fill sb with a quality: ~ the workers with energy ◇ ~ energy into the workers **2** [I, T] (of tea or herbs) soak in hot water to make a drink ▶ **infusion** /ɪnˈfjuːʒn/ n [C,U] (liquid made by soaking herbs, etc in hot water

ingenious /ɪnˈdʒiːniəs/ adj **1** (of an object, plan, etc) original and well designed **2** (of a person) having a lot of clever new ideas ▶ **ingeniously** adv ▶ **ingenuity** /ˌɪndʒəˈnjuːəti/ n [U]

ingot /ˈɪŋgət/ n (usu brick-shaped) piece of metal, eg gold or silver

ingrained /ɪnˈgreɪnd/ adj (of habits, etc) deeply fixed

ingratiate /ɪnˈgreɪʃieɪt/ v [T] (fml, disapprov) ~ yourself (with) try to make sb like you, esp sb who will be useful to you ▶ **ingratiating** adj

ingratitude /ɪnˈgrætɪtjuːd/ n [U] not feeling or showing that you are grateful for sth

ingredient /ɪnˈgriːdiənt/ n one of the parts of a mixture: the ~s of a cake

inhabit /ɪnˈhæbɪt/ v [T] live in a particular place ▶ **inhabitant** /ɪnˈhæbɪtənt/ n person living in a place

inhale /ɪnˈheɪl/ v [I, T] breathe in ▶ **inhaler** n device that produces a vapour to make breathing easier

inherent /ɪnˈhɪərənt/ adj ~(in) that is a basic or permanent part of sb/sth: ~ weaknesses in a design

inherit /ɪnˈherɪt/ v [T] **1** receive property, money, etc from sb when they die **2** receive qualities, etc from your parents, grandparents, etc ▶ **inheritance** n [C, usu sing, U] money, etc that you inherit; fact of inheriting sth ▶ **inheritor** n person who inherits sth

inhibit /ɪnˈhɪbɪt/ v [T] **1** prevent sth from happening **2** ~(from) make sb nervous or embarrassed so that they are unable to do sth ▶ **inhibited** adj unable to relax and express your feelings naturally ▶ **inhibition** /ˌɪnhɪˈbɪʃn/ n [C,U] feeling of being unable to behave naturally

inhospitable /ˌɪnhɒˈspɪtəbl/ adj not hospitable: a ~ climate

inhuman /ɪnˈhjuːmən/ adj without kindness, pity, etc ▶ **inhumanity** /ˌɪnhjuːˈmænəti/ n [U]

inhumane /ˌɪnhjuːˈmeɪn/ adj not caring about the suffering of other people; cruel ▶ **inhumanely** adv

inimitable /ɪˈnɪmɪtəbl/ adj too good or individual for anyone else to copy

initial /ɪˈnɪʃl/ adj happening at the beginning; first ● **initial** n [C, usu pl] first letter of a person's name ● **initial** v (-ll- US -l-) [I, T] sign sth with your initials ▶ **initially** /ɪˈnɪʃəli/ adv at the beginning

initiate /ɪˈnɪʃieɪt/ v [T] (fml) **1** make sth begin **2** ~(into) introduce sb into a club, group, etc ● **initiate** /ɪˈnɪʃiət/ n person who has just been initiated into a group ▶ **initiation** /ɪˌnɪʃiˈeɪʃn/ n [u]

initiative /ɪˈnɪʃətɪv/ n **1** [C] action taken to solve a difficulty **2** [U] ability to act without help: do sth on your own ~ **3** (the initiative) [sing] power or opportunity to take action: It's up to you to take the ~ and make a plan.

inject /ɪnˈdʒekt/ v [T] **1** put sth into sb with a syringe: ~ a drug into sb ◇ ~ sb with a drug **2** ~(into) add a particular quality to sth: ~ new life into the team ▶ **injection** /ɪnˈdʒekʃn/ n [C,U]

injunction /ɪnˈdʒʌŋkʃn/ n (fml) ~ (against) official order from a court of law

injure /ˈɪndʒə(r)/ v [T] hurt or damage sb/sth ▶ **injured** adj physically hurt; offended ▶ **the injured** n [pl] injured people

injury /ˈɪndʒəri/ n (pl -ies) **1** [C,U] harm done to a person's or an animal's body, eg in an accident **2** [U] esp (law) damage to a person's feelings

injustice /ɪnˈdʒʌstɪs/ n **1** [U] fact of a situation being unfair **2** [C] unfair act [IDM] **do yourself/sb an injustice** judge yourself/sb unfairly

ink /ɪŋk/ n [U,C] coloured liquid for writing, printing, etc ▶ **inky** adj black

inkling /ˈɪŋklɪŋ/ n [usu sing] vague idea

inland /ˈɪnlənd/ adj in or near the middle of a country: ~ lakes ▶ **inland** /ˌɪnˈlænd/ adv towards the middle of a country; away from the coast ■ **the Inland 'Revenue** n [sing] (in Britain) government department that collects taxes

in-laws /ˈɪn lɔːz/ n [pl] (infml) relatives by marriage

inlet /ˈɪnlet/ n strip of water reaching into the land

inmate /ˈɪnmeɪt/ n person living in a prison, mental hospital, etc

inmost /ˈɪnməʊst/ adj = INNERMOST (INNER)

inn /ɪn/ n (GB, old-fash) small old hotel or pub, usu in the country ■ **'innkeeper** n (old-fash) person who manages an inn

innards /ˈɪnədz/ n [pl] **1** parts inside the body, esp the stomach **2** parts inside a machine

innate /ɪˈneɪt/ adj (of a quality, etc) existing in a person from birth ▶ **innately** adv

inner /ˈɪnə(r)/ adj **1** inside; near to the middle **2** (of feelings) private and secret ▶ **innermost** /ˈɪnəməʊst/ adj **1** most private and secret: ~ thoughts **2** furthest inside

innings /ˈɪnɪŋz/ n (pl innings) (in cricket) time during which a team or player is batting [IDM] **have a good innings** (GB, infml) used about sb who has died to say that they had a long happy life ▶ **inning** n (in baseball) part of a game in which both teams bat

innocuous /ɪˈnɒkjuəs/ adj harmless: an ~ remark

innovate /ˈɪnəveɪt/ v [I] introduce new things, ideas or ways of doing sth ▶ **innovation** /ˌɪnəˈveɪʃn/ n **1** [U] introduction of new things, ideas, etc **2** [C] new idea, method, etc ▶ **innovative** /ˈɪnəveɪtɪv/ (GB also) /ˈɪnəvətɪv/ (also **innovatory** /ˌɪnəˈveɪtəri/) adj ▶ **innovator** n

innuendo /ˌɪnjuˈendəʊ/ n [C,U] (pl ~es or ~s) indirect remark about sb/sth, usu suggesting sth bad or rude

innumerable /ɪˈnjuːmərəbl/ adj too many to count

inoculate /ɪˈnɒkjuleɪt/ v [T] inject sb with a vaccine in order to prevent a disease: ~ sb against cholera ▶ **inoculation** /ɪˌnɒkjuˈleɪʃn/ n [C,U]

inoffensive /ˌɪnəˈfensɪv/ adj not likely to offend or upset anyone

inopportune /ɪnˈɒpətjuːn/ adj (fml) not suitable or convenient: an ~ remark/time

inordinate /ɪnˈɔːdɪnət/ adj (fml) far more than is usual or expected ▶ **inordinately** adv

inorganic /ˌɪnɔːˈɡænɪk/ adj not made of living substances: Rocks and minerals are ~.

input /ˈɪnpʊt/ n **1** [C,U] time, knowledge, etc that you put into work, etc to make it successful; act of putting sth in **2** [C] (computing) act of putting the information into a computer; the information that you put it: data ● **input** v (-tt- pt, pp input or ~ted) [T] put information into a computer

inquest /ˈɪŋkwest/ n official investigation to find out the cause of sb's death

inquire, inquiry = ENQUIRE, ENQUIRY

inquisition /ˌɪnkwɪˈzɪʃn/ n (fml) severe and detailed investigation

inquisitive /ɪnˈkwɪzətɪv/ adj (too) fond of asking questions about other people's affairs ▶ **inquisitively** adv

inroad /ˈɪnrəʊd/ n something that is achieved, esp by reducing the power or success of sth else [IDM] **make inroads into/on sth** gradually use, eat, etc more and more of sth: ~ into your savings

insane /ɪnˈseɪn/ adj mad ▶ **insanely** adv ▶ **insanity** /ɪnˈsænəti/ n [U]

insatiable /ɪnˈseɪʃəbl/ adj impossible to satisfy

inscribe /ɪnˈskraɪb/ v [T] write or cut words onto sth: ~ words on a tombstone ▶ **inscription** /ɪnˈskrɪpʃn/ n words written in the front of a book or cut in stone, etc

inscrutable /ɪnˈskruːtəbl/ adj impossible to understand; mysterious

insect /ˈɪnsekt/ n any small creature with six legs, eg an ant or a fly ▶ **insecticide** /ɪnˈsektɪsaɪd/ n [C,U] chemical used for killing insects

insecure /ˌɪnsɪˈkjʊə(r)/ adj **1** lacking confidence **2** not safe ▶ **insecurely** adv ▶ **insecurity** n [U]

insensible /ɪnˈsensəbl/ adj (fml) **1** ~ (to) not able to feel sth: ~ to pain **2** ~ (of) unaware of sth **3** unconscious ▶ **insensibility** /ɪnˌsensəˈbɪləti/ n [U]

insensitive /ɪnˈsensətɪv/ adj not realizing or caring how people feel ▶ **insensitively** adv ▶ **insensitivity** /ɪnˌsensəˈtɪvəti/ n [U]

inseparable /ɪnˈseprəbl/ adj impossible to separate: ~ friends

insert /ɪnˈsɜːt/ v [T] put or fit sth into sth: ~ a key in a lock ● **insert** /ˈɪnsɜːt/ n something put inside sth else, eg an advertisement put between the pages of a newspaper ▶ **insertion** /ɪnˈsɜːʃn/ n [C,U]

inset /ˈɪnset/ n small picture, map, etc within a larger one

inshore /ˌɪnˈʃɔː(r)/ *adj* /ˈɪnʃɔː(r)/ *adv* (of sth at sea) close to the land

inside¹ /ɪnˈsaɪd/ *n* **1** [C, usu sing] part or surface nearest to the centre **2** [sing] (*also* **insides** [pl]) (*infml*) person's stomach and bowels [IDM] **inside out 1** with the part that is usu inside facing out **2** thoroughly: *know sth ~ out* **on the inside** in an organization so that you can find out secret information ● **inside** *adj* **1** on or in the inside of sth **2** known or done by sb who is in an organization: *The robbery was an ~ job.* ▶ **insider** *n* member of an organization who can obtain special information ▶ **in,sider 'dealing** (*also* **in,sider 'trading**) *n* [U] crime of buying or selling shares in a company with the help of information known only by people who work for the business

inside² /ɪnˈsaɪd/ (*esp US* **inside of**) *prep* **1** on or to the inner side of sth/sb: *come ~ the house* **2** in less than the amount of time mentioned: *~ a year* ● **inside** *adv* **1** on or to the inside: *go ~* (= into the house) **2** (*infml*) in prison

insidious /ɪnˈsɪdiəs/ *adj* doing harm secretly ▶ **insidiously** *adv*

insight /ˈɪnsaɪt/ *n* [C,U] (instance of) understanding: *~s into his character*

insignia /ɪnˈsɪɡniə/ *n* [U, with sing or pl verb] symbol, badge or sign that shows sb's rank or membership of a group

insignificant /ˌɪnsɪɡˈnɪfɪkənt/ *adj* having little importance or value ▶ **insignificance** /-kəns/ *n* [U] ▶ **insignificantly** *adv*

insincere /ˌɪnsɪnˈsɪə(r)/ *adj* saying or doing sth that you do not really mean or believe ▶ **insincerely** *adv* ▶ **insincerity** /ˌɪnsɪnˈserəti/ *n* [U]

insinuate /ɪnˈsɪnjueɪt/ *v* [T] **1** suggest indirectly that sth unpleasant is true **2** **~ yourself into** (*fml*) gain sb's respect, affection, etc so that you can use the situation to your own advantage ▶ **insinuation** /ɪnˌsɪnjuˈeɪʃn/ *n* [C,U]

insipid /ɪnˈsɪpɪd/ *adj* (*disapprov*) **1** having almost no taste or flavour **2** not interesting or exciting

insist /ɪnˈsɪst/ *v* [I, T] **~(on) 1** demand sth strongly: *~ on going with sb* ◇ *~ that she (should) stop* **2** declare sth firmly: *He ~s that he is innocent.* ▶ **insistent** *adj* strongly insisting ▶ **insistence** *n* [U]

insofar as /ˌɪnsəˈfɑːr əz/ = IN SO FAR AS (FAR¹)

insolent /ˈɪnsələnt/ *adj* **~(to)** very rude ▶ **insolence** /-əns/ *n* [U]

insoluble /ɪnˈsɒljəbl/ *adj* **1** (of problems, etc) impossible to solve

2 (of substances) impossible to dissolve

insolvent /ɪnˈsɒlvənt/ *adj* not having enough money to pay what you owe ▶ **insolvency** /-ənsi/ *n* [U,C] (*pl* **-ies**)

insomnia /ɪnˈsɒmniə/ *n* [U] inability to sleep ▶ **insomniac** /ɪnˈsɒmniæk/ *n* person who cannot go to sleep easily

inspect /ɪnˈspekt/ *v* [T] examine sth/sb carefully ▶ **inspection** /ɪnˈspekʃn/ *n* [C,U] ▶ **inspector** *n* **1** official who inspects sth, eg schools **2** (*GB*) police officer above a sergeant in rank

inspire /ɪnˈspaɪə(r)/ *v* [T] **1** fill sb with the ability or desire to do sth **2** fill sb with feelings: *~ sb with confidence* ◇ *~ confidence in sb* ▶ **inspiration** /ˌɪnspəˈreɪʃn/ *n* **1** [U] influence producing creative ability; state of being inspired **2** [C, usu sing] person or thing that is the reason why sb creates or does sth **3** [C,U] (*infml*) sudden good idea ▶ **inspired** *adj* filled with or showing inspiration(1) ▶ **inspiring** *adj*

instability /ˌɪnstəˈbɪləti/ *n* [U] lack of stability

install /ɪnˈstɔːl/ *v* [T] **1** fix machines, furniture, etc in position **2** (*fml*) put sb in a new position of authority **3** (*fml*) make sb/yourself comfortable in a particular place ▶ **installation** /ˌɪnstəˈleɪʃn/ *n* [U,C]

instalment (*US* **-ll-**) /ɪnˈstɔːlmənt/ *n* **1** one of a number of payments spread over a period of time until sth has been paid for **2** one part of a story that appears over a period of time

instance /ˈɪnstəns/ *n* particular example or case of sth [IDM] **for instance** for example

instant /ˈɪnstənt/ *n* [C, usu sing] **1** moment: *I'll be there in an ~.* **2** particular point in time: *Come here this ~* (= immediately)! ● **instant** *adj* **1** happening immediately: *an ~ success* **2** (of food) that can be made very quickly and easily: *~ coffee* ▶ **instantly** *adv* immediately

instantaneous /ˌɪnstənˈteɪniəs/ *adj* happening or done immediately ▶ **instantaneously** *adv*

instead /ɪnˈsted/ *adv* in the place of sb/sth: *Bill was ill so I went ~.* ■ **in'stead of** *prep* in the place of sb/sth: *drink tea ~ of coffee*

instep /ˈɪnstep/ *n* top part of the foot

instigate /ˈɪnstɪɡeɪt/ *v* [T] make sth start or happen: *~ a strike/riot* ▶ **instigation** /ˌɪnstɪˈɡeɪʃn/ *n* [U] ▶ **instigator** *n*

instil (*US* **instill**) /ɪnˈstɪl/ *v* (**-ll-**) [T] **~ (in/into)** put ideas, etc into sb's mind

instinct /'mstɪŋkt/ n [C, U] natural tendency to behave in a certain way ▶ **instinctive** /m'stɪŋktɪv/ adj based on instinct: in ~ive fear of fire ▶ **instinctively** adv

institute /'mstɪtjuːt/ n (building used by an) organization with a particular purpose ● **institute** v [T] (fml) introduce a system, policy, etc or start a process

institution /ˌmstɪ'tjuːʃn/ n 1 [C] (building used by an) organization with a social purpose, eg a school or hospital 2 [C] established custom or practice: the ~ of marriage 3 [U] act of introducing a system, law, etc ▶ **institutional** /-ʃənl/ adj ▶ **institutionalize** (also **-ise**) /-ʃənəlaɪz/ v [T] 1 send sb who is not capable of living independently to live in an institution 2 make sth into an institution(2)

instruct /m'strʌkt/ v [T] (fml) 1 tell sb to do sth: ~ the child not to go out 2 teach sb sth, esp a practical skill 3 (law) employ a lawyer to represent you in court ▶ **instructive** adj giving a lot of useful information ▶ **instructor** n teacher or trainer

instruction /m'strʌkʃn/ n 1 (instructions) [pl] information on how to do sth: Follow the ~s on packet. 2 [C, usu pl] order 3 [U] act of teaching sth to sb

instrument /'mstrəmənt/ n 1 tool or device used for a particular task, esp delicate or scientific work: surgical ~s 2 = MUSICAL INSTRUMENT (MUSIC) ▶ **instrumental** /ˌmstrə-'mentl/ adj 1 ~ in important in making sth happen: You were ~al in her promotion. 2 made by or for musical instruments ▶ **instrumentalist** /ˌmstrə'mentəlɪst/ n person who plays a musical instrument

insubordinate /ˌmsə'bɔːdɪnət/ adj disobedient ▶ **insubordination** /ˌmsə-ˌbɔːdɪ'neɪʃn/ n [U, C]

insufferable /m'sʌfrəbl/ adj unbearable ▶ **behaviour**

insufficient /ˌmsə'fɪʃnt/ adj not enough ▶ **insufficiency** /-ʃənsi/ n [U] ▶ **insufficiently** adv

insular /'msjələ(r)/ adj (disapprov) only interested in your own country, ideas, etc and not in those from outside ▶ **insularity** /ˌmsjuːˈlærəti/ n [U]

insulate /'msjuleɪt/ v [T] 1 cover sth to prevent heat, electricity, etc from escaping: ~d wires 2 (written) protect sb/sth from unpleasant experiences ▶ **insulation** /ˌmsju-'leɪʃn/ n [U] (materials used in insulating sth)

insult /m'sʌlt/ v [T] be rude to sb ● **insult** /'msʌlt/ n rude remark or action ▶ **insulting** adj

insurance /m'ʃɔːrəns/ n 1 [U, C] agreement by a company or the state to pay money because of loss, illness, death, etc in return for regular payments 2 [U] money paid by or to an insurance company 3 [U, C] protection against loss, failure, etc

insure /m'ʃɔː(r)/ v [T] 1 protect sb/sth by insurance: ~ a car against fire/theft 2 (esp US) = ENSURE

insurgent /m'sɜːdʒənt/ adj rebellious ▶ **insurgent** n [usu pl] (fml) rebel soldier

insurmountable /ˌmsə'maʊntəbl/ adj (of problems or difficulties) impossible to solve or overcome

insurrection /ˌmsə'rekʃn/ n [C, U] rebellion

intact /m'tækt/ adj undamaged; complete

intake /'mteɪk/ n 1 [U, C] amount of food, drink, etc that you take into your body 2 [C] number of people taken in: last year's ~ of students 3 [C] place where liquid, air, etc enters a machine 4 [C] act of taking sth in, esp breath

intangible /m'tændʒəbl/ adj 1 that exists but is difficult to describe or understand: an ~ air of sadness 2 (business) that has no physical existence but is still valuable to a company: ~ assets/property

integer /'mtɪdʒə(r)/ n (maths) whole number, eg 1, 3, 11

integral /'mtɪgrəl/ adj necessary to make sth complete: an ~ part of the plan ▶ **integrally** adv

integrate /'mtɪgreɪt/ v [T] ~ (into/with) combine with so that it becomes fully a part of sth else 2 [I, T] (of people) mix or be together as one group ▶ **integration** /ˌmtɪ'greɪʃn/ n [U]

integrity /m'tegrəti/ n [U] 1 honesty and goodness 2 wholeness; unity

intellect /'mtəlekt/ n [U] power of the mind to reason ▶ **intellectual** /ˌmtə'lektʃuəl/ adj 1 of the intellect 2 of or interested in ideas, the arts, etc rather than practical matters ▶ **intellectual** n intellectual person ▶ **intellectually** adv

intelligence /m'telɪdʒəns/ n [U] 1 ability to learn, understand and think 2 secret information about a country's enemies; people who collect this information ▶ **intelligent** /m'telɪdʒənt/ adj clever ▶ **intelligently** adv

intelligible /m'telɪdʒəbl/ adj that can be understood ▶ **intelligibility** /-'bɪləti/ n [U] ▶ **intelligibly** adv

intend /m'tend/ v [T] have a plan, result or purpose in your mind when you do sth; mean: I ~ to leave soon.

intense /ɪnˈtens/ adj 1 extreme; very strong: ~ heat/anger 2 (of a person) serious and very emotional ▶ **intensely** adv ▶ **intensify** /-sɪfaɪ/ v (pt, pp -ied) [I, T] become or make sth greater or stronger ▶ **intensification** /ɪnˌtensɪfɪˈkeɪʃn/ n [U] ▶ **intensity** n [U] state of being intense; strength of feeling, etc

intensive /ɪnˈtensɪv/ adj concentrating effort, work, etc on one task; very thorough: an ~ search ▶ **intensively** adv

intent¹ /ɪnˈtent/ adj 1 showing strong interest and attention: an ~ look/gaze 2 ~ on determined to do sth: on becoming manager ▶ **intently** adv

intent² /ɪnˈtent/ n [U] (law) what you intend to do: shoot with ~ to kill [IDM] to all intents and purposes in the important details; almost completely

intention /ɪnˈtenʃn/ n [C,U] aim; purpose ▶ **intentional** /-ʃənl/ adj done on purpose ▶ **intentionally** adv

inter /ɪnˈtɜː(r)/ v (-rr-) [T] (fml) bury a dead person

interact /ˌɪntərˈækt/ v [I] ~(with) 1 have an effect on each other 2 (of people) communicate and work together ▶ **interaction** /-ˈækʃn/ n [U, C] ▶ **interactive** adj 1 involving people working together and influencing each other 2 (computing) allowing an exchange of information between a computer and a user

intercept /ˌɪntəˈsept/ v [T] stop sb/sth that is moving between two places ▶ **interception** /-ˈsepʃn/ n [U]

interchange /ˌɪntəˈtʃeɪndʒ/ v [I, T] (cause two people or things to) change places with each other ● **interchange** n [C,U] 1 act of sharing or exchanging sth, esp ideas or information 2 [C] place where a main road joins a motorway ▶ **interchangeable** adj

intercity /ˌɪntəˈsɪti/ adj (of transport) travelling between cities

intercom /ˈɪntəkɒm/ n system of communication using a microphone and loudspeaker, used eg in a building

intercontinental /ˌɪntəˌkɒntɪˈnentl/ adj between continents: ~ flights

intercourse /ˈɪntəkɔːs/ n [U] (fml) 1 = SEXUAL INTERCOURSE (SEXUAL) 2 (old-fash) communication between people, nations, etc

interest /ˈɪntrəst/ n 1 [sing, U] ~(in) desire to learn or know about sb/sth: lose ~ ◇ take an ~ in art 2 [U] quality that attracts attention or curiosity: an idea of ~ to us 3 [C] activity or subject which you enjoy doing or learning about: His great ~ is football. 4 [U] ~(on) money paid for the use of money: borrow money at a high rate of ~ 5 [C, usu pl] advantage for sb/sth: It is in your ~s (= It is to your advantage) to work hard. 6 [C, usu pl] share in a business 7 [C, usu pl] group of people in the same business, etc [IDM] in the interest(s) of sth in order to help or achieve sth ● **interest** v [T] attract your attention and make you feel interested ▶ **interested** adj 1 ~(in) showing interest(1) in sth: be ~ed in history 2 personally involved ▶ **interesting** adj holding your attention

interface /ˈɪntəfeɪs/ n (computing) 1 way a computer program presents information to a user, esp the layout of the screen and the menus: the user ~ 2 electrical circuit, connection or program that joins one device or system to another

interfere /ˌɪntəˈfɪə(r)/ v [I] ~(in) get involved in a situation that does not concern you, in a way that annoys other people [PV] **interfere with sth** (GB) touch a child in a sexual way **interfere with sth** 1 prevent sth from succeeding or happening as planned 2 touch, use or change sth so that it is damaged or no longer works correctly ▶ **interference** n [U] 1 act of interfering 2 interruption of a radio signal by another signal, causing unwanted extra noise

interim /ˈɪntərɪm/ adj intended to last for only a short time: ~ arrangements ▶ **interim** n [IDM] in the interim in the time between two events

interior /ɪnˈtɪəriə(r)/ n 1 [C] inside part of sth 2 (the interior) [sing] inland part of a country or continent 3 (the Interior) [sing] a country's own affairs rather than those involving other countries: the Minister of the I~ ● **interior** adj connected with the inside part of sth

interjection /ˌɪntəˈdʒekʃn/ n (gram) word or phrase, eg Ow! spoken suddenly to express an emotion

interlock /ˌɪntəˈlɒk/ v [I, T] lock or join together

interlude /ˈɪntəluːd/ n short period of time between two parts of a play, etc or two events

intermarry /ˌɪntəˈmæri/ v (pt, pp -ied) [I] marry sb of a different race or from a different country or religious group ▶ **intermarriage** /ˌɪntəˈmærɪdʒ/ n [U]

intermediary /ˌɪntəˈmiːdiəri/ n (-ies) person who passes information between two groups, esp to get agreement

intermediate /ˌɪntəˈmiːdiət/ *adj* **1** between two points or stages **2** between elementary and advanced: *an ~ course*

interminable /ɪnˈtɜːmɪnəbl/ *adj* (*disapprov*) lasting too long and therefore boring ► **interminably** *adv*

intermission /ˌɪntəˈmɪʃn/ *n* [C, U] (*esp US*) interval in a play, etc; pause

intermittent /ˌɪntəˈmɪtənt/ *adj* stopping and starting often over a period of time: *~ rain* ► **intermittently** *adv*

intern¹ /ɪnˈtɜːn/ *v* [T] put sb in prison during a war or for political reasons ► **internment** *n* [U]

intern² (*also* **interne** /ɪnˈtɜːn/ (*US*) **1** junior doctor at a hospital **2** student or graduate getting practical experience of a job ► **internship** *n*

internal /ɪnˈtɜːnl/ *adj* **1** of or on the inside: *~ injuries* (= inside the body) **2** not foreign; domestic: *~ trade* ► **internally** *adv*

international /ˌɪntəˈnæʃnəl/ *adj* of or existing between two or more countries ● **international** *n* **1** sports match with teams from two countries **2** player who takes part in a match against another country ► **internationally** *adv*

Internet /ˈɪntənet/ *n* [sing] (usu the **Internet**) (*also infml* **the Net**) international computer system connecting other networks and computers from companies, universities, etc

interplay /ˈɪntəpleɪ/ *n* [U] way in which two or more things affect each other

interpose /ˌɪntəˈpəʊz/ *v* (*fml*) **1** [I] add a question or remark into a conversation **2** [T] place sth between two people or things

interpret /ɪnˈtɜːprɪt/ *v* [T] **1** explain the meaning of sth **2** [T] **~as** understand sth in a particular way: *his silence as an expression of guilt* **3** [I] translate one language into another as you hear it ► **interpretation** /ɪnˌtɜːprɪˈteɪʃn/ *n* [U,C] explanation or understanding of sth ► **interpreter** *n* person whose job is to translate what sb is saying into another language

interrogate /ɪnˈterəgeɪt/ *v* [T] question sb closely and for a long time ► **interrogation** /ɪnˌterəˈgeɪʃn/ *n* [C,U] ► **interrogator** *n*

interrogative /ˌɪntəˈrɒgətɪv/ *adj* (*gram*) used in questions: *~ pronouns* (= eg *who, why*) ● **interrogative** *n* question word

interrupt /ˌɪntəˈrʌpt/ *v* **1** [I, T] say or do sth that stops sb speaking **2** [T]

break the continuity of sth: *~a journey* ► **interruption** /-ˈrʌpʃn/ *n* [C,U]

intersect /ˌɪntəˈsekt/ *v* **1** [I, T] (of lines, roads, etc) meet or cross each other **2** [T] (*usu passive*) divide an area by crossing it ► **intersection** /ˌɪntəˈsekʃn/ *n* **1** [C] place where roads, lines, etc meet or cross each other **2** [U] act of intersecting sth

intersperse /ˌɪntəˈspɜːs/ *v* [T] (*written*) put sth between or among other things

interval /ˈɪntəvl/ *n* **1** time between two events **2** (*GB*) short period of time between the parts of a play, etc **3** short period during which sth different happens: *It'll be cloudy with sunny ~s.*

intervene /ˌɪntəˈviːn/ *v* [I] (*fml*) **1** ~ (in) become involved in a situation to improve or help it **2** happen in a way that delays sth **3** (*fml*) exist between two events or places ► **intervention** /-ˈvenʃn/ *n* [U,C].

interview /ˈɪntəvjuː/ *n* ~(**with**) meeting at which sb, eg sb applying for a job, is asked questions ● **interview** *v* [T] ask sb questions in an interview ► **interviewer** *n* person who interviews sb

intestate /ɪnˈtesteɪt/ *adj* (*law*) not having made a will: *die ~*

intestine /ɪnˈtestɪn/ *n* [C, usu pl] long tube from the stomach to the anus ► **intestinal** *adj*

intimacy /ˈɪntɪməsi/ *n* **1** [U] state of having a close personal relationship with sb **2** [C, usu pl] thing a person says or does to sb they know very well

intimate¹ /ˈɪntɪmət/ *adj* **1** having a very close relationship: *~ friends* **2** private and personal: *~ details of her life* **3** (of knowledge) very detailed and thorough ► **intimately** *adv*

intimate² /ˈɪntɪmeɪt/ *v* [T] (*fml*) let sb know what you mean in an indirect way ► **intimation** /ˌɪntɪˈmeɪʃn/ *n* [C,U]

intimidate /ɪnˈtɪmɪdeɪt/ *v* [T] frighten or threaten sb ► **intimidation** /ɪnˌtɪmɪˈdeɪʃn/ *n* [U]

into /ˈɪntə; *before vowels* ˈɪntu:/ *prep* **1** to a position in or inside sth: *Come ~ the house.* **2** to a point at which you hit sth: *A lorry drove ~ a line of cars.* **3** during a period of time: *work long ~ the night* **4** used to show a change in state: *The fruit can be made ~ jam.* **5** used to show the result of an action: *frighten sb ~ submission* **6** used for expressing division in mathematics: *5 ~ 25 is 5* [IDM] **be into sth** (*infml*) be very interested in sth

intolerable /ɪnˈtɒlərəbl/ *adj* too bad to be endured ► **intolerably** *adv*

intolerant /ɪn'tɒlərənt/ *adj* not willing to accept ideas, etc that are different from your own ▶ **intolerance** /-əns/ *n* [U]

intonation /ˌɪntə'neɪʃn/ *n* [C, U] rise and fall of the voice in speaking

intoxicated /ɪn'tɒksɪkeɪtɪd/ *adj* (*fml*) **1** under the influence of alcohol or drugs **2** very excited by sth ▶ **intoxication** /ɪnˌtɒksɪ'keɪʃn/ *n* [U]

Intranet /'ɪntrənet/ *n* (*computing*) computer network that is private to a company, university, etc but is not connected to and uses the same software as the Internet

intransitive /ɪn'trænsətɪv/ *adj* (*gram*) (of a verb) used without an object, eg *rise* in 'Smoke rises'.

in tray /'ɪn treɪ/ *n* container on your desk for holding letters, etc that are waiting to be read or answered

intrepid /ɪn'trepɪd/ *adj* (*fml*) brave: ~ *explorers*

intricate /'ɪntrɪkət/ *adj* with many small parts put together in a complicated way ▶ **intricacy** /-kəsi/ *n* (*pl* **-ies**) **1** [U] complicated parts or details of sth **2** [U] fact of being intricate ▶ **intricately** *adv*

intrigue /ɪn'triːg/ *v* **1** [T] make sb interested or curious: ~ *sb with a story* **2** [I] (*fml*) secretly plan with other people to harm sb ● **intrigue** /'ɪntriːg/ *n* **1** [U] activity of making of secret plans to do sth bad **2** [C] secret plan or relationship ▶ **intriguing** *adj* very interesting, esp because unusual

intrinsic /ɪn'trɪnsɪk; -zɪk/ *adj* belonging to the real nature of sth/sb ▶ **intrinsically** /-kli/ *adv*

introduce /ˌɪntrə'djuːs/ *v* [T] **1** ~(**to**) make sb known to sb else by giving each person's name to the other: *I ~d Mark to Emma.* **2** be the main speaker in a television or radio show, giving details about the show and the people in it **3** make sth available for use, discussion, etc, for the first time: ~ *computers into schools*

introduction /ˌɪntrə'dʌkʃn/ *n* **1** [U] act of bringing sth into use for the first time **2** [C, U] act of introducing of one person to another **3** [C] first part of a book or speech **4** [C] textbook for people beginning to study a subject

introductory /ˌɪntrə'dʌktəri/ *adj* written or said at the beginning of sth as an introduction to what follows

introspection /ˌɪntrə'spekʃn/ *n* [U] the careful examination of your own thoughts, feelings, etc ▶ **introspective** /ˌɪntrə'spektɪv/ *adj*

introvert /'ɪntrəvɜːt/ *n* a quiet person who is more interested in their own thoughts than in spending time with other people ▶ **introverted** *adj*

intrude /ɪn'truːd/ *v* [I] ~**on** go or be somewhere where you are not invited or wanted ▶ **intruder** *n* person who enters a building or an area illegally ▶ **intrusion** /ɪn'truːʒn/ *n* [U,C] ▶ **intrusive** /ɪn'truːsɪv/ *adj* too noticeable, direct, in a way that is annoying

intuition /ˌɪntju'ɪʃn/ *n* **1** [U] ability to understand sth quickly without conscious thought **2** [C] idea that sth is true although you cannot explain why ▶ **intuitive** /ɪn'tjuːɪtɪv/ *adj* ▶ **intuitively** *adv*

inundate /'ɪnʌndeɪt/ *v* [T] **1** give or send sb so many things that they cannot deal with them all: ~*d with replies* **2** (*fml*) flood an area of land

invade /ɪn'veɪd/ *v* [T] **1** enter a country with armed forces in order to attack or occupy it **2** enter a place in large numbers: *Fans ~d the football pitch.* ▶ **invader** *n* ▶ **invasion** /ɪn'veɪʒn/ *n* [C, U]

invalid[1] /ɪn'vælɪd/ *adj* **1** not legally or officially acceptable: *an ~ passport* **2** not based on all the facts and therefore not correct: *an ~ argument* **3** (*computing*) of a type that the computer cannot recognize: ~ *characters* ▶ **invalidate** /ɪn'vælɪdeɪt/ *v* [T] **1** prove that sth is wrong **2** make sth officially invalid ▶ **invalidation** /ɪnˌvælɪ'deɪʃn/ *n* [U]

invalid[2] /'ɪnvəlɪd; -liːd/ *n* person who is weak or disabled because of illness or injury ● **invalid** *v* [T] (*GB*) ~(**out**) force sb to leave the armed forces because of illness or injury

invaluable /ɪn'væljuəbl/ *adj* having a value that is too high to be measured

invariable /ɪn'veəriəbl/ *adj* never changing ▶ **invariably** *adv* always

invasion → INVADE

invective /ɪn'vektɪv/ *n* [U] (*fml*) rude language sb uses when they are very angry

invent /ɪn'vent/ *v* [T] **1** make or design sth that did not exist before: *Who ~ed television?* **2** think of sth untrue: ~ *an excuse* ▶ **invention** /ɪn'venʃn/ *n* **1** [C] something invented **2** [U] act of inventing sth ▶ **inventive** *adj* having the ability to invent things ▶ **inventor** *n*

inventory /'ɪnvəntri/ *n* (*pl* **-ies**) detailed list of all goods or furniture in a building

inverse /ɪn'vɜːs/ *adj* opposite in amount or position to sth else ● **inverse** /'ɪnvɜːs/ *n* (**the inverse**) [sing] (*tech*) the direct opposite of sth

invert /ɪn'vɜːt/ *v* [T] turn sth upside

down or arrange sth in the opposite order ▶ **inversion** /ɪn'vɜːʃn/ n [U,C]
■ in,verted 'commas n [pl] (GB) = QUOTATION MARKS (QUOTATION)

invest /ɪn'vest/ v **1** [I, T] ~(in) use money to buy business shares, property, etc in order to make more money: ~ (money) in shares **2** [T] ~in give time, effort, etc to sth you think is good or useful: ~ your time in learning French **3** [T] ~(with) (fml) give sb power or authority [PV] **invest in sth** (infml) buy sth expensive but useful: ~ in a new car ▶ **investment** n **1** [U] act of investing money in sth **2** [C] money that you invest, or the thing that you invest in ▶ **investor** n

investigate /ɪn'vestɪɡeɪt/ v [I, T] examine the facts about sth in order to discover the truth: a murder ▶ **investigation** /ɪn,vestɪ'ɡeɪʃn/ n [C,U] ▶ **investigative** /-ɡətɪv/ adj of or concerned with investigating ▶ **investigator** n

investiture /ɪn'vestɪtʃə(r)/ n ceremony at which sb receives an official title or special powers

inveterate /ɪn'vetərət/ adj (disapprov) firmly fixed in a bad habit: an ~ liar/smoker

invigilate /ɪn'vɪdʒɪleɪt/ v [I, T] (GB) watch over students in an examination ▶ **invigilation** /ɪn,vɪdʒɪ'leɪʃn/ n [U] ▶ **invigilator** n

invigorate /ɪn'vɪɡəreɪt/ v [T] make sb feel more lively and healthy ▶ **invigorating** adj

invincible /ɪn'vɪnsəbl/ adj too strong to be defeated

inviolable /ɪn'vaɪələbl/ adj (fml) that must be respected and not attacked or destroyed: ~ rights

inviolate /ɪn'vaɪələt/ adj (fml) that has been, or must be, respected and cannot be attacked

invisible /ɪn'vɪzəbl/ adj ~(to) that cannot be seen ▶ **invisibility** /ɪn,vɪzə'bɪləti/ n [U] ▶ **invisibly** adv

invite /ɪn'vaɪt/ v [T] **1** ~(to/for) ask sb to go somewhere or to do sth: ~ sb for dinner **2** make sth, esp sth bad, likely to happen: ~ criticism ▶ **invitation** /,ɪnvɪ'teɪʃn/ n [C] ~(to) request to do sth or go somewhere: an invitation to a party **2** [U] act of inviting sb or being invited: Admission is by invitation only. ▶ **inviting** adj attractive ▶ **invitingly** adv

invoice /'ɪnvɔɪs/ n list of goods sold, work done, etc showing what you must pay ● **invoice** v [T] (business) write or send sb a bill for work you have done or goods you have provided

invoke /ɪn'vəʊk/ v [T] (fml) **1** mention or use a law, rule, etc as a reason for doing sth **2** make a request

(for help) to sb, esp a god **3** make sth appear by magic ▶ **invocation** /,ɪnvə'keɪʃn/ n [C, U] prayer or appeal for help

involuntary /ɪn'vɒləntri/ adj done without intention: an ~ movement ▶ **involuntarily** /-trəli/ adv

involve /ɪn'vɒlv/ v [T] **1** make sth a necessary condition or result: The job ~d me/my living in London. **2** include or affect sb **3** ~in make sb take part in sth ▶ **involved** adj **1** ~(in) taking part in sth; being connected with sth **2** ~(with) having a close personal relationship with sb **3** complicated ▶ **involvement** n [U,C]

invulnerable /ɪn'vʌlnərəbl/ adj that cannot be hurt or damaged

inward /'ɪnwəd/ adj **1** inside your mind: ~ thoughts **2** towards the inside or centre of sth ● **inward** (also **inwards**) adv **1** towards the inside or centre **2** towards yourself and your interests ▶ **inwardly** adv in your mind; secretly

iodine /'aɪədiːn/ n [U] dark blue liquid used in medicine and photography

ion /'aɪən/ n electrically charged particle ▶ **ionize** (also **-ise**) v [I, T] (tech) change sth or be changed into ions

iota /aɪ'əʊtə/ n [sing] very small amount

IOU /,aɪ əʊ 'juː/ n (infml) 'I owe you'; written promise to pay sb the money you owe them

IQ /,aɪ 'kjuː/ n measure of sb's intelligence: have a high/low IQ

irate /aɪ'reɪt/ adj (fml) angry

iridescent /,ɪrɪ'desnt/ adj (fml) changing colour as light falls on it from different directions

iris /'aɪrɪs/ n **1** coloured part round the pupil of the eye **2** tall plant with large bright flowers

irk /ɜːk/ v [T] (fml or lit) annoy sb ▶ **irksome** /'ɜːksəm/ adj annoying

iron¹ /'aɪən/ n **1** [U] (symb Fe) hard strong metal, used in manufacturing and building: an ~ bridge/gate ◇ (fig) She had a will of ~ (= it was very strong). **2** [C] tool with a flat metal base that can be heated to smooth clothes: a steam ~ **3** (irons) [pl] chains for a prisoner [IDM] **have several, etc irons in the fire** be involved in many different activities at the same time ■ **ironmonger** /'aɪən,mʌŋɡə(r)/ n (GB) shopkeeper who sells tools and household goods

iron² /'aɪən/ v [I, T] make clothes, etc smooth by using an iron¹(2) [PV] **iron out sth** remove any difficulties, etc affecting sth ▶ **ironing** n [U] **1** action of ironing clothes **2** clothes that

need to be ironed: *a pile of ~ing*
■ **'ironing board** *n* long narrow board on which clothes are ironed

ironic /aɪˈrɒnɪk/ (*also* **ironical** /-kl/) *adj* using or expressing irony ▶ **ironically** /-kli/ *adv*

irony /ˈaɪrəni/ *n* (*pl* **-ies**) **1** [U,C] amusing or strange aspect of an unexpected event or situation **2** [U] saying the opposite of what you really mean, often as a joke

irrational /ɪˈræʃənl/ *adj* not guided by reason: *an ~ fear of water* ▶ **irrationally** /-nəli/ *adv*

irreconcilable /ˌɪrekənˈsaɪləbl/ *adj* (*fml*) (of differences or disagreements) impossible to settle

irregular /ɪˈreɡjələ(r)/ *adj* **1** uneven; not regular **2** against the normal rules **3** (*gram*) not formed in the normal way: *~ verbs* ▶ **irregularity** /ɪˌreɡjəˈlærəti/ *n* [C,U] (*pl* **-ies**) ▶ **irregularly** *adv*

irrelevant /ɪˈreləvənt/ *adj* not important to the situation ▶ **irrelevance** /-əns/ *n* [U]

irreparable /ɪˈrepərəbl/ *adj* (of damage, an injury, etc) too bad to be put right

irreplaceable /ˌɪrɪˈpleɪsəbl/ *adj* impossible to replace if lost or damaged

irrepressible /ˌɪrɪˈpresəbl/ *adj* impossible to hold back or control

irreproachable /ˌɪrɪˈprəʊtʃəbl/ *adj* (*fml*) without fault or blame

irresistible /ˌɪrɪˈzɪstəbl/ *adj* too strong, attractive, etc to be resisted ▶ **irresistibly** *adv*

irrespective /ˌɪrɪˈspektɪv əv/ *prep* (*written*) without considering sth: *Buy it now, ~ of the cost.*

irresponsible /ˌɪrɪˈspɒnsəbl/ *adj* (*disapprov*) (of a person) not thinking enough about the effects of what they do ▶ **irresponsibility** /-ˈbɪləti/ *n* [U] ▶ **irresponsibly** *adv*

irreverent /ɪˈrevərənt/ *adj* not showing respect, esp for holy things ▶ **irreverence** /-əns/ *n* [U] ▶ **irreverently** *adv*

irrevocable /ɪˈrevəkəbl/ *adj* (*fml*) impossible to change; final: *an ~ decision*

irrigate /ˈɪrɪɡeɪt/ *v* [T] supply land with water so that crops will grow ▶ **irrigation** /ˌɪrɪˈɡeɪʃn/ *n* [U]

irritable /ˈɪrɪtəbl/ *adj* easily annoyed ▶ **irritability** /ˌɪrɪtəˈbɪləti/ *n* [U] ▶ **irritably** *adv*

irritate /ˈɪrɪteɪt/ *v* [T] **1** annoy **2** make part of the body sore ▶ **irritation** /ˌɪrɪˈteɪʃn/ *n* [U,C]

is /ɪz/ → BE

Islam /ˈɪzlɑːm/ *n* **1** [U] Muslim religion, based on the teaching of the

Prophet Muhammad **2** [sing] all Muslims ▶ **Islamic** /ɪzˈlæmɪk/ *adj*

island /ˈaɪlənd/ *n* **1** piece of land surrounded by water **2** = TRAFFIC ISLAND (TRAFFIC) ▶ **islander** *n* person living on an island

isle /aɪl/ *n* (esp in poetry and proper names) island

isn't /ˈɪznt/ is not → BE

isolate /ˈaɪsəleɪt/ *v* [T] separate sb/sth from other people or things ▶ **isolated** *adj* far from others: *an ~d cottage* ▶ **isolation** /ˌaɪsəˈleɪʃn/ *n* [U]

ISP /ˌaɪ es ˈpiː/ *abbr* Internet service provider; company that provides you with an Internet connection and services such as email

issue /ˈɪʃuː; *GB also*/ ˈɪsjuː/ *n* **1** [C] important topic for discussion **2** [C] (*infml*) problem or worry that sb has with sth **3** [C] one of a regular series of a magazine, etc **4** [U] supply and distribution of sth **5** (*law*) children of your own ● **issue** *v* [T] (*fml*) **1** make sth known formally: *~ a statement* **2** give sb to sth, esp officially: *~ a passport/visa* **3** produce sth, eg a magazine

it /ɪt/ *pron* (used as the subject or object of a v after a prep) **1** animal or thing mentioned earlier: *Where's my book. Have you seen it?* **2** baby, esp one whose sex is not known **3** used to identify a person: *'Who's that?' 'It's the postman.'* **4** used when the subject or object comes at the end of a sentence: *It's nice to see you.* **5** used when you are talking about time, distance or weather: *It's 12 o'clock.* ◇ *It's raining.* **6** used to emphasize any part of a sentence: *It was work that exhausted him.* [IDM] **that is it 1** this/that is the important point, reason, etc **2** this/that is the end: *That's it, then—we've lost the match.* **this is it 1** the expected event is going to happen: *Well, this is it! Wish me luck.* **2** this is the main point ▶ **its** /ɪts/ *det* of or belonging to a thing, animal or baby: *its tail*

italic /ɪˈtælɪk/ *adj* (of printed letters) sloping forwards: *This is ~ type.* ▶ **italics** *n* [pl] italic letters

itch /ɪtʃ/ *n* **1** [C,usu sing] feeling of irritation on the skin, causing a desire to scratch **2** [sing] (*infml*) strong desire to do sth: *have an ~ to travel* ● **itch** *v* **1** [I] have an itch(1) **2** [I] **~for/to** (*infml*) want to do sth very much: *pupils ~ing for the lesson to end* ◇ *~ing to tell her the news* ▶ **itchy** *adj* having or producing irritation on the skin: *an ~ shirt* [IDM] **(get/have) itchy feet** (*infml*) want to travel or move to a different place

it'd /ˈɪtəd/ *short for* IT HAD; IT WOULD

item /ˈaɪtəm/ *n* **1** single thing or unit

in a list, etc **2** single piece of news ▶ **itemize** (*also* **-ise**) v [T] produce a detailed list of sth: *an ~d bill*

itinerant /aɪˈtɪnərənt/ *adj* (*fml*) travelling from place to place: *~ workers*

itinerary /aɪˈtɪnərəri/ *n* (*pl* **-ies**) plan for a journey

it'll /ˈɪtl/ *short for* IT WILL

its /ɪts/ ⇒ IT

it's /ɪts/ *short for* IT IS; IT HAS

itself /ɪtˈself/ *pron* **1** used as a reflexive when the animal, thing, etc causing the action is also affected by it: *My dog hurt ~.* **2** used to emphasize an animal, a thing, etc: *The name ~ sounds foreign.* [IDM] (**all**) **by itself 1** automatically **2** alone

I've /aɪv/ *short for* I HAVE

IVF /ˌaɪ viː ˈef/ *n* [U] (*tech*) in vitro fertilization; process which fertilizes a woman's egg outside her body

ivory /ˈaɪvəri/ *n* [U] **1** creamy-white bone-like substance forming the tusks (= long teeth) of elephants **2** colour of ivory [IDM] **an ivory tower** (*disapprov*) place where people stay away from the unpleasant realities of everyday life

ivy /ˈaɪvi/ *n* [U] climbing evergreen plant with dark shiny leaves

Jj

J, j /dʒeɪ/ *n* [C,U] (*pl* **J's, j's** /dʒeɪz/) the tenth letter of the English alphabet

jab /dʒæb/ v (**-bb-**) [I, T] push a pointed object into sth with sudden force: *She ~bed him in the ribs with her finger.* ● **jab** *n* [C] **1** sudden strong hit with sth pointed **2** (*GB, infml*) injection

jabber /ˈdʒæbə(r)/ v [I, T] (*disapprov*) talk or say sth quickly and excitedly ▶ **jabber** *n* [U]

jack /dʒæk/ *n* **1** device for lifting sth heavy, esp a car **2** playing card between the ten and the queen ● **jack** *n* [PV] **jack sth in** (*GB, infml*) decide to stop doing sth, esp your job **jack sth up** lift sth, esp a vehicle, using a jack

jacket /ˈdʒækɪt/ *n* **1** short coat with sleeves **2** loose paper cover for a book **3** outer cover round a tank, pipe, etc **4** (*GB*) skin of a baked potato

jackknife /ˈdʒæknaɪf/ *n* (*pl* **-knives**) large knife with a folding blade ● **jackknife** v [I] (esp of an articulated lorry) bend sharply in the middle

jackpot /ˈdʒækpɒt/ *n* largest money prize to be won in a game of chance

Jacuzzi™ /dʒəˈkuːzi/ *n* bath with fast underwater currents of water

jade /dʒeɪd/ *n* [U] hard, usu green, stone from which jewels, etc are carved

jaded /ˈdʒeɪdɪd/ *adj* tired and lacking energy, usu after too much of sth

jagged /ˈdʒægɪd/ *adj* with rough, pointed, often sharp edges: *~ rocks*

jaguar /ˈdʒægjuə(r)/ *n* large spotted animal of the cat family, found in central America

jail /dʒeɪl/ *n* [C,U] prison ● **jail** v [T] put sb in prison

jam /dʒæm/ *n* [C] **1** [U,C] sweet food made by boiling fruit with sugar, eaten on bread **2** [C] number of people, things, etc crowded together and preventing movement: *a traffic ~* [IDM] **be in a jam** (*infml*) be in a difficult situation ● **jam** v (**-mm-**) **1** [T] push sb/sth somewhere with force or squeeze sb/sth into a small space: *~ clothes into a suitcase* **2** [I, T] (cause sth to) become unable to move or to work: *The photocopier has ~med.* **3** [T] (*tech*) send out radio signals to prevent another radio broadcast from being heard [IDM] **jam on the brake(s)** or **jam the brake(s)** on operate the brakes on a vehicle suddenly and with force

jangle /ˈdʒæŋgl/ v [I, T] (cause sth to) make a harsh sound like two pieces of metal hitting each other ● **jangle** *n* [sing] hard noise like that of metal hitting metal

janitor /ˈdʒænɪtə(r)/ *n* (*US*) = CARE-TAKER

January /ˈdʒænjuəri/ *n* [U,C] the first month of the year (See examples of use at *April*.)

jar¹ /dʒɑː(r)/ *n* **1** round glass container with a lid, used for storing food **2** a jar and what it contains: *a ~ of coffee/jam* ● **jar** *n* (**-rr-**) **1** [I, T] give or receive a sudden sharp painful knock **2** [I] *~(on)* have an unpleasant effect on sb: *Her moaning really ~s on my nerves.* **3** [I] *~(with)* be different from sth in a strange or unpleasant way

jargon /ˈdʒɑːgən/ *n* [U] technical words or expressions used by a particular profession or group of people: *medical/legal ~*

jaundice /ˈdʒɔːndɪs/ *n* [U] medical condition that makes the skin and whites of the eyes yellow ▶ **jaundiced** *adj* suspicious; bitter: *a ~d opinion*

jaunt /dʒɔːnt/ *n* (*old-fash or hum*) short journey, made for pleasure ▶ **jaunty** *adj* (**-ier, -iest**) cheerful and self-confident ▶ **jauntily** *adv*

javelin /ˈdʒævlɪn/ *n* light spear which is thrown in a sporting event

jaw /dʒɔː/ n **1** [C] either of the bone structures containing the teeth: *the lower/upper ~* **2** [sing] lower part of the face **3** (**jaws**) [pl] mouth with its bones and teeth **4** (**jaws**) [pl] part of a tool or machine that holds things tightly [IDM] **the jaws of death, defeat, etc** (*lit*) used to describe an unpleasant situation that almost happens ■ '**jawbone** n bone that forms the lower jaw

jazz /dʒæz/ n [U] type of music with strong rhythms, created by African American musicians ● **jazz** v [PV] **jazz sth up** (*infml*) make sth more lively, interesting or attractive ▶ **jazzy** adj (-**ier, -iest**) (*infml*) **1** in the style of jazz **2** brightly coloured or showy: *a ~y tie*

jealous /'dʒeləs/ adj **1** feeling angry or unhappy because sb you like or love is showing interest in sb else: *a ~ husband* **2** ~(**of**) feeling angry or unhappy because you wish you had what sb else has **3** determined to keep and protect what you have: *They're very ~ of their good reputation* (= they do not want to lose it). ▶ **jealously** adv ▶ **jealousy** n [U,C] (pl -**ies**)

jeans /dʒiːnz/ n [pl] trousers made of strong cotton, esp denim

Jeep™ /dʒiːp/ n motor vehicle for driving over rough ground

jeer /dʒɪə(r)/ v [I,T] ~(**at**) laugh rudely at sb; mock ● **jeer** n jeering remark

jelly /'dʒeli/ n (pl -**ies**) **1** [U,C] (US **jello, Jell-O**™ [U]) clear sweet soft fruit-flavoured food **2** [U] type of clear jam: *blackcurrant ~* ■ '**jellyfish** n (pl **jellyfish**) sea creature with a soft clear body which can sting

jeopardize (also -**ise**) /'dʒepədaɪz/ v [T] put sth/sb in danger ▶ **jeopardy** /'dʒepədi/ n [IDM] **in jeopardy** in a dangerous position and likely to be lost or harmed: *The success of our plan has been put in jeopardy.*

jerk /dʒɜːk/ n **1** sudden quick sharp movement **2** (*infml*) stupid person ● **jerk** v [I,T] (cause sth to) move with a jerk ▶ **jerky** adj (-**ier, -iest**) with sudden starts and stops

jersey /'dʒɜːzi/ n knitted woollen or cotton piece of clothing for the upper body, with long sleeves

Jerusalem artichoke /dʒə,ruː-sələm 'ɑːtɪtʃəʊk/ n light brown root vegetable that looks like a potato

jest /dʒest/ n (*old-fash* or *fml*) something done or said to amuse people [IDM] **in jest** as a joke ● **jest** v [I] (*fml*) joke

jet /dʒet/ n **1** [C] aircraft powered by a jet engine **2** [C] strong narrow stream of gas, liquid, etc forced out of a small opening, which is also

called a jet **3** [U] black highly-polished mineral, used in jewellery ■ ,**jet-'black** adj of a deep shiny black colour ● **jet** v (-**tt-**) [I] (*infml*) fly somewhere in a plane ■ '**jet engine** n engine that drives an aircraft forward by pushing out a stream of gases behind it ■ '**jet lag** n [U] tiredness felt after a long flight to a place where the time is different ■ **the 'jet set** n [sing] rich fashionable people who travel a lot

jettison /'dʒetɪsn/ v [T] throw away sth unwanted

jetty /'dʒeti/ n (pl -**ies**) wall or platform built out into the sea, a river, etc as a landing place for boats

Jew /dʒuː/ n person of the Hebrew people or religion ▶ **Jewish** adj

jewel /'dʒuːəl/ n **1** precious stone, eg a diamond **2** small precious stone used in a watch **3** (*infml*) person or thing that is greatly valued ▶ **jeweller** (US -**l-**) n person who sells, makes or repairs jewellery ▶ **jewellery** (also **jewelry**) /'dʒuːəlri/ n [U] ornaments, eg rings and necklaces, esp made of gold, silver, etc

jibe (also **gibe**) /dʒaɪb/ v [I] ~(**at**) make fun of sb/sth ● **jibe** n comment that makes fun of sb/sth

jiffy /'dʒɪfi/ n [C, usu sing] (*infml*) moment: *I'll be with you in a ~.*

jig /dʒɪg/ n (music for a) quick lively dance ● **jig** v (-**gg-**) [I, T] (cause sb/sth to) move up and down with short quick movements

jiggle /'dʒɪɡl/ v [I, T] (*infml*) (make sth) move quickly from side to side or up and down: *He ~d the car keys in his hands.*

jigsaw /'dʒɪɡsɔː/ n (also '**jigsaw puzzle**) picture on cardboard or wood cut into irregular shapes that has to be fitted together again

jihad /dʒɪ'hɑːd/ n holy war fought by Muslims against those who reject Islam

jilt /dʒɪlt/ v [T] end a romantic relationship with sb suddenly and unkindly

jingle /'dʒɪŋɡl/ n **1** [sing] gentle ringing sound of small bells, keys, etc **2** [C] short simple rhyme or song, esp used in advertising ● **jingle** v [I, T] (cause sth to) make a gentle ringing sound

jinx /dʒɪŋks/ n [C, sing] ~(**on**) (person or thing thought to bring) bad luck

jive /dʒaɪv/ n [sing] fast dance to music with a strong beat, esp popular in the 1950s ● **jive** v [I] dance to jazz or rock and roll music

job /dʒɒb/ n [C] **1** work for which you receive regular payment **2** particular task or piece of work: *Finding a flat to rent was quite a ~.*

3 [usu sing] responsibility or duty: *It's not my ~ to do this.* **4** (infml) criminal act, esp theft **5** item of work processed by a computer as a single unit [IDM] **just the job** (infml) exactly what was wanted or needed **make a bad, good, etc job of sth** do sth badly, well, etc ▶ **jobless** adj unemployed ■ **'job-sharing** n [U] arrangement by which two people are employed part-time to share a full-time job

jockey /'dʒɒki/ n professional rider in horse races ● **jockey** v [I] (~ **for position**) try all possible ways to gain an advantage over other people: *~ for position*

jog /dʒɒg/ v (-gg-) **1** [I] run slowly, esp for exercise **2** [T] hit sth lightly and accidentally [IDM] **jog sb's memory** help sb to remember sth [PV] **jog along** (GB, infml) continue as usual with little or no excitement ● **jog** n [sing] **1** slow run, esp for exercise **2** light push or knock ▶ **jogger** n person who jogs regularly for exercise

join /dʒɔɪn/ v **1** [T] fix or connect two or more things together **2** [I, T] (of two things or groups) come together to form one: *The two roads ~ here.* **3** [T] become a member of an organization, a company, a club, etc **4** [T] take part in sth that sb else is doing: *Please ~ us for a drink.* [IDM] **join forces (with sb)** work together to achieve a shared aim [PV] **join (in (sth)** take part in an activity ● **join** n place where two things are fixed together

joiner /'dʒɔɪnə(r)/ n skilled worker who makes wooden window frames, doors, etc of buildings ▶ **joinery** n [U] work of a joiner

joint /dʒɔɪnt/ n **1** place where two bones are joined together **2** place where two or more things are joined: *the ~s of a pipe* **3** large piece of meat **4** (infml) place where people meet to eat, drink, dance, etc **5** (infml) cigarette containing marijuana ● **joint** adj shared or done by two or more people: *~ responsibility* ◇ *a ~ account* (= a bank account in the name of more than one person) ▶ **jointly** adv ■ **joint-'stock company** (business) company that is owned by all the people who have shares in it

joist /dʒɔɪst/ n wood or steel beam supporting a floor or ceiling

joke /dʒəʊk/ n something said or done to make people laugh ● **joke** v [I] tell funny stories ▶ **joker** n **1** person who likes making jokes **2** extra playing card used in certain card games ▶ **jokingly** adv in a joking manner

jolly /'dʒɒli/ adj (-ier, -iest) happy and cheerful ● **jolly** adv (GB, old-fash, spoken) very: *a ~ good idea*

jolt /dʒəʊlt/ v [I, T] (make sth) move suddenly and roughly ● **jolt** n [C, usu sing] sudden rough movement

jostle /'dʒɒsl/ v [I, T] push roughly against sb, usu in a crowd

jot /dʒɒt/ v (-tt-) [PV] **jot sth down** write sth quickly ▶ **jotter** n small notebook

journal /'dʒɜːnl/ n **1** magazine or newspaper that deals with a particular subject: *a medical/scientific ~* **2** daily written record of events ▶ **journalism** /-nəlɪzəm/ n [U] work of writing for newspapers, magazines, television or radio ▶ **journalist** n person whose profession is journalism

journey /'dʒɜːni/ n act of travelling from one place to another ● **journey** v [I] (lit) travel

jovial /'dʒəʊviəl/ adj (written) cheerful and friendly

joy /dʒɔɪ/ n **1** [U] great happiness **2** [C] person or thing that causes you to feel very happy ▶ **joyful** adj (written) very happy; causing people to be happy ▶ **joyfully** adv ▶ **joyous** adj (lit) very happy; causing people to be happy ▶ **joyously** adv

joypad /'dʒɔɪpæd/ n device used with some computer games, with buttons for moving images on the screen

JP /ˌdʒeɪ 'piː/ abbr = JUSTICE OF THE PEACE (JUSTICE)

jubilant /'dʒuːbɪlənt/ adj (fml) very happy, esp because of a success ▶ **jubilation** /ˌdʒuːbɪ'leɪʃn/ n [U] great happiness, esp because of a success

jubilee /'dʒuːbɪliː/ n (celebration of a) special anniversary

Judaism /'dʒuːdeɪɪzəm/ n [U] religion of the Jewish people; their culture

judge /dʒʌdʒ/ n **1** public officer with authority to decide cases in a law court **2** person that decides who has won a competition **3** person able to give an opinion on the value of sth: *She's a good ~ of character.* ● **judge** v [I, T] **1** form an opinion about sb/sth **2** act as a judge in sth

judgement (also esp law **judgment**) /'dʒʌdʒmənt/ n **1** [U] ability to make sensible decisions **2** [C,U] opinion that you form after careful thought; act of making this opinion known to others: *make a fair ~ of his character* **3** [C,U] decision of a law court or judge: *The court has yet to pass ~.* (= give its decision).

judicial /dʒu'dɪʃl/ adj of or by a law court; of a judge or judgement

judiciary /dʒuˈdɪʃəri/ n [C, with sing or pl verb] (pl -ies) all the judges of a country

judicious /dʒuˈdɪʃəs/ adj (fml) showing or having good sense ▶ **judiciously** adv

judo /ˈdʒuːdəʊ/ n [U] sport in which two people fight and try to throw each other to the ground

jug /dʒʌɡ/ n (GB) 1 deep container for liquids, with a handle and a lip 2 amount of liquid contained in a jug: a ~ of milk

juggernaut /ˈdʒʌɡənɔːt/ n (GB) very large lorry

juggle /ˈdʒʌɡl/ v 1 keep objects, esp balls, in the air by throwing and catching them 2 organize information, figures, etc in the most useful or effective way ▶ **juggler** n

juice /dʒuːs/ n [U,C] liquid obtained from fruit, vegetables or meat ▶ **juicy** adj (-ier, -iest) 1 containing a lot of juice 2 (infml) interesting, esp because scandalous

jukebox /ˈdʒuːkbɒks/ n machine in a pub, etc that plays music when you put coins in it

July /dʒuˈlaɪ/ n [U,C] the seventh month of the year (See examples of use at *April*.)

jumble /ˈdʒʌmbl/ v 1 ~(together/ up) mix things together in an untidy or confused way ● **jumble** n 1 [sing] confused or untidy group of things 2 [U] (GB) goods for a jumble sale ■ **jumble sale** n (GB) sale of old unwanted goods to get money for a charity

jumbo /ˈdʒʌmbəʊ/ adj (infml) very large ● **jumbo** n (pl -s) (also **jumbo 'jet**) large plane that can carry several hundred passengers, esp a Boeing 747

jump¹ /dʒʌmp/ v 1 [I] move quickly off the ground by pushing yourself with your legs and feet: ~ up in the air 2 [T] pass over sth by jumping: ~ a wall 3 [I] move quickly and suddenly: The loud bang made me ~. 4 [I] rise suddenly by a large amount: Prices rose by 60% last year. 5 [T] (infml) attack sb suddenly **jump on the bandwagon → BAND jump the gun** do sth too soon **jump the queue** (US) **jump the line** go to the front of a queue without waiting for your turn **jump to conclusions** come to a decision about sth too quickly [PV] **jump at sth** accept an opportunity, chance, etc eagerly

jump² /dʒʌmp/ n 1 act of jumping 2 thing to be jumped over 3 ~(in) sudden rise in amount: a huge ~ in profits ▶ **jumpy** adj (-ier, -iest) (infml) nervous; anxious

jumper /ˈdʒʌmpə(r)/ n 1 (GB) =

JERSEY 2 person, an animal or an insect that jumps

junction /ˈdʒʌŋkʃn/ n place where roads or railway lines meet

juncture /ˈdʒʌŋktʃə(r)/ n (fml) particular point in an activity or series of events

June /dʒuːn/ n [U,C] the sixth month of the year (See examples of use at *April*.)

jungle /ˈdʒʌŋɡl/ n [C,U] land in a tropical country, covered with thick forest

junior /ˈdʒuːniə(r)/ adj 1 ~(to) lower in rank than sb 2 (Junior) (esp US) used after the name of a man who has the same name as his father 3 (GB) (of a school or part of a school) for children under the age of 11 or 13 ● **junior** n 1 [C] person with a low level job within an organization 2 [sing] person who is a certain number of years younger than sb else: He is three years her ~.

junk /dʒʌŋk/ n [U] old or unwanted things, usu of little value: The chair came from a ~ shop. ■ **junk bond** n (business) type of bond that pays a high rate of interest because of the risk involved ■ **junk food** n [U] (infml, disapprov) food that is thought to be bad for your health

jurisdiction /ˌdʒʊərɪsˈdɪkʃn/ n [U] (fml) legal authority

juror /ˈdʒʊərə(r)/ n member of a jury

jury /ˈdʒʊəri/ n [C, with sing or pl verb] (pl -ies) 1 group of people in a law court who decide whether the accused person is guilty or not guilty 2 group of people who decide the winner of a competition

just¹ /dʒʌst/ adj according to what is right and proper; fair: a ~ decision ▶ **justly** adv

just² /dʒʌst/ adv 1 exactly: This jacket is ~ my size. ◇ You're ~ in time. ◇ Leave everything ~ as you find it. 2 ~as at the same moment as: She arrived ~ as I did. 3 no less than; equally: It's ~ as cheap to go by plane. 4 by a small amount: I arrive ~ after nine. 5 used to say that you did sth very recently: I've ~ had dinner. 6 at this/that moment: We're ~ leaving. 7 ~ about/going to do sth used to refer to the immediate future: The water's ~ about to boil. 8 simply: Why not ~ wait and see? 9 only: There is ~ one way of saving him. 10 used in orders to get sb's attention: J~ listen to me! [IDM] **just about** (infml) almost **just now** 1 at this moment: I can't do it ~ now. 2 only a short time ago

justice /ˈdʒʌstɪs/ n 1 [U] quality of being right and fair 2 [U] the law and its administration: a court of ~ 3 [C] judge in a court of law: the Lord

Chief J~ ■ **Justice of the 'Peace** *n* judge in the lowest courts of law

justify /'dʒʌstɪfaɪ/ *v* (*pt, pp* -**ied**) [T] **1** show that sb/sth is right or reasonable **2** be a good reason for sth ► **justifiable** /ˌdʒʌstɪ'faɪəbl/ *adj* that can be justified ► **justifiably** *adv* ► **justification** /ˌdʒʌstɪfɪ'keɪʃn/ *n* [U,C] ~(**for**) acceptable reason

jut /dʒʌt/ *v* (-**tt**-) [I, T] ~(**out**) (cause sth to) stick out further than the surrounding surface

juvenile /'dʒuːvənaɪl/ *n* (*fml*) or (*law*) young person ● *adj* **1** (*fml*) or (*law*) of or suitable for young people **2** (*disapprov*) silly and childish ■ **juvenile de'linquent** *n* young person who is guilty of a crime, eg vandalism

juxtapose /ˌdʒʌkstə'pəʊz/ *v* [T] put people or things side by side, esp to show a contrast ► **juxtaposition** /ˌdʒʌkstəpə'zɪʃn/ *n* [U,C]

Kk

K /keɪ/ *abbr* (*pl* **K's**) **1** (*infml*) one thousand **2** kilometre(s) **3** (*computing*) = KILOBYTE(s)

K, k /keɪ/ *n* [C,U] (*pl* **K's, k's** /keɪz/) the eleventh letter of the English alphabet

kaleidoscope /kə'laɪdəskəʊp/ *n* **1** [C] tube containing mirrors and small pieces of coloured glass, turned to produce changing patterns **2** [sing] constantly and quickly changing pattern

kangaroo /ˌkæŋɡə'ruː/ *n* (*pl* ~**s**) Australian animal that jumps along and carries its baby in a pouch

karaoke /ˌkæri'əʊki/ *n* [U] type of entertainment in which a machine plays only the music of popular songs while people sing the words themselves

karate /kə'rɑːti/ *n* [U] Japanese system of fighting, using the hands and feet

kebab /kɪ'bæb/ *n* small pieces of meat cooked on a metal stick

keel /kiːl/ *n* wood or steel structure along the bottom of a ship ● **keel** *v* [I, T] (of a ship) fall over onto its side [PV] **keel over** fall over sideways

keen /kiːn/ *adj* **1** ~**on** having a strong interest in sth; enthusiastic or eager: *He's very ~ on tennis.* **2** ~**on** fond of sth **3** (of the senses, mind or feelings) strong; quick **4** (*lit*) (of the wind) very cold ► **keenly** *adv*

keep¹ /kiːp/ *v* (*pt, pp* **kept** /kept/) **1** [I, T] (cause sb/sth to) remain in a

state or position: *K~ (them) quiet!* ◇ *K~ off the grass!* **2** [I] ~(**on**) doing continue doing sth; do sth repeatedly: *He ~s (on) interrupting me.* **3** [T] delay sb: *You're late—what kept you?* **4** [T] continue to have sth: *Here's £5—you can ~ the change.* **5** [T] put or store sth in a particular place: *Where do you ~ the sugar?* **6** [T] own or manage a shop **7** [I] (*spoken*) used to ask or talk about sth's health: *How's she ~ing?* **8** [I] (of food) remain in good condition: *Milk doesn't ~ in hot weather.* **9** [T] not tell sb a secret **10** [T] do what you have promised to do; go where you have agreed to go: *~ a promise/ an appointment* **11** [T] write down sth as a record: *~ a diary* **12** [T] support sb financially [IDM] **keep abreast of sth** → ABREAST **keep sb at arm's length** avoid having a close relationship with sb **keep the ball rolling** → BALL **keep sb/sth at bay** → BAY **keep sb company** stay with sb so that they are not alone **keep count of sth** → COUNT² **keep your distance (from sb/sth)** **1** not go too near to sb/sth **2** avoid getting too friendly or involved with sb/sth **keep an eye on sb/sth** make sure that sb/sth is safe **keep your fingers crossed** hope that sb will be successful: *Good luck with your exam—we're ~ing our fingers crossed for you.* **keep your hair on** (GB, spoken) used to tell sb not to be angry **keep your head** → HEAD¹ **keep your head above water** deal with problems, esp financial worries, and just manage to survive **keep sth in mind** → MIND¹ **keep your mouth shut** (*infml*) not talk about sth because it is a secret **keep an open mind** → OPEN¹ **keep pace (with sb/sth)** move forward at the same speed as sb/sth **keep quiet about sth | keep sth quiet** say nothing about sth; keep sth secret **keep a straight face** → STRAIGHT² **keep a tight rein on sb/sth** control sb/sth firmly **keep your wits about you** → WIT [PV] **keep away (from sb/sth)** avoid going near sb/sth **keep sb/sth away (from sb/sth)** prevent sth/sth from going somewhere **keep sth back** (from sb) refuse to tell sb sth **keep sb down** prevent a person, group, etc from expressing themselves freely **keep sth down** not allow sth to grow or increase **keep sb from sth** prevent sb from doing sth: *~ him from leaving* **keep sth from sb** not tell sb about sth **keep in with sb** remain friendly with sb **keep on about sth** → ON¹ **keep on (at sb) (about sth/sth)** (*esp GB*) speak to sb often and in annoying way about sb/sth **keep** out (of sth) not enter a place **keep out of sth** avoid sth **keep to sth 1** avoid leaving a path or road **2** talk or write only about the subject that you are supposed to discuss: ~ *to the point* **3** do what you have promised or agreed to do: ~ *to an agreement* **keep yourself to yourself** avoid meeting people socially **keep sth to yourself** not tell other people about sth **keep sth up 1** make sth stay at a high level: ~ *prices up* ◇ ~ *your spirits up* **2** continue sth at the same, usu high, level: *K~ up the good work/K~ it up!* **3** continue to use or practise sth: *Do you still ~ up your French?* **4** maintain a house, garden, etc in good condition **keep up (with sb/ sth)** move at the same speed as sb/sth

keep² /ki:p/ n [U] (cost of) food, clothes and all the other things a person needs to live: *earn your ~* ◾ [IDM] **for keeps** (infml) for ever

keeper /'ki:pə(r)/ n **1** (esp in compounds) person whose job is to look after a building and its contents: *a shop~* **2** person whose job is to look after animals in a zoo

keeping /'ki:pɪŋ/ n [IDM] **in sb's keeping** in sb's care: *The keys are in his ~.* **in/out of keeping (with sth)** in/not in harmony with sth

keepsake /'ki:pseɪk/ n small object that sb gives you so that you will remember them

kennel /'kenl/ n [C] **1** small hut for a dog **2** (**kennels**) [with sing or pl verb] place where dogs are bred, looked after when the owner is away, etc

kept pt, pp of KEEP¹

kerb (US **curb**) /kɜːb/ n stone edge of a pavement

kernel /'kɜːnl/ n **1** inner part of a nut or seed **2** most important part of an idea, a subject, etc

kestrel /'kestrəl/ n small bird of prey of the falcon family

ketchup /'ketʃəp/ n [U] thick cold sauce made from tomatoes

kettle /'ketl/ n container with a spout, used for boiling water

key¹ /ki:/ n [C] **1** piece of metal that locks or unlocks a door, etc **2** [usu sing] ~(to) something that you are able to understand sth or achieve sth: *Diet and exercise are the ~ to good health.* **3** any of the buttons that you press to operate a computer or typewriter **4** any of the parts that you press to play a piano and some other musical instruments **5** (music) set of related notes: *the ~ of G* **6** set of answers to exercises ◾ **key** adj most important; essential: *a ~ position* ◾ **'keyboard** n set of keys on a computer, typewriter, piano or other

musical instrument ▸ **'keyboard** v [T] type information into a computer ◾ **'keyhole** n hole in a lock that you put a key in ◾ **'keynote** n central idea of a speech, book, etc ◾ **'key ring** n small ring on which keys are kept ◾ **'keyword** n **1** word that tells you the central idea or subject of sth **2** word that you type into a computer to search for information about a particular subject

key² /ki:/ v [T] ~(**in**) (computing) type information into a computer using a keyboard ◾ **,keyed 'up** adj excited or nervous

kg abbr kilogram(s)

khaki /'kɑːki/ adj greenish or yellowish-brown colour

kibbutz /kɪ'bʊts/ n (pl **~im** /,kɪbʊt-'si:m/) communal farm or factory in Israel

kick¹ /kɪk/ v **1** [T] hit sb/sth with your foot **2** [I] move your legs as if you were kicking sth **3** ~ yourself [T] (infml) be annoyed with yourself because you have done sth stupid [IDM] **kick the bucket** (infml) die **kick the habit** (infml) stop smoking, drinking alcohol, etc [PV] **kick against sth** protest about or resist sth **kick off** start **kick sb out (of sth)** (infml) make sb leave a place ◾ **'kick-off** n [C,U] start of a football match

kick² /kɪk/ n **1** [C] act of kicking sb/sth: *give sb a ~* **2** [C] (infml) strong feeling of pleasure **3** [U,sing] (infml) strength of a drug or an alcoholic drink

kid /kɪd/ n **1** [C] (infml) child or young person **2** [C] young goat **3** [U] leather made from the skin of a young goat ◾ **kid** v (-**dd**-) [I, T] (infml) tell sb sth that is not true, esp as a joke ~ sb/yourself allow sb/sth to believe sth that is not true

kidnap /'kɪdnæp/ v (-**pp**- US also -**p**-) [T] take sb away illegally and keep them prisoner, esp in order to demand money ▸ **kidnapper** n

kidney /'kɪdni/ n **1** [C] organ that removes waste products from the blood and produces urine **2** [U,C] kidney(s) of certain animals used as food

kill /kɪl/ v **1** [I, T] make sb/sth die: (infml) *He'll ~ me* (= be very angry with me) *if he finds me here.* **2** [T] destroy or spoil sth or make it stop: ~ *a rumour/story* **3** [T] (infml) hurt: *My feet are ~ing me.* [IDM] **kill two birds with one stone** achieve two aims with one action ◾ **kill** n **1** [C] act of killing, esp when an animal is killed **2** [usu sing] animal(s) killed ▸ **killer** n **killing** n act of killing sb deliberately [IDM] **make a killing** (infml) make a large profit quickly

■ **killjoy** n (disapprov) person who stops others enjoying themselves

kiln /kɪln/ n oven for baking pottery, bricks, etc

kilo /'ki:ləʊ/ n (pl ~s) kilogram

kilobyte /'kɪləbaɪt/ n (abbr **K**) 1024 bytes of computer memory or information

kilogram (GB also **-gramme**) /'kɪləgræm/ n metric unit of weight; 1000 grams

kilometre (US **-meter**) /'kɪləmi:tə(r); GB also kɪ'lɒmɪtə(r)/ n metric unit of length; 1000 metres

kilowatt /'kɪləwɒt/ n unit of electrical power; 1000 watts

kilt /kɪlt/ n tartan skirt sometimes worn by Scottish men

kind¹ /kaɪnd/ n group of people or things with similar features; sort; type: two ~s of fruit [IDM] in **kind** 1 (of payment) in goods, not money 2 (fml) with the same thing a **kind of** (infml) used to show that sth you are saying is not exact

kind² /kaɪnd/ adj friendly and thoughtful to others ■ ‚kind-'hearted adj kind and generous ▸ **kindly** adj (-ier, -iest) (infml) kind ▸ **kindly** adv 1 in a kind way 2 (oldfash, fml) used to ask or tell sb to do sth, esp when you are annoyed [IDM] **not take kindly to sth/sb** not like sth/sb ▸ **kindness** n 1 [U] quality of being kind 2 [C] kind act

kindergarten /'kɪndəgɑːtn/ n school for very young children

kindle /'kɪndl/ v [I, T] (cause a fire to) start burning 2 [T] arouse or stimulate an interest, emotion, etc

kindred /'kɪndrəd/ adj [IDM] a **kindred spirit** person whose interests, beliefs, etc are similar to your own

king /kɪŋ/ n 1 male ruler of an independent state that has a royal family 2 ~(of) the most important member of a group 3 (in chess) the most important piece 4 playing card with the picture of a king on it ■ ‚king-size (also **-sized**) adj larger than normal: a ~-size bed

kingdom /'kɪŋdəm/ n 1 country ruled by a king or queen 2 one of the three traditional divisions of the natural world: the animal, plant and mineral ~s

kink /kɪŋk/ n 1 bend or twist in sth that is usu straight 2 (infml, disapprov) something strange or abnormal in sb's character ● **kink** v [I, T] (cause sth to) develop a bend or twist ▸ **kinky** adj (-ier, -iest) (infml) strange or abnormal sexual behaviour

kiosk /'ki:ɒsk/ n small open-fronted shop where newspapers, sweets, etc are sold

kipper /'kɪpə(r)/ n salted herring (= a type of fish), dried or smoked

kiss /kɪs/ v [I, T] touch sb with your lips to show affection or as a greeting ● **kiss** n touch given with the lips [IDM] the **kiss of life** (GB) mouth-to-mouth method of helping sb to start breathing again

kit /kɪt/ n 1 [C] set of pieces to be put together to make sth 2 [C] set of tools or equipment: a first-aid ~ 3 [U] (GB) set of clothes and equipment that you use for a particular activity ● **kit** v (-tt-) [PV] **kit sb out/up (in/with sth)** provide sb with the correct clothes and/or equipment for an activity

kitchen /'kɪtʃɪn/ n room in which meals are cooked

kite /kaɪt/ n light framework covered with paper, cloth, etc, which flies in the wind

kitten /'kɪtn/ n young cat

kitty /'kɪti/ n (pl **-ies**) (infml) money collected by several people for an agreed use

kiwi /'ki:wi:/ n 1 (**Kiwi**) (infml) person from New Zealand 2 New Zealand bird that cannot fly ■ 'kiwi fruit n (pl **kiwi fruit**) (also **kiwi**) small fruit with thin hairy brown skin and soft green flesh with black seeds

km abbr (pl **km** or ~s) kilometre(s)

knack /næk/ n [sing] skill at doing a task

knackered /'nækəd/ adj (GB, sl) very tired

knead /ni:d/ v [T] 1 press and stretch bread dough with your hands 2 rub and press muscles

knee /ni:/ n 1 joint in the middle of the leg 2 part of a piece of clothing that covers the knee [IDM] **bring sb to their knees** force sb to give in ■ 'kneecap n small flat bone at the front of the knee ■ ‚knee-'deep adj up to your knees

kneel /ni:l/ v (pt, pp **knelt** /nelt/ or US ~ed) [I] ~(down) go down on your knees

knew pt of **KNOW**

knickers /'nɪkəz/ n [pl] (GB) piece of women's underwear that covers the body from the waist to the top of the legs

knick-knack /'nɪk næk/ n [C, usu pl] small ornament

knife /naɪf/ n (pl **knives** /naɪvz/) sharp blade with a handle, used for cutting ● **knife** v [T] injure sb with a knife ■ 'knife-edge n 1 sharp edge of a knife [IDM] **on a knife-edge** (of an important situation or result) very uncertain

knight /naɪt/ n 1 (in the Middle Ages) soldier of noble birth 2 (in

Britain) man to whom the title 'Sir' has been given **3** chess piece ● **knight** v [T] give sb the rank or title of a knight ▶ **knighthood** /'naɪthʊd/ n rank or title of a knight

knit /nɪt/ v (**-tt-** pt, pp **-ted**; in sense 2, usu knit) [I, T] **1** make a clothes, etc from wool or cotton thread using two long needles **2** (cause people or things to) join closely together: a closely--family **knitting** n [U] item being knitted ■ **'knitting needle** n long thin stick, used for knitting

knives plural of KNIFE

knob /nɒb/ n **1** round control button on a machine such as a television **2** round handle of a door, drawer, etc **3** small lump of sth, eg butter ▶ **knobbly** /'nɒbli/ adj (**-ier, -iest**) having small hard lumps: ~bly knees

knock[1] /nɒk/ v [I] hit a door, etc firmly to attract attention: ~ on the door **2** [T] hit sth/sth, often accidentally, with a short, hard blow **3** [T] (infml) criticize sth/sth [PV] **knock about with** sb (infml) spend a lot of time with sb/sth **knock** sb/sth **about** hit sb/sth roughly **knock** sth **back** (infml) drink sth quickly **knock** sb **down/over** hit sb and make them fall to the ground: She was ~ed down by a bus. **knock** sth **down** demolish a building **knock** sth **down (from sth) (to sth)** (infml) persuade sb to reduce the price of sth **knock** sth **off** (infml) stop work: When do you ~ off? **knock** sth **off 1** reduce the price of sth **2** (sl) steal sth **knock** sb **out 1** make sb fall asleep or become unconscious **2** make sb/yourself very tired **knock** sb **out (of sth)** defeat sb so that they cannot continue competing **knock** sth **up** make sth quickly: ~ up a meal ▶ **knocker** n metal object on the outside of a door, used for knocking[1] ■ **,knock-'kneed** adj having legs that turn inwards at the knees ■ **,knock-'on effect** n indirect result of an action ■ **'knock-out** n **1** (in boxing) blow that makes a boxer unable to get up **2** competition from which losers are eliminated **3** (infml) person or thing that is very impressive

knock[2] /nɒk/ n **1** sound of sb knocking on a door, etc **2** (infml) unfortunate experience

knot /nɒt/ n **1** fastening made by tying together pieces of string, rope, etc **2** twisted piece; tangle **3** hard round spot in a piece of wood **4** small group of people **5** unit of speed used by ships; one nautical mile per hour ● **knot** v (**-tt-**) **1** [T] fasten sth with a knot **2** [I, T] make or

form knots in sth ▶ **knotty** adj (**-ier, -iest**) **1** difficult to solve: a ~ty problem **2** (of wood) full of knots

know /nəʊ/ v (pt **knew** /njuː/ pp ~n /nəʊn/) **1** [I, T] have information in your mind: Do you ~ his address? ◇ I ~ of at least two people who did the same thing. **2** [I, T] realize, understand or be aware of sth **3** [I, T] feel certain about sth **4** [T] be familiar with a person, place, thing, etc **5** [T] be able to recognize sth/sth: I'll ~ her when I see her. **6** [T] understand and be able to use a language, skill, etc **7** [T] have personal experience of sth: a man who has ~n poverty [IDM] **be known as sth** be called or compared as sb/sth **know** sb **by sight** recognize sb without knowing them personally **know your own mind** know what you want ■ **'know-how** n [U] practical knowledge or ability

knowing /'nəʊɪŋ/ adj showing that you have information which is secret: a ~ look ▶ **knowingly** adv **1** deliberately **2** in a knowing way

knowledge /'nɒlɪdʒ/ n **1** [U, sing] information, understanding and skills gained through education or experience **2** [U] state of knowing about a particular fact or situation: done without my ~ ▶ **knowledgeable** /-əbl/ adj knowing a lot

known pp of KNOW

knuckle /'nʌkl/ n any of the joints in the fingers ● **knuckle** v [PV] **knuckle under (to** sb/sth**)** (infml) accept sb else's authority

koala /kəʊ'ɑːlə/ n Australian tree-climbing animal like a small bear

Koran /kə'rɑːn/ n (the **Koran**) [sing] the holy book of Muslims

kosher /'kəʊʃə(r)/ adj (of food) prepared according to the rules of Jewish law

kowtow /ˌkaʊ'taʊ/ v [I] ~**(to)** (infml, disapprov) show sb in authority too much respect and be too willing to obey them

kph /ˌkeɪ piː 'eɪtʃ/ abbr kilometres per hour

L l

L, l /el/ n [C,U] (pl **L's, l's** /elz/) **1** the twelfth letter of the English alphabet **2** Roman numeral for 50

L abbr **1** (esp on maps) Lake **2** (esp for sizes of clothes) large

l abbr **1** litre(s) **2** line

Lab abbr (in British politics) Labour

lab /læb/ n (infml) = LABORATORY

label /'leɪbl/ n **1** piece of paper,

cloth, etc fixed to sth to describe what it is, who owns it, etc **2** (*disapprov*) word(s) describing sb/sth in a way that is too general or unfair ● **label** v (**-ll-** *US* **-l-**) [T] **1** put a label on sth **2** describe sb/sth in a particular way, esp unfairly: *They ~led her (as) a liar.*

labor (*US*) = LABOUR ■ '**labor union** (*US*) = TRADE UNION (TRADE[1])

laboratory /ləˈbɒrətri/ n (pl **-ies**) room or building used for scientific experiments

laborious /ləˈbɔːriəs/ adj needing great effort ▶ **laboriously** adv

labour¹ (*US* **-or**) /ˈleɪbə(r)/ n **1** [U] (esp physical) work **2** [C,usu sing] (*fml*) task or period of work **3** [U] workers as a group **4** [U,C, usu sing] process of childbirth: *a woman in ~* **5** (**Labour**) [sing] = THE LABOUR PARTY ■ **the 'Labour Party** [sing, with sing or pl verb] (*GB, pol*) major political party, representing esp the interests of workers

labour² (*US* **-or**) /ˈleɪbə(r)/ v [I] **1** try hard to do sth difficult **2** do hard physical work [IDM] **labour the point** continue to repeat or explain sth already understood [PV] **labour under sth** (*fml*) believe sth that is not true ▶ **labourer** (*US* **-bor-**) n person who does heavy unskilled work

labyrinth /ˈlæbərɪnθ/ n complicated series of paths, which it is difficult to find your way through

lace /leɪs/ n **1** [U] delicate decorative cloth with an open-work design of threads **2** [C] = SHOELACE (SHOE) ● **lace** v [I, T] fasten sth or be fastened with laces **2** [T] ~(**with**) add a small amount of alcohol, a drug, etc to a drink

lacerate /ˈlæsəreɪt/ v [T] (*fml*) cut skin or flesh with sth sharp ▶ **laceration** /ˌlæsəˈreɪʃn/ n [C,U]

lack /læk/ v [T] have none or not enough of sth ▶ **lacking** adj **1** ~(**in**) having none or not enough of sth **2** not present or not available ● **lack** n [U,sing] ~(**of**) absence or shortage of sth: *a ~ of money*

lackadaisical /ˌlækəˈdeɪzɪkl/ adj (*written*) not showing enough care or attention

laconic /ləˈkɒnɪk/ adj (*fml*) using few words ▶ **laconically** /-kli/ adv

lacquer /ˈlækə(r)/ n [U] liquid used on metal or wood to give it a hard shiny surface ● **lacquer** v [T] cover sth with lacquer

lacy /ˈleɪsi/ adj (**-ier, -iest**) of or like lace(1)

lad /læd/ n [C] **1** (*old-fash*) boy; young man **2** (**the lads**) [pl] (*GB, spoken*) group of male friends: *He's*

gone out with the ~s. **3** (*GB, infml*) lively young man

ladder /ˈlædə(r)/ n **1** two lengths of wood or metal, joined together with steps or rungs, used for climbing **2** series of stages of progress in a career or an organization: *climb up the social ~* **3** (*GB*) long thin hole in women's tights or stockings ● **ladder** v [I, T] (cause tights or stockings to) develop a ladder

laden /ˈleɪdn/ adj ~(**with**) heavily loaded with sth

ladle /ˈleɪdl/ n large deep spoon for serving liquids ● **ladle** v [T] serve sth with a ladle

lady /ˈleɪdi/ n [C] (pl **-ies**) **1** (esp in polite use) woman **2** woman who has good manners **3** (*old-fash*) (in Britain) woman of good family and social position **4** (**Lady**) (in Britain) title of a woman of noble rank **5** (**a/ the ladies**) [sing] (*GB*) public toilet for women ■ **'ladylike** adj like or suitable for a lady; polite ■ **'ladyship** n (**Her/Your Ladyship**) title used when speaking to or about a Lady

lag /læg/ v (**-gg-**) **1** [I] ~(**behind**) move or develop slowly or more slowly than others **2** [T] cover pipes, etc with material to prevent heat from escaping

lager /ˈlɑːɡə(r)/ n [C,U] (glass or bottle of) light pale beer

lagoon /ləˈɡuːn/ n saltwater lake separated from the sea by sandbanks or coral reefs

laid pt, pp of LAY¹

lain pp of LIE²

lair /leə(r)/ n home of a wild animal

laity /ˈleɪəti/ n [sing, with sing or pl verb] (**the laity**) all the members of a Church who are not clergy

lake /leɪk/ n large area of water surrounded by land

lamb /læm/ n **1** [C] young sheep **2** [U] meat from a young sheep

lame /leɪm/ adj **1** (of people or animals) unable to walk well because of injury to the leg or foot **2** (of an excuse, etc) weak and hard to believe ■ **lame 'duck** n **1** person, organization, etc that is in difficulties and needs help **2** (*infml, esp US*) elected official in his/her final period of office ▶ **lameness** n [U]

lament /ləˈment/ v [I, T] express great sadness about sb/sth ● **lament** n song or poem expressing great sadness for sb/sth ▶ **lamentable** /ˈlæməntəbl/ adj unsatisfactory; regrettable ▶ **lamentably** adv

laminated /ˈlæmɪneɪtɪd/ adj made by joining several thin layers together

lamp /læmp/ n device that uses electricity, oil or gas to produce light ■ **lamp post** n (esp GB) tall post in the street with a lamp at the top ■ **lampshade** n cover placed round over a lamp

LAN /læn/ n (computing) local area network; system that connects computers inside a single building or group of nearby buildings

lance /lɑːns/ n long weapon with a pointed metal end used by people fighting on horses in the past ● **lance** v [T] cut open an infected place on sb's body with a knife in order to let out the liquid inside

land¹ /lænd/ n **1** [U] solid dry part of the earth's surface **2** [U] area of ground used for farming, etc: work on the ~ **3** [U] property in the form of land **4** (**the land**) [U] used to refer to the countryside as opposed to cities: His family had always farmed the ~. **5** [C] (lit) country or nation: see how the land lies (GB) find out about a situation ▶ **landed** adj owning a lot of land ■ **landlocked** adj almost or completely surrounded by land ■ **landmark** n **1** object easily seen and recognized from a distance **2** ~ (in) important event, discovery, etc ■ **landowner** n person who owns an area of land, esp a large area ■ **landslide** n **1** mass of earth, rock, etc that falls down the side of a mountain or cliff **2** victory by a very large majority in an election

land² /lænd/ v **1** [I] come down through the air onto the ground or another surface: The plane ~ed safely. **2** [T] bring an aircraft down to the ground in a controlled way **3** [T] put sb/sth on land from an aircraft, a boat, etc **4** [T] (infml) succeed in getting sth: ~ a job [IDM] **land on your feet** FOOT [PV] **land sb/ yourself in sth** (infml) get sb/your-self into difficulties **land up in, at …** (infml) reach a final position or situation: ~ up in jail [IDM] **land sb/ yourself with sth/sb** (infml) give sb/yourself sth unpleasant to do

landing /ˈlændɪŋ/ n **1** [C] level area at the top of a set of stairs **2** [C,U] act of bringing an aircraft to the ground after a journey: a crash ~ **3** [C] act of bringing soldiers to land in an area controlled by the enemy ■ **landing craft** n flat-bottomed boat that brings soldiers, vehicles, etc to the shore ■ **landing gear** n [U] = UNDERCARRIAGE ■ **landing stage** n platform on which people and goods are landed from a boat

landlady /ˈlændleɪdi/ n (pl -ies) **1** woman from whom you rent a room, house, etc **2** (GB) woman

who owns or manages a pub or guest house

landlord /ˈlændlɔːd/ n **1** man from whom you rent a room, house, etc **2** (GB) man who owns or manages a pub or guest house

landscape /ˈlændskeɪp/ n **1** every-thing you see when you look across a large area of land **2** painting or view of the countryside ● **land-scape** v [T] improve the appear-ance of an area of land by changing the design and planting trees, etc: ~d gardens ● **landscape** adj (com-puting) (of a document) printed so that the top of the page is one of the longer sides

lane /leɪn/ n **1** narrow country road **2** (in place names) narrow street: Mill Lane **3** part of a road that is marked for a single line of traffic: a four-~ motorway **4** route regularly used by ships or aircraft **5** marked part of track or water for each com-petitor in a race

language /ˈlæŋgwɪdʒ/ n **1** [C] sys-tem of communication in speech and writing used by people of a particular country: the English ~ **2** [U] the use by humans of a sys-tem of sounds and words to com-municate **3** [U] particular style of speaking or writing: bad/strong ~ (= words that people may consider offensive) **4** [C,U] way of express-ing ideas and feelings using move-ments, symbols and sounds: body ~ ◇ sign ~ **5** [C,U] system of symbols and rules used to operate a com-puter ■ **language laboratory** n room where foreign languages are learned by listening to tapes, etc

languid /ˈlæŋgwɪd/ adj (written) (of a person) having no energy ▶ **lan-guidly** adv

languish /ˈlæŋgwɪʃ/ v [I] (fml) **1** ~ in be forced to live and suffer in unpleasant conditions: ~ in prison **2** become weaker or fail to make progress

lank /læŋk/ adj (of hair) straight, dull and unattractive

lanky /ˈlæŋki/ adj (-ier, -iest) unattractively tall and thin

lantern /ˈlæntən/ n portable lamp with a transparent case for a can-dle or flame

lap /læp/ n **1** top part of your legs that forms a flat surface when you sit down: a baby on his ~ **2** one com-plete journey round a track or racecourse ● **lap** v (-pp-) **1** [I] (of water) make gentle splashing sounds **2** [T] (animals) drink sth with quick movements of the tongue **3** [T] (in a race) pass another competitor on a track to be one lap ahead [PV] **lap sth up** (*infml*) receive praise, news, etc eagerly

lapel /lə'pel/ n front part of the collar of a coat that is folded back

lapse /læps/ n **1** small error in behaviour, memory, etc **2** passing of a period of time ● **lapse** v [I] **1** (of a contract, an agreement, etc) be no longer valid because the period of time it lasts has come to an end **2** gradually become weaker or come to an end: *His concentration soon ~d.* **3** (**~from**) stop believing in or practising your religion: *a ~d Catholic* [PV] **lapse into sth** gradually pass into a worse or weaker state

laptop /'læptɒp/ n small computer that can work with a battery and is easily carried

larch /lɑːtʃ/ n tall deciduous tree of the pine family with small cones

lard /lɑːd/ n [U] fat of pigs, used in cooking

larder /'lɑːdə(r)/ n cupboard or small room for storing food

large /lɑːdʒ/ adj (**~r**, **~st**) more than average or usual in size; big [IDM] **at large 1** as a whole; in general: *the country at ~* **2** (of a dangerous person or animal) not captured; free **by and large** (*infml*) on the whole; generally (**as**) **large as life** (*hum*) used to show surprise at seeing sb/sth ▸ **largely** adv to a great extent; mainly ● **large-scale** adj **1** extensive: *a ~-scale search* **2** drawn or made to a large scale

lark /lɑːk/ n [C] **1** small brown songbird **2** [usu sing] (*infml*) thing that you do for fun or a joke

larva /'lɑːvə/ n (pl **-ae** /-viː/) insect in the first stage of its life

larynx /'lærɪŋks/ n (pl **larynges** /lə'rɪndʒiːz/) (*anat*) area at the top of the throat that contains the vocal cords ▸ **laryngitis** /ˌlærɪn'dʒaɪtɪs/ n [U] infection of the larynx

lascivious /lə'sɪviəs/ adj (*fml*, *disapprov*) feeling or showing sexual desire

laser /'leɪzə(r)/ n device that makes a very strong beam of controlled light (= with rays that are parallel and of the same wavelength): *a ~ beam* ■ **laser printer** n printer that produces good quality printed material by means of a laser beam

lash /læʃ/ v [I, T] **1** hit sb/sth with great force **2** [T] hit a person or an animal with a whip, rope, stick, etc **3** [T] fasten sth tightly to sth else with ropes, etc **4** [I, T] (cause sth to) move violently from side to side: *The crocodile's tail was ~ing furiously from side to side.* [PV] **lash out (at sb/sth) 1** suddenly try to hit sb

2 criticize sb/sth in an angry way ● **lash** n **1** = EYELASH (EYE) **2** hit with a whip, given as a form of punishment

lashings /'læʃɪŋz/ n [pl] (GB, *infml*) large amount of sth, esp food and drink

lass /læs/ n girl; young woman

lasso /læ'suː/ n (pl **~s** or **~es**) looped rope used for catching horses and cattle ● **lasso** v [T] catch an animal with a lasso

last¹ /lɑːst/ det **1** coming after all others: *Friday is the ~ day of the week.* **2** most recent; latest: *~ night* **3** only remaining; final: *This is our ~ bottle of milk.* **4** least likely or suitable: *She's the ~ person to trust with a secret.* [IDM] **be on your/its last legs** be very weak or in bad condition **have the last laugh** be successful over your critics, rivals, etc in the end **have the last word (on sth)** make the final remark that ends an argument **in the/as a last resort** when there are no other possible courses of action **last-ditch** final effort to be made to avoid defeat: *a ~-ditch attempt* **the last straw** → STRAW **the last word (in sth)** the most fashionable, modern, etc thing: *This car is the ~ word in luxury.* ● **last** n (**the last**) (pl **last**) **1** person or thing that comes or happens after all others **2** **~of** only remaining part or items of sth: *the ~ of the apples* [IDM] **at (long) last** after much delay, effort, etc ▸ **lastly** adv in the last place; finally

last² /lɑːst/ adv **1** after all others **2** most recently

last³ /lɑːst/ v **1** [I] continue for a period of time **2** [I, T] be enough for sb to use over a period of time: *enough food to ~ two days* ▸ **lasting** adj continuing for a long time

latch /lætʃ/ n **1** small metal bar for fastening a door or gate **2** type of lock on a door that can only be opened from the outside with a key ● **latch** v [T] fasten sth with a latch [PV] **latch on to sb** (*infml*) join sb and refuse to leave them

late /leɪt/ adj (**~r**, **~st**) **1** near the end of a period of time, a person's life, etc: *in the ~ afternoon* ◇ *She's in her ~ twenties* (= she is 28 or 29). **2** after the expected or usual time: *The train is ~.* **3** near the end of the day: *It's getting ~.* **4** no longer alive: *her ~ husband* ● **late** adv **1** after the expected or usual time: *get up ~* **2** near the end of a period of time: *as ~ as the 1990s* ▸ **lately** adv recently ▸ **latest** adj most recent or newest: *the ~st fashion* ▸ **the latest** n (*infml*) the most recent or the newest thing or piece of news: *This is the ~st in* *robot technology.* [IDM] **at the latest** no later than the time mentioned

latent /'leɪtnt/ *adj* existing but not yet active or developed: *~ talent*

lateral /'lætərəl/ *adj* of or to the side of sth

lathe /leɪð/ *n* machine that shapes pieces of wood, metal, etc by turning them against a cutting tool

lather /'lɑːðə(r)/ *n* [U] white foam produced by soap mixed with water ● **lather** v 1 [T] cover sth with lather 2 [I] produce lather

Latin /'lætɪn/ *adj, n* [U] (of the) language of ancient Rome ■ **Latin Aˈmerica** *n* Mexico and parts of Central and South America in which Spanish or Portuguese is the official language ▶ **Latin Aˈmerican** *n, adj*

latitude /'lætɪtjuːd/ *n* [U] 1 distance north or south of the equator, measured in degrees 2 (*fml*) freedom to choose what you do

latter /'lætə(r)/ *adj* near to the end of a period of time: *the ~ part of her life* ▶ **the latter** *n* the second mentioned of two things, people or groups ■ **latter-day** *adj* modern ▶ **latterly** *adv* most recently

lattice /'lætɪs/ *n* [C, U] framework of crossed wooden or metal strips

laugh /lɑːf/ *v* [I] make the sounds and movements of your face that show you are happy or think sth is funny [IDM] **be no laughing matter** be sth serious that you should not joke about **laugh your head off** → HEAD[1] [PV] **laugh at sb/sth** make sb/sth seem stupid by making jokes about them/it ● **laugh** *n* [C] 1 act or sound of laughing 2 (*a laugh*) [sing] (*infml*) amusing situation or person who is fun to be with ▶ **laughable** *adj* ridiculous ▶ **laughably** *adv* ■ **ˈlaughing stock** *n* [C, usu sing] person is made to appear foolish ▶ **laughter** *n* [U] act or sound of laughing

launch /lɔːntʃ/ *v* [T] 1 begin an activity, esp an organized one: *~ a new business* 2 make a product available to the public for the first time 3 put a ship or boat into the water, esp one that has just been built 4 send a rocket, weapon, etc into space or through water [PV] **launch out (into sth)** do sth new in your career ● **launch** *n* 1 action of launching sth; event at which sth is launched 2 large motor boat ■ **ˈlaunch pad** (*also* **ˈlaunching pad**) *n* base from which spacecraft, etc are launched

launder /'lɔːndə(r)/ *v* [T] 1 (*fml*) wash and iron clothes 2 move illegally-obtained money into foreign bank accounts or legal businesses

launderette (*also* **laundrette**) /lɔːn-'dret/ (*US* **Laundromat™** /'lɔːndrəmæt/) *n* place where you can wash and dry your clothes in coin-operated machines

laundry /'lɔːndri/ *n* (*pl* -ies) 1 [U] clothes, etc that need washing, or that are being washed: *a ~ basket/room* 2 [C] place where you send clothes, etc to be washed

laurel /'lɒrəl/ *n* evergreen bush with dark smooth shiny leaves

lava /'lɑːvə/ *n* [U] hot liquid rock that comes out of a volcano

lavatory /'lævətri/ *n* (*pl* -ies) (*fml, GB*) toilet

lavender /'lævəndə(r)/ *n* [U] 1 plant with sweet-smelling pale purple flowers 2 pale purple colour

lavish /'lævɪʃ/ *adj* 1 large in amount, or impressive and expensive: *a ~ meal* 2 generous ● **lavish** *v* [PV] **lavish sth on/upon sb/sth** give a lot of sth to sb/sth ▶ **lavishly** *adv*

law /lɔː/ *n* 1 (*also* **the law**) [U] whole system of rules that everyone in a country must obey: *Murder is against the ~.* 2 [C] rule that deals with a particular crime, agreement, etc 3 (*the law*) [sing] the police 4 [C] basic rule of action, eg in science: *the ~s of physics* [IDM] **be a law unto yourself** ignore the usual rules and conventions of behaviour **law and order** respect for the law ■ **ˈlaw-abiding** *adj* obeying the law ■ **ˈlaw court** *n* (*GB*) place where legal cases are heard and judged ▶ **lawful** *adj* (*fml*) allowed or recognized by law; legal ▶ **lawfully** *adv* ▶ **lawless** *adj* not controlled by the law ▶ **lawlessness** *n* [U] ▶ **lawsuit** *n* non-criminal case in a law court

lawn /lɔːn/ *n* area of short grass ■ **ˈlawnmower** *n* machine for cutting grass ■ **ˌlawn ˈtennis** (*fml*) = TENNIS

lawyer /'lɔːjə(r)/ *n* person who is trained and qualified to advise people about the law

lax /læks/ *adj* not strict enough; careless ▶ **laxity** *n* [U]

laxative /'læksətɪv/ *n, adj* (medicine, food or drink) that helps sb empty their bowels easily

lay[1] /leɪ/ *v* (*pt, pp* **laid** /leɪd/) 1 [T] put sb/sth in a particular position: *She laid the baby down on the bed.* 2 [T] put sth down, esp on the floor, ready to be used: *~ a carpet/cable* 3 [I, T] (of birds, insects, etc) produce eggs 4 [T] (*GB*) arrange knives, forks, plates, etc on a table ready for a meal: *to ~ the table* 5 [T] (Δ, *sl*) (esp passive) have sex with sb [IDM] **lay sth bare** (*written*) reveal sth that was secret or hidden: ~ *bare your feelings* **lay claim to sth** state that you have a right to own sth **lay down the law** tell sb what they should or should not do **lay down your life (for sb/sth)** (*lit*) die in order to save sb/sth **lay a finger on sb** harm sb **lay sb low** make sb ill or weak [PV] **lay into sb/sth** (*infml*) attack sb/sth with words or blows **lay sth off** (*infml*) stop doing or using sth harmful **lay sb off** stop employing sb because there is not enough work for them to do **lay sth on** (*GB, infml*) provide sth for sb, esp food or entertainment: ~ *on a party* **lay sb out** knock sb unconscious **lay sth out** 1 spread sth out so that it can be seen easily 2 arrange sth in a planned way: *a well laid out garden* **lay sb up** cause sb to stay in bed: *be laid up with flu* ■ **laid-back** *adj* (*sl*) happily relaxed and unworried ■ **lay-off** *n* act of dismissing a worker from a job ■ **layout** *n* way in which parts of sth are arranged according to a plan ■ **layover** *n* (*US*) = STOPOVER (STOP²)

lay² *pt of* LIE²

lay³ /leɪ/ *adj* 1 not having expert knowledge of a particular subject 2 not in an official position in the Church: *a ~ preacher* ■ **layman** (*also* **'layperson**) *n* person who does not have expert knowledge of a subject

layabout /'leɪəbaʊt/ *n* (*old-fash, GB, infml*) lazy person

lay-by /'leɪ baɪ/ *n* (*GB*) area at the side of a road where vehicles may stop

layer /'leɪə(r)/ *n* thickness of some substance or material, often one of many, on a surface: *a ~ of dust*

layman → LAY³

laze /leɪz/ *v* [I] ~ (**about/around**) relax and do very little

lazy /'leɪzi/ *adj* (-**ier**, -**iest**) 1 (*disapprov*) unwilling to work 2 showing a lack of activity ▶ **lazily** *adv* ▶ **laziness** *n* [U]

lb *abbr* (*pl* **lb**, **lbs**) one pound in weight (454 grams)

lead¹ /liːd/ *v* (*pt, pp* **led** /led/) 1 [I, T] go with or in front of a person or an animal to show the way: *The receptionist led the way to the boardroom.* 2 [I] ~ **from/to** connect one object or place to another: *the pipe ~ing from the top of the water tank* 3 [I, T] (of a road, etc) go somewhere or in a particular direction 4 [I] ~ **to** have sth as its result: *a mistake that led to his death* 5 [T] ~ **(to)** be the reason why sb does sth or thinks sth: *What led you to this conclusion?* 6 [T] have a certain kind of life: *a ~ miserable existence* 7 [I, T] be the best at sth;

be in first place 8 [I, T] control or direct sb/sth: ~ *a team of scientists* [IDM] **lead sb astray** encourage sb to do wrong [PV] **lead sb on** persuade sb to believe or do sth by making false promises, etc **lead up to sth** prepare or introduce sth ▶ **leader** *n* person who leads ▶ **leadership** *n* [U] position of being a leader; qualities of a leader ▶ **leading** *adj* most important ■ **leading 'article** (*also* **leader**) *n* (*GB*) newspaper article giving the editor's opinion ■ **leading 'question** *n* question that you ask in a particular way to get the answer you want

lead² /liːd/ *n* 1 (**the lead**) [sing] first place or position in a race or competition: *take the ~* 2 [sing] distance by which sb/sth is in front of sb/sth else: *a ~ of ten metres* 3 [sing] example or action for people to copy: *follow sb's ~* 4 [C] piece of information that might solve a crime or other problem: *The police will follow up all possible ~s.* 5 [C] (person playing the) main part in a play, etc 6 [C] strap or rope for holding and controlling a dog 7 [C] (*GB*) wire that connects a piece of electrical equipment to a source of electricity

lead³ /led/ *n* 1 [U] heavy soft greyish metal, used for water pipes, in roofing, etc 2 [C, U] thin black part of a pencil that marks paper ▶ **leaden** *adj* 1 dull, heavy or slow 2 dull grey in colour

leaf /liːf/ *n* (*pl* **leaves** /liːvz/) 1 [C] one of the usu green and flat parts of a plant growing from a stem 2 [C] sheet of paper 3 [U] metal, esp gold or silver, in the form of very thin sheets: *gold~* 4 [C] part of a table that can be lifted up to make the table bigger [IDM] **take a leaf from/out of sb's book** copy the way sb does things, because they are successful ● **leaf** *v* [PV] **leaf through sth** turn over the pages of a book, etc quickly, without reading them closely ▶ **leafy** *adj* (-**ier**, -**iest**)

leaflet /'liːflət/ *n* printed sheet of paper

league /liːg/ *n* 1 group of people or countries who have combined for a particular purpose 2 group of sports teams that play against each other 3 (*infml*) level of quality, ability, etc: *They're not in the same ~.* [IDM] **in league (with sb)** making secret plans with sb

leak /liːk/ *n* 1 small hole or crack through which liquid or gas escapes 2 liquid or gas that escapes through a hole in sth 3 deliberate act of giving secret information to the newspapers,

lean

L

244

etc: *a security* • **leak** v 1 [I] allow liquid or gas to pass through a small hole or crack 2 [I] (of liquid or gas) escape through a hole in sth 3 [T] make secret information publicly known ▶ **leakage** /'li:kɪdʒ/ n [C, U] process of leaking; amount that leaks ▶ **leaky** adj (-ier, -iest)

lean¹ /li:n/ v (pt, pp ~ed) (GB also ~ed /lent/) 1 [I] bend or move from an upright position 2 [I, T] **~against/on** (cause sth to) rest on or against sth for support: *a ladder against a wall* [PV] **lean on sb/sth 1** depend on sb/sth for help and support 2 try to influence sb by threatening them **lean to/toward/towards sth** have a tendency to prefer sth, esp an opinion ▶ **leaning** n tendency; inclination: *political ~ings*

lean² /li:n/ adj 1 (of a person or animal) thin and healthy 2 (of meat) containing little fat 3 (of a period of time) not productive: *~ years* 4 (of organizations, etc) strong and more efficient, because the number of employees has been reduced

leap /li:p/ v (pt, pp ~t /lept/ or ~ed) [I] 1 jump high or a long way 2 move quickly in the direction that is mentioned: *~ into the car* [PV] **leap at sth** accept sth eagerly: *She ~t at the chance.* • **leap** n 1 long or high jump 2 sudden large increase or change [IDM] **by/in leaps and bounds** very quickly; in large amounts ▶ **'leapfrog** n [U] game in which players jump over others' bent backs ▶ **'leapfrog** v (-gg-) [I, T] jump over sth in this way ▶ **'leap year** n one year in every four years, with an extra day (29 February)

learn /lɜ:n/ v (pt, pp ~ed /lɜ:nt/ or ~ed) 1 [I, T] gain knowledge or skill in a subject or activity: *~ Dutch ~ (how) to swim* 2 [I, T] **~of/about** become aware of sth by hearing about it from sb else: *~ of his death* 3 [T] study and repeat sth in order to be able to remember it: *~ a poem* ▶ **learned** /'lɜ:nɪd/ adj having a lot of knowledge ▶ **learner** n ▶ **learning** n [U] knowledge gained by study

lease /li:s/ n contract for the use of land, a building, etc in return for rent ▶ **lease** v [T] give or obtain the use of sth in this way ▶ **'leasehold** n [U] adj (land, etc) held on a lease

leash /li:ʃ/ n (esp US) = LEAD²(6)

least /li:st/ det, pron (usu the least) smallest in size, amount, degree, etc: *She gave (the) ~ of all* ◇ *Ignore the present.* [IDM] **not in the least** not at all: *I'm not in the ~ tired.* • **least** adv to the smallest degree: *the ~ expensive hotel* [IDM] **at least 1** not less than: *at ~ three months* 2 even

if nothing else is true: *at ~ she's reliable* **not least** especially

leather /'leðə(r)/ n [U] material from animal skins, used for making shoes, etc ▶ **leathery** adj as tough as leather

leave¹ /li:v/ v (pt, pp **left** /left/) 1 [I, T] go away from a person or place 2 [T] cause or allow sb/sth to remain in a certain condition: *~ the window open* 3 [T] cause sth to happen or remain as a result: *Blood ~s a stain.* 4 **(be left)** [T] remain to be used, sold, etc; *Is there any coffee left?* 5 [T] forget or fail to take or bring sth/sb with you: *I left my book at home.* 6 [T] (maths) have a certain amount remaining: *7 from 10 ~s 3* 7 [T] give sth to sb when you die 8 [T] allow sb to take care of sth: *We left him to do the cooking.* [IDM] **leave/let sb/sth alone** not interfere with or disturb sb/sth **leave go (of sth)** (GB, infml) stop holding on to sth **leave it at that** (infml) say or do nothing more about sth **leave sb in the lurch** (infml) fail to help sb when they are relying on you to do so [PV] **leave sb/sth behind 1** (usu passive) make much better progress than sb 2 leave a person, place or state permanently **leave off** (infml) stop doing sth: *Start reading where you left off last time.* **leave sb/sth out (of sth)** not include sb/sth in sth

leave² /li:v/ n [U] 1 time when you are allowed to be away from work for a holiday or a special reason: *maternity ~* 2 (fml) official permission to do sth

leaves plural of LEAF

lecherous /'letʃərəs/ adj (disapprov) having or showing strong sexual desire

lectern /'lektən/ n stand for holding a book, notes, etc when you are giving a talk, etc

lecture /'lektʃə(r)/ n 1 talk given for the purposes of teaching 2 long angry talk given to sb because they have done wrong • **lecture** v 1 [I] give a lecture on a particular subject 2 [T] criticize sb, or tell them how you think they should behave ▶ **lecturer** n 1 person who gives a lecture 2 (esp GB) person who teaches at a college or university ▶ **lectureship** n position as a lecturer

led pt, pp of LEAD¹

ledge /ledʒ/ n narrow shelf coming out from a wall, cliff, etc

ledger /'ledʒə(r)/ n book in which a company's accounts are kept

lee /li:/ n [sing] (fml) part of sth providing shelter against the wind

leech /li:tʃ/ n 1 small blood-sucking

worm 2 (*disapprov*) person who depends on sb else for money

leek /liːk/ n vegetable with a white stem and long green leaves

leer /lɪə(r)/ n unpleasant look that suggests sexual desire ● **leer** v [I] **~(at)** look with a sb leer

left¹ pt, pp of LEAVE¹ ■ **left-'luggage office** n (GB) place at a railway station, etc where you can pay to leave bags or suitcases for a short time ■ **'leftovers** n [pl] food that has not been eaten at the end of a meal

left² /left/ adj, adv on or towards the side of your body that is towards the west when you are facing north ● **left** n **1 (the/sb's left)** [sing] left side or direction **(the, the Left)** [sing, with sing or pl verb] political groups who support the ideas and beliefs of socialism ■ **left-hand** adj of or on the left side of sth/sb ■ **,left-'handed** adj (of a person) using the left hand more easily or usually than the right ● **leftist** n, adj (supporter) of socialism ■ **the ,left 'wing** n [sing, with sing or pl verb] supporters of a more extreme form of socialism than others in their party ▸ **left-wing** adj: --wing policies

leg /leg/ n **1** one of the long parts that connect the feet to the rest of the body **2** the leg of an animal, cooked and eaten **3** part of a pair of trousers that covers the leg: a trouser~ **4** support of a chair, table, etc **5** one section of a journey or race [IDM] **not have a leg to stand on** (*infml*) have no evidence or reason for your opinion or action

legacy /ˈlegəsi/ n (pl -ies) **1** money or property given to you by sb when they die **2** situation that exists now as a result of sth that happened in the past

legal /ˈliːgl/ adj **1** of or based on the law: my ~ adviser **2** allowed or required by law ▸ **legality** /liːˈgæləti/ n [U] fact of being legal ▸ **legally** /ˈliːgəli/ adv

legalistic /ˌliːgəˈlɪstɪk/ adj (*disapprov*) obeying the law very strictly

legalize (also **-ise**) /ˈliːgəlaɪz/ v [T] make sth legal

legend /ˈledʒənd/ n **1** [C,U] (type of) story from ancient times that may or may not be true: the ~ of Robin Hood **2** [C] famous person, esp in a particular field, who is admired by other people: He has become a ~ in his own lifetime. **3** [C] (*tech*) explanation of a map or diagram in a book ▸ **legendary** /ˈledʒəndri/ adj famous; known only in legends

legible /ˈledʒəbl/ adj clear enough to be read easily ▸ **legibly** adv

legion /ˈliːdʒən/ n **1** division of an army of the ancient Roman

army **2** large number of people ● **legion** adj (*fml*) very many ▸ **legionary** /ˈliːdʒənəri/ n (pl -ies) adj soldier who is part of a legion

legislate /ˈledʒɪsleɪt/ v [I] (*fml*) make a law affecting sth ▸ **legislation** /ˌledʒɪsˈleɪʃn/ n [U] **1** law or set of laws passed by a parliament **2** process of making laws ▸ **legislator** n (*fml*)

legislative /ˈledʒɪslətɪv/ adj connected with the act of making and passing laws: a ~ assembly

legislature /ˈledʒɪsleɪtʃə(r)/ n (*fml*) group of people with the power to make and change laws

legitimate /lɪˈdʒɪtɪmət/ adj **1** reasonable: a ~ excuse **2** allowed by law **3** (of a child) born of parents married to each other ▸ **legitimacy** /-məsi/ n [U]

legless /ˈlegləs/ adj (*infml, GB*) very drunk

leisure /ˈleʒə(r)/ n [U] free time [IDM] **at your leisure** when you are free and not in a hurry ■ **'leisure centre** n (GB) public building where people can go to do sports, etc in their free time ▸ **leisured** adj not having to work and therefore having a lot of free time ▸ **leisurely** adj, adv without hurrying: a ~ly walk

lemon /ˈlemən/ n **1** [C,U] yellow citrus fruit with a sour juice: a ~ tree **2** [U] pale yellow colour

lemonade /ˌleməˈneɪd/ n [C,U] sweet fizzy drink with a lemon flavour

lend /lend/ v (pt, pp **lent** /lent/) [T] **1** ~**(to)** give the use of sth to sb for a short time: He lent me the money. ◇ He lent it to him. **2** ~**(to)** (*written*) contribute or add sth to sth: Her presence lent dignity to the occasion. **3** **lend itself to** be suitable for sth [IDM] **lend (sb) a (helping) hand (with sth)** (*infml*) help sb with sth

length /leŋθ/ n **1** [U,C] size or measurement of sth from one end to the other **2** [U,C] amount of time that sth lasts **3** [C] extent of sth used as a measurement: swim two ~s of the pool **4** [C] long thin piece of sth: a ~ of rope [IDM] **at length 1** for a long time and in great detail **2** (*lit*) eventually **go to any, some, great, etc lengths (to do sth)** put a lot of effort into sth, esp when this seems extreme ▸ **lengthen** v [I, T] (cause sth to) become longer ▸ **'lengthways** (also **'lengthwise**) adv along the length of sth: Cut the banana in half ~ways ▸ **lengthy** adj (**-ier, -iest**) very long

lenient /ˈliːniənt/ adj not strict when punishing people ▸ **leniency** /-ənsi/ n [U] ▸ **leniently** adv

lens /lenz/ n **1** curved piece of glass or plastic that makes things look larger, smaller or clearer when you look through it: *a pair of glasses with tinted ~es* **2** = CONTACT LENS (CONTACT) **3** (*anat*) transparent part of the eye used for focusing light

lent *pt, pp of* LEND

lentil /'lentil/ *n* small green, orange or brown seed that is usu dried and eaten as food

leopard /'lepəd/ *n* large animal of the cat family with yellow fur and dark spots

leotard /'li:ata:d/ *n* close-fitting piece of clothing worn by acrobats, dancers, etc

leper /'lepə(r)/ *n* **1** person suffering from leprosy **2** person who is rejected and avoided by other people

leprosy /'leprəsi/ *n* [U] infectious disease that causes loss of feeling and which can lead to the loss of fingers, toes, etc

lesbian /'lezbiən/ *n* woman who is sexually attracted to other women ▶ **lesbian** *adj*

less /les/ *det, pron* a smaller amount of: ~ *to do than I thought* ● **less** *adv* to a smaller degree; not so much: *It rains ~ here.* [IDM] **even/much/still less** and certainly not **less and less** smaller and smaller amounts **no less than ...** used to emphasize a large amount ● **less** *prep* used before a particular amount that must be taken away from the amount just mentioned: £1000 *a month – tax*

lessen /'lesn/ *v* [I, T] (cause sth to) become smaller, weaker, less important, etc

lesser /'lesə(r)/ *adj* smaller [IDM] **the lesser of two evils** the less important of two bad choices

lesson /'lesn/ *n* **1** period of time in which sb is taught sth: *piano ~s* **2** experience that sb can learn from: *Let this be a ~ to you!*

lest /lest/ *conj* (*fml*) in order to prevent sth from happening

let /let/ *v* (-**tt**- *pt, pp* **let**) [T] **1** allow sb to do sth or sth to happen: *We – him leave.* **2** allow sb/sth to go somewhere: *~ sb into the house* **3** used for making suggestions or offers: *L–'s go!* ◇ *Here, ~ me do it.* **4** allow sb to use a house, room, etc in return for regular payments [IDM] **let alone** and certainly not: *We cannot even pay our bills, ~ alone make a profit.* **let sb/sth alone** → LEAVE¹ **let the cat out of the bag** tell a secret carelessly or by mistake **let sth drop** do or say nothing more about sth **let sth fly (at sb) (with sth)** attack sb/sth physically or with words **let sb/sth go | let go (of sb/sth)** stop holding sb/sth **let your-**

self go **1** no longer hold back your feelings **2** stop being careful about how you look, dress, etc **let your hair down** (*infml*) relax and enjoy yourself **let sb have it** (*spoken, infml*) attack sb physically or with words **let sb know** tell sb about sth **let off steam** (*infml*) release energy or anger and become less excited **let the side down** fail to give your friends, family, etc the help, support, etc they expect **let sleeping dogs lie** leave sb alone **let slip sth** accidentally reveal secret information **let sth slip (through your fingers)** miss or fail to use an opportunity **let us say** used when giving an example [PV] **let sb down** disappoint sb **let sth down 1** to lower sth **2** make clothes longer **3** (*GB*) allow air to escape from sth deliberately **let sb/yourself in for sth** involve sb/yourself in sth that is likely to be unpleasant or difficult **let sb in on sth| let sb into sth** (*infml*) allow sb to share a secret **let sb off (with sth)** not punish sb severely for sth they have done wrong **let sb off sth** allow sb not to do an unpleasant task **let sth off** fire a gun or make a bomb, etc explode **let on (to sb)** (*infml*) tell a secret: *Don't ~ on that you know.* **let sth out 1** give a cry, etc **2** make a piece of clothing looser or larger **let up** become less strong; stop: *The rain began to ~ up.* ■ **'let-down** *n* disappointment ■ **'let-up** *n* [C, U] reduction in strength, intensity, etc

lethal /'li:θl/ *adj* causing death

lethargy /'leθədʒi/ *n* [U] lack of energy or interest ▶ **lethargic** /lə-'θɑ:dʒɪk/ *adj*

let's *short for* LET US

letter /'letə(r)/ *n* **1** written message sent to sb **2** written or printed sign representing a sound ■ **'letter bomb** *n* small bomb sent to sb in an envelope ■ **'letter box** *n* **1** (*GB*) hole in a door for letters **2** box in the street or at a post office into which letters are posted ▶ **lettering** *n* [U] letters or words, esp with reference to their style and size

lettuce /'letɪs/ *n* [C, U] plant with green leaves, eaten in salads

leukaemia (*US* -**kem**-) /lu:'ki:miə/ *n* [U] serious disease in which there are too many white blood cells

level¹ /'levl/ *adj* **1** having a flat surface that does not slope **2** ~(*with*) at the same height, position, etc as another; equal: *Wales drew ~* (= made the score equal) *early in the game.* [IDM] **do/try your level best (to do sth)** do all that you can to achieve sth ■ **level 'crossing** *n* place where**

a road crosses a railway ■ ,level-
'headed *adj* sensible; calm

level² /'levl/ *n* **1** [C] amount of sth
that exists in a particular situation
at one time: *a high ~ of unemployment* **2** [C,U] particular standard or
quality: *He studied French to degree
~.* **3** [U,C] position or rank in a scale
of size or importance: *talks at management* – **4** [C,U] height of sth in
relation to the ground or to what it
used to be: *below ground ~*

level³ /'levl/ *v* (**-ll-** *US* **-l-**) [T] **1** make
sth flat or smooth **2** demolish a
building **3** ~(**at**) aim a weapon or
criticism at sb [PV] **level off/out 1**
stop rising and falling and become
horizontal **2** stay at a steady level
of development after a period of
sharp rises and falls: *Sales ~led off.*
level with sb (*infml*) speak honestly
to sb

lever /'li:və(r)/ *n* **1** handle used to
operate a vehicle or a machine **2**
bar that turns on a fixed point used
to lift things **3** action used to put
pressure on sb to do sth ● **lever** *v*
[T] move sth with a lever: *L~ it into
position.* ▸ **leverage** /'li:vərɪdʒ/ *n*
[U] **1** (*fml*) power to influence what
people do **2** (*tech*) force of a lever

levity /'levəti/ *n* [U] (*written*) lack of
respect for sth serious

levy /'levi/ *v* (*pt, pp* **-ied**) [T] demand
and collect a payment, tax, etc by
authority: *~ a tax* ● **levy** *n* (*pl* **-ies**)
sum of money that has to be paid,
esp as a tax to the government

lewd /lju:d/ *adj* referring to sex in a
rude way: *~jokes*

liability /,laɪə'bɪləti/ *n* (*pl*-ies) **1** [U]
state of being legally responsible
for sb/sth **2** [C, usu sing] (*infml*) person or thing that causes you difficulties or problems: *An old car is a
~.* **3** [C, usu pl] debt that must be paid

liable /'laɪəbl/ *adj* **1** ~(**for**) legally
responsible for paying the cost of
sth: *~ for debts* **2** ~(**to**) likely to do
sth: *~ to make mistakes* **3** ~(**to**) likely
to be affected by sth: *be ~ to injury*

liaise /li'eɪz/ *v* [I] work together with
sb and exchange information

liaison /li'eɪzn/ *n* **1** [C,U] working association between different groups
2 [C] secret sexual relationship

liar /'laɪə(r)/ *n* person who tells lies

libel /'laɪbl/ *n* [U,C] act of printing a
statement about sb that is not true
and that damages their reputation
● **libel** *v* (**-ll-** *US* **-l-**) [T] publish a
written statement about sb that is
not true ▸ **libellous** (*US* **libelous**)
/-bələs/ *adj*

liberal /'lɪbərəl/ *adj* **1** tolerant of the
beliefs or behaviour of others **2** giving or given freely: *a ~ supply*

3 (of education) giving a wide
general knowledge ■ **the ,Liberal
'Democrats** (*abbr* **Lib Dems**) *n* [pl]
one of the main British political
parties, in favour of some political
and social change but not extreme
▸ **liberalism** *n* [U] liberal opinions,
esp in politics ▸ **liberalize** (*also* **-ise**)
/'lɪbrəlaɪz/ *v* [T] (*fml*) make a law or a
political or religious system less
strict ▸ **liberally** *adv*

liberate /'lɪbəreɪt/ *v* [T] (*fml*) set
sb/sth free ▸ **liberated** *adj* free in
social and sexual matters ▸ **liberation** /,lɪbə'reɪʃn/ *n* [U]

liberty /'lɪbəti/ *n* (*pl* **-ies**) **1** [C,U]
(*fml*) right or freedom to do as you
choose **2** [U] (*fml*) state of not being
a prisoner or a slave [IDM] **at liberty**
free **take the liberty of doing sth** do
sth without permission

library /'laɪbrəri; 'laɪbri/ *n* (*pl* **-ies**)
(room or building for a) collection
of books, records, etc ▸ **librarian**
/laɪ'breəriən/ *n* person in charge of
a library

lice *plural of* LOUSE

licence (*US* **license**) /'laɪsns/ *n* [C,
U] (official paper giving) permission to do, own, etc sth: *a driving ~*

license /'laɪsns/ *v* [T] give sb official
permission to do, own, etc sth
▸ **licensee** /,laɪsən'si:/ *n* person who
has a licence, esp to sell alcohol
■ **'license number** *n* (*US*) = REGISTRATION NUMBER (REGISTRATION)

lick /lɪk/ *v* [T] **1** move your tongue
over the surface of sth in order to
eat it, make it wet or clean it: *The
dog ~ed its paw.* **2** ~(**off/up**) touch
sth lightly **3** (*infml*) easily defeat sb
[IDM] **lick your lips** → LIP ● **lick** *n*
1 [C] act of licking sth **2** [sing] small
amount of paint, etc

licorice (*esp US*) = LIQUORICE

lid /lɪd/ *n* **1** cover over a container
that can removed: *a dustbin ~*
2 = EYELID (EYE)

lie¹ /laɪ/ *v* (*pt, pp* **lied** *pp* **lying**) [I]
say or write sth that you know is
not true ● **lie** *n* statement that you
know to be untrue: *to tell a ~*

lie² /laɪ/ *v* (*pt* **lay** /leɪ/ *pp* **lain** /leɪn/
pres pt **lying**) [I] **1** (of a person or an
animal) be or put yourself in a flat
or horizontal position so that you
are not standing or sitting **2** (of a
thing) be or remain in a flat position on a surface: *Clothes lay all
over the floor.* **3** be or remain in a
particular state: *machines lying idle*
4 be situated: *The town ~s on the
coast.* **5** be spread out in a particular place **6** (of abstract things) be
found: *It does not ~ within my power
to help you.* [IDM] **lie in wait (for sb)**
be hidden, waiting to surprise sb **lie
low** (*infml*) keep quiet or hidden

take sth lying down accept an insult, unfair treatment, etc without protesting [PV] **lie behind sth** be the real reason for sth **lie down** be or get into a horizontal position, esp on a bed, in order to sleep or rest **lie with sb (to do sth)** (*fml*) be sb's duty or responsibility: *The final decision ~s with you.* ● **lie** *n* [IDM] **the lie of the land** 1 natural features of an area 2 the way a situation is now and how it is likely to develop ■ **lie-down** *n* [sing] (*GB, infml*) short rest ■ **lie-in** *n* (*GB, infml*) stay in bed later than your usual time in the morning: *have a ~-in*

lieutenant /lefˈtenənt/ (*abbr* **Lieut., Lt.**) *n* officer of middle rank in the army, navy or air force

life /laɪf/ *n* (*pl* **lives** /laɪvz/) 1 [U] ability to breathe, grow, reproduce, etc which makes people, animals and plants different from objects 2 [U,C] state of being alive as a human being; an individual person's existence: *He expects a lot from ~.* ◇ *Many lives were lost.* 3 [U] living things: *Is there ~ on Mars?* 4 [C] period between birth and death: *She spent her whole ~ in Canada.* 5 [C] period during which sth continues to exist or function: *a battery with a ~ of three years* 6 [U] punishment of being sent to prison for life: *The judge gave him ~.* 7 [U] experience and activities that are typical of all people's existences: *The dishwasher makes ~ easier for us.* 8 [U] particular way of living: *city/country ~* 9 [U] quality of being lively and exciting: *full of ~* 10 [U] living model, used as the subject in art: *a portrait drawn from ~* 11 [C] story of sb's life: *a ~ of Dante* [IDM] **come to life** become lively or active **for the life of you** (*infml*) however hard you try **the life and soul of the party, etc** (*GB, infml*) the most lively and amusing person at a party, etc **not on your life** (*spoken*) certainly not **take sb's life** kill sb **take your life in your hands** risk being killed ■ **lifebelt** (*also* **lifebuoy**) *n* floating ring for sb who has fallen into the water to hold onto ■ **lifeboat** *n* boat built to save people in danger at sea ■ **life cycle** *n* (*biol*) series of forms into which a living thing changes as it develops: *the ~ cycle of a frog* ■ **lifeguard** *n* expert swimmer employed to rescue other swimmers in danger ■ **life jacket** *n* jacket worn to keep a person afloat in water ▶ **lifeless** *adj* 1 dead 2 not lively; dull ■ **lifelike** *adj* exactly like a real person or thing: *a ~like painting* ■ **lifeline** *n* 1 rope used for rescuing sb who has fallen into the water 2 something that is very

important for sb and that they depend on ■ **lifelong** *adj* lasting all through your life ■ **life-size(d)** *adj* the same size as the person or thing really is ■ **lifespan** *n* length of time that sth is likely to live, continue, or function ■ **lifestyle** *n* way a person or group of people lives and works ■ **lifetime** *n* length of time that sb is alive

lift /lɪft/ *v* 1 [I, T] raise sb/sth or be raised to a higher level or position 2 [T] remove or end restrictions: *~ a ban* 3 [T] make sb more cheerful: *The news ~ed her spirits.* 4 [I] (of clouds, fog, etc) rise and disappear 5 [T] (*infml*) steal sth [IDM] **not lift a finger** (to) do nothing to help sb [PV] **lift off** (of a spacecraft) leave the ground and rise up into the air ● **lift** *n* 1 [C] (*GB*) machine that carries people or goods from one floor of a building to another 2 [C] (*GB*) free ride in a vehicle: *a ~ to the station* 3 [sing] feeling of being happier than before 4 [sing] act of lifting sth ■ **lift-off** *n* [C,U] act of launching a spacecraft into the air

ligament /ˈlɪgəmənt/ *n* band of strong tissue that holds bones together

light¹ /laɪt/ *n* 1 [U] energy from the sun, a lamp, etc that makes it possible to see things: *bright/dim ~* 2 [C] something, esp an electric lamp, that produces light: *turn the ~s on* 3 [sing] match or device with which you can light a cigarette: (*GB*) *Have you got a ~?* 4 [sing] expression in sb's eyes which shows what they are thinking 5 [sing] way in which sb/sth is thought about: *see things in a good ~ (= favourably)* [IDM] **bring sth/come to light** make sth/become known to people **cast/shed/throw light on sth** make sth clearer **in the light of sth** considering sth: *in the ~ of this news* **light at the end of the tunnel** something that shows you are nearly at the end of a long and difficult time ■ **light bulb** = BULB(1) ■ **lighthouse** *n* tower containing a powerful light to warn and guide ships ■ **light year** *n* 1 [C] distance that light travels in one year 2 **light years** [pl] (*infml*) a very long time

light² /laɪt/ *adj* 1 full of light; having the natural light of day: *a ~ room* 2 pale in colour: *~-blue eyes* 3 easy to lift or move; not heavy 4 of less than the usual weight, amount, force, etc: *~ rain* 5 gentle: *a ~ touch* 6 easy to do; not tiring: *~ work* 7 entertaining rather than serious or difficult: *~ reading* 8 not serious or severe: *a ~ sentence* 9 (of a meal) small in quantity and easy to digest: *a ~ snack* 10 (of drinks) low in alcohol **11** (of sleep) not deep **[IDM] make light of sth** treat sth as unimportant ■ **,light-'fingered** adj (infml) likely to steal things ■ **,light-'headed** adj feeling slightly faint ■ **,light-'hearted** adj **1** intended to be amusing rather than serious **2** cheerful ■ **light 'industry** n industry that produces small consumer goods or parts ● **lightly** adv **1** gently; with little force or effort **2** to a small degree; not much **3** not seriously **[IDM] get off/be let off lightly** (infml) manage to avoid severe punishment ▶ **lightness** n [U] ■ **'lightweight** n **1** boxer weighing between 57 and 61 kilograms **2** (infml) person of little importance or influence

light³ /laɪt/ v (pt, pp **lit** /lɪt/ or **lighted**) **1** [I, T] (cause sth to) start to burn **2** [T] give light to sth or to a place: a stage lit by spotlights ◇ well/badly lit streets **[PV] light on/upon sth** (lit) see or find sth by chance **light (sth) up 1** (infml) begin to smoke a cigarette **2** cause light to shine on sth: The fire lit up the whole sky. **3** (cause sb's face or eyes to) show happiness and excitement ▶ **lighting** n [U] arrangement or type of light in a place

lighten /'laɪtn/ v **1** [T] reduce the amount of work, debt, worry, etc that sb has: gadgets to ~ the load of domestic work **2** [I, T] (cause sth) to become brighter or lighter in colour **3** ~**(up)** [I, T] (cause sb to) feel less sad, worried or serious **4** [T] make sth lighter in weight

lighter /'laɪtə(r)/ n device for lighting cigarettes, etc

lightning /'laɪtnɪŋ/ n [U] flash of bright light in the sky, produced by electricity ● **lightning** adj very quick, brief or sudden: at ~ speed ■ **'lightning conductor** (US **'lightning rod**) n metal wire that goes from the top of a building to the ground, to prevent damage by lightning

like¹ /laɪk/ v **1** [T] find sb/sth pleasant, attractive or satisfactory; enjoy sth **2** want: Do what you ~. **3** used in negative sentences to mean 'be unwilling to do sth': I didn't ~ to stop you. **4** used with should or would to express a wish or choice politely: Would you ~ a cup of tea? ◇ I'd ~ too much about it. **[IDM] if you like** (spoken) used to politely agree to sth or to suggest sth **not like the look/sound of sb/sth** have a bad impression based on what you have seen/heard of sb/sth ● **like** n **1** (likes) [pl] the things that you like: We all have different ~s and dislikes. **2** [sing] person or thing that is similar to another: Music,

painting and the ~. ▶ **likeable** (also **likable**) adj pleasant

like² /laɪk/ prep **1** similar to sb/sth: a hat ~ mine **2** used to ask sb's opinion of sb/sth: What's his new girlfriend ~? **3** typical of sb/sth: It's just ~ him to be rude. **4** in the same way as: behave ~ children ◇ drink ~ a fish **5** for example: sports, ~ football and hockey **[IDM] like anything** (GB, infml) very much ● **like** conj (infml) **1** in the same way as **2** as if: She acts ~ she owns the place.

like³ /laɪk/ adj (fml) similar to another person or thing ■ **,like-'minded** adj having similar ideas and interests

likelihood /'laɪklihʊd/ n [U, sing] probability

likely /'laɪkli/ adj (-ier, -iest) probable or expected: ~ to rain **[IDM] a likely story** (spoken) used to show that you do not believe what sb has said ● **likely** adv **[IDM] as likely as not / most/very likely** very probably **not likely!** (spoken, esp GB) used to disagree strongly with a statement or suggestion

liken /'laɪkən/ v (fml) **~ sth/sb to sth/sb** (fml) compare one thing or person to another and say they are similar

likeness /'laɪknəs/ n [C, U] (instance of) being similar in appearance: a family ~

likewise /'laɪkwaɪz/ adv (fml) similarly; also

liking /'laɪkɪŋ/ n [sing] ~**(for)** feeling that you like sb/sth: He has a ~ for fast cars. ◇ She's taken a real ~ to him. **[IDM] to sb's liking** (fml) satisfactory

lilac /'laɪlək/ n **1** [C] bush with sweet-smelling pale purple or white flowers **2** [U] pale purple colour

lilt /lɪlt/ n [sing] pleasant rise and fall of the voice ▶ **lilting** adj

lily /'lɪli/ n (pl -ies) plant that grows from a bulb and has large usu white flowers

limb /lɪm/ n **1** leg, arm or wing **2** large branch of a tree **[IDM] out on a limb** (infml) not supported by other people

limber /'lɪmbə(r)/ v **[PV] limber up** exercise your muscles before a race, etc

limbo /'lɪmbəʊ/ n **[IDM] in limbo** in an uncertain state

lime /laɪm/ n **1** [U] white substance used in making cement **2** [C, U] (juice of a) small green fruit like a lemon but more acid **3** (also **'lime tree**) [C] tree with sweet-smelling yellow flowers ■ **'limestone** n [U] type of white stone that contains calcium, used in building

limelight /ˈlaɪmlaɪt/ n (the **lime-light**) [U] centre of public attention

limerick /ˈlɪmərɪk/ n humorous poem with five lines

limit /ˈlɪmɪt/ n **1** point or line that may not be or cannot be passed **2** greatest or smallest amount allowed or possible [IDM] **be the limit** (*old-fash, spoken*) be extremely annoying OFF LIMITS (*esp US*) = OUT OF BOUNDS (BOUNDS) **within limits** to some extent; with some restrictions: *I'm willing to help, within ~s.* ● **limit** v [T] keep sth/sb within a limit ▸ **limitation** /ˌlɪmɪˈteɪʃn/ n **1** [U] act of limiting or controlling sb/sth **2** [C] rule, fact or condition that limits sb/sth; weakness ▸ **limited** *adj* restricted; few or small ■ **limited** ˈcompany n (in Britain) company whose owners only have to pay a limited amount of its debts ▸ **limit-less** *adj* without limits

limousine /ˈlɪməziːn/ n large luxurious car with the driver's seat separated from the passengers in the back

limp¹ /lɪmp/ v [I] walk with difficulty because one leg is injured ● **limp** n [sing] limping walk: *to walk with a ~*

limp² /lɪmp/ *adj* not stiff or firm ▸ **limply** *adv*

linchpin /ˈlɪntʃpɪn/ n person or thing that is essential to an organization, plan, etc

line¹ /laɪn/ n **1** [C] long thin mark on a surface **2** [C] long thin mark on the ground to show the limit or border of sth: *~s marking a tennis court* **3** [C] mark like a line on sb's skin that people get as they get older: *the ~s on his face* **4** [C] an imaginary limit or border between one thing and another: *There's a fine ~ between showing interest and interfering.* **5** [C] overall shape; outline **6** [C] row of people or things: *customers standing in (a) ~* **7** [C, usu sing] series of people, things or events that follow one another in time: *She came from a long ~ of doctors.* **8** [C] row of words on a page **9** [C] words spoken by an actor **10** [C] length or thread, rope or wire: *a fishing ~* **11** [C] telephone connection: *I was talking to John when the ~ went dead.* **12** [C] railway track or section of a railway system **13** [C, usu sing] direction or course: *the ~ of fire* (= the direction sb is shooting in) **14** [C] course of action, behaviour or thought: *a new ~ of research* **15** [sing] type or area of business, activity or interest: *My ~ of work pays pretty well.* **16** [C] type of product: *a new ~ in coats* **17** [C] company that provides transport for people or goods: *a shipping* ~ **18** [C] series of military defences where the soldiers are fighting during a war: *He was sent to fight at the front ~.* [IDM] **be on line 1** to be working or functioning **2** using a computer; communicating with other people by computer **drop sb a line** → DROP¹ **in line for sth** likely to get sth **in line with sth** similar to sth; in accordance with sth (**put sth) on the line** (*infml*) (put sth) at risk **on the right lines** following a way that is likely to succeed **out of line (with sb/sth) 1** not forming a straight line **2** unacceptably different from others **3** (*US*) = OUT OF ORDER(3) ORDER¹ ■ **ˈline drawing** n drawing done with a pen, pencil, etc ■ **ˈline printer** n machine that prints very quickly, producing a complete line of text at a time

line² /laɪn/ v [T] **1** cover the inside surface of sth with another material: *fur-~d gloves* **2** form a layer on the inside of sth **3** form lines or rows along sth: *a road ~d with trees* **4** mark sth with lines: *~d paper* [IDM] **line your/sb's (own) pocket(s)** make yourself or sb richer, esp by being dishonest [PV] **line (sb) up** (cause people to) form a line **line sth up** (*infml*) arrange or organize sth ■ **ˈline-up** n **1** line of people formed for inspection, etc **2** set of people or things arranged for a purpose

linear /ˈlɪniə(r)/ *adj* **1** of or in lines **2** of length: *~ measurement*

linen /ˈlɪnɪn/ n [U] (cloth for making) sheets, tablecloths, etc

liner /ˈlaɪnə(r)/ n **1** large passenger ship **2** (in compounds) something put inside sth to protect it: *bin-~s*

linesman /ˈlaɪnzmən/ n (pl **-men**) (*sport*) official who says whether a ball has gone outside the limits during a game

linger /ˈlɪŋɡə(r)/ v [I] stay somewhere for a long time; be slow to leave or disappear ▸ **lingering** *adj* slow to end or disappear: *a ~ illness*

lingerie /ˈlænʒəri/ n [U] women's underwear

linguist /ˈlɪŋɡwɪst/ n **1** person who knows several foreign languages well **2** person who studies language or linguistics ▸ **linguistic** /lɪŋˈɡwɪstɪk/ *adj* of language or linguistics ▸ **linguistics** n [U] study of language

liniment /ˈlɪnəmənt/ n [C, U] liquid for rubbing on parts of the body which ache

lining /ˈlaɪnɪŋ/ n [C, U] layer of material used to cover the inside surface of sth: *a fur ~*

link /lɪŋk/ n **1** connection or relationship between two or more people or things **2** each ring of a chain ● **link** v [T] make a connection between two or more people or things [PV] **link up (with sb/sth)** join or become joined with sb/sth

linoleum /lɪˈnəʊliəm/ (GB also infml **lino** /ˈlaɪnəʊ/) n [U] type of strong material with a hard shiny surface, used for covering floors

lint /lɪnt/ n [U] soft cotton material, used for putting on wounds

lion /ˈlaɪən/ n [C] large powerful animal of the cat family [IDM] **the lion's share (of sth)** (GB) the largest or best part of sth ▶ **lioness** n female lion

lip /lɪp/ n **1** [C] either of the two soft edges of the mouth **2** [C] edge of a jug, container, etc **3** [U] (infml) rude disrespectful talk [IDM] **lick/smack your lips** (infml) show that you are looking forward eagerly to sth enjoyable **my lips are sealed** used to say that you will not repeat sb's secret to other people ■ **'lip-read** v (pt, pp **'lip-read** /-red/) [I, T] understand sb's speech by watching the movements of their lips ▶ **'lip-reading** n [U] ■ **'lip service** n [IDM] **pay lip service to sth** say that you support sth while not doing so in reality ■ **lipstick** n [C,U] (stick of) colouring for the lips

liqueur /lɪˈkjʊə(r)/ n [U,C] strong sweet alcoholic drink

liquid /ˈlɪkwɪd/ n [C,U] substance, eg water or oil, that flows freely but which is not a gas ● **liquid** adj **1** in the form of a liquid **2** easily changed into cash: ~ assets **3** (lit) clear and looking wet: ~ blue eyes **4** (lit) (of sounds) clear and flowing

liquidate /ˈlɪkwɪdeɪt/ v [T] **1** close down an unsuccessful business company **2** sell sth in order to make money, esp to pay a debt **3** destroy or remove sb/sth that causes problems ▶ **liquidation** /ˌlɪkwɪˈdeɪʃn/ n [U]

liquidize (also **-ise**) /ˈlɪkwɪdaɪz/ v [T] crush fruit, vegetables, etc into liquid ▶ **liquidizer** (also **-iser**) n electric machine for liquidizing food

liquor /ˈlɪkə(r)/ n [U] (esp US) strong alcoholic drink ■ **'liquor store** n (US) = OFF-LICENCE

liquorice /ˈlɪkərɪʃ; -rɪs/ n [U] black substance with a strong flavour, used as a sweet or in medicine

lisp /lɪsp/ n [sing] speech fault in which the sound 's' is pronounced 'th' ● **lisp** v [I, T] speak with a lisp

list /lɪst/ n [C] set of names, things, etc written down in order **2** [sing] fact of a ship leaning to one side ■ **'list price** n [usu sing] (business) price at which goods are advertised for sale, eg in a catalogue ● **list** v [T] write a list of things in

a particular order **2** [T] mention or include sth in a list **3** [I] (of a ship) lean over to one side

listless /ˈlɪstləs/ adj too tired to show interest ▶ **listlessly** adv ▶ **listlessness** n [U]

lit pt, pp of LIGHT[3]

liter (US) = LITRE

literacy /ˈlɪtərəsi/ n [U] ability to read and write

literal /ˈlɪtərəl/ adj **1** being the basic or usual meaning of a word **2** that follows the original words exactly: a ~ translation ▶ **literally** adv **1** in a literal way; exactly: The word 'planet' -ly means 'wandering body'. **2** (infml) used to emphasize the truth of sth that may seem surprising: I was -ly bored to tears.

literary /ˈlɪtərəri/ adj of literature or authors

literate /ˈlɪtərət/ adj **1** able to read and write **2** well educated; cultured

literature /ˈlɪtrətʃə(r)/ n [U] writings valued as works of art, esp novels, plays and poems **2** ~(on) pieces of writing on a particular subject

lithe /laɪð/ adj (fml) (of a person or their body) able to bend easily

litigation /ˌlɪtɪˈgeɪʃn/ n [U] (law) process of making or defending a claim in a law court

litre /ˈliːtə(r)/ n (abbr **l**) metric unit of capacity, used for measuring liquids

litter /ˈlɪtə(r)/ n **1** [U] bits of paper, bottles, etc that people have left lying in a public place **2** [C] all the young born to an animal at one time ● **litter** v [T] make a place untidy with litter ■ **'litter bin** n container for rubbish

little[1] /ˈlɪtl/ adj **1** small: ~ cups **2** young: a ~ boy **3** (of distance or time) short: wait a ~ while **4** not important: a ~ mistake

little[2] /ˈlɪtl/ det, pron **1** used with uncountable nouns to mean 'not much': There was ~ doubt in my mind. **2 (a little)** used with uncountable nouns to mean 'a small amount' or 'some': a ~ milk ● **little** adv (less, least) **1** not much; only slightly: I slept very ~ last night. ◇ (written) L~ does he know (= He doesn't know) what trouble he's in. **2 (a little)** to a small degree: She seemed a ~ (bit) afraid of going outside. [IDM] **little by little** gradually **little wonder (that …)** → WONDER

live[1] /lɪv/ v [I] have your home: ~ in Leeds **2** [I] remain alive: Doctors say he has six months to ~. **3** [I] be alive **4** [I, T] spend your life in a particular way: ~ happily **5** [I] enjoy life fully [IDM] **live (from) hand to mouth**

spend all the money you earn on basic needs such as food, without being able to save any money **live it up** (infml) enjoy yourself in an exciting way [PV] **live sth down** be able to make people forget about sth embarrassing you have done **live for sb/sth** think that sb/sth is the main purpose of or the most important thing in your life **live in/out** (of a worker or student) live at/away from the place where you work or study **live off sb/sth** receive the money you need to live from sb/sth because you do not have any yourself **live on** continue to live or exist **live on sth 1** have sth as your main food **2** have enough money for the basic things you need to live **live through sth** experience sth and survive: ~ through two wars and survive **live together** (also **live with sb**) live with sb as if you are married **live up to sth** do as well as or be as good as other people expect you to be: ~d **up to my expectations** **live with sth** accept sth unpleasant

live² /laɪv/ adj **1** living; not dead **2** (of a broadcast) sent out while the event is actually happening, not recorded first and broadcast later **3** (of a performance) given or made when people are watching, not recorded: ~ music **4** (of a wire) carrying electricity **5** still able to explode or light; ready for use: ~ ammunition **6** burning or glowing: ~ coals **7** (of a question or subject) of great interest at the present time

liveable /ˈlɪvəbl/ adj fit to live in; tolerable

livelihood /ˈlaɪvlihʊd/ n [C, usu sing] means of earning money in order to live

lively /ˈlaɪvli/ adj (-ier, -iest) full of life and activity **2** (of colours) bright ▸ **liveliness** n [U]

liven /ˈlaɪvn/ v [PV] **liven (sb/sth) up** (cause sth/sb) to become more interesting and exciting

liver /ˈlɪvə(r)/ n **1** [C] large organ in the body that cleans the blood **2** [U] animal's liver as food

lives plural of LIFE

livestock /ˈlaɪvstɒk/ n [U] farm animals

livid /ˈlɪvɪd/ adj **1** (infml) extremely angry **2** dark bluish-grey in colour

living /ˈlɪvɪŋ/ adj **1** alive now **2** used or practised now: a ~ language [IDM] **be the living image of sb** → IMAGE **within/in living memory** in the time remembered by people still alive ● **living** n **1** [sing] money to buy the things you need in life: **What do you do for a ~?** **2** [U] way or style of life: a **low standard of** ~ **3** (**the living**) [pl] people who are alive now ■ **'living**

room n room in a house where people sit together, watch TV, etc

lizard /ˈlɪzəd/ n small four-legged reptile with a long tail

load /ləʊd/ n **1** [C] thing that is carried by a person, vehicle, etc **2** [C] (esp in compounds) quantity that can be carried: bus ~s of tourists **3** [sing] (GB also **loads** (of sth)) [pl] (infml) a large number or amount of sth/sb; plenty: ~s **of money 4** [C] amount of work that a person or a machine has to do **5** [C] feeling of responsibility or worry: **Hearing they had arrived safely took a ~ off my mind.** ● **load** v **1** [I, T] put a load onto or into sth; receive a load: ~ **cargo onto a ship 2** [T] give sb a lot of things to carry **3** [T] put sth into a weapon, a camera or other piece of equipment so that it can be used **4** [I, T] put data or a program into the memory of a computer: **Wait for the game to ~.** ● **loaded** adj **1** ~ (**with**) carrying a load; full and heavy **2** (infml) very rich **3** acting either as an advantage or a disadvantage to sb in a way which is unfair **4** having more meaning than you realize at first and intended to trap you: **It was a ~ed question. 5** containing bullets, camera film, etc

loaf /ləʊf/ n (pl **loaves** /ləʊvz/) mass of shaped and baked bread ● **loaf** v [I] ~ (**about/around**) (infml) spend your time not doing anything

loan /ləʊn/ n **1** [C] money that an organization such as a bank lends and sb borrows **2** [sing] act of lending sth; state of being lent: **This painting is on loan.** ● **loan** v [T] (esp US) lend sth to sb, esp money

loath (also **loth**) /ləʊθ/ adj ~to (fml) unwilling to do sth

loathe /ləʊð/ v [T] dislike sb/sth very much ▸ **loathing** n [U] disgust ▸ **loathsome** /ˈləʊðsəm/ adj disgusting

loaves plural of LOAF

lob /lɒb/ v (-bb-) [I, T] throw or hit a ball, etc in a high curve ▸ **lob** n

lobby /ˈlɒbi/ n (pl **-ies**) **1** [C] entrance hall of a hotel, theatre, etc **2** [C, with sing or pl verb] group of people who try to influence politicians ● **lobby** v (pt, pp **-ied**) [I, T] try to persuade a politician to support or oppose a proposed law, etc

lobe /ləʊb/ n **1** = EAR LOBE (EAR) **2** part of an organ in the body, esp the lungs or brain

lobster /ˈlɒbstə(r)/ n **1** [C] shellfish with eight legs and two claws **2** [U] meat from a lobster, eaten as food

local /ˈləʊkl/ adj **1** of a particular place: ~ **news 2** affecting only a part, not the whole, of the body: a ~ anaesthetic ■ ,**local** ,**area 'network**

n = LAN ● **local** *n* [C] **1** [*usu pl*] person who lives in a particular place **2** (*Brit*, *infml*) pub near where you live ▶ **locally** *adv*

locality /ləʊ'kæləti/ *n* (*pl* **-ies**) district; place

localize (*also* **-ise**) /'ləʊkəlaɪz/ *v* [T] limit sth to a particular area: ~ *a disease*

locate /ləʊ'keɪt/ *v* [T] **1** find out the exact position of sb/sth **2** put or build sth in a particular place: *Our offices are ~d in Paris.* ▶ **location** /ləʊ'keɪʃn/ *n* place or position [IDM] **on location** (*of a film*) photographed in natural surroundings, not in a studio

loch /lɒk/ *n* (in Scotland) lake: *L~ Ness*

lock[1] /lɒk/ *v* [I, T] **1** fasten sth or be fastened with a lock **2** (cause sth to) become fixed in one position and unable to move [PV] **lock sb away/up** (*infml*) put sb in prison **lock sth away/up** put sth safely in a locked place **lock sb/yourself in/out** prevent sb/yourself from entering or leaving a place by locking the door **lock (sth) up** make a house, etc safe by locking the doors

lock[2] /lɒk/ *n* **1** device for fastening a door, etc **2** enclosed section of a canal, in which the water level can be raised or lowered **3** portion of hair that naturally hangs together [IDM] **lock, stock and barrel** including everything ■ **locksmith** *n* person who makes and mends locks

locker /'lɒkə(r)/ *n* small cupboard that can be locked, used for storing clothes, luggage, etc

locket /'lɒkɪt/ *n* piece of jewellery, worn on a chain around the neck, in which you can put a picture, piece of hair, etc

locomotive /,ləʊkə'məʊtɪv/ *n* (*fml*) railway engine

locust /'ləʊkəst/ *n* winged insect that flies in large groups and destroys crops

lodge[1] /lɒdʒ/ *n* **1** country house or cabin: *a hunting ~* **2** small house, esp at the entrance to the grounds of a large house

lodge[2] /lɒdʒ/ *v* **1** [T] make a formal statement about sth to a public organization: ~ *a complaint* **2** [I] (*old-fash*) pay to live in a room in sb's house **3** [T] provide sb with a place to sleep or live **4** [I, T] ~**in** (cause sth to) enter and become fixed in sth: *The bullet (was) ~d in his arm.* ▶ **lodger** *n* (*esp GB*) person who pays rent to live in sb's house

lodging /'lɒdʒɪŋ/ *n* **1** [U] temporary accommodation **2** [C, *usu pl*] (*old-fash*) room or rooms in sb else's house that you rent to live in

loft /lɒft/ *n* room or space under the roof of a house, used for storing things

lofty /'lɒfti/ *adj* (**-ier, -iest**) (*fml*) **1** very high **2** (of thoughts, etc) noble **3** (*disapprov*) proud

log[1] /lɒg/ *n* **1** thick piece of wood that is cut from or has fallen from a tree **2** (*also* **logbook**) official record of events during a period of time, eg a journey on a ship or plane ● **log** *v* (**-gg-**) [T] **1** put information in an official record or write a record of events **2** travel a particular distance or for a particular length of time [IDM] **log in/on** (*computing*) perform the actions that allow you to start using a computer system **log off/out** (*computing*) perform the actions that allow you to finish using a computer system

loggerheads /'lɒgəhedz/ *n* [IDM] **at loggerheads (with sb) (over sth)** in strong disagreement

logic /'lɒdʒɪk/ *n* [U] **1** science or method of organized reasoning **2** sensible reasoning: *There's no ~ in what he says.* ▶ **logical** /'lɒdʒɪkl/ *adj* **1** in accordance with logic ▶ **logically** /-kli/ *adv*

logo /'ləʊgəʊ/ *n* (*pl* **-os**) printed design or symbol that a company, organization, etc uses as its special sign

loin /lɔɪn/ *n* **1** [U,C] piece of meat from the back or sides of an animal: ~ *of pork* **2** (**loins**) [*pl*] (*lit*) person's sex organs

loiter /'lɔɪtə(r)/ *v* [I] stand or wait somewhere, esp with no obvious reason

loll /lɒl/ *v* [I] **1** lie, stand or sit in a lazy or relaxed way **2** (of the head or tongue) hang loosely

lollipop /'lɒlipɒp/ (*GB also infml* **lolly** /'lɒli/) (*pl* **-ies**) *n* large boiled sweet or piece of frozen fruit juice on a stick

lone /ləʊn/ *adj* without any other people or things

lonely /'ləʊnli/ *adj* (**-ier, -iest**) **1** sad because you have no friends or people to talk to **2** (of places) not often visited ▶ **loneliness** *n* [U]

lonesome /'ləʊnsəm/ *adj* (*esp US*) = LONELY

long[1] /lɒŋ/ *adj* (**-er** /'lɒŋgə(r)/ **-est** /'lɒŋgɪst/) having a great or a given extent in space or time: *a ~ journey* ◇ *800 metres ~* [IDM] **go a long way →** FAR[1] **in the long run** eventually; ultimately **the long and (the) short of it** all that need be said about it **long in the tooth** (*hum*) (of a person) old **not by a long chalk/shot** not nearly; not at all ■ **,long-'distance** *adj*, *adv* travelling or operating between distant places ■ **,long 'drink** *n* cold drink, served in a tall glass ■ **'long-range** *adj* of or for a long period of time or distance: *a ~-range weather forecast* ■ **,long-'sighted** *adj* not able to see things that are close to you clearly ■ **,long-'term** *adj* of or for a long period of time ■ **'long wave** *n* [U] (*abbr* **LW**) radio wave with a length of more than 1000 metres ■ **,long-'winded** *adj* (*disapprov*) (of talking or writing) too long and therefore boring

long² /lɒŋ/ *adv* (~**er** /-ŋgə(r)/ ~**est** /-ŋgɪst/) **1** for a long time: *Were you in Rome ~? ◇ I shan't be ~* (= I will come soon). **2** at a distant time: *~ ago* **3** (of duration) throughout: *all day* — [IDM] **as/so long as** on condition that/**no/any longer** used to say that sth which was possible or true before, is not now: *I can't wait any ~.* ■ **,long-'standing** *adj* that has existed for a long time: *a ~-standing arrangement* ■ **,long-'suffering** *adj* patiently bearing problems and difficulties

long³ /lɒŋ/ *v* [I] *~for*; to want sth very much: *~ for the holidays* ▶ **longing** *adj, n* [C,U] (having a) strong feeling of wanting sth/sb ▶ **longingly** *adv*

longitude /'lɒndʒɪtjuːd/ *n* [U] distance of a place east or west of Greenwich in Britain, measured in degrees

loo /luː/ *n* (*pl ~***s**) (*GB, infml*) toilet

look¹ /lʊk/ *v* **1** [I] *~(at)* turn your eyes in a particular direction **2** [I] *~(for)* try to find sb/sth **3** [I, T] pay attention to sth: *L~ where you're going!* **4** linking verb seem; appear: *~ sad/pale* **5** [I] *~as if/as though; like* seem likely: *She ~ed as if she was asleep. ◇ It ~s like rain.* **6** [I] face a particular direction: *The house ~s out over the harbour.* [IDM] **look daggers at sb** look very angrily at sb ■ **look down your nose at sb/sth** (*infml, esp GB*) behave in a way that suggests that you think you are better than sb or that sth is not good enough for you ■ **look sharp** (*GB*) hurry up/**look yourself** (not) have your usual healthy appearance **never/not look back** (*infml*) become more and more successful **not much to look at** (*infml*) not attractive [PV] **look after yourself/sb/sth** (*esp GB*) be responsible for or take care of sb/sth ■ **look ahead (to sth)** think about what is going to happen in the future **look around/round (sth)** visit a place or building, walking around it to see what is there **look at sth** examine or consider sth: *I'll ~ at your proposal tomorrow.* **look**

back (on sth) think about sth in your past **look down on sb/sth** (*infml*) think that you are better than sb/sth **look for sth** hope for sth; expect sth **look forward to sth** think with pleasure about sth that is going to happen in the future **look in (on sb)** (*GB*) make a short visit to a place, esp sb's house **look into sth** examine sth **look on** watch sth without becoming involved in it yourself **look on sb/sth as sb/sth** consider sb/sth to be sb/sth **look out** be careful **look out for sb/sth 1** try to avoid sth bad happening or doing sth bad: *You should ~ out for pickpockets.* **2** keep trying to find sth or meet sb **look sth over** examine sth to see how good, big, etc it is **look through sth** examine or read sth quickly **look to sb for sth/to do sth** rely on sb to provide or do sth **look sb up** (*infml*) visit sb, esp when you have not seen them for a long time **look sth up** look for information in a dictionary or reference book **look up to sb** admire or respect sb ● **look** *exclam* used to interrupt sb or make them listen to sth you are saying ■ **'look-in** [IDM] **(not) get a look-in** (*infml*) (not) get a chance to take part or succeed in sth ■ **lookout** *n* **1** place for watching from, esp for danger **2** person who watches for danger [IDM] **be your (own) lookout** (*GB, infml*) used to say that you do not think sb's actions are sensible, but that it is their own responsibility: *If you want to waste your money, that's your ~out.*

look² /lʊk/ *n* **1** [C, usu sing] act of looking at sth/sb: *Take a ~ at this.* **2** [C, usu sing] *~(for)* act of trying to find sth/sb **3** [I] expression or appearance: *I don't like the ~ of him.* **4** (**looks**) [pl] person's (attractive) appearance: *She's got her father's good ~s.*

loom /luːm/ *v* **1** appear in an unclear, often threatening, way [IDM] **loom large** be worrying or frightening and seem hard to avoid ● **loom** *n* machine for weaving cloth

loop /luːp/ *n* **1** shape like a circle made by a line curving right round and crossing itself **2** piece of rope, wire, etc in the shape of a curve or circle ● **loop** *v* **1** [T] bend sth into a loop **2** [I] move in a way that makes the shape of a loop

loophole /'luːphəʊl/ *n* way of escape from a legal restriction: *a legal/tax ~*

loose /luːs/ *adj* (~**r**, ~**st**) **1** not firmly

fixed where it should be; able to become separated from sth: a ~ button/tooth **2** not tied or fastened together: ~ sheets of paper **3** freed from control; not tied or shut in somewhere: The dog is too dangerous to be set ~ **4** (of clothes) not tight **5** not exact: a ~ translation **6** (old-fash) immoral [IDM] at a loose end (US also) at loose ends having nothing to do ▶ loosely adv ▶ loosen /'lu:sn/ v [I, T] become or make sth loose or less tight

loot /lu:t/ n [U] money and valuable objects taken from an enemy in war or stolen by thieves ● loot v [I, T] steal things from shops or buildings after a riot, fire, etc

lop /lɒp/ v (-pp-) [T] cut branches, etc off a tree

lop-sided /ˌlɒp'saɪdɪd/ adj with one side lower, smaller, etc than the other

lord /lɔ:d/ n [C] **1** (in Britain) nobleman **2** (Lord) [sing] (in Britain) title used by some high ranks of noblemen (= men of high social class) **3** (Lord) [sing] (in Britain) title of certain high officials: L~ Mayor **4** ((the) Lord) [sing] God; Jesus **5** (the Lords) [sing, with sing or pl verb] = THE HOUSE OF LORDS (HOUSE[1]) [IDM] (good) Lord! | Oh Lord! used to show that you are surprised, annoyed or worried about sth ▶ lordly adj too proud; arrogant ▶ lordship n (His/Your Lordship) title of respect used when speaking to a judge, bishop or lord

lorry /'lɒri/ n (pl -ies) large motor vehicle for carrying heavy loads by road

lose /lu:z/ v (pt, pp lost /lɒst/) **1** [T] become unable to find sth/sb: ~ your keys **2** [T] have sth taken away from you by death, accident, etc: ~ your job **3** [T] have less and less of sth: ~ interest in sth ◊ ~ weight **4** [T] (infml) be no longer understood by her: I'm afraid you've lost me. **5** [I, T] fail to win sth: ~ a game **6** [T] waste time or an opportunity **7** [I, T] (of a clock or watch) go too slowly or become a particular amount of time behind the correct time [IDM] lose your bearings become lost or confused lose count of sth → COUNT[2] lose face be less respected or look stupid because of sth you have done lose ground (to sb/sth) → GROUND[1] lose your head → HEAD[1] lose heart → HEART lose your heart (to sb/sth) (written) fall in love with sb/sth lose sight of sth/sb **1** no longer be able to see sb/sth **2** fail to consider or remember sth lose touch (with sb/sth) no longer have any contact with sb/sth lose your way become lost [PV] lose out (on sth) (infml) not get sth you wanted or feel you should have lose yourself in sth become so interested in sth that it takes all your attention ▶ loser n

loss /lɒs/ n **1** [U,C] state of no longer having sth or as much of sth; the process that leads to this: ~ of blood/self-control **2** [C] money lost in business **3** [C,U] death of a person: heavy ~ of life [IDM] at a loss not knowing what to say or do

lost[1] pt, pp of LOSE

lost[2] /lɒst/ adj unable to find your way; not knowing where you are **2** that cannot be found or brought back [IDM] a lost cause something that has failed or cannot succeed

lot[1] /lɒt/ pron (a lot) (also infml lots) large number or amount ● a lot of (also infml lots of) det a large number or amount of sb/sth: a ~ of people

lot[2] /lɒt/ adv (a lot) (infml) **1** (used with an adj and adv) much: I feel a ~ better. **2** (used with a v) a great amount

lot[3] /lɒt/ n **1** (the lot, the whole lot) [sing, with sing or pl verb] (infml) the whole number or amount of people or things **2** [C, with sing or pl verb] (esp GB) group or set of people or things: the next ~ of students **3** [C] object or a number of objects to be sold, esp at an auction **4** [C] area of land used for a particular purpose: a parking ~ **5** [sing] person's luck or situation in life [IDM] cast/draw lots (for sth/to do sth) choose sb to do sth by asking each person to take a piece of paper, etc from a container and the person whose paper has a special mark is chosen

loth = LOATH

lotion /'ləʊʃn/ n [C,U] liquid used for cleaning, protecting or treating the skin

lottery /'lɒtəri/ n (pl -ies) way of giving prizes to the buyers of numbered tickets chosen by chance

loud /laʊd/ adj **1** making a lot of noise **2** (of colours) too bright and lacking good taste ● loud adv in a way that makes a lot of noise or can be easily heard [IDM] loud and clear in a way that is easy to understand ▶ loudly adv ▶ loudness n [U] ■ ˌloud'speaker n part of a radio, etc that changes electrical signals into sound

lounge /laʊndʒ/ v [I] sit, stand or lie in a lazy way ● lounge n **1** room for waiting in at an airport, etc **2** (GB) room in a private house for sitting and relaxing in ■ 'lounge bar n (GB) bar in a pub or hotel that is smarter and more expensive than other bars

louse /laʊs/ n (pl **lice** /laɪs/) small insect that lives on the bodies of animals and human beings

lousy /ˈlaʊzi/ adj (-ier, -iest) (infml) very bad: ~ weather

lout /laʊt/ n (GB) rude and aggressive man or boy ▶ **loutish** adj

lovable /ˈlʌvəbl/ adj easy to love; deserving love

love /lʌv/ n **1** [U] strong feeling of deep affection for sb/sth **2** [U] strong feeling of affection and sexual attraction for sb: He's fallen in ~. **3** [U,sing] strong feeling of enjoyment that sth gives you: a ~ of music **4** [C] person or thing that you like very much **5** [U] (in tennis) score of zero points or games [IDM] **give/send my love to sb** (infml) used to send friendly greetings to sb **make love (to sb)** have sex **there's little/no love lost between A and B** they do not like each other ● **love** v [T] **1** have very strong feelings of affection for sb: ~ your wife **2** like or enjoy sth a lot: I ~ cakes. ■ **'love affair** n romantic and/or sexual relationship between two people

lovely /ˈlʌvli/ adj (-ier, -iest) **1** beautiful; attractive: a ~ woman **2** very enjoyable and pleasant: a ~ holiday ▶ **loveliness** n [U]

lover /ˈlʌvə(r)/ n **1** partner in a sexual relationship outside marriage **2** person who likes or enjoys a particular thing: a ~ of music

loving /ˈlʌvɪŋ/ adj feeling or showing love for sb/sth ▶ **lovingly** adv

low¹ /ləʊ/ adj **1** not high or tall: a ~ wall **2** below the usual height, value or amount: ~ prices **3** (of a sound) not high; not loud **4** below others in importance or quality **5** weak or depressed: feel ~ **6** not very good: have a ~ opinion of him **7** (of a person) dishonest **8** (of a gear) allowing a slower speed [IDM] **at a low ebb** in a poor or bad state ■ **'low-down** adj (infml) not fair or honest ■ **low-down** n [sing] (the **low-down)** ~on (infml) the full facts about sb/sth: She gave me the ~-down on the guests at the party. ■ **'low-key** adj not intended to attract a lot of attention ■ **'lowland** adj, n [C, usu pl] (of a) fairly flat area of land that is not very high above sea level ■ **'low-profile** adj receiving very little attention: a ~-profile campaign

low² /ləʊ/ adv at or to a low level: aim/shoot ~ ● **low** n low or lowest level or point: Shares reached a new ~ yesterday.

lower /ˈləʊə(r)/ adj at or near the bottom part of sth: the ~ lip ● **lower** v **1** [T] let or make sb/sth go down: ~ a flag **2** [I, T] (cause sth to) become less in value, quality, etc: ~ the price [PV] **lower yourself (by doing sth)** behave in a way that makes people respect you less ■ the **,lower 'class** n social class below middle class ▶ **,lower 'class** adj

lowly /ˈləʊli/ adj (-ier, -iest) low in status or importance

loyal /ˈlɔɪəl/ adj ~(to) faithful to sb/sth: ~ supporters ▶ **loyally** adv ▶ **loyalty** n (pl -ies) **1** [U] quality of being faithful to sb/sth **2** [C, usu pl] strong feeling that you want to be loyal to sb/sth

lozenge /ˈlɒzɪndʒ/ n diamond-shaped figure small sweet containing medicine

LP /ˌel ˈpiː/ abbr long-playing record; a record that plays for about 25 minutes each side and turns 33 times per minute

Ltd abbr Limited = LIMITED COMPANY (LIMIT)

lubricate /ˈluːbrɪkeɪt/ v [T] put oil, etc on sth such as the parts of a machine, to help them move smoothly ▶ **lubrication** /ˌluːbrɪˈkeɪʃn/ n [U]

lucid /ˈluːsɪd/ adj **1** easy to understand; clear **2** able to think and speak clearly ▶ **lucidity** /luːˈsɪdəti/ n [U] ▶ **lucidly** adv

luck /lʌk/ n [U] **1** good things that happen to you by chance **2** chance; the force that causes good or bad things to happen to people [IDM] **be down on your luck** (infml) have no money because of a period of bad luck **be in/out of luck** be fortunate/unfortunate ▶ **lucky** adj (-ier, -iest) having, bringing or resulting from good luck ▶ **luckily** adv

lucrative /ˈluːkrətɪv/ adj producing a large amount of money; making a large profit

ludicrous /ˈluːdɪkrəs/ adj ridiculous and unreasonable ▶ **ludicrously** adv

lug /lʌg/ v (-gg-) [T] carry or drag sth heavy with great effort

luggage /ˈlʌgɪdʒ/ n [U] bags, suitcases, etc taken on a journey

lukewarm /ˌluːkˈwɔːm/ adj **1** slightly warm **2** not enthusiastic

lull /lʌl/ n [C, usu sing] quiet period between times of activity ● **lull** v [T] make sb relaxed and calm: ~ a baby to sleep

lullaby /ˈlʌləbaɪ/ n (pl -ies) song sung to make a child go to sleep

lumbago /lʌmˈbeɪgəʊ/ n [U] pain in the lower back

lumber /ˈlʌmbə(r)/ n [U] **1** (esp US) = TIMBER(1) **2** (GB) unwanted old furniture ● **lumber** v **1** [I] move in a slow, heavy and awkward way **2** [T] ~ **(with)** (*infml*) give sb/sth unwanted to sb: *They've ~ed me with the washing-up again.* ■ **'lumberjack** *n* person whose job is to cut down trees or produce timber

luminous /'lu:mɪnəs/ *adj* giving out light; that can be seen in the dark

lump /lʌmp/ *n* **1** piece of sth hard or solid, usu without a particular shape: *a ~ of coal* **2** swelling under the skin [IDM] **have, etc a lump in your throat** feel pressure in your throat because you are very angry or emotional ● **lump** *v* [T] ~ **(together)** put or consider different things together in the same group [IDM] **lump it** (*infml*) accept sth unpleasant because there is no other choice ■ ˌ**lump 'sum** *n* amount of money paid at one time and not on separate occasions ▶ **lumpy** *adj* (**-ier, -iest**)

lunacy /'lu:nəsi/ *n* [U] behaviour that is stupid or crazy

lunar /'lu:nə(r)/ *adj* of the moon

lunatic /'lu:nətɪk/ *n* **1** person who does crazy things that are often dangerous **2** (*old-fash*) person who is mad ● **lunatic** *adj* crazy, ridiculous or extremely stupid

lunch /lʌntʃ/ *n* [U,C] meal eaten in the middle of the day ● **lunch** *v* [I] (*fml*) have lunch, esp at a restaurant

luncheon /'lʌntʃən/ *n* [C,U] (*fml*) = LUNCH

lung /lʌŋ/ *n* either of the two breathing organs in the chest

lunge /lʌndʒ/ *n, v* [I] (make a) sudden forward movement

lurch /lɜːtʃ/ *n* [C, usu sing] sudden unsteady movement ● **lurch** *v* [I] move along with a lurch

lure /lʊə(r)/ *n* [C, usu sing] attractive qualities of sth: *the ~ of adventure* ● **lure** *v* [T] persuade or trick sb to go somewhere or do sth by promising them a reward: ~ *sb into a trap*

lurid /'lʊərɪd/ *adj* (*disapprov*) **1** having unpleasantly bright colours **2** (of a story or piece of writing) shocking and violent: ~ *headlines*

lurk /lɜːk/ *v* [I] wait somewhere secretly, esp when you are going to do sth bad or illegal

luscious /'lʌʃəs/ *adj* having a very sweet pleasant taste

lush /lʌʃ/ *adj* **1** (of plants, trees, etc) growing thickly and strongly **2** beautiful and making you feel pleasure; seeming expensive

lust /lʌst/ *n* [U,C] ~ **(for)** **1** strong sexual desire **2** strong desire for or enjoyment of sth: *his ~ for power* ● **lust** *v* [PV] **lust after/for sb/sth** feel an extremely strong, esp sexual, desire for sb/sth ▶ **lustful** *adj*

lustre (*US* **luster**) /'lʌstə(r)/ *n* [U] **1** shining quality of a surface **2** quality of being special in a way that is exciting

lusty /'lʌsti/ *adj* healthy and strong

luxuriant /lʌg'ʒʊəriənt/ *adj* (of plants or hair) growing thickly and strongly ▶ **luxuriance** /-əns/ *n* [U] ▶ **luxuriantly** *adv*

luxurious /lʌg'ʒʊəriəs/ *adj* very comfortable and expensive ▶ **luxuriously** *adv*

luxury /'lʌkʃəri/ *n* (*pl* **-ies**) **1** [U] great comfort, esp in expensive surroundings: *a life of ~* **2** [C] thing that is expensive and enjoyable, but not essential

LW (*esp GB*) = LONG WAVE (LONG[1])

lying *pres part* LIE[1]

lynch /lɪntʃ/ *v* [T] kill sb, usu by hanging, without giving them a lawful trial

lyric /'lɪrɪk/ *adj* **1** (of poetry) expressing direct personal feelings **2** of or for singing ● **lyric** *n* **1** lyric poem **2** (**lyrics**) [pl] words of a song ▶ **lyrical** /-kl/ *adj* expressing strong emotion in an imaginative way ▶ **lyrically** /-kli/ *adv*

M m

M, m /em/ *n* [C,U] (*pl* **M's, m's** /emz/) **1** the thirteenth letter of the English alphabet **2** Roman numeral for 1000 **3** used with a number to show the name of a British motorway: *M1*

m (*also* **m.**) *abbr* **1** married **2** metre(s) **3** million(s)

MA /ˌem 'eɪ/ *n* Master of Arts; a second university degree in an Arts subject, or, in Scotland, a first degree

ma /mɑː/ *n* (*infml*) mother

ma'am /mæm; mɑːm/ *n* [sing] **1** (*US*) used as a polite way of addressing a woman **2** (*GB*) = MADAM

mac (*also* **mack**) /mæk/ *n* (*GB, infml*) short for MACKINTOSH

macabre /mə'kɑːbrə/ *adj* unpleasant and strange because connected with death

macaroni /ˌmækə'rəʊni/ *n* [U] pasta in the form of hollow tubes

mace /meɪs/ *n* **1** [C] ornamental stick carried by an official as a sign of authority **2** [U] dried outer covering of nutmegs, used in cooking as a spice

mach /mɑːk; mæk/ *n* [U] measurement of speed, used esp for aircraft: *M~ 2* (= twice the speed of sound)

machete /məˈʃeti/ n broad heavy knife

machine /məˈʃiːn/ n 1 piece of equipment with moving parts that uses power to perform a particular task 2 group of people that control an organization: *the party* ~ ● **machine** v [T] (tech) make sth with a machine ■ **ma'chine-gun** n gun that automatically fires many bullets one after the other very quickly ■ **ma,chine-'readable** adj (of data) in a form that a computer can understand ▸ **machinery** n [U] 1 machines as a group 2 moving parts of a machine 3 system of methods or organization of sth: *the ~ of government* ■ **ma'chine tool** n tool for cutting or shaping metal, wood, etc, driven by a machine ▸ **machinist** n person who operates a machine

macho /ˈmætʃəʊ/ adj (usu disapprov) male in an aggressive way

mackerel /ˈmækrəl/ n (pl **mackerel**) striped sea fish, eaten as food

mackintosh /ˈmækɪntɒʃ/ n (GB) coat made of rainproof material

mad /mæd/ adj (~der, ~dest) 1 mentally ill 2 (infml) very stupid; crazy 3 ~(at) (infml, esp US) angry with sb: *You're driving me ~!* 4 ~(about/on) liking sth very much: *He's ~ about football.* 5 wild and excited: *in a ~ rush* [IDM] **like crazy/mad** (infml) very fast, hard, much, etc **mad keen (on sth/sb)** (infml) very enthusiastic about sth/sb ■ **mad 'cow disease** n [U] (infml) = BSE ▸ **madly** adv 1 in a way that shows a lack of control: *rush about* ~*ly* 2 (infml) extremely: ~*ly in love* ■ **'madman** | **'madwoman** n person who is mentally ill ▸ **madness** n [U]

madam /ˈmædəm/ n [sing] (fml) used when speaking or writing to a woman in a formal or business situation

madden /ˈmædn/ v [T] make sb very angry

made pt, pp of MAKE¹

madonna /məˈdɒnə/ n 1 **the Madonna** [sing] the Virgin Mary, mother of Jesus Christ 2 (**madonna**) [C] picture or statue of the Virgin Mary

madrigal /ˈmædrɪɡl/ n song for several singers, usu without musical instruments, popular in the 16th century

maestro /ˈmaɪstrəʊ/ n (pl ~s) great performer, esp a musician

magazine /ˌmæɡəˈziːn/ n 1 weekly or monthly paper-covered publication with articles, stories, etc 2 part of a gun that holds the bullets

magenta /məˈdʒentə/ adj reddish-purple in colour ● **magenta** n [U]

maggot /ˈmæɡət/ n creature like a short worm that is the young form of a fly

magic /ˈmædʒɪk/ n [U] 1 secret power of appearing to make impossible things happen by saying special words, etc 2 art of doing tricks that seem impossible to entertain people 3 special quality that sb/sth has, that seems too wonderful to be real: *the ~ of the circus* ● **magic** adj 1 used in or using magic 2 (infml) wonderful ▸ **magical** /-kl/ adj containing or using magic; wonderful ▸ **magically** /-kli/ adv

magician /məˈdʒɪʃn/ n person who can do magic tricks

magistrate /ˈmædʒɪstreɪt/ n official who acts as a judge in the lowest courts of law

magnanimous /mæɡˈnænɪməs/ adj generous ▸ **magnanimity** /ˌmæɡnəˈnɪməti/ n [U] ▸ **magnanimously** adv

magnate /ˈmæɡneɪt/ n wealthy and powerful person, esp in business

magnesium /mæɡˈniːziəm/ n [U] (symb **Mg**) silver-white metal

magnet /ˈmæɡnət/ n [C] 1 piece of iron that attracts other metal objects towards it 2 [usu sing] person, place or thing that sb/sth is attracted to ▸ **magnetic** /mæɡˈnetɪk/ adj 1 having the qualities of a magnet 2 that people find very powerful and attractive ▸ **magnetically** /-kli/ adv ■ **mag,netic 'north** n [U] direction to which the needle on a compass points ■ **mag,netic 'tape** n [U] plastic tape on which sound, pictures or computer data can be recorded ▸ **magnetism** /ˈmæɡnətɪzəm/ n 1 physical property (= characteristic) of some metals, eg iron, that causes forces between objects, either pulling them together or pushing them apart 2 great personal attraction ▸ **magnetize** (also **-ise**) v [T] make sth magnetic

magnificent /mæɡˈnɪfɪsnt/ adj extremely attractive and impressive ▸ **magnificence** /-sns/ n [U] ▸ **magnificently** adv

magnify /ˈmæɡnɪfaɪ/ v (pt, pp **-ied**) [T] 1 make sth look bigger than it really is 2 exaggerate sth: ~ *the dangers* ▸ **magnification** /ˌmæɡnɪfɪˈkeɪʃn/ n [U] process or act of making sth look larger ■ **'magnifying glass** n lens for making objects look bigger than they really are

magnitude /ˈmæɡnɪtjuːd/ n 1 (fml) great size of sth 2 (degree of) importance of sth

magpie /ˈmæɡpaɪ/ n noisy black and white bird that likes to collect bright objects

mahogany /mə'hɒgəni/ n [U] dark brown wood used for making furniture

maid /meɪd/ n female servant in a house or hotel

maiden /'meɪdn/ n (lit) young unmarried woman ● **maiden** adj being the first of its kind: a ship's ~ voyage ■ **maiden name** n woman's family name before marriage

mail /meɪl/ n [U] 1 official system used for sending and delivering letters, packages, etc 2 letters, packages, etc that are sent and delivered by post ● **mail** v [T] (esp US) send sth to sb by post ■ **mailbox** n 1 (US) = LETTER BOX(2) (LETTER) 2 (US) = POSTBOX (POST) 3 area of a computer's memory where electronic mail messages are stored ■ **mailman** n (US) = POSTMAN (POST) ■ **mail order** n [U] system of buying and selling goods through the mail ■ **mailshot** n advertising that is sent to a large number of number of people at the same time by mail

maim /meɪm/ v [T] injure sb so seriously that some part of the body cannot be used

main¹ /meɪn/ adj being the largest or most important of its kind: the ~ purpose of the meeting ■ **mainframe** (also ,mainframe com'puter) n large powerful computer, usu the centre of a network and shared by many users ■ **mainland** n [sing] (the mainland) main area of land of a country, not including any islands near to it ▶ **mainly** adv chiefly ■ **mainspring** n 1 (written) most important part of sth or influence on sth 2 most important spring in a clock or watch ■ **mainstay** n chief support; foundation ■ **mainstream** n [sing] group of commonly accepted ideas and opinions about a subject

main² /meɪn/ n 1 [C] large pipe supplying water or gas, or large wire supplying electricity, to a building 2 (the mains) [pl] (GB) source of supply of water, gas or electricity to a building [IDM] **in the main** generally

maintain /meɪn'teɪn/ v [T] 1 make sth continue at the same level, standard, etc: ~ peaceful relations 2 keep a building, machine, etc in good condition: ~ a car 3 keep stating that sth is true: ~ your innocence 4 support sb/sth with money ▶ **maintenance** /'meɪntənəns/ n [U] 1 act of keeping sth in good condition 2 act of making a state or situation continue 3 (GB, law) money that you are legally required to pay to support sb

maisonette /,meɪzə'net/ n (GB) flat on two floors that is part of a larger building

maize /meɪz/ n [U] tall plant grown for its large yellow grains that are used for making flour or eaten as a vegetable

majesty /'mædʒəsti/ n (pl -ies) 1 [U] (written) impressive and attractive quality that sth has 2 (His/Her/Your Majesty) [C] title of respect used when speaking to or about a king or queen ▶ **majestic** /mə'dʒestɪk/ adj ▶ **majestically** /-kli/ adv

major /'meɪdʒə(r)/ adj very large or important: a ~ road ● **major** n (abbr Maj.) officer of fairly high rank in the army or the US air force ● **major** v [PV] **major in sth** (US) study sth as your main subject at college or university

majority /mə'dʒɒrəti/ n (pl -ies) 1 [sing, with sing or pl verb] ~(of) largest part of a group of people or things 2 [C] number by which votes for one side are more than those for the other side: win by a ~ of 9 votes 3 [U] (law) age at which you are legally considered to be an adult

make¹ /meɪk/ v (pt, pp made /meɪd/) 1 [T] construct, produce or prepare sth; bring sth into existence: ~ bread 2 [T] cause sth to exist, happen or be done: ~ a lot of noise ◇ ~ trouble 3 [T] cause sb/sth to be or become sth: The news made her happy. 4 [T] cause sb/sth to do sth: He ~ s me laugh. ◇ ~ sb jump 5 [T] force sb to do sth: Her parents ~ her study hard. 6 [T] elect or choose sb as sth: They made me the manager. 7 linking verb become or develop into sth: She will ~ a brilliant doctor. 8 linking verb add up to or equal sth: Two and two ~ four. 9 [T] earn or gain money: ~ a profit 10 [T] think or calculate sth to be sth: What do you ~ the time? 11 [T] manage to reach or go to a place or position: We didn't ~ Dover by 12 o'clock. [IDM] **make as if to do sth** (written) make a movement that makes it seem that you are going to do sth: She made as if to hit him. **make do (with sth)** manage with sth which is not really adequate **make it** (infml) 1 be successful in your career 2 succeed in reaching a place in time, esp when this is difficult 3 be able to be present at a place: Thanks for inviting us, but I'm afraid we won't be able to ~ it on Saturday. 4 survive after an illness, accident or difficult situation: The doctors think he's going to ~ it. **make up ground (on sb/sth)** → GROUND² **make for sb/sth 1** move towards sb/sth 2 help to make sth possible: Does exercise ~ for good health? **make sb/sth into sb/sth** change sb/sth into sb/sth: ~ the attic into a bedroom **make sth of sb/sth**

understand sb/sth: *What do you ~ of this sentence?* **make off** hurry away, esp to escape **make off with** steal sth and escape with it **make out** (*infml*) **1** manage: *How are you ~ing out in your new job?* **2** (US) kiss and touch sb in a sexual way **make sb/sth out 1** manage to see sb/sth or read or hear sth: *I can't ~ out his writing.* **2** understand sb/sth: *I just can't ~ her out.* **make sth out 1** say that sth is true when it may not be: *He ~s himself out to be cleverer than he is.* **2** write out or complete a form or document: ~ *out a cheque* **make (sth/yourself) up** put cosmetics on your/sb's face **make sth up 1** form sth: *Women ~ up 56% of the student numbers.* **2** put sth together from several different things **3** invent a story, esp in order to deceive: *She made up an excuse.* **4** complete a number or an amount required: *We need £5 to ~ up the sum.* **5** prepare a bed for use **make up (for sth) make up to sb (for sth)** compensate for sth **make up to sb** (*GB, infml, disapprov*) be pleasant to sb in order to get sth **make up (with sb)** (*GB also* **make it up**) end a quarrel with sb and become friends again ■ **'make-believe** *n* [U] imagining or pretending: *a world of ~belief* ■ **'make-up** *n* **1** [U] cosmetics **2** [sing] different qualities that combine to form a person's character **3** [sing] different things, people, etc that combine to form sth: *the ~-up of the new committee*

make² /meɪk/ *n* ~(of) named kind of product: *What ~ of car does he drive?* [IDM] **on the make** (*infml, disapprov*) trying to gain money or an advantage for yourself

maker /'meɪkə(r)/ *n* **1** [C] person, company, etc that makes or produces sth: *a decision/law ~* **2** (**the, his, your, etc Maker**) [sing] God

makeshift /'meɪkʃɪft/ *adj* used for a time because there is nothing better

making /'meɪkɪŋ/ *n* [U] act or process of making or producing sth [IDM] **be the making of sb** cause sb to succeed in or develop well **have the makings of sth** have the qualities needed to become sth

maladjusted /ˌmælə'dʒʌstɪd/ *adj* having mental and emotional problems that lead to unacceptable behaviour ► **maladjustment** /-mənt/ *n* [U]

malaria /mə'leəriə/ *n* [U] serious fever caught from mosquito bites

male /meɪl/ *adj* **1** belonging to the sex that does not give birth **2** (*biol*) (of a plant) having flowers with parts that produce pollen **3** (*tech*) (of electrical plugs, parts of tools, etc) having a part that sticks out

and is designed to fit into a hole, socket, etc ● **male** *n* male person or animal ■ **‚male 'chauvinism** *n* [U] (*disapprov*) belief held by some men that men are superior to women ■ **‚male 'chauvinist** *n* (*disapprov*) man who believes men are superior to women

malevolent /mə'levələnt/ *adj* (*fml*) wishing to do evil or cause harm to others ► **malevolence** /-əns/ *n* [U] ► **malevolently** *adv*

malformation /ˌmælfɔː'meɪʃn/ *n* [U,C] (state of having a) part of the body that is not formed correctly ► **malformed** /ˌmælˈfɔːmd/ *adj*

malfunction /ˌmælˈfʌŋkʃn/ *v* [I] (*fml*) (of a machine) fail to work correctly ► **malfunction** *n* [C,U]

malice /'mælɪs/ *n* [U] desire to harm other people ► **malicious** /mə'lɪʃəs/ *adj* ► **maliciously** *adv*

malignant /mə'lɪgnənt/ *adj* **1** (of a tumour or disease) serious and likely to cause death **2** (*fml*) having a great desire to harm others

mall /mɔːl; *GB also* mæl/ *n* (*esp US*) = SHOPPING MALL (SHOP)

malleable /'mæliəbl/ *adj* **1** (*tech*) (of metals) that can be beaten or pressed into new shapes **2** (of people, ideas, etc) easily influenced or changed

mallet /'mælɪt/ *n* hammer with a wooden head

malnourished /ˌmælˈnʌrɪʃt/ *adj* in bad health because of a lack of (the right kind of) food

malnutrition /ˌmælnjuˈtrɪʃn/ *n* [U] condition caused by a lack of (the right kind of) food

malt /mɔːlt/ *n* [U] grain, esp barley, used for making beer, whisky, etc

maltreat /ˌmælˈtriːt/ *v* [T] (*written*) be very cruel to a person or animal ► **maltreatment** *n* [U]

mama (*also* **mamma**) /'mæmə/ *n* (US) mother

mamba /'mæmbə/ *n* black or green poisonous snake

mammal /'mæml/ *n* any animal that gives birth to live babies, not eggs, and feeds its young on milk

mammoth /'mæməθ/ *n* large hairy kind of elephant, now extinct ● **mammoth** *adj* (*infml*) extremely large

man¹ /mæn/ *n* (*pl* **men** /men/) **1** [C] adult male human being **2** [U] human beings as a group: *the origins of ~* **3** [C] (*lit, old-fash*) person, either male or female: *All men must die.* **4** [C] man who comes from the place mentioned or whose job or interest is connected with the thing mentioned: *a French~* ◇ *a business~* **5** [C,*usu pl*] soldier or male worker under the authority of sb of higher rank: *officers and men* **6** [sing] (*infml spoken, esp US*) used for addressing a male person? *What's her new ~ like?* **8** [C] male person with the qualities of strength, courage, etc associated with men: *Don't give up - be a ~!* **9** [C] piece used in a game such as chess [IDM] **be your own man/ woman** act or think independently, not following others **the man (and/ or woman) in the street** the average person **man to man** between two men who are treating each other honestly and equally **to a man | to the last man** (*written*) all, without exception ■ **'manhole** *n* hole in the street that is covered with a lid, through which sb enters an underground drain, etc ▶ **manhood** *n* [U] state or qualities of being a man ■ **man-'made** *adj* made by people; artificial ■ **'manpower** *n* [U] number of people needed or available to do a job ■ **'manslaughter** *n* [U] (*law*) crime of killing sb unintentionally

man² /mæn/ *v* (*-nn-*) [T] work at a place or in charge of a place or machine; supply people to work somewhere: *Soldiers ~ned barricades around the city.*

manacle /'mænəkl/ *n* [C, usu pl] one of a pair of chains for tying a prisoner's hands or feet ● **manacle** *v* [T] tie up sb with manacles

manage /'mænɪdʒ/ *v* **1** [I, T] succeed in doing sth, esp with difficulty: *How did the prisoners ~ to escape?* **2** [I] be able to solve your problems, deal with a difficult situation, etc **3** [I] be able to live without having enough money: *I can only just ~ on my wages.* **4** [T] use money, time, information, etc in a sensible way **5** [T] control or be in charge of sth ▶ **manageable** *adj* that can be dealt with ■ **,managing di'rector** *n* (*abbr* MD) (*esp GB*) person who is in charge of a business

management /'mænɪdʒmənt/ *n* **1** [U] act of running or controlling a business, etc: *problems caused by bad ~* **2** [C, with sing or pl verb] people who manage a business, etc: *workers and ~* **3** [U] (*fml*) act or skill of dealing with people or situations successfully

manager /'mænɪdʒə(r)/ *n* person who organizes a business, sports team, etc ▶ **manageress** /,mænɪdʒə-'res/ *n* woman who is in charge of a business, etc ▶ **managerial** /,mænə-'dʒɪəriəl/ *adj* of managers

mandate /'mændeɪt/ *n* [C, usu sing] authority given to a government, trade union, etc by the people who support it ▶ **mandatory** /'mæn-

dətəri; mæn'deɪtəri/ *adj* (*fml*) required by law

mandolin /ˌmændəlɪn; ˌmændə'lɪn/ *n* musical instrument with eight metal strings

mane /meɪn/ *n* long hair on the neck of a horse or lion

maneuver (*US*) = MANOEUVRE

manfully /'mænfəli/ *adj* using a lot of effort in a brave and determined way

manger /'meɪndʒə(r)/ *n* long open box that horses or cattle can eat from

mangle /'mæŋgl/ *v* [T] (usu passive) cut or twist sth so that it is badly damaged

mango /'mæŋgəʊ/ *n* [C,U] (*pl ~es*) tropical fruit with soft orange flesh and a large stone inside

mangy /'meɪndʒi/ *adj* (*-ier, -iest*) with patches of hair, fur, etc missing; shabby

manhandle /'mænhændl/ *v* [T] **1** push, pull or handle sb roughly **2** move a heavy object using a lot of effort

mania /'meɪniə/ *n* **1** [C, usu sing, U] ~ (*for*) extremely strong desire or enthusiasm for sth **2** [U] mental illness ▶ **maniac** /-niæk/ *n* **1** (*infml*) mad person **2** person with an extremely strong desire or enthusiasm for sth ▶ **maniacal** /mə-'naɪəkl/ *adj* violent or violent

manicure /'mænɪkjʊə(r)/ *n* [C,U] care and treatment of a person's hands and nails ● **manicure** *v* [T] care for and treat your hands and nails ▶ **manicurist** *n*

manifest /'mænɪfest/ *adj* (*fml*) clear and obvious ● **manifest** *v* [T] (*fml*) show sth clearly: *The disease ~ed itself.* ▶ **manifestation** /ˌmænɪfe-'steɪʃn/ *n* [C,U] ▶ **manifestly** *adv*

manifesto /ˌmænɪ'festəʊ/ *n* (*pl ~s*) written statement of a groups beliefs and plans, esp of a political party

manifold /'mænɪfəʊld/ *adj* (*fml*) many; of many different types ● **manifold** *n* (*tech*) pipe or enclosed space with several openings for taking gases in and out of a car engine

manipulate /mə'nɪpjuleɪt/ *v* [T] **1** control or influence sb/sth, esp in a dishonest way **2** control or use sth in a skilful way ▶ **manipulation** /mə,nɪpju'leɪʃn/ *n* [C,U] ▶ **manipulative** /-lətɪv/ *adj*

mankind /mæn'kaɪnd/ *n* [U] the human race

manly /'mænli/ *adj* (*-ier, -iest*) (*approv*) having the qualities or appearance expected of a man ▶ **manliness** *n* [U]

manner /ˈmænə(r)/ n **1** [sing] (fml) way in which sth is done or happens: in a friendly ~ **2** [sing] person's way of behaving towards others: I don't like your ~. **3** (manners) [pl] polite social behaviour: to have good ~s [IDM] all manner of sb/sth (fml) many different types of people or things **in a manner of speaking** to some extent: If considered in a certain way ▶ **-mannered** (in compound adjectives) having manners of the kind stated: well ~ed

mannerism /ˈmænərɪzəm/ n particular way of speaking or behaving that sb has

manoeuvre (US **maneuver**) /məˈnuːvə(r)/ n **1** [C] movement performed with skill **2** [C,U] clever plan, action or movement, used to give sb an advantage **3** (manoeuvres) [pl] military exercises involving a large number of soldiers, ships, etc ● **manoeuvre** (US **maneuver**) v **1** [I, T] (cause sth to) move or turn skilfully **2** [T] control or influence a situation in a skilful but sometimes dishonest way ▶ **manoeuvrable** (US **maneuverable**) adj that can easily be moved into different positions

manor /ˈmænə(r)/ (also ˈ**manor house**) n large country house surrounded by land that belongs to it

mansion /ˈmænʃn/ n large grand house

mantelpiece /ˈmæntlpiːs/ n shelf above a fireplace

mantle /ˈmæntl/ n **1** [sing] ~of (lit) the responsibilities of an important job: take on the ~ of supreme power **2** [C] (lit) layer: a ~ of snow **3** [C] loose piece of clothing without sleeves, worn over other clothes, esp in the past

manual /ˈmænjuəl/ adj of, done with or controlled by the hands ● **manual** n book giving practical information or instructions ▶ **manually** adv

manufacture /ˌmænjuˈfæktʃə(r)/ v [T] make or produce goods in large quantities, using machinery ● **manufacture** n [U] process of producing goods in large quantities ▶ **manufacturer** n

manure /məˈnjuə(r)/ n [U] animal waste matter spread over the soil to help plants to grow

manuscript /ˈmænjuskrɪpt/ n **1** copy of a book, piece of music, etc before it has been printed **2** old handwritten book

many /ˈmeni/ det, pron **1** a large number of people or things: ~ people ◇ not ~ of the students ◇ I've known him for a great ~ (= very many) years. **2** (**many a**) (used with

a singular noun and v) a large number of: ~ a mother (= many mothers) [IDM] **have had one too many** (infml) be slightly drunk

map /mæp/ n drawing or plan of (part of) the earth's surface, showing countries, towns, rivers, etc [IDM] **put sth/sb on the map** make sb/sth famous or important ● **map** v (**-pp-**) [T] make a map of an area

mar /mɑː(r)/ v (**-rr-**) [T] (fml) damage or spoil sth good: a mistake that ~red his career

marathon /ˈmærəθən/ n long running race of about 42 kilometres or 26 miles ● **marathon** adj very long and needing a lot of effort: a ~ task

marauding /məˈrɔːdɪŋ/ adj (written) (of people or animals) going about searching for things to steal or people to attack ▶ **marauder**

marble /ˈmɑːbl/ n **1** [U] kind of hard stone, used, when cut and polished, for building and sculpture **2** [C] small ball of coloured glass that children roll along the ground in a game **3** (marbles) [U] game played with marbles

March /mɑːtʃ/ n [U,C] the third month of the year (See examples of use at **April**.)

march /mɑːtʃ/ v **1** [I] walk as soldiers do, with regular steps **2** [T] force sb to walk somewhere with you: They ~ed the prisoner away. ● **march** n **1** [C] organized walk by many people from one place to another, esp as a protest **2** [C] act of marching; journey made by marching **3** [sing] ~of the steady progress of sth: the ~ of time **4** [C] piece of music for marching to: a funeral ~

marchioness /ˌmɑːʃəˈnes/ n **1** woman with the same rank as a marquess **2** wife of a marquess

mare /meə(r)/ n female horse or donkey

margarine /ˌmɑːdʒəˈriːn/ n [U] food like butter, made from animal or vegetable fats

margin /ˈmɑːdʒɪn/ n **1** [C] empty space at the side or a written or printed page **2** [C,usu sing] amount of votes, time, etc by which sb wins sth: He won by a narrow ~. **3** [C] (business) = PROFIT MARGIN (PROFIT): a gross ~ of 45% **4** [C] amount of space, time, etc allowed for success or safety ▶ **marginal** /-nl/ adj small and not important: a ~al increase ▶ **marginally** /-nəli/ adv

marijuana /ˌmærəˈwɑːnə/ n [U] a drug (illegal in many countries) made from the dried leaves and flowers of the hemp plant, which is usu smoked

marina /məˈriːnə/ n small harbour for yachts and small boats

marinade /ˌmærɪˈneɪd/ n [C,U] mixture of oil, wine, herbs, etc in which meat or fish is soaked before being cooked

marinate /ˈmærɪneɪt/ (also **marin-ade**) v [I, T] (leave food to) soak in a mixture of oil, wine, herbs, etc before cooking it

marine /məˈriːn/ adj 1 of the sea and the creatures and plants that live in it: ~ life 2 of ships or trade at sea ● **marine** n soldier trained to fight on land or at sea

marionette /ˌmæriəˈnet/ n puppet moved by strings

marital /ˈmærɪtl/ adj of marriage

maritime /ˈmærɪtaɪm/ adj 1 of the sea or ships 2 (fml) near the sea

mark¹ /mɑːk/ n 1 stain, spot, etc esp that spoils the appearance of sth: dirty ~s on my shirt 2 spot or area on the body of a person or animal which helps to recognize them: a birth~ 3 written or printed symbol: punctuation ~s 4 sign that a quality or feeling exists: a ~ of respect 5 (esp GB) number or letter given to show the standard of sb's work or performance: get top ~s 6 (esp GB) model or type of a machine, etc: a M~ II engine [IDM] **make your/a mark (on sth)** become famous and successful in sth **quick/slow off the mark** fast/slow in reacting to a situation **up to the mark** as good as it/they should be

mark² /mɑːk/ v 1 [T] write or draw a symbol, line, etc on sth to give information about it: documents ~ed 'secret' 2 [I, T] (cause sth to) become spoilt or damaged: You've ~ed the table. ◇ The carpet ~s easily. 3 [T] show the position of sth or be a sign of sth: This cross ~s the place where she died. ◇ His death ~ed the end of an era. 4 [T] (esp GB) give marks to students' work 5 [T] give sb/sth a particular quality or character 6 [T] (sport) stay close to an opposing player to prevent them from getting the ball [IDM] **mark time** pass the time while you wait for sth more interesting [PV] **mark sth down/up** reduce/increase the price of sth **mark sth off** separate sth by drawing a line between it and sth else **mark sth out** draw lines to show the edges of sth **mark sb out as/for sth** make people recognize sb as special in some way ▶ **marked** adj easy to see; noticeable: a ~ed improvement ▶ **markedly** /ˈmɑːkɪdli/ adv ▶ **marker** n 1 object or sign that shows the position of sth or that sth exists 2 pen with a thick felt tip 3 (GB) person who marks examination, etc papers

▶ **marking** n 1 [usu pl] pattern of colours or marks on animals, birds or wood 2 [usu pl] lines, colours or shapes painted on roads, vehicles, etc 3 [U] activity of correcting students' exams or written work ■ **mark-up** n [C, usu sing] amount that a seller adds to a price

market /ˈmɑːkɪt/ n 1 [C] (public place for a) meeting of people in order to buy and sell goods 2 [sing] business or trade, or the amount of trade in a particular type of goods: The coffee ~ was steady. 3 [C] particular area or country in which goods might be sold: the global/domestic ~ 4 [sing] ~(for) demand: a good ~ for cars 5 (the market) [sing] people who buy and sell goods in competition with each other [IDM] **in the market for sth** interested in buying sth **on the market** available for people to buy: a product not yet on the ~ ● **market** v [T] advertise and offer a product for sale ▶ **marketable** adj easy to sell; attractive to customers or employers ■ **market 'garden** n (GB) type of farm where vegetables are grown for sale ▶ **marketing** n [U] part of business concerned with the advertising, selling, etc of a company's products ■ **'marketplace** n 1 (the marketplace) [sing] activity of buying and selling goods, services, etc 2 [C] open area in a town where a market is held ■ **market re'search** n [U] study of what people buy and use ■ **market 'share** n [U, sing] (business) amount that a company sells of its products or services compared with the competition

marksman /ˈmɑːksmən/ n (pl -men /-mən/) person skilled in shooting accurately

marmalade /ˈmɑːməleɪd/ n [U] kind of jam made from oranges

maroon /məˈruːn/ adj, n (of a) dark brownish-red colour ● **maroon** n [T] leave sb in a place that they cannot escape from

marquee /mɑːˈkiː/ n very large tent

marquess (also **marquis**) /ˈmɑːkwɪs/ n (in Britain) nobleman of high rank

marriage /ˈmærɪdʒ/ n [U,C] legal union of a man and woman as husband and wife

marrow /ˈmærəʊ/ n 1 [U] = BONE MARROW (BONE) 2 [C,U] (GB) very large oval vegetable with white flesh and stripy green skin

marry /ˈmæri/ v (pt, pp -ied) 1 [I, T] become the husband or wife of sb; get married to sb 2 [T] perform a ceremony in which a man and a woman become husband and wife: Which priest is going to ~ them? 3 [T] find a husband or wife for sb, esp your son or daughter ▶ **married** *adj* **1** (*abbr* **m**) ~(**to**) having a husband or wife **2** of marriage: *married life*

marsh /mɑːʃ/ *n* **1** area of low land that is soft and wet ▶ **marshy** *adj* (**-ier, -iest**)

marshal /ˈmɑːʃl/ *n* **1** officer of the highest rank in the British air force or army **2** official who organizes a public event, esp a sports event **3** (*US*) officer whose job is to carry out court orders ● **marshal** *v* (**-ll-** *US* **-l-**) [T] **1** gather together and organize the people or things that you need for a particular purpose **2** control or organize a large group of people

marsupial /mɑːˈsuːpiəl/ *adj, n* (of an) Australian animal, eg a kangaroo, the female of which has a pouch on its body to hold its young

martial /ˈmɑːʃl/ *adj* (*fml*) of fighting or war ■ **martial 'art** *n* [*usu pl*] fighting sport such as judo and karate ■ **martial 'law** *n* [U] situation where the army of a country controls an area rather than the police

martyr /ˈmɑːtə(r)/ *n* person who dies or suffers for their religious or political beliefs ● **martyr** *v* [T] kill sb because of their religious or political beliefs ▶ **martyrdom** /ˈmɑːtədəm/ *n* [U,C] suffering or death of a martyr

marvel /ˈmɑːvl/ *n* wonderful thing: *the ~s of modern science* ● **marvel** *v* (**-ll-** *US* **-l-**) [I] ~(**at**) (*fml*) be very surprised at sth ▶ **marvellous** (*US* **-velous**) /ˈmɑːvələs/ *adj* excellent; wonderful ▶ **marvellously** (*US* **-velously**) *adv*

Marxism /ˈmɑːksɪzəm/ *n* [U] political and economic theories of Karl Marx, on which Communism is based ▶ **Marxist** /-sɪst/ *n, adj*

marzipan /ˈmɑːzɪpæn/ *n* [U] thick paste of crushed almonds, sugar, etc

mascara /mæˈskɑːrə/ *n* [U] colour for darkening the eyelashes

mascot /ˈmæskət; -skɒt/ *n* thing, animal or person thought to bring good luck

masculine /ˈmæskjəlɪn/ *adj* **1** of like men **2** (*gram*) belonging to a particular class of nouns, pronouns, etc ▶ **masculinity** /ˌmæskju-ˈlɪnəti/ *n* [U] quality of being masculine

mash /mæʃ/ *v* [T] ~(**up**) crush food into a soft mass: *M~ the banana with a fork.* ● **mash** *n* [U] (*GB*) mashed potatoes

mask /mɑːsk/ *n* covering for part or all of the face worn to hide or protect it: (*fig*) *His behaviour is really a ~ for his shyness.* ● **mask** *v* [T] hide a feeling, smell, fact, etc so that it

cannot be easily seen or noticed ▶ **masked** *adj* wearing a mask

masochism /ˈmæsəkɪzəm/ *n* [U] practice of getting esp sexual pleasure from being physically hurt ▶ **masochist** /-kɪst/ *n* ▶ **masochistic** /ˌmæsəˈkɪstɪk/ *adj*

mason /ˈmeɪsn/ *n* person who builds in or works with stone ▶ **masonry** /-sənri/ *n* [U] the parts of a building that are made of stone

masquerade /ˌmɑːskəˈreɪd/ *v* [I] ~ **as** pretend to be sth that you are not: ~ *as a police officer* ● **masquerade** *n* (*fml*) false show

Mass (*also* **mass**) /mæs/ *n* [U,C] (esp in the Roman Catholic Church) service held in memory of the last meal of Jesus Christ

mass /mæs/ *n* **1** [C] large amount of a substance that does not have a definite shape: *a ~ of earth* **2** [*sing*] large number of: ~ *of tourists* **3** (**masses**) [*pl*] ~(**of**) (*infml*) large number or amount of sth **4** (**the masses**) [*pl*] ordinary working people **5** [U] (*physics*) amount of matter in an object ● **mass** *v* [I, T] come together or gather sb/sth together in large numbers: *The general ~ed his troops.* ■ **the mass 'media** *n* [*pl*] television, newspapers, etc ■ **mass-pro'duce** *v* [T] produce goods in very large quantities ■ **mass pro'duction** *n* [U]

massacre /ˈmæsəkə(r)/ *n* cruel killing of a large number of people ● **massacre** *v* [T] kill a large number of people cruelly

massage /ˈmæsɑːʒ/ *n* [C,U] (act of) rubbing and pressing sb's body, esp to reduce pain in the muscles or joints ● **massage** *v* [T] give a massage to sb

masseur /mæˈsɜː(r)/ *n* (*fem* **masseuse** /mæˈsɜːz/) person whose job is to give people massage

massive /ˈmæsɪv/ *adj* extremely large ▶ **massively** *adv*

mast /mɑːst/ *n* **1** tall pole on a boat or ship that supports the sails **2** tall metal tower with an aerial that sends and receives radio or television signals

master¹ /ˈmɑːstə(r)/ *n* **1** (*old-fash*) man who has people working for him, esp as servants in his home **2** ~(*written*) person who is able to control sth **3** ~**of** (*fml*) person who is very skilled at sth **4** male owner of a dog, horse, etc **5** (*GB, old-fash*) male schoolteacher **6** (**master's**) second university degree, or, in Scotland, a first degree, such as an MA **7** (**Master**) person who has a master's degree: *a M~ of Arts/Sciences* **8** captain of a ship **9** great artist **10** film, tape, etc from which copies can be made: the ~ copy ● **master** adj **1** very skilled at the job mentioned: a ~ carpenter **2** largest and/or most important: the ~ bedroom ■ '**master-mind** n [T] plan and direct a complicated project ■ '**mastermind** n intelligent person who plans and directs a complicated project ■ ˌmaster of 'ceremonies (abbr MC) n person who introduces guests or entertainers at a formal occasion ■ '**masterpiece** n work of art, eg a painting, that is the best example of the artist's work

master² /'mɑːstə(r)/ v [T] **1** learn or understand sth completely: ~ a foreign language **2** gain control of sth

masterful /'mɑːstfl/ adj able to control people or situations confidently ▶ **masterfully** /-fəli/ adv

masterly /'mɑːstəli/ adj very skilful

mastery /'mɑːstəri/ n [U] **1** great skill or knowledge **2** control or power

masturbate /'mæstəbeɪt/ v [I] give yourself sexual pleasure by rubbing your sexual organs ▶ **masturbation** /ˌmæstə'beɪʃn/ n [U]

mat /mæt/ n **1** piece of thick material or carpet used to cover part of a floor: Wipe your feet on the ~. **2** small piece of material put under a vase, hot dish, etc to protect a table ● **mat** adj (US) = MATT

matador /'mætədɔː(r)/ n bull-fighter whose task is to kill the bull

match /mætʃ/ n **1** [C] short piece of wood or cardboard used for lighting a fire, cigarette, etc **2** [C] (esp GB) sports event where people or teams compete against each other: a football ~ **3** [sing] person who is equal to sb else in skill, strength, etc: He's no ~ for her at tennis. **4** [sing] person or thing that combines well with sth else: The carpets and curtains are a good ~. ● **match** v **1** [I, T] combine well with sth: The door was painted blue to ~ the walls. **2** [T] be equal to sb/sth **3** [T] find sb/sth to go together with another person or thing ■ '**matchbox** n box for holding matches ▶ '**matchless** adj (fml) without an equal ■ '**matchmaker** n person who likes trying to arrange marriages or relationships for others

mate /meɪt/ n **1** friend, companion or person you work with or share accommodation with: He's gone out with his ~s. ◇ a flat~ **2** (GB, infml) used as a friendly way of addressing sb, esp between men **3** either of a pair of birds or animals **4** (GB) person whose job is to help a skilled worker: a plumber's ~ **5** officer in a commercial ship below the

rank of captain ● **mate** v [I, T] ~ (with) (put birds or animals together) to have sex in order to produce young

material /mə'tɪəriəl/ n **1** [U,C] cloth used for making clothes, etc **2** [C,U] substance that things can be made from: building ~s (= bricks, sand, etc) **3** [U] information or ideas for a book, etc: ~ for a newspaper article ● **material** adj **1** connected with money, possessions, etc rather than the needs of the mind or spirit: ~ comforts **2** of the physical world rather than the mind or spirit: the ~ world **3** ~(to) (law) important: ~ evidence

materialism /mə'tɪəriəlɪzəm/ n [U] (disapprov) belief that only money, possessions, etc are important ▶ **materialist** /-lɪst/ n **material-istic** /mə,tɪəriə'lɪstɪk/ adj

materialize (also **-ise**) /mə'tɪəriəlaɪz/ v [I] **1** take place or start to exist as expected or planned **2** appear suddenly and/or in a way that cannot be explained: The train failed to ~ (= it did not come).

maternal /mə'tɜːnl/ adj **1** of or like a mother **2** related through the mother's side of the family: a ~ grandfather

maternity /mə'tɜːnəti/ n [U] state of being or becoming a mother: a ~ ward/hospital (= one where women go to give birth) ■ ma'ternity leave n [U] period of time when a woman temporarily leaves her job to have a baby

mathematics /ˌmæθə'mætɪks/ (GB also infml maths /mæθs/) (US also infml math /mæθ/) n [U] science of numbers and shapes ▶ **mathematical** /-ɪkl/ adj ▶ **mathematically** /-ɪkli/ adv ▶ **mathematician** /ˌmæθəmə'tɪʃn/ n student of or expert in mathematics

matinee (also **matinée**) /'mætɪneɪ/ n afternoon performance of a play or film

matriarch /'meɪtriɑːk/ n woman who is the head of a family or social group ▶ **matriarchal** /-'ɑːkl/ adj

matriculate /mə'trɪkjuleɪt/ v [I] (fml) officially become a student at a university ▶ **matriculation** /mə,trɪkju'leɪʃn/ n

matrimony /'mætrɪməni/ n [U] (fml) state of being married ▶ **matrimonial** /ˌmætrɪ'məʊniəl/ adj

matrix /'meɪtrɪks/ n (pl matrices /'meɪtrɪsiːz/) **1** (maths) arrangement of numbers, symbols, etc in rows and columns, treated as a single quantity **2** (fml) formal social, political, etc situation from which a society or person grows or develops **3** (*tech*) mould in which sth is shaped **4** (*computing*) group of electronic circuit elements arranged in rows and columns like a grid **5** (*geol*) stratum of rock in which minerals, etc are found in the ground

matron /ˈmeɪtrən/ *n* **1** (*GB*) woman who works as a nurse in a school **2** (*GB*) (in the past) senior female nurse in charge of other nurses in a hospital **3** (*old-fash*) older married woman ▶ **matronly** *adj* (*disapprov*) (of a woman) no longer young, and rather fat

matt (*US* **mat** *also* **matte**) /mæt/ *adj* (of surfaces) not shiny

matted /ˈmætɪd/ *adj* (of hair, etc) forming a thick mass, esp because it is wet and dirty

matter¹ /ˈmætə(r)/ *n* **1** [C] affair or subject: *an important business ~* **2** (**matters**) [pl] the present situation: *To make ~s worse, I couldn't find my keys.* **3** (**the matter**) [sing] ~ (**with**) used (to ask) if sb is upset, etc or if there is a problem: *What's the ~ with her?* ◇ *Is anything the ~?* **4** [sing] situation that involves sth or depends on sth: *It's simply a ~ of letting people know in time.* ◇ *Well, that's a ~ of opinion* (= others may think differently). **5** [U] (*tech*) physical substance that everything in the world is made of **6** [U] substance or material of the kind that is mentioned: *reading ~* (= books, newspapers, etc) [IDM] **as a matter of fact** (*used for emphasis*) in reality **for that matter** (*spoken*) used to add a comment on sth you have just said (**as a matter of course** the usual and correct thing that is done **a matter of hours, minutes, etc** only a few hours, minutes, etc **no matter who, what, where, etc** used to say that sth is always true, whatever the situation is: *They don't last no ~ how careful you are.* ■ **matter-of-fact** *adj* said or done without showing any emotion

matter² /ˈmætə(r)/ *v* [I] be important or have an important effect on sb/sth: *It doesn't ~.*

matting /ˈmætɪŋ/ *n* [U] rough woven material used as a floor covering

mattress /ˈmætrəs/ *n* soft part of a bed, that you lie on

mature /məˈtjʊə(r)/ *adj* **1** (of a child or young person) behaving in a sensible way, like an adult **2** (of a person, a tree, a bird or an animal) fully grown and developed **3** (of wine or cheese) having reached its full flavour **4** (*business*) (of an insurance policy) ready to be paid

● **mature** *v* [I, T] become or make sth mature ▶ **maturity** *n* [U]

maul /mɔːl/ *v* [T] hurt sb by rough or cruel handling: *be ~ed by a lion*

mausoleum /ˌmɔːsəˈliːəm/ *n* special building made to hold the dead body of an important person or a family

mauve /məʊv/ *adj, n* [U] (of a) pale purple colour

maxim /ˈmæksɪm/ *n* saying that expresses a general truth or rule of behaviour

maximize (*also* **-ise**) /ˈmæksɪmaɪz/ *v* [T] **1** increase sth as much as possible **2** make the best use of sth

maximum /ˈmæksɪməm/ *n* [C, usu sing] greatest possible amount: *the ~ load a lorry can carry* ● **maximum** *adj* as large, fast, etc as is possible or the most that is possible or allowed

May /meɪ/ *n* [U, C] the fifth month of the year (See examples of use at **April**.)

may /meɪ/ *modal v* (*neg* **may not**) (*pt* **might** /maɪt/ *neg* **might not** *short form* **mightn't** /ˈmaɪtnt/) **1** used to say that sth is possible: *This coat ~ be Sarah's.* ◇ *He ~ have* (= Perhaps he has) *forgotten to come.* **2** (*fml*) used to ask for or give permission: *M~ I sit down?* **3** (*fml*) used to express wishes and hopes: *M~ you both be very happy!*

maybe /ˈmeɪbi/ *adv* perhaps

mayonnaise /ˌmeɪəˈneɪz/ *n* [U] thick creamy sauce made from eggs, oil and vinegar, and eaten with salads

mayor /meə(r)/ *n* head, usu elected yearly, of a city or town council ▶ **mayoress** /ˈmeəres/ *n* **1** woman who has been elected mayor **2** wife of a mayor

maze /meɪz/ *n* system of paths in a park or garden that is designed so that it is difficult to find your way through

MB (*also* **Mb**) *abbr* = MEGABYTE

MC /ˌem ˈsiː/ *abbr* **1** = MASTER OF CEREMONIES (**MASTER**) **2** (**M.C.**) (*US*) Member of Congress

MD /ˌem ˈdiː/ *abbr* **1** Doctor of Medicine **2** = MANAGING DIRECTOR (**MANAGE**)

me /miː/ *pron* (used as the object of a *v* or *prep*) person who is the speaker or writer: *Don't hit me.* ◇ *Give it to me.*

meadow /ˈmedəʊ/ *n* [C, U] field of grass

meagre (*US* **meager**) /ˈmiːgə(r)/ *adj* small in quantity and poor in quality: *a ~ income*

meal /miːl/ *n* **1** [C] occasion when food is eaten **2** [C] food that is eaten at a meal **3** [U] roughly crushed grain: *oat~*

mean¹ /miːn/ v (*pt, pp* **~t** /ment/) [T] **1** (of words, sentences, etc) have sth as an explanation: *What does this word ~?* ◇ *A green light ~s 'go'.* **2** have sth as a purpose; intend: *What do you ~ by coming (= Why did you come) so late?* ◇ *Sorry, I ~t to tell you earlier.* ◇ *Don't laugh! I ~it (= I am serious)!* ◇ *You're ~t to (= You are supposed to) pay before you come in.* **3** have sth as a result or a likely result: *This will ~ more work.* **4** ~ **to** be of value or importance to sb: *Your friendship ~s a lot to me.* [IDM] **mean business** be serious in your intentions **mean well** have good intentions, although their effect may not be good ▶ **meaning** n **1** [U, C] thing or idea that a word, sentence, etc represents **2** [U, C] things or ideas that sb wishes to communicate to sb others **3** [U] purpose, value or importance: *My life has lost all ~ing.* ▶ **meaningful** adj serious and important; full of meaning ▶ **meaningless** adj without meaning

mean² /miːn/ adj **1** not willing to give or share things, esp money **2** unkind **3** (*esp US*) likely to become angry or violent **4** (*tech*) average: *the ~ temperature* [IDM] **be no mean ...** (*approv*) used to say that sb is very good at sth ● **mean** n (*maths*) quantity between two extremes; average

meander /miˈændə(r)/ v [I] **1** (of a river, road, etc) curve a lot **2** wander about

means /miːnz/ n (*pl* **means**) **1** [C] method: *find a ~ of improving the standard of education* **2** [pl] money that a person has: *a man of ~ (= a rich man)* ◇ *Are the repayments within your ~ (= Can you afford them)?* ◇ *Try not to live beyond your ~ (= spend more than you earn).* [IDM] **by all means** (*spoken*) yes, of course **by means of sth** (*fml*) with the help of sth **by no means** (*fml*) not at all ■ '**means test** official check of sb's wealth or income to decide if they are poor enough to receive money from the government

meant *pt, pp* of MEAN¹

meantime /ˈmiːntaɪm/ n [IDM] **in the meantime** meanwhile ▶ **meantime** adv meanwhile

meanwhile /ˈmiːnwaɪl/ adv **1** while sth else is happening **2** in the time between two events

measles /ˈmiːzlz/ n [U] infectious disease, esp of children, that causes small red spots on the skin

measure¹ /ˈmeʒə(r)/ v **1** [T] find the

size, length, degree, etc of sth in standard units: *~ a piece of wood* **2** linking verb be a particular size, length, etc: *The room ~s 5 metres across.* [PV] **measure sth out** take the amount of sth you need from a larger amount **measure up (to sth/sb)** be as good, successful, etc as expected or needed ▶ **measured** adj careful ▶ **measurement** n **1** [U] act of measuring sth **2** [C, usu pl] length, width, etc that is measured: *take sb's waist ~ment*

measure² /ˈmeʒə(r)/ n **1** [C] official action done to achieve a particular purpose: *safety/security ~s* **2** [sing] degree of sth; some: *a ~ of success* **3** [sing] sign of the size or strength of sth: *a ~ of his anger* **4** [C, U] unit used for stating the size, quantity or degree of sth; system or a scale of these units: *weights and ~s* **5** [C] instrument, eg a ruler, marked with standard units: *a tape ~* [IDM] **get/take/ have the measure of sb** (*fml*) form an opinion about sb's character or abilities **made-to-measure** (*GB*) specially made for one person according to particular measurements

meat /miːt/ n **1** [U, C] flesh of animals, used as food **2** [U] important or interesting part of sth ▶ **meaty** adj (**-ier, -iest**)

mechanic /məˈkænɪk/ n worker skilled in using or repairing machines, esp car engines ▶ **mechanical** adj **1** of, connected with or produced by machines **2** (*disapprov*) done without thought; automatic ▶ **mechanically** /-kli/ adv

mechanics /məˈkænɪks/ n **1** [U] science of movement and force; science of machinery **2** [U] practical study of machinery **3** (**the mechanics**) [pl] way sth works or is done

mechanism /ˈmekənɪzəm/ n **1** set of moving parts in a machine **2** way of getting sth done

mechanize (*also* **-ise**) /ˈmekənaɪz/ v [T] change a process, so that the work is done by machines rather than people ▶ **mechanization** (*also* **-isation**) /ˌmekənaɪˈzeɪʃn/ n [U]

medal /ˈmedl/ n small round flat piece of metal, given as an honour for bravery or as a prize ▶ **medallist** (*US* **medalist**) /ˈmedəlɪst/ n person who has won a medal, esp in sport

medallion /məˈdæliən/ n piece of jewellery in the shape of a large flat coin worn on a chain around the neck

meddle /ˈmedl/ v [I] (*disapprov*) become involved in sth that does not concern you ▶ **meddler** n

media /ˈmiːdiə/ n (**the media**) [sing,

with sing or pl verb] television, radio, newspapers, etc

mediaeval = MEDIEVAL

mediate /'mi:dieɪt/ v [I] ~(between) take action to end a disagreement between two or more people or groups ▸ **mediation** /,mi:di'eɪʃn/ n [U] ▸ **mediator** n

medic /'medɪk/ n (infml) medical student or doctor

medical /'medɪkl/ adj **1** of illness and injury and their treatment: her ~ records **2** of ways of treating illness that do not involve cutting the body ● **medical** n thorough examination of your body done by a doctor, eg before you start a new job ▸ **medically** /-kli/ adv

Medicare /'medɪkeə(r)/ n [U] US government scheme providing free medical care for old people

medication /,medɪ'keɪʃn/ n [C,U] drug or medicine used to prevent or treat a disease

medicinal /mə'dɪsɪnl/ adj (used for) healing

medicine /'medsn/ n **1** [U] study and treatment of diseases and injuries **2** [U,C] substance, esp a liquid that is taken to cure an illness [IDM] **a dose/taste of your own medicine** the same bad treatment that you have given to others ■ **'medicine man** n = WITCH DOCTOR (WITCH)

medieval (also **mediaeval**) /,medi'i:vl/ adj of the Middle Ages (about AD 1000 - 1450)

mediocre /,mi:di'əʊkə(r)/ adj (disapprov) not very good ▸ **mediocrity** /-'ɒkrəti/ n [U,C] (pl -ies)

meditate /'medɪteɪt/ v [I] ~(on) think deeply, usu in silence, esp for religious reasons ▸ **meditation** /,medɪ'teɪʃn/ n [U,C]

medium /'mi:diəm/ n (pl media /'mi:diə/ or ~s) **1** way of communicating information, etc to people: an effective advertising ~ **2** something that is used for a particular person: Video is a good ~ for practising listening comprehension. **3** substance or surroundings in which sth exists **4** (pl ~s) person who claims to communicate with dead people ● **medium** adj in the middle between two sizes, amounts, etc: a man of ~ height/build ■ **'medium wave** (abbr **MW**) n [U] band of radio waves with a length of between 100 and 1000 metres

meek /mi:k/ adj quiet and always willing to do what others want ▸ **meekly** adv **meekness** n [U]

meet¹ /mi:t/ v (pt, pp met /met/) **1** [I, T] come together with sb: Let's ~ again soon. **2** [T] go to a place and wait for a particular person

to arrive **3** [I, T] see and know sb for the first time; be introduced to sb: Pleased to ~ you. **4** [T] experience sth, esp sth unpleasant: ~ your death **5** [I, T] touch sth; join: Their hands met. **6** [T] do or satisfy what is needed or what sb asks for: ~ sb's wishes **7** [T] pay sth: ~ all expenses [IDM] **meet sb halfway** make a compromise with sb **there is more to sb/sth than meets the eye** sb/sth is more complicated, interesting, etc than you might think at first [PV] **meet with sth** (esp US) meet sb, esp for discussions **meet with sth** (written) **1** be received or treated by sb in a particular way: to ~ with success/failure **2** experience sth unpleasant: ~ with an accident

meet² /mi:t/ n (esp US) sports competition event at which horse riders and dogs have raced

meeting /'mi:tɪŋ/ n occasion when people come together, esp to discuss or decide sth

megabyte /'megabaɪt/ n (abbr **MB**) unit of computer memory, equal to 2^{20} (or about 1 million) bytes

megaphone /'megəfəʊn/ n device shaped like a cone, used to make your voice sound louder

melancholy /'melənkəli; -kɒli/ n [U] (fml) deep sadness that lasts for a long time ● **melancholy** adj sad ▸ **melancholic** /,melən'kɒlɪk/ adj

mellow /'meləʊ/ adj **1** (of colour or sound) soft, rich and pleasant **2** (of a taste or flavour) smooth and pleasant **3** (of people) calm, wise and gentle because of age or experience ● **mellow** v [I, T] (cause sb/sth to) become mellow

melodrama /'melədra:mə/ n [U,C] **1** story, play, etc that is exciting and in which the characters and emotions seem too exaggerated to be real **2** events, behaviour, etc that are exaggerated or extreme ▸ **melodramatic** /,melədrə'mætɪk/ adj ▸ **melodramatically** /-kli/ adv

melody /'melədi/ n (pl -ies) tune or song ▸ **melodic** /mə'lɒdɪk/ adj of melody ▸ **melodious** /mə'ləʊdiəs/ adj having a pleasant tune

melon /'melən/ n large round juicy fruit with a hard skin

melt /melt/ v [I, T] **1** (cause sth to) become liquid as a result of heating: The sun ~ed the snow. **2** (cause a feeling, an emotion, etc to) become gentler and less strong [PV] **melt away** (cause sth to) disappear gradually **melt sth down** melt a metal object in order to use the metal again ■ **'meltdown** n [U,C] melting of the overheated centre of a nuclear reactor, causing the escape of radioactivity ■ **'melting**

pot n [usu sing] place where large numbers of people from different countries live together [IDM] **in the melting pot** likely to change; in the process of changing

member /'membə(r)/ n **1** person belonging to a group, club, etc **2** (fml) part of the body; limb ■ **Member of 'Parliament** n (abbr **MP**) elected representative in the House of Commons ▸ **membership** n [U] state of being a member of a group, club, etc **2** [C, with sing or pl verb] (number of) members of a group, club, etc

membrane /'membreɪn/ n [C,U] layer of soft thin skin-like tissue

memento /mə'mentəʊ/ n (pl **~es** or **~s**) thing that you keep to remind you of a person or place

memo /'meməʊ/ n (pl **~s**) (also fml **memorandum**) official note from one person to another in the same organization

memoir /'memwɑː(r)/ n (**memoirs**) [pl] person's written account of their own life

memorable /'memərəbl/ adj deserving to be remembered; remarkable ▸ **memorably** adv

memorandum /,memə'rændəm/ n (pl **-da** /-də/) (fml) = MEMO

memorial /mə'mɔːriəl/ n statue, stone, etc that is built to remind people of an past event or a famous person: a war ~

memorize (also **-ise**) /'meməraɪz/ v [T] learn sth well enough to remember it exactly

memory /'meməri/ n (pl **-ies**) **1** [C, U] your ability to remember things: He's got a good ~. **2** [U] period of time that sb is able to remember events **3** [C] thought of sth that you remember from the past: memories of childhood **4** [U] what is remembered about sb after their death **5** [C,U] part of a computer where information is stored; amount of space in a computer for storing information [IDM] **in memory of sb** in order that people will remember sb who has died

men plural of MAN[1]

menace /'menəs/ n **1** [C, usu sing] person or thing that will probably cause serious harm or danger **2** [U] atmosphere that makes you feel threatened **3** [C, usu sing] (infml) annoying person or thing ● **menace** v [T] threaten sth/sb ▸ **menacingly** adv

menagerie /mə'nædʒəri/ n collection of wild animals; zoo

mend /mend/ v **1** [T] repair sth damaged or broken so that it can be used again **2** [I] return to good

health [IDM] **mend your ways** stop behaving badly ● **mend** n [IDM] **on the mend** (infml, esp GB) recovering from an illness or injury

menial /'miːniəl/ adj (disapprov) (of work) not skilled or important and often boring

meningitis /,menɪn'dʒaɪtɪs/ n [U] serious illness causing inflammation of the outer part of the brain and spinal cord

menopause /'menəpɔːz/ n (**the menopause**) [sing] gradual stopping of a woman's menstruation usu at around the age of 50

menstruate /'menstrueɪt/ v [I] (fml) (of a woman) have a flow of blood from her uterus every month ▸ **menstrual** /-struəl/ adj ▸ **menstruation** /,menstru'eɪʃn/ n [U]

mental /'mentl/ adj **1** of or in the mind: a ~ illness ◇ make a ~ note of sth (= try to remember it) **2** of or concerned with illnesses of the mind: a ~ patient/hospital **3** (GB, sl) crazy ▸ **mentally** /-təli/ adv of or in the mind: ~ly ill

mentality /men'tæləti/ n [usu sing] (pl **-ies**) particular attitude or way of thinking of a person or group

menthol /'menθɒl/ n [U] substance that tastes and smells of mint, used in some medicines and as a flavouring

mention /'menʃn/ v [T] speak or write about sth/sb briefly [IDM] **don't mention it** (spoken) used as a polite answer when sb has thanked you for sth **not to mention** used to introduce extra information and to emphasize what you are saying ● **mention** n [C,U] brief reference to sth/sb

menu /'menjuː/ n **1** list of food that can be ordered in a restaurant **2** (computing) list of possible choices that are shown on a computer screen: a pull-down ~

meow (esp US) = MIAOW

MEP /,em iː 'piː/ abbr Member of the European Parliament

mercantile /'mɜːkəntaɪl/ adj (fml) of trade and commercial affairs

mercenary /'mɜːsənəri/ adj (disapprov) interested only in making money ● **mercenary** n (pl **-ies**) soldier who will fight for any country or group that offers payment

merchandise /'mɜːtʃəndaɪz/ n [U] (fml) goods bought and sold; goods for sale in a shop

merchant /'mɜːtʃənt/ n person who buys and sells goods in large quantities ● **merchant** adj concerned with the transport of goods by sea: ~ ships ■ **,merchant 'bank** n bank that deals with large businesses ■ ,merchant 'navy (US ,merchant ma'rine) n [C, with sing or pl verb] country's commercial ships and the people who work on them

mercury /'mɜːkjəri/ n [U] (symb Hg) heavy silver-coloured metal, usu in liquid form ▶ **mercurial** /mɜːˈkjʊəriəl/ adj (lit) (of a person or their moods) lively and often changing

mercy /'mɜːsi/ n (pl -ies) **1** [U] kindness or forgiveness shown to sb you have the power to punish **2** [C] event or situation to be grateful for [IDM] **at the mercy of sb/sth** powerless to prevent sb/sth from harming you ▶ **merciful** adj ready to forgive people ▶ **mercifully** /-fəli/ adv ▶ **merciless** adj showing no kindness or pity ▶ **mercilessly** adv

mere /mɪə(r)/ adj nothing more than; only: She's a ~ child. ▶ **merely** adv only; simply

merge /mɜːdʒ/ v **1** [I, T] (cause two or more things) to combine to make one thing: The two companies ~d. **2** [I] ~ (into) fade or change gradually into sth: Day ~d into night. ▶ **merger** n joining together of two or more organizations or business

meridian /məˈrɪdiən/ n one of the lines drawn from the North to the South Pole on a map of the world

meringue /məˈræŋ/ n [U,C] (small cake made from a) baked mixture of the whites of egg and sugar

merit /'merɪt/ n **1** [U] (fml) quality of being good and deserving praise **2** [C, usu pl] food feature that deserves praise or reward ■ **merit** v [T] (fml) deserve praise, attention, etc

mermaid /'mɜːmeɪd/ n (in stories) woman with a fish's tail instead of legs

merry /'meri/ adj (-ier, -iest) **1** happy and cheerful **2** (infml, esp GB) slightly drunk ▶ **merrily** adv ▶ **merriment** n [U] ■ **'merry-go-round** n revolving circular platform with wooden horses, etc on which children ride at a fairground

mesh /meʃ/ n [U,C] material made of threads of plastic rope or wire woven together like a net ■ **mesh** v [I] (written) fit together or match in a satisfactory way: Their opinions don't ~.

mesmerize (also -ise) /'mezməraɪz/ v [T] hold the attention of sb completely

mess /mes/ n **1** [C, usu sing] dirty or untidy state **2** [C, usu sing] difficult or confused situation: My life's in a ~. **3** [C] (esp US 'mess hall) room or building in which members of the armed forces eat their meals

● **mess** v [T] (infml) make sth untidy or dirty [PV] **mess about/ around 1** behave in a silly and annoying way **2** spend time doing sth for pleasure in a relaxed way **mess sb about/around** treat sb in an annoying and unfair way **mess (sth) up** spoil sth or do it badly ▶ **messy** adj (-ier, -iest)

message /'mesɪdʒ/ n **1** [C] written or spoken piece of information sent to sb or left for sb **2** [sing] central idea that a book, speech, etc tries to communicate [IDM] **get the message** (infml) understand what sb has been trying to tell you ▶ **messenger** /'mesɪndʒə(r)/ n person who takes a message to sb

Messiah /mɪˈsaɪə/ n **1** (the Messiah) [sing] (in Christianity) Jesus Christ **2** (the Messiah) [sing] (in Judaism) king sent by God who will save the Jewish people **3** [C] (messiah) leader who people believe will solve the problems of the world

met pt, pp of MEET

metabolism /məˈtæbəlɪzəm/ n [U, sing] (biol) process in the body by which food is used to supply energy ▶ **metabolic** /ˌmetəˈbɒlɪk/ adj

metal /'metl/ n [C,U] any of a kind of mineral substance such as tin, iron or gold ▶ **metallic** /məˈtælɪk/ adj

metaphor /'metəfə(r)/ n [C,U] (example of the) use of words to show sth different from the literal meaning, as in 'She has a heart of stone' ▶ **metaphorical** /ˌmetəˈfɒrɪkl/ adj ▶ **metaphorically** /-kli/ adv

mete /miːt/ v [PV] **mete sth out** (to sb) (fml) give sb a punishment

meteor /'miːtiə; -iɔː/ n piece of rock that moves through space into the earth's atmosphere, becoming bright as it burns ▶ **meteoric** /ˌmiːtiˈɒrɪk/ adj **1** achieving success very quickly: a ~ic rise to fame **2** of meteors ▶ **meteorite** /'miːtiəraɪt/ n meteor that has fallen to earth

meteorology /ˌmiːtiəˈrɒlədʒi/ n study of the weather and the earth's atmosphere ▶ **meteorological** /ˌmiːtiərəˈlɒdʒɪkl/ adj ▶ **meteorologist** n expert in meteorology

meter /'miːtə(r)/ n **1** device that measures sth: a gas ~ **2** (US) = METRE

method /'meθəd/ n **1** [C] way of doing sth **2** [U] quality of being well planned and organized ▶ **methodical** /məˈθɒdɪkl/ adj using an organized system; careful ▶ **methodically** /-kli/ adv

methodology /ˌmeθəˈdɒlədʒi/ n [C, U] (pl -ies) (fml) set of methods and principles used to perform a particular activity

meticulous /məˈtɪkjələs/ adj

showing great care and attention to detail ► **meticulously** adv

metre (US **meter**) /'miːtə(r)/ n **1** (abbr **m**) [C] metric unit of length **2** [U,C] pattern of stressed and unstressed syllables in poetry ► **metric** /'metrɪk/ adj of the metric system ■ the **'metric system** n [sing] system of measurement that uses the metre, kilogram and litre as its basic units

metropolis /mə'trɒpəlɪs/ n main or capital city of a region or country ► **metropolitan** /ˌmetrə'pɒlɪtən/ adj

mettle /'metl/ n [U] ability and determination to do sth successfully [IDM] **on your mettle** prepared to do your best, because you are being tested

mews /mjuːz/ n (pl **mews**) street of stables, converted into houses or flats

miaow (US, GB also **meow**) /mi'aʊ/ n sound made by a cat ► **miaow** v [I]

mice plural of MOUSE

mickey /'mɪki/ n [IDM] **take the mickey (out of sb)** (GB, infml) tease sb

microbe /'maɪkrəʊb/ n tiny living thing, esp one that causes disease

microchip /'maɪkrəʊtʃɪp/ n very small piece of material that has a complicated electronic circuit on it

microcosm /'maɪkrəʊkɒzəm/ n thing, place or group that has all the qualities and features of sth much larger

microfiche /'maɪkrəʊfiːʃ/ n [U,C] film on which written information is stored in very small print and which can only be read with a special machine

microfilm /'maɪkrəʊfɪlm/ n [U,C] film on which written information is stored in print of very small size

microlight /'maɪkrəʊlaɪt/ n very small light aircraft for one or two people

microphone /'maɪkrəfəʊn/ n device for recording sounds or for making your voice louder when you are speaking to an audience

microprocessor /ˌmaɪkrəʊ'prəʊsesə(r)/ n (computing) small unit of a computer that contains all the functions of the central processing unit

microscope /'maɪkrəskəʊp/ n instrument that makes very small objects appear larger ► **microscopic** /ˌmaɪkrə'skɒpɪk/ adj **1** very small **2** using a microscope

microwave /'maɪkrəweɪv/ (also fml ˌmicrowave 'oven) n type of oven that cooks or heats food very quickly using electromagnetic waves rather than heat

mid- /mɪd/ prefix in the middle of: ~-morning ◊ ~-air (= in the sky)

midday /ˌmɪd'deɪ/ n [U] 12 o'clock in the middle of the day

middle /'mɪdl/ n (the middle) [sing] position at an equal distance from all the edges or between the beginning and the end of sth ● **middle** adj position in the middle of an object, group or objects, people, etc between the beginning and the end of sth ■ **middle 'age** n [U] period of your life between the ages of about 45 and 60 ► **ˌmiddle-'aged** adj ■ the **ˌMiddle 'Ages** n [pl] in European history, the period from about AD 1000 to 1450 ■ **middle 'class** n [C, with sing or pl verb] social class whose members are neither very rich nor very poor and that includes professional and business people ► **ˌmiddle-'class** adj ■ the **ˌMiddle 'East** n [sing] area that covers SW Asia and NE Africa ■ **'middleman** n (pl **-men** /-men/) trader who buys goods from the company that makes them and sells them to sb else ■ **ˌmiddle-of-the-'road** adj (of people, policies, etc) not extreme; moderate

middling /'mɪdlɪŋ/ adj of average size, quality, etc

midge /mɪdʒ/ n small flying insect that bites humans and animals

midget /'mɪdʒɪt/ n (offens) very small person ● **midget** adj very small

Midlands /'mɪdləndz/ n (the **Midlands**) [sing, with sing or pl verb] central counties of England

midnight /'mɪdnaɪt/ n [U] 12 o'clock in the middle of the night

midriff /'mɪdrɪf/ n middle part of the body, between the waist and the chest

midst /mɪdst/ n [IDM] **in the midst of (doing)** sth in the middle of sth

midway /ˌmɪd'weɪ/ adj, adv halfway: ~ between Paris and Rome

midwife /'mɪdwaɪf/ n (pl **-wives** /-waɪvz/) person, esp a woman, trained to help women in childbirth ► **midwifery** /ˌmɪd'wɪfəri/ n [U] profession and work of a midwife

might¹ /maɪt/ modal v (neg **might not** short form **mightn't** /'maɪtnt/) **1** used as the past tense of *may* when reporting what sb has said **2** used when showing that sth is or was possible: *He ~ be at home, but I doubt it.* **3** used to make a polite suggestion: *You ~ try calling the help desk.* **4** (GB) used to ask permission politely **5** used to show that you are annoyed about sth that sb could do or could have done: *You ~ at least offer to help!*

might² /maɪt/ n [U] (fml or lit) great strength or power ► **mighty** adj (**-ier, -iest**) (esp lit) **1** powerful **2** large and impressive ● **mighty** adv (infml, esp US) very

migraine /'mi:grem; 'maɪg-/ n [U,C] very painful headache

migrate /maɪ'greɪt/ v [I] ~(from, to) **1** (of birds, etc) go from one part of the world to another regularly each year **2** (of a lot of people) move from one place to go to live in another ▶ **migrant** /'maɪgrənt/ n person or bird, etc that migrates ▶ **migration** /maɪ'greɪʃn/ n ▶ **migratory** /'maɪgrətri; maɪ'greɪtəri/ adj

mike /maɪk/ n (infml) = MICROPHONE

mild /maɪld/ adj **1** gentle; not severe: a ~ climate **2** not sharp or strong in flavour: ~ curry ▶ **mildly** adv ▶ **mildness** n

mildew /'mɪldju:/ n [U] small white fungus that grows on walls, plants, food, etc in warm moist conditions

mile /maɪl/ n unit of distance; 1760 yards (1609 metres) ▶ **mileage** /-ɪdʒ/ n **1** [C,U] distance travelled, measured in miles **2** [U] (infml) amount of advantage or use that you can get from an event or a situation: The press can't get any more ~ out of that story. ■ **milestone** (US **'milepost**) n **1** important stage or event in the development of sth **2** stone or post at the side of a road showing the distance to a place ■ **milometer** (also **mileometer**) /maɪ'lɒmɪtə(r)/ n instrument in a vehicle that records the number of miles travelled

militant /'mɪlɪtənt/ n, adj (person) supporting the use of violent methods, esp force, to achieve your aims ▶ **militancy** /-ənsi/ n [U]

military /'mɪlɪtri/ adj of or for soldiers or war ■ **the military** n [sing, with sing or pl verb] soldiers; the armed forces

militate /'mɪlɪteɪt/ v [PV] **militate against sth** (fml) prevent sth; make it difficult for sth to happen or exist

militia /mə'lɪʃə/ n [sing, with sing or pl verb] group of people trained to act as soldiers in an emergency

milk /mɪlk/ n [U] **1** white liquid produced by female mammals as food for their young **2** white juice of some trees and plants: coconut ~ ● **milk** v **1** [I, T] take milk from a cow, goat, etc **2** [T] obtain as much money, advantage, etc for yourself as you can from a situation, esp dishonestly ■ **'milkman** n (esp in Britain) person whose job is to deliver milk to customers each morning ■ **'milkshake** n drink made of milk and sometimes ice cream, with flavouring added to it ▶ **milky** adj (-ier, -iest) **1** of or like milk **2** made with a lot of milk: ~y coffee ■ **the Milky Way** n [sing] = THE GALAXY(2)

mill¹ /mɪl/ n **1** building with machinery for grinding grain into flour **2** factory that produces a particular type of material: a cotton/paper ~ **3** small machine for crushing sth: a pepper ~ [IDM] **put sb/sth through the mill** (cause sb to) have a difficult time ▶ **miller** n person who owns or runs a mill ■ **'millstone** n either of a pair of flat circular stones used, esp in the past, to crush grain [IDM] **a millstone around/round your neck** difficult problem or responsibility that seems impossible to solve or get rid of

mill² /mɪl/ v [T] crush or grind sth in a mill [PV] **mill about/around** move around aimlessly in a disorganized group

millennium /mɪ'leniəm/ n (pl **-nia** /-niə/ or **~s**) **1** [C] period of 1000 years **2** (the millennium) [sing] time when one period of 1000 years end and another begins: How did you celebrate the ~?

millet /'mɪlɪt/ n [U] type of cereal plant producing very small grain

milli- /'mɪli/ prefix (in the metric system) one thousandth: ~metre

milliner /'mɪlɪnə(r)/ n maker and seller of women's hats ▶ **millinery** n [U] (business of making or selling) women's hats

million /'mɪljən/ number **1** (abbr m) 1,000,000 **2** (a million or millions (of ...)) (infml) a very large amount: I have a ~ things to do. ▶ **millionaire** /,mɪljə'neə(r)/ n (fem **millionairess** /-'neərəs/) person who has a million pounds, dollars, etc; very rich person ▶ **millionth** ordinal number, n 1,000,000th; one of a million equal parts of sth

millipede /'mɪlɪpi:d/ n small creature like an insect with many legs

milometer → MILE

mime /maɪm/ n [U,C] (performance involving the) use of hand or body movements and facial expressions to act sth without speaking ● **mime** v [I, T] act sth using mime

mimic /'mɪmɪk/ v (pt, pp ~ked) [T] **1** copy the way sb speaks, etc in an amusing way **2** look or behave like sth else ● **mimic** n person or an animal that can copy the voice, movements, etc of others ▶ **mimicry** n [U] action or skill of mimicking sb

minaret /,mɪnə'ret/ n tall thin tower of a mosque, from which people are called to prayer

mince /mɪns/ v **1** [T] cut food, esp meat into very small pieces using a special machine (a mincer) **2** [I] walk with short quick steps, in a way that is not natural [IDM] **not mince (your) words** say sth in a direct way, even though it may offend people ● **mince** n [U] minced meat

■ 'mincemeat n [U] (esp GB) mixture of dried fruit, used esp for making pies [IDM] make mincemeat of sb (infml) defeat sb completely in a fight or argument

mind¹ /maɪnd/ n 1 [C,U] (esp GB) part of a person's brain where your thoughts are: The idea never entered my ~. ◊ She has a brilliant ~ (= She is very clever). 2 [C] very intelligent person: one of the greatest ~s of her generation 3 [U] your ability to remember things: My ~ has gone blank! [IDM] be in two minds about (doing) sth (US) be of two minds about (doing) sth feel doubtful about sth be/go out of your mind (infml) be/go mad bear/keep sb/sth in mind remember sb/sth bring/call sb/sth to mind (fml) 1 remember sb/sth 2 remind you of sb/sth have a good mind to do sth | have half a mind to do sth have a strong desire to do sth make up your mind reach a decision on sth making you worry about sth put/set/turn your mind to sth give your attention to sth take your mind off sth help you not to think about sth to my mind in my opinion your mind's eye your imagination

mind² /maɪnd/ v [I, T] 1 be upset, annoyed or worried by sth: I don't ~ the cold. 2 [I, T] used to ask permission or request sth politely: Do you ~ if I open the window? 3 [I, T] used to tell sb to be careful or warn sb of danger: M~ you don't fall! 4 [T] take care of sb/sth: ~ the baby [IDM] mind your own business not interfere in other people's affairs mind your step → STEP¹ mind you (spoken) used to add sth to what you have just said, esp sth that makes it less strong: They're separated now. M~ you, I'm not surprised—they were always arguing. never mind 1 used to tell sb not to worry or be upset 2 used to suggest that sth is not important [PV] mind out (for sb/sth) (GB, spoken) be careful ▶ minder n person whose job is to look after and protect sb: a child~er

mindful /'maɪndfl/ adj ~of (fml) conscious of sb/sth when you do sth

mindless /'maɪndləs/ adj (disapprov) done or acting without thought and for no particular reason: ~ violence 2 not needing thought

mine¹ /maɪn/ pron of or belonging to me: Is this book yours or ~? ● mine n 1 deep hole or holes under the ground where minerals such as coal, etc are dug 2 bomb that is hidden under the ground or in the sea [IDM] a mine of information (about/on sb/sth) rich source of knowledge

mine² /maɪn/ v [I, T] 1 ~(for) dig coal, etc from holes in the ground 2 [T] place mines below the surface of land or water ■ 'minefield n 1 area of land or sea where mines(2) have been hidden 2 situation that contains hidden dangers ▶ miner n person who works in a mine taking out coal, etc ■ 'minesweeper n ship used for finding and clearing away mines(2)

mineral /'mɪnərəl/ n [C,U] natural substance (eg coal or gold) taken from the earth ■ 'mineral water n [U,C] water from a spring in the ground that contains mineral salts or gases 2 [C] glass or bottle of mineral water

mineralogy /ˌmɪnə'rælədʒi/ n [U] scientific study of minerals ▶ mineralogist n student of or expert in mineralogy

mingle /'mɪŋgl/ v 1 [I, T] ~with (written) (cause sth to) combine and mix with sth else 2 [I] move among people and talk to them

mini- /'mɪni/ prefix small: a ~bus

miniature /'mɪnətʃə(r)/ adj very small; much smaller than usual: ~ roses ● miniature n very detailed painting, esp of a person ▶ miniaturize (also -ise) n [T] make a much smaller version of sth

minimal /'mɪnɪml/ adj smallest in amount or degree

minimize (also -ise) /'mɪnɪmaɪz/ v [T] reduce to the smallest possible amount, size or level

minimum /'mɪnɪməm/ n [C, usu sing] smallest possible amount, degree, etc ● minimum adj as small as possible: the ~ age

mining /'maɪnɪŋ/ n [U] process of getting coal, metals, etc from the earth

minion /'mɪniən/ n (disapprov) unimportant person in an organization who has to obey orders

minister /'mɪnɪstə(r)/ n 1 (often Minister) (GB) person at the head of a government department 2 Christian clergyman ● minister v [PV] minister to sb (fml) care for sb, esp sb who is sick or old ▶ ministerial /ˌmɪnɪ'stɪəriəl/ adj

ministry /'mɪnɪstri/ n (pl -ies) 1 [C] (GB) government department 2 (the Ministry) [sing, with sing or pl verb] (esp Protestant) ministers of religion, considered as a group: enter the ~ (= become a clergyman) 3 [C] work of a minister(2)

mink /mɪŋk/ n 1 [C] small fierce animal 2 [U] valuable shiny brown fur of the mink

minor /'maɪnə(r)/ adj not very large, important or serious: ~ injuries ◊ a ~ road ● minor n (law) person below the age of full legal responsibility

minority /mar'nɒrəti/ *n* (*pl* **-ies**) **1** [sing, with sing or *pl* verb] smaller part of a group; less than half of the people or things in a large group **2** [C] small group of people of a different race, religion, etc from the rest **3** [U] (*law*) state or time of being a minor

minster /'mɪnstə(r)/ *n* large or important church

minstrel /'mɪnstrəl/ *n* (in the Middle Ages) travelling singer

mint /mɪnt/ *n* **1** [U] plant whose leaves are used for flavouring **2** [U, C] *short for* PEPPERMINT **3** [C] place where money is made **4** (a mint) [sing] (*infml*) very large amount of money [IDM] **in mint condition** (as if) new ● **mint** *v* [T] make a coin from metal

minuet /,mɪnju'et/ *n* (music for a) slow graceful dance

minus /'maɪnəs/ *prep* **1** less: *15 ~ 9 equals 6* **2** below zero: *~ 3 degrees Celsius* **3** (*infml*) without ● **minus** (*also* **'minus sign**) *n* mathematical symbol (-) ● **minus** *adj* negative

minute[1] /'mɪnɪt/ *n* (*abbr* **min.**) **1** [C] each of the 60 parts of an hour, equal to 60 seconds **2** [sing] (*spoken*) very short time: *I'll be with you in a ~.* **3** [C] each of the 60 parts of a degree, used in measuring angles **4** (usu **the minutes**) [pl] record of what is said and decided at a meeting: *Who is going to take* (= write) *the ~s?* [IDM] **the minute/moment (that …)** as soon as … ● **minute** *v* [T] write sth down in the minutes(4)

minute[2] /maɪ'njuːt/ *adj* (**-r, -st**) **1** extremely small **2** very detailed and thorough ► **minutely** *adv*

minutiae /maɪ'njuːʃiiː/ *n* [pl] very small details

miracle /'mɪrəkl/ *n* **1** [C] act or event that does not follow the laws of nature and is believed to be caused by God **2** [sing] (*infml*) lucky thing that happens that you did not expect or think possible: *It's a ~ we weren't all killed.* **3** [C] ~ **of** wonderful example of sth: *a ~ of modern science* ► **miraculous** /mɪ'rækjələs/ *adj*

mirage /'mɪrɑːʒ; mɪ'rɑːʒ/ *n* something seen that does not really exist, esp water in the desert

mire /'maɪə(r)/ *n* [U] soft muddy ground

mirror /'mɪrə(r)/ *n* piece of glass that you can look in and see yourself ● **mirror** *v* [T] show sb/sth exactly as in a mirror

misadventure /,mɪsəd'ventʃə(r)/ *n* [U] (*GB, law*) death caused by

accident, rather than as a result of a crime **2** [C,U] (*fml*) bad luck

misappropriate /,mɪsə'prəʊprieɪt/ *v* [T] (*fml*) take sb else's money or property for yourself

misbehave /,mɪsbɪ'heɪv/ *v* [I] behave badly ► **misbehaviour** (*US* **-ior**) *n* [U]

miscalculate /,mɪs'kælkjuleɪt/ *v* [I, T] estimate amounts, etc wrongly ► **miscalculation** /-'leɪʃn/ *n* [C,U]

miscarriage /ˌmɪs'kærɪdʒ; 'mɪs'k-/ *n* [C,U] process of giving birth to a baby before it has developed enough to stay alive ■ **mis,carriage of 'justice** *n* [U,C] (*law*) incorrect legal decision

miscarry /,mɪs'kæri/ *v* (*pt, pp* **-ied**) [I] **1** give birth to a baby before it has developed enough to stay alive **2** (of a plan) fail

miscellaneous /,mɪsə'leɪniəs/ *adj* of various kinds

miscellany /mɪ'seləni/ *n* (*pl* **-ies**) collection of things of various kinds

mischance /,mɪs'tʃɑːns/ *n* [U,C] (*fml*) bad luck

mischief /'mɪstʃɪf/ *n* [U] behaviour (esp of children) that is bad, but not serious [IDM] **do yourself a mischief** (*GB, infml*) hurt yourself physically ► **mischievous** /-tʃɪvəs/ *adj* **1** enjoying playing tricks and annoying people **2** causing trouble ► **mischievously** *adv*

misconceived /,mɪskən'siːvd/ *adj* badly planned or judged

misconception /,mɪskən'sepʃn/ *n* [C,U] ~ **(about)** belief or idea that is not based on correct information

misconduct /,mɪs'kɒndʌkt/ *n* [U] (*fml*) unacceptable behaviour, esp by a professional person

misdeed /,mɪs'diːd/ *n* [C, usu pl] (*fml*) bad or evil act

miser /'maɪzə(r)/ *n* (*disapprov*) person who loves money and hates spending it ► **miserly** *adj*

miserable /'mɪzrəbl/ *adj* **1** very unhappy **2** causing unhappiness: *~ weather* **3** poor in quality: *earn a ~ wage* ► **miserably** *adv*

misery /'mɪzəri/ *n* (*pl* **-ies**) **1** [U,C] great suffering or unhappiness **2** [C] (*GB, infml*) person who is always complaining

misfire /,mɪs'faɪə(r)/ *v* [I] **1** (*infml*) (of a plan or joke) fail to have the intended effect **2** (of a gun, etc) fail to work properly

misfit /'mɪsfɪt/ *n* person who is not accepted by a group of people: *a social ~*

misfortune /,mɪs'fɔːtʃuːn/ *n* [C,U] (*written*) (instance of) bad luck

misgiving /,mɪs'gɪvɪŋ/ *n* [U,C, usu pl] feelings of doubt or anxiety

misguided /,mɪs'gaɪdɪd/ *adj* wrong

because you have understood or judged a situation badly

mishap /'mɪshæp/ n [C,U] small accident or piece of bad luck

misjudge /,mɪs'dʒʌdʒ/ v [T] **1** form a wrong opinion about a person or situation **2** estimate sth wrongly, eg time or distance, wrongly

mislay /,mɪs'leɪ/ v (pt, pp mislaid /-'leɪd/) [T] put sth down and forget where it is

mislead /,mɪs'liːd/ v (pt, pp misled /-'led/) [T] cause sb to have a wrong idea or impression about sth

mismanage /,mɪs'mænɪdʒ/ v [T] deal with or manage sth badly ► **mismanagement** n [U]

misprint /'mɪsprɪnt/ n mistake in printing

misrepresent /,mɪs,reprɪ'zent/ v [T] give false information about sb/sth ► **misrepresentation** /-zen-'teɪʃn/ n [C,U]

miss /mɪs/ v [I, T] **1** fail to hit, catch or reach, etc sth: ~ the ball/the train **2** [T] fail to see, hear or notice sth **3** [T] feel sad because of the absence of sb/sth: I'll ~ you when you go. [PV] **miss sb/sth out** (GB) include sb/sth **miss out (on sth)** fail to benefit from sth useful or enjoyable by not taking part in it ● **miss** n **1** (Miss) used before the family name when speaking to or of an unmarried woman: M~ Smith **2** failure to hit, catch or reach sth [IDM] **give sb a miss** (infml, esp GB) decide not to do sth, eat sth, etc ► **missing** adj that cannot be found; lost

missile /'mɪsaɪl/ n **1** explosive weapon sent through the air: nuclear ~s **2** object or weapon thrown or fired

mission /'mɪʃn/ n **1** [C] important official job that a person or group of people is given to do, esp abroad: a trade ~ to China **2** [C,U] work of teaching people about Christianity, esp in a foreign country; group of people who do this work **3** [C] special work you feel is your duty to do: her ~ in life ► **missionary** /'mɪʃənri/ n (pl -ies) person sent to a foreign country to teach people about Christianity ■ **'mission statement** n official statement of the aims of a company or organization

misspell /,mɪs'spel/ v (pt, pp ~t /-'spelt/ or esp US ~ed) [T] spell a word wrongly ► **misspelling** n [C,U]

misspend /,mɪs'spend/ adj (usu passive) spend time or money carelessly: his ~ youth

mist /mɪst/ n [U,C] cloud of very small drops of water in the air, making it difficult to see: hills covered in ~ ◇ (fig) She gazed at him through a

~ of tears. ● **mist** v [I, T] ~(over/up) (cause sth to) become covered with small drops of water: His glasses ~ed over. ► **misty** adj (-ier, -iest) **1** with a lot of mist: a ~y morning **2** not clear or bright: ~y memories

mistake /mɪ'steɪk/ n wrong action, idea or opinion [IDM] **by mistake** accidentally ● **mistake** v (pt mistook /mɪ'stʊk/ pp ~n /mɪ'steɪkən/) [T] not understand or judge sth/sb correctly [PV] **mistake sb/sth for sb/sth** think wrongly that sb/sth is sb/sth else: People often ~ me for my twin sister. ► **mistaken** adj wrong; not correct: ~n beliefs ► **mistakenly** adv

mistletoe /'mɪsltəʊ/ n [U] evergreen plant with white berries, used as a Christmas decoration

mistress /'mɪstrəs/ n **1** woman that a married man is having a regular sexual relationship with and who is not his wife **2** (GB) female schoolteacher **3** woman in a position of authority **4** female owner of a dog, horse, etc

mistrust /,mɪs'trʌst/ v [T] have no confidence in sb/sth ● **mistrust** n [U] lack of confidence; suspicion ► **mistrustful** adj

misty → MIST

misunderstand /,mɪsʌndə'stænd/ v (pt, pp -stood /-'stʊd/) [T] fail to understand sb/sth correctly: He ~stood the instructions and got lost. ► **misunderstanding** n [C,U] failure to understand sb/sth correctly, esp when this causes argument

misuse /,mɪs'juːz/ v [T] **1** use sth in the wrong way or for the wrong purpose: ~ your time **2** treat sb badly ● **misuse** /,mɪs'juːs/ n [U,C]: ~ of power

mitigate /'mɪtɪgeɪt/ v [T] (fml) make sth less harmful, serious, etc ► **mitigating** adj (~ circumstances/ factors) (fml, law) circumstances or factors that explain sb's actions or a crime and make them easier to understand ► **mitigation** /-'geɪʃn/ n [U]

mitre (US miter) /'maɪtə(r)/ n tall pointed hat worn by bishops

mitten /'mɪtn/ (also **mitt** /mɪt/) n kind of glove that covers the four fingers together and the thumb separately

mix /mɪks/ v **1** [I, T] (cause two or more substances to) combine, usu in a way that means they cannot easily be separated: ~ flour and water to make paste ◇ Oil and water don't ~. **2** [I] meet and talk to different people, esp at social events: He finds it hard to ~. **3** [T] combine different recordings of voices and /or instruments to produce a single piece of music

[IDM] be/get mixed up in sth (infml) be/become involved in sth bad **[PV] mix sb/sth up (with sb/sth)** confuse sb/sth with sb/sth else: *I got her ~ed up with her sister.* ● **mix** n [C,U] set of different substances to be mixed together: *a cake ~* ▶ **mixed** adj **1** of different kinds **2** of or for people of both sexes: *a ~ed school* ▶ **mixer** n machine used for mixing things ■ '**mix-up** n (infml) confused situation

mixture /ˈmɪkstʃə(r)/ n combination of different things: *a ~ of fear and sadness*

mm abbr millimetre(s)

moan /məʊn/ v [I] **1** make a long low sound of pain **2** ~(**about**) (infml) complain: *He's always ~ing about having no money.* ▶ **moan** n

moat /məʊt/ n deep wide channel filled with water that was dug around a castle

mob /mɒb/ n [C, sing, with sing or pl verb] **1** noisy disorganized crowd **2** (infml) group of criminals ● **mob** v (-**bb**-) [T] gather round sb in great numbers to in order to see them and get their attention: *a film star ~bed by his fans*

mobile /ˈməʊbaɪl/ adj that can move or be moved easily from place to place ■ ,**mobile 'phone** n telephone that does not have wires and works by radio, that you can carry around with you and use anywhere ● **mobile** n **1** ornamental hanging structure with parts that move freely in currents of air **2** (GB) = MOBILE PHONE ▶ **mobility** /məʊˈbɪləti/ n [U]

mobilize (also **-ise**) /ˈməʊbəlaɪz/ v [I, T] (cause sb/sth to) become organized or ready for service, eg in war

moccasin /ˈmɒkəsɪn/ n soft leather shoe

mock[1] /mɒk/ v [I, T] laugh at sb/sth unkindly, esp by copying what they say or do: *a ~ing smile* ▶ **mockery** n **1** [U] comments or actions intended to make sb/sth seem ridiculous **2** [sing] (disapprov) decision, etc that is a failure and not as it should be: *a ~ of a trial* **[IDM] make a mockery of sth** make sth seem ridiculous

mock[2] /mɒk/ adj not sincere: *~ horror* **2** not real: *a ~ exam*

modal /ˈməʊdl/ (also **modal 'verb, modal au'xiliary**) n (gram) verb that is used with another verb, eg *can, may* or *should* to express possibility, permission, etc

mode /məʊd/ n (fml) way in which sth is done

model[1] /ˈmɒdl/ n **1** small-scale copy of sth: *a ~ of the new airport* **2** design or kind of product: *This car is our latest ~.* **3** person or thing

of the best kind: *a ~ student* **4** person who poses for an artist or photographer **5** person who wears and shows new clothes to possible buyers: *a fashion ~*

model[2] /ˈmɒdl/ v (-**ll**- US -**l**-) **1** [I, T] show clothes, etc to possible buyers by wearing them **2** [T] create a copy of an activity, etc so that you can study it before dealing with the real thing: *The program can ~ a typical home page for you.* **3** [I, T] shape clay, etc in order to make sth **[PV] model yourself on sb** copy the behaviour of sb you like and respect in order to be like them

modem /ˈməʊdem/ n device that connects one computer system to another using a telephone line so that data can be sent

moderate[1] /ˈmɒdərət/ adj not extreme; limited ● **moderate** n person who has moderate opinions, esp in politics ▶ **moderately** adv not very; only ~ly successful

moderate[2] /ˈmɒdəreɪt/ v [I] (cause sth to) become less extreme or severe

moderation /ˌmɒdəˈreɪʃn/ n [U] quality of being reasonable and not extreme: *Alcohol should only be taken in ~* (= small quantities).

modern /ˈmɒdn/ adj **1** of the present or recent times **2** new; up-to-date ▶ **modernize** (also **-ise**) /ˈmɒdənaɪz/ v [I, T] bring sth up to date ▶ **modernization** (also **-isation**) /ˌmɒdənaɪˈzeɪʃn/ n [C, U]

modest /ˈmɒdɪst/ adj **1** not very large, expensive, important, etc: *a ~ salary* **2** (approv) not talking much about your own abilities or possessions **3** (of people, esp women) shy about showing much of the body; not intended to attract attention, esp in a sexual way: *~ behaviour* ▶ **modestly** adv ▶ **modesty** n [U]

modify /ˈmɒdɪfaɪ/ v (pt, pp -**ied**) [T] **1** change sth slightly **2** make sth less extreme: *~ your behaviour* **3** (gram) (esp of an adj or adv) describe a word or restrict its meaning in some way: *In the phrase 'walk slowly', 'slowly' modifies 'walk'.* ▶ **modification** /ˌmɒdɪfɪˈkeɪʃn/ n [C, U]

module /ˈmɒdjuːl/ n **1** independent unit in a course of study: *the biology ~ in the science course* **2** (computing) unit of a computer system or program that has a particular function **3** one of a set of parts or units that can be joined together to make a machine, a building, etc **4** independent unit of a spacecraft ▶ **modular** /-jələ(r)/ adj

mohair /ˈməʊheə(r)/ n [U] soft wool made from the fine hair of the angora goat

moist /mɔɪst/ *adj* slightly wet ▸

moisten /ˈmɔɪsn/ *v* [I, T] become or make sth moist ▸ **moisture** /ˈmɔɪstʃə(r)/ *n* [U] tiny drops of water on a surface, etc

molar /ˈməʊlə(r)/ *n* large back tooth, used for grinding and chewing food

mold, molder, mouldy (US) = MOULD, MOULDER, MOULDY

mole /məʊl/ *n* **1** small grey furry animal that lives in tunnels **2** small dark brown spot on the skin **3** employee who secretly gives information to another organization, etc ∎ **molehill** *n* small pile of earth thrown up by a mole

molecule /ˈmɒlɪkjuːl/ *n* smallest group of atoms that a particular substance can consist of ▸ **molecular** /məˈlekjələ(r)/ *adj*

molest /məˈlest/ *v* [T] attack sb, esp a child, sexually

mollusc (US **mollusk**) /ˈmɒləsk/ *n* any of a class of animals, eg oysters and snails, that have a soft body and usu a hard shell

molt (US) = MOULT

molten /ˈməʊltən/ *adj* (of metal, rock or glass) heated to a very high temperature so that it becomes liquid

mom /mɒm/ *n* (US, infml) = MUM

moment /ˈməʊmənt/ *n* **1** [C] very short period of time **2** [sing] exact point in time **3** [C] particular time for doing sth: *I'm waiting for the right ~ to tell him.* [IDM] the moment (that) → MINUTE¹ ▸ **momentary** /-məntri/ *adj* lasting for a very short time ▸ **momentarily** /-trəli/ *adv* **1** for a very short time **2** (US, spoken) very soon

momentous /məˈmentəs/ *adj* very important or serious

momentum /məˈmentəm/ *n* [U] **1** ability to keep increasing or developing: *They lost ~ in the second half.* **2** force that is gained by movement **3** (tech) quantity of movement of a moving object

mommy /ˈmɒmi/ *n* (US) = MUMMY

monarch /ˈmɒnək/ *n* king, queen, emperor or empress ▸ **monarchy** /-ki/ *n* (pl -ies) **1** (the monarchy) [U] system of rule by a monarch **2** [C] country ruled by a monarch

monastery /ˈmɒnəstri/ *n* (pl -ies) building in which monks live

monastic /məˈnæstɪk/ *adj* of monks or monasteries

Monday /ˈmʌndeɪ; -di/ *n* [C,U] the day of the week after Sunday and before Tuesday: *They're coming on ~.* ◇ *last/next ~* ◇ *The museum is closed on ~s* (= every Monday).

monetary /ˈmʌnɪtri/ *adj* of money

money /ˈmʌni/ *n* [U] **1** what you earn by working or selling things, and use to buy things **2** coins and printed paper accepted when buying and selling [IDM] **get your money's worth** get full value for the money you have spent ∎ **'money box** *n* box used for saving coins

mongrel /ˈmʌŋɡrəl/ *n* dog of mixed breed

monitor /ˈmɒnɪtə(r)/ *n* **1** television screen used to show particular kinds of information **2** screen that shows information from a computer: *a PC with a 17 inch colour ~* **3** piece of equipment used to check or record sth: *a heart ~* **4** pupil whose job is to check that sth is done fairly and honestly ● **monitor** *v* [T] watch and check sth over time to see how it develops

monk /mʌŋk/ *n* member of a male religious community living in a monastery

monkey /ˈmʌŋki/ *n* **1** small long-tailed tree-climbing animal **2** (infml) lively mischievous child

mono /ˈmɒnəʊ/ *adj, n* [U] (system of) recording or producing sound which comes from only one direction

monochrome /ˈmɒnəkrəʊm/ *adj* having only one colour or black and white

monocle /ˈmɒnəkl/ *n* single glass lens for one eye, used in the past

monogamy /məˈnɒɡəmi/ *n* [U] fact or custom of being married to only one person at a time ▸ **monogamous** /-məs/ *adj*

monogram /ˈmɒnəɡræm/ *n* two or more letters (esp a person's initials) combined in one design

monologue (US also **monolog**) /ˈmɒnəlɒɡ/ *n* long speech by one person, eg in a play

monopoly /məˈnɒpəli/ *n* (pl -ies) **1** (business) complete control of trade in particular goods or a service; type of goods or a service controlled in this way **2** complete control, possession or use of sth: *A good education should not be the ~ of the rich.* ▸ **monopolize** (also -ise) *v* [T] have or take complete control of the largest part of sth so that other people cannot share it

monorail /ˈmɒnəʊreɪl/ *n* [U] railway system using a single rail

monosyllable /ˈmɒnəsɪləbl/ *n* word with only one syllable ▸ **monosyllabic** /ˌmɒnəsɪˈlæbɪk/ *adj*

monotonous /məˈnɒtənəs/ *adj* never changing and therefore boring: *a ~ voice* ▸ **monotonously** *adv* ▸ **monotony** /-təni/ *n* [U]

monsoon /mɒnˈsuːn/ n wind which blows in S Asia, bringing heavy rains in the summer

monster /ˈmɒnstə(r)/ n **1** large ugly frightening (esp imaginary) creature **2** cruel or evil person **3** animal or thing that is large and ugly

monstrous /ˈmɒnstrəs/ adj **1** very shocking and morally wrong **2** very large, ugly and frightening ▶ **monstrosity** /mɒnˈstrɒsəti/ n (pl -ies) sth that is very large and ugly ▶ **monstrously** adv

month /mʌnθ/ n one of the twelve divisions of the year, period of about four weeks ▶ **monthly** adj, adv **1** done or happening once a month **2** paid, valid or calculated for one month ▶ **monthly** n (pl -ies) magazine published once a month

monument /ˈmɒnjumənt/ n **1** building, statue, etc to remind people of a person or event **2** very old interesting building ▶ **monumental** /ˌmɒnjuˈmentl/ adj **1** very important and influential **2** very large, good, bad, stupid, etc: a ~ failure **3** of a monument

moo /muː/ n long deep sound made by a cow ▶ **moo** v [I]

mood /muːd/ n **1** way you are feeling at a particular time: She's in a good ~ (= happy) today. **2** period of being angry or impatient **3** (gram) any of the sets of verb forms which show that sth is certain, possible, doubtful, etc: the indicative/subjunctive ~ ▶ **moody** adj (-ier, -iest) having moods that often change; bad-tempered ▶ **moodily** adv

moon¹ /muːn/ n **1** (the moon) [sing] the round object that moves round the earth and shines at night **2** [C] natural satellite that moves round a planet other than the earth [IDM] **over the moon** (infml, esp GB) extremely happy ■ **moonbeam** n ray of light from the moon ■ **moonlight** n [U] light of the moon ■ **moonlight** v (pt, pp -lighted) [I] (infml) have a second job, esp at night, in addition to your main job

moon² /muːn/ v [PV] **moon about/ around** (GB, infml) spend time doing nothing or walking about with no particular purpose

moor¹ /mɔː(r)/ n [C, usu pl] open uncultivated high land, esp covered with heather: walk on the ~s ■ **moorland** n [U, C] land consisting of moor

moor² /mɔː(r)/; mʊə(r)/ v [I, T] fasten a boat, etc to the land or to a fixed object with ropes, etc ▶ **mooring** n **1** (moorings) [pl] ropes, anchors, etc, used to moor a boat **2** [C] place where a boat is moored

moose /muːs/ n (pl moose) (US) kind of very large deer

mop /mɒp/ n **1** tool for washing floors that has a long handle and a bunch of thick strings or cloth at the end **2** mass of thick untidy hair ● **mop** v (-pp-) [T] **1** clean sth with a mop **2** wipe liquid from the surface of sth using a cloth [PV] **mop sth up** remove the liquid from sth using sth that absorbs it

mope /məʊp/ v [I] spend your time doing nothing and feeling sorry for yourself

moped /ˈməʊped/ n kind of motor-cycle with a small engine

moral /ˈmɒrəl/ adj **1** concerning principles of right and wrong: ~ standards **2** following the standards of behaviour considered acceptable and right by most people ▶ **morally** adv ■ **moral supˈport** n [U] encouragement or sympathy ● **moral** n **1** (morals) [pl] principles or standards of good behaviour **2** [C] practical lesson that a story or experience teaches you

morale /məˈrɑːl/ n [U] amount of confidence, enthusiasm, etc that a person or group has

morality /məˈræləti/ n (pl -ies) **1** [U] principles of good or right behaviour **2** [C] system of moral principles followed by a group of people

moralize (also -ise) /ˈmɒrəlaɪz/ v [I] ~(about/on) (esp disapprov) tell other people what is right or wrong

morbid /ˈmɔːbɪd/ adj having an unhealthy interest in death ▶ **morbidly** adv

more /mɔː(r)/ det, pron (used as the comparative of 'much', 'a lot of', 'many') a larger number or amount of: I need ~ time. ◇ ~ people ◇ Please tell me ~. ● **more** adv **1** used to form comparatives of adjectives and adverbs: ~ expensive ◇ talk ~ quietly to a greater extent than sth else; to a greater degree than usual: You need to sleep ~. ◇ I'll go there once ~ (= one more time). [IDM] **more and more** increasingly **more or less 1** almost **2** approximately: £20, ~ or less

moreover /mɔːrˈəʊvə(r)/ adv (fml) in addition; besides

morgue /mɔːg/ n (esp GB) building in which dead bodies are kept before a funeral

morning /ˈmɔːnɪŋ/ n [C,U] early part of the day from the time when people wake up until midday or before lunch [IDM] **in the morning** during the morning of the next day: see him in the ~ ■ **morning dress** n [U] clothes worn by a man on very formal occasions, eg weddings

moron /'mɔːrɒn/ n (infml) stupid person ▶ **moronic** /məˈrɒnɪk/ adj

morose /məˈrəʊs/ adj sad, bad-tempered and silent ● **morosely** adv

morphine /'mɔːfiːn/ n [U] powerful drug made from opium, used to reduce pain

Morse code /ˌmɔːs ˈkəʊd/ n [U] system of sending messages using short and long sounds, etc to represent letters

morsel /'mɔːsl/ n ~(of) small piece, esp of food

mortal /'mɔːtl/ adj 1 that must die 2 (lit) causing death: a ~ wound 3 extreme: In ~ fear ● **mortal** n human being ▶ **mortality** /mɔːˈtæləti/ n 1 state of being mortal and not living for ever 2 number of deaths in a particular situation or period: the infant ~ rate (= the number of babies that die at or just after birth) ▶ **mortally** /'mɔːtəli/ adv (lit) 1 resulting in death: ~ly wounded 2 extremely: ~ly offended

mortar /'mɔːtə(r)/ n 1 [U] mixture of lime, sand and water, used to hold bricks, etc together in building 2 [C] heavy gun that fires bombs and shells high into the air 3 [C] strong bowl in which substances, eg seeds and grains, can be crushed with a special tool (pestle)

mortgage /'mɔːɡɪdʒ/ n 1 legal agreement by which a bank lends you money to buy a house, etc 2 sum of money borrowed ● **mortgage** v [T] give a bank, etc the right to own your house in return for money lent

mortify /'mɔːtɪfaɪ/ v (pt, pp -ied) [T] (usu passive) make sb feel very ashamed or embarrassed ▶ **mortification** /ˌmɔːtɪfɪˈkeɪʃn/ n [U]

mortuary /'mɔːtʃəri/ n (pl -ies) 1 building or room in which dead bodies are kept before a funeral 2 (US) = FUNERAL PARLOUR (FUNERAL)

mosaic /məʊˈzeɪɪk/ n [C, U] picture or pattern made by placing together small pieces of coloured glass or stone

Moslem = MUSLIM

mosque /mɒsk/ n building in which Muslims worship

mosquito /məˈskiːtəʊ/ n (pl ~es) small flying insect that sucks blood

moss /mɒs/ n [U] (thick mass of a) small green or yellow plant that grows on damp surfaces ▶ **mossy** adj (-ier, -iest)

most /məʊst/ det, pron (used as the superlative of 'much', 'a lot of', 'many') 1 the largest in number or amount: Who will get the ~ votes? ◊ He ate the ~. 2 more than half of sb/sth; almost all of sb/sth: M~ people must pay the new tax. [IDM] at (the) most not more than ● **most** adv 1 used to form superlatives of adjectives and adverbs: the ~ expensive car 2 to the greatest degree: Children need ~ sleep. 3 (fml) very: a ~ interesting talk [IDM] most likely → LIKELY ▶ **mostly** adv mainly; generally

motel /məʊˈtel/ n hotel for people travelling by car

moth /mɒθ/ n winged insect, similar to the butterfly but flies mainly at night ■ **mothball** n small ball of a strong-smelling substance, for keeping moths out of clothes ■ **moth-eaten** adj 1 (of clothes) damaged by moths 2 (disapprov) old and in bad condition

mother /'mʌðə(r)/ n 1 female parent 2 head of a female religious community ● **mother** v [T] care for sb/sth because you are their mother or as if you were their mother ■ **mother country** n country where you were born ▶ **motherhood** n [U] ■ **mother-in-law** n (pl ~s-in-law) mother of your wife or husband ▶ **motherly** adv of or like a mother ■ **mother tongue** n language that you first learn to speak as a child

motif /məʊˈtiːf/ n theme or pattern in music or art

motion /'məʊʃn/ n 1 [U] act or process of moving or the way sth moves 2 [C] particular movement: signal with a ~ of the hand 3 [C] formal proposal to be discussed and voted on at a meeting [IDM] go through the motions (of doing sth) (infml) do sth because you have to, not because you want to set/put sth in motion start sth moving ● **motion** v [I, T] ~to signal to sb by making a movement of the hand or head ▶ **motionless** adj not moving

motivate /'məʊtɪveɪt/ v [T] 1 be the reason why sb does sth 2 make sb want to do sth ▶ **motivation** /ˌməʊtɪˈveɪʃn/ n [C, U]

motive /'məʊtɪv/ n reason for doing sth: I'm suspicious of his ~s.

motor /'məʊtə(r)/ n 1 device that changes power into movement: an electric ~ 2 (GB, old-fash) car ● **motor** adj 1 having an engine, using the power of an engine: ~ vehicles 2 of vehicles that have engines: ~ racing ● **motor** v [I] (old-fash, GB) travel by car ■ **motorbike** n = MOTORCYCLE ■ **motorcade** /'məʊtəkeɪd/ n procession of motor cars ■ **motor car** n (GB, fml) = CAR ■ **motorcycle** n road vehicle with two wheels, driven by an engine ▶ **motorcycling** n [U] sport of riding motorcycles ▶ **motorist** n person who drives a car ▶ **motorized** (also

-ised) *adj* having an engine: *a ~ wheelchair* ■ **motor racing** *n* [U] sport of racing fast cars on a special track ■ **motor scooter** *n* (*esp US*) = SCOOTER(1) ■ **motorway** *n* [C, U] (in Britain) wide road with at least two lanes in each direction, for fast traffic

motto /'mɒtəʊ/ *n* (*pl* ~**es** or ~**s**) short sentence that expresses the aims and beliefs of a person, a group, etc and is used as a rule of behaviour

mould /məʊld/ *n* **1** [C] shaped container, into which a soft or liquid substance is poured so that it sets in that shape **2** [U] fine soft grey or green substance like fur that grows on old food, etc ● **mould** *v* [T] **1** shape sth in a mould **2** strongly influence the way sb's character, etc develops ▶ **mouldy** *adj* (**-ier, -iest**) covered with or containing mould: *~y bread*

moulder /'məʊldə(r)/ *v* [I] decay slowly and steadily

moult /məʊlt/ *v* [I] **1** (of a bird) lose feathers **2** (of a dog or cat) lose hair

mound /maʊnd/ *n* **1** small hill **2** pile or heap

mount /maʊnt/ *v* **1** [T] organize and begin sth: *~ an exhibition* **2** [I] increase gradually: *~ing costs* **3** [T] go up sth or up on to sth raised: *slowly ~ the stairs* **4** [I, T] get on a bicycle, horse, etc in order to ride it **5** [T] fix sth in position: *a diamond ~ed in gold* ● **mount** *n* **1** (**Mount**) (*abbr* **Mt**) (used in place names) mountain **2** (*lit*) horse that you ride on

mountain /'maʊntən/ *n* **1** [C] very high hill, often with rocks near the top **2** [usu pl] (*infml*) very large amount or number of sth: *We made ~s of sandwiches.* [IDM] **make a mountain out of a molehill** make an unimportant matter seem important ▶ **mountaineer** /ˌmaʊntə'nɪə(r)/ *n* person who is skilled at climbing mountains ▶ **mountaineering** *n* [U] ▶ **mountainous** *adj* **1** having many mountains **2** huge: *~ous waves*

mourn /mɔːn/ *v* [I, T] ~ (**for**) feel or show sadness for sb/sth, esp sb's death ▶ **mourner** *n* ▶ **mournful** *adj* sad ▶ **mourning** *n* [U] **1** sadness that you show and feel because sb has died **2** black clothes, worn to show sadness at sb's death

mouse /maʊs/ *n* (*pl* **mice** /maɪs/) **1** small furry animal with a long tail **2** (*pl* also ~**s**) (*computing*) small device moved by hand across a surface to control the movement of the cursor on a computer screen ▶ **mousy** (also **mousey**) /'maʊsi/ *adj* (**-ier, -iest**) (*disapprov*) **1** (of

hair) of a dull brown colour **2** (of people) shy and quiet

mousse /muːs/ *n* [U,C] cold sweet dish made from cream and eggs, flavoured with fruit or chocolate

moustache /mə'stɑːʃ/ (*US* **mustache** /'mʌstæʃ/) *n* hair allowed to grow on the upper lip

mouth¹ /maʊθ/ *n* (*pl* ~**s** /maʊðz/) **1** opening in the face used for speaking, eating, etc **2** entrance or opening of sth: *the ~ of the cave* ▶ **mouthful** *n* **1** [C] amount of food, etc put into the mouth at one time **2** [sing] (*infml*) word or phrase that is too long or difficult to say ■ **mouth organ** *n* musical instrument played by passing it along the lips while blowing or sucking air ■ **mouthpiece** *n* **1** part of a musical instrument, telephone, etc that is placed in or near the mouth **2** person, newspaper, etc that expresses the opinions of others ■ **mouthwatering** *adj* (*approv*) (of food) looking or smelling delicious

mouth² /maʊð/ *v* [I, T] say sth by moving your lips but not making any sound

movable /'muːvəbl/ *adj* that can be moved from one place to another

move¹ /muːv/ *v* **1** [I, T] (cause sb/sth to) change place or position: *Don't ~ while I'm taking the photo.* **2** [I] make progress: *The company has ~d ahead of the competition.* **3** [I] ~ (**from, to**) change the place where you live, have your work, etc: *They are ~ing (house) soon.* **4** [T] cause sb to have strong feelings, esp pity: *~d by a sad film* **5** [T] (*fml*) suggest sth formally so that it can be discussed and decided [PV] **move in/out** take possession of a new/leave your old house **move off** (esp of a vehicle) start moving and leave

move² /muːv/ *n* **1** action done to achieve a purpose: *~s to end the strike* **2** change of place or position, esp in a board game: *It's your ~!* [IDM] **be on the move 1** be travelling between one place or another **2** be moving **get a move on** (*spoken*) hurry up **make a move** (*GB, infml*) begin a journey or task

movement /'muːvmənt/ *n* **1** [C,U] (act of) moving the body or part of the body **2** [C, with *sing* or *pl verb*] group of people with a shared set of aims or principles: *the peace ~* **3** [C] one of the main sections of a piece of music

movie /'muːvi/ *n* (*esp US*) **1** [C] cinema film **2** (**the movies**) [pl] the cinema

mow /məʊ/ *v* (*pt* ~**ed** *pp* ~**n** /məʊn/ or ~**ed**) [T] cut grass, etc, esp with a lawnmower [PV] **mow sb down** kill people in large numbers, using a vehicle or a gun ▶ **mower** n = LAWN-MOWER (LAWN)

MP /ˌem ˈpiː/ abbr, n (esp GB) Member of Parliament

mpg /ˌem piː ˈdʒiː/ abbr miles per gallon

mph /ˌem piː ˈeɪtʃ/ abbr miles per hour

MPV /ˌem piː ˈviː/ n multi-purpose vehicle; large car like a van

Mr /ˈmɪstə(r)/ abbr title for a man

Mrs /ˈmɪsɪz/ abbr title for a married woman

Ms /mɪz; məz/ abbr title for a married or unmarried woman

Mt abbr = MOUNT: Mt Everest

much /mʌtʃ/ det, pron A large amount or quantity of sth: I haven't got ~ money. ◇ too ~ salt ◇ How ~ is it (= What does it cost)? ◇ not much of a ... not a good ...: He's not ~ of a runner. ● **much** adj to a great degree: work ~ harder ◇ He isn't in the office ~ (= often). ◇ My new job is ~ the same as the old one. [IDM] **much as** although: M~ as I want to stay, I must go.

muck /mʌk/ n [U] **1** waste matter from farm animals; manure **2** (infml) dirt or mud ● **muck** v [PV] **muck about/around** (GB, infml) behave in a silly way **muck in** (GB, infml) work with other people to complete a task: If we all ~ in we'll soon get the job done. **muck sth up** (infml, esp GB) **1** do sth badly; spoil sth **2** make sth dirty ▶ **mucky** adj (-ier, -iest)

mucous /ˈmjuːkəs/ adj of or covered with mucus ■ **mucous 'membrane** n (anat) moist skin that lines parts of the body such as the nose and mouth

mucus /ˈmjuːkəs/ n [U] sticky liquid produced by the mucous membrane eg in the nose

mud /mʌd/ n [U] soft wet earth ▶ **muddy** adj (-ier, -iest) ■ **'mudguard** n curved cover over a wheel of a bicycle

muddle /ˈmʌdl/ n [C, usu sing] state of confusion or untidiness ● **muddle** v [T] **1** put things in the wrong order or mix them up **2** confuse sb [PV] **muddle along** (esp GB) continue doing sth with no clear plan or purpose **muddle through** achieve your aims, even though you do not really know how to do things

muesli /ˈmjuːzli/ n [U] breakfast food of grain, nuts, dried fruit, etc

muffle /ˈmʌfl/ v [T] **1** make sound quieter and less easily heard **2** wrap or cover sb/sth for warmth ▶ **muffler** n **1** (old-fash) scarf worn

round the neck for warmth **2** (US) = SILENCER (SILENCE)

mug /mʌɡ/ n **1** tall cup for drinking from, usu with straight sides and a handle **2** mug and what it contains **3** (sl) person's face **4** (infml) person who is stupid and easy to trick ● **mug** v (-gg-) [T] attack sb violently in order to steal their money ▶ **mugger** n ▶ **mugging** n [C, U]

muggy /ˈmʌɡi/ adj (-ier, -iest) (of weather) unpleasantly warm and damp

Muhammad (also **Mohammed**) /məˈhæməd/ n Arab prophet and founder of Islam

mulberry /ˈmʌlbəri/ n (pl -ies) (purple or white fruit of a) tree with broad dark green leaves

mule /mjuːl/ n animal that is half donkey and half horse, used for carrying heavy loads

mull /mʌl/ v [PV] **mull sth over** think about sth carefully: Give me time to ~ it over before deciding what to do.

mulled /mʌld/ adj (of wine) mixed with sugar and spices and heated

multi- /ˈmʌlti/ prefix (in nouns and adjectives) more than one; many: ~-million society

multilateral /ˌmʌltiˈlætərəl/ adj in which three or more countries, groups, etc take part

multimedia /ˌmʌltiˈmiːdiə/ adj (in computing) using sound, pictures and film in addition to text on a screen: the ~ industry (= producing CD-ROMs, etc)

multinational /ˌmʌltiˈnæʃnəl/ adj involving many countries ▶ **multinational** n very large powerful company that operates in many countries

multiple /ˈmʌltɪpl/ adj many in number; involving many different people or things ● **multiple** n (maths) quantity that contains another quantity an exact number of times: 28 is a ~ of 7. ■ ,multiple-'choice adj (of exam questions) with several possible answers shown from which you must choose the correct one ■ ,multiple scle'rosis /sklə'rəʊsɪs/ n (abbr **MS**) serious disease of the nervous system that causes loss of control of movement and speech

multiply /ˈmʌltɪplaɪ/ v (pt, pp -ied) [I, T] **1** add a number to itself the number of times that is mentioned: 6 multiplied by 5 is 30. **2** (cause sth to) increase in number or amount **3** (biol) (cause sth to) reproduce in large numbers: Rabbits ~ quickly. ▶ **multiplication** /-ˈkeɪʃn/ n [U, C]

multi-purpose /ˌmʌltiˈpɜːpəs/ adj

able to be used for several different purposes

multi-skilling /,mʌlti'skɪlɪŋ/ n [U] (business) fact of a person being trained in several different jobs requiring different skills

multitasking /,mʌlti'tɑːskɪŋ/ n [U] **1** (computing) ability of a computer to operate several programs at the same time **2** activity of doing several things at the same time

multitude /'mʌltɪtjuːd/ n (fml) large number of people or things

mum /mʌm/ (US **mom**) n (infml) mother ● **mum** adj [IDM] **keep mum** (infml) say nothing about sth, keep silent **mum's the word!** (infml) used to tell sb to keep sth secret

mumble /'mʌmbl/ v [I, T] speak or say sth unclearly

mummify /'mʌmɪfaɪ/ v (pt, pp -ied) [T] preserve a dead body by treating it with oils and wrapping it in cloth

mummy /'mʌmi/ n (pl -ies) **1** (US **mommy**) (infml) child's word for a mother **2** dead body that has been mummified: an Egyptian ~

mumps /mʌmps/ n [U] disease, esp of children, that causes painful swellings in the neck

munch /mʌntʃ/ v [I, T] eat sth steadily and often noisily

mundane /mʌn'deɪn/ adj not interesting or exciting

municipal /mjuːˈnɪsɪpl/ adj of a town or city with its own local government ▸ **municipality** /mjuːˌnɪsɪ-ˈpæləti/ n (pl -ies) town or city with its own local government

munitions /mjuːˈnɪʃnz/ n [pl] military supplies, esp bombs and guns

mural /'mjʊərəl/ n picture painted on a wall

murder /'mɜːdə(r)/ n **1** [U,C] crime of killing sb deliberately **2** [U] (spoken) used to describe sth difficult or unpleasant: Climbing that hill was ~. ● **murder** v [T] kill sb deliberately and illegally ▸ **murderer** n person guilty of murder ▸ **murderous** adj intending or likely to murder: a ~ous attack

murky /'mɜːki/ adj (-ier, -iest) unpleasantly dark: ~ waters of the river

murmur /'mɜːmə(r)/ v [T] say sth in a low voice: [I] make a quiet continuous sound ● **murmur** n **1** quietly spoken word(s) **2** quiet expression of feeling: He paid the extra cost without a ~ (= without complaining at all). **3** low continuous sound in the background

muscle /'mʌsl/ n [C,U] **1** (one of the pieces of) elastic tissue in the body that you tighten to produce movement **2** [U] physical strength

● **muscle** v [PV] **muscle in (on sb/sth)** (infml, disapprov) join in sth when you have no right to do so, for your own advantage

muscular /'mʌskjələ(r)/ adj **1** of the muscles **2** having large strong muscles

museum /mjuˈziːəm/ n building in which objects of art, history or science are shown

mushroom /'mʌʃrʊm/ n fungus of which some kinds can be eaten ● **mushroom** v [I] spread or grow in number quickly

music /'mjuːzɪk/ n [U] **1** sounds arranged in a way that is pleasant or exciting to listen to: listen to ~ **2** art of writing or playing music **3** written or printed signs representing the sounds to be played or sung in a piece of music ▸ **musical** /-kl/ adj **1** of music **2** fond of or skilled in music ▸ **musical** n play or film with songs and usu dancing ■ **musical 'instrument** n object used for producing musical sounds, eg a piano or a drum ▸ **musically** /-kli/ adv

musician /mjuˈzɪʃn/ n person skilled in playing music; writer of music

Muslim /'mʊzlɪm/ n person whose religion is Islam ● **Muslim** adj of Muslims or Islam

muslin /'mʌzlɪn/ n [U] thin fine cotton cloth

mussel /'mʌsl/ n kind of edible shellfish with a black shell

must /məst; strong form mʌst/ modal v (neg **must not** short form **mustn't** /'mʌsnt/) **1** used to say that sth is necessary or very important (often involving a rule or law): You ~ finish your work before you go. ◊ Visitors ~ not feed the birds. **2** used to say sth is likely or logical: You ~ be (= I am sure that you are) tired after your journey. ● **must** n (infml) thing that must be done, seen, etc: Her new film is a ~.

mustache (US) = MOUSTACHE

mustard /'mʌstəd/ n [U] yellow substance made from the seeds of a plant, used to flavour food

muster /'mʌstə(r)/ v **1** [T] find as much support, courage, etc as you can: She left the room with all the dignity she could ~. **2** [I, T] (cause people to) gather together

musty /'mʌsti/ adj (-ier, -iest) smelling damp and unpleasant because of a lack of fresh air

mutation /mjuːˈteɪʃn/ n [C,U] (biol) (instance of) change in a living thing that causes a new kind of thing to develop: genetic ~s

mute /mjuːt/ adj (written) not

speaking ● **mute** n **1** (music) device used to lessen the sound of a musical instrument **2** (old-fash) person who is unable to speak ▶ **muted** adj quiet; gentle; not bright: ~d colours

mutilate /'mju:tɪleɪt/ v [T] damage sb's body severely, esp by cutting or tearing off part of it ▶ **mutilation** /ˌmju:tɪ'leɪʃn/ n [U,C]

mutiny /'mju:təni/ n [U,C] (pl **-ies**) rebellion against authority, esp by sailors ▶ **mutineer** /ˌmju:tə'nɪə(r)/ n person who takes part in a mutiny ▶ **mutinous** /-nəs/ adj refusing to obey sb in authority: mutiny ● **mutiny** v (pt, pp **-ied**) [I] (esp of soldiers and sailors) refuse to obey sb in authority

mutter /'mʌtə(r)/ v [I, T] speak or say sth in a low quiet voice, esp because you are annoyed about sth ● **mutter** n [C, us sing] quiet sound or words that are difficult to hear

mutton /'mʌtn/ n [U] meat from a sheep

mutual /'mju:tʃuəl/ adj **1** felt or done by each towards the other: ~ affection/respect **2** shared by two or more people: a ~ friend ▶ **mutually** /-uəli/ adv

muzzle /'mʌzl/ n **1** nose and mouth of an animal **2** guard placed over the nose and mouth of an animal to prevent it from biting people **3** open end of a gun, where the bullets come out ● **muzzle** v [T] **1** put a muzzle over a dog's head **2** prevent sb from expressing their opinions freely

MW abbr = MEDIUM WAVE (MEDIUM)

my /maɪ/ det **1** of or belonging to me: Where's my hat? **2** used in exclamations to express surprise, etc: My goodness! **3** used when addressing sb to show affection: my dear

myopia /maɪ'əupiə/ n [U] (tech) inability to see clearly objects that are far away ▶ **myopic** /-'ɒpɪk/ adj

myriad /'mɪriəd/ n [U] (lit) extremely large number: a ~ of stars

myrrh /mɜ:(r)/ n [U] sticky sweet-smelling substance that comes from trees, used for making incense and perfume

myself /maɪ'self/ pron **1** (the reflexive form of I) used when the speaker or writer is also the person affected by the action: I've cut ~. **2** used to emphasize that the speaker is doing sth: I'll speak to her ~. [IDM] (**all**) **by myself 1** alone; without anyone else **2** without help

mysterious /mɪ'stɪəriəs/ adj **1** hard to understand or explain: her ~ disappearance **2** keeping things secret: He's been very ~ and not told anyone his plans. ▶ **mysteriously** adv

mystery /'mɪstri/ n (pl **-ies**) **1** [C] something that cannot be understood or explained: Her disappearance is a real ~. **2** [U] quality of being difficult to understand or explain

mystic /'mɪstɪk/ (also **mystical** /'mɪstɪkl/) adj having hidden meaning or spiritual powers ● **mystic** n person who practises mysticism ▶ **mysticism** /'mɪstɪsɪzəm/ n [U] belief that knowledge of God and real truth can be found through prayer and meditation

mystify /'mɪstɪfaɪ/ v (pt, pp **-ied**) [T] make sb confused because they do not understand sth

mystique /mɪ'sti:k/ n [U, sing] quality of mystery associated with a person or thing: The ~ surrounding the monarchy has gone for ever.

myth /mɪθ/ n [C, U] **1** (type of) story from ancient times: ancient Greek ~s **2** something that many people believe but that does not exist or is false ▶ **mythical** /-ɪkl/ adj **1** existing only in myths **2** that does not exist or is not true

mythology /mɪ'θɒlədʒi/ n [U,C] **1** group of ancient myths: Greek ~ **2** ideas or facts that many people believe but that are not true ▶ **mythological** /ˌmɪθə'lɒdʒɪkl/ adj of ancient myths

Nn

N abbr north(ern): N Yorkshire

N, n /en/ n [C,U] (pl **N's, n's** /enz/) the fourteenth letter of the English alphabet

nab /næb/ v (**-bb-**) [T] (infml) **1** catch sb doing wrong **2** take or get sth: Who ~bed my drink?

nag /næg/ v (**-gg-**) [I, T] ~(**at**) **1** keep criticizing sb or asking them to do sth **2** worry or irritate you continuously

nail /neɪl/ n **1** thin hard layer covering the outer tip of the fingers or toes **2** small thin pointed piece of metal, hit with a hammer, eg to hold pieces of wood together ● **nail** v [T] **1** fasten sth to sth with a nail or nails **2** (infml) catch sb and prove they are guilty of a crime [PV] **nail sb down** (**to sth**) force sb to say clearly what they plan to do

naive (also **naïve**) /naɪ'i:v/ adj **1** (disapprov) lacking experience of life and willing to believe that people always tell you the truth **2** (of people and their behaviour) innocent and simple ▶ **naively** adv ▶ **naivety** n [U]

naked /'neɪkɪd/ adj **1** not wearing

any clothes **2** without the usual covering: *a ~ light* [IDM] **the naked eye** normal power of the eye without the help of an instrument ▸ **nakedly** *adv* ▸ **nakedness** *n* [U]

name /neɪm/ *n* **1** [C] word(s) by which a person or thing is known: *My ~ is Tim.* **2** [usu sing] general opinion that people have of sb/sth; reputation: *She made her ~ as a writer of children's books.* **3** [C] famous person: *the big ~s in show business* [IDM] **in the name of sb/sth 1** on behalf of sb/sth **2** by the authority of sth: *I arrest you in the ~ of the law.* **make a name for yourself** become well known **take sb's name in vain** talk disrespectfully about sb ● **name** *v* [T] **1** ~ (**after**) (*US*) ~(**for**) give a name to sb/sth: *The child was ~d after his father.* **2** say the name(s) of sb/sth: *The victim has not been ~d.* **3** state sth exactly; choose sb/sth: *~ the day for the party* ■ '**name-dropping** *n* [U] (*disapprov*) mentioning the names of famous people that you know in order to impress others ▸ **nameless** *adj* **1** having no name **2** not to be mentioned or described: *~less horrors* ■ '**namesake** *n* person or thing with the same name as sb/sth else

namely /'neɪmli/ *adv* that is to say: *Only one child was missing, ~ John.*

nanny /'næni/ *n* (*pl* **-ies**) woman employed to look after children

nanny goat /'næni ɡəʊt/ *n* female goat

nap /næp/ *n* **1** [C] short sleep, esp during the day **2** [sing] surface of cloth, etc made of soft hairs usu brushed in one direction ● **nap** *v* (-**pp-**) [I] sleep for a short time, esp during the day

napalm /'neɪpɑːm/ *n* [U] petrol jelly used in bombs

nape /neɪp/ *n* [C, sing] back of the neck

napkin /'næpkɪn/ *n* piece of cloth or paper used at meals for protecting your clothes and wiping your hands and lips

nappy /'næpi/ *n* (*pl* **-ies**) piece of cloth or padding folded round a baby's bottom to absorb waste matter

narcissus /nɑːˈsɪsəs/ *n* (*pl* **narcissi** /nɑːˈsɪsaɪ/) one of several kinds of spring flower, eg daffodil

narcotic /nɑːˈkɒtɪk/ *n, adj* (kind of drug) producing sleep

narrate /nəˈreɪt/ *v* [T] (*fml*) tell a story ▸ **narration** /nəˈreɪʃn/ *n* [C, U] ▸ **narrator** *n* person who narrates

narrative /ˈnærətɪv/ *n* **1** [C] description of events, esp in a novel **2** [U] act, process of skill of telling a story

narrow /ˈnærəʊ/ *adj* **1** small in

width: *a ~ road* **2** only just achieved or avoided: *a ~ escape* **3** limited in a way that ignores important issues or the opinions of others: *a ~ view of the world* **4** limited in variety or numbers: *a ~ circle of friends* ● **narrow** *v* [I, T] become or make sth narrower ▸ **narrowly** *adv* only by a small amount: *~ly escape* ■ **narrow-'minded** *adj* (*disapprov*) not willing to consider new ideas or the opinions of others ▸ **narrowness** *n* [U]

nasal /ˈneɪzl/ *adj* of or in the nose

nasturtium /nəˈstɜːʃəm/ *n* garden plant with red, orange or yellow flowers

nasty /ˈnɑːsti/ *adj* (-**ier**, -**iest**) **1** very bad or unpleasant: *a ~ taste* **2** unkind; unpleasant: *make ~ remarks about sb* **3** dangerous or serious: *a ~ injury* ▸ **nastily** *adv* ■ **nastiness** *n* [U]

nation /ˈneɪʃn/ *n* large community of people living in a particular country under one government ■ **nation'wide** *adj, adv* over the whole of a nation

national /ˈnæʃnəl/ *adj* **1** of a particular nation; shared by a whole nation: *local and ~ news* **2** owned, controlled or supported by the federal government: *a ~ airline* ● **national** *n* (*tech*) citizen of a particular country ■ **national 'anthem** *n* official song of a nation ■ **National 'Health Service** *n* [sing] (*abbr* **NHS**) (in Britain) public service that provides medical care, paid for by taxes ■ **National In'surance** *n* [U] (*abbr* **NI**) (in Britain) system of compulsory payments made by workers to provide help for the sick, elderly or the unemployed ▸ **nationalism** *n* [U] **1** feeling that your country should be politically independent **2** love of and support for your own country ▸ **nationalist** *adj, n* ▸ **nationally** *adv* ■ **national 'service** *n* [U] period of compulsory service in the armed forces

nationality /ˌnæʃəˈnæləti/ *n* [U, C] (*pl* **-ies**) legal right of belonging to a particular nation: *a person with French ~*

nationalize (*also* **-ise**) /ˈnæʃnəlaɪz/ *v* [T] transfer a company from private to government ownership ▸ **nationalization** (*also* **-isation**) /ˌnæʃnəlaɪˈzeɪʃn/ *n* [U]

native /ˈneɪtɪv/ *n* **1** person born in a place or country **2** person who lives in a place, esp sb who has lived there a long time **3** animal or plant which occurs naturally in a place ● **native** *adj* **1** of the place of your birth: *my ~ city* **2** (of an animal or plant) found naturally in a certain area ■ **Native A'merican** *n, adj* (of a) member of any of the races of people who were the original people living in America

nativity /nə'tɪvəti/ *n* (the Nativity) [sing] birth of Jesus Christ

NATO /'neɪtəʊ/ *n* [sing] North Atlantic Treaty Organization; military association of several countries

natural /'nætʃrəl/ *adj* **1** existing in nature; not made or caused by humans: *the earth's ~ resources* (= its coal, oil, etc) **2** normal; as you would expect: *to die of ~ causes* (= of old age) **3** of the basic character of a living thing: *It's ~ for a bird to fly.* **4** born with a certain skill: *a ~ artist* **5** relaxed and not pretending to be sth/sth different ● **natural** *n* person who is very good at sth without having to learn how to do it: *That dancer is a ~.* ■ **natural 'history** *n* [U] study of plants and animals

naturalist /'nætʃrəlɪst/ *n* person who studies plants and animals

naturalize (also **-ise**) /'nætʃrəlaɪz/ *v* [T] make sb from another country a citizen of a country ▶ **naturalization** (also **-isation**) /ˌnætʃrəlaɪ'zeɪʃn/ *n* [U]

naturally /'nætʃrəli/ *adv* **1** in a way that you would expect; of course: *N~, I'll help you.* **2** without artificial help **3** as a skill from birth: *She's ~ musical.* **4** in a relaxed and normal way: *behave ~*

nature /'neɪtʃə(r)/ *n* **1** (often **Nature**) [U] all the plants, animals and things that exist in the universe and are not made by people: *the beauties of ~* **2** (often **Nature**) [U] way that things happen in the physical world when it is not controlled by people: *the forces/laws of ~* **3** [C,U] typical qualities of sb/sth: *It's her ~ to be kind.* **4** [sing] type or kind of sth: *changes of that ~* [IDM] **(get, go, etc) back to nature** return to a simple life in the country, away from civilization ■ **'nature reserve** *n* area of land where the animals and plants are protected

naught /nɔːt/ *n* = NOUGHT

naughty /'nɔːti/ *adj* (**-ier, -iest**) **1** (esp of a child) disobedient; bad **2** (*infml*) slightly rude; connected with sex ▶ **naughtily** *adv* **naughtiness** *n* [U]

nausea /'nɔːziə; -siə/ *n* [U] feeling of wanting to vomit ▶ **nauseate** /'nɔːzieɪt; 'nɔːsieɪt/ *v* [T] make sb feel that they want to vomit ▶ **nauseous** *adj*

nautical /'nɔːtɪkl/ *adj* of ships, sailors or sailing ■ **nautical 'mile** *n* measure of distance at sea; 1 852 metres

naval /'neɪvl/ *adj* of a navy

nave /neɪv/ *n* long central part of a church

navel /'neɪvl/ *n* small hollow in the middle of the stomach

navigable /'nævɪɡəbl/ *adj* (of a river, etc) wide and deep enough for ships to travel on

navigate /'nævɪɡeɪt/ *v* [I, T] find your position or the position of your ship, plane, car, etc eg by using a map ▶ **navigation** /ˌnævɪ'ɡeɪʃn/ *n* [U] ▶ **navigator** *n*

navy /'neɪvi/ *n* [C, with sing or pl verb] part of a country's armed forces that fights at sea, and the ships that it uses ■ **navy 'blue** (also **navy**) *adj* dark blue

NB /ˌen 'biː/ *abbr* (used in writing to make sb take notice of an important piece of information

near¹ /nɪə(r)/ *adj* **1** a short distance away in space or time: *Where's the ~est bank?* **2** used to describe a close family connection: *~ relations* [IDM] **a near thing** a situation in which failure or disaster is only just avoided ● **near** *v* [I, T] (*fml*) come closer to sth: *The ship is ~ing land.* ▶ **nearness** *n* [U] ■ **'nearside** *adj, n* [sing] (GB) (for a driver) (on the) side nearest the edge of the road ■ **near'sighted** (*esp US*) = SHORT-SIGHTED (SHORT)

near² /nɪə(r)/ *prep* **1** at a short distance away from sth: *Do you live ~ here?* **2** short period of time from sth ● **near** *adv* at a short distance away [IDM] **nowhere near** far from ■ **'near by** *adv* a short distance away from sb/sth: *They live ~ by.* ■ **near by** *adj* not far away ▶ **nearly** *adv* almost; not quite; not completely [IDM] **not nearly** much less than; not at all: *not ~ly enough money*

neat /niːt/ *adj* **1** tidy and in order; carefully done or arranged: *a ~ answer to the problem* **2** (of people) liking to keep things tidy and in order **3** simple but clever: *a ~ idea* **4** (esp of an alcoholic drink) not mixed with water or anything else ▶ **neatly** *adv* **neatness** *n* [U]

necessary /'nesəsəri/ *adj* that is needed for a purpose or reason: *Have you made the ~ arrangements?* ▶ **necessarily** /ˌnesə'serəli; 'nesəsərəli/ *adv* used to say that sth cannot be avoided [IDM] **not necessarily** used to say that sth is possibly true but not always

necessitate /nə'sesɪteɪt/ *v* [T] (*fml*) make sth necessary

necessity /nə'sesəti/ *n* (*pl* **-ies**) **1** [U] fact that sth must be done; need for sth **2** [C] thing that you must have and cannot manage without: *Food is a ~ of life.*

neck /nek/ *n* **1** part of the body that joins the head to the shoulders **2** part of a piece of clothing that fits around the neck **3** long narrow part of sth: *the ~ of a bottle* [IDM] **be up to your neck in sth** be very deeply involved in sth **neck and neck (with sb/sth)** level with sb in a race or competition **risk/save your neck** risk/save your life ● **neck** v [I] (*infml*) (of couples) hug and kiss each other ■ **necklace** /'neklɪs/ *n* decorative string of beads, jewels, etc worn round the neck ■ **'necktie** *n* (*old-fash*) (*US*) = TIE¹(1)

nectar /'nektə(r)/ *n* [U] sweet liquid collected by bees from plants

née /neɪ/ *adj* used after the name of a woman to give her family name before she married: *Mrs Jane Smith,~ Brown*

need¹ /niːd/ *modal v* (*pres tense, all persons neg* **need not** *short form* **needn't** /'niːdnt/) used to show what is/was necessary: *You ~n't finish that work today.* ● **need** *v* [T] **1** require sth/sb to do: *That dog ~s a bath.* **2** used to show what you should or have to do

need² /niːd/ *n* **1** [sing, U] situation when sth is necessary or must be done: *There's a ~ for more nurses.* ◊ *There's no ~ to start yet.* **2** [C, usu pl] things that sb requires in order to live comfortably: *financial/physical ~s* **3** [U] state of not having enough food, money or support: *people in ~* [IDM] **if need be** if necessary ► **needless** *adj* unnecessary [IDM] **needless to say** used to emphasize that the information you are giving is obvious ► **needlessly** *adv* ► **needy** *adj* (**-ier, -iest**) very poor

needle /'niːdl/ *n* **1** small pointed piece of steel, with a hole at the top for thread, used in sewing **2** = KNITTING NEEDLE (KNIT) **3** the thin pointed piece of steel on the end of a syringe used for giving injections: *a hypodermic ~* **4** small pointed piece of metal that touches a record that is being played ● **needle** *v* [T] (*infml*) deliberately annoy sb ■ **'needlework** *n* [U] sewing; embroidery

negation /nɪ'geɪʃn/ *n* [U] (*fml*) act of denying or refusing sth

negative /'negətɪv/ *adj* **1** bad or harmful: *have a ~ effect on sb* **2** lacking enthusiasm or hope **3** (of words, answers, etc) showing or meaning 'no' or 'not' **4** (*tech*) of the kind of electric charge carried by electrons: *a ~ charge/current* **5** less than zero ● **negative** *n* **1** word or statement that means 'no' or 'not': *He answered in the ~.* (= said 'no'). **2** photographic film with light and dark areas reversed ► **negatively** *adv*

neglect /nɪ'glekt/ *v* [T] **1** fail to take care of sb/sth: *She denied ~ing her children.* **2** not give enough atten-

tion to sth: *~ your work* **3** fail or forget to do sth ● **neglect** *n* [U] fact of neglecting sb/sth or of being neglected ► **neglectful** *adj* (*fml*) not giving enough care or attention to sb/sth

negligee (*also* **negligée**) /'neglɪʒeɪ/ *n* woman's thin light dressing gown

negligent /'neglɪdʒənt/ *adj* (*fml*) or (*law*) failing to give sb/sth enough care or attention ► **negligence** /-dʒəns/ *n* [U] ► **negligently** *adv*

negligible /'neglɪdʒəbl/ *adj* of very little importance or size

negotiable /nɪ'gəʊʃiəbl/ *adj* **1** that can be discussed or arranged before an agreement is reached **2** (*business*) that can be exchanged for money or given to sb else in exchange for money

negotiate /nɪ'gəʊʃieɪt/ *v* [I, T] **1** to reach an agreement by formal discussion **2** [T] successfully get past or over an obstacle ► **negotiation** /nɪ,gəʊʃi'eɪʃn/ *n* [C, U] ► **negotiator** *n* person who negotiates

neigh /neɪ/ *v* [I] (make the) long high sound of a horse

neighbour (*US* **-or**) /'neɪbə(r)/ *n* **1** person who lives in a house, etc near another **2** person, thing or country that is next to or near another ► **neighbourhood** *n* district; nearby area [IDM] **in the neighbourhood of** approximately ► **neighbouring** *adj* near to sth: *~ing towns* ► **neighbourliness** *n* [U] friendliness ► **neighbourly** *adj* friendly

neither /'naɪðə(r); 'niːðə(r)/ *det, pron* not one nor the other of two things or people: *N~ answer is correct.* ● **neither** *adv* **1** used to show that a negative statement is also true of sb/sth else: *She doesn't like Mozart and ~ do I.* ◊ *I've never been to Paris and ~ has she.* **2** (**neither ... nor ...**) used to show that a negative statement is true of two things: *N~ his sister nor his brother was invited.*

neon /'niːɒn/ *n* [U] (*symb* **Ne**) colourless gas used in electric lights

nephew /'nefjuː; 'nevjuː/ *n* son of your brother(-in-law) or sister(-in-law)

nepotism /'nepətɪzəm/ *n* [U] (*disapprov*) giving unfair advantages to your own family if you are in a position of power

nerve /nɜːv/ *n* **1** [C] any of the long thin threads that carry messages between the brain and parts of the body, enabling you to move, feel pain, etc **2** (**nerves**) [pl] feelings of worry or anxiety: *I need something to calm my ~s.* **3** [U] courage to do sth difficult or dangerous: *lose your ~* **4** [sing, U] (*infml*) way of behaving that people think is rude or not appropriate: *He's got a ~ asking us for money!* [IDM] **get on sb's nerves** (*infml*) annoy sb ■ **'nerve-racking** *adj* causing great worry

nervous /'nɜːvəs/ *adj* **1** ~**about/of** anxious about sth or afraid of sth **2** easily worried or frightened: *a thin, ~ woman* **3** of the body's nerves: *a ~ disorder* ■ **,nervous 'breakdown** *n* mental illness that causes depression, tiredness and weakness ▸ **nervously** *adv* ▸ **nervousness** *n* [U] ■ **'nervous system** *n* system of all the nerves in the body

nervy /'nɜːvi/ *adj* (*infml*) **1** (GB) anxious and nervous **2** (US) rude and disrespectful

nest /nest/ *n* **1** place made by a bird for its eggs **2** group of similar things (esp tables) made to fit inside each other ● **nest** *v* [I] make and use a nest ■ **'nest egg** *n* sum of money saved for future use

nestle /'nesl/ *v* **1** [I] sit or lie down in a warm or soft place: ~ (*down*) *among the cushions* **2** [T] put or hold sb/sth in a comfortable position in a warm or soft place

nestling /'nestlɪŋ/ *n* bird that is too young to leave its nest

net /net/ *n* **1** [C,U] (piece of) loose open material made of knotted string, wire, etc: ~ *curtains* ◇ *fishing* ~*s* **2** (**the Net**) [sing] (*infml*) = THE INTERNET ● **net** (GB also **nett**) *adj* remaining when nothing more is to be taken away: ~ *income* (= after tax has been paid) ● **net** *v* (**-tt-**) [T] **1** earn an amount of money as a profit after you have paid tax on it **2** catch sth (as if) with a net ■ **'netball** *n* team game in which a ball is thrown through a net on the top of a post

netting /'netɪŋ/ *n* [U] material made of string, wire, etc that is woven or tied together

nettle /'netl/ *n* common wild plant with leaves that sting if you touch them

network /'netwɜːk/ *n* **1** complex system of roads, lines, nerves, etc crossing each other **2** closely linked group of people, companies, etc **3** (*computing*) number of computers, etc linked together so that equipment and information can be shared **4** group of radio or television stations

neurology /njʊə'rɒlədʒi/ *n* [U] study of nerves and their diseases ▸ **neurologist** *n* doctor who studies and treats diseases of the nerves

neurosis /njʊə'rəʊsɪs/ *n* [C,U] (*pl* **-oses** /-əʊsiːz/) (*med*) mental illness causing strong feelings of fear or worry

neurotic /njʊə'rɒtɪk/ *adj* abnor-

mally sensitive and anxious ● **neurotic** *n* neurotic person

neuter /'njuːtə(r)/ *adj* (*gram*) neither masculine nor feminine in gender ● **neuter** *v* [T] remove the sex organs of an animal so that it cannot produce young

neutral /'njuːtrəl/ *adj* **1** not supporting either side in an argument, war, etc **2** having no clear or strong qualities: *a dull ~ colour* **3** (*chem*) neither acid nor alkaline ● **neutral** *n* **1** [U] position of the gears of a vehicle in which no power is carried from the engine to the wheels: *leave the car in ~* **2** [C] neutral person or country ▸ **neutrality** /njuː-'træləti/ *n* [U] state of not supporting either side in an argument, etc ▸ **neutralize** (*also* **-ise**) /-z/ [T] **1** stop sth from having any effect **2** (*chem*) make a substance neutral(3)

neutron /'njuːtrɒn/ *n* (*physics*) tiny particle of matter inside an atom, with no electric charge

never /'nevə(r)/ *adv* **1** not at any time; not on any occasion: *I ~ eat meat.*

nevertheless /,nevəðə'les/ *adv* (*fml*) in spite of sth you have just mentioned: *Our defeat was expected but it was disappointing ~.*

new /njuː/ *adj* **1** not existing before; recently made, introduced, etc: *a ~ film* **2** different from the previous one: *get a ~ job* **3** already existing, but not seen, experienced, etc before: *learn ~ words* **4** ~(**to**) not yet familiar with sth: *I'm ~ to this town.* **5** used in compounds to describe sth that has recently happened: *enjoying his ~-found freedom* **6** just beginning or beginning again: *He went to Australia to start a ~ life.* [IDM] **new blood → BLOOD ■ 'newcomer** *n* person who has recently arrived in a place ▸ **newly** *adv* recently: *a ~ly married couple* ■ **,newly-'wed** *n* [usu pl] person who has recently got married ■ **,new 'moon** *n* the moon appearing as a thin crescent ▸ **newness** *n* [U] ■ **,new 'year** (*also* **,New 'Year**) *n* [U,sing] the beginning of the year: *Happy New~ Year!*

news /njuːz/ *n* **1** [U] new information about sth that has happened recently: *Here's some good ~!* **2** [U] reports of recent events in newspapers or on television or radio: *He's always in the ~.* **3** (**the news**) [sing] regular television or radio broadcast of the latest news ■ **'newsagent** (*US* **'newsdealer**) *n* shopkeeper who sells newspapers, etc ■ **'newsflash** *n* short piece of important news on television or radio ■ **'newspaper** *n* printed publication, issued daily or weekly, with news, advertisements, etc

newt /njuːt/ n small lizard-like animal that can live in water or on land

next /nekst/ adj **1** coming straight after sb/sth in order, space or time: the ~ name on the list **2** the one immediately following: ~ Thursday ● **next** adv after sth else; then; afterwards: What are you going to do ~? ■ **next 'door** adv, adj in or the next house ■ **next of 'kin** n [C,U] your closest living relatives ■ **next to** prep **1** in or into a position beside sb/sth: Come and sit ~ to me. **2** almost: ~ to no time

NHS /ˌen eɪtʃ 'es/ abbr = NATIONAL HEALTH SERVICE (NATIONAL)

nib /nɪb/ n metal point of a pen

nibble /'nɪbl/ v [I,T] take small bites of sth ● **nibble** n a small bite of sth

nice /naɪs/ adj (~r, ~st) **1** pleasant, enjoyable or attractive: a ~ day **2** used before adjectives or adverbs to emphasize how pleasant sth is: I had a ~ hot bath. **3** kind; friendly: ~ neighbours **4** bad or unpleasant: You've got us into a ~ mess! **5** (fml) involving a small detail or distinction ▸ **nicely** adv in a nice way [IDM] **do nicely 1** (usu be doing nicely) be making good progress **2** be satisfactory: Tomorrow at ten will do ~ly. ▸ **niceness** n [U]

nicety /'naɪsəti/ n (pl -ies) (written) small distinction: niceties of meaning

niche /niːʃ; nɪtʃ/ n **1** comfortable or suitable role, job, etc **2** (business) opportunity to sell a product to a particular group of people: I spotted a ~ in the market. **3** small hollow place in a wall, eg for a statue

nick /nɪk/ n **1** (the ~) [sing] (GB, sl) prison or police station **2** [C] small cut in the edge or surface of sth [IDM] **in good, etc nick** (GB, infml) in good, etc condition or health **in the nick of time** (infml) at the very last moment ● **nick** v [T] **1** make a small cut in sth: He ~ed himself shaving. **2** (GB, infml) steal sth **3** (GB, infml) arrest sb

nickel /'nɪkl/ n **1** [U] (symb Ni) hard silver-white metal **2** [C] coin of the US or Canada worth 5 cents

nickname /'nɪkneɪm/ n informal name used instead of sb's real name ● **nickname** v [T] give sb a nickname to sb/sth

nicotine /'nɪkətiːn/ n [U] poisonous substance found in tobacco

niece /niːs/ n daughter of your brother(-in-law) or sister(-in-law)

night /naɪt/ n [C,U] time of darkness between one day and the next: These animals only come out at ~. [IDM] **have a good/bad night** sleep well/badly ■ **night and day | day and night** all the

time; continuously ■ **'nightclub** n place that is open until late in the evening where people can go to dance, drink, etc ■ **'nightdress** (also infml **nightie** /'naɪti/) n long loose piece of clothing, worn by a woman or girl in bed ■ **'nightfall** n [U] (fml or lit) time in the evening when it gets dark ■ **'nightlife** n [U] entertainment that is available at night ▸ **nightly** adj, adv happening every night ■ **'nightmare** n **1** frightening dream **2** (infml) very frightening or unpleasant experience ■ **night 'watchman** n (pl -men) man employed to guard a building at night

nightingale /'naɪtɪŋgeɪl/ n small bird that sings sweetly

nil /nɪl/ n [U] (esp GB) the number 0, esp as the score in some games **2** nothing

nimble /'nɪmbl/ adj (~r, ~st) **1** able to move quickly and easily **2** (of the mind) able to think and understand quickly ▸ **nimbly** adv /-bli/

nine /naɪn/ number 9 ▸ **ninth** /naɪnθ/ ordinal number, n 9th; each of nine equal parts of sth

nineteen /ˌnaɪn'tiːn/ number 19 [IDM] **talk, etc nineteen to the dozen** (GB, infml) talk, etc without stopping ▸ **nineteenth** /-'tiːnθ/ ordinal number 19th

ninety /'naɪnti/ **1** number 90 **2** (the nineties) n [pl] numbers, years or temperatures from 90 to 99 ▸ **ninetieth** ordinal number 90th

nip /nɪp/ v (-pp-) **1** [T] give sb a quick painful bite or pinch **2** [I] (GB, infml) go somewhere quickly and/ or for only a short time: I'll just ~ out to the shops. [IDM] **nip sth in the bud** stop sth in its early development ● **nip** n [C] **1** (usu sing) sharp pinch or bite **2** (infml) a feeling of cold: There's a ~ in the air. **3** (infml) small drink of strong alcohol

nipple /'nɪpl/ n **1** round point of the breast **2** something like a nipple, eg on a baby's bottle

nippy /'nɪpi/ adj (-ier, -iest) (infml) **1** quick: a ~ little car **2** (of the weather) cold

nit /nɪt/ n **1** egg of a parasitic insect that lives in human hair **2** (GB, infml) stupid person

nitrogen /'naɪtrədʒən/ n [U] (symb N) colourless gas that is found in large quantities in the earth's atmosphere

nitroglycerine (esp US **-glycerin**) /ˌnaɪtrəʊ'glɪsəriːn; -rɪn/ n [U] powerful liquid explosive

nitwit /'nɪtwɪt/ n (infml) stupid person

No. (also **no.**) abbr (pl ~s) number

no /nəʊ/ det **1** not one; not any: No child is to leave the room. ◇ She had *no money.* **2** used, eg on notices, to say that sth is not allowed: *No smoking.* **3** used to express the opposite: *He's no fool* (= He's intelligent). ● **no exclam 1** used to give a negative reply or statement: *'Would you like a drink?' 'No thanks.'* **2** used to express shock or surprise at what sb has said: *'I'm leaving.' 'No!'* ● **no adv** used before adjectives and adverbs to mean: *He's feeling no better.* ● **no n** [C] (*pl* ~**es**) **1** word or answer of 'no': *He said, 'No' twice.* **2 the noes** [pl] total number of people voting 'no' in a formal debate: *The noes have it.* ■ **,no-'claims bonus** *n* reduction in the cost of your insurance because you made no claims in the previous year ■ **,no-'go area** *n* (*esp GB*) place, esp in a city, which it is dangerous for people to enter ■ **'no-man's-land** *n* [U, sing] (in war) ground between two opposing armies ■ **no one** = NOBODY

nobility /nəʊˈbɪlətɪ/ *n* **1** (**the nobility**) [sing, with sing or pl verb] people of high social position with titles such as that of duke or duchess **2** [U] (*fml*) quality of being noble in character

noble /ˈnəʊbl/ *adj* (~**r**, ~**st**) **1** having personal qualities admired by others, eg courage and honesty: *a ~ leader* **2** impressive in appearance, size, etc **3** belonging to a family of high social rank ● **noble** *n* person of noble rank or birth ■ **'nobleman** (*fem* **'noblewoman**) *n* person of noble birth or rank ▶ **nobly** /-blɪ/ *adv*

nobody /ˈnəʊbədɪ/ (*also* **no one** /ˈnəʊ wʌn/) *pron* not anybody; no person: *N~ came to see me.* ● **nobody** *n* (*pl* -**ies**) unimportant person

nocturnal /nɒkˈtɜːnl/ *adj* **1** (of animals) active at night **2** (*written*) happening during the night: *a ~ visit*

nod /nɒd/ *v* (**-dd-**) [I, T] move your head up and down to show agreement or as a greeting [PV] **nod off** (*infml*) fall asleep ● **nod** *n* movement of the head down and up again

noise /nɔɪz/ *n* [C, U] sound, esp when loud or unpleasant ▶ **noisy** *adj* (**-ier, -iest**) making a lot of noise ▶ **noisily** *adv*

nomad /ˈnəʊmæd/ *n* member of a tribe that moves from place to place ▶ **nomadic** /nəʊˈmædɪk/ *adj*

nominal /ˈnɒmɪnl/ *adj* **1** being sth in name only; not in reality: *the ~ ruler of the country* **2** (of a sum of money) very small: *a ~ rent* **3** (*gram*) of a noun ▶ **nominally** /-nəlɪ/ *adv*

nominate /ˈnɒmɪneɪt/ *v* [T] suggest officially that sb should be chosen for a role, prize, position, etc ▶ **nomination** /ˌnɒmɪˈneɪʃn/ *n* [U, C]

nominee /ˌnɒmɪˈniː/ *n* **1** person who has been formally suggested

for a job, prize, etc **2** (*business*) person in whose name money is invested in a company, etc

non- /nɒn/ *prefix* not ● **,noncom'missioned** *adj* not having a high rank in the armed forces ■ **,non-com'mittal** *adj* not expressing an opinion or decision clearly ■ **,non-ex'ecutive** *adj* (*GB, business*) (of a company director) able to give advice at a high level but not having the power to make decisions about the company ■ **,noncon'formist** *n, adj* (person) who does not think or behave like other people ■ **,non-'fiction** *n* [U] writing that describes real facts, people and events ■ **,non-'stick** *adj* (of pans) covered with a material that prevents food from sticking during cooking ■ **,non-'stop** *adj, adv* without any stops: *a ~-stop train*

nonchalant /ˈnɒnʃələnt/ *adj* behaving in a calm and relaxed way without showing any anxiety ▶ **nonchalance** /-ləns/ *n* [U] ▶ **nonchalantly** *adv*

nondescript /ˈnɒndɪskrɪpt/ *adj* ordinary; uninteresting

none /nʌn/ *pron* not one; not any: *N~ of them has/have come back yet.* [IDM] **none the less** = NONETHELESS ● **none** *adv* **1** (**none the**) not at all: *He seems ~ the worse for their experience.* **2** (**none too**) not at all; not very: *He looked ~ too happy.*

nonentity /nɒˈnentətɪ/ *n* (*pl* -**ies**) unimportant person

nonetheless (*also* ,**none the 'less**) /ˌnʌnðəˈles/ *adv* (*written*) in spite of this fact: *She may be ill but she got the work done ~ the less.*

nonplussed /ˌnɒnˈplʌst/ *adj* very surprised and puzzled

nonsense /ˈnɒnsns/ *n* **1** [U, C, sing] foolish talk, ideas, etc **2** [U] meaningless words ▶ **nonsensical** /nɒnˈsensɪkl/ *adj* ridiculous; meaningless

noodle /ˈnuːdl/ *n* [C, usu pl] long thin strip of pasta, used esp in Chinese and Italian cooking

nook /nʊk/ *n* sheltered quiet place [IDM] **every nook and cranny** (*infml*) every part of a place

noon /nuːn/ *n* [U] 12 o'clock in the middle of the day

no one = NOBODY

noose /nuːs/ *n* loop of a rope that becomes tighter when the rope is pulled

nor /nɔː(r)/ *conj, adv* **1** (**neither ... nor ...**, **not ...: nor ...**) and not: *Neither Chris ~ his sister wanted to come.* ◇ *He can't see, ~ can he hear.* **2** used before a positive verb to agree with sth negative that has just been said: *I'm not going.' 'N~ am I.'*

norm /nɔːm/ *n* usual or expected way of behaving

normal /'nɔːml/ *adj* typical, usual or ordinary ● **normal** *n* [U] usual state or level ■ **normality** /nɔː'mæləti/ (*esp US* **normalcy** /'nɔːmlsi/) *n* [U] situation where everything is normal or as you would expect ▶ **normally** /-məli/ *adv*

north /nɔːθ/ *n* [U, sing] (*abbr* **N**) **1** (**the north**) point of the compass, to the left of a person watching the sun rise **2** (**the north, the North**) northern part of a country, a region or the world ● **north** *adj* (*abbr* **N**) **1** in or towards the north **2** (of winds) blowing from the north ● **north** *adv* towards the north ■ **north-'east** *n* [sing] *adj, adv* (*abbr* **NE**) (region or region) halfway between north and east ▶ **north-'eastern** *adj* ▶ **northerly** /'nɔːðəli/ *adj, adv* **1** in or towards the north **2** (of winds) blowing from the north ■ **northern** (*also* **Northern**) /'nɔːðən/ *adj* (*abbr* **N**) of the north part of the world or a particular country ▶ **northerner** *n* person born or living in the northern part of a country ▶ **northwards** /'nɔːθwədz/ (*also* **northward**) *adv, adj* towards the north ■ **north-'west** *n* [sing] *adj, adv* (*abbr* **NW**) (region or region) halfway between north and west ▶ **north-'western** *adj*

nose¹ /nəʊz/ *n* **1** [C] part of the face above the mouth for breathing and smelling **2** [C] front part of an aircraft, spacecraft, etc **3** ~**for** [sing] special ability for finding or recognizing sth: *a ~ for a good story* **4** [sing] sense of smell [IDM] **get up sb's nose** (*GB, infml*) annoy sb **poke/stick your nose into sth** (*infml*) interfere in sth that does not concern you **under sb's nose** (*infml*) directly in front of sb ■ **'nosebleed** *n* flow of blood from the nose ■ **'nosedive** *n, v* [I] **1** (of prices, costs, etc) (make a) sudden steep fall or drop: *Oil prices took a ~dive during the crisis.* **2** (make a) sharp vertical drop in an aircraft

nose² /nəʊz/ *v* [I, T] (cause sth to) move forward slowly and carefully [PV] **nose about/around (for sth)** look for sb, esp information about sb: *He's been nosing around in my desk.*

nosey = NOSY

nostalgia /nɒ'stældʒə/ *n* [U] feeling of sadness and pleasure when you think of happy times in the past ▶ **nostalgic** /-dʒɪk/ *adj*

nostril /'nɒstrəl/ *n* either of the two openings into the nose

nosy (*also* **nosey**) /'nəʊzi/ *adj* (**-ier, -iest**) (*infml, disapprov*) too interested

in other people's private lives ■ **,nosy 'parker** *n* (*GB, infml*) nosy person

not /nɒt/ *adv* used to form the negative of the verbs *be, do,* etc and often shortened to *n't*: *She did ~ see him.* ◊ *He warned me ~ to be late.* ◊ *Don't be late!* [IDM] **not only... (but) also** used to emphasize that sth else is also true: *She's ~ only my sister but also my best friend.* **not that** used to state that you are not suggesting sth: *She hasn't written~ ~ that she said she would.*

notable /'nəʊtəbl/ *adj* deserving to be noticed or to receive attention ● **notable** *n* important person ▶ **notably** /-bli/ *adv* especially

notary /'nəʊtəri/ *n* (*pl* **-ies**) (*also tech* **,notary 'public**) official, esp a lawyer, with authority to witness documents

notation /nəʊ'teɪʃn/ *n* [C,U] system of signs or symbols representing numbers, musical notes, etc

notch /nɒtʃ/ *n* **1** level on a scale, marking quality, etc **2** V-shaped cut in a surface ● **notch** *v* [T] **1** ~ **(up)** achieve sth such as a win or high score: *up a victory* **2** make a V-shaped cut in sth

note¹ /nəʊt/ *n* **1** [C] short piece of writing to help you remember sth: *take ~s at a lecture* **2** [C] short informal letter: *Leave a ~ about it on his desk.* **3** [C] short comment on a word, etc in a book **4** [C] piece of paper money: *a £5 ~* **5** [C] (written sign representing a) single musical sound **6** [sing] quality or tone, esp of sb's voice: *a ~ of bitterness in his voice* **7** [C] official document: *a sick ~ from your doctor* [IDM] **of note** of importance or interest **take note (of sth)** pay attention to sth ● **note** *v* [T] **1** notice or pay attention to sth [PV] **note sth down** write down sth important so that you will not forget it ■ **'notebook** *n* **1** small book for writing notes in **2** (*also* **,notebook com'puter**) small computer that you can carry with you and use anywhere ■ **noted** *adj* well known ■ **'notepaper** *n* paper for writing letters on ■ **'noteworthy** *adj* deserving to be noticed; remarkable

nothing /'nʌθɪŋ/ *pron* not anything; no single thing: *I've had ~ to eat since lunch.* ◊ *You've hurt your arm.' 'It's ~'* (= It is not important, serious, etc). [IDM] **be/have nothing to do with sb/sth** have no connection with sb/sth **for nothing 1** without payment: *He did the job for ~.* **2** with no reward or result: *All that effort was for ~!* ● **nothing but** only; no more/less than: *~ but the best* **nothing like** (*infml*) **1** not at all like: *She's ~ like her sister.* **2** not nearly:

This is ~ like as good. **there is/was nothing (else) for it (but to do sth)** there is no other action to take except the one mentioned: *There's ~ for it but to work late tonight.*

notice /ˈnəʊtɪs/ n 1 [U] fact of sb paying attention to sb/sth or knowing about sth: *Take no ~ of what he says* ◇ *It was Jo who brought the problem to my ~* (= told me about it). 2 [C] (written or printed) news or information 3 [C] warning: *give her a month's ~ to leave* [IDM] **at short notice | at a moment's notice** not long in advance; without warning ● **notice** v [I, T] see or hear sb/sth; pay attention to sb/sth ▶ **noticeable** *adj* easily noticed ■ **noticeably** *adv*

notify /ˈnəʊtɪfaɪ/ v (*pt, pp* **-ied**) [T] ~ **(of)** formally tell sb about sth: *~ the police of the accident* ▶ **notification** /ˌnəʊtɪfɪˈkeɪʃn/ n [U, C]

notion /ˈnəʊʃn/ n idea; opinion

notorious /nəʊˈtɔːriəs/ *adj* well known for sth bad: *a ~ murderer* ▶ **notoriety** /ˌnəʊtəˈraɪəti/ n [U] fame for being bad in some way ▶ **notoriously** *adv*

nougat /ˈnuːgɑː/ n [U] hard sweet made of sugar, nuts, etc

nought /nɔːt/ n 1 [U] (*esp US* **zero**) the figure 0 2 (*also* **naught**) [U] (*lit*) nothing: *All our efforts have come to ~* (= have failed).

noun /naʊn/ n (*gram*) word that refers to a person, a place or a thing, a quality or an action

nourish /ˈnʌrɪʃ/ v [T] 1 keep sb/sth alive and healthy with food 2 (*fml*) allow a feeling, etc to grow stronger ▶ **nourishment** n [U] (*fml* or *tech*) food

novel /ˈnɒvl/ *adj* new and unusual: *a ~ idea* ● **novel** n long written story ▶ **novelist** /ˈnɒvəlɪst/ n writer of novels

novelty /ˈnɒvlti/ n (*pl* **-ies**) 1 [U] quality of being new, different and interesting 2 [C] thing, person or situation that is unusual or new 3 [C] small cheap toy or decoration

November /nəʊˈvembə(r)/ n [U,C] the 11th month of the year (See examples of use at *April*.)

novice /ˈnɒvɪs/ n 1 person who is new and inexperienced in a job, activity, etc 2 person training to become a monk or nun

now /naʊ/ *adv* 1 (at) the present time: *Where are you living ~?* ◇ *From ~ on, I'll be more careful.* 2 at or from this moment, but not before: *Start writing ~.* 3 (*spoken*) used to attract attention, etc: *N~, listen to me!* [IDM] **(every) now and again/then** occasionally: *He visits me every ~ and then.* ● **now** *conj* ~ **(that)** because the thing just mentioned

is happening or has happened: *N~ (that) he's left, let's begin.*

nowadays /ˈnaʊədeɪz/ *adv* at the present time: *I don't go out much ~.*

nowhere /ˈnəʊweə(r)/ *adv* not in or to any place: *There is ~ interesting to visit in this town.* [IDM] **get (sb) nowhere** → **GET**

noxious /ˈnɒkʃəs/ *adj* (*fml*) poisonous or harmful

nozzle /ˈnɒzl/ n shaped end of a hose through which liquid is directed

nuance /ˈnjuːɑːns/ n small difference in meaning, opinion, colour, etc

nuclear /ˈnjuːkliə(r)/ *adj* using, producing or resulting from nuclear energy 2 (*physics*) of the nucleus of an atom ■ **nuclear 'energy** (*also* **nuclear 'power**) n [U] powerful form of energy produced by splitting the nuclei of atoms and used to produce electricity ■ **nuclear re'actor** n large structure used for the controlled production of nuclear energy

nucleus /ˈnjuːkliəs/ n (*pl* **nuclei** /-kliaɪ/) 1 (*physics*) central part of an atom 2 (*biol*) central part of a cell 3 central part, around which other parts are grouped: *These books form the ~ of the library.*

nude /njuːd/ *adj* not wearing any clothes ● **nude** n work of art consisting of a naked human figure [IDM] **in the nude** not wearing any clothes ▶ **nudist** n person who does not wear any clothes because they believe this is more natural: *a nudist beach* ▶ **nudity** n [U]

nudge /nʌdʒ/ v [T] push sb gently, esp with your elbow ● **nudge** n gentle push

nugget /ˈnʌgɪt/ n 1 lump of metal, esp gold 2 interesting piece of information

nuisance /ˈnjuːsns/ n [C, usu sing] annoying person, situation, etc

null /nʌl/ *adj* [IDM] **null and void** (*law*) (of an election, etc) having no legal force ▶ **nullify** /ˈnʌlɪfaɪ/ v (*pt, pp* **-ied**) [T] make sth, eg a legal agreement or order, have no effect

numb /nʌm/ *adj* unable to feel anything: *~ with cold/shock* ● **numb** v [T] make sb or a part of sb's body numb ▶ **numbness** n [U]

number /ˈnʌmbə(r)/ n 1 symbol or word representing a quantity: *3, 13 and 103 are ~s* 2 quantity or amount: *a large ~ of people* ◇ *A ~ of* (= some) *books are missing.* 3 (*GB*) issue of a magazine 4 song or dance ● **number** v [T] 1 give a number to sth as part of a series or list: *~ the pages* 2 amount to: *The crowd ~ed over 3000* 3 ~ **among** (*fml*) include sb/sth in a group

numeracy /ˈnjuːmərəsi/ n [U] good

basic knowledge of mathematics: *standards of literacy and –* ▶ **numerate** *adj* able to understand and work with numbers

numeral /'nju:mərəl/ *n* sign or symbol representing a number

numerical /nju:'merɪkl/ *adj* of or expressed in numbers ▶ **numerically** /-klɪ/ *adv*

numerous /'nju:mərəs/ *adj* (*fml*) existing in large numbers: *on ~ occasions*

nun /nʌn/ *n* member of a female religious community, living in a convent

nurse /nɜ:s/ *n* person whose job is to take care of ill or injured people, usu in a hospital ● **nurse** *v* [T] 1 take care of people who are ill, etc 2 feed a baby with milk from the breast 3 have a strong feeling in your mind for a long time: *~ feelings of revenge* 4 give special care to sb/sth: *~ young plants* ■ **nursing** *n* [U] job or skill of caring for the sick ■ **nursing home** *n* small private hospital, esp for old people

nursery /'nɜ:sərɪ/ *n* (*pl* -ies) 1 place where young children are cared for while their parents are at work 2 place where young plants are grown ■ **'nursery rhyme** *n* poem or song for young children ■ **'nursery school** *n* school for children from 2 to 5 years old

nurture /'nɜ:tʃə(r)/ *v* [T] (*fml*) 1 care for and protect a child 2 encourage the development of sb/sth

nut /nʌt/ *n* 1 small hard fruit with a hard shell that grows on some trees 2 small piece of metal with a hole through the centre for screwing onto a bolt 3 (*GB, infml*) (*also* **nutter**) crazy person [IDM] **off your nut** (*GB, spoken*) crazy ■ **'nutcase** *n* (*infml*) crazy person ■ **'nutcracker** *n* (*GB also* **nutcrackers**) [pl] tool for cracking open the shells of nuts ■ **'nutshell** *n* [IDM] (**put sth**) **in a nutshell** (say sth) in a very clear way, using few words ■ **nutty** *adj* (-ier, -iest) 1 tasting of or containing nuts 2 (*infml*) crazy

nutmeg /'nʌtmeg/ *n* [U] hard seed of an E Indian tree used in cooking as a spice, esp to flavour cakes and sauces

nutrient /'nju:triənt/ *n* (*tech*) substance needed to keep a living thing alive and help it to grow

nutrition /nju:'trɪʃn/ *n* [U] process by which living things receive the food necessary for them to be healthy ▶ **nutritional** /-ʃənl/ *adj* ▶ **nutritious** /-ʃəs/ *adj* (of food) good for you

nuts /nʌts/ *adj* (*infml*) crazy; mad

nuzzle /'nʌzl/ *v* [I, T] touch or rub sb/sth gently with the nose, esp to show affection

nylon /'naɪlɒn/ *n* [U] very strong artificial material, used in clothes, rope, etc

nymph /nɪmf/ *n* (in ancient Greek and Roman stories) spirit of nature living in rivers, trees, etc

Oo

O, o /əʊ/ *n* [C,U] (*pl* **O's, o's** /əʊz/) 1 the fifteenth letter of the English alphabet 2 (*spoken*) used to mean 'zero' when saying telephone numbers, etc

oaf /əʊf/ *n* awkward or stupid person

oak /əʊk/ (*also* **'oak tree**) *n* 1 [C] large tree with that produces small nuts (**acorns**), often eaten by animals 2 [U] hard wood of the oak tree

OAP /ˌəʊ eɪ 'pi:/ *abbr* (*GB*) old-age pensioner

oar /ɔ:(r)/ *n* long pole with a flat blade, used for rowing a boat [IDM] **put/stick your oar in** (*GB, infml*) give your opinion, advice, etc when it is not asked for

oasis /əʊ'eɪsɪs/ *n* (*pl* **oases** /-si:z/) area in a desert with water and plants

oath /əʊθ/ *n* (*pl* **~s** /əʊðz/) 1 formal promise or statement 2 (*old-fash*) swear word [IDM] **on/under oath** (*law*) having made a formal promise to tell the truth in a court of law

oats /əʊts/ *n* [pl] (grain from a) cereal plant grown as food ■ **oatmeal** *n* [U] crushed oats

obedient /ə'bi:diənt/ *adj* doing what you are told to do ▶ **obedience** /-əns/ *n* [U] ▶ **obediently** *adv*

obelisk /'ɒbəlɪsk/ *n* tall pointed stone column

obese /əʊ'bi:s/ *adj* (*fml*) (of people) very fat ▶ **obesity** *n* [U]

obey /ə'beɪ/ *v* [I, T] do what you are told or expected to do

obituary /ə'bɪtʃuərɪ/ *n* (*pl* -ies) article about sb's life, printed in a newspaper soon after they have died

object¹ /'ɒbdʒɪkt/ *n* 1 thing that can be seen or touched but is not alive 2 ~ of person or thing to which an action, feeling, etc is directed: *an ~ of pity* 3 aim or purpose: *Our ~ is to win.* 4 (*gram*) noun, phrase, etc towards which the action of a verb is directed, for example *him* and *the money* in: *Give him the money.* [IDM] **expense, money, etc is no object** to say that you are willing to spend a lot of money

object² /əb'dʒekt/ *v* [I] ~ (**to**) say that you disagree with or oppose sth

objection /əb'dʒekʃn/ n ~(to) (statement giving) reason why you dislike or are opposed to sth ▶ **objectionable** /-ʃənəbl/ adj (fml) unpleasant or offensive

objective /əb'dʒektɪv/ adj **1** not influenced by personal feelings: an ~ report **2** (phil) having existence outside the mind; real ● **objective** n something that you are trying to achieve ▶ **objectively** adv **objectivity** /ˌɒbdʒek'tɪvəti/ n [U]

obligation /ˌɒblɪ'ɡeɪʃn/ n [C,U] something that ought to be done; duty [IDM] **be under no obligation to do sth** not have to do sth

obligatory /ə'blɪɡətri/ adj (fml) that is required by law or custom

oblige /ə'blaɪdʒ/ v **1** [T] ~ sb (usu passive) force sb to do sth, by law, because it is a duty, etc: Parents are ~d to send their children to school. **2** [I, T] help sb by doing what they ask or what they want: If you need any help, I'd be happy to ~. ● **obliged** adj (fml) used to show that you are grateful to sb: I'm much ~d to you for helping us. ▶ **obliging** adj willing to help ▶ **obligingly** adv

oblique /ə'bliːk/ adj **1** indirect: an ~ reference **2** (of a line) sloping ● **oblique** n (GB) = SLASH(3) ▶ **obliquely** adv

obliterate /ə'blɪtəreɪt/ v [T] remove all signs of sth; destroy sth ▶ **obliteration** /əˌblɪtə'reɪʃn/ n [U]

oblivion /ə'blɪviən/ n [U] state of being unaware of sth or of being forgotten

oblivious /ə'blɪviəs/ adj ~of/to not aware of sth: ~ of the news

oblong /'ɒblɒŋ/ n, adj (figure) with four straight sides and angles of 90°, longer than it is wide

obnoxious /əb'nɒkʃəs/ adj very unpleasant

oboe /'əʊbəʊ/ n wooden instrument that you blow into to make sound ▶ **oboist** n oboe player

obscene /əb'siːn/ adj shocking and offensive, esp sexually ▶ **obscenely** adv ▶ **obscenity** n [C,U] (pl -ies) (instance of) obscene language or behaviour

obscure /əb'skjʊə(r)/ adj **1** not well known: an ~ poet **2** difficult to understand ● **obscure** v [T] make it difficult to see, hear or understand sth: a hill ~d by fog ▶ **obscurely** adv ▶ **obscurity** n [U] state of being obscure

observance /əb'zɜːvəns/ n **1** [U, sing] keeping of a law, custom, festival, etc **2** [C, usu pl] part of a religious ceremony

observant /əb'zɜːvənt/ adj quick at noticing things

observation /ˌɒbzə'veɪʃn/ n **1** [U,C] act of watching sb/sth carefully for a period of time: The suspect is under ~ (= watched closely by the police). ◇ She has keen powers of ~ (= the ability to notice things around her). **2** [C] comment

observatory /əb'zɜːvətri/ n (pl -ies) building in which scientists watch and study the stars, etc

observe /əb'zɜːv/ v [T] **1** see or notice sb/sth **2** watch sb/sth carefully **3** (fml) make a remark **4** (fml) obey a rule, law, etc **5** (fml) celebrate a festival, birthday, etc ▶ **observer** n **1** person who observes sb/sth **2** person who attends a meeting to listen and watch but not to take part

obsess /əb'ses/ v [T] (usu pass) completely fill your mind, so that you cannot think about anything else: be ~ed with the fear of death ▶ **obsession** /əb'seʃn/ n **1** [U] state of being obsessed **2** [C] person or thing that sb thinks about too much ▶ **obsessive** adj thinking too much about one person or thing

obsolescent /ˌɒbsə'lesnt/ adj becoming out of date ▶ **obsolescence** /ˌɒbsə'lesns/ n [U]

obsolete /'ɒbsəliːt/ adj no longer used; out of date

obstacle /'ɒbstəkl/ n something that stops progress or makes it difficult: an ~ to world peace

obstetrics /əb'stetrɪks/ n [U] branch of medicine concerned with childbirth ▶ **obstetrician** /ˌɒbstə-'trɪʃn/ n doctor trained in obstetrics

obstinate /'ɒbstɪnət/ adj **1** refusing to change your opinions, ways of behaving, etc **2** difficult to get rid of or deal with: ~ stains ▶ **obstinacy** /-nəsi/ n [U] ▶ **obstinately** adv

obstreperous /əb'strepərəs/ adj (fml) noisy and difficult to control: a class full of ~ children

obstruct /əb'strʌkt/ v [T] **1** block a road, entrance, etc **2** prevent sb/sth from doing sth or progressing: ~ justice ▶ **obstruction** /əb'strʌkʃn/ n **1** [U,C] fact of obstructing sb/sth **2** [C] something that blocks sth ▶ **obstructive** adj intending to obstruct sb/sth

obtain /əb'teɪn/ v [T] (fml) get sth: I finally managed to ~ a copy of the report. ▶ **obtainable** adj

obtrusive /əb'truːsɪv/ adj very noticeable in an unpleasant way: a modern house which is ~ in an old village ▶ **obtrusively** adv

obtuse /əb'tjuːs/ adj (fml, disapprov) slow or unwilling to understand sth ■ **ob,tuse 'angle** n angle between 90° and 180° ▶ **obtuseness** n [U]

obverse /ˈɒbvɜːs/ n [sing] **1** (fml) opposite of sth **2** (tech) side of a coin that has the head or main design on it

obvious /ˈɒbviəs/ adj easy to see or understand; clear ▶ **obviously** adv

occasion /əˈkeɪʒən/ n **1** [C] particular time when sth happens happens **2** [C] special event or celebration **3** [U,sing] (fml) time that provides a reason for sth to happen: I have had no ~ to visit them recently. [IDM] **on occasion(s)** sometimes but not often ● **occasion** v [T] (fml) cause sth

occasional /əˈkeɪʒənl/ adj happening sometimes, but not often: an ~ drink ▶ **occasionally** /-nəli/ adv

Occident /ˈɒksɪdənt/ n (the Occident) [sing] (fml) the western part of the world, esp Europe and America ▶ **occidental** /ˌɒksɪˈdentl/ adj

occult /əˈkʌlt; ˈɒkʌlt/ n (the occult) [sing] supernatural or magical powers, practices, etc ▶ **occult** adj

occupant /ˈɒkjəpənt/ n person who lives or works in a house or room ▶ **occupancy** /-pənsi/ n [U] (fml) act of living in or using a building, room, etc

occupation /ˌɒkjuˈpeɪʃn/ n **1** [C] job or profession **2** [C] activity that fills your time **3** [U] act of taking possession of a country ▶ **occupational** /-ʃənl/ adj of or connected with sb's job

occupy /ˈɒkjupaɪ/ v (pt, pp -ied) [T] **1** fill or use a space, an area or an amount of time **2** (fml) work in a room, house or building **3** take control of a country, town, etc, esp by military force ● **~ yourself** keep yourself busy **5** have an official job or position ▶ **occupier** n person who lives in a house or room

occur /əˈkɜː(r)/ v (-rr-) [i] **1** (fml) happen: The accident ~red in the rain. **2** be found somewhere; exist [PV] **occur to sb** (of an idea or thought) come into your mind: It never ~red to me that he might be lying. ▶ **occurrence** /əˈkʌrəns/ n **1** [C] event **2** [U] fact of sth happening

ocean /ˈəʊʃn/ n (Ocean) one of the very large areas of sea on the earth's surface: the Pacific O~ ▶ **oceanic** /ˌəʊʃiˈænɪk/ adj (tech)

o'clock /əˈklɒk/ adv used with the numbers 1 to 12 when telling the time, to mean an exact hour: It's 5 ~.

octagon /ˈɒktəgən/ n (geom) flat shape with eight sides and eight angles ▶ **octagonal** /ɒkˈtægənl/ adj

octane /ˈɒkteɪn/ n [U] substance found in petrol used as a measure of its quality

octave /ˈɒktɪv/ n (music) space between a note and the next one of the same name above or below it

October /ɒkˈtəʊbə(r)/ n [U,C] the tenth month of the year (See examples of use at April.)

octopus /ˈɒktəpəs/ n sea creature with a soft body and eight arms (tentacles)

odd /ɒd/ adj **1** strange; unusual **2** missing its pair or set: an ~ sock/shoe **3** (of numbers) that cannot be divided by 2: 1, 3 and 5 are ~ numbers. **4** a little more than the number mentioned: 30~ years [IDM] **the odd man/one out** person or thing that is different from the others in a group ▶ **oddity** n (pl -ies) **1** [C] strange or unusual thing or person **2** [U] quality of being strange ■ **odd** **jobs** n [pl] small jobs of various types ■ **odd-job man** n (esp GB) person paid to do odd jobs ▶ **oddly** adv strangely

oddments /ˈɒdmənts/ n [pl] small pieces of fabric, wood, etc that are left after a larger piece has been used

odds /ɒdz/ n [pl] probability or chance that sth will or will not happen: The ~ are (= It is probable that) she'll win. [IDM] **be at odds (with sb/sth)** disagree with sb; be different from sth **it makes no odds** (spoken) it is not important ■ **odds and 'ends** n [pl] (GB, infml) small items of various types

ode /əʊd/ n poem that speaks to a person or thing or celebrates an event

odious /ˈəʊdiəs/ adj (fml) extremely unpleasant

odour (US **odor**) /ˈəʊdə(r)/ n [C,U] (fml) smell

oesophagus /iˈsɒfəgəs/ n (anat) tube through which food passes from the mouth to the stomach

of /əv; strong form ɒv/ prep **1** belonging to sb; relating to sb: a friend of mine ◊ the works of Shakespeare ◊ the support of the voters **2** belonging to sth; being part of sth; relating to sth: the lid of the box ◊ a member of the team **3** coming from or living in a place: the people of Wales **4** concerning or showing sb/sth: a picture of my cat **5** used to say what sth/sb is, consists of or contains: the city of Dublin ◊ a crowd of people ◊ a bottle of lemonade **6** used with measurements and expressions of time, age, etc: 40 litres of petrol ◊ a girl of 12 ◊ the first of May **7** used to show the position of sth/sb in space or time: just south of Paris **8** used after nouns formed from verbs: the arrival of the police ◊ fear of the dark **9** used after some verbs before mentioning sth/sb involved in the action: rob sb of sth ◊ He was cleared of all blame. **10** used to give your

0 offshore

opinion of sb's behaviour: *It was kind of you to offer.*

off¹ /ɒf/ *adv* **1** away from a place; at a distance in space or time: *I must be off* (= I must leave). ◊ *The town is still 5 miles ~.* ◊ *~ to France today.* **2** used to say that sth has been removed: *take your hat ~* ◊ *He shaved his beard off.* **3** starting a race: *They're off* (= the race has begun). **4** (*infml*) cancelled: *The wedding is ~.* **5** not connected or functioning: *The electricity is ~.* ◊ *Make sure the TV is off.* **6** (*esp GB*) (of an item on a menu) no longer available: *The soup is ~.* **7** away from work: *take the day ~* • [IDM] **off and on** and **on and off** from time to time: *It rained off and on all day.*

off² /ɒf/ *adj* **1** (of food) no longer fresh: *The milk is ~.* **2** ~(**with**) (*infml, esp GB*) impolite or unfriendly: *He can be a bit ~ sometimes.* **3** (*infml*) not acceptable: *It's a bit of expecting us to work on a Sunday.* • [IDM] **do sth on the off chance** do sth even though there is only a slight possibility of success: *I went to his house on the ~ chance* (*that he'd be at home*).
■ '**off day** *n* (*infml*) day when you do not do things as well as usual ■ '**off season** *n* time of year that is less busy in business or travel

off³ /ɒf/ *prep* **1** down or away from a place or at a distance in space or time: *fall ~ a ladder* ◊ *take a packet ~ the shelf* ◊ *We're getting ~ the subject.* **2** leading away from sth: *a lane ~ the main road* **3** away from work: *He's had ten days off.* **4** (*infml*) not wanting or liking sth that you usually eat or use: *He's ~ his food.* ◊ *He's ~ drugs now* (= he no longer takes them).

offal /ˈɒfl/ *n* [U] inside parts of an animal used as food

offence (*US* -**ense**) /əˈfens/ *n* [C] ~ (**against**) illegal act **2** [U] act of upsetting or insulting sb: *I didn't mean to give ~* (= to upset you). ◊ *He's quick to take ~* (= He is easily upset).

offend /əˈfend/ *v* **1** [T] upset or insult sb **2** [T] seem unpleasant to sb: *ugly buildings that ~ the eye* **3** [I] commit a crime **4** [I] ~(**against**) (*fml*) be against what people believe is morally right ▸ **offender** *n* person who breaks the law ▸ **offending** *adj* causing a problem or difficulty

offensive /əˈfensɪv/ *adj* **1** very unpleasant; insulting: ~ *language* **2** (*fml*) used for attacking: ~ *weapons* • **offensive** *n* strong military attack [IDM] **go** (**on**) **to the offensive** / **take the offensive** start attacking sb/sth ▸ **offensively** *adv* ▸ **offensiveness** *n* [U]

offer /ˈɒfə(r)/ *v* **1** [I, T] say that you are willing to do sth for sb or give sth to

sb: *I ~ed to go first.* ◊ *They ~ed me the job.* **2** [T] make sth available or provide the opportunity for sth: *The job ~s good chances of promotion.* • **offer** *n* **1** act of offering to do sth or give sth to sb **2** something offered ▸ **offering** *n* something offered, esp to God

offhand /ˌɒfˈhænd/ *adj* (*disapprov*) not showing any interest in sb/sth • **offhand** *adv* without being able to check sth or think about it: *I can't give you my answer ~.*

office /ˈɒfɪs/ *n* **1** [C] room or building where people work, usu sitting at desks **2** [C] room or building used for a particular purpose: *a tourist ~* **3** (**Office**) [C] used in the names of some British government departments: *The Foreign O~* **4** [U, C] (work of an) important position of authority: *the ~ of president*

officer /ˈɒfɪsə(r)/ *n* **1** person in command in the armed forces: *an ~ in the navy* **2** person with authority: *a customs ~* **3** policeman or policewoman

official /əˈfɪʃl/ *adj* **1** of a position of authority or trust **2** said, done, etc publicly and with authority: *an ~ statement* • **official** *n* person in a position of authority in a large organization ▸ **officialdom** /-dəm/ *n* [U] (*disapprov*) people in positions of authority who seem more interested in following rules than in being helpful ▸ **officially** /-ʃəli/ *adv* publicly; formally

officiate /əˈfɪʃieɪt/ *v* [I] ~(**at**) perform official duties at a ceremony

officious /əˈfɪʃəs/ *adj* (*disapprov*) too eager to give orders ▸ **officiously** *adv* ▸ **officiousness** *n* [U]

offing /ˈɒfɪŋ/ *n* [IDM] **in the offing** (*infml*) likely to appear or happen soon

off-licence /ˈɒf laɪsns/ *n* (*GB*) shop where alcoholic drinks are sold to be taken away

off-line /ˌɒf ˈlaɪn/ *adj* (*computing*) not directly controlled by or connected to a computer or the Internet

off-peak /ˌɒf ˈpiːk/ *adj* in or used at a time when business is less busy: ~ *travel*

off-putting /ˈɒf pʊtɪŋ/ *adj* (*esp GB, infml*) making sb dislike; unpleasant: *His manner is very ~.*

offset /ˈɒfset/ *v* (-**tt-** *pt, pp* **offset**) use one cost, payment or situation to cancel or reduce the effect of another: *increase prices to ~ higher costs*

offshoot /ˈɒfʃuːt/ *n* **1** thing that develops from sth, esp a small organization that develops from a larger one **2** (*tech*) new stem that grows on a plant

offshore /ˌɒfˈʃɔː(r)/ *adj, adv* **1** at a

distance out to sea: *an ~ oil rig* **2** away from the land towards the sea: *~ breezes* **3** (*business*) (of money, companies, etc) kept or situated in a country that has more generous tax laws than other places

offside /ˌɒfˈsaɪd/ *adj, n* [U] **1** (*sport*) (fact of a player being) in a position in front of the ball, which is against the rules **2** (*GB*) (on) the side of a vehicle that is furthest from the edge of the road

offspring /ˈɒfsprɪŋ/ *n* (*pl* **offspring**) (*fml*) a person's child or children; young of animals

off-white /ˌɒfˈwaɪt/ *adj* very pale yellowish-white in colour

often /ˈɒfn; *also* ˈɒftən/ *adv* **1** many times; frequently: *We ~ go there.* **2** in many cases: *Old houses are ~ damp.* [IDM] **as often as not | more often than not** usually; typically | **every so often** sometimes

ogle /ˈəʊgl/ *v* [I, T] ~(at) look at sth with great sexual interest

ogre /ˈəʊgə(r)/ *n* **1** (in stories) cruel frightening giant who eats people **2** very frightening person

oh /əʊ/ *exclam* used to show surprise, fear, etc: *Oh dear!*

oil /ɔɪl/ *n* [U] any of several thick slippery liquids that burn easily, used for fuel, food, etc **2** (**oils**) [pl] coloured paint containing oil used by artists ● **oil** *v* [T] put oil on or into sth: *He ~ed the bike and pumped up the tyres.* ■ **oilfield** *n* area where oil is found in the ground or under the sea ■ **oil paint** (*also* **oil colour**) *n* [C, U] type of paint that contains oil ■ **oil painting** *n* picture painted in oil paint ■ **oil rig** (*esp US* **oil platform**) *n* large structure with equipment for getting oil from under the ground ■ **oilskin** *n* [C, U] (coat, etc made of) cloth treated with oil to make it waterproof ■ **oil slick** *n* area of oil floating on the sea ■ **oil well** *n* hole made in the ground to obtain oil ● **oily** *adj* (**-ier, -iest**) **1** of or like oil; covered with oil **2** (*disapprov*) trying to be too polite: *an ~y smile*

ointment /ˈɔɪntmənt/ *n* [C, U] smooth substance rubbed on the skin to heal a wound

OK (*also* **okay**) /əʊˈkeɪ/ *adj, adv* (*spoken*) **1** safe and well; in a calm or happy state: *Are you OK?* **2** all right; satisfactory: *Is it OK for me to go now?* ● **OK** *exclam* (*infml*) used for showing agreement: *OK, I'll do it.* ● **OK** *v* [T] (*infml*) officially agree to sth: *She filled in the claim and her manager OK'd it.* ● **OK** *n* [sing] (*infml*) permission: *wait for the OK*

old /əʊld/ *adj* **1** of a particular age: *He's 40 years ~.* ◇ *How ~ are you?* **2** having lived for a long time: *an*

~ man **3** having existed or been used for a long time: *~ shoes* **4** belonging to past times or a past time in your life: *Things were different in the ~ days.* ◇ *my ~ school* **5** known for a long time: *an ~ friend* [IDM] **(be) an old hand (at (doing) sth)** be very experienced and skilled in sth **old hat** old-fashioned and no longer interesting **an old wives' tale** (*disapprov*) old belief that has been proved not to be scientific ► **the old** *n* [pl] old people ■ **old-age 'pension** *n* (*GB*) money paid regularly by the state to people above a certain age ■ **old-age 'pensioner** (*abbr* **OAP**) *n* person who receives an old-age pension ■ **old-'fashioned** *adj* **1** not modern; out of date **2** believing in old ways, etc ■ **old 'master** *n* (picture by an) important painter, esp of the 13th - 17th centuries

olive /ˈɒlɪv/ *n* [C] (tree of S Europe with a) small green or black fruit, eaten raw or used its oil **2** [U] yellowish-green colour ■ **olive branch** *n* symbol of a wish for peace

ombudsman /ˈɒmbʊdzmən; -mæn/ *n* (*pl* -men /-mən/) government official whose job is to consider complaints about public organizations

omelette /ˈɒmlət/ *n* eggs beaten together and fried

omen /ˈəʊmən/ *n* sign of what is going to happen in the future

ominous /ˈɒmɪnəs/ *adj* suggesting that sth bad will happen ► **ominously** *adv*

omission /əˈmɪʃn/ *n* **1** [U] act of omitting sb/sth **2** [C] thing that has not been included or done

omit /əˈmɪt/ *v* (**-tt-**) (*fml*) **1** not include sb/sth either deliberately or by accident **2** ~**to** fail to do sth: *I ~ted to mention his age.*

omnibus /ˈɒmnɪbəs/ *n* **1** (*GB*) radio or television programme that combines several recent programmes in a series **2** large book containing a number of books, esp by the same writer

omnipotent /ɒmˈnɪpətənt/ *adj* (*fml*) having unlimited power ► **omnipotence** /-təns/ *n* [U]

omniscient /ɒmˈnɪsiənt/ *adj* (*fml*) knowing everything ► **omniscience** /-siəns/ *n* [U]

omnivorous /ɒmˈnɪvərəs/ *adj* (*tech*) (of animals) eating both meat and plants

on¹ /ɒn/ *adv* **1** used to show that sth continues: *They wanted the band to play on.* **2** used to show that sth moves or is sent forward: *walk on to the bus stop* ◇ *from that day on* (= from then until now) **3** on sb's body; being worn: *Put your coat on.* ◇ *He had nothing on.* **4** covering, touching or forming part of sth: *Make sure the lid is on.* **5** connected or being used: *The electricity isn't on.* ◇ *The water is on.* **6** happening: *There was a war on at the time* ◇ *What's on at the cinema?* **7** planned to take place in the future: *Have you got anything on (=* any plans for) *this weekend?* **8** on duty; working: *I'm on now until 8 in the morning.* **9** in or into a vehicle: *get on the bus* [IDM] **be/go/keep on about sth** (*infml*) talk in a boring way about sth **it isn't on** (*infml*) used to say that sth is unacceptable **on and off** → OFF¹ **on and on** without stopping

on² /ɒn/ *prep* **1** in or into a position covering, touching or forming part of a surface: *a picture on the wall* **2** supported by sth/sb: *She was standing on one foot.* ◇ *Hang your coat on the hook* **3** used to show a means of transport: *He came on the train.* **4** used to show a day or a date: *on Sunday* ◇ *on 1 May* **5** immediately after sth: *On arriving home I discovered they had gone.* **6** about sb/sth: *a lecture on Bach* **7** being carried by sb; in the possession of sb: *Have you got any money on you?* **8** used to show membership of a group: *be on the staff* **9** eating, drinking or taking sth regularly: *She lives on a diet of junk food.* ◇ *He's on antibiotics.* **10** used to show direction: *On the left/right* **11** at or near a place: *a town on the coast* **12** used to show the reason for sth: *On her advice I applied for the job.* **13** supported financially by sb: *live on a student grant* **14** by means of sth; using sth: *Most cars run on petrol.* ◇ *speak on the phone* **15** used to say who or what is affected by sth: *a tax on beer* ◇ *He's hard on his kids.* **16** used to describe an activity or state: *be on business/holiday* ◇ *be on fire* (= burning)

once /wʌns/ *adv* **1** on one occasion only; one time: *I've only been there ~.* **2** at some time in the past: *Mary ~ lived in Zambia.* [IDM] **at once 1** immediately; without delay **2** at the same time: *Don't all speak at ~!* **once again | once more** one more time; another time **once and for all** now and for the last time **once in a blue moon** (*infml*) very rarely **(every) once in a while** occasionally **once upon a time** used at the beginning of stories to mean 'a long time ago' ● **once** *conj* as soon as; when: *It's easy ~ you know how.*

oncoming /ˈɒnkʌmɪŋ/ *adj* coming towards you: *~ traffic*

one¹ /wʌn/ *number, det* **1** the number 1 **2** a certain: *~ day* **3** used for emphasis to mean 'the only one' or 'the most important one': *She is the ~ person I can trust.* **4** the same:

They all went off in ~ direction. [IDM] **(be) at one (with sb/sth)** (*fml*) be in complete agreement with sb/sth **for one** used to emphasize that sb does sth and that you believe other people do too: *I for ~ don't like it.* **one or two** a few **one up (on sb)** (*infml*) having an advantage over sb ■ **one-off** *n, adj* (thing) made or happening only once ■ **one-sided** *adj* **1** (of an argument, etc) not balanced **2** (esp in sport) with opposing players of unequal abilities ■ **one-parent 'family** *n* family in which the children live with one parent rather than two ■ **one-time** *adj* former: *her ~-time best friend, Anna* ■ **one-to-'one** (*US* **one-on-'one**) *adj, adv* between two people only: *a ~-to-~ relationship* ■ **one-'way** *adj, adv* (allowing movement) in one direction only: *a ~-way street*

one² /wʌn/ *pron* **1** used to avoid repeating a noun: *I forgot to bring a pen. Can you lend me ~?* ◇ *The small car is just as fast as the big ~.* **2** used when you are identifying the person or thing you are talking about: *Our house is the ~ with the red door.* **3** ~ **of** person or thing belonging to a particular group: *He is not ~ of my customers.* **4** person of the type mentioned: *He wanted to be at home with his loved ~s.* **5** (*fml*) used to mean 'people in general' or 'I' when the speaker is referring to him/herself: *O~ should never criticize if ~ is not sure of the facts.* ■ **one another** *pron* each other: *They don't like ~ another.*

onerous /ˈəʊnərəs/ *adj* (*fml*) needing effort; difficult

oneself /wʌnˈself/ *pron* (*fml*) **1** used as a reflexive when people in general cause an action and are also affected by an action: *wash ~* **2** used to emphasize one: *One could arrange it all ~.* [IDM] **(all) by oneself 1** alone **2** without help

ongoing /ˈɒnɡəʊɪŋ/ *adj* continuing: *~ research*

onion /ˈʌnjən/ *n* [C, U] round vegetable with a strong smell and flavour, used in cooking

online /ˌɒnˈlaɪn/ *adj* controlled by or connected to a computer or to the Internet: *an ~ ticket booking system* ▶ **online** *adv*

onlooker /ˈɒnlʊkə(r)/ *n* person who watches sth happening

only /ˈəʊnli/ *adj* **1** with no other(s) of the same group: *Jane was the ~ person able to do it.* **2** best: *He's the ~ person for the job.* ● **only** *adv* **1** nobody or nothing except: *I ~ saw Mary.* **2** in no other situation, place, etc: *Children are admitted ~ if accompanied by an adult.* [IDM] **only**

just 1 not long ago/before: *We've ~ just arrived.* **2** almost not: *We ~ just caught the train.* **only** *adv* very: *only ~ pleased to help* ● **only** *conj (infml)* except that; but: *I'd love to come, ~ I have to work.*

onrush /'ɒnrʌʃ/ *n [sing] (written)* strong movement forward

onset /'ɒnset/ *n [sing]* beginning, esp of sth unpleasant

onshore /'ɒnʃɔː(r)/ *adj, adv* towards the shore: *~ winds*

onslaught /'ɒnslɔːt/ *n ~(against/ on) (written)* strong or violent attack on sb/sth

onto (also **on to**) /'ɒntə; before vowels 'ɒntu/ *prep* to a position on: *climb ~ a horse* [IDM] **be onto sb 1** *(infml)* know about what sb has done wrong **2** be talking to sb, usu in order to ask or tell them sth **be onto sth** have information that could lead to discovering sth important

onus /'əʊnəs/ *n [sing] (fml)* responsibility: *The ~ is on you.*

onward /'ɒnwəd/ *adj (fml)* continuing or moving forward: *an ~ flight* ▶ **onwards** (*US* **onward**) *adv*: *The pool is open from 7am ~.*

ooze /uːz/ *v* **1** [I] (of thick liquids) come or flow out slowly **2** [I, T] show a particular characteristic strongly: *He ~d charm.* ● **ooze** *n* [U] soft liquid mud

opacity /əʊ'pæsəti/ *n* [U] *(tech)* fact of being difficult to see through or opaque

opal /'əʊpl/ *n* white or almost clear precious stone

opaque /əʊ'peɪk/ *adj* **1** (of glass, liquid, etc) not clear enough to see through **2** (of speech or writing) difficult to understand; not clear

open¹ /'əʊpən/ *adj* **1** not closed: *leave the door ~.* **2** spread out; with the edges apart: *The flowers were all ~.* **3** not fastened: *an ~ shirt* **4** not enclosed: *~ fields* **5** with no cover or roof: *people working in the ~ air* (= not in a building) **6** ready for business: *Are the shops ~ yet?* **7** public; free to all: *an ~ championship* **8** ~ **to** likely to suffer sth such as criticism, injury, etc: *He has laid himself wide ~ to political attack.* **9** honest; not keeping your feelings hidden **10** ~ **to** (of a person) willing to listen and think about new ideas **11** known to everyone: *an ~ secret* **12** not yet finally decided: *leave the matter ~* [IDM] **have/keep an open mind (about/on sth)** be willing to consider new ideas **with open arms** with great affection or enthusiasm ● **open** *n* [sing] **1** outdoors; in the countryside *Our home is in the ~.* **2** bring the truth out into the ~ ◇ *a problem which is out in the ~* ■ **open-'air**

adj taking place outside ■ **open-and-shut 'case** *adj* legal case that is easy to decide or solve ■ **open-'ended** *adj* without any limits or dates set in advance ■ **open-'handed** *adj* generous ● **openly** *adv* not secretly ■ **open-'minded** *adj* willing to consider new ideas ▶ **openness** *n* [U] honesty ■ **open-'plan** *adj* with no dividing walls

open² /'əʊpən/ *v* **1** [I, T] (cause sb to) move so that it is no longer closed: *The door ~ed.* ◇ *Please ~ your mouth.* **2** [T] remove the lid, undo the fastening, etc of a container to see what is inside **3** [I, T] (cause sb to) spread out or unfold: *The parachute didn't ~.* ◇ *~ a book* **4** [T] make it possible for people, cars, etc to pass through a place: *~ a new road through the forest* **5** [I, T] (cause sth to) be ready for business: *When does the bank ~?* **6** [T] start sth: *~ a bank account* [IDM] **open your/sb's eyes (to sb)** make you/sb realize the truth about sth [PV] **open up** talk freely about your feelings **open (sth) up** (cause sth to) be available for development, business, etc: *~ up possibilities*

opener /'əʊpnə(r)/ *n* (usu in compounds) tool that is used to open things: *a tin-~-er*

opening /'əʊpnɪŋ/ *n* [C] **1** space or hole that sb/sth can pass through **2** [usu sing] beginning **3** [sing] process of becoming or making sth open: *the ~ of the new library* **4** job that is available ● **opening** *adj* first: *her ~ words*

opera /'ɒprə/ *n* musical play in which most of the words are sung ▶ **operatic** /ˌɒpə'rætɪk/ *adj*

operate /'ɒpəreɪt/ *v* **1** [I] work in a particular way **2** [I, T] use or control a machine or make it work: *~ machinery* **3** [I, T] do business; direct sth: *They plan to ~ out of a new office in Leeds.* **4** [I] perform a surgical operation on sb's body ▶ **operable** /'ɒpərəbl/ *adj* (of a medical condition) that can be treated by an operation ■ **operating theatre** *n* room in a hospital used for medical operations

operation /ˌɒpə'reɪʃn/ *n* **1** [C] *(med)* process of cutting open a part of the body to remove a diseased or injured part **2** [C] organized activity: *a rescue ~* **3** [C] business or company **4** [C,U] activity as performed by a machine, esp a computer **5** [U] working of parts of a machine or system: *the ~ of the controls* **6** [C, usu pl] military activity [IDM] **in operation** working or being used: *Temporary traffic controls are in ~.* **come into operation** start working or having an effect ▶ **operational** /-ʃənl/ *adj (fml)* **1** connected with the way a business, machine, etc works **2** ready for use

operative /'ɒpərətɪv/ adj ready to be used; in use: *The law becomes ~ immediately.* ● **operative** n (tech) worker

operator /'ɒpəreɪtə(r)/ n person who works sth, esp a telephone switchboard

operetta /ˌɒpə'retə/ n short light musical comedy

opinion /ə'pɪnjən/ n **1** [C] your feelings or thought about sb/sth: *In my ~, the price is too high.* ◇ *his ~ of the new manager* **2** [U] beliefs or views of a group of people: *public ~* **3** [C] professional advice: *a doctor's ~* ▶ **opinionated** /-eɪtɪd/ adj having opinions that you are not willing to change

opium /'əʊpiəm/ n [U] drug made from poppy seeds

opponent /ə'pəʊnənt/ n person who is against another in a fight, argument or game

opportune /ˌɒpə'tjuːn/ adj (fml) **1** (of time) suitable for a purpose **2** (of action) coming at the right time

opportunism /ˌɒpə'tjuːnɪzəm/ n [U] (disapprov) practice of using situations unfairly to gain advantage for yourself ▶ **opportunist** n [C,U]

opportunity /ˌɒpə'tjuːnəti/ n [C,U] (pl -ies) favourable time or chance to do sth

oppose /ə'pəʊz/ v [T] disagree strongly with sb's plan, policy, etc ▶ **opposed** adj **~ to** disagreeing strongly with sth: *He is ~ed to our plans.* [IDM] **as opposed to** (written) in contrast to

opposite /'ɒpəzɪt/ adj **1** facing the speaker: *the house ~* (to) *mine* **2** as different as possible from sth: *in the ~ direction* ● **opposite** prep, adv on the other side of an area from sb/sth and usu facing them: *~ the station* ◇ *the person sitting ~* ● **opposite** n person or thing that is as different as possible from sb/sth else ▶ your **opposite 'number** n person who does the same job as you in an organization

opposition /ˌɒpə'zɪʃn/ n **1** [U] **~ (to)** act of strongly disagreeing with sb/sth: *strong ~ to the new law* **2** [sing, with sing or pl verb] people you are competing against in business, a competition, etc **3** [sing, with sing or pl verb] (**the Opposition**) main political party that is opposed to the government: *the leader of the O~*

oppress /ə'pres/ v [T] **1** treat sb in a cruel and unfair way, esp by not giving them the same freedom, rights, etc as others **2** make sb only able to think about sad or worrying things: *~ed by the gloomy atmos-*

-phere ▶ **oppression** /ə'preʃn/ n [U] ▶ **oppressive** adj **1** treating people in a cruel and unfair way **2** hard to bear; uncomfortable: *~ive heat* ▶ **oppressor** n cruel or unjust leader or ruler

opt /ɒpt/ v [T] **~for/against** choose to take or not to take a particular course of action: *He ~ed for a career in music.* [PV] **opt out (of sth)** choose not to take part in sth

optic /'ɒptɪk/ adj (tech) of the eye: *the ~ nerve* (= from the eye to the brain) ▶ **optical** /-kl/ adj of the sense of sight ■ ,**optical il'lusion** n something that tricks your eyes and makes you think you see sth that is not there ▶ **optician** /ɒp'tɪʃn/ n person who makes or sells glasses and contact lenses

optimism /'ɒptɪmɪzəm/ n [U] belief that good things will happen ▶ **optimist** /-mɪst/ n ▶ **optimistic** /-'mɪstɪk/ adj

optimize (also **-ise**) /'ɒptɪmaɪz/ v [T] make sth as good as it can be; use sth in the best possible way

optimum /'ɒptɪməm/ adj most favourable; best: *the ~ price*

option /'ɒpʃn/ n **1** [U] freedom to choose what you do **2** [C] something that you can choose to have or do **3** right to buy or sell sth at some time in the future: *share ~s* (= right to buy shares in a company) **4** (computing) one of the choices you can make when using a computer program ▶ **optional** /-ʃənl/ adj that you can choose to do or have if you want to

opulent /'ɒpjələnt/ adj (fml) showing signs of great wealth ▶ **opulence** /-ləns/ n [U]

or /ɔː(r)/ conj **1** used to introduce an alternative: *Is it green or blue?* ◇ *Do you want tea, coffee or milk?* **2** (also **or else**) if not; otherwise: *Turn the heat down or it'll burn.* **3** in other words: *It weighs one pound, or about 450 grams.* [IDM] **or so** about: *We stayed there an hour or so.*

oral /'ɔːrəl/ adj **1** spoken, not written: *an ~ test* **2** of, by or for the mouth: *~ medicine* ● **oral** n a spoken exam, esp in a foreign language ▶ **orally** adv

orange /'ɒrɪndʒ/ n [C,U] round thick-skinned juicy reddish-yellow fruit ● **orange** adj bright reddish-yellow in colour

orang-utan /ɔːˌræŋu'tæn; ə'ræŋuːtæn/ n large ape with long arms and reddish hair

oration /ɔː'reɪʃn/ n (fml) formal public speech

orator /'ɒrətə(r)/ n (fml) person who makes formal public speeches

▶ **oratory** /'brətri/ n [U] art of skilful public speaking

orbit /'ɔːbɪt/ n **1** curved path of a planet or satellite round the earth, sun, etc **2** area of influence ● **orbit** v [I, T] move in an orbit round sth: *The earth takes a year to ~ the sun.* ▶ **orbital** /-tl/ adj

orchard /'ɔːtʃəd/ n piece of land on which fruit trees are grown

orchestra /'ɔːkɪstrə/ n [C, with sing or pl verb] group of people playing different musical instruments together ▶ **orchestral** /ɔː'kestrəl/ adj ▶ **orchestrate** /-strert/ v [T] **1** arrange a piece of music to be played by an orchestra **2** organize a complicated plan very carefully or secretly ▶ **orchestration** /,ɔːkɪ'streɪʃn/ n [C, U]

orchid /'ɔːkɪd/ n plant with flowers of brilliant colours and unusual shapes

ordain /ɔː'deɪn/ v [T] **1** make sb a member of the clergy **2** (fml) (of God, the law, etc) order or command sth

ordeal /ɔː'diːl; 'ɔːdiːl/ n difficult or unpleasant experience

order¹ /'ɔːdə(r)/ n **1** [U] way in which people or things are arranged in relation to one another: *names in alphabetical ~* ◇ *arranged in ~ of size* **2** [U] state of being carefully arranged: *It was time she put her life in ~.* **3** [U] state that exists when people obey laws, rules or authority: *The army was sent to restore ~.* ◇ *The chairman called them to ~* (= ordered them to obey the rules of the meeting). **4** [C] command given by sb in authority **5** [C, U] request to supply goods: *Send the shop your ~ for books* **6** [C] goods supplied in response to a particular order: *Your ~ will arrive tomorrow.* **7** [C] formal written instruction for sb to be paid money **8** [C] (badge, etc worn by) group of people who are specially honoured: *~s and medals* [IDM] **in order** as it should be; valid: *Your passport is in ~.* **in order that** (fml) so that sth can happen **in order to do sth** with the purpose of doing sth **of/in the order of** about: *It will cost in the ~ of £60.* **of the highest/first order** of the highest quality or degree **on order** asked for, but not yet supplied: *The machines are still on ~.* **out of order 1** (of a machine, etc) not working properly **2** not arranged correctly or neatly: *The papers are all out of ~.* **3** (infml) behaving in a way that is not acceptable or right: *You were well out of ~ - taking it without asking.* **4** (fml) not allowed by the rules of a formal meeting: *His objection was ruled out of ~.* **be in/take (holy) orders** be/become a priest

order² /'ɔːdə(r)/ v **1** [T] tell sb to do sth: *He ~ed the soldiers to attack.* **2** [I, T] ask for goods or services to be supplied: *to ~ a dessert* **3** [T] (fml) organize or arrange sth [PV] **order sb about/around** keep telling sb what to do in an unkind way

orderly /'ɔːdəli/ adj **1** carefully arranged; tidy **2** well behaved; peaceful ▶ **orderliness** n [U] ● **orderly** n (pl -ies) hospital worker

ordinal /'ɔːdɪnl/ (also ,ordinal 'number) n number, eg *first*, *second* and *third*, showing order in a series

ordinary /'ɔːdnri/ adj normal, usual [IDM] **out of the ordinary** unusual ▶ **ordinarily** /-rəli/ adv usually

ordination /,ɔːdɪ'neɪʃn/ n [C, U] ceremony of making a person a member of the clergy

ore /ɔː(r)/ n [U, C] rock or earth from which metal can be obtained

organ /'ɔːɡən/ n **1** part of the body that has a particular purpose: *the sense ~s* (= the eyes, ears, etc) **2** large musical instrument from which sounds are produced by air forced through pipes **3** (fml) official organization which has a special purpose: *the ~s of government* **4** (fml) newspaper, etc that supplies information about a particular group or organization ▶ **organist** n person who plays the organ

organic /ɔː'ɡænɪk/ adj **1** (of food, farming methods, etc) produced without using chemicals **2** produced by or from living things **3** (fml) consisting of related parts ▶ **organically** /-kli/ adv

organism /'ɔːɡənɪzəm/ n **1** (usu very small) living thing **2** (fml) system with parts dependent on each other

organization (also -isation) /,ɔːɡənaɪ'zeɪʃn/ n **1** [C] group of people who form a business, club, etc to achieve a particular aim **2** [U] act of making arrangements or preparations for sth

organize (also -ise) /'ɔːɡənaɪz/ v [T] **1** make preparations for sth: *~ a party* **2** arrange sth into a particular structure or order: *~ your time*

orgasm /'ɔːɡæzəm/ n point of feeling greatest sexual pleasure

orgy /'ɔːdʒi/ n (pl -ies) wild party with a lot of drinking and sexual activity

Orient /'ɔːrient/ n [sing] (lit) (the Orient) the eastern part of the world, esp China and Japan ▶ **oriental** /,ɔːri'entl/ adj of or from the eastern part of the world

orient /'ɔːrient/ (GB also **orientate** /'ɔːriəntert/) v [T] **1** ~ (to/towards) (usu passive) direct sb/sth towards a particular purpose: *Our company is ~d towards exports.* **2 ~ yourself** find your position in relation to your surroundings ► **orientation** /ˌɔːriənˈteɪʃn/ *n* [U, C]

orifice /ˈɒrɪfɪs/ *n* (*fml*) hole or opening, esp in the body

origin /ˈɒrɪdʒɪn/ *n* [C,U] (*also* **origins** [pl]) **1** starting point or cause of sth **2** person's social and family background: *people of Polish ~*

original /əˈrɪdʒənl/ *adj* **1** existing at the beginning of a period, process or activity: *Go back to your ~ plan.* **2** newly created; fresh: *~ designs* **3** able to produce new and interesting ideas: *an ~ thinker* **4** painted, written, etc by the artist rather than copied ● **original** *n* the earliest form of sth, from which copies can be made ► **originality** /əˌrɪdʒəˈnæləti/ *n* [U] quality of being new and interesting ► **originally** /-nəli/ *adv* used to describe the situation that existed at the beginning of a period or activity, esp before sth was changed: *His shirt was ~ly white.*

originate /əˈrɪdʒɪneɪt/ *v* (*fml*) **1** begin **2** [T] create sth new ► **originator** *n*

ornament /ˈɔːnəmənt/ *n* (*fml*) **1** [C] object that is beautiful rather than useful **2** [U] use of objects, designs, etc as decoration ● **ornament** /-ment/ *v* [T] (*fml*) add decoration to sth ► **ornamental** /ˌɔːnəˈmentl/ *adj*

ornate /ɔːˈneɪt/ *adj* having a lot of decoration ► **ornately** *adv*

ornithology /ˌɔːnɪˈθɒlədʒi/ *n* [U] study of birds ► **ornithologist** *n*

orphan /ˈɔːfn/ *n* child whose parents are dead ● **orphan** *v* [T] (*usu* passive) make a child an orphan ► **orphanage** /ˈɔːfənɪdʒ/ *n* home for children whose parents are dead

orthodox /ˈɔːθədɒks/ *adj* (having opinions that are) generally accepted or approved ► **orthodoxy** *n* [U,C] (*pl* **-ies**)

orthography /ɔːˈθɒɡrəfi/ *n* [U] (*fml*) system of spelling in a language

orthopaedics (*US* **-pedics**) /ˌɔːθəˈpiːdɪks/ *n* [U] branch of medicine that deals with problems and diseases of bones ► **orthopaedic** (*US* **-pedic**) *adj*

oscillate /ˈɒsɪleɪt/ *v* [I] (*fml*) **1 ~ (between A and B)** keep changing between extremes of feeling or opinion: *Her mood ~d between elation and depression.* **2** (*physics*) keep moving from one position to another and back again ► **oscillation** /ˌɒsɪˈleɪʃn/ *n* [U,C] (*fml*)

ostensible /ɒˈstensəbl/ *adj* given as a reason, etc though perhaps not the real one ► **ostensibly** /-əbli/ *adv*

ostentation /ˌɒstenˈteɪʃn/ *n* [U] (*disapprov*) show of wealth, importance, etc in order to impress people ► **ostentatious** /ˌɒstenˈteɪʃəs/ *adj*

ostracize (*also* **-ise**) /ˈɒstrəsaɪz/ *v* [T] (*fml*) exclude sb from a social group; refuse to meet or talk to sb

ostrich /ˈɒstrɪtʃ/ *n* very large African bird with a long neck and long legs, that cannot fly

other /ˈʌðə(r)/ *adj, pron* **1** used to refer to a person or thing additional to that already mentioned: *Tim, John and two ~ students were there.* **2** (**the, my, your, etc other**) used to refer to the second of two people or things: *Pull the cork out with your ~ hand.* **3** used to refer to the remaining people or things in a group: *I went swimming with the ~s played tennis.* ◊ *The ~ teachers are from Brunei.* **4** (**the other**) used to refer to a place, direction, etc that is the opposite to where you are, are going, etc: *He works on the ~ side of town.* **[IDM] other than** except: *We're away in June, but ~ than that we'll be around all summer.*

otherwise /ˈʌðəwaɪz/ *adv* **1** used to state what the result would be if the situation were different: *Shut the window, ~ it'll get too cold in here.* **2** apart from that: *The rent is high, but ~ the room is satisfactory.* **3** in a different way to the way mentioned; differently

otter /ˈɒtə(r)/ *n* fur-covered animal that lives in rivers and eats fish

ouch /aʊtʃ/ *exclam* used to express sudden pain: *Ouch! That hurt!*

ought to /ˈɔːt tə; *before vowels and finally* ˈɔːt tuː/ *modal v* (*neg* **ought not to** *or* **oughtn't to**) **1** used to say what is the right thing to do: *You ~ to apologize.* **2** used to say what you advise or recommend: *You ~ to see a doctor about that cough.* **3** used to say what has probably happened or is probably true: *She started early, so she ~ to be here by now.*

ounce /aʊns/ *n* **1** (*abbr* **oz**) [C] unit of weight; one sixteenth of a pound, equal to 28.35 grams **2** [*sing*] **~(of)** (*infml*) very small amount of sth

our /ɑː(r); ˈaʊə(r)/ *det* of or belonging to us: *~ house* ► **ours** /ɑːz; ˈaʊəz/ *pron* the one(s) that belong to us: *He's a friend of ~s.*

ourselves /ɑːˈselvz; aʊəˈselvz/ *pron* **1** (*the reflexive form of* **we**) used when you and others cause and are affected by an action: *We dried ~.* **2** used to emphasize *we* or *us*: *We saw the crash ~.* **[IDM] (all) by ourselves 1** alone **2** without any help

oust /aʊst/ *v* [T] **~(from)** (*written*) force sb to leave a job, etc

out /aʊt/ *adv, prep* **1 ~(of)** away from the inside of a place or thing: *go*

~ for some fresh air ◇ walk ~ of the room ◇ He opened the box and ~ jumped a frog. **2** ~(of) (of people) not at home or at a place of work: I phoned her but she was ~. ◇ He's ~ of the office this morning. **3** ~(of) away from the edge of a place: Do not lean ~ of the window. **4** ~(of) a long or particular distance away from a place or from land: The boats were all ~ at sea. ◇ a mile ~ of Hull **5** ~(of) used to show that sth is removed from a place, job, etc: This detergent is good for getting stains ~. **6** ~of used to show that sth comes from or is obtained from sth/sb: made ~ of wood ◇ Drink ~ of the bottle. **7** ~ of without: He's been ~ of work for months. **8** ~of not or no longer in the state or condition mentioned: Stay ~ of trouble. **9** ~(of) no longer involved in sth: He'll be ~ (= out of prison) on bail in no time. **10** ~of used to show the reason why sth is done: I asked ~ of curiosity. **11** ~of from a particular number or set: in nine cases ~ of ten **12** (of the tide) away from the shore **13** available to everyone; known by everyone: The secret is ~. **14** clearly and loudly: shout ~ **15** (sport) (in cricket, baseball, etc) no longer batting **16** (sport) (of a ball) outside the line **17** not correct or exact; wrong: I'm ~ in my calculations. **18** not fashionable: Short skirts are ~. **19** (of fire, lights, etc) no longer burning **20** (GB, infml) on strike **21** to the end; completely: I'm tired ~. [IDM] be ~ for sth/to do sth be trying to get or do sth: I'm not ~ to change the world! ■ ,out-and-'out adj complete

outboard /'aʊtbɔːd/ adj (tech) on, towards or near the outside of a ship or aircraft ■ ,outboard 'motor n engine that you can fix to the back of a small boat

outbreak /'aʊtbreɪk/ n sudden start of sth unpleasant: the ~ of war

outbuilding /'aʊtbɪldɪŋ/ n building separate from the main building

outburst /'aʊtbɜːst/ n sudden strong expression, esp of anger

outcast /'aʊtkɑːst/ n person sent away from home or society

outcome /'aʊtkʌm/ n effect or result

outcrop /'aʊtkrɒp/ n (geol) large mass of rock that sticks out of the ground

outcry /'aʊtkraɪ/ n (pl -ies) strong public protest

outdated /,aʊt'deɪtɪd/ adj no longer useful because of being old-fashioned

outdo /,aʊt'duː/ v (third pers sing pres tense **-does** /-'dʌz/ pt **-did** /-'dɪd/ pp **-done** /-'dʌn/) [T] (written) do more or better than sb else: Not to be outdone, she tried again.

outdoor /'aʊtdɔː(r)/ adj done or situated outside rather than in a building ▶ **outdoors** /,aʊt'dɔːz/ adv outside, rather than in a building

outer /'aʊtə(r)/ adj **1** on the outside of sth: ~ walls **2** furthest from the inside or centre of sth: the ~ suburbs ▶ **outermost** /'aʊtəməʊst/ adj furthest from the inside or centre ■ ,outer 'space = SPACE(4)

outfit /'aʊtfɪt/ n [C] **1** clothing or equipment needed for a particular occasion or purpose **2** [with sing or pl verb] (infml) organization or group of people

outflank /,aʊt'flæŋk/ v [T] go round the side of an enemy in order to attack them

outgoing /'aʊtgəʊɪŋ/ adj **1** friendly **2** leaving: the ~ president ▶ **outgoings** n [pl] (GB) amount of money that a person or business has to spend regularly, eg every month

outgrow /,aʊt'grəʊ/ v (pt **-grew** /-'gruː/ pp **-grown** /-'grəʊn/) [T] **1** grow too big for to be able to wear or fit into sth **2** stop doing sth or lose interest in sth as you grow older

outhouse /'aʊthaʊs/ n small building next to the main building

outing /'aʊtɪŋ/ n trip made for pleasure

outlandish /aʊt'lændɪʃ/ adj (usu disapprov) strange or extremely unusual: ~ clothes ▶ **outlandishly** adv

outlaw /'aʊtlɔː/ v [T] make sth no longer legal: ~ the selling of guns ● **outlaw** n (esp in the past) person who has broken the law and is hiding to avoid being caught

outlay /'aʊtleɪ/ n amount of money spent in order to start a new project, etc

outlet /'aʊtlet/ n **1** way of expressing or making good use of strong feelings or energy: sport is a good ~ for aggression **2** (business) shop that sells goods made by a particular company or of a particular type: The business has 34 retail ~s. **3** (esp US) shop that sells goods of a particular make at reduced prices **4** pipe or hole through which liquid or gas can flow out

outline /'aʊtlaɪn/ n **1** description of the main facts involved in sth: an ~ of the plan **2** line that goes round the edge of sth, showing its main shape ● **outline** v [T] **1** give a short description of sth **2** show or mark the outer edge of sth

outlive /,aʊt'lɪv/ v [T] live longer than sb: ~ your children

outlook /'aʊtlʊk/ n **1** person's

attitude to life and the world **2** what seems likely to happen

outlying /ˈaʊtlaɪŋ/ *adj* far from a centre or city: ~ *villages*

outmoded /ˌaʊtˈməʊdɪd/ *adj* (*disapprov*) no longer fashionable

outnumber /ˌaʊtˈnʌmbə(r)/ *v* [T] be greater in number than sb/sth

out of date ▷ DATE[1]

outpatient /ˈaʊtpeɪʃnt/ *n* person who goes to a hospital for treatment, but does not stay there

outpost /ˈaʊtpəʊst/ *n* **1** small military observation post far from the main army **2** small town in a lonely part of a country

output /ˈaʊtpʊt/ *n* [sing] **1** quantity of goods, etc produced **2** (*computing*) information, results, etc produced by a computer **3** power, energy, etc produced by a piece of equipment

outrage /ˈaʊtreɪdʒ/ *n* **1** [U] strong feeling or shock and anger **2** [C] act or event of great violence and cruelty that shocks people and makes them angry ● **outrage** *v* [T] make sb very shocked and angry ▶ **outrageous** /aʊtˈreɪdʒəs/ *adj* **1** very shocking and unacceptable **2** very unusual ▶ **outrageously** *adv*

outright /ˈaʊtraɪt/ *adv* **1** openly and honestly: *I told him ~ what I thought.* **2** clearly and completely: *He won ~.* **3** not gradually; immediately: *be killed ~* ● **outright** *adj* complete and total: *an ~ ban/rejection*

outset /ˈaʊtset/ *n* [IDM] **at/from the outset (of sth)** at/from the beginning of sth

outshine /ˌaʊtˈʃaɪn/ *v* (*pt, pp* **outshone** /-ˈʃɒn/) [T] (*written*) be much better than sb/sth: *She ~s all her friends at games.*

outside /ˌaʊtˈsaɪd/ *n* [C, usu sing] outer side or surface of sth: *the ~ of the house* ● **outside** /ˈaʊtsaɪd/ *adj* **1** of, on or facing the outer side **2** not included in or connected with your group, organization, etc: ~ *help* **3** used to say that sth is very unlikely: *an ~ chance* ● **outside** /ˌaʊtˈsaɪd/ (*esp US* **outside of**) *prep* **1** on or to a place on the outside of sth: ~ *the bank* **2** away from or not in a particular place: *We live in a village just ~ Bath.* **3** not part of sth: ~ *my areas of responsibility* **4** (**outside of**) apart from: *no interests ~ of his work* ● **outside** /ˌaʊtˈsaɪd/ *adv* on or to the outside of sth; in the open air: *Please wait ~.*

outsider /ˌaʊtˈsaɪdə(r)/ *n* **1** person who is not a member of or not accepted by a group of people **2** horse, team, etc that is not expected to win a competition

outsize /ˈaʊtsaɪz/ *adj* (esp of clothing) larger than the standard sizes

outskirts /ˈaʊtskɜːts/ *n* [pl] outer areas of a city or town

outsmart /ˌaʊtˈsmɑːt/ *v* [T] gain an advantage over sb by being cleverer than them

outsource /ˈaʊtsɔːs/ *v* [I, T] (*business*) arrange for sb outside a company to do work or provide goods for that company ▶ **outsourcing** *n* [U]

outspoken /aʊtˈspəʊkən/ *adj* saying exactly what you think, even if this shocks people

outstanding /aʊtˈstændɪŋ/ *adj* **1** extremely good; excellent **2** very obvious or important **3** (of payment, work, problems, etc) not yet paid, done or solved ▶ **outstandingly** *adv* **1** used to emphasize the good quality of sth **2** extremely well

outstay /aʊtˈsteɪ/ *v* [IDM] **outstay your welcome** stay somewhere as a guest longer than you are wanted

outstrip /aʊtˈstrɪp/ *v* (**-pp-**) [T] be or become better, larger, more important, etc than sb/sth: *Demand is ~ping production.*

outward /ˈaʊtwəd/ *adj* **1** of or on the outside: *an ~ appearance* **2** going away from a particular place: *the ~ journey* ▶ **outwardly** *adv* on the surface; in appearance ▶ **outwards** (*also* **outward**) *adv* towards the outside; away from the centre or a particular point

outweigh /ˌaʊtˈweɪ/ *v* [T] be greater or more important than sth

outwit /ˌaʊtˈwɪt/ *v* (**-tt-**) [T] defeat or gain an advantage over sb by doing sth clever

outwork /ˈaʊtwɜːk/ *n* [U] (*GB, business*) work that is done by people at home ▶ **outworker** *n*

oval /ˈəʊvl/ *n, adj* (shape) like an egg

ovary /ˈəʊvəri/ *n* (*pl* **-ies**) either of the two organs in women and female animals that produce eggs

ovation /əʊˈveɪʃn/ *n* enthusiastic clapping by an audience as a sign of their approval

oven /ˈʌvn/ *n* enclosed box-like space in which food is cooked

over[1] /ˈəʊvə(r)/ *prep* **1** resting on the surface of and partly or completely covering sth/sb: *She put a blanket ~ the sleeping child.* **2** in a position higher than but not touching sth/sb: *They held an umbrella ~ her.* **3** from one side of sth to the other: *a bridge ~ the river* **4** on the far or opposite side of sth: *I live ~ the road.* **5** so as to cross sth and be on the other side: *jump ~ the wall* **6** in or on all or most parts of sth: *travel all ~ the world* ◇ *books all ~ the floor* **7** more than a particular time, amount, etc: *wait for ~ an hour* **8** used to show that sb has control or authority: *rule ~ an* empire **9** during sth: *discuss sth ~ lunch* **10** because of sth: *an argument ~ money* **11** using sth; by means of sth: *She wouldn't tell me ~ the phone.* [IDM] **over and above** in addition to sth **over sb's head** → HEAD¹

over² /ˈəʊvə(r)/ *adv* **1** outwards and downwards from an upright position: *knock a vase ~* **2** from one side to another side: *She turned ~ onto her front.* **3** across a road, open space, etc: *I went ~* (= across the room) *and asked his name.* **4** so as to cover sth/sth completely: *paint sth ~* **5** above; more: *children of 14 and ~* **6** remaining; not used or needed: *the food left ~* **7** again: (*esp US*) *do it ~* **8** ended: *The meeting is ~.* [IDM] **(all) over again** once more from the beginning **over and over (again)** many times

over³ /ˈəʊvə(r)/ *n* (in cricket) series of six balls bowled in succession to the same bowler

over- *prefix* **1** more than usual; too much: *~eat ◇ ~work* **2** across; above: *~cast ◇ ~hang*

overall /ˌəʊvərˈɔːl/ *adj, adv* including or considering everything: *the ~ cost* ● **overall** /ˈəʊvərɔːl/ *n* **1** [C] (*GB*) loose coat worn over other clothes to protect them from dirt, etc **2** (**overalls**) [pl] (*GB*) one-piece garment covering the body and legs, worn over other clothing by workers doing dirty work

overawe /ˌəʊvərˈɔː/ *v* [T] (*usu passive*) impress sb so much that they feel nervous or frightened

overbalance /ˌəʊvəˈbæləns/ *v* [I] fall over

overbearing /ˌəʊvəˈbeərɪŋ/ *adj* (*disapprov*) forcing others to do what you want

overboard /ˈəʊvəbɔːd/ *adv* over the side of a ship into the water

overcast /ˌəʊvəˈkɑːst/ *adj* (of the sky) covered with cloud

overcharge /ˌəʊvəˈtʃɑːdʒ/ *v* [I, T] charge sb too high a price for sth

overcoat /ˈəʊvəkəʊt/ *n* thick warm coat

overcome /ˌəʊvəˈkʌm/ *v* (*pt* **-came** /-ˈkeɪm/ *pp* **-come**) [T] **1** succeed in dealing with a problem that has prevented you from achieving sth: *She overcame injury to win the race.* **2** (*written*) defeat sb **3** be strongly affected by sth: *be ~ with grief*

overcrowded /ˌəʊvəˈkraʊdɪd/ *adj* with too many people in a place ▸ **overcrowding** /-dɪŋ/ *n* [U]

overdo /ˌəʊvəˈduː/ *v* (*third pers sing pres tense* **-does** /-ˈdʌz/; *pt* **-did** /-ˈdɪd/; *pp* **-done** /-ˈdʌn/) [T] do sth too much; exaggerate sth [IDM] **overdo it/things** work, etc too hard or for too long

overdose /ˈəʊvədəʊs/ *n* [C, *usu sing*] too much of a drug taken at one time

overdraft /ˈəʊvədrɑːft/ *n* amount of money by which a bank account is overdrawn

overdrawn /ˌəʊvəˈdrɔːn/ *adj* **1** (of a person) having taken more money out of your bank account than you have in it **2** (of an account) with more money taken out than was paid in or left in

overdrive /ˈəʊvədraɪv/ *n* [C, U] extra high gear in a vehicle, used when driving at high speeds

overdue /ˌəʊvəˈdjuː/ *adj* not paid, arrived, returned, etc by the right or expected time

overflow /ˌəʊvəˈfləʊ/ *v* [I, T] **1** flow over the edges of sth: *The river has ~ed it banks.* **2** (of a room, etc) go beyond the limits of a room, etc ● **overflow** /ˈəʊvəfləʊ/ [U, *sing*] **1** number of people or things that do not fit into the space available **2** action of liquid flowing out of a container that is already full; liquid that flows out

overgrown /ˌəʊvəˈɡrəʊn/ *adj* covered with plants that are growing thickly in an uncontrolled way

overhang /ˌəʊvəˈhæŋ/ *v* (*pt, pp* **-hung** /-ˈhʌŋ/) [I, T] stick out over and above sth else ● **overhang** /ˈəʊvəhæŋ/ *n* [C, *usu sing*] part of sth that overhangs

overhaul /ˌəʊvəˈhɔːl/ *v* [T] examine a machine, system, etc thoroughly and repair any faults: *the ~ engine* ● **overhaul** /ˈəʊvəhɔːl/ *n* thorough examination of a machine or system

overhead /ˈəʊvəhed/ *adj* above your head; raised above the ground: *~ wires* ● **overhead** /ˌəʊvəˈhed/ *adv* above your head; in the sky: *aircraft flying ~*

overheads /ˈəʊvəhedz/ *n* [pl] regular business expenses, eg rent, salaries and insurance

overhear /ˌəʊvəˈhɪə(r)/ *v* (*pt, pp* **-heard** /-ˈhɜːd/) [T] hear what sb is saying without them knowing

overjoyed /ˌəʊvəˈdʒɔɪd/ *adj* extremely happy

overland /ˈəʊvəlænd/ *adj, adv* across the land; by land, not by sea or air

overlap /ˌəʊvəˈlæp/ *v* (**-pp-**) [I, T] partly cover sth by going over its edge: (*fig*) *These two subjects ~.* ● **overlap** /ˈəʊvəlæp/ *n* [C, U] part that overlaps

overleaf /ˌəʊvəˈliːf/ *adv* (*written*) on the other side of the page

overload /ˌəʊvəˈləʊd/ *v* [T] **1** put too great a weight on sth **2** put too great a demand on a computer, an electrical system, etc, causing it to fail

0

overlook /ˌəʊvəˈlʊk/ v [T] **1** fail to see or notice sth **2** see sth wrong or bad but decide to ignore it: ~ *a fault* **3** have a view of a place from above

overmanned /ˌəʊvəˈmænd/ adj (of a company, office, etc) having more workers than are needed ▶ **overmanning** n [U]

overnight /ˌəʊvəˈnaɪt/ adv **1** during or for the night: *stay* ~ **2** (*infml*) suddenly or quickly: *become a success* ~ ● **overnight** /ˈəʊvənaɪt/ adj: *an* ~ *bag*

overpass /ˈəʊvəpɑːs/ n (US) = FLY-OVER

overpower /ˌəʊvəˈpaʊə(r)/ v [T] defeat sb by using greater strength ▶ **overpowering** adj very strong or powerful: *an* ~*ing smell*

overrate /ˌəʊvəˈreɪt/ v [T] have too high an opinion of sth

overreach /ˌəʊvəˈriːtʃ/ v ~ **yourself** fail by trying to achieve more than is possible

overreact /ˌəʊvəriˈækt/ v [I] react too strongly, esp to sth unpleasant

override /ˌəʊvəˈraɪd/ v (pt -**rode** /-ˈrəʊd/ pp -**ridden** /-ˈrɪdn/) [T] **1** use your authority to reject sb's decision, order, etc **2** be more important than sth ▶ **overriding** adj more important than anything else

overrule /ˌəʊvəˈruːl/ v [T] decide against sth already decided by using your higher authority

overrun /ˌəʊvəˈrʌn/ v (pt -**ran** /-ˈræn/ pp -**run**) [T] **1** spread over and occupy an area quickly: *a house* ~ *by insects* **2** [I, T] take more time or money than was intended: *The meeting might* ~.

overseas /ˌəʊvəˈsiːz/ adj, adv to, of, or in foreign countries, esp those separated from your country by the sea

oversee /ˌəʊvəˈsiː/ v (pt -**saw** /-ˈsɔː/ pp -**seen** /-ˈsiːn/) [T] watch over sb's work to see that it is done properly ▶ **overseer** /ˈəʊvəsiːə(r)/ n

overshadow /ˌəʊvəˈʃædəʊ/ v [T] **1** make sb/sth seem less important or successful **2** throw a shadow over sth

overshoot /ˌəʊvəˈʃuːt/ v (pt, pp -**shot** /-ˈʃɒt/) [T] go further than a place where you intended to stop or turn

oversight /ˈəʊvəsaɪt/ n [C, U] careless failure to notice sth

oversleep /ˌəʊvəˈsliːp/ v (pt, pp -**slept** /-ˈslept/) [I] sleep longer than you intended

overspill /ˈəʊvəspɪl/ n [U, sing] (GB) people who move out of a crowded city to an area where there is more space

overstep /ˌəʊvəˈstep/ v (-**pp**-) [T] go beyond the normal accepted limit

overt /əʊˈvɜːt/ adj (fml) done or shown openly ▶ **overtly** adv

overtake /ˌəʊvəˈteɪk/ v (pt -**took** /-ˈtʊk/ pp -**taken** /-ˈteɪkən/) **1** [I, T] go past a moving vehicle or person ahead of you **2** [T] (of unpleasant events) affect sb suddenly and unexpectedly

overthrow /ˌəʊvəˈθrəʊ/ v (pt -**threw** /-ˈθruː/ pp -**thrown** /-ˈθrəʊn/) [T] remove a government, ruler, etc from power ▶ **overthrow** /ˈəʊvəθrəʊ/ n [C, usu sing]

overtime /ˈəʊvətaɪm/ n [U] time spent at work in addition to your usual working hours

overtone /ˈəʊvətəʊn/ n [C, usu pl] something suggested but not expressed openly

overture /ˈəʊvətjʊə(r)/ n musical introduction to an opera or ballet [IDM] **make overtures (to sb)** try to begin a friendly or business relationship with sb

overturn /ˌəʊvəˈtɜːn/ v **1** [I, T] (cause sth to) turn upside down or on its side **2** [T] officially decide that a legal decision, etc is not correct, and make it no longer valid

overview /ˈəʊvəvjuː/ n general description of sth

overweight /ˌəʊvəˈweɪt/ adj (of people) too heavy or fat

overwhelm /ˌəʊvəˈwelm/ v [T] (usu passive) have such a strong emotional effect on sb that it is difficult for them to resist: ~*ed by the beauty of the landscape* **2** defeat sb completely

overwork /ˌəʊvəˈwɜːk/ v [I, T] (cause sb to) work too hard ▶ **overwork** n [U]

overwrite /ˌəʊvəˈraɪt/ v (pt -**wrote** /-ˈrəʊt/ pp -**written** /-ˈrɪtn/) [T] (computing) replace information on the screen or in a file by putting new information over it

overwrought /ˌəʊvəˈrɔːt/ adj nervous, anxious and upset

ovulate /ˈɒvjuleɪt/ v [I] (of a woman or female animal) produce an egg (**ovum**) from an ovary ▶ **ovulation** /ˌɒvjuˈleɪʃn/ n

ovum /ˈəʊvəm/ n (pl **ova** /ˈəʊvə/) (biol) female cell that can develop into a new individual

ow /aʊ/ exclam used to express sudden pain: *Ow! That hurt!*

owe /əʊ/ v [T] **1** have to return money that you have borrowed or pay for sth you have already received: *I* ~ *him £10.* **2** ~ **to** feel that you ought to do sth for sb or give them sth, esp because you are grateful to them: *I* ~ *a debt of gratitude to all my family.*

owing /ˈəʊɪŋ/ adj still to be paid ∎ **owing to** prep because of

owl /aʊl/ n bird of prey with large round eyes, that hunts at night

own¹ /əʊn/ adj, pron belonging to the person mentioned: his ~ room ◇ a room of his ~ [IDM] **get your own back (on sb)** (infml) harm sb **on your own 1** alone **2** without help

own² /əʊn/ v [T] possess sth ~ a house [PV] **own up (to sth/to doing sth)** (infml) admit that you are to blame for sth ▸ **owner** n ▸ **ownership** n [U]

ox /ɒks/ n (pl ~en /ˈɒksn/) fully grown castrated bull

oxygen /ˈɒksɪdʒən/ n [U] gas without colour, taste or smell, present in the air and necessary for life

oyster /ˈɔɪstə(r)/ n large flat shellfish

oz abbr ounce(s)

ozone /ˈəʊzəʊn/ n [U] **1** (chem) poisonous form of oxygen **2** (infml) fresh air at the seaside ∎ **ozone-ˈfriendly** adj not containing substances that will damage the ozone layer ∎ **ozone layer** n [sing] layer of ozone high above the earth's surface that helps to protect the earth from the sun's harmful rays

Pp

P, p /piː/ n [C,U] (pl **P's, p's** /piːz/) the sixteenth letter of the English alphabet

p abbr **1** (infml) penny; pence **2** (pl **pp**) page

PA /ˌpiː ˈeɪ/ n (esp GB) personal assistant; person who works as a secretary for just one person

p.a. abbr per year (from Latin 'per annum')

pace /peɪs/ n **1** [sing,U] speed at which sb/sth walks, runs or moves **2** [C] (length of a) single step in walking or running **3** [U] rate of progress ∎ **pace** v **1** [I, T] walk up and down in a small area many times **2** [T] set the speed at which sth happens or develops [PV] **pace sth out/off** measure sth by taking regular steps across it ∎ **'pace-maker** n electronic device placed inside a person's body to help their heart beat regularly

pacifism /ˈpæsɪfɪzəm/ n [U] belief that all war is wrong ▸ **pacifist** /-ɪst/ n

pacify /ˈpæsɪfaɪ/ v (pt, pp **-ied**) [T] make sb who is angry calm ▸ **pacification** /ˌpæsɪfɪˈkeɪʃn/ n [U] ▸ **pacifier** n (US) = DUMMY(2)

pack¹ /pæk/ n **1** [I, T] load sth, eg clothes, etc into a bag for a trip away from home: ~ a suitcase **2** [T] put sth into

a container so that it can be transported, sold, etc: I carefully ~ed the gifts. **3** [T] cover or protect sth with material, to prevent damage: plates ~ed in newspaper **4** [I, T] ~ (into) fill a space with a lot of people or things: Crowds ~ed (into) the theatre. [PV] **pack sth in** (infml) stop doing sth **pack sb off (to …)** (infml) send sb away **pack up** (infml, esp GB) (of a machine) stop working properly **pack (sth) up 1** put your possessions into a bag, etc and leave **2** (GB, infml) stop doing sth, esp a job ▸ **packed** adj full of people

pack² /pæk/ n **1** (esp US) container that holds a number of things or an amount of sth, ready to be sold: a ~ of gum/cigarettes **2** number of things wrapped or tied together, esp for carrying **3** group of wild animals: a ~ of wolves **4** group of people or things: a ~ of fools/lies **5** complete set of playing cards

package /ˈpækɪdʒ/ n **1** = PARCEL **2** (US) (contents of a) box, bag, etc in which things are wrapped or packed **3** (also **package deal**) set of items or ideas that must be bought or accepted together: a benefits ~ **4** (also **'software package**) (computing) set of related programs, sold and used as a single unit: The system came with a database software ~. ∎ **package** v [T] put sth into a box, bag, etc to be sold or transported ∎ **'package holiday/tour** n holiday arranged by a company at a fixed price which includes the cost of travel, hotels, etc

packet /ˈpækɪt/ n **1** (GB) small container in which goods are packed for selling: a ~ of cigarettes/crisps **2** [sing] (infml) large amount of money **3** (computing) piece of information that forms part of a message sent through a computer network

packing /ˈpækɪŋ/ n [U] **1** process of packing goods **2** material used for packing delicate objects, to protect them

pact /pækt/ n agreement

pad¹ /pæd/ n **1** thick piece of soft material, used eg for absorbing liquid, protecting or cleaning sth: shin/shoulder ~s **2** number of sheets of paper fastened together: a sketch ~ **3** soft fleshy part under the foot of a dog, fox, etc **4** flat surface from which spacecraft are launched or take off

pad² /pæd/ v (**-dd-**) **1** [T] put a layer of soft material in or on sth to protect it or change its shape: a ~ded jacket **2** [I] walk with quiet steps [PV] **pad sth out** make sth, eg an article longer by adding unnecessary parts ▸ **padding** n [U] **1** soft material used to pad sth **2** unnecessary material in a book, speech, etc

paddle /'pædl/ n **1** [C] short pole with a wide flat part at one or both ends, used to move a small boat through water **2 (a paddle)** [sing] act of walking in shallow water with bare feet: *Let's go for a ~.* ● **paddle** v **1** [I, T] move a boat with a paddle **2** [I] walk with bare feet in shallow water

paddock /'pædək/ n field where horses are kept

paddy /'pædi/ n (pl -ies) (also 'paddy field) field in which rice is grown

padlock /'pædlɒk/ n lock with a curved bar that forms a loop when closed ● **padlock** v [T] fasten a gate, bicycle, etc with a padlock

paediatrics /ˌpiːdiˈætrɪks/ n [U] branch of medicine concerned with children and their diseases ▸ **paediatrician** /ˌpiːdiəˈtrɪʃn/ n doctor who specializes in paediatrics

pagan /'peɪɡən/ n person who holds beliefs about a part of any of the world's main religions ▸ **pagan** adj: *~ festivals* ▸ **paganism** n [U]

page /peɪdʒ/ n **1** (abbr p) one side or both sides of a sheet of paper in a book, etc **2** section of data or information that can be shown on a computer screen at any one time **3** (GB) = PAGEBOY **4** (in the Middle Ages) boy who worked for a knight while training to become a knight himself

pageant /'pædʒənt/ n **1** public entertainment in which historical events are acted **2** (US) competition for young women in which their beauty, personal qualities, etc are judged: *a beauty ~* ▸ **pageantry** n [U] impressive and colourful events and ceremonies

pageboy /'peɪdʒbɔɪ/ n (GB) small boy who helps or follows a bride during a marriage ceremony

pagoda /pəˈɡəʊdə/ n religious building in India or E Asia, in the form of a tower with several levels

paid pt, pp of PAY¹

pail /peɪl/ n (US) = BUCKET

pain /peɪn/ n **1** [U,C] feelings of suffering that you have in your body when you are hurt or ill: *a ~ in her leg* ◇ *He was in a lot of ~.* **2** [U,C] mental or emotional suffering: *the ~ of separation* **3** [C] (infml) very annoying person or thing [IDM] **a pain in the neck** (infml) very annoying person or thing ● **pain** v [T] cause sb pain ▸ **pained** adj unhappy and upset: *a ~ed look* ▸ **painful** adj causing pain ▸ **painless** adj not causing pain

pains /peɪnz/ n [pl] [IDM] **take (great) be at pains to do sth** make a great

effort to do sth ■ **'painstaking** adj very careful; thorough

paint /peɪnt/ n **1** [U] coloured liquid that is put on a surface **2 (paints)** [pl] set of tubes of paint: *oil ~s* ● **paint** v **1** [T] cover a surface or an object with paint: *~ the door* **2** [I, T] make a picture or design using paints: *~ flowers* **3** [T] give a particular impression of sb/sth: *The article ~s them as a gang of criminals.* [IDM] **paint the town red** (infml) go out and enjoy yourself ▸ **painting** n **1** [C] picture that has been painted **2** [U] action or skill of painting ▸ **paintwork** n [U] painted surface

painter /'peɪntə(r)/ n **1** person whose job is painting walls, buildings, etc: *He's a ~ and decorator.* **2** artist who paints pictures

pair /peə(r)/ n **1** [C] two things of the same kind: *a ~ of shoes* **2** [C] object made of two parts joined together: *a ~ of trousers/scissors* **3** [C, with sing or pl verb] two people closely connected, eg a married couple ● **pair** v [I, T] ~ **(off)** (cause) people or things to form groups of two

pajamas (esp US) = PYJAMAS

pal /pæl/ n (infml) friend

palace /'pæləs/ n large splendid house, esp the official home of a king, queen or president

palaeontology (esp US paleo-) /ˌpæliɒnˈtɒlədʒi; ˌpeɪl-/ n [U] study of fossils ▸ **palaeontologist** (esp US paleo-) /-dʒɪst/ n

palatable /'pælətəbl/ adj **1** having a pleasant taste **2** ~ **(to)** pleasant or acceptable to sb: *The truth is not always very ~.*

palate /'pælət/ n [C] **1** top part of the inside of the mouth **2** [usu sing] sense of taste

palatial /pəˈleɪʃl/ adj like a palace; very large and impressive: *a ~ hotel*

palaver /pəˈlɑːvə(r)/ n [U, sing] (infml) unnecessary trouble; fuss

pale /peɪl/ adj (~r, ~st) **1** (of a person or their face) having little colour; whiter than usual because of illness, shock, etc **2** light in colour; not bright: *~ blue eyes* ● **pale** v [I] **1** become pale **2** seem less important when compared with sth else: *Compared to your problems mine ~ into insignificance.* ● **pale** n [IDM] **beyond the pale** considered unacceptable ▸ **paleness** n [U]

paleo- (esp US) = PALAEO-

palette /'pælət/ n board on which an artist mixes colours

paling /'peɪlɪŋ/ n fence made of pointed pieces of wood

pall /pɔːl/ v [I] ~ **(on)** become less interesting to sb over time because they have done or seen it too much

● **pall** n [C] **1** [usu sing] thick dark cloud of sth: a ~ of smoke **2** cloth spread over a coffin ■ **'pall-bearer** n person who walks beside or helps to carry the coffin at a funeral

pallet /'pælət/ n large flat frame for carrying heavy goods, lifted by a fork-lift truck

pallid /'pælɪd/ adj pale; looking ill ▶ **pallor** /'pælə(r)/ n [U]

palm /pɑːm/ n **1** inner surface of the hand **2** (also **'palm tree**) tree growing in warm climates, with no branches and a large mass of leaves at the top ● **palm** v [PV] **palm sth off (on/onto sb)** (infml) get rid of sth unwanted by persuading sb to accept it: She's always ~ing off the worst jobs on me.

palmist /'pɑːmɪst/ n person who claims to be able to tell sb's future by looking at the palm of their hand ▶ **palmistry** n [U] skill of a palmist

palmtop /'pɑːmtɒp/ n small computer that can be held in the palm of one hand

palpable /'pælpəbl/ adj (fml) clear to the mind; obvious ▶ **palpably** /-əbli/ adv

palpitate /'pælpɪteɪt/ v [I] (of the heart) beat very fast and/or irregularly, esp because of fear or excitement ▶ **palpitations** /ˌpælpɪ'teɪʃnz/ n [pl] physical condition in which your heart beats rapidly and irregularly

paltry /'pɔːltri/ adj (-ier, -iest) very small; worthless

pamper /'pæmpə(r)/ v [T] take care of sb very well

pamphlet /'pæmflət/ n thin book with a paper cover

pan /pæn/ n **1** metal container with a handle, used for cooking: a frying ~ **2** amount contained in a pan: a ~ of boiling water **3** bowl of a toilet ● **pan** v (-nn-) **1** [T] (infml) strongly criticize sth, eg a play or a film **2** [I, T] turn a television or video camera to follow a moving object or to film a wide area **3** [I] (~ for) wash small stones in a dish in order to find gold [PV] **pan out** (infml) (of events) develop in a particular way: How did things ~ out?

panacea /ˌpænə'siːə/ n something that will solve all the problems of a situation

panache /pæ'næʃ/ n [U] confident stylish manner

pancake /'pænkeɪk/ n thin flat round cake of batter fried on both sides

pancreas /'pæŋkriəs/ n part of the body that produces substances which help in the digestion of food

panda /'pændə/ n large bear-like black and white animal from China

pandemonium /ˌpændə'məʊniəm/ n [U] wild and noisy disorder

pander /'pændə(r)/ v [PV] **pander to sth/sb** (disapprov) to satisfy a weak or bad desire or sb who has one: ~ to sb's whims/wishes

pane /peɪn/ n sheet of glass in a window

panel /'pænl/ n **1** square or rectangular piece of wood, glass or metal that forms part of a door or wall **2** group of speakers who discuss topics of interest, esp on a radio or television programme **3** flat board in a vehicle or piece of machinery for controls and instruments: a control/display ~ ● **panel** v (-ll- US -l-) [T] cover or decorate a surface with panels: The walls were ~led in oak. ▶ **panelling** (US -l-) n [U] series of panels on a wall, etc

pang /pæŋ/ n sudden strong feeling of pain, guilt, etc

panic /'pænɪk/ n [U,C] sudden uncontrollable feeling of great fear ● **panic** v (-ck-) [I, T] (cause sb to) feel panic ▶ **panicky** adj (infml) feeling or showing panic ■ **'panic-stricken** adj filled with panic

pannier /'pæniə(r)/ n one of a pair of bags on either side of the back wheel of a bicycle or motorcycle

panorama /ˌpænə'rɑːmə/ n view of a wide area ▶ **panoramic** /-'ræmɪk/ adj

pansy /'pænzi/ n (pl -ies) small garden plant with brightly coloured flowers

pant /pænt/ v [I] breathe with short quick breaths ● **pant** n [C, usu pl] short quick breath

panther /'pænθə(r)/ n **1** black leopard **2** (US) = PUMA

panties /'pæntiz/ n (esp US) = KNICKERS

pantomime /'pæntəmaɪm/ n [C,U] funny play for children, based on a fairy tale, with music and dancing, esp at Christmas

pantry /'pæntri/ n (pl -ies) cupboard or small room in a house where food is kept

pants /pænts/ n [pl] **1** (GB) men's underpants; women's knickers **2** (esp US) trousers

papacy /'peɪpəsi/ n (the papacy) [sing] position or authority of the Pope ▶ **papal** /'peɪpl/ adj of the Pope

paper /'peɪpə(r)/ n **1** [U] substance in thin sheets used for writing, printing or drawing on or wrapping things in **2** [C] newspaper **3** (papers) [pl] official documents **4** [C] (GB) set of exam questions **5** [C] academic article **6** [C] (US) piece of written work done by a student ● **paper** v [T] cover the walls of a room with wallpaper ■ **'paperback** n [C,U] book with a thick paper cover ■ '**paper boy**, '**paper girl** *n* boy or girl who delivers newspapers to people's houses ■ '**paper clip** *n* piece of bent wire, used to hold sheets of paper together ■ '**paperweight** *n* small heavy object put on top of loose papers to keep them in place ■ '**paperwork** *n* [U] writing letters and reports, filling in forms, etc

paprika /'pæprɪkə/ *n* [U] red powder of a sweet pepper, used in cooking

par /pɑː(r)/ *n* [U,C] **1** (in golf) average number of hits necessary to hit the ball into a hole or complete the course **2** (*also* '**par value**) (*business*) value that a share in a company had originally [IDM] **below/under par** (*infml*) less well than usual **on a par with sb/sth** equal in quality, importance, etc to sb/sth

parable /'pærəbl/ *n* (esp in the Bible) simple story that teaches a moral lesson

parachute /'pærəʃuːt/ *n* umbrella-shaped device by which sb may fall slowly and safely to the ground from an aircraft ● **parachute** *v* [I, T] jump or drop sth from an aircraft using a parachute ▶ **parachutist** *n* person who jumps from a plane using a parachute

parade /pə'reɪd/ *n* **1** procession **2** formal gathering of soldiers in order to march in front of people ● **parade** *v* **1** [I] walk somewhere in a formal group of people, to celebrate or protest about sth **2** [I] walk around in a way that makes people notice you **3** [I, T] show sb/sth in public so that people can see them/it: ~ *your wealth* **4** [I, T] (cause soldiers to) gather together to march in front of people

paradise /'pærədaɪs/ *n* **1** (often **Paradise**) [U] heaven **2** [U,C] place or state of perfect happiness

paradox /'pærədɒks/ *n* statement which seems to contain two opposite facts but is or may be true ▶ **paradoxical** /ˌpærə'dɒksɪkl/ *adj* ▶ **paradoxically** /-kli/ *adv*

paraffin /'pærəfɪn/ *n* [U] oil obtained from petroleum, used as a fuel

paragliding /'pærəɡlaɪdɪŋ/ *n* [U] sport in which you jump from a high place, wearing something like a parachute, and are carried along by the wind

paragon /'pærəɡən/ *n* ~ (**of**) person who is a perfect example of a quality: *She is a ~ of virtue.*

paragraph /'pærəɡrɑːf/ *n* division of a piece of writing, started on a new line

parakeet /'pærəkiːt/ *n* small long-tailed parrot

parallel /'pærəlel/ *adj* **1** (of lines) always at the same distance from

each other **2** very similar ● **parallel** *n* **1** [C, U] person or thing that is exactly similar to another **2** [C, usu pl] comparison or similarity: *draw a ~ between A and B* ● **parallel** *v* [T] be equal or similar to sth

parallelogram /ˌpærə'leləɡræm/ *n* (*geom*) four-sided figure with its opposite sides parallel to each other

paralyse (*US* -**lyze**) /'pærəlaɪz/ *v* [T] **1** make sb unable to fell or move all or part of their body **2** prevent sth from functioning normally: *The city was ~d by the railway strike.*

paralysis /pə'ræləsɪs/ *n* [U] **1** loss of feeling in or control of part of the body **2** total inability to move, act or function, etc ▶ **paralytic** /ˌpærə-'lɪtɪk/ *adj* **1** (*GB, infml*) very drunk **2** (*fml*) suffering from paralysis

parameter /pə'ræmɪtə(r)/ *n* [C, usu pl] something that decides or limits how sth can done

paramilitary /ˌpærə'mɪlətri/ *adj* (of a military force) organized like but not part of an official army

paramount /'pærəmaʊnt/ *adj* (*fml*) more important than anything else

paranoia /ˌpærə'nɔɪə/ *n* [U] mental illness in which sb believes that other people want to harm them ▶ **paranoid** /'pærənɔɪd/ *n, adj* (person) suffering from paranoia

parapet /'pærəpɪt/ -pet- *n* low protective wall at the edge of a roof, bridge, etc

paraphernalia /ˌpærəfə'neɪliə/ *n* [U] many small articles of different kinds

paraphrase /'pærəfreɪz/ *v* [T] express what sb has said or written using different words ▶ **paraphrase** *n* different

parascending /'pærəsendɪŋ/ *n* [U] sport in which you wear a parachute and are pulled along behind a boat so that you rise up into the air

parasite /'pærəsaɪt/ *n* **1** animal or plant that lives on and gets food from another **2** person supported by others, giving nothing in return ▶ **parasitic** /ˌpærə'sɪtɪk/ *adj*

parasol /'pærəsɒl/ *n* umbrella used for giving shade from the sun

paratroops /'pærətruːps/ *n* [pl] soldiers trained to drop from an aircraft using parachutes ▶ **paratrooper** /-pə(r)/ *n*

parcel /'pɑːsl/ *n* (*esp GB*) something wrapped up for carrying and sending by post ● **parcel** *v* (-**ll**- *US* -**l**-) [T] ~ (**up**) wrap sth up and make it into a parcel [PV] **parcel sth out** divide sth into parts

parched /pɑːtʃt/ *adj* **1** very dry, because of a lack of water **2** (*infml*) very thirsty

parchment /'pɑːtʃmənt/ n [U] **1** material made from animal skin for writing on **2** thick yellowish type of paper

pardon /'pɑːdn/ n **1** [C] official decision not to punish sb for a crime **2** [U] (fml) act of forgiving sb for sth: He asked her ~ for deceiving her ● pardon v [T] **1** officially allow sb to leave prison and/or avoid punishment **2** forgive sb for sth ● pardon exclam (esp US ,pardon 'me) used to ask sb to repeat sth because you did not hear or understand it ▸ pardonable adj that can be forgiven

pare /peə(r)/ v [T] **1** ~ (off/away) cut away the outer part, edge or skin of sth **2** ~ (back/down) gradually reduce the size or amount of sth

parent /'peərənt/ n father or mother ▸ parental /pə'rentl/ adj

parenthesis /pə'renθəsɪs/ n [C] (pl -eses /-əsiːz/) **1** additional sentence or phrase within another sentence, separated off using brackets, commas or dashes **2** [usu pl] (US or fml) = BRACKET

parish /'pærɪʃ/ n area that has its own church and priest ▸ parishioner /pə'rɪʃənə(r)/ n person living in a parish, esp one who goes to church regularly

parity /'pærəti/ n [U] (fml) state of being equal

park /pɑːk/ n public garden or area of ground for public use ● park v [I, T] stop and leave a vehicle in a place for a time ■ 'parking meter n machine beside the road that you put money into when you park your car near it ■ 'parking lot n (US) = CAR PARK ■ 'parkland n [U] open area of grass and trees

parliament /'pɑːləmənt/ n [C, with sing or pl verb] group of people that make the laws of a country ▸ parliamentary /ˌpɑːlə'mentri/ adj

parlour (US -lor) /'pɑːlə(r)/ n **1** (old-fash) sitting room **2** (in compounds) (esp US) shop: a beauty/an ice-cream ~

parochial /pə'rəʊkiəl/ adj **1** (fml) of a church parish **2** (disapprov) only concerned with small issues that happen in your local area

parody /'pærədi/ n (pl -ies) **1** [C, U] piece of writing intended to amuse by imitating the style of sb else **2** [C] (disapprov) something that is such a bad example of sth that it seems ridiculous: The trial was a ~ of justice. ● parody v (pt, pp -ied) [T] copy the style of sb/sth in order to make people laugh

parole /pə'rəʊl/ n [U] permission given to a prisoner to leave prison before the end of their sentence on

condition that they behave well: She was released on ~. ▸ parole v [T]

paroxysm /'pærəksɪzəm/ n (written) sudden attack or burst of anger, pain, etc

parquet /'pɑːkeɪ/ n [U] floor covering made of flat pieces of wood fixed together

parrot /'pærət/ n tropical bird with a curved beak and bright feathers ● parrot v [T] (disapprov) repeat what sb else has said without thinking about what it means

parry /'pæri/ v (pt, pp -ied) **1** turn aside or avoid a blow, question, etc ▸ parry n

parsimonious /ˌpɑːsɪ'məʊniəs/ adj (fml, disapprov) extremely unwilling to spend money

parsley /'pɑːsli/ n [U] small plant with curly leaves used for flavouring and decorating food

parsnip /'pɑːsnɪp/ n [C, U] long pale yellow root vegetable

parson /'pɑːsn/ n parish priest ▸ parsonage /-ɪdʒ/ n parson's house

part¹ /pɑːt/ n **1** ~ (of) some but not all of thing: We spent (a) ~ of our holiday in Paris. **2** piece of a machine: spare ~s **3** area of a country, town, etc **4** section of a book, television series, etc: The final ~ will be shown next Sunday evening. **5** person's share in an activity; actor's role in a play, film, etc **6** (music) melody for a particular voice or instrument **7** (US) = PARTING [IDM] for the most part mostly; usually **be, have, their, etc part** speaking for myself, etc **in part** to some extent **on sb's part** made or done by sb **take part (in sth)** be involved in sth **take sb's part** (GB) support sb, eg in an argument ● part adv (often in compounds) consisting of two things; partly: She's ~ French, ~ English. ▸ partly adv to some extent; not completely ▸ ,part of 'speech n (gram) one of the classes of words, eg noun or verb ■ ,part-'time adj, adv working only a part of the day or week

part² /pɑːt/ v **1** [I, T] (fml) separate; leave sb: The clouds ~ed. ◇ He has ~ed from his wife. **2** [T] prevent sb from being with sb else: I hate being ~ed from the children. **3** [T] divide your hair into two sections with a comb, creating a line on the top of your head [IDM] part company (with/from sb) **1** leave sb; end a relationship with sb **2** disagree with sb about sth [PV] part with sth give sth to sb, esp sth you would prefer to keep: Read the contract before ~ing with any money. ▸ parting n [U, C] act of leaving a person or place **2** [C] (US part) line where the hair is parted: a side ~

partake /pɑːˈteɪk/ v (pt **-took** /-ˈtʊk/ pp **-taken** /-ˈteɪkən/) [I] (fml) ~of eat or drink sth

partial /ˈpɑːʃl/ adj **1** not complete or whole: only a ~ success **2** ~to (old-fash) liking sth very much **3** ~(towards) (disapprov) unfairly showing favour to one person or side ▸ **partiality** /ˌpɑːʃiˈæləti/ n **1** [U] (disapprov) unfair support of one person or side **2** [C, usu sing] fondness for sth ▸ **partially** /ˈpɑːʃəli/ adv not completely; partly

participate /pɑːˈtɪsɪpeɪt/ v [I] ~(in) take part or become involved in an activity ▸ **participant** /-pənt/ n person who participates in sth ▸ **participation** /pɑːˌtɪsɪˈpeɪʃn/ n [U]

participle /ˈpɑːtɪsɪpl/ n (gram) form of a verb: 'Sinking' and 'sunk' are the present and past ~s of 'sink'.

particle /ˈpɑːtɪkl/ n **1** very small piece of sth: dust ~s **2** (gram) adverb or preposition that can combine with a verb to make a phrasal verb

particular /pəˈtɪkjələ(r)/ adj **1** relating to one individual person or thing and not others: in this ~ case **2** greater than usual; special: of ~ interest **3** ~(about) very definite about what you like and careful about what you choose [IDM] in particular (esp fml): I like these flowers in ~. ● **particular** n [C, usu pl] (fml) fact or detail, esp one that is written down: The nurse asked me for my ~s (= my name, address, etc). ▸ **particularly** adv especially

partisan /ˌpɑːtɪˈzæn/ n **1** strong supporter of a particular leader, group, etc **2** member of an unofficial armed force in a country occupied by enemy soldiers ● **partisan** adj showing too much support for one person, cause, etc

partition /pɑːˈtɪʃn/ n **1** [C] thin wall that separates one part of a room from another **2** [U] division of a country into two or more countries: the ~ of Germany after the war ● **partition** v [T] divide sth into two parts [PV] **partition off** separate sth with a partition

partner /ˈpɑːtnə(r)/ n **1** person you are married to or have a sexual relationship with **2** one of the people who owns a business and shares the profits, etc **3** person you are doing an activity with, eg dancing or playing a game ● **partner** v [T] be sb's partner in a dance, game, etc ▸ **partnership** n **1** [U] state of being a partner in business: be in/go into ~ship **2** [C,U] (state of having) a relationship between two people, organizations, etc

partook pt of PARTAKE

partridge /ˈpɑːtrɪdʒ/ n bird with brown feathers, a round body and a short tail that is hunted for food or sport

party /ˈpɑːti/ n [C] (pl **-ies**) **1** (also **Party**) [with sing or pl verb] group of people with the same political aims: the Labour P~ **2** social occasion, often in sb's home: a birthday ~ **3** [with sing or pl verb] group of people doing sth together, eg travelling: a ~ of tourists **4** (fml) one of the people or groups involved in a legal agreement or dispute: the innocent ~ [IDM] **be (a) party to sth** (fml) be involved in or support sth ■ **party 'line** n [sing] official opinions of a political party

pass¹ /pɑːs/ v **1** [I, T] move past or to the other side of sb/sth: ~ the house **2** [I, T] (cause sb/sth to) go or move in the direction mentioned: He ~ed through Oxford on his way to London. **3** [T] give sth to sb: Please ~ me the butter. **4** [I, T] (sport) kick, hit, etc the ball, etc to a player on your own side **5** [I] ~from; to/into change from one state or condition to another **6** [I] (of time) go by **7** [T] spend time **8** [I] come to an end: wait for the storm to ~ **9** [I, T] reach the required standard in an exam **10** [T] test sb and decide they have reached the required standard **11** [T] accept a proposal, law, etc by voting **12** [T] be allowed: I don't like it that I'll let it ~. **13** [T] say or state sth, esp officially: ~ sentence on a prisoner [IDM] **pass the time of day (with sb)** greet sb and have a short conversation with them ■ **pass water** (fml) urinate [PV] **pass away** die **pass by (sb/sth)** go past **pass sb/sth by** happen without affecting sb/sth **pass for/as sb/sth** be accepted as sb/sth: He could ~ for a Frenchman. **pass off** (GB) (of an event) take place and be completed **pass sb/yourself/sth off as sb/sth** pretend that sb/sth is sth they are not **pass on** = PASS AWAY **pass sth on (to sb)** give sth to sb else **pass out** faint **pass sb over** not choose sb for a job **pass over sth** ignore or avoid sth **pass sth up** (infml) not take advantage of sth ■ **,passer-'by** n (pl **passers-by**) person who is going past sb/sth by chance

pass² /pɑːs/ n **1** (esp GB) successful result in an exam **2** official document or ticket showing that you have the right to enter a building, travel on a train, etc **3** (sport) act of kicking, hitting, etc the ball to a player on your own side **4** road or way over or through mountains [IDM] **make a pass at sb** (infml) try to start a sexual relationship with sb ■ **'password** n secret word or phrase that you need to know to be allowed to enter a place, use a computer, etc

passable /ˈpɑːsəbl/ adj **1** fairly good, but not excellent **2** (of a road, etc) open to traffic ▸ **passably** /-əbli/ adv

passage /ˈpæsɪdʒ/ n [C] (also **passageway** /ˈpæsɪdʒweɪ/) narrow way through sth; corridor: *underground ~s* **2** [C] short section from a book, piece of music, etc **3** [sing] (lit) process of time passing: *the ~ of time* **4** [C] journey by ship **5** [C, usu sing] way through sth: *clear a ~ through the crowd*

passenger /ˈpæsɪndʒə(r)/ n person travelling in a bus, train, plane, etc other than the crew

passing /ˈpɑːsɪŋ/ adj lasting only for a short time and then disappearing: *a ~ thought* ● **passing** n [U] **1** process of time going by **2** [sing] (fml) fact of sth ending or of sb dying **3** [sing] (fml) act of making sth law [IDM] **in passing** done or said while giving your attention to sth else

passion /ˈpæʃn/ n **1** [C, U] strong feeling of love, hate, anger, etc **2** [U] ~(for) very strong sexual love **3** [sing] ~for strong liking for sth: *a ~ for books* ▸ **passionate** /ˈpæʃənət/ adj showing passion ▸ **passionately** adv

passive /ˈpæsɪv/ adj **1** accepting what happens or what people do without trying to change anything or oppose them **2** (gram) relating to the verb form used when the subject is affected by the action of the verb, as in 'She was bitten by a dog' ● **passive** (also **passive voice**) n [sing] (gram) form of a verb used when the subject is affected by the action of the verb ▸ **passively** adv ▸ **passiveness** n [U]

Passover /ˈpɑːsəʊvə(r)/ n [U] Jewish religious festival

passport /ˈpɑːspɔːt/ n **1** official document to be carried by a traveller abroad **2** ~to thing that makes sth possible: *a ~ to success*

past¹ /pɑːst/ adj **1** gone by in time; of the time before the present: *in ~ years* **2** (gram) (of a verb form) showing a state or action in the past: *a ~ participle* ● **past** n **1** (the past) [sing] (things that happened in) the time before the present **2** [C] person's past life or career **3** (the past) (also the ˌpast ˈtense) [sing] (gram) form of a verb used to describe actions in the past: *The ~ (tense) of 'take' is 'took'*. ■ **the ˌpast ˈperfect** (also the ˌpast ˈperfect ˈtense) n [sing] (gram) verb form which expresses an action completed before a particular time in the past, formed in English with *had* and a past participle

past² /pɑːst/ prep **1** later than sth; after: *~ midnight* **2** on or to the other side of sb/sth: *She walked ~ the church*. **3** above or further than a

particular point or stage: *I'm ~ caring* (= I no longer care) *what happens.* [IDM] **past it** (GB, infml) too old to do what you used to be able to do ● **past** from one side of sth to the other **2** used to describe time passing: *A week went ~ and nothing happened.*

pasta /ˈpæstə/ n [U] Italian food made from flour, eggs and water and cut into various shapes

paste /peɪst/ n **1** [sing] soft wet mixture, usu made of powder and a liquid: *Mix the flour and water to a smooth ~.* **2** [C] (esp in compounds) mixture of meat or fish for spreading on bread: *fish ~* **3** [U] type of glue used for sticking paper to things: *wallpaper ~* ● **paste** v **1** [T] stick sth to sth else using glue or paste **2** [I, T] (computing) copy or move text into a document from another place: *It's quicker to cut and ~ than to retype it.*

pastel /ˈpæstl/ n **1** [U] soft coloured chalk, used for drawing pictures **2** (pastels) [pl] small sticks of chalk **3** [C] picture drawn with pastels **4** [C] pale delicate colour

pasteurize (also **-ise**) /ˈpɑːstʃəraɪz/ v [T] heat a liquid, esp milk, in order to remove bacteria: *~d milk*

pastille /ˈpæstəl/ n small sweet that you suck, esp one containing medicine for a sore throat

pastime /ˈpɑːstaɪm/ n something that you enjoy doing when you are not working

pastor /ˈpɑːstə(r)/ n Christian clergyman in charge of a church

pastoral /ˈpɑːstərəl/ adj **1** of the work of a priest or teacher, giving advice on personal matters **2** of country life or the countryside

pastry /ˈpeɪstri/ n (pl -ies) **1** [U] mixture of flour, fat and water baked in an oven and used for pies, etc **2** [C] small cake made using pastry

pasture /ˈpɑːstʃə(r)/ n [C, U] (area of) land covered with grass for cattle

pasty¹ /ˈpeɪsti/ adj (-ier, -iest) pale; looking unhealthy: *a ~ white skin*

pasty² /ˈpæsti/ n (pl -ies) small pie containing meat and vegetables

pat /pæt/ v (-tt-) [T] touch sb/sth gently several times with your open hand, esp to show affection ● **pat** n **1** gentle tap with your open hand **2** small soft, lump of butter ● **pat** adj (disapprov) too quick, easy or simple: *a ~ answer*

patch /pætʃ/ n **1** small area of sth that is different from the area around it: *a bald ~ on the top of his head* **2** small piece of material put over a hole or damaged place **3** piece of material worn to protect an injured eye **4** area of land, esp one used for growing vegetables or fruit: *a vegetable ~* [IDM] **be** much less good, attractive, etc than sb/sth else ○ *patch* v [T] cover a hole, esp in clothes, with a piece of material [PV] **patch sth/sb up 1** repair sth quickly **2** treat sb's injuries, esp quickly **3** settle a quarrel ○ **'patchwork** n **1** [U] material in which different small pieces of cloth are sewn together **2** [sing] thing that is made up of many different pieces or parts ○ **patchy** *adj* (**-ier, -iest**) uneven in quality

pâté /'pæteɪ/ n [U] soft paste of meat or fish

patent /'peɪtnt; 'pæt-/ n [C,U] official right to be the only person to make or sell a new invention ○ **patent** *adj* /'peɪtnt/ **1** connected with a patent: *~ laws* **2** (of a product) made or sold by a particular company: *~ medicines* **3** (*fml*) used to emphasize that sth bad is very clear and obvious ○ **patent** *v* /'peɪtnt/ [T] obtain a patent for an invention ■ **,patent 'leather** n [U] leather with a hard shiny surface ▶ **patently** *adv* (*fml*) without doubt; clearly

paternal /pə'tɜ:nl/ *adj* **1** of or like a father **2** related through the father's side of the family: *my ~ grandfather* ▶ **paternally** *adv*

paternity /pə'tɜ:nəti/ n [U] (*written*) fact of being the father of a child

path /pɑ:θ/ n **1** (also **'pathway**) way or track made for or by people walking **2** line along which sth moves

pathetic /pə'θetɪk/ *adj* **1** making you feel pity or sadness: *a ~* **2** (*infml, disapprov*) weak, useless and unsuccessful: *a ~ attempt* ▶ **pathetically** /-kli/ *adv*

pathology /pə'θɒlədʒi/ n [U] study of diseases ▶ **pathological** /ˌpæθə-'lɒdʒɪkl/ *adj* **1** not reasonable or sensible; impossible to control: *~ical fear* **2** of or caused by disease or illness (*tech*) of disease or illness ▶ **pathologist** n expert in pathology

pathos /'peɪθɒs/ n [U] (in writing, speech and plays) power to produce feelings of pity or sadness

patience /'peɪʃns/ n [U] **1** ~ (**with**) ability to stay calm and accept delay or annoyance without complaining **2** ability to spend a lot of time doing sth difficult that needs lot of attention **3** (*GB*) card game for one player

patient /'peɪʃnt/ n person receiving medical treatment ○ **patient** *adj* having or showing patience ▶ **patiently** *adv*

patio /'pætiəʊ/ n (pl **~s**) paved area next to a house where people can sit, eat, etc outdoors

patriarch /'peɪtriɑ:k/ n **1** male head of a family or tribe **2** (**Patriarch**) title of a most senior priest in the Orthodox or Roman Catholic Church ▶ **patriarchal** /ˌpeɪtri'ɑ:kl/ *adj*

patriot /'peɪtriət; 'pæt-/ n person who loves their country and is ready to defend it ▶ **patriotic** /ˌpeɪtri'ɒtɪk; ˌpæt-/ *adj* ▶ **patriotism** n [U] love of your country and willingness to defend it

patrol /pə'trəʊl/ v (**-ll-**) [I, T] go round an area or building at regular times to protect or guard it ○ **patrol** n **1** [U] act of patrolling a place: *soldiers on ~* **2** [C] group of soldiers, vehicles, etc that patrol an area

patron /'peɪtrən/ n **1** person who gives money and support to an artist, a writer or an organization: *a wealthy ~ of the arts* **2** (*fml*) regular customer at a shop, restaurant, etc ▶ **patronage** /'pætrənɪdʒ/ n [U] **1** support, esp financial, given by a patron: *her ~age of the arts* **2** system by which sb gives help or a job to sb in return for their support ■ **,patron 'saint** n Christian saint believed to protect a particular group of people or place

patronize (also **-ise**) /'pætrənaɪz/ v [T] **1** (*disapprov*) treat sb in a way that shows you think sb is not very intelligent, experienced, etc **2** (*fml*) be a regular customer of a shop, restaurant, etc ▶ **patronizing** (also **-ising**) *adj*

patter /'pætə(r)/ n **1** [sing] sound made by sth repeatedly hitting a surface quickly and lightly: *the ~ of rain on the roof* **2** [U, sing] fast talk, eg of entertainers or salespeople ○ **patter** v [I] make quick light sounds

pattern /'pætn/ n **1** regular way in which sth happens or is done: *the usual ~ of events* **2** regular arrangement of lines, shapes, etc, as a decorative design **3** design or instructions from which sth is to be made: *a knitting ~* ○ **pattern** v [PV] **pattern sth on sth** (*US* **pattern sth after sth**) (usu passive) use sth as a model for sth; copy sth: *a new approach ~ed on Japanese ideas* ▶ **patterned** *adj* ~ (**with**) decorated with a pattern

paucity /'pɔ:səti/ n [sing] (*fml*) small amount; lack of sth

paunch /pɔ:ntʃ/ n fat stomach

pause /pɔ:z/ n short stop or interval in action or speech: *a ~ in the conversation* ○ **pause** v [I] stop talking or doing sth for a short time

pave /peɪv/ v [T] cover a path, etc with flat stones or bricks [IDM] **pave the way (for sb/sth)** create a situation in which sb will be able to do

sth or sth can happen ■ **'paving stone** *n* flat piece of stone used for making pavements

pavement /'peɪvmənt/ *n* paved path at the side of a road for people to walk on

pavilion /pə'vɪliən/ *n* **1** temporary building used at public events and exhibitions **2** (*GB*) building next to a sports ground, used by players and spectators

paw /pɔː/ *n* animal's foot with claws ● **paw** *v* ~(at) **1** [I, T] (of an animal) touch or scratch sth repeatedly with a paw **2** [T] touch sb in a rough sexual way

pawn /pɔːn/ *n* **1** least valuable chess piece **2** person whose actions are controlled by more powerful people ● **pawn** *v* [T] leave an object with a pawnbroker in exchange for money lent ■ **'pawnbroker** *n* person who lends money in exchange for articles left with them, which they can sell if you do not pay the money back

pay¹ /peɪ/ *v* (*pt, pp* **paid** /peɪd/) **1** [I, T] give money to sb for goods, services, etc: ~ *him for the bread* **2** [T] give sb money that you owe them: ~ *the rent* **3** [I, T] produce some advantage or profit for sb: *It's hard to make farming ~.* ◇ *It ~s to be honest.* **4** [I] suffer or be punished for your beliefs or actions: *You'll ~ for that remark!* **5** [T] used with some nouns to show that you are giving or doing the thing mentioned: ~ *attention to sth* ◇ ~ *a visit* [IDM] **pay lip service to** → LIP **pay through the nose (for sth)** (*infml*) pay too much money for sth **pay your respects (to sb)** (*fml*) visit sb or send greetings as a sign of respect for them: *Many came to ~ their last respects* (= by attending sb's funeral). **pay your way** pay for everything yourself without having to rely on anyone else's money **put paid to sth** destroy or ruin sth [PV] **pay sb back (sth)** return money to sb that you have borrowed from them **pay sb back (for sth)** punish sb for making you or sb else suffer **pay off** (*infml*) be successful **pay sb off 1** pay sb what they have earned and tell them to leave their job **2** (*infml*) give money to sb to prevent them from doing sth **pay sth off** finish paying money owed for sth **pay sth out 1** pay a large sum of money for sth **2** pass a length of rope through your hands **pay up** pay in full the money that is owed ■ **,paid-'up** *adj* having paid all the money necessary to be a member of a club or an organization ▶ **payable** *adj* that must or can be paid ▶ **payee** /,peɪ'iː/ *n* (*tech*) person that money or a cheque is paid to ▶ **payer** *n* person

who pays or has to pay for sth ▶ **payment** *n* **1** [U] act of paying sb/sth or being paid **2** [C] amount of money (to be) paid ■ **'pay-off** *n* (*infml*) **1** payment of money to sb so that they will not cause you any trouble **2** advantage or reward from sth you have done

pay² /peɪ/ *n* [U] money paid for regular work ■ **'payload** *n* (*tech*) amount carried in an aircraft or other vehicle ■ **'pay packet** *n* envelope containing your wages; amount that sb earns ■ **'payphone** *n* coin-operated telephone ■ **'payroll** *n* list of people employed and paid by a company

PC /,piː'siː/ *abbr* **1** personal computer; a small computer designed for one person to use at work or home: *software for* ~ **2** (*GB*) Police Constable; police officer of the lowest rank **3** = POLITICALLY CORRECT (POLITICAL)

PDA /,piː diː 'eɪ/ *abbr* personal digital assistant; hand-held computer for storing information and accessing the Internet

PE /,piː 'iː/ *n* [U] physical education; sport and exercise taught in schools

pea /piː/ *n* round green seed eaten as a vegetable

peace /piːs/ *n* **1** [U, sing] situation or a period of time in which there is no war or violence in a country: ~ *talks* ◇ *A UN force has been sent in to keep the* ~ (= prevent people from fighting). **2** [U] state of being calm or quiet: *He just wants to be left in* ~. ◇ *I need some* ~ *and quiet.* **3** [U] state of living in friendship with sb without arguing [IDM] **make (your) peace with sb** end an argument with sb, esp by apologizing ▶ **peaceable** *adj* not involving or causing argument or violence ▶ **peaceful** *adj* **1** not involving war, violence or argument **2** quiet and calm ▶ **peacefully** *adv* ▶ **peacefulness** *n* [U] ■ **'peacetime** *n* [U] time when a country is not at war

peach /piːtʃ/ *n* round juicy fruit with soft yellowish-red skin and a rough stone inside ● **peach** *adj* pinkish-orange in colour

peacock /'piːkɒk/ *n* large male bird with blue and green tail feathers

peahen /'piːhen/ *n* female of a peacock

peak /piːk/ *n* **1** point when sb/sth is best, most successful, strongest, etc: *Traffic reaches a* ~ *between 8 and 9 in the morning.* **2** pointed top of a mountain **3** pointed front part of a cap ● **peak** *v* [I] reach the highest point or value ● **peak** *adj* at its highest level; busiest: *the* ~ *season* ▶ **peaked** *adj* having a peak

peal /piːl/ *n* **1** loud sound or series of sounds: ~*s of laughter/thunder*

2 loud ringing of bells ● **peal** v [I] (of bells) ring loudly

peanut /'piːnʌt/ n **1** [C] nut that grows underground in a thin shell **2** (peanuts) [pl] (*infml*) very small amount of money

pear /peə(r)/ n yellow or green fruit that is narrow at the top and wide at the bottom ■ '**pear-shaped** adj shaped like a pear [IDM] **go pear-shaped** (*GB, infml*) go wrong

pearl /pɜːl/ n small hard shiny white jewel that grows inside an oyster

peasant /'peznt/ n **1** (esp in the past) person who works on the land **2** (*infml, disapprov*) person who is rude or uneducated ▶ **peasantry** n [sing, with sing or pl verb] all the peasants of a country

peat /piːt/ n [U] partly decayed plant material, used in gardening or as a fuel ▶ **peaty** adj

pebble /'pebl/ n small stone made smooth and round by water ▶ **pebbly** adj

peck /pek/ v [I, T] (of a bird) hit sth with the beak **2** [T] (*infml*) kiss sb lightly and quickly: *He ~ed her on the cheek.* ● **peck** n **1** (*infml*) light quick kiss **2** act or pecking sb/sth

peckish /'pekɪʃ/ adj (*GB, infml*) slightly hungry

peculiar /pɪ'kjuːliə(r)/ adj **1** strange or unusual, esp in a way that is unpleasant or worrying **2** ~(to) belonging only to a particular person, time, place, etc: *an accent ~ to the West of the country* **3** (*GB, infml*) unwell ▶ **peculiarity** /pɪ,kjuːli-'ærəti/ n (pl -ies) **1** [C] strange or unusual feature or habit **2** [C] feature belonging to a particular person, thing, place, etc **3** [U] quality of being strange ▶ **peculiarly** adv **1** very; more than usually **2** odd

pedagogue /'pedəgɒg/ n (*old-fash* or *fml*) teacher ▶ **pedagogy** /'pedə-gɒdʒi/ n [U] (*tech*) study of teaching methods ▶ **pedagogic** /,pedə-'gɒdʒɪk/ (*also* **pedagogical** /-ɪkl/) ▶ **pedagogically** /-kli/ adv

pedal /'pedl/ n flat bar that drives or controls a machine (eg a bicycle) when pressed down by the foot ● **pedal** v (**-ll-** *US also* **-l-**) [I, T] ride a bicycle somewhere; turn or press the pedals on a bicycle, etc

pedant /'pednt/ n (*disapprov*) person who is too concerned with small details and rules ▶ **pedantic** /pɪ-'dæntɪk/ adj ▶ **pedantically** /-kli/ adv

peddle /'pedl/ v [I, T] go from house to house trying to sell goods ▶ **peddler** n **1** (*US*) = PEDLAR **2** person who sells illegal drugs

pedestal /'pedɪstl/ n base of a pillar, for a statue [IDM] **put/place sb**

on a pedestal admire sb so much that you do not notice their faults

pedestrian /pə'destriən/ n person who is walking in the street and not travelling in a vehicle ● **pedestrian** adj **1** of or for pedestrians **2** not interesting; dull ■ **pe,destrian 'crossing** n part of a road where vehicles stop to allow people to cross

pediatrician (*US*) = PAEDIATRICIAN

pediatrics (*US*) = PAEDIATRICS

pedigree /'pedɪgriː/ n **1** [C] official record of the animals from which an animal has been bred **2** [C,U] person's (esp impressive) family history or background ● **pedigree** (*US* pedigreed) adj (of an animal) descended from a known line of ancestors of the same breed

pedlar /'pedlə(r)/ n (in the past) person who went from house to house trying to sell small objects

pee /piː/ v [I] (*infml*) pass waste liquid from your body ● **pee** n (*infml*) **1** [sing] act of urinating **2** [U] urine

peek /piːk/ v [I] ~**(at)** (take a) quick look at sth secretly

peel /piːl/ v **1** [T] take the skin off fruit or vegetables: *~ the potatoes* **2** [I, T] (cause sth to) come off in layers: *The paint is ~ing.* ◇ *Carefully ~ away the lining paper.* ● **peel** n [U] skin of fruit, etc: *lemon ~*

peep /piːp/ v [I] **1** ~**(at)** look quickly and secretly at sth, esp through a small opening ● **peep** n **1** [C, usu sing] quick or secret look at sth **2** [sing] (*infml*) sound made by sb, esp in sleep: *We didn't hear a ~ out of him all night.* **3** [C] short high sound

peer /pɪə(r)/ n [C] **1** [usu pl] person of the same age or social status as you **2** (in Britain) member of the nobility ● **peer** v [I] ~**(at)** look closely or carefully at sth, esp when you cannot see it clearly ▶ **peerage** /'pɪərɪdʒ/ n **1** [sing] all the peers as a group **2** [C] rank of a peer(2) or peeress ▶ **peeress** /'pɪəres/ n female peer(2) ■ '**peer group** n group of people of the same age or social status

peeved /piːvd/ adj (*infml*) annoyed ▶ **peevish** /'piːvɪʃ/ adj easily annoyed; bad-tempered ▶ **peevishly** adv

peg /peg/ n **1** short thin piece of wood, metal or plastic, used to hang things on or for fastening sth **2** = CLOTHES PEG (CLOTHES) ● **peg** v (**-gg-**) **1** [T] fasten sth with pegs **2** [T] (*usu passive*) fix or keep prices, wages, etc at a particular level [PV] **peg out** (*GB, infml*) die

pejorative /pɪ'dʒɒrətɪv/ adj (*fml*) expressing criticism

Pekinese /,piːkɪ'niːz/ n small dog with short legs and long silky hair

pelican /'pelɪkən/ n large water-bird with a big beak for storing fish to eat ■ **pelican 'crossing** n (in Britain) place on a road where you can stop the traffic and cross by operating a set of traffic lights

pellet /'pelɪt/ n 1 small hard ball made from soft material 2 small metal ball, fired from a gun

pelmet /'pelmɪt/ n strip of wood or fabric above a window to hide the curtain rail

pelt /pelt/ v 1 [T] ~(with) attack sb by throwing things at them 2 [I] ~(down) (of rain) fall very heavily 3 [I] (infml) run somewhere very fast ● **pelt** n animal's skin with the fur on it [IDM] (at) full pelt as fast as possible

pelvis /'pelvɪs/ n (anat) wide curved set of bones at the bottom of the body that forms the hips and spine and are connected to ▶ **pelvic** /-vɪk/ adj

pen /pen/ n 1 instrument for writing with ink 2 small enclosed piece of land for keeping farm animals in ● **pen** v (-nn-) [T] 1 (fml) write sth 2 ~(in/up) shut an animal or a person in a small space ■ '**penfriend** (also '**penpal**) n person that you make friends with by writing letters, often sb you have never met ■ '**penknife** n (pl -knives) small knife with folding blades ■ '**pen-name** n name used by a writer instead of their real name

penal /'piːnl/ adj of the punishment of criminals: reform of the ~ system

penalize (also -**ise**) /'piːnəlaɪz/ v [T] (usu passive) 1 ~(for) punish sb for breaking a rule or law 2 cause sb to suffer a disadvantage

penalty /'penəlti/ n (pl -ies) 1 ~(for) punishment for breaking a law, rule or contract: the death ~ 2 ~(of) disadvantage suffered as a result of sth 3 (sport) advantage given to a player or team when the other side breaks a rule 4 (in football) free kick at the goal by the attackers

penance /'penəns/ n [C,U] ~(for) act that you give yourself to do to show that you are sorry for sth you have done wrong

pence plural of PENNY

penchant /'pɒ̃ʃɒ̃/ n [sing] ~for (written) liking for sth

pencil /'pensl/ n [C,U] narrow piece of wood, containing a black or col-oured substance, used for writing or drawing ● **pencil** v (-ll- US -l-) [T] write or draw sth with a pencil [PV] **pencil sth/sb in** write down details of an arrangement with sb that you know may have to be changed later

pendant /'pendənt/ n piece of jew-ellery that hangs from a chain worn round the neck

pending /'pendɪŋ/ adj (fml) 1 wait-ing to be decided 2 going to hap-pen soon ● **pending** prep (fml) until sth happens

pendulum /'pendjələm/ n weight hung so that it can swing freely, esp in a clock

penetrate /'penɪtreɪt/ v 1 [I, T] go into or through sth: The snow ~d the holes in his shoes. 2 [T] see into or through sth: ~ the darkness ▶ **pene-trating** adj 1 (of sb's eyes or the way they look at you) making you feel uncomfortable 2 (of a sound) loud and hard 3 showing that you have understood sth quickly ▶ **penetra-tion** /ˌpenɪ'treɪʃn/ n [U]

penguin /'peŋgwɪn/ n black and white Antarctic seabird that uses its wings for swimming

penicillin /ˌpenɪ'sɪlɪn/ n [U] anti-biotic medicine

peninsula /pə'nɪnsjələ/ n area of land almost surrounded by water ▶ **peninsular** adj

penis /'piːnɪs/ n sex organ of a man or male animal

penitent /'penɪtənt/ adj feeling or showing that you are sorry for hav-ing done wrong ▶ **penitence** /-təns/ n [U]

penitentiary /ˌpenɪ'tenʃəri/ n (pl -ies) (US) prison

pennant /'penənt/ n long narrow pointed flag, used on a ship for signalling, etc

penniless /'peniləs/ adj having no money

penny /'peni/ n (pl **pennies** or **pence** /pens/) 1 (abbr p) small British coin and unit of money. There are 100 pence in one pound (£1). 2 (before 1971) British coin worth one twelfth of a shilling [IDM] **the penny drops** (esp GB, infml) used to say that sb has finally real-ized or understood sth

pension¹ /'penʃn/ n [C,U] money paid regularly by a government or company to sb who is too old or ill to work ● **pension** v [PV] **pension sb off** allow or force sb to retire and pay them a pension ▶ **pensionable** adj giving sb the right to receive a pension ▶ **pensioner** n person receiving a pension, esp because they have retired from work

pension² /'pɒsjɒ̃/ n small, usu cheap, hotel in some European countries, esp France

pensive /'pensɪv/ adj thinking deeply about sth ▶ **pensively** adv

pentagon /'pentəgən/ n 1 [C] (geom) flat shape with five sides and five angles 2 (**the Pentagon**) [sing] the headquarters of the US Defense Department ▶ **pentagonal** /pen'tægənl/ adj

pentathlon /pen'tæθlən/ n sports contest in which each competitor takes part in five events

penthouse /'penthaʊs/ n expensive and comfortable flat or set of rooms at the top of a tall building

pent up /,pent 'ʌp/ adj (of feelings) that cannot be expressed: ~ anger

penultimate /pen'ʌltɪmət/ adj (written) just before the last one; last but one

penury /'penjəri/ n [U] (fml) state of being extremely poor ▸ **penurious** /pə'njʊəriəs/ adj

people /'piːpl/ n 1 [pl] persons in general: How many ~ were at the party? 2 [C] nation; race: the ~s of Asia 3 [pl] persons who live in a particular place: the ~ of London 4 (**the people**) [pl] ordinary persons without special rank or position ● **people** v [T] (written) live in a place or fill it with people

pep /pep/ n [U] energy and enthusiasm ● **pep** v (-pp-) [PV] **pep sb/sth up** (infml) make sb/sth more interesting or full of energy ■ '**pep pill** n (infml) pill taken to make you feel happier or livelier ■ '**pep talk** n (infml) short speech intended to encourage you to work harder, try to win, etc

pepper /'pepə(r)/ n 1 [U] grey powder made from dried berries (**peppercorns**), used for giving a hot flavour to food 2 [C] hollow fruit, usu red, green or yellow, eaten as a vegetable either raw or cooked: green ~s ● **pepper** v [T] put pepper on food [PV] **pepper sb/sth with sth** (usu passive) hit sb/sth with a series of small objects, esp bullets ■ ,**peppercorn** 'rent n (GB) very low rent

peppermint /'pepəmɪnt/ n 1 [U] type of mint grown for its strong-tasting oil 2 [C] sweet flavoured with peppermint oil

per /pə(r); strong form pɜː(r)/ prep for each: £60 ~ person ~ day ■ **per annum** /,pər 'ænəm/ (abbr **p.a.**) adv for each year: He earns over $80 000 ~ annum. ■ ,**per 'cent** adv for or in each hundred: a five ~ cent wage increase ■ **per se** /,pɜː 'seɪ/ adv by itself

perceive /pə'siːv/ v [T] (written) notice or become aware of sth; think of sth in a particular way

percentage /pə'sentɪdʒ/ n 1 [C, with sing or pl verb] rate, number or amount of sth, expressed as if it is part of a total which is 100; part or share of a whole: pay a ~ of your earnings in tax 2 [usu sing] share of the profits of sth

perceptible /pə'septəbl/ adj (fml) great enough to be noticed: a ~ change in colour ▸ **perceptibly** adv

perception /pə'sepʃn/ n (fml) 1 [U] ability to perceive sth 2 [C] way of seeing or understanding sth

perceptive /pə'septɪv/ adj (fml) quick to notice or understand things ▸ **perceptively** adv

perch /pɜːtʃ/ v 1 [I] ~(on) (of a bird) land and stay on a branch, etc 2 [I, T] ~(on) (cause sb to) sit on sth, esp on the edge of it: I ~ed myself on a high stool at the bar. 3 [T] be placed on the top or edge of sth ● **perch** n 1 place, eg a branch, where a bird rests 2 (infml) high seat or position 3 (pl **perch**) freshwater fish, sometimes eaten as food

percolate /'pɜːkəleɪt/ v 1 [I] (of a liquid, gas, etc) move gradually through a surface that has very small holes in it 2 [I] gradually become known or spread through a group or society ▸ **percolator** n coffee pot in which boiling water percolates through ground coffee beans

percussion /pə'kʌʃn/ n [U] musical instruments, eg drums, that you play by hitting them

perennial /pə'reniəl/ adj 1 continuing for a long time; happening again and again: a ~ problem 2 (of a plant) living for more than two years ● **perennial** n perennial plant ▸ **perennially** adv

perfect¹ /'pɜːfɪkt/ adj 1 having everything necessary; complete and without faults: in ~ condition 2 completely correct; exact: The dress is a ~ fit. 3 the best of its kind 4 excellent; very good: ~ weather 5 total: a ~ stranger 6 (gram) of a tense formed with have and a past participle, eg I have eaten ▸ **perfectly** adv in a perfect way; completely

perfect² /pə'fekt/ v [T] make sth perfect or as good as you can

perfection /pə'fekʃn/ n [U, sing] 1 state of being perfect: The fish was cooked to ~. 2 act of making sth perfect ▸ **perfectionist** /-ʃənɪst/ n person who is not satisfied with anything less than perfection

perfidious /pə'fɪdiəs/ adj (lit) that cannot be trusted

perforate /'pɜːfəreɪt/ v [T] make a hole or holes through sth ▸ **perforation** /,pɜːfə'reɪʃn/ n [C,U] small hole in a surface, often one of a series of small holes

perform /pə'fɔːm/ v 1 [T] do sth, eg a piece of work: ~ a task 2 [I, T] entertain an audience by playing music, acting in a play, etc 3 [I] work or function in the way that is mentioned: This new car ~s well. ▸ **performance** n 1 [C] act of performing a play, concert, etc **2** [U] way of performing sth **3** how well or badly you do sth or sth works ▶ **performer** n person who sings, acts, etc in front of an audience

perfume /ˈpɜːfjuːm/ n [C,U] liquid, often made from flowers, that you put on your skin to make yourself smell nice ● **perfume** v [T] (*lit*) give a sweet smell to sth

perfunctory /pəˈfʌŋktəri/ *adj* (*fml*) done as a duty or habit, without real care or interest ▶ **perfunctorily** /-trəli/ *adv*

perhaps /pəˈhæps; præps/ *adv* possibly; it may be (that): P~ the weather will improve tomorrow.

peril /ˈperəl/ n (*fml* or *lit*) **1** [U] serious danger **2** [C,usu pl] fact of sth being dangerous or harmful: *warning about the ~s of drug abuse* ▶ **perilous** *adj* ▶ **perilously** *adv*

perimeter /pəˈrɪmɪtə(r)/ n **1** outside edge of an enclosed area of land **2** (*maths*) total length of the outside edge of a shape

period /ˈpɪəriəd/ n **1** particular length of time **2** (time allowed for a) lesson at school, college, etc **3** monthly flow of blood from a woman's body **4** (US) = FULL STOP (FULL) ▶ **periodic** /ˌpɪəriˈɒdɪk/ *adj* happening fairly often and regularly ▶ **periodical** /-kl/ n magazine that is published at regular intervals ▶ **periodically** /-kli/ *adv* fairly often

peripatetic /ˌperipəˈtetɪk/ *adj* (*fml*) going from place to place, esp to work: *a ~ music teacher*

periphery /pəˈrɪfəri/ n [usu sing] (pl -ies) (*fml*) outer edge of a particular area ▶ **peripheral** /-rəl/ *adj* **1** (*fml*) not as important as the main aim, part, etc of sth: ~ *information* **2** (*tech*) of the outer edge of an area **3** (*computing*) (of equipment) connected to a computer

periscope /ˈperɪskəʊp/ n instrument with mirrors, for seeing things at a higher level, used esp in submarines

perish /ˈperɪʃ/ v [I] **1** (*fml* or *lit*) die; be destroyed **2** (of material such as rubber) rot ▶ **perishable** *adj* (of food) likely to go bad quickly ▶ **perishables** n [pl] (often pl) types of food that go bad quickly ▶ **perishing** *adj* (GB, *infml*) extremely cold

perjure /ˈpɜːdʒə(r)/ v ~ **yourself** (*law*) tell a lie in a court of law ▶ **perjury** n [U]

perk /pɜːk/ n [C,usu pl] something you receive as well as your wages for doing a particular job: *Free health insurance and a car are the ~s of the job.* ● **perk** v [PV] **perk (sb/sth) up** become or make sb/sth more cheer-

ful or lively ▶ **perky** *adj* (-ier, -iest) (*infml*) cheerful and full of energy

perm /pɜːm/ n **1** putting of artificial curls into the hair ● **perm** v [T] give sb's hair a perm

permanent /ˈpɜːmənənt/ *adj* lasting for a long time or for ever ▶ **permanence** /-əns/ n [U] ▶ **permanently** *adv*

permeate /ˈpɜːmieɪt/ v [I, T] (*fml*) enter and spread to every part of sth ▶ **permeable** /-miəbl/ *adj* (*tech*) ~(to) allowing a liquid or gas to pass through

permissible /pəˈmɪsəbl/ *adj* (*fml*) that is allowed

permission /pəˈmɪʃn/ n [U] act of allowing sb to do sth

permissive /pəˈmɪsɪv/ *adj* allowing great freedom of behaviour, esp in sexual matters: *the ~ society* ▶ **permissiveness** n [U]

permit /pəˈmɪt/ v (-tt-) [T] (*fml*) allow sb to do sth or allow sth to happen ● **permit** /ˈpɜːmɪt/ n official written paper that allows sb to do sth: *a work ~*

permutation /ˌpɜːmjuˈteɪʃn/ n [C, usu pl] any of the different ways in which a set of things can be arranged

pernicious /pəˈnɪʃəs/ *adj* (*fml*) very harmful

pernickety /pəˈnɪkəti/ *adj* (*infml*, *disapprov*) worrying too much about small unimportant details

perpendicular /ˌpɜːpənˈdɪkjələ(r)/ *adj* ~(to) at an angle of 90° to another line or surface; upright ● **perpendicular** n [sing] (**the perpendicular**) line, position or direction that is exactly perpendicular

perpetrate /ˈpɜːpətreɪt/ v [T] (*fml*) commit a crime or do sth wrong or evil ▶ **perpetrator** n

perpetual /pəˈpetʃuəl/ *adj* **1** continuous **2** frequently repeated, in a way which is annoying: *their ~ complaints* ▶ **perpetually** /-tʃuəli/ *adv*

perpetuate /pəˈpetʃueɪt/ v [T] make sth bad continue for a long time ▶ **perpetuation** n,petʃuˈeɪʃn/ n [U]

perplex /pəˈpleks/ v [T] (usu passive) make sb feel puzzled or confused, because they do not understand sth: *They were ~ed by her response.* ▶ **perplexity** /-əti/ n [U] state of feeling perplexed

per se = PER

persecute /ˈpɜːsɪkjuːt/ v [T] treat sb cruelly or unfairly, esp because of their race, religion or political beliefs ▶ **persecution** /ˌpɜːsɪˈkjuːʃn/ n [C,U] ▶ **persecutor** n

persevere /ˌpɜːsɪˈvɪə(r)/ v [I] (*approv*) ~(in/with) continue doing sth in spite of difficulties: *You have to ~ with difficult students.* ▶ **perseverance** n [U]

persist /pəˈsɪst/ v [I] **1** ~(in/with)

continue to do sth in spite of opposition, in a way that can seem unreasonable: *He will ~ in thinking I don't like him.* **2** continue to exist: *If the symptoms ~, see a doctor.* ▶ **persistence** *n* [U] ▶ **persistent** *adj* determined to do sth, esp when others are against you: continuing; repeated: *a ~ent cough* ▶ **persistently** *adv*

person /'pɜ:sn/ *n* (*pl* **people** /'pi:pl/ or, esp in formal use **persons**) **1** human being: *You're just the ~ we need.* **2** (*gram*) any of the three classes of personal pronouns: *the first ~* (= I, we) ◇ *the second ~* (= you) ◇ *the third ~* (= he, she, it, they) [IDM] **in person** actually present; yourself: *The actress will be there in ~.*

personable /'pɜ:sənəbl/ *adj* having a pleasant appearance or manner: *a ~ young woman*

personage /'pɜ:sənɪdʒ/ *n* (*fml*) important or famous person

personal /'pɜ:sənl/ *adj* **1** your own; not of or belonging to anyone else: *~ belongings* **2** not of your professional life; private: *receive a ~ phone call at work* **3** critical of a person: *~ remarks* **4** of the body: *~ cleanliness* ▶ **personally** *adv* **1** used to show that you are giving your own opinion: *P~ly, I think you're crazy!* **2** doing sth yourself **3** privately ■ **,personal as'sistant** *n* = PA ■ **,personal com'puter** *n* = PC(1) ■ **,personal 'pronoun** *n* (*gram*) pronoun *I, she, you*, etc

personality /ˌpɜ:sə'næləti/ *n* (*pl* **-ies**) **1** [C, U] person's character: *a strong ~* **2** [C] famous person, esp from entertainment, sport, etc

personify /pə'sɒnɪfaɪ/ *v* (*pt, pp* **-ied**) [T] **1** be a good example of a quality: *She ~ kindness.* **2** show or think of an object, quality, etc as a person ▶ **personification** /pəˌsɒnɪfɪ'keɪʃn/ *n* [U, C]

personnel /ˌpɜ:sə'nel/ *n* **1** [pl] all the people who work for an organization **2** [U, with sing or pl verb] department in a company, etc that deals with employees and their problems: *a ~ manager*

perspective /pə'spektɪv/ *n* **1** [C] way of thinking about sth **2** [U] ability to think about problems, etc in a reasonable way without exaggerating their importance: *Try to keep these issues in ~.* **3** [U] art of drawing things so as to give the impression of depth and distance

Perspex™ /'pɜ:speks/ *n* [U] strong plastic often used instead of glass

perspire /pə'spaɪə(r)/ *v* [I] (*fml*) sweat ▶ **perspiration** /ˌpɜ:spə'reɪʃn/ *n* [U]

persuade /pə'sweɪd/ *v* **1** make sb do sth by giving them good reasons for doing it: *They ~d him to try again.* **2** make sb believe sth that is true

persuasion /pə'sweɪʒn/ *n* **1** [U] act of persuading sb to do sth or believe sth **2** [C, U] set of beliefs

persuasive /pə'sweɪsɪv/ *adj* able to persuade sb to do sth: *She can be very ~ when she wants.* ▶ **persuasively** *adv*

pert /pɜ:t/ *adj* cheeky; disrespectful: *a ~ reply* ▶ **pertly** *adv*

pertain /pə'teɪn/ *v* [I] (*fml*) **~to** be connected with or belong to sth

pertinent /'pɜ:tɪnənt/ *adj* (*fml*) relevant

perturb /pə'tɜ:b/ *v* [T] (*fml*) make sb very worried

peruse /pə'ru:z/ *v* [T] (*fml*) read sth, esp carefully ▶ **perusal** *n* [U, sing]

pervade /pə'veɪd/ *v* [T] (*fml*) spread through every part of sth

pervasive /pə'veɪsɪv/ *adj* present or felt everywhere

perversion /pə'vɜ:ʃn/ *n* **1** [U,C] behaviour, esp sexual behaviour, that people think is not normal or acceptable **2** [U] act of changing sth good into sth bad: *the ~ of justice*

pervert /pə'vɜ:t/ *v* [T] **1** change a system, etc in a bad way so that it is not what it should be: *~ the course of justice* **2** affect sb in a way that makes them behave in an immoral way ● **pervert** /'pɜ:vɜ:t/ *n* person whose sexual behaviour is considered to be unnatural

pessimism /'pesɪmɪzəm/ *n* [U] belief that bad things will happen ▶ **pessimist** /-mɪst/ *n* ▶ **pessimistic** /ˌpesɪ'mɪstɪk/ *adj*

pest /pest/ *n* **1** insect or animal that destroys plants, food, etc **2** (*infml*) annoying person

pester /'pestə(r)/ *v* annoy or bother sb constantly

pesticide /'pestɪsaɪd/ *n* [C, U] chemical substance used for killing pests, esp insects

pestle /'pesl/ *n* stick with a thick end used for crushing things in a bowl (**mortar**)

pet /pet/ *n* **1** animal, eg a cat or dog, that you keep at home as a companion **2** person treated as a favourite: *She's the teacher's ~.* ● **pet** *v* (*-tt-*) **1** [T] (*esp US*) treat a child or an animal lovingly, esp by stroking them **2** [I] (*infml*) (of two people) kiss and touch each other in a sexual way ■ **'pet name** *n* name you use for sb instead of their real name, as a sign of affection

petal /'petl/ *n* delicate coloured part of a flower

peter /'piːtə(r)/ v [PV] **peter out** gradually come to an end

petition /pə'tɪʃn/ n **1** ~ (against/for) written request to sb in authority that is signed by many people **2** (law) official document asking a court of law to take legal action ● **petition** v [I, T] (fml) make a formal request to sb in authority

petrify /'petrɪfaɪ/ v (pt, pp -ied) **1** [T] (usu passive) frighten sb very much **2** [I, T] (cause sth to) change into stone

petrol /'petrəl/ n [U] (GB) liquid obtained from petroleum, used as fuel in car engines, etc ■ **petrol station** n (GB) place at the side of a road where you take your car to buy petrol, oil, etc

petroleum /pə'trəʊliəm/ n [U] mineral oil that comes from underground

petticoat /'petɪkəʊt/ n (old-fash) piece of women's underwear, worn under a dress or skirt

petty /'peti/ adj (-ier, -iest) (disapprov) **1** small and unimportant: ~ squabbles ◇ ~ crime (= that is not very serious) **2** concerned with unimportant matters; unkind ► **pettiness** n [U] ■ ,petty 'cash n [U] money kept in an office for small payments ■ ,petty 'officer n sailor of middle rank in the navy

petulant /'petjələnt/ adj bad-tempered in a childish way ► **petulance** /-əns/ n [U] ► **petulantly** adv

pew /pjuː/ n long wooden seat in a church

pewter /'pjuːtə(r)/ n [U] grey metal made by mixing tin with lead

phallus /'fæləs/ n image of the penis ► **phallic** /'fælɪk/ adj

phantom /'fæntəm/ n **1** ghost **2** unreal or imagined thing

pharaoh /'feərəʊ/ n king of ancient Egypt

pharmaceutical /,fɑːmə'sjuːtɪkl/ adj of the making of drugs and medicines

pharmacist /'fɑːməsɪst/ n person trained to sell and prepare medicines in a shop

pharmacy /'fɑːməsi/ n (pl -ies) **1** [C] (part of a) shop where medicines are sold **2** [U] study of the preparation of drugs and medicines

phase /feɪz/ n **1** stage of development **2** shape that the moon appears to have at a particular time ● **phase** v [T] arrange to do sth in stages over a period of time [PV] **phase sth in/out** begin/stop using sth gradually

PhD /,piː eɪtʃ 'diː/ abbr Doctor of Philosophy; university degree of a very high level

pheasant /'feznt/ n [C, U] large bird

with a long tail, often shot for food; meat from this bird

phenomenal /fə'nɒmɪnl/ adj very great or impressive: ~ success ► **phenomenally** /-nəli/ adv: ~ly successful

phenomenon /fə'nɒmɪnən/ n (pl -mena /-mɪnə/) **1** fact or event in nature or society, esp one that is not fully understood **2** person or thing that is very successful or impressive

philanthropy /fɪ'lænθrəpi/ n [U] giving of money and other help to people in need ► **philanthropic** /,fɪlən'θrɒpɪk/ adj ► **philanthropist** /fɪ'lænθrəpɪst/ n

philately /fɪ'lætəli/ n (tech) collection and study of postage stamps

philistine /'fɪlɪstaɪn/ n (disapprov) person who does not like or understand art, literature, music, etc

philosopher /fə'lɒsəfə(r)/ n **1** person who studies or writes about philosophy **2** person who thinks deeply about things

philosophy /fə'lɒsəfi/ n (pl -ies) **1** [U] study of nature and the meaning of existence, how people should live, etc **2** [C] set or system of beliefs ► **philosophical** /,fɪlə'sɒfɪkl/ adj **1** of philosophy **2** (approv) ~(about) having a calm attitude towards failure, disappointment, etc ► **philosophically** /-kli/ adv ► **philosophize** (also -ise) /-faɪz/ v [I] talk about sth in a serious way, esp when others find it boring

phlegm /flem/ n [U] **1** thick yellowish-green substance that forms in the nose and throat, esp when you have a cold **2** (written) ability to remain calm in a difficult situation ► **phlegmatic** /fleg'mætɪk/ adj not easily made angry or upset

phobia /'fəʊbiə/ n strong unreasonable fear or hatred of sth

phone /fəʊn/ n **1** [U,C] (also telephone) (machine used in a) system for talking to sb else over long distances using wires or radio: make a ~ call **2** [C] the part of the telephone that you hold in your hand and speak into: He put the ~ down. [IDM] **be on the phone** be using the telephone ● **phone** v [I, T] (GB also **phone up**) make a telephone call to sb ■ **'phone book** n = TELEPHONE DIRECTORY (TELEPHONE) ■ **'phone booth** n partly-enclosed place, containing a telephone, in a hotel, restaurant, etc ■ **'phone box** n small enclosed unit, containing a public telephone, in the street, at a station, etc ■ **'phone-in** n radio or television programme in which telephoned questions and answers from the public are broadcast ■ **'phone number** = TELEPHONE NUMBER (TELEPHONE)

phonetic /fə'netɪk/ adj **1** using

special symbols to represent each different speech sound: *the International P- Alphabet* **2** (of a spelling system) that closely matches the sounds represented **3** of the sounds of human speech ▸ **phonetically** /-kli/ *adv* ▸ **phonetician** /ˌfəʊnəˈtɪʃn; fɒn-/ *n* expert in phonetics ▸ **phonetics** *n* [U] study of speech sounds

phoney (*esp US* **phony**) /ˈfəʊni/ *adj* (**-ier, -iest**) (*infml, disapprov*) false, and trying to deceive people ● **phoney** (*also* **phony**) *n* phoney person or thing

phonology /fəˈnɒlədʒi/ *n* [U] (*ling*) (study of) the speech sounds of a particular language: *English ~* ▸ **phonological** /ˌfəʊnəˈlɒdʒɪkl/ *adj*

phosphorescent /ˌfɒsfəˈresnt/ *adj* (*tech*) producing a faint light without heat, esp in the dark ▸ **phosphorescence** /-ns/ *n* [U]

phosphorus /ˈfɒsfərəs/ *n* [U] (*symb* **P**) poisonous, pale yellow substance that shines in the dark

photo /ˈfəʊtəʊ/ *n* (*pl* **~s**) = PHOTOGRAPH ■ **,photo 'finish** *n* end of a race in which the leading competitors are so close together that a photograph is needed to show the winner

photocopy /ˈfəʊtəʊkɒpi/ *n* (*pl* **-ies**) photographic copy of a document, etc ● **photocopy** *v* (*pt, pp* **-ied**) make a photocopy of sth ▸ **photocopier** /-piə(r)/ *n* machine for photocopying documents, etc

photogenic /ˌfəʊtəʊˈdʒenik/ *adj* looking attractive in photographs

photograph /ˈfəʊtəgrɑːf/ *n* picture made by using a camera that has film sensitive to light inside it ● **photograph** *v* [T] take a photograph of sb/sth ▸ **photographer** /fəˈtɒɡrəfə(r)/ *n* person who takes photographs, esp as a job ▸ **photographic** /ˌfəʊtəˈɡræfik/ *adj* ▸ **photography** /fəˈtɒɡrəfi/ *n* [U] art or process of taking photographs

phrasal /ˈfreɪzl/ *adj* of or connected with a phrase ■ **,phrasal 'verb** *n* (*gram*) verb combined with an adverb and/or preposition, to give a new meaning: *'Blow up' and 'look forward to' are ~ verbs.*

phrase /freɪz/ *n* **1** (*gram*) group of words without a finite verb, esp one that forms part of a sentence **2** group of words which have a particular meaning when used together ● **phrase** *v* [T] say or write sth in a particular way: *a badly ~d example* ■ **'phrase book** *n* book containing common expressions translated into another language, esp for people visiting a foreign country

phraseology /ˌfreɪziˈɒlədʒi/ *n* [U] (*fml*) choice or style of words

physical /ˈfizikl/ *adj* **1** of the body:

~ exercise/fitness **2** of things that can be touched or seen: *the ~ world* **3** of the laws of nature: *a ~ impossibility* ■ **,physical edu'cation** *n* = PE ■ **,physical ge'ography** *n* [U] study of the natural features on the surface of the earth ▸ **physically** /-kli/ *adv*

physician /fiˈzɪʃn/ *n* (*fml, esp US*) doctor, esp one specializing in general medicine

physicist /ˈfizisist/ *n* scientist who studies physics

physics /ˈfiziks/ *n* [U] scientific study of matter and energy

physiology /ˌfiziˈɒlədʒi/ *n* [U] scientific study of the normal functions of living things ▸ **physiological** /ˌfiziəˈlɒdʒikl/ *adj* ▸ **physiologist** *n* scientist who studies physiology

physiotherapy /ˌfiziəʊˈθerəpi/ *n* [U] treatment of disease, esp in the joints or muscles by exercises, massage and the use of water and heat ■ **physiotherapist** *n*

physique /fiˈziːk/ *n* general appearance and size of a person's body

piano /piˈænəʊ/ *n* (*pl* **~s**) large musical instrument in which metal strings are struck by hammers operated by pressing black and white keys ▸ **pianist** /ˈpiːənist/ *n* person who plays the piano

piccolo /ˈpikələʊ/ *n* (*pl* **~s**) musical instrument like a small flute

pick¹ /pik/ *v* [T] **1** choose sb/sth from a group of people or things: *P~ a number between 1 and 10.* **2** take flowers, fruit, etc from the plant or tree where they are growing: *~ strawberries* **3** pull or remove sth or small pieces of sth from sth else, esp with your fingers: *~ your teeth* [IDM] **pick and choose** choose only the things that you like or want very much **pick sb's brains** (*infml*) ask sb a lot of questions because they know more about the subject than you do **pick a fight/quarrel (with sb)** deliberately start a fight or argument with sb **pick holes in sth** find faults in sth such as a plan, suggestion, etc **pick a lock** open a lock without a key **pick sb's pocket** steal money, etc from sb's pocket [PV] **pick at sth 1** eat food in very small amounts **2** pull or touch sth several times: *He tried to undo the knot by ~ing at it with his fingers.* **pick on sb** treat sb unfairly by criticizing or punishing them: *He's always ~ing on me.* **pick sb/sth out 1** choose sb/sth carefully from a group of people or things **2** recognize sb/sth clearly in a large group **pick up 1** get better, stronger, etc; improve **2** start again; continue: *Let's ~ up where we left off yesterday.* **pick sb up 1** go somewhere in your car to collect sb **2** allow sb to get into your vehicle and take them somewhere **3** take hold of sb and lift them up **4** (*infml, disapprov*) talk to sb you do not know, to try to start a sexual relationship **5** (*infml*) (of the police) arrest sb **pick sth up 1** learn a skill, foreign language, etc by chance rather than by making a deliberate effort **2** take hold of sth and lift it up **3** get or obtain sth **4** receive a radio signal ► **picker** *n* person or machine that picks fruit, etc ► **pickings** *n* [pl] money or profits that can be easily or dishonestly obtained ■ **pickpocket** *n* person who steals from people's pockets ■ **pickup** *n* (*also* **'pickup truck**) small van or truck with low sides and no roof at the back **2** (*disapprov*) person who meets sb for the first time **3** part of a record player that holds the needle

pick² /pɪk/ *n* **1** [sing] ~ (of) the best or most suitable one, chosen from a group of things: *take your* ~ **2** [sing] (**the pick of sth**) the best thing(s) in a group **3** [C] = PICKAXE

pickaxe (*US* **pickax** /ˈpɪkæks/) *n* large tool with a curved metal bar that has two sharp ends, used for breaking up roads, rocks, etc

picket /ˈpɪkɪt/ *n* **1** worker or group of workers standing outside a place of work esp during a strike to try to persuade others not to enter ● **picket** *v* [I, T] stand outside a place to protest about sth or to persuade people to join a strike: *a factory*

pickle /ˈpɪkl/ *n* **1** [C, U, usu pl] vegetable that has been preserved in vinegar or salt water **2** [U] (*GB*) thick spicy sauce, often sold in jars, served with meat, cheese, etc [IDM] **in a pickle** (*infml*) in a difficult or unpleasant situation ● **pickle** *v* [T] preserve food in vinegar or salt water

picnic /ˈpɪknɪk/ *n* informal meal eaten outdoors ● **picnic** *v* (**-ck-**) [I] have a picnic ► **picnicker** *n*

pictorial /pɪkˈtɔːriəl/ *adj* of or using pictures

picture /ˈpɪktʃə(r)/ *n* **1** painting, drawing, etc, that shows a scene, a person or thing **2** photograph **3** image on a television screen **4** description that gives you an idea in your mind of what sth is like **5** mental image or memory of sth **6** [sing] (**the picture**) the general situation concerning sb/sth **7** film or movie: *The movie won nine awards, including Best P-.* **8** (**the pictures**) (*GB, old-fash*) [pl] cinema: *go to the* ~*s* [IDM] **be the picture of health, etc** look very healthy, etc **get the picture** (*spoken*) understand a situation **put/keep sb in the picture** (*infml*) give sb the information they need to be able to understand a situation ● **picture** *v* [T] **1** imagine sth: *He* ~*d himself*

as *a rich man* **2** show sb/sth in a photograph or picture

picturesque /ˌpɪktʃəˈresk/ *adj* **1** attractive to look at: *a* ~ *fishing village* **2** (of language) very descriptive

pidgin /ˈpɪdʒɪn/ *n* simple form of a language, used together with words from a local language

pie /paɪ/ *n* [C, U] meat or fruit covered with pastry and baked in a dish

piebald /ˈpaɪbɔːld/ *adj* (of a horse) having black and white patches of irregular shape

piece¹ /piːs/ *n* **1** [C] ~(of) amount of sth that has been cut or separated from the rest: *a* ~ *of cake/paper* **2** [C, usu pl] one of the bits or parts that sth breaks into or is made of: *There were tiny* ~*s of glass on the floor.* ◇ *I took the clock to* ~*s* **3** [C] single item or example of sth: *a* ~ *of furniture* ◇ *a* ~ *of news/advice* **4** [C] single item of writing, art, music, etc **5** [C] coin: *a ten-pence* ~ **6** [C] small object used in a board game: *a chess* ~ [IDM] **give sb a piece of your mind** (*infml*) tell sb that you disapprove of their behaviour or are angry with them **go to pieces** (*infml*) be so upset or afraid that you lose control of yourself **(all) in one piece** (*infml*) safe and unharmed, eg after a dangerous experience **a piece of cake** (*infml*) thing that is very easy to do ■ **'piecework** *n* [U] work paid for by the amount done and not by the hours worked

piece² /piːs/ *v* [PV] **piece sth together** put the parts of sth together to make it complete

piecemeal /ˈpiːsmiːl/ *adj* (*often disapprov*) done or happening gradually at different times rather than carefully planned ● **piecemeal** *adv*

pier /pɪə(r)/ *n* **1** long structure built out into the sea, often with places of entertainment on it **2** (*tech*) pillar supporting a bridge, etc

pierce /pɪəs/ *v* **1** [I, T] make a small hole in sth or go through sth, with a sharp object **2** [T] ~(**through**) (*lit*) (of light or sound) be suddenly seen or heard ► **piercing** *adj* **1** (of eyes) searching **2** (of sound) sharp and unpleasant **3** (of the wind) cold and very strong ► **piercingly** *adv*

piety /ˈpaɪəti/ *n* [U] strong religious beliefs and behaviour

pig /pɪg/ *n* **1** fat short-legged animal with pink, black or brown skin, kept on farms for its meat **2** (*infml, disapprov*) greedy, dirty or rude person ► **piggy** *n* (*pl* **-ies**) (*infml*) child's word for a pig ■ **'piggy bank** *n* small container, esp one shaped like a pig, used by children for saving money in ■ **,pig-'headed** *adj* refusing to change your opinion or actions; stubborn ■ **'pigsty** *n* (*pl* **-ies**) **1** [C] small building for pigs **2** [*sing*] (*infml*) very dirty or untidy room or house ■ **'pigtail** *n* length of plaited hair that hangs down from the back of the head

pigeon /'pɪdʒɪn/ *n* fat grey bird of the dove family ■ **'pigeonhole** *n* one of a series of small open box-like sections for letters or messages ■ **'pigeonhole** *v* [T] **1** decide that sth belongs to a particular class or group **2** decide to deal with sth later or to forget it ■ **'pigeon-toed** *adj* having toes that turn inwards

piglet /'pɪglət/ *n* young pig

pigment /'pɪgmənt/ *n* [U,C] **1** substance existing naturally in people, animals and plants that gives their skin, leaves, etc a particular colour **2** coloured powder that is mixed with a liquid to make paint, etc ▶ **pigmentation** /,pɪgmen'teɪʃn/ *n* [U] natural colouring

pigmy = PYGMY

pike /paɪk/ *n* **1** (*pl* **pike**) large freshwater fish **2** long wooden spear, used by soldiers in the past

pilchard /'pɪltʃəd/ *n* small sea fish eaten as food

pile /paɪl/ *n* **1** [C] number of things lying one upon another: *a ~ of papers* **2** [C, *usu pl*] (*infml*) *~s of work to do* **3** [U, *sing*] soft surface of threads or loops on a carpet or some fabrics **4** [C] large wooden, metal or stone post that is fixed into the ground to support a building, etc [IDM] **make a/your pile** (*infml*) earn a lot of money ● **pile** *v* [T] put things one on top of the other; form a pile: *~ the books on the table* **2** [T] load sth with sth: *The table was ~d high with boxes.* **3** [I] (*infml*) (of a number of people) go somewhere quickly without order or control: *When the bus finally arrived, we all ~d on.* [PV] **pile up** increase in quantity or amount: *The work is ~ing up.* ■ **'pile-up** *n* road crash involving several vehicles crashing into each other

piles /paɪlz/ *n* [pl] = HAEMORRHOIDS

pilfer /'pɪlfə(r)/ *v* [I, T] steal things of little value

pilgrim /'pɪlgrɪm/ *n* person who makes a journey to a holy place ▶ **pilgrimage** /-ɪdʒ/ *n* [C,U] journey made by a pilgrim

pill /pɪl/ *n* **1** [C] small round piece of medicine that you swallow **2** (**the pill**) [*sing*] pill taken regularly as a form of birth control

pillage /'pɪlɪdʒ/ *v* [I, T] (*fml*) steal things from a place, esp in a war, using violence

pillar /'pɪlə(r)/ *n* **1** tall upright post of stone, etc as a support for part of a building **2** strong supporter of sth; important member of sth

pillion /'pɪliən/ *n* seat for a passenger behind the driver of a motor cycle

pillory /'pɪləri/ *v* (*pt, pp* **-ied**) [T] (*written*) criticize sth strongly in public

pillow /'pɪləʊ/ *n* soft cushion used for supporting the head in bed ● **pillow** *v* [T] (*lit*) rest sth, esp your head, on an object ■ **'pillowcase** (*also* **'pillowslip**) *n* fabric cover for a pillow

pilot /'paɪlət/ *n* **1** person who operates the controls of an aircraft, esp as a job **2** person who guides a ship into or out of a harbour ● **pilot** *v* [T] **1** act as a pilot of sth; guide sth/sb **2** test a new product, idea, etc ● **pilot** *adj* used for testing sth: *a ~ scheme* ■ **'pilot light** *n* small flame that burns all the time on a gas cooker, etc and lights a larger flame

pimp /pɪmp/ *n* man who controls prostitutes, finds customers for them and makes a profit from them

pimple /'pɪmpl/ *n* small sore spot on the skin ▶ **pimply** *adj*

PIN /pɪn/ *n* (*also* **'PIN number**) *n* personal identification number; number given to you by a bank so that you can use a plastic card to take out money from a cash machine

pin¹ /pɪn/ *n* **1** short thin pointed piece of metal with a round head, used for fastening things together ■ **'pincushion** *n* small cushion used for sticking pins in when they are not being used ■ **'pinpoint** *v* [T] discover or describe sth exactly ■ **,pins and 'needles** *n* [pl] uncomfortable feeling in a part of your body, esp when you have been sitting or lying in an awkward position ■ **'pinstripe** *adj* (of fabric) with very narrow stripes

pin² /pɪn/ *v* (**-nn-**) [T] **1** fasten sth with a pin **2** make sb unable to move by holding them or pressing them against sth: *He ~ned him against a wall.* [IDM] **pin (all) your hopes on sb/sth** rely on sb/sth completely for success or help [PV] **pin sb down** make sb make a decision or state their intentions clearly **pin sth down** explain or understand sth exactly: *The cause of the disease is difficult to ~ down.* ■ **'pin-up** *n* picture of an attractive person, eg a film star, for pinning on a wall

pinafore /'pɪnəfɔː(r)/ *n* loose sleeveless garment worn over a dress to keep it clean

pincer /'pɪnsə(r)/ *n* **1** (**pincers**) [pl] tool used for holding things tightly and pulling out nails **2** [C] curved claw of a shellfish

pinch /pɪntʃ/ *v* **1** [T] press sth tightly between your thumb and finger or two surfaces **2** [I] be too tight: *These*

shoes ~. **3** [T] (*infml*) steal sth ● **pinch**
n **1** act of squeezing a part of sb's
skin between your thumb and finger
2 amount that you can hold between
your thumb and finger: *a ~ of salt*
[IDM] **at a pinch** (*US*) **in a pinch** if
necessary **feel the pinch** (*infml*) not
have enough money **take sth with a
pinch of salt** be careful about believing that sth is completely true

pine /paɪn/ *n* **1** (*also* '**pine tree**) [C,U]
tall evergreen tree with leaves like
needles **2** (*also* '**pinewood**) [U] pale
soft wood of the pine tree ● **pine** *v* [I]
1 be very unhappy because sb has
gone away or has died [PV] **pine for
sb/sth** want or miss sb/sth very much

pineapple /ˈpaɪnæpl/ *n* [C,U] large
juicy tropical fruit with sweet yellow flesh

ping /pɪŋ/ *v* [I] *n* (make a) short high
ringing noise

ping-pong /ˈpɪŋpɒŋ/ *n* [U] = TABLE
TENNIS (TABLE)

pinion /ˈpɪnjən/ *v* [T] hold or tie sb,
esp their arms, so that they can-
not move

pink /pɪŋk/ *adj* of a pale red colour
● **pink** *n* [U,C] pale red colour

pinnacle /ˈpɪnəkl/ *n* [C] **1** [*usu sing*] ~
(**of**) most important or successful
part of sth: *the ~ of her career*
2 pointed stone decoration on a
roof **3** high pointed piece of rock

pinpoint → PIN¹

pinstripe → PIN¹

pint /paɪnt/ *n* **1** measure for liquids;
one eighth of a gallon (0·568 litre in
the UK and 0·473 litre in the US)
2 (*GB*) pint of beer, esp in a pub

pioneer /ˌpaɪəˈnɪə(r)/ *n* **1** ~ **in/of** person who is first to study a new
area of knowledge **2** one of the first
people to go into a new land or area
● **pioneer** *v* [T] be one of the first
people to do, discover or use sth new

pious /ˈpaɪəs/ *adj* having or showing a deep respect for God and
religion ▸ **piously** *adv*

pip /pɪp/ *n* small seed, eg of an apple,
orange or grape ● **pip** *v* (**-pp-**) [T]
(*GB, infml*) beat sb in a race, etc by
only a small amount: *He was ~ped
at/to the post for the top award.*

pipe¹ /paɪp/ *n* **1** [C] tube through
which liquids or gases can flow **2** [C]
narrow tube with a bowl at one end,
used for smoking tobacco **3** [C]
musical instrument consisting of a
tube with holes for the fingers **4** (**pipes**) [*pl*] = BAG-
PIPES ■ '**pipedream** impossible idea
or plan ■ '**pipeline** *n* system of connected pipes, usu underground, for
carrying oil or gas [IDM] **in the pipeline** being prepared; about to happen

pipe² /paɪp/ *v* **1** [T] carry water, gas,
etc in pipes **2** [I, T] play music on a

pipe or the bagpipes **3** speak or
sing in a high voice [PV] **pipe down**
(*infml, spoken*) be less noisy; stop
talking **pipe up** (**with sth**) (*infml*)
begin to speak ■ ,**piped** '**music** *n* [U]
recorded music played continu-
ously in large shops, stations, etc

piper /ˈpaɪpə(r)/ *n* person who plays
music on a pipe or the bagpipes

piping /ˈpaɪpɪŋ/ *n* [U] pipe or system
of pipes ● **piping** *adj* (of a person's
voice) high ■ ,**piping** '**hot** *adj* (of
liquids or food) very hot

piquant /ˈpiːkənt/ *adj* (*written*) **1**
having a pleasantly strong or spicy
taste **2** exciting and interesting
▸ **piquancy** /-ənsi/ *n* [U] (*written*)

pique *n* /piːk/ [U] annoyance and
bitterness because your pride has
been hurt ● **pique** *v* [T] (*fml*) make
sb annoyed and upset

piracy /ˈpaɪrəsi/ *n* [U] **1** crime of
attacking ships and stealing from
them **2** act of making illegal copies
of video tapes, CDs, etc

piranha /pɪˈrɑːnə/ *n* small S American freshwater fish that eats live
animals

pirate /ˈpaɪrət/ *n* **1** (*esp in the past*)
person who robs other ships at sea
2 person who makes illegal copies of
video tapes, computer programs, etc
● **pirate** *v* [T] copy and sell sb's work
or a product without permission

pirouette /ˌpɪruˈet/ *n* ballet dancer's
fast turn or spin on one foot ● **pirouette** *v*; [I] *She ~d across the stage.*

piss /pɪs/ *v* [I] (△, *sl*) urinate [PV] **piss
off** (*esp GB*) go away ● **piss** *n* (△,
sl) urine [IDM] **take the piss (out of
sb/sth)** make fun of sb ▸ **pissed** *adj*
1 (*GB, △, sl*) drunk **2** (*US,sl*) very
angry or annoyed

pistol /ˈpɪstl/ *n* small gun held in
one hand

piston /ˈpɪstən/ *n* round plate or
short cylinder that moves up and
down inside a tube, used in engines,
pumps, etc

pit /pɪt/ *n* **1** [C] large deep hole in
the ground **2** [C] large hole in the
ground from which minerals are dug
out: *a gravel ~* **3** [C] = COAL MINE (COAL) **4** [C]
hollow mark left on the skin by some
diseases, eg chickenpox **5** [C] (*esp
US*) = STONE(3) **6** (**the pits**) [*pl*] (*US* **the
pit** [C]) (in motor racing) place near a
race track where cars stop for fuel,
etc during a race **7** [C] space in front
of the stage for the orchestra [IDM] **be
the pits** (*infml*) be very bad or the
worst example of sth **the pit of your/
the stomach** the bottom of the stomach where fear is thought to be felt
● **pit** *v* (**-tt-**) [T] (*usu passive*) make
marks or holes on the surface of sth
[PV] **pit sb/sth against sb/sth** test sb

or their strength, intelligence, etc in a contest against sb/sth else

pitch¹ /pɪtʃ/ *n* **1** [C] area of ground with lines marked for playing football, cricket, etc **2** [sing, U] degree or strength of a feeling or activity; the highest point of sth: *a frenetic ~ of activity* **3** [sing, U] how high or low a sound is, esp a musical note **4** [C, usu sing] talk or arguments used by a person trying to sell things or persuade people to do sth: *an aggressive sales* ~ **5** [C] (in baseball) act of throwing the ball; way in which it is thrown **6** [U] black substance that is sticky when hot and hard when cold, used for making roofs, etc waterproof **7** [C] (*GB*) place where a street trader does business ▪ **,pitch-'black** *adj* completely black or dark

pitch² /pɪtʃ/ *v* **1** [T] throw sb/sth in the direction or that way that is mentioned **2** [i] fall heavily in a particular direction **3** [i] (of a ship or aircraft) move up and down on the water or in the air **4** [T] set sth at a particular level **5** [i, T] try to persuade sb to buy sth, give you sth or make a business deal with you sb **6** [T] produce a sound or piece of music at a particular level **7** [T] set up a tent [PV] **pitch in** (**with sb/sth**) (*infml*) join in and help with an activity, by doing some of the work or by giving money, etc **pitch into sb** (*infml*) attack or criticize sb ▪ **,pitched 'battle** *n* fierce violent fight ▪ **'pitchfork** *n* farm tool in the shape of a fork with a long handle, for lifting hay, etc

pitcher /pɪtʃə(r)/ *n* **1** (*US*) = JUG **2** (*GB*) large clay container with two handles, used esp in the past for holding liquids **3** (in baseball) player who throws the ball to the batter

piteous /pɪtiəs/ *adj* (*lit*) deserving or causing pity: *a ~ cry* ▶ **piteously** *adv*

pitfall /pɪtfɔːl/ *n* hidden or unexpected difficulty or danger

pith /pɪθ/ *n* [U] soft white substance under the skin of oranges, etc and in the stems of some plants ▶ **pithy** *adj* (**-ier, -iest**) (*approv*) short, but full of meaning: *~ remarks* ▶ **pithily** *adv*

pitiable /pɪtiəbl/ *adj* **1** deserving or causing you to feel pity **2** not deserving respect ▶ **pitiably** *adv*

pitiful /pɪtɪfl/ *adj* **1** deserving or causing you to feel pity **2** not deserving respect: *a ~ excuse* ▶ **pitifully** *adv*

pitiless /pɪtɪləs/ *adj* showing no pity or mercy; cruel ▶ **pitilessly** *adv*

pittance /pɪtns/ *n* [usu sing] very small amount of money

pity /pɪti/ *n* **1** [U] feeling of sympathy and sadness for the sufferings or troubles of others: *I had ~ on her and lent her the money.* **2** [sing] something that is sad and

unfortunate: *It's a ~ (that) the weather isn't better.* [IDM] **more's the pity** (*infml*) unfortunately ● **pity** *v* (*pt, pp* **-ied**) [T] feel pity for sb

pivot /pɪvət/ *n* **1** central pin or point on which sth turns or balances **2** central or most important person or thing ● **pivot** *v* [i] (**cause sth to**) turn or balance on a central pivot ▶ **pivotal** *adj* (*written*) of great importance because other things depend on it

pixel /pɪksl/ *n* (*computing*) any of the small individual areas on a computer screen, which together form the whole display

pixie /pɪksi/ *n* (in stories) small creature with pointed ears that has magic powers

pizza /piːtsə/ *n* [C, U] flat round piece of dough covered with tomatoes, cheese, etc and baked in an oven

placard /plækɑːd/ *n* large notice that is shown publicly

placate /pləkeɪt/ *v* [T] make sb feel less angry about sth

place¹ /pleɪs/ *n* **1** [C] particular position or area: *Is this the ~ where it happened?* **2** [C] particular city, town, building, etc: *Canada is a big ~.* **3** [C] building or area used for a particular purpose: *a meeting ~* **4** [C] seat or position kept for or occupied by sb: *I've saved you a ~ next to me.* ◇ *I laid a ~ for them at the table.* **5** [sing] ~ (**in**) role or importance of sb/sth in a particular situation **6** [C] opportunity to take part in sth, esp to study at a school, etc: *get a ~ at university* **7** [C] natural or correct position for sth: *Put everything away in the right ~.* **8** [sing] house or flat; a person's home: *What about dinner at my ~?* **9** [C, usu sing] position among the winners in a race or competition **10** (**Place**) [sing] used as part of the name of a short street or square [IDM] **all over the place** (*GB also*) **all over the shop** (*US also*) **all over the lot** (*infml*) **1** everywhere **2** untidy; not well organized **in/out of place 1** in/not in the correct position **2** suitable/unsuitable: *His remarks were out of ~.* **in place of sb/sth** instead of sb/sth **in the first, second, etc place** used to introduce the different points you are making in an argument **put sb in their place** make sb feel stupid or embarrassed for being too confident **take place** happen **take the place of sb/sth** replace sb/sth

place² /pleɪs/ *v* [T] **1** put sth in a certain place **2** put sb/yourself in a particular situation: *to ~ sb under arrest* **3** recognize sth/sth and be able to identify them/it: *I know her face, but I can't ~ her.* **4** give instructions about sth or make a request for sth to happen: *to ~ a bet/an* order ▸ **placement** n [U] **1** act of finding sb a job or place to live **2** act of placing sth/sb somewhere

placenta /plə'sentə/ n (anat) material inside the womb during pregnancy, through which the baby is fed

placid /'plæsɪd/ adj calm; not easily angered ▸ **placidly** adv

plagiarize (also **-ise**) /'pleɪdʒəraɪz/ v [T] (disapprov) copy another person's work, words, ideas, etc and pretend that they are your own ▸ **plagiarism** /-rɪzəm/ n [U]

plague /pleɪg/ n **1** [C,U] infectious disease that kills a lot of people **2** [C] large numbers of an animal or insect that come into an area and cause great damage: a ~ of locusts ● **plague** v [T] ~(**with**) **1** cause pain or trouble to sb/sth over a period of time: to be ~d by doubts **2** annoy sb continually with sth

plaice /pleɪs/ n [C,U] (pl **plaice**) flat sea fish eaten as food

plaid /plæd/ n [C,U] (long piece of) woollen cloth with a pattern of coloured stripes or squares

plain¹ /pleɪn/ adj **1** easy to see or understand: I made it – that he should leave. **2** not trying to trick anyone; honest and direct: He has a reputation for – speaking. **3** not decorated or complicated: ~ food ◇ available in ~ or printed cotton **4** not beautiful or attractive: a ~ girl [IDM] **be plain sailing** be simple and free from trouble ● **plain** adv (infml) used to emphasize how bad, stupid, etc sth is: ~ stupid/wrong ■ **plain-'clothes** adj (of a police officer) wearing ordinary clothes when on duty, not in uniform ▸ **plainly** adv ▸ **plainness** n [U]

plain² /pleɪn/ n large area of flat land

plaintiff /'pleɪntɪf/ n (law) person who brings a legal action against sb

plaintive /'pleɪntɪv/ adj (written) sounding sad ▸ **plaintively** adv

plait /plæt/ v [T] twist three or more pieces of hair, rope, etc together to make one long piece ● **plait** n length of sth, esp hair, that has been plaited

plan /plæn/ n **1** arrangement for doing sth, considered in advance; intention: make ~s for the holidays ◇ detailed map of a building, town, etc: a street ~ **2** (tech) detailed drawing of a machine, building, etc ■ diagram showing how sth will be arranged: a seating ~ ● **plan** v (**-nn-**) [I, T] make a plan of or for sth ▸ **planner** n person who plans sth, esp how land is to be used in a town: a town ~ner

plane /pleɪn/ n **1** flying vehicle with wings and one or more engines **2** (geom) flat or level surface **3** level of thought, existence or development **4** tool with a blade set in a flat sur-

face, used for making wood smooth **5** (also usu **'plane tree**) tree with broad leaves and thin bark ● **plane** adj (tech) completely flat; level ● **plane** v [T] make a piece of wood smoother or flatter with a plane

planet /'plænɪt/ n large round object in space that moves around a star (eg the sun) and receives light from it ▸ **planetary** /-tri/ adj

plank /plæŋk/ n long flat piece of wood ▸ **planking** n [U] planks used to make a floor, etc

plankton /'plæŋktən/ n [U] very small plants and animals that live near the surface of the sea

plant¹ /plɑːnt/ n **1** [C] living thing that grows in the earth, with a stem, leaves and roots **2** [C] factory **3** [U] machinery used in an industrial process

plant² /plɑːnt/ v [T] **1** put plants, seeds, etc in the ground to grow **2** place sth or yourself firmly in position **3** ~(**on**) (infml) hide sth, esp sth illegal, in sb's possessions to make that person seem guilty of a crime **4** send sb to join a group secretly, as a spy ▸ **planter** n **1** attractive container to grow a plant in **2** person who owns or manages a plantation

plantation /plɑːn'teɪʃn/ n large area of land, esp in a hot country, planted with trees or crops, eg sugar, coffee or rubber

plaque /plæk; GB also plɑːk/ n **1** [C] flat piece of stone, metal, etc fixed on a wall in memory of sb/sth **2** [U] harmful substance that forms on the teeth

plasma /'plæzmə/ n [U] (med) clear liquid part of blood, in which the blood cells, etc float

plaster /'plɑːstə(r)/ n **1** [U] mixture of lime, sand and water that is put on walls and ceilings to give them a smooth surface **2** [U] (also **plaster of 'Paris**) white powder mixed with water that becomes very hard when dry, used for holding broken bones in place: Her leg is still in ~. **3** [C] (GB also **'sticking plaster**) (small strip of) fabric that can be stuck to the skin to protect a small wound or cut ● **plaster** v [T] **1** cover a wall, etc with plaster **2** cover sb/sth with a wet or sticky substance: hair ~ed with oil ■ **'plaster cast** n **1** case made of plaster of Paris, used to hold a broken bone in place **2** copy of sth that is made from plaster of Paris ▸ **plastered** adj (infml) drunk ▸ **plasterer** n person whose job is to put plaster on walls and ceilings

plastic /'plæstɪk/ n [U,C] light, chemically produced material that can be formed in shapes and is used to make different objects and fabrics

● **plastic** adj **1** made of plastic: a ~ bag/cup **2** (of materials) easily formed into different shapes ▶ **plasticity** /plæˈstɪsəti/ n [U] ■ **plastic surgery** n [U] medical operations to repair injury to a person's skin, or to improve their appearance

Plasticine™ /ˈplæstəsiːn/ n [U] (GB) soft coloured substance like clay, used by children for making models

plate /pleɪt/ n **1** [C] flat, usu round, dish that you put food on **2** [C] amount of food that you can put on a plate **3** [C] flat thin sheet of metal **4** [usu pl] sheets of metal or plastic at the front and back of a vehicle with numbers and letters on them **5** [U] gold or silver articles, eg spoons and dishes **6** [C] photograph used as a picture in a book, esp one that is printed separately **7** [C] sheet of metal from which the pages of a book are printed [IDM] **hand sth to sb on a plate** (infml) give sth to sb without the person concerned making any effort **have enough/a lot/too much on your plate** (infml) have a lot of work or problems, etc to deal with ● **plate** v [T] cover another metal with a thin layer of gold, silver, etc ■ **plate glass** n [U] clear glass made in large thick sheets

plateau /ˈplætəʊ/ n (pl -eaux or ~s /-təʊz/) **1** large area of high level ground **2** time of little or no change after a period of growth: Prices have reached a ~.

platform /ˈplætfɔːm/ n **1** raised surface beside the track at a railway station **2** flat raised surface for speakers or performers **3** main aims and plans of a political party, esp as stated before an election **4** type of computer system or the software that is used: a multimedia ~

plating /ˈpleɪtɪŋ/ n [U] (esp thin) covering of gold, silver, etc

platinum /ˈplætɪnəm/ n [U] very valuable greyish white metal, used for jewellery, etc

platitude /ˈplætɪtjuːd/ n (fml) statement that is obviously true but not at all new or interesting

platonic /pləˈtɒnɪk/ adj (of love or friendship between two people) close and deep, but not sexual

platoon /pləˈtuːn/ n small group of soldiers, commanded by a lieutenant

platter /ˈplætə(r)/ n large plate that is used for serving food

platypus /ˈplætɪpəs/ n (,duck-billed ˈplatypus) furry Australian animal with a beak like a duck, which lays eggs and feeds its young on milk

plausible /ˈplɔːzəbl/ adj reasonable; likely to be true ▶ **plausibly** adv

play[1] /pleɪ/ v **1** [I, T] do things for pleasure, as children do; enjoy yourself, rather than work **2** [I, T] ~ (at) pretend to be or do sth for amusement **3** [I, T] take part in a game or sport; compete against sb in a game **4** [T] make contact with the ball and hit or kick it in the way mentioned **5** [T] move a piece in chess **6** [I, T] (in card games) put a card face upwards on the table **7** [I, T] perform on a musical instrument: to ~ the piano **8** [T] make a tape, CD, etc produce sound **9** [T] act in a play, film, etc; act the role of sb **10** [T] pretend to be sth you are not: I decided it was safer to ~ dead. **11** [T] (~ a part/role) (in) have an effect on sth **12** [I] move quickly and lightly: sunlight ~ing on the lake [IDM] **play ball (with sb)** (infml) be willing to work with other people in a helpful way **play it by ear** (fml) decide how to deal with a situation as it develops rather than by making plans in advance: We'll ~ it by ear depending on the weather. **play your cards right** act in the most effective way to get sth that you want **play it cool** (infml) deal with a situation calmly, without getting excited **play for time** try to gain time by delaying **play the game** behave fairly and honestly **play gooseberry** (GB) be the unwanted third person when two lovers want to be alone together **play (merry) hell with sth** (GB, infml) affect sth badly **play into sb's hands** do sth that gives your opponent an advantage **play a part (in sth)** be involved in sth **play second fiddle (to sb/sth)** be treated as less important than sb/sth; have a less important position than sb/sth else **what is sb playing at?** used to ask angrily about what sb is doing [PV] **play along (with sb/sth)** pretend to agree with sb/sth **play at (doing) sth** (disapprov) do sth with little seriousness or interest **play sth back (to sb)** allow the material recorded on a tape, video, etc to be heard or seen **play sth down** try to make sth seem less important than it is **play A off against B** put two people in competition with each other, esp to get an advantage for yourself **play on/upon sth** take advantage of sb's feelings, etc: The advert ~s on people's fears. **play (sb) up** (infml, esp GB) cause sb pain or problems **play sth up** try to make sth seem more important than it is ■ **ˈplayback** n [U] act of playing music, showing a film or listening to a telephone message before it has been recorded before ■ **ˈplaying card** n any of a set of 52 cards with numbers and pictures printed on one side, used for various games ■ **ˈplaying field** n large area of grass on which people play sports ■ **'play-off** n game or a series of games between two players who are level, to decide the winner

play² /pleɪ/ n 1 [U] things that people, esp children, do for pleasure 2 [C] story written to be performed by actors in a theatre, on television or on the radio: a Shakespeare ~ 3 [U] playing of a game or sport: Rain stopped ~. 4 [U] possibility of free and easy movement: a lot of ~ in the rope 5 [U] activity or operation of sth: The crisis has brought new factors into ~. 6 [U] (lit) light quick movement: the ~ of sunlight on water [IDM] **a play on words** = PUN ■ **'play-acting** n [U] behaviour that seems sincere when in fact the person is pretending ■ **'playboy** n rich man who spends his time enjoying himself ■ **'playground** n outdoor area where children can play, esp at a school ■ **'playgroup** n [C,U] place where children below school age go regularly to play together and to learn through playing ■ **'playhouse** n used in names of theatres ■ **'playmate** n friend with whom a child plays ■ **'playpen** n small portable enclosure in which a baby can play ■ **'plaything** n toy or thing that you treat like a toy, without really caring about them/it 1 2 (old-fash) toy ■ **'playwright** /'pleɪraɪt/ n person who writes plays

player /'pleɪə(r)/ n 1 person who plays a game 2 company or person involved in a particular area of business or politics 3 machine for reproducing sound or pictures that have been recorded on cassettes, discs, etc: a CD/DVD ~ 4 person who plays a musical instrument: a trumpet ~

playful /'pleɪfl/ adj 1 full of fun; wanting to play 2 not serious ▶ **playfully** adv ▶ **playfulness** n [U]

plaza /'plɑːzə/ n (esp US) small shopping centre, sometimes also with offices

plc (also **PLC**) /ˌpiː el 'siː/ abbr (GB) public limited company; (used after the name of a company or business)

plea /pliː/ n 1 (fml) ~(for) urgent emotional request: ~s for mercy 2 (law) statement made by sb or for sb who is accused of a crime: a ~ of not guilty

plead /pliːd/ v (pt, pp **ed** US **pled** /pled/) 1 [I] ~(with) make repeated serious requests to sb 2 [T] (law) state officially in court that you are guilty or not guilty of a crime 3 [T] (law) present a case in a court of law 4 [T] ~(for) offer sth as an excuse for sth

pleasant /'pleznt/ adj 1 enjoyable, pleasing or attractive 2 friendly ▶ **pleasantly** adv ▶ **pleasantness** n [U]

pleasantry /'plezntri/ n (pl **-ies**) (fml) polite friendly remark

please /pliːz/ exclam used as a polite way of asking for sth or telling sb to do sth: Come in, ~. ● **please** v 1 [I, T] make sb happy 2 [I] choose or want to do sth: He does as he ~s. ▶ **pleased** adj happy or satisfied: She was very ~ with her exam results. ▶ **pleasing** adj ~(to) giving pleasure or satisfaction

pleasure /'pleʒə(r)/ n 1 [U] feeling of happiness or enjoyment 2 [C] thing that makes you happy or satisfied: It's a ~ helping you. ▶ **pleasurable** /-ərəbl/ adj (fml) giving enjoyment ▶ **pleasurably** adv ■ **'pleasure boat** n boat used for short pleasure trips

pleat /pliːt/ n permanent fold in a piece of fabric, made by sewing the top or side of the fold ● **pleated** adj having pleats: a ~ed skirt

plebeian /plə'biːən/ n, adj (disapprov) (member) of the lower social classes

plectrum /'plektrəm/ n (pl **-s** or **-tra** /-trə/) small piece of plastic, metal, etc for plucking the strings of a guitar, etc

pled (US) pt, pp of PLEAD

pledge /pledʒ/ n 1 serious promise 2 sum of money or sth valuable that you leave with sb to prove that you will pay back money owed ● **pledge** v [T] 1 (make sb or yourself) formally promise to give or do sth: The government has ~d itself to fight poverty. 2 leave sth with sb as a pledge(2)

plenary /'pliːnəri/ adj (of a meeting) attended by all who have the right to attend: a ~ session

plentiful /'plentɪfl/ adj available or existing in large quantities: a ~ supply ▶ **plentifully** adv

plenty /'plenti/ pron, adv ~(of) as much as or more than is needed; a lot: There's ~ of time before we go.

pleurisy /'plʊərəsi/ n [U] serious illness that affects the inner covering of the chest and lungs

pliable /'plaɪəbl/ adj 1 easy to bend without breaking 2 (of people) easy to influence and control

pliant /'plaɪənt/ adj (written) 1 (of a person or their body) soft and giving way to sb 2 easy to influence and control

pliers /'plaɪəz/ n [pl] tool used for holding small things or for bending or cutting wire

plight /plaɪt/ n [sing] serious and difficult situation

P

plimsoll /ˈplɪmsəl/ n (GB) light rubber-soled canvas sports shoe

plinth /plɪnθ/ n square base on which a column or statue stands

plod /plɒd/ v (-dd-) walk slowly with heavy steps, esp because you are tired ▶ **plodder** n person who works steadily and slowly but with no imagination

plonk /plɒŋk/ v [T] ~ (**down**) (infml) **1** put sth down on sth, esp noisily or carelessly: P~ it (down) on the chair. **2** ~ **yourself** sit or lie down heavily or in relaxed way ● **plonk** n [U] (infml, esp GB) cheap wine of poor quality

plop /plɒp/ n short sound like that of a small object dropping into water ● **plop** v (-pp-) [I] fall or drop sth, making a plop

plot /plɒt/ n **1** [C,U] series of events which form the story of a film, novel, etc **2** [C] secret plan made by several people, to do sth wrong or illegal **3** [C] small piece of land ● **plot** v (-tt-) [I, T] **1** make a secret plan to harm sb, esp a government or its leader **2** [T] mark sth on a map, eg the position or course of sth **3** [T] make a line by joining points on a graph ▶ **plotter** n

plough (US **plow**) /plaʊ/ n large farming tool for breaking and turning over soil ● **plough** (US **plow**) v [I, T] dig and turn over a field, etc with a plough [PV] **plough sth back** (**in/into sth**) put money made as profit back into a business in order to improve it **plough into sb/sth** crash violently into sb/sth **plough** (**your way**) **through sth** make slow and difficult progress through sth

ploy /plɔɪ/ n something said or done to gain an advantage over sb else

pluck /plʌk/ v [T] **1** pull out hairs with your fingers or with tweezers: ~d eyebrows **2** pull the feathers off a dead bird, eg a chicken **3** play a musical instrument, esp the guitar, by pulling the strings with your fingers **4** (lit) remove sb from a dangerous place or situation: Survivors were ~ed to safety by a helicopter. [IDM] **pluck up courage** (**to do sth**) make yourself do sth even though you are afraid [PV] **pluck at sth** hold sth with the fingers and pull it gently ● **pluck** n [U] (old-fash, infml) courage ▶ **plucky** adj (-ier, -iest) having a lot of courage and determination

plug /plʌg/ n **1** device with metal pins for connecting a piece of equipment to the electricity supply **2** piece of rubber or plastic that fits tightly into a hole in a bath or sink **3** piece of favourable publicity for a product on radio or television ● **plug** v (-gg-) [T] fill a hole

with sth **2** (infml) give praise or attention to a new book, film, etc, to encourage people to read it, see it, etc [PV] **plug away** (**at sth**) continue working hard at sth **plug sth in** connect sth to the electricity supply ■ **'plughole** n hole in a bath, sink, etc into which a plug fits

plum /plʌm/ n round sweet smooth-skinned fruit with a stone in the middle ● **plum** adj (GB) considered good and desirable: a ~ job

plumage /ˈpluːmɪdʒ/ n [U] feathers on a bird's body

plumb /plʌm/ v [T] (lit) try to understand sth completely [IDM] **plumb the depths of sth** be or experience an extreme example of sth unpleasant ● **plumb** adv exactly: ~ in the middle ■ **'plumb line** n piece of string with a weight tied to one end, used esp for testing whether a wall is vertical

plumber /ˈplʌmə(r)/ n person whose job is to fit and repair water pipes

plumbing /ˈplʌmɪŋ/ n [U] **1** system of water pipes, tanks, etc in a building **2** work of a plumber

plume /pluːm/ n **1** cloud of sth that rises into the air **2** large feather

plummet /ˈplʌmɪt/ v [I] fall suddenly and quickly from a high level: House prices have ~ed.

plump /plʌmp/ adj having a soft, round body; slightly fat ● **plump** v [T] ~ (**up**) make sth larger, softer and rounder: ~ up the pillows [PV] **plump for sth** (infml) choose sb/sth ▶ **plumpness** n [U]

plunder /ˈplʌndə(r)/ v [I, T] steal things from a place, esp during a war ● **plunder** n [U] **1** act of plundering **2** things that have been stolen, esp during a war

plunge /plʌndʒ/ v [I, T] (cause sb/sth to) move suddenly forwards and/or downwards: plunge her ~d into the river. ◇ He ~d his hands into his pockets. ● **plunge** n [C, usu sing] sudden movement downwards or away from sth; decrease [IDM] **take the plunge** (infml) finally decide to do sth important or difficult ▶ **plunger** n part of a piece of equipment that can be pushed down

pluperfect /ˌpluːˈpɜːfɪkt/ n (gram) = THE PAST PERFECT (PAST¹)

plural /ˈplʊərəl/ n [usu sing] adj (gram) (form of a word) used for referring to more than one: The ~ of 'child' is 'children'.

plus /plʌs/ prep **1** used when the two numbers or amounts mentioned are being added together: One ~ three is three. **2** as well as sth/sb; and also sth/sb ● **plus** n **1** (infml) advantage; good thing **2** (also **'plus**

sign) mathematical symbol (+) ● **plus** *adj* above zero; positive

plush /plʌʃ/ *adj* (*infml*) smart, expensive and comfortable

plutonium /pluː'təʊniəm/ *n* [U] (*chem*) (*symb* **Pu**) radioactive element used in nuclear reactors and weapons

ply /plaɪ/ *v* (*pt, pp* **plied**) [I, T] (*lit*) (of ships, etc) go regularly along a route: *ferries that ~ between the islands* [IDM] **ply your trade** (*written*) do your work or business [PV] **ply sb with sth 1** keep giving sb large amounts of food and drink **2** keep asking sb questions ● **ply** *n* [U] (esp in compounds) measurement of wool, rope, wood, etc that tells you how thick it is ■ **'plywood** *n* [U] board made by sticking thin layers of wood on top of each other

PM /ˌpiː 'em/ *abbr* (*infml, esp GB*) Prime Minister

p.m. /ˌpiː 'em/ *abbr* after 12 o'clock noon

pneumatic /njuː'mætɪk/ *adj* **1** filled with air: *a ~ tyre* **2** worked by air under pressure: *a ~ drill*

pneumonia /njuː'məʊniə/ *n* [U] serious illness affecting the lungs

PO /ˌpiː 'əʊ/ *abbr* **1** = POST OFFICE (POST¹) **2** = POSTAL ORDER (POSTAL) ■ **ˌP'O box** (*also* **'post office box**) *n* used as a kind of address, so that mail can be sent to a post office where it is kept until it is collected

poach /pəʊtʃ/ *v* **1** [T] cook fish or an egg without its shell in water that is boiling gently **2** [I, T] illegally hunt animals, birds or fish on sb else's property **3** [T] take from sb/sth dishonestly; steal sth ▶ **poacher** *n* person who illegally hunts animals, birds or fish on sb else's property

pocket /'pɒkɪt/ *n* [C] **1** small bag sewn into a piece of clothing so that you can carry things in it **2** small bag or container fastened to sth so that you can put things in it, eg in a car door or handbag **3** [usu sing] amount of money that you have to spend: *He had no intention of paying out of his own ~.* **4** small separate group or area [IDM] **in/out of pocket** (*esp GB*) having gained/lost money as a result of sth ● **pocket** *v* [T] **1** put sth into your pocket **2** keep or take sth, esp money, that does not belong to you ■ **'pocketbook** *n* **1** (*US*) used to refer to the financial situation of a person or country **2** (*esp GB*) small notebook ■ **'pocket money** *n* [U] small amount of money that parents give their children, usu every week

pockmark /'pɒkmɑːk/ *n* hollow mark on the skin, often caused by disease or infection ■ **'pock-**

marked *adj* covered with hollow marks or holes: *a ~-marked face*

pod /pɒd/ *n* long thin case filled with seeds that develops from the flowers of some plants, esp peas and beans

podgy /'pɒdʒi/ *adj* (**-ier, -iest**) (of a person) short and fat

poem /'pəʊɪm/ *n* piece of writing arranged in lines, usu with a regular rhythm and often with a pattern of rhymes

poet /'pəʊɪt/ *n* writer of poems ■ **Poet Laureate** /ˌpəʊɪt 'lɒriət/ *n* (esp in Britain) poet officially chosen to write poems for the country's special occasions, paid by the government and the king or queen

poetic /pəʊ'etɪk/ (*also* **poetical** /-ɪkl/) *adj* **1** of poetry **2** like poetry, esp because it shows imagination and deep feeling ▶ **poetically** /-kli/ *adv*

poetry /'pəʊətri/ *n* [U] **1** collection of poems; poems in general **2** graceful quality: *the ~ of dance*

poignant /'pɔɪnjənt/ *adj* causing deep sadness: *~ memories* ▶ **poignancy** /-jənsi/ *n* [U] ▶ **poignantly** *adv*

point¹ /pɔɪnt/ *n* **1** [C] thing that sb says or writes giving their opinion or stating a fact: *OK, you've made your ~ (= I take your ~ = understand and accept what you are saying).* **2** (usu **the point**) [sing] main idea: *come to/get to the ~ ◇ see/miss the ~ of a joke ◇ That's beside the ~* (= not relevant). **3** [U, sing] purpose or aim of sth: *There's no ~ in going now.* **4** [C] particular quality or feature that sb/sth has: *Tidiness is not his strong ~.* **5** [C] particular time or stage of development: *We were on the ~ of giving up.* **6** [C] particular place or area: *No parking beyond this ~.* **7** [C] one of the marks of direction around a compass **8** [C] individual unit that adds to a score in a game or sports competition: *We won by six ~s.* **9** [C] mark or unit on a scale of measurement: *boiling ~* **10** [C] dot in writing or printing; full stop or marker of decimals **11** [C] sharp end of sth: *the ~ of a pin/pencil* **12** [C] narrow piece of land that extends into the sea **13** [C] (GB) electrical socket in a wall, etc **14** (**points**) [pl] (GB) movable rails by which a train can move from one track to another [IDM] **make a point of doing sth** make a special effort to do sth **point of view** opinion that sb has about sth **to the point** expressed in a simple, clear way

point² /pɔɪnt/ *v* **1** [I, T] **~ (at/to/ towards)** stretch out your finger or sth held in your hand to show sb where a person or thing is **2** [T] **~ at** aim sth at sb/sth: *a gun at sb* **3** [T] put cement between the bricks of a wall [PV] **point sth out (to sb)** draw sb's attention to sth ▶ **pointed** *adj* **1** having a sharp end **2** directed in a clear, often critical way, at a particular person: *~ remarks* ▶ **pointedly** *adv*

point-blank /ˌpɔɪnt ˈblæŋk/ *adj, adv* **1** (of a shot) fired with the gun (almost) touching the person or thing it is aimed **2** directly and rather rudely: *He refused ~.*

pointer /ˈpɔɪntə(r)/ *n* **1** (*infml*) piece of advice **2** thin piece of metal, plastic, etc that points to numbers on a dial or scale **3** stick used to point to things on a map or a picture on a wall **4** short-haired hunting dog

pointless /ˈpɔɪntləs/ *adj* having no purpose; not worth doing ▶ **pointlessly** *adv*

poise /pɔɪz/ *n* [U] **1** calm and confident manner and self-control **2** balanced control of movement ● **poise** *v* [I, T] hold or hold sth steady in a particular position ▶ **poised** *adj* **1** in a position that is completely still but ready to move at any moment **2** ~ (**for/to**) ready for sth or to do sth

poison /ˈpɔɪzn/ *n* [C,U] substance causing death or harm if absorbed by a living thing ● **poison** *v* [T] **1** give poison to sb; put poison on sth **2** (*written*) have a bad effect on sth ▶ **poisonous** *adj*

poke /pəʊk/ *v* [I, T] **1** quickly push your fingers or another object into sb/sth **2** put or move sth somewhere with a small quick movement: *P~ your head out of the window.* [IDM] **poke fun at sb/sth** make sb appear foolish **poke your nose into sth** → NOSE¹ ● **poke** *n* action of poking sth into sb/sth

poker /ˈpəʊkə(r)/ *n* **1** [U] card game played for money **2** [C] metal stick used for moving coal in a fire

poky /ˈpəʊki/ *adj* (**-ier, -iest**) (*infml*) **1** (of a room or building) too small **2** (*also* **pokey**) (*US*) very slow and annoying

polar /ˈpəʊlə(r)/ *adj* **1** of or near the North or South Pole **2** (*fml*) directly opposite ■ **polar bear** *n* white bear that lives near the North Pole ▶ **polarity** /pəˈlærəti/ *n* [U] (*fml*) state of having two opposite qualities or tendencies

polarize (*also* **-ise**) /ˈpəʊləraɪz/ *v* [I, T] (cause people to) separate into two groups with completely opposite opinions: *an issue that ~d public opinion* ▶ **polarization** (*also* **-isation**) /ˌpəʊləraɪˈzeɪʃn/ *n* [U]

pole /pəʊl/ *n* **1** long thin piece of wood or metal, used as a support **2** either of the two ends of the Earth's axis: *the North/South P~* **3** (*physics*)

either of the ends of a magnet or the positive or negative points of an electric battery [IDM] **be poles apart** be widely separated; have no shared interests ■ **the 'pole vault** *n* [sing] sporting event in which people try to jump over a high bar using a long pole to support them ▶ **'pole-vaulter** *n* ▶ **'pole-vaulting** *n* [U]

polecat /ˈpəʊlkæt/ *n* **1** small European wild animal with an unpleasant smell **2** (*US*) = SKUNK

police /pəˈliːs/ *n* (**the police**) [pl] (members of an) official organization whose job is to keep public order, prevent and solve crime, etc ● **police** *v* [T] keep order in a place ■ **po,lice 'constable** *n* (*abbr* **PC**) (in Britain and some other countries) a police officer of the lowest rank ■ **po'lice force** *n* police organization of a country or region ■ **po'liceman** *n* / **po'lice officer** / **po'licewoman** *n* member of a police force ■ **po'lice station** *n* office of a local police force

policy /ˈpɒləsi/ *n* [C,U] (*pl* **-ies**) **1** plan of action agreed or chosen by a political party, a business, etc: *the Government's foreign ~* **2** written insurance contract

polio /ˈpəʊliəʊ/ *n* [U] serious infectious disease affecting the central nervous system, often causing paralysis

polish /ˈpɒlɪʃ/ *v* [T] **1** make sth smooth and shiny by rubbing it **2** ~ (**up**) improve sth [PV] **polish sth off** (*infml*) finish sth, esp food, quickly ● **polish** *n* **1** [U] substance used when rubbing a surface to make it smooth and shiny **2** [sing] act of polishing sth **3** [U] high quality of performance achieved with great skill ▶ **polished** *adj* **1** shiny as a result of polishing **2** elegant, confident and/or highly skilled

polite /pəˈlaɪt/ *adj* having or showing good manners ▶ **politely** *adv* ▶ **politeness** *n* [U]

politic /ˈpɒlətɪk/ *adj* (*fml*) (of actions) sensible; wise

political /pəˈlɪtɪkl/ *adj* **1** of the state, government or public affairs: *~ prisoners* **2** of politics; of political parties **3** (of people) interested in politics ▶ **politically** /-kli/ *adv* ■ **po,litically cor'rect** *adj* (*abbr* **PC**) used to describe language that deliberately avoids offending particular groups of people

politician /ˌpɒləˈtɪʃn/ *n* person whose job is connected with politics

politics /ˈpɒlətɪks/ *n* **1** [U, with *sing* or *pl* verb] activities of government; political affairs **2** [pl] person's political views **3** [U] study of government

polka /ˈpɒlkə/ *n* (music for a) fast dance, popular in the 19th century

poll /pəʊl/ n 1 [C] survey of public opinion 2 [C] (also **the polls** [pl]) election 3 [sing] number of votes given in an election ● **poll** v [T] 1 receive a certain number of votes in an election 2 ask a large number of members of the public what they think about sth ■ **'polling booth** n small, partly enclosed space in a polling station where people vote by marking a card, etc ■ **'polling station** n building where people go to vote in an election

pollen /'pɒlən/ n [U] fine usu yellow powder formed on flowers that fertilizes other flowers

pollinate /'pɒləneɪt/ v [T] put pollen into a flower or plant so that it produces seeds ▸ **pollination** /ˌpɒlə'neɪʃn/ n [U]

pollute /pə'luːt/ v [T] make dirty or harmful substances to land, air, water, etc: a river ~d with toxic waste ▸ **pollution** /pə'luːʃn/ n [U]

polo /'pəʊləʊ/ n [U] ball game played on horseback with long-handled hammers ■ **'polo neck** n (piece of clothing with) a high round collar that is folded over

polyester /ˌpɒli'estə(r)/ n [U,C] artificial fabric used for making clothes

polygamy /pə'lɪgəmi/ n [U] (tech) custom of having more than one wife at the same time

polygon /'pɒlɪgən/ n (geom) figure with five or more straight sides

polystyrene /ˌpɒli'staɪriːn/ n [U] very light soft plastic, used for making containers, etc: ~ cups

polythene /'pɒliθiːn/ (US **polyethylene**) n [U] strong thin plastic, used esp for making bags or wrapping things

polyunsaturated /ˌpɒliʌn'sætʃəreɪtɪd/ adj (esp of vegetable fats) having a chemical structure that does not help cholesterol to form in the blood

pomegranate /'pɒmɪgrænɪt/ n thick-skinned round fruit with a reddish centre full of seeds

pomp /pɒmp/ n [U] impressive clothes, decorations, music, etc at an official ceremony

pompous /'pɒmpəs/ adj (disapprov) full of self-importance ▸ **pomposity** /pɒm'pɒsəti/ n [U] ▸ **pompously** adv

poncho /'pɒntʃəʊ/ n (pl ~s) piece of cloth with a hole for the head, worn as a cloak

pond /pɒnd/ n small area of water: a fish ~

ponder /'pɒndə(r)/ v [I, T] (written) think about sth carefully

ponderous /'pɒndərəs/ adj (written) 1 (disapprov) (of speech or writing) too slow; serious and dull 2 moving slowly and heavily ▸ **ponderously** adv

pong /pɒŋ/ v [I] n (GB, infml) (make a) strong unpleasant smell

pontoon /pɒn'tuːn/ n 1 [C] boat or structure, esp supporting a bridge 2 [U] (GB) kind of card game

pony /'pəʊni/ n (pl -ies) small horse ■ **'ponytail** n hair tied at the back of the head so that it hangs down

poodle /'puːdl/ n small dog with thick curly hair

pool /puːl/ n 1 [C] = SWIMMING POOL (SWIM) 2 [C] small area of water 3 [C] small amount of liquid or light lying on a surface: a ~ of blood 4 [C] common supply of goods, services or people, shared among many: a ~ of cars used by the firm's sales staff 5 [U] game for two people played with 16 coloured balls on a table, often in pubs and bars 6 (**the pools**) [pl] = FOOTBALL POOLS (FOOT) ● **pool** v [T] collect money, information, etc from different people so that it can be shared

poor /pɔː(r)/ adj 1 having very little money 2 showing pity and sympathy: P~ Lisa is ill. 3 low in quality: be in ~ health 4 having very small amounts of sth: soil ~ in nutrients

poorly /'pɔːli; 'pɔːli/ adj (GB, infml) ill ● **poorly** adv in a way that is not satisfactory

pop¹ /pɒp/ n 1 [U] (also **'pop music**) modern popular music with a strong rhythm: rock, ~ and soul 2 [sing] (infml, esp US) used as a word for 'father' 3 [C] short sharp explosive sound ● **pop** adj of or in the style of modern popular music

pop² /pɒp/ v (-pp-) 1 [I, T] (cause sth to) make a short explosive sound 2 [I] (GB, infml) go somewhere quickly, suddenly or for a short time: She's just ~ped out to the shops. 3 [I] suddenly appear, esp when not expected: The menu ~s up when you double-click on the icon. ■ **'popcorn** n [U] type of food made from grains of maize, heated until they burst open ■ **'pop-eyed** adj (infml) with eyes wide open with surprise ■ **'pop-up** adj (computing) that can be brought to the screen quickly, while you are working on another document: a ~-up menu/window

pope /pəʊp/ n (the Pope) head of the Roman Catholic Church

poplar /'pɒplə(r)/ n tall straight tree

poppy /'pɒpi/ n (pl -ies) plant with large red flowers

populace /'pɒpjələs/ n (the populace) [sing] (fml) all the ordinary people in a country

popular /ˈpɒpjələ(r)/ adj 1 ~(with) liked or enjoyed by many people 2 of or relating to ordinary people: ~ *culture/fiction* 3 of beliefs, opinions, etc shared by many people ► **popularity** /ˌpɒpjuˈlærəti/ n [U] ► **popularize** (*also* **-ise**) v [T] (*written*) make a lot of people know about sth and enjoy it ► **popularly** adv

populate /ˈpɒpjuleɪt/ v [T] (*usu passive*) live in an area and form its population

population /ˌpɒpjuˈleɪʃn/ n (number of) people living in a particular country, city, etc

porcelain /ˈpɔːsəlɪn/ n [U] (articles made of) fine china

porch /pɔːtʃ/ n covered entrance to a building

porcupine /ˈpɔːkjupaɪn/ n animal with long pointed spikes on its back

pore /pɔː(r)/ n 1 tiny hole in your skin, that sweat can pass through ● **pore** v [PV] **pore over sth** look at or read sth carefully

pork /pɔːk/ n [U] meat from a pig

pornography /pɔːˈnɒɡrəfi/ (*also infml* **porn**) n [U] (*disapprov*) books, films, etc that show sexual activity in order to cause sexual excitement ► **pornographic** /ˌpɔːnəˈɡræfɪk/ (*also infml* **porno**) adj

porous /ˈpɔːrəs/ adj allowing liquid or air to pass through

porpoise /ˈpɔːpəs/ n sea animal like a small dolphin

porridge /ˈpɒrɪdʒ/ n [U] soft food made by heating crushed oats in water or milk

port /pɔːt/ n 1 [C] town or city with a harbour 2 [C,U] place where ships load and unload goods or shelter from storms 3 [U] strong sweet dark red wine made in Portugal 4 [U] left side of a ship or aircraft when it is facing forward

portable /ˈpɔːtəbl/ adj that is easy to carry or move

portal /ˈpɔːtl/ n website used as a point of entry to the Internet, where information will be collected that will be useful to a person interested in particular kinds of things: *a business ~*

porter /ˈpɔːtə(r)/ n 1 person whose job is to carry luggage, eg at a railway station 2 person whose job is to be on duty at the entrance of a hotel, etc

portfolio /pɔːtˈfəʊliəʊ/ n (*pl* **~s**) 1 flat case for carrying documents, drawings, etc 2 (*business*) set of shares owned by a person or an organization 3 position and duties of a government minister

porthole /ˈpɔːthəʊl/ n round window in the side of a ship or aircraft

portion /ˈpɔːʃn/ n 1 part or share of sth larger 2 amount of food for one person

portly /ˈpɔːtli/ adj (**-ier, -iest**) (esp of an older man) rather fat

portrait /ˈpɔːtreɪt, -trət/ n 1 painting, drawing or photograph of a person 2 detailed description of sb/sth ● **portrait** adj (*computing*) (of a document) printed so that the top of the page is one of the shorter sides

portray /pɔːˈtreɪ/ v [T] 1 make sb/sth in a picture; describe sb/sth in a piece of writing 2 describe or show sb/sth in a particular way 3 act a particular role in a film or play ► **portrayal** n [C,U]

pose /pəʊz/ v 1 [T] create a threat, problem, etc that has to be dealt with 2 [T] (*fml*) ask a question 3 [i] ~(**for**) sit or stand in a particular position, to be photographed, drawn, etc 4 [i] ~ **as** pretend to be sb/sth ● **pose** n 1 position in which sb stands, sits, etc, esp when being photographed, drawn, etc 2 (*disapprov*) way of behaving that is intended to impress and is not sincere ► **poser** n 1 (*infml*) difficult question 2 (*disapprov*) person who behaves in a way that is intended to impress other people

posh /pɒʃ/ adj (*infml*) elegant and expensive

position /pəˈzɪʃn/ n 1 [C,U] place where sb/sth is 2 [U] place where sb/sth is meant to be; the correct place: *Is everybody in* ~? 3 [C,U] way in which sb is sitting or standing or in which sth is arranged: *lie in a comfortable* ~ 4 [C, *usu* sing] situation or condition that sb is in: *I am not in a* ~ *to help you.* 5 [C] opinion or attitude 6 [C,U] person or an organization's level of importance in relation to others 7 [C] (*fml*) job ● **position** v [T] put sb/sth in a particular position

positive /ˈpɒzətɪv/ adj 1 thinking about what is good in a situation: *a* ~ *attitude* 2 useful; good 3 (of a person) certain and confident: *I'm* ~ *he's here.* 4. (*infml*) complete; real: *a* ~ *pleasure* 5 clear and definite: ~ *proof* 6 (*maths*) (of a number) greater than zero 7 (*tech*) (of the kind of electric charge carried by protons ► **positively** adv definitely; really

possess /pəˈzes/ v [T] 1 (*fml*) have or own sth 2 (*usu* passive) (*lit*) (of a feeling, etc) control sb's mind: *~ed by jealousy* ► **possessor** n (*fml*) owner

possession /pəˈzeʃn/ n 1 [U] (*fml*) state of having or owning sth 2 [C, *usu* pl] thing that you own or have with you at one time

possessive /pəˈzesɪv/ adj 1 unwilling to share what you own with others 2 (*gram*) of or showing

possession: *'Yours' is a ~ pronoun.*
▶ **possessively** *adv* ▶ **possessive-ness** *n* [U]

possibility /ˌpɒsə'bɪlətɪ/ *n* (*pl* **-ies**)
1 [U] state of being possible **2** [C]
something that may happen

possible /'pɒsəbl/ *adj* **1** that can be
done; that can exist **2** reasonable;
acceptable ● **possible** *n* person or
thing that might be chosen for sth
▶ **possibly** *adv* **1** perhaps **2** reasonably: *I'll come as soon as I ~ can.*

post¹ /pəʊst/ *n* **1** [U] official system
used for sending and delivering
letters, parcels, etc **2** [C,U] (one collection or delivery of) letters, parcels, etc **3** [C] job **4** [C] place where
sb, esp a soldier, is on duty **5** [C]
upright piece of wood, metal, etc
supporting or marking sth **6** (**the post**) [sing] place where a race finishes ■ **'postbox** *n* (*GB*) public box
in the street that you put letters in
when you send them ■ **'postcard** *n*
card for sending messages by post
without an envelope ■ **'postcode** *n*
(*GB*) group of letters and numbers
used as part of an address, to make
delivery easier ■ **post-'haste** *adv*
(*lit*) very quickly ■ **'postman** |
'postwoman *n* person whose job is
to collect and deliver letters, etc
■ **'postmark** *n* official mark on a
letter, etc, giving the place and date
of posting ■ **'post office** *n* building
where postal business takes place
■ **'post office box** = PO BOX (PO)

post² /pəʊst/ *v* [T] **1** send a letter, etc
to sb by post **2** (*usu passive*) send
sb to a place for a period of time as
part of their job **3** put a soldier, etc,
in a particular place to guard a
building or an area **4** put a notice,
etc in a public place so that people
can see it **5** announce sth publicly
or officially: *The aircraft and its
crew were ~ed missing.* ■ **'Post-it™**
(*also* **Post-it note**) *n* small piece of
coloured sticky paper that you use
for writing a note on

postage /'pəʊstɪdʒ/ *n* [U] amount
charged for the sending of a letter,
etc by post ■ **'postage stamp** *n* (*fml*)
= STAMP¹(1)

postal /'pəʊstl/ *adj* of the post; by
post: *~ services* ■ **'postal order** *n*
written form for money, to be
cashed at a post office

post-date /ˌpəʊst 'deɪt/ *v* [T] write a
date on a cheque that is later than
the actual date so that the cheque
cannot be cashed until then

poster /'pəʊstə(r)/ *n* large printed
notice or picture

posterior /pɒ'stɪərɪə(r)/ *adj* (*tech*)
situated behind or at the back of
the sth

posterity /pɒ'sterətɪ/ *n* [U] (*fml*)
future generations

postgraduate /ˌpəʊst'grædʒuət/ *n*
person already holding a first
degree and who is doing advanced
study or research

posthumous /'pɒstjʊməs/ *adj*
happening after a person has died
▶ **posthumously** *adv*

post-mortem /ˌpəʊst 'mɔːtəm/ *n* **1**
medical examination of a body to
find the cause of death **2** review of
an event after it has happened

postpone /pə'spəʊn/ *v* [T] arrange
for sth to happen at a later time
than originally planned: *The match
was ~d because of the rain.* ▶ **postponement** *n* [C,U]

postscript /'pəʊstskrɪpt/ *n* (*abbr*
PS) extra message written at the
end of a letter

posture /'pɒstʃə(r)/ *n* **1** [U] position
in which you hold your body when
standing, sitting, etc **2** [C] attitude
of mind

posy /'pəʊzɪ/ *n* (*pl* **-ies**) small bunch
of flowers

pot¹ /pɒt/ *n* **1** [C] round container,
esp one used for cooking things in:
~s and pans **2** [C] container of various kinds, made for a particular purpose: *a coffee/plant ~* **3** [C] amount
contained in a pot **4** [U] (*infml*) =
MARIJUANA [IDM] **go to pot** (*infml*) be
spoilt or ruined **pots of money** (*GB*,
infml) very large amount of money
take pot luck accept whatever is
available, without any choice ■ **potbellied** *adj* having a fat stomach
■ **pothole** *n* **1** large hole in a road
made by rain and traffic **2** deep hole
worn in rock by water ■ **'pot-holing** *n*
[U] = CAVING ■ **'potshot** *n* (*infml*) carelessly aimed shot

pot² /pɒt/ *v* (**-tt-**) [T] put a plant into a
flowerpot filled with soil ▶ **potted**
adj **1** planted in a pot **2** (of a book,
etc) in a short simple form: *a ~ted
history* **3** (of cooked meat or fish)
preserved in a small container

potassium /pə'tæsɪəm/ *n* [U] (*symb*
K) soft silver-white metal

potato /pə'teɪtəʊ/ *n* [C,U] (*pl* **~es**)
round vegetable, with a brown or
red skin, that grows underground

potent /'pəʊtnt/ *adj* powerful: *~
arguments/drugs* ▶ **potency** /-tnsɪ/
n [U] ▶ **potently** *adv*

potential /pə'tenʃl/ *adj* that can
develop into sth or be developed in
the future ● **potential** *n* [U] **1** possibility of sth happening or being
developed or used **2** qualities that
exist and can be developed ▶ **potentiality** /pə,tenʃɪ'ælətɪ/ *n* (*pl* **-ies**)
(*fml*) power or quality that can be
developed ▶ **potentially** /-ʃəlɪ/ *adv*

P

potion /ˈpəʊʃn/ n (lit) drink of medicine, poison, or magical liquid

potter /ˈpɒtə(r)/ v [I] move around in an unhurried relaxed way, doing small unimportant tasks: *I spent the day ~ing around the house.*
● **potter** n person who makes clay pots by hand ▶ **pottery** n (pl -ies) **1** [U] (pots, dishes, etc made of) baked clay **2** [C] place where clay pots and dishes are made

potty /ˈpɒti/ adj (-ier, -iest) (GB, infml) crazy ● **potty** n (pl -ies) (infml) bowl that young children use as a toilet

pouch /paʊtʃ/ n **1** small usu leather bag carried in a pocket or on a belt **2** pocket of skin on the stomach of some female animals, eg kangaroos

poultry /ˈpəʊltri/ n **1** [pl] chickens, ducks, etc **2** [U] meat from chickens, ducks, etc

pounce /paʊns/ v [I] ~(on) make a sudden forward attack on sb/sth: *The lion crouched ready to ~.* [PV] **pounce on/upon sth** quickly notice sth that sb has said or done, esp in order to criticize it

pound[1] /paʊnd/ n **1** unit of money in Britain; 100 pence **2** unit of money of several other countries. **3** (abbr **lb**) measure of weight; 16 ounces (0·454 kilogram) **4** place where lost dogs are kept until claimed by their owners ■ **'pound sign** n **1** symbol (£) that represents a pound in British money **2** (US) = HASH(3)

pound[2] /paʊnd/ v [I, T] hit sth/sb hard many times **2** [T] (of sb's heart) beat quickly and loudly **3** [T] hit sth many times to break it into pieces: *The seeds were ~ed to a fine powder.*

pour /pɔː(r)/ v **1** [I, T] (cause a liquid to) flow in a continuous stream: *P~ the sauce over the pasta.* **2** [I] (of rain) fall heavily **3** [I] come or go somewhere continuously in large numbers: *In summer tourists ~ into London.* [IDM] **pour cold water on sth** → COLD[1] [PV] **pour sth out** express your feelings fully, esp after keeping them hidden: *~ out your troubles*

pout /paʊt/ v [I] push your lips forward, esp to show you are annoyed ▶ **pout** n

poverty /ˈpɒvəti/ n [U] state of being poor ■ **'poverty-stricken** adj extremely poor

powder /ˈpaʊdə(r)/ n [U,C] dry mass of fine particles ● **powder** v [T] put powder on sth: *She ~ed her face and put on lipstick.* ▶ **powdered** adj in the form of a powder ■ **'powder room** n polite word for a women's toilet in a hotel, etc ▶ **powdery** adj of or like powder

power /ˈpaʊə(r)/ n **1** [U] ability to control people or things **2** [U] political control of a country: *seize/lose ~* **3** [U] (in people) ability or opportunity to do sth **4** [U] (also **powers**) [pl] particular ability of the body or mind: *the ~ of speech* **5** (**powers**) [pl] all the abilities of the body or mind **6** [U,C, usu pl] right or authority to do sth **7** [C] country, etc with great influence in world affairs: *a world ~* **8** [U] energy or force that can be used to do work: *nuclear ~* ● **power** v [T] supply a machine or vehicle with the energy that makes it work: *~ed by electricity* ■ **'power station** n building where electricity is produced ■ **'power steering** (GB also **power-assisted 'steering**) n [U] (in a vehicle) system that uses power from the engine to help the driver change direction

powerful /ˈpaʊəfl/ adj having great power, influence or strength ▶ **powerfully** adv

powerless /ˈpaʊələs/ adj without power to control sth; unable to do sth: *~ to act* ▶ **powerlessness** n [U]

pp abbr **1** pages **2** (esp GB) used in front of a person's name when sb signs a business letter on his/her behalf: *pp Mike Holland*

PR /ˌpiː ˈɑː(r)/ abbr public relations

practicable /ˈpræktɪkəbl/ adj (fml) able to be done; likely to succeed ▶ **practicability** /-ˈbɪləti/ n [U]

practical /ˈpræktɪkl/ adj **1** concerned with real situations rather than ideas or theories **2** sensible, useful or suitable **3** (of a person) sensible and realistic **4** (of a person) good at making or repairing things ▶ **practicality** /ˌpræktɪˈkæləti/ n [C,U] (pl -ies) ■ **practical 'joke** n trick played on sb ▶ **practically** /-kli/ adv **1** almost: *no time left* **2** in a realistic or sensible way

practice /ˈpræktɪs/ n **1** [U] action rather than ideas: *put a plan into ~* **2** [U,C] usual way of doing sth; procedure or custom: *standard ~* **3** [U,C] (time spent) doing an activity regularly or training regularly to improve your skill: *football ~* **4** [U,C] (place of) work or the business of some professional people, eg doctors and lawyers [IDM] **in practice** in reality **be/get out of practice** to get less good at sth because you have not spent time doing it recently

practise (US -ice) /ˈpræktɪs/ v **1** [I, T] do sth repeatedly or regularly to improve your skill: *~ your English* **2** [T] do sth regularly as part of your normal behaviour: *a practising Catholic* **3** [I, T] ~(as) work as a doctor, lawyer, etc [IDM] **practise what you preach** do what you advise others to do ▶ **practised** adj experienced; skilled

practitioner /præk'tɪʃənə(r)/ n 1 (tech) person who works in a profession, esp medicine 2 (fml) person who regularly does an activity, esp one requiring skill

pragmatic /præg'mætɪk/ n solving problems in a sensible and practical way

prairie /'preəri/ n [C,U] large flat area of grass-covered land in North America

praise /preɪz/ v [T] 1 express your approval or admiration for sb/sth 2 worship God ● **praise** n [U] expression of praise ■ **praiseworthy** adj deserving praise

pram /præm/ n small vehicle on four wheels for a baby to go out in, pushed by hand

prance /prɑːns/ v [I] 1 move quickly with exaggerated steps 2 (of a horse) move with high steps

prank /præŋk/ n trick that is played on sb as a joke

prattle /'prætl/ v [I] talk a lot about unimportant things ▶ **prattle** n [U]

prawn /prɔːn/ n edible shellfish that turns pink when cooked

pray /preɪ/ v [I] 1 speak to God, to give thanks or to ask for help 2 hope very much that sth will happen: Let's just ~ for good weather.

prayer /preə(r)/ n 1 [C] words which you say to God 2 [C] fixed form of words that you say when you speak to God 3 [U] act or habit of praying

preach /priːtʃ/ v 1 [I, T] give a religious talk in a church service 2 [T] try to persuade people to accept a particular religion, way of life, etc 3 [I] give sb unwanted advice on morals, behaviour, etc ▶ **preacher** n Christian who preaches at a church service or religious meeting

preamble /pri'æmbl; 'pri:æmbl/ n [C,U] introduction, esp to a formal document

precarious /prɪ'keəriəs/ adj not safe or certain; dangerous ▶ **precariously** adv

precaution /prɪ'kɔːʃn/ n action taken in advance to avoid danger or trouble: take ~s against illness ▶ **precautionary** adj

precede /prɪ'siːd/ v [T] come or go before sth/sb in time, place or order: She ~d me in the job.

precedence /'presɪdəns/ n [U] right to come before sb/sth in importance: take ~ over all others

precedent /'presɪdənt/ n [C,U] earlier decision or action that is taken as a rule for the future: set a ~

precinct /'priːsɪŋkt/ n 1 [C] (GB) commercial area of a town where cars cannot go: a shopping ~ 2 [C] (US) division of a city, county, etc 3 [usu pl] area around a place or a building, often enclosed by a wall

precious /'preʃəs/ adj 1 of great value 2 (disapprov) (of people and their behaviour) formal, exaggerated and unnatural ● **precious** adv (infml) very: ~ little time

precipice /'presəpɪs/ n very steep cliff

precipitate /prɪ'sɪpɪteɪt/ v [T] 1 (fml) make sth, esp sth bad, happen sooner than it should: Illness ~d her death. 2 ~ into force sb/sth into a particular state ● **precipitate** n [C,U] (chem) solid substance that has been separated from a liquid in a chemical process ● **precipitate** /prɪ'sɪpɪtət/ adj (fml) (of an action or a decision) too hurried ▶ **precipitation** /prɪ,sɪpɪ'teɪʃn/ n 1 [U] fall of rain, snow, etc 2 [U,C] (chem) chemical process in which solid matter is separated from a liquid

precipitous /prɪ'sɪpɪtəs/ adj (fml) dangerously high or steep

precis /'preɪsiː/ n (pl precis /-si:z/) short version of a speech or piece of writing that gives the main points or ideas

precise /prɪ'saɪs/ adj 1 clear and accurate 2 exact 3 showing care about small details ▶ **precisely** adv 1 exactly 2 (spoken) used to emphasize that you agree with a statement

precision /prɪ'sɪʒn/ n [U] exactness and accuracy

preclude /prɪ'kluːd/ v [T] (fml) ~ (from) prevent sth from happening or sb from doing sth

precocious /prɪ'kəʊʃəs/ adj (of a child) having developed particular abilities at a younger age than usual ▶ **precociously** adv ▶ **precociousness** n [U]

preconceived /,priːkən'siːvd/ adj (of an opinion) formed in advance, before gaining enough knowledge ▶ **preconception** /-'sepʃn/ n preconceived idea

precursor /priː'kɜːsə(r)/ n (fml) ~ (of/to) something that comes before and leads to sth more important

predatory /'predətri/ adj 1 (tech) (of animals) living by killing and eating other animals 2 (written) (of people) using weaker people for their own advantage ▶ **predator** /'predətə(r)/ n predatory animal or person

predecessor /'priːdɪsesə(r)/ n person who did a job before sb else

predestined /,priː'destɪnd/ adj already decided by God or by fate

predicament /prɪ'dɪkəmənt/ n difficult or unpleasant situation

P

predicate /'predɪkət/ n (gram) part of a statement that says sth about the subject, eg 'is short' in 'Life is short.'

predicative /prɪ'dɪkətɪv/ adj (gram) (of an adjective) coming after a verb

predict /prɪ'dɪkt/ v [T] say that sth will happen in the future ▸ **predictable** adj that can be predicted ▸ **prediction** /-'dɪkʃn/ n [C,U] (act of making a) statement saying what you think will happen

predispose /ˌpriːdɪ'spəʊz/ v [T] (fml) influence sb so they are likely to think or behave in a particular way ▸ **predisposition** /-dɪspə'zɪʃn/ n

predominant /prɪ'dɒmɪnənt/ adj 1 most obvious or noticeable 2 having more power or influence than others ▸ **predominance** /-nəns/ n [sing, U] ▸ **predominantly** adv mostly; mainly

predominate /prɪ'dɒmɪneɪt/ v [i] 1 be greater in amount or number than sth/sb else 2 have the most influence or importance

pre-eminent /pri'emɪnənt/ adj (fml) more important, more successful or of a higher standard than others ▸ **pre-eminence** /-nəns/ n [U] ▸ **pre-eminently** adv to a very great degree; especially

pre-empt /pri'empt/ v [T] prevent sth from happening by taking action to stop it ▸ **pre-emption** n [U] (business) opportunity given to one person or group to buy goods, shares, etc before they are offered to others ▸ **pre-emptive** adj done to stop sb taking action: a ~ive attack/strike

preen /priːn/ v 1 ~ yourself spend a lot of time making yourself look attractive and then admiring your appearance 2 [I, T] (of a bird) clean and smooth its feathers with its beak

prefabricated /ˌpriː'fæbrɪkeɪtɪd/ adj (esp of a building) made in sections that can be put together later

preface /'prefəs/ n introduction to a book ● **preface** v [T] ~(with) begin by saying or doing sth

prefect /'priːfekt/ n 1 (in some British schools) older pupil who has authority over younger pupils 2 (in France) chief administrative officer of an area

prefer /prɪ'fɜː(r)/ v (-rr-) [T] choose one thing rather than sth else because you like it better: I ~ tea to coffee. [IDM] **prefer charges against sb** → CHARGE² ▸ **preferable** /'prefrəbl/ adj more attractive or suitable ▸ **preferably** adv

preference /'prefrəns/ n 1 [U,sing] ~(for) liking for sb/sth more than sth else 2 [C] thing that is liked better or best [IDM] **give (a) preference to sb/sth** treat sb/sth in a way that gives them an advantage over others: P~ will be given to graduates.

preferential /ˌprefə'renʃl/ adj giving an advantage to a particular person or group: get ~ treatment

prefix /'priːfɪks/ n (gram) letter or group of letters, eg pre- or un-, placed in front of a word to change its meaning ● **prefix** v [T] add letters or numbers to the beginning of a word or number

pregnant /'pregnənt/ adj 1 (of a woman or female animal) having a baby or young animal in the womb 2 (fml) full of a quality or feeling ▸ **pregnancy** /-nənsi/ n [U,C] (pl -ies)

prehistoric /ˌpriːhɪ'stɒrɪk/ adj of the time before recorded history ▸ **prehistory** /pri'hɪstri/ n [U]

prejudge /ˌpriː'dʒʌdʒ/ v [T] (fml) make a judgement about sth before knowing all the facts

prejudice /'predʒudɪs/ n [U,C] unfair dislike of sb/sth [IDM] **without prejudice (to sth)** (law) without affecting any other legal matter ● **prejudice** v [T] 1 influence sb so that they have an unfair opinion of sb/sth 2 (fml) have a harmful effect on sth ▸ **prejudicial** /ˌpredʒu'dɪʃl/ adj

prelate /'prelət/ n (fml) priest of high rank

preliminary /prɪ'lɪmɪnəri/ adj coming first: a ~ study/report ● **preliminary** n (pl -ies) action or event done in preparation for sth

prelude /'preljuːd/ n 1 short, esp introductory, piece of music 2 (written) action, event, etc that acts as an introduction to another

premarital /ˌpriː'mærɪtl/ adj before marriage: ~ sex

premature /'premətʃə(r)/ adj happening before the normal or expected time ▸ **prematurely** adv

premeditated /ˌpriː'medɪteɪtɪd/ adj (of a crime or bad action) planned in advance: ~ murder

premier /'premiə(r)/ adj most important, famous or successful ● **premier** n used esp in newspapers, etc to mean 'prime minister' ▸ **premiership** n [sing]

premiere /'premieə(r)/ n first public performance of a play or film

premise /'premɪs/ n (fml) statement on which reasoning is based

premises /'premɪsɪz/ n [pl] building and land near to it that a business owns or uses: The company is looking for larger ~.

premium /'priːmiəm/ n 1 money paid for an insurance policy 2 extra payment added to the basic rate

premonition /ˌpriːmə'nɪʃn; ˌprem-/

n feeling that sth unpleasant is going to happen

preoccupation /pri,ɒkjuˈpeɪʃn/ *n* **1** [U] state of thinking about sth continuously **2** [C] something that a person thinks about all the time

preoccupy /priˈɒkjupaɪ/ *v* (*pt, pp* -ied) [T] take all the attention of sb

preparation /ˌprepəˈreɪʃn/ *n* **1** [U] ~(for) act of getting ready for sth or making sth ready: *work done without* ~ **2** [C, usu pl] things you do to get ready for sth or to make sth ready **3** [C] mixture that has been prepared for use as medicine, food, etc

preparatory /priˈpærətri/ *adj* (*fml*) done in order to prepare for sth ■ **pre'paratory school** (*also* '**prep school**) *n* **1** (in Britain) private school for children aged between 7 and 13 **2** (in the USA) (usu private) school that prepares students for college

prepare /prɪˈpeə(r)/ *v* [I, T] get or make sth ready to be used to do sth ► **prepared** *adj* **1** ~(for) ready and able to deal with sth **2** willing to do sth: *How much are you ~d to pay?*

preposition /ˌprepəˈzɪʃn/ *n* (*gram*) word, eg *in, from or to,* used before a noun or pronoun to show place, position, time or method ► **prepositional** /-ʃənl/ *adj*

preposterous /prɪˈpɒstərəs/ *adj* completely unreasonable; ridiculous ► **preposterously** *adv*

prerogative /prɪˈrɒgətɪv/ *n* (*fml*) right or privilege of a particular person or group

Presbyterian /ˌprezbɪˈtɪəriən/ *n, adj* (member of) a Church governed by officials of equal rank

prescribe /prɪˈskraɪb/ *v* [T] **1** (of a doctor) tell sb to take medicine or to have treatment: *She ~d antibiotics.* **2** state with authority what should be done

prescription /prɪˈskrɪpʃn/ *n* **1** [C] doctor's written instruction for a medicine **2** [C] medicine that your doctor ordered for you **3** [U] act of prescribing medicine

prescriptive /prɪˈskrɪptɪv/ *adj* (*fml*) telling people what should be done

presence /ˈprezns/ *n* [U] **1** fact of being present in a place **2** (*approv*) person's appearance and manner

present¹ /ˈpreznt/ *adj* **1** existing or happening now: *the ~ government* **2** being in a particular place: *Were you ~ at the meeting?* ● **present** *n* **1** [C] thing that you give to sb as a gift **2** (usu **the present**) [sing] the time now: *I'm sorry, he's out at ~ (= now).* **3** (**the present**) (*also* **present 'tense**) [usu sing] (*gram*) verb form that expresses an action happening now or at the time of speaking ■ **the ,present 'perfect** *n* [sing] (*gram*) verb form which expresses an action done in a time period up to the present, formed in English with *have/has* and a past participle

present² /prɪˈzent/ *v* [T] **1** ~(with, to) give sth to sb, esp formally: ~ *her with a book* ◊ ~ *it to her* **2** show or offer sth for people to consider: *a report* **3** show or describe sth/sb from a particular point of view or in a certain way **4** ~ **with** cause sth to happen or be experienced: *Your request shouldn't ~ us with any problems.* **5** (of an opportunity, etc) suddenly happen **6** introduce the different sections of a radio or television programme **7** produce a show, play, etc for the public **8** ~ **(to)** (*fml*) introduce sb to sb, esp of higher rank **9** ~ **yourself** officially appear somewhere ► **presenter** *n* person who introduces the different sections of a radio or television programme

presentable /prɪˈzentəbl/ *adj* fit to appear or be shown in public

presentation /ˌpreznˈteɪʃn/ *n* **1** [U] act of showing sth or giving sth to sb **2** [U] way in which sth is presented; appearance **3** [C] meeting at which sth is presented

presently /ˈprezntli/ *adv* **1** (*esp US*) now **2** (*written*) soon: *I'll see you ~.*

preservative /prɪˈzɜːvətɪv/ *n* [C,U] substance used to prevent food and wood from decaying ► **preservative** *adj*

preserve /prɪˈzɜːv/ *v* [T] **1** keep sth in an unchanged condition **2** prevent food, etc from decaying, esp by treating it in some way **3** keep sb/sth alive, or safe from harm or danger ● **preserve** *n* [C, usu pl, U] preserved fruit; jam ► **preservation** /ˌprezəˈveɪʃn/ *n* [U]

preside /prɪˈzaɪd/ *v* [I] ~(over/at) be in charge of a formal meeting

presidency /ˈprezɪdənsi/ *n* (*pl* -ies) [usu sing] **1** job of being president of a country or organization **2** period of time that sb is president

president /ˈprezɪdənt/ *n* **1** (*also* **President**) leader of a republic, esp the US **2** person in charge of some organizations, clubs, etc ► **presidential** /ˌprezɪˈdenʃl/ *adj*

press¹ /pres/ *v* **1** [T] push sth closely and firmly against sth **2** [I, T] push or squeeze part of a device, etc to make it work: ~ *a button/key/switch* **3** [I] (of a crowd) move in the direction that is mentioned by pushing: *The crowd ~ed forward.* **4** try repeatedly to persuade or force sb to do sth **5** [T] make sth flat and smooth by using a hot iron **6** [T] squeeze the juice out of fruit or vegetables by using force or weight [IDM] **press charges against sb** → CHARGE² [PV] **press ahead/on (with sth)** continue doing sth in a determined way; hurry forward **press for sth** keep asking for sth ▶ **pressed** adj ~(**for**) have barely enough of sth, esp time or money ▶ **pressing** adj urgent: ~ing business

press² /pres/ n **1** (**the press, the Press**) [sing, with sing or pl verb] (writers for) newspapers and magazines **2** [sing, U] type or amount of reports that newspapers write about sb/sth: The airline has had a bad ~. **3** [C,U] machine for printing books, newspapers, etc; process of printing them: Prices are correct at the time of going to ~. **4** [C] business that publishes and prints books: Oxford University P~ **5** [C] machine for pressing sth: a trouser ~ **6** [C, usu sing] act of pushing sth with your hand or with a tool ■ '**press conference** n meeting at which a politician, etc answers reporters' questions

pressure /'preʃə(r)/ n **1** [U] force or weight with which sth presses against sth else: the ~ of her hand on his head **2** [U,C] (amount of) force produced by a gas or liquid in an enclosed space: air ~ **3** [U] strong persuasion **4** [U] worry caused by the need to achieve or behave in a certain way: The ~ of work is making me ill. ■ '**pressure cooker** n airtight pot in which food is cooked quickly by steam ■ '**pressure group** n organized group of people who try to persuade the government, etc to act in a certain way

pressurize (also **-ise**) /'preʃəraɪz/ v [T] **1** ~(**into**) use forceful influence to persuade sb to do sth **2** keep a cabin in an aircraft, etc at a constant air pressure

prestige /pre'stiːʒ/ n [U] respect or admiration caused by sb's success, status, etc ▶ **prestigious** /-'stɪdʒəs/ adj respected and admired as very important

presumably /prɪ'zjuːməbli/ adv used to say that you think sth is probably true

presume /prɪ'zjuːm/ v **1** [T] suppose that sth is true **2** [I] (fml) behave in a way that shows a lack or respect: I wouldn't ~ to advise you.

presumption /prɪ'zʌmpʃn/ n **1** [C] something thought to be true or probable **2** [U] (fml) disrespectful behaviour

presumptuous /prɪ'zʌmptʃuəs/ adj too confident, in a way that shows a lack of respect

presuppose /ˌpriːsə'pəʊz/ v [T] (fml) **1** accept sth as true and act on that basis **2** depend on sth in order

to exist or be true ▶ **presupposition** /-sʌpə'zɪʃn/ n [C,U] (fml)

pretence (US **-tense**) /prɪ'tens/ n [C,U] act of pretending sth

pretend /prɪ'tend/ v [I, T] behave in a way that is intended to make people believe that sth is true when in reality it is not

pretension /prɪ'tenʃn/ n [C, usu pl, U] act of trying to appear more important, intelligent, etc than you really are

pretentious /prɪ'tenʃəs/ adj (disapprov) trying to appear more important, intelligent, etc than you really are ▶ **pretentiously** adv ▶ **pretentiousness** n [U]

pretext /'priːtekst/ n reason that is not true

pretty /'prɪti/ adv fairly; very: I'm ~ sure he'll come back. [IDM] **pretty much/well** (spoken) almost; almost completely ● **pretty** adj (**-ier, -iest**) pleasing and attractive: a ~ girl ▶ **prettily** adv ▶ **prettiness** n [U]

prevail /prɪ'veɪl/ v [I] (fml) **1** exist or happen without trouble **2** win [PV] **prevail on/upon sb to do sth** (fml) persuade sb to do sth ▶ **prevailing** adj **1** (written) most common or general **2** (of winds) most frequent

prevalent /'prevələnt/ adj existing generally; common ▶ **prevalence** /-əns/ n [U]

prevent /prɪ'vent/ v [T] stop sb from doing sth; stop sth from happening ▶ **prevention** /-'venʃn/ n [U] ▶ **preventive** (also **preventative** /-'ventətɪv/) adj intended to prevent sth from happening: ~ive medicine

preview /'priːvjuː/ n showing of a film, play, etc in private before it is shown to the public ● **preview** v [T] see a film, play, etc before the public and write an account of it for a newspaper, etc

previous /'priːviəs/ adj happening or existing before sth else: the ~ day ▶ **previously** adv

prey /preɪ/ n [U] animal, bird, etc killed by another for food ● **prey** v [IDM] **prey on sb's mind** worry sb greatly **prey on/upon sb/sth** hunt and catch an animal, etc as prey

price /praɪs/ n **1** [C] amount of money that you have to pay for sth **2** [sing] what must be done or experienced to obtain sth: a small ~ to pay for freedom ● **price** v [T] fix the price of sth ▶ **priceless** adj **1** extremely valuable **2** (infml) very funny

prick¹ /prɪk/ v **1** [T] make a very small hole in sth with a sharp point **2** [I, T] (cause sb to) feel a sharp pain in the skin [IDM] **prick (up) your ears 1** (of an animal) raise its ears **2** (of a person) listen carefully

prick² /prɪk/ n **1** (△, sl) penis **2** (△, sl) offensive word for an unpleasant man **3** act of pricking with sth **4** pain caused by a sharp point

prickle /'prɪkl/ n **1** small sharp point growing on a plant or on the skin of an animal **2** slight stinging feeling on the skin ● **prickle** v [I, T] give sb an unpleasant feeling on their skin ► **prickly** adj (-ier, -iest) **1** covered with prickles **2** (infml) (of a person) easily annoyed

pride /praɪd/ n **1** [U] feeling of satisfaction that you get from doing sth well **2** [U, sing] person or thing that gives you a feeling of satisfaction or pleasure: Their daughter was their ~ and joy. **3** [U] self-respect **4** [U] (disapprov) too high an opinion of yourself **5** [C] group of lions ● **pride** v [PV] **pride yourself on (doing)** sth be proud of sth

priest /priːst/ n clergyman of the Christian Church ► **the priesthood** n [sing] position of being a priest

prig /prɪg/ n (disapprov) very moral person who disapproves of others' behaviour ► **priggish** adj

prim /prɪm/ adj (~mer, ~mest) easily shocked by anything rude: ~ and proper

primary /'praɪməri/ adj **1** main; most important; first **2** developing or happening first ► **primarily** /praɪˈmerəli; ˈpraɪmərəli/ adv mainly ● **primary** n (pl -ies) (in the US) election in which voters choose candidates for a future election ■ **primary colour** (US **primary color**) n red, yellow or blue ■ **primary school** n (in Britain) school for children aged between 5 and 11

primate /'praɪmeɪt/ n **1** any animal that belongs to the group of mammals that includes humans, apes and monkeys **2** archbishop

prime /praɪm/ adj **1** main; most important; basic **2** of the best quality ■ **prime minister** n chief minister in a government ● **prime** n [sing] time in your life when you are strongest or most successful: in the ~ of life ● **prime** v [T] **1** supply sb with information in advance **2** cover wood with primer

primer /'praɪmə(r)/ n special paint put on wood, metal, etc before the main layer

primeval (also **primaeval**) /praɪˈmiːvl/ adj very ancient

primitive /'prɪmətɪv/ adj **1** belonging to a simple society with no industry, etc: ~ tribes **2** of an early stage of the development of humans or animals: ~ man **3** simple and old-fashioned

primrose /'prɪmrəʊz/ n wild plant with pale yellow flowers in spring

prince /prɪns/ n **1** male member of a royal family, esp the son of a king or queen **2** male royal ruler of a small country ► **princely** adj **1** generous **2** of or for a prince

princess /ˌprɪnˈses/ n **1** female member of a royal family, esp the daughter of a king or queen **2** wife of a prince

principal /'prɪnsəpl/ adj most important; main ● **principal** n [C] **1** head of a college or school **2** [usu sing] money lent to sb, on which interest is paid ► **principally** /-pli/ adv mainly

principality /ˌprɪnsɪˈpæləti/ n (pl -ies) country ruled by a prince

principle /'prɪnsəpl/ n [C, usu pl, U] **1** moral rule or strong belief that influences your actions: It's against my ~s. ◇ I wouldn't wear fur on ~. **2** [C] basic general truth: the ~ of justice [IDM] **in principle** concerning the basic idea, but perhaps not the details

print¹ /prɪnt/ v **1** [T] produce letters, etc on paper using a machine that puts ink on the surface **2** [T] produce books, etc by printing them in large quantities **3** [T] produce a photograph from photographic film **4** [I, T] write without joining the letters together [PV] **print sth off/out** produce a document or information from a computer in printed form ► **printer** n **1** machine for printing text on paper, esp one attached to a computer **2** person or company that prints books, etc ■ **printout** n [C, U] printed paper produced from a computer

print² /prɪnt/ n **1** [U] letters, words, etc in printed form **2** [C, usu pl] mark left on a surface: finger~s **3** [C] picture made by printing from an ink-covered surface **4** [C] photograph printed from a negative [IDM] **in/out of print** (of a book) available/no longer available

prior /'praɪə(r)/ adj earlier in time, order or importance: a ~ engagement ■ **prior to** prep (fml) before sth

priority /praɪˈɒrəti/ n (pl -ies) **1** [C] something that you think is more important than other things **2** [U] right of being more important

prise (esp US **prize**) /praɪz/ v [T] use force to separate sth from sth else

prism /'prɪzəm/ n transparent block of glass that separates light into the colours of the rainbow

prison /'prɪzn/ n [C, U] building in which criminals are kept as a punishment ► **prisoner** n person kept in prison ■ **prisoner of war** n soldier caught by the enemy in war

P

privacy /'prɪvəsi/ n [U] state of being alone and undisturbed

private /'praɪvət/ adj 1 of or for the use of one person or group, not the public 2 that you do not want other people to know about; secret 3 not organized or managed by the government; independent: a ~ school 4 not connected with your work; personal: your ~ life 5 where you are not likely to be disturbed; quiet ● **private** n soldier of the lowest rank in the army [IDM] **in private** with no one else present ▶ **privately** adv

privatize (also -**ise**) /'praɪvətaɪz/ v [T] transfer a company from state to private ownership ▶ **privatization** (also -**isation**) /ˌpraɪvətaɪ'zeɪʃn/ n [U]

privet /'prɪvɪt/ n [U] evergreen bush often used for hedges

privilege /'prɪvəlɪdʒ/ n 1 [C,U] special right or advantage that a particular person or group has 2 [sing] opportunity that gives you great pleasure: a ~ to hear him sing ▶ **privileged** adj having special rights and advantages

prize /praɪz/ n award given for winning a competition, doing good work, etc ● **prize** adj good enough to win a prize: ~ cattle ● **prize** v [T] 1 value sth highly 2 (US) = PRISE

pro /prəʊ/ n (pl ~**s**) (infml) person who works as a professional, esp in a sport [IDM] **the pros and cons** advantages and disadvantages of sth

pro- /prəʊ; prə/ prefix in favour of; supporting: pro-democracy

probability /ˌprɒbə'bɪləti/ n (pl -**ies**) 1 [U,C] how likely sth is to happen: There is a ~ that you will win. 2 [C] thing that is likely to happen [IDM] **in all probability** (written) it is very likely that

probable /'prɒbəbl/ adj likely to happen or be true ▶ **probably** adv

probation /prə'beɪʃn/ n [U] (law) 1 system that allows a person who has committed a crime not to go to prison if they behave well and for a set time report to an official (**a probation officer**) regularly over a period of time: He was put on ~. 2 time of training when you start a new job to see if you are suitable

probe /prəʊb/ v [I,T] 1 ask questions in order to find out secret information 2 examine sth, esp with a long thin instrument ● **probe** n 1 ~ (into) careful investigation of sth 2 spacecraft used for obtaining information 3 long thin metal tool used by doctors for examining the body

problem /'prɒbləm/ n thing that is difficult to deal with or understand ▶ **problematic** /ˌprɒblə'mætɪk/ adj full of problems

procedure /prə'siːdʒə(r)/ n [C,U] usual or proper way of doing sth ▶ **procedural** adj

proceed /prə'siːd/ v [i] 1 ~ (with/to) continue; go on 2 (fml) move on or go in the direction that is mentioned

proceedings /prə'siːdɪŋz/ n [pl] (fml) 1 legal action against sb: divorce ~ 2 written report of a meeting, etc

proceeds /'prəʊsiːdz/ n [pl] money obtained from sth; profits

process /'prəʊses/ n 1 series of things that are done in order to achieve sth: We're in the ~ of selling our house. 2 method of doing or making sth, esp one used in industry ● **process** v [T] 1 treat raw material, food, etc in order to change it, preserve it, etc: ~ed food 2 deal officially with a document, request, etc: ~ an application 3 perform a series of operations on data in a computer ▶ **processor** n 1 machine or person that processes things 2 (computing) part of a computer that controls all the other parts of a system

procession /prə'seʃn/ n line of people, vehicles, etc moving along, esp as part of a ceremony

proclaim /prə'kleɪm/ v [T] (fml) publicly and officially tell people about sth important ▶ **proclamation** /ˌprɒklə'meɪʃn/ n [C,U] (act of making an) official public statement about sth important

procure /prə'kjʊə(r)/ v [T] (fml) obtain sth, esp with difficulty

prod /prɒd/ v (-**dd**-) 1 [I, T] push sb/sth with your finger or a pointed object 2 [T] try to make sb do sth, esp when they are unwilling ● **prod** n

prodigal /'prɒdɪgl/ adj (fml, disapprov) spending money wastefully

prodigious /prə'dɪdʒəs/ adj very large or powerful and causing surprise or admiration ▶ **prodigiously** adv

prodigy /'prɒdədʒi/ n (pl -**ies**) young person who is unusually intelligent or skilful for their age

produce /prə'djuːs/ v [T] 1 make things to be sold; manufacture 2 grow or make sth as part of a natural process 3 cause a particular result or effect 4 show sth or make sth appear from somewhere 5 be in charge of a play, film, etc for the public to see ● **produce** /'prɒdjuːs/ n [U] things that have been made or grown, esp by farming

producer /prə'djuːsə(r)/ n 1 person, company or country that grows or makes food, goods or materials 2 person who is in charge of making a play, film, etc

product /ˈprɒdʌkt/ n [C] **1** thing that is grown or produced, usu for sale **2** result of a process **3** (maths) quantity obtained by multiplying one number by another

production /prəˈdʌkʃn/ n **1** [U] process of growing or making food, goods or materials **2** [U] quantity of goods produced **3** [C,U] (act of preparing a) play, film, etc for the public

productive /prəˈdʌktɪv/ adj **1** making goods or growing crops, esp in large quantities **2** doing or achieving a lot: a ~ meeting ▶ **productively** adv

productivity /ˌprɒdʌkˈtɪvəti/ n [U] rate of producing goods: P~ has fallen sharply.

profane /prəˈfeɪn/ adj **1** (fml) showing disrespect for God or holy things: ~ language **2** (tech) not connected with religion; secular ▶ **profanity** /prəˈfænəti/ n [C,U] (pl -ies) (instance of) profane behaviour or language

profess /prəˈfes/ v [T] (fml) **1** claim sth, often falsely: I don't ~ to be an expert. **2** state openly that you have a particular belief, etc **3** belong to a particular religion ▶ **professed** adj (fml) **1** (falsely) claimed **2** self-declared

profession /prəˈfeʃn/ n **1** type of job that needs special knowledge, eg medicine or law **2** statement about what you believe, feel or think about sth

professional /prəˈfeʃənl/ adj **1** of a profession(1) **2** showing that sb is well trained and highly skilled **3** doing sth as a paid job rather than as a hobby: a ~ golfer ▶ **professional** n professional person ▶ **professionalism** n [U] skill or qualities of a professional ▶ **professionally** /-ʃənəli/ adv

professor /prəˈfesə(r)/ n university teacher of the highest rank ▶ **professorial** /ˌprɒfəˈsɔːriəl/ adj ▶ **professorship** n position of a professor

proffer /ˈprɒfə(r)/ v [T] (fml) offer sth to sb

proficient /prəˈfɪʃnt/ adj (written) able to do sth well because of training and practice ▶ **proficiency** /-nsi/ n [U]

profile /ˈprəʊfaɪl/ n **1** side view of the human face **2** description of sb/sth that gives useful information

profit /ˈprɒfɪt/ n [C,U] **1** money that you make in business, etc or by selling things **2** [U] (fml) advantage that you get from doing sth ■ '**profit margin** n difference between the cost of buying or producing sth and the price that it is sold for ● **profit** v [I] ~ by/from gain an advantage or benefit from sth ▶ **profitable** adj that makes or is likely to make money **2** that gives sb a useful result: a ~ discussion ▶ **profitably** /-əbli/ adv

profound /prəˈfaʊnd/ adj **1** deep; very great: a ~ effect **2** showing or needing great knowledge or thought ▶ **profoundly** adv deeply

profuse /prəˈfjuːs/ adj (fml) produced in large amounts ▶ **profusely** adv /-ˈfjuːʒn/ n [sing, with sing or pl verb, U] (fml) very large quantity of sth: a ~ of flowers ◇ flowers growing in ~

program /ˈprəʊɡræm/ n **1** (computing) set of instructions for a computer **2** (US) = PROGRAMME ● **program** v (-mm- US also -m-) [T] **1** (computing) give a set of instructions to a computer to make it perform a particular task **2** (US) = PROGRAMME ▶ **programmer** n person whose job is writing programs for a computer

programme /ˈprəʊɡræm/ n **1** plan of what is to be done: a ~ of modernization **2** television or radio broadcast **3** list of items in eg a concert or course of study ● **programme** v [T] **1** plan for sth to happen **2** give a machine instructions to do a particular task: ~ the VCR

progress /ˈprəʊɡres/ n [U] **1** process of improving or developing or nearing the achievement of sth **2** forward movement [IDM] **in progress** (fml) happening at this time ● **progress** /prəˈɡres/ v [I] make progress

progression /prəˈɡreʃn/ n **1** [U] process of progressing **2** [C] number of things that come in a series

progressive /prəˈɡresɪv/ adj **1** favouring new, modern ideas: ~ policies **2** happening or developing steadily ● **progressive** n person in favour of new, modern ideas ▶ **progressively** adv

prohibit /prəˈhɪbɪt/ v [T] (fml) **1** stop sth from being done or used, esp by law **2** make sth impossible to do

prohibition /ˌprəʊɪˈbɪʃn/ n **1** [U] act of prohibiting sth **2** [C] law or rule that forbids sth

prohibitive /prəˈhɪbətɪv/ adj **1** (of prices) so high that people cannot afford to buy or do it **2** preventing people from doing sth ▶ **prohibitively** adv

project¹ /ˈprɒdʒekt/ n planned piece of work designed to find information about sth or to produce sth new

project² /prəˈdʒekt/ v **1** [T] plan sth for a time in the future **2** [T] estimate sth, based on known facts: ~ the population growth **3** [T] ~ **on(to)** cause light, a film, etc to appear on a screen or surface **4** [I] stick out beyond a surface **5** [T] present sb/sth/yourself to others in a way that gives a good impression

projectile /prə'dʒektaɪl/ n (fml) object fired from a gun or thrown as a weapon

projection /prə'dʒekʃn/ n **1** estimate that is based on known facts **2** [U] act of projecting an image of sth onto a surface **3** [C] something that sticks out from a surface

projector /prə'dʒektə(r)/ n apparatus for projecting pictures onto a screen

the proletariat /,prəʊlə'teəriæt/ n [sing, with sing or pl verb] (tech) the class of ordinary working people

proliferate /prə'lɪfəreɪt/ v [I] (written) increase rapidly in number or amount ▶ **proliferation** /prə,lɪfə'reɪʃn/ n [U]

prolific /prə'lɪfɪk/ adj (of a writer, artist, etc) producing many works

prologue (US also **-log**) /'prəʊlɒg/ n introductory speech, etc at the beginning of a play, book or film

prolong /prə'lɒŋ/ v [T] make sth last longer ▶ **prolonged** adj continuing for a long time

promenade /,prɒmə'nɑːd/ n paved area for walking next to the beach at a seaside town

prominent /'prɒmɪnənt/ adj **1** important or well known **2** noticeable **3** sticking out from sth ▶ **prominence** n [U,sing] state of being important, well known or noticeable ▶ **prominently** adv

promiscuous /prə'mɪskjuəs/ adj (disapprov) having many sexual partners ▶ **promiscuity** /,prɒmɪs'kjuːəti/ n [U] ▶ **promiscuously** adv

promise /'prɒmɪs/ n [C] statement telling sb that you will definitely do or not do sth ● **promise** v [I, T] tell sb that you definitely do or not do sth **2** [T] make sth seem likely to happen: It ~s to be a hot day. ▶ **promising** adj likely to succeed

promontory /'prɒməntri/ n (pl -ies) long narrow area of high land that goes out into the sea

promote /prə'məʊt/ v [T] **1** help sb to happen or develop **2** advertise a product or service **3** move sb to a higher rank or more senior job ▶ **promoter** n person who organizes or supports sth

promotion /prə'məʊʃn/ n [C,U] **1** (instance of) promoting sb/sth **2** advertising or other activity to increase the sales of sth

prompt¹ /prɒmpt/ adj done or acting without delay: a ~ reply ▶ **promptly** adv ▶ **promptness** n [U]

prompt² /prɒmpt/ v **1** [T] cause sb to decide to do sth; cause sth to happen **2** [I, T] remind an actor of the words if they forget during a performance of a play ● **prompt** n **1** word(s) said to an actor to remind them what to say next **2** (computing) sign on a screen that shows that the computer has finished doing sth and is ready for more instructions ▶ **prompter** n person who prompts actors

prone /prəʊn/ adj **1** ~ **to** likely to suffer from sth or do sth bad: ~ to infection ◇ accident-~ **2** (fml) lying flat, face downwards

prong /prɒŋ/ n thin pointed part of a fork

pronoun /'prəʊnaʊn/ n (gram) word, eg hers or it used instead of a noun

pronounce /prə'naʊns/ v [T] **1** make the sound of a word or letter **2** state sth officially ▶ **pronounced** adj very noticeable ▶ **pronouncement** n formal official statement

pronunciation /prə,nʌnsi'eɪʃn/ n [U,C] way in which a language or a particular word or sound is spoken

proof /pruːf/ n **1** [U,C] information, documents, etc that show that sth is true **2** [U] process of testing whether sth is true **3** [C, usu pl] copy of printed material which is produced so that mistakes can be corrected **4** [U] standard of strength of alcoholic drink

-proof /pruːf/ adj (in compounds) that can resist sth or protect against the thing mentioned: bullet~ glass

prop /prɒp/ n [C] **1** piece of wood, metal, etc used to support sth **2** person or thing that helps or supports sb/sth **3** [usu pl] small object used by actors during a performance ● **prop** v (-pp-) [T] ~(up) support or keep sth in position

propaganda /,prɒpə'gændə/ n [U] (disapprov) information spread in order to gain support for a political leader, party, etc

propagate /'prɒpəgeɪt/ v **1** [T] (fml) spread an idea, a belief, etc among many people: ~ ideas **2** [I, T] (tech) produce new plants from a parent plant ▶ **propagation** /-'geɪʃn/ n [U]

propel /prə'pel/ v (-ll-) [T] move, drive or push sb/sth forward or in a particular direction ▶ **propeller** n blades that turn, to move a ship, helicopter, etc

propensity /prə'pensəti/ n (pl -ies) ~(for/to) (fml) natural tendency to do sth

proper /'prɒpə(r)/ adj **1** (esp GB) right, appropriate or correct **2** (GB, spoken) real; satisfactory: We've not had a ~ holiday in years. **3** socially and morally acceptable **4** according to the exact meaning of the word ▶ **properly** *adv* correctly ● **'proper noun** (*also* **'proper name**) *n* (*gram*) name of a particular person, place, etc, written with a capital letter

property /'prɒpəti/ *n* (*pl* **-ies**) **1** [U] thing(s) owned by sb; possession(s) **2** [C,U] area of land and buildings **3** [C, usu pl] (*fml*) quality or characteristic that sth has: *the chemical properties of the metal*

prophecy /'prɒfəsi/ *n* (*pl* **-ies**) **1** [C,U] statement that sth will happen in the future **2** [U] power of saying what will happen in the future

prophesy /'prɒfəsaɪ/ *v* (*pt, pp* **-ied**) [I, T] say what will happen in the future (done in the past using religious or magic powers)

prophet /'prɒfɪt/ *n* **1** person sent by God to teach people and give them messages **2** person who claims to know what will happen in the future ▶ **prophetic** /prə'fetɪk/ *adj*

propitious /prə'pɪʃəs/ *adj* (*fml*) favourable

proportion /prə'pɔːʃn/ *n* **1** [C, with sing or pl verb] part or share of a whole **2** [U] relationship of one thing to another in quantity, size, etc: *The room is very long in ~ to* (= relative to) *its width.* **3** [U,C] the correct relationship in size, etc between one thing and another **4** (**proportions**) [pl] measurements or size of sth: *a room of generous ~s* ▶ **proportional** *adj* of an appropriate size, etc in comparison with sth

proposal /prə'pəʊzl/ *n* **1** formal suggestion or plan **2** offer of marriage

propose /prə'pəʊz/ *v* **1** [T] (*fml*) suggest a plan, idea, etc **2** [T] intend to do sth **3** [I, T] ~ (**to**) ask sb to marry you

proposition /ˌprɒpə'zɪʃn/ *n* **1** idea or plan that is suggested, esp in business **2** thing that you intend to do; task to be dealt with **3** (*fml*) statement that expresses an opinion ● **proposition** *v* [T] say to sb in a direct way that you would like to have sex with them

proprietary /prə'praɪətri/ *adj* made by a particular company and sold under a trade name

proprietor /prə'praɪətə(r)/ *n* (*fml*) owner of a business, hotel, etc

propriety /prə'praɪəti/ *n* (*fml*) correct social and moral behaviour

propulsion /prə'pʌlʃn/ *n* [U] (*tech*) force that drives sth forward

pro rata /ˌprəʊ 'rɑːtə/ *adv, adj* calculated according to how much of sth has been used, the amount of work done, etc

prosaic /prə'zeɪɪk/ *adj* (*written*) uninteresting; dull

proscribe /prə'skraɪb/ *v* [T] (*fml*) forbid sth by law

prose /prəʊz/ *n* [U] writing that is not poetry

prosecute /'prɒsɪkjuːt/ *v* [I, T] officially charge sb with a crime in a court of law ▶ **prosecution** /ˌprɒsɪ'kjuːʃn/ *n* **1** [U,C] process of trying to prove in a court of law that sb is guilty of a crime; process of being charged with a crime **2** (**the prosecution**) [sing, with sing or pl verb] lawyer(s) that prosecute sb in a court of law ▶ **prosecutor** *n*

prospect¹ /'prɒspekt/ *n* **1** [U,sing] ~ (**of**) possibility that sth will happen **2** [sing] idea of what might or will happen in the future **3** (**prospects**) [pl] chances of success

prospect² /prə'spekt/ *v* [I] ~ (**for**) search an area for oil, gold, etc ▶ **prospector** *n*

prospective /prə'spektɪv/ *adj* wanting or likely to be or do sth

prospectus /prə'spektəs/ *n* **1** printed leaflet advertising a school, college, etc **2** (*business*) document giving information about a company's shares before they are offered for sale

prosper /'prɒspə(r)/ *v* [I] succeed, esp financially ▶ **prosperity** /prɒ'sperəti/ *n* [U] success or wealth ▶ **prosperous** /'prɒspərəs/ *adj* successful; rich

prostitute /'prɒstɪtjuːt/ *n* person who has sex for money ● **prostitute** *v* [T] ~ **yourself/sth** use your skills or abilities to earn money doing sth that others feel is unworthy of you ▶ **prostitution** /ˌprɒstɪ'tjuːʃn/ *n* [U]

prostrate /'prɒstreɪt/ *adj* lying on the ground, face downwards ● **prostrate** /prə'streɪt/ *v* ~ **yourself** lie on the ground, face downwards

protagonist /prə'tæɡənɪst/ *n* (*fml*) **1** main person in a play or real event **2** active supporter of a movement, idea, etc

protect /prə'tekt/ *v* [T] keep sb/sth safe from harm, injury, etc ▶ **protection** /prə'tekʃn/ *n* **1** [U] act of protecting sth/sb; state of being protected **2** [C] thing that protects sth/sb against sth ▶ **protective** *adj* **1** providing or intended to provide protection: *~ clothing* **2** ~(**of/towards**) wishing to protect sb/sth ▶ **protector** *n* person or thing that protects

protectorate /prə'tektərət/ *n* country that is controlled and protected by a more powerful country

protégé /'prɒteʒeɪ/ *n* person helped and guided by sb important and influential

protein /'prəʊtiːn/ *n* [C,U] natural substance found in meat, eggs, fish, etc which is essential to good health

protest¹ /ˈprəʊtest/ n [C,U] statement or action that shows strong disapproval or disagreement

protest² /prəˈtest/ v [I, T] **1** ~(**about/against/at**) show your strong disapproval or disagreement of sb/sth **2** [T] say firmly that sth is true, esp against opposition: *He -ed his innocence.* ▸ **protester** n person who makes a public protest

Protestant /ˈprɒtɪstənt/ n, adj (member) of any of the Christian groups that separated from the Roman Catholic Church in the 16th century

protocol /ˈprəʊtəkɒl/ n **1** [U] system of fixed rules and formal behaviour used at official meetings **2** [C] (*computing*) set of rules that control the way data is sent between computers

proton /ˈprəʊtɒn/ n (*physics*) tiny particle of matter inside an atom, with a positive electric charge

prototype /ˈprəʊtətaɪp/ n first design of sth, eg of an aircraft, from which others are developed

protracted /prəˈtræktɪd/ adj lasting for a long time

protractor /prəˈtræktə(r)/ n instrument for measuring and drawing angles

protrude /prəˈtruːd/ v [I, T] (cause sth to) stick out ▸ **protrusion** /-ˈtruːʒn/ n [C,U]

protuberance /prəˈtjuːbərəns/ n (*fml*) round part that sticks out of a surface

proud /praʊd/ adj **1** having a feeling of satisfaction from doing sth well or owning sth **2** (*disapprov*) having too high an opinion of yourself **3** having self-respect ▸ **proudly** adv

prove /pruːv/ v (pp ~d US ~n /ˈpruːvn/) **1** [T] use evidence to show sth to be true **2** linking verb be seen or found to be sth: *The opposition -d too strong for him.*

proverb /ˈprɒvɜːb/ n well-known phrase or sentence that states the truth or gives advice, eg *Waste not, want not.* ▸ **proverbial** /prəˈvɜːbiəl/ adj **1** of or expressed in a proverb **2** well known

provide /prəˈvaɪd/ v [T] **1** ~(**for**) give sth to sb or make it available for them to use [PV] **provide for sb** supply sb with the things that they need to live, eg food and clothing **provide for sth** (*fml*) make preparations to deal with sth that might happen

provided /prəˈvaɪdɪd/ (*also* **providing**) conj ~(**that**) if; on condition that

providence /ˈprɒvɪdəns/ n [U] the care and kindness of God or fate ▸ **providential** /ˌprɒvɪˈdenʃl/ adj (*fml*) fortunate

province /ˈprɒvɪns/ n **1** [C] main administrative division of a country **2** (**the provinces**) [pl] (*GB*) all the parts of a country outside the capital city **3** [sing] (*fml*) person's particular area of knowledge or responsibility ▸ **provincial** adj **1** of a province(1) or the provinces(2) **2** (*disapprov*) unwilling to consider new ideas or things ▸ **provincial** n (*disapprov*) person from the provinces(2)

provision /prəˈvɪʒn/ n **1** [U] act of providing sb with what they want or need **2** [U] ~(**for**) preparation for future needs **3** (**provisions**) [pl] food supplies **4** [C] conditions in a legal document

provisional /prəˈvɪʒənl/ adj for the present time only and likely to be changed in the future ▸ **provisionally** /-nəli/ adv

provocation /ˌprɒvəˈkeɪʃn/ n **1** act of doing or saying sth deliberately in order to make sb angry **2** [C] something said or done in order to provoke sb

provocative /prəˈvɒkətɪv/ adj intended to cause anger, argument, etc **2** intended to cause sexual desire ▸ **provocatively** adv

provoke /prəˈvəʊk/ v [T] **1** cause a particular feeling or reaction **2** deliberately do sth to annoy sb

prow /praʊ/ n (*lit*) pointed front part of a ship

prowess /ˈpraʊes/ n [U] (*fml*) great skill at doing sth

prowl /praʊl/ v [I] ~(**about/around**) move about an area quietly, looking for food, sth to steal, etc ● **prowl** n [IDM] (**be/go**) **on the prowl** (of an animal or a person) moving quietly, hunting or looking for sth

proximity /prɒkˈsɪməti/ n [U] (*fml*) nearness

proxy /ˈprɒksi/ n (pl -ies) **1** [U] authority to act for another person, esp to vote **2** [C] person given this authority

prude /pruːd/ n (*disapprov*) person easily shocked by sexual matters ▸ **prudish** adj

prudent /ˈpruːdnt/ adj careful and sensible ▸ **prudence** /-dns/ n [U] ▸ **prudently** adv

prune¹ /pruːn/ n dried plum ● **prune** v [T] **1** cut off some of the branches of a tree or bush to encourage further growth **2** cut out unnecessary parts from sth

pry /praɪ/ v (pt, pp **pried** /praɪd/) [I] ~(**into**) try to find out about sb's private life

PS /ˌpiː ˈes/ *abbr* postscript; something written at the end of a letter to add sth you have forgotten to say

psalm /sɑːm/ *n* religious song or poem, esp one of those in the Bible

pseudonym /ˈsjuːdənɪm/ *n* name that sb, esp a writer, uses, instead of their real name

psyche /ˈsaɪki/ *n* (*fml*) the mind; your deepest feelings

psychedelic /ˌsaɪkəˈdelɪk/ *adj* 1 (of drugs) causing sb to see sth that isn't there 2 having very bright colours and strange patterns

psychiatry /saɪˈkaɪətri/ *n* [U] study and treatment of mental illness ▶ **psychiatric** /ˌsaɪkiˈætrɪk/ *adj* ▶ **psychiatrist** /saɪˈkaɪətrɪst/ *n* doctor trained in psychiatry

psychic /ˈsaɪkɪk/ *adj* 1 (*also* **psychical** /ˈsaɪkɪkl/) connected with or having strange powers of the mind that are not able to be explained by natural laws 2 of the mind rather than the body

psychoanalysis /ˌsaɪkəʊəˈnæləsɪs/ *n* [U] method of treating some mental illnesses by looking at and discussing the effects of events in the patient's life as possible causes ▶ **psychoanalyse** /ˌsaɪkəʊˈænəlaɪz/ *v* [T] treat sb using psychoanalysis ▶ **psychoanalyst** /-ˈænəlɪst/ *n* person who treats patients using psychoanalysis

psychology /saɪˈkɒlədʒi/ *n* [U] scientific study of the mind and how it influences behaviour ▶ **psychological** /ˌsaɪkəˈlɒdʒɪkl/ *adj* ▶ **psychologist** *n* student of or expert in psychology

psychopath /ˈsaɪkəpæθ/ *n* person suffering from a severe mental illness that causes them to behave violently ▶ **psychopathic** /-ˈpæθɪk/ *adj*

pt *abbr* 1 part 2 pint 3 point 4 (**Pt.**) (esp on a map) port

PTO /ˌpiː tiː ˈəʊ/ *abbr* (*GB*) (written at the bottom of a page to show that there is more on the other side) please turn over

pub /pʌb/ *n* (*GB*) building where alcoholic drinks are sold and drunk

puberty /ˈpjuːbəti/ *n* [U] stage at which a person becomes physically able to have children

pubic /ˈpjuːbɪk/ *adj* of or near the sexual organs

public /ˈpʌblɪk/ *adj* 1 of or for people in general 2 of or provided by the government: ~ *money* ◇ *a* ~ *library* 3 known to many people; not secret [IDM] **in the public eye** often seen on television and often mentioned in newspapers, etc ● **public** *n* [sing, with sing or pl verb] 1 (**the public**) ordinary people in society in general 2 group of people who share an interest or are involved in the same activity: *the reading* ~ [IDM] **in public** when other people, esp strangers, are present ■ , **public 'bar** *n* (*GB*) bar in a pub with simple and less comfortable furniture than the other bars ■ , **public 'company** (, **public 'limited company**) (*US* , **public corpo'ration**) (*abbr* **plc**, **PLC**) *n* business company that sells shares in itself to the public ■ , **public con'venience** *n* (*GB*) toilet which the public may use ■ , **public 'house** *n* (*fml*) = PUB ▶ **publicly** *adv* ■ , **public re'lations** *n* 1 [U] (*abbr* PR) business of obtaining good public opinion of an organization 2 [pl] relationship between an organization and the public ■ , **public 'school** *n* (in Britain) private secondary school for fee-paying pupils

publication /ˌpʌblɪˈkeɪʃn/ *n* 1 [U] act of publishing sth 2 [C] book, magazine, etc

publicity /pʌbˈlɪsəti/ *n* [U] 1 attention that is given to sb/sth by newspapers, television, etc 2 information that attracts public attention to sth; advertising

publicize (*also* -**ise**) /ˈpʌblɪsaɪz/ *v* [T] make sth known to the public; advertise sth

publish /ˈpʌblɪʃ/ *v* [T] 1 print and offer a book, etc for sale to the public 2 (*fml*) make sth known to the public ▶ **publisher** *n* person or company that publishes books, etc

pucker /ˈpʌkə(r)/ *v* [I, T] (cause sth to) form small folds or lines

pudding /ˈpʊdɪŋ/ *n* [C, U] (*GB*) 1 sweet dish eaten at the end of a meal 2 sweet or savoury food made with flour and baked, boiled or steamed

puddle /ˈpʌdl/ *n* small pool of water, esp rain

puff¹ /pʌf/ *v* 1 [I, T] smoke a pipe, cigarette, etc 2 [I, T] (cause smoke, steam, etc to) blow out in clouds [I] (*infml*) breathe loudly and quickly [PV] **puff (sth) out/up** (cause sth to) swell ▶ **puffed** *adj* (*GB*, *infml*) breathing with difficulty

puff² /pʌf/ *n* 1 act of breathing in smoke from a cigarette, etc 2 small amount of air, smoke, etc that is blown from somewhere ■ , **puff 'pastry** *n* [U] light pastry that forms many layers when baked ▶ **puffy** *adj* (-**ier**, -**iest**) (of eyes, faces, etc) looking swollen

puffin /ˈpʌfɪn/ *n* N Atlantic seabird with a large brightly coloured beak

pull¹ /pʊl/ *v* [I, T] hold sth firmly and use force in order to move it towards yourself or in a particular direction: ~ *the door shut* ◇ *You push and I'll* ~.

P

2 [T] remove sth from a place by pulling: ~ (*out*) *a tooth* **3** [T] damage a muscle, etc by using too much force [IDM] **pull faces/a face (at sb)** → FACE **pull a fast one (on sb)** (*sl*) trick sb **pull your finger out** → FINGER **pull sb's leg** (*infml*) play a joke on sb by making them believe sth untrue **pull your socks up** (*GB, infml*) try to improve your work or behaviour **pull sth to pieces** criticize sth strongly **pull your weight** do your fair share of the work [PV] **pull away (from sth)** (of a vehicle) start moving **pull sth down** destroy a building completely **pull in (to sth) 1** (of a train) enter a station **2** (*GB*) (of a vehicle) move to the side of the road and stop **pull sth off** (*infml*) succeed in doing sth difficult **pull out** (of a vehicle) move away from the side of the road **pull (sb/sth) out (of sth)** (cause sb/sth to) withdraw from sth: ~ *out of a race* **pull over** (of a vehicle) move to the side of the road and stop **pull (sb) through** (help sb to) get better after a serious illness, operation, etc **pull together** act, work, etc together with other people in an organized way and without fighting **pull yourself together** take control of your feelings and behave calmly **pull up** (of a vehicle) stop **pull sb up** (*GB, infml*) criticize sb for sth they have done ■ **pull-down 'menu** *n* (*computing*) list of possible choices that appears on a computer screen when you select its title

pull² /pʊl/ *n* **1** [C] act of pulling sth **2** [sing] force or attraction: *the ~ of the river current* **3** [U] (*infml*) power and influence over other people **4** [C, usu sing] difficult walk up a steep hill

pullet /ˈpʊlɪt/ *n* young hen

pulley /ˈpʊli/ *n* device with a wheel and rope, used for lifting things

pullover /ˈpʊləʊvə(r)/ *n* (*esp GB*) knitted piece of clothing for the upper body, pulled on over the head

pulp /pʌlp/ *n* **1** soft white substance that is made by crushing sth, esp wood fibre used for making paper **2** soft part inside some fruit and vegetables ● **pulp** *v* [T] crush or beat sth so that it becomes soft and wet

pulpit /ˈpʊlpɪt/ *n* raised enclosed platform in a church, from which a priest speaks

pulsate /pʌlˈseɪt/ *v* [I] move or shake with a strong regular action ► **pulsation** /-ˈseɪʃn/ *n* [C, U]

pulse /pʌls/ *n* **1** [C, usu sing] regular beating of the arteries as the blood is pumped through them **2** [sing] regular beat in music ● **pulse** *v* [I] move, beat or flow with a strong regular movements or sounds

pulverize (*also* **-ise**) /ˈpʌlvəraɪz/ *v* [T] **1** (*fml*) crush sth to a fine powder **2** (*infml*) defeat or destroy sb/sth completely

puma /ˈpjuːmə/ *n* large American wild animal of the cat family

pump /pʌmp/ *n* **1** machine for forcing liquid, gas or air into, out of or through sth **2** (*GB*) light soft shoe worn for dancing or exercise ● **pump** *v* **1** [T] force air, gas or liquid to flow in a particular direction: *The heart ~s blood around the body.* **2** [I] work like a pump; beat **3** [I, T] (cause sth to) move quickly up and down or in and out **4** [T] (*infml*) try to get information from sb by asking them a lot of questions

pumpkin /ˈpʌmpkɪn/ *n* [C, U] large round vegetable with thick orange skin

pun /pʌn/ *n* humorous use of words that sound the same or have two meanings, eg 'The soldier laid down his *arms*' ● **pun** *v* (*-nn-*) [I] make a pun

punch /pʌntʃ/ *v* [T] **1** hit sb/sth with your fist **2** make a hole in sth with a **punch**(3) or some other sharp object ● **punch** *n* **1** [C] hard hit made with the fist **2** [U] power to interest people **3** [C] tool or machine for cutting holes in paper, etc: *a hole ~* **4** [U] drink made of wine or spirits mixed with sugar, lemon, spice, etc ■ **'punch-up** *n* (*GB, infml*) physical fight

punctual /ˈpʌŋktʃuəl/ *adj* happening or doing sth at the arranged or correct time; not late ► **punctuality** /-tʃuˈælətɪ/ *n* [U] ► **punctually** *adv*

punctuate /ˈpʌŋktʃueɪt/ *v* **1** [T] ~ (**with/by**) (*usu passive*) interrupt sth at intervals **2** [I, T] divide writing into sentences and phrases by using full stops, question marks, etc ► **punctuation** /ˌpʌŋktʃuˈeɪʃn/ *n* [U] (practice of putting) marks such as full stops and commas in a piece of writing

puncture /ˈpʌŋktʃə(r)/ *n* small hole in a tyre made by a sharp point ● **puncture** *v* [I, T] get or make a small hole in sth

pundit /ˈpʌndɪt/ *n* person who knows a lot about a subject and often talks about it in public; expert: *political ~s*

pungent /ˈpʌndʒənt/ *adj* having a strong taste or smell

punish /ˈpʌnɪʃ/ *v* [T] make sb suffer because they have broken the law or done sth wrong ► **punishing** *adj* long and difficult and making you work so hard you become tired ► **punishment** *n* **1** [U,C] act or way of punishing sb **2** [U] rough treatment

punitive /'pju:nətɪv/ adj (fml) intended as punishment; harsh or severe

punk /pʌŋk/ n 1 [U] (also ,punk 'rock') loud and aggressive rock music popular in the late 1970s and early 1980s 2 [C] (also ,punk 'rocker') person who likes punk rock and wears leather clothes, metal chains and has brightly coloured hair 3 [C] (US, infml, disapprov) rude or violent young man or boy

punnet /'pʌnɪt/ n small square basket used as a container for fruit

punt /pʌnt/ n long shallow flat-bottomed boat moved along by a long pole ● **punt** v [I] travel in a punt, esp for pleasure

punter /'pʌntə(r)/ n (GB, infml) 1 customer 2 person who bets money on horse races

puny /'pju:ni/ adj (-ier, -iest) (disapprov) small and weak

pup /pʌp/ n = PUPPY 2 young of various animals, eg seals

pupil /'pju:pl/ n 1 person being taught, esp a child in a school 2 small round black area at the centre of the eye

puppet /'pʌpɪt/ n 1 doll that can be made to move, eg by pulling strings attached to parts of its body or by putting your hand inside it 2 (disapprov) person or group whose actions are controlled by another

puppy /'pʌpi/ n (pl -ies) young dog

purchase /'pɜ:tʃəs/ v [T] (fml) buy sth ● **purchase** n (fml) 1 [U] act or process of buying sth 2 [C] something bought ▶ **purchaser** n (fml) person who buys sth

pure /pjʊə(r)/ adj (~r, ~st) 1 not mixed with any other substance; with nothing added 2 not containing harmful substances; clean 3 complete; total: They met by ~ chance. 4 without evil thoughts or actions; morally good 5 (of colour, sound or light) very clear; perfect 6 concerned with theory only; not practical: ~ science ▶ **purely** adv only; completely

purée /'pjʊəreɪ/ n [U, C] smooth thick liquid made by crushing cooked vegetables, fruit, etc in a little water

purgatory /'pɜ:ɡətri/ n [U] 1 (in Roman Catholic teaching) place after death in which the soul has to be purified by suffering 2 (spoken, hum) any state or place of suffering

purge /pɜ:dʒ/ v [T] 1 ~ (of/from) remove unwanted people from a political party, etc: a party of extremists ◇ ~ extremists from the party 2 ~(of/from) (written) make yourself/sth pure by getting rid of bad thoughts ● **purge** n act of purging(1)

purify /'pjʊərɪfaɪ/ v (pt, pp -ied) [T] make sth/sb pure ▶ **purification** /ˌpjʊərɪfɪ'keɪʃn/ n [U]

purist /'pjʊərɪst/ n person who has strong opinions about what is correct in language, art, etc

puritan /'pjʊərɪtən/ adj, n 1 (disapprov) (of a) person who is very strict in morals 2 (**Puritan**) (of a) member of a Protestant group in the 16th and 17th centuries who wanted simpler forms of church ceremony ▶ **puritanical** /ˌpjʊərɪ-'tænɪkl/ adj (disapprov)

purity /'pjʊərəti/ n [U] state of being pure

purl /pɜ:l/ n [U] stitch used in knitting ▶ **purl** v [I, T]

purple /'pɜ:pl/ adj having the colour of red and blue mixed together

purpose /'pɜ:pəs/ n 1 [C] reason for which sth is done or made 2 [U] ability to form plans and carry them out [IDM] **on purpose** deliberately ▶ **purposeful** adj showing purpose(2)

purr /pɜ:(r)/ v [I] (of a cat) make a low vibrating sound expressing pleasure ▶ **purr** n [sing]

purse /pɜ:s/ n 1 (esp GB) small bag for carrying money, cards, etc, used esp by women 2 (US) = HANDBAG (HAND¹) 3 (sport) sum of money given as a prize in a boxing match ● **purse** v [T] (~ your lips) form your lips into a tight round shape, eg to show disapproval

purser /'pɜ:sə(r)/ n officer on a ship responsible for taking care of the passengers, and for the ship's accounts

pursue /pə'sju:/ v [T] (fml) 1 do sth to try to achieve sth over a period of time: a goal/an objective 2 continue to discuss or be involved in sth: ~ your legal action 3 follow or chase sb/sth in order to catch them ▶ **pursuer** n (written)

pursuit /pə'sju:t/ n (fml) 1 [U] act of pursuing sth/sb 2 [C, usu pl] hobby; leisure activity

purvey /pə'veɪ/ v [T] (fml) supply sth, esp food ▶ **purveyor** n

pus /pʌs/ n [U] thick yellowish liquid formed in an infected wound

push¹ /pʊʃ/ v [I, T] 1 use force on sth in order to move it forward, away or to a different position: ~ a bike up the hill ◇ ~ your way through the crowd 2 [T] try to persuade sb to do sth that they may not want to do 3 [T] (infml) sell illegal drugs [PV] **push sb about/around** (infml) give orders to sb in a rude or unpleasant way **push (sb) for sth** repeatedly ask for sth or try to make sth happen: They're ~ing for a ban on GM foods. **push off** (GB, spoken) go away ■ 'push-button adj operated by pressing buttons with your fingers ■ '**pushchair** n small folding seat on wheels for a baby ▶ **pushed** adj 1 ~ **to** having difficulty doing sth: *be hard ~ed to finish on time* 2 ~ (**for**) not having enough of sth: *be ~ed for time* ▶ **pusher** n (infml) person who sells illegal drugs

push[2] /pʊʃ/ n [C, usu sing] **1** act of pushing sth/sb **2** great effort or attack [IDM] **give sb/get the push** (GB, infml) dismiss sb/be dismissed from your job

pussy /'pʊsi/ n (pl -ies) (also '**pussy cat**) child's word for a cat

put /pʊt/ v (pt, pp **put** pres pt **~ting**) [T] **1** move sth/sb into a particular place or position: *She ~ the book on the table.* ◇ *Her family ~ her in a nursing home.* **2** write sth or make a mark on sth: *P~ your name here.* **3** bring sb/sth into the state or condition mentioned: *Don't ~ yourself at risk.* **4** express sth in a particular way: *She ~ it very politely.* [IDM] **put your cards on the table** → CARD **put the clock back** → CLOCK **put it to sb that ...** suggest sth to sb to see if they can argue against it **put your oar in** → OAR **put sth right** → RIGHT[1] **put sb/sth to rights** → RIGHT[3] **put sth about** (GB, infml) cause rumours, etc to pass from one person to another **put yourself/sth across/over** (**to sb**) communicate your ideas, feelings, etc well to sb **put sth aside 1** ignore or forget sth, usu a feeling or difference of opinion: *~ aside your differences* **2** save money for a particular purpose **put sth at sth** calculate sb/sth to be a particular age, amount, etc: *I ~ the possible cost at £500.* **put sth away** put sth in its usual place: *~ the cup away in the cupboard* **put sth back 1** return sth to its usual place: *~ the book back on the shelf* **2** move sth to a later time or date: *~ the meeting back by one hour* **3** move the hands of a clock to show the correct earlier time **put sb by** = PUT STH ASIDE(2) **put sb down** (infml) make sb look or seem stupid, esp in front of other people **put sth down 1** stop holding sth and place it on a table, etc **2** write sth **3** pay part of the cost of sth: *~ down a 5% deposit* **4** stop sth by force: *~ down a rebellion* **5** kill a sick animal put sth **down to sth** consider that sth is caused by sth: *I ~ his failure down to laziness.* **put sth forward 1** move sth to an earlier time or date **2** move the hands of a clock to show the correct later time **3** suggest sth for discussion: *~ forward a new idea* **put sth in 1** install equipment or furniture: *~ central heating in* **2** spend a lot of time or make a lot of effort doing sth: *~ in ten hours' work* **put yourself/**

sb/sth **in for sth** enter yourself/sb/ sth for a competition **put sb off 1** cancel a meeting, etc you have made with sb **2** make sb dislike sb/sth or not trust them/it **3** distract sb from sth: *Don't ~ me off when I'm trying to concentrate.* **put sb off sth/sb** make sb lose enthusiasm for or interest in sth/sb **put sth off** change sth to a later time or date **put sth on 1** dress yourself in sth: *~ a coat on* **2** apply sth to your skin, face, etc **3** switch on a piece of equipment: *~ on the television* ◇ *~ on some music* **4** become heavier or fatter: *~ on a stone (in weight)* **5** provide sth specially: *~ on extra trains* **6** produce or present a play, show, etc: *~ on a play* **put sb out 1** cause inconvenience to sb: *I hope my visit won't ~ you out.* **2** (**be put out**) be upset or offended **put sth out 1** take sth outside your house and leave it, eg for sb to collect **2** stop sth from burning or shining: *~ out the lights* **3** publish or broadcast sth: *~ out a warning* **put yourself/sth over** (**to sb**) = PUT YOURSELF/STH ACROSS (TO SB) **put sb/sth through** (**to sb**) connect sb by telephone **put sth to sb 1** offer a suggestion to sb so that they can accept or reject it **2** ask sb a question **put sth up 1** show a level of skill, determination, etc, in a fight or contest: *~ up a fight* **put sb up** let sb stay at your home **put sb up 1** raise sth: *~ your hand up* **2** build sth or place sth somewhere: *~ a tent up* **3** increase sth: *~ up the rent* **4** provide or lend money **put sth up** (**at ...**) (esp GB) stay somewhere for the night **put sb up to sth** (infml) encourage sb to do sth wrong **put up with sb/sth** accept sb/sth annoying, unpleasant, etc without complaining: *~ up with bad behaviour* ■ '**putdown** n remark intended to make sb look or feel stupid

putrefy /'pju:trɪfaɪ/ v (pt, pp **-ied**) [I] (fml) decay and smell very bad ▶ **putrefaction** /,pju:trɪ'fækʃn/ n [U]

putrid /'pju:trɪd/ adj rotten and bad-smelling

putt /pʌt/ v [I, T] (in golf) hit the ball gently along the ground

putter /'pʌtə(r)/ v [I] (US) = POTTER

putty /'pʌti/ n [U] soft paste used for fixing glass in window frames

puzzle /'pʌzl/ n **1** game, etc that you have to think about carefully in order to answer it or do it: *a crossword ~* **2** something difficult to understand or explain ● **puzzle** v [T] make sb feel confused because they do not understand sth: *What ~s me is why he didn't return my call.* [PV] **puzzle sth out** find the answer to sth by thinking hard **puzzle**

over/about sth think hard about sth in order to understand it

PVC /ˌpiː viː ˈsiː/ n [U] strong plastic material

pygmy (also **pigmy**) /ˈpɪɡmi/ n (pl -ies) **1** (Pygmy) member of a race of very short people living in parts of Africa and SE Asia **2** (disapprov) very small person or animal

pyjamas /pəˈdʒɑːməz/ n [pl] loose jacket and trousers worn in bed

pylon /ˈpaɪlən/ n tall steel structure for carrying electric cables

pyramid /ˈpɪrəmɪd/ n **1** structure with a square base and sloping sides meeting at a point, one built in ancient Egypt **2** pile of objects in the shape of a pyramid

pyre /ˈpaɪə(r)/ n high pile of wood for burning a dead body on

python /ˈpaɪθən/ n large tropical snake that kills animals by twisting its body tightly round them

Q q

Q, q /kjuː/ n [C,U] (pl **Q's, q's** /kjuːz/) the seventeenth letter of the English alphabet

quack /kwæk/ n **1** sound that a duck makes **2** (infml, disapprov) person who dishonestly claims to have medical knowledge ● **quack** v [I] make the sound of a duck

quad /kwɒd/ n short for QUADRANGLE **2** short for QUADRUPLET

quad bike /kwɒd baɪk/ n motorcycle with four large tyres, used for riding over rough ground ▶ '**quad biking** n [U] activity or sport of riding a quad bike

quadrangle /ˈkwɒdræŋɡl/ n open square area with buildings round it, esp in a school or college

quadruped /ˈkwɒdruped/ n (tech) any creature with four feet

quadruple /kwɒˈdruːpl/ v [I, T] become or make sth four times bigger ● **quadruple** /ˈkwɒdrupl/ adj, det **1** consisting of four parts, people or groups **2** being four times as much or as many

quadruplet /ˈkwɒdruplət; kwɒˈdruːplət/ n one of four babies born to the same mother at one time

quagmire /ˈkwæɡmaɪə(r); GB also ˈkwɒɡ-/ n **1** area of soft wet ground **2** difficult or dangerous situation

quail /kweɪl/ n [C,U] (meat of a) small brown bird, whose meat and eggs are used for food ● **quail** v [I] (lit) feel or show that you feel very afraid

quaint /kweɪnt/ adj attractive in an unusual or old-fashioned way ▶ **quaintly** adv

quake /kweɪk/ v [I] shake; tremble

qualification /ˌkwɒlɪfɪˈkeɪʃn/ n **1** [C,usu pl] exam that you have passed or course of study that you have completed successfully **2** skill or type of experience needed for a particular job **3** [C,U] information added to a statement that modifies or limits it: accept an offer with ~s **4** [U] fact of passing an exam, etc

qualify /ˈkwɒlɪfaɪ/ v (pt, pp -ied) **1** [I, T] have or give sb the qualities, training, etc that are necessary or suitable for sth: She'll ~ as a doctor next year. **2** [T] add sth to a previous statement to make it less general or extreme ▶ **qualified** adj **1** have the necessary qualifications **2** limited in some way: qualified approval

qualitative /ˈkwɒlɪtətɪv/ adj concerned with how good sth is, rather than how much of it there is

quality /ˈkwɒləti/ n (pl -ies) **1** [U,C] (high) standard; how good or bad sth is **2** [C] typical part of sb/sth's character

qualm /kwɑːm/ n feeling of doubt about whether what you are doing is right

quandary /ˈkwɒndəri/ n (pl -ies) state of not being able to decide what to do

quantitative /ˈkwɒntɪtətɪv/ adj concerned with the amount or number of sth rather than how good it is

quantity /ˈkwɒntəti/ n [C,U] (pl -ies) (esp large) amount or number of sth

quarantine /ˈkwɒrəntiːn/ n [U] period when a person or animal is separated from others to prevent the spread of a disease ● **quarantine** v [T] put an animal or person in quarantine

quarrel /ˈkwɒrəl/ n **1** [C] angry argument **2** [U] reason to disagree with sb/sth ● **quarrel** v (-ll- US -l-) [I] ~(with) have an angry argument or disagreement ▶ **quarrelsome** /-səm/ adj (of a person) liking to argue with others

quarry /ˈkwɒri/ n (pl -ies) **1** [C] place where stone, slate, etc is dug out of the ground **2** [sing] animal or person that is being hunted or followed ● **quarry** v (pt, pp -ied) [T] dig stone, etc from a quarry

quart /kwɔːt/ n measure for liquids, equal to 2 pints (1.14 litres) in the UK and 0.94 of a litre in the US

quarter /ˈkwɔːtə(r)/ n **1** [C] one of four equal parts of sth; ¼ **2** [C] 15 minutes: a ~ to four ◇ (US) a ~ of four ◇ a ~ past six ◇ (US) a ~ after six **3** [C] period of three months **4** [C] part of a town or city: the historic

~ **5** [C] person or group from which help or information may come **6** [C] coin of the US and Canada worth 25 cents **7** (**quarters**) [pl] accommodation, esp for soldiers: *married ~s* ● **quarter** *v* [T] **1** divide sth into four parts **2** (*fml*) provide sb with a place to eat and sleep ■ **,quarter-'final** *n* one of four matches in a competition, whose four winners play in the semi-finals ■ **'quartermaster** *n* army officer in charge of stores and accommodation

quarterly /'kwɔːtəli/ *adj, adv* (happening or produced) every three months: *I pay my bills ~.* ● **quarterly** *n* (*pl* -ies) magazine, etc published four times a year

quartet /kwɔː'tet/ *n* (music for) four players or singers

quartz /kwɔːts/ *n* [U] hard mineral used in making very accurate clocks

quash /kwɒʃ/ *v* [T] **1** (*law*) officially say that a legal decision is no longer valid or correct: *an appeal* **2** (*written*) stop sth from continuing

quaver /'kweɪvə(r)/ *v* [I, T] (of sb's voice) shake because the person is afraid ● **quaver** *n* [C, usu sing] shaking sound in sb's voice

quay /kiː/ *n* platform in a harbour where boats come to load, etc

queasy /'kwiːzi/ *adj* (-ier, -iest) feeling sick; wanting to vomit

queen /kwiːn/ *n* **1** female ruler of an independent state that has a royal family **2** wife of a king **3** woman thought to be the best in a particular group or area **4** (in chess) the most powerful piece **5** playing card with a picture of a queen on it **6** egg-producing female of bees, ants, etc ■ **,queen 'mother** *n* mother of a ruling king or queen

queer /kwɪə(r)/ *adj* **1** (*old-fash*) strange or unusual **2** (∆, *sl*) homosexual ● **queer** *n* (∆, *sl*) homosexual man

quell /kwel/ *v* [T] put an end to sth

quench /kwentʃ/ *v* [T] **1** satisfy your thirst by drinking **2** (*written*) put out a fire

query /'kwɪəri/ *n* (*pl* -ies) question ● **query** *v* (*pt, pp* -ied) [T] **1** express doubt about whether sth is correct or not **2** (*written*) ask a question

quest /kwest/ *n* (*fml*) long search

question[1] /'kwestʃən/ *n* **1** [C] sentence, phrase, etc that asks for information **2** [C] matter that needs to be discussed or dealt with **3** [U] doubt: *His honesty is beyond ~.* [IDM] **in question 1** that is being discussed **2** in doubt; uncertain **out of the question** impossible ■ **'question mark** *n* mark (?) written at the end of a question

question[2] /'kwestʃən/ *v* [T] **1** ask sb questions about sth, esp officially

2 express your doubts about sth ▸ **questionable** *adj* that can be doubted

questionnaire /ˌkwestʃə'neə(r)/ *n* ~(**on**/**about**) list of questions to be answered to give information

queue /kjuː/ *n* line of people, cars, etc waiting for sth or to do sth ● **queue** *v* [I] wait in a queue

quibble /'kwɪbl/ *v* [I] argue about small unimportant details ● **quibble** *n* argument about a small point

quiche /kiːʃ/ *n* [C, U] open pie with a filling of eggs, cheese, etc

quick /kwɪk/ *adj* **1** done with speed; taking or lasting a short time **2** moving or doing sth fast: *a ~ learner/worker* [IDM] **be quick on the uptake** → UPTAKE **have a quick temper** become angry easily **quick off the mark** → MARK[1] ● **quick** *adv* quickly; fast ● **quick** *n* (**the quick**) [sing] soft sensitive flesh below the fingernails ▸ **quickly** *adv* ▸ **quickness** *n* [U] ■ **,quick-'witted** *adj* able to think quickly; clever

quicken /'kwɪkən/ *v* [I, T] (*written*) become or make sth quicker

quicksand /'kwɪksænd/ *n* [U, C] loose wet deep sand that you sink into if you walk on it

quid /kwɪd/ *n* (*pl* **quid**) (*GB, infml*) one pound in money

quiet /'kwaɪət/ *adj* **1** making little noise **2** without many people or much noise or activity: *a ~ life* **3** (of a person) not talking very much ● **quiet** *n* [U] state of being calm without much noise [IDM] **on the quiet** secretly ▸ **quieten** /-tn/ *v* [I, T] (*GB*) ~(**down**) become or make sb/sth calmer or less noisy ▸ **quietly** *adv* ▸ **quietness** *n* [U]

quill /kwɪl/ *n* **1** large feather **2** (*also* ˌquill 'pen) pen made from a quill feather **3** one of the long sharp spines on a porcupine

quilt /kwɪlt/ *n* **1** decorative padded cover for a bed: *a patchwork ~* **2** (*GB*) = DUVET ▸ **quilted** *adj* having two layers of cloth filled with soft material

quin /kwɪn/ (*US* **quint** /kwɪnt/) (*infml*) *n* = QUINTUPLET

quinine /kwɪ'niːn/ *n* [U] drug from the bark of a S American tree, used in the past to treat malaria

quintet /kwɪn'tet/ *n* (music for) five players or singers

quintuplet /'kwɪntjuplət; kwɪn-'tjuːplət/ *n* one of five babies born to the same mother at one time

quip /kwɪp/ *n* quick and clever remark ● **quip** *v* (-**pp**-) [I] make a quip

quirk /kwɜːk/ *n* **1** strange aspect of sb's personality **2** strange thing that happens, esp accidentally

R

quit /kwɪt/ v (**-tt-** pt, pp quit GB also **~ted**) [I, T] (infml) **1** leave your job, school, etc **2** (esp US) stop doing sth

quite /kwaɪt/ adv **1** to some degree; fairly: ~ hot **2** to the greatest possible degree; completely: ~ delicious **3** (also fml **quite so**) (GB) used to show you agree with sb [IDM] **quite a/the sth** used to show that a person or thing is unusual in some way: There's ~ a story about how they met

quiver /ˈkwɪvə(r)/ v [I] shake slightly ● **quiver** n **1** slight movement in part of your body **2** case for carrying arrows

quiz /kwɪz/ n (pl ~zes) game in which people are asked questions to test their knowledge ● **quiz** v (**-zz-**) [T] ask sb a lot of questions in order to get information

quizzical /ˈkwɪzɪkl/ adj (of an expression) showing that you are surprised or amused ▸ **quizzically** /-kli/ adv

quoit /kɔɪt/ n [C] ring thrown onto a small post in the game of quoits **2** (**quoits**) [U] game in which rings are thrown onto a small post

quota /ˈkwəʊtə/ n limited number or share that is officially allowed

quotation /kwəʊˈteɪʃn/ n **1** [C] group of words taken from a play, speech, etc **2** [U] act of repeating sth that another person has said **3** [C] statement of how much money a piece of work will cost ■ **quo'tation marks** n [pl] punctuation marks (' ' or " ") used at the beginning and end of a quotation(1)

quote /kwəʊt/ v [I, T] **1** repeat the exact words that another person has said or written **2** [T] mention an example of sth to support a statement **3** [T] tell a customer how much you will charge for a job or service ● **quote** n [infml] **1** [C] = QUOTATION(1) **2** [C] = QUOTATION(3) **3** (**quotes**) [pl] = QUOTATION MARKS (QUOTATION)

quotient /ˈkwəʊʃnt/ n (maths) number obtained by dividing one number by another

Rr

R, r /ɑː(r)/ n [C, U] (pl **R's, r's** /ɑːz/) the eighteenth letter of the English alphabet

R & B /ˌɑːr ən ˈbiː/ abbr = RHYTHM AND BLUES

rabbi /ˈræbaɪ/ n Jewish spiritual leader; teacher of Jewish law

rabbit /ˈræbɪt/ n small animal with long ears that lives in a hole in the ground ● **rabbit** v [PV] **rabbit on (about sb/sth)** (GB, infml) talk continuously about unimportant or uninteresting things

rabble /ˈræbl/ n large noisy crowd of people ■ **'rabble-rouser** n person who makes speeches to crowds of people intending to make them angry or excited

rabid /ˈræbɪd/ adj **1** (disapprov) having violent or extreme feelings or opinions **2** suffering from rabies

rabies /ˈreɪbiːz/ n [U] disease of dogs and other animals causing madness and death

race¹ /reɪs/ n **1** [C] competition of speed, eg in running **2** [sing] situation in which a number of people, groups, etc are competing, esp for political power: the arms ~ **3** (**the races**) [pl] series of horse races that happen at one place **4** [C, U] one of the main groups into which humans can be divided according to their physical differences, eg colour of skin **5** [C] group of people with the same history, language, etc, **6** [C] breed or type of animal or plant ■ **,race re'lations** n [pl] relationships between people of different races in the same community

race² /reɪs/ v **1** [I, T] **~(against)** compete against sb/sth in a race or races **2** [T] make an animal or a vehicle compete in a race **3** [I, T] (cause sb/sth to) move very fast ■ **'racecourse** n track where horses race ■ **'racehorse** n horse that is trained to run in races ■ **'racetrack** n **1** track for races between runners, cars, bicycles, etc **2** (US) = RACECOURSE

racial /ˈreɪʃl/ adj **1** happening or existing between people of different races: ~ discrimination **2** of race¹(4) ▸ **racially** adv

racism /ˈreɪsɪzəm/ n [U] (disapprov) unfair treatment of other races; belief that some races of people are better than others ▸ **racist** adj, n

rack /ræk/ n **1** framework, usu of metal or wooden bars, for holding things or hanging things on **2** shelf over the seats in a train, aeroplane, etc for light luggage: a luggage ~ [IDM] **go to rack and ruin** get into a bad condition ● **rack** v (often passive) cause sb to suffer great pain [IDM] **rack your brains** try very hard to think of sth

racket /ˈrækɪt/ n [C] **1** [sing] (infml) loud noise **2** (infml) dishonest way of getting money **3** (also **racquet**) piece of sports equipment used for hitting the ball in tennis, squash, etc **4** (**rackets**) (also **racquets**) [U] game played with a ball in a court with four walls ▸ **racketeer** /ˌrækəˈtɪə(r)/ n person involved in a racket(2)

racy /'reɪsi/ adj (-ier, -iest) lively, amusing and perhaps about sex

radar /'reɪdɑ:(r)/ n [U] equipment or system for showing the position of solid objects on a screen by using radio waves

radiant /'reɪdiənt/ adj 1 showing great happiness, love or health: ~ *beauty* 2 sending out rays of light or heat ► **radiance** /-əns/ n [U] ► **radiantly** adv

radiate /'reɪdieɪt/ v [I, T] 1 (of a person) send out a particular quality or emotion: *She ~s confidence.* 2 send out rays of light or heat

radiation /,reɪdi'eɪʃn/ n 1 [U,C] powerful and dangerous rays sent out from a radioactive substance 2 [U] heat, energy, etc, sent out in the form of rays

radiator /'reɪdieɪtə(r)/ n 1 apparatus, esp a set of pipes, used for heating a room 2 device for cooling the engine of a vehicle

radical /'rædɪkl/ adj 1 basic; thorough and complete 2 new, different and likely to have a great effect 3 favouring thorough political or social change ● **radical** n person with radical(3) opinions ► **radically** /-kli/ adv

radii plural of RADIUS

radio /'reɪdiəʊ/ n (pl ~s) 1 [U,sing] (activity of broadcasting) programmes for people to listen to 2 [C] piece of equipment for listening to radio broadcasts 3 [U] process of sending and receiving messages through the air using electromagnetic waves ● **radio** v [I, T] send a message to sb by radio

radioactive /,reɪdiəʊ'æktɪv/ adj sending out energy in the form of rays that can be harmful ► **radioactivity** /-æk'tɪvəti/ n [U]

radiography /,reɪdi'ɒɡrəfi/ n [U] process or job of taking X-ray photographs ► **radiographer** /-fə(r)/ n person working in a hospital whose job is to take X-ray photographs

radiology /,reɪdi'ɒlədʒi/ n [U] study and use of different types of radiation in medicine ► **radiologist** n

radish /'rædɪʃ/ n small crisp red or white root vegetable with a strong taste, eaten raw in salads

radium /'reɪdiəm/ n (symb Ra) radioactive chemical element used in the treatment of some diseases

radius /'reɪdiəs/ n (pl radii /-diaɪ/) 1 (length of a) straight line from the centre of a circle to the side 2 circular area measured from a central point: *within a two-mile ~ of the factory*

raffia /'ræfiə/ n [U] soft fibre from the leaves of a type of palm tree, used for making mats, etc

raffle /'ræfl/ n way of getting money (esp for charity) by selling numbered tickets that may win prizes ● **raffle** v [T] offer sth as a prize in a raffle

raft /rɑ:ft/ n 1 flat floating structure of logs fastened together, used as a boat 2 small inflatable boat ► **rafting** n [U] sport or activity of travelling down a river on a raft: *We went white-water ~ing in Vermont.*

rafter /'rɑ:ftə(r)/ n large sloping piece of wood that supports a roof

rag /ræɡ/ n 1 [C,U] piece of old torn cloth 2 [C] (infml, disapprov) newspaper 3 [U,C] (GB) amusing public event held by students to collect money for charity [IDM] **in rags** wearing very old torn clothes

rage /reɪdʒ/ n [U,C] feeling of violent anger that is difficult to control [IDM] **be all the rage** (infml) be very popular and fashionable ● **rage** v [I] 1 show that you are very angry with sb or with sth, esp by shouting 2 (of storms) continue in a violent way

ragged /'ræɡɪd/ adj 1 (of clothes) old and torn 2 (of people) wearing old or torn clothes 3 rough; uneven ► **raggedly** adv

ragtime /'ræɡtaɪm/ n [U] popular 1920s jazz music

raid /reɪd/ n 1 short surprise attack on an enemy position 2 surprise visit by the police looking for criminals or illegal goods 3 attack on a building, etc in order to commit a crime: *a bank ~* ● **raid** v [T] make a raid on sb/sth ► **raider** n person who makes a raid(3) on a place

rail /reɪl/ n 1 [C] wooden or metal bar put round sth as a barrier or for support 2 [C] bar fixed to the wall for hanging things on: *a towel ~* 3 [C, usu pl] steel bar on which trains run 4 [U] railways as a means of transport: *travel by ~* ● **rail** v [PV] **rail sth in/off** surround/separate sth with rails ■ **railing** n [C, usu pl] fence made of upright metal bars ■ **railroad** n (US) = RAILWAY ■ **railway** n 1 track on which trains run 2 system of such tracks, with the trains, etc

rain /reɪn/ n [U,sing] water that falls in drops from the clouds ● **rain** v 1 [I] (used with *it*) fall as rain: *It ~ed all day.* 2 [I, T] ~(**down/on**) (cause sth to) fall on sb/sth in large quantities [PV] **be rained off** (US **be rained out**) (of an event) be cancelled or have to stop because of rain ■ **rainbow** /'reɪnbəʊ/ n curve of many colours seen in the sky when the sun shines through rain ■ **raincoat** n light waterproof coat ■ **rainfall** n [U] amount of rain that falls in a certain area during a particular time ■ 'rainforest n thick forest in tropical areas with heavy rainfall

rainy /'reɪni/ adj (-ier, -iest) having or bringing a lot of rain [IDM] save, keep, etc sth for a rainy day save sth, esp money, for a time when you will really need it

raise /reɪz/ v [T] **1** lift or move sth to a higher level **2** increase the amount or level of sth: ~ sb's hopes (= make sb more hopeful) ◇ ~ your voice (= speak louder) **3** bring or collect money or people together: ~ money for charity ◇ ~ an army **4** bring sth up for discussion or discussion: ~ a new point **5** cause or produce sth; make sth appear: ~ doubts **6** (esp US) look after a child or young animal until it is able to take care of itself **7** breed farm animals; grow crops [IDM] raise hell (infml) protest angrily about sth ▶ raise the roof (cause sb to) make a lot of noise in a building, eg by cheering ● raise n (US) = RISE² (3)

raisin /'reɪzn/ n dried sweet grape

rake /reɪk/ n garden tool with a long handle and a row of metal points at the end ● rake v [I, T] pull a rake over a surface in order to level it or to remove sth: She ~d the leaves into a pile. [PV] rake sth in (infml) earn a lot of money: She's really raking it in! rake sth up (infml, disapprov) remind people of sth unpleasant that happened in the past ▶ 'rake-off n (infml) (usu dishonest) share of profits

rally /'ræli/ n (pl -ies) **1** large public meeting, esp one held to support a particular idea or political party **2** (GB) race for motor vehicles on public roads **3** long series of hits of the ball in tennis, etc ● rally v (pt, pp -ied) **1** [I, T] (cause people to) come together to help or support sb/sth **2** [I] become healthier, stronger, etc after a period of illness, weakness, etc [PV] rally round/around (sb) (of a group of people) work together to help sb in a time of need

RAM /ræm/ n [U] random-access memory; computer memory in which data can be changed and which can be looked at in any order

ram /ræm/ n **1** male sheep **2** = BATTERING RAM (BATTER) ● ram (-mm-) v [T] **1** (of a vehicle) drive into or hit another vehicle with force, or ram sth deliberately **2** push sth somewhere with force

ramble /'ræmbl/ n long walk for pleasure ● ramble v [I] **1** walk for pleasure, esp in the countryside **2** talk about sb/sth in a confused way, esp for a long time **3** (of a plant) grow wildly ▶ rambler n ▶ rambling adj **1** (esp of buildings) extending in many

directions irregularly **2** (of speech or writing) long and confused

ramification /ˌræmɪfɪ'keɪʃn/ n [C, usu pl] one of the large number of complicated and unexpected results of an action or decision

ramp /ræmp/ n **1** slope that joins two parts of a road, building, etc when one is higher than the other **2** (US) = SLIP ROAD (SLIP¹)

rampage /ræm'peɪdʒ/ v [I] move through a place wildly, usu causing damage ● rampage n [usu sing] sudden period of wild or violent behaviour, often causing damage: Football fans went on the ~ in the city.

rampant /'ræmpənt/ adj **1** (of sth bad) spreading uncontrollably **2** (of plants) growing very fast

rampart /'ræmpɑːt/ n wide bank of earth built to defend a fort, etc

ramshackle /'ræmʃækl/ adj (of a house or vehicle) almost collapsing

ran pt of RUN¹

ranch /rɑːntʃ/ n large farm, esp in the US, where cattle are bred ▶ rancher n person who owns or manages a ranch

rancid /'rænsɪd/ adj (of fatty foods) tasting or smelling bad because no longer fresh

rancour (US -cor) /'ræŋkə(r)/ n [U] (fml) feelings of hatred because you think sb has done sth unfair to you ▶ rancorous /-kərəs/ adj

random /'rændəm/ adj done, chosen, etc without a definite plan or pattern ● random n [IDM] at random without thinking or deciding in advance what is going to happen ■ random 'access n [U] (computing) ability in a computer to go straight to data items without having to read through items stored previously ■ random-access 'memory n [U] (computing) = RAM ▶ randomly adv

randy /'rændi/ adj (-ier, -iest) (infml, GB) sexually excited

rang pt of RING¹

range¹ /reɪndʒ/ n [C, usu sing] group or set of similar things; variety: sell a wide ~ of books [C, usu sing] limits between which sth varies **3** [C, U] distance over which sth can be seen or heard **4** [C, U] distance over which a gun or other weapon can hit things: shot him at close ~ **5** [C] line or group of mountains or hills **6** [C] area of land where people practise shooting

range² /reɪndʒ/ v [I] vary between limits: Prices ~ from £70 to £100. **2** [T] (fml) arrange people or things in a particular position or order [PV] range over sth include a variety of different subjects

ranger /'reɪndʒə(r)/ n person whose

job is to take care of a forest or large park

rank¹ /ræŋk/ n **1** [U,C] position sb has in an organization or in society **2** [C,U] position sb has in the army, navy, etc **3** (**the ranks**) [pl] ordinary soldiers, not officers **4** [C] line or row of people or things: *a taxi ∼* ● **rank** v [I, T] be or put sth/sb in a certain position or class: *∼ among the world's best* ■ **the ,rank and 'file** n [sing, with sing or pl verb] ordinary members of an organization, not its leaders

rank² /ræŋk/ *adj* **1** smelling bad **2** (of sth bad) complete **3** (of plants) growing too thickly

rankle /ˈræŋkl/ v [I] cause lasting bitterness or anger

ransack /ˈrænsæk/ v [T] search a place thoroughly leaving it very untidy

ransom /ˈrænsəm/ n money paid to set a prisoner free ● **ransom** v [T] get the freedom of sb by paying a ransom

rant /rænt/ v [I] speak or complain about sth loudly and angrily

rap /ræp/ n **1** [C] quick sharp hit or knock **2** [U] type of modern music with a fast rhythm and words which are spoken fast [IDM] **take the rap (for sb/sth)** (*infml*) be punished, esp for sth you have not done ● **rap** v (**-pp-**) [I, T] hit sth lightly and quickly

rape /reɪp/ v [T] force sb to have sex with you when they do not want to by threatening them or using violence ● **rape** n [C,U] **1** crime of forcing sb to have sex with you, esp using violence **2** (*lit*) act of spoiling or destroying an area ▸ **rapist** n

rapid /ˈræpɪd/ adj done or happening very quickly ▸ **rapidity** /rəˈpɪdəti/ n [U] ▸ **rapidly** adv ▸ **rapids** n [pl] part of a river where the water flows very fast, usu over rocks

rappel /ræˈpel/ (*US*) v = ABSEIL

rapport /ræˈpɔː(r)/ n [sing, U] friendly relationship and understanding

rapt /ræpt/ adj (*written*) so deep in thought that you are not aware of other things

rapture /ˈræptʃə(r)/ n [U] (*fml*) great happiness [IDM] **be in, go into, etc raptures (about/over sb/sth)** feel great pleasure or enthusiasm for sb/sth ▸ **rapturous** adj: *rapturous applause*

rare /reə(r)/ adj (**∼r**, **∼st**) **1** not common **2** (of meat) lightly cooked ▸ **rarely** adv rashness n [U]

rarefied /ˈreərɪfaɪd/ adj understood by only a small group of people who share a particular area of knowledge **2** (of air) containing less oxygen than usual

raring /ˈreərɪŋ/ adj **∼to** (*infml*) very keen to do sth

rarity /ˈreərəti/ n (*pl* **-ies**) **1** [C] unusual, and therefore interesting, person or thing **2** [U] quality of being rare

rascal /ˈrɑːskl/ n **1** naughty child **2** (*old-fash*) dishonest man

rash /ræʃ/ n **1** [C] area of red spots on a person's skin, caused by illness or a reaction to sth **2** [sing] series of unpleasant things that happen over a short period of time: *a ∼ of strikes* ● **rash** adj acting or done without care about or careful thought ▸ **rashly** adv ▸ **rashness** n [U]

rasher /ˈræʃə(r)/ n thin slice of bacon

rasp /rɑːsp/ n **1** [sing] unpleasant harsh sound **2** [C] metal tool used for making rough surfaces smooth ● **rasp** v [I, T] say sth in an unpleasant harsh voice

raspberry /ˈrɑːzbəri/ n (*pl* **-ies**) **1** small dark red berry that grows on bushes **2** (*infml*) rude noise made by sticking out the tongue and blowing

rat /ræt/ n **1** animal like, but larger than, a mouse **2** (*infml*) unpleasant or disloyal person [IDM] **the rat race** (*disapprov*) endless competition for success ● **rat** v (**-tt-**) [PV] **rat on sb** (*infml*) tell sb in authority about sth wrong that sb else has done ▸ **ratty** adj (**-ier**, **-iest**) (*GB, infml*) irritable

rate¹ /reɪt/ n [C] **1** measure of the speed at which sth happens: *a ∼ of 3 miles per hour* **2** measure of the number of times sth happens or exists in a period of time: *the birth/divorce ∼* **3** fixed price that is charged or paid for sth: *postage ∼s* **4** (**rates**) [pl] (in Britain) local tax paid by businesses for land and buildings that they use [IDM] **at any rate** (*spoken*) whatever happens **at this/that rate** (*spoken*) if things continue

rate² /reɪt/ v [T] **1** consider sb/sth in the way that is mentioned: *He is generally ∼d as one of the best players.* **2** place sb/sth in a position on a scale in relation to other similar people or things **3** deserve to be treated in a particular way: *The film didn't ∼ a mention in the press.*

rather /ˈrɑːðə(r)/ adv **1** fairly; to some degree: *They were ∼ surprised.* **2** used to correct sth you have said or to clarify sth: *last night, or ∼ early this morning* [IDM] **would rather...** (**than**) would prefer to: *I'd ∼ walk than go by bus.*

ratify /ˈrætɪfaɪ/ v (*pt, pp* **-ied**) [T] make an agreement officially valid by voting for or signing it ▸ **ratification** /ˌrætɪfɪˈkeɪʃn/ n [U]

rating /ˈreɪtɪŋ/ n **1** [C,U] grade or position of quality **2** [pl] figures showing the popularity of television programmes **3** [C] (*GB*) sailor in the navy who is not an officer

ratio /ˈreɪʃiəʊ/ *n* (*pl* ~**s**) relationship between two amounts: *The ~ of men to women was 3 to 1.*

ration /ˈræʃn/ *n* **1** [C] fixed amount of food, fuel, etc allowed to one person, eg during a war **2** (**rations**) [*pl*] fixed amount of food given regularly to soldiers ● **ration** *v* [T] limit the amount of sth that sb is allowed to have

rational /ˈræʃnəl/ *adj* **1** based on reason rather than emotions **2** (of a person) able to think clearly ▶ **rationally** /-ʃnəli/ *adv*

rationale /ˌræʃəˈnɑːl/ *n* (*fml*) reasons which explain a decision, course of action, belief, etc

rationalize (*also* **-ise**) /ˈræʃnəlaɪz/ *v* **1** [I, T] think and offer reasons for sth that seems unreasonable **2** [T] make changes to a system, business, etc to make it more efficient, esp by spending less money ▶ **rationalization** (*also* **-isation**) /ˌræʃnəlaɪˈzeɪʃn/ *n* [C, U]

rattle /ˈrætl/ *v* **1** [I, T] (cause sth to) make a series of short loud sounds **2** [T] (*infml*) make sb nervous [PV] **rattle sth off** repeat sth from memory without having to think too hard ● **rattle** *n* **1** rattling sound **2** baby's toy that produces a rattling sound ■ **rattlesnake** *n* poisonous American snake that makes a rattling noise with its tail

ratty → RAT

raucous /ˈrɔːkəs/ *adj* sounding loud and harsh ▶ **raucously** *adv*

ravage /ˈrævɪdʒ/ *v* [T] badly damage sth ▶ **ravages** (**the ravages of sth**) *n* [*pl*] the destruction caused by sth

rave /reɪv/ *v* [I] ~ **about** (*infml*) talk with great enthusiasm about sth **2** shout loudly or angrily at sb ● **rave re'view** *n* newspaper or magazine article that praises a new film, book, etc ▶ **raving** *adv, adj* completely (mad)

raven /ˈreɪvn/ *n* large black bird like a crow ● **raven** *adj* (*lit*) (of hair) shiny and black

ravenous /ˈrævənəs/ *adj* very hungry ▶ **ravenously** *adv*

ravine /rəˈviːn/ *n* deep narrow steep-sided valley

ravish /ˈrævɪʃ/ *v* [T] (*lit*) **1** (of a man) force a woman to have sex **2** (*esp passive*) give sb great pleasure ▶ **ravishing** *adj* very beautiful

raw /rɔː/ *adj* **1** not cooked **2** in the natural state: *~ materials* **3** (of people) not experienced **4** (of skin) sore and painful **5** (of the weather) very cold

ray /reɪ/ *n* **1** narrow line of light,

heat, etc **2** ~ (**of**) small amount of sth good: *a ~ of hope*

rayon /ˈreɪɒn/ *n* [U] smooth fabric used for making clothes

raze /reɪz/ *v* [T] (*usu passive*) destroy a building, town, etc completely

razor /ˈreɪzə(r)/ *n* instrument used for shaving: *a cut-throat/disposable ~*

Rd *abbr* (in written addresses) Road

re /riː/ *prep* (*written*) used at the beginning of an email, letter, etc to introduce the subject that it is about

re- /riː/ *prefix* again: *refill*

reach /riːtʃ/ *v* **1** [T] arrive at a place; achieve an aim: *~ London* ◇ *~ an agreement* **2** [I, T] stretch out your hand or arm to touch or take sth: *He ~ed for his gun.* ◇ *Can you ~ the book on the top shelf?* **3** [I, T] go as far as sth: *The water ~es (down) to the river.* **4** [T] communicate with sb, esp by telephone ● **reach** *n* **1** [*sing, U*] distance that can be reached: *Medicines should be kept out of ~ of children.* **2** [C, *usu pl*] part of a river

react /riˈækt/ *v* [I] **1** ~ (**to**) behave differently as a result of sth **2** ~ (**with**) (*chem*) have an effect on another substance [PV] **react against sth/sb** behave in a certain way in opposition to sth

reaction /riˈækʃn/ *n* **1** [C, U] what you do, say or think as a result of sth that has happened **2** [U] opposition to political or social change **3** [C] (*chem*) change caused in a substance by the effect of another ▶ **reactionary** /-ʃənri/ *n, adj* (*pl* -**ies**) (person) opposed to political or social change

reactor /riˈæktə(r)/ *n* = NUCLEAR REACTOR (NUCLEAR)

read /riːd/ *v* (*pt, pp* **read** /red/) **1** [I, T] look at and understand sth written or printed: *Can you ~ music?* **2** [I, T] go through written words, etc in silence or aloud to others: *~ a book* **3** [T] understand sth: *~ sb's thoughts* **4** [I] (of a piece of writing) have sth written on it; give a particular impression when read: *The sign ~s 'No Entry'.* ◇ *Her reports always ~ well.* **5** [T] (of measuring instruments) show a certain weight, pressure, etc **6** [T] study a subject at university **7** [T] (of a computer or the user) take information from a disk [IDM] **read between the lines** find a meaning that is not openly stated ▶ **readable** *adj* that is easy or pleasant to read ■ **read-only 'memory** *n* [U] (*computing*) = ROM ■ **'read-out** *n* (*computing*) display of information on a computer screen

reader /ˈriːdə(r)/ *n* **1** person who reads **2** book that gives students practice in reading **3** (*usu* **Reader**) (in Britain) senior university teacher ▶ **readership** n [sing] number or type of people who read a particular newspaper, etc

reading /'riːdɪŋ/ n 1 [C] act of reading sth 2 [C] books, articles, etc that are intended to be read: *light ~* (= not serious)*~* 3 [C] way in which sth is understood: *My ~ of the situation is...* 4 [C] amount, etc shown on a measuring instrument 5 [C] (GB) (in Parliament) one of three stages of debate before a bill(2) becomes law

ready /'redi/ adj (-ier, -iest) 1 ~for/to prepared and fit for action or use: *~ for action* ◇ *~ to act* 2 easily available: *a ~ source of income* 3 willing 4 ~to likely to do sth: *She looked ~ to collapse.* 5 quick and clever: *a ~ answer* ▶ **readily** adv 1 quickly and easily 2 without hesitation ■ **readiness** n [U] ● **ready** adj already done: *~-cooked meals* ● **ready** n [IDM] **at the ready** available to be used immediately ■ **ready-made** adj ready to use or wear immediately

real /rɪəl/ adj 1 existing as a fact 2 true or actual 3 genuine and not false or artificial ● **real** adv (US, infml) very ■ **real estate** n [U] (esp US) 1 property in the form of land and buildings 2 business of selling houses or land ■ **real estate agent** n = ESTATE AGENT (ESTATE)

realism /'rɪəlɪzəm/ n [U] 1 acceptance of the facts of a situation 2 (in art and literature) showing of things as they are in real life ▶ **realist** n ▶ **realistic** /ˌrɪə'lɪstɪk/ adj

reality /ri'æləti/ n (pl -ies) 1 [U] true situation and the problems that actually exist in life 2 [C] something actually seen or experienced: *the realities of war* [IDM] **in reality** in actual fact

realize (also -ise) /'rɪəlaɪz/ v [T] 1 understand or become aware of sth 2 make sth, eg plans or fears, happen 3 (fml) be sold for a particular amount of money ▶ **realization** (also -isation) /ˌrɪəlaɪ-'zeɪʃn, rɪəl-/ n [U]

really /'rɪəli, 'rɪəli/ adv 1 in reality; truly 2 used to emphasize an adjective or adverb: *I'm ~ sorry.* 3 (spoken) used to show interest, surprise, etc at what sb is saying

realm /relm/ n 1 area of interest or knowledge 2 (fml) kingdom

Realtor™ /'rɪəltə(r)/ n (US) = ESTATE AGENT (ESTATE)

reap /riːp/ v 1 [T] obtain sth good, esp as a result of hard work 2 [I, T] cut and collect a crop, esp corn

rear¹ /rɪə(r)/ n (usu the rear) [sing] back part of sth ● **rear** adj at or near the back of sth ■ **the 'rearguard**

n soldiers protecting the back part of an army

rear² /rɪə(r)/ v 1 [T] look after young children or animals until they are fully grown 2 [T] breed or keep animals, eg on a farm 3 [I] ~(up) (of a horse) raise itself on its back legs

reason¹ /'riːzn/ n 1 [C] cause or an explanation for sth that has happened or that sb has done 2 [C] fact that makes it right or fair to do sth 3 [U] power of the mind to think logically, etc: *lose your ~* (= go mad) 4 [U] what is possible practical or right: *He needs a job and is willing to do anything within ~.*

reason² /'riːzn/ v 1 [I] form a judgement about sth after careful thought 2 [I] use your power to think and understand sth [PV] **reason with sb** talk to sb in order to persuade them to be more sensible ▶ **reasoning** n [U] opinions and ideas based on logical thinking

reasonable /'riːznəbl/ adj 1 fair; sensible 2 not too expensive ▶ **reasonably** adv 1 quite 2 in a reasonable way

reassure /ˌriːə'ʃɔː(r)/ v [T] remove sb's worries ▶ **reassurance** n [U, C]

rebate /'riːbeɪt/ n part of tax, rent, etc paid back

rebel /'rebl/ n 1 person who fights against the government 2 person who opposes authority ● **rebel** /rɪ'bel/ v (-ll-) [I] ~(against) fight against or refuse to obey an authority, eg a government ▶ **rebellion** /rɪ'beljən/ n [C,U] act of rebelling ▶ **rebellious** adj

reboot /ˌriː'buːt/ v [I, T] (computing) (cause a computer to) switch off and then start again immediately

rebound /rɪ'baʊnd/ v 1 [I] bounce back after hitting sth 2 ~(on) (fml) have unpleasant effects on the doer 3 (business) (of prices, shares, etc) rise again after falling ● **rebound** /'riːbaʊnd/ n [IDM] **on the rebound** while you are sad and confused, esp after a relationship has ended

rebuff /rɪ'bʌf/ n (fml) unkind refusal or answer ▶ **rebuff** v [T]

rebuke /rɪ'bjuːk/ v [T] (fml) speak severely to sb for doing sth wrong ▶ **rebuke** n [C,U]

recall /rɪ'kɔːl/ v [T] 1 remember sth; remind sb of sth 2 order sb/sth to return or be returned ● **recall** /rɪ'kɔːl; also 'riːkɔːl/ n 1 ability to remember sth 2 [sing] official order for sb/sth to return or be given back

recap /'riːkæp/ v (-pp-) [I, T] short for RECAPITULATE

recapitulate /ˌriːkə'pɪtʃuleɪt/ v [I, T] (fml) repeat the main points of what has been said, decided, etc ► **recapitulation** /ˌriːkəˌpɪtʃuˈleɪʃn/ n [C, U]

recede /rɪˈsiːd/ v [I] 1 move gradually away or back 2 slope backwards

receipt /rɪˈsiːt/ n 1 [C] piece of paper showing that goods or services have been paid for 2 [U] (fml) act of receiving sth 3 (**receipts**) [pl] money received by a business, bank or government

receivable /rɪˈsiːvəbl/ adj (business) (of bills, accounts, etc) for which money has not yet been received

receive /rɪˈsiːv/ v [T] 1 get or accept sth sent or offered 2 experience or be given a particular type of treatment or injury: I ~d a warm welcome from the crowd. 3 accept sb as a member or visitor 4 change broadcast signals into sounds or pictures ► **receiver** n 1 part of a telephone that is held to the ear 2 piece of radio or television equipment that changes broadcast signals into sounds or pictures 3 (law) official chosen to take charge of a company that is bankrupt 4 person who buys or accepts stolen goods

recent /ˈriːsnt/ adj that happened, began, etc a short time ago ► **recently** adv not long ago

receptacle /rɪˈseptəkl/ n (fml) container

reception /rɪˈsepʃn/ n 1 part of a hotel, office building, etc where visitors are received 2 [C] formal social occasion: a wedding ~ 3 [sing] type of welcome that is given to sb: be given a warm ~ 4 [U] quality of radio or television signals received ► **receptionist** /-ʃənɪst/ n person whose job is to deal with visitors to a hotel, office building, etc

receptive /rɪˈseptɪv/ adj willing to consider new ideas

recess /rɪˈses/ n 1 [C, U] period of time when work is stopped 2 [C] area of a room where part of a wall is set back 3 [C, U usu pl] secret or hidden part of a place

recession /rɪˈseʃn/ n 1 [C, U] difficult time for the economy of a country: The economy is in deep ~. 2 [U] (fml) backward movement of sth

recipe /ˈresəpi/ n 1 set of instructions for preparing a food dish 2 way of achieving sth: a ~ for disaster

recipient /rɪˈsɪpiənt/ n (fml) person who receives sth

reciprocal /rɪˈsɪprəkl/ adj given and received in return: ~ trade agreements ► **reciprocally** /-kli/ adv

reciprocate /rɪˈsɪprəkeɪt/ v [I, T] (fml) behave or feel towards sb in the same way as they behave or feel towards you

recital /rɪˈsaɪtl/ n performance of music or poetry by one person or a small group

recite /rɪˈsaɪt/ v [T] 1 say a poem, etc aloud from memory 2 say aloud a list or series of things ► **recitation** /ˌresɪˈteɪʃn/ n [C, U]

reckless /ˈrekləs/ adj not caring about danger or the effects of sth ► **recklessly** adv ► **recklessness** n [U]

reckon /ˈrekən/ v [T] 1 (infml) think sth: I ~ we ought to go now. 2 calculate an amount, a number, etc [PV] **reckon on sth** rely on sth happening **reckon with sb/sth** consider or treat sb/sth as important: a force to be ~ed with (= that cannot be ignored) 2 consider sth as a possible problem: I didn't ~ with getting caught in so much traffic. ► **reckoning** n [U, C] 1 calculation 2 time when sb's actions will be judged and they may be punished: the day of ~ing

reclaim /rɪˈkleɪm/ v [T] 1 ask for sth to be given back 2 make land suitable for use ► **reclamation** /ˌrekləˈmeɪʃn/ n [U]

recline /rɪˈklaɪn/ v [I] (fml) lie back or down

recluse /rɪˈkluːs/ n person who lives alone and avoids other people

recognize (also **-ise**) /ˈrekəgnaɪz/ v [T] 1 know again sb/sth that you have seen, heard, etc before 2 admit that sth exists or is true: They ~d the need to take the problem seriously. 3 accept and approve of sb/sth officially: refuse to ~ a new government 4 give sb official thanks for sth they have done ► **recognition** /ˌrekəgˈnɪʃn/ n [U] ► **recognizable** adj

recoil /rɪˈkɔɪl/ v [I] 1 (written) move back suddenly in fear, dislike, etc 2 (of a gun) move back quickly when fired ► **recoil** /ˈriːkɔɪl/ n [U, sing]

recollect /ˌrekəˈlekt/ v [I, T] remember sth ► **recollection** /ˌrekəˈlekʃn/ n 1 [U] ability to remember sth; act of remembering 2 [C] thing that you remember from the past

recommend /ˌrekəˈmend/ v [T] 1 praise sb/sth as suitable for a job/purpose: Can you ~ a good hotel? 2 advise sb; advise sb to do sth: I ~ leaving/you leave early. ► **recommendation** /-menˈdeɪʃn/ n [C, U]

recompense /ˈrekəmpens/ v [T] (fml) reward sb for work; repay sb for losses or harm ● **recompense** n [sing, U] (fml) reward or repayment

reconcile /ˈrekənsaɪl/ v [T] 1 find a way of dealing with two more ideas, etc that seem to be opposed to each other 2 make people become friends again after an argument 3 ~ sb/yourself (to) make sb/yourself accept an unpleasant situation ► **reconciliation** /ˌrekənsɪliˈeɪʃn/ n [U, C]

reconnaissance /rɪˈkɒnɪsns/ n

reed

[C, U] act of getting information about an area for military purposes

reconnoitre (*US* **-ter**) /ˌrekə-ˈnɔɪtə(r)/ *v* [I, T] get information about an area for military purposes, by using soldiers, planes, etc

record¹ /ˈrekɔːd/ *n* 1 [C] written account of facts, events, etc 2 [C] round flat piece of plastic on which sound has been recorded 3 [C] the best result or level ever achieved: *a new world ~ in the 100 metres* ◇ *~ profits* 4 [sing] known facts about sb's character or past [IDM] **off the record** unofficial and not for publication **on record** officially noted ■ **'record player** *n* machine for producing sound from records(2)

record² /rɪˈkɔːd/ *v* 1 [T] keep a permanent account of facts or events by writing them down, filming them, etc 2 [I, T] make a copy of music, a film, etc by storing it on tape or a disc to listen to or watch again 3 [T] (of a measuring instrument) show a particular measurement or amount

recorder /rɪˈkɔːdə(r)/ *n* 1 machine for recording sounds or pictures or both 2 musical instrument played by blowing into one end 3 (*GB*) judge in certain law courts in Britain and the US

recording /rɪˈkɔːdɪŋ/ *n* sounds or pictures recorded on a tape or disc

recount¹ /rɪˈkaʊnt/ *v* [T] (*fml*) tell sb about sth, esp sth you have experienced

recount² /ˌriːˈkaʊnt/ *v* [T] count sth again, esp votes ▶ **recount** /ˈriːkaʊnt/ *n*

recoup /rɪˈkuːp/ *v* [T] get back money that you have spent or lost

recourse /rɪˈkɔːs/ *n* [U] fact of having to, or being able to, use sth that can provide help in a difficult situation: *The government, when necessary, has ~ to the armed forces.*

recover /rɪˈkʌvə(r)/ *v* 1 [I] ~(**from**) get well again after an illness, etc ● **well** 2 [T] get back sth lost or stolen 3 [T] get control of yourself, your senses, etc again: *to ~ consciousness* ▶ **recovery** *n* [U, C, usu sing]

recreation /ˌrekriˈeɪʃn/ *n* [C, U] (form of) play or amusement or way of spending your free time

recrimination /rɪˌkrɪmɪˈneɪʃn/ *n* [C, usu pl, U] (act of) accusing and blaming each other

recruit /rɪˈkruːt/ *n* 1 new member of the armed forces or the police 2 person who joins an organization, company, etc ● **recruit** *v* [T] find sb to join a company, the armed forces, etc ▶ **recruitment** *n* [U]

rectangle /ˈrektæŋgl/ *n* flat four-sided shape with four angles of 90° ▶ **rectangular** /rekˈtæŋgjələ(r)/ *adj*

rectify /ˈrektɪfaɪ/ *v* (*pt, pp* **-ied**) [T] put sth right: *~ an error*

rector /ˈrektə(r)/ *n* Anglican priest in charge of a parish ▶ **rectory** /ˈrektəri/ *n* (*pl* **-ies**) rector's house

rectum /ˈrektəm/ *n* (*anat*) lower end of the large intestine

recuperate /rɪˈkuːpəreɪt/ *v* [I] ~ (**from**) (*fml*) become strong again after an illness, etc ▶ **recuperation** /rɪˌkuːpəˈreɪʃn/ *n* [U]

recur /rɪˈkɜː(r)/ *v* (**-rr-**) [I] happen again ▶ **recurrence** /rɪˈkʌrəns/ *n* [C, U] repetition ▶ **recurrent** /rɪˈkʌrənt/ *adj*

recycle /ˌriːˈsaɪkl/ *v* [T] treat sth already used so that it can be used again

red /red/ *adj* (**~der, ~dest**) 1 of the colour of blood 2 (of the face) bright red or pink, because of embarrassment or anger 3 (of hair) reddish-brown 4 (*infml, pol*) having very left-wing political opinions ■ **red 'herring** *n* unimportant fact, event, etc that takes people's attention away from the main point ■ **red 'tape** *n* [U] unnecessary official rules that cause delay ● **red** *n* 1 [C, U] the colour of blood: *dressed in ~* 2 [C, U] red wine 3 [C] (*infml, pol*) person with very left-wing political opinions [IDM] **be in the red** (*infml*) owe money to the bank ■ **'redhead** *n* person who has red hair ■ **red-'hot** *adj* so hot that it glows red

redden /ˈredn/ *v* [I, T] become or make sth red

redeem /rɪˈdiːm/ *v* [T] 1 make sth seem less bad: *a film with no ~ing features* 2 buy sth back by payment ▶ **redemption** /rɪˈdempʃn/ *n* [U]

redouble /ˌriːˈdʌbl/ *v* [T] increase or strengthen sth: *~ your efforts*

redress /rɪˈdres/ *v* [T] (*fml*) correct sth that is wrong or unfair [IDM] **redress the balance** make a situation equal or fair again ● **redress** *n* [U] (*fml*) payment, etc to compensate for sth wrong that has happened to sb

reduce /rɪˈdjuːs/ *v* [T] make sth less or smaller in size, price, etc [PV] **reduce sb/sth** (**from sth**) **to** (**doing**) **sth** force sb/sth into a certain state or condition: *He was ~d to tears.* ▶ **reduction** /rɪˈdʌkʃn/ *n* 1 [C, U] (instance of) reducing sth: *~s in price* 2 [C] small copy of a picture, map, etc

redundant /rɪˈdʌndənt/ *adj* 1 (*GB*) (of a person) dismissed from a job because no longer needed 2 not needed or useful ▶ **redundancy** /-dənsi/ *n* [C, U] (*pl* **-ies**)

reed /riːd/ *n* 1 tall plant like grass

that grows near water **2** (in some wind instruments) piece of cane or metal that vibrates to produce sound

reef /riːf/ n **1** line of rocks, sand, etc just below or above the surface of the sea

reek /riːk/ n [sing] strong unpleasant smell ● **reek** v [I] ~ (**of**) smell unpleasantly of sth

reel /riːl/ n **1** cylinder on which thread, wire, film, etc is wound **2** length of thread, film, etc on one reel **3** (music for a) fast Scottish, Irish or American dance ● **reel** v [I] **1** move unsteadily, eg because you are drunk **2** feel very shocked or upset about sth [PV] **reel sth in/out** wind sth on/off a reel: *I slowly ~ed the fish in.* **reel sth off** say sth quickly without having to think about it

refectory /rɪˈfektri/ n (pl -ies) large dining room, eg in a college

refer /rɪˈfɜː(r)/ v (-rr-) [PV] **refer to sb/sth** (**as sth**) mention or speak about sb/sth **refer to sb/sth 1** describe or be connected to sb/sth **2** look at sth or ask a person for information: *You may ~ to your notes if you want.* **refer sb/sth to sb/sth** send sth to sb/sth for help, advice or a decision: *My GP ~red me to a specialist.*

referee /ˌrefəˈriː/ n **1** (sport) official who controls the game in some sports **2** (GB) person who agrees to write a reference(3) for you

reference /ˈrefrəns/ n [C,U] **1** (act of) referring to sb/sth **2** [C] number, word or symbol telling you where information may be found **3** [C] letter giving information about sb's character and abilities, esp for a new employer [IDM] **in/with reference to** (written) used to say what you are writing or talking about ■ **'reference book** n book, eg a dictionary or an encyclopedia, looked at for finding information

referendum /ˌrefəˈrendəm/ n (pl -dums or -da) n [C,U] direct vote by all the people on a political question

refine /rɪˈfaɪn/ v [T] **1** make a substance pure **2** improve sth by making small changes to it ▶ **refined** adj **1** (of a substance) made pure: *~d sugar* **2** (of a person) well educated and polite ▶ **refinement** n **1** [C] small change or addition to sth that improves it **2** [U] process of refining sth **3** [U] quality of being well educated and polite ▶ **refinery** n (pl -ies) factory where oil, sugar, etc is refined

reflate /ˌriːˈfleɪt/ v [I, T] increase the amount of money in an economy ▶ **reflation** /ˌriːˈfleɪʃn/ n [U]

reflect /rɪˈflekt/ v **1** [T] throw back an image, heat, sound, etc from a surface

2 [T] show the nature of sth or sb's attitude: *The book faithfully ~s his ideas.* **3** [I] ~(**on**) think deeply about sth [PV] **reflect well, badly, etc on sb/sth** make sb/sth appear to be good, bad, etc to other people ▶ **reflector** n surface that reflects light

reflection /rɪˈflekʃn/ n **1** [C] reflected image, eg in a mirror **2** [U] reflecting of light, heat, etc **3** [C,U] deep thought: *on ~* (= after thinking very carefully)

reflex /ˈriːfleks/ n (also **'reflex action**) sudden unintended movement, eg sneezing, made in response to sth

reflexive /rɪˈfleksɪv/ n, adj (gram) (word) showing that the action of the verb is performed on the subject: *a ~ verb* ◊ *In 'I cut myself', 'myself' is a ~ pronoun.*

re-form /ˌriːˈfɔːm/ v [I, T] (cause sth to) form again

reform /rɪˈfɔːm/ v [I, T] **1** improve a system, organization, etc by making changes to it **2** (cause sb to) behave better than before ● **reform** n [U,C] change or improvement made to a social system, organization, etc ▶ **reformer** n person who works to achieve social and political change

reformation /ˌrefəˈmeɪʃn/ n **1** [U] (fml) act of improving or changing sb/sth **2** (**the Reformation**) [sing] 16th century religious movement that led to the forming of the Protestant Churches

refract /rɪˈfrækt/ v [T] (physics) make a ray of light bend where it enters water, glass, etc ▶ **refraction** /-kʃn/ n [U]

refrain /rɪˈfreɪn/ v [I] ~(**from**) (fml) not do sth ● **refrain** n lines of a song that are repeated

refresh /rɪˈfreʃ/ v [T] make sb feel less tired or hot [IDM] **refresh your/ sb's memory** remind yourself/sb of sth by referring to notes, etc ■ **re'fresher course** n course providing training on new ideas and developments in your job ▶ **refreshing** adj **1** pleasantly new or different **2** making you feel less tired or hot ▶ **refreshment** n **1** (**refreshments**) [pl] food and drink **2** (fml) fact of making sb feel stronger

refrigerate /rɪˈfrɪdʒəreɪt/ v [T] make food, etc cold in order to keep it fresh or preserve it ▶ **refrigeration** /rɪˌfrɪdʒəˈreɪʃn/ n [U] ▶ **refrigerator** n (fml) = FRIDGE

refuel /ˌriːˈfjuːəl/ v (-ll- US -l-) [I, T] fill sth or be filled with fuel: *The plane landed to ~.*

refuge /ˈrefjuːdʒ/ n [C,U] (place giving) protection from danger, trouble, etc

refugee /ˌrefjuˈdʒiː/ n person forced

to leave their country, esp because of political or religious beliefs

refund /ˈriːfʌnd/ *n* repayment ● **refund** /rɪˈfʌnd/ *v* [T] pay back money to sb

refusal /rɪˈfjuːzl/ *n* [C,U] (instance of) refusing to do, give or accept sth

refuse[1] /rɪˈfjuːz/ *v* [I, T] not give, accept or do sth: ~ *to help*

refuse[2] /ˈrefjuːs/ *n* [U] waste; rubbish

regain /rɪˈɡeɪn/ *v* [T] get sth back; recover sth: ~ *your strength*

regal /ˈriːɡl/ *adj* typical of a king or queen

regalia /rɪˈɡeɪliə/ *n* [U] special clothes worn or objects carried at official ceremonies

regard[1] /rɪˈɡɑːd/ *v* [T] **~as** think about sb/sth in a particular way: *She is ~ed as the best teacher in the school.* [IDM] **as regards sb/sth** concerning sb/sth ▶ **regarding** *prep* concerning sb/sth; about sb/sth

regard[2] /rɪˈɡɑːd/ *n* **1** [U] attention to or concern for sb/sth: *with no ~ for safety* **2** [U] (*fml*) respect for sb: *have a high ~ for sb* (**regards**) [pl] kind wishes [IDM] **in/with regard to** sth concerning sb/sth; about sb/sth ▶ **regardless of** *prep* paying no attention to sth

regatta /rɪˈɡætə/ *n* meeting for boat races

regency /ˈriːdʒənsi/ *n* (*pl* **-ies**) **1** (period of) government by a regent (= person who rules a country in place of the king or queen) **2** (**Regency**) [sing] period 1811-20 in Britain

regenerate /rɪˈdʒenəreɪt/ *v* [I, T] give new strength or life to sth/sb ▶ **regeneration** /rɪˌdʒenəˈreɪʃn/ *n* [U]

regent /ˈriːdʒənt/ *n* person who rules instead of a king or queen who is too young, ill, etc

reggae /ˈreɡeɪ/ *n* [U] West Indian popular music and dance

regime /reɪˈʒiːm/ *n* (system of) government

regiment /ˈredʒɪmənt/ *n* large group of soldiers commanded by a colonel ▶ **regimental** /ˌredʒɪˈmentl/ *adj* ▶ **regimented** *adj* (*disapprov*) involving strict discipline and/or organization

region /ˈriːdʒən/ *n* **1** large area of land **2** division of a country [IDM] **in the region of** about; approximately ▶ **regional** *adj*

register /ˈredʒɪstə(r)/ *n* **1** [C] (book containing an) official list of names, etc **2** [C] range of the voice or a musical instrument **3** [C,U] (*ling*) level of language (formal or informal) used in a piece of writing or speech ● **register** *v* **1** [I, T] record your/sb's/sth's name on an official list **2** [I, T] make your opinion know officially or publicly **3** [I, T] (of measuring instruments) show an amount **4** [I, T] (*fml*) show or express a feeling **5** [T] send sth by post, paying extra to protect it against loss

registrar /ˌredʒɪˈstrɑː(r)/ *n* keeper of official records

registration /ˌredʒɪˈstreɪʃn/ *n* [U,C] act of making an official record of sb/sth ■ **regi'stration number** (*also* **registration**) (*GB*) [C] numbers and letters on a vehicle used to identify it

registry office /ˈredʒɪstri ˌɒfɪs/ *n* place where civil marriages take place and where births, marriages and deaths are officially recorded

regret[1] /rɪˈɡret/ *v* (**-tt-**) [T] be sorry or sad about sth: *Later, I ~ted my decision to leave.* ▶ **regrettable** *adj* that is or should be regretted ▶ **regrettably** *adv*

regret[2] /rɪˈɡret/ *n* [U,C] feeling of sadness at the loss of sth or because of sth you have done ▶ **regretful** *adj* sad; sorry

regular /ˈreɡjələ(r)/ *adj* **1** happening, coming, etc repeatedly at times or places that are the same distance apart: ~ *breathing* **2** usual or normal **3** evenly shaped: *a face with ~ features* **4** (esp of verbs, nouns) changing their form in the same way as other verbs, nouns **5** belonging to the permanent armed forces: *a ~ soldier* ● **regular** *n* **1** customer who often goes to a shop, pub, restaurant, etc: *He's one of our ~s.* **2** professional soldier ▶ **regularity** /ˌreɡjuˈlærəti/ *n* [U] ▶ **regularly** *adv* at regular times or intervals

regulate /ˈreɡjuleɪt/ *v* [T] **1** control sth by means of rules **2** control the speed, pressure, etc in a machine

regulation /ˌreɡjuˈleɪʃn/ *n* **1** [C, usu pl] official rule or order **2** [U] controlling sth by means of rules ● **regulation** *adj* as required by rules: *in ~ uniform*

rehabilitate /ˌriːəˈbɪlɪteɪt/ *v* [T] help sb who has been imprisoned or ill live a normal life again ▶ **rehabilitation** /ˌriːəˌbɪlɪˈteɪʃn/ *n* [U]

rehearse /rɪˈhɜːs/ *v* [I, T] practise a play, music, etc for public performance ▶ **rehearsal** *n* [C,U]

reign /reɪn/ *n* (period of) rule of a king or queen ● **reign** *v* [i] **1** be king or queen **2** (*lit*) (of a feeling, an idea or atmosphere) be the most obvious feature: *Silence ~ed.*

reimburse /ˌriːɪmˈbɜːs/ *v* [T] (*fml*) pay back money to sb that they have spent or lost ▶ **reimbursement** *n* [U]

rein /reɪn/ *n* [C, usu pl] long narrow strap for controlling a horse

reincarnate /ˌriːɪnˈkɑːneɪt/ *v* [T]

(usu passive) bring sb back in another body after death ▶ **reincarnation** /ˌriːɪnkɑːˈneɪʃn/ n [U,C]

reindeer /ˈreɪndɪə(r)/ n (pl **reindeer**) large deer with antlers, living in cold northern regions

reinforce /ˌriːɪnˈfɔːs/ v [T] make sth stronger ▶ **reinforcement** n **1** (**reinforcements**) [pl] extra soldiers or police officers sent to a place when needed **2** [U,sing] act of making sth stronger

reinstate /ˌriːɪnˈsteɪt/ v [T] give back a job or position that has been taken away from sb ▶ **reinstatement** n [U]

reiterate /riˈɪtəreɪt/ v [T] (fml) repeat sth several times ▶ **reiteration** /riˌɪtəˈreɪʃn/ n [sing]

reject /rɪˈdʒekt/ v [T] **1** refuse to accept sth/sb **2** send sth back or throw sth away as not good enough ● **reject** /ˈriːdʒekt/ n person or thing that has been rejected ▶ **rejection** /rɪˈdʒekʃn/ n [U,C]

rejoice /rɪˈdʒɔɪs/ v [I] (fml) express great happiness about sth ▶ **rejoicing** n [U] happiness; joy

rejuvenate /rɪˈdʒuːvəneɪt/ v [T] make sb/sth look or feel younger and more lively ▶ **rejuvenation** /rɪˌdʒuːvəˈneɪʃn/ n

relapse /rɪˈlæps/ v [I] go back into a previous or worse state after making an improvement ▶ **relapse** n

relate /rɪˈleɪt/ v [T] **1** ~(to) show or make a connection between two people or things **2** ~(to) give a spoken or written report of sth; tell a story [PV] **relate to sth/sb 1** be connected with sth/sb **2** be able to understand and sympathize with sb/sth ▶ **related** adj of the same family or group; connected

relation /rɪˈleɪʃn/ n **1** (**relations**) [pl] way in which two people, countries, etc behave towards or deal with each other **2** [U,C] way in which two or more things are connected: *The fee bears no ~ to the amount of work involved.* **3** [C] member of your family ▶ **relationship** n **1** [C] way in which two people, countries, etc behave towards or deal with each other **2** [C] loving and/or sexual friendship between two people **3** [C,U] connection between two or more things

relative /ˈrelətɪv/ adj considered in relation to sth else **2** ~to (fml) with reference to sth **3** (gram) referring to an earlier noun, sentence, or part of a sentence: *a ~ clause/pronoun* ● **relative** n member of your family ▶ **relatively** adv to a fairly large degree; quite: *~ cheap food*

relax /rɪˈlæks/ v **1** [I] rest while you are doing sth enjoyable, esp after

work **2** [I, T] become or make sb calmer and less worried **3** [T] allow rules, etc to become less strict ▶ **relaxation** /ˌriːlækˈseɪʃn/ n **1** [U] ways of resting and enjoying yourself **2** [C] something pleasant you do in order to rest, esp after work ▶ **relaxed** adj calm and not worried

relay /ˈriːleɪ/ n **1** (also '**relay race**) race in which each member of a team runs, swims, etc one section of the race **2** fresh set of people or animals that replace others that are tired or have finished a period of work **3** electrical device that receives radio and television signals and sends them on again ● **relay** /ˈriːleɪ; also rɪˈleɪ/ v [T] receive and send on a message or broadcast

release /rɪˈliːs/ v [T] **1** set sb/sth free **2** allow news, etc to become known; make sth available **3** move sth from a fixed position: *~ the brake* ● **release** n **1** [U,sing] act of releasing sb/sth **2** [C] thing that is made available to the public, esp a new CD or film

relegate /ˈrelɪɡeɪt/ v [T] give a lower or less important position, rank, etc than before ▶ **relegation** /ˌrelɪˈɡeɪʃn/ n

relent /rɪˈlent/ v [I] become less strict or harsh ▶ **relentless** adj constant; harsh

relevant /ˈreləvənt/ adj connected with what is being discussed ▶ **relevance** /-əns/ n [U] ▶ **relevantly** adv

reliable /rɪˈlaɪəbl/ adj that can be trusted to do sth well ▶ **reliability** /rɪˌlaɪəˈbɪləti/ n [U] ▶ **reliably** adv

reliant /rɪˈlaɪənt/ adj ~on dependent on sb/sth ▶ **reliance** /rɪˈlaɪəns/ n [U] dependence

relic /ˈrelɪk/ n **1** something remaining from an earlier time **2** part of the body or sth that belonged to a holy person and is deeply respected

relief /rɪˈliːf/ n **1** [U,sing] lessening or ending of suffering, worry, etc: *pain* **2** [U] food, money, medicine, etc given to people in need **3** [C] person that replaces another when they have finished working for the day **4** [U,C] (way of) carving, etc in which the design stands out from a flat surface ■ **relief map** n map showing the height of hills, etc by shading or colour

relieve /rɪˈliːv/ v [T] **1** reduce or remove an unpleasant feeling or pain **2** make sth less boring, by introducing sth different **3** replace sb who is on duty [PV] **relieve sb of sth** (fml) take a responsibility or job away from sb: *He was ~d of his duties.* ▶ **relieved** adj no longer anxious

religion /rɪˈlɪdʒən/ n **1** [U] belief in

and worship of God or gods **2** [C] particular system of faith and worship based on such belief

religious /rɪˈlɪdʒəs/ adj **1** of religion **2** (of a person) believing in and practising a religion ▶ **religiously** adv regularly

relinquish /rɪˈlɪŋkwɪʃ/ v [T] (fml) stop having sth, esp unwillingly: ~ control

relish /ˈrelɪʃ/ v [T] get pleasure from sth: I don't ~ the idea of getting up so early. ● **relish 1** [U] (written) great enjoyment **2** [U,C] sauce, etc added to food to give it more flavour

reluctant /rɪˈlʌktənt/ adj unwilling ▶ **reluctance** /-əns/ n [U] ▶ **reluctantly** adv

rely /rɪˈlaɪ/ v (pt, pp -ied) [I] ~ **on** need or depend on sb/sth; trust sb/sth

remain /rɪˈmeɪn/ v (fml) **1** linking verb continue to be sth: ~ silent **2** [I] still be present after other people/ things have gone or been dealt with: Not much ~ed of the house after the fire. ◊ She ~ed in the house after her friends had left. **3** [I] still need to be done or dealt with: There are only a couple of jobs ~ing now. ▶ **remainder** n [sing, with sing or pl verb] (written) people, things or time that is left ▶ **remains** n [pl] **1** ~ (**of**) parts that are left after others have been eaten, removed, etc **2** (fml) dead body

remand /rɪˈmɑːnd/ v [T] send an accused person away from a court to wait for their trial at a later date ● **remand** n [U] (GB) process of keeping sb in prison while they are waiting for trial: He is currently being held on ~.

remark /rɪˈmɑːk/ v [I, T] ~(**on**) say or write a comment about sb/sth: They all ~ed on his youth. ● **remark** n something said or written which expresses an opinion, thought, etc ▶ **remarkable** adj unusual or surprising ▶ **remarkably** adv

remedial /rɪˈmiːdiəl/ adj aimed at solving a problem, esp by correcting sth that has been done wrong

remedy /ˈremədi/ n [C,U] (pl -ies) **1** way of putting sth right **2** cure ● **remedy** v (pt, pp -ied) [T] correct or improve sth

remember /rɪˈmembə(r)/ v **1** [I, T] have or keep an image in your memory; bring back to your mind a fact, etc that you knew **2** [T] give money, a present, etc to sb: She always ~s my birthday. [PV] **remember me to sb** used to ask sb to give your greetings to sb else ▶ **remembrance** /-brəns/ n (fml) **1** [U] act of remembering a past event or a person who is dead **2** [C] (fml) object that causes you to remember sb/sth

remind /rɪˈmaɪnd/ v [T] help sb to remember sth important that they must do: R- me to buy some more milk, will you? [PV] **remind sb of sb/sth** cause sb to think about sb/sth similar: You ~ me of your father when you do that. ▶ **reminder** n something, eg a letter, that causes a person to remember sth

reminisce /ˌremɪˈnɪs/ v [I] ~(**about**) talk about a happy time in your past ▶ **reminiscence** n [C,pl] remembered experiences ▶ **reminiscent** adj ~**of** reminding you of sb/sth

remission /rɪˈmɪʃn/ n [U,C] **1** period during which a serious illness improves for a time: The patient is in ~. **2** (GB) shortening of the time sb spends in prison, because of good behaviour **3** (fml) act of reducing or cancelling the amount of money sb has to pay

remit /ˈriːmɪt; rɪˈmɪt/ n [usu sing] (GB) area of activity over which a person or group has authority, control or influence ● **remit** /rɪˈmɪt/ v (-tt-) [T] (fml) **1** send money to a person or place **2** cancel or free sb from a debt or punishment ▶ **remittance** n sum of money remitted

remnant /ˈremnənt/ n small part of sth that is left

remonstrate /ˈremənstreɪt/ v [I] ~(**with**) (fml) protest or complain about sb/sth

remorse /rɪˈmɔːs/ n [U] ~(**for**) feeling of being extremely sorry for sth wrong that you have done ▶ **remorseful** adj ▶ **remorseless** adj (written) **1** unpleasant and not stopping **2** cruel and without pity

remote /rɪˈməʊt/ adj (~**r**, ~**st**) **1** ~ (from) far away from places where people live **2** far away in time **3** (of a computer, etc) that you can connect to from far away, using an electronic link **4** ~(**from**) very different from sth **5** (of a person) unfriendly; not interested in others **6** very small: a ~ possibility ■ re,mote con'trol n **1** [U] ability to control an apparatus from a distance using radio or electrical signals **2** [C] device that allows you to operate a television, etc from a distance ▶ **remotely** adv to a very small degree ▶ **remoteness** n [U]

remove /rɪˈmuːv/ v [T] **1** take sth away or off **2** get rid of sth: ~ stains/ doubts **3** dismiss sb from a job [IDM] **be far, further, furthest removed from sth** be very different from sth ▶ **removal** n **1** [U] act of removing sth/sb **2** [C] (GB) act of moving furniture, etc to a different home ▶ **remover** n [C,U]: a stain ~ er

remunerate /rɪˈmjuːnəreɪt/ v [T] (fml) pay sb for work done ▶ **remuneration** /rɪˌmjuːnəˈreɪʃn/ n

[C, U] ▶ **remunerative** /-ərətɪv/ *adj* profitable

renaissance /rɪˈneɪsns/ *n* [sing] **1 (the Renaissance)** renewed interest in art and literature in Europe in the 14th-16th centuries **2** any similar renewed interest in sth

renal /ˈriːnl/ *adj* (anat) of the kidneys

render /ˈrendə(r)/ *v* [T] (fml) **1** cause sb/sth to be in a particular state or condition: *The shock ~ed him speechless.* **2** give sb sth: *a reward for services ~ed* **3** perform sth **4** translate sth ▶ **rendering** *n* performance

rendezvous /ˈrɒndɪvuː; deɪ-/ *n* (pl rendezvous /-vuːz/) **1** (place chosen for) a meeting **2** place where people often meet ● **rendezvous** *v* [I] meet at an arranged time and place

rendition /renˈdɪʃn/ *n* (fml) performance

renegade /ˈrenɪgeɪd/ *n* (fml, disapprov) person who leaves one political or religious group to join another

renew /rɪˈnjuː/ *v* [T] **1** begin sth again: *~ a friendship* **2** make sth valid for a further period of time: *~ a passport* **3** emphasize sth by stating or saying it again **4** replace sth old or damaged with sth new of the same kind ▶ **renewable** *adj* (of energy and natural resources) that is replaced naturally and can be used without the risk of finishing it all: *~able sources of energy such as wind and solar power* ▶ **renewal** *n* [C, U]

renounce /rɪˈnaʊns/ *v* [T] (fml) **1** formally give up a title, position, etc **2** state publicly that you will no longer have anything to do with sb/sth: *~ your faith*

renovate /ˈrenəveɪt/ *v* [T] repair and paint an old building, etc so that it is in good condition again ▶ **renovation** /ˌrenəˈveɪʃn/ *n* [U, C]

renown /rɪˈnaʊn/ *n* [U] (fml) fame ▶ **renowned** *adj* famous

rent /rent/ *n* **1** [U, C] money paid regularly for the use of a house, etc **2** [C] torn place in a piece of material or clothing ● **rent** *v* [I, T] **1** pay money for the use of a house, etc **2** [T] **~(out)** allow sth to be used in return for payment of rent ▶ **rental** *n* amount of rent paid

renunciation /rɪˌnʌnsiˈeɪʃn/ *n* [U] (fml) act of renouncing sth

reorganize (also **-ise**) /riˈɔːgənaɪz/ *v* [I, T] change the way in which sth is organized ▶ **reorganization** (also **-isation**) /riˌɔːgənaɪˈzeɪʃn/ *n* [U, C]

Rep. *abbr* (US) Republican

rep /rep/ *n* (infml) **1** [C] = REPRESENTATIVE(2) **2** [U] = REPERTORY

repair /rɪˈpeə(r)/ *v* [T] mend sth broken, damaged or torn ● **repair**

n [C, U] act of repairing sth: *The building was in need of ~.* [IDM] **in good, bad, etc** repair (fml) in a good, bad, etc condition

reparation /ˌrepəˈreɪʃn/ *n* (fml) money given or sth done to compensate for loss or damage

repatriate /ˌriːˈpætrieɪt/ *v* [T] **1** send or bring sb back to their own country **2** (business) send money or profits back to your own country ▶ **repatriation** /ˌriːˌpætriˈeɪʃn/ *n* [U]

repay /rɪˈpeɪ/ *v* (pt, pp repaid /rɪˈpeɪd/) [T] **1** pay back money borrowed **2** give sth to sb or do sth in return for sth they have done for you ▶ **repayment** *n* [C, U]

repeal /rɪˈpiːl/ *v* [T] end a law officially ▶ **repeal** *n* [U]

repeat /rɪˈpiːt/ *v* **1 ~ sth/yourself** say or write sth again or more than once **2** [T] do or produce sth again or more than once ● **repeat** *n* sth that is repeated ▶ **repeated** *adj* done again and again ▶ **repeatedly** *adv*

repel /rɪˈpel/ *v* (-ll-) [T] **1** drive, push or keep sb/sth away **2** make sb feel horror and disgust ▶ **repellent** *adj* causing great dislike ▶ **repellent** *n* [U, C] substance that repels insects

repent /rɪˈpent/ *v* [I, T] **~(of)** (fml) feel and show you are sorry about sth wrong you have done ▶ **repentance** *n* [U] ▶ **repentant** *adj*

repercussion /ˌriːpəˈkʌʃn/ *n* [C, usu pl] indirect and usu bad result of an action or event

repertoire /ˈrepətwɑː(r)/ *n* all the plays, songs, etc that an actor or musician can perform

repertory /ˈrepətri/ *n* [U] performance of several plays for a short time using the same actors: *a ~ company*

repetition /ˌrepəˈtɪʃn/ *n* [C, U] (act of) repeating sth ▶ **repetitive** /rɪˈpetətɪv/ *adj* saying or doing the same thing many times, so that it becomes boring

rephrase /ˌriːˈfreɪz/ *v* [T] say sth again, using different words

replace /rɪˈpleɪs/ *v* [T] **1** be used instead of sth/sb else; do sth instead of sb/sb else **2** put a new thing in the place of an old, broken, etc one **3** put sth back in its place ▶ **replacement** *n* **1** [U] act of replacing one thing with another **2** [C] person or thing that replaces another

replay /ˌriːˈpleɪ/ *v* [T] **1** (GB, sport) play a sports match again because the previous game was a draw **2** play part of a film, tape, etc again ● **replay** /ˈriːpleɪ/ *n* **1** replayed sports match, part of a tape, etc

replenish /rɪˈplenɪʃ/ *v* [T] (fml) make sth full again

replica /ˈreplɪkə/ *n* exact copy

reply /rɪˈplaɪ/ v (pt, pp -ied) [I, T] say sth as an answer to sb/sth ● **reply** n (pl -ies) act of replying to sb/sth

report¹ /rɪˈpɔːt/ v 1 [I, T] give an account of sth heard, seen, done, etc, esp for a newspaper 2 [T] ~(to) tell sb in authority about a crime, an accident, etc or about sth bad that has happened 3 [I] ~to/for tell sb that you have arrived, eg for work or for a meeting with sb ■ re,ported 'speech n [U] = INDIR-ECT SPEECH (INDIRECT) ▶ **reporter** n person who reports news for a newspaper or on radio or television

report² /rɪˈpɔːt/ n 1 written or spoken account of sth heard, seen, done, etc 2 (GB) written statement about a pupil's work and behaviour 3 story or piece of information that may or may not be true 4 (written) sound of a gun being fired

repose /rɪˈpəʊz/ v [I] (lit) lie or rest in a particular place ● **repose** n [U] (lit) state of rest

reprehensible /ˌreprɪˈhensəbl/ adj (fml) morally wrong; deserving criticism

represent /ˌreprɪˈzent/ v [T] 1 act or speak officially on behalf of sb: ~ the Queen 2 linking verb be sth: This figure ~s an increase of 10%. 3 show sb/sth, esp in a picture 4 be a sign or example of sth 5 describe sb/sth in a particular way ▶ **representation** /ˌreprɪzenˈteɪʃn/ n [U,C]

representative /ˌreprɪˈzentətɪv/ n 1 person chosen to speak or act for sb else or on behalf of a group of people 2 (also infml rep) person who works for a company and travels around selling its products ▶ **representative** adj 1 typical of a particular group of people 2 of a system of government in which a small number of people make decisions for a larger group

repress /rɪˈpres/ v [T] 1 try not to have or show an emotion, etc 2 use political force to control a group of people and restrict their freedom ▶ **repression** /rɪˈpreʃn/ n [U] ▶ **repressive** adj harsh or cruel

reprieve /rɪˈpriːv/ v [T] delay or cancel punishment, esp execution ● **reprieve** n 1 order for the delay or cancelling of punishment, esp execution 2 delay before sth bad happens

reprimand /ˈreprɪmɑːnd/ v [T] (fml) express strong official disapproval of sb or their actions ▶ **reprimand** n

reprisal /rɪˈpraɪzl/ n (written) violent act towards sb because of sth bad they have done towards you

reproach /rɪˈprəʊtʃ/ v [T] ~(for) blame or criticize sb for a wrong action: The captain's behaviour is above/beyond ~ (= cannot be criticized). ● **reproach** n 1 [U] blame or criticism for sth 2 [C] word or remark expressing blame or criticism

reproduce /ˌriːprəˈdjuːs/ v 1 [T] make a copy of a picture, piece of text, etc 2 [I, T] produce babies or young ▶ **reproduction** /-ˈdʌkʃn/ n [C,U] ▶ **reproductive** /-ˈdʌktɪv/ adj of or for reproduction of young

reproof /rɪˈpruːf/ n [C,U] (fml) (remark expressing) blame or disapproval

reprove /rɪˈpruːv/ v [T] (fml) tell sb that you do not approve of sth they have done

reptile /ˈreptaɪl/ n cold-blooded egg-laying animal, eg a lizard or snake ▶ **reptilian** /repˈtɪliən/ adj

republic /rɪˈpʌblɪk/ n country governed by a president and politicians elected by the people and where there is no king or queen ▶ **republican** adj of or supporting the principles of a republic ▶ **republican** n 1 person favouring republican government 2 (Republican) (US) member of the Republican party

repudiate /rɪˈpjuːdieɪt/ v [T] (fml) refuse to accept sth ▶ **repudiation** /rɪˌpjuːdiˈeɪʃn/ n [U]

repugnant /rɪˈpʌɡnənt/ adj (fml) causing a feeling of strong dislike or disgust ▶ **repugnance** /-nəns/ n [U]

repulse /rɪˈpʌls/ v [T] (fml) 1 make sb feel disgust or strong dislike 2 drive back an enemy 3 refuse to accept sb's help, etc ▶ **repulsion** /rɪˈpʌlʃn/ n [U] 1 strong feeling of dislike or disgust 2 (physics) tendency of objects to push each other away ▶ **repulsive** adj very unpleasant

reputable /ˈrepjətəbl/ adj having a good reputation

reputation /ˌrepjuˈteɪʃn/ n [C,U] opinion people have of sb/sth, based on what has happened in the past

repute /rɪˈpjuːt/ n [U] (fml) opinion people have of sb/sth ▶ **reputed** adj generally thought to be sth, although this is not certain: He is ~d to be the best heart surgeon in the country. ▶ **reputedly** adv

request /rɪˈkwest/ n 1 [C,U] act of politely asking for sth: make a ~ for more money 2 [C] thing that you formally ask for ● **request** v [T] (fml) ask for sth politely

require /rɪˈkwaɪə(r)/ v [T] (fml) 1 need sth; depend on sth: My car ~s some attention. 2 (usu passive) make sb do sth, esp because it is necessary according to a law or set of rules: You are ~d to pay the fine. ▶ **requirement** n something required

requisite /ˈrekwɪzɪt/ n, adj (fml)

(something) necessary for a particular purpose

rescue /'reskju:/ v [T] save sb/sth away from a dangerous or harmful situation ● **rescue** n [C,U] (instance of) saving sb/sth from danger

research /rɪ'sɜːtʃ/ n [U,C] ~ (**into/on**) detailed study of a subject to discover new facts about it ● **research** /rɪ'sɜːtʃ/ v [I,T] study sth carefully to find out new facts about it ► **researcher** n

resemble /rɪ'zembl/ v [T] look like or be similar to another person or thing ► **resemblance** n [C,U] fact of being or looking like sb/sth

resent /rɪ'zent/ v feel bitter and angry about sth: ~ *his success* ► **resentful** adj ► **resentment** n [U,C]

reservation /ˌrezə'veɪʃn/ n **1** arrangement to keep sth for sb, eg a seat in a train, a room in a hotel, etc **2** [C,U] feeling of doubt about a plan or idea: *I have a few ~s about the plan.* **3** (also **reserve**) [C] area of land in the US that is kept separate for Native Americans to live in

reserve /rɪ'zɜːv/ v [T] **1** ask for a seat, table, room, etc to be used for you or sb else at a future time: ~ *a table for three at eight o'clock* **2** keep sth for sb/sth, so that it cannot be used by any other person ● **reserve** n **1** [C] supply of sth kept for use when needed **2** [C] piece of land kept for a particular purpose: *a nature ~* **3** [U] quality sb has when they do not talk easily about their feelings, etc **4** [C] extra player in a team who plays if another player cannot **5** (**the reserve**) [sing] (also **the reserves** [pl]) extra military force kept back for use when needed [IDM] **in reserve** available for use if needed ► **reserved** adj slow to show your feelings or opinions; shy

reservoir /'rezəvwɑː(r)/ n artificial lake where water is stored

reside /rɪ'zaɪd/ v [I] (*fml*) live in a particular place [PV] **reside in sb/sth** be in sb/sth; be caused by sth

residence /'rezɪdəns/ n (*fml*) **1** [C] (esp large or impressive) house **2** [U] state of living in a particular place: *The Queen is in ~.*

resident /'rezɪdənt/ n, adj (person) living in a place ► **residential** /ˌrezɪ'denʃl/ adj **1** (of an area of a town) having houses, not offices or factories **2** (of a job, course, etc) offering accommodation

residue /'rezɪdjuː/ n (*tech*) small amount of sth that remains after most has been taken away or used ► **residual** /rɪ'zɪdjuəl/ adj remaining at the end of a process

resign /rɪ'zaɪn/ v [I, T] give up your job, position, etc [PV] **resign yourself to sth** accept sth unpleasant without complaining ► **resigned** adj accepting sth unpleasant without complaining

resignation /ˌrezɪg'neɪʃn/ n **1** [C,U] (act or formal written statement of) resigning from your job **2** [U] state of being resigned to an unpleasant situation

resilient /rɪ'zɪliənt/ adj **1** able to recover quickly after sth unpleasant, eg shock, injury, etc **2** (of a substance) able to return quickly to its original shape after being bent, etc ► **resilience** /-əns/ n [U]

resin /'rezɪn/ n [C,U] **1** sticky substance that is produced by some trees **2** similar man-made plastic substance

resist /rɪ'zɪst/ v [T] **1** refuse to accept sth and try to stop it from happening: ~ *change* **2** fight back when attacked; use force to stop sth from happening **3** not be damaged or harmed by sth ► **resistance** n **1** [U,sing] (action of) resisting sb/sth **2** [U,sing] opposing force: *wind ~* **3** (**the Resistance**) [sing, with sing or pl verb] secret organization that opposes the enemy in a country controlled by the enemy ► **resistant** adj not affected by sth; able to resist sth

resistor /rɪ'zɪstə(r)/ n device that reduces the power in an electric circuit

resolute /'rezəluːt/ adj (*fml*) determined; firm ► **resolutely** adv

resolution /ˌrezə'luːʃn/ n **1** [C] formal decision at a meeting **2** [U] act of solving or settling a problem or dispute **3** [U] quality of being resolute **4** [C] firm decision to do or not do sth: *I made a New Year's ~ to lose weight.* **5** [U,sing] (power of a computer screen, printer, etc to give a clear image: *high-~ graphics*

resolve /rɪ'zɒlv/ v [T] (*fml*) **1** find a satisfactory solution to a problem, etc **2** make a firm decision to do sth ● **resolve** n [C,U] (*fml*) strong determination

resonant /'rezənənt/ adj (*fml*) (of sound) deep, clear and lasting a long time ► **resonance** /-əns/ n [U]

resort /rɪ'zɔːt/ v [PV] **resort to sth** make use of sth as a means of achieving sth, when nothing else is available: *We had to ~ to using untrained staff.* ● **resort** n popular holiday centre: *a seaside ~*

resound /rɪ'zaʊnd/ v [I] **1** (of a sound, voice, etc) fill a place with sound **2** ~ (**with**) (of a place) be filled with sound ► **resounding** adj **1** very great: *a ~ing success* **2** loud and clear: *~ing cheers*

resource /rɪˈsɔːs; -ˈzɔːs/ n [C, usu pl] **1** supply of raw materials, etc that a country can use to bring wealth **2** thing that can be used for help when needed ▸ **resourceful** adj (approv) good at finding ways of solving difficulties ▸ **resourcefully** adv

respect /rɪˈspekt/ n **1** [U, sing] ~(for) admiration for sb/sth **2** [U, sing] ~(for) consideration for sb/sth: show ~ for her wishes **3** [C] particular aspect or detail of sth: In some ~s, I agree with you. [IDM] **pay your respects (to sb)** → PAY[1] **with respect to sth** (fml) concerning sth ● **respect** v [T] admire sb/sth; treat sb/sth with consideration

respectable /rɪˈspektəbl/ adj **1** socially acceptable **2** fairly good: a ~ income ▸ **respectability** /rɪˌspektə-ˈbɪləti/ n [U]

respectful /rɪˈspektfl/ adj showing respect ▸ **respectfully** adv

respective /rɪˈspektɪv/ adj of, for or belonging to each one separately ▸ **respectively** adv in the order mentioned

respiration /ˌrespəˈreɪʃn/ n [U] (fml) act of breathing ▸ **respiratory** /rəˈspɪrətri; ˈrespərətri/ adj connected with breathing

respite /ˈrespaɪt/ n [U, sing] short rest from sth difficult or unpleasant

resplendent /rɪˈsplendənt/ adj (fml) very bright; splendid

respond /rɪˈspɒnd/ v [I] ~(to) **1** answer sb/sth **2** act in answer to sb/sth **3** react favourably to sth: ~ to treatment

response /rɪˈspɒns/ n [C, U] **1** answer **2** action done in answer to sth

responsibility /rɪˌspɒnsəˈbɪləti/ n (pl -ies) **1** [U, C] duty to deal with or take care of sth/sb **2** [U] blame for sth bad that has happened

responsible /rɪˈspɒnsəbl/ adj **1** ~(for) having to look after sb/sth or do sth as a duty: ~ for cleaning the car **2** ~(for) being the cause of sth bad: Who's ~ for this mess? **3** ~(to) having to report to sb in authority and explain your actions to them **4** trustworthy **5** (of a job) having important duties ▸ **responsibly** adv

responsive /rɪˈspɒnsɪv/ adj reacting quickly and positively to sth

rest[1] /rest/ n **1** (**the rest (of sth)**) [sing] the remaining part of sth **2** (**the rest (of sth)**) [pl] the others **3** [C, U] period of relaxing or sleeping **4** [C] object used to support sth: an arm~ **5** [C, U] (music) (sign showing) a pause between notes [IDM] **at rest 1** (tech) not moving **2** dead and therefore free from worry ▸ **restful** adj relaxing and peaceful ▸ **restless**

adj unable to stay still or be happy where you are ▸ **restlessly** adv

rest[2] /rest/ v [I, T] relax, sleep or do nothing; not use a part of your body for some time **2** [I, T] ~**on/against** lean sth on sth [IDM] **rest assured (that …)** (fml) used to emphasize that what you are saying will definitely happen **rest on your laurels** (disapprov) be so satisfied with your success that you do nothing more [PV] **rest on/upon sb/sth 1** depend on sth **2** look at sb/sth **rest with sb (to do sth)** (fml) be the responsibility of sb

restaurant /ˈrestrɒnt/ n place where meals can be bought and eaten

restitution /ˌrestɪˈtjuːʃn/ n [U] (fml) giving back sth stolen, etc to its owner or paying money for damage

restive /ˈrestɪv/ adj (fml) unable to be still; unwilling to be controlled

restoration /ˌrestəˈreɪʃn/ n **1** [U, C] act of restoring sth **2** (**the Restoration**) [sing] period just after 1660 in Britain

restorative /rɪˈstɔːrətɪv/ adj bringing back health and strength

restore /rɪˈstɔː(r)/ v [T] **1** bring back a situation or feeling that existed before **2** bring sb/sth back to a former state or position **3** repair an old building, picture, etc so that it looks as good as it did originally **4** (fml) give sth that was lost or stolen back to sb ▸ **restorer** n person who restores old buildings, etc

restrain /rɪˈstreɪn/ v [T] **1** stop sb/sth from doing sth, esp by using physical force ▸ **restrained** adj controlled; calm ▸ **restraint** /rɪˈstreɪnt/ n **1** rule, fact, etc that limits or controls what people can do **2** [U] act of controlling or limiting sth **3** [U] quality of behaving calmly and with control

restrict /rɪˈstrɪkt/ v [T] limit sth; stop sb/sth from moving freely ▸ **restriction** /rɪˈstrɪkʃn/ n [C, U] ▸ **restrictive** adj

result /rɪˈzʌlt/ n **1** [C, U] something that happens because of an action or event **2** [C] final score in a game; marks in an examination **3** [C] answer to a mathematical calculation ● **result** v [I] ~**(from/from)** happen because of sth else that happened first [PV] **result in sth** make sth happen ▸ **resultant** adj (fml) caused by the thing just mentioned

resume /rɪˈzjuːm/ v **1** [I, T] begin sth again after stopping **2** (~ **your seat/place/position**) [T] go back to the seat or place that you had before

résumé /ˈrezjumeɪ/ n **1** summary **2** (US) = CURRICULUM VITAE

resumption /rɪˈzʌmpʃn/ n [U, sing] (fml) act of beginning sth again after stopping

resurrect /ˌrezəˈrekt/ v [T] bring sth back into use ▸ **resurrection** /ˌrezəˈrekʃn/ n **1** (**the Resurrection**) [sing] (in Christianity) coming back to life of Jesus after his death; time when all dead people will become alive again **2** [U,sing] new beginning for sth which is old or has disappeared

resuscitate /rɪˈsʌsɪteɪt/ v [T] (fml) bring sb back to consciousness ▸ **resuscitation** /rɪˌsʌsɪˈteɪʃn/ n [U]

retail /ˈriːteɪl/ n [U] selling of goods to the public, usu through shops ▸ **retail** adv ● **retail** v **1** [T] sell goods to the public **2** [I] ~ **at/for** (business) be sold at a particular price ▸ **retailer** n person or business that sells goods to the public

retain /rɪˈteɪn/ v [T] (fml) **1** keep sth; continue to hold or contain sth **2** obtain the services of a lawyer by payment ▸ **retainer** n **1** fee paid to sb to make sure they will be available to do work when they are needed **2** (GB) reduced rent paid to reserve a flat, etc when you are not there **3** (old-fash) servant

retaliate /rɪˈtælieɪt/ v [I] repay an injury, insult, etc with a similar one ▸ **retaliation** /rɪˌtæliˈeɪʃn/ n [U]

retard /rɪˈtɑːd/ v [T] (fml) make the development of sth slower

retch /retʃ/ v [I] try to vomit but without bringing up anything

retention /rɪˈtenʃn/ n [U] (fml) action of retaining sth

retentive /rɪˈtentɪv/ adj (of the memory) able to remember things well

reticent /ˈretɪsnt/ adj saying little; not saying all that is known ▸ **reticence** /-sns/ n [U]

retina /ˈretɪnə/ n (pl ~**s** or -**ae** /-niː/) part of the eye at the back of the eyeball, sensitive to light

retinue /ˈretɪnjuː/ n [C, with sing or pl verb] group of people travelling with an important person

retire /rɪˈtaɪə(r)/ v **1** [I] ~ (**from**) stop doing your job, esp because you have reached a particular age or you are ill **2** [T] tell sb they must stop doing their job **3** [I] (fml) leave a place, esp to go somewhere quiet **4** [I] (lit) go to bed ▸ **retired** adj having retired from work ▸ **retirement** n [U] ▸ **retiring** adj preferring not to spend time with other people

retort /rɪˈtɔːt/ v [T] reply to a comment quickly or angrily ● **retort** n [C, U] quick or angry reply

retrace /rɪˈtreɪs/ v [T] go back along the route you have taken: She began to ~ her steps towards the house.

retract /rɪˈtrækt/ v [I, T] **1** take back a statement, offer, etc **2** draw sth in or back: A cat can ~ its claws. ▸ **retractable** adj ▸ **retraction** n [C, U]

retread /ˈriːtred/ n tyre made by putting a new rubber surface on an old tyre

retreat /rɪˈtriːt/ v [I] (esp of an army) go back ● **retreat** n [C, U] **1** act of retreating **2** (place for) a period of quiet and rest

retribution /ˌretrɪˈbjuːʃn/ n [U] (fml) severe punishment for sth seriously wrong that sb has done

retrieve /rɪˈtriːv/ v [T] (fml) **1** bring or get sth back **2** (computing) find and get back data that has been stored in a computer's memory **3** make a bad situation better ▸ **retrieval** n [U] act of retrieving sth ▸ **retriever** n dog trained to find and bring back shot birds, etc

retrograde /ˈretrəgreɪd/ adj (fml, disapprov) going back to an earlier worse condition

retrogressive /ˌretrəˈgresɪv/ adj (fml, disapprov) returning to old-fashioned ideas or methods instead of making progress

retrospect /ˈretrəspekt/ n [IDM] **in retrospect** looking back on a past event ▸ **retrospective** adj **1** looking back on the past **2** (of a new law or decision) intended to take effect from a particular date in the past

return[1] /rɪˈtɜːn/ v **1** [I] come or go back: ~ home **2** [T] give, send or put sth back: ~ damaged goods to the shop ◇ He didn't ~ my call. **3** [I] go back to an activity you were doing earlier or a previous state **4** [T] give a decision about sth in a court of law: The jury ~ed a verdict of guilty. **5** [T] (GB) elect sb to a political position **6** [T] (business) give a particular amount of money as a profit or loss: to ~ a high rate of interest

return[2] /rɪˈtɜːn/ n **1** [sing] act of returning to a place **2** [U,sing] action of giving, putting or sending sth/sb back **3** [U,C] amount of profit that you get from sth **4** [C] official report or statement: fill in a tax ~ **5** [C] (also re**turn 'ticket**) (GB) ticket for a journey to a place and back again [IDM] **in return (for sth)** in exchange or as a payment for sth

reunion /riːˈjuːniən/ n **1** [C] meeting of former friends, colleagues, etc who have not seen one another for a long time **2** [C, U] coming together again after a separation

Rev. (GB also **Revd**) abbr Reverend

rev /rev/ v (-**vv**-) [I, T] ~ (**up**) increase the speed of an engine: ~ the car (up)

reveal /rɪˈviːl/ v [T] **1** make sth known to sb: ~ a secret **2** allow sth to be seen

revel /ˈrevl/ v (-**ll**- US -**l**-) [PV] **revel in sth** enjoy sth very much

revelation /ˌrevəˈleɪʃn/ n **1** [U]

making known of sth secret **2** [C] something (esp surprising) that is revealed

revenge /rɪ'vendʒ/ *n* [U] punishment or injury done to sb because they have made you suffer ● **revenge** *v* [PV] **revenge yourself on sb** punish or hurt sb because they have made you suffer

revenue /'revənju:/ *n* [U,C] income, especially as received by the government

reverberate /rɪ'vɜ:bəreɪt/ *v* [i] (of sound) echo again and again ▶ **reverberation** /rɪ,vɜ:bə'reɪʃn/ *n* **1** [C] loud noise that echoes **2** (**reverberations**) [pl] (usu unpleasant) effects of sth that happens that spread among a large number of people

revere /rɪ'vɪə(r)/ *v* [T] (*fml*) have great respect for sb/sth

reverence /'revərəns/ *n* [U] great respect

reverend /'revərənd/ *n* (*abbr* **Rev.**) (title of a) member of the clergy

reverent /'revərənt/ *adj* feeling or showing great respect for sb/sth ▶ **reverently** *adv*

reversal /rɪ'vɜ:sl/ *n* [C,U] complete change of sth so that it is the opposite of what it was

reverse /rɪ'vɜ:s/ *v* **1** [T] make sth the opposite of what it was: *~ a decision* **2** [T] turn sth the other way round **3** [I, T] (cause a vehicle to) move backwards [IDM] **reverse (the) charges** (*GB*) make a telephone call that will be paid for by the person receiving the call ● **reverse** *n* **1** (**the reverse**) [sing] the opposite **2** [C] the back of a coin, etc **3** (*also* re,verse 'gear) [U] mechanism used to make a vehicle move backwards: *put the car into ~ (gear)* ● **reverse** *adj* opposite in position or order

revert /rɪ'vɜ:t/ *v* [i] ~ **to** go back to a former state, owner or kind of behaviour

review /rɪ'vju:/ *v* **1** consider or examine sth again: *~ the past/a decision* **2** [I, T] write a report of a book, film, etc, giving your opinion of it **3** [T] officially inspect a group of soldiers, etc ● **review** *n* **1** [U,C] examination of sth, with the intention of changing it if necessary **2** [C,U] article in a newspaper, etc that gives an opinion of a new book, film, etc **3** [C] inspection of military forces ▶ **reviewer** *n* person who writes reviews(2)

revise /rɪ'vaɪz/ *v* **1** [T] change your opinions or plans, eg because of sth you have learned **2** [T] examine sth again and correct or improve it **3** [I, T] ~ (**for**) (*GB*) go over work already done to prepare for an examination ▶ **revision** /rɪ'vɪʒn/ *n*

1 [C,U] (act of) revising sth **2** [C] corrected version

revitalize (*also* **-ise**) /,ri:'vaɪtəlaɪz/ *v* [T] put new life or strength into sth

revive /rɪ'vaɪv/ *v* **1** [I, T] become, or make sb/sth become, conscious or healthy and strong again **2** [T] bring sth into use again: *~ old customs* ▶ **revival** *n* [C,U]

revoke /rɪ'vəʊk/ *v* [T] (*fml*) officially cancel sth so that it is no longer valid

revolt /rɪ'vəʊlt/ *v* **1** [i] ~ (**against**) take violent action against people in power **2** [T] cause sb to feel horror or disgust ▶ **revolt** *n* [C,U] protest against those authority ▶ **revolting** *adj* extremely unpleasant

revolution /,revə'lu:ʃn/ *n* **1** [C,U] complete change in the system of government, esp by force **2** [C,U] complete change in conditions or ways of doing things: *the computer ~* **3** [C,U] one complete circular movement around a point ▶ **revolutionary** *adj* **1** of a political revolution **2** involving a great or complete change: *a ~ary idea* ▶ **revolutionary** *n* (*pl* **-ies**) person who supports a revolution, esp a political one ▶ **revolutionize** (*also* **-ise**) /-ʃənaɪz/ *v* [T] completely change the way sth is done

revolve /rɪ'vɒlv/ *v* [i] ~ (**around**) go round sth in a circle [PV] **revolve around/round sb/sth** have sb/sth as the main interest or subject: *The story ~s around the old man.*

revolver /rɪ'vɒlvə(r)/ *n* small gun with a revolving container for bullets

revue /rɪ'vju:/ *n* show in a theatre, with dances, songs and jokes

revulsion /rɪ'vʌlʃn/ *n* [U,sing] feeling of disgust or horror

reward /rɪ'wɔ:d/ *n* [C,U] something given in return for services or for bringing back stolen property ● **reward** *v* [T] give sth to sb because they have done sth good, worked hard, etc ▶ **rewarding** *adj* (of an activity, etc) worth doing; satisfying

rewind /,ri:'waɪnd/ *v* (*pt, pp* **rewound** /-'waʊnd/) [I, T] cause a tape, film, etc to go back to the beginning

rhapsody /'ræpsədi/ *n* (*pl* **-ies**) **1** piece of music in irregular form **2** (*written*) expression of great delight

rhetoric /'retərɪk/ *n* [U] **1** (*disapprov*) speech or writing intended to influence people, but that is insincere **2** (*fml*) art of using words impressively in speech and writing ▶ **rhetorical** /rɪ'tɒrɪkl/ *adj* **1** (of a question) asked only for effect, not to get an answer **2** intended to influence people, but not completely honest

rheumatism /'ru:mətɪzəm/ *n* [U] disease causing pain and stiffness

rhino

in the muscles and joints ▶ **rheumatic** /ru'mætɪk/ *adj, n*

rhino /'raɪnəʊ/ *n* (*pl* ~s) (*infml*) = RHINOCEROS

rhinoceros /raɪ'nɒsərəs/ *n* large heavy thick-skinned animal with one or two horns on its nose

rhododendron /,rəʊdə'dendrən/ *n* bush with large red, purple, pink or white flowers

rhubarb /'ru:bɑ:b/ *n* [U] (garden plant with) thick reddish stems that are cooked and eaten like fruit

rhyme /raɪm/ *v* [I] (of words or lines of a poem) end with the same sound: *'Fall'* ~*s with* '*wall'.* ● **rhyme** *n* **1** [U] (use of) rhyming words at the end of lines in poetry **2** [C] word that rhymes with another word **3** [C] short rhyming poem

rhythm /'rɪðəm/ *n* **1** [C,U] regular pattern of beats or movements **2** [C] regular pattern of changes or events: *the ~ of the tides* ▶ **rhythmic(al)** /'rɪðmɪk(l)/ *adj* ■ **rhythm and 'blues** *n* [U] (*abbr* R&B) type of music that is a mixture of blues and jazz and has a strong rhythm

rib /rɪb/ *n* **1** [C] one of the curved bones that go from the backbone to the chest **2** [U,C] way of knitting that produces raised lines ▶ **ribbed** *adj* (of fabric) having raised lines

ribbon /'rɪbən/ *n* [C,U] narrow strip of material used to tie things or for decoration

rice /raɪs/ *n* [U] white or brown grain that is cooked and eaten

rich /rɪtʃ/ *adj* **1** having a lot of money or property **2** ~**in** containing or providing a large supply of sth: *soil ~ in minerals* **3** (of food) containing a lot of fat, oil, eggs, etc **4** (of colours, sounds, smells and tastes) strong or deep; very beautiful or pleasing **5** (*lit*) expensive and beautiful: ~ *fabrics* ● **rich** *n* [pl] **1** (**the rich**) rich people **2** (**riches**) wealth ▶ **richly** *adv* ▶ **richness** *n* [U]

rickety /'rɪkəti/ *adj* likely to break or collapse

rickshaw /'rɪkʃɔ:/ *n* small light vehicle with two wheels that is pulled by sb walking

ricochet /'rɪkəʃeɪ/ *v* (*pt, pp* **-t-** or **-tt-**) [I] (of a moving object) hit a surface and bounce away from it at an angle ▶ **ricochet** *n* [C,U]

rid /rɪd/ *v* (**-dd-**, *pt, pp* **rid**) [IDM] **get rid of sb/sth** make yourself free of sb/sth that you do not want; throw sth away [PV] **rid sb/sth of sth** (*written*) remove sth/sb that is causing a problem from a place, group, etc

riddance /'rɪdns/ *n* [U] [IDM] **good riddance (to sb/sth)** unkind way of

saying that you are pleased sb/sth has gone: *He's going and good ~ to him!*

ridden *pp* of RIDE[1]

riddle /'rɪdl/ *n* **1** difficult or amusing question **2** mysterious event or situation that you cannot explain ● **riddle** *v* [T] ~**with** (*usu passive*) make a lot of holes in sb/sth: (*fig*) ~*d with bullets*

ride¹ /raɪd/ *v* (*pt* **rode** /rəʊd/ *pp* **ridden** /'rɪdn/) **1** [I, T] sit on a horse, bicycle, etc and control it as it moves **2** [I] travel in a vehicle, esp as a passenger **3** [I, T] float on water or air: *surfers riding the waves* [PV] **ride up** (of clothing) gradually move upwards, out of position ▶ **rider** *n* **1** person who rides a horse, bicycle, etc **2** additional remark following a statement

ride² /raɪd/ *n* short journey on a horse or bicycle or in a car, etc [IDM] **take sb for a ride** (*infml*) cheat or trick sb

ridge /rɪdʒ/ *n* **1** long narrow piece of high land **2** raised line where two sloping surfaces meet

ridicule /'rɪdɪkju:l/ *n* [U] unkind comments that make fun of sb ● **ridicule** *v* [T] make sb/sth look silly

ridiculous /rɪ'dɪkjələs/ *adj* very silly or unreasonable: *He looks ~ in that hat.* ▶ **ridiculously** *adv*

rife /raɪf/ *adj* (of sth bad) widespread; common

rifle /'raɪfl/ *n* gun with a long barrel, fired from the shoulder ● **rifle** *v* [T] ~**(through)** search quickly through sth in order to find or steal sth

rift /rɪft/ *n* **1** serious disagreement between people **2** large crack in the ground, rocks or cloud

rig /rɪɡ/ *v* (**-gg-**) [T] **1** arrange or influence sth dishonestly for your own advantage: *an election ~* **2** fit a ship with ropes, sails, etc [PV] **rig sth up** make or build sth quickly using whatever materials are available ● **rig** *n* **1** large piece of equipment for taking oil or gas out of the land or sea: *an oil ~* **2** way that a ship's masts, sails, etc are arranged ▶ **rigging** *n* [U] ropes, etc that support a ship's masts and sails

right¹ /raɪt/ *adj* **1** morally correct or acceptable: *I hope we're doing the ~ thing.* **2** true or correct: *the ~ answer* **3** most suitable: *the ~ person for the job* **4** in a normal or satisfactory condition: *That milk doesn't smell ~.* **5** of, on or towards the side of the body that is towards the east when a person faces north: *my ~ hand* [IDM] **(not) in your right mind** (not) mentally normal **on the right track** = TRACK **put/set sth right** correct sth or deal with a problem ■ **'right angle** *n* angle of 90° ▶ **right-angled** *adj* ▶ **rightly**

right² /raɪt/ *adv* **1** exactly; directly: *Put it ~ in the middle.* **2** all the way; completely: *Go ~ to the end of the road.* **3** (*infml*) immediately: *I'll be ~ with you* (= I am coming very soon). **4** correctly **5** on or to the right side: *turn ~* ◇ [IDM] **right away/off** immediately; without delay **right now** at this moment; immediately

right³ /raɪt/ *n* **1** [U,C] what is morally good or correct: *He knew he was in the ~* (= had justice on his side). **2** [C,U] moral or legal claim to get sth or to behave in a particular way: *You have no ~ to be here.* ◇ *animal ~s campaigners* ◇ *By ~s* (= if justice were done) *half the money should be mine.* **3** (**rights**) [pl] the authority to perform, publish, film, etc a particular work: *He sold the ~s for $2 million.* **4** (**the/sb's right**) [sing] right side or direction **5** (**the right, the Right**) [sing, with sing or pl verb] political groups that most strongly support the capitalist system [IDM] **in your own right** because of your own personal qualifications or efforts **put/set sb/sth to rights** correct sb/sth; put things in order ■ **right-hand** *adj* on the right side of sth ■ **right-'handed** *adj* (of a person) using the right hand for writing, using tools, etc ■ **right-hand 'man** *n* [sing] main helper and supporter ■ **right of 'way** *n* [C] (legal permission to use a path that goes across private land **2** [U] (in road traffic) the right to go first ■ **the right 'wing** *n* [sing, with sing or pl verb] part of a political party whose members are least in favour of social change ■ **right-'wing** *adj*

right⁴ /raɪt/ *v* [T] return sb/sth/yourself to the normal, upright position: *The ship ~ed herself.* [IDM] **right a wrong** do sth to correct an unfair situation or sth bad that you have done

righteous /'raɪtʃəs/ *adj* (*fml*) morally right and good ▶ **righteously** *adv* **righteousness** *n* [U]

rightful /'raɪtfl/ *adj* (*fml*) that is correct, right or legal: *the ~ owner* ▶ **rightfully** *adv*

rigid /'rɪdʒɪd/ *adj* **1** strict; unwilling or difficult to change **2** stiff and difficult to bend ▶ **rigidity** /rɪ'dʒɪdəti/ *n* [U] ▶ **rigidly** *adv*

rigorous /'rɪgərəs/ *adj* **1** careful and detailed **2** strict; severe ▶ **rigorously** *adv*

rigour (*US* **-or**) /'rɪgə(r)/ *n* **1** [U] fact of paying great attention to detail **2** [U] strictness; severity **3** (**the rigours of sth**) [pl] the difficulties and unpleasant conditions of sth

rim /rɪm/ *n* edge of sth circular: *the ~ of a cup* ● **rim** *v* (**-mm-**) [T] (*fml*) form an edge round sth

rind /raɪnd/ *n* [U,C] hard outer covering of certain fruits, cheese or bacon

ring¹ /rɪŋ/ *v* (*pt* **rang** /ræŋ/ *pp* **rung** /rʌŋ/) **1** [I, T] ~ (**up**) telephone sb/sth: *I'll ~ you* (*up*) *later.* **2** [I, T] (cause a bell to) produce a sound: *~ the doorbell* ◇ *R~ for the nurse if you need her.* **3** [I] ~ (**with**) (*lit*) be full of a sound [IDM] **ring a bell** (*infml*) remind one of sth **ring true/hollow/false** give the impression of being sincere/true or not sincere/true [PV] **ring off** (*GB*) end a telephone conversation **ring out** be heard loudly and clearly ● **ring** *n* **1** [C] sound of a bell **2** [sing] particular quality that sounds, sounds, etc have: *a ~ of truth* [IDM] **give sb a ring** (*GB, infml*) make a telephone call to sb

ring² /rɪŋ/ *n* **1** circular metal band worn on a finger **2** circular band of any kind of material: *a key ~* **3** circle: *The children stood in a ~.* **4** group of people working together, often illegally: *a spy ~* **5** enclosed area in which animals or people perform or compete, with seats around it for an audience: *a circus ~* ● **ring** *v* (*pt, pp* **~ed**) [T] **1** surround sb/sth **2** draw a circle around sth ■ **ringleader** *n* (*esp lit*) person who leads others in doing sth wrong ■ **ring road** *n* road built around a town

ringlet /'rɪŋlət/ *n* [C, usu *pl*] long hanging curl of hair

rink /rɪŋk/ *n* specially prepared area of ice for skating: *ice/skating ~*

rinse /rɪns/ *v* [T] wash sth in clean water: *R~ the pasta with boiling water.* ● **rinse** *n* **1** [C] act of rinsing sth **2** [C,U] liquid for colouring the hair

riot /'raɪət/ *n* **1** [C] noisy violent behaviour by a crowd **2** [sing] ~ **of** collection of a lot of different types of the same thing: *a ~ of colour* [IDM] **run riot** → RUN¹ ● **riot** *v* [I] behave in a violent way in a public place, often as a protest ▶ **rioter** *n* ▶ **riotous** *adj* disorderly; wild

rip /rɪp/ *v* (**-pp-**) [I, T] tear sth or become torn, often suddenly or violently [PV] **rip sb off** (*infml*) cheat sb, by charging them too much money, etc ● **rip** *n* long tear in fabric, paper, etc ■ **'ripcord** *n* string that you pull to open a parachute ■ **'rip-off** *n* (*infml*) something that is not worth what you pay for it

ripe /raɪp/ *adj* (**~r, ~st**) **1** (fully grown and) ready to be eaten: *apples/ cheese* **2** ~ **for** ready or suitable for sth to happen ▶ **ripeness** *n* [U]

ripen /'raɪpən/ *v* [I, T] become or make ripe

ripple /ˈrɪpl/ n **1** very small wave or movement on the surface of water **2** short sound of quiet laughter, etc ● **ripple** v [I, T] (cause sth to) move in ripples

rise¹ /raɪz/ v (pt rose /rəʊz/ pt ~n /ˈrɪzn/) [I] **1** come or go upwards **2** (written) get up from a lying, sitting or kneeling position: He always rose (= got out of bed) early. **3** (of the sun, moon, etc) appear above the horizon **4** increase in amount or number: Prices have continued to ~. **5** become more successful, important, powerful, etc **6** get stronger: The wind is rising. **7** (fml) rebel against sb/sth **8** slope upwards: rising ground **9** (of a river) start [PV] **rise to sth** show that you are able to deal with an unexpected situation, problem, etc: He was determined to rise to the challenge. **2** react when sb is deliberately trying to make you angry ▶ **rising** n armed rebellion

rise² /raɪz/ n **1** [C] increase in number, amount or level **2** [C] (GB) increase in wages **3** [sing] upward movement or progress: his ~ to power **4** [C] small hill [IDM] **give rise to sth** (fml) cause sth to happen or exist

risk /rɪsk/ n **1** [C,U] possibility of danger or of sth bad happening in the future **2** [C] ~(to) person or thing that is likely to cause problems or danger in the future [IDM] **at risk (from/of sth)** in danger of sth unpleasant happening **do sth at your own risk** do sth so dangerous and agree to take responsibility for anything bad that happens **run the risk (of doing sth)** | **take a risk** do sth even though you know that sth bad could happen to you: ● **risk** v [T] **1** put sth in danger **2** take the chance of sth bad happening to you: ~ getting wet [IDM] **risk your neck** → NECK ▶ **risky** adj (-ier, -iest) dangerous

risotto /rɪˈzɒtəʊ/ n [C,U] (pl ~s) Italian dish of rice cooked with vegetables, etc

rissole /ˈrɪsəʊl/ n small flat mass of minced meat, etc that is fried

rite /raɪt/ n traditional, esp religious, ceremony [IDM] **rite of passage** ceremony or event that marks an important stage in sb's life

ritual /ˈrɪtʃuəl/ n [C,U] **1** series of actions regularly followed, esp as part of a religious ceremony **2** something done regularly and always in the same way ● **ritual** adj of or done as a ritual

rival /ˈraɪvl/ n person, company or thing that competes with another in sport, business, etc ● **rival** v (-ll- US also -l-) [T] be as good, impressive, etc as sb/sth else ▶ **rivalry** n [C,

U] (pl -ies) competition between two people, companies, etc

river /ˈrɪvə(r)/ n large natural stream of water flowing to the sea

rivet /ˈrɪvɪt/ n metal pin used to fasten pieces of metal, leather, etc together ● **rivet** v [T] **1** hold sb's attention completely **2** fasten sth with rivets ▶ **riveting** adj (approv) so interesting that it holds your attention completely

road /rəʊd/ n **1** hard surface built for vehicles to travel on the way to achieving sth: be on the ~ to success ■ **'roadblock** n barrier placed across the road by the police or army ■ **'road hog** n (infml) careless driver ■ **'roadworks** n [pl] (GB) (area where there are) repairs being done to the road ■ **'roadworthy** adj (of a vehicle) fit to be driven on roads

roam /rəʊm/ v [I, T] walk or travel about with no clear purpose

roar /rɔː(r)/ n deep loud sound (like that) made by a lion ● **roar** v **1** [I] make a deep loud sound **2** [I, T] shout sth very loudly **3** [I] laugh very loudly ▶ **roaring** adj (infml) **1** noisy **2** (of a fire) burning with a lot of flames and heat [IDM] **do a roaring trade (in sth)** (infml) sell a lot of sth very quickly **roaring drunk** extremely drunk and noisy

roast /rəʊst/ v [T, I] cook food, esp meat, in an oven or over a fire; be cooked in this way ● **roast** adj cooked in an oven or over a fire: ~ potatoes ● **roast** n **1** large piece of roasted meat: the Sunday ~ **2** (US) party held in sb's garden at which food is cooked over an open fire

rob /rɒb/ v (-bb-) [T] steal money or property from a person or place ▶ **robber** n person who robs sb/sth ▶ **robbery** n [C,U] (pl -ies) crime of stealing money or goods from a bank, shop, etc, esp using violence

robe /rəʊb/ n long loose garment

robin /ˈrɒbɪn/ n small brown bird with a red breast

robot /ˈrəʊbɒt/ n machine that can do certain human tasks automatically

robust /rəʊˈbʌst/ adj strong; healthy ▶ **robustly** adv ▶ **robustness** n [U]

rock¹ /rɒk/ n **1** [U,C] hard solid material that forms part of the earth's surface **2** [C] mass of rock standing above the earth's surface or in the sea **3** [C] large stone **4** [U] (also **'rock music**) type of loud modern music with a strong beat, played on electric guitars, etc **5** [U] (GB) hard stick-shaped sweet [IDM] **on the rocks 1** (of a relationship or a business) likely to fail soon **2** (of a drink) served with ice but no water ■ **rock and roll** (also **rock'n' roll**) n [U] type of music popular in the

1950s ■ ,rock-'bottom n [U] lowest point ▶ rockery n (pl -ies) part of a garden with small rocks and plants

rock² /rɒk/ v [I, T] move gently backwards and forwards or from side to side **2** [T] (*written*) shock sb/sth very much [IDM] **rock the boat** (*infml*) spoil a calm situation ▶ **rocker** n **1** one of the two curved pieces of wood on the bottom of a rocking chair **2** = ROCKING CHAIR [IDM] **be off your rocker** (*spoken*) be crazy ■ '**rocking chair** n chair fitted with rockers that make it move backwards and forwards

rocket /'rɒkɪt/ n **1** [C] tube-shaped device filled with fast-burning fuel that is used to launch a missile or spacecraft **2** [C] firework that shoots high into the air **3** [U] (*GB*) plant with long green leaves that have a strong flavour and are eaten raw in salads ● **rocket** v [I] increase quickly and suddenly; move very fast: *Prices are ~ing.*

rocky /'rɒki/ (-**ier**, -**iest**) *adj* **1** of rock; full of rocks **2** difficult and not certain to continue: *a ~ marriage*

rod /rɒd/ n long thin straight piece of wood, metal, etc: *a fishing ~*

rode *pt of* RIDE¹

rodent /'rəʊdnt/ n small animal, eg a rat, with strong sharp front teeth

rodeo /rəʊ'deɪəʊ/ n (pl ~s) (esp in the US) contest of skill in catching cattle with a rope, riding wild horses, etc

roe /rəʊ/ n **1** [U] mass of fish eggs, eaten as food **2** [C] = ROE DEER ■ '**roe deer** n (pl **roe deer**) small European and Asian deer

rogue /rəʊg/ n (*hum*) person who behaves badly but in a harmless way ▶ **roguish** *adj* (of a person) pleasant and amusing but looking as if they might do sth wrong

role /rəʊl/ n **1** function or importance of sb/sth **2** actor's part in a play ■ '**role model** n person that you admire and try to copy ■ '**role-play** n learning activity in which you behave as sb else would behave in certain situations ▶ **role-play** v [I, T]

roll¹ /rəʊl/ v **1** [I, T] (make a round object) move along by turning over and over **2** [I, T] (cause sth to) turn over and over while remaining in the same place: *a dog ~ing in the mud* **3** [I, T] (cause sth to) move smoothly (on wheels or as a ball): *The clouds ~ed away.* ◇ *The car began to ~ back down the hill.* **4** [I, T] ~ (**up**) make sth/yourself into the shape of a ball or tube: *~ up a carpet* ◇ *The hedgehog ~ed up into a ball.* **5** [T] make sth flat, by pushing sth heavy over it: *~ pastry* **6** [I] make a long continuous sound: *The thunder ~ed in the distance.* [IDM] **be rolling in**

money/it (*infml*) have a lot of money [PV] **roll in** (*infml*) arrive in large quantities **roll up** (*infml*) arrive

roll² /rəʊl/ n **1** something made into a tube: *a ~ of film* **2** (also ,**bread** '**roll**) small rounded portion of bread for one person **3** rolling movement **4** official list of names: *the electoral ~* **5** long deep sound: *the ~ of drums*

roller /'rəʊlə(r)/ n **1** tube-shaped object for pressing sth, smoothing sth, etc ■ **Rollerblade™** (*US* **Roller Blade™**) n boot with a line of small wheels attached to the bottom ▶ **Rollerblade** v [I] ■ '**roller skate** n boot with two pairs of small wheels attached to the bottom ■ '**roller skate** v [I] move over a hard surface wearing roller skates

rolling /'rəʊlɪŋ/ *adj* rising and falling gently: *– hills/waves* ■ '**rolling pin** n wooden or glass tube-shaped kitchen utensil for flattening pastry

ROM /rɒm/ n [U] (*computing*) read-only memory; computer memory that contains data that cannot be changed or removed

Roman /'rəʊmən/ n, *adj* (citizen) of Rome, esp ancient Rome ■ ,**Roman** '**Catholic** n, *adj* (member) of the Christian Church that has the Pope as its leader ▶ ,**Roman Ca'tholicism** n [U] ■ ,**Roman** '**numeral** n letter, eg V, L or M, or group of letters, eg IV, used to represent a number

romance /rəʊ'mæns/ n **1** [C] love affair **2** [U] love or the feeling of being in love **3** [U] feeling of excitement and adventure **4** [C] story of love, adventure, etc

romantic /rəʊ'mæntɪk/ *adj* **1** of or having feelings of love **2** of or suggesting love, adventure and excitement: *a ~ journey* **3** not practical; very imaginative and emotional ● **romantic** n imaginative person whose hopes and ideas may not be realistic ▶ **romantically** /-kli/ *adv* ▶ **romanticism** /rəʊ'mæntɪsɪzəm/ n [U] romantic feelings, attitudes, etc ▶ **romanticize** (also -**ise**) /rəʊ'mæntɪsaɪz/ v [I, T] make sth seem more attractive or interesting than it really is

romp /rɒmp/ v [I] play happily and noisily ● **romp** n

roof /ruːf/ n **1** top covering of a building, car, etc **2** upper part: *the ~ of the mouth* ▶ **roof** v [T] cover sth with a roof ▶ **roofing** n [U] material for making roofs ■ '**roof rack** n metal frame fixed on top of a car, used for carrying large objects

rook /rʊk/ n **1** large black bird like a crow **2** = CASTLE(2)

room /ruːm; rʊm/ n **1** [C] part of a building with its own walls, ceiling and door **2** [U] empty space that can be used for a particular purpose: *Is there ~ for me in the car?* **3** [U] possibility of sth happening; opportunity to do sth: *~ for improvement* ▶ **roomy** *adj* (**-ier, -iest**) having plenty of space

roost /ru:st/ *n* place where birds sleep ● **roost** *v* [I] (of a bird) rest or go to sleep somewhere

rooster /'ru:stə(r)/ *n* (*esp US*) = COCK¹(1)

root¹ /ru:t/ *n* **1** [C] part of a plant that is in the soil and takes in water and food from the soil **2** [C] base of a hair, tooth, etc **3** [C, usu sing] main cause or origin of sth: *Is money the ~ of all evil?* **4** (**roots**) [pl] feelings or connections you have with the place in which you grew up **5** [C] (*ling*) form of a word on which other forms are based [IDM] **take root** become established

root² /ru:t/ *v* **1** [I, T] (cause a plant to) grow roots **2** [I] search for sth by turning things over [PV] **root sth⇔out** find the person or thing that is causing a problem and remove or get rid of them ▶ **rooted** *adj* **1** in or developing from or being strongly influenced by sth: *His problems are deeply ~ed in his childhood experiences.* **2** firmly fixed in one place [IDM] **rooted to the spot** so frightened or shocked that you cannot move

rope /rəʊp/ *n* [C,U] (piece of) very thick strong string [IDM] **show sb/know/learn the ropes** (*infml*) show sb/know/learn how a particular job should be done ● **rope** *v* [T] tie sth/sb with a rope [PV] **rope sb in| rope sb into sth** persuade sb to join in an activity or to help to do sth **rope sth⇔off** separate one area from another with ropes ▶ **ropy** (*also* **ropey**) *adj* (**-ier, -iest**) (*GB, infml*) poor in quality, health, etc

rosary /'rəʊzəri/ *n* (*pl* **-ies**) **1** [C] string of beads used by some Roman Catholics for counting prayers **2** (**the Rosary**) [sing] set of prayers said while counting the rosary beads

rosé /'rəʊzeɪ/ *n* [U] pink wine

rose¹ *pt of* RISE¹

rose² /rəʊz/ *n* **1** [C] (bush which produces a) flower with a sweet smell **2** [U] pink colour

rosette /rəʊ'zet/ *n* circular decoration made of ribbon, worn by supporters of a political party, etc

roster /'rɒstə(r)/ *n* list of people's names and their duties

rostrum /'rɒstrəm/ *n* (*pl* **~s** *or* **-tra** /-trə/) raised platform for a public speaker

rosy /'rəʊzi/ *adj* (**-ier, -iest**) **1** pink and pleasant in appearance:

~ cheeks **2** likely to be good or successful: *a ~ future*

rot /rɒt/ *v* (**-tt-**) [I, T] (cause sth to) decay naturally and gradually ● **rot** *n* **1** process of decaying **2** (**the rot**) used to describe the fact that a situation is getting worse

rota /'rəʊtə/ *n* (*GB*) list of jobs to be done and the people who will do them in turn

rotary /'rəʊtəri/ *adj* moving round a central point

rotate /rəʊ'teɪt/ *v* [I, T] **1** (cause sth to) move or turn around a central point (cause sth/sb to) regularly change around: *We ~ the night shift.* ▶ **rotation** /-'teɪʃn/ *n* **1** [U] action of rotating: *the rotation of the Earth* **2** [C] one complete turn

rotor /'rəʊtə(r)/ *n* rotating part of a machine, esp on a helicopter

rotten /'rɒtn/ *adj* **1** decayed **2** (*infml*) very bad; terrible

rough¹ /rʌf/ *adj* **1** (of a surface) not level or smooth **2** not exact; not in detail: *a ~ guess/sketch* **3** not gentle or careful; violent **4** (of the sea) having large waves ● **rough** *n* **1** (**the rough**) [sing] part of a golf course where the grass is long **2** [C] (*tech*) first version of a drawing or design, done without much detail [IDM] **in rough** (*esp GB*) not complete; unfinished ▶ **rough-and-ready** *adj* not carefully made but good enough for particular situation ▶ **roughly** *adv* **1** approximately: *It will cost ~£100.* **2** using force ▶ **roughness** *n* [U]

rough² /rʌf/ *v* [IDM] **rough it** (*infml*) live without the normal comforts [PV] **rough sb⇔up** (*infml*) hurt sb by hitting them ● **rough** *adv* using force or violence [IDM] **live/sleep rough** live or sleep outdoors, usu because you have no home

roughen /'rʌfn/ *v* [I, T] become or make sth rough

roulette /ru:'let/ *n* [U] gambling game played with a small ball on a revolving wheel

round¹ /raʊnd/ *adj* **1** shaped like a circle or a ball; curved **2** (of a number) expressed to the nearest 10, 100, etc ▶ **roundly** *adv* forcefully ▶ **roundness** *n* [U] (*written*) ■ **,round 'trip** *n* [C, U] journey to a place and back again ■ **,round-'shouldered** *adj* with shoulders that are bent forward

round² /raʊnd/ *adv* **1** moving in a circle; on all sides of sb/sth: *spin ~* ◇ *The hands of a clock go ~.* ◇ *A crowd gathered ~.* **2** in a circle or curve to face the opposite way: *Turn your chair ~.* **3** at various places in an area: *People stood ~ waiting for something to happen.* **4** to the other side of sth: *We walked ~ to the back of the house.* **5** from one place, person, etc to another: *Pass these papers* ~. **6** (*infml*) to or at sb's house: *I'll be ~ in an hour.*

round³ /raʊnd/ n **1** set of events forming part of a process: *the next ~ of talks* **2** stage in a sports competition **3** stage in a boxing or wrestling game **4** complete game of golf **5** regular route taken by sb delivering or collecting sth: *a postman's ~* **6** number of drinks bought by one person for all the others in a group **7** (*GB*) whole slice of bread; sandwich made from two whole slices of bread **8** bullet

round⁴ /raʊnd/ *prep* **1** in a circle: *The earth moves ~ the sun.* **2** on, to or from the other side of sth: *walk ~ the corner* **3** surrounding sth/sb: *a wall ~ the house* **4** in or to many parts of sth: *look ~ the shop* [IDM] **round here** near where you are now or where you live

round⁵ /raʊnd/ *adv* **1** go round a corner, bend, etc **2** make sth into a round shape [PV] **round sth off (with sth)** complete sth satisfactorily **round sb/sth up 1** find and bring people, animals or things together: *~ up cattle* **2** increase sth to the nearest whole number

roundabout /'raʊndəbaʊt/ n (*GB*) **1** road junction where vehicles must go round a circle **2** = MERRY-GO-ROUND (MERRY) ● **roundabout** *adj* indirect: *a ~ route*

rounders /'raʊndəz/ n [U] (*GB*) team game played with a bat and a ball

rouse /raʊz/ v [T] **1** (*fml*) wake sb up **2** cause sb to be more active, interested, etc: *a rousing speech*

rout /raʊt/ v [T] defeat sb easily and completely ● **rout** n [sing] complete defeat

route /ru:t/ n way from one place to another ● **route** v [T] send sb/sth by a particular route

routine /ru:'ti:n/ n [C,U] regular way of doing things ● **routine** *adj* **1** regular or normal **2** (*disapprov*) ordinary and boring

row¹ /rəʊ/ n **1** line of people or things: *We sat in a ~ at the back of the room.* **2** journey in a rowing boat: *We went for a ~ on the lake.* [IDM] **in a row** happening one after another without interruption: *This is her third win in a ~.* ● **row** v [I, T] move a boat through the water using oars ■ **rowing boat** (*US* **rowboat**) n small open boat that you row with oars

row² /raʊ/ n **1** [C] serious disagreement; noisy argument **2** [sing] loud unpleasant noise ● **row** v [I] (*GB*) have a noisy argument

rowdy /'raʊdi/ *adj* (**-ier, -iest**) (of people) noisy and rough

royal /'rɔɪəl/ *adj* of or belonging to a

king or queen ● **royal** n [C, usu *pl*] (*infml*) member of a royal family ■ **,royal 'blue** *adj* deep bright blue ▶ **royalist** n person who supports rule by a king or queen

royalty /'rɔɪəlti/ n (*pl* **-ies**) **1** [U] royal person or people **2** [C] payment to an author, etc for every copy of a book, etc that is sold

RSI /ˌɑːr es 'aɪ/ n [U] repetitive strain injury; pain and swelling, esp in the arms and hands, caused by performing the same movement many times in a job or an activity

RSVP /ˌɑːr es viː 'piː/ *abbr* (on an invitation) please reply

rub /rʌb/ v (**-bb-**) [I, T] move your hand, a cloth, etc backwards and forwards over a surface **2** [I] (of a surface) move backwards and forwards many times against sth, esp causing pain: *My shoes are ~bing.* **3** [I] spread a liquid or other substance over a surface while pressing firmly: *She ~bed the lotion into her skin.* [IDM] **rub sb up the wrong way** (*infml*) annoy sb [PV] **rub sb/yourself/sth down** rub the skin of a person, horse, etc hard with sth to make it dry and clean **rub sth down** make sth smooth by rubbing it with a special material **rub it/sth in** (*infml*) remind sb of sth unpleasant **rub sth off (sth)** remove sth or be removed by rubbing: *R~ the dirt off your trousers.* **rub sth out** remove pencil marks, etc by using a rubber ● **rub** n [C, usu *sing*] act of rubbing a surface

rubber /'rʌbə(r)/ n **1** [U] strong elastic substance used for making tyres, etc **2** (*GB*) [C] piece of rubber for removing pencil marks from paper, etc **3** [C] (in some card games or sports) competition consisting of a series of games between the same players ■ **,rubber 'band** n thin circular strip of rubber, used for keeping papers, etc together

rubbish /'rʌbɪʃ/ n [U] **1** (*esp GB*) things that you throw away **2** nonsense ▶ **rubbishy** *adj* (*GB, infml*) of very poor quality

rubble /'rʌbl/ n [U] bits of broken stone, rocks or bricks

ruby /'ru:bi/ n (*pl* **-ies**) dark red precious stone

rucksack /'rʌksæk/ n large bag carried on the back by walkers and climbers

rudder /'rʌdə(r)/ n flat hinged piece at the back of a boat or aircraft, used for steering

ruddy /'rʌdi/ *adj* (**-ier, -iest**) **1** (of sb's face) looking red and healthy **2** (*lit*) red in colour ● **ruddy** *adj, adv* (*GB, infml*) mild swear word used to show annoyance: *You're a ~ fool!*

rude /ru:d/ *adj* (**-r, -st**) **1** not polite

2 connected with sex or the body in a way people find offensive **3** (written) sudden and unexpected: *a ~ reminder* ▶ **rudely** *adv* ▶ **rudeness** *n* [U]

rudiments /'ruːdɪmənts/ *n* [pl] (*fml*) most basic facts of a subject ▶ **rudimentary** /ˌruːdɪ'mentri/ *adj* (*fml*) **1** simple; basic **2** undeveloped

ruffle /'rʌfl/ *v* [T] **1** disturb the smooth surface of sth: *He ~d her hair affectionately.* **2** upset or annoy sb

rug /rʌg/ *n* **1** thick piece of material, like a small carpet, for covering part of a floor **2** small blanket

rugby /'rʌgbi/ *n* [U] kind of football played with an oval ball that may be kicked or carried

rugged /'rʌgɪd/ *adj* **1** (of a landscape) uneven; rocky **2** (of a man's face) having strong, attractive features

rugger /'rʌgə(r)/ *n* [U] (*infml, esp GB*) = RUGBY

ruin /'ruːɪn/ *v* [T] **1** destroy or spoil sth **2** cause sb to lose all their money ● **ruin** *n* **1** [U] destruction **2** [U] fact of having no money, of having lost your job, etc: *Drink led to his ~.* **3** [C, usu pl] parts of a building that remain after it has been destroyed: *the ~s of an old castle* [IDM] **in ruins** destroyed or severely damaged: *The scandal left his reputation in ~s.* ▶ **ruined** *adj* partly destroyed ▶ **ruinous** *adj* causing ruin

rule /ruːl/ *n* **1** [C] statement of what may, must or must not be done **2** [C] habit; usual way sth happens: *I go to bed early, as a ~.* **3** [U] government: *under foreign ~* [IDM] **a rule of thumb** rough practical way of doing or measuring sth ● **rule** *v* **1** [I, T] have authority over a country, group of people, etc **2** [T] give an official decision about sth: *The judge ~d in his favour.* **3** [T] draw a line with a ruler [IDM] **rule the roost** (*infml*) be the most powerful member of a group [PV] **rule sb/sth out** state that sth is not possible or that sb/sth is not suitable ▶ **ruler** *n* **1** person who rules or governs **2** straight piece of wood, plastic, etc used for drawing straight lines or for measuring ▶ **ruling** *n* official decision

rum /rʌm/ *n* [U] alcoholic drink made from sugar cane

rumble /'rʌmbl/ *v* [I, T] *v* [U, C] (make a) deep heavy continuous sound

rummage /'rʌmɪdʒ/ *v* [I] turn things over carelessly while looking for sth

rumour (*US* **-or**) /'ruːmə(r)/ *n* [C, U] (piece of) information spread by being talked about but not certainly true ▶ **rumoured** (*US* **-ored**) *adj* reported as a rumour

rump /rʌmp/ *n* **1** [C] area of flesh at the top of the back legs of a four-legged animal **2** (ˌrump 'steak) [C, U] (piece of) good quality beef cut from the rump of a cow

rumple /'rʌmpl/ *v* [T] make sth creased or untidy

rumpus /'rʌmpəs/ *n* [usu sing] (*infml*) noisy quarrel or disturbance

run¹ /rʌn/ *v* (**-nn-** *pt* **ran** /ræn/ *pp* **run**) **1** [I] move using your legs, going faster than when you walk **2** [T] cover a certain distance by running **3** [I] practise running as a sport: *I go ~ning every morning.* **4** [I, T] take part in a race: *~ the marathon* **5** [T] control or manage a business, etc: *~ a hotel* **6** [I, T] (cause sth to) operate or function: *I can't afford to ~ a car any more.* ◇ *The heater ~s on electricity.* **7** [I] (of buses, etc) travel on a particular route **8** [T] (*infml*) drive sb to a place in a car: *I'll ~ you home.* **9** [I] move, esp quickly, in a particular direction: *The car ran off the road into a ditch.* **10** [T] move sth in a particular direction: *~ a comb through your hair* **11** [I, T] (cause sth to) lead or stretch from one place to another: *The road ~s parallel to the river.* **12** [I] continue for a time without stopping: *The play ran for six months.* **13** [T] bring sth into a country illegally and secretly: *~ drugs* **14** [I, T] (cause liquid to) flow: *a river that ~s into the sea* ◇ *I'll ~ you a bath.* **15** [I] (of colour) spread **16** (usu used with *adj*) become different in a particular (esp bad) way: *Supplies are ~ning low.* ◇ *We're ~ning short of milk.* **17** [T] publish an item or a story in a newspaper, etc **18** [I] ~**for** (*esp US*) be a candidate in an election for a political position: *~ for president* [IDM] **run amok** suddenly become angry or excited and start behaving violently **run in the family** → FAMILY **run its course** → COURSE **run for it** run in order to escape from sb/sth **run high** (of feelings) be strong and angry or excited **run riot/wild** behave in a very free and uncontrolled way **run the risk (of doing sth)** → RISK **run to seed** → SEED [PV] **run across sb/sth** meet sb or find sth by chance **run after sb/sth** chase sb/sth **2** (*infml*) try to have a romantic relationship with sb **run along** (*old-fash*) go away **run away (from sb/sth)** leave a place suddenly; escape from sb/sth **run away with you** (of a feeling) control you completely **run away/off with sb** leave your home, husband, wife, etc to have a relationship with sb else **run (sth) down 1** (cause sth to) lose power or stop working **2** (cause sth to) stop functioning gradually or become smaller in size: *The company is being ~ down.* **run sb/sth down 1** hit and injure sb/sth with a vehicle **2** criticize sb/sth in an unkind way **run into sb** meet sb by chance **run**

into sth experience difficulties unexpectedly **run sth off** copy sth on a machine **run out** become no longer valid **run out (of sth)** use up or finish a supply of sth **run sb/sth over** (of a vehicle or its driver) knock down and drive over sb/sth **run through sth 1** (written) pass quickly through sth **2** discuss, read or examine sth quickly **3** perform, act or practise sth **run to sth 1** be of a particular size or amount **2** (of money) be enough for sth: *Our funds won't ~ to a trip abroad this year.* **run sth up 1** allow a bill, debt, etc to reach a total: ~ *up big debts* **2** make a piece of clothing quickly **3** raise sth, esp a flag **run up against sth** experience a difficulty ■ **runaway** *adj* **1** (of a person) having left without telling anyone **2** out of control ■ **'runaway** *n* child who has left home without telling anyone ■ **run-'down** *adj* **1** (of a building, etc) in bad condition **2** (of a person) tired, esp from working too hard ■ **'run-up n** [sing] period of time leading up to an event

run² /rʌn/ *n* **1** [C] act of running on foot **2** [C] journey in a car, train, etc **3** [C] period of sth good or bad happening: *a ~ of bad luck* **4** [C] series of performances of a play or film **5** [sing] strong demand for sth **6** [sing] enclosed space for domestic animals **7** [C] point scored in cricket or baseball [IDM] **on the run** trying to escape ■ **run-of-the-'mill** *adj* ordinary, with no interesting features

rung¹ *pp of* RING¹

rung² /rʌŋ/ *n* step on a ladder

runner /'rʌnə(r)/ *n* **1** person or animal that runs, esp in a race **2** smuggler: *a gun ~* **3** thin strip on which sth slides or moves: *the ~s of a sledge* ■ **runner 'bean** *n* climbing plant with a long flat green bean container, eaten as a vegetable ■ **runner-'up** (*pl* **,runners-'up**) *n* person who finishes second in a race

running /'rʌnɪŋ/ *n* [U] **1** action or sport of running **2** activity of managing or operating sth [IDM] **make the running** (GB, *infml*) set the pace or standard ● **running** *adj* **1** in succession: *win the championship three years ~* **2** (of water) flowing; supplied to a building **3** continuous: *a ~ battle*

runny /'rʌni/ *adj* (-ier, -iest) (*infml*) **1** (of the eyes or nose) producing liquid **2** more liquid than usual

runway /'rʌnweɪ/ *n* surface along which aircraft take off and land

rupture /'rʌptʃə(r)/ *n* **1** (*med*) breaking or bursting of sth inside the body; hernia: *the ~ of a blood vessel* **2** (*fml*) ending of friendly relations between people, countries, etc ● **rupture** *v* **1** [I, T] (*med*) (cause sth to) burst or break apart inside the body **2** [T] (written) end good relations with sb

rural /'rʊərəl/ *adj* in or of the countryside

ruse /ruːz/ *n* trick

rush¹ /rʌʃ/ *v* **1** [I, T] move or do sth with great speed, often too fast **2** [I, T] do or force sb to do sth too quickly **3** [T] try to attack or capture sb/sth suddenly [IDM] **be rushed off your feet** be extremely busy ● **rush** *n* **1** [sing] sudden movement forward made by a lot of people or things **2** [sing, U] situation in which you are in a hurry and need to do things quickly: *I can't stop—I'm in a ~.* **3** [sing, U] (period of) great activity: *the Christmas ~* **4** [sing] sudden demand for goods, etc **5** [C, usu pl] tall plant like grass that grows near water ■ **'rush hour** *n* busy period when many people are travelling to or from work

rusk /rʌsk/ *n* hard crisp biscuit for babies to eat

rust /rʌst/ *n* [U] reddish-brown substance formed on metal by the action of water and air ● **rust** *v* [I, T] (cause sth to) become covered in rust ● **rusty** *adj* (-ier, -iest) **1** covered with rust **2** (*infml*) showing lack of recent practice: *My tennis is a bit ~ y these days.*

rustle /'rʌsl/ *v* **1** [I, T] (cause sth dry and light to) make a sound like paper, leaves, etc moving or rubbing together **2** [T] steal farm animals [PV] **rustle sth up (for sb)** (*infml*) make or find sth quickly for sb: ~ *up a meal* ● **rustle** *n* [sing] light dry sound

rut /rʌt/ *n* **1** deep track made by a wheel in soft ground **2** fixed and boring way of life: *be in a ~* ● **rutted** *adj* (of a road or path) having deep tracks made by wheels

ruthless /'ruːθləs/ *adj* (*disapprov*) without pity; cruel ● **ruthlessly** *adv*

rye /raɪ/ *n* [U] (grain of a) cereal plant used for making flour and whisky

Ss

S *abbr* south(ern): *S Yorkshire*

S, s /es/ *n* [C,U] (*pl* **S's, s's** /'esɪz/) the nineteenth letter of the English alphabet

sabbath /'sæbəθ/ (the **Sabbath**) *n* [sing] the day of rest, Sunday for Christians, Saturday for Jews

sabotage /'sæbətɑːʒ/ *n* [U] deliberate damaging of an enemy's or rival's equipment, plans, etc ● **sabotage** *v* [T] secretly damage or spoil a machine, a car, sb's plans, etc ▶ **saboteur** /ˌsæbə'tɜː(r)/ n person who commits sabotage

sabre (US **saber**) /'seɪbə(r)/ n heavy sword with a curved blade

saccharin /'sækərɪn/ n [U] very sweet substance used in place of sugar

sachet /'sæʃeɪ/ n small paper or plastic packet for holding sugar, shampoo, etc

sack¹ /sæk/ n (contents of a) large bag of strong material for carrying coal, potatoes, etc [IDM] **get the sack | give sb the sack** be dismissed/ dismiss sb from a job ■ **'sackcloth** (also **sacking**) n [U] rough material for making sacks ▶ **'sackful** n amount held by a sack

sack² /sæk/ v [T] **1** (infml, esp GB) dismiss sb from a job **2** (of an army, etc in the past) steal or destroy property in a captured city, etc

sacrament /'sækrəmənt/ n Christian ceremony, eg baptism or confirmation ▶ **sacramental** /ˌsækrə'mentl/ adj

sacred /'seɪkrɪd/ adj **1** connected with religion or with God: a ~ shrine **2** very important and treated with great respect

sacrifice /'sækrɪfaɪs/ n **1** [U] fact of giving sth valuable to you for a good purpose **2** [C] valuable thing that you give up for a good purpose: make ~ **3** [C,U] ~(to) act of offering sth valuable to a god ● **sacrifice** v ~ (to) **1** [T] give up sth that is valuable to you for a good purpose: ~ a career to have a family **2** [I, T] kill an animal or a person in order to please a god ▶ **sacrificial** /ˌsækrɪ'fɪʃl/ adj

sacrilege /'sækrəlɪdʒ/ n [U, sing] disrespectful treatment of a holy thing or place ▶ **sacrilegious** /ˌsækrɪ'lɪdʒəs/ adj

sad /sæd/ adj (~der, ~dest) unhappy or causing sorrow: a ~ person/song ▶ **sadden** v [T] (fml) (often passive) make sb sad: ~dened by his death ▶ **sadly** adv unfortunately: S~ly, we have no more money. **2** in a sad way: smile ~ly ▶ **sadness** n [U]

saddle /'sædl/ n leather seat for a rider on a horse, bicycle, etc [IDM] **in the saddle 1** in a position of authority and control **2** riding a horse ● **saddle** v [T] put a saddle on a horse [PV] **saddle sb with sth** give sb an unpleasant task, etc: I was ~d with cleaning the car. ■ **'saddlebag** n bag attached to a saddle

sadism /'seɪdɪzəm/ n [U] (getting sexual pleasure from) cruelty to other people ▶ **sadist** n person who gets pleasure from hurting others ▶ **sadistic** /sə'dɪstɪk/ adj

sae /ˌes eɪ 'iː/ abbr stamped addressed envelope, usually sent to sb when you want a reply

safari /sə'fɑːri/ n [C,U] journey to hunt or watch wild animals, esp in Africa: on ~ in Kenya

safe¹ /seɪf/ adj (~r, ~st) **1** ~ (from) protected from danger and harm: ~ from attack **2** not likely to lead to physical harm or danger: a ~ speed **3** not hurt, damaged, lost, etc: They turned up ~ and sound. **4** (of a place, etc) giving protection from danger, harm, etc **5** careful: a ~ driver [IDM] **(as) safe as houses** as very safe **play (it) safe** be careful; avoid risks ■ **,safe 'keeping** n [U] fact of sth being in a safe place: Put it in your pocket for ~ keeping. **2** fact of sb/sth being taken care of by a trusted person ▶ **safely** adv

safe² /seɪf/ n very strong box with a lock, for keeping valuable objects in

safeguard /'seɪfgɑːd/ n ~(against) something that prevents harm, damage, etc ● **safeguard** v [T] ~ (against) protect sth from loss, harm or damage; keep sth safe

safety /'seɪfti/ n [U] state of being safe; freedom from danger ■ **'safety belt** n = SEAT BELT (SEAT) ■ **'safety pin** n pin with a point bent backwards towards the head, that is covered when closed so it cannot hurt you ■ **'safety valve** n device which lets gas, liquid, etc escape if the pressure gets too high **2** harmless way of letting out anger, etc

sag /sæg/ v (-gg-) [I] **1** sink or curve down under weight or pressure **2** hang unevenly

saga /'sɑːɡə/ n **1** long story full of adventures about people who lived a long time ago **2** long story about events over a period of many years

sage /seɪdʒ/ n **1** [U] herb used for flavouring food **2** [C] (fml) very wise person ● **sage** adj (lit) wise

said pt, pp of SAY

sail¹ /seɪl/ n **1** [C,U] strong cloth used for catching the wind and moving a boat along **2** [sing] trip on a boat: go for a ~ **3** [C] arm of a windmill [IDM] **set sail (from/for ...)** begin a trip by sea

sail² /seɪl/ v **1** [I] travel on water in a ship, yacht, etc **2** [I, T] control a boat or ship: Can you ~ (a yacht)? **3** [I] begin a journey on water **4** [T] move quickly and smoothly in a particular direction [PV] **sail through (sth)** pass an exam, etc easily ▶ **sailing** n [U] sport of travelling in a boat with sails: go ~ing ■ **'sailing boat** (US **'sailboat**) (also **'sailing ship**) n boat or ship that uses sails ▶ **sailor** n member of a ship's crew; person who sails a boat

saint /seɪnt; *or before names* snt/ *n* (*abbr* **St**) person recognized as holy by the Christian Church because of the way they have lived or died ▸ **saintly** *adj* (-**ier**, -**iest**) very holy and good

sake /seɪk/ *n* [IDM] **for God's, goodness', heaven's, etc sake** used before or after an action or request to express anger, etc: *For goodness' ~ hurry up!* **for the sake of sb/sth | for sb/sth's sake** in order to help sb/sth or because you like sb/sth: *Please do it for my ~.*

salad /'sæləd/ *n* [C,U] **1** mixture of raw vegetables, eg lettuce, cucumber and tomato **2** food served with salad: *a cheese ~* ■ **salad dressing** *n* [U,C] sauce of oil, vinegar, etc put on salads

salami /sə'lɑːmi/ *n* [U] large spicy sausage served cold in slices

salary /'sæləri/ *n* (*pl* -**ies**) (usu monthly) payment for a job ▸ **salaried** *adj* receiving a salary

sale /seɪl/ *n* **1** [U,C] act of selling sth or being sold **2** [C] period when goods are sold at a lower price than usual: *buy a dress in the ~s* [IDM] **for sale** available to be bought: *They've put their house up for ~.* **on sale 1** (of goods in shops, etc) available to be bought **2** (*esp US*) being offered at a reduced price ■ **salesman** *n* (*pl* -**men**) ('**salesperson** *n* (*pl* -**people**) ('**saleswoman** *n* (*pl* -**women**) person who sells goods ■ **salesmanship** *n* [U] skill in persuading people to buy things

saline /'seɪlaɪn/ *adj* containing salt

saliva /sə'laɪvə/ *n* [U] liquid produced in your mouth to help you to swallow food

sallow /'sæləʊ/ *adj* (of sb's skin or face) having an unhealthy yellow colour

salmon /'sæmən/ *n* (*pl* **salmon**) [C, U] large fish with silver skin and pink flesh that is used for food ■ **salmon** 'pink *adj* orange-pink in colour, like the flesh of a salmon

salmonella /ˌsælmə'nelə/ *n* [U] type of bacteria that causes food poisoning

salon /'sælɒn/ *n* shop that gives customers hair or beauty treatment

saloon /sə'luːn/ *n* **1** (*also* **sa'loon car**) (*GB*) car with four doors and a boot which is separated from the rest of the interior **2** (*also* **sa'loon bar**) (*GB*) = LOUNGE BAR (LOUNGE) **3** bar where alcoholic drinks were sold in the western US in the past **4** large comfortable room on a ship, used by the passengers to relax

salt /sɔːlt/ *n* **1** [U] white substance obtained from mines and sea water, used to flavour food **2** [C] chemical compound of a metal and an acid [IDM] **the salt of the earth** good and honest people ▸ take sth with a pinch of salt → PINCH ● **salt** *v* [T] put salt in or on food ■ **'salt cellar** (*US* '**salt shaker**) *n* small container for salt ▸ **salty** *adj* (-**ier**, -**iest**)

salute /sə'luːt/ *n* action of raising your right hand to the side of your head as a sign of respect, esp in the armed forces ● **salute** *v* **1** [I,T] give sb a salute **2** [T] (*fml*) express admiration for sth

salvage /'sælvɪdʒ/ *n* [U] **1** act of saving things that have been or might be lost or damaged, esp in an accident **2** things that are saved from a disaster or an accident ● **salvage** *v* [T] save sth from loss, wreckage, etc

salvation /sæl'veɪʃn/ *n* [U] **1** (in Christianity) state of being saved from evil **2** way of protecting sth from danger, disaster, etc

same /seɪm/ *adj* **1** exactly the one(s) referred to; not different: *We've lived in the ~ house for ten years.* **2** exactly like the one(s) mentioned: *The ~ thing happened to me last week.* ● **same** *pron* (**the same**) **1** the same thing(s): *I would do the same~.* **2** the same number, colour, size, etc: *I'd like one the ~ as yours.* [IDM] **all/just the same** in spite of this: *She's quite old, but very lively all the ~.* **be all the same to sb** → ALL **same here** (*spoken*) used to say that sth is also true of you: *'I'm hungry.' 'S~ here.'* ● **same** *adv* (usu **the same**) in the same way: *Babies all look the ~ to me.* ▸ **sameness** *n* [U] being the same; lack of variety

samosa /sə'məʊsə/ *n* spicy Indian food consisting of a triangle of pastry filled with meat or vegetables

sample /'sɑːmpl/ *n* one of a number of people or things, or part of a whole, used for showing what the rest is like: *wallpaper ~s* ● **sample** *v* [T] test a small amount of sth to see what it is like: *~ our new wine*

sanatorium /ˌsænə'tɔːriəm/ *n* (*pl* ~s *or* -**ria** /-riə/) place like a hospital for treating people who are or have been ill

sanctimonious /ˌsæŋktɪ'məʊniəs/ *adj* (*disapprov*) showing that you feel morally better than others ▸ **sanctimoniously** *adv*

sanction /'sæŋkʃn/ *n* **1** [C,usu pl] official order that limits trade, etc with a country in order to make it obey a law: *economic ~s* **2** [U] (*fml*) official permission or approval for sth ● **sanction** *v* [T] give permission for sth to happen

sanctity /'sæŋktɪti/ *n* [U] holiness

sanctuary /'sæŋktʃuəri/ *n* (*pl* -**ies**) **1** [C] area where wild birds or animals are protected and encouraged to breed **2** [C,U] (place offering) safety and protection from arrest, attack, etc: *be offered ~* **3** [C] holy building or part of it that is considered the most holy

sand /sænd/ n **1** [U] substance consisting of fine grains of rock, found on beaches, in deserts, etc on a beach **2** [U,C, usu pl] large area of sand on a beach ● **sand** v [T] ~(**down**) smooth sth by rubbing it with sandpaper: ~ (*down*) *the wood* ■ **'sandbag** n bag filled with sand, used for stopping floods, water, etc ■ **'sandcastle** n pile of sand made to look like a castle, usu by a child on a beach ■ **'sand dune** n = DUNE ■ **'sandpaper** n [U] strong paper with sand glued to it, used for rubbing surfaces smooth ■ **'sandstone** n [U] type of stone formed from sand, used in building ▶ **sandy** *adj* (**-ier, -iest**) **1** covered with or containing sand **2** (of hair) yellowish-red

sandal /sændl/ n type of open shoe attached to the foot by straps

sandwich /sænwɪdʒ/ n two slices of bread with meat, salad, etc between them: *a cheese ~* ● **sandwich** v [T] put sth/sb between two other people or things

sane /seɪn/ adj (**~r, ~st**) **1** having a healthy mind **2** sensible and reasonable: *a ~ policy*

sang *pt of* SING

sanitary /sænətri/ adj **1** free from dirt that might cause disease: *poor ~ conditions* **2** clean; not likely to cause health problems ■ **'sanitary towel** (US **'sanitary napkin**) n pad of cotton wool, used by a woman during her period(3)

sanitation /ˌsænɪˈteɪʃn/ n [U] systems that keep places clean, esp by removing human waste

sanity /sænəti/ n the quality of having a normal healthy mind

sank *pt of* SINK

sap /sæp/ v (**-pp-**) [T] make sth/sb weaker; destroy sth gradually ● **sap** n [U] liquid in a plant or tree that carries food to all its parts ▶ **sapling** n young tree

sapphire /sæfaɪə(r)/ n bright blue precious stone ● **sapphire** adj bright blue in colour

sarcasm /sɑːkæzəm/ n [U] (use of ironic remarks, intended to hurt sb's feelings) ▶ **sarcastic** /sɑːˈkæstɪk/ adj ▶ **sarcastically** /-kli/ adv

sardine /ˌsɑːˈdiːn/ n small young sea fish that is either eaten fresh or preserved in tins [IDM] (**packed, crammed, etc**) **like sardines** (*infml*) pressed tightly together

sari /sɑːri/ n dress worn esp by Indian women made of a long piece of cloth wrapped round the body

sarong /səˈrɒŋ/ n long piece of fabric wrapped around the body from the waist, worn in Indonesia and Malaysia

sash /sæʃ/ n **1** long piece of cloth worn round the waist or over the shoulder **2** either of a pair of windows that slide up and down inside the main frame ■ **ˌsash 'window** n window with two frames that slide up and down

sat *pt, pp of* SIT

Satan /seɪtn/ n the Devil ▶ **satanic** (*also* **Satanic**) /səˈtænɪk/ adj

satchel /sætʃəl/ n bag with a long strap for carrying school books

satellite /sætəlaɪt/ n **1** electronic device that is sent into space and moves around the earth or another planet. It is used for communicating by radio, television, etc and for providing information: ~ *television/TV* **2** natural object that moves around a larger natural object in space **3** town, country or organization that depends on another larger or more powerful one: ~ *states* ■ **'satellite dish** n piece of equipment that receives signals from a satellite

satin /sætɪn/ n [U] silk material that is shiny on one side

satire /sætaɪə(r)/ n **1** [U] way of criticizing a person, idea or institution, using humour to show their faults: *political ~* **2** [C] piece of writing that uses this type of criticism ▶ **satirical** /səˈtɪrɪkl/ adj ▶ **satirize** (*also* **-ise**) /sætəraɪz/ v [T] make fun of sb/sth using satire

satisfaction /ˌsætɪsˈfækʃn/ n **1** [U] feeling of being contented: *get ~ from your work* **2** [C] something that makes sb contented **3** [U] (*fml*) acceptable way of dealing with a complaint, etc

satisfactory /ˌsætɪsˈfæktəri/ adj good enough for a particular purpose; acceptable: ~ *progress* ▶ **satisfactorily** /-tərəli/ adv

satisfy /sætɪsfaɪ/ v (*pt, pp* **-ied**) [T] **1** give sb what they want or need; make sb pleased **2** provide what is wanted, needed or asked for: ~ *sb's hunger/curiosity* **3** give sb proof that sth is true ▶ **satisfied** adj contented

saturate /sætʃəreɪt/ v [T] **1** make sth completely wet **2** (*usu pass*) fill sth/sb completely so that it is impossible to add any more ▶ **saturated** adj **1** completely wet **2** (*chem*) (of butter, oils, etc) containing fats that are not easily processed by the body when eaten ▶ **saturation** /-ˈreɪʃn/ n [U]

Saturday /sætədeɪ; -di/ n [U,C] the seventh day of the week, next after

Friday (See examples of use at *Monday*.)

sauce /sɔːs/ n [C,U] thick liquid that is served with food to give it flavour ▶ **saucy** adj (-ier, -iest) rude ▶ **saucily** adv

saucepan /'sɔːspən/ n deep metal cooking pot with a lid and a handle

saucer /'sɔːsə(r)/ n small shallow dish on which a cup stands

sauna /'sɔːnə; also 'saʊnə/ n (period of sitting in a) very hot room filled with steam

saunter /'sɔːntə(r)/ v [I] walk in a slow relaxed way ▶ **saunter** n [sing]

sausage /'sɒsɪdʒ/ n [C,U] mixture of chopped meat, flavouring, etc inside a tube of thin skin

savage /'sævɪdʒ/ adj 1 fierce and violent: *a ~ animal* 2 involving very strong criticism: *a ~ attack on the education system* ● **savage** v [T] 1 (of an animal) attack sb violently: *~d by a dog* 2 (*written*) criticize sb/sth severely ▶ **savagely** adv ▶ **savagery** n [U] cruel and violent behaviour

save /seɪv/ v 1 [T] ~ (**from**) keep sb/sth safe from harm, loss, etc: *~ sb's life* 2 [I, T] ~ (**up**; **for**) keep sth, esp money for future use: *~ (up) for a new car* ◇ *S~ some cake for me!* 3 [T] make sth unnecessary: *That will ~ you a lot of trouble.* 4 [T] in football, etc) stop the ball going into the net [IDM] **save (sb's) face** (help sb to) avoid embarrassment **save your neck** → NECK ● **save** n (in football, etc) act of stopping a goal being scored ▶ **saving** n 1 [C] amount saved: *a saving of £5* 2 (**savings**) [pl] money saved ■ '**savings account** n bank account in which interest is paid on money saved

saviour (US **-or**) /'seɪvjə(r)/ n 1 person who saves sb/sth from danger 2 (**the Saviour**) Jesus Christ

savour (US **-or**) /'seɪvə(r)/ v 1 enjoy the full taste of sth: *~ the wine* 2 enjoy a feeling or an experience thoroughly: *~ your freedom* ● **savour** n [usu sing] taste or smell

savoury (US **-ory**) /'seɪvəri/ adj having a taste that is salty not sweet ● **savoury** n [usu pl] (pl **-ies**) savoury dish

saw¹ pt of SEE¹

saw² /sɔː/ n tool which has a long blade with sharp teeth, for cutting wood, metal, etc ● **saw** v (pt **~ed** pp **~n** /sɔːn/, US also **~ed**) [I, T] use a saw to cut sth [PV] **saw sth up** (**into sth**) cut sth into pieces with a saw ■ '**sawdust** n [U] tiny pieces of wood that fall from wood as it is sawn ■ '**sawmill** n factory where wood is cut into boards

saxophone /'sæksəfəʊn/ n curved metal musical instrument, often used for jazz

say /seɪ/ v (pt, pp **said** /sed/) [T] 1 speak or tell sth to sb, using words 2 give an opinion on sth 3 suggest or give sth as an example or a possibility: *You could learn the basics in, let's ~, two months.* 4 make sth clear by words, gestures, etc: *His angry glance said it all.* 5 (of sth written or that can be seen) give particular information: *The book doesn't ~ where he was born.* [IDM] **go without saying** be very obvious **that is to say** in other words **you can say that again** I agree with you completely ● **say** n [sing, U] right to influence sth by giving your opinion before a decision is made: *have no ~ in what happens* [IDM] **have your say** express your opinion ▶ **saying** n well-known phrase or statement

scab /skæb/ n 1 dry crust that forms over a wound 2 (*infml, disapprov*) worker who refuses to join a strike

scaffold /'skæfəʊld/ n 1 platform on which criminals are executed 2 framework of poles and boards round a building for workers to stand on ▶ **scaffolding** n [U] framework of poles and boards round a building for workers to stand on

scald /skɔːld/ v [T] burn yourself with hot liquid or steam ● **scald** n injury to the skin from hot liquid or steam ▶ **scalding** adj very hot

scale¹ /skeɪl/ n 1 [sing, U] relative size, extent, etc of sth: *riots on a large ~* 2 [C] range or levels or numbers used for measuring sth: *a salary ~* 3 [C] regular series of marks on an instrument used for measuring 4 (**scales**) (US also **scale**) [pl] instrument for weighing people or things: *bathroom ~s* 5 [C] relation between the actual size of sth and its size on a map, diagram, etc that represents it 6 [C] (*music*) series of notes arranged in order of pitch 7 [C] one of the thin pieces of hard material that cover fish, snakes, etc 8 [U] (*GB*) chalky substance left inside kettles, water pipes, etc ▶ **scaly** adj (-ier, -iest)

scale² /skeɪl/ v 1 [T] (*written*) climb to the top of sth high 2 [T] remove the scales from a fish [PV] **scale sth up/down** increase/decrease the size or number of sth

scallop /'skɒləp/ n shellfish with two fan-shaped shells

scalp /skælp/ n skin and hair on top of the head ● **scalp** v [T] cut the scalp off sb

scalpel /'skælpəl/ n small light knife used by surgeons

scamper /'skæmpə(r)/ v [I] run quickly like a child or small animal

scampi /'skæmpi/ n [U, with sing or pl verb] (GB) large prawns

scan /skæn/ v (-nn-) **1** [T] examine sth closely: ~ the horizon **2** [T] look at a document, etc quickly but not thoroughly: ~ the newspapers **3** [T] get an image of an object, part of sb's body, etc on a computer by passing X rays, etc over it in a special machine **4** [I] (of poetry) have a regular rhythm [PV] **scan sth into sth/scan sth in** (computing) pass an electronic beam over sth in order to put it into the computer's memory ● **scan** n medical test in which a machine produces a picture of the inside of the body: do/have a brain ~ ▶ **scanner** n **1** device for examining or recording sth using beams of light sound or X-rays **2** machine which uses X-rays, etc to produce a picture of the inside of the body

scandal /'skændl/ n **1** [C,U] action or behaviour that offends or shocks people **2** [U] talk which damages a person's reputation ▶ **scandalize** (also **-ise**) /-dəlaɪz/ v [T] do sth that people find very shocking ▶ **scandalous** adj

scant /skænt/ adj (fml) hardly any; not enough ▶ **scantily** adv ▶ **scanty** adj (-ier, -iest) very small in size or amount

scapegoat /'skeɪpgəʊt/ n person blamed for the wrong acts of another

scar /skɑː(r)/ n **1** mark left on the skin by a wound that has healed **2** permanent mental suffering after a bad experience ● **scar** v (-rr-) [T] leave a scar on sb

scarce /skeəs/ adj (~r, ~st) less than is needed; hard to find ▶ **scarcely** adv almost not; barely: ~ enough food ▶ **scarcity** n [U,C] (pl **-ies**) lack of sth

scare /skeə(r)/ v **1** [T] frighten sb **2** [I] become frightened: He ~s easily. ● **scare** n feeling or state of fear: a bomb/health ~ **1** ▶ **'scarecrow** n figure dressed in old clothes, to scare birds away from crops ▶ **scary** /'skeəri/ adj (-ier, -iest) (infml) frightening

scarf /skɑːf/ n (pl **scarves** /skɑːvz/ or **~s**) piece of material worn round the neck or over the hair

scarlet /'skɑːlət/ adj bright red in colour **1** ,**scarlet 'fever** n serious infectious disease that causes red marks on the skin

scathing /'skeɪðɪŋ/ adj criticizing sb/ sth very severely ▶ **scathingly** adv

scatter /'skætə(r)/ v **1** [T] throw or drop things in different directions: ~ seed **2** [I, T] (cause people or animals to) move quickly in various directions **1** ,**scatterbrain** n (infml) person who cannot concentrate for long or forgets things quickly

▶ **scatterbrained** adj ▶ **scattered** adj spread over a wide area

scavenge /'skævɪndʒ/ v [I, T] **1** search through rubbish for things that can be used or eaten **2** (of animals or birds) eat dead animals that have been killed by a car, etc ▶ **scavenger** n animal, bird or person that scavenges

scenario /sə'nɑːriəʊ/ n (pl **~s**) **1** imagined series of future events: a nightmare ~ **2** written outline of a play, film, etc

scene /siːn/ n [C] **1** place where sth happens: the ~ of the crime **2** incident in real life: ~s of horror during the fire **3** place represented on the stage in a theatre, etc **4** division of play or opera **5** (**the scene**) particular area of activity or way life: the fashion ~ **6** view that you see **7** (usu sing) loud embarrassing argument: make a ~ [IDM] **behind the scenes 1** behind the stage of a theatre **2** in secret ▶ **scenery** n [U] **1** natural features of an area, eg mountains **2** painted background used on a theatre stage ▶ **scenic** /'siːnɪk/ adj having beautiful natural scenery

scent /sent/ n **1** [U,C] pleasant smell **2** [U,C, usu sing] smell left behind by a person or animal and that other animals can follow **3** [U] (esp GB) perfume [IDM] **on the scent (of sth)** close to discovering sth ● **scent** v [T] **1** find sth by using the sense of smell **2** (written) suspect the presence of sth: ~ danger **3** give sth a particular, pleasant smell: ~ed paper

sceptic (US **sk-**) /'skeptɪk/ n person who usu doubts that a statement, claim, etc is true ▶ **sceptical** adj ▶ **scepticism** /'skeptɪsɪzəm/ n [U, sing] attitude of doubting that claims or statements are true

sceptre (US **-er**) /'septə(r)/ n decorated rod carried by a king or queen as a symbol of power

schedule /'ʃedjuːl/ n **1** [C,U] plan that lists all the work that you have to do and when you must do each thing: production ~s ◇ on/behind ~ (= on time/not on time) **2** [C] (US) = TIMETABLE (TIME¹) ● **schedule** v [T] arrange for sth to happen at a particular time

scheme /skiːm/ n **1** plan or system for doing or organizing sth: a ~ for raising money **2** ordered arrangement: a colour ~ **3** secret or dishonest plan ● **scheme** v [T] make secret plans to do sth ▶ **schemer** n (disapprov) person who plans secretly to do sth for their own advantage

schizophrenia /ˌskɪtsə'friːniə/ n [U] illness in which the mind becomes separated from actions

▶ **schizophrenic** /ˌskɪtsə'frenɪk/ adj, n (person) with schizophrenia

scholar /'skɒlə(r)/ n 1 person who knows a lot about an academic subject 2 student who has been given a scholarship to attend school or university ▶ **scholarly** adj ▶ **scholarship** n 1 [C] payment given to sb by an organization to help pay for their education 2 [U] serious study of an academic subject

school /skuːl/ n 1 [C,U] place where children go to be educated or where people go to learn a particular skill: All children should go to ~ (= attend) ~. ◇ primary/public ~ ◇ a driving/riding ~ 2 [U] process of learning in a school; time during your time when you go to a school: Is she old enough for ~? 3 [U] time during the day when children are working in a school: S~ starts at 9 am. 4 (**the school**) [sing] all the children and staff in a school 5 [U] (US, infml) (time spent at) college or university 6 [C] department of a university: medical ~ 7 [C] group of artists, writers, etc: the Dutch ~ of painting 8 [C] large number of fish swimming together ● **school** v [T] (fml) ~ (**in**) train sb/yourself/an animal to do sth ▶ **schooling** n [U] education ■ **school-'leaver** n (GB) person who has just left school ■ **'schoolmaster** ('schoolmistress) n teacher in a school, esp a private school

schooner /'skuːnə(r)/ n 1 sailing ship with two or more masts 2 tall glass for sherry or beer

science /'saɪəns/ n 1 [U] knowledge about the structure and behaviour of the natural and physical world, based on facts that you can prove, eg by experiments 2 [U, C] particular branch of knowledge, eg physics ■ ,**science 'fiction** n [U] fiction dealing with future scientific discoveries, imaginary worlds, etc ▶ **scientific** /ˌsaɪən'tɪfɪk/ adj ▶ **scientifically** /-klɪ/ adv ▶ **scientist** /'saɪəntɪst/ n expert in one or more of the sciences

scintillating /'sɪntɪleɪtɪŋ/ adj very clever, amusing and interesting

scissors /'sɪzəz/ n [pl] instrument with two blades, used for cutting paper, cloth, etc: a pair of ~

scoff /skɒf/ v [I] ~ (**at**) talk about sb/sth in a way that shows you think they are stupid or ridiculous

scold /skəʊld/ v [I, T] (fml) speak angrily to sb, esp a child

scone /skɒn/ n small cake made with fat and flour and eaten with butter

scoop /skuːp/ n 1 tool like a large spoon, used for picking up flour, grain, etc or for serving ice cream 2 piece of exciting news obtained by one newspaper, etc before its rivals ● **scoop** v [T] 1 ~ (**up**) move or lift sth with a scoop or sth like a scoop 2 ~ (**up**) move or lift sb/sth with a quick continuous movement

scooter /'skuːtə(r)/ n 1 (also '**motor scooter**) light motorcycle with a small engine and a cover to protect the rider's legs 2 child's vehicle with two wheels, moved by pushing one foot against the ground

scope /skəʊp/ n [U] 1 opportunity to achieve sth: ~ for improvement 2 range of things that a subject, an organization, etc deals with

scorch /skɔːtʃ/ v 1 [T] burn the surface of sth by making it too hot 2 [I, T] (cause sth to) become dry and brown, esp from the heat of the sun or from chemicals: ~ed grass ■ '**scorch mark** n brown mark made on a surface by burning

score[1] /skɔː(r)/ n 1 [C] (record of) points, goals, etc in a game 2 [C] copy of written music 3 [C] set or group of twenty 4 (**scores**) [pl] (infml) very many 5 [C] cut in a surface, made with a sharp tool [IDM] **on that/this score** as far as that/this is concerned **settle an old score** have your revenge

score[2] /skɔː(r)/ v 1 [I, T] win points, goals, etc in a game 2 [T] make a record of the points, goals, etc won in a game 3 [I, T] gain marks in a test or an exam; succeed 4 [T] write music: ~d for the piano 5 [T] make a cut or mark on a surface ▶ **scorer** n 1 (in sports) player who scores points, goals, etc 2 person who keeps a record of the points, etc scored

scorn /skɔːn/ n [U] strong feeling that sb/sth is stupid or not good enough ● **scorn** v [T] 1 feel or show that you do not respect sb/sth 2 refuse sth proudly: ~ sb's advice ▶ **scornful** adj ▶ **scornfully** adv

scorpion /'skɔːpiən/ n small animal with claws and a poisonous sting in its tail

Scotch /skɒtʃ/ n [C,U] (type or glass of) Scottish whisky ■ '**Scotch tape**™ n (US) = SELLOTAPE™

scot-free /ˌskɒt 'friː/ adj (infml) unpunished: escape ~

scoundrel /'skaʊndrəl/ n (old-fash) person without moral principles

scour /'skaʊə(r)/ v [T] 1 search a place thoroughly: ~ the area for the child 2 clean a surface by rubbing it hard with rough material ▶ **scourer** (also '**scouring pad**) n small ball of wire or stiff plastic used for cleaning pans

scourge /skɜːdʒ/ n (written) cause of great suffering: the ~ of war

scout /skaʊt/ n 1 (**the Scouts**) [pl] organization originally for boys, that trains young people in practical skills **2** [C] member of the Scouts **3** person, aircraft, etc sent ahead to get information about the enemy ● **scout** v [I, T] ~ (around/for) search an area in order to find sth

scowl /skaʊl/ n angry look or expression ● **scowl** v [I] ~ (at) look at sb/sth angrily

scrabble /'skræbl/ v [I] ~ (around/about/for) try to do sth in a hurry, often by moving your hands or feet about quickly: *She ~d around in her bag for her glasses.*

scraggy /'skrægi/ adj (-ier, -iest) (disapprov) thin and not looking healthy

scram /skræm/ v (-mm-) [I] (old-fash, sl) go away quickly

scramble /'skræmbl/ v **1** [I] move quickly, often with difficulty, using your hands to help you **2** [I] ~ (for) push, fight or compete with others for sth: *~ for the best seats* **3** [T] beat and cook eggs **4** [T] mix up a telephone or radio message so that only people with special equipment can understand it ● **scramble** n **1** [sing] difficult walk or climb over rough ground **2** [sing] ~ (for) rough struggle: *a ~ for seats* **3** [T] motorbike race over rough ground

scrap /skræp/ n **1** [C] small piece of sth, esp paper, fabric, etc: *a ~ of paper* ◊ (fig) *~s of news* **2** [U] unwanted things: *metal* **3** [C] (infml) short fight or quarrel ● **scrap** v (-pp-) **1** [T] cancel or get rid of sth useless **2** [I] (infml) fight with sb ■ '**scrapbook** n book of blank pages on which newspaper articles, etc are pasted ■ '**scrap heap** n pile of unwanted things, esp metal [IDM] **on the scrap heap** (infml) no longer wanted or useful ▶ **scrappy** adj (-ier, -iest) not well organized

scrape /skreɪp/ v **1** [T] remove sth from a surface by moving sth sharp like a knife across it: *She ~d the mud off her boots.* **2** [T] cut sth accidentally so that it gets damaged or hurt: *~ your arm on the wall* **3** [I, T] (cause sth to) make an unpleasant noise by rubbing against sth: *Don't ~ your chairs on the floor.* **4** [T] ~ (out) make a hole in the ground [IDM] **scrape (the bottom of) the barrel** (disapprov) have to use whatever people or things you can get because nothing better is available [PV] **scrape sth together/up** obtain or collect sth together, but with difficulty ● **scrape** n **1** [sing] action or sound of one thing scraping against another **2** injury or mark made by scraping sth against sth rough **3** (old-fash) difficult situation

scratch¹ /skrætʃ/ v **1** [I, T] rub your skin with your nails, to stop it itch-ing **2** [I, T] cut or damage your skin or the surface of sth with sth sharp **3** [T] remove sth by rubbing it with sth sharp: *They ~ed lines in the dirt to mark out a pitch.* [IDM] **scratch the surface (of sth)** deal with, understand, or find out only a small part of a subject or problem

scratch² /skrætʃ/ n **1** [C] mark, cut or sound made by scratching **2** [sing] act of scratching a part of your body when it itches [IDM] **from scratch** at the beginning **up to scratch** good enough ▶ **scratchy** adj **1** making the skin itch **2** (of a record) sounding bad because of scratches

scrawl /skrɔːl/ v [I, T] write sth quickly or carelessly ● **scrawl** n [C, sing] (piece of) untidy handwriting

scream /skriːm/ v **1** [I] give a long sharp cry of fear, pain, anger, etc **2** [T] shout sth in a loud, high voice because of fear, pain, etc ● **scream** n loud sharp cry made by sb who is frightened, excited, etc

screech /skriːtʃ/ v **1** [I, T] make a loud high unpleasant sound; say sth using this sound **2** [I] (of a vehicle) make a loud high unpleasant noise as it moves ● **screech** n [sing] screeching cry or sound: *a ~ of brakes*

screen /skriːn/ n **1** [C] flat surface on a television, computer, etc on which you see pictures or information **2** [C] large flat surface that films or pictures are shown on **3** [sing, U] films shown in a cinema or on television in general **4** [C] upright piece of furniture that can be moved to divide a room or to keep one area separate **5** [C] something that hides or protects sb/sth: *a ~ of trees around the house* **6** [C] (esp US) frame with wire netting fastened on a window or a door ● **screen** v [T] **1** hide or protect sb/sth with a screen **2** examine sb/sth for defects, diseases, etc **3** show a film etc on a screen ■ '**screenplay** n script for a film

screw /skruː/ n **1** [C] metal pin with a spiral groove cut round its length, used to fasten things together **2** [C] act of turning a screw **3** [sing] (△, sl) act of having sex **4** [C] propeller of a ship [IDM] **have a screw loose** be slightly strange in your behaviour ● **screw** v **1** [T] fasten one thing to another with a screw **2** [T] twist sth round in order to fasten it in place: *~ the lid on* **3** [I] be attached by screwing: *The lid simply ~s on.* **4** [I, T] (△, sl) have sex with sb [PV] **screw (sth) up** (sl) do sth badly or spoil sth **screw your eyes/face up** tighten the muscles of your eyes/face because of bright light, pain, etc ■ '**screwdriver** n tool for turning a screw ■ '**screwed-up** adj (infml) upset and confused

scribble /'skrɪbl/ v [I, T] write sth quickly and carelessly: ~ (a note) on an envelope ● draw meaningless marks on paper, etc ● **scribble** n **1** [U, sing] careless and untidy writing **2** [C] something scribbled

scribe /skraɪb/ n person who made copies in writing before printing was developed

scrip /skrɪp/ n (business) extra share in a business, given out instead of a dividend

script /skrɪpt/ n **1** [C] written text of a play, speech, film, etc **2** [U] handwriting **3** [U,C] system of writing ● **script** v [T] write the script of a film, etc ■ **'scriptwriter** n person who writes scripts for radio, films, etc

scripture /'skrɪptʃə(r)/ n **1** (Scripture) [U] (also the Scriptures) [pl] the Bible **2** (scriptures) [pl] holy books of a particular religion ▸ **scriptural** adj

scroll /skrəʊl/ n **1** long roll of paper for writing on **2** design like a scroll, cut in stone ● **scroll** v [I, T] (computing) move text on a computer screen up or down so that you can read different parts of it: ~ down the page ■ **'scroll bar** (computing) strip at the edge of a computer screen that you use to scroll through a file with, using a mouse

scrounge /skraʊndʒ/ v [I, T] (infml, disapprov) get sth from sb by asking them for it rather than by paying for it: ~ (£10) off a friend ▸ **scrounger** n

scrub /skrʌb/ v (-bb-) [I, T] **1** clean sth by rubbing it hard, usu with a brush and soap and water **2** [T] (infml) cancel sth ● **scrub** n **1** act of scrubbing sth **2** [U] (land covered with) low trees and bushes ■ **'scrubbing brush** (US **'scrub brush**) n stiff brush for scrubbing floors, etc

scruff /skrʌf/ n (esp GB, infml) a dirty or untidy person [IDM] **by the scruff of the/sb's neck** roughly holding the back of an animal's or a person's neck ▸ **scruffy** adj (-ier, -iest) (infml) dirty and untidy

scruple /'skru:pl/ n [C,U] feeling that prevents you from doing sth that you think may be morally wrong: have no ~s about doing sth

scrupulous /'skru:pjələs/ adj **1** paying great attention to small details **2** very honest ▸ **scrupulously** adv

scrutinize (also **-ise**) /'skru:tənaɪz/ v [T] (written) look at or examine sb/sth carefully

scrutiny /'skru:təni/ n (pl -**ies**) [C,U] (fml) careful and thorough examination

scuba-diving /'sku:bə daɪvɪŋ/ n [U] sport or activity of swimming underwater using special breathing equipment. This consists of a container of air which you carry on your back and a tube through which you breathe the air.

scuff /skʌf/ v **1** [T] mark a smooth surface when you rub it against sth rough: ~ your shoes **2** [I, T] drag your feet along the ground when walking

scuffle /'skʌfl/ n [I] ~(with) (of two or more people) fight or struggle with each other ▸ **scuffle** n

sculpt = SCULPTURE

sculptor /'skʌlptə(r)/ n (fem **sculptress**) n person who makes sculptures

sculpture /'skʌlptʃə(r)/ n **1** [C,U] work of art that is a solid figure or object made by carving or shaping wood, stone, etc **2** [U] art of making sculptures ● **sculpture** (also **sculpt** /skʌlpt/) v [I, T] make a sculpture

scum /skʌm/ n **1** layer of bubbles or dirt that forms on the surface of a liquid **2** [pl] (infml) insulting word for people that you strongly disapprove of

scurry /'skʌri/ v (pt, pp -**ied**) [I] run with short quick steps: Ants scurried around the crumbs of food. ▸ **scurry** n [sing]

scythe /saɪð/ n tool with a long handle and a curved blade, used for cutting grass, etc ● **scythe** v [T] cut grass, corn, etc with a scythe

sea /si:/ n **1** (the sea) [U] salt water that covers most of the earth's surface: to travel by ~ **2** [C] (in proper names) particular area of the sea, sometimes surrounded by land **3** [C] (also **seas** [pl]) movement of the waves of the sea: a rough/calm ~ **4** [sing] ~of large amount of sth covering a large area: a ~ of corn [IDM] **at sea 1** on a ship, etc on the sea **2** confused and not knowing what to do **go to sea** become a sailor **put (out) to sea** leave a port on a ship, boat, etc ■ **'seaboard** n part of a country that is along its coast ■ **'seafaring** /-feərɪŋ/ adj, n [U] (of) work or travel on the sea ■ **'seafood** n [U] fish, shellfish, etc from the sea used as food ■ **'sea front** [sing] part of a town facing the sea ■ **'seagoing** adj (of ships) built for crossing the sea ■ **'seagull** n = GULL ■ **'sea horse** n small fish with a head like a horse ■ **'sea legs** [pl] ability to travel on a ship without being seasick ■ **'sea level** n [U] level of the sea used as a basis for measuring the height of land: 50 metres above ~ level ■ **'sea lion** n large seal ■ **'seaman** n sailor ■ **'seamanship** n [U] skill in sailing a boat or ship ■ **'seashore** n [usu sing] land close along the edge of the sea ■ **'seasick** adj feeling sick from the motion of a ship ■ **'seaside** n [sing] (esp GB) place by the sea, esp a holiday resort ■ **'seaward** adj, adv towards the sea ■ **'seaweed** n [U] plant growing in the sea, esp on rocks at its edge ■ **'seaworthy** adj (of a ship) in a suitable condition to sail

seal /siːl/ n **1** [C] sea animal that eats fish and swims around coasts **2** [C] official design or mark, stamped on a document to show that it is genuine **3** [sing] thing that makes sth definite: The project has been given the PM's ~ of approval (= official approval). **4** [C] substance that prevents gas, liquid, etc escaping through a crack **5** [C] piece of wax, etc that is placed across a letter or box and which has to be broken before the letter or box can be opened ● **seal** v [T] **1** close an envelope by sticking the edges of the opening together **2** close a container tightly or fill a crack, etc **3** (written) make sth definite, so that it cannot be changed: ~ a bargain ◇ ~ sb's fate [PV] **seal sth off** (of the police, army) prevent people from entering an area: Police ~ed off the building.

seam /siːm/ n **1** line where two edges of cloth, etc are joined together **2** layer of coal, etc in a mine

seance /'seɪɒns/ n meeting where people try to talk to the spirits of the dead

search /sɜːtʃ/ v [I, T] look carefully for sb/sth; examine a particular place when looking for sb/sth: ~ (her pockets) for money **2** [T] examine sb's clothes, etc in order to find sth they may be hiding: The youths were arrested and ~ed. ● **search** n **1** attempt to find sth: She went out in ~ of (= looking for) a drink. **2** (computing) act of looking for information in a computer database or network: do a ~ on the Internet ▶ **searching** adj (of a book, a question, etc) trying to find out the truth about sth ■ **'searchlight** n powerful light that can be turned in any direction ■ **'search party** n group of people formed to search for sb/sth ■ **'search warrant** n official document allowing a building, etc to be searched by police, etc

season /'siːzn/ n **1** any of the four main periods of the year: spring, summer, autumn and winter **2** period when something typically happens: the rainy ~ [IDM] **in/out of season** (of fruit, etc) available/not available ● **season** v [T] ~ (with) flavour food with salt, pepper, etc ▶ **seasonable** /-əbl/ adj usual or suitable for the time of year ▶ **seasonal** adj happening or needed during a particular season: ~ trade ▶ **season-**

ally adv ▶ **seasoned** adj **1** (of a person) having a lot of experience of sth **2** (of food) flavoured with salt, pepper, etc **3** (of wood) made suitable for use by being left outside ▶ **seasoning** n [U] herb, spice, etc used to season food ■ **'season ticket** n ticket that can be used many times within a stated period of time

seat /siːt/ n **1** place where you can sit, eg a chair: Please take a ~ (= sit down). **2** the part of a chair, etc on which you actually sit **3** place where you pay to sit in a bus, train, theatre, etc: There are no ~s left for the concert. **4** official position as a member of a council, parliament, etc **5** (fml) ~of place where an activity goes on: the ~ of government **6** the part of the body on which a person sits ● **seat** v [T] **1** (fml) give sb a place to sit: Please be ~ed (= sit down). **2** have enough seats for a particular number of people: The cinema ~s 200. ■ **'seat belt** n strap fastened across a passenger in a car or aircraft ▶ **seating** n [U] seats

secateurs /ˌsekə'tɜːz/ n [pl] strong scissors used in the garden for cutting small branches, etc

secede /sɪ'siːd/ v [I] (fml) ~**(from)** (of a state, country, etc) officially leave an organization and become independent ▶ **secession** /sɪ'seʃn/ n [U] fact of an area or group becoming independent

secluded /sɪ'kluːdɪd/ adj not visited by many people: isolated ▶ **seclusion** /sɪ'kluːʒn/ n [U] privacy

second¹ /'sekənd/ det, ordinal number **1** next after the first in a series; 2nd: the ~ person to come ◇ He was the ~ to arrive. **2** next in order of importance, size, etc: As a dancer, he is ~ to none (= nobody is a better dancer than he is). **3** another; additional: a ~ home ● **second** adv after one other person or thing in order of importance: come ~ in a race ■ **,second 'best** n [U] adj next after the best ■ **,second-'class** adj, adv of or by a class not as good as the best ■ **,second-'hand** adj, adv **1** not new; previously owned by somebody else **2** (of news, etc) obtained from a source other than the origin ▶ **secondly** adv used to introduce the second of a list of points you want to make ■ **,second 'nature** n [U] habit that has become instinctive ■ **,second-'rate** adj not of the best quality

second² /'sekənd/ n **1** [C] sixtieth part of a minute **2** (also infml **sec**) very short time: Wait a ~! **3** [C] (symb ') sixtieth part of a degree(1) **4** (**seconds**) [pl] (spoken) second helping of food **5** [C, usu pl] item sold at a lower price than usual because it is imperfect **6** [C] *(GB)* level of university degree at British universities ■ **'second hand** *n* hand on a watch or clock recording seconds

second³ /'sekənd/ *v* [T] (in a meeting) officially state that you support a proposal ▸ **seconder** *n* person who seconds a proposal at a meeting

second⁴ /sɪ'kɒnd/ *v* [T] *(esp GB)* ~ (from; to) send an employee to another department, country, etc, to do a different job for a short period of time ▸ **secondment** *n* [C,U]

secondary /'sekəndri/ *adj* **1** less important than sth else: *of ~ inter-est* **2** developing from something else: *a ~ infection* **3** connected with teaching children of 11 - 18 years

secrecy /'si:krəsi/ *n* [U] keeping secrets; state of being secret

secret /'si:krət/ *adj* **1** (to be) kept from the knowledge or view of others: *~ information* **2** not declared or admitted: *a ~ admirer* **3** (of places) quiet and unknown; secluded ● **secret** *n* **1** [C] something that is known about by only a few people **2** (usu **the secret**) [sing] best way or the only way to achieve sth: *the ~ of her success* **3** [usu *pl*] thing that is not fully understood: *the ~s of the universe* [IDM] **in secret** without other people knowing about it ■ **,secret 'agent** *n* member of a secret service; spy ▸ **secretly** *adv* ■ **,secret 'service** *n* [usu *sing*] government department concerned with spying

secretariat /,sekrə'teəriət; -iæt/ *n* administrative department of a large political or international organization

secretary /'sekrətri/ *n* **1** employee who types letters, makes arrangements and appointments, etc **2** official of a society, club, etc in charge of writing letters, keeping records, etc ▸ **secretarial** /,sekrə'teəriəl/ *adj* ■ **Secretary of 'State** *n* **1** *(GB)* head of an important government department **2** *(US)* head of the department that deals with foreign affairs

secrete /sɪ'kri:t/ *v* [T] **1** (of the body) produce a liquid, eg saliva **2** *(fml)* hide sth: *~ money in a drawer* ▸ **secretion** /sɪ'kri:ʃn/ *n* *(tech)* **1** [U] process of secreting liquids **2** [C] liquid produced in the body

secretive /'si:krətɪv/ *adj* liking to hide your thoughts, feelings, etc from other people ▸ **secretively** *adv*

sect /sekt/ *n* small group of people sharing the same religious beliefs ▸ **sectarian** /sek'teəriən/ *adj* of a sect

section /'sekʃn/ *n* **1** any of the parts into which something is divided **2** department in an organization, institution, etc **3** drawing or dia-

gram of something seen as if cut through from top to bottom ▸ **sectional** *adj* **1** of one particular part within a community or an organization **2** made of separate sections

sector /'sektə(r)/ *n* **1** part of an area of activity, esp of a country's economy: *the private/public ~* **2** division of an area, esp for control of military operations

secular /'sekjələ(r)/ *adj* not religious or spiritual: *~ education*

secure /sɪ'kjʊə(r)/ *adj* **1** free from worry, doubt, etc **2** likely to continue or be successful for a long time: *a ~ job* **3** ~ (against/from) safe **4** unlikely to move, fall down, etc: *a ~ foothold* ● **secure** *v* [T] **1** *(fml)* obtain or achieve sth: *~ a job* **2** close sth tightly: *~ all the doors* **3** ~ (against) protect sth so that it is safe ▸ **securely** *adv*

security /sɪ'kjʊərəti/ *n* (*pl* **-ies**) **1** [U] measures to protect a country, building or person against attack, danger, etc: *tight ~ at the airport* **2** [U] protection against sth bad that might happen in the future **3** [U,C] valuable item, eg a house, used as a guarantee that a loan will be repaid **4** (**securities**) [*pl*] documents showing ownership of property

sedan /sɪ'dæn/ *n (US)* = SALOON(1)

sedate /sɪ'deɪt/ *adj* calm and dignified ▸ **sedately** *adv*

sedation /sɪ'deɪʃn/ *n* [U] treatment using sedatives

sedative /'sedətɪv/ *n, adj* (drug) used to calm the nerves or make sb sleep

sedentary /'sedntri/ *adj* **1** (of work) done sitting down **2** (of people) spending much of their time seated

sediment /'sedɪmənt/ *n* [U] solid material that settles at the bottom of a liquid ▸ **sedimentary** /-'mentri/ *adj*

seduce /sɪ'dju:s/ *v* [T] **1** persuade sb to have sex with you **2** persuaded sb to do sth they would not usu want to do ▸ **seduction** /sɪ'dʌkʃn/ *n* [C,U] ▸ **seductive** /sɪ'dʌktɪv/ *adj* very attractive

see¹ /si:/ *v* (*pt* **saw** /sɔ:/ *pp* **~n** /si:n/) **1** [T] (often with *can, could*) become aware of sb/sth by using the eyes: *He couldn't ~ her in the crowd.* **2** [T] (often with *can, could*) have or use the power of sight: *It was dark so I couldn't ~ much.* **3** [T] watch a film, TV programme, etc: *Did you ~ the film on TV last night?* **4** [T] (used in orders) look at sth to find information: *S~ page 4.* **5** [T] meet sb by chance: *Guess who I saw last night?* **6** [T] visit sb; consult sb: *Come and ~ us again soon.* ◇ *You should ~ a doctor about that cough.* **7** [T] understand sth: *He didn't ~ the joke.* **8** [T] find sth out by looking, asking or

waiting: *I'll go and ~ if she's there.*
9 [I] find out or decide sth by thinking or considering: *'Can I go to the party?' 'We'll ~* (= I'll decide later).
10 [T] make sure of sth: *~ that the windows are shut* **11** [T] go with sb to help or protect them: *I'll ~ you home.* [IDM] **you see** (*spoken*) used when you are explaining sth to sb (**not**) **see eye to eye with sb** (not) agree with sb **see for yourself** check sth yourself in order to be convinced **see how the land lies** → LAND[1] **seeing is believing** (*spoken*) you need to actually see something to believe it exists or happens **see the light** **1** finally understand and accept sth **2** begin to believe in a religion **see red** (*infml*) become very angry **see sense** become reasonable **seeing things** (*infml*) think you can see sth that is not really there [PV] **see about sth** deal with sth **see sth in sb/sth** find sb/sth interesting or attractive **see sb off** go to a station, etc to say goodbye to sb who is leaving **see through sb/sth** realize the truth about sb/sth so that you are not deceived **see sth through** continue with sth until it is finished **see to sth** deal with sth

see[2] /siː/ *n* (*fml*) district or office of a bishop

seed /siːd/ *n* **1** [C,U] small hard part of a plant from which a new plant can grow **2** [C] (*US* = PIP **3** [C, usu *pl*] origin of a development, etc: *the ~s of doubt* **4** [C] (esp in tennis) one of the best players in a competition, given a position in a list [IDM] **go/run to seed 1** (of a plant) stop flowering as seed is produced **2** (of a person) begin to look untidy, old, etc ● **seed** *v* [I] (of a plant) produce seed **2** [T] plant seeds in an area of ground **3** [T] (esp in tennis) make sb a seed in a competition ▸ **seedless** *adj* (of fruit) having no seeds ▸ **seedling** *n* young plant grown from a seed

seedy /ˈsiːdi/ *adj* (-**ier**, -**iest**) (*disapprov*) dirty and unpleasant, possibly connected with immoral activities ▸ **seediness** *n* [U]

seek /siːk/ *v* (*pt, pp* **sought** /sɔːt/) (*fml*) **1** [I, T] look for sb/ sth **2** [T] try to obtain or achieve sth: *~ to end the conflict* **3** [T] ask sb for sth: *~ advice* ▸ **seeker** *n* (used in compounds) person trying to find or get the thing mentioned: *job/asylum ~s*

seem /siːm/ *v* [I] give the appearance of being or doing sth: *This book ~s interesting.* ▸ **seeming** *adj* (*fml*) appearing to be sth that may not be true: *a ~ing contradiction* ▸ **seemingly** *adv*

seen *pp* of SEE[1]

seep /siːp/ *v* [I] (of liquids) come slowly through sth: *water ~ing through the cracks* ▸ **seepage** /-ɪdʒ/ *n* [U] process of seeping through sth

see-saw /ˈsiː sɔː/ *n* **1** [C] long plank supported in the middle, with a person sitting at each end, rising and falling in turn **2** [sing] situation in which things keep changing from one state to another and back again ● **see-saw** *v* [I] keep changing from one state, emotion, etc to another and back again

seethe /siːð/ *v* [I] **1** be angry about sth but try not to show it: *~ing (with rage) at his behaviour* **2** (*written*) (of a place) be full of a lot of people or animals moving around

segment /ˈseɡmənt/ *n* **1** part of something, esp of a circle, marked off or cut off **2** section of an orange, lemon, etc

segregate /ˈseɡrɪɡeɪt/ *v* [T] keep people of a different race, etc apart from the rest of the community ▸ **segregation** /ˌseɡrɪˈɡeɪʃn/ *n* [U]

seismic /ˈsaɪzmɪk/ *adj* of earthquakes

seize /siːz/ *v* [T] **1** take hold of sb/sth suddenly and with force **2** be quick to make use of a chance, an opportunity, etc: *~d the chance to get revenge* [PV] **seize up** (of machinery) become stuck and stop working

seizure /ˈsiːʒə(r)/ *n* **1** [C,U] (act of) using force to take sth from sb **2** [C] (*old-fash*) sudden attack of illness

seldom /ˈseldəm/ *adv* not often; rarely

select /sɪˈlekt/ *v* [T] choose sth carefully from a group of people or things ● **select** *adj* **1** carefully chosen as the best of a larger group **2** (of a society, club, etc) used by people with a lot of money or a high social position ▸ **selection** /-kʃn/ *n* **1** [U] process of choosing sth/sth **2** [C] group of selected things; number of things from which to select ▸ **selective** *adj* **1** affecting only a small number of people or things from a larger group **2** tending to choose carefully

self /self/ (*pl* **selves** /selvz/) *n* [C, U] your own nature; your personality

self- /self/ *prefix* of, to or by yourself or itself ■ **self-as'sured** *adj* confident ■ **self-'catering** *adj* (of holiday accommodation) with no meals provided, so you must cook for yourself ■ **self-'centred** *adj* thinking too much about yourself and not about the needs of others ■ **self-'confident** *adj* confident in your own ability ▸ **self-confidence** *n* [U] ■ **self-'conscious** *adj* nervous or embarrassed because you are aware of being watched by others ▸ **self-consciousness** *n* [U]

■ ,self-con'tained *adj* **1** not needing or depending on others **2** (*GB*) (of a flat) having its own kitchen, bathroom and entrance ■ ,self-con'trol *n* [U] ability to remain calm and not show your emotions ■ ,self-de'fence (*US* -defense) *n* [U] something you do to protect yourself when being attacked, criticized, etc ■ ,self-em'ployed *adj* working for yourself and not employed by a company, etc ■ ,self-es'teem *n* [U] feeling of being happy with your own character and abilities ■ ,self-'evident *adj* obvious; without need for proof ■ ,self-'help *n* [U] relying on your own efforts and abilities to achieve things, without the help of others ■ ,self-im'portant *adj* (*disapprov*) having too high an opinion of yourself ▶ ,self-im'portance *n* [U] (*disapprov*) ■ ,self-in'dulgent *adj* (*disapprov*) allowing yourself to have or do things that you like, esp when you do this too often ▶ ,self-in'dulgence *n* [U] ■ ,self-'interest *n* [U] (*disapprov*) fact of sb only considering their own interests and of not caring about things that would help others ■ ,self-'pity *n* [U] (*disapprov*) feeling of pity for yourself ■ ,self-re'liant *adj* not depending on others ■ ,self-re'liance *n* [U] ■ ,self-re'spect *n* [U] feeling of pride in yourself that you say, do, etc is right and good ■ ,self-'righteous *adj* (*disapprov*) convinced that what you say and do is always morally right, and that other people are wrong ■ ,self-'sacrifice *n* [U] (*approv*) giving up things you have or want in order to help others ■ 'selfsame *adj* (*written*) identical ■ ,self-'satisfied *adj* (*disapprov*) too pleased with yourself and your achievements ■ ,self-'service *n* [U] system in which buyers collect goods themselves and pay at a special desk ■ ,self-suf'ficient *adj* able to do or produce everything you need ■ ,self-'willed *adj* (*disapprov*) determined to do what you want without caring about others

selfish /'selfɪʃ/ *adj* (*disapprov*) thinking mainly of yourself and your own needs, not of others ▶ **selfishly** *adv* ▶ **selfishness** *n* [U]

sell /sel/ *v* (*pt, pp* **sold** /səʊld/) **1** [I, T] give sth to sb in exchange for money **2** [T] offer sth for people to buy: *Do you ~ stamps?* **3** [I] be bought in the way or numbers mentioned; be offered at the price mentioned: *Does this book ~ well?* **4** [T] make people want to buy sth: *Scandals ~ newspapers.* **5** [T] persuade sb to accept sth as good, useful, true, etc: *~ sb an idea* **6** [T] **~ yourself** present yourself, your ideas, etc in a way which is attractive to others **7** [T] **~ yourself**

(*disapprov*) accept money, etc for doing something bad [IDM] **sell sb/ yourself short** not value sb/yourself highly enough **sell your soul (to the devil)** do sth dishonourable for money [PV] **sell sth off** sell sth cheaply because you want to get rid of them **sell sth out 1** sell all of sth, eg tickets **2** be disloyal to sb/sth **sell (sth) up** sell your house, business, etc, usu when retiring

Sellotape™ /'seləʊteɪp/ *n* [U] (*GB*) thin, clear, sticky plastic tape used for joining, mending, etc its name

selves *plural of* SELF

semantics /sɪ'mæntɪks/ *n* [U] (*ling*) study of the meanings of words

semaphore /'seməfɔː(r)/ *n* [U] system of sending signals by holding two flags in various positions ● **semaphore** *v* [I, T] send a message by semaphore

semblance /'sembləns/ *n* [sing, U] **~ of** (*written*) appearance: *create a/ some ~ of order*

semen /'siːmen/ *n* [U] whitish liquid containing sperm, produced by the sex organs of men and male animals

semi- /'semi/ *prefix* half; partly: *~- literate* ■ 'semicircle *n* (*geom*) half a circle ■ 'semicolon *n* the punctuation mark (;) ■ ,semicon'ductor *n* solid substance that conducts electricity in certain conditions ■ ,semi-de'tached *adj* (*GB*) (of a house) joined to another on one side by a shared wall ■ ,semi-'final *n* either of two matches before the final ■ ,semi-'skimmed *adj* (*GB*) (of milk) that has had half the fat removed

seminar /'semɪnɑː(r)/ *n* small group of students meeting for study

senate /'senət/ *n* (usu the Senate) **1** [sing] upper house of the law-making bodies in the US, France, etc **2** [C, usu sing, U] governing council of some universities ▶ **senator** (often **Senator**) *n* member of a senate

send /send/ *v* (*pt, pp* **sent** /sent/) **1** [T] cause sth to go or be taken to a place, esp by post, radio, etc: *~ a letter/an email* **2** tell sb sth by sending them a message: *My parents ~ their love.* **3** tell sb to go somewhere or to do sth: *~ the kids to bed* **4** cause sth/sb to move quickly: *The punch sent him flying.* **5** make sb react in a particular way: *~ sb to sleep* [PV] **send away (to sb) (for sth)** = SEND OFF (FOR STH) **send for sb/sth** ask or order that sb should come, or sth be brought to you: *~ for a doctor* **send off (for sth)** write and ask for sth to be sent to you by post **send sth out 1** send sth to a lot of different people or places: *~ out wedding invitations* **2** produce sth, eg light, a signal, etc: *The sun ~s out light.* **send sb/sth up** (*GB, infml*) copy sb/sth in a way that makes them/it seem funny ■ **'send-off** *n* (*infml*) occasion when people gather to say goodbye to sb

senile /'si:naɪl/ *adj* weak in body or mind as a result of old age ▶ **senility** /sə'nɪləti/ *n* [U]

senior /'si:niə(r)/ *adj* **1** ~(to) higher in rank or status than others **2** (**Senior**) used after the name of a man who has the same name as his son, to avoid confusion ● **senior** *n* **1** [*sing*] person who is older than sb else: *He is three years her* ~. **2** [*C*, *usu pl*] older school pupil ■ **,senior 'citizen** *n* older person, esp sb who has retired from work ▶ **seniority** /,si:ni'ɒrəti/ *n* [U] fact of being older or of higher rank than others

sensation /sen'seɪʃn/ *n* **1** [*C*,*U*] feeling; the ability to feel **2** [*C*] (cause of) great excitement, surprise, etc ▶ **sensational** *adj* **1** causing great excitement or interest **2** (*infml*) wonderful; very good

sense /sens/ *n* **1** [*C*] one of the five powers (sight, hearing, smell, taste and touch) by which a person is conscious of things **2** [*C*] feeling about sth important: *a* ~ *of dread* **3** [*sing*] understanding of the value or importance of sth: *a* ~ *of humour* **4** [U] good practical judgement: *There's no* ~ *in doing that.* **5** (**senses**) [*pl*] normal state of mind; ability to think clearly: *take leave of your* ~*s* (= go mad) **6** [*C*] meaning of a word; way of understanding sth [IDM] **make sense 1** have a meaning that can be understood **2** be a sensible thing to do **3** be easy to understand or explain **make sense of sth** understand sth difficult ● **sense** *v* [T] become aware of sth even though you cannot see it, hear it, etc: ~ *danger*

senseless /'sensləs/ *adj* **1** (*disapprov*) foolish **2** unconscious ▶ **senselessly** *adv*

sensibility /,sensə'bɪləti/ *n* [U,C] ability to experience and understand deep feelings, esp in the arts **2** (**sensibilities**) [*pl*] person's feelings

sensible /'sensəbl/ *adj* **1** having or showing good sense(4); practical: *a* ~ *person/idea* **2** (*lit*) aware of sth ▶ **sensibly** *adv*

sensitive /'sensətɪv/ *adj* **1** ~(to) aware of and able to understand other people's feelings: *a* ~ *friend* **2** easily offended or upset: ~ *about his baldness* **3** requiring great care: *a politically* ~ *issue* **4** ~(to) reacting quickly or more than usual to sth: ~ *skin* ◇ ~ *to light* **5** (of instruments) able to measure very small changes ▶ **sensitivity** /,sensə'tɪvəti/ *n* [U] quality or degree of being sensitive

sensitize (*also* -**ise**) /'sensətaɪz/ *v*

[T] ~(to) make sb/sth more aware of sth, esp a problem or sth bad

sensual /'senʃuəl/ *adj* **1** enjoying physical, esp sexual, pleasures **2** suggesting an interest in physical, esp sexual, pleasure ▶ **sensuality** /-'æləti/ *n* [U] enjoyment of sensual pleasures

sensuous /'senʃuəs/ *adj* giving pleasure to the senses ▶ **sensuously** *adv* ▶ **sensuousness** *n* [U]

sent *pt*, *pp* of SEND

sentence /'sentəns/ *n* **1** [C] (*gram*) group of words that express a statement, question, etc **2** [C,U] punishment given by a court of law: *a jail/prison* ~ ● **sentence** *v* [T] state that sb is to have a certain punishment: ~ *sb to death*

sentiment /'sentɪmənt/ *n* **1** [C,U] (*fml*) attitude or opinion, esp one based on emotions **2** [U] (*disapprov*) feelings of pity, romantic love, etc, which may be too strong

sentimental /,sentɪ'mentl/ *adj* **1** of the emotions, rather than reason **2** (*disapprov*) producing too much emotion ▶ **sentimentality** /-'tæləti/ *n* [U] (*disapprov*) the quality of being too sentimental ▶ **sentimentally** *adv*

sentry /'sentri/ *n* (*pl* -**ies**) soldier whose job is to guard sth

separate¹ /'seprət/ *adj* **1** ~(from) forming a unit by itself; not joined to sth else: ~ *rooms* **2** different: *on three* ~ *occasions* ▶ **separately** *adv*

separate² /'sepəreɪt/ *v* [I, T] (cause people or things to) move apart; divide into different parts or groups **2** [I] stop living together as a couple with your husband, wife or partner ▶ **separation** /-'reɪʃn/ *n* **1** [U,*sing*] act of separating sb/sth; state of being separated **2** [C] period of living apart from sb **3** [C] legal agreement by a married couple to live apart

September /sep'tembə(r)/ *n* [U,C] ninth month of the year (See examples of use at *April*.)

septic /'septɪk/ *adj* infected with harmful bacteria: *a* ~ *wound*

sepulchre (*US* **sepulcher**) /'seplkə(r)/ *n* (*old-fash*) tomb, esp one cut in rock

sequel /'si:kwəl/ *n* ~(to) **1** [C] book, film, etc continuing the story of an earlier one **2** [*usu sing*] thing that happens after or as a result of an earlier event

sequence /'si:kwəns/ *n* [C,U] set of events, actions, etc which have a particular order

sequin /'si:kwɪn/ *n* small shiny disc sewn onto clothing as decoration

serene /sə'ri:n/ *adj* calm and peaceful ▶ **serenely** *adv* ▶ **serenity** /sə'renəti/ *n* [U]

sergeant /'sɑːdʒənt/ n 1 member of one of the middle ranks in the army and the air force, below an officer 2 (in Britain) police officer below an inspector in rank 3 (in the US) police officer just below a lieutenant or captain

serial /'sɪəriəl/ n story, etc broadcast or published in parts ● **serial** *adj* of or forming a series ▸ **serialize** (*also* **-ise**) /-aɪz/ v [T] produce a story, etc in parts for the television, a magazine, etc ■ **'serial number** n number put on a product, eg a camera or television, to identify it

series /'sɪəriːz/ n (*pl* **series**) group of related things, events, etc, occurring one after the other

serious /'sɪəriəs/ *adj* 1 bad or dangerous: *a ~ illness* 2 needing careful thought; important 3 not joking; thoughtful: *a ~ face* 4 ~ (**about**) sincere about sth: *Are you ~ about this plan?* ▸ **seriously** *adv* ▸ **seriousness** n [U]

sermon /'sɜːmən/ n speech on religious or moral matters, esp one given in a church

serpent /'sɜːpənt/ n (*lit*) snake

serrated /sə'reɪtɪd/ *adj* having a series of sharp points on the edge like a saw

serum /'sɪərəm/ (*pl* **sera** /-rə/ *or* **~s**) n [C,U] (*med*) (injection of) liquid which fights disease or poison: *snakebite ~*

servant /'sɜːvənt/ n person who works in sb's house and cooks, cleans, etc for them

serve /sɜːv/ v 1 [I, T] give food or drink to sb at a meal 2 [I, T] attend to customers in a shop 3 [T] be useful to sb in achieving sth 4 [T] provide an area or group of people with sth needed: *This bus ~s our area.* 5 [I] ~ (**as**) be suitable for a particular purpose: *This room ~s as a study.* 6 [T] work or perform duties for sb/sth: *~ on a committee* 7 [T] spend a period of time in prison: *~ a life sentence* 8 [T] (*law*) deliver an official document to sb, esp one ordering them to appear in court 9 [I, T] (in tennis, etc) start playing by throwing the ball in the air and hitting it [IDM] **it serves sb right (for doing sth)** (of bad luck, etc) be deserved by sb ● **serve** n (in tennis, etc) action of serving the ball to your opponent ▸ **server** n 1 (*computing*) computer or program that manages information or devices shared by several computers connected in a network 2 (*sport*) person who is serving, eg in tennis ▸ **serving** n amount of food for one person

service /'sɜːvɪs/ n 1 [C] system or business that meets public needs: *a bus ~* 2 (*also* **Service**) [C] organiza-

tion or a company that provides sth for the public or does sth for the government 3 [U] serving of customers in hotels, restaurants and shops 4 [U] work that sb does for an organization, etc: *ten years' ~ in the army* 5 [U] work done by a vehicle: *This car has given good ~.* (= has been reliable) 6 [C,U] maintenance or repair of a vehicle to keep it operating well 7 [C, usu *pl*] particular skills or help that a person is able to offer 8 [C, usu *pl*, U] (work done by people in) the army, the navy and the air force 9 [C] religious ceremony 10 (**services**) [*sing*, with *sing* or *pl* verb] (*GB*) place beside a motorway where you can stop for petrol, food, etc 11 [C] (in tennis, etc) act or way of serving the ball 12 [C] complete matching set of plates, dishes, etc [IDM] **at sb's service** ready to help sb **be of service** (*to sb*) (*fml*) be useful or helpful ● **service** v [T] maintain and repair a car, machine, etc to keep it operating well ▸ **serviceable** *adj* suitable to be used ■ **'service charge** n additional charge on a bill for service in a restaurant, etc ■ **'serviceman** n (*pl* **-men** *fem* **'servicewoman** *pl* **-women**) person serving in the armed forces ■ **'service station** n = PETROL STATION

serviette /ˌsɜːvi'et/ n piece of cloth or paper used at meals for protecting your clothes and wiping your hands and lips

session /'seʃn/ n 1 period spent in one activity: *a recording ~* 2 meeting or series of meetings of a parliament, law court, etc 3 (in Scotland) school or university year

set[1] /set/ n 1 [C] group of similar things of the same kind that belong together 2 [C, with *sing* or *pl* verb] group of people who spend a lot of time together and have similar interests 3 [C] television or radio receiver 4 [C] scenery for a play, film, etc 5 [C] division of a match in tennis, volleyball, etc 6 [C] act of styling hair

set[2] /set/ v (*pt*, *pp* **set**, *-tt-*) 1 [T] put sth/sth in a particular place or position: *~ a tray down on the table* 2 [T] cause sth/sth to be in a particular state; start sth happening: *~ a prisoner free* ◇ *~ sb thinking* 3 [T] (*usu* passive) place the action of a play, film or novel in a particular place, time, etc: *The film is ~ in London in the 1960s.* 4 [T] prepare sth so that it is ready for use or in position: *~ the alarm clock for 7 o'clock* 5 [T] arrange plates, knives, forks, etc on a table ready for a meal 6 [T] put a precious stone into a piece of jewellery 7 [T] arrange or fix sth: *~ a date for the wedding* 8 [T] fix sth so that others copy it or try to achieve it: *~ a new fashion/record* ◇ *~ a good example*

9 [T] give sb a piece of work, a task, etc: ~ *an examination* **10** [I] become firm or hard: *The cement has ~.* **11** [T] put a broken bone into the right position to mend **12** [T] ~ **(to)** write music to go with words **13** [I] (of the sun or moon) go down [IDM] **set eyes on sb/sth see sb/sth** enter or visit a place **set light/fire to sth | set sth on fire** cause sth to start burning **set your heart on sth | have your heart set on sth** want sth very much **set your mind to sth →** MIND¹ **set sth right →** RIGHT¹ **set sb/sth to rights →** RIGHT¹ **set sail (from/for ...)** begin a journey by sea **set the scene (for sth)** create a situation in which sth can happen or develop **set sb's teeth on edge** (of a sound or taste) make sb feel physically uncomfortable [PV] **set about sth** start doing sth **set sb back sth** (*infml*) cost sb a particular amount of money **set sth/sb back** delay the progress of sth/sb by a particular time **set sth back (from sth)** place sth, esp a building, at a distance from sth **set in** start and seem likely to continue **set sth off** begin a journey, etc **set sth off 1** cause a bomb, etc to explode **2** start a process or series of events **3** make sth look attractive: *This colour ~s off her eyes.* **set on/upon sb** attack sb **set out 1** begin a journey, etc **2** begin a job, task, etc with a particular goal **set sth out 1** arrange or display things **2** present ideas, facts, etc in an orderly way: ~ *out your ideas in an essay* **set sth up 1** build sth or put sth somewhere: *The police ~ up roadblocks.* **2** arrange for sth to happen **3** create sth or start it: ~ *up a business* **set (yourself) up (as sb)** start running a business ■ **'setback** *n* something that delays progress or development ■ **'set-up** *n* (*infml*) **1** way of organizing sth, system **2** situation in which sth makes it seem that you have done something wrong

set³ /set/ *adj* **1** in a particular position **2** planned; fixed and unlikely to change: *We always follow a ~ pattern.* ◇ *have ~ ideas about sth* ◇ *As people get older, they get more ~ in their ways.* **3** (of a restaurant meal) having a fixed price and limited choice of dishes: *a ~ menu/lunch* **4** (*infml*) ready or likely to do sth: ~ *for go* [IDM] **be set on (doing) sth** be determined to do sth: *She's ~ on winning.* ■ **set book** *n* (*GB*) book that students must study for an exam

set square /'set skweə(r)/ *n* triangular instrument used for drawing lines at certain angles

settee /se'ti:/ *n* (*GB*) = SOFA

setter /'setə(r)/ *n* breed of long-haired dog

setting /'setɪŋ/ *n* **1** surroundings: *a rural ~* **2** place and time at which the action of film, play or book takes place **3** height, speed, etc at which a machine, etc is or can be set

settle /'setl/ *v* **1** [T] put an end to an argument or disagreement: ~ *an argument* **2** [T] decide or arrange sth finally **3** [I, T] make a place your permanent home **4** [I, T] make sb/yourself comfortable: ~*d (back) in the chair* **5** [I, T] (cause sb to) become calm: ~ *sb's nerves* **6** [I] ~ **(on/over)** fall from above and come to rest on sth: *The bird ~d on a branch.* **7** [I, T] (cause sth to) sink slowly down: *dust settling on the floor* ◇ *The rain ~d the dust.* **8** [I, T] ~**(up)** pay a debt [PV] **settle down 1** get into a comfortable position, either sitting or lying **2** start to have a quieter way of life, living in one place **settle (down) to sth** begin to give your attention to sth **settle for sth** accept sth that is not quite what you want **settle in** move into a new house, job, etc and start to feel comfortable there **settle on sth** decide to have sth ▶ **settled** *adj* not likely to change or move: ~*d weather* ▶ **settler** *n* person who goes to live in a new country or region

settlement /'setlmənt/ *n* **1** [C,U] (action of reaching an) official agreement that ends an argument **2** [C] (*law*) (document stating the) conditions on which money or property is given to sb: *a divorce ~* **3** [U,C] process of people settling in a place; place where they settle

seven /'sevn/ *number* **7** ▶ **seventh** /'sevnθ/ *ordinal number, n* 7th; the fraction ¹/₇; one of seven equal parts of sth

seventeen /,sevn'ti:n/ *number* **17** ▶ **seventeenth** /,sevn'ti:nθ/ *ordinal number* 17th

seventy /'sevnti/ **1** *number* **70 2 (the seventies)** *n* [pl] numbers, years or temperatures from 70 to 79 ▶ **seventieth** /'sevntiəθ/ *ordinal number* 70th

sever /'sevə(r)/ *v* **1** [T] cut a part of sth from the rest: ~ *a limb from the body* **2** [T] end sth: ~ *relations with sb*

several /'sevrəl/ *det, pron* more than two but not very many

severe /sɪ'vɪə(r)/ *adj* **1** very bad, difficult, intense, etc: *a ~ storm* **2** stern; strict: ~ *discipline* ▶ **severely** *adv* ▶ **severity** /sɪ'verəti/ *n* [U]

sew /səʊ/ *v* (*pt ~ed pp ~n* /səʊn/) [I, T] make stitches with a needle and thread; fasten cloth, etc with stitches [PV] **sew sth up 1** join or mend sth by sewing **2** (*infml*) arrange sth satisfactorily: *They have the election ~n up* (= they will win).

sewage /'su:ɪdʒ/ *n* [U] used water

and human waste carried away from houses and factories by sewers

sewer /'suːə(r)/ n underground pipe that carries sewage away from houses and factories

sewn pt of SEW

sex /seks/ n **1** [U,C] state of being male or female **2** [C] group of all male or all female people: *a member of the opposite* ~ **3** [U] (sexual activity leading to and including) sexual intercourse ► **sexy** adj (-ier, -iest) sexually attractive ► **sexily** adv ► **sexiness** n [U]

sexism /'seksɪzəm/ n [U] unfair treatment of people (esp women) because of their sex ► **sexist** adj, n.

sextant /'sekstənt/ n instrument for measuring the altitude of the sun, etc

sexton /'sekstən/ n person who takes care of a church, churchyard, etc

sexual /'sekʃuəl/ adj of sex or the sexes ■ ,**sexual** ha'**rassment** n [U] comments about sex, physical contact, etc in the workplace, that a person finds annoying and offensive ■ ,**sexual** 'intercourse n [U] physical union of two people often leading to the production of children ► **sexuality** /-'æləti/ n [U] feelings and activities connected with a person's sexual desires ► **sexually** adv

shabby /'ʃæbi/ adj (-ier, -iest) **1** in poor condition; poorly dressed **2** (of behaviour) unfair; mean ► **shabbily** adv

shack /ʃæk/ n small, crudely built shed or house

shackle /'ʃækl/ n [C, usu pl] **1** one of a pair of metal rings linked by a chain, for fastening a prisoner's wrists or ankles **2** ~(of) (fml) anything that prevents freedom of action ● **shackle** v [T] **1** put shackles on sb **2** prevent sb from acting freely

shade /ʃeɪd/ n **1** [U] area that is dark and cool because the sun's light does not get to it: *sit in the* ~ **2** [C] thing that reduces light: *a lamp-* ~ **3** [C] ~(of) (depth of) colour: *four* ~*s of blue* **4** [C, usu sing] different kind or level of opinion, feeling, etc: ~*s of meaning* **5** (written) a little; slightly: *a* ~ *warmer* **6** (shades) [pl] (infml) = SUNGLASSES ● **shade** v [T] **1** prevent direct light from reaching sth: ~ *your eyes* **2** cover a light to reduce brightness **3** darken parts of a drawing, etc [PV] **shade into** sth change gradually into sth else: *green shading into blue*

shadow /'ʃædəʊ/ n **1** [C,U] dark shape that sb/sth's form makes on a surface when they are between the light and the surface: *The ship's sail cast a* ~ *on the water.* **2** [U] (also **shadows** [pl]) darkness in a place or on sth **3** [sing] a very small amount

of sth: *not a* ~ *of doubt* **4** [sing] strong (usu bad) influence of sb/sth **5** (shadows) [pl] dark areas under sb's eyes, because they are tired, etc ● **shadow** v [T] follow sb and watch sb closely and often secretly ► **shadowy** adj **1** dark and full of shadows **2** not clear; mysterious

shady /'ʃeɪdi/ adj (-ier, -iest) **1** giving shade from sunlight; situated in the shade **2** (infml) not entirely honest: *a* ~ *character*

shaft /ʃɑːft/ n **1** long, narrow, usu vertical passage in a building or underground, eg for entering a mine: *a lift* ~ **2** long narrow part of an arrow, hammer, golf club, etc **3** metal bar joining parts of a machine or engine together **4** either of two poles between which a horse is fastened to a cart, etc **5** (lit) narrow beam of light

shaggy /'ʃægi/ adj (-ier, -iest) **1** (of hair, fur, etc) long and untidy **2** having long untidy hair, fur, etc

shake¹ /ʃeɪk/ v (pt shook /ʃʊk/ pp ~n /'ʃeɪkən/) **1** [I, T] (cause sb/sth to) move quickly from side to side or up and down **2** [I] ~(with) make short quick movements that you cannot control, eg because you are afraid **3** [I] (of sb's voice) sound unsteady, usu because you are afraid, etc **4** [T] shock or upset sb very much: *We were* ~*n by his death.* [IDM] **shake hands (with sb)** | **shake sb's hand** take sb's hand and move it up and down as a greeting **shake your head** move your head from side to side to indicate 'no' or to show doubt, etc [PV] **shake sb/sth off** free yourself of sb/sth **shake sth up** make important changes in an organization, etc to make it more efficient ■ '**shake-up** n major reorganization of a company, etc ► **shakily** /-ɪli/ adv ► **shaky** adj (-ier, -iest) **1** (of a person) shaking and weak because of illness, etc **2** not firm or safe; not certain

shake² /ʃeɪk/ n [C, usu sing] act of shaking sb/sth

shale /ʃeɪl/ n [U] soft stone that splits easily

shall /ʃəl; strong form ʃæl/ modal v (neg **shall not** short form **shan't** /ʃɑːnt/ pt **should** /ʃʊd/ neg **should not** short form **shouldn't** /ˈʃʊdnt/) **1** (old-fash) used with *I* and *we* to talk about the future: *I shan't be gone long.* **2** used in questions with *I* and *we* for making offers or suggestions or asking for advice: *S- I open the window?* ◇ *What* ~ *we do tonight?*

shallot /ʃə'lɒt/ n kind of small onion

shallow /'ʃæləʊ/ adj **1** not deep: *a* ~ *river* **2** (disapprov) not serious: *a* ~ *thinker* ► **shallowness** n [U] ► **shallows** n [pl] shallow place in a river, etc

sham /ʃæm/ n (disapprov) **1** [sing] situation, feeling, system, etc that is not as good or true as it seems to be **2** [C] person who pretends to be sth they are not **3** [U] pretence ● **sham** adj not genuine but intended to seem real: a ~ marriage ● **sham** v (-mm-) [I, T] pretend sth.: ~ illness

shamble /ˈʃæmbl/ v [I] walk without lifting your feet properly

shambles /ˈʃæmblz/ n [sing] (infml) (a shambles) situation or scene of disorder or confusion

shame /ʃeɪm/ n **1** [U] feelings of guilt, sadness, etc that you have when you know you have done wrong: feel ~ at having told a lie **2** [U] (fml) ability to feel ashamed for sth you have done: He has no ~. **3** (a shame) [sing] used to say that sth is a cause for feeling sad or disappointed: It's/ What a ~ you can't come. **4** [U] loss of respect caused when you do sth wrong: bring ~ on your family [IDM] put sb/sth to shame be much better than sb/sth ● **shame** v [T] **1** (written) make sb feel ashamed **2** (fml) make sb feel they have lost honour or respect [PV] shame sb into doing sth cause sb to do do sth by making them feel ashamed not to do them ▶ **shamefaced** /ˌʃeɪmˈfeɪst/ adj looking ashamed ▶ **shameful** adj that should make you feel ashamed ▶ **shamefully** /-fəli/ adv ▶ **shameless** adj (disapprov) not feeling ashamed of sth you have done

shampoo /ʃæmˈpuː/ n **1** [C,U] liquid soap used for washing hair; a similar liquid used for cleaning carpets, etc **2** [U] act of washing your hair using shampoo ● **shampoo** v [T] wash hair or carpets with shampoo

shamrock /ˈʃæmrɒk/ n [C,U] small plant with three leaves on each stem, the national emblem of Ireland

shandy /ˈʃændi/ n [C,U] drink of beer mixed with lemonade

shan't shall not → SHALL

shanty town /ˈʃænti taʊn/ n town or part of a town where poor people live in very bad conditions

shape /ʃeɪp/ n **1** [C,U] outer form or outline of sth: a round ~ **2** [U] physical condition of sb/sth: She's in good ~. [IDM] get/knock/lick sth into shape make sth more acceptable, organized or successful take shape develop and become more complete ● **shape** v [T] **1** make sth into a particular shape: S~ the dough into a ball. **2** have an influence on the way that sb/sth develops [PV] shape up develop satisfactorily: Our plans are shaping up well. ▶ **shapeless** adj having no definite shape ▶ **shapely** adj (-ier, -iest)

(esp of a woman's body) having an attractive curved shape

share /ʃeə(r)/ n **1** [C, usu sing] part of something divided between two or more people **2** [sing] ~(of) part that sb has in an activity that involves several people: your ~ of the blame **3** [C] ~(in) one of the equal parts into which the capital of a company is divided and which people buy as a way of investing money ● **share** v **1** [I, T] ~(with) have or use sth at the same time as sb else: a house with sb **2** [T] ~(out) divide sth between two or more people **3** [I, T] have the same feelings, experiences, etc as sb else: a view that is widely ~d ▶ '**shareholder** n owner of shares in a company ▶ '**share-out** n [usu sing] act of dividing sth between two or more people

shark /ʃɑːk/ n **1** large and sometimes dangerous fish **2** (infml, disapprov) person who is dishonest in business

sharp /ʃɑːp/ adj **1** having a fine cutting edge or point: a ~ knife **2** sudden: a ~ rise/fall **3** well defined; clear: a ~ outline **4** (of people or their mind, eyes, etc) quick to notice things **5** critical or harsh: ~ words **6** (of sounds) loud and high **7** causing a cutting or piercing feeling: a ~ wind/ pain **8** (of bends, etc) changing direction suddenly **9** (of tastes) strong and slightly bitter **10** (of clothes or the way sb dresses) fashionable and new **11** (music) half a tone higher than the note before it **12** (music) above the correct pitch ● **sharp** n (music) (symb #) note played half a tone higher than the note named ● **sharp** adv **1** exactly: at seven o'clock ~ **2** suddenly: turn ~ left **3** above the correct pitch ▶ **sharpen** v [I, T] (cause sth to) become sharp ▶ **sharpener** n tool or machine that makes things sharp ▶ **sharply** adv

shatter /ˈʃætə(r)/ v **1** [I, T] (cause sth to) suddenly break into small pieces **2** [I, T] (cause sb's feelings, hopes or beliefs to) be completely destroyed: All my illusions were ~ed. ▶ **shattered** adj **1** shocked and upset **2** (GB, infml) very tired

shave /ʃeɪv/ v **1** [I, T] cut hair off the face, etc with a razor **2** [T] cut a small amount off a price, etc [PV] shave sth off sth remove a thin layer from a surface ● **shave** n act of shaving the face ▶ **shaven** /ˈʃeɪvn/ adj with all the hair shaved off ▶ **shaver** n electric razor ▶ **shavings** n [pl] thin pieces of wood which have been shaved off

shawl /ʃɔːl/ n large piece of material worn over a woman's shoulders or head or wrapped round a baby

she /ʃiː/ pron (used as the subject of a v) female person or animal

sheaf /ʃiːf/ n (pl **sheaves** /ʃiːvz/) **1** corn, etc tied into a bundle after it has been cut **2** bundle of papers, etc tied together

shear /ʃɪə(r)/ v (pt **~ed** pp **shorn** /ʃɔːn/ or **~ed**) [T] cut the wool off a sheep ▶ **shears** n [pl] garden tool like a large pair of scissors: a pair of ~

sheath /ʃiːθ/ n (pl **~s** /ʃiːðz/) cover for the blade of a knife, etc

sheathe /ʃiːð/ v [T] (lit) put sth into a sheath

sheaves plural of SHEAF

she'd /ʃiːd/ short for SHE HAD; SHE WOULD

shed /ʃed/ n small building, usually of wood, used for storing things, etc ● **shed** v (pt, pp **shed** pres pt **-dd-**) [T] **1** get rid of sth no longer wanted **2** let sth fall; drop sth: Flowers ~ their petals. ◇ The lorry ~ its load. **3** send light over sth **4** (fml) allow liquid to pour out: ~ tears (= cry)

sheep /ʃiːp/ n (pl **sheep**) grass-eating animal kept for food and for its wool ■ '**sheepdog** n dog trained to look after sheep ■ '**sheepskin** n [U,C] the skin of a sheep with the wool still on it ▶ **sheepish** adj looking or feeling embarrassed because you have done sth silly

sheer /ʃɪə(r)/ adj **1** used to emphasize the size, degree or amount of sth **2** complete: ~ nonsense **3** very steep: a ~ drop **4** (of cloth, etc) very thin and light ● **sheer** adv straight up or down

sheet /ʃiːt/ n **1** piece of thin fabric used on a bed to lie on or under **2** flat thin piece of a material: a ~ of glass/paper **3** wide flat area of water, ice, etc ■ '**sheet music** n [U] music printed on single sheets

sheikh (also **sheik**) /ʃeɪk; ʃiːk/ n Arab prince or ruler

shelf /ʃelf/ n (pl **shelves** /ʃelvz/) **1** flat board of wood, etc attached to a wall, etc for things to stand on **2** (geol) piece of rock like a shelf on a cliff face or underwater

she'll /ʃiːl/ short for SHE WILL

shell /ʃel/ n **1** hard outer covering of eggs, nuts and some animals, eg snails **2** metal case filled with explosives, to be fired from a large gun **3** walls or outer structure of sth, eg an empty or ruined building [IDM] **come out of your shell** become less shy, quiet, etc ● **shell** v **1** [I, T] fire shells at sth **2** [T] remove the shell from nuts, peas, etc [PV] **shell (sth) out (for sth)** (infml) pay a lot of money for sth ■ '**shellfish** n (pl **shellfish**) creature with a shell that lives

in water, esp one of the types that can be eaten, eg a crab

shelter /ˈʃeltə(r)/ n **1** [U] fact of having a place to live or stay **2** [U] protection from rain, danger or attack **3** [C] building, etc that gives people shelter ● **shelter** v **1** [T] give sb/sth a place where they are protected from the weather or danger **2** [I] find a place that gives you shelter: ~ from the rain under a tree

shelve /ʃelv/ v [T] **1** delay dealing with a problem, project, etc **2** put books, etc on a shelf **3** [I] (of land) slope downwards

shelves plural of SHELF

shepherd /ˈʃepəd/ (fem **shepherdess** /ˈʃepəˈdes/ old-fash) n person who takes care of sheep ● **shepherd** v [T] guide sb or a group of people somewhere ■ **shepherd's pie** n [C,U] (GB) dish of finely chopped meat with mashed potato on top

sheriff /ˈʃerɪf/ n (in US) chief law officer in a county

sherry /ˈʃeri/ n [U] strong yellow or brown wine, originally from southern Spain

shied pt, pp of SHY²

shield /ʃiːld/ n **1** piece of metal, etc carried by soldiers n the past to protect the body when fighting **2** person or thing used to protect sb/sth, esp by forming a barrier **3** drawing or model of a shield showing a coat of arms ● **shield** v [T] protect sb/sth from danger, harm or sth unpleasant

shift /ʃɪft/ n **1** [C] ~ (in) change in position or direction **2** [C] (period worked by) a group of workers which starts work as another group finishes: be on the day/night ~ **3** [U] mechanism on a computer keyboard that allows capital letters, etc to be typed: a ~ key ● **shift** v **1** [I, T] (cause sth to) change position or direction **2** [T] (infml) remove sth: ~ a stain

shifty /ˈʃɪfti/ adj (**-ier, -iest**) not to be trusted

shimmer /ˈʃɪmə(r)/ v [I] shine with a soft light

shin /ʃɪn/ n front part of the leg below the knee ● **shin** v (**-nn-**) (US **shinny**) [PV] **shin up/down sth** climb up or down sth quickly

shine /ʃaɪn/ v (pt, pp **shone** /ʃɒn/ or, in sense 3 **~d**) **1** [I] give out or reflect light **2** [T] shine the light from a lamp, etc in a particular direction **3** [T] (infml) polish sth: ~ shoes **4** [I] very good at sth ● **shine** n [sing] brightness that sth has when light is reflected on it ▶ **shiny** adj (**-ier, -iest**) smooth and bright

shingle /ˈʃɪŋgl/ n [U] area of small stones on a beach

ship¹ /ʃɪp/ n large boat that carries people or goods by sea ■ **'shipmate** n sailor belonging to the same crew ■ **'shipshape** adj clean and tidy ■ **'shipwreck** n [U, C] loss or destruction of a ship at sea because of a storm, etc ● **'shipwreck** v [T] (**be shipwrecked**) be left somewhere after your ship has been lost or destroyed ■ **'shipyard** n place where ships are built

ship² /ʃɪp/ v (**-pp-**) [T] transport or send sb/sth, esp by ship ► **shipment** n [U] process of sending goods from one place to another 2 [C] load of goods shipped ► **shipper** n person or company that arranges for goods to be shipped ► **shipping** n [U] all the ships of a country, port, etc

shirk /ʃɜːk/ v [I, T] try to avoid work, duty, etc, esp through laziness ► **shirker** n

shirt /ʃɜːt/ n piece of clothing worn esp by men, for the upper part of the body, with sleeves and buttons

shirty /'ʃɜːti/ adj (**-ier, -iest**) (GB, infml) annoyed; angry

shit /ʃɪt/ n (Δ, sl) 1 [U] solid waste matter passed from the bowels 2 [sing] act of emptying the bowels 3 [C] (disapprov) unpleasant person [IDM] **not give a shit** (**about sb/sth**) not care at all about sb/sth ● **shit** v (**-tt-**, pp **shat**/ʃæt/ shitted) (Δ, sl) pass solid waste matter from the bowels ● **shit** exclam (Δ, sl) swear word used to show that you are angry ► **shitty** adj (**-ier, -iest**) (Δ, sl) unpleasant; very bad

shiver /'ʃɪvə(r)/ v [I] ~ (**with**) shake slightly, esp with cold or fear ● **shiver** n act of shivering ► **shivery** adj

shoal /ʃəʊl/ n great number of fish swimming together

shock /ʃɒk/ n 1 [U, C] (medical condition or unpleasant feeling caused by a) sudden surprise, fear, worry, etc 2 [C] violent shaking movement, caused by an earthquake, explosion, etc 3 [C] effect caused by an electric current passing through the body ● **shock** v [T] 1 surprise and upset sb 2 offend and disgust sb ► **shocking** adj 1 that offends or upsets people: ~ing behaviour 2 (infml) very bad

shod pt, pp of SHOE

shoddy /'ʃɒdi/ adj (**-ier, -iest**) of poor quality: ~ work

shoe /ʃuː/ n outer covering of leather, etc for the foot, which does not reach above the ankle [IDM] **be in sb's shoes | put yourself in sb's shoes** be in, or imagine yourself to be in, another person's situation ● **shoe** v (pt, pp **shod** /ʃɒd/) fit a horse with horseshoes ■ **'shoelace** n material

like string for fastening a shoe ■ **'shoestring** n [IDM] **on a shoestring** (infml) with a very small amount of money

shone pt, pp of SHINE

shoo /ʃuː/ exclam used to tell an animal or a child to go away ● **shoo** v [T] make animals, etc go away by saying 'shoo'

shook pt of SHAKE¹

shoot¹ /ʃuːt/ v (pt, pp **shot** /ʃɒt/) 1 [I, T] aim and fire with (sth from) a gun or other weapon 2 [T] kill or wound a person or an animal in this way 3 [I, T] (cause sb/sth to) move suddenly or quickly: Pain shot up his arm. ◇ He shot out his hand. 4 [I] make a film or photograph of sth 5 [I] (in football, etc) try to score a goal [IDM] **shoot your mouth off** (**about sth**) (infml) talk indiscreetly about sth ■ **shooting 'star** n small meteor

shoot² /ʃuːt/ n 1 young growth on a plant 2 occasion when sb takes professional photographs: a fashion- 3 group of people shooting animals or birds for sport

shop /ʃɒp/ n 1 (esp GB) (part of a) building where goods are sold 2 place where things are repaired or made, esp part of a factory [IDM] **talk shop** talk about your work ● **shop** v (**-pp-**) 1 [I] go to the shops to buy things: ~ for presents 2 [T] (GB, infml) give information about sb, esp to the police [PV] **shop around** (**for sth**) search carefully for goods giving the best value ■ **'shop assistant** n person serving in a shop ■ **,shop 'floor** n [sing] area in a factory where goods are made ■ **'shopkeeper** n owner of a (small) shop ■ **'shoplifter** n person who steals things from shops ► **'shoplifting** n [U] ► **shopper** n ► **shopping** n [U] act of shopping: go ~ping 2 goods bought from shops ■ **'shopping mall** (esp US) large group of shops built together under one roof and closed to traffic ■ **,shop 'steward** n official of a branch of a trade union elected by the workers

shore /ʃɔː(r)/ n land along the edge of the sea or a lake ● **shore** [PV] **shore sth up** support part of a building, etc with large pieces of wood or metal

shorn pp of SHEAR

short¹ /ʃɔːt/ adj 1 measuring or covering a small length or distance: He had ~ hair. 2 (of a person) small in height 3 lasting or taking a small amount of time: the ~est day of the year 4 ~ (**of**) not having enough of sth; lacking sth: ~ of money 5 ~**on** (infml) lacking in a certain quality: ~ on tact 6 ~ (**of**) less than the number, amount or distance mentioned: five miles ~ of our destination 7 ~ (**with**) (of a person) rude to sb: I was a *little ~ with her.* **[IDM] for short** as an abbreviation **in short** briefly **in the short term** ▸ TERM **little/nothing short of sth** almost sth ■ **'shortbread** *n* [U] crumbly biscuit made with a lot of butter ■ **short-'change** *v* [T] cheat sb, esp by giving them too little change ■ **short 'circuit** *n* electrical fault causing current to flow the wrong way ■ **short-'circuit** *v* [I, T] (cause sth to) have a short circuit ■ **'shortcoming** *n* (usu pl) fault in sb's character, a plan, system, etc ■ **short 'cut** (also **'short cut**) **1** route taken to shorten a journey, etc **2** way of doing sth more quickly, efficiently, etc ■ **'shortfall** *n* amount of sth that is less than is needed ■ **'shorthand** *n* [U] system of writing quickly using special symbols ■ **short-'handed** *adj* not having enough workers, helpers, etc ■ **'shortlist** *n* [usu sing] list of candidates, eg for a job, selected from a larger group, from which the final choice is to be made ▸ **shortlist** *v* [T] ■ **short-'lived** *adj* lasting only for a short time ■ **shortness** *n* [U] ■ **short 'sight** *n* [U] inability to see distant objects clearly ■ **short-'sighted** *adj* **1** unable to see distant objects clearly **2** not thinking about the possible future effects of sth ■ **short-'tempered** *adj* easily annoyed ■ **short-'term** *adj* of or for a short period of time ■ **short 'wave** *n* [U] (abbr **SW**) radio wave with a wavelength of less than 100 metres

short² /ʃɔːt/ *adv* before the agreed or natural time: *a career tragically cut ~ by illness* **[IDM] go short (of)** not have enough of sth **short of (doing) sth** without (doing) sth; unless sth happens: *do anything ~ of murder*

short³ /ʃɔːt/ *n* **1** small strong alcoholic drink **2** short film **3** = SHORT CIRCUIT (SHORT¹)

shortage /'ʃɔːtɪdʒ/ *n* [C, U] lack of sth; state of not having enough of sth

shorten /'ʃɔːtn/ *v* [I, T] (cause sth to) become shorter: *~ a dress*

shortly /'ʃɔːtli/ *adv* **1** soon: *We'll leave ~.* **2** in an angry impatient way: *speak ~ to sb*

shot¹ /ʃɒt/ *n* (~at) **1** act of firing a gun, etc; sound of this **2** person who shoots a gun well, badly, etc: *a good/ bad ~* **3** remark, etc aimed against sb/sth that you are arguing or competing with **4** (*infml*) attempt; try: *have a ~ at solving the problem* **5** throw, kick, stroke, etc of the ball in certain sports: *a ~ at goal* **6** photograph; scene in a film **7** (*infml*) small injection of a drug, etc: *a ~ of morphine* **[IDM] like a shot** very quickly **not by a long shot** → LONG¹ **a shot in the arm** something that gives fresh

energy to sb/sth ■ **a shot in the dark** answer, etc that is risked in the hope that it may be right ■ **'shotgun** *n* long gun used esp for shooting birds and animals ■ **the 'shot-put** (also **'shot-putting**) *n* [sing] contest in which athletes throw a heavy metal ball as far as possible

should¹ /ʃəd; *strong form* ʃʊd/ *modal v* (*neg* **should not** *short form* **shouldn't** /'ʃʊdnt/) **1** used to show what is right, appropriate, etc, esp when criticizing sb: *You ~ have been more careful.* **2** used to give or ask for advice: *S~ I apologize to him?* **3** used to say you expect sth is true or will happen: *We ~ arrive before dark.* **4** used to say that sth expected has not happened: *He ~ be here by now.* **5** (*GB, fml*) used after *I* or *we* instead of *would* to say what you would do if sth else happened first **6** (*fml*) used to refer to a possible event or situation: *If she ~ come back, please tell me.* **7** used in a *that* clause after certain adjs: *I'm anxious that we ~ allow plenty of time.* **8** (*GB*) used to make polite requests: *I ~ like to make a phone call, please.* **9** used with questions words to express lack of interest, disbelief, etc: *How ~ I know?*

should² *pt of* SHALL

shoulder /'ʃəʊldə(r)/ *n* **1** either of the two parts of the body between the top of each arm and the neck **2** part of a piece of clothing which covers the shoulder **3** part of sth, eg a bottle or mountain, shaped like a shoulder **[IDM] shoulder to shoulder (with sb) 1** side by side **2** working, fighting, etc together ▸ **shoulder** *v* [T] **1** accept the responsibility for sth: *~ the responsibility/blame for sth* **2** push sb/sth out of your way with your shoulder: *~ sb aside* **3** carry sth on the shoulder ■ **'shoulder blade** *n* either of the flat bones of the upper back

shouldn't *short for* SHOULD NOT

shout /ʃaʊt/ *n* loud cry of anger, fear, etc ■ **shout** *v* [I, T] say sth in a loud voice; speak angrily to sb: *Don't ~ at me!* ◇ *~ (out) orders* **[PV] shout sb down** shout in order to prevent sb being heard ▸ **shouting** *n* [U] shouts

shove /ʃʌv/ *v* [I, T] push sb/sth roughly **[PV] shove up** (*GB, spoken*) move in order to make a space for sb to sit down: *S~ up so I can sit down.* ● **shove** *n* [usu sing] strong push

shovel /'ʃʌvl/ *n* tool like a spade, used for moving earth, stones, coal, etc ■ **shovel** *v* (**-ll-**, *US* **-l-**) **1** lift or move sth with a shovel

show¹ /ʃəʊ/ *v* (*pt* **~ed**; *pp* **~n** /ʃəʊn/) **1** [T] make sth clear; prove sth: *The figures ~ that our efforts are false.* **2** [T] let sb see sth: *~ your ticket at the gate* **3** [T] help sb to do sth by letting them watch you or by explaining it: She ~ed me how to do it. **4** [T] point to sth: S~ me which one you want. **5** [T] lead or guide sb to a place: S~ her in. **6** [T] make it clear that you have a particular quality: She ~ed great courage. **7** [T] behave in a particular way towards sb: He ~ed me great kindness. **8** [I, T] be visible; allow sth to be seen: Black doesn't ~ the dirt. [IDM] **it goes to show** used to say that sth proves sth **show your face** appear among friends or in public **show your hand/cards** reveal your intentions [PV] **show off** (infml, disapprov) try to impress people with your wealth, ability, etc **show up** (infml) arrive: All the guests ~ed up. **show (sth) up** (cause sth) to become visible: The lines ~ed up in the light. ▶ **showing** n **1** [C] act of showing a film **2** [usu sing] performance: the company's poor ~ing ■ **'show-off** n (infml, disapprov) person who tries to impress people with his/her wealth, ability, etc

show² /ʃəʊ/ n **1** [C] theatre performance, esp one containing singing and dancing **2** [C] programme on television or the radio **3** [C, U] collection of things for public display: a fashion ~ ◇ The latest computers will be on ~ at the exhibition. **4** [C] action or behaviour that shows how you feel: a ~ of emotion **5** [U, sing] insincere act: Her grief is all ~. ◇ She does it for ~. **6** [C] colourful or pleasing sight: all the ~ of the circus **7** [C, usu sing] (infml) effort: put up a good ~ [IDM] **a show of hands** raising of hands to vote for or against sth ■ **'show business** n [U] business of entertaining the public ■ **'show-down** n argument, fight, etc that will settle a disagreement ■ **'show-jumping** n [U] sport of riding a horse and jumping over fences as quickly as possible ■ **'showroom** n large shop where goods, esp cars or electrical goods, are put on display ▶ **showy** adj (-ier, -iest) intended to attract attention

shower /ˈʃaʊə(r)/ n **1** (room or part of a room containing a) device which sprays water from above for people to wash under **2** act of washing yourself with a shower: (esp GB) have a ~ ◇ (esp US) take a ~ **3** short period of rain **4** fall of a large number of things: a ~ of stones ● **shower** v **1** [I] wash yourself under a shower **2** [I, T] ~ (with, down, on) (cause sth to) fall onto sth/sb, esp in a lot of small pieces **3** [T] ~ (with, on) give a lot of sth to sb: ~ sb with presents ▶ **showery** adj (of the weather) with frequent showers of rain

shown pt, pp of SHOW¹

shrank pt of SHRINK

shrapnel /ˈʃræpnəl/ n [U] pieces of metal from an exploding bomb

shred /ʃred/ n [C] **1** [usu pl] small thin piece torn or cut from sth **2** [usu sing] ~**of** very small amount of sth: not one ~ of proof ● **shred** v (-dd-) [T] cut or tear sth into small pieces ■ **'shredder** n machine that tears paper into pieces so that nobody can read what was printed on it

shrewd /ʃruːd/ adj having or showing sound judgement and common sense: a ~ guess ▶ **shrewdly** adv

shriek /ʃriːk/ v **1** [I] give a loud high shout, eg because you are excited **2** [T] say sth in a loud high voice ● **shriek** n loud high shout: a ~ of pain/delight

shrill /ʃrɪl/ adj (of sounds or voices) unpleasantly high and loud ▶ **shrillness** n [U]

shrimp /ʃrɪmp/ n **1** small shellfish, pink when boiled **2** (US) = PRAWN

shrine /ʃraɪn/ n **1** place where people come to worship because it is connected with a holy person or an event **2** any place associated with a deeply respected person, activity, etc

shrink /ʃrɪŋk/ v (pt shrank /ʃræŋk/ or shrunk /ʃrʌŋk/; pp shrunk) **1** [I, T] (cause sth) to become smaller: My shorts shrank in the wash. **2** [I] move back or away from sth out of fear or disgust [PV] **shrink from sth** be unwilling to do sth ▶ **shrinkage** /-ɪdʒ/ n [U] process or amount of shrinking ■ **shrunken** /ˈʃrʌŋkən/ adj that has become smaller (and less attractive)

shrivel /ˈʃrɪvl/ v (-ll-, US -l-) [I, T] ~ (up) (cause sth to) become dry and wrinkled from heat, cold or old age

shroud /ʃraʊd/ n **1** cloth wrapped round a dead body **2** thing that covers and hides sth: a ~ of mist ● **shroud** v [T] (usu passive) cover or hide sth: be ~ed in mystery

shrub /ʃrʌb/ n plant with a woody stem, lower than a tree ▶ **shrubbery** n [C, U] (pl -ies) area planted with shrubs

shrug /ʃrʌg/ v (-gg-) [I, T] lift your shoulders slightly to express doubt, etc [PV] **shrug sth off** treat sth as unimportant ▶ **shrug** n [usu sing]

shrunk pt, pp of SHRINK

shrunken → SHRINK

shudder /ˈʃʌdə(r)/ v [I] shake with fear, disgust, etc ● **shudder** n [usu sing] strong shaking movement

shuffle /ˈʃʌfl/ v **1** [I] walk without lifting your feet properly **2** [I, T] move from one foot to another because of embarrassment, etc **3** [T] mix up playing cards to change their order ● **shuffle** n [usu sing]

1 slow shuffling walk **2** act of mixing playing cards before a game

shun /ʃʌn/ v [T] (**-nn-**) (*written*) avoid sb/sth

shunt /ʃʌnt/ v **1** [I, T] move trains, etc from one track to another **2** [T] (*disapprov*) move sb/sth to a different place

shush /ʃʊʃ/ *exclam* used to tell sb to be quiet

shut /ʃʌt/ v (**-tt-**, *pt, pp* **shut**) [I, T] **1** (cause sth to) become closed: ~ *a book* ◇ *The window won't ~* (*GB*) (cause a shop, etc to) stop being open for business: *What time does the baker's ~?* [IDM] **shut your eyes to sth** deliberately ignore sth **shut up shop** close a business; stop trading, etc [PV] **shut (sth) down** cause a factory, etc to) stop working **shut sth off** stop the supply of gas, water, etc **shut sb/sth off from sth** separate sb/sth from sth **shut (sb) up** (*infml*) (cause sb to) stop talking **shut sth up** close a room, house, etc ■ '**shutdown** *n* act of closing a factory, business or switching off a large machine

shutter /ʃʌtə(r)/ *n* **1** wooden or metal cover for a window **2** part of a camera that opens to let light pass through the lens ► **shuttered** *adj* with shutters closed

shuttle /ʃʌtl/ *n* **1** aircraft, bus, etc that travels regularly between two places **2** device for carrying thread in a sewing machine, etc ● **shuttle** v [I] travel between two places frequently **2** [T] carry people between two places, making regular journeys backwards and forwards ■ '**shuttlecock** *n* cork with feathers in it, used in badminton

shy¹ /ʃaɪ/ *adj* **1** (of people) nervous or embarrassed about meeting others **2** (of animals) easily frightened ► **shyly** *adv* ► **shyness** *n* [U]

shy² /ʃaɪ/ v (*pt, pp* **shied** /ʃaɪd/) [I] (esp of a horse) turn away suddenly in fear [PV] **shy away (from sth)** avoid doing sth because you are frightened

Siamese twin /ˌsaɪəmiːz 'twɪn/ *n* one of two people born with their bodies joined together

sibilant /sɪbɪlənt/ *adj* (*lit*) making an 's' or a 'sh' sound

sibling /sɪblɪŋ/ *n* (*fml*) brother or sister

sick /sɪk/ *adj* **1** ill: *care for ~ people in hospital* **2** likely to vomit: *feel ~* **3** ~ **of** (*infml*) bored with or annoyed about sth that has been happening for a long time: *I'm ~ and tired of his lies.* **4** (*infml*) (esp of humour) cruel or offensive: ~ *jokes* [IDM] **be worried sick** | **be sick with worry** be very worried ● **sick** *n* **1** [U] (*GB*) vomit **2** (**the sick**) [pl] people who are ill ■ '**sick**

leave *n* [U] permission to be absent from work, etc because of illness

sicken /sɪkən/ v **1** make sb feel disgusted: *Violence ~s him.* **2** [I] ~ (**for**) begin to be ill ► **sickening** *adj* disgusting

sickle /sɪkl/ *n* short tool with a curved blade for cutting grass

sickly /sɪkli/ *adj* (**-ier, -iest**) **1** often ill **2** looking ill: *a ~ complexion* **3** making you feel sick: *a ~ sweet smell*

sickness /sɪknəs/ *n* **1** [C,U] (type of) illness or disease **2** [U] feeling that you are going to vomit; the fact of vomiting

side¹ /saɪd/ *n* **1** either of the two halves of a surface, an object or an area: *the left-hand ~ of the road* **2** any flat surface that is not the top, bottom, front or back **3** part of sth near the edge and away from the centre: *parked at the ~ of the road* **4** left or right part of a body: *a pain in your ~* **5** either surface of a piece of paper, etc **6** either of two opposing groups of people in games, war, etc **7** one of the opinions held by sb in an argument, a business arrangement, etc **8** aspect of sth: *study all ~s of a question* [IDM] **get on the right/wrong side of sb** please/displease sb **on/from all sides** in/from all directions **on the big, small, etc side** slightly too big, small, etc **onto one side 1** out of your way **2** to be dealt with later **side by side** close together **take sides** support sb in a dispute ■ '**sideboard** *n* cupboard with drawers for holding plates, etc ■ '**sideboards** | '**sideburns** *n* [pl] hair that grows down the sides of a man's face in front of the ears ■ '**side effect** *n* indirect, usu bad effect of a drug ■ '**sidelight** *n* either of a pair of two small lights at the front of a car ■ '**sideline** *n* **1** job that is not your main occupation **2** (**sidelines**) [pl] lines forming the edge of a sports field ■ '**sidelong** *adj* to or from the side: *a ~ glance* ■ '**side road** *n* minor road ■ '**sidestep** v (**-pp-**) **1** [I, T] avoid answering a question **2** [I, T] avoid a blow, etc by stepping to one side ■ '**sidetrack** v [T] turn sb's attention away from more important matters ■ '**sidewalk** *n* (*US*) = PAVE- MENT ■ '**sideways** *adv* to, towards or from the side

side² /saɪd/ v [PV] **side with sb (against sb/sth)** support one person or group in an argument against sb else

siding /saɪdɪŋ/ *n* short railway track off the main lines

siege /siːdʒ/ *n* [C,U] (act of) surrounding a city, etc with armed forces to capture it [IDM] **lay siege**

to sth begin a siege of a town, building, etc

sieve /sɪv/ *n* frame with wire netting through which flour, etc is passed to separate coarse grains from fine grains ● **sieve** *v* [T] put sth through a sieve

sift /sɪft/ *v* **1** [T] put flour or some other fine substance through a sieve **2** [T] examine sth very carefully: ~ *(through) the evidence*

sigh /saɪ/ *v* **1** [I] take a deep breath, expressing sadness, tiredness, relief, etc **2** [T] say sth with a sigh ● **sigh** *n* act or sound of sighing

sight /saɪt/ *n* **1** [U] act of seeing sb/sth: *I faint at the ~ of blood.* ◇ *The soldiers have orders to shoot on ~* (= as soon as they see sb). **2** [U] range within which sb/sth can be seen: *The end is in ~* (= will happen soon). ◇ *Keep out of ~.* **4** [C] thing seen or worth seeing **(sights)** [pl] famous buildings, etc of a place: *the ~s of London* **5** [C] device that helps you aim a gun, etc **7 (a sight)** [sing] (*infml*) person or thing that looks ridiculous, dirty, etc [IDM] **a sight for sore eyes** (*spoken*) something very pleasing to see ● **sight** *v* [T] (*written*) suddenly see sth, esp sth you have been looking for ▸ **sighted** *adj* able to see; not blind ▸ **sighting** *n* instance of sb/sth being seen ■ **'sightseeing** *n* [U] activity of visiting interesting buildings, etc as a tourist

sign /saɪn/ *n* **1** thing that shows that sb/sth exists or is present: *Headaches may be a ~ of stress.* **2** notice, board, etc that gives a warning, direction, advertises a business, etc: *a road ~* **3** movement of the hand, head, etc to tell sb sth **4** mark or symbol used to represent sth [IDM] **a sign of the times** event, etc typical of its period ● **sign** *v* [I, T] **1** write your name on sth **2** use sign language to communicate with sb [PV] **sign sth away** give away property, etc by signing a document **sign off** end a letter **2** end a broadcast **sign on** (*GB*) officially register as unemployed **sign (sb) on/up** (cause sb to) sign an agreement to work for sb ■ **'sign language** *n* [U,C] system of communicating with people who cannot hear, using the hands ■ **'signpost** *n* sign at the side of a road giving information about the direction of places

signal /ˈsɪɡnəl/ *n* **1** movement or sound that gives sb information, instructions, a warning, etc: *A red light is a danger ~.* **2** event, action, etc that shows that sth exists or is likely to happen: *Chest pains can be a warning ~ of heart problems.* **3** device which gives information to train drivers **4** message sent or

received by radio waves ● **signal** *v* (**-ll-**, *US* **-l-**) **1** [I, T] make a movement or sound to give sb a message, an order, etc **2** [T] be a sign that sth exists or is likely to happen ■ **'signal box** *n* building beside a railway, from which rail signals are operated

signatory /ˈsɪɡnətri/ *n* (*pl* **-ies**) person, country, etc that has signed an agreement

signature /ˈsɪɡnətʃə(r)/ *n* person's name as they usually write it, eg at the end of a letter ■ **'signature tune** *n* short tune that introduces a broadcast or performer

significance /sɪɡˈnɪfɪkəns/ *n* [U] meaning; importance ▸ **significant** *adj* **1** having a special meaning; important **2** full of meaning: *a ~ look* ▸ **significantly** *adv*

signify /ˈsɪɡnɪfaɪ/ *v* (*pt, pp* **-ied**) **1** [T] be a sign of sth; mean sth **2** [T] make your intentions, views, etc known **3** [I] (*fml*) be of importance; matter

silence /ˈsaɪləns/ *n* **1** complete lack of noise or sound **2** period of not speaking or answering questions: *They finished their meal in total ~.* ● **silence** *v* [T] make sb/sth silent ▸ **silencer** *n* device for reducing the noise that a vehicle or gun makes

silent /ˈsaɪlənt/ *adj* **1** (of a person) saying little or nothing **2** making little or no sound; where there is little or no sound **3** (of a letter in a word) written but not pronounced ▸ **silently** *adv*

silhouette /ˌsɪluˈet/ *n* dark outline of sb/sth against a lighter background ● **silhouette** *v* [T] (usu passive) make sth appear as a silhouette: *trees ~d against the sky*

silicon /ˈsɪlɪkən/ *n* [U] (*symb* **Si**) chemical element found in rocks and sand, used in making glass and transistors ■ **silicon 'chip** *n* very small piece of silicon used to carry a complicated electronic circuit

silk /sɪlk/ *n* [U] (material made from) fine, soft thread produced by silkworms ▸ **silken** *adj* soft, smooth and shiny like silk ■ **'silkworm** *n* (= creature like a worm) that produces silk thread ▸ **silky** *adj* (**-ier, -iest**) soft, shiny and smooth like silk

sill /sɪl/ *n* flat shelf at the base of a window

silly /ˈsɪli/ *adj* (**-ier, -iest**) showing a lack of thought or good sense; foolish ▸ **silliness** *n* [U]

silt /sɪlt/ *n* [U] sand, mud, etc left behind by moving water ● **silt** *v* [PV] **silt (sth) up** (cause sth to) become blocked with silt

silver /ˈsɪlvə(r)/ *n* **1** [U] (*symb* **Ag**) shiny white precious metal **2** articles, coins, etc of silver **3** the colour of silver ● **silver** adj made of or looking like silver ■ **silver 'jubilee** n 25th anniversary of an important event ■ **silver 'medal** n medal given to the person who wins the second place in a competition ■ **silver-'plated** adj (of spoons, dishes, etc) covered with a thin layer of silver ■ **silversmith** n person who makes or sells silver articles ■ **silver 'wedding** n 25th anniversary of a wedding ▶ **silvery** adj like silver

similar /'sɪmələ(r)/ adj ~(to) like sb/sth but not exactly the same ▶ **similarly** adv

similarity /ˌsɪmə'lærəti/ n (pl -ies) 1 [U, sing] state of being like sb/sth but not exactly the same 2 [C] similar feature, characteristic, etc

simile /'sɪməli/ n [C, U] (tech) word or phrase that compares sth to sth else, eg *as white as snow*

simmer /'sɪmə(r)/ v 1 [I, T] (cause sth to) boil gently 2 [I] ~with be almost unable to control an emotion: *~ing with anger* [PV] **simmer down** become calm after being angry

simple /'sɪmpl/ adj 1 easily understood; not difficult: *a ~ problem* 2 plain: *~ food* consisting of only a few parts; not complicated in structure: *~ forms of life* 4 (of a person) ordinary; not special: *a ~ country girl* 5 (of a person) not very intelligent; not mentally normal 6 (gram) used to describe the present or past tense of a verb that is formed without an auxiliary verb, eg *I love him.* ▶ **simply** adv 1 used to emphasize how easy or basic sth is: *Simply add hot water and stir.* 2 absolutely 3 in a way that is natural and plain

simplicity /sɪm'plɪsəti/ n [U] quality of being easy to understand or use [IDM] **be simplicity itself** be very easy

simplify /'sɪmplɪfaɪ/ v (pt, pp -ied) [T] make sth easier to do or understand ▶ **simplification** /-fɪ'keɪʃn/ n [C, U]

simulate /'sɪmjuleɪt/ v [T] 1 pretend to have a particular feeling: *~ interest* 2 create particular conditions that exist in real life for training or study purposes ▶ **simulation** n [C, U]

simultaneous /ˌsɪml'teɪniəs/ adj happening or done at the same time ▶ **simultaneously** adv

sin /sɪn/ n 1 [C] offence against God's laws 2 [U] act of breaking a religious or moral law ● **sin** v (pt **sang** /sæŋ/; pp **sung** /sʌŋ/) 1 [I, T] make musical sounds with your voice in the form of a song or tune [I] make a high ringing sound ▶ **singer** n ▶ **singing** n [U]

singe /sɪndʒ/ v [I, T] (cause the surface of sth to) be blackened by burning

single /'sɪŋgl/ adj 1 only one: *a ~ apple* 2 (of a person) not married 3 for the use of one person: *a ~ bed* 4 (GB) (of a ticket) for a journey to a place but not back again [IDM] (in) **single file** (in) one line, one behind the other ● **single** n 1 (GB) ticket allowing travel to a place but not back again 2 [C] tape, CD, etc with only one song on each side 3 (**singles**) [U] (esp in tennis) game with one person on each side ● **single** v [PV] **single sb/sth out** (for sth/as sb/sth) choose sb/sth from a group for special attention ■ **single-'handed** adj, adv (done) by one person without help ■ **single-'minded** adj giving all your attention, energy, etc to one aim ■ **single 'parent** n parent caring for a child on their own ▶ **singly** /'sɪŋgli/ adv one at a time

singsong /'sɪŋsɒŋ/ n 1 [C] informal occasion at which people sing songs together 2 [sing] way of speaking with a rising and falling rhythm

singular /'sɪŋgjələ(r)/ adj 1 (gram) referring to one person: *a ~ verb* 2 (fml) very great or obvious 3 (lit) unusual; strange ● **singular** n (gram) form of a noun or verb that refers to one person or thing ▶ **singularly** adv (fml) very; in an unusual way

sinister /'sɪnɪstə(r)/ adj suggesting evil or danger: *a ~ place*

sink /sɪŋk/ v (pt **sank** /sæŋk/, pp **sunk** /sʌŋk/) 1 [I] go down below the surface or towards the bottom of a liquid or sth soft 2 [T] cause a boat or ship so that it goes below the surface of the sea, etc 3 [I] move slowly downwards: *She sank to the ground.* ◇ *The building is ~ing.* 4 [I] decrease in value, strength, etc 5 [T] make a deep hole in the ground: *a well* [PV] **sink in/into sth** 1 (of words, etc) be fully understood 2 (of liquids) go down into another substance ● **sink**

sth into sth invest a lot of money in sth ● **sink** n large open container in a kitchen with taps, used for washing the dishes in

sinuous /'smjuəs/ adj curving; twisting

sinus /'saɪnəs/ n hollow space in the bones of the head behind the nose

sip /sɪp/ v (-pp-) [I, T] drink sth, taking a very small amount each time ● **sip** n very small amount of a drink that you take into your mouth

siphon (also **syphon**) /'saɪfn/ n tube used for moving liquid from one container to another, using pressure from the atmosphere ● **siphon** v [T] 1 move a liquid from one container to another using a siphon 2 (infml) remove money from one place to another, esp illegally

sir /sɜː(r)/ n 1 (fml) used as a polite way of addressing a man: Can I help you, ~? 2 (**Dear Sir/Sirs**) used at the beginning of a formal business letter 3 (**Sir**) used before the name of a knight or baronet

sire /'saɪə(r)/ n (tech) male parent of an animal, esp a horse ● **sire** v [T] be the male parent of an animal, esp a horse

siren /'saɪrən/ n device for producing a loud noise as a signal or warning: an ambulance ~

sirloin /'sɜːlɔɪn/ (also **sirloin 'steak**) n [C,U] good quality beef that is cut from a cow's back

sister /'sɪstə(r)/ n 1 girl or woman who has the same mother and father as another person 2 (**Sister**) (GB) senior hospital nurse 3 (**Sister**) female member of a religious group, esp a nun 4 fellow woman ▶ **sisterhood** n 1 [U] close relationship between women with shared ideas and aims 2 [C, with sing or pl verb] group of women living together in a religious community ▶ **sisterly** adj of or like a sister

sit /sɪt/ v (-tt- pt, pp sat /sæt/) 1 [I] rest your bottom with your back upright 2 [T] put sb in a sitting position: She sat the child on the chair. 3 [I] (of objects) be in a particular place: The box sat unopened on a shelf. 4 [I] have an official position as sth or as a member of sth: She ~s on several committees. 5 [I] (of a parliament, law court, etc) meet in order to do official business 6 [I, T] ~ (**for**) (GB) do an exam [IDM] **sit on the fence** avoid becoming involved in deciding or influencing sth **sit tight** 1 stay where you are 2 refuse to take action, etc [PV] **sit about/around** spend time doing sth not very useful **sit back** relax and do nothing: ~ back and watch television **sit for sb/sth** be a model for an artist or a photographer **sit in on sth** attend a class, discussion, etc as an observer **sit on sth** (infml) have received a letter, report, etc from sb and then not replied or taken any action concerning it **sit up** not go to bed until later than usual **sit (sb) up** (cause sb to) take a sitting position ■ '**sit-in** n act of occupying a building, etc as a protest

sitcom /'sɪtkɒm/ n [C] regular programme on television that shows the same characters in different amusing situations

site /saɪt/ n 1 place where a building, etc is or will be situated 2 place where sth happened or that is used for sth: a caravan ~ 3 (computing) place on the Internet where a company, an organization, etc puts information ● **site** v [T] build or position sth in a particular place

sitting /'sɪtɪŋ/ n 1 time during which a parliament or law court meets 2 time when a meal is served in a hotel, etc to a group of people at the same time 3 act of posing for a portrait or photograph [IDM] **sitting duck** person or thing that is easy to attack ■ '**sitting room** n (GB) room in a house where people sit together, watch TV, etc

situate /'sɪtʃueɪt/ v [T] (fml) build sth in a particular position ▶ **situated** adj in a particular place or position: The hotel is beautifully ~d in a quiet spot near the river. 2 (fml) (of a person, an organization, etc) in the stated circumstances

situation /ˌsɪtʃu'eɪʃn/ n 1 all the circumstances and things happening at a certain time and in a certain place 2 (written) position of a town, building, etc 3 (old-fash) job ■ **situation 'comedy** n [C,U] (fml) = SITCOM

six /sɪks/ number 6 [IDM] **at sixes and sevens** (infml) in confusion ▶ **sixth** /sɪksθ/ ordinal number, n 6th; the fraction ⅙; each of six equal parts of sth

sixteen /ˌsɪks'tiːn/ number 16 ▶ **sixteenth** /ˌsɪks'tiːnθ/ ordinal number

sixty /'sɪksti/ 1 number 60 2 (the **sixties**) n [pl] numbers, years or temperatures from 60 to 69 ▶ **sixtieth** /'sɪkstiəθ/ ordinal number

size /saɪz/ n 1 [U,C] how large a person or thing is 2 [C] standard measurement of clothes, shoes, etc: ~ five shoes ● **size** v [T] mark the size of sth [PV] **size sb/sth up** (infml) form a judgement of sb/sth ▶ **sizeable** /-əbl/ adj fairly large

sizzle /'sɪzl/ v [I], n (make the) hissing sound of sth cooking in fat

skate /skeɪt/ n 1 = ICE SKATE (ICE¹) 2 = ROLLER SKATE (ROLLER) [IDM] **get/put your skates on** (infml) hurry up ● **skate** v [I] move on skates

[IDM] **be skating on thin ice** be taking a risk [PV] **skate over/round sth** avoid talking about sth directly ■ **'skateboard** *n* short, narrow board with small wheels at each end, for standing and riding on for fun ► **skater** *n*

skeleton /'skelɪtn/ *n* **1** structure of bones that supports the body **2** main structure that supports a building, etc **3** basic outline of a plan, etc **4** smallest number of people needed to provide a service, etc: *a ~ staff* [IDM] **a skeleton in the cupboard** secret which you are ashamed of ■ **'skeleton key** *n* key that opens several different locks

skeptic, skeptical, skepticism (*US*) = SCEPTIC, SCEPTICAL, SCEPTICISM

sketch /sketʃ/ *n* **1** simple drawing that is done quickly and without detail **2** short funny scene on television, in the theatre, etc **3** short description of sth ● **sketch** *v* [I, T] make a quick drawing of sb/sth **2** give a general description of sth ► **sketchy** *adj* (-ier, -iest) not done thoroughly; lacking detail

skewer /'skjuːə(r)/ *n* pointed wood or metal pin for holding meat, vegetables, etc together during cooking ● **skewer** *v* [T] push a skewer into sth

ski /skiː/ *n* long narrow strip of wood, etc attached to special boots for moving over snow ● **ski** *v* (*pt, pp* **skied**; *pres pt* **~ing**) move over snow on skis, esp as a sport: *go ~ing* ► **skier** *n*

skid /skɪd/ *n* uncontrollable sideways sliding movement of a vehicle on ice ● **skid** *v* (**-dd-**) [I] (usu of a vehicle) move sideways or forwards in an uncontrollable way

skies plural of SKY

skilful (*US* **skillful**) /'skɪlfl/ *adj* good at sth, esp sth that requires special ability: *a ~ player* ► **skilfully** *adv*

skill /skɪl/ *n* [C,U] ability to do sth well ► **skilled** *adj* ~ (**in/at**) **1** having enough ability, experience, etc to be able to do sth well **2** (of a job) needing special abilities or training: *~ed work*

skim /skɪm/ *v* (**-mm-**) **1** [T] remove fat, cream, etc from the surface of a liquid **2** [I, T] move lightly over a surface, barely touching it **3** [I, T] ~ (**through**) read sth quickly

skin /skɪn/ *n* **1** [U,C] layer of tissue that covers the body **2** [C,U] skin of a dead animal, used for making leather, etc **3** [C,U] outer layer of some fruit and vegetables **4** [C,U] thin layer that forms on the surface of some liquids, eg boiled milk [IDM] **by the skin of your teeth** by a very narrow margin **get under sb's skin** (*infml*) annoy sb **it's no skin off my, your,**

his, etc **nose** (*infml*) it does not matter to me, you, him, etc **make your skin crawl** make you feel afraid or disgusted (**nothing but/all/only**) **skin and bone** (*infml*) extremely thin ● **skin** *v* [T] (**-nn-**) take the skin off an animal, a fruit or a vegetable ■ **,skin-'deep** *adj* (of a feeling, etc) not deep or lasting ■ **'skinflint** (*disapprov*) person who does not like spending money ■ **'skinhead** *n* young person with very short hair, esp one who is violent ■ **,skin'tight** *adj* (of clothing) fitting very closely to the body ► **skinny** *adj* (**-ier, -iest**) (*disapprov*) very thin

skint /skɪnt/ *adj* (*GB, infml*) having no money

skip /skɪp/ *v* (**-pp-**) **1** [I] move forwards lightly and quickly making a little jump with each step **2** [I] jump over a rope swung under your feet as you jump **3** [T] not do sth that you usually do or should do: *to ~ lunch/a class* **4** [T] leave out sth that would normally be the next thing you would do, read, etc: *~ part of the book* **5** [I] move from one place to another quickly **6** [I, T] leave a place quickly or secretly: *~ the country* ● **skip** *n* **1** skipping movement **2** large metal container for rubbish, etc

skipper /'skɪpə(r)/ *n* captain of a small ship or a sports team ● **skipper** *v* [T] be the captain of a ship or team

skirt /skɜːt/ *n* piece of women's clothing that hangs from the waist ● **skirt** *v* [T] **1** be or go round the edge of sth: *a wood ~ing the field* **2** avoid talking about a subject, esp because it is embarrassing ■ **'skirting board** *n* [U] narrow piece of wood fixed along the bottom of the walls in a house

skittle /'skɪtl/ *n* **1** [C] wooden or plastic object used in the game of skittles **2** (**skittles**) [U] game in which players try to knock over as many skittles as possible by rolling a ball at them

skulk /skʌlk/ *v* [I] hide or move around, trying not to be seen

skull /skʌl/ *n* bone structure that forms the head

skunk /skʌŋk/ *n* small N American animal that sends out a strong smell when attacked

sky /skaɪ/ *n* [C,U] (*pl* **skies** /skaɪz/) the space above the earth, where we see clouds, the sun, moon and stars ■ **'skydiving** *n* [U] sport in which you jump from a plane and fall for as long as you safely can before opening your parachute ■ **,sky-'high** *adj* very high; too high ■ **'skylark** *n* small bird that sings as it flies high in the sky ■ **'skylight** *n* window in a sloping roof ■ **'skyline** *n* [C, usu sing] outline of buildings, hills, etc against the sky ■ **'skyscraper** *n* very tall building

slab /slæb/ *n* thick flat piece of stone, etc

slack /slæk/ *adj* **1** not stretched tight: *a ~ rope* **2** (of business) not having many customers or sales; not busy: *Trade is ~.* **3** (*disapprov*) giving little care, attention or energy to a task ● **slack** *v* [I] work less hard than you should do or than you usu do [PV] **slack off** (on sth) do sth more slowly or with less energy than before ● **slack (the slack)** *n* [U] part of a rope that is hanging loosely [IDM] **take up the slack 1** improve the way money or people are used in an organization **2** tighten a rope ▶ **slacker** *n* (*infml, disapprov*) person who is lazy and avoids work ▶ **slackness** *n* [U]

slacken /'slækən/ *v* [I, T] **1** ~ (off/up) (cause sth to) gradually become slower, less active, etc **2** (cause sth to) become less tight

slag /slæg/ *n* **1** [U] waste matter remaining when metal has been removed from rock **2** [C] (*GB, sl*) offensive word for a woman, used to suggest that she has a lot of sexual partners ● **slag** *v* (**-gg-**) [PV] **slag sb off** (*GB, sl*) say cruel or critical things about sb ■ **'slag heap** *n* large pile of slag (= waste matter) from a mine

slam /slæm/ *v* (**-mm-**) **1** [I, T] (cause sth to) shut with great force **2** [T] throw or knock sth somewhere with great force: *a book against the wall* **3** [T] (*infml*) criticize sth/sb very strongly ● **slam** *n* noise of sth being slammed

slander /'slɑːndə(r)/ *n* [U,C] (offence of) saying sth false about sb that damages their reputation ● **slander** *v* [T] say sth false about sb ▶ **slanderous** *adj*

slang /slæŋ/ *n* [U] very informal words and expressions used in spoken conversation, esp by a particular group of people

slant /slɑːnt/ *v* [I, T] (cause sth to) slope in a certain direction **2** [T] (*often disapprov*) present information from a particular point of view, esp unfairly ● **slant** *n* **1** sloping position **2** point of view

slap /slæp/ *v* (**-pp-**) [T] **1** hit sb/sth with the palm of the hand **2** put sth on a surface carelessly, esp because you are angry: ~ *paint onto the wall* ● **slap** *n* action of hitting sb/sth with the palm of the hand [IDM] **a slap in the face** action seemingly intended as a deliberate insult to sb ● **slap** *adv* (*also* **slap 'bang**) (*infml*) straight: *The car ran ~ into the wall.*

slapdash /'slæpdæʃ/ *adj* done or

doing things too carelessly and quickly

slapstick /'slæpstɪk/ *n* [U] comedy in which people fall over, knock each other down, etc

slap-up /'slæp ʌp/ *adj* (*GB, infml*) (of a meal) large and very good

slash /slæʃ/ *v* [T] **1** make a long cut with a sharp object, esp in a violent way **2** reduce sth by a large amount: ~ *prices* ● **slash** *n* **1** sharp movement made with a knife, etc in order to cut sb/sth **2** long narrow wound or cut **3** symbol (/) used to show alternatives, as in 'lunch and/or dinner'

slat /slæt/ *n* thin, narrow piece of wood, metal, etc

slate /sleɪt/ *n* **1** [U] dark grey stone that splits easily into thin, flat layers **2** [C] small thin piece of slate used for covering roofs ● **slate** *v* [T] (*written*) criticize sth severely, esp in a newspaper

slaughter /'slɔːtə(r)/ *n* [U] **1** killing of animals for their meat **2** cruel killing of many people at once ● **slaughter** *v* [T] **1** kill an animal, usu for its meat **2** kill a large number of people or animals violently **3** (*infml*) defeat sb/sth completely in a game, competition, etc ■ **'slaughterhouse** *n* place where animals are killed for food

slave /sleɪv/ *n* **1** person who is legally owned by and forced to work for another **2** ~ (to/of) person controlled by a habit, etc: *a ~ to drink* ● **slave** *v* [I] work very hard: ~ *away in the kitchen* ▶ **slavery** *n* [U] **1** state of being a slave **2** system of using slaves

slaver /'slævə(r)/ *v* [I] (usu of an animal) let saliva run out of the mouth, esp because of hunger or excitement

slavish /'sleɪvɪʃ/ *adj* (*disapprov*) lacking originality or independence: *a ~ copy* ▶ **slavishly** *adv*

slay /sleɪ/ *v* (*pt* **slew** /sluː/; *pp* **slain** /sleɪn/) [T] (*lit* or *US*) kill sb/sth violently

sledge /sledʒ/ (*also* **sled** /sled/) *n* vehicle for travelling over snow, with long strips of wood or metal instead of wheels

sledgehammer /'sledʒhæmə(r)/ *n* heavy hammer with a long handle

sleek /sliːk/ *adj* **1** smooth and shiny: ~ *hair* **2** (*often disapprov*) looking well dressed and rich

sleep[1] /sliːp/ *v* (*pt, pp* **slept** /slept/) **1** [I] rest with your eyes closed and your mind and body not active **2** [T] have enough beds for a particular number of people: *a flat that ~s six* [IDM] **sleep like a log/baby** (*infml*) sleep well **sleep tight** (*spoken*) used to wish sb a good night's sleep [PV] **sleep around** (*infml, disapprov*) have sex with a lot of people **sleep in**

sleep until after the time you usu get up in the morning **sleep sth off** recover from drunkenness, etc by sleeping **sleep on sth** leave a problem, etc to the next day **sleep through sth** not be woken by a noise **sleep together**(**sleep with sb** (*infml*) have sex with sb ● **sleeper** n **1** person who sleeps **2** (bed in a) sleeping car **3** beam of wood supporting the rails of a railway track ■ '**sleeping bag** n thick warm bag for sleeping in, eg when camping ■ '**sleeping car** n railway carriage fitted with beds ■ '**sleeping pill** (*also* '**sleeping tablet**) n pill containing a drug that helps sb to sleep ▸ **sleepy** adj (**-ier, -iest**) **1** needing or ready for sleep **2** (of places, etc) without much activity: *a ~ little town* ▸ **sleepily** adv

sleep² /sliːp/ n **1** [U] condition when the body is at rest with the eyes closed, mostly at night: *It's late—go to ~.* **2** [sing] period of sleep [IDM] **put sb to sleep** (*infml*) make sb unconscious before an operation by using an anaesthetic **put sth to sleep** kill a sick or injured animal by giving it drugs so that it dies without pain ▸ **sleepless** adj

sleet /sliːt/ n [U] falling snow mixed with rain ● **sleet** v (used with *it*) fall as sleet: *It's ~ing outside.*

sleeve /sliːv/ n **1** part of a piece of clothing that covers the arm **2** stiff envelope for a record [IDM] **have/keep sth up your sleeve** keep a plan, idea, etc secret until you need it

sleigh /sleɪ/ n sledge (= vehicle that slides over snow), esp one pulled by horses

sleight /slaɪt/ n [IDM] **sleight of hand** skilful movements of your hand that others cannot see

slender /'slendə(r)/ adj **1** (*approv*) (of people) slim **2** thin or narrow **3** small in amount or size: *to win by a ~ margin* ▸ **slenderness** n [U]

slept pt, pp of SLEEP¹

slice /slaɪs/ n **1** thin flat piece cut off sth, esp bread or meat **2** (*infml*) part or share of sth: *a ~ of the credit* **3** utensil with a wide blade for cutting or lifting sth, eg cooked fish [IDM] **a slice of life** film, play or book that gives a realistic view of ordinary life ● **slice** v **1** [I, T] (~ (**up**)) cut sth into pieces **2** [I] cut sth easily (as if) with a sharp blade: *a knife slicing through butter*

slick /slɪk/ adj **1** done (often) smoothly and efficiently **2** (*disapprov*) (of people) speaking easily and smoothly but in a way that seems insincere **3** smooth and slippery

slide¹ /slaɪd/ v (pt, pp **slid** /slɪd/) **1** [I, T] (cause sth to) move smoothly over a smooth or wet surface **2** [I, T]

(cause sth to) move quickly and quietly so as not to be noticed **3** [I] move gradually into a worse situation: *He began to let things ~* (= neglect things). ■ '**slide rule** n instrument like a ruler with a part that slides, used for calculating numbers

slide² /slaɪd/ n **1** [C, sing] change to a lower or worse situation **2** [C] structure with a steep slope for children to play on **3** [C] picture on photographic film projected onto a screen **4** [C] glass plate on which sth is examined under a microscope

slight¹ /slaɪt/ adj **1** not serious or important: *a ~ headache* **2** small and thin in size [IDM] **not in the slightest** not at all ▸ **slightly** adv **1** a little: *feel ~ly better* **2** slenderly: *a ~ly built boy* ▸ **slightness** n [U]

slight² /slaɪt/ v [T] treat sb rudely and without respect; insult sb ● **slight** n critical or offensive remark

slim /slɪm/ adj (**-mer, -mest**) **1** (*approv*) not fat or thick; slender **2** small: *a ~ chance of success* ● **slim** v (**-mm-**) [I] eat less, etc to reduce your weight ▸ **slimmer** n person who is slimming ▸ **slimness** n [U]

slime /slaɪm/ n [U] any unpleasant thick liquid substance ▸ **slimy** adj (**-ier, -iest**) **1** like or covered with slime **2** (*infml, disapprov*) polite, friendly, etc in a way that is not sincere or honest

sling /slɪŋ/ n band of material looped round an object, eg a broken arm, to support or lift it ● **sling** v (pt, pp **slung** /slʌŋ/) [T] (*infml*) throw sth/sb carelessly or with force

slink /slɪŋk/ v (pt, pp **slunk** /slʌŋk/) [I] move as if you do not want to be seen or are ashamed

slip¹ /slɪp/ v (**-pp-**) **1** [I] slide accidentally and (almost) fall: *He ~ped (over) in the mud.* **2** [I] slide out of position or out of your hand: *The plate ~ped from my hand.* **3** [I, T] (cause sth to) move quietly and quickly, without being seen: *He ~ped the coin into his pocket.* **4** [I] fall to a lower level; become worse **5** [I, T] put clothes on or take them off easily and quickly: *~ on a coat* [IDM] **let slip sth** accidentally reveal secret information **let sth slip (through your fingers)** miss or fail to use an opportunity **slip your mind** (of sb's name, etc) be forgotten [PV] **slip up** (*infml*) make a careless mistake ■ '**slip road** n (GB) road for joining or leaving a motorway ■ '**slipstream** n [sing] stream of air behind a fast-moving vehicle ■ '**slip-up** n (*infml*) careless mistake

slip² /slɪp/ n **1** small mistake **2** small piece of paper **3** act of slipping **4** piece of women's underwear, worn under a dress or a skirt [IDM] **give sb the slip** (*infml*) escape from sb

slipper /ˈslɪpə(r)/ *n* loose soft shoe worn in the house

slippery /ˈslɪpəri/ *adj* (**-ier**, **-iest**) **1** (*also infml* **slippy**) difficult to hold, stand or move on, because it is smooth, wet or polished **2** (*infml*) (of people) that you cannot trust **3** (*infml*) (of problems, etc) difficult to deal with [IDM] **the/a slippery slope** course of action that can easily lead to serious problems or disaster

slipshod /ˈslɪpʃɒd/ *adj* done or doing things without care

slit /slɪt/ *n* long narrow cut, tear or opening ● **slit** *v* (**-tt-**, *pt, pp* **slit**) [T] make a slit in sth

slither /ˈslɪðə(r)/ *v* [I] move somewhere smoothly, often close to the ground

sliver /ˈslɪvə(r)/ *n* long thin piece of sth: *a ~ of glass*

slob /slɒb/ *n* (*infml, disapprov*) dirty, untidy, lazy person

slog /slɒg/ *v* (**-gg-**) [I] (*infml*) **1** work hard and steadily at sth boring or difficult: ~ (*away*) *at sth* **2** walk somewhere with difficulty: ~ *up the hill* ● **slog** *n* [U,C, usu sing] period of hard work or effort

slogan /ˈsləʊgən/ *n* easily remembered phrase used in advertising

slop /slɒp/ *v* (**-pp-**) **1** [I] (of a liquid) move around in a container, often so that some liquid spills over the edge **2** [T] cause sth to spill: *Don't ~ the water all over the floor!* ● **slop** *n* [U] (*also* **slops** [pl]) **1** waste food, sometimes fed to animals **2** dirty waste water

slope /sləʊp/ *n* **1** [C] area of rising or falling ground **2** [C, usu sing] area of land that is part of a mountain or hill: *ski ~s* **3** [sing, U] amount by which sth slopes ● **slope** *v* [I] be at an angle; have a slope [PV] **slope off** (*GB, infml*) go somewhere quietly, esp to avoid sth/sb

sloppy /ˈslɒpi/ *adj* (**-ier**, **-iest**) **1** that shows a lack of care, thought or effort: ~ *work* **2** (of clothes) loose and shapeless **3** (*infml*) romantic in a silly way: *a ~ love story* **4** containing too much liquid ▶ **sloppily** *adv* ▶ **sloppiness** *n* [U]

slosh /slɒʃ/ *v* **1** [I, T] (cause liquid to) move about noisily or spill over the edge of sth: ~ *water all over the floor* **2** [I] walk noisily in water or mud ▶ **sloshed** *adj* (*sl*) drunk

slot /slɒt/ *n* **1** narrow opening: *put a coin in the ~* **2** position, time or opportunity for sb/sth in a plan, schedule, etc: ~ *s for advertisements on television* ● **slot** *v* (**-tt-**) [T] make

a slot for sth; place sth in a slot [PV] **slot sb/sth in** manage to find a position, time or opportunity for sb/sth

sloth /sləʊθ/ *n* **1** [C] S American animal that lives in trees and moves very slowly **2** [U] (*fml*) laziness ▶ **slothful** *adj*

slouch /slaʊtʃ/ *v* [I] stand, sit or move in a lazy way ● **slouch** *n* [sing] slouching posture, walk, etc [IDM] **be no slouch** (*infml*) be very good at sth

slovenly /ˈslʌvnli/ *adj* untidy; dirty ▶ **slovenliness** *n* [U]

slow¹ /sləʊ/ *adj* **1** taking a long time; not fast: *a ~ vehicle* **2** not acting immediately **3** not quick to learn: *a ~ child* **4** not very busy; containing little action: *Sales are ~ this month.* **5** (of a watch or clock) showing a time earlier than the correct time [IDM] **be slow on the uptake** ⇒ UPTAKE **slow off the mark** ⇒ MARK¹ ● **slow** *adv* at a slow speed: ~ *-moving traffic* [IDM] **go slow (on sth)** show less enthusiasm for achieving sth ■ **slowcoach** (*US* **'slowpoke**) *n* (*infml*) person who moves, works, etc too slowly ▶ **slowly** *adv* ▶ **slowness** *n* [U]

slow² /sləʊ/ *v* [I, T] ~(**down/up**) (cause sth/sb to) go at a slower speed or be less active ■ **slowdown** *n* **1** reduction of speed or activity **2** (*US*) = GO-SLOW (GO¹)

sludge /slʌdʒ/ *n* [U] (anything resembling) thick soft wet mud

slug /slʌg/ *n* **1** small soft creature like a snail but without a shell **2** (*infml*) small amount of a strong alcoholic drink **3** (*infml, esp US*) bullet ● **slug** *v* (**-gg-**) [T] (*infml*) hit sb/sth hard

sluggish /ˈslʌgɪʃ/ *adj* moving, reacting or working more slowly than normal ▶ **sluggishly** *adv*

sluice /sluːs/ *n* (*also* **'sluice gate**) sliding gate for controlling the flow of water in a canal, etc ● **sluice** *v* [T] wash sth with a stream of water

slum /slʌm/ *n* very poor area of a city where the houses are dirty and in bad condition ● **slum** *v* (**-mm-**) [I] (*infml*) spend time in places that are much worse than you are used to [IDM] **slum it** accept conditions that are worse than those you are used to

slumber /ˈslʌmbə(r)/ *v* [I] (*lit*) sleep ● **slumber** *n* [U,C, usu sing] (*lit*) sleep

slump /slʌmp/ *v* [I] **1** fall in price, value, number, etc suddenly and steeply **2** sit or fall down heavily ● **slump** *n* sudden fall in prices, trade, etc

slung *pt, pp* of SLING

slur /slɜː(r)/ *v* (**-rr-**) [T] **1** pronounce words in a way that is not clear, usu because you are drunk or tired **2** damage sb's reputation by making false statements about them ● **slur** *n* damaging remark: *a ~ on her name*

slush /slʌʃ/ *n* [U] **1** melting, dirty snow **2** (*infml, disapprov*) silly sentimental stories, films, etc ■ **'slush fund** *n* (*disapprov*) money kept for illegal purposes, esp in politics ▶ **slushy** *adj* (**-ier, -iest**)

slut /slʌt/ *n* (*disapprov, offens*) **1** woman who has many sexual partners **2** lazy or untidy woman ▶ **sluttish** *adj*

sly /slaɪ/ *adj* acting or done in a secret and dishonest way ● **sly** *n* [IDM] **on the sly** secretly ▶ **slyly** *adv* ▶ **slyness** *n* [U]

smack /smæk/ *n* **1** [C] (sound of a) sharp hit given with your open hand **2** [C] (*infml*) loud kiss **3** [U] (*infml*) the drug heroin ● **smack** *vb* suddenly and forcefully: *run ~ into a wall* ● **smack** *v* **1** [T] hit sb with your open hand **2** [I, T] (cause sth to) hit sth with a lot of force and a loud noise [IDM] **smack your lips** → LIP [PV] **smack of sth** seem to contain or involve an unpleasant quality

small /smɔːl/ *adj* **1** not large in size, number, degree, amount, etc: *a ~ house* **2** young: *~ children* **3** unimportant; slight: *a ~ problem* **4** not doing business on a large scale: *~ businesses* [IDM] **look/feel small** look/feel stupid, weak, ashamed, etc **the small hours** period of time very early in the morning, some time after midnight **small wonder (that …)** → WONDER ■ **,small 'fortune** *n* [usu sing] a lot of money ● **small** *n* [sing] **the ~ of the/sb's back** the lower part of the back where it curves in ■ **'small arms** *n* [pl] weapons carried in the hand ■ **'smallholding** *n* (*GB*) small piece of land used for farming ■ **,small-'minded** *adj* (*disapprov*) mean and selfish ▶ **smallness** *n* [U] ■ **'smallpox** *n* [U] serious infectious disease that leaves permanent scars on the skin ■ **'small talk** *n* [U] polite conversation about everyday social matters

smart¹ /smɑːt/ *adj* **1** clean and neat; well dressed: *a ~ appearance/person* **2** (*esp US*) intelligent: *a ~ answer* **3** connected with fashionable or rich people: *a ~ restaurant* **4** quick or hard: *We set off at a ~ pace.* ▶ **smarten** /ˈsmɑːtn/ *v* [PV] **smarten (yourself/sb/sth) up** make yourself/sb/sth look neater and more attractive ▶ **smartly** *adv* ▶ **smartness** *n* [U]

smart² /smɑːt/ *v* [I] feel a sharp stinging pain: *The smoke made my eyes ~.*

smash /smæʃ/ *v* **1** [I, T] (cause sth to) break violently into small pieces: *~ a cup on the floor* **2** [I, T] (cause sth to) move with great force against sth solid: *They ~ed into the wall.* **3** [T] hit

sth/sb very hard **4** [T] defeat or destroy sth/sb ● **smash** *n* **1** [sing] sound or act of breaking sth noisily into pieces **2** (*GB*) [C] accident in which one vehicle hits another: *a car ~* **3** [C] (in tennis) hard, downward stroke **4** (*also* **,smash 'hit**) [C] play, song, etc that is suddenly very successful ▶ **smashing** *adj* (*old-fash, GB, infml*) very good

smattering /ˈsmætərɪŋ/ *n* [sing] **~ of** small amount of sth, esp knowledge of a language: *a ~ of French*

smear /smɪə(r)/ *v* [T] **1** cover a surface with an oily or soft substance: *His face was ~ed with blood.* **2** damage sb's reputation by saying untrue things about them ● **smear** *n* **1** oily or dirty mark **2** untrue remark about sb that is intended to damage their reputation, esp in politics: *a ~ campaign* **3** small amount of a substance taken from the body, to be tested for disease

smell¹ /smel/ *v* (*pt, pp* **smelt** /smelt/ *or* **smelled**) **1** [I] **~(of)** have a particular smell: *good/of soap* **2** [T] (often with *can, could*) notice or recognize a particular smell: *Can you ~ gas?* **3** [T] put your nose near sth to test its smell: *~ the flowers* **4** [I] have a bad smell: *Your feet ~.* **5** [I] have the power of smelling: *Can birds ~?* [IDM] **smell a rat** (*infml*) suspect that sth is wrong

smell² /smel/ *n* **1** [C,U] quality of sth that people and animals detect through their noses **2** [sing] unpleasant smell: *What a ~!* **3** [U] ability to sense things with the nose **4** [C] act of smelling sth: *Have a ~ of this.* ▶ **smelly** *adj* (**-ier, -iest**) (*infml*) having an unpleasant smell

smile /smaɪl/ *n* expression of the face with the corners of the mouth turned up, showing amusement, happiness, etc ● **smile** *v* [I] make a smile appear on your face ▶ **smilingly** *adv*

smirk /smɜːk/ *v, n* (give a) silly self-satisfied smile

smithereens /ˌsmɪðəˈriːnz/ *n* [pl] [IDM] **smash, blow, etc sth to smithereens** destroy sth completely by breaking it into pieces

smitten /ˈsmɪtn/ *adj* **~(with/by)** **1** suddenly feeling that you are in love with sb: *I'm rather ~ with her.* **2** severely affected by a feeling, disease, etc

smock /smɒk/ *n* loose comfortable piece of clothing like a long shirt

smog /smɒg/ *n* [U,C] mixture of fog and smoke

smoke¹ /sməʊk/ *n* **1** [U] usu white, grey or black vapour produced by sth burning **2** [C] act of smoking a cigarette, etc [IDM] **go up in smoke** **1** be completely burned **2** result in failure ■ **'smokescreen** *n* **1** something you do or say in order to hide your real intentions **2** cloud of smoke used to hide soldiers, ships, etc during a battle ▶ **smoky** *adj* (**-ier, -iest**)

smoke² /sməʊk/ *v* **1** [I, T] breathe smoke from a cigarette; etc; use cigarettes, etc as a habit **2** [I] produce smoke **3** [T] preserve meat or fish with smoke [PV] **smoke sb/sth out** fill a place with smoke to force sb/sth out ▶ **smoker** *n* person who smokes tobacco regularly ▶ **smoking** *n* [U] activity of smoking cigarettes, etc

smooth /smuːð/ *adj* **1** (of a surface) completely flat and even, without any lumps, holes, etc: ~ *skin* **2** (of a liquid) free from lumps **3** happening or continuing without any problems **4** (of movement) even and regular: *a* ~ *ride* **5** (*disapprov*) (of a person, esp a man) polite and pleasant, but seeming insincere **6** (of sounds or tastes) pleasant and not bitter or harsh ● **smooth** *v* [T] make sth smooth [PV] **smooth sth over** make problems, etc seem less important ▶ **smoothly** *adv* ▶ **smoothness** *n* [U]

smother /'smʌðə(r)/ *v* [T] **1** kill sb by covering their face so that they cannot breathe **2** ~(**with/in**) cover sth/sb thickly or with too much of sth: *a cake* ~*ed in cream* ◇ *She* ~*ed him with kisses.* **3** prevent sth from developing or being expressed: ~ *a yawn* **4** put out a fire by covering it with sth

smoulder (*US* **smol-**) /'sməʊldə(r)/ *v* [I] burn slowly without flame: ~*ing ashes* ◇ (*fig*) *Hate* ~*ed within her.*

smudge /smʌdʒ/ *n* dirty mark ● **smudge** *v* [T] **1** touch or rub sth, esp wet ink or paint, so that it is no longer clear **2** (of wet ink, etc) become blurred: *Her lipstick had* ~*d.*

smug /smʌg/ *adj* (**-ger, -gest**) (*disapprov*) too pleased with yourself ▶ **smugly** *adv* ▶ **smugness** *n* [U]

smuggle /'smʌgl/ *v* [T] take goods, people, etc illegally or secretly into or out of a place or country: ~ *drugs into the country* ◇ *a letter into prison* ▶ **smuggler** *n* ▶ **smuggling** *n* [U]

smut /smʌt/ *n* **1** [U] (*infml*) vulgar stories, pictures, etc about sex **2** [C] small piece of dirt, soot, etc ▶ **smutty** *adj* (**-ier, -iest**)

snack /snæk/ *n* small quick meal, usu eaten instead of or between main meals

snag /snæg/ *n* **1** hidden or unexpected difficulty **2** sharp or rough piece of an object that sticks out ● **snag** *v* (**-gg-**) [T] (cause sth to) catch or tear on sth rough or sharp

snail /sneɪl/ *n* small soft animal that moves very slowly and has a shell on its back

snake /sneɪk/ *n* reptile with a very long thin body and no legs [IDM] **a snake (in the grass)** (*disapprov*) person who pretends to be a friend but who cannot be trusted ● **snake** *v* [I] follow a twisting path

snap /snæp/ *v* (**-pp-**) **1** [I, T] (cause sth to) break suddenly with a sharp noise **2** [I, T] (cause sth to) open or close with a sudden sharp noise: *His eyes* ~*ped open.* **3** [I, T] ~(**at**) (say sth in an impatient, usu angry, voice **4** [I] ~(**at**) (of dogs, etc) try to bite sb/sth: *The dog* ~*ped at her ankles.* **5** [I, T] (*infml*) take a photograph **6** [I] suddenly be unable to control your feelings any longer: *My patience finally* ~*ped.* [IDM] **snap your fingers** make a clicking noise with your fingers to attract attention, etc [PV] **snap out of it/sth** (*infml*) get out of a bad, unhappy, etc mood [PV] **snap sth up** buy sth quickly and eagerly ● **snap** *n* **1** sudden sharp noise, esp made by sth breaking **2** (*also* 'snapshot') photograph, usu one taken quickly **3** sudden short period of cold weather ● **snap** *adj* done quickly, without careful thought: ~ *a decision* ▶ **snappy** *adj* (**-ier, -iest**) **1** (of a remark, title, etc) clever, amusing and short **2** (*infml*) attractive and fashionable **3** speaking to people bad-tempered

snare /sneə(r)/ *n* **1** trap for catching small animals and birds **2** situation which traps sb ● **snare** *v* [T] catch sth, esp an animal, in a snare

snarl /snɑːl/ *v* **1** [I] (of dogs, etc) show the teeth and growl **2** [I, T] speak or say sth in an angry voice [PV] **snarl (sth) up** (*infml*) (cause sth) to become confused or tangled ● **'snarl-up** *n* (*GB, infml*) situation in which traffic is unable to move ● **snarl** *n* act or sound of snarling

snatch /snætʃ/ *v* **1** [I, T] (try to) take sb/sth suddenly or steal sth: ~ *the child from her father* **2** [T] take or get sth quickly, usu because there is not much time: ~ *some sleep* ● **snatch** *n* **1** short part of a conversation or some music that you hear: ~*es of conversation* **2** act of moving your hand quickly to take or steal sth: *a bag* ~

sneak /sniːk/ *v* **1** [I] go somewhere quietly and secretly: ~ *past sb* **2** [T] do sth or take sb/sth secretly: ~ *money from the box* **3** [I] (*old-fash*) tell an adult that another child has done sth wrong ● **sneak** *n* (*old-fash*) person who sneaks(3) ▶ **sneaker** *n* (*US*) = TRAINER(1) (TRAIN). ▶ **sneaking** *adj* secret: *a* ~*ing respect for sb* ◇ *a* ~*ing suspicion* ▶ **sneaky** *adj* (**-ier, -iest**) (*infml*) done or acting in a secret and sometimes dishonest way

sneer /snɪə(r)/ v [I] ~ (at) show that you have no respect for sb/sth by your expression or words ● **sneer** n sneering look, smile, etc

sneeze /sniːz/ v [I] have air come noisily and uncontrollably through through your nose and mouth, eg because you have a cold [IDM] **not to be sneezed at** (infml) good enough to be accepted ● **sneeze** n act of sneezing or the noise you make when sneezing

sniff /snɪf/ v **1** [I] draw in air through the nose, producing a sound **2** [I, T] ~ (at) breathe air in through the nose in order to smell sth: ~ (at) the roses [IDM] **not to be sniffed at** good enough to be accepted [PV] **sniff sb/sth out** discover or find sb/sth by looking ● **sniff** n act of sniffing

snigger /'snɪgə(r)/ n quiet unpleasant laugh ● **snigger** v [I] ~ (at) laugh in a quiet unpleasant way

snip /snɪp/ v (-pp-) [I, T] cut sth with scissors using short quick strokes ● **snip** n **1** [C] act or sound of cutting sth with scissors **2** (a **snip**) [sing] (GB, infml) thing that is cheap and good value: It's ~ at only £10

snipe /snaɪp/ v [I] **1** shoot at sb from a hiding place **2** criticize sb unpleasantly ► **sniper** n person who shoots at sb from a hidden position

snippet /'snɪpɪt/ n small item of news, information, etc: ~s of gossip

snivel /'snɪvl/ v (-ll- US -l-) [I] cry or complain in a miserable way

snob /snɒb/ n (disapprov) person who respects social position or wealth too much ● **snob** n [U] behaviour of a snob ► **snobbish** adj

snog /snɒg/ v (-gg-) [I, T] (GB, infml) (of two people) kiss each other, esp for a long time

snooker /'snuːkə(r)/ n [U] game played with 15 red balls and 7 of other colours on a long table ● **snooker** v [T] place sb in a difficult position

snoop /snuːp/ v [I] ~ (around/round) find out private things about sb, esp by looking secretly around a place

snooze /snuːz/ v [I] n (infml) (take a) short sleep, esp during the day

snore /snɔː(r)/ v [I] breathe noisily while sleeping ● **snore** n sound of snoring

snorkel /'snɔːkl/ n tube that allows a swimmer to breathe air while under water ● **snorkel** v (-ll- US -l-) [I] swim with a snorkel

snort /snɔːt/ v **1** [I] force air out loudly through the nose, esp to show that you are angry or amused **2** [T] (sl) take drugs by breathing

them in through the nose ● **snort** n act or sound of snorting

snout /snaʊt/ n nose of an animal, esp a pig

snow¹ /snəʊ/ n [U] frozen water falling from the sky in soft, white flakes, or a mass of this on the ground, etc ■ **'snowball** n ball of snow for throwing in play ■ **'snowball** v [I] grow quickly in size, importance, etc ■ **'snowboarding** n [U] sport of moving over snow on a long board called a **snowboard** ■ **'snowdrift** n deep pile of snow that has been blown together by the wind ■ **'snowdrop** n type of small white spring flower ■ **'snowman** n figure of a man made from snow ■ **'snowplough** (US -**plow**) n vehicle or machine for pushing snow off roads, etc ■ **'snowstorm** n heavy fall of snow, esp with a strong wind

snow² /snəʊ/ v [I] (used with it) fall as snow: It ~ed all day. [PV] **be snowed in/up** be unable to leave a place because of heavy snow **be snowed under (with sth)** have more things, esp work, than you feel able to deal with: He is ~ed under with work. ► **snowy** adj (-ier, -iest)

snub /snʌb/ v (-bb-) [T] insult sb by ignoring them when you meet ● **snub** n deliberately rude action or comment ● **snub** adj (of a nose) short, flat and turned up at the end ► **snub-'nosed** adj

snuff /snʌf/ n [U] powdered tobacco that is sniffed into the nose ● **snuff** v [T] ~ (**out**) put out a candle by pinching the flame with your fingers or by covering it with sth [IDM] **snuff it** (sl) die [PV] **snuff sth out** (written) put an end to sth

snug /snʌg/ adj **1** warm and comfortable **2** tight-fitting: a ~ jacket ► **snugly** adv

snuggle /'snʌgl/ v [I] ~ (**up/down**) lie or get close to sb for warmth or affection

so¹ /səʊ/ adv **1** to such a great degree: not so big as I thought **2** very: I'm so glad to see you. **3** used to refer back to sth already mentioned: 'Is he coming?' 'I hope so.' **4** also: You are young and so am I. **5** (spoken) used to agree that sth is true: 'It's Friday today, not Thursday.' 'So it is.' **6** (spoken) used to show sb how to do sth or how sth happened: Stand with your arms out, so. [IDM] **and so on/and so forth** used at the end of a list to show that it continues in the same way **so as to do sth** with the intention of doing sth: He drove fast so as not to be late. **so much for sth** nothing further needs to be said or done about sth **so much so that** to such an extent that ■ **'so-and-so** n (infml) **1** some person or other **2** annoying and unpleasant person: *That ~ so lied to me.* ■ **,so-'called** adj used to show that you do not think the word being used is appropriate: *Her so-called friends refused to help her.*

so² /səʊ/ conj **1** used to show the reason for sth: *He was hurt so I helped him.* **2** used to show the result of sth: *Nothing more was heard from her so people thought she was dead.* **3** ~ **(that) ...** used to show the purpose of sth: *I gave you a map so (that) you wouldn't get lost.* **4** used to introduce the next part of a story: *So she went and told the police.* [IDM] **so what?** (spoken) used when sth doesn't matter?: *'She lied to me.' 'So what?'*

soak /səʊk/ v **1** [T] put sth in liquid for a time so that it becomes completely wet: ~ *the beans overnight* **2** [I] become completely wet by being put in liquid for a time: *I'm going to ~ in a hot bath.* **3** [T] make sb/sth completely wet: *The rain ~ed the spectators.* [PV] **soak sth up** take in or absorb liquid: *Paper ~s up water.* ● **soak** n act of soaking sth/sb ▶ **soaked, soaking** adj completely wet

soap /səʊp/ n **1** [U] substance used with water for washing your body **2** [C] = SOAP OPERA ● **soap** v [T] rub yourself/sb/sth with soap ■ **'soap opera** n [C,U] story about the lives and problems of a group of people which is broadcast several times a week on the radio or TV ▶ **soapy** adj

soar /sɔ:(r)/ v **1** rise very quickly: ~*ing prices* **2** (of birds, etc) fly or go high up in the air

sob /sɒb/ v (**-bb-**) [I] cry noisily, taking sudden sharp breaths [PV] **sob your heart out** cry noisily for a long time ● **sob** n act or sound of sobbing ■ **'sob story** n (disapprov) story that sb tells you just to make you feel sorry for them

sober /'səʊbə(r)/ adj **1** not drunk **2** serious and responsible: *a ~ person* ● **sober** v [I, T] (cause sb to) behave or think in a more serious and sensible way [PV] **sober (sb) up** (cause sb) to become no longer drunk ▶ **soberly** adv

soccer /'sɒkə(r)/ n [U] = FOOTBALL(1)

sociable /'səʊʃəbl/ adj liking company or friendly

social /'səʊʃl/ adj **1** of society and the way it is organized: ~ *reforms* **2** of your position in society: ~ *class* **3** of activities in which people meet each other for pleasure: *a busy ~ life* **4** (of animals, etc) living in groups **5** = SOCIABLE ■ **,social 'science** n [C,U] subjects concerning society within society, eg sociology, economics ■ **,social se'curity** n [U] government

payments to help the unemployed, disabled, etc ■ **'social worker** n person employed to provide help and advice on health, housing, social security, etc ▶ **socially** adv

socialism /'səʊʃəlɪzəm/ n [U] political and economic theory that land, industries, etc should be owned by the state ▶ **socialist** adj, n

socialize (also **-ise**) /'səʊʃəlaɪz/ v [I] mix socially with others

society /sə'saɪəti/ n (pl **-ies**) **1** [U] people in general, living together in communities **2** [C,U] particular community of people **3** [C] organization of people with a common interest: *a drama ~* **4** [U] the group of people in a country who are rich, fashionable and powerful: *a ~ wedding* **5** [U] (fml) state of being with other people

sociology /,səʊsi'ɒlədʒi/ n [U] study of the nature and growth of society and social behaviour ▶ **sociologist** n expert in sociology ▶ **sociological** /-'lɒdʒɪkl/ adj

sock /sɒk/ n **1** piece of clothing worn over the foot and ankle, esp inside a shoe **2** (infml) hard blow, esp with the fist ● **sock** v [T] (infml) hit sb hard

socket /'sɒkɪt/ n **1** device in a wall that you put a plug into in order to connect electrical equipment to the power supply **2** curved hollow space in which sth fits or turns

sod /sɒd/ (△, sl) **1** used to refer to, a person you are annoyed with **2** thing that causes problems

soda /'səʊdə/ n **1** [U] = SODA WATER **2** (US) [U,C] sweet fizzy drink made with soda water flavoured with fruit **3** [U] chemical substance used for making soap, glass, etc ■ **'soda water** n [U,C] (glass of) water containing a gas to make it bubble

sodden /'sɒdn/ adj very wet

sodium /'səʊdiəm/ n [U] (symb **Na**) soft silver-white metal found naturally only in compounds, eg salt

sofa /'səʊfə/ n long comfortable seat with raised ends and back for two or more people

soft /sɒft/ adj **1** not hard or stiff: *a ~ pillow* **2** (of surfaces) smooth and pleasant to touch: ~ *skin* **3** (of light or colours) not too bright or strong **4** (of sounds) not too loud **5** (of outlines) not having sharp angles or hard edges **6** ~**(on)** (too) kind and gentle: *Don't be too ~ on the class.* **7** (disapprov) too easy: *a ~ job* **8** (infml, disapprov) weak and lacking in courage **9** (infml, disapprov) stupid or crazy [IDM] **have a soft spot for sb/sth** (infml) like sb/sth ■ **,soft-'boiled** adj (of eggs) boiled for a short time so that the yellow part (**yolk**) stays soft

■ ,soft 'drink n cold drink that does not contain alcohol ■ ,soft 'drug n illegal drug (eg cannabis) but likely to cause addiction ■ ,soft-'hearted adj kind, sympathetic and emotional ▶ **softly** adv ▶ **softness** n [U] ■ ,soft-'pedal v (-ll-, US -l-) [I, T] (infml) treat sth as less important than it really is ■ ,soft-'soap v [T] (infml) persuade sb to do sth by saying nice things to them ■ 'software n [U] programs, etc used to operate a computer

soften /'sɒfn/ v [I, T] (cause sth) to become softer **2** [T] make sth easier to accept: try to ~ the shock [PV] **soften sb up** (infml) try to persuade sb to do sth for you by being very nice first

soggy /'sɒgi/ adj (-ier, -iest) very wet or heavy with water

soil /sɔɪl/ n [C, U] upper layer of earth in which plants grow ● **soil** v [I, T] (fml) (cause sth) to become dirty

sojourn /'sɒdʒən/ n (lit) temporary stay in a place

solace /'sɒləs/ n [C, U] (fml) (thing that gives) comfort or relief from sadness, etc

solar /'səʊlə(r)/ adj of the sun: ~ power ■ **the solar system** n [sing] the sun and its planets

sold pt, pp of SELL

solder /'səʊldə(r)/ n [U] type of metal which melts easily, used for joining together harder metals, etc ● **solder** v [T] join pieces of metal with solder ■ 'soldering iron n tool that is heated and used for joining metals together

soldier /'səʊldʒə(r)/ n member of an army ● **soldier** v [PV] **soldier on** continue with what you are doing in spite of difficulties

sole¹ /səʊl/ adj **1** only; single: the ~ owner **2** not shared: have ~ responsibility ▶ **solely** adv not; not involving sb/sth else

sole² /səʊl/ n **1** [C] bottom surface of the foot or a shoe **2** [U,C] (pl sole) flat sea fish used for food ● **sole** v [T] repair a shoe by replacing the sole

solemn /'sɒləm/ adj **1** not happy or smiling **2** done in a serious, formal way: a ~ promise ▶ **solemnly** adv ▶ **solemnity** /sə'lemnəti/ n (pl -ies) (fml) **1** [U] quality of being solemn **2** (solemnities) [pl] (fml) formal things people do at a serious event

solicit /sə'lɪsɪt/ v **1** [I, T] ~(for) (fml) ask for sth, eg support, money, etc **2** [I, T] (of a prostitute) offer sex to sb for money

solicitor /sə'lɪsɪtə(r)/ n (GB) lawyer who prepares legal documents, advises clients, etc

solid /'sɒlɪd/ adj **1** not in the form of a liquid or gas: Water becomes ~ when it freezes. **2** having no holes or spaces inside **3** strong and well made **4** that you can rely on: ~ arguments **5** of the same substance throughout: ~ gold **6** (infml) without a pause; continuous: sleep ten hours ~ **7** (geom) (of a shape) having length, width and height; not flat **8** in complete agreement: The workers were ~ on this issue. ● **solid** n **1** substance or object that is solid, not a liquid or gas **2** (geom) shape with length, width and height ▶ **solidly** adv ▶ **solidity** /sə'lɪdəti/ n [U]

solidarity /,sɒlɪ'dærəti/ n [U] ~ (with) support by one person or group for another because they share feelings, opinions, aims, etc

solidify /sə'lɪdɪfaɪ/ v (pt, pp -ied) [I, T] (cause sth) to become solid or firm

solitaire /,sɒlɪ'teə(r)/ n **1** [U] (US = PATIENCE(3)) **2** [C] (piece of jewellery with a) single jewel: a ~ ring

solitary /'sɒlətri/ adj **1** done alone, without other people **2** remote **3** only one; single: a ~ visitor

solitude /'sɒlɪtjuːd/ n [U] state of being alone

solo /'səʊləʊ/ n (pl ~s) piece of music, dance, etc (to be) performed by one person: a clarinet ~ ● **solo** adj, adv **1** done by one person alone, without any help: a ~ flight **2** done alone, or performed as a musical solo: music for ~ flute ▶ **soloist** n person who performs alone

solstice /'sɒlstɪs/ n time at which the sun is furthest north or south of the equator

soluble /'sɒljəbl/ adj **1** that can be dissolved in liquid **2** (fml) (of a problem) that can be solved ▶ **solubility** /-'bɪləti/ n [U]

solution /sə'luːʃn/ n **1** [C] ~(to) way of dealing with a problem or difficult situation **2** [C] ~(to) answer to a puzzle **3** [C,U] liquid in which sth is dissolved **4** [U] process of dissolving a solid or gas in a liquid

solve /sɒlv/ v [T] find the answer to a problem, etc ▶ **solvable** adj

solvent /'sɒlvənt/ adj having enough money to pay your debts ● **solvent** n [U,C] liquid able to dissolve another substance ▶ **solvency** /-ənsi/ n [U] (written) state of not being in debt

sombre (US **somber**) /'sɒmbə(r)/ adj **1** dark coloured or dull: ~ colours **2** serious and sad: a ~ mood ▶ **sombrely** adv ▶ **sombreness** n [U]

some¹ /sʌm; weak form səm/ det **1** an unspecified number or amount of: Have ~ milk. ◇ ~ children **2** unknown or not named: She's living at ~ place in Surrey. **3** approximately: ~ twenty years ago **4** large amount of: for ~ time

some² /sʌm/ pron **1** an unspecified number or amount: S~ of these *books are quite useful.* **2** part of an amount or number: *S~ of the guests didn't stay for long, but most did.*

somebody /'sʌmbədi/ (also **someone** /'sʌmwʌn/) *pron* **1** an unknown or unnamed person: *There's ~ at the door.* **2** an important person: *She really thinks she's ~.*

somehow /'sʌmhaʊ/ *adv* **1** in some way; by some means: *We'll get there ~.* **2** for some reason: *S~ I just don't think she'll come back.*

someone = SOMEBODY

somersault /'sʌməsɔːlt/ *n* movement in which sb turns over completely, with their feet over their head ● **somersault** *v* [I] turn over completely in the air

something /'sʌmθɪŋ/ *pron* **1** an unknown or unnamed thing: *I want ~ to eat.* ◇ *The car hit a tree or ~.* **2** (*infml*) a significant thing: *I'm sure she knows ~ about this.* **3** (*infml*) used to show that a description or an amount, etc is not exact: *a new comedy aimed at thirty~s* (= people between 30 and 40 years old) ◇ *It looks ~ like a melon.*

sometime /'sʌmtaɪm/ *adv* at an unspecified point in time: *~ in May*

sometimes /'sʌmtaɪmz/ *adv* occasionally: *I ~ receive letters from him.*

somewhat /'sʌmwɒt/ *adv* quite; rather: *I was ~ surprised.*

somewhere /'sʌmweə(r)/ (*US* **someplace**) *adv* in, at or to an unknown or unnamed place: *It's ~ near here.* [IDM] **get somewhere** ⇒ GET

son /sʌn/ *n* **1** male child of a parent **2** used as a form of address by an older man to a younger man or boy: *What's your name, ~?* ■ **'son-in-law** *n* (*pl* **'sons-in-law**) husband of your daughter

sonata /sə'nɑːtə/ *n* music for one or two instruments, usu with three or four parts

song /sɒŋ/ *n* **1** [C] short piece of music with words that you sing **2** [U] songs in general; music for singing [IDM] **for a song** (*infml*) at a very low price ■ **a song and dance (about sth)** unnecessary fuss

sonic /'sɒnɪk/ *adj* (*tech*) relating to sound or the speed of sound

sonnet /'sɒnɪt/ *n* poem containing 14 lines with 10 syllables each

soon /suːn/ *adv* **1** a short time from now; a short time after sth else has happened: *We will ~ be home.* **2** early; quickly: *How ~ can you be ready?* ◇ *Please send it as ~ as possible.* [IDM] **no sooner ... than ...** (*written*) used to say that sth happens immediately after sth else: *No ~er had she arrived than she had to leave again.* **the sooner the better** as quickly as pos-

sible I, etc **would sooner do sth (than sth else)** prefer to do sth (than do sth else): *I'd sooner die than marry you.*

soot /sʊt/ *n* [U] black powder produced when wood, coal, etc is burnt ▶ **sooty** *adj* (**-ier, -iest**) covered with or black with soot

soothe /suːð/ *v* [T] **1** make sb who is upset, etc feel calmer **2** make a painful part of your body feel more comfortable ▶ **soothing** *adj*

sop /sɒp/ *n* something offered to please sb who is angry, disappointed, etc

sophisticated /sə'fɪstɪkeɪtɪd/ *adj* **1** having or showing experience of the world and culture **2** (of a machine, system, etc) complicated and refined: *~ weapons* ▶ **sophistication** /sə‚fɪstɪ'keɪʃn/ *n* [U]

soppy /'sɒpi/ *adj* (**-ier, -iest**) (*infml*) silly and sentimental

soprano /sə'prɑːnəʊ/ *n* (*pl* **~s**) *adj* (music for, or singer with) the highest singing voice of women

sorcerer /'sɔːsərə(r)/ (*fem* **sorceress** /-əs/) *n* (in stories) person with magic powers, helped by evil spirits ▶ **sorcery** *n* [U] magic that uses evil spirits

sordid /'sɔːdɪd/ *adj* **1** immoral or dishonest **2** very dirty and unpleasant

sore /sɔː(r)/ *adj* **1** (of a part of the body) painful, and often red, esp because of infection **2** (*esp US, infml*) upset and angry: *feel ~* [IDM] **a sore point** subject that makes you feel angry or upset when it is mentioned **stand/stick out like a sore thumb** be very noticeable in an unpleasant way ● **sore** *n* painful infected area on the skin ▶ **sorely** *adv* greatly: *~ly needed* ▶ **soreness** *n* [U]

sorrow /'sɒrəʊ/ *n* [C,U] feeling of great sadness because sth very bad has happened ● **sorrow** *v* [I] (*lit*) ~ **(at/over)** feel or express great sadness ▶ **sorrowful** *adj*

sorry /'sɒri/ *adj* (**-ier, -iest**) **1** feeling sad and sympathetic: *I'm ~ to hear that your father's ill.* **2** feeling sad and ashamed about sth that has been done: *She was ~ for her past crimes.* **3** feeling disappointment and regret: *I was genuinely ~ to leave.* **4** poor and causing pity: *in a ~ state* [IDM] **be/feel sorry for sb** feel pity or sympathy for sb **I'm sorry** (*spoken*) **1** used when you are apologizing for sth **2** used for disagreeing with sb **3** used for introducing bad news: *I'm ~ to tell you that you've failed.* ● **sorry** *exclam* **1** used for apologizing for sth: *S~ I'm late.* **2** (*GB*) used for asking sb to repeat sth that you have not heard

sort¹ /sɔːt/ *n* group of people or things that are alike in some way

[IDM] **out of sorts** feeling ill or upset

sort of (infml) to some extent: ~ *of pleased that it happened*

sort² /sɔːt/ v [T] ~ (**out**) arrange things in groups or in a particular order: ~ (**out**) *the good and bad apples* [PV] **sort sth out** (infml) **1** put sth in good order **2** deal with a problem

SOS /ˌes əʊ 'es/ n [sing] urgent message for help sent by radio, etc

so-so /ˌsəʊ 'səʊ/ adj, adv (infml) average; neither very well nor very badly: '*How are you feeling?*' '*So-so.*'

soufflé /'suːfleɪ/ n [C,U] dish of eggs, milk, cheese, etc beaten together and baked until it rises

soul /səʊl/ n **1** [C] spiritual part of a person, believed to exist after death **2** [C,U] emotional and intellectual energy: *put* ~ *into your work* **3** [sing] perfect example of a good quality: *She's the* ~ *of discretion.* **4** [C] person: *not a* ~ *to be seen* **5** [U] = soul music ■ 'soul-destroying adj (of work) very dull and boring ▶ soulful adj showing deep feeling ▶ soulfully adv ▶ soulless adv (of a person) feeling no emotion ■ 'soul music n [U] type of music that expresses strong emotions, made popular by African American musicians ■ 'soul-searching n [U] careful examination of your thoughts and feelings

sound¹ /saʊnd/ adj **1** sensible; that can be relied on: *a man of* ~ *judgement* **2** good and thorough: *She has a* ~ *grasp of the issues.* **3** in good condition; not hurt or damaged: *I arrived home safe and* ~. **4** deep: *be a* ~ *sleeper* ● **sound** adv deeply: ~ *asleep* ▶ **soundly** adv deeply or well ▶ **soundness** n [U]

sound² /saʊnd/ n [C,U] something you can hear: *the* ~ *of drums* [sing] idea or impression that you get from sb/sth from what sb says or what you read: *I don't like the* ~ *of him.* ■ 'sound barrier n point at which an aircraft's speed equals that of sound ■ 'sound effect n [usu pl] sound other than speech or music used in a film, play, etc ■ 'sound-proof adj made so that sound cannot pass through it or into it ■ soundproof v [T] make a room, etc soundproof ■ 'soundtrack n music, etc used in a film

sound³ /saʊnd/ v [I] give a certain impression: *His story* ~*s genuine.* **2** [I,T] (cause sth to) produce a sound: ~ *the alarm* **4** [T] (tech) pronounce sth: *Don't* ~ *the 'b' in 'dumb'.* **5** [I,T] (tech) measure the depth of the sea or a lake with a weighted line [PV] **sound off (about sth)** (infml) express your opinions loudly or aggressively **sound sb**

out (about/on sth) try to find out what sb thinks about sth

soup /suːp/ n [U] liquid food made by cooking meat, vegetables, etc together in water

sour /'saʊə(r)/ adj **1** having a sharp bitter taste **2** not fresh: ~ *milk* **3** not cheerful; bad-tempered [IDM] **go/turn sour** stop being pleasant or satisfactory ● **sour** v [T] (cause sth to) become sour ▶ **sourly** adv ▶ **sourness** n [U]

source /sɔːs/ n place, person or thing that you get sth from or where sth starts: *renewable energy* ~*s* ◇ *the* ~ *of a river* ● **source** n [T] (business) ~ (**from**) get sth from a particular source

south /saʊθ/ n [U,sing] (abbr S) **1** (**the south**) point of the compass, to the right of a person facing the sunrise **2** (**the south, the South**) southern part of a country, region or the world ● **south** adj (abbr S) **1** in or towards the south **2** (of winds) from the south ● **south** adv towards the south ■ 'south-'east n [sing], adj, adv (abbr SE) (direction or region) halfway between south and east ▶ ,south-'eastern adj ▶ southerly /'sʌðəli/ adj, adv **1** in or towards the south **2** (of winds) from the south ▶ southern (also Southern) /'sʌðən/ adj of or in the south part of the world or a region ▶ southerner n person born or living in the southern part of a country ▶ southward /'saʊθwəd/ adj towards the south ▶ southward(s) adv ■ ,south-'west n [sing], adj, adv (abbr SW) (direction or region) halfway between south and west ▶ ,south-'western adj

souvenir /ˌsuːvə'nɪə(r)/ n thing kept as a reminder of a person, a place or an event

sovereign /'sɒvrɪn/ n (fml) king or queen ● **sovereign** adj **1** (of a country or state) free to govern itself; independent **2** having complete power ▶ **sovereignty** /'sɒvrənti/ n [U] complete power to govern a country

sow¹ /saʊ/ n adult female pig

sow² /səʊ/ v (pt ~ed; pp ~n /səʊn/ or ~ed) **1** [I,T] plant or spread seeds in or on the ground **2** [T] introduce or spread feelings, etc: ~ *discontent*

soya bean /'sɔɪə biːn/ n type of bean grown as food and for its oil

spa /spaː/ n a spring of mineral water

space /speɪs/ n **1** [U] amount of an area or a place that is empty and available for use: *There's not enough* ~ *here.* **2** [C] area or place that is empty: *a parking* ~ **3** [C,U] large area of land that has no buildings on it **4** (also **outer space**) [U] the universe outside the earth's atmosphere

5 [C, usu sing] period of time: *within the ~ of a day* **6** [U] whole area in which all things exist and move **[IDM] look/ stare/gaze into space** look straight ahead of you without looking at a particular thing, usu because you are thinking about sth ● **space** v [T] ~ (**out**) arrange things so that they have regular spaces between them ■ '**space-age** adj (infml) very modern ■ '**spacecraft** n (pl **spaceship**) n vehicle for travelling in space ■ '**space shuttle** n spacecraft designed to be used, eg for travelling between the earth and a space station ■ '**space station** n large structure that is sent into space and remains there as a base for people working in space

spacial adj = SPATIAL

spacious /'speɪʃəs/ adj having a lot of space ▶ **spaciousness** n [U]

spade /speɪd/ n **1** long-handled tool with a flat blade and sharp edge for digging **2** playing card with black figures shaped like leaves ■ '**spadework** n [U] hard work done as preparation for sth else

spaghetti /spə'geti/ n [U] long thin pieces of pasta that look like string

spam /spæm/ n [U] (infml) advertising material sent by email to people who have not asked for it ▶ **spamming** n [U] practice of sending mail, esp advertisements, through the Internet to a large number of people

span /spæn/ n **1** time that sth lasts or is able to continue: *the ~ of a person's life* **2** range or variety of sth **3** distance or part between the supports of a bridge or an arch ● **span** v (**-nn-**) [T] **1** last all through a period of time; cover sth: *a life ~ning fifty years* **2** stretch right across sth

spaniel /'spænjəl/ n breed of dog with long ears that hang down

spank /spæŋk/ v [T] hit sb, esp a child, several times on their bottom as a punishment ▶ **spank** n

spanner /'spænə(r)/ (US **wrench**) n tool for holding and turning nuts onto bolts, etc

spar /spɑː(r)/ v (**-rr-**) [I] **1** ~(**with**) practise boxing **2** argue, usu in a friendly way

spare¹ /speə(r)/ adj **1** additional to what is needed: *two ~ chairs* **2** kept in case you need to replace the one you usually use; extra: *a ~ key/tyre* **3** (of time) free from work **4** (written) (of people) thin ● **spare** (also ,**spare** '**part**) n [usu pl] new part for a car, machine, etc used to replace an old or broken part ■ ,**spare** '**tyre** (US =**tire**) n extra wheel for a

spare² /speə(r)/ v [T] **1** be able to give money, time, etc for a purpose: *Can you ~ me a few minutes?* ◊ *You should*

~ *a thought for* (= think about) *those who clean up after you.* **2** ~ *sb/ yourself* (**from**) save sb/yourself from having to go through an unpleasant experience **3** (lit) allow sb/sth to escape harm, damage or death: *a prisoner's life* **4** do sth well without limiting the time, money or effort involved. *No expense was ~d* (= no money at all was spent). ▶ **sparing** adj careful to give or use only a little of sth ▶ **sparingly** adv

spark /spɑːk/ n [C] **1** tiny flash of light produced by sth burning or an electric current being broken **2** [usu sing] small amount of a quality or feeling: *not a ~ of decency in him* ● **spark** v [T] ~(**off**) cause sth to start or develop, esp suddenly **2** [I] produce sparks ■ '**spark plug** (also '**sparking plug**) n device for lighting the fuel in an engine

sparkle /'spɑːkl/ v [I] shine brightly with flashes of light: *(fig) Her conversation ~d.* ● **sparkle** n [C, U] act of sparkling: *(fig) a performance lacking in ~* ▶ **sparkling** /'spɑːklɪŋ/ adj

sparrow /'spærəʊ/ n common small brown and grey bird

sparse /spɑːs/ adj not crowded or thick: *a ~ population* ▶ **sparsely** adv ▶ **sparseness** n [U]

spasm /'spæzəm/ n **1** [C, U] sudden uncontrollable tightening of a muscle **2** [C] sudden strong feeling or reaction ▶ **spasmodic** /-'mɒdɪk/ adj **1** done or happening at irregular intervals **2** (tech) caused or affected by spasms ▶ **spasmodically** adv

spat pt, pp of SPIT²

spate /speɪt/ n [sing] large number of usu unpleasant things coming all at once: *a ~ of robberies*

spatial /'speɪʃl/ adj (fml or tech) of or concerning space ▶ **spatially** adv

spatter /'spætə(r)/ v **1** [T, I] cover sb/sth with drops of liquid, dirt, etc **2** [I] fall on a surface in drops ● **spatter** n [sing] shower of drops of liquid

spatula /'spætjələ/ n tool with a flat flexible blade used for mixing and spreading things

spawn /spɔːn/ n [U] eggs of fish and frogs ● **spawn** v **1** [I, T] (of fish or frogs) lay eggs **2** [T] cause sth to develop or be produced

speak /spiːk/ v (pt **spoke** /spəʊk/; pp **spoken** /'spəʊkən/) **1** [I] talk to sb about sth; use your voice to say sth: *I was ~ing to her about my plans.* ◊ *Please ~ more slowly.* **2** [I] be able to use a language: ~ *French* **3** [I] make a speech to an audience **4** [T] say or state sth: ~ *the truth* **[IDM] be on speaking terms (with sb)** be willing to be friendly towards sb, esp after an argument **speak your mind** express your opinion openly

[PV] **speak for sb** state the views or wishes of a person or group **speak out (against sth)** state your opinions publicly, in opposition to sth **speak up 1** speak more loudly **2** say what you think, esp to support or defend sb/sth ▶ **speaker** n **1** person who makes a speech **2** person who speaks a particular language: *a French -er* **3** part of a radio or piece of musical or computing equipment that the sound comes out of

spear /spɪə(r)/ n weapon with a metal point on a long shaft
● **spear** v [T] push or throw a spear through sth/sb ■ **'spearhead** n person or group that begins an activity or leads an attack ■ **spearhead** v [T] begin an activity or lead an attack

spearmint /'spɪəmɪnt/ n [U] kind of mint used esp in making sweets

special /'speʃl/ adj **1** of a particular kind; not common **2** adj of or for a certain person or purpose **3** exceptional in amount, degree, etc: *~ treatment* ● **special** n **1** thing that is not usually available but is provided on one occasion: *a television ~ about the elections* **2** (US, infml) reduced price in a shop ▶ **specialist** n person who is an expert in a particular country, profession, etc ▶ **specially** adv particularly

speciality /ˌspeʃi'æləti/ (esp US **specialty**) n (pl -ies) **1** type of food or product that a restaurant or place is famous for **2** sb's special interest, skill, subject, etc

specialize (also -ise) /'speʃəlaɪz/ v [I] **~(in)** become an expert in a particular area of work, study or business: *~ in modern history* ▶ **specialization** (also -isation) /ˌspeʃəlaɪ'zeɪʃn/ n [U]

species /'spiːʃiːz/ n (pl **species**) group into which animals, plants, etc that are able to breed with each other are divided

specific /spə'sɪfɪk/ adj **1** detailed and precise: *~ instructions* **2** relating to one particular thing, etc: *for a ~ purpose* ▶ **specifically** /-kli/ adv

specification /ˌspesɪfɪ'keɪʃn/ n [C, U] detailed description of how sth is, or should be, designed or made

specify /'spesɪfaɪ/ v (pt, pp -ied) [T] state details, materials, etc clearly and precisely

specimen /'spesɪmən/ n **1** small amount of sth that shows what the rest is like: *a ~ of her work* **2** small quantity of blood, etc taken from sb to be tested for disease

speck /spek/ n small spot; tiny piece of dirt, etc

speckle /'spekl/ n [usu sing] small spot, espe one of many, on feathers, etc ▶ **speckled** adj

spectacle /'spektəkl/ n **1** (spec-

tacles) [pl] (fml) = GLASSES **2** [C, U] impressive and exciting performance or event **3** [C] impressive sight or view

spectacular /spek'tækjələ(r)/ adj very impressive ▶ **spectacularly** adv

spectator /spek'teɪtə(r)/ n person watching a show or sports event

spectrum /'spektrəm/ n [usu sing] (pl **-tra** /-trə/) **1** image of a band of colours as seen in a rainbow **2** (written) wide range of related qualities, ideas, etc: *a ~ of opinions*

speculate /'spekjuleɪt/ v [I, T] **1** form opinions without having complete knowledge **2** [I] buy and sell goods, shares, etc, hoping to make a profit but risking loss ▶ **speculation** /-'leɪʃn/ n [C, U] ▶ **speculative** adj

sped pt, pp of SPEED

speech /spiːtʃ/ n **1** [C] formal talk given to an audience: *make a ~* **2** [U] power, act or way of speaking ▶ **speechless** adj unable to speak, eg because of deep feeling

speed /spiːd/ n [C, U] rate at which sb/sth moves: *a ~ of 10 kilometres an hour* ◇ *travelling at full ~* **2** [U] quickness of movement: *move with great ~* ● **speed** v (pt, pp **sped** /sped/ or **~ed**) **1** [I] (written) go quickly **2** [I] drive faster than the speed allowed by law [PV] **speed (sth) up** (cause sth to) go faster: *~ up production* **2** ▶ **speedometer** /spiː'dɒmɪtə(r)/ n instrument showing the speed of a vehicle, etc ■ **'speedway** n [C, U] (track used for) racing motorbikes ▶ **speedy** adj (**-ier**, **-iest**) quick

spell¹ /spel/ n **1** short period of time during which sth lasts: *a ~ of warm weather* **2** period spent doing a certain activity: *a ~ at the wheel* (= driving) **3** (condition produced by) words supposed to have magic power: (fig) *under the ~ of a fascinating man* ■ **'spellbound** adj with the attention held (as if) by a magic spell

spell² /spel/ v (pt, pp **spelt** /spelt/ or **~ed**) **1** [I, T] say or write the letters of a word in the correct order **2** [T] (of letters) form words when in a particular order: *C-A-T ~s cat* **3** [T] mean sth, usu sth bad, as a result: *The crop failure spelt disaster for farmers.* [PV] **spell sth out** make sth easy to understand ■ **'spell check** (also **'spellchecker**) n computer program that checks your writing to see if your spelling is correct ▶ **spell check** v [T] ▶ **spelling** n **1** [U] act of forming words correctly from individual letters; ability to do this **2** [C] way in which a word is spelt

spelunking /spɪ'lʌŋkɪŋ/ n [U] (US) = CAVING

spend /spend/ v (pt, pp **spent** /spent/) **1** [I, T] **~(on)** pay out money for goods, services, etc **2** [T] use time for a purpose; pass time: *a week in hospital* **3** [T] use energy, effort, etc until it has all been used: *your energy cleaning the house* ■ '**spend-thrift** *n* (*disapprov*) person who wastes money ► **spent** *adj* used up

sperm /spɜːm/ *n* [C] male sex cell which fertilizes a female egg

spew /spjuː/ *v* [I, T] (cause sth to) come out in a stream

sphere /sfɪə(r)/ *n* **1** completely round solid shape **2** range of interests, activities, influence, etc ► **spherical** /sferɪkl/ *adj* round

spice /spaɪs/ *n* **1** [C, U] one of various types of powder or seed that come from plants and are used in cooking **2** [U] extra interest or excitement: *add ~ to a story* ● **spice** *v* [T] add spice to sth ► **spicy** (**-ier, -iest**) **1** containing spice **2** exciting and slightly shocking

spick /spɪk/ *adj* [IDM] **spick and span** clean and tidy

spider /spaɪdə(r)/ *n* small creature with eight legs, esp one that spins a web to trap insects ► **spidery** *adj* long and thin, like the legs of a spider: *~y handwriting*

spied *pt, pp* of SPY

spike /spaɪk/ *n* [C] **1** thin object with a sharp point **2** [usu pl] metal spike attached to the sole of a running shoe, etc **3** long pointed group of flowers that grow together on a single stem ● **spike** *v* [T] **1** push a sharp piece of metal, wood, etc into sb/sth **2** add alcohol, poison or a drug to sb's drink or food without knowing ► **spiky** *adj* (**-ier, -iest**)

spill /spɪl/ *v* (*pt, pp* **spilt** /spɪlt/ *or* **~ed**) [I, T] (cause liquid or powder to) run over the side of the container [IDM] **spill the beans** (*infml*) reveal a secret

spin /spɪn/ *v* (**-nn-**, *pt, pp* **spun** /spʌn/) **1** [I, T] (cause sth to) turn round and round quickly **2** [I, T] make thread from wool, cotton, etc by twisting it **3** [T] (of a spider or silkworm) produce thread from its body to make a web or cocoon: *Spiders ~ webs.* **4** [T] (*infml*) compose a story [PV] **spin sth out** make sth last as long as possible ● **spin** *n* **1** [C, U] very fast turning movement **2** [sing, U] (*infml*) way of presenting information, esp in a way that makes you or your ideas seem good **3** [C] short ride in a car for pleasure [IDM] **in a (flat) spin** very confused, worried or excited ■ '**spin doctor** *n* (*infml*) person whose job is to present information to the public about a politician, etc in the most positive way possible ■ '**spin 'dryer** (*also* **~ drier**) *n* (*GB*) machine that spins

clothes to dry them ■ '**spin-off** *n* product, etc resulting indirectly from another activity

spinach /spɪnɪdʒ/ *n* [U] plant with large green leaves, cooked and eaten as a vegetable

spinal /spaɪnl/ *adj* (*anat*) of the spine(1)

spindle /spɪndl/ *n* **1** thin rod for winding thread by hand in spinning **2** bar on which part of a machine turns ► **spindly** /spɪndli/ *adj* (**-ier, -iest**) long and thin

spine /spaɪn/ *n* **1** row of small bones that are connected together down the middle of the back **2** sharp point on some animals and plants, eg the cactus **3** part of the cover of a book where the pages are joined together ■ '**spine-chilling** *adj* very frightening ► **spineless** *adj* (*disapprov*) cowardly ► **spiny** *adj* (**-ier, -iest**) (of animals or plants) having sharp points

spinster /spɪnstə(r)/ *n* (*old-fash*, *often disapprov*) unmarried woman

spiral /spaɪrəl/ *n* **1** curve winding round a central point: *A snail's shell is a ~.* **2** continuous harmful increase or decrease in sth ● **spiral** *adj* moving in a continuous curve winding round a central point: *a ~ staircase* ● **spiral** *v* (**-ll-**, *US* **-l-**) **1** move in a spiral **2** increase rapidly

spire /spaɪə(r)/ *n* pointed tower, esp of a church

spirit /spɪrɪt/ *n* **1** [U, C] person's thoughts and feelings or soul **2** (*spirits*) [pl] state of mind: *in high ~s* (= happy) **3** [C] person: *What a generous ~!* **4** [U] courage or energy: *act with ~* **5** [sing] mental attitude; state of mind: *It depends on the ~ in which it was done.* **6** [U] real meaning or purpose of sth **7** [C] soul without a body; ghost **8** [C, usu sing] strong alcoholic drink, eg whisky [IDM] **in spirit** in your thoughts ● **spirit** *v* [T] take sth/sb away quickly or mysteriously ► **spirited** *adj* lively, brave, etc ► **high-low- ed**

spiritual /spɪrɪtʃuəl/ *adj* **1** connected with the human spirit rather than the body **2** religious ● **spiritual** *n* religious song as originally sung by black slaves in the US ► **spiritually** *adv*

spit[1] /spɪt/ *n* **1** [U] saliva **2** [C] narrow point of land jutting out into the sea, etc **3** [C] metal spike which holds meat, etc for roasting

spit[2] /spɪt/ *v* (**-tt-**, *pt, pp* **spat** /spæt/) **1** [T] force liquid, food, etc from the mouth **2** [I] force saliva out of your mouth, often as a sign of lack of respect **3** [T] say sth angrily: *He was ~ting abuse at the judge.* **4** [I] (used with *it*) rain lightly [IDM] **be the spitting image of sb** → IMAGE

spite /spaɪt/ *n* [U] feeling of wanting to hurt or upset sb: *do sth out of* – [IDM] **in spite of sth** without being prevented by the conditions mentioned: *They went out in* ~ *of the rain.* ● **spite** *v* [T] deliberately annoy or upset sb ► **spiteful** *adj* unkind

splash /splæʃ/ *v* **1** [I] (of liquid) fall noisily onto a surface **2** [T] make sb/sth wet by throwing liquid: ~ *water on the floor* **3** [I] move through water making drops fly everywhere: *People were ~ing around in the pool.* [PV] **splash sth across/over sth** put a photograph, news story, etc in a place where it will be easily noticed **splash out (on sth)** (*infml*) spend a lot of money on sth ● **splash** *n* sound or act of, or mark made by, splashing

spleen /spliːn/ *n* organ that controls the quality of the blood in the body

splendid /ˈsplendɪd/ *adj* **1** very impressive: *a* ~ *view* **2** (*old-fash*) excellent ► **splendidly** *adv*

splendour (*US* **-dor**) /ˈsplendə(r)/ *n* [U] grand and impressive beauty

splice /splaɪs/ *v* [T] join two pieces of a rope, film, tape, etc together

splint /splɪnt/ *n* piece of wood or metal tied to a broken arm or leg to keep it still and in position

splinter /ˈsplɪntə(r)/ *n* sharp piece of wood, glass, etc broken from a larger piece ● **splinter** *v* [I, T] (cause sth to) break into splinters ■ **splinter group** *n* (esp in politics) group that has separated from a larger one

split /splɪt/ *v* (-tt-, *pt, pp* **split**) **1** [I, T] (cause a group of people to) divide into separate or opposing parts: *Arguments* ~ *the group.* **2** [I] divide sth into parts and share it with others: ~ *the profits* **3** [I, T] (cause sth to) tear along a straight line: *The box* ~ *(open).* **4** [T] cut sb's skin and make it bleed **5** [I] ~ **(from/with sb)** leave sb and stop having a relationship with them: *He* ~ *with his wife in June.* [IDM] **split hairs** pay too much attention in an argument to small differences **split your sides (laughing/with laughter)** laugh very much [PV] **split up (with sb)** stop having a relationship with sb ● **split** *n* **1** [C] separation or division **2** [C] crack or tear made by splitting **3** (**the splits**) [pl] act of sitting with the legs stretched in opposite directions: *a gymnast doing the* ~*s* ■ **split 'second** *n* very short moment

splutter /ˈsplʌtə(r)/ *v* **1** [I, T] speak quickly and with difficulty, because you are angry or embarrassed **2** [I] make a series of short explosive sounds: *The fire* ~*ed.* ● **splutter** *n* short explosive sound

spoil /spɔɪl/ *v* (*pt, pp* ~**t** or ~**ed**) **1** [T] ruin the value or pleasure of sth: *Rain* ~*ed our holiday.* **2** [T] harm the character of a child by lack of discipline **3** [T] make sb/yourself happy by doing sth special **4** [I] (of food, etc) become bad ● **the spoils** *n* [pl] (*fml*) stolen goods, profit, etc ■ **spoilsport** *n* person who ruins others' enjoyment

spoke[1] /spəʊk/ *n* rod connecting the centre of a wheel to the edge

spoke[2] *pt of* SPEAK

spoken *pp of* SPEAK

spokesman /ˈspəʊksmən/ (*pl* **-men**) (*also* **spokesperson**) (*pl* **-people**) (*fem* **spokeswoman**) (*pl* **-women**) *n* person speaking as the representative of a group, etc

sponge /spʌndʒ/ *n* **1** [C, U] (piece of a) soft light substance that is full of holes and can hold water easily **2** [C] simple sea animal with a body full of holes from which natural sponge is obtained **3** [C, U] (*GB*) = SPONGE CAKE ● **sponge** *v* **1** [T] wipe sb/yourself/sth with a sponge **2** [T] remove sth using a wet cloth or sponge **3** [I] (*infml, disapprov*) get money, food, etc from people without offering anything in return: ~ *money off/from your friends* ■ **sponge cake** *n* [C, U] (*GB*) soft light cake ► **spongy** *adj* (**-ier, -iest**)

sponsor /ˈspɒnsə(r)/ *n* **1** person, company, etc that pays for an event **2** person or company that supports sb by paying for their training or education ● **sponsor** *v* [T] **1** pay for an event, a programme, etc as a way of advertising **2** pay sb money if they do sth for charity ► **sponsorship** *n* [U]

spontaneous /spɒnˈteɪniəs/ *adj* done, happening, etc naturally and not planned: *a* ~ *offer of help* ► **spontaneity** /ˌspɒntəˈneɪəti/ *n* [U] ► **spontaneously** *adv*

spoof /spuːf/ *n* (*infml*) humorous copy of a film, TV programme, etc

spooky /ˈspuːki/ *adj* (**-ier, -iest**) (*infml*) frightening

spool /spuːl/ *n* reel for thread, film, tape, etc

spoon /spuːn/ *n* utensil with a shallow bowl on a handle, used for putting food, eg soup, into the mouth ● **spoon** *v* [T] lift and move food with a spoon ■ **spoon-feed** *v* [T] (*disapprov*) teach people sth in a way that does not make them think for themselves

sporadic /spəˈrædɪk/ *adj* occurring only occasionally ► **sporadically** /-kli/ *adv*

spore /spɔː(r)/ *n* (*biol*) small cell

like a seed produced by some plants, eg mushrooms

sport /spɔːt/ n 1 [U] activity done for pleasure or exercise, usu according to rules 2 [C] particular form of sport: water ~s [IDM] **be a (good) sport** (infml) be generous, cheerful and pleasant ● **sport** v [T] have or wear sth proudly: ~ a new beard ▸ **sporting** adj 1 of sport 2 fair and generous in your treatment of others [IDM] **a sporting chance** a reasonable chance of success ■ '**sports car** n low fast car, often with a roof that can be folded back ■ '**sportsman** (pl **-men**) | '**sportswoman** (pl **-women**) n person who takes part in sport ■ '**sportsmanship** n quality of being fair and generous, esp in sport ▸ **sporty** adj (-ier, -iest) good at or liking sport

spot /spɒt/ n 1 small egg-round mark of a different colour from the surface it is on 2 small dirty mark on sth 3 small red infected mark on the skin 4 place: a secluded ~ 5 (infml) ~ of small amount: a ~ of tea [IDM] in a (tight) **spot** (infml) in a difficult situation **on the spot** 1 immediately: an on-the-~ parking fine 2 actual place where sth is happening ● **spot** v (-tt-) [T] see or notice sb/sth [IDM] **be spotted with** sth be covered with small round marks of sth ▸ **spotless** adj completely clean ▸ **spotted** adj marked with spots ▸ **spotty** adj (-ier, -iest) (of a person) having a lot of spots on the skin

spotlight /'spɒtlaɪt/ n (lamp used for sending a) strong light directed at a particular place ● **spotlight** v [T] (pt, pp **spotlit** /-lɪt/ or, in sense 2 **~ed**) 1 shine a spotlight on sb/sth: a spotlit stage 2 direct attention at a problem, situation, etc

spouse /spaʊs/ n (fml or law) husband or wife

spout /spaʊt/ n pipe through which liquid pours: a ~ on a teapot [IDM] **be/go up the spout** (GB, sl) be/go wrong; be spoilt ● **spout** v [I, T] (cause liquid to) come out of sth with great force 2 (infml, disapprov) speak a lot about sth; repeat sth in a boring or annoying way

sprain /spreɪn/ v [T] injure a joint in your body by suddenly twisting it: ~ an ankle ▸ **sprain** n

sprang pt of SPRING²

sprawl v /sprɔːl/ [I] 1 sit or lie with your arms and legs spread out in a relaxed or awkward way 2 spread untidily over a large area ● **sprawl** n [C, usu sing, U] large area covered with buildings that spreads into the countryside in an ugly way: urban ~

spray /spreɪ/ n 1 [U, C] liquid sent through the air in tiny drops 2 [U, C] substance that is forced out of a

container, eg an aerosol, in the form of tiny drops: hair~ 3 [C] device or container that turns liquid into tiny drops 4 [C] small branch of a tree or plant, esp for decoration ● **spray** v [I, T] cover sb/sth with very small drops of liquid

spread /spred/ v (pt, pp **spread**) 1 [T] extend the surface of sth by unfolding it: The bird ~ its wings. 2 [T] put a substance on a surface: ~ butter on bread 3 [I, T] (cause sth to) become more widely known, felt, etc: ~ disease 4 [T] extend over an area or period of time ● **spread** n 1 [U] growth or increase of sth: the rapid ~ of the disease 2 [U,C] soft food that you put on bread 3 [usu sing] extent or width of sth 4 [C] (infml) a lot of food ■ **spread-eagled** adj in a position with your arms and legs spread out ■ '**spreadsheet** n computer program for displaying and changing rows of figures

sprightly /'spraɪtli/ adj (-ier, -iest) lively and active ▸ **sprightliness** n [U]

spring¹ /sprɪŋ/ n 1 [U,C] season of the year between winter and summer, when plants begin to grow 2 [C] length of coiled wire which returns to its shape after being pulled or pressed: bed ~s 3 [U] ability of a spring to return to its original position 4 [C] place where water comes naturally to the surface from under the ground 5 [C] quick sudden jump ■ ,**spring-'clean** v [T] clean a house, etc thoroughly, including the parts you do not usu clean ▸ ,**spring 'clean** n [sing] ▸ **springy** adj (-ier, -iest) returning quickly to the original shape when pushed, pulled, etc

spring² /sprɪŋ/ v (pt **sprang** /spræŋ/; pp **sprung** /sprʌŋ/) 1 [I] jump or move suddenly: ~ (up) from your chair ◊ The door sprang open. 2 [T] ~ (on) do sth, ask sth or say sth that sb is not expecting: She sprang the news on me. [IDM] **spring a leak** (of a boat, etc) begin to leak [PV] **spring from** sth have sth as a source or an origin **spring up** appear or develop quickly

sprinkle /'sprɪŋkl/ v [T] throw small pieces of sth or drops of liquid on sth ▸ **sprinkler** /-klə(r)/ n device for sprinkling water in drops on grass, plants, etc

sprint /sprɪnt/ v [I] run at full speed ● **sprint** n fast run ▸ **sprinter** n

sprout /spraʊt/ v [I, T] produce leaves, etc or begin to grow: (fig) houses ~ing ⊘ on the edge of town ● **sprout** n 1 = BRUSSELS SPROUT 2 new part of a plant

sprung pp of SPRING²

spun pp of SPIN

spur /spɜː(r)/ n 1 sharp pointed

object worn on the heel of a rider's boot, used to make the horse go faster **2** thing that encourages sb to try or work harder [IDM] **on the spur of the moment** suddenly and without planning in advance ● **spur** v (**-rr-**) [T] ~ (**on**) encourage sb to do sth or try harder to achieve sth

spurn /spɜːn/ v [T] reject or refuse sb, an offer, etc

spurt /spɜːt/ v **1** [I, T] (cause liquids, etc to) come out in a sudden burst **2** [I] make a sudden effort in a race, contest, etc ● **spurt** n **1** sudden burst of energy, speed, etc **2** sudden rush of liquid, etc

sputter /'spʌtə(r)/ v [I] make a series of spitting sounds

spy /spaɪ/ n (pl **-ies**) person who tries to get secret information about another country, organization, or person ● **spy** v (pt, pp **-ied**) **1** [I, T] ~ (**on**) watch secret information about sb/sth **2** [T] (lit or fml) suddenly see or notice sb/sth

squabble /'skwɒbl/ v [I], n (have a) quarrel, usu about sth unimportant

squad /skwɒd/ n [C, with sing or pl verb] small group of people working as a team: a football ~

squadron /'skwɒdrən/ n [C, with sing or pl verb] group of military aircraft or ships

squalid /'skwɒlɪd/ adj (disapprov) **1** dirty and unpleasant **2** morally bad

squall /skwɔːl/ n **1** sudden violent wind **2** loud cry, esp from a baby ● **squall** v [I] cry noisily

squalor /'skwɒlə(r)/ n [U] dirty and unpleasant conditions

squander /'skwɒndə(r)/ v [T] ~ (**on**) waste time, money, etc in a stupid or careless way

square[1] /skweə(r)/ adj **1** having four straight equal sides and four angles of 90° **2** forming an angle of 90°: ~ corners **3** equal to a square with sides of a stated length: six metres ~ **4** (infml) having paid all the money owed to sb: Here's the £10 I owe you—now we're ~. **5** (sport) (of two teams) having the same number of points **6** honest; fair: ~ dealings [IDM] **a square meal** a satisfying meal ● **square** adv directly; not at an angle ▶ **squarely** adv **1** directly; not at an angle or to one side: I looked her ~ly in the eye. **2** directly or exactly; without any uncertainty ■ **square 'root** n (maths) number which when multiplied by itself gives a particular number: The ~ root of 4 is 2.

square[2] /skweə(r)/ n **1** shape or area with four equal sides and four angles of 90° **2** four-sided open area in a town **3** result when a number is multiplied by itself [IDM] **back to square one** a return to the

situation you were in at the beginning of a project, task, etc

square[3] /skweə(r)/ v **1** [T] ~ (**off**) make sth have straight edges and corners **2** [T] multiply a number by itself **3** [T] make sth straight or level **4** [T] (infml) bribe sb [PV] **square (sth) with sth** make two ideas, facts or situations agree or be consistent with each other: ~ the theory with the facts **square up (with sb)** pay money that you owe

squash /skwɒʃ/ v **1** [T] press sth so that it becomes soft, damaged or flat **2** [I, T] push sth/sth or yourself into a space that is too small: ~ ten people into a car **3** [T] stop sth from continuing; destroy sth because it is a problem for you ● **squash** n **1** [U] game for two players, played with rackets and a rubber ball in a walled court **2** [U,C] (GB) drink made from fruit juice **3** [C,U] (pl squash or ~es) type of vegetable that grows on the ground, eg a pumpkin or marrow **4** [sing] (infml) crowd of people squashed together

squat /skwɒt/ v (**-tt-**) [I] **1** sit with your legs bent under your body **2** occupy empty buildings, land, etc without permission ● **squat** adj short and wide or fat ● **squat** n building occupied by squatters ▶ **squatter** n person who lives in a building, etc without permission and without paying rent

squawk /skwɔːk/ v [I] **1** (of birds) make a loud harsh sound **2** speak in a loud sharp voice because you are angry, surprised, etc▶ **squawk** n

squeak /skwiːk/ v [I, T] n (make a) short high sound that is not very loud ▶ **squeaky** adj (**-ier, -iest**)

squeal /skwiːl/ n long high cry or sound ● **squeal** v [I] **1** make a long high sound **2** (infml, disapprov) give information, esp to the police about sth illegal sb has done

squeamish /'skwiːmɪʃ/ adj easily made sick by unpleasant sights or situations, esp the sight of blood **2** easily shocked, offended, etc

squeeze /skwiːz/ v **1** [T] press sth firmly, esp with your fingers: ~ a sponge **2** [T] ~ (**from/out of**) get liquid out of sth by pressing or twisting it hard **3** [I, T] force sb/sth/yourself into or through a small space: ~ into the back seat [PV] **squeeze sth out of/from sb** get sth by putting pressure on sb, using threats, etc ● **squeeze** n **1** [C, usu sing] act of pressing sth **2** [sing] condition of being squeezed **3** [C, usu sing] (difficulty caused by a) reduction in the amount of money, jobs, etc available

squelch /skweltʃ/ v [I] make a sucking sound as when feet are lifted from mud ● **squelch** n squelching sound

squid /skwɪd/ n [C,U] sea creature with ten long arms around its mouth

squint /skwɪnt/ v 1 look at sth with your eyes partly shut 2 (GB) (of an eye) look in a different direction from the other eye ● **squint** n [C, usu sing] disorder of the eye muscles which causes each eye to look in a different direction

squirm /skwɜːm/ v [I] 1 move by twisting the body about 2 feel embarrassment or shame

squirrel /ˈskwɪrəl/ n small bushy-tailed animal with red or grey fur

squirt /skwɜːt/ v [I, T] force liquid, gas, etc out in a thin fast stream through a narrow opening: be forced out in this way 2 [T] hit sb/sth with a stream of water, gas, etc ● **squirt** n thin fast stream of a liquid

St abbr 1 (used in addresses) Street 2 Saint

stab /stæb/ v (-bb-) [I, T] 1 push a pointed weapon into sb, killing or injuring them 2 make a short, forceful movement with a finger, etc [IDM] **stab sb in the back** betray sb ● **stab** n 1 act of stabbing sb/sth 2 sudden sharp pain 3 attempt to do sth: have a ~ at sth ► **stabbing** adj (of pain) very sharp and sudden

stable¹ /ˈsteɪbl/ adj 1 firmly fixed; not likely to move, change or fail 2 (of a person) calm and reasonable; balanced ► **stability** /stəˈbɪləti/ n [U] ► **stabilize** (also **-ise**) /ˈsteɪbəlaɪz/ v [I, T] (cause sth to) become firm, steady and unlikely to change ► **stabilizer** (also **-iser**) n device that keeps sth stable

stable² /ˈsteɪbl/ n building in which horses are kept ● **stable** v [T] put or keep a horse in a stable

stack /stæk/ n [C] 1 (usu neat) pile: a ~ of books 2 pile of hay, straw, etc stored in the open 3 tall chimney or group of chimneys 4 (**stacks**) [pl] (infml) ~(of) large number of ● **stack** v 1 arrange things in a pile 2 fill sth with piles of things

stadium /ˈsteɪdiəm/ n (pl ~s or **-dia** /-diə/) n large sports ground, with seats for spectators

staff /stɑːf/ n 1 [C, usu sing] all the workers employed in an organization considered as a group 2 (US) people who work at a school or university, but who do not teach students 3 [C, with sing or pl verb] group of senior army officers 4 [C] strong stick used as a support when walking ● **staff** v [T] (provide people to) work in an institution, company, etc

stag /stæg/ n male deer

stage /steɪdʒ/ n 1 period or step in development, growth, etc: at an early ~ in her life 2 [C] separate part of a process, etc is divided into 3 [C] raised platform on which actors perform plays 4 **the stage** [sing] acting as a profession: go on the ~ (= be an actor) 5 [sing] place where important things happen, esp in politics ● **stage** v [T] produce a performance of a play, etc ■ **stagecoach** n vehicle pulled by horses, which was used in the past to carry passengers ■ **stage 'manager** n person in charge of a theatre stage

stagger /ˈstægə(r)/ v 1 [I] walk unsteadily 2 [T] shock or surprise sb very much 3 [T] arrange events, etc so that they do not happen together ► **stagger** n

stagnant /ˈstægnənt/ adj 1 (of air or water) not moving and therefore smelling bad 2 not developing, growing or changing

stagnate /stægˈneɪt/ v [I] 1 stop developing or making progress 2 be or become stagnant ► **stagnation** /-ʃn/ n [U]

staid /steɪd/ adj (of appearance, behaviour, etc) dull, quiet and serious

stain /steɪn/ v 1 leave marks on sth that are difficult to remove 2 [I] become marked 3 [T] colour wood, fabric, etc ● **stain** n 1 [C] dirty mark that is difficult to remove 2 [U] liquid used for colouring wood, etc 3 [C] thing that harms sb's reputation, etc ■ **stained 'glass** n [U] pieces of coloured glass, often used to make patterns in windows ■ **stainless 'steel** adj type of steel that does not rust

stair /steə(r)/ n 1 (**stairs**) [pl] set of steps built between two floors inside a building: a flight of ~s 2 one of a series of steps: sitting on the bottom ~ ■ **staircase** n [C] ■ **stairway** n set of stairs inside a building

stake /steɪk/ n 1 [C] strong pointed wooden or metal post pushed into the ground to support sth, etc 2 [C] money that sb invests in a company: I have a ~ in the company's success. 3 [C, usu pl] sum of money risked or gambled [IDM] **at stake** that can be won or lost, depending on the success of a particular action ● **stake** v [T] 1 risk money or sth important on the result of sth 2 support sth with a stake [IDM] **stake (out) a/your claim (to/for/on sth)** say or show publicly that you think sth should be yours [PV] **stake sth out** (infml) watch a place secretly, esp for signs of illegal activity

stale /steɪl/ adj 1 (of food, etc) not fresh 2 no longer interesting because too well known 3 no longer able to do sth well because you have been doing the same thing for too long ▶ **staleness** n [U]

stalemate /'steɪlmeɪt/ n [C,U] **1** position in chess in which no further move can be made **2** stage in an argument, etc in which no further discussion seems possible

stalk /stɔːk/ n thin stem that supports a flower, leaf or fruit and joins it to another part of the plant ● **stalk** v **1** [I, T] move slowly and quietly towards an animal or a person, in order to kill, catch or harm it or them: *He ~ed his victim as she was walking home.* **2** [T] illegally follow and watch sb over a long period of time **3** [I] walk in an angry or proud way ▶ **stalker** n **1** person who follows and watches another person over a long period of time **2** person who follows an animal in order to kill it

stall /stɔːl/ n [C] **1** compartment for one animal in a stable **2** table or small open shop, etc from which things are sold in the street **3** (**the stalls**) [pl] seats in a theatre nearest the stage ● **stall** v **1** [I, T] (cause a vehicle or an engine to) stop suddenly because of lack of power or speed **2** [I] delay doing sth so that you have more time **3** [T] make sb wait so that you have more time to do sth

stallion /'stæliən/ n male horse, esp one used for breeding

stamina /'stæmɪnə/ n [U] energy and strength to work hard, run long distances, etc

stammer /'stæmə(r)/ v [I, T] speak with difficulty, repeating sounds or words before saying them correctly ● **stammer** n [sing] tendency to stammering speech

stamp¹ /stæmp/ n **1** (also fml **'postage stamp**) small piece of printed paper stuck on envelopes, parcels, etc to show that postage has been paid: *a ~ album* **2** [U] tool for printing the date or a mark on a surface **3** words, design, etc made by stamping sth on a surface **4** small piece of paper stuck on a document to show that an amount of money has been paid **5** act of stamping with the foot

stamp² /stæmp/ v [I, T] put your foot down with force on the ground, etc **2** [T] **~A on B; ~B with A** print a design, the date, etc onto sth using a special tool **3** [T] make a feeling show clearly on sb's face, their actions etc: *The crime had revenge ~ed all over it.* **4** [T] stick a stamp on a letter or parcel [PV] **stamp sth out** get rid of sth bad, unpleasant or dangerous, esp by using force

stampede /stæm'piːd/ n sudden rush of people or animals, eg through fear ● **stampede** v [I, T]

(cause animals or people to) move in a stampede

stance /stæns/ n **1** way of standing, esp when striking the ball in golf, cricket, etc **2** attitude, opinion: *her ~ on nuclear arms*

stand¹ /stænd/ n **1** [usu sing] attitude or opinion **2** [C] strong effort to defend yourself or your opinion: *make a ~ against job losses* **3** [C] table or upright structure where things are sold or displayed **4** [C] piece of furniture for holding a particular type of thing: *a music ~* **5** [C] building where people stand or sit to watch sports contests, etc [sing = WIT-NESS BOX (WITNESS)] ■ **'standpoint** n [usu sing] point of view

stand² /stænd/ v (pt, pp **stood** /stʊd/) **1** [I] be on your feet; be upright **2** [I] get up onto your feet from another position **3** [T] put sth/sb in an upright position: *~ the ladder against the wall* **4** [I] be in a certain place, condition or situation: *the house ~s on the corner* **5** [I] be a particular height: *She ~s five foot six.* **6** [I] **~at** be at a particular level, amount, height, etc **7** [I] (of an offer, decision, etc) be still valid: *My decision ~s.* **8** [T] (used esp with *can't*, *couldn't*) strongly dislike sb/sth: *I can't ~ her brother.* **9** [T] be able to survive or tolerate sth without being harmed or damaged: *His heart won't ~ the strain.* **10** [T] buy a drink or meal for sb: *~ sb a meal* **11** [I] **~ (for/as)** be a candidate in an election: *~ for parliament* [IDM] **it stands to reason** (*infml*) it must be obvious to any sensible person who thinks about it **stand a chance (of doing sth)** have the possibility of succeeding or achieving sth **stand fast/firm** refuse to move back; refuse to change your opinions **stand your ground** → GROUND¹ **stand on your own (two) feet** be independent **stand out like a sore thumb** → SORE [PV] **stand by 1** be present while sth bad happens without doing anything **2** be ready for action **stand by sb** help or support sb, esp in a difficult situation **stand by sth** still believe sth you said, decided or agreed earlier **stand down** resign from a job, etc; withdraw **stand for sth 1** be an abbreviation or symbol for sth: *PO ~s for Post Office.* **2** (**not stand for sth**) not tolerate sb/sth: *She won't ~ for disobedience.* **stand in (for sb)** take the place of sb **stand out (as sth)** be much better or more important than sb/sth **stand out (from/against sth)** be easily seen; be noticeable **stand sb up** (*infml*) deliberately not meet sb you have arranged to meet **stand up for sb/sth** support or defend sb/sth **stand up to sb** resist sb **stand up to sth** remain in good condition in spite of hard use, etc ■ **'standby** n person or thing to be used as a substitute, esp in case of emergency [IDM] **on standby** ready to do sth immediately if needed or asked ■ **'stand-in** n person who does sb's job for them for a short time ■ **standoffish** /-'ɒfɪʃ/ adj (infml) (of people) unfriendly

standard /'stændəd/ n **1** thing used as a measure **2** (normal or expected) level of quality: the ~ of her school work **3** special flag ● **standard** adj of the normal or usual kind: ~ sizes of paper ▶ **standardize** (also **-ise**) v [T] make sth conform to a fixed standard of size, shape, quality, etc ■ **'standard lamp** n tall lamp with a base on the floor ■ **standard of 'living** n level of comfort, wealth, etc enjoyed by a particular group of people

standing /'stændɪŋ/ n [U] **1** position or reputation of sb within a group of people or an organization **2** period of time sth has existed: debts of long ~ ● **standing** adj permanent and established: a ~ joke

stank pt of STINK

stanza /'stænzə/ n group of lines in a poem

staple n **1** small piece of bent wire for holding sheets of paper together **2** main article or product ● **staple** v [T] fasten or secure sth with a staple(1) ● **staple** adj forming the main part of sth: Their ~ diet is rice. ▶ **stapler** n device for putting staples into paper, etc

star /stɑː(r)/ n **1** large ball of burning gas seen as a point of light in the sky at night **2** figure with five or more points resembling a star, often used to show quality **3** famous singer, actor, etc **4** planet or force believed to influence a person's life: born under a lucky ~ ● **star** v (-rr-) **1** [I] be the main actor in a film, etc **2** [T] (of a film, etc) have sb as the main actor ▶ **stardom** n [U] status of being a star(3) ■ **'starfish** n sea animal shaped like a star ▶ **starry** adj

starboard /'stɑːbəd/ n [U] right side of a ship or an aircraft when it is facing forward

starch /stɑːtʃ/ n [U] **1** white, tasteless food substance found in potatoes, rice, etc **2** starch in powdered form or as a spray, used for making clothes, etc stiff ● **starch** v [T] make clothes, sheets, etc stiff using starch ▶ **starchy** adj (-ier, -iest)

stare /steə(r)/ v [I] ~ (at) look at sb/sth for a long time ● **stare** n staring, often unfriendly, look

stark /stɑːk/ adj **1** looking severe, without colour or decoration **2** unpleasant and impossible to avoid: the ~ reality of life in prison **3** clearly very different to sth: in ~ contrast ● **stark** adv completely: ~ naked

starling /'stɑːlɪŋ/ n common small bird with dark shiny feathers

starry → STAR

start¹ /stɑːt/ n **1** [C, usu sing] point at which sth begins; act of beginning sth **2** (**the start**) [sing] place where a race begins **3** [C, usu sing] amount of time or distance that sb has as an advantage over others in a race **4** [C, usu sing] sudden movement of the body because of surprise, fear, etc

start² /stɑːt/ v **1** [I, T] begin doing sth **2** [I, T] (cause sb) to start happening: When does the class ~? ◇ ~ a fire **3** [I, T] (cause a machine or vehicle to) begin running. The car won't ~. **4** [I, T] ~ (**up**) (cause sth to) begin to exist: ~ a business **5** [I] ~ (**out**) begin a journey [IDM] **start the ball rolling** → BALL [PV] **start sb off** to move **start sb off** (**on sth**) cause sb to begin doing sth **start out** begin to do sth, esp in business or work ▶ **starter** n **1** (esp GB) first course of a meal **2** person, horse, car, etc that starts a race **3** device to start an engine [IDM] **for starters** (spoken) first of all

startle /'stɑːtl/ v [T] shock or surprise sb

starve /stɑːv/ v [I, T] (cause sb to) suffer or die from hunger [IDM] **be starving** (**for sth**) | **be starved** (infml) feel very hungry [PV] **starve sb/sth of sth** not give sb that is needed: Her children were ~d of love. ▶ **starvation** /-'veɪʃn/ n [U]

state¹ /steɪt/ n **1** [C] condition of a person or thing: a poor ~ of health **2** (also **State**) [C] country **3** (also **State**) [C] organized political community forming part of a larger country: Ohio is a ~ in America. **4** (also the **State**) [U, sing] government of a country **5** [U] very formal ceremony: buried in ~ ● **state** (also **State**) adj **1** of the state(4) **2** connected with the leader of a country attending an official ceremony **3** of a particular state(3), esp in the US: ~ police ▶ **stately** adj (-ier, -iest) impressive in size, appearance or manner ■ **stately 'home** n (GB) large, impressive house of historical interest

state² /steɪt/ v [T] formally write or say sth, esp clearly and fully ▶ **statement** n **1** formal account of events, views, etc **2** financial report: a bank ~ment

statesman /'steɪtsmən/ n (pl -men) wise, experienced and respected political leader ▶ **'statesmanship** n [U] skill in managing state affairs

static /'stætɪk/ adj not moving ● **static** n [U] **1** atmospheric disturbance affecting radio broadcasts

2 (also ,static elec'tricity) electricity which collects on the surface of objects

station /'steɪʃn/ n **1** place where trains stop so that people can get on and off **2** building, etc where a service is organized: *a bus* ~ **3** radio or TV company ● **station** v [T] send sb, esp from one of the armed forces, to work in a certain place ■ 'station wagon n (US) = ESTATE CAR (ESTATE)

stationary /'steɪʃənri/ adj not moving: ~ *traffic*

stationer /'steɪʃənə(r)/ n person who owns or manages a shop selling paper, envelopes, etc for writing ► **stationery** /-ʃənri/ n [U] materials for writing and for using in an office

statistics /stə'tɪstɪks/ n **1** [pl] information shown as numbers **2** [U] the science of collecting and explaining statistics ► **statistical** /-kl/ adj ► **statistically** /-kli/ adv ► **statistician** /,stætɪ'stɪʃn/ n expert in statistics

statue /'stætʃuː/ n figure of a person, an animal, etc in wood, stone, bronze, etc ► **statuette** /,stætʃu'et/ n small statue

stature /'stætʃə(r)/ n [U] (*written*) **1** importance gained from achievement or ability **2** (person's) size or height

status /'steɪtəs/ n [U] person's legal, social or professional position ■ 'status symbol n item showing sb's importance, wealth, etc

status quo /,steɪtəs 'kwəʊ/ n [sing] the situation as it is now

statute /'stætʃuːt/ n law passed by a parliament, council, etc ► **statutory** /-tri/ adj fixed or required by law

staunch /stɔːntʃ/ adj (of a supporter, etc) loyal ► **staunchly** adv

stave /steɪv/ v (pt, pp ~d or stove /stəʊv/) [PV] **stave sth in** break or damage sth by making part of it fall inwards **stave sth off** (pt, pp ~d) delay danger, etc

stay /steɪ/ v [I] **1** be or remain in the same place or condition: ~ *at home* ◇ ~ *sober* **2** live in a place temporarily as a guest or visitor: ~ *at a hotel* [IDM] **stay clear (of sb/sth)** → CLEAR¹ **stay put** (*infml*) remain where you are or where sb/sth is [PV] **stay up** not go to bed ● **stay** n **1** period of staying; visit: *a long ~ in hospital* ► rope or wire supporting a ship's mast, a pole, etc [IDM] **a stay of execution** (*law*) delay in carrying out the order of a court ■ 'staying power n [U] = STAMINA

steadfast /'stedfɑːst/ adj firm and unchanging ► **steadfastly** adv

steady /'stedi/ adj (-ier, -iest) **1** even and regular: *a ~ speed* **2** firmly fixed and not interrupted: *a ~ job/income* **3** firmly fixed or supported; not

moving: *hold the ladder* ~ **4** (of a person) reliable: *a ~ worker* ● **steady** adv steadily ● **steady** v (-ied) [I, T] (cause sb/sth/yourself to) stop moving, shaking or falling ► **steadily** adv in a regular way

steak /steɪk/ n [C, U] (thick slice of) meat or fish

steal /stiːl/ v (pt **stole** /stəʊl/, pp **stolen** /'stəʊlən/) **1** [I, T] ~ (from) take sb's property without permission **2** [I] move secretly and quietly **3** [T] obtain sth suddenly or secretly: ~ *a kiss* [IDM] **steal the show** attract the most attention

stealth /stelθ/ n [U] fact of doing sth in a quiet or secret way ► **stealthy** adj (-ier, -iest)

steam /stiːm/ n [U] **1** hot gas that water changes into when it boils **2** power produced from steam under pressure, used to operate engines, etc: ~ *power* [IDM] **run out of steam** (*infml*) lose energy and enthusiasm and stop doing sth ● **steam** v **1** [I] send out steam **2** [T] move, work, etc by steam power **3** [T] cook food over boiling water so that it cooks in the steam [PV] **steam (sth) up** (cause sth to) become covered with steam ■ **steamer** n **1** boat or ship driven by steam **2** vessel in which food is steamed ■ 'steamroller n slow heavy vehicle used for flattening new roads ► **steamy** adj

steel /stiːl/ n [U] hard metal made from iron and carbon, used for knives, machinery, etc ● **steel** v [T] ~ **yourself (for/against sth)** prepare yourself to deal with sth unpleasant: *She ~ed herself for disappointment.*

steep¹ /stiːp/ adj **1** (of a slope) rising or falling sharply **2** (*infml*) (of a price or demand) too much; unreasonable ► **steeply** adv ► **steepness** n [U]

steep² /stiːp/ v [IDM] **be steeped in sth** (*written*) have a lot of a particular quality: *a city ~ed in history* [PV] **steep sth in sth** leave food in a liquid for a long time to flavour it **steep yourself in sth** (*written*) spend time thinking or learning about sth

steeple /'stiːpl/ n tall pointed tower of the roof of a church ■ 'steeple-chase n race for horses or athletes with obstacles such as fences and water to jump over ■ 'steeplejack n person who repairs steeples, tall chimneys, etc

steer /stɪə(r)/ v [I, T] direct the course of a boat, car, etc [IDM] **steer clear (of sb/sth)** → CLEAR¹ ■ 'steering wheel n wheel used for controlling the direction that a vehicle goes in

stem /stem/ n **1** main long thin part of a plant above the ground **2** long thin part like a stem, eg on a wine glass ● **stem** v [T] (-mm-) stop sth that is flowing from spreading or increasing [PV] **stem from sth** be the result of sth

stench /stentʃ/ n strong, very unpleasant smell

stencil /'stensl/ n 1 thin sheet of metal, etc with letters or designs cut in it 2 letters, etc made by putting ink, etc through holes in a stencil ▶ **stencil** v (-ll-, US -l-) [I, T] produce letters, etc with a stencil

step¹ /step/ n [C] 1 act of lifting your foot and putting it down in order to walk; sound this makes 2 way that sb walks: I heard her ~ on the stair. 3 distance covered when you take a step 4 one of a series of actions done to achieve sth or that form part of process: take ~s to help sb ○ I'll explain it to you ~ by ~. 5 flat place for the foot when going from one level to another: A flight of ~s led up to the door. 6 (steps) [pl] =STEPLADDER [IDM] **in/out of step (with sb/sth)** 1 putting/not putting your feet down at the same time as others 2 agreeing/not agreeing with others' ideas **mind/watch your step** 1 walk carefully 2 behave carefully ▪ **'stepladder** n folding ladder with steps

step² /step/ v (-pp-) 1 [I] lift your foot and move it in a particular direction or put it on or in sth 2 move a short distance [IDM] **step on it** (spoken) go faster or hurry **step out of line** behave badly or break the rules [PV] **step aside/down** resign from a position or job, esp so sb else can have it **step in** help sb in a dispute or difficult situation **step sth up** increase sth ▪ **'stepping stone** n 1 one of a line of flat stones used to cross a stream, etc 2 stage towards achieving sth

step- /step-/ prefix related as a result of one parent marrying again: ~mother

stereo /'steriəʊ/ n 1 [C] machine that plays CDs, cassettes, the radio, etc that has two separate speakers 2 [U] system for playing recorded music, in which the sound is directed through two channels: broadcast in ~ ▶ **stereo** adj: ~ sound

stereotype /'steriətaɪp/ n fixed idea of what sb/sth is like

sterile /'steraɪl/ adj 1 not able to produce children or young 2 clean and free from bacteria 3 having no result: a ~ argument 4 (of land) not able to produce crops ▶ **sterility** /stə'rɪləti/ n [U] ▶ **sterilize** (also -ise) /'sterəlaɪz/ v [T] 1 kill the bacteria in sth 2 make a person or animal unable to have babies or young

sterling /'stɜːlɪŋ/ n [U] money system of Britain ● **sterling** adj (fml) of excellent quality

stern /stɜːn/ adj severe, strict or

serious ▶ **sternly** adv ● **stern** n back end of a ship

steroid /'steroɪd; 'stɪər-/ n powerful chemical produced in the body or taken as a drug

stethoscope /'steθəskəʊp/ n instrument for listening to the beating of the heart, etc

stew /stjuː/ v [T] cook sth slowly in liquid in a closed dish ● **stew** n [C, U] dish of stewed meat, etc [IDM] **get (yourself)/be in a stew (about/over sth)** (infml) become/feel very nervous or upset about sth

steward /'stjuːəd/ n (fem **stewardess** /ˌstjuːə'des/) person who takes care of passengers on a ship, an aircraft or a train 2 person who helps to organize a large public event, eg a race

stick¹ /stɪk/ n 1 [C] small thin piece of wood that has fallen from a tree 2 [C] =WALKING STICK (WALK¹) 3 [C] long thin piece of sth: a ~ of chalk 4 [U] (GB, infml) criticism or harsh words: The referee got a lot of ~ for his decision.

stick² /stɪk/ v (pt, pp **stuck** /stʌk/) 1 [I, T] (cause sth) to be pushed into sb/sth, usu a sharp object to) be pushed into sth: ~ the knife into the cheese 2 [I, T] (cause sth to) be fixed to sth else, esp with glue 3 [T] (infml) put sth somewhere, esp quickly or carelessly: S~ it in the bag. 4 [I] become fixed in one position and impossible to move: The key stuck in the lock. 5 [T] (GB, infml) tolerate sb/sth unpleasant: I can't ~ this job any longer. [IDM] **stick your neck out** (infml) take risks about your future **stick your nose into sth →** NOSE¹ **stick your oar in →** OAR **stick out like a sore thumb →** SORE **stick to sth** continue doing or using sth and not want to change it **stick up** point upwards or be above a surface **stick up for sb/yourself/sth** defend or support sb/yourself/sth ▶ **sticker** n sticky label ▪ **'sticking plaster** n [C, U] =PLASTER(3) ▪ **'stick-in-the-mud** n (infml, disapprov) person who refuses to try anything new ▪ **sticky** adj (-ier, -iest) 1 like or covered with glue 2 (infml) difficult: a ~ situation

[PV] **stick at sth** keep on with sth **stick by sb** continue to support sb **stick (sth) out** (cause sth to) be further out than sth else or come through sth else: ~ your tongue out **stick it/sth out** (infml) continue to the very end **stick to your guns** (infml) refuse to change your mind about sth [PV] **stick around** (infml) not go away

stiff /stɪf/ adj 1 not easily bent, folded, etc: ~ cardboard 2 hard to stir, move, etc: a ~ paste 3 more difficult than usual: a ~ climb ◇ a ~ breeze 4 (of a person) not friendly or relaxed [IDM] **(keep) a**

stiff upper lip keep calm and hide your feelings in spite of pain or difficulty ● **stiff** *adv* (*infml*) very much: *bored ~* ▸ **stiffly** *adv* ▸ **stiffness** *n* [U]

stiffen /'stɪfn/ *v* [I, T] become or make sth difficult to bend, move, etc

stifle /'staɪfl/ *v* 1 [T] prevent sth from happening: *~ a yawn* 2 [I, T] (cause sb to) have difficulty breathing

stigma /'stɪgmə/ *n* [U,C, usu sing] mark of shame

stile /staɪl/ *n* step used to climb over a fence, etc

stiletto /stɪ'letəʊ/ *n* (*pl* -os or -oes) woman's shoe with a very high narrow heel; heel on such a shoe

still¹ /stɪl/ *adv* 1 up to now or the time mentioned and not finishing: *She is ~ busy.* 2 in spite of what has just been said: *It's raining. S~, we must go shopping.* 3 even: *Tom is tall, but Mary is ~ taller.*

still² /stɪl/ *adj* 1 not moving; calm and quiet: *Keep ~ while I brush your hair.* 2 (*GB*) (of a drink) not containing bubbles of gas ● **still** *v* [I, T] (*lit*) become or make sth calm or quiet ● **still** *n* 1 photograph of a scene from a film 2 equipment for making strong alcoholic drinks ■ **'stillborn** *adj* 1 born dead 2 not successful; not developing

stilt /stɪlt/ *n* one of two poles with a support for the foot, used for walking raised above the ground

stilted /'stɪltɪd/ *adj* (of speech, behaviour, etc) stiff and unnatural

stimulant /'stɪmjələnt/ *n* drink, drug, etc that increases bodily or mental activity

stimulate /'stɪmjuleɪt/ *v* [T] 1 make sth develop; encourage sth: *~ discussion* 2 make sb interested and excited about sth ▸ **stimulating** *adj* ▸ **stimulation** /ˌstɪmju'leɪʃn/ *n* [U]

stimulus /'stɪmjələs/ *n* (*pl* -li /-laɪ/) something that stimulates sb/sth: *a ~ to hard work*

sting /stɪŋ/ *v* (*pt, pp* **stung** /stʌŋ/) 1 [I, T] (of an insect or a plant) touch your skin or make a small hole in it so that you feel a sharp pain 2 [I, T] (cause sb to) feel a sharp pain: *The smoke made my eyes —.* 3 [T] make sb feel angry or upset ● **sting** *n* 1 sharp, often poisonous organ of some insects, eg bees 2 wound made when an insect stings you 3 any sharp pain

stingy /'stɪndʒi/ *adj* (**-ier, -iest**) (*infml*) unwilling to spend or give money, etc ▸ **stinginess** *n* [U]

stink /stɪŋk/ *v* (*pt* **stank** /stæŋk/ or **stunk** /stʌŋk/; *pp* **stunk**) [I] 1 have a strong unpleasant smell 2 seem very bad or dishonest [PV] **stink sth out** fill a place with a bad smell ● **stink** *n* (*infml*) 1 very unpleas-

ant smell 2 [*sing*] lot of trouble and anger about sth: *kick up a ~* (= complain a lot and cause trouble)

stint /stɪnt/ *v* [I, T] **~(on)** give sb only a small amount of sth ● **stint** *n* fixed amount of work, etc

stipulate /'stɪpjuleɪt/ *v* [T] state sth as a necessary condition ▸ **stipulation** /ˌstɪpju'leɪʃn/ *n* [C, U]

stir /stɜː(r)/ *v* (**-rr-**) 1 [T] mix a liquid by moving a spoon, etc round and round in it 2 [I, T] (cause sb/sth to) move 3 [T] excite sb or make them feel sth strongly: *a book that ~s the imagination* 4 [I, T] (*GB, infml*) try to cause trouble [PV] **stir sb up** encourage sb to do sth ● **stir** *n* [*sing*] excitement or shock ▸ **stirring** *adj* exciting

stirrup /'stɪrəp/ *n* one of two metal rings attached to a horse's saddle which support the rider's feet

stitch /stɪtʃ/ *n* 1 [C] single passing of a needle and thread through cloth, etc to join or decorate sth, or through skin to close a wound 2 [C] one turn of the wool round the needle in knitting 3 [C,U] style of sewing or knitting that you use to get the pattern you want 4 [C, usu *sing*] pain in the side caused by running [IDM] **in stitches** (*infml*) laughing a lot **not have a stitch on** | **not be wearing a stitch** be naked ● **stitch** *v* [T] sew sth

stoat /stəʊt/ *n* small brown furry animal, larger than a rat

stock¹ /stɒk/ *n* 1 [C, U] supply of goods available for sale in a shop 2 [C, U] **~(of)** supply of sth available for use 3 [C, usu *pl, U*] share in a company, issued in fixed amounts, bought as a way of investing money 4 [U] = LIVE-STOCK 5 [U] liquid in which bones, etc have been cooked, used for soup, etc [IDM] **in/out of stock** available/not available to buy **take stock (of sth)** review a situation ● **stock** *adj* not interesting because it has been used too often: *a ~ phrase* ■ **'stockbroker** *n* person who buys and sells stocks(3) and shares for other people ■ **'stock exchange** *n* place where stocks(3) are bought and sold ■ **'stock market** *n* business of buying and selling shares in companies and the place where this is done ■ **'stockpile** *v* [T] buy large quantities of sth and keep it for use in the future ▸ **'stockpile** *n* ■ **stock-'still** *adv* without moving at all ■ **'stock-taking** *n* [U] process of making a list of all the goods in a shop or business

stock² /stɒk/ *v* [T] 1 (of a shop) keep a supply of a particular type of goods to sell 2 fill sth with food, books, etc [PV] **stock up (on/with sth)** buy a lot of sth to use later

stockade /stɒ'keɪd/ *n* tall strong fence, built for defence

stocking /'stɒkɪŋ/ n either of a pair of thin coverings for a woman's feet and legs

stocky /'stɒki/ adj (-ier, -iest) (of a person) short, with a strong, solid body ► **stockily** adv

stodge /stɒdʒ/ n [U] (sl) heavy solid food ► **stodgy** adj (-ier, -iest) 1 heavy and solid 2 dull

stoic /'stəʊɪk/ n person who suffers without complaint ► **stoical** adj ► **stoically** /-kli/ adv ► **stoicism** /'stəʊɪsɪzəm/ n [U] patient suffering, etc

stoke /stəʊk/ v [T] ~ (up; with) add fuel to a fire, etc ■ **stoker** n person whose job is to add fuel to a fire, etc, esp on a ship or steam train

stole[1] /stəʊl/ n wide band of fabric, etc worn around the shoulders

stole[2] pt of STEAL

stolen pp of STEAL

stomach /'stʌmək/ n 1 organ in the body where food is digested 2 front part of the body below the chest [IDM] **have no stomach for sth** 1 not want to eat sth 2 not have the desire or courage to do sth: *have no ~ for a fight* ● **stomach** v [T] approve of and be able to enjoy sth

stone /stəʊn/ n 1 [U] solid mineral substance found in the ground, used for building 2 [C] piece of rock 3 [C] jewel 4 [C] hard seed of some fruits, eg the cherry 5 [C] (pl **stone**) unit of weight, 14 pounds (6.35 kilograms) 6 [C] piece of hard material that can form in a body organ: *kidney ~s* [IDM] **a stone's throw** a short distance away ● **stone** v [T] throw stones at sb/sth ■ the '**Stone Age** n [sing] early period in human history when tools, etc were made of stone ► **stoned** adj (sl) under the influence of drugs or alcohol ■ ,**stone 'deaf** adj completely unable to hear

stony /'stəʊni/ adj (-ier, -iest) 1 having a lot of stones 2 hard and unsympathetic ► **stonily** /-ɪli/ adv

stood pt, pp of STAND[2]

stool /stuːl/ n small seat without a back

stoop /stuːp/ v [I] bend your body forwards and downwards [PV] **stoop to sth** lower your standards to do sth wrong ● **stoop** n [sing] stooping position

stop[1] /stɒp/ n 1 act of stopping or stopping sth: *The car came to a ~. It's time to put a ~ to the violence.* 2 place at which buses, etc stop regularly 3 (GB) = FULL STOP (FULL)

stop[2] /stɒp/ v (-pp-) 1 [I, T] (cause sb/sth to) no longer move or function: *We decided to ~ for the night.* ◊ *The engine ~ped.* ◊ *He was ~ped by the police.* 2 [I, T] (make sb/sth) no

longer continue to do sth: (spoken) *S~ it! You're hurting me.* ◊ *The phone never ~s ringing.* 3 [I, T] (cause sth to) end or finish 4 [T] prevent sb from doing sth or sth from happening: *~ her (from) leaving* 5 [I] (GB, infml) stay somewhere for a short time 6 [T] prevent money from being paid: *a ~ cheque* [PV] **stop off (at/in …)** make a short visit somewhere during a trip ■ **stop over (at/in …)** stay somewhere for a short time during a journey ■ '**stopcock** n tap that controls the flow of liquid or gas through a pipe ■ '**stopgap** n temporary substitute ■ '**stopover** n short stay somewhere between two parts of a journey ► **stoppage** /-pɪdʒ/ n period when work is stopped ► **stopper** n object that fits into the top of a bottle to close it ■ ,**stop 'press** n [U] late news added to a newspaper

storage /'stɔːrɪdʒ/ n [U] 1 (space used for) keeping sth in a place until it is needed 2 (computing) process of keeping information, etc on a computer; way in which it is kept

store /stɔː(r)/ n 1 large shop selling many different types of goods 2 (US) any shop, large or small 3 quantity of sth kept for use as needed 4 place where things are kept [IDM] **in store (for sb)** waiting to happen to sb: *What's in ~ for us today?* **set/put (great, etc) store by sth** consider sth to be important ● **store** v [T] 1 ~ (away/up) put sth somewhere and keep it for future use 2 keep information or facts in a computer or your brain

storey /'stɔːri/ n floor or level of a building

stork /stɔːk/ n large, long-legged wading bird

storm /stɔːm/ n 1 period of very strong winds, rain, etc 2 violent show of feeling: *a ~ of protest* [IDM] **take sth/sb by storm** 1 be extremely successful very quickly 2 capture a building by violent attack ● **storm** v [T] 1 suddenly attack a place 2 [I] speak, move, etc angrily ► **stormy** adj (-ier, -iest)

story /'stɔːri/ n (pl **-ies**) 1 description of past or imaginary events 2 news report 3 (infml) lie 4 (US) = STOREY

stout /staʊt/ adj 1 (of a person) rather fat 2 strong and thick 3 (fml) determined and brave ● **stout** n [U, C] strong dark beer ► **stoutly** adv

stove /stəʊv/ n closed apparatus burning wood, coal, etc used for cooking, etc

stow /stəʊ/ v [T] ~ (away) put sth in a safe place ■ '**stowaway** n person who hides on a ship or an aircraft to avoid paying

straddle /ˈstrædl/ v [T] sit or stand with one of your legs on either side of sth/sb

straight¹ /streɪt/ adv 1 not in a curve or at an angle; in a straight line: walk ~ 2 by a direct route; immediately: Come ~ home. 3 into or into a level or upright position: Sit up ~. 4 honestly, directly: Tell her ~ what you think. [IDM] **go straight** (infml) stop being a criminal and live an honest life ■ **straight a'way** adv immediately

straight² /streɪt/ adj 1 not bent or curved: a ~ line 2 level, upright or parallel to sth 3 clean and neat 4 honest and direct 5 (US) (of alcoholic drinks) not mixed with water or anything else 6 (infml) = HETERO-SEXUAL [IDM] **keep a straight face** stop yourself from smiling or laughing ● **straight** n straight part of a race-track or road ► **straightness** n [U]

straighten /ˈstreɪtn/ v [I, T] make sth or become level, tidy, etc

straightforward /ˌstreɪtˈfɔːwəd/ adj 1 easy to understand or do 2 honest ► **straightforwardly** adv

strain¹ /streɪn/ n 1 [U,C] pressure on sb/sth because they have too much to do or deal with; the problems and anxiety that this produces: a marriage under great ~ 2 [U,C] pressure put on sth when a physical force stretches or pushes it: put ~ on a rope 3 [C,U] injury caused by stretching a muscle too much 4 [C] type of a virus, an insect, etc

strain² /streɪn/ v 1 injure a muscle, etc by stretching it too much 2 [I,T] make the greatest possible effort to do sth: I ~ed my ears (= listened very hard) to hear what he was saying. 3 [T] force or push sth beyond a normal or acceptable limit 4 [T] pass food, etc through a sieve, cloth, etc to separate the solid part from the liquid ► **strained** adj forced and unnatural ► **strainer** n C of small kitchen utensil with a lot of small holes in it for straining tea, etc

strait /streɪt/ n [C] 1 (also **straits** [pl]) narrow stretch of water connecting two seas (**straits** [pl]) difficulty, esp because of lack of money: The firm is in dire ~s.

straitjacket /ˈstreɪtdʒækɪt/ n jacket with long sleeves tied round a violent person to prevent movement

strait-laced (also **straight-laced**) /ˌstreɪt ˈleɪst/ adj (disapprov) morally strict or serious

strand /strænd/ n 1 single piece of thread, wire, hair, etc 2 one of the different parts of an idea, plan, story, etc

stranded /ˈstrændɪd/ adj in a helpless position, unable to move, etc

strange /streɪndʒ/ adj 1 not familiar, unknown 2 unusual; odd: What ~ ideas you have! ► **strangely** adv ► **strangeness** n [U] ► **stranger** n 1 person you do not know 2 person in a place they have not been in before

strangle /ˈstræŋɡl/ v [T] kill sb by squeezing their throat ■ **'strangle-hold** n [sing] strong hold on sb/sth: They have a ~hold on the economy. ► **strangler** n

strap /stræp/ n strip of leather, plastic, etc used for fastening or support ● **strap** v (-pp-) [T] fasten, carry or hold sth in place with a strap ► **strapping** adj (of people) big and strong

strata plural of STRATUM

strategic /strəˈtiːdʒɪk/ adj 1 done as part of a plan meant to achieve a purpose or gain an advantage 2 connected with getting an advantage in a war ► **strategically** /-kli/ adv

strategy /ˈstrætədʒi/ n 1 [C] plan intended to achieve a particular purpose 2 [U] (skill in) planning sth, esp the movement of armies in war ► **strategist** n person skilled in strategy

stratosphere /ˈstrætəsfɪə(r)/ n [sing] layer of the atmosphere between about 10 and 50 km above the earth

stratum /ˈstrɑːtəm/ n (pl -ta /-tə/) 1 (geol) horizontal layer of rock, etc in the earth 2 (written) class in a society

straw /strɔː/ n 1 [U] dry, cut stems of wheat, barley, etc 2 [C] single stem or piece of straw 3 [C] thin tube of plastic, etc that you suck a drink through [IDM] **the last/final straw** last in a series of bad events that finally makes a situation intolerable

strawberry /ˈstrɔːbəri/ n (pl -ies) (plant with) small juicy red fruit with tiny seeds on its surface

stray /streɪ/ v [I] move away from the right path, etc ● **stray** adj 1 (of animals) lost from home: a ~ dog 2 separated from other things or people of the same kind ● **stray** n animal or person that has got lost or separated from others

streak /striːk/ n 1 long thin line that is a different colour from the rest 2 bad quality in sb's character: a ~ of cruelty 3 brief period: a ~ of good luck ● **streak** v 1 [T] mark sth with streaks 2 [I] move very fast ► **streaky** adj (-ier, -iest) marked with streaks

stream /striːm/ n 1 small narrow river 2 steady flow of people, liquid, things, etc: a ~ of abuse 3 (esp GB) group of pupils with the same level of ability ● **stream** v [I] 1 flow as a stream 2 move freely, esp in the wind or water: with her long hair ~ing ► **streamer** n long narrow ribbon of paper ■ **'streamline** v [T] 1 give sth a smooth even shape so that it moves easily through air and water **2** make a system, etc more efficient, esp in a way that saves money

street /striːt/ n road with houses and buildings on one or both sides [IDM] **streets ahead of sb/sth** (*infml*) much better or more advanced than sb/sth else (**right**) **up your street** (*infml*) in your area of interest, etc ■ '**streetcar** n (*US*) = TRAM

strength /streŋθ/ n **1** [U] quality or degree of being strong **2** [C] way in which sb/sth is strong, effective, etc: *Her intelligence is one of her ~s.* **3** [U] number of people available: *The army is below ~.* [IDM] **on the strength of sth** because sb has been influenced by sth: *buy it on the ~ of his advice*

strenuous /ˈstrenjuəs/ adj needing great effort ▶ **strenuously** adv

stress /stres/ n **1** [U,C] pressure or worry caused by the problems in sb's life **2** [U,C] pressure put on sth that can damage it or make it lose shape **3** [U] emphasis: *She lays great ~ on punctuality.* **4** [U,C] (*ling*) extra force used when speaking a particular word or syllable ● **stress** v [T] **1** emphasize a fact, an idea, etc **2** (*ling*) give extra force to a word or syllable when saying it

stretch /stretʃ/ v **1** [T] make sth wider, longer or looser by pulling it **2** [I] (be able to) be stretched **3** [I, T] put your arms or legs out straight and tighten your muscles **4** [I] extend over an area: *fields ~ing for miles* **5** [T] make use of all sb's skills, intelligence, etc [IDM] **stretch your legs** (*infml*) go for a short walk after sitting for some time [PV] **stretch (yourself) out** lie at full length ● **stretch** n **1** [C] area of land or water **2** [C] continuous period of time: *ten hours at a ~* **3** [C, U] act of stretching a part of your body **4** [U] ability to stretch, eg of a rope ▶ **stretchy** adj (*-ier, -iest*) that can be made longer or wider without breaking or tearing

stretcher /ˈstretʃə(r)/ n frame covered with canvas for carrying sb who is sick or injured

stricken /ˈstrɪkən/ adj ~(**by/with**) affected or overcome by sth bad: *~ with terror*

strict /strɪkt/ adj **1** that must be obeyed exactly: *a ~ diet* **2** demanding that rules, esp rules of behaviour, should be obeyed: *a ~ teacher* **3** exactly defined: *the ~ sense of a word* ▶ **strictly** adv ● **strictness** n [U]

stride /straɪd/ v (*pt* **strode** /strəʊd/) (not used in the perfect tenses) [I] walk with long steps: *We strode across the snowy fields.* ● **stride** n long step [IDM] **take sth in your**

stride accept and deal with sth difficult without letting it worry you too much

strident /ˈstraɪdnt/ adj (esp of a voice) loud and insistent: *~ protests*

strife /straɪf/ n [U] (*fml* or *lit*) state of conflict

strike¹ /straɪk/ v (*pt, pp* **struck** /strʌk/) **1** [T] hit sb/sth hard **2** [T] attack sb/sth, esp suddenly **3** [T] (of a thought or an idea) come into sb's mind suddenly: *An awful thought has just struck me.* **4** [T] give sb a certain impression: *She ~s me as a clever girl.* **5** [T] put sb suddenly into a particular state: *struck dumb* **6** [I] (of workers) refuse to work as a protest **7** [T] produce a flame by rubbing sth against a surface: *~ a match* **8** [I, T] show the time by making a ringing noise, etc: *The clock struck (four).* **9** [T] discover gold, etc by digging or drilling [IDM] **strike a bargain/deal** make an agreement with sb in which both sides have an advantage **strike a chord (with sb)** say or do sth that makes people feel sympathy or enthusiasm **strike it rich** become suddenly rich [PV] **strike sb/sth off (sth)** remove sb/sth's name from sth, eg a list **strike out 1** start being independent **2** (*US, infml*) fail or be unsuccessful **strike up sth (with sb)** begin a friendship, conversation, etc

strike² /straɪk/ n **1** act of stopping work for a period of time as a protest: *Firefighters are threatening to come out on ~.* **2** military attack **3** sudden discovery of sth valuable, esp oil

striking /ˈstraɪkɪŋ/ adj attracting attention, beautiful

string¹ /strɪŋ/ n **1** [C,U] (length of) fine cord for tying things, etc **2** [C] series of things threaded on a string: *a ~ of beads* **3** [C] series of things or people coming one after another: *a ~ of accidents* **4** (*computing*) [C] series of characters ie (letters, numbers, etc) **5** [C] stretched piece of wire on a musical instrument **6** (**the strings**) [pl] the players of string instruments in an orchestra [IDM] (**with**) **no strings (attached)** with no special conditions or restrictions ▶ **stringy** adj (*-ier, -iest*) like string

string² /strɪŋ/ v (*pt, pp* **strung** /strʌŋ/) [T] **1** tie or hang sth in place, esp as a decoration **2** put a series of small objects on string, etc **3** put a string or strings on a violin, tennis racket, etc [PV] **string along (with sb)** go somewhere with sb for a while **string sb along** (*infml*) allow sb to believe sth that is not true **string sth out** make sth last longer than expected or necessary ■ **,strung 'up** adj (*GB, infml*) (of a person) tense and nervous

stringent /'strɪndʒənt/ adj (of rules, etc) very strict ▸ **stringently** adv

strip /strɪp/ v (-pp-) **1** [I, T] take off clothes, coverings, parts, etc **2** [T] ~ (**down**) separate a machine, etc into parts to be cleaned or repaired **3** [T] ~of take sth from sb as a punishment: ~ sb of his liberty ● **strip** n **1** long narrow piece of material, land, etc ■ 'strip cartoon = COMIC STRIP (COMIC) ▸ **stripper** n person who performs a striptease ■ 'striptease n [C, U] entertainment in which a person takes their clothes off in front of an audience

stripe /straɪp/ n **1** long narrow band on a surface that is different in colour, material, etc **2** (often a V-shaped) badge worn on a uniform, showing rank ▸ **striped** (also **stripy**, **stripey**) adj having stripes

strive /straɪv/ v (pt **strove** /strəʊv/; pp **striven** /'strɪvn/) [I] (fml) try very hard to achieve sth: ~ to succeed

strode pt of STRIDE

stroke¹ /strəʊk/ n [C] **1** act of hitting a ball, eg in tennis, cricket **2** single movement of the arm when hitting sb/sth **3** any of a series of repeated movements in swimming or rowing **4** [usu sing] act of moving your hand gently over a surface **5** mark made by moving a pen or brush across a surface **6** ~(**of**) single successful action or event **7** sound made by a bell **8** sudden serious illness when a blood vessel in the brain bursts [IDM] **at a (single) stroke | at one stroke** with a single immediate action

stroke² /strəʊk/ v [T] move your hand gently over a surface, sb's hair, etc

stroll /strəʊl/ n slow relaxed walk ● **stroll** v [I] walk somewhere in a slow relaxed way ▸ **stroller** n **1** person enjoying a relaxed walk **2** (US) = PUSHCHAIR (PUSH¹)

strong /strɒŋ/ adj (~er /-ŋgə(r)/ ~est /-ŋgɪst/) **1** having great power **2** having a powerful effect on the mind or body: a ~ drug **3** able to resist attack or influence: a ~ will **4** not easily hurt, broken, changed, etc **5** having the stated number: an army 2000 ~ **6** having a lot of a flavour: ~ cheese **7** (of a drink) containing a lot of a substance: ~ coffee [IDM] **be strong on sth 1** be good at sth **2** have a lot of sth **going strong** (infml) continuing to be healthy, active or successful ■ 'stronghold n **1** place where a cause has strong support **2** castle ▸ **strongly** adv

strove pt of STRIVE

struck pt, pp of STRIKE¹

structural /'strʌktʃərəl/ adj of the way sth is built or organized ▸ **structurally** adv

structure /'strʌktʃə(r)/ n **1** [C, U] way in which the parts of sth are put together, etc **2** [C] thing built of parts, esp a building ● **structure** v [T] arrange or organize sth

struggle /'strʌgl/ v [I] **1** try hard to do sth or move somewhere when it is difficult: ~ to earn a living **2** fight against sb/sth **3** fight sb or try to get away from them: How did she manage to ~ free? ● **struggle** n **1** [C] hard fight **2** [sing] something that is difficult for you to do or achieve

strum /strʌm/ v [I, T] ~(**on**) play a guitar, etc by moving your fingers across the strings

strung pt, pp of STRING²

strut /strʌt/ v (-tt-) [I] walk in a proud, angry, etc way ● **strut** n piece of wood or metal to strengthen a framework

stub /stʌb/ n **1** short remaining end of a pencil, cigarette, etc **2** piece of a cheque left in the book ● **stub** v (-bb-) [T] accidentally hit your toe against sth [PV] **stub sth out** put out a cigarette, etc by pressing it against sth hard

stubble /'stʌbl/ n [U] **1** lower stems of corn, etc, left in the ground after harvest **2** short growth of beard ▸ **stubbly** /-bli/ adj

stubborn /'stʌbən/ adj **1** having a strong will; too determined **2** difficult to move, remove, cure, etc: a ~ cough ▸ **stubbornly** adv ▸ **stubbornness** n [U]

stubby /'stʌbi/ adj (-ier, -iest) short and thick

stuck¹ pt, pp of STICK²

stuck² /stʌk/ adj **1** unable to move or continue **2** ~**with** (infml) unable to get rid of sb/sth that you do not want: ~ with sb all day [IDM] **get stuck in (to sth)** (infml) begin to do sth enthusiastically

stud /stʌd/ n **1** [C] small piece of jewellery pushed through a hole in your ear, nose, etc **2** [C] small round piece of metal attached to sth, esp for decoration **3** [C, usu pl] one of several metal or plastic objects on the sole of a football boot, etc **4** [C, U] animal, esp a horse, kept for breeding; place where such animals are kept **5** [C] (infml) man regarded as a good sexual partner ▸ **studded** adj decorated with small raised pieces of metal

student /'stju:dnt/ n **1** (GB) person who is studying at a college or university **2** (US) person studying at secondary school **3** any person interested in a particular subject

studio /'stju:diəʊ/ n (pl ~ s) **1** workroom of a painter, photographer, etc

2 room(s) where films, or radio or television programmes are made

studious /'stju:dias/ *adj* spending a lot of time studying or reading ▸ **studiously** *adv*

study¹ /'stʌdi/ *n* (*pl* **-ies**) **1** [U] (*also* **studies** [pl]) process of learning sth **2** [C] piece of research that examines a subject in detail: *a ~ of the country's economy* **3** [C] room used for reading, writing, etc **4** [C] drawing or painting of sth, esp one done for practice **5** [C] piece of music played as an exercise

study² /'stʌdi/ *v* (*pt, pp* **ied**) **1** [I, T] give time and attention to learning sth **2** [T] watch or look at sb/sth carefully to find out sth

stuff¹ /stʌf/ *n* [U] (*infml*) **1** used to refer to a substance, material, group of objects, etc when you do not know the name: *What's this sticky ~ on the carpet?* ◇ *Where's all my ~ (= possessions)?* **2** used to refer generally to things people do, say, think, etc: *I've got loads of ~ to do today.* [IDM] **do your stuff** (*infml*) show what you can do

stuff² /stʌf/ *v* [T] **1** fill sth tightly with sth **2** fill a vegetable, chicken, etc with another type of food **3** (*infml*) fill yourself/sb with food **4** fill the body of a dead animal with material to give it the original shape [IDM] **get stuffed** (*GB, spoken*) used to tell sb rudely to go away or that you do not want sth ▸ **stuffing** *n* [U] **1** mixture of food used to stuff sth **2** soft material used to fill cushions, toys, etc

stuffy /'stʌfi/ *adj* (**-ier, -iest**) **1** (of a room) not having enough fresh air **2** (*infml*) formal and dull ▸ **stuffiness** *n* [U]

stumble /'stʌmbl/ *v* [I] **1** hit your foot against sth and almost fall **2** make a mistake or mistakes as you speak [PV] **stumble across/on/upon sth** discover sth/sb unexpectedly ■ **'stumbling block** *n* something that prevents progress

stump /stʌmp/ *n* **1** part of a tree left in the ground after the rest has been cut down, etc **2** something left after the main part has been cut or broken off **3** (in cricket) one of the three upright pieces of wood at which the ball is aimed ● **stump** *v* **1** [T] (*infml*) ask sb a question that is too difficult for them to answer **2** [I] walk in a noisy heavy way ▸ **stumpy** *adj* (**-ier, -iest**) short and thick

stun /stʌn/ *v* (**-nn-**) [T] **1** make sb unconscious by hitting them on the head **2** shock sb so much that they cannot think or speak **3** impress sb very much ▸ **stunning** *adj* very attractive

stung *pt, pp* of STING

stunk *pp* of STINK

stunt /stʌnt/ *n* **1** dangerous thing done as entertainment, esp as part of a film **2** thing done to attract attention ● **stunt** *v* [T] stop or slow the growth or development of sth ■ **'stuntman | 'stuntwoman** *n* person employed to do dangerous scenes in place of an actor in a film, etc

stupendous /stju:'pendəs/ *adj* amazingly large, good, etc ▸ **stupendously** *adv*

stupid /'stju:pɪd/ *adj* showing a lack of intelligence or good sense ▸ **stupidity** /-'pɪdəti/ *n* [C, U] ▸ **stupidly** *adv*

stupor /'stju:pə(r)/ *n* [C, U] condition of being almost unconscious from shock, drink, etc

sturdy /'stɜːdi/ *adj* (**-ier, -iest**) strong and solid ▸ **sturdily** /-ɪli/ *adv*

stutter /'stʌtə(r)/ *v* [I, T], *n* = STAMMER

sty /staɪ/ *n* **1** (*pl* **sties**) = PIGSTY (PIG) **2** (*also* **stye**) (*pl* **sties** or **styes**) inflamed swelling of the eyelid

style /staɪl/ *n* [C, U] particular way in which sth is done **2** [C] design of sth, esp clothes **3** [U] quality of being fashionable and elegant **4** [C, U] features of a book, painting, building, etc that make it typical of an author, period, etc: *a fine example of Gothic ~* [IDM] **be more sb's style** be what sb prefers or what suits sb: *Big cars are more my ~.* ● **style** *v* [T] design, make or shape sth in a particular way ▸ **stylish** *adj* (*approv*) fashionable ▸ **stylist** *n* person who styles people's hair ▸ **stylistic** /-'lɪstɪk/ *adj* of the style an artist uses in a particular piece of art, writing or music ▸ **stylized** (*also* **-ised**) *adj* drawn, written, etc in a way that is not natural or realistic

stylus /'staɪləs/ *n* **1** needle used for reproducing sound from records **2** (*computing*) pointing device shaped like a pen for use with palmtops, etc

suave /swɑːv/ *adj* confident, elegant and polite, sometimes in a way that seems insincere

sub /sʌb/ *n* (*infml*) **1** short for SUBMARINE **2** substitute, esp in cricket or football

subconscious /,sʌb'kɒnʃəs/ *adj* of feelings that influence your behaviour, even though you are not aware of them ● **subconscious** *n* [sing] (**the/your ~**) part of your mind containing feelings you are not aware of ▸ **subconsciously** *adv*

subcontinent /,sʌb'kɒntɪnənt/ *n* large land mass forming part of a continent

subdivide /,sʌbdɪ'vaɪd/ *v* [I, T] divide sth again into smaller parts ▸ **subdivision** /-'dɪvɪʒn; ,sʌbdɪ'vɪʒn/ *n* [C, U]

subdue /səb'dju:/ *v* [T] **1** bring sb/sth under control, esp by using force

2 calm or control your feelings

subject¹ /'sʌbdʒɪkt; 'dʒekt/ n **1** thing or person being discussed, described or dealt with: *the ~ of the book* **2** area of knowledge studied in a school, etc **3** *(gram)* noun or phrase which comes before a verb and which performs the action of that verb or is described by it, eg *the book* in *The book is green.* **4** person who has the right to belong to a country

subject² /səb'dʒekt/ v [T] *(fml)* bring a nation or group under your control, esp by using force [PV] **subject sb/sth to sth** *(written)* make sb/sth experience sth unpleasant: *~ sb to criticism* ▶ **subjection** /-ʃn/ n [U]

subject³ /'sʌbdʒɪkt; 'dʒekt/ *~to* **1** likely to be affected by sth, esp sth bad: *~ to frequent colds* **2** depending on sth to be completed or agreed: *~ to confirmation* **3** under the authority of sth/sb: *~ to the law*

subjective /səb'dʒektɪv/ *adj* **1** influenced by personal feelings **2** *(phil)* having no existence outside the mind; imaginary ▶ **subjectively** *adv* ▶ **subjectivity** /-'tɪvəti/ n [U]

sublet /ˌsʌb'let/ v (**-tt-**, *pt, pp* **sublet**) [I, T] (of a tenant) rent a house, flat, etc to sb else

sublime /sə'blaɪm/ *adj* of the greatest and highest kind ▶ **sublimely** *adv*

submarine /ˌsʌbmə'riːn/ n ship that can travel under water

submerge /səb'mɜːdʒ/ v [I, T] **1** (cause sth to) go under water **2** [T] *(written)* hide ideas, feelings, etc completely ▶ **submersion** /səb-'mɜːʃn/ n [U]

submission /səb'mɪʃn/ n **1** [U] acceptance of sb's power over you **2** [U,C] (act of presenting sb in authority with) a document, proposal, etc for consideration

submissive /səb'mɪsɪv/ *adj* always willing to obey others ▶ **submissively** *adv* ▶ **submissiveness** n [U]

submit /səb'mɪt/ v (**-tt-**) *~(to) to sth* **1** [T] give a document, proposal, etc to sb in authority so they can study or consider it **2** [I] accept the power of sb/sth over you

subordinate /sə'bɔːdɪnət/ *adj* **1** lower in rank **2** of less importance ● **subordinate** n person who is lower in rank or position than sb else ● **subordinate** /sə'bɔːdɪneɪt/ v [T] *~(to)* treat sb/sth as less important than sb else

subscribe /səb'skraɪb/ v *~(to) to sth* **1** pay money once a year to receive regular copies of a newspaper, etc **2** agree to pay a sum of money regularly to be a member of an organization, charity, etc [PV] **subscribe to sth** *(fml)* agree with an opinion, theory, etc ▶ **subscriber** n ▶ **subscription** /səb'skrɪpʃn/ n [C,U] money paid to a charity, to receive a magazine regularly, to belong to a club, etc

subsequent /'sʌbsɪkwənt/ *adj* *~ (to)* following ▶ **subsequently** *adv* afterwards

subservient /səb'sɜːviənt/ *adj* *(disapprov)* too willing to obey others ▶ **subservience** /-əns/ n [U]

subside /səb'saɪd/ v [I] **1** (of water, etc) return to the normal level **2** (of land or a building) sink lower **3** become less strong, active, loud, etc ▶ **subsidence** /-ns; 'sʌbsɪdns/ n [C,U] (instance of) subsiding(2)

subsidiary /səb'sɪdiəri/ *adj* connected with sth but less important than it: *a ~ role* ● **subsidiary** n (pl **-ies**) company controlled by another larger company

subsidy /'sʌbsədi/ n (pl **-ies**) money granted, esp by a government, to help an industry, a charity, etc ▶ **subsidize** (*also* **-ise**) /'sʌbsɪdaɪz/ v [T] give a subsidy to sb or an organization to help pay for sth

subsist /səb'sɪst/ v [I] manage to stay alive, esp with little food and money ▶ **subsistence** n [U] state of having just enough money to stay alive

substance /'sʌbstəns/ n **1** [C,U] type of solid, liquid or gas that has particular qualities **2** [U] *(written)* quality of being based on facts or the truth: *a speech with little ~* **3** [U] most important or main part of sth

substantial /səb'stænʃl/ *adj* **1** large: *a ~ amount* **2** solidly built ▶ **substantially** *adv* very much **2** mainly

substantiate /səb'stænʃieɪt/ v [T] prove a claim, etc by giving facts

substitute /'sʌbstɪtjuːt/ n person or thing taking the place of another ● **substitute** v [I, T] *~(for)* serve or use sb/sth instead of sb/sth else ▶ **substitution** /ˌsʌbstɪ'tjuːʃn/ n [U,C]

subsume /səb'sjuːm/ v [T] *(fml)* include sth in a group and not consider it separately

subterfuge /'sʌbtəfjuːdʒ/ n [U,C] *(fml)* secret, usu dishonest, way of behaving or doing sth

subterranean /ˌsʌbtə'reɪniən/ *adj* *(fml)* under the ground

subtitle /'sʌbtaɪtl/ n [C] **1** [usu pl] words printed on a film, translating the dialogue, giving the dialogue for deaf viewers, etc **2** secondary title of a book, etc

subtle /'sʌtl/ *adj* **1** not very noticeable or obvious: *a ~ difference* **2** clever: *a ~ plan* **3** good at noticing and understanding things ▶ **subtlety** n [U,C] (pl **-ies**) ▶ **subtly** /'sʌtli/ *adv*

subtract /səb'trækt/ v [T] *~(from)* take a number or amount away from another number or amount ▶ **subtraction** /-ʃn/ n [U,C]

suburb /'sʌbɜːb/ n residential area of a town away from the centre ▶ **suburban** /sə'bɜːbən/ adj ▶ **suburbia** /sə'bɜːbiə/ n [U] (life lived by people in) suburbs

subvert /səb'vɜːt/ v [T] (fml) try to destroy the authority of a political, religious, etc system ▶ **subversion** /-ʃn/ n [U] ▶ **subversive** adj trying to subvert sth

subway /'sʌbweɪ/ n 1 pedestrian tunnel beneath a road, etc 2 (US) underground railway system in a city

succeed /sək'siːd/ v 1 [I] ~(in) achieve what you are trying to achieve or do well in your job, etc: ~ in winning the race 2 [T] come next after sb/sth and take their/its place or position: ~ sb as president 3 [I] ~ (to) gain the right to sth when sb dies

success /sək'ses/ n 1 [U] achievement of your aims, fame, wealth, etc 2 [C] person or thing that succeeds ▶ **successful** adj ▶ **successfully** adv

succession /sək'seʃn/ n 1 [C, usu sing] series of people or things that follow each other in time or order: They had three children in quick ~. 2 [U] regular pattern of one thing happening after another ▶ **successive** adj coming one after the other ▶ **successor** n person or thing that follows another

succinct /sək'sɪŋkt/ adj expressed briefly and clearly ▶ **succinctly** adv ▶ **succinctness** n

succulent /'sʌkjələnt/ adj 1 (of fruit and meat) juicy and delicious 2 (of plants) thick and fleshy

succumb /sə'kʌm/ v [I] ~(to) (fml) stop resisting temptation, illness, etc

such /sʌtʃ/ det, pron 1 of the type already mentioned: ~ countries as France ◇ He said he didn't have time or made some ~ excuse. 2 of the type that you are just going to mention: There is no ~ thing as a free lunch. 3 used to emphasize the degree of sth: Don't be in ~ a hurry. [IDM] **as such** as the word is usually understood **such as** for example ■ **'such-and-such** pron, det used for referring to sb/sth without saying exactly what it is ■ **'suchlike** pron, det (things) of the same kind

suck /sʌk/ v 1 [T] take liquid, air, etc into your mouth using the lips 2 [T] hold a sweet, etc in the mouth and lick it with your tongue 3 [T] (of a pump, etc) take liquid, air, etc out of sth 4 [T] pull sb/sth with great force in one direction: The current ~ed her under the water. ● **suck** n [usu sing] act of sucking ▶ **sucker** n 1 (infml) person easily tricked or persuaded

to do sth 2 ~**for** (infml) person who likes sb/sth very much: a ~er for old films 3 organ on the body of some animals that enables them to stick to a surface 4 rubber disc that sticks to a surface when you press against it

suckle /'sʌkl/ v [T] feed a baby or young animal with milk from the breast

suction /'sʌkʃn/ n [U] process of causing a vacuum, esp so that two surfaces stick together

sudden /'sʌdn/ adj happening unexpectedly and quickly ▶ **suddenly** adv ▶ **suddenness** n [U]

suds /sʌdz/ n [pl] mass of bubbles that forms on soapy water

sue /suː; sjuː/ v [I, T] make a legal claim against sb in a court of law

suede /sweɪd/ n [U] soft leather with one rough side

suet /'suːɪt; 'sjuːɪt/ n [U] hard animal fat used in cooking

suffer /'sʌfə(r)/ v 1 [I] ~(from) be badly affected by a disease, pain, sadness, etc 2 [T] experience sth unpleasant, eg injury, defeat or loss 3 [I] become worse: Her work ~ed when she was ill. [IDM] **not suffer fools gladly** have little patience with people you think are stupid ▶ **suffering** n [U] (also **sufferings**) [pl] physical or mental pain

suffice /sə'faɪs/ v [I] (fml) be enough for sb/sth

sufficient /sə'fɪʃnt/ adj enough ▶ **sufficiency** /-nsi/ n [sing] (fml) sufficient quantity ▶ **sufficiently** adv

suffix /'sʌfɪks/ n (gram) letter or group of letters added to the end of a word to change its meaning

suffocate /'sʌfəkeɪt/ v 1 [I, T] (cause sb to) die from not being able to breathe air 2 (be suffocating) [I] be very hot with very little fresh air: Open a window. It's suffocating in here! ▶ **suffocation** /ˌsʌfə'keɪʃn/ n [U]

sugar /'ʃʊɡə(r)/ n [U] sweet substance obtained from various plants ● **sugar** v [T] add sugar to sth ■ **'sugar cane** n [U] tall tropical grass from which sugar is made ▶ **sugary** adj 1 containing sugar; sweet 2 (disapprov) too sentimental

suggest /sə'dʒest/ v [T] 1 put forward an idea or plan for consideration 2 put an idea into sb's mind ▶ **suggestion** /-tʃən/ n 1 [C] idea, plan, etc that you mention for sb to think about 2 [U, C, usu sing] reason to think that sth, esp sth bad, is true ▶ **suggestive** adj making sb think about sth, esp about sex ▶ **suggestively** adv

suicide /'suːɪsaɪd; 'sjuː-/ n 1 [C, U] act of killing yourself deliberately: commit ~ 2 [U, C, usu sing] action likely to ruin your career, position in society, etc

3 [C] (*fml*) person who commits suicide ► **suicidal** /-'saidl/ *adj* **1** wanting to kill yourself **2** likely to lead to death or disaster

suit¹ /su:t; sju:t/ *n* **1** jacket and trousers (or skirt) of the same material **2** set of clothing worn for a particular activity **3** any of the four sets of playing cards (spades, hearts, diamonds, clubs) ► **suitcase** *n* case for carrying clothes, etc when travelling

suit² /su:t; sju:t/ *v* **1** [I,T] be convenient or useful for sb/sth **2** [T] (esp of clothes, colours, etc) make you look attractive: *Blue ~s you*. [IDM] **suit yourself** (*infml*) do as you want ► **suitable** /'su:təbl; 'sju:-/ *adj* right or appropriate for a purpose ► **suitably** *adv* ► **suitability** /ˌsu:tə-'bɪləti/ *n* [U] ► **suited** *adj* right or appropriate for sth/sth

suite /swi:t/ *n* **1** set of matching pieces of furniture **2** set of rooms, eg in a hotel **3** piece of music in three or more parts

sulk /sʌlk/ *v* [I] (*disapprov*) refuse to speak because you are annoyed with sb ► **sulky** *adj* (-ier, -iest)

sullen /'sʌlən/ *adj* (*disapprov*) silent and bad-tempered ► **sullenly** *adv* ► **sullenness** *n* [U]

sulphur (*US* **sulfur**) /'sʌlfə(r)/ *n* (*symb* **S**) yellow element that burns with a bright flame ■ **sulphuric acid** (*US* **sulfuric ~**) /ˌsʌlˌfjʊərɪk 'æsɪd/ *n* [U] (*chem*) (*symb* H₂SO₄) strong colourless acid

sultan /'sʌltən/ *n* ruler of certain Muslim countries

sultana /sʌl'tɑːnə/ *n* small dried grape without seeds, used in cakes, etc

sultry /'sʌltri/ *adj* (-ier, -iest) **1** (of the weather) hot and uncomfortable **2** (*written*) (of a woman) sexually attractive

sum /sʌm/ *n* **1** amount of money **2** total obtained by adding together two or more numbers or amounts **3** simple problem that involves calculating numbers ● **sum** *v* (-mm-) [PV] **sum** (**sth**) **up** give a summary of sth **sum sb/sth up** form or express an opinion of sb/sth

summary /'sʌməri/ *n* (*pl* -ies) short statement giving only the main points of sth ● **summary** *adj* **1** (*fml*) giving the main points only; brief **2** done without delay: *a ~ execution* ► **summarize** (*also* -ise) /-raiz/ *v* [T] make a summary of sth

summer /'sʌmə(r)/ *n* [C,U] warmest season of the year ► **summery** *adj* like or suitable for summer

summit /'sʌmɪt/ *n* **1** highest point of sth, esp a mountain **2** meeting of two or more heads of government

summon /'sʌmən/ *v* [T] **1** (*fml*) order sb to appear in a court of law **2** (*fml*) order sb to come to you **3** ~ (**up**) make an effort to find a quality within yourself: ~ (*up*) *all your courage*

summons /'sʌmənz/ *n* (*pl* ~es /-zɪz/) order to appear in a court of law ● **summons** *v* [T] order sb to appear in a court of law

sun /sʌn/ *n* **1** (**the sun, the Sun**) [sing] star round which the earth moves and which gives it heat and light **2** (usu **the sun**) [sing, U] light and heat from the sun **3** [C] any star around which planets move [IDM] **under the sun** used to emphasize that you are talking about a large number of things ● **sun** *v* (-nn-) [T] ~ **yourself** lie in the sun ■ **sunbathe** *v* [I] sit or lie in the sun ■ **sunbeam** *n* ray of sunlight ■ **sunburn** *n* [U] painful red skin caused by too much time spent in the sun ■ **sunburnt** *adj* suffering from sunburn ■ **sunglasses** *n* [pl] glasses with dark lenses to protect the eyes from the sun ■ **sunlight** *n* [U] light from the sun ► **sunny** *adj* (-ier, -iest) **1** bright with sunlight **2** cheerful ■ **sunrise** *n* [U] dawn ■ **sunshade** *n* object like an umbrella to keep off the sun ■ **sunshine** *n* [U] light and heat of the sun ■ **sunstroke** *n* [U] illness caused by spending too much time in the sun ■ **suntan** *n* browning of the skin caused by exposure to sunlight

Sunday /'sʌndeɪ; -di/ *n* [U,C] the first day of the week, next after Saturday (See examples of use at *Monday*.)

sundry /'sʌndri/ *adj* (*fml*) various ► **sundries** *n* [pl] (*written*) various small items

sung *pp* of **SING**

sunk *pt, pp* of **SINK**

sunken /'sʌŋkən/ *adj* **1** that has fallen to the bottom of the sea **2** (of eyes or cheeks) hollow **3** lower than the surrounding area

super /'su:pə(r); 'sju:-/ *adj* (*infml*) excellent

superb /su:'pɜːb; sju:-/ *adj* excellent ► **superbly** *adv*

supercomputer /'su:pəkəm-pju:tə(r); 'sju:-/ *n* powerful computer with a large amount of memory and a very fast central processing unit

superficial /ˌsu:pə'fɪʃl; ˌsju:-/ *adj* **1** of or on the surface only: not thorough or deep: *a ~ knowledge* ► **superficiality** /ˌsu:pəˌfɪʃi'æləti/ *n* [U] ► **superficially** *adv*

superfluous /su:'pɜːfluəs; sju:-/ *adj* more than you need or want ► **superfluously** *adv*

superhighway /ˌsu:pəhaɪweɪ; 'sju:-/ *n* way of quickly sending information such as video, sound and pictures through a computer network, esp the Internet: *the information* ~

superhuman /,su:pə'hju:mən; ,sju:-/ *adj* having much greater power, knowledge, etc than is normal

superimpose /,su:pərɪm'pəʊz; ,sju:-/ *v* [T] ~(on) put one image on top of another

superintend /,su:pərɪn'tend; ,sju:-/ *v* [I, T] (*fml*) be in charge of sth and make sure everything is working, being done, etc as it should be ● **superintendent** *n* **1** person who superintends sth/sb **2** senior police officer

superior /su:'pɪərɪə(r); sju:-/ *adj* **1** higher in rank, importance, quality, etc **2** (*disapprov*) showing that you think you are better than others ● **superior** *n* person of higher rank, status or position ► **superiority** /su:,pɪərɪ'ɒrətɪ; n [U]

superlative /su:'pɜːlətɪv; sju:-/ *adj* **1** excellent **2** (*gram*) of adjectives or adverbs, expressing the highest degree, eg *best, worst, most* ● **superlative** *n* superlative form of an adjective or adverb

supermarket /'su:pəmɑːkɪt; 'sju:-/ *n* large shop selling food, household goods, etc

supernatural /,su:pə'nætʃrəl; ,sju:-/ *adj* seeming magical, etc because it cannot be explained by the laws of science

superpower /'su:pəpaʊə(r); 'sju:-/ *n* one of the most powerful nations in the world

supersede /,su:pə'si:d/ *v* [T] take the place of sth/sb

supersonic /,su:pə'sɒnɪk; ,sju:-/ *adj* faster than the speed of sound

superstar /'su:pəstɑː(r)/ *n* very famous performer

superstition /,su:pə'stɪʃn; ,sju:-/ *n* [U,C] (idea, practice, etc based on) the belief that particular events bring good or bad luck ► **superstitious** *adj*

supervise /'su:pəvaɪz; 'sju:-/ *v* [I, T] be in charge of sb/sth and make sure everything is done correctly ► **supervision** /,su:pə'vɪʒn/ *n* [U] ► **supervisor** *n* person who supervises sb/sth

supper /'sʌpə(r)/ *n* [C, U] last meal of the day

supple /'sʌpl/ *adj* easily bent; not stiff ► **suppleness** *n* [U]

supplement /'sʌplɪmənt/ *n* **1** thing added to sth else to improve or complete it **2** additional section of a book, newspaper, etc ● **supplement** /'sʌplɪment/ *v* [T] ~(with) add sth to sth else ► **supplementary** /-'mentrɪ/ (*US* **supplemental** /-'mentl/) *adj* additional

supply /sə'plaɪ/ *v* (*pt, pp* **-ied**) [T] provide sb/sth with sth that they need or want, esp in large quantities: ~ *gas to a house* ◊ ~ *sb with food* ● **supply** *n* (*pl* **-ies**) **1** [C] amount of sth that is provided or available to use **2** [pl] things such as food, medicines, fuel, etc needed by a group of people, eg an army: *food supplies* **3** [U] act of supplying sth ► **supplier** *n* person or company that supplies goods, etc

support /sə'pɔːt/ *v* [T] **1** help or encourage sb/sth by showing that you agree with them/it, by giving money, etc: ~ *a political party* **2** provide sb with what is necessary to live, esp money: ~ *a family* **3** hold sth/sb in position; prevent sth/sb from falling **4** help to show that sth is true **5** (*GB*) like a particular sports team, watch their games, etc ● **support** *n* **1** [U] encouragement and help you give to sb/sth **2** [U] sympathy and help that you give to sb in a difficult situation **3** [C] thing that supports sth ► **supporter** *n* person who gives encouragement ► **supportive** *adj* giving encouragement, help, etc

suppose /sə'pəʊz/ *v* [T] **1** think or believe that sth is true or possible: *There's no reason to* ~ *she's lying.* **2** pretend sth is true; imagine what would happen if sth were true: *Let us* ~*, for example, that you have lost your passport.* [IDM] **be supposed to do/be sth** be expected or required to do/be sth according to a rule, an arrangement, etc: *I'm* ~*d to make coffee for the visitors.* **not be supposed to do sth** not be allowed to do sth ► **supposedly** /-ɪdlɪ/ *adv* according to what is generally thought or believed ► **supposing** *conj* used to ask sb to imagine that sth is true

supposition /,sʌpə'zɪʃn/ *n* **1** [C] idea that you think is true but cannot prove **2** [U] act of believing or claiming sth to be true

suppress /sə'pres/ *v* [T] **1** put an end to sth, often by force: ~ *a revolt* **2** prevent sth from being known: ~ *the truth* ► **suppression** /-'ʃn/ *n* [U]

supreme /su:'pri:m; sju:-/ *adj* **1** highest in rank or position **2** greatest in degree ► **supremacy** /su:'preməsɪ; sju:-/ *n* [U] ► **supremely** *adv*

surcharge /'sɜːtʃɑːdʒ/ *n* payment additional to the usual charge

sure /ʃɔː(r)/ *adj* **1** confident that you know sth or that you are right: *Are you* ~ *you don't mind?* **2** ~ *of* certain that you will receive sth or that sth will happen **3** ~ *to* certain to do sth or to happen: *He's* ~ *to be late.* **4** reliable: *a* ~ *cure for colds* [IDM] **be sure to do sth** used to tell sb to do sth **make sure (of sth/that …)** **1** do sth in order to be certain that sth else happens

2 check that sth is true or has been done ● **sure** adv (infml, esp US) **1** used to say 'yes' to sb **2** used to emphasize what you are saying: It ~ is cold! [IDM] **sure enough** as was expected: I said he would be late and ~ enough, he was. ▶ **surely** adv **1** used for expressing hope, certainty, etc: S-ly not! **2** (fml) certainly

surety /'ʃʊərəti; 'ʃɔːr-/ n (pl -ies) [C, U] (law) **1** money given as a promise that you will pay a debt, appear in court, etc **2** person responsible for the conduct or debt(s) of another

surf /sɜːf/ n [U] large waves in the sea, and the white foam that they produce as they fall on the shore ● **surf** v [I, T] take part in the sport of riding on waves on a surfboard **2** [T] ~ **the net/Internet** use the Internet ■ **'surfboard** n long narrow board used for surfing ▶ **surfing** n [U] **1** sport of riding on top of the waves using a board **2** activity of looking at different things on the Internet

surface /'sɜːfɪs/ n **1** [C] outside or top layer of sth **2** [C, usu sing] top layer of an area of water **3** [sing] outward appearance of sb/sth ● **surface** v **1** [I] come up to the surface of water **2** [I] suddenly appear or become obvious **3** [I] (infml) wake up or get up **4** [T] put a surface on a path, road, etc ■ **'surface mail** n [U] letters, etc sent by land or sea, not by air

surfeit /'sɜːfɪt/ n [usu sing] ~ (of) (fml) too much of sth

surge /sɜːdʒ/ v **1** [I] move forward or upward like waves **2** fill sb with a strong feeling ● **surge** n **1** sudden increase **2** sudden forward or upward movement

surgeon /'sɜːdʒən/ n doctor who performs surgical operations

surgery /'sɜːdʒəri/ n (pl -ies) **1** [U] medical treatment of injuries and diseases by cutting open the body **2** [C] place where a doctor, dentist, etc sees their patients

surgical /'sɜːdʒɪkl/ adj of, by or for surgery ▶ **surgically** /-kli/ adv

surly /'sɜːli/ adj (-ier, -iest) bad-tempered and rude ▶ **surliness** n [U]

surmount /sə'maʊnt/ v [T] (fml) **1** deal successfully with a difficulty, etc **2** (usu passive) be placed on top of sth: a church ~ed with a tower

surname /'sɜːneɪm/ n name shared by all the members of a family

surpass /sə'pɑːs/ v [T] (fml) do or be better than sb/sth

surplus /'sɜːpləs/ n amount of money, etc beyond what is needed

surprise /sə'praɪz/ n [U,C] (usu pleasant feeling caused by) sth sudden or unexpected [IDM] **take sb by surprise** surprise sb by happening unexpectedly ● **surprise** v [T] **1** cause sb to feel surprised **2** attack, discover, etc sb suddenly and unexpectedly: ~ a burglar ▶ **surprised** adj feeling or showing surprise ▶ **surprising** adj ▶ **surprisingly** adv

surrender /sə'rendə(r)/ v **1** [I, T] ~ (**yourself**) (**to**) stop fighting against an enemy, etc and allow yourself to be caught, etc **2** [T] give up sth/sb when you are forced to [PV] **surrender (yourself) to sth** (fml) allow a feeling, habit, etc to control your actions ▶ **surrender** n [U, sing] act of surrendering

surround /sə'raʊnd/ v [T] be or move all around sb/sth ● **surround** n (usu decorative) edge or border ▶ **surrounding** adj that is near or around sth ▶ **surroundings** n [pl] everything around sb/sth

surveillance /sɜː'veɪləns/ n [U] close watch kept on sb suspected of doing wrong, etc: under ~

survey /sə'veɪ/ v [T] **1** look at or study the whole of sth **2** measure and make a map of an area of land, etc **3** (GB) examine a building to make sure it is in good condition ● **survey** /'sɜːveɪ/ n **1** investigation of the opinions, behaviour, etc of a group of people **2** act of examining and measuring an area of land to make a map of it **3** (GB) examination of the condition of a building **4** general view or study of sth ▶ **surveyor** /sə'veɪə(r)/ n person whose job is to examine buildings and record the details of areas of land

survival /sə'vaɪvl/ n **1** [U] state of continuing to live or exist, despite danger **2** [C] thing that has survived from an earlier time

survive /sə'vaɪv/ v [I, T] continue to live or exist (longer than sb/sth): ~ an accident ◇ She ~d her husband. ▶ **survivor** n person who continues to live, despite almost being killed

susceptible /sə'septəbl/ adj **1** ~ **to** likely to be affected by sb/sth: ~ to cold **2** easily influenced ▶ **susceptibility** /sə,septə'bɪləti/ n [U]

suspect /sə'spekt/ v [T] **1** think that sth is possible: We ~ that he's dead. **2** feel doubt about sb/sth: ~ the truth of her statement **3** ~ (**of**) feel that sb is guilty of sth: ~ sb of lying ● **suspect** /'sʌspekt/ n person suspected of doing wrong, etc ● **suspect** /'sʌspekt/ adj not to be relied on or trusted

suspend /sə'spend/ v [T] **1** ~ (**from**) hang sth from sth else: ~ a lamp from the ceiling **2** delay sth: ~ judgement **3** ~ (**from**) officially prevent sb from doing their job, going to school, etc for a time: They ~ed the two boys from school.

suspenders /sə'spendəz/ n [pl] **1** (GB) short elastic straps for holding up stockings or socks **2** (US) = BRACES (BRACE(3))

suspense /sə'spens/ n [U] uncertainty or worry about what may happen

suspension /sə'spenʃn/ n [U,C] **1** act of suspending sb from their job, etc or of delaying sth **2** springs, etc that support a car so the driver cannot feel bumps in the road ■ **su'spension bridge** n bridge hanging on steel cables attached to towers

suspicion /sə'spɪʃn/ n [U,C] feeling that sth is wrong, sb has done wrong, etc: *arrested on ~ of murder* **2** feeling that sth is true, though you have no proof **3** [sing] small amount of sth: *a ~ of sadness* ▸ **suspicious** adj having or causing suspicion ▸ **suspiciously** adv

sustain /sə'steɪn/ v [T] **1** keep sb/sth alive or in existence **2** (fml) suffer: *~ an injury* **3** (fml) support a weight

sustenance /'sʌstənəns/ n [U] (fml) (nourishing quality of) food or drink

SW abbr = SHORT WAVE (SHORT)

swab /swɒb/ n piece of cotton wool, etc used for cleaning wounds, taking a sample for testing, etc ● **swab** v (-bb-) [T] clean a wound, etc with a swab

swagger /'swægə(r)/ v [I] (disapprov) walk or behave in a proud and confident way ● **swagger** n [sing] (disapprov) way of walking that seems too confident

swallow /'swɒləʊ/ v **1** [I,T] take food, etc to go down your throat **2** [T] ~(up) use up sth completely: *earnings ~ed up by bills* **3** [T] accept that sth is true; believe sth: *I'm not ~ing that story!* **4** [T] hide your feelings **5** [T] accept an insult, etc without complaining ● **swallow** n **1** small bird with a forked tail **2** act of swallowing or amount swallowed

swam pt of SWIM

swamp /swɒmp/ n [C,U] (area of) soft wet land ● **swamp** v [T] **1** make sb have more of sth than they can deal with: *~ed with requests* **2** fill or cover sth with water ▸ **swampy** adj (-ier, -iest) having swamps

swan /swɒn/ n large white water bird with a long thin neck ● **swan** v (-nn-) [I] (GB, infml, disapprov) go around enjoying yourself in a way that annoys others or makes them jealous ■ **'swansong** n [sing] last performance or last work of a musician, poet, etc

swanky /'swæŋki/ adj (-ier, -iest) (infml, disapprov) fashionable and expensive

swap (also **swop**) /swɒp/ v (-pp-) [I, T]
~(with) give sth to sb in exchange for sth else: *~ seats with sb* ● **swap** n act of swapping or sth swapped

swarm /swɔːm/ n large group of insects, esp bees ● **swarm** v [I] move in large numbers [PV] **swarm with sb/sth** be full of people or things: *beaches ~ing with people*

swat /swɒt/ v (-tt-) [T] hit sth, esp an insect, with a flat object

sway /sweɪ/ v **1** [I, T] (cause sth to) move from side to side **2** [T] persuade sb to believe sth or do sth ● **sway** n [U] **1** movement from side to side **2** (lit) power or influence over sth

swear /sweə(r)/ v (pt **swore** /swɔː(r)/; pp **sworn** /swɔːn/) **1** [I] ~(at) use offensive or rude words, usu because you are angry **2** [T] make a serious promise to do sth: *She made him ~ not to tell anyone.* **3** [I, T] say or promise sth solemnly, esp in a court of law [PV] **swear by sth** be certain that sth is good or useful **swear sb in** make sb promise to do sth correctly, be loyal to a country, etc ■ **'swear word** n rude or offensive word

sweat /swet/ n **1** [U] liquid which comes through the skin when you are hot, nervous etc **2** [usu sing] state of being covered with sweat **3** [U] hard work or effort ● **sweat** v [I] **1** produce sweat **2** (infml) be worried or nervous [IDM] **sweat blood** (infml) work very hard ■ **'sweatshirt** n long-sleeved cotton sweater ▸ **sweaty** adj (-ier, -iest) (causing sb to be) hot and covered with sweat

sweater /'swetə(r)/ n knitted woollen or cotton piece of clothing for the upper body

swede /swiːd/ n [C,U] large round yellow root vegetable

sweep¹ /swiːp/ v (pt, pp **swept** /swept/) **1** [T] clear dust, dirt, etc using a brush, broom, etc **2** [T] carry or move sb/sth quickly: *The sea swept him along.* **3** [I, T] (of weather, fire, etc) pass quickly over an area: *A huge wave swept (over) the deck.* **4** [I] move in a proud way **5** [I] form a long smooth curve: *The coast ~s northwards.* [IDM] **sweep sb off their feet** make sb suddenly fall in love with you **sweep sth under the carpet** hide sth embarrassing or scandalous ▸ **sweeper** n person or thing that sweeps ▸ **sweeping** adj **1** having a wide effect: *~ing changes* **2** too general: *a ~ing statement*

sweep² /swiːp/ n **1** [C] act of cleaning a room, etc with a broom **2** [C] smooth curving movement **3** [U] range of an idea, piece of writing, etc: *the broad ~ of a novel* **4** [C] movement over an area, eg to search for sth **5** [C] = CHIMNEY SWEEP (CHIMNEY)

sweet /swiːt/ adj **1** tasting like sugar

2 smelling pleasant: *Don't the roses smell ~!* **3** pleasant or attractive: *a ~ face* **4** fresh and pure: *the ~ smell of the countryside* **5** lovable: *a ~ little boy* [IDM] **have a sweet tooth** (infml) like food that contains a lot of sugar ● **sweet** n **1** small piece of sweet food, eg boiled sugar, chocolate, etc **2** dish of sweet food ■ **'sweetcorn** n [U] type of maize with sweet yellow seeds ▶ **sweeten** v [I, T] become or make sth sweet ▶ **sweetener** n substance used to make food taste sweeter ■ **'sweetheart** n [sing] used to address sb in a way that shows affection ▶ **sweetly** adv ▶ **sweetness** n [U] ■ **'sweet-talk** v [T] ~ **(into)** try to persuade sb to do sth by saying nice things to them

swell /swel/ v (pt **swelled** /sweld/; pp **swollen** /ˈswəʊlən/ or **swelled**) [I, T] **1** (cause sth to) become greater in size, thickness, quantity, etc: *a swollen ankle* **2** (cause sth to) curve outwards ● **swell** n [sing] slow rise and fall of the sea's surface ▶ **swelling** n swollen place on the body

swelter /ˈsweltə(r)/ v [I] be uncomfortably hot

swept pt, pp of SWEEP[1]

swerve /swɜːv/ v [I] change direction suddenly: *The car ~d to avoid her.* ▶ **swerve** n

swift[1] /swɪft/ adj quick, prompt: *a ~ reply* ▶ **swiftly** adv ▶ **swiftness** n [U]

swift[2] /swɪft/ n small bird similar to a swallow

swig /swɪg/ v (-gg-) [T] (infml) drink sth in large amounts

swill /swɪl/ v [T] **1** clean sth by pouring large amounts of water in, on or through it **2** (infml) drink sth in large amounts: *~ tea* ● **swill** n [U] waste food that is given to pigs to eat

swim /swɪm/ v (-mm- pt **swam** /swæm/; pp **swum** /swʌm/) **1** [I, T] (of a person) move through water using the arms and legs: *to ~ the Channel* **2** [I] spend time swimming for pleasure: *I go ~ming twice a week.* **3** [I] (of a fish, etc) move through or across water **4** [I] ~ **(in/with)** seem to be covered with liquid **5** [I] seem to be moving around: *His head swam.* ● **swim** n [sing] period of time during which you swim: *go for a ~* [IDM] **in the swim (of things)** (infml) involved in things that are happening ▶ **swimmer** n person who swims ■ **'swimming costume** | **'swimsuit** n piece of clothing worn by women and girls for swimming ■ **'swimming pool** n area of water that has been created for people to swim in ■ **'swimming trunks** n [pl] shorts worn by boys and men for swimming

swindle /ˈswɪndl/ v [T] get money, etc from sb by cheating ● **swindle** n [usu sing] situation in which sb uses illegal methods to get money

from sb/sth ▶ **swindler** n person who gets money, etc by swindling

swing /swɪŋ/ v (pt, pp **swung** /swʌŋ/) [I, T] **1** (cause sth to) move backwards and forwards while hanging from a fixed point: *~ your arms* **2** (cause sth to) turn or change direction quickly: *~ round the corner* **3** (cause sb/sth to) change from one opinion, mood, etc to another: *a speech that ~s the voters* [IDM] **swing into action** start doing sth quickly ● **swing** n **1** [C] swinging movement or rhythm **2** [C] change from one opinion or situation to another **3** [C] seat hanging from a bar, etc for swinging on **4** [U] type of jazz with a smooth rhythm, played in the 1930s [IDM] **go with a swing** be lively and enjoyable **swings and roundabouts** (GB, infml) situation in which there are gains and losses

swingeing /ˈswɪndʒɪŋ/ adj (GB, written) large in amount, etc; severe

swipe /swaɪp/ v **1** [I, T] hit sb/sth with your hand, etc by swinging your arm **2** [T] (infml) steal sth **3** [T] pass a credit card, etc through a special machine that is able to read the information stored on it ● **swipe** n swinging blow ■ **'swipe card** n plastic card with information recorded on it which can only be read by an electronic device: *Access to the building is by ~ card only.*

swirl /swɜːl/ v [I, T] (cause air, water, etc to) move or flow with twists and turns ● **swirl** n swirling movement or pattern

swish /swɪʃ/ v [I, T] (cause sth to) move through the air with a hissing sound ● **swish** n [sing] movement or sound made by sth moving quickly ● **swish** adj (infml) fashionable or expensive

switch /swɪtʃ/ n **1** device for making and breaking an electrical circuit: *a light ~* **2** change from one thing to another: *a ~ from gas to electricity* ● **switch** v **1** [I, T] (cause sth to) change from one thing to another: *~ to using gas* **2** [T] exchange one thing for another: *~ the dates of the exams* [PV] **switch sth off/on** turn a light, machine, etc off/on by pressing a button or switch ■ **'switchboard** n central part of a telephone system used by a company, etc where calls are answered and put through to the appropriate person, etc

swivel /ˈswɪvl/ v (-ll-, US -l-) [I, T] (cause sth to) turn (as if) on a central point: *~ (round) in your chair*

swollen pp of SWELL

swoop /swuːp/ v [I] (of a bird or plane) fly downwards suddenly, esp in order to attack sb/sth: (fig) *Police ~ed (on the house) at dawn.*

● **swoop** n **1** swooping movement **2** sudden attack

swop = SWAP

sword /sɔːd/ n weapon with a long steel blade fixed in a handle ■ **'swordfish** n large sea fish with a long thin pointed upper jaw

swore pt of SWEAR

sworn[1] pp of SWEAR

sworn[2] /swɔːn/ adj **1** made after you have promised to tell the truth: a ~ statement **2** (~ enemies) people, countries, etc that hate each other

swum pp of SWIM

swung pt, pp of SWING

syllable /'sɪləbl/ n unit into which a word can be divided, usu containing a vowel: 'Table' has two ~s. ▶ **syllabic** /sɪ'læbɪk/ adj

syllabus /'sɪləbəs/ n list of subjects, etc in a course of study

syllogism /'sɪlədʒɪzəm/ n logical argument in which a conclusion is drawn from two statements

symbol /'sɪmbl/ n sign, mark, object, etc that represents sth: The dove is a ~ of peace. ▶ **symbolic** /sɪm'bɒlɪk/ adj of or used as a symbol ▶ **symbolically** adv ▶ **symbolism** /'sɪmbəlɪzəm/ n [U] (use of) symbols ▶ **symbolize** (also **-ise**) /'sɪmbəlaɪz/ v [T] be a symbol of sth

symmetry /'sɪmətri/ n [U] **1** exact match in size and shape of the two halves of sth **2** quality of being very similar or equal ▶ **symmetric** /sɪ'metrɪk/ (also **symmetrical** /-ɪkl/) adj

sympathetic /ˌsɪmpə'θetɪk/ adj **1** kind to sb who is hurt or sad; showing understanding and care: ~ looks **2** showing that you approve of sb/sth or that you share their views **3** (of a person) easy to like: a ~ character in a novel ▶ **sympathetically** /-kli/ adv

sympathize (also **-ise**) /'sɪmpəθaɪz/ v [I] ~(with) **1** feel sorry for sb; show that you understand their problems **2** support sb/sth ▶ **sympathizer** (also **-iser**) n person who supports a cause, party, etc

sympathy /'sɪmpəθi/ n (pl **-ies**) [U, C, usu pl] **1** (capacity for) sharing or understanding the feelings of others **2** act of showing support for or approval of an idea, cause, etc

symphony /'sɪmfəni/ n (pl **-ies**) long musical composition, usu in three or four parts, for an orchestra

symptom /'sɪmptəm/ n **1** change in the body that is a sign of illness **2** sign, usu of sth bad: ~s of discontent ▶ **symptomatic** /-'mætɪk/ adj being a sign of an illness or problem

synagogue /'sɪnəgɒg/ n building used by Jews for religious worship and teaching

synchronize (also **-ise**) /'sɪŋkrə-naɪz/ v [I, T] (cause sth to) happen at the same time or move at the same speed as sth else: ~ watches

syndicate /'sɪndɪkət/ n group of people or companies that join together for business ● **syndicate** /'sɪndɪkeɪt/ v [T] (usu passive) sell an article, a photograph, etc to several different newspapers, etc

syndrome /'sɪndrəʊm/ n (med) set of symptoms which are a sign of an illness, etc

synonym /'sɪnənɪm/ n word with the same meaning as another ▶ **synonymous** /sɪ'nɒnɪməs/ adj

synopsis /sɪ'nɒpsɪs/ n (pl **-opses** /-siːz/) summary or outline of a book, play, etc

syntax /'sɪntæks/ n [U] (ling) (rules for) making sentences out of words and phrases ▶ **syntactic** /sɪn'tæktɪk/ adj of syntax

synthesis /'sɪnθəsɪs/ n [U,C] (pl **-theses** /-siːz/) combining of separate parts to make a single whole ▶ **synthetic** /sɪn'θetɪk/ adj artificial, not natural: ~ fabric ▶ **synthesize** (also **-ise**) /'sɪnθəsaɪz/ v [T] make sth by combining separate things ▶ **synthetically** /sɪn'θetɪkli/ adv

syphilis /'sɪfɪlɪs/ n [U] serious venereal disease

syphon = SIPHON

syringe /sɪ'rɪndʒ/ n device with a needle for injecting liquids into the body, etc ● **syringe** v [T] clean sth with a syringe

syrup /'sɪrəp/ n [U] thick sweet liquid

system /'sɪstəm/ n **1** [C] organized set of ideas, etc: a ~ of government **2** [C] group of parts that are connected or work together **3** [sing] human or animal body, when considered as the organs and processes that make it function ▶ **systematic** /ˌmætɪk/ adj based on order, following a fixed plan ▶ **systematically** /-kli/ adv

T t

T, t /tiː/ n [C,U] (pl **T's**, **t's** /tiːz/) the twentieth letter of the English alphabet ■ **T-shirt** /n informal shirt with short sleeves and no buttons

ta /tɑː/ exclam (GB, sl) thank you

tab /tæb/ n small piece of cloth, paper, etc that sticks out from the edge of sth, used to give information about it, or to hold it, pull it, etc

tabby /'tæbi/ n (pl **-ies**) (also **'tabby cat**) cat with grey or brown fur and dark stripes

table /'teɪbl/ n **1** piece of furniture with a flat top on legs **2** list of facts

T

or figures arranged in columns or rows ■ **table** v [T] present sth formally for discussion ■ **'tablecloth** n cloth for covering a table, esp during meals ■ **'tablespoon** n large spoon for serving food ■ **'tablespoonful** n amount contained in a tablespoon ■ **'table tennis** n [U] indoor game in which a small light ball is hit over a low net on a table

tablet /'tæblət/ n 1 small piece of medicine 2 small bar of soap 3 flat piece of stone, etc with words cut into it

tabloid /'tæblɔɪd/ n newspaper with small pages, short news articles and many pictures of famous people

taboo /tə'buː/ n (pl ~s) something that is forbidden because of a strong religious or social custom ► **taboo** adj: in the days when sex was a ~ subject ■ **taboo words** n [pl] words that many people consider offensive or shocking

tabulate /'tæbjuleɪt/ v [T] arrange facts, figures, etc in a table ► **tabulation** /-'leɪʃn/ n [U]

tacit /'tæsɪt/ adj understood without being said: ~ agreement ► **tacitly** adv

tack /tæk/ n 1 [U,sing] course of action: change ~ 2 [C] small nail with a flat head 3 [C] long loose stitch ● **tack** v [T] sew sth together with loose stitches

tackle /'tækl/ v 1 [T] deal with a problem, piece of work, etc 2 [T] speak to sb frankly about sth 3 [I, T] (in football, etc) try to take the ball away from sb 4 [T] deal with sb violent or threatening, eg a thief ● **tackle** n 1 [C] act of tackling sb in football, etc 2 [U] equipment needed for a certain sport, esp fishing

tacky /'tæki/ adj (-ier, -iest) (infml) cheap and in bad taste: ~ jewellery

tact /tækt/ n [U] skill of not offending people by saying or doing the right thing ► **tactful** adj having or showing tact ► **tactfully** adv ► **tactless** adj ► **tactlessly** adv

tactic /'tæktɪk/ n 1 [C, usu pl] method used to achieve sth 2 (**tactics**) [pl] art of arranging and moving armies in a battle ► **tactical** adj of tactics: a ~al move ► **tactician** /tæk'tɪʃn/ n expert in tactics

tadpole /'tædpəʊl/ n small creature that grows into a frog or toad

tag /tæg/ n 1 [C] small piece of paper, fabric, etc attached to sth to show its cost, owner, etc 2 [U] (GB) game in which one child chases and tries to touch another ● **tag** v (-gg-) [T] fasten a tag to sth ► [PV] **tag along (behind/with)** go somewhere with sb, esp uninvited

tail /teɪl/ n 1 [C] long movable part at the end of the body of an animal, bird, etc 2 [C] part of sth that sticks out at the back like a tail: the ~ of an aircraft 3 (**tails**) [U] side of a coin without a person's head on it 4 [C] (infml) person employed to follow sb ● **tail** v [T] follow sb closely to watch what they do ► [PV] **tail away/off** become gradually less or quieter ■ **'tailback** n long line of traffic reaching back along a road ■ **'tail light** n red light at the back of a car, bus, etc ■ **'tailpipe** n (esp US) = EXHAUST(2) ■ **'tail wind** n wind blowing from behind a moving vehicle, etc

tailor /'teɪlə(r)/ n maker of men's clothes, eg coats and jackets ● **tailor** v [T] 1 make or adapt sth for a particular purpose, person, etc 2 cut out and sew sth: a well-~ed suit ■ **tailor-'made** adj 1 perfectly suitable: a ~-made course of study 2 (of clothes) made by a tailor for a particular person

taint /teɪnt/ v [T] spoil sth by adding a bad quality ● **taint** n [sing] trace of a bad quality

take¹ /teɪk/ v (pt took /tʊk/; pp ~n /'teɪkən/) 1 [T] carry sth/sb or cause sb to go from one place to another: T~ an umbrella with you. ◊ She took a friend home. 2 [T] get hold of or reach sb/sth: ~ her hand ◊ She took him in her arms. 3 [T] remove and use sth, esp without permission or by mistake; steal sth: Who has ~n my bicycle? 4 [T] get sth from a certain source: This line is ~n from a poem by Keats. 5 [T] capture a place or person; get control of sth: He was ~n prisoner. 6 [T] (fml) buy a newspaper or magazine regularly: He ~s The Times. 7 [T] eat or drink, etc sth: Do you ~ sugar in your tea? 8 [T] find out and record sth; write sth down: ~ notes ◊ ~ the names of the volunteers 9 [T] photograph sb/sth 10 [T] test or measure sth: ~ sb's pulse/temperature 11 [T] accept or receive sth: ~ advice ◊ ~ the blame ◊ Will you ~ £450 for the car? 12 [T] be able to bear sth: He can't ~ being criticized. 13 [T] react to sth/sb in the way stated: I wish you'd ~ me seriously. 14 [T] consider sth/sth to be sth/sth: What do you ~ me for? 15 [T] have a particular feeling, opinion, etc: ~ pleasure in being cruel 16 [T] used with nouns to show that a specific action is being performed: ~ a bath/walk/holiday 17 [T] need or require a particular amount of time: The work took four hours. 18 [T] wear a particular size in clothes or shoes: What size shoes do you ~? 19 [T] have enough space for sth/sb; be able to hold a certain quantity: The car ~s five people. 20 [T] do an exam or a test: ~ a driving test 21 [T] be the teacher in a class: She ~s us for

French. **22** [T] study a subject at school, college, etc **23** [T] use a means of transport, a road, etc: ~ *a bus into town* ◇ = (= turn into) *the first road on the left* **24** [I] be successful; work: *The smallpox injection did not ~.* [IDM] **take heart →** **HEART** **take it on/upon yourself to do sth** decide to do sth without asking permission or advice **take it/a lot out of sb** make sb very tired **take its course → COURSE** [PV] **take sb aback** shock and surprise sb **take after sb** be like your mother or father in appearance or character **take sth apart** separate the parts of a machine, etc **take sth away 1** subtract one amount from another: *T- 5 from 10, and that leaves 5.* **2** buy a meal at a restaurant and take it somewhere else to eat **3** cause sth to disappear: *a pill to ~ the pain away* **take sb/sth away** remove sb/sth from a place **take sb/sth back 1** admit that sth you have said is wrong **2** agree to receive sb/sth back: *This shop only ~s goods back if you have your receipt.* **take sb back (to ...)** cause sb to remember sth **take sth down 1** remove a structure by separating it into pieces **2** make a written record of sth **take sb in** deceive sb: *Don't be ~n in by him.* **take sth in 1** absorb sth into the body, eg by breathing **2** make a piece of clothing narrower or tighter **3** include or cover sth: *The trip took in several cities.* **4** take notice of sth with your eyes **5** understand and remember sth: *I couldn't ~ in everything she said.* **take off 1** (of an aircraft) leave the ground **2** (of a project, etc) become successful **take sth off** (*infml*) imitate sb **take sth (sth) 1** remove clothes, etc: *~ off your coat* **2** take time as a break from work: *a week off to go on holiday* **3** stop a public service, TV programme, etc **4** deduct an amount from the total: *~ 50p off the price* **take sth on** begin to have a quality, appearance, etc **take sb on 1** decide to do work, etc **take sb on 1** accept sb as an opponent **2** employ sb **take sb/sth on** (of a vehicle, aircraft, etc) allow passengers, fuel, cargo, etc to be loaded **take sb out** go to a restaurant, etc with sb you have invited: *~ her out to dinner* **take sth out 1** remove or extract a part of the body: *~ out a tooth* **2** obtain an official document for payment: *~ out a licence* **take it/sth out on sb** (*infml*) show your anger, etc by being unkind to sb, although it is not their fault **take over (from sb)** begin to have control of sb else's duties, responsibilities, etc **take sth**

over gain control of a business, company, etc, esp by buying shares **take to sth 1** go away to a place, esp to escape from danger: *~ to the woods to avoid capture* **2** begin to do sth as a habit; develop an ability for sth: *I took to cycling ten miles a day.* **take to sb/sth** begin to like sb/sth **take sth up 1** shorten a piece of clothing **2** learn or start to do sth, esp for pleasure: *~ up cycling/chess* **3** continue sth unfinished **4** occupy time or space: *This table ~s up half the room.* **5** accept an offer **take up with sb** (*infml*) begin to be friendly with sb, esp sb with a bad reputation **take sth up with sb** speak or write to sb about sth **be taken with sb/sth** find sb/sth interesting or attractive ▶ **takeaway** (*US* **'takeout**) *n* **1** restaurant from which food is taken to be eaten somewhere else **2** meal bought at this type of restaurant: *have a ~away* ■ **take-off** *n* **1** start of a flight, when an aircraft leaves the ground **2** imitation of sb ■ **'takeover** *n* act of taking over a business, etc

take² /teɪk/ *n* period of filming without stopping

taker /'teɪkə(r)/ *n* person who accepts an offer

takings /'teɪkɪŋz/ *n* [pl] amount of money that a shop, theatre, etc receives

talcum powder /'tælkəm paʊdə(r)/ *n* [U] perfumed powder for the skin

tale /teɪl/ *n* **1** story: *~s of adventure* **2** report or account of sth **3** lie: *Don't tell ~s.*

talent /'tælənt/ *n* [C, U] natural ability to do sth well: *have a ~ for music* ▶ **talented** *adj* having talent; skilled

talk¹ /tɔːk/ *v* **1** [I] say things; speak to give information: *He was ~ing to a friend.* **2** [I, T] discuss sth: *This is serious. We need to ~.* ◇ *We ~ed politics all evening.* **3** [I] say words in a language: *Can the baby ~ yet?* **4** [I] gossip **5** [I] give information to sb, esp unwillingly: *Has the prisoner ~ed yet?* [PV] **talk down to sb** speak to sb as if they were less important or intelligent than you **talk sb into/out of sth** persuade sb to do/not to do sth **talk sth over (with sb)** discuss sth thoroughly ▶ **talkative** /'tɔːkətɪv/ *adj* liking to talk a lot ▶ **talker** *n* ■ **'talking point** *n* subject for discussion ■ **'talking-to** *n* [sing] (*infml*) serious talk with sb who has done sth wrong

talk² /tɔːk/ *n* **1** [C, U] conversation or discussion **2** (**talks**) [pl] formal discussions between governments, etc: *peace ~s* **3** [C] speech or lecture on a particular subject **4** [U] (*infml*) words that are spoken but without facts, etc to support them: *Don't pay any attention to him. He's all ~.*

tall /tɔːl/ *adj* **1** of more than average height **2** of the height that is mentioned: *Tim is six feet ~.* [IDM] **be a tall order** (*infml*) be very difficult to do **a tall story** (*infml*) a story that is difficult to believe

tally /'tælɪ/ *n* (*pl* **-ies**) record of money spent, points scored in a game, etc ● **tally** *v* (*pt, pp* **-ied**) [I] ~ (**with**) be the same as or match another person's account, another set of figures, etc

talon /'tælən/ *n* curved claw of a bird, eg an eagle

tambourine /ˌtæmbə'riːn/ *n* small shallow drum with metal discs round the edge, shaken or hit with the hand

tame /teɪm/ *adj* (**~r, ~st**) **1** (of animals) trained to live with people; not wild or fierce: *a ~ monkey* **2** (*infml*) not interesting or exciting: *The film has a rather ~ ending.* **3** (*infml*) (of a person) easily controlled ● **tame** *v* [T] make sth tame or easy to control: *~ a lion* ▶ **tamely** *adv* ▶ **tameness** *n* [U] ▶ **tamer** *n* person who tames animals: *a lion ~r*

tamper /'tæmpə(r)/ *v* [I] ~**with** interfere with or change sth without authority

tampon /'tæmpɒn/ *n* piece of cotton material that a woman puts inside her vagina to absorb blood during her period(3)

tan /tæn/ *n* **1** [C] brown colour of the skin from sunlight **2** [U] yellowish brown colour ● **tan** *v* (**-nn-**) **1** [I, T] make animal skins into leather **2** [I, T] (cause skin to) go brown from sunlight [IDM] **tan sb's hide** (*infml*) beat sb hard

tandem /'tændəm/ *n* bicycle for two riders [IDM] **in tandem (with sb/sth)** working closely together with sb/sth

tandoori /tæn'dʊəri/ *n* [C, U] (dish of meat, etc in the) style of Indian cooking using a clay oven

tang /tæŋ/ *n* [C, *usu sing*] strong sharp taste or smell

tangent /'tændʒənt/ *n* a straight line that touches a curve but does not cross it [IDM] **fly/go off at a tangent** change suddenly from one line of thought, action, etc to another

tangerine /ˌtændʒə'riːn/ *n* kind of small sweet orange

tangible /'tændʒəbl/ *adj* **1** that can clearly be seen to exist: *~ proof* **2** that you can touch and feel ▶ **tangibly** *adv*

tangle /'tæŋɡl/ *n* **1** [C] confused mass of string, hair, etc **2** [*sing*] confused state: *in a ~* ● **tangle** *v* [I, T] (cause sth to) become twisted into a confused mass: *~d hair* [PV] **tangle with sb/sth** become involved in a fight or argument with sb

tango /'tæŋɡəʊ/ *n* (*pl* **~s**) (music for a) South American dance

tank /tæŋk/ *n* **1** large container for liquid or gas **2** armoured fighting vehicle with guns

tankard /'tæŋkəd/ *n* large metal mug for beer

tanker /'tæŋkə(r)/ *n* ship, lorry, etc that carries large quantities of liquid or gas

tantalize (*also* **-ise**) /'tæntəlaɪz/ *v* [T] tease sb by offering sth that they want and then not allowing them to have it

tantamount /'tæntəmaʊnt/ *adj* ~ **to** having the same effect as sth

tantrum /'tæntrəm/ *n* outburst of bad temper, esp by a child

tap /tæp/ *n* **1** device for controlling the flow of liquid or gas from a pipe or container **2** light hit with your hand or fingers [IDM] **on tap** available to be used at any time ● **tap** *v* (**-pp-**) **1** [I, T] hit sth/sb quickly and lightly: *~ sb on the back* **2** [T] make use of a source of energy, knowledge, etc that already exists: *~ a country's resources* **3** [T] fit a device to a telephone so that sb's calls can be listened to secretly **4** [T] draw liquid from sth ■ **'tap-dance** *n* [U,C] style of dancing in which you make tapping steps on the floor with special shoes

tape /teɪp/ *n* **1** [U] long narrow strip of magnetic material used for recording sounds, pictures, etc **2** [C] cassette that contains sounds (and pictures) that have been recorded: *a blank ~* **3** [C, U] (piece of) narrow strip of material: *sticky ~* **4** [C] piece of tape stretched across the place where a race will finish ● **tape** *v* [T] **1** record sound, etc on magnetic tape **2** fasten sth by sticking or tying it with tape [IDM] **have (got) sb/sth taped** (*GB, infml*) understand sb/sth fully ■ **'tape measure** *n* strip of cloth or thin metal, marked for measuring things ■ **'tape recorder** *n* apparatus for recording and playing sound on magnetic tape

taper /'teɪpə(r)/ *v* [I, T] (cause sth to) become gradually narrower [PV] **taper off** gradually become less in number ● **taper** *n* long thin candle

tapestry /'tæpəstri/ *n* [C, U] (*pl* **-ies**) (piece of) heavy cloth with a picture or pattern woven into it, used for covering walls

tar /tɑː(r)/ *n* [U] thick black sticky substance, hard when cold, used for making roads, preserving wood, etc ● **tar** *v* (**-rr-**) [T] cover sth with tar [IDM] **be tarred with the same brush (as sb)** be thought to have the same fault, etc as sb else

tarantula /tə'ræntjələ/ *n* large hairy poisonous spider

target /'tɑːgɪt/ n 1 [C,U] result that you try to achieve: *achieve a sales ~* 2 [C] object or person aimed at when attacking 3 [C] object that people practise shooting at ● **target** v [T] aim sth at sb/sth

tariff /'tærɪf/ n 1 tax on goods coming into a country 2 list of prices for rooms, meals, etc in a hotel

Tarmac™ /'tɑːmæk/ n [U] mixture of tar and broken stones for making road surfaces (**the tarmac**) area covered with Tarmac, esp at an airport

tarnish /'tɑːnɪʃ/ v 1 [I, T] (esp of metal surfaces) (cause sth to) lose brightness: *Brass ~es easily.* 2 [T] lessen the quality of sb's reputation

tarpaulin /tɑː'pɔːlɪn/ n [C,U] (piece of) waterproof cloth

tart /tɑːt/ n 1 open pie containing jam or fruit 2 (*GB, infml, disapprov*) sexually immoral girl or woman ● **tart** v [PV] **tart yourself up** (*GB, infml*) make yourself attractive by putting on nice clothes, etc **tart sth up** (*GB, infml*) decorate or improve the appearance of sth ● **tart** *adj* 1 having an unpleasant sour taste 2 (of remarks, etc) quick and unkind: *a ~ reply* ▸ **tartly** *adv* ▸ **tartness** n [U]

tartan /'tɑːtn/ n [U,C] (woollen cloth with a) pattern of coloured stripes crossing each other, esp of a Scottish clan

tartar /'tɑːtə(r)/ n [U] hard substance that forms on the teeth

task /tɑːsk/ n piece of (esp hard or unpleasant) work that has to be done [IDM] **take sb to task (for/over sth)** criticize sb strongly for sth they have done ■ **'task force** n group of people organized for a special (esp military) purpose ■ **'taskmaster** n person who gives others work to do, often work that is difficult

tassel /'tæsl/ n bunch of threads tied at one end, hanging as decoration from sth

taste¹ /teɪst/ n 1 [U] quality that different foods and drinks have that allows you to recognize them when you put them in your mouth: *a sweet/sour ~* 2 [U] sense that allows you to recognize a food or drink in your mouth 3 [C, usu sing] small quantity of food or drink 4 [U] person's ability to choose things that others recognize as being of good quality or appropriate: *Your choice of colours shows good ~.* 5 [C, U] personal liking [IDM] **be in good/ bad; etc taste** be tasteful/offensive, etc **a taste of your own medicine** → MEDICINE ▸ **tasteful** *adj* showing good taste(4) ▸ **tastefully** *adv* ▸ **tasteless** *adj* 1 (of food) having no flavour 2 showing bad taste(4) ▸ **taste-**

lessly *adv* ▸ **tasty** *adj* (**-ier**, **-iest**) having a pleasant flavour

taste² /teɪst/ v 1 *linking verb* **~(of)** have a particular flavour: *~ bitter/ sweet* 2 [T] be able to recognize flavours in food and drink 3 [T] test the flavour of sth: *She ~d the soup.* 4 [T] have a short experience of sth: *~ freedom*

tatters /'tætəz/ n [pl] [IDM] **in tatters** 1 torn in many places 2 ruined ▸ **tattered** *adj* old and torn; in bad condition

tattoo /tə'tuː/ n (*pl* **~s**) 1 picture or design marked permanently on sb's skin by making holes with a needle and filling them with coloured ink 2 outdoor show by members of the armed forces, with music, marching, etc ● **tattoo** v [T] mark sb's skin with a tattoo

taught *pt, pp* of TEACH

taunt /tɔːnt/ v [T] say unkind or insulting words to sb in order to upset them ● **taunt** n taunting remark

taut /tɔːt/ *adj* tightly stretched ▸ **tautly** *adv* ▸ **tautness** n [U]

tautology /tɔː'tɒlədʒi/ n [C,U] (*pl* **-ies**) unnecessary repeating of the same thing in different ways ▸ **tautological** /-'lɒdʒɪkl/ *adj*

tavern /'tævən/ n (*lit*) pub; inn

tawny /'tɔːni/ *adj* brownish-yellow

tax /tæks/ n [C,U] money that has to be paid to a government for public services ● **tax** v [T] 1 put a tax on sb/sth 2 require sb to pay a tax 3 need a lot of physical or mental effort: *~ sb's patience* ▸ **taxable** *adj* (of money) that you have to pay tax on: *~able income* ▸ **taxation** /-'seɪʃn/ n [U] (system of) raising money by taxes ■ **tax-'free** *adj* on which tax need not be paid ▸ **taxpayer** n person who pays taxes, esp income tax

taxi /'tæksi/ n (*also* **taxicab**) car with a driver which may be hired ● **taxi** v [I] (of an aircraft) move along the ground before or after flying ■ **'taxi rank** n place where taxis wait to be hired

tea /tiː/ n 1 [U] dried leaves of a bush grown in China, India, etc 2 [U,C] hot drink made by pouring boiling water onto tea leaves 3 [U,C] hot drink made by pouring boiling water onto the leaves of other plants: *mint ~* 4 [C,U] light early evening meal ■ **'tea bag** n small paper bag containing tea leaves ■ **'tea caddy** /-kædi/ (*pl* **-dies**) n small tin in which tea is kept ■ **'tea chest** n (*GB*) large light wooden box in which tea is packed ■ **'tea cosy** n (*pl* **-ies**) cover to keep a teapot warm ■ **'teacup** n cup from which tea is drunk ■ **'teapot** n container in which tea is made and served ■ **'tea set** (*also* **'tea service**) n set of cups, plates, etc for serving tea ■ **'teaspoon** *n* small spoon for stirring tea ■ **'teaspoonful** *n* amount contained in a teaspoon ■ **'teatime** *n* [U] (*GB*) time at which tea is served ■ **'tea towel** (*also* **'tea cloth**) *n* cloth used for drying washed dishes and cutlery

teach /tiːtʃ/ *v* (*pt, pp* **taught** /tɔːt/) [I, T] gives lessons to sb; give sb knowledge, skill, etc: *He taught them art.* ◇ *a child (how) to swim* ▶ **teacher** *n* person who teaches, esp in a school ▶ **teaching** *n* **1** [U] work of a teacher: *earn a living by ~ing* **2** [C, usu pl, U] ideas of a particular person or group: *the ~ings of Lenin*

teak /tiːk/ *n* [U] strong hard wood of a tall Asian tree

team /tiːm/ *n* [C, with sing or pl verb] **1** group of people playing on the same side in a game: *a football ~* **2** group of people working together: *a ~ of surgeons* ● **team** *v* [I] **~ up (with)** work together with another person or group ■ **team 'spirit** *n* [U] (*approv*) desire and willingness of people to work together as a team ■ **'teamwork** *n* [U] organized cooperation

tear¹ /teə(r)/ *v* (*pt* **tore** /tɔː(r)/, *pp* **torn** /tɔːn/) **1** [T] damage sth by pulling it apart or into pieces or by cutting it on sth sharp: *~ a sheet of paper* **2** [I] become torn: *This cloth ~s easily.* **3** [T] remove sth from sth else by pulling it forcefully: *~ a page out of a book* **4** [I] move somewhere very quickly: *We tore home.* **5** [T] badly affect or damage sth: *a country torn by civil war* [IDM] **be torn between A and B** be unable to choose between two things or people [PV] **tear sth down** pull or knock down a building, wall, etc **tear sth up** tear a piece of paper into small bits ● **tear** *n* hole made in sth by tearing ■ **'tearaway** *n* (*infml*) young person who is difficult to control

tear² /tɪə(r)/ *n* [C, usu pl] drop of liquid that comes from your eye when you cry: *She left the room in ~s* (= crying). ■ **'teardrop** *n* single tear ■ **'tearful** *adj* crying or likely to cry ▶ **tearfully** *adv* ■ **'tear gas** *n* [U] gas that stings the eyes, used by the army, etc ■ **'tear jerker** *n* (*infml*) story, film, etc likely to make people cry

tease /tiːz/ *v* [I, T] laugh at sb and make fun of them playfully or unkindly ● **tease** *n* person who likes teasing people ▶ **teaser** *n* (*infml*) difficult problem or question

teat /tiːt/ *n* **1** rubber end on a baby's feeding bottle **2** animal's nipple

tech /tek/ *n* (*infml*) short for TECHNICAL COLLEGE (TECHNICAL)

technical /'teknɪkl/ *adj* **1** concerned with the practical use of machinery,

methods, etc in science or industry **2** concerned with the skills needed for a particular job, subject, etc **3** of a particular subject: *the ~ terms of physics* **4** in a strict legal sense ■ **,technical 'college** *n* college that teaches practical skills ▶ **technicality** /ˌtekni'kæləti/ *n* (*pl* **-ies**) technical point or small detail, esp one that seems unfair ▶ **technically** /-kli/ *adv*

technician /tek'nɪʃn/ *n* person with a practical, mechanical or industrial skill

technique /tek'niːk/ *n* [C] way of doing sth, esp one that needs special skills **2** [U, sing] skill with which sb is able to do sth practical

technocrat /'teknəkræt/ *n* expert in science, engineering, etc who has a lot of power in politics and/or industry

technology /tek'nɒlədʒi/ *n* study and use of science for practical tasks in industry, business, etc ▶ **technological** /-'lɒdʒɪkl/ *adj* ▶ **technologist** *n* expert in technology

teddy bear /'tedi beə(r)/ *n* soft furry toy bear

tedious /'tiːdiəs/ *adj* long and boring: *a ~ lecture* ◇ *~ work* ▶ **tediously** *adv*

tee /tiː/ *n* **1** (*golf*) flat area from which a player starts at each hole **2** piece of wood, plastic, etc on which you put a golf ball before you hit it ● **tee** *v* [PV] **tee off** hit a golf ball from a tee **tee (sth) up** prepare to hit a golf ball by placing it on a tee

teem /tiːm/ *v* [I] (used *with it*) (of rain) fall very heavily [PV] **teem with sth** be full of animals, people, etc moving around

teenage /'tiːneɪdʒ/ *adj* (for people who are) between 13 and 19 years old: *~ fashions*

teenager /'tiːneɪdʒə(r)/ *n* person who is between 13 and 19 years old

teens /tiːnz/ *n* [pl] years of a person's life when they are between 13 and 19 years old: *Both girls are in their ~.*

teeter /'tiːtə(r)/ *v* [I] stand or move unsteadily

teeth *plural of* TOOTH

teethe /tiːð/ *v* [I] (of a baby) grow its first teeth ■ **'teething troubles** *n* [pl] problems that occur when first using a new system

teetotal /ˌtiː'təʊtl/ *adj* never drinking alcohol ▶ **teetotaller** *n*

telecommunications /ˌtelikəˌmjuːnɪ'keɪʃnz/ *n* [pl] technology of sending signals, images and messages over long distances by radio, television, satellite, etc

telegram /'teligræm/ *n* message sent by telegraph and then printed

telegraph /'teligrɑːf/ *n* [U] method of sending messages over long distances, using wires that carry electrical signals ● **telegraph** v [I, T] send a message by telegraph ▶ **telegraphic** /-'græfɪk/ adj

telemarketing /'telɪmɑːkɪtɪŋ/ n [U] = TELESALES

telepathy /tə'lepəθi/ n [U] direct communication of thoughts from one person to another without using speech, writing, etc ▶ **telepathic** /ˌtelɪ'pæθɪk/ adj

telephone /'telɪfəʊn/ n [C,U] (machine used in) system for talking to sb over long distances using wires or radio ● **telephone** v [I, T] (fml, esp GB) speak to sb by telephone ■ **'telephone booth** n = PHONE BOOTH (PHONE) ■ **'telephone box** n = PHONE BOX (PHONE) ■ **'telephone directory** n book that lists the names, addresses and telephone numbers of people in a particular area ■ **'telephone exchange** n place where telephone calls are connected ■ **'telephone number** n number of a particular telephone, that you use when you make a call to it

telephonist /tə'lefənɪst/ n person whose job is to handle telephone connections in an office or at a telephone exchange

telephoto lens /ˌtelɪfəʊtəʊ 'lenz/ n special lens that produces a large clear picture of a distant object being photographed

telesales /'teliseɪlz/ n [U] method of selling things and taking orders for sales by telephone

telescope /'telɪskəʊp/ n long tube-shaped instrument with lenses, for making distant objects appear nearer and larger ● **telescope** v [I, T] become or make sth shorter by sliding sections inside one another ▶ **telescopic** /-'skɒpɪk/ adj

teletext /'telɪtekst/ n [U] computerized service providing information on television screens

television /'telɪvɪʒn/ n (abbr **TV**) **1** [C] (also **'television set**) piece of electrical equipment with a screen on which you can watch moving pictures and sounds **2** [U] programmes broadcast on television **3** [U] system, process or business of broadcasting television programmes ▶ **televise** /'telɪvaɪz/ v [T] broadcast sth on television

telex /'teleks/ n **1** [U] system of sending typed messages round the world by telephone lines **2** [C] message sent by telex ● **telex** v [T] send a message by telex

tell /tel/ v (pt, pp **told** /təʊld/) **1** [T] make sth known to sb in words: *I told her my name.* **2** [T] give information about sth **3** [I] (infml) reveal a secret: *You promised not to ~.* **4** [T] order or

advise sb to do sth: *I told them to go.* **5** [I, T] know, see or judge sth correctly: *I think he's happy - it's hard to ~.* **6** [I] ~ **(on)** have an effect on sb/sth, esp a bad one: *All this hard work is ~ing on him.* [IDM] **all told** with all the people or things counted **I told you (so)** (infml) I warned you that this would happen **tell tales (about sth/on sb)** tell sb about sth that another person has done wrong **tell the time** read the time from a clock, etc [PV] **tell A and B apart** be able to see the difference between A and B **tell sb off (for doing sth)** (infml) speak angrily to sb for doing sth wrong **tell on sb** (infml) inform against sb: *John told on his sister.* ▶ **teller** n **1** person who receives and pays out money in a bank **2** person who counts votes, esp in a parliament ▶ **telling** adj effective: *a ~ing remark*

telltale /'telteɪl/ n (disapprov) child who tells an adult what another child has done wrong ● **telltale** adj showing that sth exists or has happened: *a ~ blush*

telly /'teli/ n [C,U] (pl **-ies**) (infml) short for TELEVISION

temerity /tə'merəti/ n [U] (fml) extremely confident and rude behaviour: *He had the ~ to call me a liar.*

temp /temp/ n **1** (infml) person, esp a secretary, employed for a short time

temper /'tempə(r)/ n **1** [C, usu sing, U] fact of becoming angry very easily: *He's got a quick ~.* **2** [C, usu sing] short period of feeling very angry: *fly into a ~* **3** [C] state of the mind: *be in a foul ~.* [IDM] **keep/lose your temper (with sb)** manage/fail to control your anger ● **temper** v [T] make sth less extreme: *justice ~ed with mercy* ▶ **-tempered** (used to form compound adjectives) having a certain temper: *a bad--ed man*

temperament /'temprəmənt/ n [U, C] person's character shown in the way they behave or react to sb/sth ▶ **temperamental** /-'mentl/ adj **1** having a tendency to become angry, etc easily: *Children are often ~al.* **2** connected with sb's personality ▶ **temperamentally** /-təli/ adv

temperate /'tempərət/ adj **1** (tech) (of climate) free from extremes of heat and cold **2** (fml) behaving in a calm controlled way

temperature /'temprətʃə(r)/ n [C, U] **1** measurement in degrees of how hot or cold sth is **2** measurement of how hot sb's body is: *Does he have a ~ = is it higher than normal because of illness?)*

tempest /'tempɪst/ n (fml) violent storm ▶ **tempestuous** /-'pestʃuəs/ adj stormy, violent: (fig) *a ~uous love affair*

temple /'templ/ n 1 building used in the worship of a god or gods, esp in the Hindu and Buddhist religions 2 flat part on each side of the forehead

tempo /'tempəʊ/ n (pl ~s; or, in sense 1 **tempi** /'tempiː/) 1 (tech) speed or rhythm of a piece of music 2 speed of any movement or activity: the ~ of city life

temporal /'tempərəl/ adj (fml) 1 of the real physical world, not spiritual matters 2 of or limited by time

temporary /'temprəri/ adj lasting for only a short time ▶ **temporarily** /'temprərəli; tempə'rerəli/ adv

tempt /tempt/ v [T] 1 attract sb or make sb want to do or have sth 2 (try to) persuade sb to do sth, esp sth wrong or unwise: Nothing would ~ me to live here. ▶ **temptation** /temp'teɪʃn/ n 1 [C,U] desire to do or have sth that you know is bad or wrong 2 [C] thing that tempts you ▶ **tempting** adj attractive: a ~ing offer

ten /ten/ number 10 ▶ **tenth** ordinal number, n 10th; the fraction ¹⁄₁₀, each of ten equal parts of sth

tenable /'tenəbl/ adj 1 (of an opinion) that can be reasonably defended 2 (of a job or position) that can be held for the stated time

tenacious /tə'neɪʃəs/ adj very determined to get or keep sth ▶ **tenacity** /tə'næsəti/ n [U]

tenant /'tenənt/ n person who pays rent for the use of a building, land, etc ▶ **tenancy** /-ənsi/ n (pl -ies) 1 [C] period of time that you rent a house, land, etc for 2 [C,U] right to live or work in a house, etc that you rent

tend /tend/ v 1 [I] ~ **to** be likely to do sth: He ~s to make too many mistakes. 2 [T] care for sb/sth: shepherds ~ing their sheep

tendency /'tendənsi/ n (pl -ies) 1 way a person or thing is likely to behave or act: a ~ to talk too much 2 new custom that is starting to develop: an increasing ~ for parents to help at school

tender¹ /'tendə(r)/ adj 1 gentle, kind and loving 2 (of food) easy to bite through or cut 3 (of part of the body) painful to touch 4 easily hurt or damaged ▶ **tenderly** adv ▶ **tenderness** n [U]

tender² /'tendə(r)/ v 1 [I] ~ (**for**) make a formal offer to do work at a stated price: ~ for the construction of the new motorway 2 [T] (fml) offer or give sth to sb: He ~ed his resignation. ● **tender** n formal offer to do work at a stated price

tendon /'tendən/ n strong band of tissue that joins a muscle to a bone

tenement /'tenəmənt/ n large building, esp in a poor part of a city, divided into flats

tenet /'tenɪt/ n (fml) principle; belief

tenner /'tenə(r)/ n (GB, infml) £10 (note)

tennis /'tenɪs/ n [U] game for two or four players who hit a ball across a net with a racket ■ **'tennis court** n marked area on which tennis is played

tenor /'tenə(r)/ n 1 [C] (man with a) singing voice with a range just below the lowest woman's voice 2 [sing] musical part written for a tenor voice 3 [sing] (fml) (**the tenor of sth**) general meaning of sth ● **tenor** adj (of a musical instrument) with a range of notes similar to that of a tenor voice: a ~ saxophone

tenpin bowling /,tenpɪn 'bəʊlɪŋ/ n [U] game in which a ball is rolled towards ten bottle-shaped objects, in order to knock them down

tense¹ /tens/ adj (~r, ~st) 1 nervous and worried 2 stretched tightly ● **tense** v [I, T] make your muscles tight and stiff, esp because you are not relaxed: He ~d his muscles. ▶ **tensely** adv

tense² /tens/ n (gram) verb form that shows the time of the action or state: the present/past/future ~

tension /'tenʃn/ n 1 [U,C, usu pl] situation in which people do not trust each other or feel unfriendly towards each other: political ~(s) 2 [U] mental, emotional or nervous strain 3 [U] state or degree of being stretched: the ~ of the rope

tent /tent/ n shelter made of nylon, etc that is supported by poles and ropes and is used esp for camping

tentacle /'tentəkl/ n long thin part of certain creatures (eg an octopus) used for feeling, holding, etc

tentative /'tentətɪv/ adj made or done to test sth; not definite: make a ~ offer ▶ **tentatively** adv

tenterhooks /'tentəhʊks/ n [pl] [IDM] (**be) on tenterhooks** (be) in a state of anxious waiting

tenth → TEN

tenuous /'tenjuəs/ adj so weak or uncertain that it hardly exists

tepid /'tepɪd/ adj slightly warm

term /tɜːm/ n 1 [C] word or phrase used as the name of sth: technical ~s 2 [C,U] (esp GB) division of the school or university year: summer/ spring ~ 3 [C] fixed period of time: the president's ~ of office [IDM] in the long/short/medium term used to describe what will happen a long, short, etc time in the future ● **term** v [T] (fml) use a particular name or word to describe sb/sth

terminal /'tɜːmɪnl/ n 1 building(s)

for passengers or goods, esp at an airport or port **2** (*computing*) piece of equipment that joins the user to a central computer system **3** (*tech*) point at which connections can be made in an electric circuit ● **terminal** *adj* (of an illness) that will cause death and cannot be cured ▶ **terminally** /-nəli/ *adv*

terminate /'tɜːmɪneɪt/ *v* [I, T] come or bring sth to an end ▶ **termination** /,tɜːmɪ'neɪʃn/ *n* [U,C] (*fml*) ending of sth: *the termination of a contract*

terminology /,tɜːmɪ'nɒlədʒi/ *n* [U] (*pl* -**ies**) special words and expressions used in a particular subject

terminus /'tɜːmɪnəs/ *n* (*pl* -**ni** /-naɪ/ or ~**es**) last station or stop at the end of a railway line or bus route

termite /'tɜːmaɪt/ *n* insect that eats wood

terms /tɜːmz/ *n* [pl] **1** conditions of an agreement or a contract **2** conditions of sale or payment **3** way of expression: *I'll explain this in general ~ first.* [IDM] **be on good, friendly, bad, etc terms** (with sb) have a good, friendly, bad etc relationship with sb **come to terms with sth** learn to accept sth unpleasant or difficult **in terms of sth** concerning sth

terrace /'terəs/ *n* **1** [C] long row of houses joined together in one block **2** [C] flat area outside a house, restaurant, etc **3** (**terraces**) [pl] (*GB*) wide steps where spectators can stand at a football ground, etc **4** [C] one of a series of flat areas of ground that are cut into a hillside like steps ▶ **terraced** *adj* formed into terraces: ~*d houses* ◇ *a ~d hillside*

terrain /tə'reɪn/ *n* [C,U] (*written*) area of land: *hilly ~*

terrestrial /tə'restriəl/ *adj* **1** (*tech*) of or living on the land **2** (of our planet Earth) **3** (of television and broadcasting systems) operating on earth rather than from a satellite

terrible /'terəbl/ *adj* **1** causing great fear, harm or unhappiness: *a ~ war/ accident* **2** unhappy or ill **3** (*infml*) very bad: *What ~ food!* ▶ **terribly** *adv* (*infml*) extremely: *terribly busy*

terrier /'teriə(r)/ *n* kind of small lively dog

terrific /tə'rɪfɪk/ *adj* **1** (*infml*) excellent; wonderful **2** very large; very great: *a ~ amount of work* ▶ **terrifically** /-kli/ *adv* extremely

terrify /'terɪfaɪ/ *v* (*pt, pp* -**ied**) [T] make sb feel very frightened: *I'm terrified of dogs.*

territorial /,terə'tɔːriəl/ *adj* of land or territory

territory /'terətri/ *n* [C,U] (*pl* -**ies**) **1** area of land under the control of a ruler, country, etc: *Spanish ~* **2** area

of land claimed and defended by one person or animal **3** area for which sb is responsible

terror /'terə(r)/ *n* **1** [U] feeling of extreme fear **2** [C] person, thing or situation that makes you very afraid ▶ **terrorism** /-rɪzəm/ *n* [U] use of violence for political purposes ▶ **terrorist** *adj, n* ▶ **terrorize** (*also* -**ise**) *v* [T] use threats or violence to make people do as they are told

terse /tɜːs/ *adj* using few, often unfriendly, words ▶ **tersely** *adv* ▶ **terseness** *n* [U]

test /test/ *n* **1** examination of a person's knowledge or ability: *an intelligence ~* ◇ *a driving ~* **2** medical examination to discover what is wrong with you, etc: *a blood ~* **3** experiment to discover whether sth works, etc: *a nuclear ~* ● **test** *v* [T] check how well sth works or examine sb's health or mental abilities ■ '**test match** *n* international cricket or rugby match ■ '**test tube** *n* small glass tube, closed at one end, used in chemical experiments

testament /'testəmənt/ *n* (*fml*) **1** [C, usu sing, U] ~ (**to**) thing that clearly shows or proves sth **2** [C] (**Testament**) either of the two main divisions of the Bible: *the New T~* **3** = WILL³(5)

testicle /'testɪkl/ *n* either of the two glands of the male sex organ that produce sperm

testify /'testɪfaɪ/ *v* (*pt, pp* -**ied**) [I, T] make a statement that sth happened or that sth is true, esp in a law court

testimonial /,testɪ'məʊniəl/ *n* **1** formal written statement, often by a former employer, about sb's character, abilities, etc **2** thing given to sb to show honour or thanks

testimony /'testɪməni/ *n* [U,C] (*pl* -**ies**) formal statement of truth, esp in a law court

tetanus /'tetənəs/ *n* [U] serious disease, caused by infection of a cut, causing muscles to become stiff

tête-à-tête /,teɪt ɑː 'teɪt/ *n* private conversation between two people

tether /'teðə(r)/ *n* rope or chain used to tie an animal to sth ● **tether** *v* [T] tie an animal to sth so that it cannot move very far

text /tekst/ *n* **1** [U] main printed part of a book or magazine **2** [U] any form of written material: *a computer that can process ~* **3** [C] (*infml*) = TEXT MESSAGE **4** [C] written form of a speech, play, article, etc **5** [C] book, play, etc that is studied **6** [C] short passage of the Bible, etc as the subject of a sermon ● **text** *v* [I, T] send sb a written message using a mobile phone: *I'll ~ you when I get in.*

■ **'textbook** n book that teaches a particular subject, used in schools, etc ■ **'text message** (also **informl text**) n written message sent from one mobile phone to another ▶ **'text messaging** n [U] ■ **textual** /'tekstʃuəl/ adj (written) of or in a text

textile /'tekstaɪl/ n [C, usu pl] any type of fabric made by weaving

texture /'tekstʃə(r)/ n [C, U] way a surface or fabric feels or looks, eg how rough or smooth it is

than /ðən; rare strong form ðæn/ conj, prep **1** used for introducing the second part of a comparison: Sylvia is taller ~ me. **2** used after more or less and before expressions of time, distance, etc: It cost more ~ £100. ◇ It's less ~ a mile to the station.

thank /θæŋk/ v [T] tell sb that you are grateful for sth [IDM] no, thank you used for refusing an offer politely **thank you** used to show that you are grateful for sth or to accept an offer ▶ **thankful** adj grateful ▶ **thankfully** adv ▶ **thankless** adj unpleasant or difficult to do and unlikely to bring any thanks: a ~less task ▶ **thanks** n [pl], exclam (words or actions) used to show that you are grateful for sth [IDM] thanks to sb/sth because of sb/sth ■ **thanks'giving** n **1** [U,C] (Thanks'giving (Day)) public holiday in the US and Canada **2** [U] (fml) expression of thanks to God

that /ðæt/ det, pron (pl **those** /ðəʊz/) **1** used to refer to a person or thing that is not near the speaker: Look at ~ man over there. **2** used to refer to sb/sth that has already been mentioned or is known about: Have you forgotten about ~ money I lent you last week? **3** (fml) used for referring to people or things of a particular type: Those present were in favour of change. **4** used to introduce a part of a sentence which refers to the person, thing or time you have been talking about: Where's the letter ~ came yesterday? ◇ The pen (~) you gave me is a nice one. [IDM] that is (to say) used to say what sth means or to give more information ● **that** adv to that degree; so: The film wasn't ~ bad. ● **that** conj used after some verbs, adjectives and nouns to introduce a new part of the sentence: She said (~) the story was true.

thatch /θætʃ/ n [C, U] roof covering of dried straw, reeds, etc ● **thatch** v [T] cover a roof, etc with a thatch

thaw /θɔː/ v **1** [I, T] (cause ice and snow to) melt **2** [I, T] (cause frozen food, etc to) become liquid or soft again: Leave the meat to ~. **3** [I] become friendlier and less formal ● **thaw** n [C, usu sing] (warm weather causing) thawing

the /ðə; ði; strong form ðiː/ definite article **1** used for referring to a particular thing: T~ sky was blue. ◇ Please close ~ window. **2** all the people, things, etc of the stated kind: T~ dog is a popular pet. **3** used for referring to a member or nationality: ~ rich ◇ ~ French **4** used before certain geographical names: ~ Mediterranean ◇ ~ Atlantic (Ocean) **5** used with musical instruments: play ~ piano **6** (used with a unit of measurement) every: paid by ~ hour **7** used with a superlative: ~ best day of your life [IDM] the more, less, etc . . . , the more, less, etc . . . used to show that two things change to the same degree: T~ more I read, ~ less I understand.

theatre (US **theater**) /'θɪətə(r)/ n **1** [C] building in which plays are performed **2** (**the theatre**) [sing] work of acting in, producing, etc plays **3** [C] hall or room for lectures **4** [C, U] (GB) = OPERATING THEATRE (OPERATE) ■ **'theatregoer** n person who frequently sees plays at the theatre ▶ **theatrical** /θi'ætrɪkl/ adj **1** of the theatre **2** (of behaviour) exaggerated in order to attract attention

theft /θeft/ n [U, C] (crime of) stealing sth from a person or place

their /ðeə(r)/ det of or belonging to them: They have lost ~ dog. ▶ **theirs** /ðeəz/ pron of or belonging to them: That dog is ~s, not ours.

them /ðəm; strong form ðem/ pron **1** (used as the object of a v or prep) people, animals or things mentioned earlier: Give ~ to me. ◇ Did you eat all of ~? **2** used instead of him or her: If anyone comes, ask ~ to wait.

theme /θiːm/ n **1** subject of a talk, book, etc **2** repeated tune in a piece of music ■ **'theme park** n large park which has machines for people to ride on which are based on a single idea ■ **'theme music/song/tune** n music played at the beginning and end of a film, TV programme, etc

themselves /ðəm'selvz/ pron **1** used as a reflexive when the people or animals doing an action are also affected by it: They hurt ~. **2** used for emphasis: They ~ have often made that mistake. [IDM] (all) by themselves **1** alone **2** without help

then /ðen/ adv **1** at that time: I was still unmarried ~. **2** next; after that: We stayed in Rome and ~ in Naples. **3** used to show the logical result of sth: If you miss that train – you'll have to get a taxi. **4** and also: There's the soup to heat, – there's the bread to butter.

thence /ðens/ adv (old-fash or fml) from that place

theology /θi'ɒlədʒi/ n [U] study of

religion ▸ **theologian** /θiːəˈləʊdʒən/ n ▸ **theological** /ˌθiːəˈlɒdʒɪkl/ adj

theorem /ˈθɪərəm/ n mathematical statement that can be proved by reasoning

theory /ˈθɪəri/ n (pl -ies) 1 [C,U] formal set of ideas intended to explain sth happens or exists: *Darwin's ~ of evolution* 2 [U] principles on which a particular subject is based ▸ **theoretical** /ˌθɪəˈretɪkl/ adj

therapeutic /ˌθerəˈpjuːtɪk/ adj designed to help treat an illness

therapy /ˈθerəpi/ n [U] treatment of a physical problem or an illness ▸ **therapist** n

there /ðeə(r)/ adv 1 (there is, are, was, were, etc) used to show that sth exists or happens: *T~'s a pub round the corner.* 1 in, at or to that place or position: *We'll soon be ~.* ◇ *I took one look at the car and offered to buy it ~ and then/and then ~* (= immediately). 2 at that point (in a story, etc): *Don't stop ~!* 3 used for calling attention to sth: *T~'s the bell for lunch.* ● **there** exclam used to express satisfaction that you were right about sth or to show that sth annoys you: *T~! You've woken the baby!* [IDM] **there, there!** used to persuade a small child to stop crying

thereabouts /ˌðeərəˈbaʊts/ adv near that place, number, year, etc

thereafter /ˌðeərˈɑːftə(r)/ adv (fml) after that

thereby /ˌðeəˈbaɪ/ adv (fml) by that means; in that way

therefore /ˈðeəfɔː(r)/ adv for that reason

thereupon /ˌðeərəˈpɒn/ adv (fml) immediately; because of that

thermal /ˈθɜːml/ adj 1 (tech) of or caused by heat 2 (of clothes) designed to keep you warm in cold weather

thermometer /θəˈmɒmɪtə(r)/ n instrument for measuring temperature

Thermos™ (also **Thermos flask**) /ˈθɜːməs flɑːsk/ n type of vacuum flask

thermostat /ˈθɜːməstæt/ n device that automatically keeps a building, engine, etc at an even temperature

thesaurus /θɪˈsɔːrəs/ n (pl -es or -ri /-raɪ/) book of words grouped together according to their meanings

these plural of THIS

thesis /ˈθiːsɪs/ n (pl **theses** /ˈθiːsiːz/) 1 long piece of writing on a subject, done as part of a university degree 2 statement or theory supported by arguments

they /ðeɪ/ pron (used as the subject of a v) 1 people, animals or things mentioned earlier 2 used instead of *he* or *she* to refer to a person whose sex is unknown: *If anyone comes late, ~'ll have to wait.* 3 people in general: *T~ say we're going to have a hot summer.*

they'd /ðeɪd/ short for THEY HAD, THEY WOULD

they'll /ðeɪl/ short for THEY WILL

they're /ðeə(r)/ short for THEY ARE

they've /ðeɪv/ short for THEY HAVE

thick /θɪk/ adj 1 having a large distance between opposite sides or surfaces: *a ~ slice of bread* ◇ *a wall 2 feet ~* 2 growing closely together in large numbers: *~ hair* ◇ *a ~ forest* 3 (of a liquid) not flowing very easily 4 difficult to see through; difficult to breathe in: *a ~ fog* 5 (GB, infml) slow to learn or understand things ● **thick** adv thickly: *spread the butter too ~* [IDM] **thick and fast** quickly and in large quantities ● **thick** n [U] [IDM] **in the thick of sth** involved in the busiest part of sth **through thick and thin** even when there are problems or difficulties ▸ **thicken** v [I, T] become or make sth thick: *~en the soup* ▸ **thickly** adv ▸ **thickness** n 1 [U] size of sth between opposite surfaces or sides: *4 centimetres in ~ness* 2 [C] layer of sth ■ ˌ**thickˈset** adj (esp of a man) having a strong heavy body ■ ˌ**thick-ˈskinned** adj not sensitive to criticism, etc

thicket /ˈθɪkɪt/ n mass of trees or bushes growing closely together

thief /θiːf/ n (pl **thieves** /θiːvz/) person who steals sth from another person or place ▸ **thieving** /ˈθiːvɪŋ/ n [U] (infml) act of stealing things

thigh /θaɪ/ n part of the human leg between the knee and the hip

thimble /ˈθɪmbl/ n small cap of metal or plastic worn over the end of the finger to protect it when sewing

thin /θɪn/ adj (~ner, ~nest) 1 having a small distance between opposite sides or surfaces 2 (of a person or part of the body) not fat 3 not growing closely together or in large amounts: *~ hair* 4 containing more liquid than is normal or expected: *~ soup* 5 easy to see through: *a ~ mist* 6 weak; feeble: *a ~ excuse* [IDM] **the thin end of the wedge** event or action that is the beginning of sth more serious or unpleasant ● **thin** adv thinly: *cut the bread too ~* ● **thin** v (-nn-) [I, T] become or make sth thin ▸ **thinly** adv ▸ **thinness** n [U]

thing /θɪŋ/ n 1 [C] any unnamed object: *What is that ~ on the table?* 2 (**things**) [pl] personal possessions, clothes, etc: *Bring your swimming ~s.* 3 (**a thing**) [sing] used with negatives to mean 'anything': *I haven't got a ~ to wear.* 4 [C] fact, event, situation or action: what sb says or thinks: *A terrible ~ happened last night.* ◇ *There's another ~ I want to ask you.*

5 (things) [pl] general situation as it affects sb: *Hi Mike. How are ~s?* **6** [C, usu sing] what is needed or socially acceptable behaviour: *do/say the right/wrong ~* **7** [C] (with an adjective) (spoken) used to talk to or about a person or animal, to show how you feel about them: *She's a sweet little ~.* [IDM] **for one thing** used for introducing a reason **have a thing about sb/sth** (infml) have a strong like or dislike of sb/sth in a way that seems strange **the thing is** (spoken) used to introduce an important fact, reason or explanation

think /θɪŋk/ v (pt, pp **thought** /θɔːt/) **1** [T] have a particular idea or opinion about sth/sb; believe sth: *Do you ~ it's going to rain?* **2** [I] use your mind to form opinions, make decisions, etc **3** [I, T] imagine sth: *I can't ~ why he came.* **4** [T] expect sth: *The job took longer than we thought.* **5** [I, T] have sth as a plan or intention: *I ~ I'll go for a swim.* [IDM] **think aloud** say what your thoughts are as you have them **think better of it/of doing sth** decide not to do sth after thinking further about it **think nothing of (doing) sth** consider an activity to be normal or easy **think the world, highly, a lot, not much, poorly, little, etc of sb/sth** have a very good, bad, etc opinion of sb/sth: *I don't ~ much of her idea.* [PV] **think about/of sb/sth 1** consider sb/sth when you are doing or planning sth **2** consider doing sth **think of sth/sb 1** have an image or idea of sth/sb in your mind: *When I said that I wasn't ~ing of anyone in particular.* **2** have an idea in your imagination: *Can you ~ of a way to raise money?* **3** (used esp with *can*) remember sth: *I can't ~ of her name.* **4** imagine sth: *Just ~ of the expense!* **5** consider sth/sb in a particular way: *I ~ of this place as my home.* **think sth out/through** consider sth carefully and thoroughly **think sth over** consider sth carefully before reaching a decision **think sth up** invent or devise a plan, etc ● **think** n [sing] [IDM] **have a think (about sth)** (infml) think carefully about sth ▶ **thinker** n person who thinks seriously about things or in a particular way: *a quick ~*

thinking /ˈθɪŋkɪŋ/ n [U] process of thinking; opinions about sth ● **thinking** adj intelligent

third /θɜːd/ ordinal number, n 3rd; the fraction ⅓; each of three equal parts of sth ■ **third deˈgree** n [sing] [IDM] **give sb the third degree** (infml) question sb for a long time; use threats or violence to get information from sb ▶ **thirdly** adv ■ **third ˈparty** n (fml or law) person other than the two main people involved

■ **third party inˈsurance** n [U] insurance that covers you if you injure sb or damage their property ● **the ˌthird ˈperson** n [sing] (gram) set of pronouns and verb forms used by a speaker to refer to other people or things: *'They are' is the ~ person plural of the verb 'to be'.* ■ **third-ˈrate** adj of very poor quality ● **the ˌThird ˈWorld** n [sing] way of referring to the developing countries of the world in Africa, Asia and Latin America

thirst /θɜːst/ n **1** [U, sing] feeling of needing or wanting a drink **2** [sing] ~ **(for)** strong desire for sth: *a ~ for knowledge* ● **thirst** v [PV] **thirst for sth** (lit) be very eager for sth: *~ for revenge* ▶ **thirsty** adj (-ier, -iest) feeling or causing thirst

thirteen /ˌθɜːˈtiːn/ number 13 ▶ **thirteenth** /-ˈtiːnθ/ ordinal number

thirty /ˈθɜːti/ number **1** 30 **2 (the thirties)** n [pl] numbers, years or temperatures from 30 to 39 ▶ **thirtieth** /ˈθɜːtiəθ/ ordinal number

this /ðɪs/ det, pron (pl **these** /ðiːz/) **1** (being) the person or thing nearby, named or understood: *Is ~ your bag?* **2** used for introducing sb or for showing sth to sb: *Jo, ~ is Pete.* **3** (infml) used when you are telling a story or telling sb about sth: *Then ~ man came in.* ● **this** adv to this degree; so: *It was about ~ high.*

thistle /ˈθɪsl/ n wild plant with prickly leaves and esp purple flowers

thong /θɒŋ/ n **1** narrow strip of leather used to fasten sth **2** piece of underwear for men or women that has only a very narrow strip of fabric at the back

thorn /θɔːn/ n **1** [C] sharp pointed part on the stem of some plants, eg roses **2** [C, U] tree or bush that has thorns [IDM] **a thorn in sb's flesh/side** person or thing that constantly annoys sb ▶ **thorny** adj (-ier, -iest) **1** causing difficulty or disagreement: *a ~y problem* **2** having thorns

thorough /ˈθʌrə/ adj **1** done completely and carefully **2** (of a person) doing work carefully, with attention to detail ■ **thorough-ˈgoing** adj (written) very thorough; complete: *a ~going revision* ▶ **thoroughly** adv ▶ **thoroughness** n [U]

thoroughbred /ˈθʌrəbred/ n, adj (animal, esp a horse) of pure breed

thoroughfare /ˈθʌrəfeə(r)/ n (fml) public road or street

those plural of THAT

though /ðəʊ/ conj **1** in spite of the fact that: *They bought the car, even ~ they couldn't really afford it.* **2** and yet; but: *It's possible, ~ unlikely.* ● **though** adv however

thought¹ pt, pp of THINK

thought² /θɔːt/ *n* **1** [C] something that you think of or remember **2** [U] power or process of thinking **3** [C] feeling of care or worry **4** [U,C] intention or hope of doing sth **5** [U] particular way of thinking: *modern scientific ~s* ▸ [IDM] **have second thoughts** change your opinion after thinking about sth again **on second thoughts** used to say that you have changed your mind ▸ **thoughtful** *adj* **1** quiet, because you are thinking **2** (*approv*) showing that you think about other people ▸ **thoughtfully** *adv* ▸ **thoughtless** *adj* not caring for other people, selfish ▸ **thoughtlessly** *adv*

thousand /ˈθaʊznd/ *number* **1** 1000 **2** (**a thousand** or **thousands** (**of**)) (*infml*) large number: *There were ~s of people there.* ▸ **thousandth** /ˈθaʊznθ/ *ordinal number*

thrash /θræʃ/ *v* **1** [T] beat a person or an animal with a stick, whip, etc **2** [I, T] (cause sth to) move about violently: *He ~ed about in the water.* **3** [T] defeat sb very easily in a game [PV] **thrash sth out** discuss a problem thoroughly in order to decide sth ▸ **thrashing** *n* **1** beating **2** defeat

thread /θred/ *n* **1** [C,U] (length of) cotton, silk, wool, etc used in sewing **2** [C] line of thought connecting parts of a story **3** [C] raised spiral line round a screw or bolt ● **thread** *v* [T] **1** put a thread through a narrow opening or hole: ~ *a needle* **2** join objects, eg beads, together by passing sth long and thin through them **3** pass film, tape, etc into position in a machine [IDM] **thread your way through sth** move carefully through sth ■ **'threadbare** *adj* (of cloth) worn

threat /θret/ *n* **1** [C,U] statement of an intention to punish or harm sb **2** [U,C, usu sing] possibility of trouble, danger or disaster **3** [C] person or thing likely to cause trouble or danger: *He is a ~ to society.*

threaten /ˈθretn/ *v* **1** [T] make a threat or threats against sb; use sth as a threat: *They ~ed to kill all the passengers.* **2** [I, T] seem likely to happen or cause sth unpleasant: *Danger ~ed.* **3** [T] be a danger to sb ▸ **threatening** *adj* ▸ **threateningly** *adv*

three /θriː/ *number* 3 ■ **three-di'mensional** *adj* having length, breadth and depth

thresh /θreʃ/ *v* [T] separate grains of corn, etc from the rest of the plant, using a machine or by beating

threshold /ˈθreʃhəʊld/ *n* (*fml*) **1** floor at the bottom of a doorway, considered as the entrance to a building or room **2** point of beginning sth: *on the ~ of a new career*

threw *pt* of THROW

thrift /θrɪft/ *n* [U] (*approv*) careful use of money ▸ **thrifty** *adj* (**-ier, -iest**)

thrill /θrɪl/ *n* **1** strong feeling of excitement or pleasure **2** sudden strong feeling that produces a physical effect ● **thrill** *v* [T] excite or please sb very much ▸ **thriller** *n* book, play or film with an exciting story, esp about crime or spying

thrive /θraɪv/ *v* [I] grow well and strong; prosper: *a thriving business*

throat /θrəʊt/ *n* **1** tube in the neck that takes food and air into the body **2** front part of the neck

throb /θrɒb/ *v* (**-bb-**) [I] (of the heart, pulse, etc) beat, esp more quickly and strongly than usual ▸ **throb** *n*

throes /θrəʊz/ *n* [pl] [IDM] **in the throes of (doing) sth** in the middle of a difficult activity

thrombosis /θrɒmˈbəʊsɪs/ (*pl* **-ses** /-siːz/) *n* [C,U] serious medical condition caused by a thick mass of blood forming in a blood vessel or the heart

throne /θrəʊn/ *n* **1** [C] special chair used by a king or queen in official ceremonies **2** (**the throne**) [sing] position of being king or queen

throng /θrɒŋ/ *n* (*fml*) large crowd of people ● **throng** *v* [I, T] go somewhere or be present somewhere in large numbers

throttle /ˈθrɒtl/ *v* [T] attack or kill sb by squeezing their throat to stop them breathing ● **throttle** *n* device controlling the flow of fuel into an engine

through /θruː/ *prep* **1** from one end or side of sth/sb to the other: *The train went ~ the tunnel.* ◇ *The bullet went straight ~ him.* **2** from the beginning to the end of an activity, situation or period of time: *She won't live ~ the night.* **3** past a barrier, stage or test: *He drove ~ a red light.* ◇ *smuggle drugs ~ customs* **4** (*US*) (also *infml* **thru**) *until,* 'and including: *Monday ~ Thursday* **5** by means of; because of: *The accident happened ~ lack of care.* ● **through** *adv* **1** from one end or side of sth to the other: *Put the coffee in the filter and let the water run ~.* **2** from the beginning to the end of sth **3** past a barrier, stage or test: *Our team is ~ to the semi-finals.* **4** connected by telephone: *I tried to ring you but I couldn't get ~.* [IDM] **through and through** completely ▸ **through** *adj* **1** allowing a direct journey: *a ~ train* **2** ~(**with**) (*esp US*) used to show you have finished using sth or have ended a relationship with sb

throughout /θruːˈaʊt/ *prep, adv* **1** in or into every part of sth: *They're sold ~ the world.* **2** during the whole period of time of sth: *I watched the film and cried ~.*

throw /θrəʊ/ *v* (*pt* **threw** /θru:/; *pp* **~n** /θrəʊn/) **1** [T] send sth through the air with some force, esp by moving the arm **2** [T] put sth in a particular place quickly and carelessly **3** [T] move sth suddenly and forcefully: *I threw open the windows.* **4** [T] move (a part of) your body suddenly and forcefully: ~ *up your hands in horror* **5** [T] make sb fall to the ground **6** [T] cause sb/sth to be in a certain state: *Hundreds were ~n out of work.* **7** [T] direct sth at sb/sth: *She threw me an angry look.* ◇ *The trees threw long shadows on the grass.* **8** [T] (*infml*) confuse, upset or surprise sb: *The interruptions threw him.* **9** [T] (*tech*) make a clay pot, etc on a potter's wheel **10** [T] move a switch, etc to operate sth **11** [T] (**throw a party**) give a party [IDM] **throw cold water on sth** → COLD¹ **throw a fit** → FIT² **throw sb in at the deep end** (*infml*) ask sb to do sth new and difficult for which they are unprepared **throw in the towel** admit defeat **throw light on sth** → LIGHT¹ **throw your weight about/around** (*infml*) use your position of power aggressively in order to achieve what you want [PV] **throw sth away| throw sth out 1** get rid of sth unwanted **2** fail to make use of sth; waste sth **throw sth in** include sth with what you are selling, without increasing the price **throw yourself/sth into sth** become involved in an activity with enthusiasm **throw sth/sb out** manage to get rid of sth/sb that is annoying you, etc **throw sb out (of ...)** force a troublemaker to leave a place **throw sth out 1** reject a plan, idea, etc **2** = THROW STH AWAY **throw sth together** make or produce sth quickly **throw sth up 1** make people vomit sth **2** leave your job ● **throw** *n* **1** act of throwing sth, esp a ball or dice **2** distance over which sth is thrown **3** loose cover for a sofa, etc ▶ **thrower** *n*

thru (*US*) = THROUGH

thrush /θrʌʃ/ *n* bird with a brown back and brown spots on its chest

thrust /θrʌst/ *v* (*pt, pp* **thrust**) [I, T] push sth suddenly and forcefully in a particular direction ● **thrust** *n* **1** (**the thrust**) [sing] main point of an argument, etc **2** [C] sudden strong movement that pushes sth/sb forward **3** [U] (*tech*) force produced by an engine to push a plane, etc forward

thud /θʌd/ *n* dull sound of a heavy object hitting sth ● **thud** *v* (**-dd-**) [I] strike or fall with a thud

thug /θʌg/ *n* violent and dangerous person

thumb /θʌm/ *n* short thick finger set apart from the other four [IDM] **thumbs up/down** used to show that sth has been accepted/rejected **under sb's thumb** (of a person) completely controlled by sb ● **thumb** *v* [T] ask for a free ride from passing motorists by signalling with your thumb: *to ~ a lift* [PV] **thumb through sth** turn the pages of a book quickly to get a general idea of it ■ **'thumbnail** *n* nail at the tip of the thumb ■ **,thumbnail 'sketch** *n* very short description of sth ■ **'thumbtack** *n* (*US*) = DRAWING PIN (DRAWING)

thump /θʌmp/ *v* **1** [I, T] hit sth hard, esp with your fist **2** [I] beat strongly: *His heart ~ed with fear.* ● **thump** *n* (noise of a) heavy blow

thunder /'θʌndə(r)/ *n* [U] **1** loud noise that follows a flash of lightning **2** loud noise like thunder: *the ~ of guns* ● **thunder** *v* [I] (used with *it*) sound with thunder: *It's been ~ing all night.* **2** [I] move somewhere very fast, often with a loud noise **3** [T] say sth in a loud angry voice ■ **'thunderbolt** *n* (*written*) flash of lightning that comes at the same time as the noise of thunder and that hits sth ■ **'thunderclap** *n* loud crash of thunder ▶ **thunderous** *adj* very loud: *~ous applause* ■ **'thunderstorm** *n* storm of lightning, thunder and heavy rain

Thursday /'θɜːzdeɪ; -di/ *n* [U, C] fifth day of the week, next after Wednesday (See examples of use at *Monday*.)

thus /ðʌs/ *adv* (*fml*) **1** in this way; like this **2** as a result of this

thwart /θwɔːt/ *v* [T] (*fml*) prevent sb or their plans from succeeding

thyme /taɪm/ *n* [U] kind of herb used in cooking

thyroid /'θaɪrɔɪd/ (*also* **'thyroid gland**) *n* gland in the neck that affects the body's growth

tiara /ti'ɑːrə/ *n* piece of jewellery like a small crown, worn by a woman

tic /tɪk/ *n* sudden unconscious moving of the muscles, esp in the face

tick /tɪk/ *n* **1** (*GB*) mark (✓) showing that sth is correct or has been dealt with **2** small bloodsucking insect **3** (*also* **ticking**) light repeated sound of a clock or watch **4** (*GB*) (*infml*) moment: *I'll be with you in a ~.* ● **tick** *v* **1** (of a clock, etc) make short light repeated sounds **2** [T] ~(**off**) put a mark (✓) next to an item on a list, an answer, etc [IDM] **what makes sb tick** what makes sb behave in the way they do [PV] **tick sb off** (*infml*) speak angrily to sb because they have done sth wrong **tick over** keep working or operating steadily

ticket /'tɪkɪt/ *n* **1** printed piece of

card or paper that gives you the right to travel on a bus, enter a cinema, etc **2** label attached to sth in a shop, etc giving the price or size of sth **3** official notice of an offence against traffic laws: *a parking ~*

tickle /'tɪkl/ v **1** [T] touch part of sb's body lightly, esp so as to make them laugh **2** [I, T] have or cause an itching feeling in a part of the body: *My throat ~s.* **3** [T] amuse and interest sb ■ **tickle** *n* [usu sing] act or feeling of tickling ▸ **ticklish** *adj* **1** (of a person) sensitive to being tickled **2** (*infml*) (of a problem) needing to be dealt with carefully

tidal /'taɪdl/ *adj* of or caused by tides ■ **tidal wave** *n* very large ocean wave

tide /taɪd/ *n* **1** [C,U] regular rise and fall in the level of the sea **2** [U] flow of water that happens as the sea rises and falls: *Beware of strong ~s.* **3** [C, usu sing] direction in which opinions, events, etc seem to be moving ■ **tide** *v* [PV] **tide sb over (sth)** help sb through a difficult period by providing what they need ■ **tidemark** *n* highest point reached by a tide on a beach

tidings /'taɪdɪŋz/ *n* [pl] (*old-fash*) news

tidy /'taɪdi/ *adj* (-**ier**, -**iest**) **1** neat; orderly: *a ~ room/girl* **2** (*infml*) (of an amount of money) fairly large: *a ~ sum of money* ▸ **tidily** *adv* ▸ **tidiness** *n* [U] ■ **tidy** *v* (*pt, pp* -**ied**) [I, T] make sth look neat by putting things where they belong: *~ (up) the room*

tie¹ /taɪ/ *v* (*pres pt* **tying** /'taɪŋ/) **1** [T] fasten sth to sth or hold things together using string, rope, etc: *A label was ~d to the handle.* ◇ *~ (up) a parcel* **2** [T] make a knot in a piece of string, ribbon, etc: *~ your shoelaces* **3** [I] be closed or fastened with a knot, etc: *Does this dress ~ in front?* **4** [T] connect or link sb/sth closely with sb/sth else **5** [T] (*~to*) restrict sb and make them unable to do everything they want: *be ~d by a contract/ promise* **6** [I, T] (of two teams, etc) have the same number of points: *The two teams ~d.* [PV] **tie sb down (to (doing) sth)** limit sb's freedom **tie in (with sth)** match or agree with sth **tie sb up 1** tie sb's arms or legs with rope so that they cannot move or escape **2** (*infml*) (usu passive) cause sb to be busy: *I'm a bit ~d up now; can you call back later?* **tie sth up** invest money so that it is not easily available for use

tie² /taɪ/ *n* **1** long narrow strip of material worn round the neck, esp by men, with a knot at the front **2** piece of string or wire, used for fastening or tying sth **3** strong connection between people and organizations: *family ~s* **4** thing that limits

sb's freedom of action **5** equal score in a game, etc ■ **tiebreaker** *n* way of deciding the winner when competitors have the same score

tier /tɪə(r)/ *n* row or layer of sth that has several rows or layers placed one above the other

tiff /tɪf/ *n* slight argument

tiger /'taɪgə(r)/ *n* large fierce animal of the cat family, yellowish with black stripes ■ **tigress** /'taɪgrəs/ *n* female tiger

tight /taɪt/ *adj* **1** held or fixed in position firmly; difficult to move or undo. *u ~ knot* **2** (of clothes) fitting closely: *These shoes are too ~.* **3** strict and firm: *Security is ~ at the airport.* **4** with people or things packed closely together **5** difficult to manage because there is not enough of sth, esp money or time: *a ~ schedule* **6** (*GB, infml, disapprov*) unwilling to spend money; not generous **7** (-**tight**) made so that sth cannot get in or out: *air-~* [IDM] **a tight spot/corner** a very difficult or dangerous situation ● **tight** *adv* tightly: *The bags are packed ~.* ▸ **tighten** *v* [I, T] (cause sth to) become tighter: *~ (up) the screws* ■ **tight-fisted** *adj* (*infml*) unwilling to spend money ▸ **tightly** *adv* ▸ **tightness** *n* [U] ■ **tightrope** *n* tightly stretched high rope on which acrobats perform ● **tights** *n* [pl] piece of clothing made of very thin fabric that fits closely over a woman's hips, legs and feet

tile /taɪl/ *n* thin usu square piece of baked clay or other material for covering roofs, walls and floors [IDM] **have a night on the tiles** (*GB, infml*) stay out late enjoying yourself ● **tile** *v* [T] **1** cover a surface with tiles: *a ~d bathroom* **2** (*computing*) arrange several windows on a computer screen

till¹ *conj, prep* = UNTIL

till² /tɪl/ *n* drawer or box for money in a shop, bank, etc ● **till** *v* [T] prepare and use land for growing crops

tiller /'tɪlə(r)/ *n* handle used for turning the rudder of a boat

tilt /tɪlt/ *v* [I, U] (cause sth to) move into a position with one side or end higher than the other ● **tilt** *n* sloping position [IDM] **(at) full tilt** as fast as possible

timber /'tɪmbə(r)/ *n* **1** [U] trees grown to be used in building, etc **2** [U] wood prepared for use in building, etc **3** [C, usu pl] wooden beam used in building a house or ship ▸ **timbered** *adj* built of wooden beams

time¹ /taɪm/ *n* **1** [U] what is measured in minutes, days, etc: *As other ~ went by we saw less of each other.* **2** [U] the time shown on a clock in minutes and hours: *What ~ is it?*

453

T

3 [U,C] time when sth happens or when sth should happen: *It's ~ for lunch.* ◇ *What ~ do you finish work?* **4** [U] an amount of time; the amount of time available to work, rest, etc: *He never takes any ~ off* (= time spent not working). ◇ *What a waste of ~!* **5** (a time) [sing] period of time during which you do sth or sth happens: *I lived in Egypt for a ~.* ◇ *Her parents died a long ~ ago.* **6** [U,pl] period of time; age: *in prehistoric ~s* **7** [C] occasion: *He failed the exam three ~s.* **8** [C] how long sb takes to run a race or complete an event: *The winner's ~ was 11.6 seconds.* **9** [U] (*music*) speed of a piece of music: *dance in ~ to the music* [IDM] **ahead of your time** having advanced or new ideas that other people use or copy later **all the time, the whole time** during the whole period or time **at all times** always **at one time** at a period of time in the past **at a time** separately **at times** sometimes **behind the times** old-fashioned in your ideas, methods, etc **do time** (*infml*) spend time in prison **for the time being** for a short period of time but not permanently **from time to time** occasionally **have no time for sb/sth** dislike sb/sth **have the time of your life** (*infml*) enjoy yourself very much **in time** after a period of time when a situation has changed **it's about/high time** (*spoken*) used to say that you think sb should do sth soon: *It's high ~ you went to bed.* **on time** not late or early; punctual(ly) **take your time** use as much time as you need without hurrying **time after time | time and (time) again** often; on many or all occasions ■ **'time bomb** *n* bomb set to explode at a certain time ■ **'time limit** *n* period of time during which sth must be done ▶ **times** *prep* (*maths*) multiplied by sth: *5 ~s 2 is 10.* **2** *n* [pl] used in comparisons to show how much more, better, etc sth is than sth else: *three ~s as long as sth* ■ **'timescale** *n* period of time it takes for sth to happen or be completed ■ **'timeshare** (*also* **timesharing**) *n* [U] arrangement in which a holiday home is owned by several people who use it for a short time each year ■ **'time switch** *n* switch that can be set to operate automatically at a certain time ■ **'timetable** *n* **1** list showing the times at which trains, buses, etc depart or arrive **2** list showing the times at which the various subjects are taught at school

time² /taɪm/ *v* [T] **1** choose the time or moment for sth: *She ~ed her arrival for shortly after 3.* **2** measure the time taken for sth to happen or for sb to do sth ▶ **timer** *n*

device used to measure the time that sth takes; device that starts or stops a machine working at a particular time ▶ **timing** *n* [U] (skill in) choosing the best moment to do sth

timely /'taɪmli/ *adj* (**-ier, -iest**) occurring at just the right time

timid /'tɪmɪd/ *adj* shy and not brave or self-confident ▶ **timidity** /tɪ'mɪdəti/ *n* [U] ▶ **timidly** *adv*

tin /tɪn/ *n* **1** [U] (*symb* Sn) soft silver-white metal **2** (*also* **tin can**) [C] (*GB*) metal container for food: *a ~ of beans* ▶ **tinned** *adj* (of food) preserved in a can: *~ned peaches* ■ **'tinfoil** *n* [U] very thin sheets of metal, used for wrapping food in ▶ **tinny** *adj* (**-ier, -iest**) (*disapprov*) (of a sound) light, high and unpleasant ■ **'tin-opener** *n* (*GB*) tool for opening tins of food

tinge /tɪndʒ/ *v* [T] **~(with)** **1** add a small amount of colour to sth **2** add a small amount of a particular emotion or quality to sth: *admiration ~d with envy* ● **tinge** *n* **1** (usu sing) small amount of a colour, feeling or quality: *a ~ of sadness in her voice*

tingle /'tɪŋɡl/ *v* [I] **1** (of a part of your body) feels as if a lot of small sharp points are pushing into it **2** **~ with** feel an emotion strongly: *~ with excitement* ● **tingle** *n* [C, usu sing] tingling feeling

tinker /'tɪŋkə(r)/ *v* [I] **~(with)** make small changes to sth to repair it, esp in way that may not be helpful

tinkle /'tɪŋkl/ *v* [I] make a series of light high ringing sounds ● **tinkle** *n* [usu sing] tinkling sound

tinsel /'tɪnsl/ *n* [U] strip or thread of shiny material used as a Christmas decoration

tint /tɪnt/ *n* (esp pl) shade of colour ● **tint** *v* [T] add a small amount of colour to sth

tiny /'taɪni/ *adj* (**-ier, -iest**) extremely small

tip /tɪp/ *n* **1** thin pointed end of sth: *the ~s of your fingers* **2** small part put on or over the end of sth: *a stick with a rubber ~* **3** small piece of advice about sth practical **4** small amount of extra money given to sb who has done a service: *leave the waiter a ~* **5** (*GB*) place where you can take rubbish and leave it **6** (*GB, infml, disapprov*) untidy place [IDM] **on the tip of your tongue** just about to be remembered or spoken **the tip of the iceberg** small sign of a much larger problem ● **tip** *v* (**-pp-**) **1** [I, T] (cause sth to) move so that one end or side is higher than the other **2** [T] (esp *GB*) make sth come out of a container or its position by holding or lifting it at an angle **3** (*GB*) [I, T] leave rubbish somewhere outdoors in order to get rid of it **4** [I, T] give a tip(4) to sb: *~ the* *waiter* **5** say in advance that sb/sth will be successful **6** [T] cover the end or edge of sth with a colour, substance, etc: *~ped cigarettes* [PV] **tip sb off** *(about sth)* *(infml)* warn sb that sth, esp sth illegal is about to happen ■ **'tip-off** *n* secret warning ■ **,tip-'top** *adj (infml)* excellent

tipple /ˈtɪpl/ *n (infml)* alcoholic drink
tipsy /ˈtɪpsi/ *adj* (**-ier**, **-iest**) *(infml)* slightly drunk
tiptoe /ˈtɪptəʊ/ *n* [IDM] **on tiptoe/tiptoes** standing or walking on the front part of your foot, with your heels off the ground: *stand on ~ to see over sb's head* ● **tiptoe** *v* [I] walk quietly: *She ~d out.*
tire¹ /ˈtaɪə(r)/ *v* [I, T] (cause sb to) become tired: *The long walk ~d them (out).* ▸ **tired** *adj* **1** feeling that you need rest or sleep **2** *~of* bored with sth/sb: *I'm ~d of watching television.* ▸ **tiredness** *n* [U] ▸ **tireless** *adj (approv)* putting a lot of hard work and energy into sth over a long time ▸ **tiresome** *adj* annoying or boring
tire² (*US*) = TYRE
tissue /ˈtɪʃuː/ *n* **1** [U] (*also* **tissues** [pl]) mass of cells that form the different parts of humans, animals and plants: *nerve ~* **2** [C] piece of soft paper used as a handkerchief **3** [U] (*also* **'tissue paper**) very thin soft paper, used esp for wrapping things
tit /tɪt/ *n* **1** (⚠, *sl*) woman's breast **2** small bird of various kinds [IDM] **tit for tat** situation in which you do sth bad to sb because they have done the same to you
titbit /ˈtɪtbɪt/ *n* **1** small tasty piece of food **2** small piece of gossip, etc
titillate /ˈtɪtɪleɪt/ *v* [T] excite sb, esp sexually
title /ˈtaɪtl/ *n* **1** [C] name of a book, play, picture, etc **2** [C] word, eg *Lord, Mrs* or *Professor*, used for showing sb's rank, profession, marital status, etc **3** [C] position of being the winner of a competition **4** [U,C] (*law*) right to own sth ▸ **titled** *adj* having a title such as Lord, Lady, etc ■ **'title deed** *n* legal document proving that sb is the owner of a house, etc **title role** *n* part in a play, etc that is used as the title
titter /ˈtɪtə(r)/ *v* [I] give a nervous or silly little laugh ▸ **titter** *n*
TNT /ˌtiː en ˈtiː/ *n* [U] powerful explosive
to¹ */before consonants* tə; *before vowels* tu; *strong form* tuː/ *prep* **1** in the direction of sth: *walk to the shops* **2** situated in the direction mentioned from sth: *Place the cursor to the left of the first word.* **3** as far as: *Her hair fell to her waist.* **4** reaching a particular state: *rise to power*

5 used to show the end or limit of a range or period of time: *from May to July* **6** before the start of sth: *It's ten (= minutes) to three.* **7** used to show the person or thing that receives sth: *I gave it to Peter.* **8** used to show a relationship between one person or thing and another: *She's married to Mark.* ◊ *the key to the door* **9** used to show a comparison or ratio: *I prefer tea to coffee.* ◊ *We won by 6 goals to 3.*
to² */before consonants* tə; *before vowels* tu; *strong form* tuː/ (used before the simple form of a v to form the infinitive) **1** used to show purpose or intention: *I went out to buy food.* **2** used to show the result of sth: *It was too hot to go out.* **3** used to show the cause of sth: *I'm sorry to hear that.* **4** used to show an action that you want or are advised to do: *I'd love to go to Paris.* **5** used instead of the whole infinitive: *'Will you come?' 'I hope to.'*
to³ /tuː/ *adv* (of a door) in or into a closed position: *Push the door to.* [IDM] **to and fro** backwards and forwards
toad /təʊd/ *n* animal like a frog
toadstool /ˈtəʊdstuːl/ *n* kind of fungus, esp one that is poisonous
toast /təʊst/ *n* **1** [U] slices of bread that have been made brown by heating them on both sides **2** [C] act of a group of people wishing sb happiness, success, etc by drinking a glass of sth, especially alcohol, at the same time: *propose a ~ to sb* ● **toast** *v* **1** [T] wish happiness, success, etc to sb by drinking wine, etc: *~ the bride and bridegroom* **2** [I, T] (cause sth, esp bread, to) turn brown by heating it in a toaster, etc **3** [T] warm a part of your body by placing it near a fire ▸ **toaster** *n* electrical machine for toasting bread
tobacco /təˈbækəʊ/ *n* [U] (plant having) leaves that are dried and used for smoking in cigarettes, pipes, etc ▸ **tobacconist** /-kənɪst/ *n* shop or person that sells tobacco, cigarettes, etc
toboggan /təˈbɒɡən/ *n* long narrow sledge (= vehicle that slides over snow) used for sliding down slopes ● **toboggan** *v* [I] travel down a slope on snow using a toboggan
today /təˈdeɪ/ *adv, n* [U] **1** (on) this day **2** (at) this present time: *the young people of ~*
toddle /ˈtɒdl/ *v* [I] (esp of a young child) walk with short unsteady steps ▸ **toddler** *n* small child that has just learned to walk
to-do /təˈduː/ *n* [C, usu sing] (*pl* **~s**) *(infml)* unnecessary excitement or anger about sth
toe /təʊ/ *n* **1** one of the five small

parts that stick out from the foot **2** part of a sock, shoe, etc that covers the toes [IDM] **keep sb on their toes** make sure that sb is ready for action by doing things that they are not expecting ● **toe** v [IDM] **toe the line** obey orders ■ **'toenail** n hard layer covering the end of your toe

toffee /'tɒfɪ/ n [C,U] (piece of) hard sticky sweet made by heating sugar, butter, etc

together /tə'geðə(r)/ adv **1** with each other: They went for a walk ~. **2** so that two or more things touch or are joined with each other: Tie the ends ~. **3** in or into agreement **4** at the same time: They both spoke ~. [IDM] **together with** including; in addition to ● **together** adj (infml, approv) (of a person) well organized and confident ▸ **togetherness** n [U] feeling of friendliness or love

toggle /'tɒgl/ v [I] (computing) press a key or set of keys on a computer keyboard in order to move from one program, etc to another

toil /tɔɪl/ v [I] (fml) work hard and/or for a long time ● **toil** n [U] (fml) hard, unpleasant and tiring work

toilet /'tɔɪlət/ n (room containing a bowl used for receiving and taking away waste matter from the body ■ **'toilet paper** n [U] paper used for cleaning your bottom after you have used the toilet ▸ **toiletries** n [pl] things, eg soap and toothpaste, that you use for cleaning your teeth, etc ■ **'toilet roll** n roll of toilet paper

token /'təʊkən/ n **1** round flat piece of metal used instead of a coin to operate some machines, etc **2** (GB) piece of paper that you pay for and that sb can exchange for goods in a shop: a book ~ **3** symbol or sign: a ~ of my affection ● **token** adj small; not serious: a ~ gesture

told pt, pp of TELL

tolerate /'tɒləreɪt/ v [T] **1** allow sb to do sth that you disagree with or dislike: I won't ~ such behaviour. **2** accept sb/sth unpleasant without protesting: ~ heat/noise ▸ **tolerable** /-rəbl/ adj fairly good; that can be tolerated ▸ **tolerably** adv fairly ▸ **tolerance** /-rəns/ n [U] willingness or ability to tolerate sb/sth: religious/racial tolerance ▸ **tolerant** /-rənt/ adj able to accept what other people say or do even if you do not agree with it ▸ **toleration** /-'reɪʃn/ n [U] action or practice of tolerating sb/sth

toll /təʊl/ n **1** [C] money that you pay to use a particular road or bridge **2** [C] amount of damage or the number of deaths caused by a war, disaster, etc: the death ~ has now reached 7000 **3** [sing] sound of a bell ringing

with slow regular strokes ● **toll** v [I, T] (of a bell) ring slowly and repeatedly, esp as a sign that sb has died

tomato /tə'mɑːtəʊ/ n (pl **~es**) (plant with a) soft red fruit eaten raw or cooked as a vegetable

tomb /tuːm/ n place, esp with a stone monument, where a dead body is buried ■ **'tombstone** n stone monument over a tomb

tomboy /'tɒmbɔɪ/ n young girl who enjoys games and activities traditionally associated with boys

tomcat /'tɒmkæt/ n male cat

tomorrow /tə'mɒrəʊ/ adv, n [U] **1** (on) the day after today **2** (in) the near future

ton /tʌn/ n **1** [C] unit for measuring weight, 2240 pounds in Britain, 2000 pounds in the USA **2** (**tons**) [pl] (infml) a lot: ~s of money

tone¹ /təʊn/ n **1** [C] quality of sb's voice, esp expressing a particular emotion: speaking in hushed ~s **2** [sing] general quality or character of sth, eg a piece of writing: the serious ~ of the article **3** [C] quality of a sound, esp that of a musical instrument **4** [C] shade of a colour **5** [C] signal on a telephone line: the dialling ~ **6** [C] (music) one of the five longer differences in pitch between one note and the next ■ **'tone-'deaf** adj unable to hear the differences between musical notes

tone² /təʊn/ v **1** [T] ~(**up**) make your muscles, skin, etc firmer and stronger: Exercise ~s up the body. **2** [I] ~(**in; with**) match the colour of sth [PV] **tone sth down** cause sth to become less forceful or intense

tongs /tɒŋz/ n [pl] tool with two long parts joined at one end, used for picking up and holding things

tongue /tʌŋ/ n **1** [C] soft part in the mouth that moves around, used for talking, tasting, licking, etc **2** [U,C] tongue of some animals, cooked and eaten **3** [C] (fml) language **4** [sing] particular way of speaking: He has a sharp ~. **5** [C] long narrow piece of leather under the laces on a shoe [IDM] **with your tongue in your cheek | with tongue in cheek** saying sth that you do not intend to be taken seriously; joking ■ **'tongue-tied** adj unable to speak because of shyness or nervousness ■ **'tongue-twister** n word or phrase that is difficult to say

tonic /'tɒnɪk/ n **1** (also **'tonic water**) [U,C] clear fizzy drink, often mixed with a strong alcoholic drink, eg gin **2** [C,U] medicine that gives strength or energy **3** [C,U] liquid that you put on your hair or skin to make it healthier

tonight /təˈnaɪt/ *adv, n* [U] (during the) evening or night of today

tonnage /ˈtʌnɪdʒ/ *n* [U,C] amount of cargo a ship can carry

tonne /tʌn/ *n* metric unit of weight; 1000 kilograms

tonsil /ˈtɒnsl/ *n* either of the two small organs at the back of the throat ▶ **tonsillitis** /ˌtɒnsəˈlaɪtɪs/ *n* [U] painful swelling of the tonsils

too /tuː/ *adv* **1** to a higher degree than is allowed or desirable: *You're driving ~ fast!* **2** in addition; also: *She plays the guitar and sings ~.*

took *pt of* TAKE¹

tool /tuːl/ *n* instrument that you hold in your hand and use for working on sth

toot /tuːt/ *n* short high sound from a car horn or whistle ● **toot** *v* [I, T] (cause sth to) make a short high sound

tooth /tuːθ/ *n* (*pl* **teeth** /tiːθ/) **1** any of the hard white objects in the mouth, used for biting and chewing food **2** narrow pointed part that sticks out of an object, eg on a comb or saw [IDM] **get your teeth into sth** (*infml*) put a lot of effort or enthusiasm into sth ■ **toothache** *n* [U,C, usu sing] pain in a tooth or teeth ■ **toothbrush** *n* brush for cleaning your teeth ▶ **toothed** /tuːθt/ *adj* having teeth ▶ **toothless** *adj* ■ **toothpaste** *n* [U] substance that you put on a brush and use to clean your teeth ■ **toothpick** *n* short pointed piece of wood, etc, used for removing food from between your teeth

top¹ /tɒp/ *n* **1** [C] highest part or point of sth: *at the ~ of the hill* **2** [C] upper flat surface of sth: *the ~ of the table* **3** [sing] highest or most important rank or position **4** [C] thing that you put on the end of sth to close it: *a pen/bottle* ~ **5** [C] piece of clothing worn on the upper part of the body **6** [C] toy that spins on its pointed end [IDM] **at the top of your voice** as loudly as you can **from top to bottom** very thoroughly **get on top of sb** (*infml*) be too much for sb to manage or deal with **on top of sth 1** in addition to sth **2** in control of a situation **on top of the world** very happy or proud **over the top** ~, **OTT** (*esp GB, infml*) unacceptably extreme or exaggerated: *His performance in the film is a bit over the ~.* ● **top** *adj* highest in position, rank or degree: *a room on the ~ floor ◇ at ~ speed* ■ **top brass** *n* [sing, with sing or pl verb] (*infml*) people in the most important positions in a company, etc ■ **top dog** *n* [usu sing] (*infml*) person, group, etc that is better than all the others, esp in a competition ■ **top 'hat** *n* man's tall formal black or grey hat ■ **top-'heavy** *adj* too heavy at the top ▶ **top-less** *adj, adv* (of a woman) with the breasts bare ■ **topmost** *adj* (*written*) highest ■ **top 'secret** *adj* needing to be kept completely secret ■ **topsoil** *n* [U] layer of soil nearest the surface

top² /tɒp/ *v* (-**pp**-) [T] **1** be higher than an amount: *Exports have ~ped £100m.* **2** be in the highest position: *a cake ~ped with icing* **4** ~ **yourself** (*GB, infml*) kill yourself deliberately [PV] **top sth up** fill up a partly empty container: ~ *up sb's drink*

topic /ˈtɒpɪk/ *n* subject for discussion or study ▶ **topical** *adj* of present interest: ~*al issues*

topple /ˈtɒpl/ *v* [I, T] (cause sth to) become unsteady and fall: (*fig*) *The crisis ~d the government.*

torch /tɔːtʃ/ *n* **1** (*GB*) small electric light held in the hand **2** piece of wood soaked in oil, etc for carrying as a light ■ **torchlight** *n* [U] light of torch or torches

tore *pt of* TEAR¹

torment /ˈtɔːment/ *n* [U,C] (person or thing that causes) extreme suffering ● **torment** /tɔːˈment/ *v* [T] **1** (*written*) make sb suffer very much **2** annoy sb in a cruel way ▶ **tormentor** *n*

torn *pp of* TEAR²

tornado /tɔːˈneɪdəʊ/ *n* (*pl* ~**es**) violent destructive storm with circular winds

torpedo /tɔːˈpiːdəʊ/ *n* (*pl* ~**es**) long narrow bomb that travels underwater and is used for destroying ships ● **torpedo** *v* [T] attack and destroy sth (as if) with a torpedo

torrent /ˈtɒrənt/ *n* **1** large amount of water moving very quickly **2** large amount of sth that comes suddenly and violently: *a ~ of abuse* ▶ **torrential** /təˈrenʃl/ *adj* (of rain) falling in large amounts

torso /ˈtɔːsəʊ/ *n* (*pl* ~**s**) main part of the human body, not including the head, arms or legs

tortoise /ˈtɔːtəs/ *n* slow-moving animal with a hard shell ■ **tortoise-shell** *n* [U] hard yellow and brown shell of some turtles, used for making ornaments

tortuous /ˈtɔːtʃuəs/ *adj* **1** full of bends **2** not direct; complicated

torture /ˈtɔːtʃə(r)/ *v* **1** cause extreme pain to sb as a punishment or to force them to say sth ● **torture** *n* **1** [U] act of torturing sb **2** [C,U] (*infml*) (thing that causes) mental or physical suffering ▶ **torturer** *n*

Tory /ˈtɔːri/ *n* (*pl* -**ies**), *adj* (member) of the Conservative Party

toss /tɒs/ *v* **1** [T] throw sth lightly or

carelessly **2** [T] move your head suddenly upwards, esp to show annoyance **3** [I, T] (cause sb/sth to) move restlessly from side to side: *I kept ~ing and turning all night.* **4** [I, T] shake or turn food in order to cover it with oil, butter, etc: *~ a salad* **5** [I, T] decide sth by throwing a coin and guessing which side will be on top when it falls: *Let's ~ to see who goes first.* ● **toss** *n* act of tossing sth: *with a ~ of her head* ▸ **'toss-up** *n* [sing] even chance

tot /tɒt/ *n* **1** (*infml*) very small child **2** (*esp GB*) small amount of alcoholic drink ● **tot** *v* (**-tt-**) [PV] **tot sth up** (*infml*) add up numbers to make a total

total /ˈtəʊtl/ *n* complete number or amount: *The repairs come to over £500 in ~.* ● **total** *adj* complete: *the ~ profit* ● **total** *v* (**-ll-**, *US also* **-l-**) [T] **1** reach a particular total: *The number of visitors ~ed 15 000.* **2** ~ (**up**) add up the numbers of sth/sb and get a total ▸ **totality** /-ˈtæləti/ *n* [C,U] (*fml*) whole amount; state of being complete or whole ▸ **totally** *adv* completely: *~ly blind*

totalitarian /təʊˌtæləˈteəriən/ *adj* (*disapprov*) (of a system of government) in which there is only one political party that has complete power and control over the people

totter /ˈtɒtə(r)/ *v* [I] **1** walk or move unsteadily **2** be weak and seem likely to fall

touch[1] /tʌtʃ/ *v* **1** [I, T] put your hands or fingers onto sb/sth: *The dish is hot—don't ~ (it)!* **2** [I, T] (of two or more things, surfaces, etc) be or come so close together that there is no space between: *The two wires ~ed.* **3** [T] eat, drink or use sth: *He hasn't ~ed any food for two days.* **4** [T] cause sb to feel upset or sympathetic: *We were greatly ~ed by your thoughtfulness.* **5** [T] be as good as sb in skill, quality, etc: *No one can ~ him as an actor.* [IDM] **touch wood** touch sth made of wood to avoid bad luck [PV] **touch down** (of an aircraft) land **touch sth off** make sth begin, esp a violent situation **touch on/upon sth** mention sth briefly **touch sth up** improve sth by changing or adding to it slightly ■ **'touchdown** *n* [C,U] moment when a plane or spacecraft lands ■ **touched** *adj* feeling happy and grateful ■ **touching** *adj* causing feelings of pity or sympathy ■ **'touch screen** *n* (*computing*) display device which allows you to use a computer by touching areas on the screen

touch[2] /tʌtʃ/ *n* **1** [U] sense that enables you to be aware of things when you put your hands on them **2** [C, usu sing] act of putting your

hands or fingers on sb/sth **3** [sing] way sth feels when you touch it: *The material has a velvety ~.* **4** [C] small detail: *put the finishing ~es to the project* **5** [sing] way of doing sth: *Her work has that professional ~.* **6** [C, usu sing] ~of very small amount: *a ~ of frost in the air* **7** [U] (in football/rugby) part of the pitch outside the sidelines: *The ball is in ~.* [IDM] **be, get, keep, etc in touch (with sb)** communicate with sb ■ **touch-and-'go** *adj* uncertain; risky

touchy /ˈtʌtʃi/ *adj* (**-ier, -iest**) easily offended

tough /tʌf/ *adj* **1** having or causing difficulties: *a ~ problem* **2** very firm; severe: *~ laws to deal with terrorism* **3** strong enough to deal with difficult situations **4** (of meat) difficult to cut and chew **5** not easily cut or broken [IDM] **tough luck** (*infml*) used to show sympathy for sb unfortunate that has happened to sb ▸ **toughen** /ˈtʌfn/ *v* [I, T] become or make sth/sb stronger ▸ **toughness** *n* [U]

toupee /ˈtuːpeɪ/ *n* small wig worn on a bald part of a man's head

tour /tʊə(r)/ *n* **1** journey made for pleasure during which several places are visited: *a round-the-world ~* **2** act of walking around a town, building, etc in order to visit it: *I went on a guided ~* (= by sb who knows the place) *of the palace.* **3** official series of visits to different places by a sports team, famous person, etc ● **tour** *v* [I, T] travel around a place, eg to perform, advertise sth, etc ▸ **tourism** /-rɪzəm/ *n* [U] business of providing hotels, special trips, etc for tourists ▸ **tourist** *n* person who visits places for pleasure

tournament /ˈtɔːnəmənt/ *n* series of games or contests: *a chess ~*

tourniquet /ˈtʊənɪkeɪ/ *n* bandage twisted tightly round an injured arm or leg to stop it bleeding

tout /taʊt/ *v* **1** [I, T] try to get people to buy your goods or services, esp in an annoyingly direct way **2** [T] (*GB*) sell tickets for sports matches, etc at very high prices ● **tout** *n* person who buys tickets for sports events, etc and then sells them at a higher price

tow /təʊ/ *v* [T] pull a car or boat behind another vehicle, using a rope, chain, etc ● **tow** *n* act of towing a vehicle [IDM] **in tow** (*infml*) following closely behind ■ **'towpath** *n* path along the bank of a canal or river

towards /təˈwɔːdz/ (*also* **toward** /təˈwɔːd/) *prep* **1** in the direction of sb/sth: *walk ~ the door* **2** getting closer to achieving sth: *steps ~ unity* **3** close(r) to a point in time: *~ the end of the 19th century* **4** in relation to sb/sth: *friendly ~ tourists*

5 with the aim of obtaining sth: *The money will go ~ a new car.*

towel /ˈtaʊəl/ *n* piece of fabric or paper for drying things, esp your body ▸ **towelling** (*-l- US*) *n* [U] thick soft cloth used for making towels

tower /ˈtaʊə(r)/ *n* tall narrow (part of a) building, esp of a church or castle [IDM] **a tower of strength** person who can be relied on for help or support ● **tower** *v* [PV] **tower over/above sb/sth** be much higher or taller than sb/sth ■ **'tower block** *n* (*GB*) very tall block of flats or offices ▸ **towering** *adj* very tall; very great

town /taʊn/ *n* **1** [C] place with many buildings and houses, larger than a village **2** [sing] all the people who live in a particular town **3** [U] main business or shopping area of a town: *I gave her a lift into ~.* **4** [U] particular town where sb works or lives or one which has just been referred to: *I'll be in ~ again next week.* **5** [sing, U] life in towns as opposed to life in the country [IDM] **go to town (on sth)** (*infml*) do sth with great energy or enthusiasm **(out) on the town** (*infml*) visiting restaurants, clubs, etc for entertainment, esp at night ■ **,town 'hall** *n* buildings with the offices of the town's local government ■ **'town-ship** *n* (in South Africa in the past) a town where black citizens live

toxic /ˈtɒksɪk/ *adj* (*fml*) containing poison; poisonous

toy /tɔɪ/ *n* thing for children to play with ● **toy** *v* [PV] **toy with sth** consider an idea or plan, but not seriously **2** play with sth and move it around carelessly: *~ with a pencil*

trace /treɪs/ *v* [T] **1** discover or find sb/sth after looking for them/it carefully: *I cannot ~ the letter.* **2** find the origin or cause of sth **3** describe a process or the development of sth **4** follow the shape or outline of sth; draw a line or lines on sth **5** copy sth by drawing on transparent paper placed over it ● **trace** *n* **1** [C,U] mark, sign, etc that shows that sb/sth was present in a place: *~s of an ancient civilization* ◊ *disappear without ~* **2** [C] very small amount of sth: *~s of poison in his blood* ▸ **tracing** *n* copy of a drawing, map, etc made by tracing(s) it ■ **'tracing paper** *n* [U] transparent paper used for making tracings

trachea /trəˈkiːə/ *n* (*pl ~s* or, in scientific use, *~e* /-kiː/) (*anat*) tube that carries air to the lungs

track /træk/ *n* **1** [C] rough path or road **2** [C, usu pl] series of marks left by a moving vehicle, a person or an animal **3** [C,U] rails that a train moves along **4** [C] course or circuit

for racing **5** [C] piece of music or song on a record, CD or tape [IDM] **(be) hot on sb's/sth's tracks** thinking in the right/wrong way **keep/lose track of sb/sth** have/not have information about what is happening or where sb/sth is **make tracks** (*spoken*) leave a place **on the right/wrong track** thinking in the right/wrong way **stop/halt sb in their tracks** | **stop/halt/freeze in your tracks** (*infml*) suddenly make sb stop by frightening or surprising them; suddenly stop because sth has frightened or surprised you: *The horse stopped dead in its ~.* ● **track** *v* [T] find sb/sth by following the marks, signs, etc they have left behind [PV] **track sb/sth down** find sb/sth after searching in different places ▸ **tracker** *n* ■ **'track record** *n* past achievements of a person or organization ■ **'tracksuit** *n* loose warm suit worn by athletes, esp during training

tract /trækt/ *n* **1** (*tech*) system of connected organs or tubes in the body: *the respiratory ~* **2** large area of land **3** short article on a religious, political or moral subject

traction engine /ˈtrækʃn endʒɪn/ *n* large vehicle, driven by steam, used in the past for pulling heavy loads

tractor /ˈtræktə(r)/ *n* motor vehicle used for pulling farm machinery

trade¹ /treɪd/ *n* **1** [U] business of buying, selling or exchanging goods or services **2** [C] particular type or area of business: *She's in the drug ~.* **3** [U,C] job, esp one needing training and skill with the hands: *a carpenter by ~.* ■ **trademark** (*abbr TM*) *n* name or symbol used on a product by a manufacturer ■ **'trade name** *n* = BRAND NAME (BRAND) ■ **'tradesman** *n* person, eg a shopkeeper, who sells goods ■ **,trade 'union** *n* organization of workers, formed to protect their interests and get better working conditions ■ **,trade 'unionist** *n* member of a trade union

trade² /treɪd/ *v* **1** [I, T] *~(in)* buy and sell things **2** [T] *~(for)* exchange sth for sth else: *to ~ secrets* [PV] **trade sth in (for sth)** give sth used in part payment for sth new **trade on sth** take unfair advantage of sth ▸ **trader** *n*

tradition /trəˈdɪʃn/ *n* [C,U] (set of) customs, beliefs or practices passed down from one generation to the next ▸ **traditional** /-ʃənl/ *adj* ▸ **traditionally** *adv*

traffic /ˈtræfɪk/ *n* [U] **1** vehicles on a road at a particular time **2** movement of ships or aircraft along a route **3** movement of people or goods from one place to another: *commuter ~* **4** *~(in)* illegal trade in sth ● **traffic** *v* (*-ck-*) [PV] **traffic in**

sth buy and sell sth illegally ▶ **trafficker** n ■ **'traffic island** n raised area for pedestrians in the middle of a busy road ■ **'traffic jam** n long line of vehicles on a road that cannot move or cannot move very slowly ■ **'traffic light** n [C, usu pl] set of coloured lights that control the flow of traffic at a road junction ■ **'traffic warden** n person whose job is to check that people do not park their cars in the wrong place

tragedy /'trædʒədi/ n (pl **-ies**) [C,U] **1** very sad event or situation, esp one involving death **2** serious play with a sad ending; plays of this type

tragic /'trædʒɪk/ adj **1** making you feel very sad, usu because sb has died: a ~ accident **2** connected with tragedy(2) ▶ **tragically** -/kli/ adv

trail /treɪl/ n **1** line, signs, series of marks, etc left by sb/sth showing where they have been **2** path through the countryside ● **trail** v **1** [I, T] (cause sth to) be pulled along behind sb/sth, usu along the ground **2** [I] walk slowly because you are tired or bored, esp behind sb else **3** [I] ~(**by/in**) lose in a game, etc **4** [T] follow sb/sth by looking for signs they have left behind **5** [I] (of plants) grow along the ground or hang down loosely [IDM] ➔ **hot on sb's/sth's trail** → HOT ▶ **trailer** n **1** truck or container with wheels, that is pulled along by another vehicle **2** (US) vehicle without an engine, that can be pulled by a car or truck or used as a home when it is parked **3** series of short pieces from a new film, shown to advertise it

train¹ /treɪn/ n **1** line of carriages or trucks joined together and pulled along by a railway engine **2** number of people or animals moving in a line **3** series of connected things: a ~ of thought **4** part of a long dress that spreads out on the ground behind the wearer

train² /treɪn/ v **1** [I, T] receive or give sb teaching, practice or exercise: ~ a football team **2** [T] make a plant grow in a certain direction: ~ roses up a wall [PV] **train sth at/on sb/sth** (written) aim a gun, camera, etc at sb/sth ▶ **trainee** /,treɪ'ni:/ n person being taught how to do a particular job ▶ **trainer** n [C] **1** [usu pl] shoe worn for sports or as a piece of informal clothing **2** person who trains people or animals ▶ **training** n [U] preparation; practice

traipse /treɪps/ v [I] (infml) walk in a tired way

trait /treɪt/ n particular quality in your personality

traitor /'treɪtə(r)/ n person who betrays your country, friends, etc

tram /træm/ n passenger vehicle powered by electricity that runs on rails set in the road

tramp /træmp/ v [I, T] walk with heavy or noisy steps, esp for a long time ● **tramp** n [C] **1** person with no house or job who travels from place to place **2** [sing] **(the tramp of sb/sth)** sound of sb's heavy footsteps

trample /'træmpl/ v **1** [I, T] ~(**on/ over**) step heavily on sb/sth so that you crush or harm them/it with your feet **2** [I] ~(**on/over**) ignore sb's rights or feelings and treat them as if they were unimportant

trampoline /'træmpəliːn/ n strong cloth held by springs in a frame, on which gymnasts jump up and down

trance /trɑːns/ n sleep-like condition of the mind

tranquil /'træŋkwɪl/ adj (fml) calm; quiet ▶ **tranquillity** (US also -l-) /-'kwɪləti/ n [U] calm quiet state ▶ **tranquillize** (also -ise) (US also -l-) v [T] make a person or animal calm, esp by giving them a drug ▶ **tranquillizer** (also -iser) n (US also -l-) drug used to reduce anxiety ▶ **tranquilly** adv

transact /træn'zækt/ v [T] (fml) do business with a person or an organization ▶ **transaction** /-'zækʃn/ n **1** [C] piece of business done between people **2** [U] (fml) ~ **of** process of doing sth

transatlantic /,trænzət'læntɪk/ adj of travelling or communications across the Atlantic Ocean

transcend /træn'send/ v [T] (fml) be or go beyond the usual limits of sth: ~ human knowledge

transcontinental /,trænz,kɒntɪ'nentl/ adj crossing a continent

transcribe /træn'skraɪb/ v [T] **1** record thoughts, speech or data in written form **2** (tech) show the sounds of speech using a phonetic alphabet: ~d in phonetic symbols **3** arrange a piece of music so that it can be played by a different instrument, etc ▶ **transcript** /'trænskrɪpt/ n written or printed copy of words that have been spoken ▶ **transcription** /-'skrɪpʃn/ n [U, C]

transfer¹ /træns'fɜː(r)/ v (**-rr-**) [I, T] move from one place, job, etc to another: He was ~red to the sales department. **2** [T] give the possession of sth to sb else ▶ **transferable** adj that can be transferred(2): This ticket is not ~able. ▶ **transference** /'trænsfərəns/ n [U]

transfer² /'trænsfɜː(r)/ n **1** [U,C] (instance of) moving sb/sth from one place, job, etc to another **2** [C] design that can be transferred from one surface and stuck onto another

transfix /træns'fiks/ v [T] (*fml*) (usu passive) make sb unable to move, think or speak because of fear, astonishment, etc

transform /træns'fɔːm/ v [T] completely change the appearance or character of sth ▶ **transformation** /-'meɪʃn/ n [C,U] ▶ **transformer** n apparatus that changes the voltage of an electric current

transfusion /træns'fjuːʒn/ n [C,U] act or process of putting one person's blood into sb else's body

transgress /trænz'gres/ v [I, T] (*fml*) go beyond the limit of what is morally or legally acceptable ▶ **transgression** /-'greʃn/ n [C, U]

transient /'trænziənt/ adj lasting for only a short time

transistor /træn'zɪstə(r)/ ·'sɪst-/ n 1 small electronic device used in computers, radios, etc for controlling the electric current 2 (also **tran,sistor 'radio**) small radio with transistors

transit /'trænzɪt/ n [U] process of travelling or being moved from one place to another: *goods damaged in ~*

transition /træn'zɪʃn/ ·'sɪʃn/ n [U,C] (instance of) changing from one state or condition to another ▶ **transitional** /-ʃənl/ adj

transitive /'trænsətɪv/ adj (*gram*) (of a verb) used with a direct object, eg *washed* in 'He washed the cups.'

transitory /'trænsətri/ adj lasting for only a short time

translate /træns'leɪt/ v [I, T] 1 put sth written or spoken into a different language: ~ *(the book) from French into Russian* 2 ~(**into**) (cause sth to) be changed into a different form: ~ *words into action* ▶ **translation** /-'leɪʃn/ n [C,U] ▶ **translator** n

translucent /træns'luːsnt/ adj allowing light to pass through, but not transparent

transmission /trænz'mɪʃn/ n (*fml*) 1 [U] act of passing sth from one person, place or thing to another: *the ~ of the disease* 2 [C] television or radio broadcast 3 [U,C] parts of a vehicle that pass power to the wheels

transmit /træns'mɪt/ v (-tt-) [T] 1 send an electronic signal, radio or television broadcast, etc 2 pass sth from one person to another: *sexually ~ted diseases* ▶ **transmitter** n device that transmits radio or television signals

transnational /,trænz'næʃnəl/ ,træns-/ adj (*business*) operating in or between many different countries, without being based in any particular one

transparent /træns'pærənt/ adj 1 (of glass, plastic, etc) allowing you to see through it: *Glass is ~.* 2 easily understood; obvious ▶ **transparency** /-rənsi/ n (pl -ies) 1 [C] small piece of photographic film in a frame 2 [U] quality of being transparent ▶ **transparently** adv

transplant /træns'plɑːnt; trænz-/ v [T] 1 take an organ, skin, etc from one person, animal, part of the body, etc and put it into or onto another 2 move a growing plant and plant it somewhere else 3 (*fml*) move sb/sth to a different place or environment ● **transplant** /'trænsplɑːnt; 'trænz-/ n 1 [C,U] medical operation in which a damaged organ, etc is replaced with another: *have a heart ~* 2 plant, etc that is used in a transplant operation

transport /træn'spɔːt/ v [T] move goods or people from one place to another ● **transport** /'trænspɔːt/ (*esp US* **transportation** /,trænspɔː-'teɪʃn/) n [U] 1 (system for) carrying people or goods from one place to another 2 [U] vehicle or method of travel ▶ **transporter** n large vehicle used for carrying cars

transpose /træn'spəʊz/ v [T] 1 (*fml*) change the order of two or more things 2 (*fml*) move sth to a different place or change sth into a different form 3 (*music*) write or play a piece of music in a different key[5] (5) ▶ **transposition** /,trænspə'zɪʃn/ n [C, U]

transverse /'trænzvɜːs/ adj (*tech*) situated across sth

transvestite /trænz'vestaɪt/ n person who enjoys wearing the clothes of the opposite sex

trap /træp/ n 1 device for catching animals 2 plan for catching or deceiving sb 3 light two-wheeled carriage 4 (*sl*) mouth ● **trap** v (-pp-) [T] 1 keep sb in a dangerous place, etc that they want to get out of but cannot 2 catch an animal in a trap 3 trick or deceive sb ▶ **'trapdoor** n small door in a floor or ceiling ▶ **trapper** n person who catches animals

trapeze /trə'piːz/ n bar hung from two ropes, used by acrobats for swinging on

trash /træʃ/ n [U] 1 (*US*) = RUBBISH 2 (*infml*) material, writing, etc of very low quality ▶ **'trash can** n (*US*) = DUSTBIN (DUST) ▶ **trashy** adj (-ier, -iest) (*infml*) of very low quality

trauma /'trɔːmə/ n 1 [U] emotional shock producing a lasting harmful effect 2 [C,U] (*infml*) very upsetting, unpleasant experience ▶ **traumatic** /trɔː'mætɪk/ adj

travel /'trævl/ v (-ll-, *US* -l-) [I, T] 1 go from one place to another, esp over a long distance: ~ *abroad/across Africa/around the world* 2 [I] move or go at a particular speed or in a particular direction: *Light ~s faster than*

T

sound. ● **travel** n 1 [U] act or activity of travelling: *space ~ 2 (travels)* [pl] time spent travelling, esp for pleasure ■ **'travel agent** n person whose job is to make arrangements for people wanting to travel ▶ **travelled** (*US* **-l-**) *adj* (of a person) having travelled the amount mentioned: *a well-~ writer* ▶ **traveller** (*US* **-l-**) n **1** person who is travelling or who often travels **2** (*GB*) person who does not live in one place, but who travels around, esp as part of a group ■ **'traveller's cheque** n cheque that can be exchanged abroad for the money of the country you are in

traverse /trə'vɜːs/ v [T] (*fml*) cross an area of land or water

travesty /'trævəsti/ n (*pl* **-ies**) very bad imitation or representation of sth: *a ~ of justice*

trawl /trɔːl/ v [I, T] fish with a large wide net dragged along the bottom of the sea ▶ **trawler** n fishing boat used for trawling

tray /treɪ/ n flat piece of wood, plastic, etc, used for carrying things, esp food

treacherous /'tretʃərəs/ *adj* **1** disloyal or deceitful **2** dangerous: *~ tides* ▶ **treacherously** *adv* ▶ **treachery** /-tʃəri/ n [U, C] *of betrayal*

treacle /'triːkl/ n [U] thick sticky liquid made from sugar

tread /tred/ v (*pt* **trod** /trɒd/; *pp* **trodden** /'trɒdn/) **1** [I] put your foot down while stepping or walking **2** [T] press or crush sth with your feet **3** [I, L] (*lit*) walk somewhere [IDM] **tread on sb's toes** (*infml*) offend sb **tread water** keep yourself upright in water by moving your legs up and down ● **tread** n [sing] **1** way sb walks or the sound sb makes when they walk **2** [C, U] raised pattern on a tyre of a vehicle **3** [C] upper surface of a step or stair

treason /'triːzn/ n [U] crime of betraying your country, eg by helping its enemies ▶ **treasonable** /-zənəbl/ *adj*: *a ~able offence*

treasure /'treʒə(r)/ n **1** [U] collection of gold and silver, jewels, etc **2** [C] highly valued object or person ● **treasure** v [T] have or keep sth that is extremely valuable to you ▶ **treasurer** n person in charge of the money, accounts, etc of an organization ■ **'treasure trove** /trəʊv/ n [U] treasure found hidden and claimed by no one

treasury /'treʒəri/ n (**the Treasury**) [sing, with sing or pl verb] government department that controls public money

treat /triːt/ v [T] **1** behave in a particular way towards sb/sth: *They ~ their children badly.* **2** consider or deal with sth in a particular way: *~ it as a joke* **3** give medical care to a person, an injury, etc: *~ a patient* **4** use a chemical substance to clean, protect, preserve, etc sth: *~ crops with insecticide* **5** pay for sth that sb/you will enjoy and that they/you do not usu have or do ● **treat** n sth very pleasant or enjoyable, esp sth that you give sb or do for them

treatise /'triːtɪs; -tɪz/ n long formal written work on one subject

treatment /'triːtmənt/ n [U,C] way of treating a person or thing: *medical ~*

treaty /'triːti/ n (*pl* **-ies**) formal agreement between countries: *a peace ~*

treble /'trebl/ *det* three times as much or as many: *He earns ~ my salary.* ● **treble** n **1** [U] high tones or part in music or a sound system **2** [C] (boy who sings with) a child's high voice ● **treble** v [I, T] become or make sth three times as much or as many ● **treble** *adj* high in tone: *a ~ recorder*

tree /triː/ n tall plant with a wooden trunk and branches ▶ **treeless** *adj* without trees

trek /trek/ v (**-kk-**) [I], n (make a) long hard journey, esp on foot

trellis /'trelɪs/ n light wooden framework used for supporting climbing plants

tremble /'trembl/ v [I] **1** shake uncontrollably from fear or cold **2** shake slightly: *The leaves ~d in the breeze.* **3** be very anxious ● **tremble** n [C, usu sing] feeling, movement or sound of trembling: *a ~ in her voice*

tremendous /trə'mendəs/ *adj* **1** very great: *a ~ explosion* **2** extremely good ▶ **tremendously** *adv*

tremor /'tremə(r)/ n **1** small earthquake: *earth ~s* **2** slight shaking movement in a part of your body

trench /trentʃ/ n long narrow channel dug in the ground, eg for drainage or to protect soldiers

trend /trend/ n general change or development: *the ~ towards smaller families* ■ **'trendsetter** n person who starts a new fashion or makes it popular ▶ **trendy** *adj* (**-ier, -iest**) (*infml*) very fashionable

trespass /'trespəs/ v [I] **~(on)** go on sb's private land without their permission ▶ **trespass** n [C, U] ▶ **trespasser** n

trestle /'tresl/ n wooden or metal structure with legs, used for supporting a flat surface ■ **'trestle table** n table supported on trestles

trial /'traɪəl/ n [C, U] examination in a law court before a judge (and jury) to decide if sb is guilty or innocent: *He's on ~ for murder.* **2** [C, U] (act of) testing how good sth is **3** [C] cause of worry or difficulty [IDM] **trial and error** process of solving a problem by trying various methods until you find one that is successful ■ **trial 'run** n test of how well sth new works

triangle /'traɪæŋgl/ n flat shape with three straight sides and three angles ▶ **triangular** /-'æŋgjələ(r)/ adj

tribe /traɪb/ n group of people of the same race, customs, language, etc living in a particular area, often under the rule of a chief ▶ **tribal** adj ■ **'tribesman** n **'tribeswoman** n member of a tribe

tribunal /traɪ'bju:nl/ n type of court with the authority to settle certain kinds of problems

tributary /'trɪbjətri/ n (pl -ies) river or stream that flows into a larger river or a lake

tribute /'trɪbju:t/ n [C,U] act, statement or gift intended to show your respect or admiration for sb: pay ~ to her courage

trick /trɪk/ n **1** something done to deceive sb or to annoy them as a joke: play a ~ on sb **2** clever or skilful action intended to entertain people: conjuring ~s **3** way of doing sth that works perfectly **4** cards played or won in one round of a game [IDM] **do the trick** (infml) succeed in doing what is needed or wanted ● **trick** v [T] deceive sb: He was ~ed into giving away all his money. ▶ **trickery** n [U] (written) deception; cheating ▶ **tricky** adj (-ier, -iest) **1** difficult to do or deal with: a ~ position **2** (of a person) deceitful

trickle /'trɪkl/ v [I] flow in a thin stream: Tears ~d down her cheek. ● **trickle** n slow or thin flow of sth: a ~ of blood

tricycle /'traɪsɪkl/ n vehicle like a bicycle, but with one wheel at the front and two behind

tried pt, pp of TRY¹

trifle /'traɪfl/ n **1** (a trifle) [sing] slightly **2** [C] thing of little value or importance **3** [C,U] sweet dish made of cream, cake, jelly, etc ● **trifle** v [I] [PV] **trifle with sb/sth** (fml) treat sb/sth without genuine respect ▶ **trifling** adj unimportant

trigger /'trɪgə(r)/ n part of a gun that you press in order to fire it ● **trigger** v [T] ~ (**off**) make sth happen suddenly

trill /trɪl/ n **1** repeated short high sound made, eg by sb's voice or a bird **2** (music) quick repeated playing of two different notes ● **trill** v [I, T] sound or sing sth with a trill

trilogy /'trɪlədʒi/ n (pl -ies) group of three related books, plays, etc

trim /trɪm/ v (-mm-) [T] **1** make sth neater, smaller, better, etc by cutting parts from it **2** decorate sth, esp around its edges ● **trim** n [C, usu sing] act of cutting a small amount

off sth, esp hair [IDM] **in** (**good, etc**) **order** ● **trim** adj (~mer, ~mest) (approv) **1** (of a person) looking slim and attractive **2** neat and tidy ▶ **trimming** n **1** (trimmings) [pl] extra things that it is traditional to have with a meal, etc: roast beef with all the ~mings (= vegetables, sauce, etc) **2** [U,C, usu sing] material used to decorate sth, eg along its edges

trimester /traɪ'mestə(r)/ n (US) = TERM(2)

trinity /'trɪnəti/ n [sing] (**the Trinity**) (in Christianity) union of Father, Son and Holy Spirit as one God

trinket /'trɪŋkɪt/ n small piece of jewellery, etc of little value

trio /'triːəʊ/ n (pl ~s) **1** group of three people or things **2** (music for) a group of three players or singers

trip /trɪp/ n **1** (usu short) journey to a place and back again, esp for pleasure **2** (sl) experience caused by taking a drug causing hallucinations **3** act of falling over ● **trip** v (-pp-) **1** [I] ~ (**over/up**) catch your foot on sth and fall over **2** [T] ~ (**up**) catch sb's foot and make them fall or almost fall **3** [I] (lit) move with quick light steps [PV] **trip** (**sb**) **up** (deliberately cause sb to) make a mistake ▶ **tripper** n person visiting a place for a short time for pleasure

tripartite /traɪ'pɑːtaɪt/ adj (fml) having three parts or groups

tripe /traɪp/ n [U] **1** lining of a cow's or pig's stomach, used as food **2** (infml) nonsense

triple /'trɪpl/ adj having three parts or involving three people or groups ● **triple** v [I, T] become or make sth three times as much or as many

triplet /'trɪplət/ n one of three children born to the same mother at one time

triplicate /'trɪplɪkət/ n [IDM] **in triplicate 1** done three times **2** (of documents) copied twice, so that there are three copies in total

tripod /'traɪpɒd/ n support with three legs, eg for a camera

trite /traɪt/ adj uninteresting and not original

triumph /'traɪʌmf/ n **1** [C] great achievement or success **2** [U] feeling of joy and satisfaction that you get from a great success or victory ● **triumph** v [I] ~ (**over**) defeat sb/sth; be successful ▶ **triumphal** /-'ʌmfl/ adj done to celebrate a great success or victory ▶ **triumphant** /-'ʌmfənt/ adj showing great joy and satisfaction because you have triumphed ▶ **triumphantly** adv

trivia /'trɪviə/ n [U] unimportant matters, details or information

trivial /'trɪvɪəl/ adj not important or serious; not worth considering ▶ **triviality** /-'æləti/ n [C,U] (pl -ies) ▶ **trivialize** (also -**ise**) v [T] make sth seem important, etc than it really is

trod pt of TREAD

trodden pp of TREAD

trolley /'trɒli/ n 1 small vehicle with wheels that is pushed by hand and used for carrying things: a super-market ~ 2 small table on wheels for serving food 3 (US) = TRAM

trombone /trɒm'bəʊn/ n brass musical instrument with a sliding tube ▶ **trombonist** n person who plays the trombone

troop /truːp/ n 1 (troops) [pl] soldiers, esp in a large group 2 [C] group of people or animals ● **troop** v [I] walk somewhere together as a group ▶ **trooper** n soldier of low rank in the part of an army that uses tanks or horses

trophy /'trəʊfi/ n (pl -ies) 1 prize given for winning a competition 2 something kept as a reminder of a victory or success

tropic /'trɒpɪk/ n 1 [C, usu sing] one of the two imaginary lines drawn around the earth 23°26' north (the **Tropic of Cancer**) or south (the **Tropic of Capricorn**) of the equator 2 (**the tropics**) [pl] area between the two tropics, which is the hottest part of the world ▶ **tropical** adj of the tropics

trot /trɒt/ v (-**tt**-) 1 [I] (of a horse or its rider) move fairly quickly, at a speed faster than a walk but slower than a gallop 2 [I] run with short steps [PV] **trot sth out** (infml, disapprov) give the same facts, explanations, etc for sth that have often been used before: ~ out the same old excuses ● **trot** n [sing] trotting speed [IDM] **on the trot** (infml) one after the other

trouble /'trʌbl/ n 1 [C,U] (situation causing a) problem, worry or difficulty: You shouldn't have expected ~ finding the house. 2 [U] illness; pain: heart ~ 3 [U] something that is wrong with a machine, vehicle, etc: engine ~ 4 [U] situation that is difficult or dangerous; situation in which you might be criticized or punished: A yachtsman got into ~ off the coast and had to be rescued. ◇ He's always in ~ with the police. 5 [U,sing] angry or violent situation: the ~s in Northern Ireland 6 [U] extra work or effort: I don't want to put you to any ~. ● **trouble** v 1 [T] make sb worried or upset 2 [T] (fml) (used in polite requests) disturb sb because you want to ask them sth: I'm sorry to ~ you, but could you tell me the way to the station? 3 [I] (fml) make an effort;

bother ▶ **troubled** adj worried ■ '**troublemaker** n person who causes trouble ▶ **troublesome** adj causing trouble, pain, etc over a long time

trough /trɒf/ n 1 long narrow container for animals to feed or drink from 2 low area between two waves 3 area of low air pressure

troupe /truːp/ n [C, with sing or pl verb] group of actors, dancers, etc

trousers /'traʊzəz/ n [pl] (esp GB) piece of clothing that covers the body from the waist down and is divided into two to cover each leg separately: a pair of ~

trout /traʊt/ n [C,U] (pl **trout**) common freshwater fish that is used for food

trowel /'traʊəl/ n 1 small garden tool with a curved blade 2 small tool with a flat blade, used for spreading cement, etc

truant /'truːənt/ n child who stays away from school without permission: play ~ (= be a)~ ▶ **truancy** /-ənsi/ n [U]

truce /truːs/ n agreement between enemies to stop fighting for a period of time

truck /trʌk/ n 1 (esp US) = LORRY 2 (GB) open railway vehicle for carrying goods or animals 3 vehicle that is open at the back, esp for carrying goods, etc: a farm ~ [IDM] **have/want no truck with sb/sth** refuse to deal with sb/sth; refuse to consider sth

trudge /trʌdʒ/ v [I, T] walk slowly or with difficulty ● **trudge** n [C,usu sing] long tiring walk

true /truː/ adj (-**r**, -**st**) 1 connected with facts rather than things that have been invented or guessed: Is it ~ she's leaving? 2 real: my ~ feelings for you 3 faithful; loyal: a ~ friend 4 being an accurate version or copy of sth: a ~ copy [IDM] **come true** (of a hope, dream, etc) become reality **true to form** behaving as you would expect sb to behave, esp when this is annoying ● **true** n [IDM] **out of true** not straight or in the correct position

truly /'truːli/ adv 1 sincerely: feel ~ grateful 2 really: a ~ brave action

trump /trʌmp/ n (also '**trump card**) (in some card games) card of a suit that is chosen to have a higher value in a game [IDM] **come up/turn up trumps** (infml) be unexpectedly helpful or generous ● **trump** v [T] (in some games) play a trump card that beats sb else's card [PV] **trump sth up** (usu passive) invent a false accusation: ~ed-up charges ■ '**trump card** n 1 = TRUMP 2 something that gives you an advantage over others

trumpet /'trʌmpɪt/ n brass musical instrument with a long curved

tube that you blow into ● **trumpet**
v 1 [I, T] declare sth loudly 2 [I] (of
an elephant) make a loud noise
▶ **trumpeter** *n* trumpet player

truncate /trʌŋˈkeɪt/ *v* [T] shorten
sth by cutting off the top or end

truncheon /ˈtrʌntʃən/ *n* (*esp GB*)
short thick stick carried as a
weapon by a police officer

trundle /ˈtrʌndl/ *v* [I, T] (cause sth
to) roll or move somewhere slowly
and noisily

trunk /trʌŋk/ *n* 1 [C] thick main stem
of a tree 2 [C] (*US*) = BOOT(2) 3 [C]
long nose of an elephant 4 (**trunks**)
[pl] shorts worn by men or boys for
swimming 5 [C] large strong box for
storing or transporting clothes, etc
6 [C, *usu sing*] human body apart from
the head, arms and legs ■ **trunk
road** *n* (*GB*) important main road

truss /trʌs/ *v* [T] 1 tie up sb's arms
and legs so that they cannot move
2 tie the legs and wings of a
chicken, etc before cooking it
● **truss** *n* 1 padded belt worn by sb
suffering from a hernia 2 framework supporting a roof, bridge, etc

trust[1] /trʌst/ *n* 1 [U] ~ (**in**) belief that
sb/sth is good, sincere, etc and will
not try to harm or deceive you 2 [C]
(*law*) (arrangement for the) holding
and managing of money or property
for others: *money kept in a* ~ 3 [C]
(*law*) organization, etc that invests
money that is given or lent to it and
uses the profits to help a charity [IDM]
take sth on trust believe sth without
proof ▶ **trusting** *adj* ready to trust
others ▶ **trustworthy** *adj* reliable
▶ **trusty** *adj* (-**ier**, -**iest**) (*old-fash or
hum*) that you have had a long time
and have always been able to rely on

trust[2] /trʌst/ *v* 1 have confidence
in sb; believe that sb is good, sincere, etc. *You can* ~ *me.* 2 believe
that sth is true or correct or can be
relied on: *He* ~*ed his judgement.*
3 (*fml*) hope and expect that sth is
true: *I* ~ *you are well.*

trustee /trʌˈstiː/ *n* person or organization that has control of money, etc
that has been put into a trust for sb

truth /truːθ/ *n* (*pl* ~**s** /truːðz/) 1 [sing]
the true facts about sth, rather than
things that have been invented or
guessed: *tell the* ~ 2 [U] quality or
state of being based on fact: *There's
not a grain of* ~ *in what he says.* 3 [C]
fact that is generally accepted as
true: *scientific* ~*s* ▶ **truthful** *adj* (of
a person) saying only what is true
2 (of a statement) giving only the
true facts about sth ▶ **truthfully** *adv*
▶ **truthfulness** *n* [U]

try[1] /traɪ/ *v* (*pt, pp* tried) 1 [I] make an
attempt to or get sth: *He tried to
escape.* 2 [T] use, do or test sth to see

if it is satisfactory, enjoyable, etc:
Have you tried this new soap? 3 [T] ~
(**for**) examine and decide a case in a
law court: *He was tried for murder.*
[IDM] **tried and tested/trusted** (*US*)
tried and true that you have used or
relied on successfully in the past **try
your hand (at sth)** attempt to do sth
try it on (with sb) (*GB, infml*) behave
badly towards sb or try to get sth
from them, even though this will
make them angry **try sb's patience**
make sb feel impatient [PV] **try sth
on** put on a piece of clothing to see if
it fits and how it looks **try sb/sth out
(on sb)** test or use sb/sth to see how
good or effective they are ▶ **trying**
adj annoying or difficult to deal with

try[2] /traɪ/ *n* (*pl* -**ies**) 1 [*usu sing*]
attempt 2 (in rugby) points scored
by a player touching the ball down
behind the opponents' goal

tsar /zɑː(r)/ *n* title of the emperor of
Russia in the past ▶ **tsarina** /zɑː-
ˈriːnə/ *n* title of the empress of
Russia in the past

tsetse fly /ˈtsetsi flaɪ/ *n* African fly
that bites humans and animals and
can cause a serious disease called
'sleeping sickness'

T-shirt → T, τ

tub /tʌb/ *n* 1 open container, used
for washing clothes in, etc 2 small
plastic or paper container with a
lid, used for food, etc: *a* ~ *of
margarine* 3 (*esp US*) = BATH

tuba /ˈtjuːbə/ *n* brass musical
instrument that you play by blowing and that produces low notes

tubby /ˈtʌbi/ *adj* (-**ier**, -**iest**) (*infml*)
(of a person) short and fat

tube /tjuːb/ *n* 1 [C] long hollow pipe
of rubber, plastic, etc, esp for carrying liquids 2 [C] soft metal or plastic container for pastes, paints, etc
3 [C] hollow tube-shaped organ in
the body 4 (**the tube**) [sing] (*GB*) (in
London) underground railway sys-
tem ▶ **tubing** *n* [U] metal, plastic, etc
in the shape of a tube ▶ **tubular**
/ˈtjuːbjələ(r)/ *adj* made of or shaped
like tubes

tuber /ˈtjuːbə(r)/ *n* short thick
rounded part of an underground
stem on some plants, eg potatoes

tuberculosis /tjuːˌbɜːkjuˈləʊsɪs/ *n*
[U] serious infectious
disease that affects the lungs

TUC /ˌtiː juː ˈsiː/ *abbr* Trades Union
Congress; organization to which
many British trade unions belong

tuck /tʌk/ *v* [T] 1 push the loose ends
of sth into sth else so that it is tidy: *He
*~*ed his shirt into his trousers.* 2 put
sth in a tidy, comfortable or hidden
position [PV] **tuck in/ tuck into sth**
(*infml*) eat food eagerly **tuck sb in/up**
make sb feel comfortable in bed by

pulling the covers up around them ● **tuck** n **1** fold sewn into a piece of clothing **2** medical operation in which skin and/or fat is removed, to make sb look thinner or younger

Tuesday /'tjuːzdeɪ; -di/ n [C,U] the third day of the week, next after Monday (See examples of use at *Monday*.)

tuft /tʌft/ n bunch of hair, grass, etc

tug /tʌg/ v (-gg-) [I, T] ~(at) pull sth hard, often several times ● **tug** n **1** (*also* **'tugboat**) small powerful boat that pulls ships into harbours **2** sudden hard pull

tuition /tjuˈɪʃn/ n [U] (*fml*) (fee for) teaching sth: *have private ~*

tulip /'tjuːlɪp/ n large brightly coloured spring flower, shaped like a cup, on a tall stem

tumble /'tʌmbl/ v **1** [I, T] (cause sb to) fall downwards **2** [I] ~(down) fall suddenly and dramatically **3** [I] move or fall somewhere in a relaxed, uncontrolled way [PV] **tumble to sth/sb** (*infml*) suddenly understand sth ● **tumble** n [C, usu sing] fall ■ **'tumble-down** adj falling to pieces ■ **'tumble-'dryer** | **,tumble-'drier** n machine for drying washed clothes

tumbler /'tʌmblə(r)/ n straight-sided drinking glass

tummy /'tʌmi/ n (pl **-ies**) (*infml*) stomach

tumour (*US* **-or**) /'tjuːmə(r)/ n mass of diseased cells growing in the body

tumult /'tjuːmʌlt/ n [U,C, usu sing] (*fml*) **1** noisy confusion involving a large number of people **2** confused state ▶ **tumultuous** /tjuːˈmʌltʃuəs/ adj (*fml*) very loud; involving strong feelings, esp of approval: *~uous applause*

tuna /'tjuːnə/ n [C,U] (pl **tuna** or **~s**) large sea fish eaten as food

tune /tjuːn/ n series of musical notes that are sung or played in a particular order [IDM] **be in/out of tune (with sb/sth)** be/not be in agreement with sb/sth **in/out of tune** be/not be singing or playing the correct musical notes to sound pleasant **to the tune of sth** (*infml*) used to emphasize how much money sth cost: *I was fined to the ~ of £1000.* ● **tune** v [T] **1** adjust a musical instrument to the correct pitch **2** adjust an engine so that it runs smoothly **3** ~(in) adjust the controls on a radio or television so that you can receive a particular programme or channel [PV] **tune in (to sth)** listen to or watch a radio or television programme ▶ **tuneful** adj having a pleasant tune ▶ **tunefully** adv ▶ **tuner** n person who tunes musical instruments, esp pianos ■ **'tuning fork** n small steel fork that produces a certain musical note when you hit it

tunic /'tjuːnɪk/ n **1** loose piece of clothing covering the body down to the knees, as worn in ancient Greece **2** (*GB*) tightly fitting jacket worn as part of a uniform by police officers, soldiers, etc

tunnel /'tʌnl/ n underground passage, eg for a road or railway ● **tunnel** v (-ll-, *US* -l-) [I, T] dig a tunnel under or through the ground

turban /'tɜːbən/ n head covering worn by a Muslim or Sikh man, consisting of a long cloth wound round the head

turbine /'tɜːbaɪn/ n engine driven by a wheel that is turned by a current of water, steam, air or gas

turbulent /'tɜːbjələnt/ adj confused; violent or uneven: *~ passions/seas* ▶ **turbulence** /-ləns/ n [U]

tureen /tjuˈriːn; təˈ-/ n large deep dish from which soup or vegetables are served

turf /tɜːf/ n (pl **-s** or **turves**) **1** [C,U] (cut piece of) short grass and the surface layer of soil held together by its roots **2** (**the turf**) [sing] sport of horse racing ● **turf** v [T] cover an area of ground with turf [PV] **turf sb out (of sth)** | **turf sb off (sth)** (*GB, infml*) force sb to leave a place, an organization, etc

turkey /'tɜːki/ n **1** [C] large bird, used for food **2** [U] meat from a turkey

turmoil /'tɜːmɔɪl/ n [U, sing] state of confusion or disorder

turn¹ /tɜːn/ v **1** [I, T] (cause sth to) move around a central point: *The earth ~s around the sun.* ◇ *~ a key in a lock* [I, T] move (a part of) your body so as to face or start moving in a different direction: *She ~ed to look at me.* ◇ *Don't ~ your back on me!* **3** [I, T] (cause sth/sb to) change the direction it/they are facing or moving in: *She ~ed the jumper inside out.* **4** [I] (of a road or river) curve in a particular direction **5** [T] aim or point sth in a particular direction: *She ~ed her attention back to her work.* **6** (usu used with an adj) (cause sth to) change into a particular state or condition: *The milk has ~ed sour.* ◇ *She's just ~ed 50.* **7** [I, T] ~(**from**) **into** (cause sth to) pass from one state to another: *Caterpillars ~ into butterflies.* [IDM] **be well, badly, etc turned out** be well, badly, etc dressed **not turn a hair** show no emotion when sth shocking, surprising, etc happens **turn your back on sb/sth** reject sb/sth that you have previously been connected with **turn a blind eye (to sth)** pretend not to notice sth bad that is happening **turn the clock back →** **CLOCK** **turn a deaf ear (to sb/sth)** ignore or refuse to listen to sb/sth **turn your hand to sth** begin to learn a practical skill **turn your nose up at sth** (*infml*) refuse sth, esp because you do not think it is good enough for you **turn over a new leaf** change your way of life to become a better, more responsible person **turn the tables (on sb)** gain an advantage over sb who had an advantage over you **turn tail** turn and run away **turn up trumps** → TRUMP [PV] **turn sth against sb** (cause sb to) become unfriendly or opposed to sth **turn sb away (from sth)** refuse to allow sb to enter a place **turn (sb/sth) back** return the way you have come; make sb/sth do this **turn sb/sth down** refuse sb, their offer, etc **turn sth down** adjust a cooker, radio, etc to reduce the heat, sound, etc it produces **turn in** (*infml*) go to bed; her feet ~ in. **turn sb in** (*infml*) take sb to the police to be arrested **turn sb off** (*infml*) cause sb to be bored or not sexually excited **turn sth off** stop the flow or operation of sth: ~ *off the tap* **turn on sb** suddenly attack sb **turn sb on** (*infml*) make sb excited or interested, esp sexually **turn sth on** start the flow or operation of sth: ~ *on the radio* **turn out 1** be present at an event **2** happen in the way that is mentioned: *Everything ~ed out well.* **turn sth out 1** switch a light or fire off **2** empty sth, esp to clean it: ~ *out the cupboards* **3** produce sth: *The factory ~s out 900 cars a week.* **turn sth over 1** make sth change position so that the other side is facing upwards or outwards **2** think carefully about sth **3** do business worth the amount that is mentioned **turn sth/sb over to sb** give up control of sth/sb to sb: *The thief was ~ed over to the police.* **turn to sb/sth** go to sb/sth for help, advice, etc **turn up 1** (of a person) appear **2** (of an opportunity) happen, esp by chance **turn (sth) up** (cause sth to) be found: *The book you've lost will probably ~ up somewhere.* **turn sth up** adjust a cooker, radio, etc to increase the heat, sound, etc ■ **'turn-off** *n* road that leads away from a main road ■ **'turnout** *n* [C, *usu sing*, U] number of people who attend an event ■ **'turnover** *n* [*sing*] amount of business done by a company: *Their annual ~over is £10 million.* ■ **'turn-up** *n* [C] **1** [*usu pl*] folded-up end of a trouser leg **2** (*infml*) surprising and unexpected event: *He offered to help? That's a ~-up for the books!*

turn² /tɜːn/ *n* **1** act of turning sth/sb around **2** change of direction in a vehicle, on a road, etc **3** time when sb in a group of people should or is allowed to do sth: *It's your ~ to choose.*

4 unusual or unexpected change in what is happening: *Business was taken a ~ for the worse.* **5** short performance or piece of entertainment **6** (*old-fash*) feeling of illness [IDM] **at every turn** everywhere or every time you try to do sth **done to a turn** (*GB*) (of food) cooked just long enough **in turn 1** one after the other **2** as a result of sth in a series of events **speak/talk out of turn** say sth that you should not because it is the wrong time or it offends **take turns (in sth/to do sth) | take it in turns** do sth one after the other: *The children took it in ~s to play on the swing.*

turning /'tɜːnɪŋ/ *n* road that leads off another ■ **'turning point** *n* time at which an important change happens

turnip /'tɜːnɪp/ *n* [C, U] round white, or white and purple, root vegetable

turnpike /'tɜːnpaɪk/ *n* (*US*) road which drivers have to pay to use

turnstile /'tɜːnstaɪl/ *n* entrance gate that turns in a circle when pushed and allows one person through at a time

turntable /'tɜːnteɪbl/ *n* flat circular surface that turns round, on which a record is placed in a record player

turpentine /'tɜːpəntaɪn/ *n* [U] strong-smelling colourless liquid used for cleaning off or thinning paint

turquoise /'tɜːkwɔɪz/ *adj* greenish-blue in colour ● **turquoise** *n* [C, U] type of greenish-blue precious stone

turret /'tʌrət/ *n* **1** small tower on top of a building **2** small metal tower on a ship, plane or tank that can usu turn around and from which guns are fired

turtle /'tɜːtl/ *n* large reptile with a hard round shell, that lives in the sea

tusk /tʌsk/ *n* either of a pair of very long pointed teeth of an elephant and some other animals

tussle /'tʌsl/ *v* [I], *n* (have a) rough fight or argument

tut /tʌt/ (*also* **tut-'tut**) *exclam* used for showing disapproval, annoyance, etc

tutor /'tjuːtə(r)/ *n* **1** private teacher, esp one who guides the studies of a student **2** (*GB*) university teacher who guides the studies of a student ● **tutor** *v* [I, T] teach sb or work as a tutor ► **tutorial** /tjuː'tɔːriəl/ *n* teaching period for a small group of students ● **tutorial** *adj* connected with the work of a tutor

tuxedo /tʌk'siːdəʊ/ *n* (*pl* ~**s**) (*US*) = DINNER JACKET (DINNER)

TV /ˌtiː 'viː/ *n* [C, U] television

twang /twæŋ/ *n* **1** used to describe a way of speaking, esp one in which the sounds are produced through the nose **2** sound made when a tight string is pulled and released ● **twang** *v* [I, T] (cause sth to) make a twang(2)

tweak /twiːk/ v [T] **1** pull or twist sth: ~ *a child's nose* **2** make slight changes to a machine, system, etc to improve it ▶ **tweak** n [sing]

tweed /twiːd/ n **1** [U] thick woven woollen fabric that has small spots of different coloured thread in it **2** (**tweeds**) [pl] clothes made of tweed

tweet /twiːt/ n short high sound made by a small bird

tweezers /ˈtwiːzəz/ n [pl] small tool with two long thin parts joined at one end, used for pulling out or picking up very small things

twelve /twelv/ *number* **12** ▶ **twelfth** /twelfθ/ *ordinal number*

twenty /ˈtwenti/ *number* **1** 20 **2** (**the twenties**) [pl] numbers, years or temperatures from 20 to 29 ▶ **twentieth** /ˈtwentiəθ/ *ordinal number*

twice /twaɪs/ *adv* two times: *I've read this book ~.* ◊ *Your room is as big as mine.*

twiddle /ˈtwɪdl/ v [I, T] twist or turn sth with your fingers, often because you are nervous or bored

twig /twɪg/ n small thin piece of a branch of a bush or tree ● **twig** v (-gg-) [I, T] (GB, infml) suddenly realize or understand sth

twilight /ˈtwaɪlaɪt/ n [U] (time of) faint light just after sunset

twill /twɪl/ n [U] strong woven fabric with diagonal lines

twin /twɪn/ n either of two children born to the same mother at one time ● **twin** *adj* similar, one of a matching pair: ~ *beds* (= two single beds)

twine /twaɪn/ n [U] strong string ● **twine** v [I, T] (cause sth to) twist or wind around sth

twinge /twɪndʒ/ n **1** sudden sharp pain **2** ~ (**of**) sudden short feeling of an unpleasant emotion: *a ~ of guilt*

twinkle /ˈtwɪŋkl/ v [I] **1** shine with an unsteady light: *stars twinkling in the sky* **2** (of sb's eyes) look bright with happiness or amusement ▶ **twinkle** n [sing]: *a ~ in her eyes*

twirl /twɜːl/ v [I, T] (cause sb/sth to) move or spin round and round **2** [T] curl or twist sth with your fingers ● **twirl** n action of a person spinning around once

twist /twɪst/ v **1** [I, T] (cause sth to) bend or turn into a particular shape: *The car was a pile of ~ed metal.* **2** [I, T] turn your body, or a part of your body, around: *She ~ed (her head) round.* **3** [T] turn sth around in a circle with your hand: *I nervously ~ed the ring on my finger.* **4** [I] (of a road or river) have many bends **5** [T] injure part of your body, esp your ankle, wrist or knee, by bending it awkwardly **6** [T] wind sth around or through an object: *The phone cable*

has got ~ed (= wound round itself). **7** [T] deliberately change the meaning of what sb has said: ~ *the facts* [IDM] **twist sb's arm** (infml) persuade or force sb to do sth **twist sb round your little finger** (infml) get sb to do anything you want ● **twist** n **1** action of turning sth with your hand or turning a part of your body **2** unexpected change or development in a story or situation: *by a strange ~ of fate* **3** thing that has been twisted into a particular shape: *mineral water with a ~ of lemon*

twit /twɪt/ n (GB, infml) silly or annoying person

twitch /twɪtʃ/ n small sudden uncontrollable movement of the muscles ● **twitch** v [I] (cause a part of the body to) make a sudden quick movement **2** [I, T] give sth a short sharp pull; be pulled in this way

twitter /ˈtwɪtə(r)/ v [I] **1** (of a bird) make short high sounds **2** talk quickly in an excited or nervous way ▶ **twitter** n [sing]

two /tuː/ *number* **2** [IDM] **put two and two together** guess the truth from what you see, hear, etc ■ **two-faced** *adj* (infml, disapprov) deceitful or insincere ■ **twofold** *adj*, *adv* **1** having two parts **2** twice as many or as much ■ **two-way** *adj* allowing movement or communication in two directions

tying ▷ TIE¹

type /taɪp/ n **1** [C] (one of a) group of things or people with certain features in common; kind or sort: *many different ~s of computers* **2** [U] letters that are printed or typed: *italic ~* ● **type** v [I, T] write sth using a word processor or typewriter ■ **typecast** /ˈtaɪpkɑːst/ v (pt, pp **typecast**) [T] (usu passive) constantly give an actor the same kind of part to play ■ **typescript** n [C,U] typed copy of sth ■ **typewriter** n machine that prints letters on paper by means of keys that are pressed with the fingers ▶ **typing** n [U] activity or job of using a typewriter or word processor to write sth ▶ **typist** n person whose job is to type letters, etc in an office

typhoid /ˈtaɪfɔɪd/ n [U] serious infectious disease that causes fever and sometimes death

typhoon /taɪˈfuːn/ n very violent tropical storm

typhus /ˈtaɪfəs/ n [U] serious infectious disease causing fever and purple spots on the body

typical /ˈtɪpɪkl/ *adj* having the usual qualities of a particular thing or person: *a ~ case* ▶ **typically** /-kli/ *adv*

typify /'tɪpɪfaɪ/ v (pt, pp **-ied**) [T] be a typical feature or example of sth

typist → TYPE

tyrannical /tɪ'rænɪkl/ adj of or like a tyrant

tyrannize (also **-ise**) /'tɪrənaɪz/ v [I, T] ~**(over)** (written) use your power to treat sb cruelly and unfairly

tyranny /'tɪrəni/ n [U] unfair or cruel use of power or authority

tyrant /'taɪrənt/ n person who has complete power in a country and uses it in a cruel and unfair way

tyre /'taɪə(r)/ n thick rubber ring that fits around the edge of a wheel of a bicycle, car, etc

Uu

U, u /juː/ n [C,U] (pl **U's, u's** /juːz/) the twenty-first letter of the English alphabet ● **'U-turn** n **1** turn of 180° that a vehicle makes so that it can move forward in the opposite direction **2** (infml) complete change in policy or behaviour

ubiquitous /juː'bɪkwɪtəs/ adj (fml) seeming to be present everywhere; very common

udder /'ʌdə(r)/ n part of a cow, goat, etc that produces milk

UFO /juː ef 'əʊ; 'juːfəʊ/ n (pl ~**s**) Unidentified Flying Object, esp a spacecraft believed to have come from another planet

ugh /ɜː; ʊx/ exclam used for expressing disgust: *Ugh! What a horrible smell!*

ugly /'ʌgli/ adj (**-ier, -iest**) **1** unpleasant to look at **2** threatening, likely to be violent ▶ **ugliness** n [U]

UK /juː 'keɪ/ abbr United Kingdom

ulcer /'ʌlsə(r)/ n open sore area on the skin or inside the body ▶ **ulcerate** /'ʌlsəreɪt/ (med) v [I, T] (cause sth to) become covered with ulcers

ulterior /ʌl'tɪəriə(r)/ adj (of a reason for doing sth) hidden: *an ~ motive*

ultimate /'ʌltɪmət/ adj last, final or most extreme ▶ **ultimately** adv in the end

ultimatum /ˌʌltɪ'meɪtəm/ n (pl ~**s** or **-ta** /-tə/) final statement of conditions to be agreed to without discussion: *issue an ~*

ultrasound /'ʌltrəsaʊnd/ n **1** [U] sound that is higher than human beings can hear **2** [U,C] medical process that produces an image of what is inside your body: *have an ~ scan*

ultraviolet /ˌʌltrə'vaɪələt/ adj (physics) of or using electromagnetic waves that are just shorter than those of violet light in the spectrum and that cannot be seen: *~ rays* (= that cause the skin to go darker)

umbilical cord /ˌʌm.bɪlɪkl 'kɔːd/ n tube that joins an unborn baby to its mother

umbrella /ʌm'brelə/ n **1** folding frame covered with cloth, used as a protection from rain **2** thing that contains or includes many different parts or elements

umpire /'ʌmpaɪə(r)/ n (in tennis, baseball, etc) person who sees that rules are obeyed ● **umpire** v [I, T] act as an umpire in a game

umpteen /ˌʌmp'tiːn/ det (infml) very many: *read ~ books on the subject* ▶ **umpteenth** /-'tiːnθ/ det: *for the ~th time*

UN /juː 'en/ abbr United Nations

unable /ʌn'eɪbl/ adj ~**to** not having the skill, strength, knowledge, etc to do sth

unaccountable /ˌʌnə'kaʊntəbl/ adj (fml) that cannot be explained ▶ **unaccountably** adv

unaccustomed /ˌʌnə'kʌstəmd/ adj (fml) **1** ~**to** not in the habit of doing sth; not used to sth: *~ to speaking in public* **2** unusual

unanimous /ju'nænɪməs/ adj in or showing complete agreement: *a ~ decision* ▶ **unanimity** /ˌjuːnə'nɪməti/ n [U] (written)

unanswerable /ʌn'ɑːnsərəbl/ adj that cannot be questioned or disagreed with

unarmed /ˌʌn'ɑːmd/ adj without weapons

unassuming /ˌʌnə'sjuːmɪŋ/ adj not attracting attention to yourself; modest

unattached /ˌʌnə'tætʃt/ adj **1** not married or involved in a romantic relationship **2** not connected with a particular group or organization

unattended /ˌʌnə'tendɪd/ adj not looked after; alone: *~ luggage*

unavoidable /ˌʌnə'vɔɪdəbl/ adj impossible to avoid or prevent

unaware /ˌʌnə'weə(r)/ adj ~**(of)** not knowing or realizing that sth exists or is happening ▶ **unawares** /-'weəz/ adv when not expected: *catch/take sb ~s* (= surprise sb)

unbalanced /ˌʌn'bælənst/ adj slightly crazy; mentally ill

unbearable /ʌn'beərəbl/ adj that cannot be tolerated or endured ▶ **unbearably** adv

unbeatable /ʌn'biːtəbl/ adj that cannot be beaten: *~ value for money*

unbelievable /ˌʌnbɪ'liːvəbl/ adj that cannot be believed; astonishing ▶ **unbelievably** adv

unborn /ˌʌn'bɔːn/ adj not yet born

unbroken /ʌn'brəʊkən/ adj not interrupted or disturbed: *~ sleep*

unbutton /ʌnˈbʌtn/ v [T] undo the buttons on a piece of clothing

uncalled for /ʌnˈkɔːld fɔː(r)/ adj (of behaviour or remarks) not fair or appropriate

uncanny /ʌnˈkæni/ adj (-ier, -iest) strange and difficult to explain

unceremonious /ˌʌnˌserəˈməʊniəs/ adj (written) done roughly and rudely ▸ **unceremoniously** adv

uncertain /ʌnˈsɜːtn/ adj 1 not sure; doubtful: *be ~ about what to do* 2 likely to change; not reliable: *~ weather* ▸ **uncertainly** adv ▸ **uncertainty** n [C, U] (pl **-ies**)

uncharitable /ʌnˈtʃærɪtəbl/ adj unkind or unfair

unchecked /ˌʌnˈtʃekt/ adj not controlled or stopped

uncivilized (also **-ised**) /ʌnˈsɪvəlaɪzd/ adj (of behaviour, etc) rude

uncle /ˈʌŋkl/ n brother of your father or mother; husband of your aunt

uncomfortable /ʌnˈkʌmftəbl/ adj 1 (of clothes, furniture, etc) not letting you feel physically comfortable 2 embarrassed; not relaxed ▸ **uncomfortably** adv

uncommon /ʌnˈkɒmən/ adj not existing in large numbers or in many places ▸ **uncommonly** adv (fml) extremely; unusually

uncompromising /ʌnˈkɒmprəmaɪzɪŋ/ adj unwilling to change your opinions, decisions, etc

unconcerned /ˌʌnkənˈsɜːnd/ adj not interested or worried

unconditional /ˌʌnkənˈdɪʃənl/ adj without conditions or limits: *~ love*

unconscious /ʌnˈkɒnʃəs/ adj 1 in a state like sleep because of injury or illness: *She was knocked ~.* 2 (of feelings, thoughts, etc) happening without your realizing or being aware; not deliberate: *~ impulses* 3 not aware of sb/sth ▸ **unconsciously** adv

uncool /ˌʌnˈkuːl/ adj (infml) not considered acceptable by fashionable young people

uncountable /ʌnˈkaʊntəbl/ adj (gram) (of nouns) that cannot be made plural or used with *a* or *an*, eg *water, bread* and *information*

uncouth /ʌnˈkuːθ/ adj (of a person or their behaviour) rude or socially unacceptable

uncover /ʌnˈkʌvə(r)/ v [T] 1 remove sth that is covering sth 2 discover sth secret or hidden

undaunted /ˌʌnˈdɔːntɪd/ adj (written) not discouraged or afraid

undecided /ˌʌndɪˈsaɪdɪd/ adj not having decided sth; not certain

undeniable /ˌʌndɪˈnaɪəbl/ adj true or certain; that cannot be denied ▸ **undeniably** adv

under /ˈʌndə(r)/ prep 1 below sth: *Have you looked ~ the bed?* 2 covered by sth: *Most of the iceberg is ~ the water.* 3 less than; younger than: *~ £50* 4 used to say who or what controls, governs or manages sb/sth: *She has a staff of 19 working ~ her.* 5 according to an agreement, a law or system: *~ the terms of the contract* 6 experiencing a particular process; affected by sth: *a hotel ~ construction* ◇ *You'll be ~ anaesthetic so you won't feel anything.* 7 using a particular name: *She wrote ~ the name of George Eliot.* ● **under** adv in or to a lower place, esp under water

under- prefix 1 (in nouns and adjectives) below: *an ~current* 2 (in adjectives and verbs) not enough: *~ripe*

underarm /ˈʌndərɑːm/ adj 1 connected with a person's armpit: *~ deodorant* 2 (sport) (of the way a ball is thrown) with the hand kept below the level of the shoulder ▸ **underarm** adv

undercarriage /ˈʌndəkærɪdʒ/ n the part of an aircraft, including its wheels, that supports it when it is landing and taking off

undercharge /ˌʌndəˈtʃɑːdʒ/ v [I, T] charge too little for sth, usu by accident

underclothes /ˈʌndəkləʊðz/ n [pl] (fml) = UNDERWEAR

undercover /ˌʌndəˈkʌvə(r)/ adj, adv working or done secretly, esp as a spy

undercurrent /ˈʌndəkʌrənt/ n hidden thought or feeling: *an ~ of bitterness*

undercut /ˌʌndəˈkʌt/ v (-tt-, pt, pp **-cut**) [T] sell goods or services at a lower price than your competitors

underdeveloped /ˌʌndədɪˈveləpt/ adj (of a country) having few industries and a low standard of living

underdog /ˈʌndədɒg/ n person, etc thought to be in a weaker position, and so unlikely to win a competition

underdone /ˌʌndəˈdʌn/ adj (esp of meat) not completely cooked

underestimate /ˌʌndərˈestɪmeɪt/ v [T] 1 think or guess that the amount, cost or size of sth is smaller than it really is 2 not realize how good, strong, determined, etc sb really is: *~ the enemy's strength*

underfed /ˌʌndəˈfed/ adj having had too little food to eat

underfoot /ˌʌndəˈfʊt/ adv under your feet: *The grass was wet ~.*

undergo /ˌʌndəˈgəʊ/ v (pt **-went** /-ˈwent/, pp **-gone** /-ˈgɒn/) [T] experience sth, esp a change or sth unpleasant

undergraduate /ˌʌndəˈgrædʒuət/ n university or college student studying for their first degree

underground /ˈʌndəgraʊnd/ adj **1** under the surface of the ground **2** operating secretly and often illegally, esp against a government ● **underground** n [sing] **1** (the Underground) (GB) underground railway system in a city **2** (the underground) [with sing or pl verb] secret political organization ● **underground** /ˌʌndəˈgraʊnd/ adv **1** under the surface of the ground **2** in or into a secret place in order to hide from the police, etc: He went ~ to avoid arrest.

undergrowth /ˈʌndəgrəʊθ/ n [U] bushes and plants growing thickly under trees

underhand /ˌʌndəˈhænd/ adj done secretly and dishonestly

underlie /ˌʌndəˈlaɪ/ v (pt -lay /-ˈleɪ/ pp -lain /-ˈleɪn/ pres p lying) [T] (fml) to be the basis or cause of sth

underline /ˌʌndəˈlaɪn/ v [T] **1** draw a line under a word, sentence, etc **2** emphasize that sth is important

undermanned /ˌʌndəˈmænd/ adj not having enough workers to be able to function well

undermine /ˌʌndəˈmaɪn/ v [T] **1** gradually weaken sth, esp sb's confidence or authority: Repeated failure ~d his confidence. **2** make sth weaker at the base, eg by digging under it

underneath /ˌʌndəˈniːθ/ prep, adv under or below sth else

underpants /ˈʌndəpænts/ n [pl] **1** (GB) piece of men's underwear worn under their trousers **2** (US) piece of underwear worn by men or women under trousers, a skirt, etc

underpass /ˈʌndəpɑːs/ n road or path that goes under a railway, another road, etc

underprivileged /ˌʌndəˈprɪvəlɪdʒd/ adj not having the standard of living, rights, etc enjoyed by others in society

underrate /ˌʌndəˈreɪt/ v [T] not recognize how good, important, etc sb/sth really is

underscore /ˌʌndəˈskɔː(r)/ v (esp US) = UNDERLINE

underside /ˈʌndəsaɪd/ n side or surface that is underneath

the undersigned /ˌʌndəˈsaɪnd/ n (pl the undersigned) (fml) the person who has signed that particular document: We, the ~ agree to...

understand /ˌʌndəˈstænd/ v (pt, pp -stood /-ˈstʊd/) [I, T] **1** know or realize the meaning of words, a language, what sb says, etc: She can ~ French perfectly. **2** [T] know or realize how or why sth happens, works, etc: I don't ~ why she was fired. **3** [I, T] know sb's character well: No one ~s me. **4** [I, T] (fml) have been told: I ~ that you wish to leave. [IDM] make

yourself understood make your meaning clear ▶ **understandable** adj seeming normal and natural; that can be understood ▶ **understandably** adv ▶ **understanding** n **1** [U, sing] knowledge **2** [C, usu sing] informal agreement **3** [U] sympathy ▶ **understanding** adj sympathetic and willing to forgive others

understate /ˌʌndəˈsteɪt/ v [T] state that sth is smaller, less important or less serious than it really is: ~ the extent of the problem ▶ **understatement** /ˈʌndəsteɪtmənt/ n [C, U]

understudy /ˈʌndəstʌdi/ n (pl -ies) actor who learns the part of another actor in a play so that they can play that part if necessary

undertake /ˌʌndəˈteɪk/ v (pt -took /-ˈtʊk/, pp -n /-ˈteɪkən/) (fml) **1** [T] make yourself responsible for sth and start doing it **2** [I] ~ to agree or promise to do sth ▶ **undertaking** n **1** important and/or difficult task or project **2** (fml) promise or agreement to do sth

undertaker /ˈʌndəteɪkə(r)/ n person whose job is to arrange funerals

undertone /ˈʌndətəʊn/ n ~(of) hidden meaning or feeling [IDM] in an undertone in a quiet voice

undervalue /ˌʌndəˈvæljuː/ v [T] not recognize how good, valuable or important sb/sth really is

underwater /ˌʌndəˈwɔːtə(r)/ adj, adv found, used or happening below the surface of water

underwear /ˈʌndəweə(r)/ n [U] clothing worn next to the skin and under other clothes

underworld /ˈʌndəwɜːld/ n [sing] **1** people and activities involved in crime in a particular place **2** (the underworld) (in mythology) home of the dead

underwrite /ˌʌndəˈraɪt/ v (pt -wrote /-ˈrəʊt/, pp -written /-ˈrɪtn/) [T] (tech) accept financial responsibility for sth so that you will pay money in case of loss or damage ▶ '**underwriter** n person or organization that underwrites insurance policies, esp for ships

undesirable /ˌʌndɪˈzaɪərəbl/ adj not wanted or approved of; likely to cause trouble ● **undesirable** n [C, usu pl] person who is not wanted in a particular place

undeveloped /ˌʌndɪˈveləpt/ adj (of a place, land, etc) not yet used for agriculture, industry, building, etc

undies /ˈʌndiz/ n [pl] (infml) = UNDERWEAR

undo /ʌnˈduː/ v (pt -did /-ˈdɪd/, pp -done /-ˈdʌn/) [T] **1** open sth that is fastened, wrapped or tied: ~ a button/zip **2** destroy the effect of sth: *He undid all my good work.* ▶ **undoing** n [sing] cause of sb's failure

undoubted /ʌnˈdaʊtɪd/ adj certain; accepted as true ▶ **undoubtedly** adv

undress /ʌnˈdres/ v [I, T] take off your clothes; remove sb else's clothes ▶ **undressed** adj not wearing any clothes

undue /ˌʌnˈdjuː/ adj (fml) too much: ~ *with haste* ▶ **unduly** adv

undulate /ˈʌndjuleɪt/ v [I] move up and down gently like a wave: *The road ~s through the hills.*

undying /ʌnˈdaɪɪŋ/ adj (fml) that will last for ever: ~ *love*

unearth /ʌnˈɜːθ/ v [T] **1** find sth in the ground by digging **2** discover sth by chance or after searching for it: ~ *the truth*

unearthly /ʌnˈɜːθli/ adj unnatural and therefore frightening [IDM] **at an unearthly hour** (infml) very early, esp when this is annoying

uneasy /ʌnˈiːzi/ adj (-ier, -iest) worried or anxious ▶ **uneasily** adv ▶ **uneasiness** n [U]

uneconomic /ˌʌnˌiːkəˈnɒmɪk, ˌʌnˌek-/ adj not producing profit

unemployed /ˌʌnɪmˈplɔɪd/ adj not having a job ▶ **the unemployed** n [pl] unemployed people ▶ **unemployment** /-ˈplɔɪmənt/ n [U]

unequal /ʌnˈiːkwəl/ adj **1** in which people are treated differently or have different advantages in a way that seems unfair **2** ~ (in) different in size, amount, etc **3** ~to (fml) not capable of doing sth ▶ **unequally** adv

unequivocal /ˌʌnɪˈkwɪvəkl/ adj (fml) having a completely clear meaning ▶ **unequivocally** adv

uneven /ʌnˈiːvn/ adj **1** not level or smooth **2** varying in quality

unexpected /ˌʌnɪkˈspektɪd/ adj causing surprise because it is not expected ▶ **unexpectedly** adv

unfailing /ʌnˈfeɪlɪŋ/ adj (approv) that you can rely on to always be there and always be the same

unfair /ˌʌnˈfeə(r)/ adj ~(on/to) not right or just: ~ *remarks/competition* ▶ **unfairly** adv

unfaithful /ʌnˈfeɪθfl/ adj ~(to) having sex with sb who is not your husband, wife or usual partner

unfamiliar /ˌʌnfəˈmɪliə(r)/ adj **1** ~ (to) that you do not know or recognize **2** ~with not having any knowledge or experience of sth: *I'm ~ with this type of equipment.*

unfasten /ʌnˈfɑːsn/ v [T] undo sth that is fastened

unfinished /ʌnˈfɪnɪʃt/ adj not complete: *We have some ~ business.*

unfit /ʌnˈfɪt/ adj **1** not of an acceptable standard; not suitable: ~ *for human consumption* **2** not capable

of doing sth, eg because of illness **3** (of a person) not in good physical condition because you have not taken exercise

unfold /ʌnˈfəʊld/ v [I, T] **1** (cause sth folded to) become open or flat **2** (cause sth to) gradually be made known: *as the story ~ed*

unforeseen /ˌʌnfɔːˈsiːn/ adj unexpected

unforgettable /ˌʌnfəˈɡetəbl/ adj that cannot be easily forgotten

unfortunate /ʌnˈfɔːtʃənət/ adj **1** unlucky **2** that makes you feel sorry: *an ~ remark* ▶ **unfortunately** adv

unfounded /ʌnˈfaʊndɪd/ adj not based on facts

unfriendly /ʌnˈfrendli/ adj (-ier, -iest) not kind or pleasant to sb

unfurl /ʌnˈfɜːl/ v [I, T] (cause sth that is curled or rolled tightly to) open: *The leaves slowly ~ed.*

unfurnished /ʌnˈfɜːnɪʃt/ adj (of a rented room, etc) without furniture

ungainly /ʌnˈɡeɪnli/ adj moving in a way that is not graceful

ungodly /ʌnˈɡɒdli/ adj (old-fash) not showing respect for God; wicked [IDM] **at an ungodly hour** very early or very late and therefore annoying

ungrateful /ʌnˈɡreɪtfl/ adv not expressing thanks for sth that sb has done for you

unguarded /ʌnˈɡɑːdɪd/ adv careless, esp in speech

unhappy /ʌnˈhæpi/ adj (-ier, -iest) not happy; sad ▶ **unhappily** adv ▶ **unhappiness** n [U]

unhealthy /ʌnˈhelθi/ adj (-ier, -iest) **1** not having or showing good health **2** harmful to your health

unheard-of /ʌnˈhɜːd ɒv/ adj that has never been known or done; very unusual

unicorn /ˈjuːnɪkɔːn/ n (in stories) white horse with a long straight horn on its forehead

unidentified /ˌʌnaɪˈdentɪfaɪd/ adj not recognized or known; not identified

uniform /ˈjuːnɪfɔːm/ n [C, U] special set of clothes worn by all members of an organization or group, eg the army or schoolchildren ● **uniform** adj not varying; regular ▶ **uniformed** adj: ~*ed police officers* ▶ **uniformity** /-ˈfɔːməti/ n [U, sing]

unify /ˈjuːnɪfaɪ/ v (pt, pp -ied) [T] join people, things, parts of a country, etc together to form a single unit ▶ **unification** /ˌjuːnɪfɪˈkeɪʃn/ n [U]

unilateral /ˌjuːnɪˈlætrəl/ adj done by one member of a group or organization without the agreement of the other members: *a ~ decision*

union /ˈjuːniən/ n **1** [C] = TRADE UNION (TRADE[1]) **2** [C] club or association

3 [C] group of countries or states **4** [U, sing] (fml) act of joining or state of being joined together: a summit to discuss economic and monetary ■ the ˌUnion ˈJack n [sing] national flag of the United Kingdom

unique /juːˈniːk/ adj **1** being the only one of its kind **2** very special or unusual: a ~ singing voice **3** ~(to) belonging to or connected with one particular person, place or thing: The koala is ~ to Australia. ▶ **uniquely** adv

unisex /ˈjuːnɪseks/ adj designed to be used by both men and women

unison /ˈjuːnɪsn/ n [IDM] **in unison (with sb/sth) 1** done or said at the same time **2** (of people or organizations) working together or in agreement with each other

unit /ˈjuːnɪt/ n **1** single thing, person or group **2** (business) single item of the type of product that a company sells: What's the ~ cost? **3** group of people with a specific job or function: the university research ~ **4** small machine that has a special function or is part of a larger machine: the central processing ~ of a computer **5** standard of measurement: The metre is a ~ of length.

unite /juˈnaɪt/ v [I, T] (cause people or things to) join together or become one with others ■ the Uˌnited ˈKingdom n [sing] (abbr (the) UK) England, Scotland, Wales and Northern Ireland ■ the Uˌnited ˈNations n [sing, with sing or pl verb] association of many countries which works for peace, better conditions, etc

unity /ˈjuːnəti/ n [U, sing] state of being in agreement and working together

universal /ˌjuːnɪˈvɜːsl/ adj done by or involving all the people in the world or in a particular group ▶ **universally** adv

universe /ˈjuːnɪvɜːs/ n (the universe) [sing] everything that exists in space, including all the stars and planets

university /ˌjuːnɪˈvɜːsəti/ n [C, U] (pl -ies) institution for advanced teaching and research

unkempt /ˌʌnˈkempt/ adj not kept tidy: ~ hair

unkind /ˌʌnˈkaɪnd/ adj unpleasant or unfriendly; slightly cruel

unknown /ˌʌnˈnəʊn/ adj not known or identified

unleaded /ˌʌnˈledɪd/ adj (of petrol) not containing lead and therefore less harmful to the environment

unleash /ʌnˈliːʃ/ v [T] (fml) suddenly release a powerful force

unless /ənˈles/ conj if ... not: You will fail ~ you work harder.

unlike /ˌʌnˈlaɪk/ adj, prep different from a particular person or thing

unlikely /ʌnˈlaɪkli/ adj **1** not likely to happen; not probable: He's ~ to get better. **2** not the person, thing or place that you would normally expect: an ~ candidate for the job

unload /ˌʌnˈləʊd/ v **1** [I, T] remove things from a vehicle or ship; empty the contents of sth **2** [T] ~ (on/onto) (fml) pass the responsibility for sb/sth to sb else

unlock /ˌʌnˈlɒk/ v [T] open a door, etc using a key

unlucky /ʌnˈlʌki/ adj having or bringing bad luck

unmanned /ˌʌnˈmænd/ adj (of a machine, vehicle or place) not having or needing a person to control or operate it

unmask /ˌʌnˈmɑːsk/ v [T] show the true character of sb

unmentionable /ʌnˈmenʃənəbl/ adj too shocking or embarrassing to be spoken about

unmistakable /ˌʌnmɪˈsteɪkəbl/ adj that cannot be mistaken for sb/sth else ▶ **unmistakably** adv

unmitigated /ʌnˈmɪtɪɡeɪtɪd/ adj (fml) completely bad: an ~ disaster

unmoved /ˌʌnˈmuːvd/ adj not feeling any pity or sympathy: He was ~ by her tears.

unnatural /ʌnˈnætʃrəl/ adj **1** not natural or normal: an ~ silence **2** not expected or acceptable: ~ behaviour

unnecessary /ʌnˈnesəsəri/ adj not needed; more than is needed ▶ **unnecessarily** adv

unnerve /ˌʌnˈnɜːv/ v [T] cause sb to lose confidence or courage

unnoticed /ˌʌnˈnəʊtɪst/ adj not seen or noticed

unobtrusive /ˌʌnəbˈtruːsɪv/ adj (fml) not attracting unnecessary attention

unofficial /ˌʌnəˈfɪʃl/ adj without the approval or permission of sb in authority

unpalatable /ʌnˈpælətəbl/ adj **1** (of facts, ideas, etc) unpleasant and not easy to accept: his ~ views **2** not pleasant to taste

unpleasant /ʌnˈpleznt/ adj not pleasant or nice; not kind, friendly or polite ▶ **unpleasantness** n [U]

unprecedented /ʌnˈpresɪdentɪd/ adj never having happened or been done before

unpredictable /ˌʌnprɪˈdɪktəbl/ adj that cannot be predicted: I never know how she will react, she's so ~.

unprintable /ʌnˈprɪntəbl/ adj (of words, etc) too offensive or shocking to be printed

unqualified /ˌʌnˈkwɒlɪfaɪd/ adj **1** not qualified for a job: ~ to teach **2** not limited; complete: an ~ disaster

unquestionable /ʌnˈkwestʃənəbl/

adj that cannot be doubted; certain ▶ **unquestionably** *adv*

unravel /ʌnˈrævl/ *v* (**-ll-**, *US* **-l-**) **1** [I, T] (cause sth woven or knotted to) separate into threads **2** [T] explain sth that is difficult to understand or mysterious: *~ a mystery*

unreal /ʌnˈrɪəl/ *adj* **1** so strange that it is more like a dream than reality **2** not related to reality: *~ expectations* ▶ **unreality** /ˌʌnrɪˈæləti/ *n* [U]

unreasonable /ʌnˈriːznəbl/ *adj* not reasonable or fair

unreliable /ˌʌnrɪˈlaɪəbl/ *adj* that cannot be trusted or depended on

unremitting /ˌʌnrɪˈmɪtɪŋ/ *adj* never relaxing or stopping

unrest /ʌnˈrest/ *n* [U] political situation in which people are angry and likely to fight or protest

unrivalled (*US* **-l-**) /ʌnˈraɪvld/ *adj* better or greater than any other

unroll /ʌnˈrəʊl/ *v* [I, T] (cause sth to) open from a rolled state and become flat

unruffled /ʌnˈrʌfld/ *adj* (of a person) calm

unruly /ʌnˈruːli/ *adj* not easy to control

unsavoury (*US* **-vory**) /ˌʌnˈseɪvəri/ *adj* unpleasant or offensive; not considered morally acceptable: *Her friends are all ~ characters.*

unscathed /ʌnˈskeɪðd/ *adj* not harmed

unscrupulous /ʌnˈskruːpjələs/ *adj* without moral principles; not honest or fair

unseat /ˌʌnˈsiːt/ *v* [T] **1** remove sb from a position of power **2** cause sb to fall off a horse, etc

unseemly /ʌnˈsiːmli/ *adj* (*old-fash*) (of behaviour, etc) not polite or suitable

unsettle /ʌnˈsetl/ *v* [T] make sb feel upset or worried, esp because a situation has changed: *Changing schools might ~ the kids.*

unsightly /ʌnˈsaɪtli/ *adj* not pleasant to look at

unsound /ˌʌnˈsaʊnd/ *adj* **1** not acceptable; not holding acceptable views: *politically ~* **2** (of a building, etc) in poor condition; weak **[IDM] unsound mind** (*law*) mentally ill

unspeakable /ʌnˈspiːkəbl/ *adj* that cannot be described in words, usu because it is so bad

unstuck /ˌʌnˈstʌk/ *adj* **[IDM] come unstuck 1** become separated from sth it was stuck to **2** (*infml*) (of a person, plan, etc) fail completely, with bad results

unswerving /ʌnˈswɜːvɪŋ/ *adj* strong and not changing: *~ loyalty*

unthinkable /ʌnˈθɪŋkəbl/ *adj* impossible to imagine or accept

untidy /ʌnˈtaɪdi/ *adj* (**-ier**, **-iest**) not neat or ordered

untie /ʌnˈtaɪ/ *v* (*pt, pp* **~d** *pres pt* **untying**) [T] undo a knot in sth; undo sth that is tied

until /ənˈtɪl/ (*also* **till** /tɪl/) *prep, conj* up to the point in time or the event mentioned: *Wait ~ the rain stops.*

untold /ˌʌnˈtəʊld/ *adj* (*fml*) too great to be measured

untoward /ˌʌntəˈwɔːd/ *adj* (*fml*) unexpected or unfortunate

unused¹ /ˌʌnˈjuːzd/ *adj* never having been used; not being used at the moment

unused² /ˌʌnˈjuːst/ *adj* **~to** not having much experience of sth; not used to sth: *She was ~ to talking about herself.*

unusual /ʌnˈjuːʒuəl/ *adj* different from what is usual or normal; interesting because it is different ▶ **unusually** *adv*

unveil /ʌnˈveɪl/ *v* [T] **1** remove a covering from a painting, statue, etc so that it can be seen for the first time **2** introduce a new plan, product, etc to the public for the first time

unwarranted /ʌnˈwɒrəntɪd/ *adj* (*fml*) not deserved or justified

unwieldy /ʌnˈwiːldi/ *adj* difficult to move or control, because it is large or heavy

unwind /ˌʌnˈwaɪnd/ *v* (*pt, pp* **-wound** /-ˈwaʊnd/) **1** [I, T] undo sth that has been wrapped into a ball or around sth **2** [I] (*infml*) relax

unwitting /ʌnˈwɪtɪŋ/ *adj* (*written*) not aware of what you are doing or the situation you are involved in ▶ **unwittingly** *adv*

unwrap /ʌnˈræp/ *v* (**-pp-**) [T] take off the paper, etc that covers or protects sth

up /ʌp/ *adv* **1** towards or in a higher position: *He jumped up from his chair.* **2** to or at a higher level: *She turned the volume up.* ◇ *Prices are going up.* **3** to the place where sth is: *A car drove up and he got in.* **4** to or at an important place: *go up to London* **5** to a place in the north of a country: *He's moved up north.* **6** into pieces or parts: *tear the paper up* **7** completely: *The stream has dried up.* **8** out of bed: *Is Pete up yet?* **9** (*spoken*) used to say that sth is happening: *What's up?* **[IDM] be up to sb** sb's duty or responsibility; be for sb to decide **up against sth** (*infml*) facing difficulties or problems **up and down 1** moving upwards and downwards: *The boat bobbed up and down in the water.* **2** backwards and forwards: *walk up and down* **3** sometimes good and sometimes bad **up for sth 1** on offer for sth; being considered for sth **2** willing to take part in an activity: *We're going clubbing. Are you up for it?* **up to sth 1** as far as a particular number, level, etc: *My car takes up to four people.* **2** until sth: *up to now* **3** as high or as good as sth **4** capable of sth: *She's not up to the job.* ● **up** *prep* **1** to or in a higher position: *climb up the stairs* **2** along or further along a road, etc: *There's another telephone box up the road.* ● **up** *adj* **1** directed or moving upwards: *the up escalator* **2** (*infml*) cheerful **3** (of a computer system) working ● **up** *v* (**-pp-**) **1** (*infml*) (**up and ...**) suddenly or do sth unexpected: *He just upped and left without telling anyone.* **2** [T] increase the price or amount of sth: *The buyers upped their offer.* ■ **up-and-'coming** *adj* (*infml*) likely to be successful and popular in the future ■ **ups and 'downs** *n* [pl] mixture of good and bad experiences

upbringing /ˈʌpbrɪŋɪŋ/ *n* [*sing*, U] way in which a child is cared for and taught how to behave while it is growing up

update /ˌʌpˈdeɪt/ *v* [T] **1** make sth more modern **2** give sb the most recent information about sth

upheaval /ʌpˈhiːvl/ *n* [C, U] big change that causes a lot of confusion, worry and problems

uphill /ˌʌpˈhɪl/ *adv* towards the top of a hill or slope ● **uphill** *adj* **1** sloping upwards **2** difficult to win; requiring a lot of effort: *an ~ battle/task*

uphold /ʌpˈhəʊld/ *v* (*pt*, *pp* -**held** /-ˈheld/) [T] **1** support sth: *~ the law* **2** confirm a legal decision

upholster /ʌpˈhəʊlstə(r)/ *v* [T] cover a chair, etc with soft material (**padding**) and fabric ▶ **upholsterer** *n* ▶ **upholstery** *n* [U] materials used in upholstering

upkeep /ˈʌpkiːp/ *n* [U] cost or process of keeping sth in good condition: *the ~ of a house*

upland /ˈʌplənd/ *n* [C, usu pl] area of high land situated away from the coast

upload /ˌʌpˈləʊd/ *v* [T] (*computing*) move data to a larger computer system from a smaller one ● **upload** /ˈʌpləʊd/ *n* [U] (*computing*) act or process of uploading

upmarket /ˌʌpˈmɑːkɪt/ *adj* (*infml*) designed for or used by people who belong to a high social class: *an ~ restaurant*

upon /əˈpɒn/ *prep* (*fml*) = ON²

upper /ˈʌpə(r)/ *n* at or near the top of sth; situated above sth else: *the ~ lip.* [IDM] **gain, get, have, etc the upper hand** get an advantage over sb so that you are in control ● **upper** *n* top part of a shoe attached to the

sole ■ **the ˌupper 'class** *n* social group considered to have the highest social status and more money and/or power than others ▶ **upper 'class** *adj* ■ **uppermost** *adj* (*written*) **1** higher or nearer the top than other things **2** more important than other things: *These thoughts were ~most in his mind at the time.* ■ **'uppermost** *adv* (*written*) in the highest position; facing upward

upright /ˈʌpraɪt/ *adj* **1** (of a person) not lying down, and with the back straight **2** placed in a vertical position **3** (of a person) moral and honest ● **upright** *n* piece of wood, metal or plastic that is placed vertically in order to support sth

uprising /ˈʌpraɪzɪŋ/ *n* fighting by ordinary people against those in power

uproar /ˈʌprɔː(r)/ *n* [U, sing] (outburst of) noise and excitement or anger ▶ **uproarious** /ʌpˈrɔːriəs/ *adj* (*written*) very noisy

uproot /ˌʌpˈruːt/ *v* [T] **1** pull a tree, etc out of the ground **2** ~ **yourself**/**sb** (cause sb to) leave a place where you/they have lived for a long time

upset /ʌpˈset/ *v* (**-tt-**, *pt*, *pp* upset) [T] **1** make sb feel worried, unhappy or annoyed: *be ~ by the bad news* **2** cause sth to go wrong: *~ all our plans* **3** make sb feel sick after they have eaten or drunk sth: *Milk ~s her stomach.* **4** cause sth to fall over by hitting it accidentally: *~ a glass of water* ● **upset** *adj* unhappy or disappointed because of sth unpleasant that has happened ● **upset** /ˈʌpset/ *n* **1** [C] situation in which there are unexpected problems or difficulties **2** [C] illness in the stomach causing sickness and diarrhoea: *a stomach ~* **3** [U, C] feelings of unhappiness and disappointment

upshot /ˈʌpʃɒt/ *n* (**the upshot**) [*sing*] ~(of) final result of a series of events

upside down /ˌʌpsaɪd ˈdaʊn/ *adv*, *adj* in a position with the top to the bottom usu is: *The canoe floated ~ in the river.* [IDM] **turn sth upside down 1** make a place untidy when looking for sth **2** cause large changes and confusion in a person's life: *His death turned her world ~.*

upstage /ˌʌpˈsteɪdʒ/ *v* [T] attract attention away from sb else and onto yourself

upstairs /ˌʌpˈsteəz/ *adv*, *adj* to or on a higher floor

upstanding /ˌʌpˈstændɪŋ/ *adj* (*fml*) behaving in a moral and honest way

upstart /ˈʌpstɑːt/ *n* (*disapprov*) person who has just started a new job but who behaves as if they are more important than other people

upstream /ˌʌpˈstriːm/ *adv* along a

river; in the opposite direction from the way the water flows

uptake /ˈʌpteɪk/ n [IDM] **be quick/slow on the uptake** be quick/slow to understand sth

uptight /ˌʌpˈtaɪt/ adj (infml) anxious and/or angry about sth

up to date /ˌʌp tə ˈdeɪt/ adj **1** modern; fashionable: This technology is bang up to date. **2** having all the most recent information: up-to-date records

upward /ˈʌpwəd/ adj pointing towards or facing a higher place ▶ **upwards** (esp US **upward**) adv **1** towards a higher place or position **2** towards a higher place or amount or price

uranium /juˈreɪniəm/ n [U] (symb **U**) radioactive metal used in producing nuclear energy

urban /ˈɜːbən/ adj of a town or city ▶ **urbanized** (also **-ised**) adj (of an area, country, etc) having a lot of towns, streets, factories, etc, rather than countryside

urge /ɜːdʒ/ v [T] **1** try hard to persuade sb to do sth: They ~d her to come back soon. **2** recommend sth strongly: ~ caution **3** (written) use force to make a person or an animal move more quickly ● **urge** n strong desire to do sth: a sudden ~ to run away

urgent /ˈɜːdʒənt/ adj needing to be dealt with immediately ▶ **urgency** /-dʒənsi/ n [U] ▶ **urgently** adv

urine /ˈjʊərɪn/ n [U] liquid waste that is passed from the body ▶ **urinate** /-eɪt/ v [I] pass urine from the body

URL /ˌjuː ɑːr ˈel/ abbr (computing) uniform/universal resource locator; address of a World Wide Web page

urn /ɜːn/ n **1** container for holding the ashes of a dead person **2** large metal container for serving tea or coffee

US /ˌjuː ˈes/ abbr United States of America): a US citizen

us /əs; strong form ʌs/ pron (used as the object of a v or prep; me and another or others; me and you

USA /ˌjuː es ˈeɪ/ abbr United States of America: visit the ~

usage /ˈjuːsɪdʒ/ n **1** [U,C] way in which words are used in a language: a guide to modern English ~ **2** [U] fact of sth being used; how much sth is used: Car ~ is predicted to increase.

use¹ /juːz/ v (pt, pp ~**d** /juːzd/) [T] **1** do sth with a machine, a method, an object, etc for a particular purpose: Can I ~ your phone? **2** take a particular amount of a liquid, substance, etc in order to achieve or make sth: This type of heater ~s a lot of electricity. **3** (disapprov) take advantage of sb unfairly; exploit sb

[PV] **use sth up** finish sth completely ▶ **usable** adj ▶ **user** n person or thing that uses sth

use² /juːs/ n **1** [U, sing] act of using sth; state of being used: The 12th-century chapel is still in ~ today. **2** [C,U] purpose for which sth is used; way in which sth is or can be used: a tool with many ~s **3** [U] right or opportunity to use sth, eg sth that belongs to sb else: You can have the ~ of my car. **4** [U] ability to use your mind or body: He lost the ~ of his legs. [IDM] **be of use** (to sb) (fml) be useful ● **come into/go out of use** start/stop being used **it's no use (doing sth) | What's the use (of doing sth)?** used to say that there is no point in doing sth because it will not be successful: It's no ~ —I can't persuade her. **make use of sth/sb** use sth/sb, esp in order to gain an advantage ▶ **useful** /-sfl/ adj that can help you to do or achieve what you want ▶ **usefully** adv ▶ **usefulness** n [U] ▶ **useless** adj **1** not useful **2** (infml) not very good at sth: I'm ~less at maths. ▶ **uselessly** adv

used¹ /juːst/ adj ~**to** familiar with sth; in the habit of doing sth: You will soon be/get ~ to the weather.

used² /juːzd/ adj that has belonged to or been used by sb before: ~ cars

used to /ˈjuːst tu:; before vowels and finally ˈjuːst tu/ modal v used to say that sth happened frequently or continuously during a period in the past: I ~ play football when I was a boy.

usher /ˈʌʃə(r)/ n person who shows people where to sit in a church, public hall, etc ● **usher** v [T] take or show sb where they should go [PV] **usher sb in** (fml) make sth new appear or make sth new begin ▶ **usherette** /ˌʌʃəˈret/ n (esp GB) woman whose job is to lead people to their seats in a theatre or cinema

usual /ˈjuːʒuəl/ adj existing, done, happening, etc most often: We'll meet at the ~ place. ▶ **usually** adv in the way that is usual or most normal; most often: I ~ly walk to work.

usurp /juːˈzɜːp/ v [T] (fml) take sb's position and/or power without having the right to do this ▶ **usurper** n

utensil /juːˈtensl/ n tool that is used in the house: kitchen ~s

uterus /ˈjuːtərəs/ n (anat) = WOMB

utility /juːˈtɪləti/ n (pl -ies) **1** [C] public service such as an electricity, water or gas supply **2** [U] (fml) quality of being useful **3** [C] (computing) piece of computer software that performs a particular task ■ **u'tility room** n room in a private house which contains equipment such as a washing machine, freezer, etc

utilize (also **-ise**) /ˈjuːtəlaɪz/ v [T] (fml) use sth, esp for a practical purpose ▸ **utilization** (*also* **-isation**) /-'zeɪʃn/ *n* [U]

utmost /'ʌtməʊst/ *adj* greatest; most extreme: *of the ~ importance* ● **utmost** *n* [sing] the greatest amount possible: *I will do my ~* (= try as hard as possible) *to persuade her.*

utter /'ʌtə(r)/ *adj* complete; total: *~ darkness* ● **utter** *v* [T] (*fml*) make a sound with your voice; say sth: *to ~ a groan* ▸ **utterance** /-rəns/ *n* [U,C] (*fml*) spoken word or words ▸ **utterly** *adv* completely

U-turn → U,u

V v

V, v /viː/ *n* [C,U] (*pl* **V's, v's** /viːz/) **1** the twenty-second letter of the English alphabet **2** Roman numeral for 5 **3** volt(s)

v *abbr* **1** (*also* **vs**) (in sport or a legal case) versus (= against) **2** (*infml*, *written*) very

vacancy /'veɪkənsi/ *n* (*pl* **-ies**) **1** job that is available for sb to do **2** room that is available in a hotel, etc

vacant /'veɪkənt/ *adj* **1** not filled or occupied; empty **2** showing no sign that the person is thinking of anything: *a ~ expression*

vacate /və'keɪt/ *v* [T] (*fml*) leave a building, seat, etc empty; make sth available for sb else

vacation /və'keɪʃn/ *n* **1** [C] period when universities are closed **2** [U, C] (*US*) = HOLIDAY

vaccinate /'væksɪneɪt/ *v* [T] *~ (against)* protect sb against a disease by injecting them with a vaccine ▸ **vaccination** /ˌvæksɪ'neɪʃn/ *n* [C,U]

vaccine /'væksiːn/ *n* [C,U] substance that is put into the blood and that protects the body from a disease

vacuum /'vækjuəm/ *n* [C] (*pl* **~s**) **1** space that is completely empty of all matter or gases **2** [*usu sing*] situation in which sb/sth is missing or lacking: *a ~ in his life since his wife died* **3** [*usu sing*] act of cleaning sth with a vacuum cleaner ● **vacuum** *v* [I, T] clean sth with a vacuum cleaner ▪ **'vacuum cleaner** *n* electrical machine that sucks up dirt and dust from floors ▪ **'vacuum flask** *n* container with a vacuum between its two walls, used for keeping liquids hot or cold

vagabond /'vægəbɒnd/ *n* (*old-fash*) person who has no home or job and who travels around

vagina /və'dʒaɪnə/ *n* (*anat*) passage from the outer female sex organs to the womb

vagrant /'veɪgrənt/ *n* (*fml* or *law*) person who has no home or job,

esp who begs ▸ **vagrancy** /-rənsi/ *n* [U]

vague /veɪg/ *adj* (*~r, ~st*) **1** not clear in a person's mind **2** not having or giving enough information about sth ▸ **vaguely** *adv* ▸ **vagueness** *n* [U]

vain /veɪn/ *adj* **1** unsuccessful: *a ~ attempt* **2** (*disapprov*) too proud of your own appearance, abilities, etc **|in vain** unsuccessfully ▸ **vainly** *adv*

vale /veɪl/ *n* (in poetry or place names) valley

valentine /'væləntaɪn/ *n* **1** (*also* **'valentine card**) card sent to sb you love on St Valentine's Day (14th February) **2** person that you send a valentine to

valet /'væleɪ; 'vælɪt/ *n* **1** man's personal male servant **2** (*GB*) hotel employee whose job is to clean the clothes of hotel guests **3** (*esp US*) person who parks your car for you at a hotel or restaurant

valiant /'væliənt/ *adj* very brave ▸ **valiantly** *adv*

valid /'vælɪd/ *adj* **1** that is legally and officially acceptable: *The ticket is ~ until 1st May.* **2** based on what is logical or true **3** (*computing*) that is accepted by the system: *a ~ password* ▸ **validate** *v* [T] (*fml*) make sth valid ▸ **validity** /və'lɪdəti/ *n* [U]

valley /'væli/ *n* low land between hills or mountains, often with a river

valour (*US* **-or**) /'vælə(r)/ *n* [U] (*lit*) great courage, esp in war

valuable /'væljuəbl/ *adj* **1** worth a lot of money **2** very useful: *~ advice* ▸ **valuables** *n* [*pl*] valuable things, esp jewellery

valuation /ˌvæljuˈeɪʃn/ *n* **1** [U] professional judgement about how much money sth is worth **2** [C] estimated value that has been decided on

value /'væljuː/ *n* **1** [U,C] amount of money sth is worth **2** [U] worth of sth compared with its price: *This large packet is good ~ at 99p.* **3** [U] quality of being useful or important: *the ~ of regular exercise* **4** (**values**) [*pl*] principles: *high moral ~s* ● **value** *v* [T] **1** think that sb/sth is important: *I really ~ her as a friend.* **2** decide that sth is worth a particular amount of money ▪ **value 'added tax** *n* [U] = VAT ▸ **valueless** *adj* (*fml*) without value or worth ▸ **valuer** *n* person whose job is to estimate how much property, land, etc is worth

valve /vælv/ *n* **1** device for controlling the flow of a liquid or gas in one direction only **2** structure in the heart that lets blood flow in one direction only

vampire /'væmpaɪə(r)/ *n* (in stories)

dead person who sucks the blood of living people

van /væn/ n covered vehicle with no side windows, used for carrying goods

vandal /'vændl/ n person who commits acts of vandalism ▸ **vandalism** /-dəlizəm/ n [U] crime of deliberately damaging public property, etc ▸ **vandalize** (also **-ise**) /-dəlaiz/ v [T] deliberately damage or destroy public property, etc

vanguard /'vænɡɑːd/ n (**the vanguard**) [sing] **1** leaders of a movement in society, eg in politics, art, industry, etc **2** front part of an advancing army

vanilla /və'nɪlə/ n [U] flavouring that comes from a plant and is used in sweet foods, eg ice cream

vanish /'vænɪʃ/ v [I] **1** disappear suddenly **2** stop existing: *Her hopes of finding a new job have vanished.*

vanity /'vænəti/ n [U] **1** (*disapprov*) too high an opinion of oneself: *She had no personal ~* (= about her appearance). **2** (*lit*) quality of being unimportant

vanquish /'væŋkwɪʃ/ v [T] (*lit*) defeat sb completely

vaporize (also **-ise**) /'veipəraiz/ v [I, T] (cause sth to) turn into gas

vapour (*US* **-or**) /'veipə(r)/ n [C,U] mass of very small drops of liquid in the air, eg steam: *water ~*

variable /'veəriəbl/ adj often changing; likely to change ● **variable** n situation, number or quantity that can vary or be varied ▸ **variably** adv

variant /'veəriənt/ adj, n (being a) different form of sth: *~ spellings*

variation /ˌveəri'eɪʃn/ n [C, U] change, esp in the amount or level of sth: *~(s) in temperature* **2** [C] (*music*) repetition of a simple tune in a different form

varicose vein /ˌværɪkəʊs 'veɪn/ n swollen painful vein, esp in the leg

varied /'veərid/ adj **1** of many different types **2** not staying the same, but changing often: *a ~ life*

variety /və'raɪəti/ n (pl **-ies**) **1** [sing] (of) several different sorts of the same thing: *a wide ~ of interests* **2** [U] quality of not being the same: *a life full of ~* **3** [C] type: *rare varieties of birds* **4** [U] entertainment with singing, dancing, comedy, etc: *a ~ act*

various /'veəriəs/ adj several different: *This dress comes in ~ colours.* ◇ *She took the job for ~ reasons.* **2** (*fml*) having many different features ▸ **variously** adv

varnish /'vɑːnɪʃ/ n [U,C] liquid used for giving a) hard shiny sur-

face on wood, etc ● **varnish** v [T] put varnish on the surface of sth

vary /'veəri/ v (pt, pp **-ied**) **1** [I] be different in size, amount, etc: *Car prices ~ greatly.* **2** [I, T] (cause sth to) change or be different according to the situation: *~ your route*

vase /vɑːz/ n container made of glass, etc, used esp for holding cut flowers

vast /vɑːst/ adj extremely large: *a ~ desert* ▸ **vastly** adv: *~ly improved* ▸ **vastness** n [U]

VAT /ˌviː eɪ 'tiː; væt/ abbr value added tax; tax added to the price of goods or services

vat /væt/ n large container for holding liquids, esp in industrial processes

vault /vɔːlt/ n **1** room with thick walls, esp in a bank, where valuable things are kept safe **2** room under a church or cemetery, used for burying people **3** arched roof **4** jump made by vaulting ● **vault** v [I, v] *~(over)* jump over sth using your hands or a pole to push you: *~ (over) a wall*

VCR /ˌviː siː 'ɑː(r)/ abbr = VIDEO CASSETTE RECORDER (VIDEO)

VD /ˌviː 'diː/ abbr = VENEREAL DISEASE

VDU /ˌviː diː 'juː/ n visual display unit; machine with a screen like a television that displays information from a computer

veal /viːl/ n [U] meat from a calf (= a young cow)

veer /vɪə(r)/ v [I] change direction

vegetable /'vedʒtəbl/ n plant, eg potato, bean or onion, eaten as food: *root ~s, such as carrots* ◇ *a ~ garden/patch*

vegetarian /ˌvedʒə'teəriən/ n person who does not eat meat or fish ▸ **vegetarian** adj: *a ~ restaurant*

vegetate /'vedʒəteɪt/ v [I] (of a person) spend time doing very little and feeling bored

vegetation /ˌvedʒə'teɪʃn/ n [U] (*written*) plants in general

veggie /'vedʒi/ n, adj (GB, infml) = VEGETARIAN

vehement /'viːəmənt/ adj (*written*) showing very strong feelings, esp anger ▸ **vehemence** /-məns/ n [U] ▸ **vehemently** adv

vehicle /'viːəkl/ n **1** something such as a car, bus or lorry that carries people or goods from place to place **2** *~ (for)* means of expressing or achieving a particular sth: *Art may be a ~ for propaganda.*

veil /veɪl/ n **1** [C] covering for a woman's face **2** [sing] (*written*) something that hides sth else: *a ~ of mist* ● **veil** v [T] **1** cover your face with a veil **2** [U] cover sth with sth else that hides it partly or completely

vein /veɪn/ n **1** [C] any of the tubes that carry blood from all parts of the body to the heart **2** [C] thin line in a leaf or an insect's wing **3** [C] layer of metal or mineral in rock: a ~ of gold **4** [sing] particular style or manner: in a comic ~

velocity /vəˈlɒsəti/ n [U,C] (pl -ies) (fml or physics) speed

velvet /ˈvelvɪt/ n [U] cloth made of cotton, silk, etc with a thick soft surface on one side ▸ **velvety** adj: ~ soft like velvet

vendetta /venˈdetə/ n a long bitter quarrel between families who try to harm or kill each other

vending machine /ˈvendɪŋ məʃiːn/ n machine from which you can buy cigarettes, drinks, etc by putting coins into it

vendor /ˈvendə(r)/ n **1** person who sells food, sweets, newspapers, etc, usu outside on the street **2** (law) person who is selling a house or other property

veneer /vəˈnɪə(r)/ n **1** [C,U] thin layer of wood or plastic glued to the surface of cheaper wood **2** [sing] ~(of) false outer appearance: a ~ of politeness ● **veneer** v [T] cover the surface of sth with a veneer of wood, etc

venerable /ˈvenərəbl/ adj (fml) deserving respect because of age, importance, etc

venerate /ˈvenəreɪt/ v [T] (fml) feel and show great respect for sb/sth ▸ **veneration** /ˌvenəˈreɪʃn/ n [U]

venereal disease /vəˌnɪəriəl dɪˈziːz/ n [C,U] (abbr VD) any disease caught by having sex with an infected person

vengeance /ˈvendʒəns/ n [U] (fml) act of punishing or harming sb in return for what they have done to you [IDM] **with a vengeance** (infml) to a greater degree than is expected or usual

vengeful /ˈvendʒfl/ adj (fml) showing a desire for revenge

venison /ˈvenɪsn; -zn-/ n [U] meat from a deer

venom /ˈvenəm/ n **1** [U] poison of certain snakes, spiders, etc **2** (written) strong bitterness or hate ▸ **venomous** adj: a ~ous snake/glance

vent /vent/ n hole for air, gas, liquid to pass through [IDM] **give (full) vent to sth** (fml) express a feeling, esp anger, strongly: give ~ to your feelings ● **vent** v [T] (written) ~(on) express feelings, esp anger, strongly: He ~ed his anger on his brother.

ventilate /ˈventɪleɪt/ v [T] allow fresh air to enter and move around a room, building, etc ▸ **ventilation** /ˌventɪˈleɪʃn/ n [U] ▸ **ventilator** n **1** device or opening for letting fresh air come into a room **2** piece of equipment

that helps sb to breathe by pumping air in and out of their lungs

ventriloquist /venˈtrɪləkwɪst/ n person who can make their voice appear to come from another person

venture /ˈventʃə(r)/ n business project or activity, esp one that involves taking risks: The project is a joint ~. ● **venture** v **1** [I] go somewhere even though you know it might be dangerous or unpleasant **2** [T] (fml) say or do sth carefully, esp because it might offend sb **3** [T] risk losing sth valuable or important if you are not successful at sth ■ **'venture capital** n [U] (business) money lent to sb to buy buildings, equipment, etc when they start a business

venue /ˈvenjuː/ n place where people meet for an organized event, eg a concert

veranda (also **verandah**) /vəˈrændə/ n (esp GB) platform with an open front and a roof, built along one side of a house

verb /vɜːb/ n (gram) word or phrase that expresses an action (eg eat), an event (eg happen) or a state (eg exist)

verbal /ˈvɜːbl/ adj **1** relating to words: Applicants must have good ~ skills. **2** spoken, not written: a ~ agreement **3** (gram) relating to verbs: a ~ noun ▸ **verbally** /-bəli/ adv in spoken words

verbose /vɜːˈbəʊs/ adj (fml, disapprov) using more words than are needed ▸ **verbosity** /vɜːˈbɒsəti/ n [U]

verdict /ˈvɜːdɪkt/ n **1** decision reached by a jury in a law court: return a ~ of guilty/not guilty **2** ~(on) opinion or decision formed after you have tested or considered sth

verge /vɜːdʒ/ n piece of grass at the edge of a path or road [IDM] **on/to the verge of (doing) sth** very near to the moment when sb does sth or sth happens: He was on the ~ of tears. ● **verge** v [PV] **verge on sth** be very close to an extreme state or condition

verify /ˈverɪfaɪ/ v (pt, pp -ied) [T] make sure that sth is true ▸ **verifiable** adj ▸ **verification** /ˌverɪfɪˈkeɪʃn/ n [U]

veritable /ˈverɪtəbl/ adj (fml or hum) rightly named; real: a ~ liar

vermin /ˈvɜːmɪn/ n [pl] **1** small animals or insects that are harmful to crops, birds and other animals **2** (disapprov) people who are harmful to society

vernacular /vəˈnækjələ(r)/ adj, n [sing] (in or of the) language spoken in a particular area or by a particular group

versatile /ˈvɜːsətaɪl/ adj having many different skills or uses ▸ **versatility** /-ˈtɪləti/ n [U]

verse /vɜːs/ n 1 [U] writing arranged in lines, each having a regular pattern 2 [C] unit in a poem or song 3 [C] short numbered division of a chapter in the Bible

versed /vɜːst/ adj ~ in (fml) knowledgeable about or skilled in sth: He had become well ~ in employment law.

version /ˈvɜːʃn/ n 1 copy of sth that is slightly different from the original: the film ~ of the play 2 description of an event, etc from the point of view of one person: There were three ~s of what happened.

versus /ˈvɜːsəs/ prep (abbr v, vs) against: England – Brazil

vertebra /ˈvɜːtɪbrə/ n (pl -brae /-briː/) any of the small bones that are connected together to form the backbone ▶ **vertebrate** /ˈvɜːtɪbrət/ n, adj (tech) (animal) having a backbone

vertical /ˈvɜːtɪkl/ adj (of a line, pole, etc) going straight up or down from a level surface or from top to bottom in a picture, etc: the ~ axis of the graph ● **vertical** n vertical line or position ▶ **vertically** /-kli/ adv

vertigo /ˈvɜːtɪɡəʊ/ n [U] feeling of dizziness and fear, caused by looking down from a high place

very /ˈveri/ adv 1 to a great degree; extremely: ~ little/quickly 2 used to emphasize a superlative or before own: the ~ best quality ◇ his ~ own car (= belonging to him and nobody else) [IDM] **very likely** ⇒ LIKELY ● **very** adj 1 actual: This is the ~ book I want! 2 extreme: at the ~ end 3 used to emphasize a noun: The ~ thought of it upsets me.

vessel /ˈvesl/ n 1 (fml) large ship or boat 2 (old-fash or tech) container used for holding liquids, eg a cup

vest /vest/ n 1 (GB) piece of underwear worn under a shirt, etc to keep the skin 2 special piece of clothing that covers the upper body: a bullet-proof ~ 3 (US) = WAISTCOAT (WAIST) ● **vest** v [PV] **vest sth in sb/sth** (law) of power, responsibility, etc) belong to sb/sth legally **vest sb/sth in sb/sth vest sth with sth** (fml) 1 give sb the legal right or power to do sth: the authority ~ed in her 2 make sb the legal owner of land or property ■ **vested interest** n ~(in) personal reason for wanting sth to happen, esp because you benefit from it

vestige /ˈvestɪdʒ/ n (fml) 1 small remaining part of sth 2 used in negative sentences to say that not even a small amount of sth exists: not a ~ of truth in the report

vet /vet/ n 1 doctor skilled in the treatment of sick animals ● **vet** v (-tt-) [T] find out about sb's past life and career in order to decide if they are suitable for a particular job

veteran /ˈvetərən/ n person with long experience, eg as a soldier ■ **veteran 'car** n car made before 1916, esp before 1905

veterinarian /ˌvetərɪˈneəriən/ n (US) = VET

veterinary /ˈvetnri; ˈvetrənəri/ adj connected with caring for the health of animals ■ **'veterinary surgeon** n (GB, fml) = VET

veto /ˈviːtəʊ/ n (pl -es) 1 [C, U] official right to refuse to allow sth to be done, esp a law being passed 2 [C] ~(on) occasion when sb refuses to allow sth to be done ● **veto** v [T] stop sth from happening or being done by using your official authority: ~ a proposal

vex /veks/ v [T] (old-fash or fml) annoy or worry sb ▶ **vexation** /vek-ˈseɪʃn/ n [C, U]

via /ˈvaɪə/ prep 1 through a place 2 by means of a particular person, system, etc: I heard about the sale – Jim.

viable /ˈvaɪəbl/ adj (esp of a plan or business) capable of succeeding ▶ **viability** /-ˈbɪləti/ n [U]

viaduct /ˈvaɪədʌkt/ n long high bridge carrying a road or railway across a valley

vibrate /vaɪˈbreɪt/ v [I, T] (cause sth to) move from side to side very quickly and with small movements: The house ~s whenever a heavy lorry passes. ▶ **vibration** /-ˈbreɪʃn/ n [C, U]

vicar /ˈvɪkə(r)/ n Anglican priest in charge of a church and the area around it (parish) ▶ **vicarage** /ˈvɪkərɪdʒ/ n vicar's house

vice /vaɪs/ n 1 [U] criminal activities that involve sex or drugs: plain-clothes detectives from the ~ squad 2 [C, U] evil or immoral behaviour or quality in sb's character: (hum) Cigarettes are my only ~. 3 [C] tool with two metal jaws that hold sth firmly

vice- /vaɪs/ prefix next in rank to sb and able to represent sb and act for them: ~-president

vice versa /ˌvaɪs ˈvɜːsə/ adv the other way round: We gossip about them and ~ (= they gossip about us).

vicinity /vəˈsɪnəti/ n (the vicinity) [sing] area around a particular place

vicious /ˈvɪʃəs/ adj acting or done with evil intentions; cruel and violent ■ **vicious 'circle** n [sing] situation in which one problem causes another problem, which then makes the first problem worse ▶ **viciously** adv

victim /ˈvɪktɪm/ n person who has been attacked, injured or killed as the result of a crime, disease, accident, etc: ~s of the flood ▶ **victimize** (also **-ise**) v [T] make sb suffer unfairly ▶ **victimization** (*also* **-isation**) /ˌvɪktɪmaɪˈzeɪʃn/ n [U]

victor /ˈvɪktə(r)/ n (*lit*) winner

victory /ˈvɪktəri/ n [C,U] (*pl* **-ies**) success in a game, an election, a war, etc ▶ **victorious** /vɪkˈtɔːriəs/ *adj* having won a victory

video /ˈvɪdiəʊ/ n (*pl* ~s) 1 [U,C] (box containing a) type of magnetic tape used for recording moving pictures and sound 2 [C] copy of a film, programme, etc that is recorded on videotape 3 [C] (*GB*) = VIDEO RECORDER ● **video** v [T] record a television programme using a video recorder; film sb/sth using a video camera ■ **'video camera** special camera for making video films ■ **video cas'sette recorder** (*abbr* **VCR**) (*also* **'video recorder**) n machine for recording and playing video and TV programmes on video ■ **'videoconferencing** n [U] system enabling people in different parts of the world to have a meeting by watching and listening to each other using video screens ■ **'videotape** n [U,C] = VIDEO(1)

vie /vaɪ/ v (*pres pt* **vying** /ˈvaɪɪŋ/) [I] ~ **with** compete with sb

view¹ /vjuː/ n 1 [C] personal opinion about sth; attitude towards sth: *In my* ~, *nurses deserve better pay.* 2 [U,sing] used when you are talking about whether you can see sth or whether sth can be seen in a particular situation: *The lake soon came into* ~. 3 [C] what can be seen from a place: *a wonderful* ~ *from the top of the mountain* [IDM] **in full view** (**of sb/sth**) completely visible; directly in front of sb/sth ▶ **in view of sth** considering sth: *In* ~ *of the weather, the event will be held indoors.* ▶ **on view** being shown in public ▶ **with a view to** (**doing**) **sth** (*fml*) with the intention of doing sth ■ **'viewdata** n [U] information system in which computer data is sent along telephone lines and shown on a television screen ■ **'viewfinder** n part of a camera that you look through to see the area that you are photographing ■ **'viewpoint** n way of thinking about a subject

view² /vjuː/ v [T] 1 think about sb/sth in a particular way: ~ *the problem with some concern* 2 look at sth carefully 3 (*fml*) watch television, a film, etc ▶ **viewer** n person watching television

vigil /ˈvɪdʒɪl/ n [C,U] period of time when people stay awake, esp at night, to watch a sick person, say prayers, etc: *His mother kept a round-the-clock* ~ *at his bedside.*

vigilant /ˈvɪdʒɪlənt/ *adj* (*fml*) very careful to notice any signs of

danger or trouble ▶ **vigilance** /-əns/ n [U] ▶ **vigilantly** adv

vigilante /ˌvɪdʒɪˈlænti/ n member of a group who try to prevent crime or punish criminals in their community, esp because they think the police are not doing this

vigour (*US* **-or**) /ˈvɪɡə(r)/ n [U] energy, force or enthusiasm ▶ **vigorous** *adj* strong or energetic ▶ **vigorously** adv

vile /vaɪl/ *adj* (~**r**, ~**st**) 1 (*infml*) very unpleasant: ~ *weather* 2 (*fml*) wicked; completely unacceptable ▶ **vilely** /ˈvaɪlli/ adv

villa /ˈvɪlə/ n (*GB*) house for holiday makers, eg in the countryside: *rent a* ~ *in Tuscany*

village /ˈvɪlɪdʒ/ n very small town situated in a country area ▶ **villager** n person who lives in a village

villain /ˈvɪlən/ n 1 main bad character in a story, play, etc 2 (*GB, infml*) criminal [IDM] **the villain of the piece** (*hum*) person or thing to be blamed for a problem, damage, etc

vindicate /ˈvɪndɪkeɪt/ v [T] (*fml*) 1 prove that sth is true or that you were right to do sth 2 prove that sb is not guilty of sth ▶ **vindication** /-ˈkeɪʃn/ n [C,U]

vindictive /vɪnˈdɪktɪv/ *adj* wanting to harm or upset sb who has harmed you ▶ **vindictively** adv ▶ **vindictiveness** n [U]

vine /vaɪn/ n climbing plant, esp one that produces grapes as its fruit ■ **vineyard** /ˈvɪnjəd/ n area of land planted with vines for making wine

vinegar /ˈvɪnɪɡə(r)/ n [U] bitter liquid made from malt, wine, etc, used to add flavour to food or to preserve it ▶ **vinegary** *adj*

vintage /ˈvɪntɪdʒ/ n year in which a particular wine was made ● **vintage** *adj* 1 old and of very high quality 2 (*GB*) (of a vehicle) made between 1917 and 1930

vinyl /ˈvaɪnl/ n [U,C] kind of strong flexible plastic

viola /viˈəʊlə/ n stringed musical instrument slightly larger than a violin

violate /ˈvaɪəleɪt/ v [T] 1 (*fml*) go against or refuse to obey a law, an agreement, etc 2 (*fml*) disturb or not respect sb's peace, privacy, etc 3 damage or destroy a holy place ▶ **violation** /-ˈleɪʃn/ n [U,C]

violent /ˈvaɪələnt/ *adj* 1 involving or caused by physical force: *a* ~ *attack* 2 showing or caused by very strong emotion: *a* ~ *argument* 3 very strong and sudden: *a* ~ *thunderstorm* ▶ **violence** /-ləns/ n [U] 1 violent behaviour 2 physical or emotional force or energy ▶ **violently** adv

violet /ˈvaɪələt/ n 1 [C] small plant with sweet-smelling purple or white flowers 2 [U] bluish-purple colour

violin /ˌvaɪəˈlɪn/ n stringed musical instrument held under the chin and played with a bow ▶ **violinist** n violin player

VIP /ˌviː aɪ ˈpiː/ n Very Important Person; famous or important person who is treated in a special way

viper /ˈvaɪpə(r)/ n poisonous snake

viral → VIRUS

virgin /ˈvɜːdʒɪn/ n person who has never had sex ● **virgin** adj 1 pure or natural and not changed, touched or spoiled: ~ *snow* 2 with no previous experience ▶ **virginity** /vəˈdʒɪnəti/ n [U] state of being a virgin

virile /ˈvɪraɪl/ adj having the strength and (esp sexual) energy considered typical of men ▶ **virility** /vəˈrɪləti/ n [U]

virtual /ˈvɜːtʃuəl/ adj 1 almost or very nearly the thing described: *The deputy manager is the ~ head of the business.* 2 made to appear to exist by the use of computer software: ~ *memory/space* ▶ **virtually** /ˈvɜːtʃuəli/ adv 1 in every important respect; almost or very nearly 2 by the use of computer software that makes sth appear to exist ■ **virtual re'ality** n [U] images created by a computer that appear to surround the person looking at them and seem almost real

virtue /ˈvɜːtʃuː/ n 1 [U] (fml) behaviour or attitudes that show high moral standards 2 [C] particular good quality or habit: *Patience is a ~.* 3 [C,U] attractive or useful quality: *The great ~ of the plan is its cheapness.* [IDM] **by/in virtue of sth** (fml) by means of or because of sth ▶ **virtuous** adj morally good

virus /ˈvaɪrəs/ n 1 tiny living thing that causes infectious disease 2 (infml) disease caused by a virus 3 instructions hidden within a computer program that are designed to cause faults or destroy data ▶ **viral** /ˈvaɪrəl/ adj like or caused by a virus: *a viral infection*

visa /ˈviːzə/ n official mark put on a passport allowing the owner to visit or leave a country

viscount /ˈvaɪkaʊnt/ n (in Britain) nobleman of a rank below an earl and above a baron ▶ **viscountess** n 1 woman who has the rank of a viscount 2 wife of a viscount

vise (US) = VICE(3)

visible /ˈvɪzəbl/ adj that can be seen ▶ **visibility** /ˌvɪzəˈbɪləti/ n [U] condition of the light or weather for seeing things clearly over a distance ▶ **visibly** adv clearly

vision /ˈvɪʒn/ n 1 [U] ability to see; area that you can see from a particular position 2 [C] idea or picture in your imagination: ~*s of great wealth* 3 [U] wisdom in planning the future: *problems caused by lack of ~*

visionary /ˈvɪʒənri/ adj 1 (approv) original and showing vision(3) 2 relating to dreams or strange experiences ● **visionary** n (pl **-ies**) person who has the ability to think about or plan the future in an intelligent, imaginative way

visit /ˈvɪzɪt/ v 1 [I, T] go to see a person or place for a period of time: ~ *a friend/Rome* 2 [T] make an official visit to sb, eg to carry out checks or give advice [PV] **visit with sb** (US) spend time with sb, esp talking socially ● **visit** n act or time of visiting sb/sth: *pay a ~ to a friend* ▶ **visitor** n person who visits a person or place

visor /ˈvaɪzə(r)/ n movable part of a helmet, covering the face

vista /ˈvɪstə/ n 1 (fml) (lit) beautiful view 2 (written) range of things that might happen in the future: *This job will open up new ~s for her.*

visual /ˈvɪʒuəl/ adj of or connected with seeing or sight ■ **visual 'aid** n [usu pl] picture, video, etc used in teaching to help people understand sth ■ **visual dis'play unit** n (computing) = VDU ▶ **visualize** (also **-ise**) v [T] form a mental picture of sb/sth ▶ **visually** adv

vital /ˈvaɪtl/ adj 1 necessary or very important: *a ~ part of the machine* 2 connected with or necessary for staying alive 3 (written) (of a person) full of energy and enthusiasm ▶ **vitality** /vaɪˈtæləti/ n [U] energy and enthusiasm ▶ **vitally** /ˈvaɪtəli/ adv extremely; in an essential way ■ **vital sta'tistics** n [pl] 1 figures that show the numbers of births and deaths in a country 2 (esp GB, infml) measurements of a woman's chest, waist and hips

vitamin /ˈvɪtəmɪn/ n natural substance found in food that is an essential part of what humans and animals eat to help them stay healthy

vitriolic /ˌvɪtriˈɒlɪk/ adj (fml) (of language or comments) very angry and bitter

vivacious /vɪˈveɪʃəs/ adj (approv) having a lively and attractive personality ▶ **vivaciously** adv ▶ **vivacity** /vɪˈvæsəti/ n [U]

vivid /ˈvɪvɪd/ adj 1 (of memories, a description, etc) producing very clear pictures in your mind: *a ~ description* 2 (of light, colours, etc) very bright ▶ **vividly** adv

vivisection /ˌvɪvɪˈsekʃn/ n [U]

experiments on living animals for scientific research

vixen /ˈvɪksn/ n female fox

vocabulary /vəˈkæbjələri/ (pl -ies) n 1 [C,U] all the words that a person knows or uses: the ~ of a three-year-old 2 [C] all the words in a language 3 [C,U] list of words with their meanings, esp in a book for learning a foreign language

vocal /ˈvəʊkl/ adj 1 connected with the voice 2 expressing your opinions freely and loudly ● **vocal** ~s n (usu pl) part of a piece of music that is sung, rather than played on an instrument: backing ~s ■ ˌvocal ˈcords n [pl] thin strips of muscle in the throat that move to produce the voice ▶ **vocalist** /-kəlɪst/ n singer ▶ **vocally** /-kəli/ adv

vocation /vəʊˈkeɪʃn/ n [C,U] 1 (fml) type of work or way of life that you believe is esp suitable for you: She believes that she has found her true ~ in life. 2 belief that a particular type of work or way of life is esp suitable for you ▶ **vocational** /-ʃənl/ adj connected with the skills, knowledge, etc that you need to do a particular job: ~al training

vociferous /vəˈsɪfərəs/ adj (fml) expressing your opinions in a loud and confident way: a ~ group of demonstrators ▶ **vociferously** adv

vodka /ˈvɒdkə/ n [U] strong Russian alcoholic drink

vogue /vəʊg/ n [C,U] fashion for sth: a new ~ for low-heeled shoes

voice /vɔɪs/ n 1 [C,U] sounds produced through the mouth by a person speaking or singing: recognize sb's ~ ◇ He's lost his ~ (= he cannot speak). 2 [U, sing] (right to express) your opinion: They should be allowed a ~ in deciding their future. ● **voice** v [T] tell people your feelings or opinions about sth

void /vɔɪd/ n [C] (fml) [usu sing] large empty space ● **void** adj 1 ~ of (fml) completely lacking sth 2 (law) (of a contract, etc) not valid or legal ● **void** v [T] (law) state officially that sth is no longer valid

volatile /ˈvɒlətaɪl/ adj likely to change (in mood or behaviour) suddenly and unexpectedly

vol-au-vent /ˈvɒl ə vɒ̃/ n small light pastry case filled with meat, fish, etc in a cream sauce

volcano /vɒlˈkeɪnəʊ/ n (pl -es or ~s) mountain with an opening (crater) through which hot melted rock, gas, etc are forced out ▶ **volcanic** /-ˈkænɪk/ adj

volition /vəˈlɪʃn/ n [U] (fml) power to choose sth freely or to make your own decisions: He left of his own ~ (= because he wanted to).

volley /ˈvɒli/ n 1 (in tennis, football, etc) hit or kick of the ball before it touches the ground 2 many bullets, stones, etc that are fired or thrown at the same time ● **volley** v [I, T] (in some sports) hit or kick the ball before it touches the ground: He ~ed the ball into the back of the net. ■ **volleyball** n [U] game in which a ball is thrown over a net

volt /vəʊlt/ n (abbr V) unit for measuring the force of an electric current ▶ **voltage** n [U,C] electrical force measured in volts

voluble /ˈvɒljʊbl/ adj (fml) talking a lot ▶ **volubly** adv

volume /ˈvɒljuːm/ n 1 [U,C] amount of space occupied by a substance 2 [C,U] amount of sth: The ~ of exports fell last month. 3 [U] amount of sound produced by a radio, television, etc: the ~ control on the TV 4 [C] (fml) book, esp one of a series

voluminous /vəˈluːmɪnəs/ adj (fml) 1 (of clothing) very large; using a lot of material: a ~ skirt 2 (of writing) very long and detailed

voluntary /ˈvɒləntri/ adj 1 done willingly, without being forced: Attendance is ~. 2 (of work) done without payment: a ~ organization ▶ **voluntarily** /-trəli/ adv

volunteer /ˌvɒlənˈtɪə(r)/ n 1 person who offers to do sth without being forced or paid 2 person who chooses to join the armed forces without being forced to join ● **volunteer** v 1 [I, T] offer to do sth without being forced or paid to do it 2 [T] suggest sth or tell sb sth without being asked 3 [I] ~ **for** join the armed forces voluntarily

voluptuous /vəˈlʌptʃuəs/ adj (written) 1 (of a woman) having a full and sexually desirable figure 2 (lit) giving you physical pleasure ▶ **voluptuously** adv

vomit /ˈvɒmɪt/ v [I, T] bring food from the stomach back out through the mouth ● **vomit** n [U] food from the stomach that has been vomited

vote /vəʊt/ n 1 [C] formal choice that you make in an election or at a meeting in order to choose sb or decide sth 2 [C] ~(on) occasion when a group of people vote on sth: have/take a ~ on an issue 3 (the vote) [sing] total number of votes in an election: She obtained 40% of the ~. 4 (the vote) [sing] right to vote in political elections ● **vote** v 1 [I, T] formally express an opinion, support for sb, etc by marking a paper or raising your hand: ~ for/against sb ◇ ~ on the suggestion 2 [T] suggest sth or support a suggestion that sb has made ▶ **voter** n

vouch /vaʊtʃ/ v [PV] **vouch for sb**
say that sb will behave well and
that you will be responsible for
their actions **vouch for sth** say that
you believe that sth is true or good
because you have evidence for it

voucher /ˈvaʊtʃə(r)/ n piece of
paper that can be exchanged for
certain goods or services

vow /vaʊ/ n formal and serious
promise, esp a religious one, to do
sth ● **vow** v [I, T] make a formal
promise to do sth or a formal statement that sth is true

vowel /ˈvaʊəl/ n **1** speech sound in
which the mouth is open and the
tongue is not touching the top of
the mouth, the teeth, etc **2** letter
that represents a vowel sound, eg
a, e, i, o, and *u*

voyage /ˈvɔɪdʒ/ n (*written*) long
journey, esp by sea or in space
● **voyage** v [I] (*lit*) travel, esp in a
ship ▸ **voyager** n

vs *abbr* (*US*) = VERSUS

vulgar /ˈvʌlɡə(r)/ *adj* **1** showing a
lack of good taste; not polite, elegant or well behaved **2** rude and
likely to offend ▸ **vulgarity** /vʌl-
ˈɡærəti/ n [U]

vulnerable /ˈvʌlnərəbl/ *adj* weak
and easily hurt physically or emotionally ▸ **vulnerability** /ˌvʌlnərə-
ˈbɪləti/ n [U]

vulture /ˈvʌltʃə(r)/ n **1** large bird
that eats the flesh of dead animals
2 person who hopes to gain from
the troubles or suffering of others

vying *pres part of* VIE

W w

W *abbr* **1** west(ern): *W Yorkshire*
2 watt(s)

W, w /ˈdʌblju/ n [C, U] (*pl* W's, w's
/ˈdʌblju:z/) the twenty-third letter
of the English alphabet

wacky /ˈwæki/ *adj* (**-ier, -iest**)
(*infml*) funny or amusing in a
slightly crazy way

wad /wɒd/ n **1** thick pile of papers,
banknotes, etc folded or rolled
together **2** mass of soft material: *a
~ of cotton wool*

waddle /ˈwɒdl/ v [I] walk with short
steps, swinging from side to side,
like a duck ▸ **waddle** n [sing]

wade /weɪd/ v [I] walk with an effort
through sth, esp water or mud [PV]
wade in|wade into sth (*infml*) enter
a fight, discussion or argument in a
forceful or insensitive way **wade
through sth** deal with or read sth
that is boring and takes a lot of time
■ **'wading bird** (*also* 'wader) n long-

legged bird that feeds in shallow
water

wafer /ˈweɪfə(r)/ n **1** thin crisp light
biscuit, eaten with ice cream **2** very
thin round piece of special bread
given by a priest during Communion

waffle /ˈwɒfl/ n **1** [C] small crisp
pancake with a pattern of raised
squares **2** [U] (*GB, infml*) language
that uses a lot of words but does
not say anything important or
interesting ● **waffle** v [I] (*GB, infml,
disapprov*) talk or write using a lot
of words but without saying anything important or interesting

waft /wɒft/ v [I, T] (cause sth to)
move gently through the air: *The
scent ~ed into the room.* ▸ **waft** n

wag /wæɡ/ v (**-gg-**) [I, T] (cause sth
to) move from side to side: *The dog
~ged its tail.* ▸ **wag** n

wage /weɪdʒ/ n [C] (*also* **wages** [pl])
regular amount of money that you
earn, usu every week, for work or
services: *fight for higher ~s* ◇ *a
~ increase* ● **wage** v [T] ~(**against/on**)
begin and continue a war, campaign,
etc: *~ a war on poverty*

wager /ˈweɪdʒə(r)/ n, v [I, T] (*old-
fash or fml*) = BET

waggle /ˈwæɡl/ v [I, T] (cause sth to)
move with short movements from
side to side or up and down

wagon /ˈwæɡən/ n **1** railway truck
for carrying goods **2** (*GB also* **wag-
gon**) vehicle with four wheels,
pulled by horses and used for
carrying heavy loads

wail /weɪl/ v [I] **1** make a long loud
high cry, esp because you are sad
or in pain: *a ~ing child* **2** (of things)
make a long high sound: *~ing
sirens* ● **wail** n long loud high cry

waist /weɪst/ n **1** area around the
middle of the body between the ribs
and the hips **2** part of a piece of
clothing that covers the waist
■ **'waistcoat** n (*GB*) short piece of
clothing with buttons down the front
but no sleeves, often worn under a
man's jacket ■ **'waistline** n measurement of the body around the waist

wait /weɪt/ v **1** [I] ~(**for**) stay where
you are or delay doing sth until
sb/sth comes or sth happens: *We had
to ~ an hour for the train.* ◇ *I'm ~ing to
see the manager.* **2** [T] ~(**for**) hope or
watch for sth to happen, esp for a
long time: *He is ~ing for his opportunity.* **3** [I] be left to be dealt with at a
later time: *The matter isn't urgent; it
can ~.* [IDM] **I, they, etc can't wait/can
hardly wait** used when you are
emphasizing that sb is very excited
about sth or keen to do it: *I can't ~ to
tell her the news!* **wait and see** used to
tell sb to be patient and wait to find
out about sth later **wait on sb** hand

and foot (*disapprov*) do everything that sb wants [PV] **wait on sb** act as a servant to sb, esp by serving food to them **wait up (for sb)** wait for sb to come home before you go to bed ● **wait** *n* [C,*usu sing*] act or time of waiting: *We had a long ~ for the bus.* ▸ **waiter** (*fem* **waitress** /ˈweɪtrəs/) *n* person whose job is to serve customers at their tables in a restaurant, etc ■ **'waiting list** *n* list of people who will be served, treated, etc later ■ **'waiting room** *n* room where people can sit while they are waiting, eg for a train or to see a doctor

waive /weɪv/ *v* [T] choose not to insist on a rule or right in a particular situation: *~ a fee*

wake¹ /weɪk/ *v* (*pt* **woke** /wəʊk/, *pp* **woken** /ˈwəʊkən/) [I, T] **~ (up)** (cause sb to) stop sleeping: *What time did you ~ up?* [IDM] **your waking hours** time when you are awake [PV] **wake up to sth** become aware of sth; realize sth

wake² /weɪk/ *n* **1** occasion before a funeral when people gather to remember the dead person **2** track left on the surface of water by a moving ship [IDM] **in the wake of sb/sth** coming after or following sb/sth

waken /ˈweɪkən/ *v* [I, T] (*written*) (cause sb to) wake from sleep

walk¹ /wɔːk/ *v* **1** [I] move or go somewhere by putting one foot in front of the other on the ground, but without running **2** [T] go somewhere with sb on foot, esp to make sure they get there safely: *I'll ~ you home.* **3** [T] take an animal for a walk, for food [PV] **walk away/off with sth** (*infml*) **1** win sth easily **2** steal sth **walk into sth** (*infml*) **1** become caught in an unpleasant situation, esp because you are careless: *~ into a trap* **2** get a job very easily **walk out** (*infml*) (of workers) go on strike **walk out (of sth)** leave a meeting, etc, esp in order to show your disapproval **walk out (on sb)** (*infml*) suddenly leave sb that you are having a relationship with: *How could he ~ on me when he knew I was pregnant?* **walk (all) over sb** (*infml*) treat sb badly ■ **'walkabout** *n* (*GB*) occasion when an important person walks among ordinary people to meet and talk to them ▸ **walker** *n* ■ **'walking stick** *n* stick that you carry and use as a support when walking ■ **'Walkman™** *n* (*pl* **~s**) small cassette or CD player with headphones that you carry with you and use while you are moving around ■ **'walk-on** *adj* (of a part in a play) small and with no words to say ■ **'walkout** *n* sudden strike by workers ■ **'walkover** *n* easy victory

walk² /wɔːk/ *n* **1** [C] journey on foot,

usu for pleasure or exercise: *My house is a five-minute ~ from the shops.* **2** [C] path or route for walking **3** [sing] way of walking: *a slow ~* [IDM] **a walk of life** person's job or position in society

walkie-talkie /ˌwɔːki ˈtɔːki/ *n* (*infml*) small radio that you can carry with you and use to send or receive spoken messages

wall /wɔːl/ *n* **1** long upright solid structure of stone, brick, etc that surrounds, divides or protects sth **2** any of the upright sides of a room or building **3** something that forms a barrier or prevents progress: *Investigators were confronted by a ~ of silence.* **4** outer layer of sth hollow, eg an organ of the body: *the abdominal ~* [IDM] **go to the wall** (*infml*) (of a company or organization) fail because of lack of money **up the wall** (*infml*) crazy or angry. *Dad will go up the ~ if I'm late.* ● **wall** *v* [T] surround an area, town, etc with a wall or walls: *a ~ed garden* [PV] **wall sth/sb in** surround sth/sb with a wall or barrier **wall sth off** separate one place or area from another with a wall **wall sth up** block sth with a wall or bricks ■ **'wallflower** *n* garden plant with sweet-smelling flowers ■ **'wallpaper** *n* [U] paper, usu with a coloured design, for covering the walls of a room ● **'wallpaper** *v* [T] cover the walls of a room with wallpaper ■ **,wall-to-'wall** *adj* covering the floor of a room completely

wallet /ˈwɒlɪt/ *n* small flat case, esp for carrying paper money and credit cards

wallop /ˈwɒləp/ *v* [T] (*infml*) hit sb/sth very hard ▸ **wallop** *n* [sing]

wallow /ˈwɒləʊ/ *v* [I] **~ (in)** **1** (of animals or people) roll about in mud, water, etc **2** take pleasure in sth: *~ in luxury/self-pity*

Wall Street /ˈwɔːl striːt/ *n* [U] US financial centre and stock exchange in New York City

wally /ˈwɒli/ *n* (*pl* **-ies**) (*GB*, *infml*) stupid person

walnut /ˈwɔːlnʌt/ *n* **1** [C] (tree producing a) large nut with a hard round shell in two halves **2** [U] brown wood of the walnut tree, used for making furniture

walrus /ˈwɔːlrəs/ *n* large sea animal with thick fur and two long outer teeth (**tusks**)

waltz /wɔːls/ *n* (music for a) graceful ballroom dance ● **waltz** *v* [I] **1** dance a waltz **2** (*infml*) walk or go somewhere in a very confident way: *I don't like him ~ing into the house as if he owns it.*

WAN /wæn/ *n* (*pl* **~s**) (*computing*) wide area network; system in which computers in different places are connected, usu over a large area

wan /wɒn/ *adj* (*written*) looking pale and weak

wand /wɒnd/ *n* long thin stick used by a magician

wander /ˈwɒndə(r)/ *v* **1** [I, T] walk around a place with no special purpose: *~ round the town* ◇ *~ the streets* **2** [I] (of sb's thoughts) move away from the subject ▶ **wanderer** *n* ■ **wanderings** *n* [pl] (*written*) journeys from place to place

wane /weɪn/ *v* [I] **1** gradually become weaker or less important **2** (of the moon) appear slightly smaller each day after being round and full ● **wane** *n* [sing] [IDM] **on the wane** (*fml*) becoming smaller, less important or less common

wangle /ˈwæŋɡl/ *v* [T] ~ (**from/out of**) (*infml*) get sth that you mean to get by persuading sb or by a clever plan: *~ an extra week's holiday*

want¹ /wɒnt/ *v* **1** [I, T] have a desire or wish for sth: *They ~ a new car.* ◇ *I ~ to go home.* **2** [I, T] (*infml*) need sth: *The grass ~s cutting.* **3** [I] ~ **to** (*infml*) used to give advice to sb, meaning *should*: *You ~ to be more careful.* **4** [T] feel sexual desire for sb **5** [T] (*fml*) lack sth [PV] **want for sth** (esp in negative sentences) (*fml*) lack sth that you really need: *They ~ for nothing.* ▶ **wanted** *adj* being searched for by the police in connection with a crime: *America's most ~ed man* ■ **wanting** *adj* ~ (**in**) (*fml*) **1** not having enough of sth **2** not good enough: *The new system was tried and found ~ing.*

want² /wɒnt/ *n* **1** [C, usu pl] thing that you need or want **2** [U, sing] ~ **of** (*fml*) lack of sth: *die for ~ of water*

WAP /wæp/ *abbr* wireless application protocol; technology that links devices such as mobile phones to the Internet: *a ~ phone*

war /wɔː(r)/ *n* [C, U] **1** (instance or period of) armed fighting between countries: *the First World W~* ◇ *at ~* **2** struggle or competition: *a trade ~* ◇ *~ on drugs* [IDM] **have been in the wars** (*spoken*) have been injured in a fight or an accident ■ **warfare** *n* [U] activity of fighting war: *chemical ~fare* ■ **war game** *n* practice battle used as a training exercise ■ **warhead** *n* explosive front end of a missile ■ **warlike** *adj* (*fml*) **1** aggressive and wanting to fight **2** connected with fighting ■ **warpath** *n* [IDM] (**be/go**) **on the warpath** (*infml*) be angry and wanting to fight or punish sb ■ **warring** *adj* involved in a war: *~ring tribes* ■ **warship** *n* ship used in war ■ **wartime** *n* [U] period of war

warble /ˈwɔːbl/ *v* [I, T] (esp of a bird) sing with rapidly changing notes ▶ **warbler** *n* bird that warbles

ward /wɔːd/ *n* **1** separate room in a hospital for people with the same type of medical condition **2** (in Britain) division of a local government area **3** (*law*) person, usu a child, under the protection of a guardian ▶ **ward** *v* [PV] **ward sth/sb off** protect or defend yourself from danger, illness, attack, etc

warden /ˈwɔːdn/ *n* person responsible for taking care of a particular place and for making sure rules are obeyed: *the ~ of a youth hostel*

warder /ˈwɔːdə(r)/ *n* (*fem* **wardress** /ˈwɔːdrəs/) (*GB*) guard in a prison

wardrobe /ˈwɔːdrəʊb/ *n* [C] **1** tall cupboard for hanging clothes in **2** [usu sing] the clothes that a person has **3** [usu sing] department in a TV or theatre company that takes care of the clothes that the actors wear

ware /weə(r)/ *n* **1** [U] (in compounds) manufactured goods of the type mentioned: *silver~* **2** (**wares**) *n* [pl] (*old-fash*) things that sb is selling ■ **warehouse** *n* large building for storing goods

warm /wɔːm/ *adj* **1** fairly hot; between cool and hot: *~ water* **2** (of clothes, buildings, etc) keeping you warm or staying warm in cold weather: *a ~ jumper* **3** friendly and enthusiastic: *a ~ welcome* **4** (of colours) creating a comfortable feeling or atmosphere ● **warm** *v* [I, T] (cause sth/sb to) become warm(er) [PV] **warm to/towards sth/sb 1** begin to like sth/sb **2** become more interested in sth **warm up** prepare for physical exercise or a performance by doing gentle exercises or practice **warm (sb/sth) up** (cause sb/sth to) become more lively or enthusiastic ■ **warm-blooded** *adj* (of animals) having a constant body temperature ■ **warm-hearted** *adj* (of a person) kind ▶ **warmly** *adv* ■ **warmth** *n* [U] state or quality of being warm

warn /wɔːn/ *v* [T] tell sb in advance about a possible danger or difficulty: *I ~ed her that it would cost a lot.* ◇ *They were ~ed not to climb the mountain in bad weather.* ▶ **warning** *n* **1** [C, U] statement, event, etc telling sb that sth bad may happen in the future: *He didn't listen to my ~ing.* **2** [C] statement telling sb that they will be punished if they continue to behave in a certain way ▶ **warning** *adj*: *~ing signs of trouble ahead*

warp /wɔːp/ *v* [I, T] **1** (cause sth to) become bent or twisted: *Some wood ~s in hot weather.* **2** [T] influence sb so that they behave in an unacceptable or shocking way: *a ~ed mind*

warrant /'wɒrənt/ n legal document giving sb authority to do sth: a ~ for his arrest ● **warrant** v [T] (fml) make sth necessary or appropriate in a particular situation ▸ **warranty** n [C,U] (pl -ies) written agreement in which a company promises to repair or replace a product if there is a problem

warren /'wɒrən/ n (also 'rabbit warren) **1** system of holes and underground tunnels where wild rabbits live **2** (disapprov) building or part of a city which many narrow passages or streets

warrior /'wɒrɪə(r)/ n (fml) (esp in the past) soldier; fighter

wart /wɔːt/ n small hard lump on the skin

wary /'weəri/ adj (-ier, -iest) looking out for possible danger or difficulty ▸ **warily** adv

was /wəz; strong wɒz/ third pers sing pres tense of BE

wash¹ /wɒʃ/ v **1** [T] make sth/sb clean using water and usu soap: ~ your hands/clothes **2** ~ (yourself) [I, T] make yourself clean using water and usu soap: I had to ~ and dress in a hurry. **3** [I] (of clothes, fabrics etc) be able to be washed without damage: Does this sweater ~ well? **4** [I, T] (of water) flow or carry sth/sb in a particular direction: Pieces of the wreckage were ~ed ashore. [IDM] **wash your hands of sb/sth** refuse to be involved with or responsible for sb/sth **sth won't/doesn't wash (with sb)** used to say that sb's explanation, excuse, etc is not valid or acceptable: That excuse just won't ~ with me. [PV] **wash sb/sth away** (of water) remove or carry sth/sb away to another place **wash sth down (with sth) 1** clean sth large or a surface with a lot of water **2** drink sth while or after eating food: We had bread and cheese ~ed down with beer. **wash sth out 1** wash the inside of sth to remove dirt, etc **2** remove a substance from sth by washing **3** (of rain) make a game, an event, etc end early or prevent it from starting **wash (sth) up 1** wash plates, glasses, etc after a meal ▸ **washable** adj that can be washed without being damaged ■ 'wash-basin n bowl with taps that is fixed to a wall in a bathroom, used for washing your hands and face ■ washed 'out adj **1** (of fabric or colours) no longer brightly coloured **2** (of a person) pale and tired ■ ,washing-'up n [U] (GB) (act of washing the) dirty plates, glasses, pans, etc left after a meal ■ washing-'up liquid n [U] (GB) liquid soap for washing dishes, pans, etc ■ 'washout n (infml) complete failure

wash² /wɒʃ/ n **1** [C, usu sing] act of cleaning sb/sth using water and usu soap: give the car a good ~ **2** (**the wash**) [sing] (sound made by the) movement of water caused by a passing boat

washer /'wɒʃə(r)/ n **1** small flat ring of metal, plastic, etc for making a screw or joint tight **2** (infml) = WASHING MACHINE (WASHING)

washing /'wɒʃɪŋ/ n [U] **1** act of washing sth: I do the ~ = wash the clothes) in our house. **2** clothes, sheets, etc that are waiting to be washed or that have been washed: hang the ~ out on the line ■ 'washing machine n electric machine for washing clothes ■ 'washing powder n [U] soap in the form of powder for washing clothes

wasn't /'wɒznt/ → BE

wasp /wɒsp/ n flying insect with black and yellow stripes and a sting in its tail

wastage /'weɪstɪdʒ/ n [U, sing] fact of losing or destroying sth, esp because it has been used carelessly **1** [U] amount of sth that is wasted **3** [U] reduction in numbers of employees or students: natural ~

waste¹ /weɪst/ v [T] **1** use more of sth than is necessary or useful **2** not make good or full use of sth/sb: ~ an opportunity [PV] **waste away** (of a person) become thin and weak

waste² /weɪst/ n **1** [U, sing] ~(of) act of using sth in a careless or unnecessary way: a ~ of time/money ◇ I hate to see good food go to ~ (= be thrown away). **2** [U] materials that are no longer needed and are thrown away: industrial ~ **3** (**wastes**) [pl] large area of land where there are few people, animals or plants: the frozen ~s of Siberia ● **waste** adj **1** (of land) not suitable for building or growing things on and therefore not used: ~ ground **2** no longer useful and to be thrown away: ~ paper ▸ **wasteful** adj causing waste: ~ful processes ▸ **wastefully** adv ■ ,waste-'paper basket n container for waste paper

watch¹ /wɒtʃ/ v **1** [I, T] look at sb/sth carefully for a period of time **2** [T] take care of sth for a short time: Can you ~ my bags for me while I go to the loo? **3** [T] (infml) be careful about sth: ~ your head on the low ceiling [IDM] **watch your step** → STEP¹ [PV] **watch out** (spoken) used to warn sb about sth dangerous **watch over sb/sth** (fml) take care of sb/sth; protect and guard sb/sth ▸ **watcher** n person who watches and studies sb/sth regularly

watch² /wɒtʃ/ n **1** [C] small clock worn on the wrist **2** [sing, U] act of watching sb/sth carefully in case of danger or problems: *keep (a) close ~ on her* **3** [C,U] fixed period of time, usu while others are asleep, during which sb watches for any danger so that they can warn others; the person who does this: *I'm on first ~.* [IDM] **be on the watch (for sb/sth)** looking carefully for sb/sth, esp in order to ward off danger: *Be on the ~ for thieves.* ■ **'watchdog** *n* person or group of people whose job is to protect people's rights ▶ **watchful** *adj* paying attention to what is happening in case of danger, accidents, etc ■ **'watchword** *n* word or phrase that expresses sb's beliefs or attitudes

water¹ /ˈwɔːtə(r)/ *n* **1** [U] clear colourless liquid that falls as rain, is found in rivers, etc and is used for drinking **2** [U] area of water, esp a lake, river, etc: *He fell into the ~.* **3** (**waters**) [pl] the water in a particular lake, river, sea or ocean **4** [U] surface of a mass of water: *She dived under the ~.* **5** (**waters**) [pl] area of sea or ocean belonging to a particular country: *in British ~s* ■ **'water cannon** *n* machine that produces a powerful jet of water, used for breaking up crowds ■ **'water closet** *n* (*abbr* **WC**) (*old-fash*) toilet ■ **'watercolour** (*US* **-color**) *n* **1** (**watercolours**) [pl] paints that you mix with water, not oil, and use for painting pictures **2** [C] picture painted with these paints ■ **'watercress** *n* [U] plant that grows in running water, with leaves used as food ■ **'waterfall** *n* place where a stream or river falls from a high place ■ **'waterfront** *n* [C, usu sing] part of a town or area that is next to water, eg in a harbour ■ **'waterhole** (also **'watering hole**) *n* place in a hot country, where animals go to drink ■ **waterlogged** /-lɒɡd/ *adj* **1** (of soil, a field, etc) extremely wet **2** (of a boat) full of water ■ **'watermark** *n* design in some kinds of paper that can be seen when the paper is held up to the light ■ **'watermelon** *n* [C,U] large round dark green fruit with red flesh and black seeds ■ **'watermill** *n* mill next to a river in which the machinery for grinding grain into flour is driven by the power of the water turning a wheel ■ **'waterproof** /-pruːf/ *adj, n* coat that does not let water through ▶ **'waterproof** *v* [T] make sth waterproof ■ **'watershed** *n* **1** event or period of time that marks an important change **2** line of high land separating river systems ■ **'waterside** *n* [sing] edge of a river, lake, etc ■ **'waterski** *v* [I] ski on water while being pulled along by a boat ▶ **'waterskiing** *n* [U] ■ **'water table** *n* level below which the ground is

filled with water ■ **'watertight** *adj* **1** that does not allow water to get in or out **2** (of an excuse, plan, argument, etc) containing no mistakes, faults or weaknesses ■ **'waterway** *n* river, canal, etc along which boats can travel ■ **'waterworks** *n* [C, with sing or pl verb] building with pumping machinery, etc for supplying water to an area [IDM] **turn on the waterworks** (*infml, disapprov*) start crying

water² /ˈwɔːtə(r)/ *v* **1** [T] pour water on plants, etc: *~ the lawn* **2** [I] (of the eyes) become full of tears **3** [I] (of the mouth) produce saliva **4** [T] give water to an animal to drink [PV] **water sth down 1** make a liquid weaker by adding water **2** change a speech, piece of writing, etc to make it less offensive ■ **'watering can** *n* container with a long spout, used for watering plants

watery /ˈwɔːtəri/ *adj* **1** containing too much water **2** (of colours) pale; weak

watt /wɒt/ *n* unit of electrical power

wave /weɪv/ *v* **1** [I, T] move your hand or arm from side to side in the air to attract attention, as a greeting, etc **2** [I, T] show where sth is, show sb where to go, etc by moving your hand in a particular direction: *The guard ~d us on.* **3** [T] hold sth in your hand and move it from side to side: *~ a flag* **4** [I] move freely and gently, while one end or side is held in position: *branches ~ing in the wind* [PV] **wave sth aside/ away** not accept sth because you do not think it is important ● **wave** *n* **1** raised line of water that moves across the surface of the sea, etc **2** sudden increase in a particular feeling or activity: *a ~of panic* **3** movement of your arm or hand from side to side: *with a ~ of his hand* **4** form in which heat, sound, light, etc is carried: *radio ~s* **5** (of hair) slight curl ■ **'wavelength** *n* **1** distance between two similar points on a wave of energy, eg light or sound **2** size of a radio wave used by a particular radio station, etc ▶ **wavy** *adj* (-**ier**, -**iest**) having curves; not straight: *a wavy line* ◇ *wavy hair*

waver /ˈweɪvə(r)/ *v* [I] **1** be or become weak or unsteady **2** hesitate when making a decision **3** move unsteadily

wax /wæks/ *n* [U] soft easily-melted sticky or oily substance used for making candles, polish, etc ● **wax** *v* **1** [T] polish or cover sth with wax **2** [T] remove hair from a part of the body using wax **3** [I] (of the moon) seem to get gradually bigger until its full form is visible **4** [I] (*~ lyrical, eloquent, etc*) (*written*) become lyrical, eloquent, etc when speaking or writing

way¹ /weɪ/ *n* **1** [C] method, style or manner of doing sth: *the best ~ to help* people ◊ the rude ~ in which he spoke to us **2** (ways) [pl] habits: *She is not going to change her ~s.* **3** [C, usu sing] route or road that you take in order to reach a place: *ask sb the ~ to the airport* **4** [C, usu sing] route along which sb/sth is moving or that sb/sth would take if there was nothing stopping them/it: *Get out of my ~! I'm in a hurry.* **5** [C] road, path, etc **6** [C, usu sing] (in a) particular direction: *He went the other ~.* **7** [sing] distance or period of time between two points: *It's a long ~ to London.* **8** [C] particular aspect of sth: *In some ~s, I agree with you.* **9** [sing] particular condition or state: *The economy's in a bad ~.* [IDM] **by the way** (spoken) used to introduce a new subject when talking **by way of sth** (fml) as a form of sth: *say something by ~ of introduction* **get/have your (own) way** get or do what you want, esp when sb has tried to stop you **give way** break or fall down **give way (to sb/sth) 1** stop resisting sth; agree to do sth that you do not want to do: *give ~ to their demands* **2** (GB) allow sb/sth to be or go first: *Give ~ to traffic coming from the right.* **3** be replaced by sth **go out of your way (to do sth)** make a special effort to do sth **go your own way** do what you want **in the/sb's way** stopping sb from moving or doing sth **make way (for sb/sth)** allow sb/sth to pass **(there is) no way** (infml) used to say that there is no possibility that you will do sth or that sth will happen **on your/the/its way 1** going or coming **2** during the journey **out of the way 1** no longer blocking sb/sth or causing inconvenience: *I moved my legs out of the ~ to let her get past.* **2** finished **3** far from a town or city **4** unusual **under way** having started and making progress **way of life** typical beliefs, habits and behaviour of a person or group

way² /weɪ/ *adv* (used with a preposition or an adverb) very far; by a large amount: *She finished the race ~ ahead of the others.* ■ **way-'out** *adj* (infml) unusual or strange

waylay /ˈweɪleɪ/ *v* (*pt, pp* **-laid** /-'leɪd/) [T] stop sb from going somewhere, esp in order to talk to them or attack them

wayward /ˈweɪwəd/ *adj* (written) difficult to control: *a ~ child*

WC /ˌdʌblju: 'si:/ *abbr* (GB) (on signs and doors in public places) water closet; toilet

we /wi:/ *pron* (used as the subject of a v) I and another person or other people: *We are all going to visit him.*

weak /wi:k/ *adj* **1** not physically strong: *still ~ after his illness* **2** easily bent, broken or defeated: *a ~ joint/*

team **3** easy to influence; not having much power: *a ~ leader* **4** not good at sth: *~ at mathematics* **5** not convincing: *a ~ argument* **6** not easily seen or heard: *~ sound/light* **7** containing a lot of water: *~ tea* ▶ **weaken** *v* [I, T] become or make sb/sth weak ■ **weak-'kneed** *adj* (infml) lacking courage or strength ▶ **weakling** *n* (disapprov) weak person ▶ **weakly** *adv* ▶ **weakness** *n* **1** [U] lack of strength, power or determination **2** [U] fault or defect: *We all have our little ~nesses.* **3** [C, usu sing] difficulty in resisting sth/sb that you like very much: *a ~ for cream cakes*

wealth /welθ/ *n* **1** [U] large amount of money, property, etc that a person or country owns **2** [U] state of being rich **3** [sing] **~of** large amount of sth: *a ~ of information* ▶ **wealthy** *adj* (**-ier, -iest**) rich

wean /wi:n/ *v* [T] gradually stop feeding a baby with its mother's milk and start giving it solid food [PV] **wean sb off/from sth** cause sb to stop doing sth gradually

weapon /ˈwepən/ *n* something, eg a gun, bomb or sword, used in fighting ▶ **weaponry** *n* [U]

wear¹ /weə(r)/ *v* (*pt* **wore** /wɔ:(r)/ *pp* **worn** /wɔ:n/) **1** [T] have sth on your body as a piece of clothing, an ornament, etc: *~ a dress* **2** [T] have your hair in a particular style; have a beard or moustache **3** [T] have a particular expression on your face: *a ~ smile* **4** [I, T] (cause sth to) become thinner, smoother or weaker through continuous use or rubbing: *The carpets are starting to ~.* **5** [I] stay in good condition after being used for a long time: *These shoes have worn well.* **6** [T] (infml) accept or allow sth [PV] **wear (sth) away** (cause sth to) become thinner, smoother, etc by continuously using or rubbing it **wear (sth) down** (cause sth to) become gradually smaller, smoother, etc **wear sb/sth down** gradually make sb/sth weaker or less determined **wear off** gradually disappear or stop **wear on** (written) (of time) pass, esp slowly **wear (sth) out** (cause sth to) become useless because of constant wear or use **wear yourself/sb out** make yourself/sb feel very tired

wear² /weə(r)/ *n* [U] **1** (in compounds) clothes for a particular purpose or occasion: *mens~* **2** fact of wearing sth: *clothes for everyday ~* **3** amount or type of use that sth has over time: *There's a lot of ~ in these shoes yet* **4** damage or loss of quality from use: *The carpet is showing signs of ~.* [IDM] **wear and tear**

damage to objects, furniture, etc caused by normal use

weary /ˈwɪəri/ *adj* (**-ier, -iest**) very tired ▶ **wearily** *adv* ▶ **weariness** *n* [U] ● **weary** *v* (*pt, pp* **-ied**) [I, T] ~(**of**) become or make sb feel tired

weasel /ˈwiːzl/ *n* small wild animal with reddish-brown fur

weather¹ /ˈweðə(r)/ *n* [U] condition of sun, wind, temperature, etc at a particular place and time [IDM] **under the weather** (*infml*) slightly ill ■ **'weather-beaten** *adj* (of a person or their skin) rough and damaged because the person spends a lot of time outside ■ **'weather forecast** *n* description on the TV, etc of what the weather will be like tomorrow, etc ■ **'weatherman** (*pl* **-men** /-men/) (*fem* **'weathergirl**) *n* (*infml*) person on the TV or radio who tells people what the weather will be like ■ **'weatherproof** *adj* that keeps out rain, wind, etc ■ **'weathervane** *n* metal object on the roof of a building that turns round to show the direction of the wind

weather² /ˈweðə(r)/ *v* [I, T] (cause sth to) change shape or colour because of the effect of the sun, rain, etc **2** [T] come safely through a difficult experience: ~ *a storm/crisis*

weave /wiːv/ *v* (*pt* **wove** /wəʊv/ or in sense 4 ~**d**) (*pp* **woven** /ˈwəʊvn/ or in sense 4 ~**d**) **1** [I, T] make fabric, a carpet, a basket, etc by crossing threads or strips across, over and under each other **2** [T] make sth by twisting flowers, pieces of wood, etc together: ~ *flowers into a garland* **3** [T] compose a story **4** [I, T] move along by twisting and turning to avoid obstructions: ~ *through the traffic* ● **weave** *n* way in which threads are arranged in a piece of woven fabric ▶ **weaver** *n* person whose job is weaving fabric

web /web/ *n* **1** [C] net of fine threads made by a spider **2** (**the Web**) [sing] = WORLD WIDE WEB (WORLD) **3** [C] complicated pattern of closely-connected things **4** [C] skin that joins the toes of ducks, frogs, etc ▶ **webbed** *adj* (of a bird or animal) having pieces of skin between the toes ■ **'webcam** (*also* **'Webcam**) *n* (*computing*) video camera connected to a computer so that its images can be seen by Internet users ■ **'webcast** *n* (*computing*) live video broadcast of an event sent out on the Internet ■ **'webmaster** *n* (*computing*) person responsible for particular pages of information on the World Wide Web ■ **'website** *n* (*computing*) place connected to the Internet, where a company, organization, etc puts

information that can be found on the World Wide Web

wed /wed/ *v* (*pt, pp* **~ded** or **wed**) [I, T] (*old-fash*) marry

we'd /wiːd/ = WE HAD, WE WOULD

wedding /ˈwedɪŋ/ *n* marriage ceremony ■ **'wedding ring** *n* ring worn to show that you are married

wedge /wedʒ/ *n* **1** piece of wood, metal, etc with one thick end and one thin pointed end, used for splitting sth or to keep two things separate **2** something shaped like a wedge: *a ~ of cake* ● **wedge** *v* [T] put or squeeze sth into a narrow space to fix it in place: ~ *the door open*

wedlock /ˈwedlɒk/ *n* [U] (*old-fash*) or (*law*) state of being married

Wednesday /ˈwenzdeɪ; -di/ *n* [C, U] the fourth day of the week, next after Tuesday (See examples of use at *Monday*.)

wee /wiː/ *adj* (*infml*) very little ● **wee** *n* **1** [sing] act of passing liquid waste from the body: *do/have a ~* **2** [U] urine ▶ **wee** *v* [I]

weed /wiːd/ *n* **1** wild plant growing where it is not wanted, eg in a garden **2** (*GB, infml*) thin weak person ● **weed** *v* [I, T] remove weeds from the ground [PV] **weed sth/sb out** get rid of sth/sb: ~ *out the lazy students* ▶ **weedy** *adj* (**-ier, -iest**) **1** (*GB, infml*) having a thin weak body **2** full of weeds

week /wiːk/ *n* **1** period of seven days, esp from Monday to Sunday **2** period spent at work in a period: *a 35-hour ~* [IDM] **week after week | week in, week out** every week ■ **'weekday** *n* any day except Saturday and Sunday ■ **'week'end** *n* Saturday and Sunday ▶ **weekly** *adj, adv* happening or appearing every week or once a week ▶ **weekly** *n* (*pl* **-ies**) newspaper or magazine that is published once a week

weep /wiːp/ *v* (*pt, pp* **wept** /wept/) [I, T] (*fml*) cry ▶ **weeping** *adj* (of some trees) with branches that hang downwards

weigh /weɪ/ *v* **1** *linking verb* have a certain weight: ~ *10 kilograms* **2** [T] measure how heavy sb/sth is: *She ~ed herself on the scales.* **3** [T] ~(**up**) consider sth carefully before deciding sth: ~ *up the pros and cons* **4** [I] have an influence on sb's opinion or the result of sth: *His past record ~s heavily against him.* [IDM] **weigh anchor** lift an anchor out of the water before sailing away [PV] **weigh sb/sth down 1** make sb/sth heavier so they are not able to move easily **2** make sb feel worried or depressed **weigh in (with sth)** (*infml*) join in a discussion, argument, etc by saying sth important

weigh on sb make sb anxious or worried **weigh sth out** measure an amount of sth by weight

weight /weɪt/ *n* **1** [U,C] how heavy sb/sth is, which can be measured in kilograms, etc: *I've put on* ~. ◇ *She wants to lose* ~ (= become less heavy or fat). **2** [U] fact of being heavy **3** [C] heavy object **4** [sing] great responsibility or worry: *The news was certainly a* ~ *off my mind* (= I did not have to worry about it any more). **5** [U] importance, influence or strength: *opinions that carry* ~ **6** [C,U] unit or system of units by which weight is measured **7** [C] piece of metal known to weigh a particular amount: *a 100-gram* ● **weight** *v* [T] ~ (**down**) attach a weight to sth to keep it in position or to make it heavier ▶ **weighted** *adj* ~ **towards/against/in favour of** arranged in such a way that one person or thing has an advantage/a disadvantage ▶ **weightless** *adj* having no weight ■ **weightlifting** *n* [U] sport of lifting heavy weights ▶ **weightlifter** *n* ▶ **weighty** *adj* (**-ier, -iest**) (*fml*) **1** important and serious **2** heavy

weir /wɪə(r)/ *n* wall across a river to control its flow

weird /wɪəd/ *adj* **1** (*infml*) unusual or different; not normal **2** (*written*) strange; unnatural: ~ *shrieks* ▶ **weirdly** *adv* ▶ **weirdness** *n* [U]

welcome /ˈwelkəm/ *v* [T] **1** greet sb in a friendly way when they arrive somewhere **2** be pleased to receive or accept sth: *The decision has been* ~*d by everyone.* ● **welcome** *exclam* used as a greeting to a person who is arriving: *W*~ *home!* ● **welcome** *n* [C,U] greeting or reception ● **welcome** *adj* **1** received with or giving pleasure: *a* ~ *change* **2** ~ **to** used to say that you are very happy for sb to do sth if they want to: *You're* ~ *to use my car.* [IDM] **you're welcome** (*esp US*) used as a polite reply when sb thanks you for sth

weld /weld/ *v* [T] join pieces of metal together by heating their edges and pressing them together ● **weld** *n* joint made by welding ▶ **welder** *n* person whose job is welding metal

welfare /ˈwelfeə(r)/ *n* [U] health, comfort and happiness ■ **welfare 'state** (**the ˌWelfare 'State**) *n* [usu sing] system of social services for people who are ill, unemployed, old, etc paid for by the government

well¹ /wel/ *exclam* used to express hesitation, surprise, acceptance, etc: *W*~,... ◇ *I don't know about that.* ◇ *W*~, ~, *so you've come at last!* ◇ *Oh, very* ~ *then, if you insist.* ● **well** *adj* (**better** /ˈbetə(r)/ **best** /best/) **1** in

good health: *feel/get* ~ **2** in a satisfactory state or condition: *All is not* ~ *at home.* **3** advisable; a good idea: *It would be* ~ *to start early.*

well² /wel/ *adv* (**better** /ˈbetə(r)/ **best** /best/) **1** in a good, right or satisfactory way: *The children behaved* ~. **2** thoroughly and completely: *Shake the mixture* ~. **3** to a great extent or degree: *drive at* ~ *over the speed limit* **4** (**can/could well**) easily: *She can* ~ *afford it.* **5** (**can/could/may/might well**) probably: *You may* ~ *be right.* **6** (**can/could/may/might well**) with good reason: *I can't very* ~ *leave him now.* [IDM] **as well** (**as sb/sth**) in addition to sb/sth; too **be well out of sth** (*infml*) be lucky that you are not involved in sth **do well** be successful **do well to do sth** be sensible or wise to do sth **may/might (just) as well do sth** do sth because it seems best in the situation you are in, although you may not really want to do it **well and truly** (*infml*) completely **well done** used to express admiration for what sb has done **well in** (**with sb**) (*infml*) be good friends with sb, esp sb important **well off 1** having a lot of money **2** in a good situation ■ **well ad'vised** *adj* acting in the most sensible way ■ **well-being** *n* [U] state of being comfortable, healthy or happy ■ **well 'bred** *adj* having or showing good manners ■ **well con'nected** *adj* (*fml*) (of a person) having important or rich friends or relatives ■ **well 'done** *adj* (of food, esp meat) cooked thoroughly ■ **well 'earned** *adj* much deserved ■ **well 'heeled** *adj* (*infml*) rich ■ **well in'formed** *adj* having or showing wide knowledge ■ **well in'tentioned** *adj* intending to be helpful, but not always succeeding ■ **well 'known** *adj* known about by a lot of people; famous: *a* ~-*known actor* ■ **well 'meaning** *adj* = WELL INTENTIONED ■ **well-nigh** /ˈnaɪ/ *adv* (*fml*) almost ■ **well 'read** *adj* having read many books; knowledgeable ■ **well 'spoken** *adj* having a way of speaking that is considered correct or elegant ■ **well 'timed** *adj* done or happening at the right time or at an appropriate time ■ **well-to-'do** *adj* rich ■ **well-wisher** *n* person who wishes another success, happiness, etc

well³ /wel/ *n* **1** deep hole in the ground from which people obtain water **2** = OIL WELL (OIL) **3** narrow space in a building for a staircase or lift ● **well** *v* [I] ~ (**up**) (of a liquid) rise to the surface of sth and start to flow: *Tears* ~*ed up in his eyes.*

we'll /wiːl/ = WE SHALL, WE WILL

wellington /ˈwelɪŋtən/ (*also* ˌwel-lington 'boot) (*also infml* **welly**) *n* waterproof rubber boot that reaches to the knee

welter /'weltə(r)/ *n* [sing] (*fml*) large and confusing amount of sth

wend /wend/ *v* (*old-fash* or *lit*) move slowly somewhere: *He ~ed his way home.*

went *pt of* GO[1]

wept *pt, pp of* WEEP

were /wə(r)/; *strong form* WE:(r)/ *pt of* BE

we're /wɪə(r)/ *short for* WE ARE (BE)

weren't /wɜːnt/ = WERE NOT (BE)

werewolf /'weəwʊlf/ *n* (*pl* -wolves /-wʊlvz/) (in stories) person who sometimes turns into a wolf, esp when the moon is full

west /west/ *n* [U,sing] (*abbr* W) **1** (*the* west) direction that you look towards to see the sun set; one of the four points of the compass **2** (*the* West) Europe and N America, contrasted with eastern countries **3** (*the* West) (*US*) western side of the US ● **west** *adj* (*abbr* W) **1** in or towards the west **2** (of winds) blowing from the west ● **west** *adv* towards the west ■ '**westbound** *adj* travelling towards the west: *~bound traffic* ▶ **westerly** *adj* **1** in or towards the west **2** (of winds) blowing from the west ▶ **westward(s)** *adv, adj* towards the west

western /'westən/ *adj* (*abbr* W) (*also* **Western**) of the west part of the world or a particular country ● **western** *n* film or book about life in the western US in the 19th century, usu involving cowboys ▶ **westerner** *n* person who comes from or lives in the western part of the world, esp western Europe or N America ▶ **westernize** (*also* **-ise**) *v* [T] bring ideas or ways of life that are typical of western Europe and N America to other countries

wet /wet/ *adj* (~**ter**, ~**test**) **1** covered or soaked with liquid, esp water: *~ grass/hair* ◇ *My shirt was ~ through* (= completely wet). **2** (of weather, etc) with rain: *a ~ climate* **3** (of paint, cement, etc) not dry or solid **4** (*GB, infml, disapprov*) (of a person) lacking a strong character: *Don't be such a ~!* ● **wet** *v* (-**tt**-; *pt, pp* **wet** or ~**ted**) [T] make sth wet ■ '**wet suit** *n* rubber clothing worn by underwater swimmers to keep warm

we've /wiːv/ *short for* WE HAVE

whack /wæk/ *v* [T] (*infml*) hit sb/sth very hard ● **whack** *n* [C,usu sing] (*infml*) **1** (sound made by the) act of hitting sb/sth very hard **2** (*GB*) share

of sth; amount of sth [IDM] **out of whack** (*esp US, infml*) (of a system or machine) not working as it should because its parts are not working together correctly ▶ **whacked** *adj* (*GB, infml*) very tired ▶ **whacking** (*also* **whacking great**) *adj* (*GB, infml*) used to emphasize how big or how much sth is ▶ **whacky** = WACKY

whale /weɪl/ *n* very large sea animal hunted for its oil and meat [IDM] **have a whale of a time** (*infml*) enjoy yourself very much ▶ **whaler** *n* **1** ship used for hunting whales **2** person who hunts whales ▶ **whaling** *n* [U] activity or business of hunting and killing whales

wharf /wɔːf/ *n* (*pl* ~**s** *or* **wharves** /wɔːvz/) flat structure built beside the sea or a river where boats can be tied up and goods unloaded

what /wɒt/ *pron, det* **1** used in questions to ask for particular information about sb/sth: *W~ time is it?* ◇ *W~ are you reading?* **2** the thing(s) that: *Tell me ~ happened next.* **3** used to say that you think that sth is especially good, bad, etc: *W~ a good idea!* [IDM] **what about …** ➤ ABOUT **what for?** for what purpose or reason?: *W~ is this tool used for?* ◇ *W~ did you do that for?* **what if …** ? what would happen if … ? **what is more** used to add a point that is even more important **what's what** (*spoken*) what things are useful, important, etc **what with sth** used to list the various reasons for sth

whatever /wɒt'evə(r)/ *det, pron* **1** any or every; anything or everything: *You can eat ~ you like.* **2** used when you are saying that it does not matter what sb does, or what happens, because the result will be the same: *Keep calm, ~ happens.* **3** used in questions to show surprise or confusion: *W~ do you mean?* ● **whatever** (*also* **whatsoever**) *adv* (used for emphasis) at all; not of any kind: *no doubt ~*

wheat /wiːt/ *n* [U] (plant producing) grain from which flour is made

wheedle /'wiːdl/ *v* [I, T] (*disapprov*) persuade sb to give you sth or do sth by saying nice things that you do not mean: *She ~d the money out of her brother.*

wheel /wiːl/ *n* **1** [C] one of the circular objects under a car, bicycle, etc that turns when it moves **2** [C, usu sing] the circular object used to steer a car, etc or ship: *A car swept past with Jon at the ~.* ● **wheel** *v* **1** [T] push or pull sth that has wheels **2** [I] move or turn in a circle [IDM] **wheel and deal** do a lot of complicated deals in business or politics, often dishonestly ■ '**wheelbarrow** *n* small open container with one wheel and two handles, that you use outside to carry things ■ **'wheelchair** *n* chair with wheels for sb who is unable to walk ▶ **-wheeled** (forming compound adjectives) having the number of wheels mentioned: *a three- ~ed vehicle*

wheeze /wiːz/ *v* [I] breathe noisily and with difficulty ● **wheeze** *n* high whistling noise that your chest makes when you cannot breathe easily ▶ **wheezy** *adj* (**-ier, -iest**)

whelk /welk/ *n* small shellfish that can be eaten

when /wen/ *adv* **1** (used in questions) at what time; on what occasion: *W~ did you come?* **2** used after an expression of time to mean *at or on which: Sunday is the day ~ few people work.* ◇ *Her last visit to the town was in May, ~ she saw the new hospital.* ● **when** *pron* what/which time: *'I've got a new job.' 'Since ~?'* ● **when** *conj* **1** at or during the time that: *It was raining ~ we arrived.* **2** after: *Call me ~ you've finished.* **3** considering that; although: *Why buy a new car ~ your present one runs well?*

whence /wens/ *adv* (old-fash) from where

whenever /wen'evə(r)/ *conj* **1** at any time that; on any occasion that: *Ask for help ~ you need it.* **2** every time that: *I go ~ I can.* ● **whenever** *adv* (used in questions to show surprise) when

where /weə(r)/ *adv* **1** (used in questions) in or to what place or situation: *W~ does he live?* **2** (used after words or phrases that refer to a place or situation) at, in or to which place: *one of the few countries ~ people drive on the left* ● **where** *conj* (in) the place or situation in which: *Put it ~ we can all see it.* ■ **'whereabouts** *adv* used to ask the general area where sb/sth is: *W~abouts did you find it?* ● **'whereabouts** *n* [U, with sing or pl verb] place where sb/sth is: *Her ~abouts is/are unknown.* ■ **where'as** *conj* used to compare or contrast two facts: *He gets to work late every day ~ she is always early.* ■ **where'by** *adv* (fml) by which; because of which: *the system ~ the taxes are paid* ■ **whereu'pon** *conj* (written) and then; as a result of this

wherever /weər'evə(r)/ *conj* **1** in any place: *I'll find him, ~ he is.* **2** in all places that; everywhere: *Crowds of people queue to see her ~ she goes.* ● **wherever** *adv* (used in questions for showing surprise) where

wherewithal /'weəwɪðɔːl/ *n* (**the wherewithal**) [sing] the money,

things or skill needed for a purpose: *Does he have the ~ to buy a car?*

whet /wet/ *v* (**-tt-**) increase your desire for or interest in sth: *The book will ~ your appetite for more of her work.*

whether /'weðə(r)/ *conj* used to express a doubt or a choice between two possibilities: *I don't know ~ to accept or refuse.*

which /wɪtʃ/ **1** *pron, det* used in questions to ask sb to be exact about one or more people or things from a limited number: *W~ way shall we go - up the hill or along the road?* **2** used to be exact about the thing(s) that you mean: *Houses ~ overlook the sea cost more.* **3** used to give more information about sth: *His best film, ~ won several awards, was about Gandhi.*

whichever /wɪtʃ'evə(r)/ *det, pron* **1** used to say what feature or quality is important in deciding sth: *Choose ~ brand you prefer.* **2** used to say that it does not matter which, as the result will be the same: *W~ way you travel, it is expensive.*

whiff /wɪf/ *n* **1** slight smell **2** slight sign or feeling of sth

while /waɪl/ *conj* **1** during the time that sth is happening: *Her parents died ~ she was still at school.* **2** at the same time as sth else is happening **3** used to contrast two things: *She likes tea, ~ I prefer coffee.* **4** although: *W~ I want to help, I don't think I can.* ● **while** *n* [sing] period of time: *for a long ~* ● **while** *v* [PV] **while sth away** spend time in a pleasant, lazy way

whilst /waɪlst/ *conj* (*fml*) = WHILE

whim /wɪm/ *n* [C, U] sudden wish to do or have sth, esp when it is unnecessary

whimper /'wɪmpə(r)/ *v* [I] make low weak crying noises ▶ **whimper** *n*

whimsical /'wɪmzɪkl/ *adj* unusual and not serious in a way that is either amusing or annoying

whine /waɪn/ *n* long high unpleasant sound or cry ● **whine** *v* [I] **1** complain in an annoying, crying voice: *a child that never stops whining* **2** make a long high unpleasant sound: *The dog was whining to come in.*

whinny /'wɪni/ *n* (*pl* **-ies**) quiet sound made by a horse of a horse ▶ **whinny** *v* (*pt, pp* **-ied**) [I]

whip¹ /wɪp/ *n* **1** [C] piece of leather or rope fastened to a handle, used for hitting people or animals **2** [C] (member of a political party who gives an) order to members to attend and vote in a debate

whip² /wɪp/ *v* (**-pp-**) **1** [T] hit a person or an animal hard with a whip **2** [I, T] (cause sth to) move quickly and suddenly: *A branch ~ped across* the car window. **3** [T] remove or pull sth quickly and suddenly: *He ~ped out a knife.* **4** [T] stir cream, etc very quickly until it becomes stiff [PV] **whip sb/sth up 1** try to make people excited or feel strongly about sth **2** quickly make a meal or sth to eat ▶ **whipping** *n* [C, usu sing] act of hitting sb with a whip, as a punishment ■ '**whip-round** *n* (*GB, infml*) money given by a group of people in order to buy sth for sb

whirl /wɜːl/ *v* **1** [I, T] (cause sb/sth to) move around quickly in a circle **2** spin; feel confused: *Her mind was ~ing.* ● **whirl** *n* [sing] **1** movement of sth spinning around: (*fig*) *Her mind was in a ~* (= a state of confusion). **2** number of events or activities happening one after another [IDM] **give sth a whirl** (*infml*) try sth to see if you like it or can do it ■ '**whirlpool** *n* strong circular current of water ■ '**whirlwind** *n* **1** tall column of quickly circulating air **2** situation in which a lot of things happen very quickly ▶ **whirlwind** *adj* happening very fast: *a ~wind romance*

whirr (*esp US* **whir**) /wɜː(r)/ *n* [C, usu sing] continuous low sound of a machine working or a bird's wings moving quickly ● **whirr** (*esp US* **whir**) *v* [I] make a continuous low sound like the parts of a machine moving

whisk /wɪsk/ *v* [T] **1** beat eggs, cream, etc into a stiff light mass **2** take sb/sth somewhere very quickly and suddenly: *They ~ed him off to prison.* ● **whisk** *n* kitchen utensil for beating eggs, etc

whisker /ˈwɪskə(r)/ *n* **1** [C] long stiff hair near the mouth of a cat, etc **2** (**whiskers**) [pl] hair on the side of a man's face

whisky (*US* **whiskey**) /ˈwɪski/ *n* [U, C] (*pl* **-ies**) strong alcoholic drink made from grain

whisper /ˈwɪspə(r)/ *v* [I, T] speak very quietly to sb so that others cannot hear what you are saying **2** [I] (*written*) (of leaves, the wind, etc) make a soft quiet sound ● **whisper** *n* **1** low quiet voice or the sound it makes **2** (*also* **whispering**) (*written*) soft sound

whist /wɪst/ *n* [U] card game for two pairs of players

whistle /ˈwɪsl/ *v* **1** instrument that produces a clear high sound, esp as a signal **2** sound you make by forcing your breath out when your lips are closed **3** high loud sound produced by air or steam being forced through a small opening ● **whistle** *v* [I, T] make the high sound or a musical tune by forcing your breath out when your lips are

closed **2** [I] (of a kettle or other machine) make a high sound **3** [I] move quickly with a whistling sound: *The bullets ~d past us.*

white /waɪt/ *adj* (**~r, ~st**) **1** having the colour of fresh snow or milk **2** of a pale-skinned race of people **3** (of the skin) pale because of illness or emotion **4** (*GB*) (of tea or coffee) with milk added ● **white** *n* **1** [U] colour of fresh snow or milk **2** [C, usu pl] member of a race of people who have pale skin **3** [C, U] part of an egg that surrounds the yellow part (**yolk**) **4** [C, usu pl] white part of the eye ■ **white-'collar** *adj* of office workers, not manual workers ■ **white 'elephant** *n* [usu sing] something expensive but useless ■ **white 'lie** *n* small harmless lie ▶ **whiten** *v* [I, T] become or make sth white or whiter ▶ **whiteness** *n* [U, sing] ■ **whitewash** *n* **1** [U] mixture of lime or chalk and water, used for painting walls **2** [U, sing] (*disapprov*) attempt to hide unpleasant facts about sb/sth ■ **whitewash** *v* [T] **1** cover a wall, etc with whitewash **2** (*disapprov*) try to hide unpleasant facts about sb/sth ■ **white 'water** *n* [U] part of a river that looks white because the water is moving very fast over rocks: *~-water rafting*

whittle /ˈwɪtl/ *v* [I, T] shape a piece of wood by cutting small pieces from it [PV] **whittle sth away** make sth gradually decrease in value or amount: *The value of our savings is being slowly ~d down by inflation.* **whittle sth down** reduce the size or number of sth

whizz (*esp US* **whiz**) /wɪz/ *v* [I] (*infml*) **1** move very quickly, making a high continuous sound: *A bullet ~ed past me.* **2** do sth very quickly

whizz-kid (*esp US* **whiz-kid**) /ˈwɪz kɪd/ *n* (*infml*) person who is very good and successful at sth, esp at a young age

whizzy /ˈwɪzi/ *adj* (*infml*) having features that make use of advanced technology: *a ~ new mobile phone*

who /huː/ *pron* **1** used in questions to ask about the name, identity or function of sb: *W~ is the woman in the black hat?* ◇ *W~ are you phoning?* **2** used to show which person or people you mean: *The people ~ called yesterday want to buy the house.* **3** used to give more information about sb: *My husband, ~ has been ill, longs to see you.*

whoever /huːˈevə(r)/ *pron* **1** the person or people who: *W~ says that is a liar.* ◇ *You must speak to ~ is the head of the department.* **2** used to say that it does not matter who, since the result will be the same: *W~ rings, I don't want to speak to them.* **3** (used

in questions for showing surprise:
who: W~ heard of such a thing!

whole /həʊl/ *adj* **1** full; complete: *He told us the ~ story.* **2** not broken or damaged: *She swallowed the sweet ~.* [IDM] **go the whole hog** (*infml*) do sth thoroughly ● **whole** *n* **1** [C] thing that is complete in itself: *Four quarters make a ~.* **2** (**the whole**) [sing] **~of** all that there is of sth: *the ~ of her life* [IDM] **on the whole** considering everything; in general ■ ‚whole-ˈhearted *adj* (*approv*) complete and enthusiastic ■ ‚whole-ˈheartedly *adv* ■ ˈwholemeal *adj* containing whole grains of wheat, etc, including the husk: *~meal flour/bread* ■ ‚whole ˈnumber *n* (*maths*) number that consists of one or more units, with no fractions ▶ **wholly** *adv* completely: *I'm not wholly convinced.*

wholesale /ˈhəʊlseɪl/ *adj, adv* **1** of goods that are bought and sold in large quantities, esp so they can be sold again to make a profit **2** (esp of sth bad) happening or done to a very large number of people or things: *the ~ slaughter of animals* ▶ **wholesaler** *n* trader who sells goods wholesale

wholesome /ˈhəʊlsəm/ *adj* **1** good for your health **2** morally good

whom /huːm/ *pron* (*fml*) used instead of 'who' as the object of a verb or preposition: *W~ did she invite?* ◇ *The person to ~ this letter is addressed died two years ago.*

whoop /wuːp/ *n* loud cry of happiness or excitement ● **whoop** *v* [I] shout loudly because you are happy or excited: *~ing with joy*

whooping cough /ˈhuːpɪŋ kɒf/ *n* [U] infectious disease, esp of children, that makes them cough and have difficulty breathing

whore /hɔː(r)/ *n* (*old-fash*) female prostitute

whose /huːz/ *det, pron* **1** used in questions to ask who sth belongs to: *W~ (house) is that?* **2** used to say which person or thing you mean: *He's a man ~ opinion I respect.* **3** used to give more information about a person or thing: *Isobel, ~ brother he was, had heard the story before.*

why /waɪ/ *adv* **1** used in questions to ask the reason for or purpose of sth: *W~ are you late?* **2** used to give or talk about a reason: *That's ~ she left so early.* [IDM] **why not?** used to make or agree to a suggestion: *W~ not write to him?*

wick /wɪk/ *n* burning piece of string, etc in a candle or oil lamp [IDM] **get on sb's wick** (*GB, infml*) annoy sb

wicked /ˈwɪkɪd/ *adj* **1** morally bad **2** (*infml*) slightly bad but in a way that

is amusing and/or attractive: *a ~ grin* **3** dangerous, harmful or powerful **4** (*sl*) very good: *Their new song's ~.* ▶ **wickedly** *adv* ▶ **wickedness** *n* [U]

wicker /ˈwɪkə(r)/ *n* [U] thin sticks of wood woven together to make baskets, etc ■ ˈwickerwork *n* [U] baskets, furniture, etc made of wicker

wicket /ˈwɪkɪt/ *n* **1** (in cricket) set of three sticks (**stumps**) at which the ball is bowled **2** area of grass between the two wickets

wide /waɪd/ *adj* (**~r, ~st**) **1** measuring a lot from one side to the other: *a ~ river* **2** measuring a particular distance from one side to the other: *12 metres ~* **3** including many different things: *a ~ range of interests* **4** far from what is aimed at: *His shot was ~ (of the target).* [IDM] **give sb/sth a wide berth** not to go too near sb/sth; avoid sb/sth ● **wide** *adv* as far or fully as possible: *He was ~ awake.* ◇ *The door was ~ open.* ■ ‚wide-ˈeyed *adj* **1** with your eyes fully open because of fear, surprise, etc **2** inexperienced; naive ▶ **widely** *adv* **1** by a lot of people; in or to many places: *It is ~ly known that...* ◇ *He has travelled ~ in Asia.* **2** to a large degree; a lot: *Prices vary ~ly from shop to shop.* ▶ **widen** *v* [I, T] become or make sth wider ■ ˈwidespread *adj* existing or happening over a large area

widow /ˈwɪdəʊ/ *n* woman whose husband has died ● **widow** *v* [T] (*usu passive*) cause to become a widow or widower ▶ **widower** *n* man whose wife has died

width /wɪdθ; wɪtθ/ *n* [U, C] measurement from one side of sth to the other; how wide sth is

wield /wiːld/ *v* [T] **1** have and use power, authority, etc **2** hold sth, ready to use it as a weapon or tool: *~ an axe*

wife /waɪf/ *n* (*pl* **wives** /waɪvz/) woman that a man is married to

wig /wɪg/ *n* piece of artificial hair that is worn on the head

wiggle /ˈwɪgl/ *v* [I, t] (cause sth to) move from side to side or up and down in short quick movements: *~ your toes* ▶ **wiggle** *n*

wigwam /ˈwɪgwæm/ *n* type of tent used by Native Americans in the past

wild /waɪld/ *adj* **1** living or growing in natural conditions; not kept in a house or on a farm: *~ animals/plants* **2** (of land) in its natural state; not changed by people **3** lacking discipline or control: *The boy is ~ and completely out of control.* **4** full of very strong feeling: *~ applause/cheers* **5** not carefully planned; not sensible or accurate: *a ~ guess* **6** **~about** (*infml*) very enthusiastic about sb/sth **7** affected by storms and strong winds: ~ *weather* [IDM] **run wild** → RUN¹ ● **wild** n **1** (the wild) [sing] natural environment that is not controlled by people **2** (the wilds) [pl] area of a country far from towns and cities ■ **'wild card** n **1** (in card games) card that has no value of its own and takes the value of any card the player chooses **2** (*computing*) symbol that has no meaning of its own and can represent any letter ■ **wildcat 'strike** n sudden unofficial strike by workers ■ **wild 'goose chase** n (*infml*) search for sth that is impossible for you to find and so wastes your time ■ **'wildlife** n [U] wild animals, birds, etc ▸ **wildly** adv **1** in a way that is not controlled **2** extremely: *The story had been ~ly exaggerated.* ▸ **wildness** n

wilderness /'wɪldənəs/ n [C, usu sing] large uncultivated area of land [IDM] **in the wilderness** no longer in an important position, esp in politics

wiles /waɪlz/ n [pl] clever tricks intended to deceive sb

wilful (*US also* **willful**) /'wɪlfl/ adj (*disapprov*) **1** (of sth bad) done deliberately though you know it is wrong **2** determined to do what you want; not caring about what others want ▸ **wilfully** adv

will¹ /wɪl/ *modal* v (*short form* **'ll** /l/ neg **will not** *short form* **won't** /wəʊnt/ pt **would** /wʊd/ *short form* **'d** /d/ neg **would not** *short form* **wouldn't** /'wʊdnt/) **1** used for talking about or predicting the future: *You'll be in time if you hurry.* ◇ *How long ~ you be staying in Paris?* **2** used for showing that sb is willing to do sth: *They won't lend us any more money.* **3** used for asking sb to do sth: *W~ you come this way please?* **4** used for ordering sb to do sth: *W~ you be quiet!* **5** used for stating what you think is probably true: *That ~ be the postman at the door.* **6** used for stating that is generally true: *If it's made of wood, then it ~ float.* **7** used for describing habits: *She would sit there, hour after hour, doing nothing.* ◇ *He'~ smoke between courses at dinner* (= it annoys you).

will² /wɪl/ v [T] **1** use the power of your mind to do sth or to make sth happen: *She ~ed her eyes to stay open.* **2** (*fml*) formally give your property or possessions to sb after you die, by means of a will

will³ /wɪl/ n **1** (*also* **'will power**) [C,U] ability to control your thoughts and actions to achieve what you want to do: *He has an iron ~/a ~ of iron.* **2** [U,C] strong determination to do sth that you want: *the ~ to live* **3** [sing] what sb wants to happen in a particular situation:

(*fml*) *It is God's ~.* **4** [C] legal document saying what is to happen to sb's property and money after they die: *to make a ~* [IDM] **at will** whenever or wherever you like

willing /'wɪlɪŋ/ adj **1 ~(to)** not objecting to doing sth; having no reason for not doing sth: *I'm perfectly ~ to discuss the problem.* **2** ready or pleased to help; done enthusiastically: ~ *helpers* ▸ **willingly** adv ▸ **willingness** n [U]

willow /'wɪləʊ/ n tree with thin flexible branches

wilt /wɪlt/ v [I] **1** (of plants) bend, lose their freshness and begin to die **2** (*infml*) become weak or tired or less confident

wily /'waɪli/ adj (**-ier, -iest**) clever at getting what you want, esp by deceiving people

wimp /wɪmp/ n (*infml, disapprov*) person who is not strong, brave or confident

win /wɪn/ v (**-nn- pt, pp won** /wʌn/) v **1** [I, T] be the most successful in a game, competition, etc **2** [T] get sth as a result of a competition, race, election, etc **3** [T] achieve or get sth that you want, esp by your own efforts: *try to ~ support for your proposals* [IDM] **win (sth) hands down** (*infml*) win easily [PV] **win sb around/over/round (to sth)** get sb's support by persuading them that you are right ● **win** n success; victory ▸ **winner** n ▸ **winning** adj **1** that wins or has won sth **2** attractive; pleasing: *a ~ning smile* ▸ **winnings** n [pl] money won in a competition, etc

wince /wɪns/ v [I] show pain, distress, etc by a sudden slight movement of the face ▸ **wince** n [C, usu sing]

winch /wɪntʃ/ n machine for lifting or pulling heavy weights using a rope or chain ● **winch** v [T] move by using a winch

wind¹ /wɪnd/ n **1** (*also* **the wind**) [C, U] air that moves quickly as a result of natural forces: *gale-force ~s* **2** [U] gas that forms in the stomach and causes discomfort **3** [U] breath that you need when you do exercises: *I need time to get my ~ back after running so far.* [IDM] **get wind of sth** (*infml*) hear about sth secret or private **put the wind up sb** (*GB, infml*) make sb frightened ● **wind** v [T] make sb unable to breathe for a short time ■ **'windfall** n **1** amount of money that sb/sth wins or receives unexpectedly **2** fruit, esp an apple, blown off a tree by the wind ■ **'wind instrument** n musical instrument (eg an oboe) that you blow into to produce sounds ■ **'windmill** n **1** building with machinery for grinding grain into flour that is driven by the power of the wind turning long arms (**sails**) **2** tall thin structure with parts that turn round, used to change wind power into electricity ■ **'windpipe** n passage for air from the throat to the lungs ■ **'windscreen** (US **'windshield**) n window across the front of a motor vehicle ■ **'windscreen wiper** (US **'windshield wiper**) n blade with a rubber edge that moves across a windscreen to make it clear of rain ■ **'windsurfing** n [U] sport of sailing on water standing on a long narrow board with a sail ▸ **'windsurfer** n ■ **'windswept** adj **1** (of a place) not protected against strong winds **2** looking as though you have been in a strong wind: ~*swept hair* ▸ **windy** adj (-ier, -iest) with a lot of wind: *a ~y day*

wind² /waɪnd/ v (pt, pp **wound** /waʊnd/) **1** [I, T] (of a road, river, etc) have many bends and twists: *The river ~s (its way) through the countryside.* **2** [T] wrap or twist sth around itself or sth else **3** [T] ~(**up**) make a clock, etc work by turning a key, handle, etc to tighten the spring **4** [I, T] ~**forward/back** operate a tape, film, etc so that it moves nearer to its ending or starting position: *He wound the tape back to the beginning.* [PV] **wind down 1** (*infml*) (of a person) rest or relax after a period of activity **2** (of a machinery) go slowly and then stop **wind sth down 1** bring a business, an activity, etc to an end gradually over a period of time **2** make sth move downwards by turning a handle, etc: ~ *the window down* **wind up** (*infml*) (of a person) find yourself in a particular place or situation: *We eventually wound up in a little cottage by the sea.* **wind (sth) up** bring a speech, meeting, etc to an end, **wind sb up** (*infml*) deliberately say or do sth to annoy sb **wind sth up 1** stop running a company, business, etc and close it completely **2** make sth, eg a car window, move upwards by turning a handle, etc

window /'wɪndəʊ/ n **1** opening (usu filled with glass) in a wall, vehicle, etc to let in light and air **2** glass at the front of a shop and the area behind it where the goods are displayed **3** area within a frame on a computer screen, in which a particular program is operating or in which information of a particular type is shown ■ **'window box** n long narrow box outside a window, in which flowers are grown ■ **'window dressing** n [U] act of arranging goods attractively in a shop window ■ **'window-shopping** n [U] looking at goods in shop windows, usu without intending to buy

■ **'window sill** n narrow shelf below a window, either inside or outside

wine /waɪn/ n [U,C] alcoholic drink made from grapes or other fruit ● **wine** v [IDM] **wine and dine** (**sb**) entertain sb or be entertained by going to restaurants, enjoying good food and drink, etc

wing /wɪŋ/ n **1** [C] one of the parts of the body of a bird or insect that it uses for flying **2** [C] one of the long flat surfaces that stick out from the sides of a plane and support it in flying **3** [C] part of a large building that sticks out from the main part: *add a new ~ to a hospital* **4** [C] (GB) part of a car above the wheel **5** [C] one section of an organization or whose members share the same opinions: *the left/right* ~ **6** [C] (in football, hockey, etc) far left or right side of the sports field **7** (**the wings**) [pl] sides of the stage in a theatre that are hidden from the audience [IDM] **take sb under your wing** take care of and help sb less experienced than you are ● **wing** v [I, T] (*lit*) fly somewhere [IDM] **wing it** (*infml*) do sth without planning or preparing at first ▸ **winged** adj having wings ▸ **winger** n (in football, hockey, etc) attacking player who plays towards the side of the pitch ■ **'wingspan** n distance between the end of one wing and the end of the other when the wings are fully extended

wink /wɪŋk/ v [I] **1** ~(**at**) close one eye and open it again quickly **2** (*written*) shine with an unsteady light; flash on and off ● **wink** n act of winking, esp as a signal to sb [IDM] **have forty winks** (*infml*) sleep for a short time, esp during the day **not get/have a wink of sleep** | **not sleep a wink** not be able to sleep

winkle /'wɪŋkl/ n small shellfish, like a snail, that can be eaten

winner, winning → WIN

winter /'wɪntə(r)/ n [U,C] coldest season of the year ● **winter** v [I] (*fml*) spend the winter somewhere ■ **'winter 'sports** n [pl] sports that people do on snow or ice ▸ **wintry** /-tri/ adj

wipe /waɪp/ v [T] rub a surface with a cloth, your hand, etc, or rub sth against a surface, in order to remove dirt or liquid from it: ~ *the dishes with a cloth* ◇ ~ *your feet on the mat* ◇ *Use that cloth to ~ up the mess.* [PV] **wipe sb/sth out** destroy or remove sb/sth completely: *War ~d out whole villages.* ● **wipe** n act of cleaning sth with a cloth

wire /'waɪə(r)/ n **1** [C,U] (piece of) metal in the form of a thin thread **2** [C] (*infml, esp US*) = TELEGRAM tele-gram ● **wire** v [T] **1** connect a building, piece of equipment, etc to an electricity supply, using wires **2** connect sth/sb to a piece of equipment, esp using a tape recorder or computer system **3** (US) send sb a message by telegram ▶ **wiring** n [U] **1** system of wires that supply electricity to a building, etc ■ **wiry** adj **1** (of a person) thin but strong **2** strong and rough, like wire

wireless /'waɪələs/ n (old-fash) radio ● **wireless** adj lacking or not needing wires

wisdom /'wɪzdəm/ n [U] **1** ability to make sensible decisions and give good advice because of the experience and knowledge that you have **2** ~of how sensible sth is ■ **'wisdom tooth** n any of the four large back teeth that do not grow until you are an adult

wise /waɪz/ adj (~r, ~st) having or showing experience, knowledge and common sense [IDM] **be none the wiser | not be any the wiser** knowing no more than before ▶ **wisely** adv

wish /wɪʃ/ v **1** [T] want sth to happen or be true even though it is unlikely or impossible: I ~ I was/were taller. ◇ She ~ed she hadn't eaten so much. **2** [T] ~**to** (fml) want to do sth; want sth to happen: I ~ to speak to the manager. **3** [I] ~(**for**) think very hard that you want sth, esp sth that can only be achieved by good luck or magic: He has everything he could possibly ~ for. **4** [T] say that you hope sb will be happy, lucky, etc: ~sb good luck/a happy birthday ● **wish** n [C] **1** desire or longing for sth: I have no ~ to interfere, but... **2** [C] thing that you want to have or to happen **3** (wishes) [pl] used esp in a letter or card to say that you hope sb will be happy, successful, etc: Dad sends his best ~es. ■ **,wishful 'thinking** n [U] belief that sth will come true simply because you wish it

wishy-washy /'wɪʃi wɒʃi/ adj (infml, disapprov) weak or feeble; not firm or clear

wisp /wɪsp/ n **1** small thin piece of hair, grass, etc **2** long thin line of smoke or cloud ▶ **wispy** adj: ~y hair

wistful /'wɪstfl/ adj feeling sadly about sth that you would like to have, esp sth in the past that you can no longer have ▶ **wistfully** /-fəli/ adv

wit /wɪt/ n **1** [C,U,sing] (person who has the) ability to say or write things that are both clever and amusing **2** (wits) [pl] your ability to think quickly and clearly and to make good decisions [IDM] **be at your wits' end** be so worried by a problem that you do not know what to do next **be frightened/scared/terrified out of your wits** be very frightened **have/**

keep your wits about you be alert and ready to act ▶ **witticism** /'wɪtɪsɪzəm/ n clever and amusing remark ▶ **witty** adj (-ier, -iest) able to say or write clever, amusing things ▶ **wittily** adv

witch /wɪtʃ/ n woman believed to have evil magic powers ■ **'witchcraft** n [U] use of magic powers, esp evil ones ■ **'witch doctor** n person believed to have special magic powers to heal people ■ **'witch-hunt** n attempt to find and punish people with ideas that are thought to be unacceptable or dangerous to society

with /wɪð; wɪθ/ prep **1** in the company or presence of sb/sth: live ~ your parents ◇ leave a child ~ a babysitter **2** having or carrying sth: a coat ~ two pockets ◇ a girl ~ blue eyes **3** using sth: cut it ~ a knife **4** used to say what bits, covers, etc sth: Fill the bottle ~ water. **5** in opposition to sb/sth; against sth/sb: argue ~ Rosie **6** concerning; in the case of: be patient ~ them **7** used to show the way in which sb does sth: He behaved ~ great dignity. **8** because of; as a result of: tremble ~ fear **9** because of sth and as it happens: Skill comes ~ experience. **10** in the same direction as sth: sail ~ the wind **11** in spite of sth: W~ all her faults, I still love her. [IDM] **be with me/you** (infml) be able to understand what sb is talking about: I'm afraid I'm not quite ~ you. **be with sb (on sth)** support sb and agree with what they say: We're all ~ you on this one. **with it** (infml) **1** fashionable **2** understanding what is happening around you

withdraw /wɪð'drɔː; wɪθ'd-/ v (pt -drew /-'druː/ pp ~n /-'drɔːn/) **1** [I, T] (cause sb/sth to) move back or away from a place or situation: ~ troops from the battle **2** [T] stop giving or offering sth to sb: The drug was ~n from sale. **3** [I, T] (cause sb/sth to) stop taking part in or being a member of an organization: calls for Britain to ~ from the EU **4** [T] take money out of a bank account ▶ **withdrawal** /-'drɔːəl/ n [C,U] (act of) withdrawing ■ **with'drawal symptoms** n [pl] unpleasant effects experienced by a person who has stopped taking a drug they are addicted to ▶ **withdrawn** adj (of a person) unusually quiet and shy

wither /'wɪðə(r)/ v **1** [I, T] (cause a plant to) dry up and die **2** [I] become less or weaker, esp before disappearing completely: All our hopes just ~ed away. ▶ **withering** adj making sb feel silly or ashamed: a ~ing look

withhold /wɪð'həʊld; wɪθ'h-/ v (pt, pp -**held** /-'held/) [T] (fml) ~(**from**) refuse to give sth to sb: ~ permission

within /wɪ'ðɪn/ *prep* not further than sth; inside: ~ *seven days* ◇ *the city walls* ● **within** *adv* inside

without /wɪ'ðaʊt/ *prep* **1** not having, experiencing or showing sth: *You can't buy things ~ money.* **2** not in the company of sb: *Don't go ~ me.* **3** used with the *-ing* form to mean 'not': *He left ~ saying goodbye.*

withstand /wɪð'stænd; wɪθ's-/ *v* (*pt, pp* -**stood** /-'stʊd/) [T] (*fml*) be strong enough not to be hurt or damaged by extreme conditions, the use of force, etc: ~ *an attack*

witness /'wɪtnəs/ *n* **1** person who sees an event take place and is able to describe it **2** person who gives evidence in a law court **3** person who signs a document to confirm that another person's signature is real **4** (*fml*) sign or proof ● **witness** *v* [T] **1** see sth happen because you are there when it happens: ~ *an accident* **2** be present when an official document is signed ■ '**witness box** (*US* '**witness stand**) *n* place in a court of law where people stand to give evidence

witticism, witty ➪ WIT

wives *plural of* WIFE

wizard /'wɪzəd/ *n* **1** man believed to have magic powers **2** person who is very good at sth: *a financial ~*

wizened /'wɪznd/ *adj* (*written*) looking smaller and having wrinkles because of old age

wobble /'wɒbl/ *v* [I, T] (cause sth) to move from side to side unsteadily ➤ **wobbly** *adj* (*infml*) unsteady: *a wobbly chair*

woe /wəʊ/ *n* (*old-fash* or *hum*) **1** (**woes**) [pl] troubles and problems that sb has **2** [U] great unhappiness ➤ **woeful** *adj* **1** very bad or serious **2** (*lit*) very sad

wok /wɒk/ *n* large bowl-shaped Chinese cooking pan

woke *pt of* WAKE¹

woken *pp of* WAKE¹

wolf /wʊlf/ *n* (*pl* **wolves** /wʊlvz/) fierce wild animal of the dog family ● **wolf** *v* [T] ~ (**down**) (*infml*) eat sth quickly and greedily

woman /'wʊmən/ *n* (*pl* **women** /'wɪmɪn/) **1** [C] adult female human being **2** [U] women in general **3** [C] woman who comes from the place mentioned, does the job mentioned, etc: *a business~*, does the job mentioned, etc: *a business~* ➤ **womanhood** *n* [U] (*fml*) state or qualities of being a woman ➤ **womanizer** (*also* -**iser**) *n* (*disapprov*) man who has sexual relationships with many different women ➤ **womanly** *adj* (*approv*) (of a woman) behaving, dressing, etc in the way that is expected of a woman ■ ,**Women's Libe'ration** (*also infml*

Women's Lib) *n* [U] movement that aimed to achieve the same social and economic rights for women as men

womb /wuːm/ *n* organ in a woman's body in which a baby develops before it is born

won *pt, pp of* WIN

wonder /'wʌndə(r)/ *v* **1** [I, T] feel curious about sth; ask yourself about sth: *I ~ who she is.* **2** [I] used to make polite requests: *I ~ if you can help me.* **3** [I] ~ (**at**) (*fml*) be very surprised by sth: *She ~ed at her own stupidity.* ● **wonder** *n* **1** [U] feeling of surprise and admiration **2** [C] thing or quality in sth that fills you with surprise and admiration: *the ~s of modern medicine* ◇ *a drug* [IDM] **do/work wonders** have a very good effect or result **it's a wonder** (**that**) … (*spoken*) it is surprising or strange: *It's a ~ that they weren't all killed.* (**it's**) **no/little/small wonder** (**that**) … it is not surprising ➤ **wonderful** *adj* very good, pleasant or enjoyable ➤ **wonderfully** *adv*

wonky /'wɒŋki/ *adj* (*GB, infml*) unsteady; not straight

won't /wəʊnt/ *short for* WILL NOT (WILL¹)

woo /wuː/ *v* [T] **1** try to get the support of sb: ~ *voters* **2** (*old-fash*) (of a man) try to persuade a woman to marry him

wood /wʊd/ *n* **1** [U,C] hard material that the trunk and branches of a tree are made of **2** [C] (*also* **woods** [pl]) area of trees, smaller than a forest [IDM] **not out of the wood(s)** (*infml*) not yet free from difficulties or problems ➤ **wooded** *adj* covered with trees ➤ **wooden** *adj* **1** made of wood **2** not showing enough natural expression, emotion or movement ■ '**woodland** *n* [U] land covered with trees ➤ '**woodpecker** *n* bird with a long sharp beak that makes holes in tree trunks to find insects ■ '**woodwind** *n* [sing, with sing or pl verb] (players of) wind instruments, eg the flute and the clarinet ■ '**woodwork** *n* [U] **1** parts of a building made of wood **2** activity or skill of making things from wood ■ '**woodworm** *n* [U, C] (damage caused by a a) small worm that eats wood ➤ **woody** *adj* (-**ier**, -**iest**) **1** of or like wood **2** covered with trees: *a ~y hillside*

woof /wʊf/ *exclam* (*infml*) word used to describe the sound made by a dog

wool /wʊl/ *n* [U] **1** soft hair of sheep and some other animals **2** thread or cloth made from animal's wool, used for knitting ➤ **woollen** (*US* -**l-**) *adj* made of wool ➤ **woollens** (*US* -**l-**) *n* [pl] clothes made of wool ➤ **woolly** (*US also* -**l-**) *adj* (-**ier**, -**iest**) **1** made of or looking like wool **2** (of

W

people or their ideas) confused; not clear ▶ **woolly** n (pl -**ies**) (infml) woollen sweater

word /wɜːd/ n **1** [C] written or spoken unit of language **2** [C] thing that you say; remark or statement: Have a ~ with Mick and see what he thinks. ◇ Don't say a ~ about it. **3** [sing] promise that you will do sth or that sth is true: I give you my ~ that I will come back. ◇ You'll just have to take my ~ for it (= believe me). **4** [sing] piece of information or news: If ~ gets out about the affair, he'll have to resign. [IDM] **by word of mouth** because people tell each other and not because they read about it **have/exchange words (with sb) (about sth)** argue or quarrel with sb **in other words** used to introduce an explanation of sth **in a word** (spoken) used for giving a very short, usu negative, answer or comment **(not) in so/as many words** (not) using the exact words sb said, but suggested indirectly **say/give the word** give an order; make a request: Just say the ~, and I'll go. **too funny, silly, etc for words** (infml) extremely funny, silly, etc **word for word** in exactly the same words ● **word** v [T] express sth in words ▶ **wording** n [U,C, usu sing] words used in a piece of writing or speech ■ **word-perfect** adj able to say sth from memory without making any mistakes ■ **word processing** n [U] use of a computer to create, store and print a piece of text, usu typed in from a keyboard ■ **word processor** n computer that runs a word processing program and is usu used for writing letters, reports, etc ▶ **wordy** adj (-**ier**, -**iest**) using too many words, esp formal ones

wore pt of WEAR¹

work¹ /wɜːk/ v [I, T] do sth that requires mental or physical effort, esp as part of a job: I've been ~ing hard all day. ◇ Doctors often ~ long hours. **2** [I] have a job: She ~s for an engineering company. **3** [I] ~ (for) make efforts to achieve sth: a politician who ~s for peace **4** [T] manage or operate sth to gain benefit from it: ~ the land (= grow crops on it, etc) **5** [T] function; operate: The lift is not ~ing. **6** [T] make a machine, device, etc operate: Do you know how to ~ the coffee machine? **7** [I] have the desired result; be successful: Will your plan ~? **8** [T] make a material into a particular shape or form by pressing, stretching, etc: clay/dough **9** [I, T] move or pass to a particular place or state, usu gradually: He ~ed his way to the top of his profession. ◇ The screw had ~ed loose. [IDM] **work to rule** follow the rules of your job strictly in

order to cause delay, as a form of protest against your employer, etc **work wonders** → WONDER [PV] **work sth off** get rid of sth by using physical effort: He ~ed off his anger by digging the garden. **work out 1** train the body by physical exercise **2** develop in a successful way: Things ~ed out well for us. **work out (at sth)** be equal to a particular amount: The total ~s out at £180. **work sb out** (infml) understand sb's character **work sth out 1** calculate sth: ~ out the new price **2** find the answer to sth; solve sth: ~ out a problem **3** plan or think of sth: ~ out a new scheme **work sb/yourself up (into sth)** make sb/yourself reach a state of great excitement, anger, etc **work sth up** develop or improve sth with some effort: I can't ~ up any enthusiasm for his idea. **work up to sth** develop or move gradually towards sth ■ **worker** n person who works ■ **workout** n period of physical exercise ■ **work-to-rule** n act or working strictly according to the rules to cause delay, etc, as a protest

work² /wɜːk/ n **1** [U] the job that a person does esp in order to earn money: He's been looking for ~ for a year. ◇ to be in/out of ~ (= have/not have a job) **2** [U] the duties you have and the activities you do as part of your job: Police ~ is mainly routine. **3** [U] tasks that need to be done: I've plenty of ~ for you to do. **4** [U] place where you do your job: I go to ~ at 8 o'clock. **5** [U] use of physical strength or mental power in order to do or make sth: Do you like hard ~? **6** [U] thing produced as a result of work: an artist whose ~ I admire **7** [C] piece of writing, art, music etc: the ~s of Shakespeare **8** (**works**) [pl] activities involving building or repair: road~ **9** (**works**) [C, with sing or pl verb] place where industrial processes are carried out: a gas~ **10** (**the works**) [pl] moving parts of a machine, etc [IDM] **at work 1** having an effect on sth **2** ~ (**on sth**) busy doing sth **get to work** begin **have your work cut out** have sth difficult to do, esp in the available time ■ **workbench** n long heavy table used for working with tools, etc ■ **workbook** n book with questions to be answered, usu in the spaces provided ■ **workforce** n [C, with sing or pl verb] total number of workers in a factory, industry, etc ■ **workload** n amount of work to be done by sb ■ **workman** n man whose job involves work with his hands ■ **workmanlike** adj done well; skilful ■ **workmanship** n [U] skill with which sb makes sth ■ **work of art** n excellent painting, sculpture, etc ■ **workshop** n **1** room or building where things are made or repaired

2 period of group discussion and practical work ■ **'work-shy** adj (GB, disapprov) not wanting to work; lazy ■ **'workstation** n desk and computer at which a person works ■ **'worktop** n flat surface in a kitchen, on which food is prepared

workable /'wɜːkəbl/ adj (of a system, an idea, etc) that can be used successfully: a ~ plan

workaholic /ˌwɜːkə'hɒlɪk/ n (infml) person who finds it difficult to stop working

working /'wɜːkɪŋ/ adj **1** having a paid job: the ~ population **2** of or for work: ~ hours/clothes **3** good enough, esp as a basis for further improvement: a ~ knowledge of Russian [IDM] **in running/working order** (esp of machines) working well ● **working** n [C, usu sing] **1** way a machine, organization, etc operates **2** parts of a mine or quarry where coal, metal, etc has been dug from the ground ■ **,working 'capital** n [U] (business) money that is needed to run a business rather than to buy buildings, equipment, etc at the beginning ■ the **,working 'class** n social class whose members do not have much money, etc and are usu employed to do manual work ■ **,working-'class** adj ■ **'working party** n group of people that study and report on a subject

world /wɜːld/ n **1** (the world) [sing] the earth, its countries and people **2** [C, usu sing] particular part of this: the French-speaking ~ **3** [C] planet: There may be other ~s out there. **4** [C] people or things of a certain kind or area of activity: the insect ~ ⋄ the ~ of sport **5** [sing] person's environment, experiences, friends, etc: Parents are the most important people in a child's ~. **6** [sing] our society; all the people in the world: I don't want the whole ~ to know about it. **7** [sing] (of a future human existence: this ~ and the next (= life on earth and after death)) [IDM] **do sb/sb the world of good** make sb feel much better; improve sth **how, why, etc in the world** (infml) used for emphasis and to show surprise or annoyance: How in the ~ did you manage to do it? **out of this world** (infml) absolutely wonderful **a/the world of difference** (infml) used to emphasize how much difference there is between two things ■ **,world-'class** adj as good as the best in the world ■ **,world-'famous** adj known throughout the world ● **worldly** adj (written) **1** of material, not spiritual, things **2** having a lot of experience of life ▸ **worldliness** n [U] ■ **,world 'power** n country with great influence on international politics ■ **,world 'war** n war involving many important countries ■ **'worldwide** adj, adv happening all over the world ■ the **,World Wide 'Web** (also the Web) (abbr WWW) n [sing] international multimedia system of sound, pictures and video for finding information on the Internet

worm /wɜːm/ n **1** small long thin creature with no bones or legs: birds looking for ~s **2** young form of an insect **3** (infml, disapprov) weak worthless person ● **worm** v [I, T] use a twisting and turning movement, esp to move through a narrow place: He ~ed his way through the narrow tunnel. [PV] **worm your way/ yourself into sth** (disapprov) make sb like you or trust you, in order to gain some personal advantage

worn¹ pp of WEAR¹

worn² /wɔːn/ adj damaged by use or wear ■ **,worn 'out** adj **1** (of a thing) badly damaged and no longer usable **2** (of a person) extremely tired

worry /'wʌri/ v (pt, pp -ied) **1** [I, T] ~ (about) (cause sb/yourself to) be anxious about sb/sth: Don't ~ about me. I'll be fine. ⋄ What worries me is how I'm going to get home. **2** [T] annoy or disturb sb **3** [T] (of a dog) attack animals by chasing and/or biting them ▸ **worried** adj anxious; troubled ● **worry** n (pl -ies) **1** [U] state of worrying about sth **2** [C] something that worries you ▸ **worrying** adj that makes you worry

worse /wɜːs/ adj comparative of BAD **1** of poorer quality or lower standard; less good: Her work is bad, but his is ~. **2** more serious or severe: an even ~ tragedy **3** more ill or unhappy: She got ~ in the night. ● **worse** adv comparative of BADLY **1** less well: She cooks badly, but I cook ~. **2** more seriously or severely: It's raining ~ than ever. [IDM] **be worse off** be poorer, unhappier, etc than before or than sb else ● **worse** n [U] more problems or bad news [IDM] **be none the worse (for sth)** not be harmed by sth **the worse for wear** (infml) worn, damaged or tired ▸ **worsen** v [I, T] (cause sth to) become worse than it was before

worship /'wɜːʃɪp/ n [U] **1** practice of showing respect for God or a god by saying prayers, etc **2** strong feeling of love and respect for sb/sth ● **worship** v (-pp- US -p-) **1** [I, T] show respect for God or a god, by going to church, praying, etc **2** [T] love and admire sb very much ▸ **worshipper** (US -p-) n

worst /wɜːst/ adj superlative of BAD of the poorest quality or lowest standard; worse than any other person or thing of a similar kind: the ~ storm for years ● **worst** adv superlative of BADLY most badly or seriously ● **worst** n **(the worst)** [sing] the worst part, state, event, etc [IDM] at (the) worst used for saying what is the worst thing that can happen **if the worst comes to the worst** if the situation becomes too difficult or dangerous

worth /wɜːθ/ adj **1** having a value in money, etc: a car ~ £55000 **2** used to recommend the action mentioned because you think it may be useful, enjoyable, etc: The book is ~ reading. **3** important, good or enjoyable enough to make sb feel satisfied, esp when effort is involved: The job is hard work but it's ~ it. [IDM] **for all sb/it is worth** (infml) making every effort worth your while interesting or useful for sb to do ● **worth** n [U] **1** amount of sth that a person can buy with a certain sum of money: a pound's ~ of apples **2** financial, practical or moral value of sb/sth ▶ **worthless** adj **1** having no value **2** (of a person) having no good qualities ■ **worth while** adj useful or interesting, and worth the time, money or effort spent

worthy /ˈwɜːði/ adj (-ier, -iest) **1** ~ (of) deserving sth: ~ of blame **2** deserving respect

would /wəd; strong form wʊd/ modal v (short form **'d** /d/; neg **would not** short form **wouldn't** /ˈwʊdnt/) **1** used as the past form of will when reporting what sb said or thought: He said he ~ be here at nine o'clock. **2** used for describing the result of sth imagined: She'd look better with short hair. **3** used for making polite requests: W~ you open a window, please? **4** used in offers or invitations: W~ you like a sandwich? **5** used to say what you like, love, hate, etc: I'd love a cup of coffee. **6** used to give advice: I ~n't drink any more, if I were you. ■ **would-be** adj used to describe sb who is hoping to become the type of person mentioned: -- be parents

wound[1] /wuːnd/ n injury to the body, esp one made with a weapon: a bullet ~ ● **wound** v [T] **1** injure part of the body **2** hurt sb's feelings

wound[2] /waʊnd/ pt, pp of WIND[2]

wove pt of WEAVE

woven pp of WEAVE

wow /waʊ/ exclam (infml) used for to express great surprise or admiration

wrangle /ˈræŋgl/ n [i] n (take part in) an angry argument that lasts for a long time

wrap /ræp/ v (-pp-) [T] cover sth completely in material; fold sth round sth/sb: ~ (up) a parcel ◇ W~ the bandage round your leg. [IDM] **be wrapped up in sb/sth** (infml) that you do not pay enough attention to

others [PV] **wrap (sb/yourself) up** put warm clothes on sb/yourself **wrap sth up** (infml) complete a task, agreement, etc ● **wrap** n piece of fabric that a woman wears around her shoulders ▶ **wrapper** n piece of paper wrapped round sth, eg a sweet or newspaper ▶ **wrapping** n [C,U] something used for covering or packing sth

wrath /rɒθ/ n [U] (old-fash or fml) extreme anger

wreak /riːk/ v [T] (fml) do great damage or harm to sb/sth

wreath /riːθ/ n (pl ~s /riːðz/) circle of flowers and leaves, esp one placed on a grave as sign of respect for sb who has died

wreathe /riːð/ v [T] (written) (usu passive) ~(in/with) cover or surround sth: hills ~d in mist

wreck /rek/ n [C] **1** ship that has sunk or been very badly damaged **1** car, plane, etc that has been very badly damaged in an accident **2** [usu sing] (infml) person who is in a bad physical or mental condition ● **wreck** v [T] **1** damage or destroy sth **2** spoil sth completely: The weather ~ed all our plans. ▶ **wreckage** n [U] remains of a vehicle, etc that has been badly damaged or destroyed

wren /ren/ n very small brown bird

wrench /rentʃ/ v [T] **1** twist or pull sth/sb/yourself violently: ~ the door open **2** twist or injure a part of your body ● **wrench** n **1** [C] (esp US) metal tool for holding or turning things **2** [sing] sad and painful separation **3** [C,usu sing] sudden and violent twist or pull

wrestle /ˈresl/ v [i] **1** ~(with) fight sb by holding them and trying to throw them to the ground **2** ~with struggle to deal with a problem ▶ **wrestler** n person who wrestles as a sport

wretch /retʃ/ n unfortunate or unpleasant person

wretched /ˈretʃɪd/ adj **1** feeling ill or unhappy: His toothache made him feel ~. **2** extremely bad or unpleasant **3** extremely annoying ▶ **wretchedly** adv ▶ **wretchedness** n [U]

wriggle /ˈrɪgl/ v [i, T] move with quick short twists and turns: Stop wriggling and sit still! [PV] **wriggle out of (doing) sth** (infml) avoid doing sth unpleasant ▶ **wriggle** n

wring /rɪŋ/ v (pt, pp **wrung** /rʌŋ/) [T] **1** ~(out) twist and squeeze sth wet to get the water out of it **2** twist a bird's neck in order to kill it [IDM] **wring your hands** squeeze and twist your hands because you are sad, anxious, etc [PV] **wring sth from/out of sb** obtain sth from sb with difficulty ▶ **wringer** n machine for wringing clothes that are wet ■ **wringing** 'wet *adj* very wet

wrinkle /'rɪŋkl/ *n* [C, usu *pl*] small fold or line in the skin, esp caused by age ● **wrinkle** *v* [I, T] (cause sth to) form wrinkles ▶ **wrinkly** *adj*

wrist /rɪst/ *n* joint between the hand and the arm ■ **'wristwatch** *n* watch that you wear on your wrist

writ /rɪt/ *n* legal document ordering sb to do or not to do sth

write /raɪt/ *v* (*pt* **wrote** /rəʊt/ *pp* **written** /'rɪtn/) **1** [I, T] mark letters or numbers on a surface, esp with a pen or pencil **2** [T] produce sth in written form so that people can read, perform or use it, etc: ~ *a report/novel* **3** [I, T] put information, greetings, etc in a letter and then send it to sb: *She promised to* ~ *to me every week.* **4** [T] put information in the appropriate places on a cheque or form **5** (*computing*) record data in the memory of a computer [IDM] **be written all over sb's face** (of a feeling) be very obvious from the expression on sb's face [PV] **write sth down** write sth on paper to remember or record it **write off/ away (to sb/sth) (for sth)** write a letter to an organization, etc to order sth, ask for information, etc **write sb/sth off 1 ~ (as)** decide that sb/sth is a failure and not worth paying attention to sth **2** (*business*) cancel a debt **3** (*GB*) damage sth, esp a vehicle, so badly that it is not worth repairing **write sth out** write sth in full **write sth up** write a full written record of sth ■ **'write-off** *n* **1** (*GB*) vehicle so badly damaged that it is not worth repairing **2** (*business*) act of cancelling a debt and accepting that it will never be paid ■ **'write-up** *n* article giving sb's opinion of a new book, play, etc in a newspaper

writer /'raɪtə(r)/ *n* **1** person whose job is writing books, stories, etc **2** person who has written a particular thing: *the ~ of this article*

writhe /raɪð/ *v* [I] twist or move your body about, esp because you are in pain

writing /'raɪtɪŋ/ *n* **1** [U] activity of writing **2** [U] books, articles, etc in general **3** (**writings**) [pl] written works of an author **4** [U] person's handwriting ■ **'writing paper** *n* [U] (usu good quality) paper for writing letters on

written *pp* of WRITE

wrong /rɒŋ/ *adj* **1** not true or correct; mistaken: *a ~ answer* ◇ *prove that sb is* ~ **2** causing problems or difficulties; not as it should be: *What's* ~ *with your car?* **3** not suitable, right or what you need: *catch the* ~ *train* **4** not morally right or honest:

It is ~ *to steal.* ● **wrong** *adv* in a way that produces a result that is not correct or that you do not want: *You've spelt my name* ~. [IDM] **go wrong 1** make a mistake **2** (of a machine) stop working correctly **3** experience problems or difficulties ● **wrong** *n* **1** [U] behaviour that is not honest or morally acceptable: *know the difference between right and* ~ **2** [C] (*fml*) dishonest or illegal act [IDM] **in the wrong** responsible for an accident, mistake, etc **on the wrong track →** TRACK ● **wrong** *v* [T] (usu *passive*) (*fml*) treat sb badly or unfairly ■ **wrongdoer** *n* person who does sth dishonest or illegal ■ **'wrongdoing** *n* [U] ▶ **wrongful** *adj* (*law*) not fair, morally right or legal: *She sued her employer for ~ful dismissal.* ▶ **wrongfully** *adv* ▶ **wrongly** *adv*

wrote *pt* of WRITE

wrought iron /ˌrɔːt 'aɪən/ *n* [U] form of iron used to make decorative fences, gates, etc

wrung *pt, pp* of WRING

wry /raɪ/ *adj* **1** showing that you are both amused and disappointed or annoyed: *a ~ face* **2** amusing in an ironic way: *a ~ smile* ▶ **wryly** *adv*

WWW /ˌdʌblju: dʌblju: 'dʌblju:/ *abbr* = THE WORLD WIDE WEB (WORLD)

WYSIWYG /'wɪziwɪg/ *abbr* (*computing*) what you see is what you get; what you see on the computer screen is exactly the same as will be printed

X x

X, x /eks/ *n* [C, U] (*pl* **X's, x's** /'eksɪz/) **1** the twenty-fourth letter of the English alphabet **2** Roman numeral for 10 **3** (*maths*) unknown quantity **4** used to represent a kiss at the end of a letter, etc

xenophobia /ˌzenə'fəʊbiə/ *n* [U] (*disapprov*) great dislike or fear of foreigners

Xerox™ /'zɪərɒks/ *n* **1** process for producing copies of letters, documents, etc using a special machine **2** copy made using Xerox ▶ **xerox** *v* [T] make a copy of a letter, document, etc by using Xerox

Xmas /'krɪsməs; 'eksməs/ *n* [C, U] (*infml, written*) used as a short way of writing 'Christmas'

X-ray /'eks reɪ/ *n* [C] **1** [usu *pl*] type of radiation that can pass through objects and make it possible to see inside them **2** photograph made by X-rays: *a chest* ~ ● **X-ray** *v* [T] photograph and examine bones and organs inside the body, using X-rays

xylophone /'zaɪləfəʊn/ n musical instrument with a row of wooden bars that are hit with small wooden hammers

Y y

Y, y /waɪ/ n [C,U] (pl **Y's, y's** /waɪz/) the twenty-fifth letter of the English alphabet ■ **'Y-fronts**™ n [pl] (GB) men's underpants with an opening in the front sewn in the form of an inverted Y

yacht /jɒt/ n large sailing boat, often with an engine and a place to sleep on board, used for pleasure trips and racing ▸ **yachting** n [U] sport or activity of sailing or racing yachts

yam /jæm/ n [C,U] large root of a tropical plant that is cooked as a vegetable

Yank /jæŋk/ n (GB, infml often disapprov) person from the US

yank /jæŋk/ v [I, T] (infml) pull sb/sth hard, quickly and suddenly

yap /jæp/ v (-**pp**-) **1** [I] (of small dogs) make short sharp barks **2** (infml) talk in a silly, noisy and usu irritating way

yard /jɑːd/ n **1** (GB) area outside a building, usu with a hard surface and a surrounding wall **2** (US = GARDEN(1) **3** (usu in compounds) area of land used for a special purpose or business: a boat~ **4** (abbr **yd**) unit for measuring length equal to 3 feet (0.9144 of a metre) ■ **'yardstick** n standard for judging how good or successful sth is

yarn /jɑːn/ n **1** [U] thread that has been spun for knitting, weaving, etc **2** [C] (infml) long story

yawn /jɔːn/ v [I] **1** open your mouth wide and breathe in deeply, usu because you are tired or bored **2** (of a large hole or empty space) be very wide and often frightening: a ~ing gap ● **yawn** n act of yawning

yd abbr (pl ~**s**) = YARD

yeah /jeə/ exclam (infml) yes

year /jɪə(r); also jɜː(r)/ n [C] **1** period of 365 days (or 366) from 1 January to 31 December: The museum is open all (the) ~ round (= during the whole year). **2** period of 12 months, measured from any particular time **3** period of 12 months connected with a particular activity: the financial/school ~ **4** (esp GB) (at a school, etc) level that you stay in for one year: She was in my ~ at school. **5** [usu pl] age; time of life: He was 14 ~s old when it happened. [IDM] **year in, year out | year after year** every year

for many years ▸ **yearly** adj, adv (happening) every year or once a year

yearn /jɜːn/ v [I] ~**for/to** (lit) want sth very much: He ~ed for his home. ▸ **yearning** n [C,U] (written) strong and emotional desire

yeast /jiːst/ n [C,U] fungus used in making beer and wine, or to make bread rise

yell /jel/ v [I, T] shout loudly ● **yell** n loud shout

yellow /'jeləʊ/ adj **1** of the colour of lemons or butter **2** (infml, disapprov) easily frightened ● **yellow** n [U,C] the colour of lemons or butter ● **yellow** v [I, T] (cause sth to) become yellow: The papers had ~ed with age. ▸ **yellowish** adj yellow ■ **'Yellow 'Pages**™ (US also **'yellow 'pages**) n [with sing or pl verb] telephone directory listing companies, etc by the service they provide

yelp /jelp/ v [I] n (make a) short sharp cry, esp of pain

yen /jen/ n [C] **1** (pl **yen**) unit of money in Japan **2** [usu sing] strong desire: I've always had a ~ to travel.

yes /jes/ exclam used when accepting, agreeing, etc: Y~, I'll come with you. ● **yes** n answer that shows you agree with an idea, a statement, etc

yesterday /'jestədeɪ; -di/ adv, n [U] **1** (on) the day before today **2** (in) the recent past

yet /jet/ adv **1** used in negative sentences and questions to talk about sth that has not happened but that you expect to happen: They haven't come ~. ◇ I have ~ to meet him (= I have not met him yet). **2** at some future time: She may surprise us all ~. **3** used to emphasize an increase in number, amount or the number of times sth happens: ~ another government report **4** still: I have ~ to meet him. (= I have still not met him.) [IDM] **as yet** until now/then ● **yet** conj in spite of what has just been said: a clever ~ simple idea

yew /juː/ n [C,U] **1** (also **'yew tree**) small tree with dark green leaves and red berries **2** wood of the yew

yield /jiːld/ v **1** [T] produce or provide sth, eg a profit, result or crop: The tax increase would ~ £10 million a year. **2** [I] ~(**to**) stop resisting sth/sb; agree to do sth that you do not want to do: ~ to temptation **3** [T] (fml) allow sb to win, have or take control of sth that has been yours up until now ● **yield** n [C,U] total amount of crops, profits, etc produced: a ~ of three tonnes of wheat per hectare ▸ **yielding** adj **1** (of a substance) soft and easy to bend **2** (of a person) willing to do what others want

yippee /jɪˈpiː/ *exclam* (*infml*) used to express pleasure or excitement

yodel /ˈjəʊdl/ *v* (**-ll-** *US* **-l-**) [I, T] sing or call in the traditional Swiss way, with frequent changes from the normal voice to high notes

yoga /ˈjəʊɡə/ *n* [U] **1** Hindu philosophy that teaches you how to control your body and mind **2** system of exercises for your body and for controlling your breathing

yoghurt /ˈjɒɡət/ *n* [U,C] thick white liquid food made by adding bacteria to milk and often flavoured with fruit

yoke /jəʊk/ *n* **1** [C] piece of wood placed across the necks of two oxen so that they can pull heavy loads **2** [sing] (*fml*) harsh treatment or control: *freed from the ~ of slavery*

yokel /ˈjəʊkl/ *n* (*hum* or *disapprov*) person from the countryside

yolk /jəʊk/ *n* [C,U] yellow part of an egg

yonder /ˈjɒndə(r)/ *adj, adv* (*old-fash*) (that is) over there

you /juː/ *pron* (used as the subject of a v or as the object of a v or prep) **1** person or people being spoken to or written to **2** used for referring to people in general: *It's easier to cycle with the wind behind ~.*

you'd /juːd/ *short for* YOU HAD, YOU WOULD

you'll /juːl/ *short for* YOU WILL

young /jʌŋ/ *adj* (~**er** /-ŋɡə(r)/ ~**est** /-ŋɡɪst/) having lived or existed for a short time: *a ~ woman/nation* ● **young** *n* [pl] **1** young animals or birds; offspring **2** (**the young**) young people as a group ▶ **youngish** *adj* fairly young ▶ **youngster** /-stə(r)/ *n* (*infml*) young person or child

your /jɔː(r)/ *adj* belonging to you: *How old are ~ children?* ▶ **yours** /jɔːz/ *pron* **1** of or belonging to you: *Is this book ~?* **2** (usu **Yours**) used at the end of a letter before signing your name: *Y~s faithfully/sincerely/truly*

you're /jʊə(r); jɔː(r)/ = YOU ARE (BE)

yourself /jɔːˈself/ *pron* (*pl* **-selves** /-ˈselvz/) **1** used as a reflexive when the person or people doing sth are also the person or people affected by it: *Have you hurt ~?* **2** used for emphasis: *You did it yourselves?* **1** alone **2** without help ● *You said so ~.* [IDM] **(all) by yourself/yourselves 1** alone **2** without help

youth /juːθ/ *n* (*pl* ~**s** /juːðz/) **1** [U] time or state of being young: *in my ~* **2** [C] young man **3** (also **the youth**) [pl] young people considered as a group ▶ **youthful** *adj* young; seeming young: *a ~ful appearance* **youth hostel** *n* building that provides cheap and simple accommodation to young people who are travelling

you've /juːv/ *short for* YOU HAVE

yuck /jʌk/ *exclam* (*infml*) used to express disgust

yuppie /ˈjʌpi/ *n* (*infml* often *disapprov*) young professional person, esp one who is ambitious and earns a lot of money

Z z

Z, z /zed/ *n* (*pl* **Z's, z's** /zedz/) the twenty-sixth letter of the English alphabet

zany /ˈzeɪni/ *adj* (**-ier, -iest**) (*infml*) strange or unusual in an amusing way

zeal /ziːl/ *n* [U,C] (*written*) energy and enthusiasm ▶ **zealous** /ˈzeləs/ *adj* (*written*) full of zeal

zealot /ˈzelət/ *n* often (*disapprov*) person who is very enthusiastic about sth, esp religion or politics

zebra /ˈzebrə; ˈziːbrə/ *n* African wild animal like a horse with black and white stripes on its body ■ **zebra 'crossing** *n* (*GB*) area on the road marked with black and white stripes where people may cross

zenith /ˈzenɪθ/ *n* (*fml*) highest point of sth

zero /ˈzɪərəʊ/ *number* **1** 0; nought **2** temperature, pressure, etc that is equal to zero on a scale: *The temperature was ten degrees below ~ (= -10°C).* **3** lowest possible amount or level; nothing at all ● **zero** *v* [PV] **zero in on sb/sth 1** fix all your attention of the person or thing mentioned **2** aim a gun, etc at the person or thing mentioned ■ **'zero hour** *n* [U] time when an important event, an attack, etc is to start

zest /zest/ *n* **1** [sing,U] enjoyment and enthusiasm **2** [U,sing] quality of being interesting and enjoyable **3** [U] outer skin of an orange or lemon

zigzag /ˈzɪɡzæɡ/ *n* line that turns right and left at sharp angles ● **zigzag** *v* (**-gg-**) [I] move forward with sudden sharp turns first to the left and then to the right: *The path ~s up the cliff.*

zinc /zɪŋk/ *n* [U] (*symb* Zn) bluish-white metal

zip (also **'zip fastener**) /zɪp/ *n* device for fastening clothes, bags, etc, consisting of two rows of metal or plastic teeth that you can pull together to close sth or pull apart to open it ● **zip** *v* (**-pp-**) [T] **1** open or close sth with a zip **2** (*computing*) make computer files, etc smaller so that they use less space on a disk,

etc ■ 'Zip code n (US) = POSTCODE
(POST¹) ▶ zipper n (esp US) = ZIP

zither /'zɪðə(r)/ n flat musical
instrument with many strings

zodiac /'zəʊdiæk/ n (**the zodiac**)
[sing] imaginary band in the sky
containing the positions of the sun,
moon and planets, divided into
twelve equal parts: the signs of the ~

zombie /'zɒmbi/ n (infml) person
who seems only partly alive, without any feeling or interest in what
is happening

zone /zəʊn/ n area or region with
particular features or uses: a time ~
◇ a nuclear-free ~

zoo /zu:/ n (pl ~s) park where living
animals are kept for people to look
at ■ 'zookeeper n person who
works in a zoo taking care of the
animals

zoology /zəʊˈɒlədʒi; zuˈɒl-/ n [U] scientific study of animals and their
behaviour ▶ **zoological** /ˌzəʊə-
ˈlɒdʒɪkl; ˌzuːəˈl-/ adj ▶ **zoologist** n
student of or expert in zoology

zoom /zu:m/ v [I] **1** move or go
somewhere very fast **2** (of prices,
etc) increase suddenly and sharply
[PV] **zoom in/out** (of a camera)
show the object that is being
photographed from closer/further
away, using a zoom lens ■ 'zoom
lens n camera lens that can make
the object being photographed
appear bigger or smaller

zucchini /zuˈkiːni/ n (pl **zucchini** or
~s) (US) = COURGETTE

Common irregular verbs

(Where two forms are given, consult the entry to see if there is a difference in meaning)

Infinitive	Past Tense	Past Participle	Infinitive	Past Tense	Past Participle
arise	arose	arisen	forecast	forecast/~ed	forecast/~ed
awake	awoke	awoken	foresee	foresaw	foreseen
be	was/were	been	foretell	foretold	foretold
bear	bore	borne	forget	forgot	forgotten
beat	beat	beaten	forgive	forgave	forgiven
become	became	become	forgo	forwent	forgone
begin	began	begun	forsake	forsook	forsaken
bend	bent	bent	freeze	froze	frozen
beset	beset	beset	get	got	got/gotten
bet	bet	bet	give	gave	given
bid	bid/bade	bid/bidden	go	went	gone
bite	bit	bitten	grind	ground	ground
bleed	bled	bled	grow	grew	grown
blow	blew	blown	hang	hung/~ed	hung/~ed
break	broke	broken	have	had	had
breed	bred	bred	hear	heard	heard
bring	brought	brought	hide	hid	hidden
broadcast	broadcast	broadcast	hit	hit	hit
build	built	built	hold	held	held
burn	burnt/~ed	burnt/~ed	hurt	hurt	hurt
burst	burst	burst	keep	kept	kept
buy	bought	bought	kneel	knelt	knelt
cast	cast	cast	knit	~ted/knit	~ted/knit
catch	caught	caught	know	knew	known
choose	chose	chosen	lay[1]	laid	laid
cling	clung	clung	lead[1]	led	led
come	came	come	lean	~ed/leant	~ed/leant
cost	cost/~ed	cost/~ed	leap	leapt/~ed	leapt/~ed
creep	crept	crept			
cut	cut	cut	learn	learnt/~ed	learnt/~ed
deal	dealt	dealt	leave	left	left
dig	dug	dug	lend	lent	lent
do[1]	did	done	let	let	let
draw	drew	drawn	lie[2]	lay	lain
dream	dreamt/~ed	dreamt/~ed	light	lit/~ed	lit/~ed
			lose	lost	lost
drink	drank	drunk	make	made	made
drive	drove	driven	mean	meant	meant
dwell	dwelt	dwelt	meet	met	met
eat	ate	eaten	mislay	mislaid	mislaid
fall	fell	fallen	mislead	misled	misled
feed	fed	fed	misspell	misspelt/~ed	misspelt/~ed
feel	felt	felt			
fight	fought	fought	mistake	mistook	mistaken
find	found	found	mow	mowed	mown
flee	fled	fled	outdo	outdid	outdone
fling	flung	flung	outgrow	outgrew	outgrown
fly	flew	flown	outshine	outshone	outshone
forbid	forbade	forbidden			

Common irregular verbs

Infinitive	Past Tense	Past Participle	Infinitive	Past Tense	Past Participle
overcome	overcame	overcome	speak	spoke	spoken
overdo	overdid	overdone	speed	sped/~ed	sped/~ed
overhang	overhung	overhung	spend	spent	spent
overhear	overheard	overheard	spell	spelt/~ed	spelt/~ed
override	overrode	overridden	spill	spilt/~ed	spilt/~ed
overrun	overran	overrun	spin	spun	spun
oversee	oversaw	overseen	spit	spat	spat
overshoot	overshot	overshot	spread	spread	spread
oversleep	overslept	overslept	spring	sprang	sprung
overtake	overtook	overtaken	stand	stood	stood
overthrow	overthrew	overthrown	stink	stank/stunk	stunk
partake	partook	partaken			
pay	paid	paid	stride	strode	___
put	put	put	strike	struck	struck
quit	quit	quit	string	strung	strung
read	read	read	strive	strove	striven
repay	repaid	repaid	swear	swore	sworn
rewind	rewound	rewound	sweep	swept	swept
rid	rid	rid	swell	swelled	swollen/~ed
ride	rode	ridden	swim	swam	swum
ring[1]	rang	rung	swing	swung	swung
rise	rose	risen	take	took	taken
run	ran	run	teach	taught	taught
saw	sawed	sawn	tear	tore	torn
say	said	said	tell	told	told
see	saw	seen	think	thought	thought
seek	sought	sought	throw	threw	thrown
sell	sold	sold	tread	trod	trodden
send	sent	sent	typecast	typecast	typecast
set	set	set	undercut	-cut	-cut
sew	~ed	sewn	undergo	-went	-gone
shake	shook	shaken	underlie	-lay	-lain
shear	sheared	shorn/~ed	understand	-stood	-stood
shed	shed	shed	undertake	-took	-taken
shine	shone	shone	underwrite	-wrote	-written
shit	shat/~ted	shat/~ted	undo	undid	undone
shoe	shod	shod	unwind	unwound	unwound
shoot	shot	shot	upset	upset	upset
show	showed	shown	wake	woke	woken
shrink	shrank	shrunk	waylay	waylaid	waylaid
shut	shut	shut	wear	wore	worn
sing	sang	sung	weave	wove	woven
sink	sank	sunk	wed	~ded/wed	~ded/wed
sit	sat	sat	weep	wept	wept
slay	slew	slain	win	won	won
sleep	slept	slept	wind	wound	wound
slide	slid	slid	withdraw	withdrew	withdrawn
sling	slung	slung	withhold	withheld	withheld
slink	slunk	slunk	withstand	withstood	withstood
slit	slit	slit	wring	wrung	wrung
smell	smelt/~led	smelt/~led	write	wrote	written
sow	sowed	sown/~ed			

Help with spelling and pronunciation

It is sometimes difficult to find a word in the dictionary if you do not know how the first sound is written. Here are the most common difficulties:

The first letter is silent

wh- is sometimes pronounced /h-/ as in *who, whole*.

wr- is pronounced /r-/ as in *write, wrist*.

kn- is pronounced /n-/ as in *knife, know*.

ho- is sometimes pronounced /ɒ-/ as in *honest, honour*.

ps- is pronounced /s-/ as in *psychology*.

pn- is pronounced /n-/ as in *pneumonia*.

The second letter is silent

wh- is sometimes pronounced /w-/ as in *which, whether*.

gu- is sometimes pronounced /g-/ as in *guest, guess*.

gh- is pronounced /g-/ as in *ghastly, ghost*.

bu- is sometimes pronounced /b-/ as in *build, buoy*.

The first two letters have a special sound

ph- is pronounced /f-/ as in *phonetics, photo*.

qu- is nearly always pronounced /kw-/ as in *question, quick*.

ch- is sometimes pronounced /k-/ as in *chaos, chorus*.

Remember

c- can be /k-/ as in *call* or /s-/ as in *centre*.

g- can be /g-/ as in *good* or /dʒ-/ as in *general*

If you have looked for a word in the dictionary and cannot find it, here is a list for you to use as a guide:

If the sound is:	look at this possible spelling:	as in the following words:
/f-/	ph-	photo
/g-/	gh-	ghost or
	gu-	guest
/h-/	wh-	who, whole
/k-/	ch-	character
/kw-/	qu-	quick
/n-/	kn-	knife or
	pn-	pneumonia
/r-/	wr-	write
/s-/	c-	centre or
	ps-	psychology
/dʒ-/	j-	job or
	g-	general
/ʃ-/	sh-	shop or
	ch-	chalet
/iː/	ea-	each
/ɪ/	e-	enjoy
/e/	a-	any
/ɑː/	au-	aunt
/ɒ/	ho-	honest
/ɔː/	au-	author or
	oa-	oar
/ə/	a-	awake or
	o-	obey
/ɜː/	ear-	early or
	ir-	irk
/eɪ/	ai-	aim or
		eight
/əʊ/	oa-	oath
/aɪ/	ei-	either
/juː/	eu-	Europe